W9-DFI-962

ScottForesman

EXPLORING MATHEMATICS

AUTHORS

L. Carey Bolster
Coordinator of Mathematics
Baltimore County Public Schools
Towson, Maryland

Clem Boyer
Coordinator of Mathematics, K-12
District School Board of Seminole County
Sanford, Florida

Thomas Butts
Associate Professor,
Mathematics Education
University of Texas at Dallas
Richardson, Texas

Mary Cavanagh
Math/Science Coordinator
Solana Beach School District
Solana Beach, California

Marea W. Channel
Mathematics Resource Teacher
Los Angeles Unified School District
Los Angeles, California

Warren D. Crown
Associate Professor of
Mathematics Education, Rutgers,
The State University of New Jersey
New Brunswick, New Jersey

Jan Fair
Mathematics Department
Allan Hancock College
Santa Maria, California

Robert Y. Hamada
District Mathematics Specialist, K-12
Los Angeles Unified School District
Los Angeles, California

Margaret G. (Peggy) Kelly
Associate Professor
California State University, San Marcos
San Marcos, California

Miriam Leiva
Professor of Mathematics
University of North Carolina at Charlotte
Charlotte, North Carolina

Mary Montgomery Lindquist
Callaway Professor of Mathematics Education
Columbus College
Columbus, Georgia

William B. Nibbelink
Professor, Division of Early Childhood and
Elementary Education, University of Iowa
Iowa City, Iowa

Linda Proudfit
University Professor of Mathematics
and Computer Education, Governors State
University, University Park, Illinois

Cathy Rahlfs
Mathematics Coordinator
Humble Independent School District
Humble, Texas

Rosie Ramirez
Assistant Principal
Highland Elementary School
Silver Spring, Maryland

Jeanne F. Ramos
Assistant Principal
Nobel Middle School
Northridge, California

Gail Robinette
Vice-Principal
Fresno Unified School District
Fresno, California

David Robitaille
Head, Department of Mathematics
and Science Education
University of British Columbia
Vancouver, British Columbia,
Canada

James E. Schultz
Project LITMUS
University of Georgia
Athens, Georgia

Richard Shepardson
Professor, Division of Early Childhood
and Elementary Education
University of Iowa
Iowa City, Iowa

Jane Swafford
Professor of Mathematics
Illinois State University, Normal, Illinois

Benny Tucker
Dean, School of Education and Human Studies
Union University
Jackson, Tennessee

John Van de Walle
Professor of Education
Virginia Commonwealth University
Richmond, Virginia

David E. Williams
Former Director of Mathematics Education
School District of Philadelphia
Philadelphia, Pennsylvania

Robert J. Wisner
Professor of Mathematics
New Mexico State University
Las Cruces, New Mexico

Multicultural Reviewers

Cherry McGee Banks
University of Washington
Seattle, Washington

Armando Ayala
Director of Bilingual Education
Placer County, California

Diane Deckert Jost
Field Museum of Natural History, Chicago, Illinois

Patricia Locke
(Ta Wacin Waste Win)
Lakota, Chippewa Educator
Wakpala, South Dakota

Vicky Owyang Chan
Multicultural Educator
Fremont, California

Seree Weroha
Kansas State University, Manhattan, Kansas

Efrain Melendez
Dakota School, Los Angeles, California

Linda Skinner
Choctaw Educator, Edmond, Oklahoma

ScottForesman

A Division of HarperCollins*Publishers*

Editorial Offices: Glenview, Illinois   Regional Offices: Sunnyvale, California • Tucker, Georgia • Glenview, Illinois • Oakland, New Jersey • Dallas, Texas

CONSULTANTS

Reading
Robert A. Pavlik
Professor, Reading/Language Arts Department
Cardinal Stritch College
Milwaukee, Wisconsin

At-Risk Students
Edgar G. Epps
Marshall Field Professor of Urban Education
Department of Education
University of Chicago
Chicago, Illinois

Limited-English-Proficient Students
Walter Secada
Department of Curriculum and Instruction
University of Wisconsin
Madison, Wisconsin

Mainstreaming
Roxie Smith
Associate Provost
Northwestern University
Evanston, Illinois

Gifted Students
Christine Kuehn Ebert
Associate Professor of Education
University of South Carolina
Columbia, South Carolina

Junior High School
Edward A. Silver
Professor of Cognitive Studies and
Mathematics Education
University of Pittsburgh
Pittsburgh, Pennsylvania

CRITIC READERS

Susan Gail Blumenthal
Quail Valley Middle School
Missouri City, Texas

Van Campbell
Central Middle School
Columbus, Indiana

Sister Carole Cierniak
Our Lady of Perpetual Help School
Glenview, Illinois

Charleen M. DeRidder
Knox County Schools
Knoxville, Tennessee

Amy H. Dudley
Haggard Middle School
Plano, Texas

Linda Hayden
Timberland Junior High School
Pennington, New Jersey

Diana D. Heafey
St. Brendan School
San Francisco, California

Les Leibovitch
Van Nuys Middle School
Los Angeles, California

Patty McGuffey
Central Intrermediate School
Brownsville, Texas

Melleretha Moses-Johnson
School District of the City of Saginaw
Saginaw, Michigan

Theresa Frazier Norris
Crest Hills Middle School
Cincinnati, Ohio

Jean Reherman
Taft Middle School
Oklahoma City, Oklahoma

Nelda J. Reynolds
HaHom Middle School
Fort Worth, Texas

Linda A. Tangretti
Greensburg Salem School District
Greensburg, Pennsylvania

Acknowledgments appear after the index.

ISBN: 0-673-45527-0

78910-RRW-0099989796

Contents

Chapter 1 Getting Started

Chapter 2 Tables, Expressions, and Equations

Chapter 3 Dividing Whole Numbers and Decimals

Chapter 4 Geometry

Chapter 5 Number Theory

Chapter 6 Fraction Computation

Chapter 7 Measurement

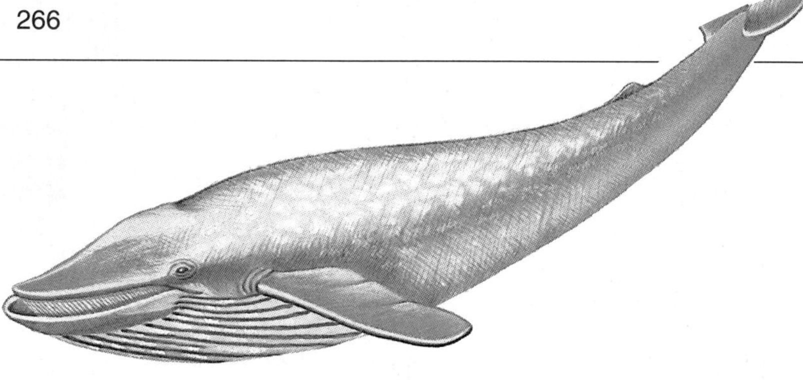

Chapter 8 Relating Ratio, Proportion, and Percent

Chapter 9 Percent

Chapter 10 Geometry and Measurement

Chapter 11 Statistics

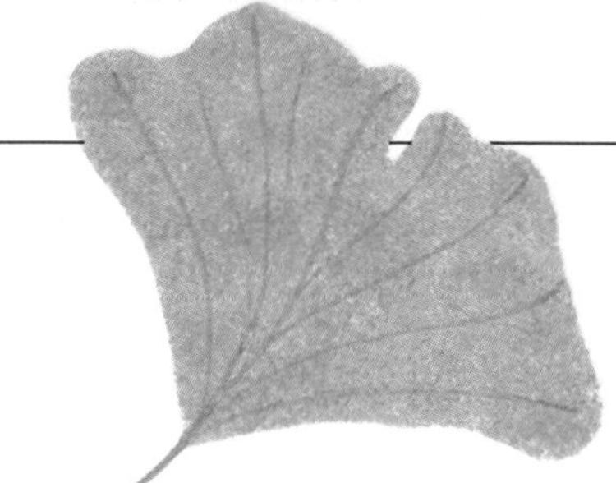

Chapter 12 Probability

Chapter 13 Integers and Rational Numbers

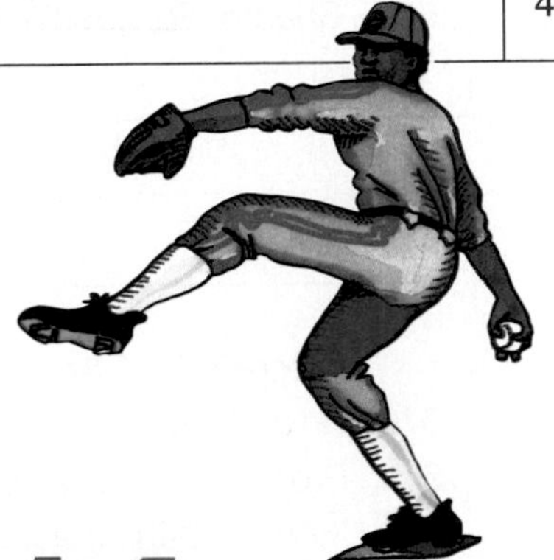

Chapter 14 Expressions and Equations with Rational Numbers

Chapter 15 Graphing Equations and Inequalities

Review

Independent Study Handbook

WELCOME TO

EXPLORING MATHEMATICS

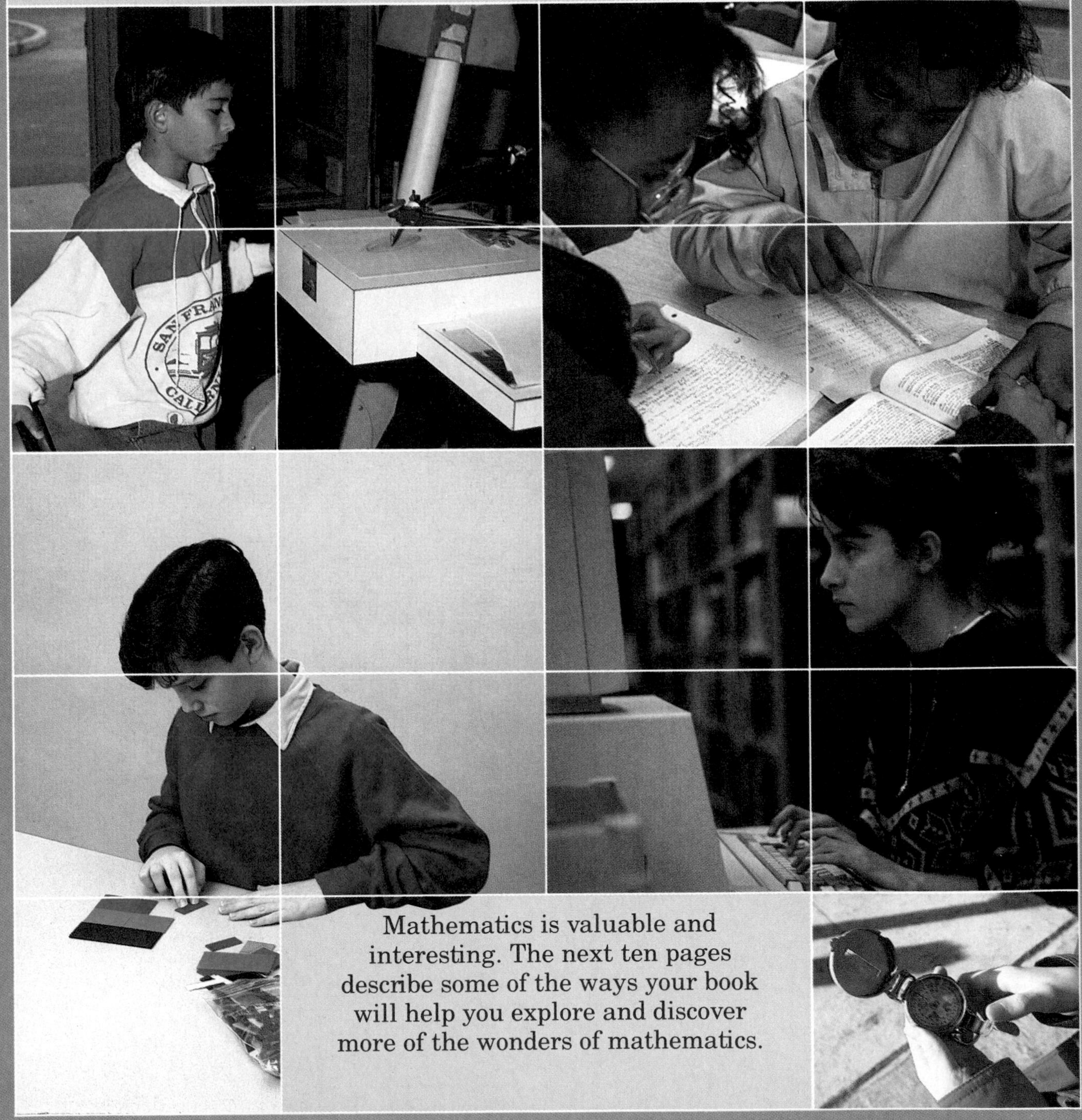

Mathematics is valuable and interesting. The next ten pages describe some of the ways your book will help you explore and discover more of the wonders of mathematics.

Your book will help you build your

Math Power

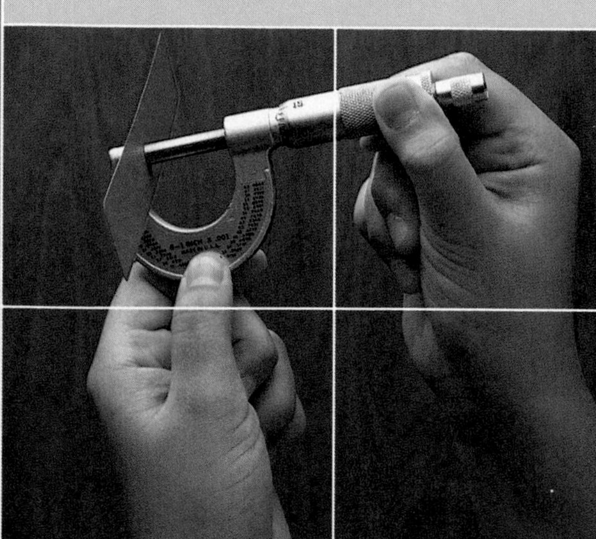

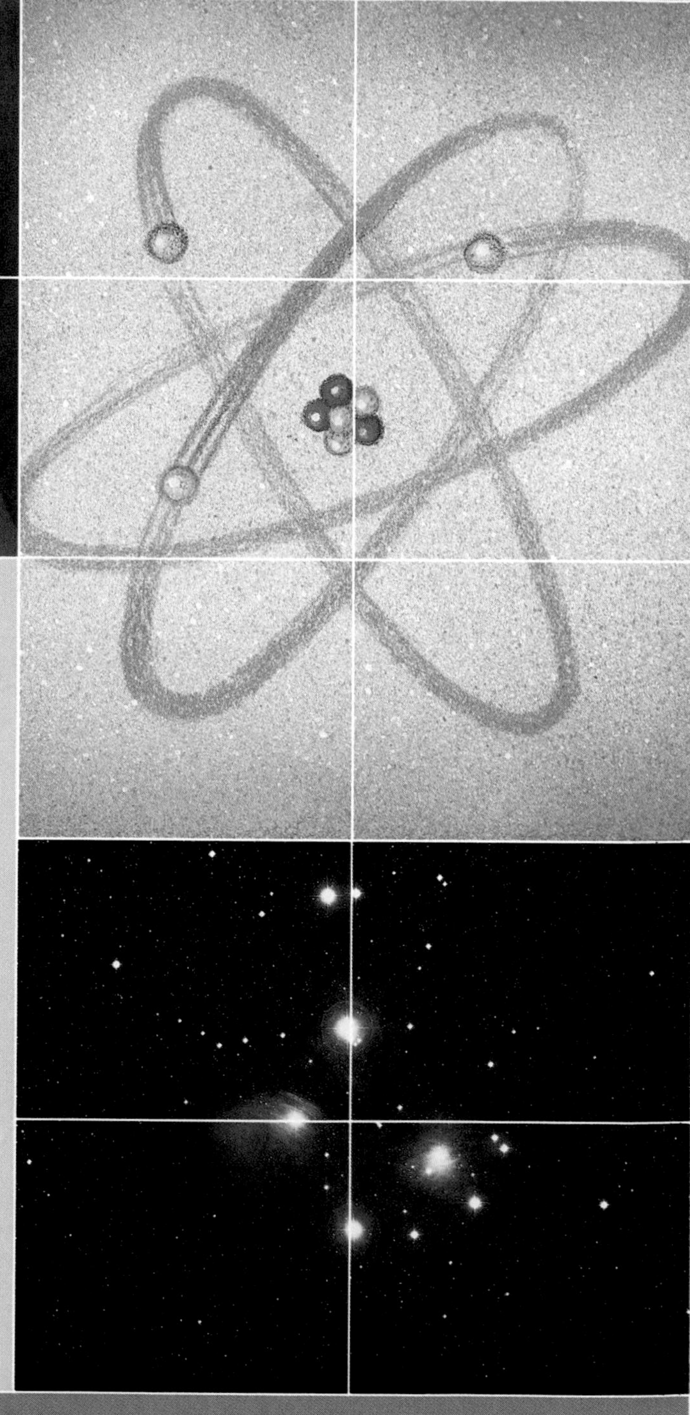

Build your math power by doing

Problem Solving and Critical Thinking

You'll need to use math to solve problems all your life. So, as you solve problems in your book, you will do more than find answers, you will also learn how to think mathematically.

In Chapter 1, tell the page numbers where these first occur.

1 "Problem-Solving Guide"
- Understand
- Plan and Solve
- Look Back

2 "Tips for Problem Solvers"

3 An exercise called "Critical Thinking"

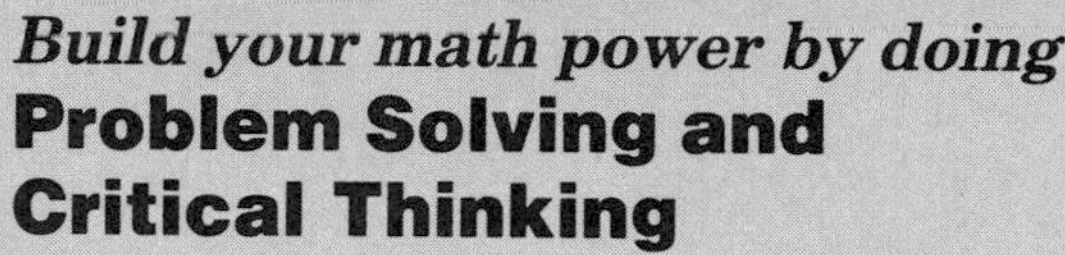

Build your math power by looking for
Connections

Your book will help you explore connections between mathematics, the real world, and other school subjects. Multicultural connections show the part mathematics plays in many cultures and societies.

4 On what page does "Multicultural Connection" first appear at the top?

5 On page 13, find a problem which involves a consumer decision.

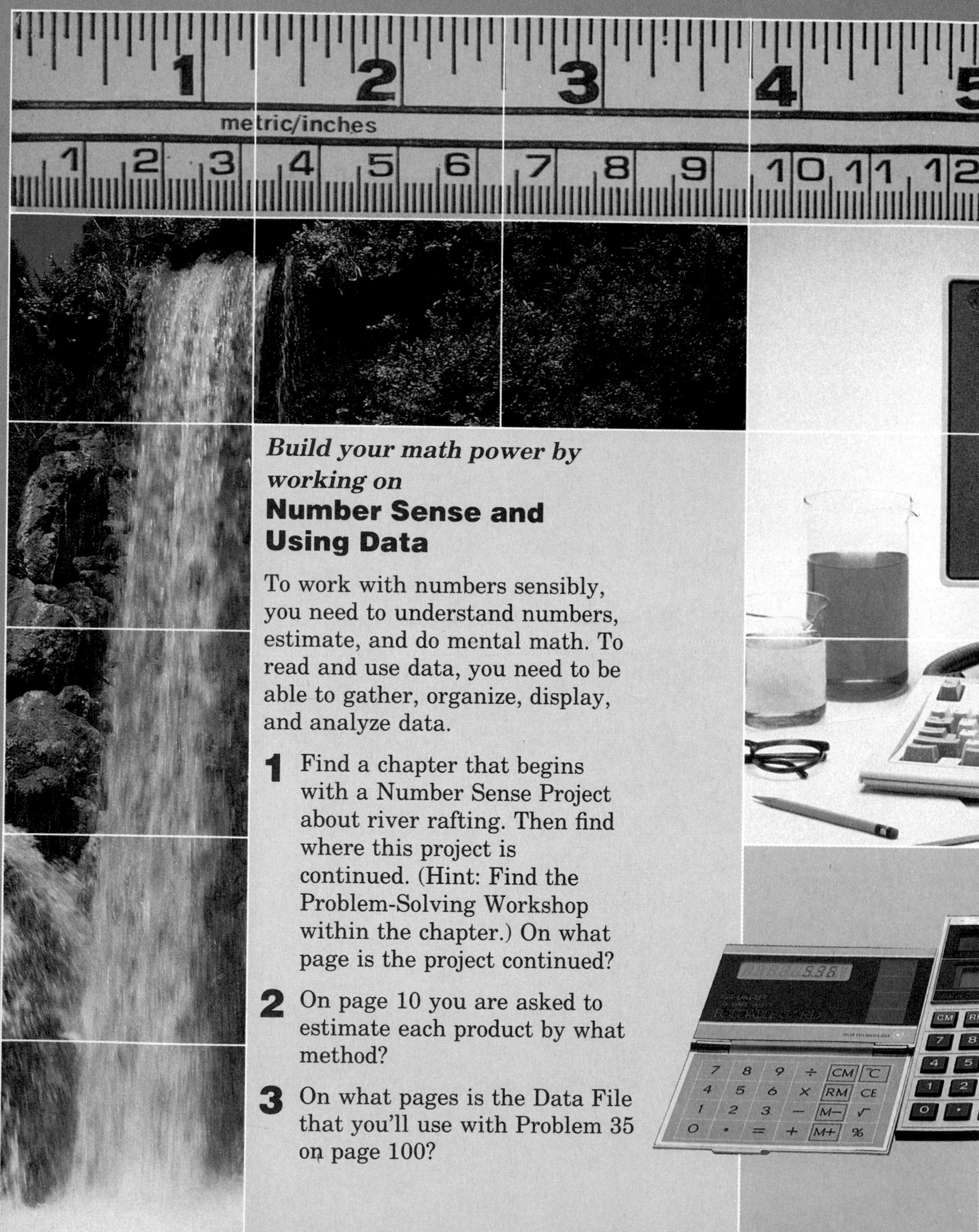

Build your math power by working on
Number Sense and Using Data

To work with numbers sensibly, you need to understand numbers, estimate, and do mental math. To read and use data, you need to be able to gather, organize, display, and analyze data.

1 Find a chapter that begins with a Number Sense Project about river rafting. Then find where this project is continued. (Hint: Find the Problem-Solving Workshop within the chapter.) On what page is the project continued?

2 On page 10 you are asked to estimate each product by what method?

3 On what pages is the Data File that you'll use with Problem 35 on page 100?

Build your math power by using

Calculators and Computers

Calculators and computers can help you solve problems and learn mathematics. It's important to know when calculators can help you and when they are not needed.

4 On page 24, what reason is given to use a calculator to perform the given computation?

5 On page 43, which problem suggests you use a calculator?

6 What pages in the Independent Study Handbook explain how to use a calculator?

7 On page 201, what math topic does a computer help you learn?

Use your book to help you

Do Your Best

To do your best

Expect to Succeed

When you want to learn something, it helps to believe in yourself. Whether you are learning a sport, a musical instrument, or mathematics, a positive attitude can make a big difference.

To do your best

Build Your Understanding

When you understand what you're doing, you do it better and remember it longer. So it pays to study the "Build Understanding" part of the lessons.

1 On page 114, why is it easy to see what new math words are being taught?

To do your best, learn ways to do
Independent Study

One of the most important things you can learn from a math book is how to learn math even when a teacher is not there to help.

2 On page 8, look to the right of the words "Check Understanding." On what page can you find another example for that lesson?

3 On page 9, look to the right of the word "Practice." On what page can you find more practice for that lesson?

4 There is an Independent Study Handbook in the back of your book. On what page does the "Math Study Skills" section begin?

5 Name the first and last words defined in the glossary on page 589.

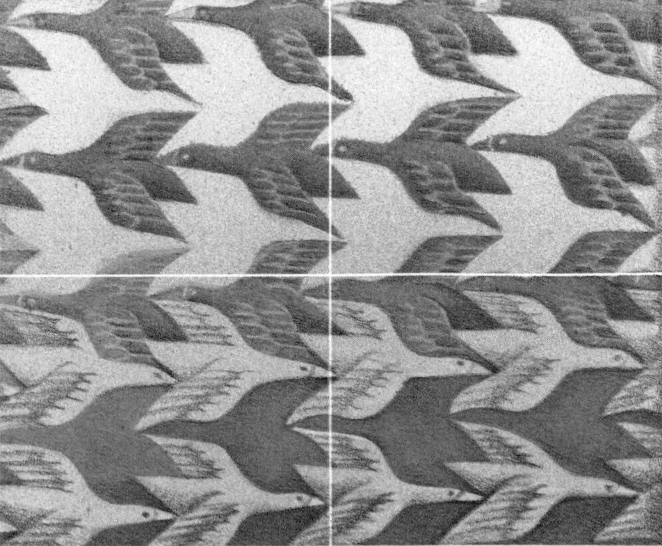

Your book will help you experience

Active Learning

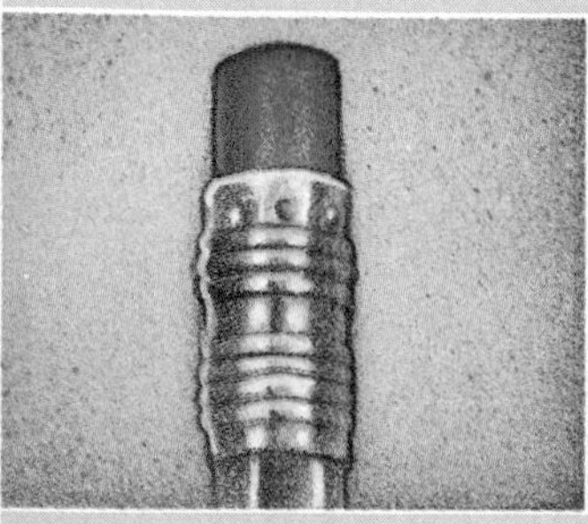

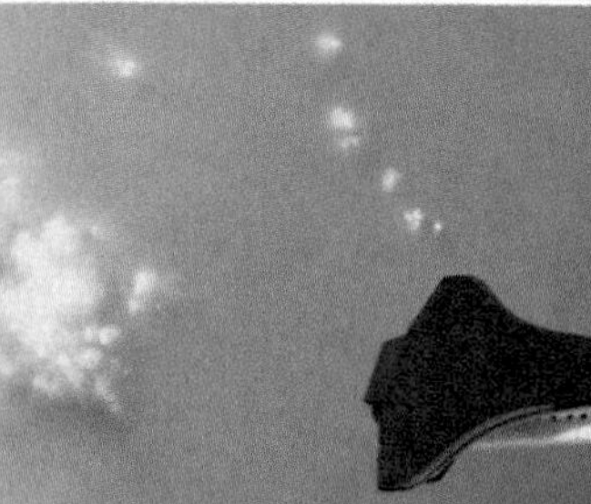

You'll learn math by doing

Math Activities

Activities help you understand math. Some activities use materials that help you show numbers, measure objects, do experiments, explore shapes, and solve problems.

1 What materials are needed to do the Practice problems on page 138?

2 Draw one-half of a circle using the "Math Sketcher" (or a compass). Then draw one-fourth of a circle.

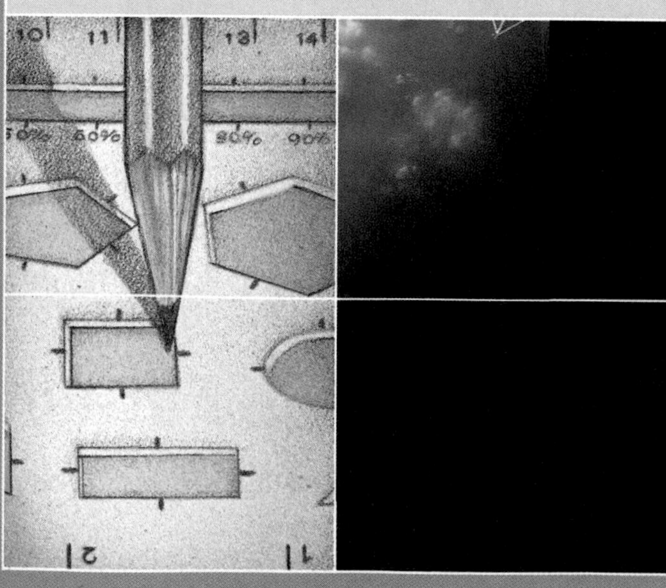

Doing math includes

Reading, Writing Talking, Listening

Reading, writing, talking, and listening in math class will help you think mathematically.

3 In Chapter 3, tell the page numbers where these first occur.

"Talk About Math"

"Write About Math"

A good way to learn is by
Working in Groups

In real life, and in math class, people can often solve problems better by working together.

4 How many students should work together in a group to do the "Divide and Conquer" activity on page 214?

5 In the "Explore As a Team" on page 134, what is the "Tip for Working Together"?

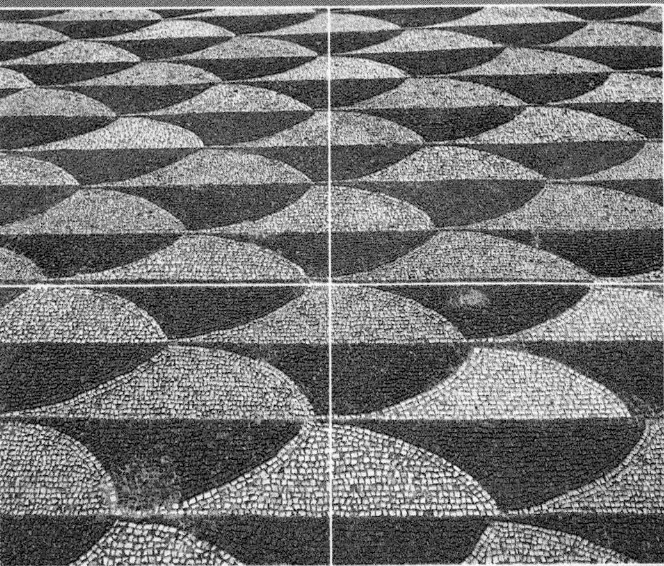

To have a math adventure, catch the spirit of
Exploration

Be a Math Explorer and discover new things. Look for patterns, check out your hunches, and try different approaches to problems.

6 On what page in Chapter 4 are you invited to explore regular polygons?

7 In the "Explore Math" on page 21, what type of computation are you asked to explore for patterns?

A key ingredient to learning math is

Enjoying Math

Your book will help you

Enjoy Math at School

The explorations in your book will help you enjoy and discover the wonders of math.

1 In Chapter 4, what lesson involves exploring beautiful, geometric patterns in a quilt?

2 Use dot paper or grid paper to explore geometric patterns which could be used in a quilt. Find a pattern which repeats itself and covers an area using more than one geometric shape.

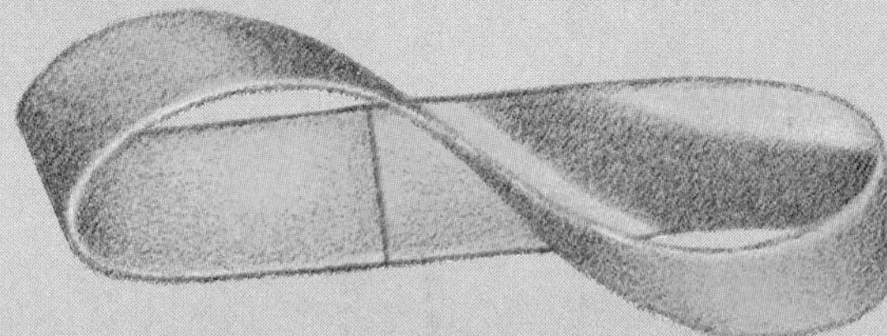

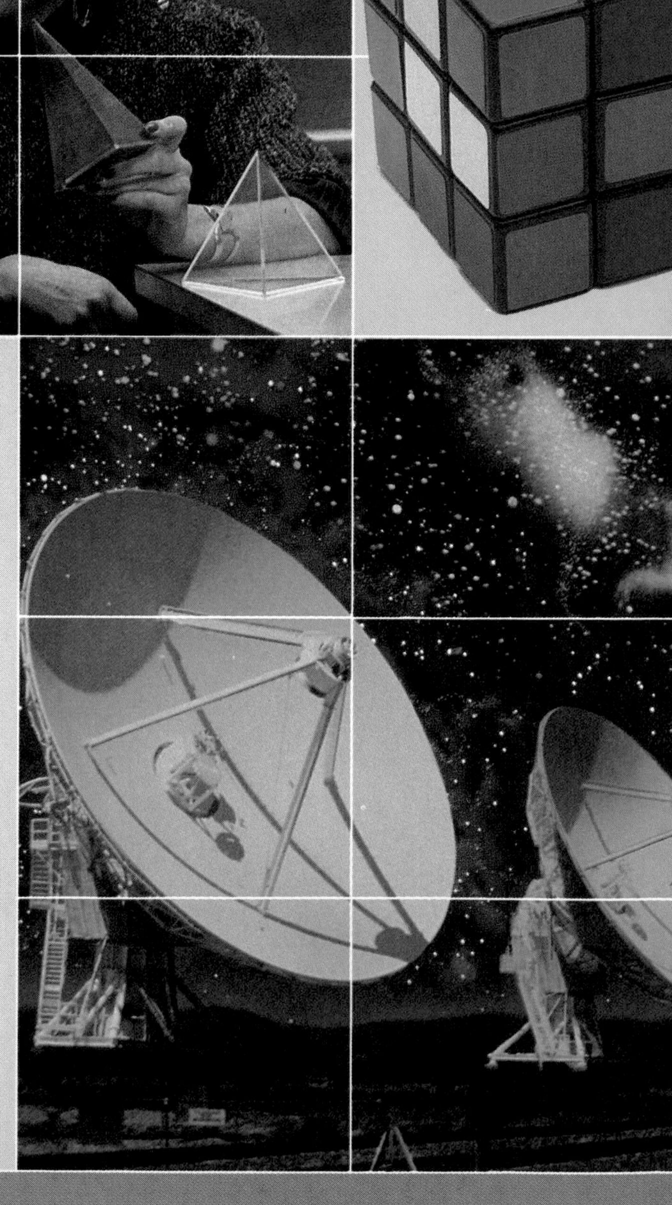

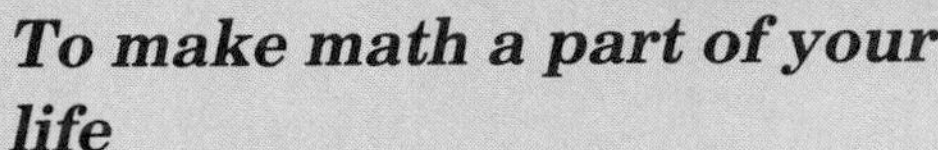

To make math a part of your life

Enjoy Math at Home

Outside of school, share math ideas with others and continue to explore math your whole life.

3 In the Math-at-Home activity on page 313, where will you be when you are doing this suggested activity?

4 What materials do you need in order to make the geometric models shown in the Problem-Solving Workshop in Chapter 10?

5 Play a game with a family member. To help build thinking skills, choose a strategy game like checkers, chess or cribbage; to sharpen number, computation, money, and other math skills, play darts, dominoes, or a boardgame that involves numbers or money.

Getting Started

Did You Know: There are about 49 million dogs and 58 million cats in the United States. About 37% (37 out of 100) of the households in this country have dogs and 30% (30 out of 100) have cats.

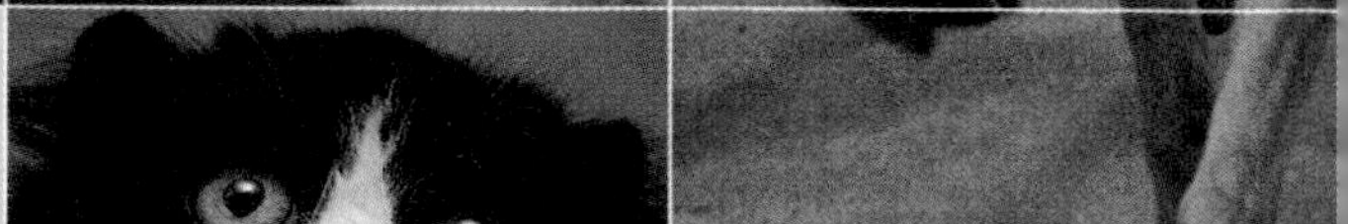

Number-Sense Project

Estimate

Out of 100 households in your neighborhood, how many do you think have dogs? cats? both a cat and a dog?

Gather Data

Survey 20 households in your neighborhood. Keep track of the number that have a dog, a cat, and both a dog and a cat.

Analyze and Report

Combine your results with those of 4 other students. How do your percents compare with those for the United States? Can you give any reasons why they might be different?

Using Numbers

Build Understanding

Suppose you were to broadcast the sports news over your school radio station. In the copy, the boxed numbers are correct but are in an inappropriate form. How can you change each boxed number so your audience will better understand this story about a football game?

Before an estimated crowd of [57,832], the San Francisco [$\frac{98}{2}$]ers defeated the Houston Oilers by a score of [28.00 to 21.00]. The quarterback Lewis completed [60% of 20] passes. With [$2\frac{2}{3}$] minutes left, Rowan scored the winning touchdown on a [$\frac{72}{36}$]-yard plunge on the [4] down to cap a [162-foot] drive.

Boxed Number	Appropriate Form	Reason
57,832	58,000	An estimate of a large crowd would probably be given to the nearest thousand.
$\frac{98}{2}$	49	The team name uses the number 49.
28.00 to 21.00	28 to 21	Whole numbers are used to give the number of points scored.
60% of 20	12 of 20	The number of passes completed is easier to understand.
$2\frac{2}{3}$	2:40	Time is kept on a digital clock.
$\frac{72}{36}$	2	A whole number is appropriate when there are no fractional parts.
4	4th	When a number is used to order, it is given a name that indicates the position.
162-foot	54-yard	Football fields are measured in yards.

■ **Talk About Math** In football, whole numbers are used to keep score. What sports use decimal scoring? Why?

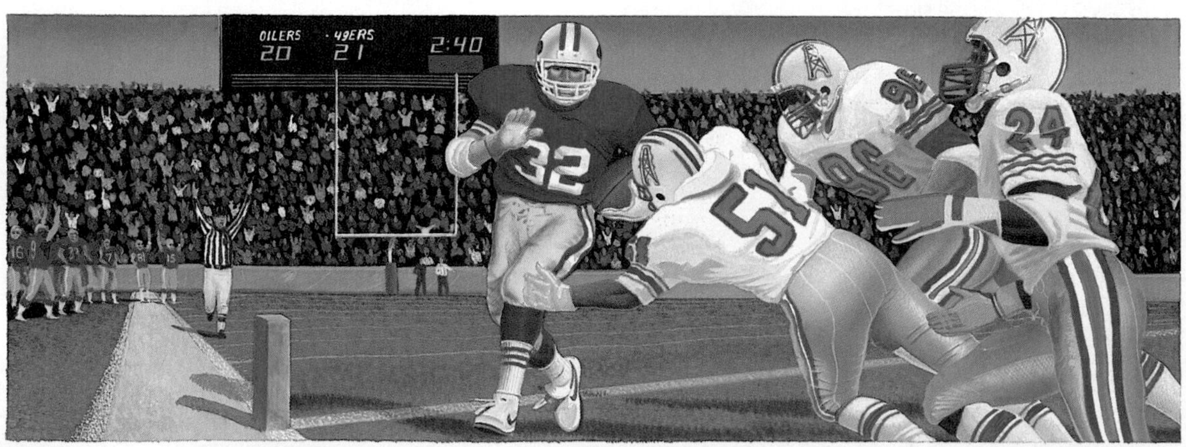

Check Understanding

For another example, see Set A, pages 30–31.

Tell what each number means.

1. 5:08 **2.** 5/08/91 **3.** $0.58 **4.** 58% **5.** $\frac{5}{8}$

Choose the best form of the number 1 in each sentence.

6. Students chanted, "We're number *1, 1:00, 1.00*."

7. All team members had a grade point average above $\frac{5}{5}$, *1.0, 100%*.

Practice

For More Practice, see Set A, pages 32–33.

Choose the best form of the number 1 in each sentence.

8. Today at *1:00, 100%, 1.0* P.M., students attended a pep rally.

9. The band played the school march in $\frac{4}{4}$, *100%, 1* time.

Name the form (whole number, fraction, mixed numbers, decimal, percent) of each number. Give an example.

10. Average yearly rainfall in Santa Fe, New Mexico:

11. Average January temperature in Nome, Alaska

12. Time of 200-meter dash

13. Length of broad jump

14. Calories in a piece of fruit

15. Amount of an ingredient in a recipe: ▒ cups ▒ teaspoons

16. The amount of weight a twelve year old might gain in one month

17. The rate of sales tax in the state of Illinois

Problem Solving

A radio reporter might give information about the following topics. First choose the correct alternative(s). Then formulate a general rule about how the numbers are determined in the given situation.

18. The interstate routes that run north-south: I-75, I-44, I-3.5, I-51A

19. Zip codes: 60513-1050, 1258, $342\frac{1}{2}$, 05412

20. Telephone area codes: 312, 213, 713, 1.23

21. The intensity of an earthquake on the Richter scale: 3.2, 5.6, 15.2, 132.7

22. **Critical Thinking** Write a paragraph about sports in which you use numbers in at least 3 different forms.

Using a Problem-Solving Guide

Build Understanding

This problem-solving guide will help you solve the kinds of problems you will find in this book.

The ***digital sum*** of 342 is 3 + 4 + 2, or 9. How many 3-digit numbers have a digital sum of 5?

Understand
QUESTION
FACTS
KEY IDEA

Plan and Solve
STRATEGY
ANSWER

Look Back
SENSIBLE ANSWER
ALTERNATE APPROACH

Understand
QUESTION
What are you asked to find?

FACTS
What facts are given?

KEY IDEA
How are the facts and question related?

Plan and Solve
STRATEGY
What can you do to solve the problem?

ANSWER
Give the answer in a sentence.

Look Back
SENSIBLE ANSWER
Did you check your work?

ALTERNATE APPROACH
Is there another way to get the same answer?

Understand

QUESTION How many 3-digit numbers qualify?

FACTS The digital sum of a number is the sum of its digits.

KEY IDEA List all possible numbers. Use an organized method.

Plan and Solve

STRATEGY Try to *make a table* and *find a pattern.*

Hundreds digit	Numbers	How many?
5	500	1
4	410, 401	2
3	320, 311, 302	3
2	230, 203, 221, 212	4
1	140, 104, 113, 131, 122	5

ANSWER There are 15 numbers.

Look Back

SENSIBLE ANSWER The answer seems sensible since the table follows a pattern.

ALTERNATE APPROACH Start with the smallest such number. Continue as in the first solution.

■ **Write About Math** What pattern do you see in the table on page 6? How can a pattern help you solve problems like this?

Check Understanding

Consider 3-digit numbers that have a digital sum of 8.

1. What is the greatest such number?

2. List any other numbers that have the same hundreds digit.

3. How many such numbers have 7 as the hundreds digit?

4. How many 3-digit numbers have a digital sum of 8?

Practice

One example of a 2-digit number with two different digits in decreasing order is 98. Answer these questions about other such numbers.

5. What is the least number with 2 digits in decreasing order?

6. List any other numbers with a tens digit of one that fit these conditions.

7. How many numbers in the 20s fit these conditions? in the 30s? 40s?

8. Describe the pattern you see in Exercises 5–7.

9. How many 2-digit numbers are there with two different digits in decreasing order?

Use the problem-solving guide to solve these problems.

10. How many 2-digit numbers contain at least one 7?

11. How many 3-digit numbers contain at least one 7?

List the whole numbers from 1 to 100 in order to form one huge number.

123456789101112 99100

The digit "2" is in the 15th place. What digit is in the given place?

12. 17th **13.** 21st **14.** 99th **15.** 187th

16. How many digits are in this large number?

17. How many times does the digit "3" appear in this large number?

Multiplying Decimals

Build Understanding

Mangoes are grown mainly in Southeast Asia, Central and South Africa, and Central and South America. They are shipped to your supermarket in refrigerated containers.

Item	Price per pound
jicama	\$0.79
papaya	\$1.89
daikon	\$0.99
kiwi	\$0.98
mangoes	\$1.39
okra	\$0.79
eggplant	\$1.99

You want to buy 2.5 pounds of mangoes using the per pound prices in the table. Find the cost.

Since you know the price per pound (\$1.39) and the number of pounds (2.5), you multiply.

First estimate: $2.5 \times 1.39 \rightarrow 3 \times 1 = 3$

Paper and Pencil

```
   1.39  ← 2 decimal places
 ×  2.5  ← 1 decimal place
   ----
    695
   278
  -----
  3.475  ← 3 decimal places
```

Calculator

Press: 2.5 [×] 1.39 [=]

Display: 3.475

Stores usually round prices up to the next whole cent. So, the price of the mangoes is \$3.48.

Mangoes are very rich in vitamin A. One mango has twenty times as much vitamin A as an orange of the same size.

Talk About Math Explain two ways you could decide how to place the decimal point in the example above: first, by using the estimate; and, second, by counting decimal places in the factors.

Check Understanding

For another example, see Set B, pages 30–31.

Estimate to place the decimal point in each product.

1. $15.2 \times 4.5 = 684$ **2.** $8.7 \times 0.85 = 7395$ **3.** $4.2 \times 100 = 4200$

Mental Math Multiply using mental math.

4. 0.3×100 **5.** $0.05 \times 1{,}000$ **6.** 15.27×100 **7.** 1.67×0.001

Choose paper and pencil or calculator to multiply.

8. 480×3.9 **9.** 0.6×0.7 **10.** 73.2×8 **11.** 503.82×0.005

Practice

For More Practice, see Set B, pages 32–33.

Use the table on page 8. Find the price of each of the following. Round up to the next whole cent.

12. 1.2 lb of papaya

13. 3.58 lb of jicama

14. 3.72 lb of daikon

15. 3 lb of eggplant

16. 2.92 lb of kiwi

17. 0.97 lb of okra

18. 2.2 lb of mangoes and 1.5 lb of kiwi

19. 1.25 lb of eggplant and 2.45 lb of okra

20. 3.88 lb of jicama and 4.56 lb of daikon

Choose paper and pencil or calculator to multiply.

21. $\begin{array}{r} 0.01 \\ \times\ 10 \\ \hline \end{array}$

22. $\begin{array}{r} 70 \\ \times\ 0.8 \\ \hline \end{array}$

23. $\begin{array}{r} 1.07 \\ \times\ 0.97 \\ \hline \end{array}$

24. $\begin{array}{r} 0.204 \\ \times\ 5.78 \\ \hline \end{array}$

25. 390×2.7

26. 0.8×0.3

27. 76.7×7

28. 207.65×0.008

29. 8.65×4.5

30. 0.463×24

31. 15.5×1.425

32. 3.64×0.92

33. 9.27×2.31

34. 1.3×3.24

35. 3×1.124

36. 7.541×4.2

37. 3.025×1.11

38. 0.005×10.03

39. 2.134×45

40. 101×4.789

Problem Solving

Use the table on page 8. Solve each problem. Round up to the next whole cent.

41. Iyo buys 2.4 pounds of daikon (a large, white Japanese radish). She shreds the daikon to make a nest for small slices of raw fish. How much does she spend?

42. Okra is native to the tropical parts of Africa. It is used in soups and stews. Raul buys 1.6 pounds of okra and 3.68 pounds of jicama for dinner. How much does he spend?

43. Koyi is making “Terong Balado,” a Southeast Asian eggplant dish, for 8 people. If 0.6 pound of eggplant is used per person, will 5 pounds be enough?

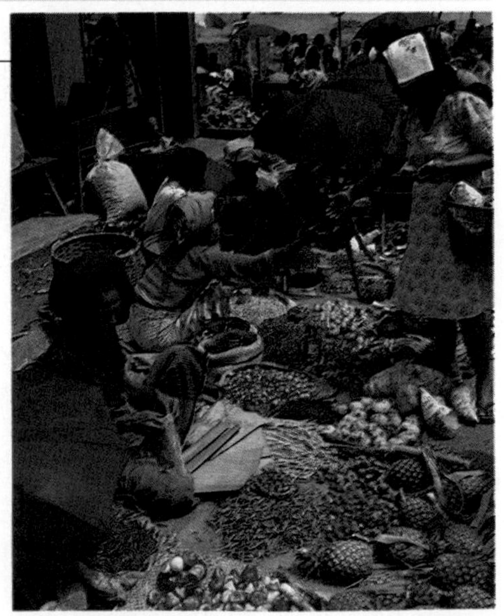

This open market in Sumatra sells pale green eggplants; limes; sweet oranges; and black, mushroomlike djamur kuping, or “cloud ears.”

Estimating Sums, Differences, and Products

Build Understanding

ACTIVITY

A. Up or Down?
Groups: Partners

a. With a partner, copy the table and estimate each product by ***rounding***. Then find each actual product.

Problem	Estimated Product	Actual Product
86 × 18	▦	▦
57 × 49	▦	▦
77 × 35	▦	▦

b. For each exercise, are both numbers rounded up or rounded down? Compare the estimated products to the actual products. Circle the greater product.

c. Try three more pairs of numbers for which both numbers are rounded up. Will the estimated product always be greater than the actual product when both numbers are rounded up? Why?

d. Now find the estimated and actual products for 34 × 63; 52 × 41; 84 × 72. What happens when both numbers are rounded down? What can you say about the relationship between the estimated and actual products?

e. Predict how the estimated product will compare to the actual product when the first number is rounded up and the second is rounded down. Test your prediction with three pairs of numbers.

B. Estimate the costs of a trip by using ***front-end*** estimation. First, add the tens digits. Then add the ones digits and adjust the estimate.

Meals	**\$44.95 →**	**40**
Car repair	**\$39.95 →**	**30**
Gas/oil	**\$29.95 →**	**+20**
		90

4 + 9 + 9 is more than 20.
90 + 20 = 110

The estimated cost is \$110.

C. Estimate 23 × 64 × 4.

Use ***compatible numbers*** to estimate. Substitute numbers that are close to the original numbers so that you can do the arithmetic mentally.

23 × 64 × 4 → 25 × 64 × 4 = 100 × 64, or 6,400

E. Estimate the total meal costs for four days. Use ***clustering*** to estimate the sum.

Mon.	**$17.55**
Tues.	**$16.95**
Wed.	**$16.50**
Thurs.	**$17.25**

All the prices are close to $17.00. The 4 addends cluster around 17.

4 × 17 = 68

The estimated cost is $68.00.

F. Estimate 22 + 16.

Compare the numbers to the ***reference point*** 25 which you can work with mentally.

22 < 25
16 < 25

So the sum of 22 + 16 is less than 50.

D. Estimate 133.2 − 14.9 by ***rounding to the same place.***

$$\begin{array}{rcr} 133.2 & \rightarrow & 130 \\ -\ 14.9 & \rightarrow & -\ 10 \\ \hline & & 120 \end{array}$$

Nine out of ten adults in the United States are licensed drivers, each of whom travels over 9,000 miles per year on this country's 4 million miles of paved and unpaved roads.

Talk About Math Describe how you can round both numbers up and both numbers down to get a range when estimating a sum or a product.

Check Understanding

For another example, see Set C, pages 30–31.

Describe the method that was used to estimate each sum or difference.

1. 289 + 303 + 325
a. 200 + 300 + 300
b. 3 × 300

2. 7,230 + 5,520
a. 12,000
b. 13,000

3. 736 − 498
a. 200
b. 300

Choose the most reasonable product. Explain your choice.

4. (91)(29)
a. 263
b. 2,639
c. 26,390

5. 4.23 × 6
a. 2.538
b. 25.38
c. 253.8

6. 0.25 × 7.5
a. 0.187
b. 1.875
c. 18.7

Practice

For More Practice, see Set C, pages 32–33.

Use rounding to estimate each answer.

7. 12.049 + 3.27 **8.** 23.228 − 6.93 **9.** 6.2 × 7.74

10. 122.397 − 21.701 **11.** 9.87 × 7.84 **12.** 12.654 + 17.15

Use front-end digits to estimate each answer.

13. 137 + 425 **14.** 3,424 + 7,486 **15.** 119 + 8,298

16. 440 − 328 **17.** 98,802 − 43,315 **18.** 63,690 − 2,414

Use compatible numbers to estimate each answer.

19. 24 × 21 **20.** 15 × 39 **21.** 27 × 119 **22.** (19)(17)(5)

23. 11 × 29 **24.** 98 × 27 **25.** (2)(48)(78) **26.** (6)(21)(51)

Use clustering to estimate each sum.

27. 15.83 + 16.011 + 15.5 **28.** 0.921 + 0.9 + 1.1 + 1.335

29. 115 + 97 + 106 + 99 **30.** 47 + 44 + 42 + 30

Use a reference point to estimate each answer. Fill in the blanks.

31. 255 + 264
more than ▒

32. $80.00 − $36.00
less than ▒
more than ▒

33. $400.00 − $172.00
between ▒ and ▒

34. 221 − 138
less than ▒
more than ▒

35. 3,021 − 168
between ▒ and ▒

36. $2.76 + $3.28
more than ▒

Estimate each answer. Name the method you used.

37. 173 + 421 + 348 **38.** 6,278 + 6,589 + 5,893 **39.** 28.4 − 3.9

40. 24 × 78 × 4 **41.** 28 + 31 + 29 + 33 **42.** 4.23 × 8.821

43. $21.24 + $18.78 **44.** (41)(251)(14) **45.** 1.1 + 7.68 + 9.12 + 2.3

Mixed Practice Use any method to estimate each answer. Name the method you used. Then, use paper and pencil or a calculator to compute each answer exactly.

46. 9,213 − 2,043 − 1,154 **47.** 123 + 78 + 197 **48.** 7 × 28 × 11

49. 242 + 261 + 253 + 248 **50.** 123,987 + 226,063 **51.** 24.3 × 3.6 × 9.74

Problem Solving

Solve each problem.

52. The cost of a train ticket for an adult is $18.50. If children ride for half price, estimate the cost of tickets for 1 adult and 3 children.

53. Four friends shared the following expenses for a weekend trip: $42.50, $6.31, $2.80, $14.76, $12.93. Estimate how much each paid.

54. Lise has planned a 4-day vacation. The airline ticket agent tells her that the airfare is $230.40 if she stays for 5 days or $288 for 4 days. Her expenses for the extra day will be $35. Estimate to determine how much Lise will save by extending her vacation.

55. Sal and 3 friends are sharing travel expenses equally. They have $49 left and 350 miles to go to reach their destination. Tolls will cost $12. They can drive 18 miles on a gallon of gas. If they have to pay $1.15 per gallon of fuel, do they have enough money to buy $5 tickets to a game and still reach their destination?

Midchapter Checkup

Name the form of the number you would use in each situation. Give an example.

1. Batting average
2. Sales tax rate
3. Your height
4. TV schedule

Multiply.

5. 1.2×3.8
6. 0.18×50
7. 148.2×1.5
8. 0.48×0.015

Estimate each answer. Name the method you used.

9. 36×52
10. $31.9 + 32.5 + 31.7$
11. $92 - 39$
12. $5{,}090 + 2{,}890 + 6{,}663$
13. 4.1×7
14. $(1.8)(23)(4)$

Explore as a Team

Play "Guess the Number" with another person.

1. One person thinks of a number and writes it on a piece of paper and stores it away. (For the first few games, use 2-digit numbers. After you have mastered the rules, use 3-digit numbers.)

2. The second player guesses the number. The first player then must tell two things: (1) how many digits in the guess are correct, and (2) how many digits are in the correct place.

The second player keeps track of these responses by recording them in a chart. (See the example game at the right.)

3. The game continues until the second player guesses the number.

4. After you have played several games, discuss the reasoning you used in different situations. Did some strategies work better than others? Give examples.

5. Keep a record of how many guesses it took on each game. Watch for improvement!

No. of Guess	Guess	Correct Digits	Correct Places
1.	36	0	0
2.	84	1	0
3.	20	1	0
4.	98	0	0
5.	40	1	1
6.	42	2	2

"4" or "8" is correct but not in the correct position.

This tells you "8" is not correct digit in step 2.

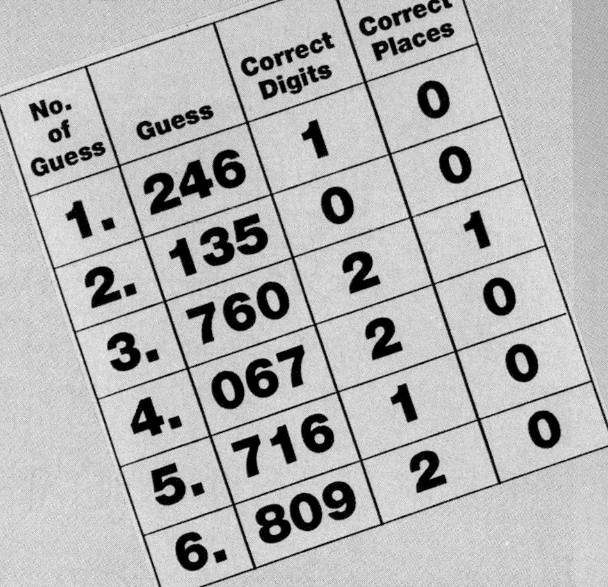

No. of Guess	Guess	Correct Digits	Correct Places
1.	246	1	0
2.	135	0	0
3.	760	2	1
4.	067	2	0
5.	716	1	0
6.	809	2	0

MATH laugh

I told my friend a joke about decimals, but he didn't get the point.

TIPS FOR WORKING TOGETHER

Help keep your group on task.

Explore with a computer

Use the *Graphing and Probability Workshop Project* for this activity.

During a 30-minute network news program the newscasters report on many different topics. They may spend 3 minutes reporting international news and 8 minutes on local news.

1. At the computer, view data for a newscast as a bar graph. Then use the *Transform Option* to list the data as percents.

2. Compare the percent of time spent on each topic. Change the data in the table so that 30% of the program is spent on local news.

Topic	Minute
International News	3
National News	3
Local News	8
Sports	5
Weather	5
Commercials	6

Number-Sense Project

Look back at pages 2-3.

1. What percent of the households in the United States have a dog? A cat?

2. Notice that there are more cats than dogs in the United States, but fewer households have cats. Explain how this could be possible.

3. If 12% of the households in the United States have both a dog and a cat, can you tell what percent of the households have a dog but not a cat?

Critical-Thinking Activity

What coins does Ty have in each pocket?

1. In his coat pocket, he has 19 coins that total $1.00. There are twice as many pennies as dimes.

2. In his pants pocket he has 16 coins. There are three different types of coins. The total is $1.00.

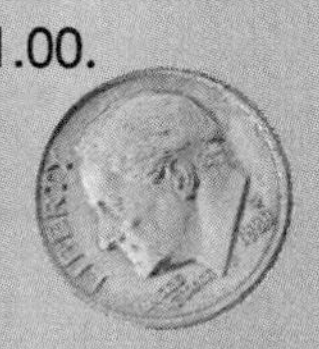

ALGEBRA

Mental Math Strategies

The following properties can help you do many computations easily.

Commutative Properties of Addition and Multiplication

The order of the numbers can be changed without changing the sum or the product. $a + b = b + a$ $a \times b = b \times a$

Associative Properties of Addition and Multiplication

The grouping of the numbers can be changed without changing the sum or the product. $(a + b) + c = a + (b + c)$ $(a \times b) \times c = a \times (b \times c)$

Distributive Property

Multiplication distributes over addition. $a \times (b + c) = (a \times b) + (a \times c)$

A. The chart shows the number of tickets sold by seventh graders. How many did they sell for the first performance?

Show Tickets Sold		
Home Room Teacher	First Performance	Second Performance
Mr. Tanzi	54	117
Ms. Kline	91	83
Mr. Gomez	46	83
Mrs. McDuff	95	91

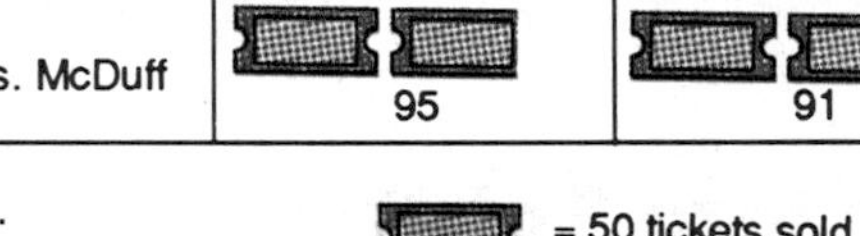

= 50 tickets sold

You can add 54 + 91 + 46 + 95 mentally by ***looking for special numbers***. The commutative and associative properties let you add the numbers in any convenient order. It helps to keep a "running total."

54 + 91 + 46 + 95

54 + 46, or 100 Use 54 + 46 to get 100.

+ 90 + 90, or 280 Next add the tens from 91 and 95.

+ 1 + 5, or 286 Then add the remaining ones.

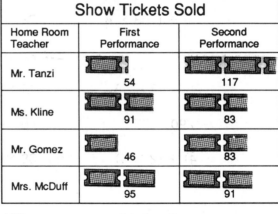

The students sold 286 tickets for the first performance.

B. You can subtract mentally by using ***compensation.***

345 − 290 290 is 10 less than 300.

345 − 300 + 10 = 55 Subtract 300. Then add 10.

C. Multiply by ***breaking apart*** the numbers and using the distributive property.

$$\begin{aligned} 6 \times 46 &= 6 \times (40 + 6) \\ &= (6 \times 40) + (6 \times 6) \\ &= 240 + 36 = 276 \end{aligned}$$

Talk About Math Add zero to three different numbers. What do you notice about the sums? Multiply three different numbers by zero. What do you notice about the products?

Check Understanding

For another example, see Set D, pages 30–31.

1. Subtract by using compensation: 204 − 150.

2. Multiply by breaking apart numbers and using the distributive property: 4 × 64.

3. Add by looking for special numbers: 19 + 37 + 11 + 23.

Practice

For More Practice, see Set D, pages 32–33.

Find each answer. Compute mentally.

4. 23 + 35

5. 347 + 236

6. 5 × 37

7. 190 + (153 + 10)

8. (46 × 8) + (46 × 2)

9. 72 − 25

10. 357 − 198

11. 6,005 − 3,995

12. 25 + 93 + 7 + 53

13. (97 × 4) + (103 × 4)

14. 27 + 85 + 13 − 5

15. 203 + 18 − 53

16. 32 × 12 − 14

17. 2,137 + 313

18. 287 − 98 + 21

19. 34 + 28 + 18 + 15

20. 42 × 8

21. 50 × 13

22. 580 − 290

23. 450 + (50 + 263)

24. 92 − 28

25. (23 × 4) + (2 × 4)

26. 38 × 5

27. 38 + 7 + 16 + 5 − 6

Problem Solving

Solve each problem mentally. Refer to Example A on page 16.

28. Which homerooms were the top two ticket sellers for the two performances? Together, how close were they to selling 400 tickets?

29. At $6.00 per ticket, what was the total amount of ticket sales for the first performance?

Skills Review

Review, pages 564–565

Compute. Tell whether you use paper and pencil or a calculator.

1. 499 + 527

2. 28,321 − 9,047

3. 635,448 + 109,379

4. 533 × 7

5. 5,031 × 6

6. 512 × 6 × 8

Using Division

Build Understanding

A math class took a survey of their own TV viewing habits. The table shows the number of hours per week that each student watches TV. What is the average number of hours per week that the boys in this class watch TV?

Since you want to find the average number of hours per boy, you divide the boys' total time of 192 hours by the number of boys (9).

First, estimate by rounding.
192 ÷ 9 → 190 ÷ 10 = 19

Paper and Pencil

$$\begin{array}{r} 2 \\ 9\overline{)192} \\ \underline{18} \\ 1 \end{array}$$

Divide (19 ÷ 9).
Multiply.
Subtract and compare.

$$\begin{array}{r} 2 \\ 9\overline{)192} \\ \underline{18} \\ 12 \end{array}$$

Bring down.

$$\begin{array}{r} 21 \text{ R3} \\ 9\overline{)192} \\ \underline{18} \\ 12 \\ \underline{9} \\ 3 \end{array}$$

Divide (12 ÷ 9).
Multiply.
Subtract and compare.

Weekly TV Viewing

Boys	Hours	Girls	Hours
Al	23	Aimee	22
Bob	21	Sabena	10
Carlos	19	Carmen	30
Erik	11	Dawn	24
Lloyd	13	Greta	21
Juan	24	Lori	20
Sumi	18	Naomi	17
Tom	33	Aiko	15
Kiyo	30	Trish	14
Total	192	Total	173

Press: 192 ÷ 9 = **Display:** *21.333333*

The answer, 21 R3, can be written as the mixed number, $21\frac{1}{3}$. The answer is close to the estimate of 19, so the answer is reasonable. The boys watch TV an average of $21\frac{1}{3}$ hours per week.

■ **Write About Math** Explain how the mixed number $21\frac{1}{3}$ is found from the answer 21 R3.

Check Understanding

For another example, see Set E, pages 31–32.

Complete each division by using the given computation.

1. $8 \times 9 = 72$
$72 \div 8 = ▒$

2. $8 \times 9 = 72$
$72 \div 9 = ▒$

3. $5 \times 17 = 85$
$85 \div 5 = ▒$

4. $5 \times 17 + 2 = 87$
$87 \div 5 = ▒$ R ▒

5. $7 \times 21 = 147$
$147 \div 7 = ▒$

6. $7 \times 21 + 3 = 150$
$150 \div 7 = ▒$ R ▒

Estimation Estimate each quotient.

7. $4\overline{)83}$

8. $130 \div 6$

9. $\frac{4,366}{9}$

10. $\frac{56,483}{8}$

11. Use the table on page 18. How would you find the average weekly TV viewing time for the girls?

12. **Calculator** Use a calculator to show that in the example the remainder, $\frac{1}{3}$, is equal to the decimal part of the calculator display.

Number Sense Answer the following without doing any computing.

13. Would the girls' average weekly TV viewing time be greater or less than the boys' average? How can you tell?

14. How would the average for the whole class compare to the boys' average and the girls' average?

What operation would you use to find each of the following?

15. The total weekly TV viewing time for Al and Aimee

16. How many hours per day Greta watches TV

17. How many hours per week Sumi watches TV if he watches 4 hours per day

18. How many more hours per week Bob watches TV than Sabena

Practice

For More Practice, see Set E, pages 32–33.

Use the table on page 18. Find the average number of hours per day that each person below spends watching television. Round to the nearest whole number.

19. Sumi **20.** Aimee **21.** Tom **22.** Carmen

Divide. Choose paper and pencil or a calculator.

23. $93 \div 5$ **24.** $739 \div 2$ **25.** $961 \div 4$ **26.** $9{,}731 \div 6$

27. $6\overline{)705}$ **28.** $5\overline{)2{,}439}$ **29.** $5\overline{)12{,}046}$ **30.** $4\overline{)14{,}790}$

31. $\frac{641}{3}$ **32.** $\frac{26{,}543}{7}$ **33.** $\frac{15{,}326}{5}$ **34.** $\frac{6{,}142}{4}$

35. $854 \div 5$ **36.** $3{,}452 \div 3$ **37.** $7{,}253 \div 6$ **38.** $2{,}802 \div 9$

Mixed Practice List the numbers in order from least to greatest.

39. 50,063 50,036 50,066 **40.** 0.098 0.101 0.089 0.099

Compute. **Remember** to watch the signs.

41. $\begin{array}{r} 556 \\ +458 \\ \hline \end{array}$ **42.** $\begin{array}{r} 1{,}014 \\ -\ 556 \\ \hline \end{array}$ **43.** $\begin{array}{r} 2{,}511 \\ \times\ \ 9 \\ \hline \end{array}$ **44.** $\begin{array}{r} 56.02 \\ -39.03 \\ \hline \end{array}$

45. $\begin{array}{r} 1{,}705 \\ \times\ \ 6 \\ \hline \end{array}$ **46.** $\frac{10{,}230}{6}$ **47.** $\begin{array}{r} 39.03 \\ +16.99 \\ \hline \end{array}$ **48.** $\frac{22{,}600}{9}$

49. $\begin{array}{r} 3{,}217 \\ -\ 732 \\ \hline \end{array}$ **50.** $\begin{array}{r} 56.04 \\ +18.27 \\ \hline \end{array}$ **51.** $\frac{92{,}923}{7}$ **52.** $\begin{array}{r} 3{,}257 \\ \times\ \ 8 \\ \hline \end{array}$

Problem Solving

Use the table on page 18. Find the weekly average for each group described below. Round to the nearest whole number.

53. The four boys and four girls whose weekly viewing times are the highest

54. The four boys and four girls whose weekly viewing times are the lowest

55. The girls **56.** The class

Don't give up. Some problems take longer than others.

Critical Thinking Without computing, answer each question.

57. If Tom transferred to another school, would the boys' weekly average go up or down?

58. If Sabena transferred to another school, would the girls' average go up or down?

59. If a new boy who watched TV 25 hours per week joined the class, would the boys' weekly average go up or down?

60. If Lori cut her weekly viewing time to 10 hours, but Sabena increased hers to 20 hours, what would happen to the girls' weekly average?

61. If Carlos increased his weekly viewing time to 24 hours, but Tom decreased his viewing time to 22 hours, would the boy's weekly average go up or down?

62. Find the dividends.

$$\begin{array}{r} 123{,}456{,}789 \\ 2\overline{)\square\square\square{,}\square\square\square{,}\square\square\square} \end{array}$$

$$\begin{array}{r} 123{,}456{,}789 \\ 3\overline{)\square\square\square{,}\square\square\square{,}\square\square\square} \end{array}$$

Explore ________ Math

Study each set of division exercises below. Find each quotient.

63. $6\overline{)30}$ $60\overline{)300}$ $600\overline{)3{,}000}$

64. $5\overline{)25}$ $50\overline{)250}$ $500\overline{)2{,}500}$

65. $7\overline{)42}$ $70\overline{)420}$ $700\overline{)4{,}200}$

66. $4\overline{)24}$ $40\overline{)240}$ $400\overline{)2{,}400}$

67. What pattern do you see in each set?

68. Write three division problems that follow the pattern.

Now study each set of division exercises. Find each missing number.

69. $\begin{array}{r} 3 \\ 8\overline{)\square} \end{array}$ $\begin{array}{r} 3 \\ 80\overline{)\square} \end{array}$ $\begin{array}{r} 3 \\ 800\overline{)\square} \end{array}$

70. $\begin{array}{r} 4 \\ \square\overline{)36} \end{array}$ $\begin{array}{r} 4 \\ \square\overline{)360} \end{array}$ $\begin{array}{r} 4 \\ \square\overline{)3{,}600} \end{array}$

Use Data from a Graph

Understand
QUESTION
FACTS
KEY IDEA

Plan and Solve
STRATEGY
ANSWER

Look Back
SENSIBLE ANSWER
ALTERNATE APPROACH

Build Understanding

A bar graph often makes it easy to compare events and predict trends. This bar graph shows the population growth of North America. What is the projected increase in population between 1988 and 2010?

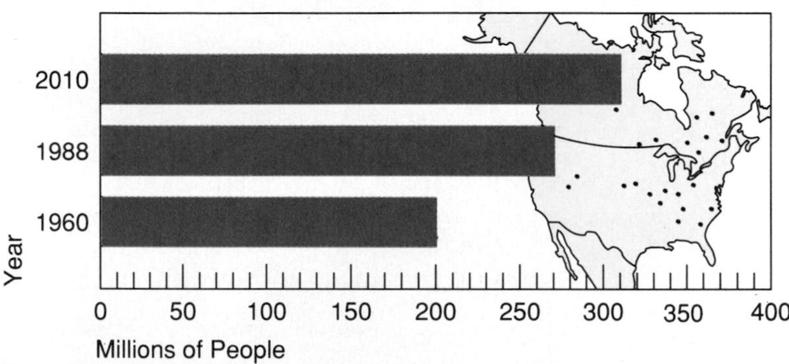

Understand QUESTION How much greater will the population be in 2010 than in 1988?

FACTS The graph shows that the population in 1988 was about 270 million and the projected population for 2010 is about 310 million.

KEY IDEA Since you want to find how much more one number is than another, subtract.

Plan and Solve STRATEGY Use numbers from the graph to solve the problem by computing.

310 million − 270 million = 40 million

ANSWER Between 1988 and 2010, the population of North America is projected to increase by 40 million.

Look Back SENSIBLE ANSWER You can use the graph to solve the problem without computing. Count four 10-million units between 1988 and 2010. A population increase of 40 million people is reasonable.

Talk About Math
Explain how you would show a population of 205 million on the graph above.

Check Understanding

Millions of people produce tons of garbage. The pictograph shows the amount of garbage collected in 5 cities in 1980. How many pounds of garbage per person did the European cities generate during the entire year?

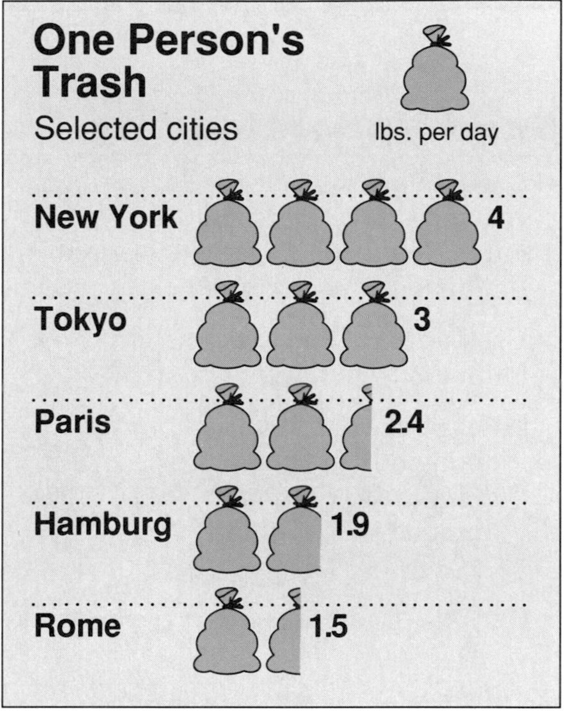

Source: *Time*, January 2, 1989

1. What are the European cities?
2. How much garbage per person did each European city generate daily?
3. Will you need more than one operation to solve the problem?
4. How will you find the amount of daily garbage per person these cities generated altogether?
5. How will you find the amount of garbage per person they generated for one year? Compute to solve the problem.

Practice

Use Data Use data from a graph to solve each problem.

6. What was the average annual population growth between 1960 and 1988? Refer to the graph on page 22.
7. **Visual Thinking** Did the projected rate of population growth increase or decrease from 1988 to 2010 compared to 1960–1988? Explain your answer.
8. During what years did carbon emissions decrease?
9. Estimate the average yearly increase in carbon emissions between 1960 and 1988.

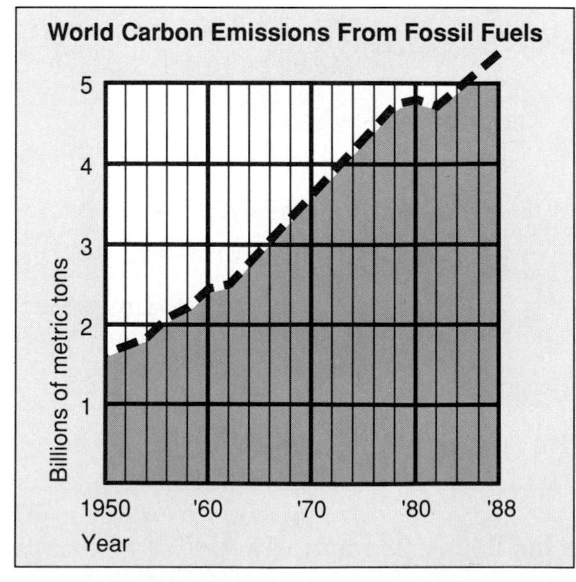

Choose a Computation Method

Build Understanding

A. Carlotta uses a mileage chart when she visits customers. How many miles would she have to drive from Indianapolis to the three cities in Ohio?

Use paper and pencil to record numbers from another source.

Mileage-chart distances:
Indianapolis to Cincinnati 109
Cincinnati to Columbus 106
Columbus to Cleveland +141
356

Carlotta would have to drive 356 miles.

TO \ FROM	Chicago, Ill.	Cincinnati, Ohio	Cleveland, Ohio	Columbus, Ohio	Detroit, Mich.	Indianapolis, Ind.
Chicago, Ill.	–	324	341	359	293	184
Cincinnati, Ohio	324	–	239	106	255	109
Cleveland, Ohio	341	239	–	141	167	295
Columbus, Ohio	359	106	141	–	185	173
Detroit, Mich.	293	255	167	185	–	277
Duluth, Minn.	496	797	847	815	756	686
Evansville, Ind.	297	236	490	344	436	164

B. Carlotta has to fill out the expense report shown. Her meals were $6.80, $5.87, $5.16, $8.59, and $14.10. What were her total expenses?

Calculator Use a calculator because there are several computations.

Expenses from Indianapolis, IN
to Cleveland, OH and return.
Transportation by car
(____ mi @ $ .21 per mi): $ ____
Meals: 2 Breakfasts, $ ____
2 Lunches, 1 Dinner $ ____
Hotel: Royal Hotel, 1 night $ 59.90
Miscellaneous: Parking $ 4.50
TOTAL: $ ____

Use the total miles driven from Example A. Add the distance from Cleveland back to Indianapolis, 295 miles. Multiply by $0.21 per mile to find the total transportation cost.

Press: 356 [+] 295 [×] .21 [=]

Display: *136.71*

Now add to find the total expenses.

Press: 136.71 [+] 6.80 [+] 5.87 [+] 5.16 [+] 8.59 [+] 14.10 [+] 4.50 [+] 59.90 [=]

Display: *241.63*

Her total expenses were $241.63.

C. Find 356 − 28 mentally. Use *compensation*.

356 − 30 + 2 = (356 − 30) + 2 = 326 + 2 = 328

28 is 2 less than 30.
Subtract 30. Then add 2.

■ **Talk About Math** In Example A, what factors other than distance from Indianapolis might Carlotta consider when deciding which city to visit first?

Check Understanding

For another example, see Set F, pages 30–31.

Tell which computation method (mental math, paper and pencil, or calculator) you would use to solve each exercise. Then solve.

1. 345 + 542 **2.** 429,583 − 28,070 **3.** 57 ÷ 3 **4.** 72 × 3

Practice

For More Practice, see Set F, pages 32–33.

Choose mental math, paper and pencil, or a calculator. Tell which method you chose.

5. 46 × 89 **6.** 83 × 7 **7.** 23 + 35 **8.** 0.93 + 3.036 **9.** 90 ÷ 6

10. 144 ÷ 4 **11.** 946 − 576 **12.** 600 ÷ 120 **13.** 40 × 250 **14.** 0.02 × 31

15. 67 ÷ 8 **16.** 45 × 11 **17.** 999 − 723 **18.** 0.6 × 90 **19.** 72 ÷ 0.08

20. 12.8 + 45.25 **21.** 75 × 20 + 35 **22.** 3.35 + 12.5

23. 32 × 18 − 37 **24.** 15 + 22 + 31 + 10 **25.** 7.32 − 2.0124

26. 298 − 150 **27.** 1,500 ÷ 300 **28.** 3.2 × 3.0

29. (16 + 14) × 4 **30.** 24 − 12 + 15 + 27 **31.** 1.5 × 6 × 11

32. (16.20 + 8.37 − 2.98) × 1.5 **33.** (24.0 + 12.6 + 0.31) × 8

Problem Solving

Solve each problem. Tell which computation method you used. See the chart on page 24.

34. Which city, Cincinnati or Cleveland, is farther from Evansville? How many miles farther away is it?

35. Which is the shorter trip, a. or b.? How much shorter?
a. Cleveland to Chicago to Duluth
b. Indianapolis to Detroit to Chicago

36. On another business trip, Carlotta drove from Chicago to Cincinnati and then from Cincinnati to Detroit. How many miles did she drive?

37. Which town is closer to Columbus—Cleveland or Detroit? How many miles closer is it?

Choose an Operation

Understand
QUESTION
FACTS
KEY IDEA

Plan and Solve
STRATEGY
ANSWER

Look Back
SENSIBLE ANSWER
ALTERNATE APPROACH

Build Understanding

In New York City, the holiday programs at Radio City Music Hall are legendary. The list gives facts about the theater and the annual holiday programs performed there.

During the week of December holidays, the show is performed four times each day except Monday. If every performance is sold out, how many people saw the show on Friday? during the entire week?

To solve the problem, you can use the problem-solving guide.

Understand QUESTION What was the total audience on Friday? for the entire week (6 days)?

FACTS There were 4 shows each day for 6 days. All seats were filled at each show. Radio City has 6,000 seats.

Plan and Solve STRATEGY Use the strategy *choose an operation*. Since the same number of people were at each show, you can multiply.

Seats filled daily: **6,000 × 4 = 24,000**

Seats filled weekly: **24,000 × 6 = 144,000**

ANSWER On Friday, 24,000 people saw the show; during the week, 144,000 people saw the show.

Look Back ALTERNATE APPROACH There were 6 × 4 = 24 shows during the week.

Seats filled weekly: **6,000 × 24 = 144,000**

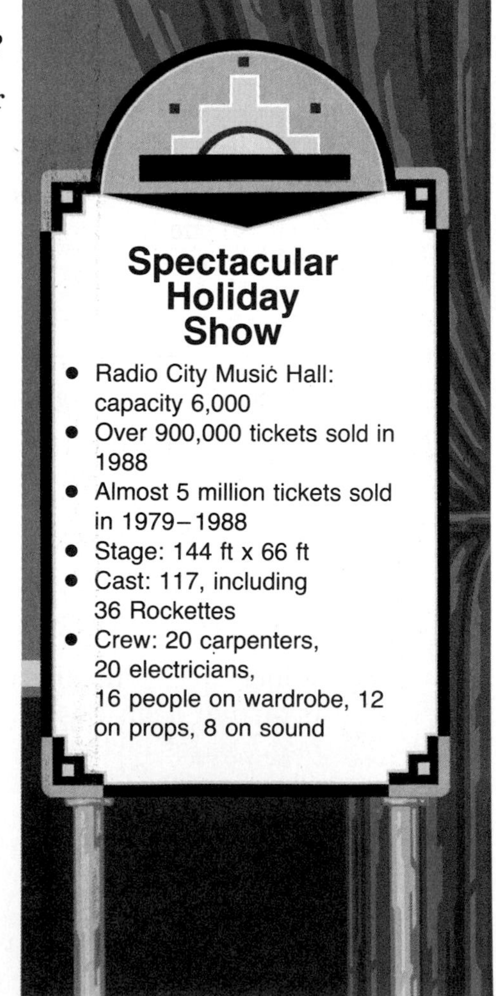

Spectacular Holiday Show
• Radio City Music Hall: capacity 6,000
• Over 900,000 tickets sold in 1988
• Almost 5 million tickets sold in 1979–1988
• Stage: 144 ft x 66 ft
• Cast: 117, including 36 Rockettes
• Crew: 20 carpenters, 20 electricians, 16 people on wardrobe, 12 on props, 8 on sound

■ **Talk About Math** Explain how you could use addition to solve the problem above.

Check Understanding

Many people work behind the scenes on the Radio City show. How large is this crew? Refer to the list on page 26.

1. Where can you find the data you need?
2. What kind of workers made up the crew?
3. How many people in each job worked on the show?
4. Is the cast part of the crew?
5. Which operation will you use to find the total number of workers?
6. Compute to solve the problem.

Practice

Tell which operation to use. Then solve the problem.

7. The Radio City cast rehearsed nine days in a studio and five days on stage. How long was the rehearsal time?
8. **Use Data** Use the table on page 236 to solve. The stage has a 3-ton curtain. If the curtain parts in the center, how many pounds pull to each side?
9. What is the area of the stage floor? Refer to the list on page 26.
10. If the show sold 20,000 tickets a day for 2 weeks, how many tickets would be sold?

Choose a ________ Strategy

Black and Red Bike Bells Every black bicycle in the school yard has a bike bell. Half of all the red bikes have bells. Half of all the bikes with bells are black. There are 40 red bikes and 30 black bikes. How many bikes with bells are neither black nor red?

11. How many red bikes have bells?
12. If there are 30 black bikes and half of all the bikes with bells are black, how many bikes have bells?
13. How many bikes with bells are either black or red?
14. How many bikes with bells are neither black nor red?

Skills Review

Name the form of the number you would use in each situation. Give an example.

1. average travel speed
2. time to run a 100 meter dash
3. length of a movie

Multiply.

4. 12 × 1.2
5. 6.7 × 3.4
6. 246.3 × 25
7. 0.033 × 0.78

Estimate each answer.

8. 48 × 21
9. 505 − 288
10. 4 × 24 × 8
11. $65.18 + $24.77
12. 483 + 515 + 495 + 502 + 511

Use mental math to find each answer.

13. 29 + 17 + 71
14. 32 × 3
15. 816 − 202
16. 460 − 232

Divide.

17. 73 ÷ 5
18. $\frac{2{,}808}{3}$
19. $8\overline{)11{,}992}$
20. 594 ÷ 9

Choose mental math, paper and pencil, or calculator to compute.

21. 116.4 + 22.5
22. 245.7 − 132.5
23. 12 × 36 × 9
24. 6,666 ÷ 6
25. 421 + 9.25
26. 277 × 14.5
27. 24,114 ÷ 3
28. 2,612.4 − 933.1
29. 1.15 × 6.03
30. 212.63 + 11.91

Problem-Solving Review

Solve each problem.

31. Sally earns $5.15 an hour at the Grocery Basket. This week she worked 16.5 hours. How much did she earn? Round your answer to the nearest cent.

32. The *City Times* has 36,425 readers. The *Evening News* has 52,904 readers. Estimate how many more readers the *Evening News* has.

33. A bowling league has teams of 4 players each. How many teams can be formed if 132 bowlers sign up for the league?

34. The Chans drove to Boston for a vacation. They drove for 18 hours at an average speed of 53 miles per hour. Estimate how far they drove.

35. Half of the students and half of the adults attending the Art Fair entered drawings. Half of the remaining adults entered pottery. No students entered pottery. Altogether, 50 students and 80 adults attended the fair. How many students and teachers had not entered a drawing or pottery?

36. **Data File** Use the data on pages 108–109. Compare the cost of shipping 9,820 ton-miles of cargo by airplane and by motor truck.

37. **Make a Data File** Use a world almanac to find the record 24-hour precipitation in these states: Maine, Florida, Texas, Missouri, California, Washington, and your state (if it is not one of the states listed). Display the data you gather on a bar graph.

Cumulative Skills Review • Chapter 1

Cumulative Skills REVIEW

Name the form of the number you would use in each situation. Give an example.

1. Cost of a pair of shoes
2. Part of an orange that is water
3. Amount of fabric needed for a shirt
4. Water temperature
5. Length of a vacation
6. Pages in a book

Find each product.

7. 3.25×16
8. 8.6×0.4
9. 1.55×22
10. 0.002×39
11. 506×6.3
12. 0.3×0.5
13. 4.02×1.1
14. $3{,}207 \times 2.34$

Estimate each answer.

15. $5 \times 19 \times 21$
16. $314 + 2{,}707$
17. 52% of \$59.20
18. $61.92 - 42.06$
19. $5.6 + 6.2 + 5.8$
20. 78×83
21. $590.87 - 278.91$
22. 34% of \$17.98
23. $90{,}402 - 55{,}116$
24. \$489.38 + \$518.74 + \$502.10 + \$495.67

Use mental math to find each answer.

25. $460 - 222$
26. 4×42
27. $699 + 238$
28. 25×8
29. $26 + 64 + 74$
30. $909 - 319$
31. $3 \times 3 \times 5 \times 6$
32. $800 - 561$

Divide.

33. $98 \div 2$
34. $4\overline{)586}$
35. $\frac{23{,}180}{3}$
36. $700 \div 5$
37. $\frac{5{,}084}{9}$
38. $217 \div 7$
39. $6\overline{)10{,}002}$
40. $\frac{5{,}000}{4}$

Choose mental math, paper and pencil, or calculator to compute.

41. $452 + 7.19$
42. $15 \times 8 \times 90$
43. $674 + 392$
44. 65×39
45. $4{,}040 \div 8$
46. $5{,}923 \div 3$
47. $45 + 55 + 27$
48. $7{,}202 - 1{,}865$
49. $77 + 2.78$
50. $93 + 67 + 21$
51. 381×102
52. $15{,}936 \div 3$
53. $1{,}876 - 742$
54. $3{,}621 + 32.32$
55. $4{,}000 \div 7$
56. $30 \times 5 \times 6$
57. $(6 \times 19) + (6 \times 6)$
58. $14 + 101 + 6 + 99 + 73 + 7$
59. $4 \times 1{,}206 \times 25$
60. $(13 \times 14) + (13 \times 6)$

Independent Study RETEACHING

Reteaching

Set A pages 4–5

Numbers should be used in an appropriate form. For example, only one form of the number 11 is appropriate in this sentence.

Celia is *11.0, 11, 11:00* years old.

The appropriate form for age is the whole number 11.

Remember, use the form of the number—whole number, fraction, decimal, percent, digital time—that matches the situation.

Choose the appropriate form of the number.

1. He wears a size *7, $\frac{14}{2}$, 7.0* shoe.
2. Today's maximum temperature was *65′, 65°, 65% of 100°.*
3. Toby paid *\$8$\frac{99}{100}$, 899¢, \$8.99* for that new cassette tape.
4. Angie lives about *3 miles, 3.0 miles, 15,000 feet* from school.

Set B pages 8–9

In multiplication with decimals, you need to know where to put the decimal point in the product. To find 9.2 × 4.7, estimate first.

$$9.2 \times 4.7 \approx 9 \times 5 = 45$$

Then multiply and use your estimate to locate the decimal point.

9.2	1 decimal place
× 4.7	1 decimal place
644	Count and add
368	decimal places:
43.24	1 + 1 = 2 2 decimal places

The estimate is 45. So the answer is 43.24. Use a calculator to check:

9.2 [×] 4.7 [=] *43.24*

Remember, you can count and add the decimal place in the factors to find the decimal places in the product.

Estimate to place the decimal point in the product.

1. 13.6 × 2.1 = 2856
2. 28.17 × 3.8 = 107046
3. 7.4 × 0.37 = 2738

Use mental math to find the products.

4. 10 × 0.39
5. 1.57 × 100
6. 0.001 × 2.5
7. 25.68 × 1,000
8. 0.0017 × 10,000
9. 6.802 × 0.01

Set C pages 10–13

You can estimate 53 × 39 × 2 by using compatible numbers.

53 × 39 × 2 Think: 50 × 2 = 100
39 × 100 = 3,900

Or, you can estimate by rounding.

53 × 39 × 2 Think: 50 × 2 = 100
40 × 100 = 4,000

The actual product is 4,134. In this case, rounding gives a closer estimate.

Remember, choose an estimation strategy that is convenient for the problem.

1. Estimate by using front-end digits: 78.18 + 63.46 + 19.96.
2. Estimate by using clustering: 3.06 + 2.98 + 3.11.
3. Estimate by using the reference point of 100: 98 + 93.
4. Estimate by using rounding: 249.18 − 104.63.
5. Estimate by using compatible numbers: 4 × 67 × 26.

Set D pages 16–17

The properties of addition and multiplication can help you solve problems mentally. Add 79 + 16 + 21.

The associative and commutative properties let you add numbers in a convenient order.

Think: 79 = 70 + 9   21 = 20 + 1
9 + 1 = 10   70 + 20 = 90
10 + 90 = 100
100 + 16 = 116

The sum is 116.

Remember, look for special numbers —numbers whose sum is a multiple of 10— when you do mental math.

1. Subtract by using compensation: 602 − 450.
2. Multiply by breaking apart numbers and using the distributive property: 9 × 38.
3. Add by looking for special numbers: 37 + 22 + 93 + 18.

Find each answer mentally.

4. 54 × 9
5. 7,300 − 2,500
6. 11 + 55 + 45 + 39
7. 8 × 93

Set E pages 18–21

Multiplication facts (such as 7 × 3 = 21) and estimation can help you divide. Find 239 ÷ 7. Estimate: 210 ÷ 7 = 30.

```
   34R1
7)239
  21
   29
   28
    1
```

Think: 7 × 3 = 21; the first digit in the quotient is 3.
Think: 7 × 4 = 28; the next digit is 4.
Think: 1 is less than 7; 1 is the remainder.

The answer is 34 R1, or $34\frac{1}{7}$. The answer is close to the estimate of 30.

Remember, use basic facts and estimation to find each quotient. Name the multiplication fact you would use to find the first digit of the quotient.

1. 74 ÷ 3
2. 178 ÷ 5
3. 8)497
4. 6)451

Estimate the quotient for each exercise. Then divide.

5. Exercise 1
6. Exercise 2
7. Exercise 3
8. Exercise 4

Set F pages 24–25

To solve problems faster, choose the most efficient computation method before you begin.

First decide which exercises could be computed mentally.

Next select a calculator for exercises requiring more difficult or a greater number of computations.

Solve remaining problems using paper and pencil.

Remember, begin by choosing the most efficient computation method.

Tell which computation method—mental math, paper and pencil, or calculator—you would use to solve the problem. Then solve.

1. 563 + 297
2. 75 × 4
3. 38.1 + 29.2 − 16.4
4. 100 ÷ 0.1
5. 1,346 + 14
6. 913 − 845
7. 17 × 2.5 × 91.3 × 4
8. 18 + 20 + 22 + 56 + 44

Independent Study MORE PRACTICE

More Practice

Set A pages 4–5

Name the form of the number you would use in each situation. Give an example. Answers may vary.

1. flight departure at an airport

2. average annual snowfall

3. bus arrival at a bus station

4. Olympic ski-jumping record

5. estimated distance in miles

6. football player's uniform number

7. weight of a person

8. data from a circle graph

9. commuter train schedule

10. weight of an apple

11. length of a swimming pool

12. length of a ladder

13. average monthly rainfall

14. cost of quart of juice

Set B pages 8–9

Choose paper and pencil or calculator to multiply.

1. 6.57×28

2. 5.5×0.9

3. 2.29×0.66

4. 0.131×7.62

5. 401×3.5

6. 0.5×0.9

7. 72.4×8

8. 302.58×0.2

9. 34.2×16.5

10. 0.029×1.63

11. 816.03×42.5

12. 0.31×0.06

13. 4.06×2.6

14. 0.649×3.8

15. 4.085×0.27

16. 71.5×0.19

17. 7.008×4.5

18. 213.6×44

19. 6.01×7.6

20. $5{,}812 \times 3.53$

Set C pages 10–13

Estimate each answer. Name the method you used.

1. \$15.10 + \$14.95 + \$14.75

2. 379 + 6,108

3. 52 × 19

4. 73.17 − 4.55

5. 1,951 + 1,894

6. 862 − 253

7. 831.55 + 109 + 222.06

8. 0.706 − 0.099

9. 32% of \$5.98

10. 58 × 789

11. 2 × 18 × 49

12. 292 + 309 + 287 + 315

13. 9.87 + 10.2 + 9.92

14. 87,642 − 38,991

15. 24% of \$11.75

16. 4.6 + 5.2 + 4.9

17. 614 − 330

18. 80.2 − 16.8

19. 4 × 26 × 17

20. 281 + 5,210

21. 46% of \$21.50

Set D pages 16–17

Find each answer. Compute mentally.

1. 180 + 793 **2.** 595 + 641 **3.** 550 − 297

4. 9 × 48 **5.** 95 × 6 **6.** 6 × 73

7. 2 × 3 × 8 × 5 **8.** 25 + 64 + 11 + 64 **9.** 900 − 486

10. 654 + 549 **11.** 7 × 490 **12.** 617 − 209

13. 8 × 299 **14.** 72 + 36 + 28 + 14 **15.** 6 × 43

16. 34 + 16 + 76 + 24 **17.** 6 × 51 **18.** 531 − 119

19. 8 × 498 **20.** 270 + 685 **21.** 500 − 207

22. 5 × 46 **23.** 18 + 82 + 68 **24.** 750 − 192

Set E pages 18–21

Choose paper and pencil or calculator to divide.

1. 85 ÷ 7 **2.** 208 ÷ 6 **3.** 340 ÷ 3 **4.** 1,837 ÷ 5

5. $4\overline{)999}$ **6.** $2\overline{)7{,}315}$ **7.** $8\overline{)19{,}123}$ **8.** $5\overline{)42{,}003}$

9. $\frac{524}{8}$ **10.** $\frac{3{,}535}{2}$ **11.** $\frac{44{,}688}{5}$ **12.** $\frac{90{,}111}{4}$

13. 755 ÷ 4 **14.** 161 ÷ 7 **15.** 500 ÷ 8 **16.** 32,050 ÷ 4

17. $\frac{4{,}257}{9}$ **18.** $\frac{8{,}108}{5}$ **19.** $\frac{3{,}606}{4}$ **20.** $\frac{7{,}154}{8}$

21. 3,061 ÷ 8 **22.** 249 ÷ 5 **23.** 880 ÷ 7 **24.** 293 ÷ 4

25. $3\overline{)13{,}409}$ **26.** $9\overline{)654}$ **27.** $6\overline{)20{,}613}$ **28.** $4\overline{)8{,}902}$

29. $\frac{716}{5}$ **30.** $\frac{5{,}094}{8}$ **31.** $\frac{2{,}910}{5}$ **32.** $\frac{8{,}785}{3}$

Set F pages 24–25

Choose mental math, paper and pencil, or calculator to compute. Tell which method you chose.

1. 2,654.11 − 881.3 **2.** 83 + 6.12 **3.** 5,045 ÷ 5 **4.** 91 × 35

5. 6 × 28 × 904 **6.** 47 + 18 + 59 **7.** 8,351 ÷ 7 **8.** 654 + 549

9. 24 + 8.03 **10.** 249 × 108 **11.** 34 + 87 + 66 **12.** 14 × 82 × 73

13. 18,074 ÷ 6 **14.** 724 + 678 **15.** 6,010.07 − 919.6 **16.** 110 + 101.6

Enrichment

The Binary System

Binary numbers have widespread applications in computers and switching networks. A switch is either open or closed; these possibilities can be represented by using 0 and 1. This allows for an entire circuit to be represented by a binary number. Circuits can then be analyzed by operating on these numbers mathematically.

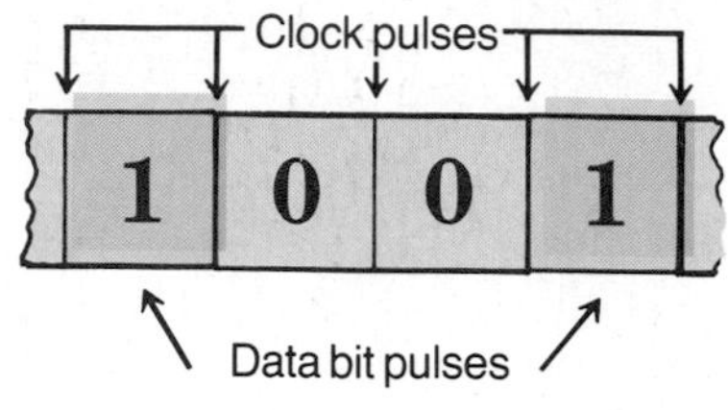

Frequency Modulation encoding (FM)

To encode data on disks, computers use pulses (1) and lack of pulses (0) as recording information.

Our decimal system of numeration is based on the number 10. Each place in a decimal number has a value 10 times the value of the place to its right. The *binary system* of numeration is based on the number 2. Each place in a binary number has a value 2 times the value of the place to its right.

Use subscripts to distinguish binary numbers from decimal numbers.

$11{,}010_2$ = 1 sixteen + 1 eight + 0 fours + 1 two + 0 ones = 26_{10}

Use the following method to write 75_{10} in binary notation.

	64	32	16	8	4	2	1
75 contains one 64, with 11 left over.	1	0	0				
11 contains one 8, with 3 left over.	1	0	0	1	0		
3 contains one 2, with 1 left over.	1	0	0	1	0	1	1

$75_{10} = 1{,}001{,}011_2$

1. What are the values of the next 3 places to the left of the sixteens place in a binary number?

Find the value of each number in decimal notation.

2. 101_2 **3.** $11{,}111_2$ **4.** $100{,}001_2$ **5.** $10{,}101{,}010_2$ **6.** 1_2

7. $10{,}001_2$ **8.** $1{,}000{,}101_2$ **9.** $1{,}011{,}011_2$ **10.** $10{,}010_2$ **11.** $1{,}010{,}000_2$

Write in binary notation.

12. 6_{10} **13.** 15_{10} **14.** 64_{10} **15.** 103_{10} **16.** 207_{10}

17. 23_{10} **18.** 32_{10} **19.** 42_{10} **20.** 54_{10} **21.** 12_{10}

Chapter 1 Review/Test

1. What does the number 0.73 mean?

2. Choose the best form of the numbers to report a baseball score.

a. Lions 8.00; Cougars 3.00
b. Lions $\frac{16}{2}$; Cougars $\frac{6}{3}$
c. Lions 8; Cougars 3

Multiply.

3. $\begin{array}{r} 60 \\ \times\ 0.4 \\ \hline \end{array}$

4. 0.9×0.7

5. Chris bought 1.08 pounds of fish for dinner at $4.49 per pound. How much did he spend?

Estimate each answer.

6. 5,983 + 2,198 + 4,427

7. 687 + 704 + 693

8. Jack wants to rent a video for $3.95 and buy 2 pounds of popcorn at $0.89 a pound. He has $6.00. Estimate to decide if he has enough money.

Find each answer. Compute mentally.

9. 5×43

10. $286 - 197$

11. $(108 \times 3) + (92 \times 3)$

12. Which is *not* an answer to $5\overline{)23}$?

a. 4 R3
b. 4.3333333
c. $4\frac{3}{5}$

13. Find the average of 27, 29, and 37.

14. Which problem would be easiest to solve with mental computation?

a. 41×99
b. 43×94
c. 47×91

15. Tell which operation to use. Then solve the problem.

Phil had a roll of wire 450 feet long. He used 125 feet of the wire. How much wire does he have left?

The graph shows the total number of points scored by Hill School's basketball team in the years 1986 to 1990. Use it for Exercises 16 and 17.

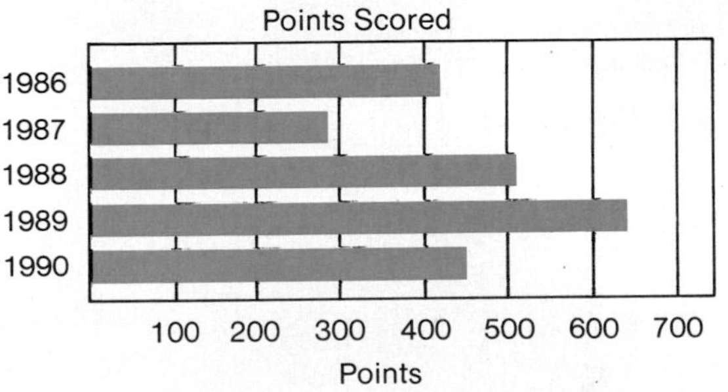

16. About how many more points did the team score in its highest scoring year than in its lowest scoring year?

17. Choose the best estimate of the average number of points scored by the team per year.

a. 400 **b.** 460 **c.** 560

18. **Write About Math** Lynn estimates the answer for 4,647 + 3,145 in two different ways and gets 7,700 and 7,800. Which is the better estimate? Explain how you can tell which is better without computing the actual answer.

Tables, Expressions, and Equations

2

Did You Know: The general rule for determining the angle of window glazing in greenhouses designed for winter use is to add 15 degrees (15°) to the latitude of the location. The latitude of your location is its distance north of the equator measured in degrees.

Estimate
Latitudes in the continental United States range from about 25° N in the Florida Keys to 49° N on the Canadian border. Estimate the latitude of your area.

Gather Data
Find the latitude of your area and 5 other cities in the United States.

Analyze and Report
Determine the angle of window glazing in greenhouses in your area and in each of the other cities.

ALGEBRA

Using Tables

Build Understanding

ACTIVITY

A. "Setting" the Table

Groups: With a partner

A group of hikers at Loon Lake made a table to show the distance they planned to hike for the first 2 days of a 4-day hike.

Day	Total miles from starting point
1	10
2	20
3	
4	

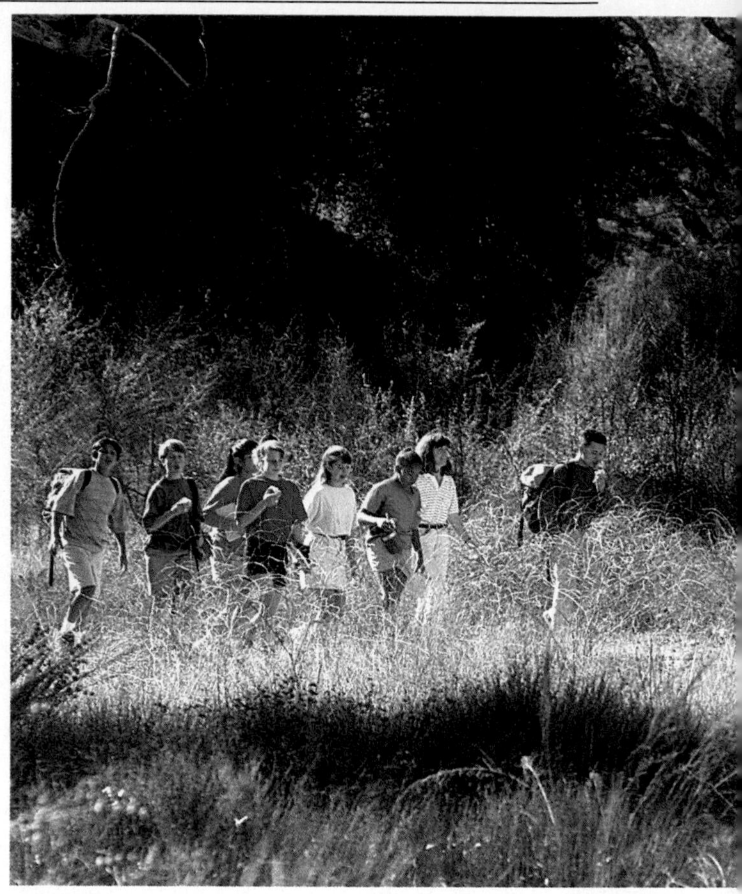

a. Continue the table for the next 2 days, assuming the hikers will continue at the same rate.

b. About how long will it take them to hike 30 miles?

c. About how long will it take them to hike 35 miles?

B. The camp cook at Loon Lake prepares 8 sandwiches for each hiker on a 4-day hike. How many sandwiches would the cook need to prepare for 5 hikers? 6 hikers?

Number of hikers	1	2	3	4	5	6
Number of sandwiches	8	16	24	32	40	48

You can tell from the table that the cook would need to prepare 40 sandwiches for 5 hikers and 48 sandwiches for 6 hikers.

C. Two families rented mountain bikes and rode 24 miles to a campground at Possum Peak. The Clarks left at 9:00 A.M. and traveled 6 miles per hour for 2 hours. After a 1-hour rest, they continued to travel 6 miles per hour until they reached the campground. The Mitzes left at 10:00 A.M. and traveled 8 miles per hour until they arrived at Possum Peak.

When did each family arrive at the campground?

You can make a table showing the distance covered by each family at the end of every hour.

You can see from the table that the Clarks covered the 24 miles to the campground by the end of the fifth hour, or by 2:00 P.M. The Mitzes covered the 24 miles to the campground by the end of the fourth hour, or by 1:00 P.M.

	Miles covered	
Hour	Clarks	Mitzes
0	0	0
1	6	0
2	12	8
3	12	16
4	18	24
5	24	24

Write About Math Describe the relationship between the number of hikers and the number of sandwiches in Example B.

Check Understanding

For another example, see Set A, pages 66–67.

This table shows the distance a group of hikers at Loon Lake planned to hike by the end of each day of a 5-day hike.

Day	Miles hiked
1	10
2	20
3	30
4	40
5	50

1. About how long did the hikers think it would take to hike 30 miles?

2. About how long did the hikers think it would take to hike 45 miles?

3. How many miles did the hikers plan to hike each day?

4. If the hikers continued to cover the same distance each day, how many miles would they have hiked at the end of the seventh day?

Practice

For More Practice, see Set A, pages 68–69.

Complete each table.

Hikers	Canteens
1	1
2	2
3	3
4	**5.**
6.	5
7.	6
7	**8.**

Hikers	Boots
0	0
1	2
2	4
3	**9.**
4	**10.**
11.	10
12.	12
7	**13.**

People	Ants
0	0
1	200
2	400
3	**14.**
15.	800
16.	1,000
6	**17.**
18.	1,400

People	Tents
3	1
6	2
9	3
19.	4
15	**20.**
18	**21.**
22.	7

Distance canoeing	9	10	13	40	**23.**
Distance to campsite	20	21	24	**24.**	39

Children	5	6	7	**25.**	**26.**	10	20
Adults	2	3	**27.**	5	6	**28.**	**29.**

Campers	14	35	42	**30.**	**31.**	70	91
Campfires	2	5	**32.**	7	9	**33.**	**34.**

Number of people in family	1	2	3	4	5	**35.**	**36.**
Entrance + 1-week camping fee	25	45	65	**37.**	**38.**	145	205

39. Critical Thinking How many campfires do you think would be needed for 20 campers? Explain.

Problem Solving

The Riveras backpacked 10 miles to Hollow Point, a remote campground. They left at 9:00 A.M. and hiked at the rate of 2 miles per hour. They stopped at the end of 2 hours for a 1-hour break. The Frost family also hiked the 10 miles to Hollow Point. Leaving at 10:00 A.M., they were able to travel at the rate of $2\frac{1}{2}$ miles per hour. After two hours of hiking, they rested for an hour and then continued their pace.

TIPS FOR PROBLEM SOLVERS
Compare problems to help you relate new problems to ones you've solved before.

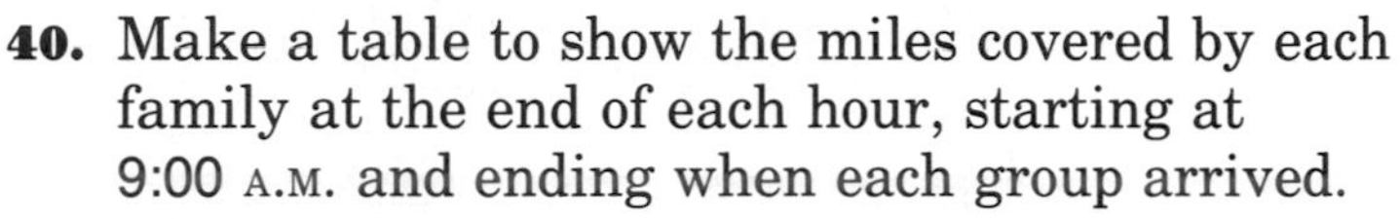

40. Make a table to show the miles covered by each family at the end of each hour, starting at 9:00 A.M. and ending when each group arrived.

41. At what time were the Riveras halfway to the campground?

42. Did the Riveras or the Frosts arrive at Hollow Point first? How much earlier did they arrive?

43. At 2:15 P.M., a group of backpackers is 15 miles from the camp. They can hike back at 3 miles per hour, but need an hour to pack. They do not want to be on the trail after 8:00 P.M. Make a table to help decide whether or not they should wait until morning to return.

The graph at the right shows the elevation above base camp for a group of campers on a 10-day outing.

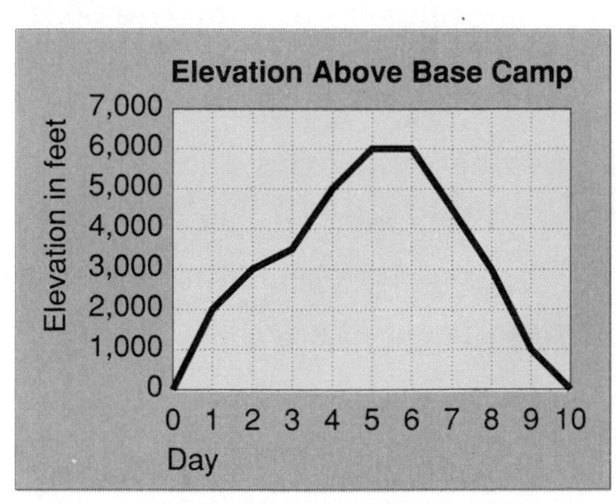

44. How high above base camp was the group after the first day?

45. What was the highest elevation reached by the campers?

46. On which days did they end the day's hike at elevation 3,000 ft above base camp?

Skills Review

Review, page 566

Add or subtract.

1. 0.72 + 0.91

2. 6.3 + 0.713

3. 5.32 − 2.83

4. 41.73 + 4.123

5. 8.01 + 64.2

6. 3.116 + 1.711

7. 53.98 − 5.398

8. 1,970.9 + 129.4

9. 1,813.38 − 42.584

ALGEBRA

Evaluating Expressions: One Operation

Build Understanding

A. Mr. Steele is the manager of the Loon Lake Campground. He uses a computer spreadsheet to keep a record of how much campers owe him. The cost is \$7 per night for each campsite.

The total cost in column C can be represented by the ***expression*** $7 \times n$, or $7n$, where n is a ***variable*** standing for the number of nights.

A variable is a letter or symbol that stands for a number. An expression uses numbers, variables, and operation symbols to represent a value. The value of an expression changes as the value of the variable changes.

Campground		
A	B	C
Campsite	Nights	Cost
1	2	14
2	5	35
3	1	7
4	6	42

B. If the campers at campsite 36 stay for 6 nights, what amount will the computer calculate in column C?

Evaluate the expression $7n$, using 6 as the value of the variable n.

$7n$ Cost per night × number of nights

7(6) Substitute 6 for n.

42 Multiply.

The computer prints 42 as the campers' cost for 6 nights.

C. Evaluate $c - 1.25$ when c is 17.5.

$c - 1.25$

17.5 − 1.25 Substitute 17.5 for c.

16.25 Subtract.

■ **Talk About Math** If Mr. Steele raises the cost per night for each campsite, would this change the value in column B of the spreadsheet? in column C? Explain your answer.

Check Understanding

For another example, see Set B, pages 66–67.

Copy and complete the table to evaluate the expression $50 - m$ for the indicated values of the variable m.

Number of miles hiked, m	10	2.5	25	40	5	32	12.5
Miles remaining, $50 - m$	40	47.5	**1.**	**2.**	**3.**	**4.**	**5.**

Practice

For More Practice, see Set B, pages 68–69.

Copy and complete each table for Exercises 6–25.

d	1	2	4	5	10	**10.**
$1 + d$	2	**6.**	**7.**	**8.**	**9.**	15

k	0	2	4	5	10	**15.**
$4k$	0	**11.**	**12.**	**13.**	**14.**	32

t	10	11	12	15	20	**20.**
$t - 4$	6	**16.**	**17.**	**18.**	**19.**	28

w	0	2	4	8	10	**25.**
$w \div 2$	0	**21.**	**22.**	**23.**	**24.**	14

Evaluate each expression when $y = 4$.

26. $3y$ **27.** $6 + y$ **28.** $y + 25$ **29.** $19 - y$ **30.** $y \div 5$

Evaluate each expression when $r = 25$.

31. $3r$ **32.** $r + 17$ **33.** $92 - r$ **34.** $\frac{175}{r}$ **35.** $12r$

Evaluate each expression when $z = \frac{1}{3}$.

36. $2z$ **37.** $z + \frac{2}{3}$ **38.** $z \div 3$ **39.** $3 + z$ **40.** $4 \div z$

Number Sense Answer each question.

41. If y is greater than 1, is $2y$ greater than, less than, or equal to 2?

42. If $2c$ is less than 10, can c be greater than 2?

43. **Calculator** Evaluate $\frac{n}{9}$ when n is 1, 2, 3, 4, and 5. Then guess the answer for $n = 6$. Check your guess. Use the same procedure for $\frac{n}{11}$.

Problem Solving

Golden Age Campers (over 60 years of age) pay only $5 per night, or $5n$. Find the cost for Golden Agers who camp the given number of nights.

44. 4 nights **45.** 9 nights **46.** 14 nights

47. If the Golden Agers paid $60 to camp, how many nights did they camp?

48. One group of Golden Agers rented a stove for $15 and camped 7 nights. How much did they pay in total?

Critical Thinking Answer each question.

49. When does $3x + 4y$ have the same value as $7x$?

50. When does $2x$ have the same value as $4y$?

ALGEBRA

Writing Expressions: One Operation

Build Understanding

On August 20, 1977, the *Voyager 2* spacecraft was launched from Cape Canaveral to explore the solar system.

A. The chart shows the names of the planets on *Voyager's* course, the date of *Voyager's* closest encounter with each planet, and the distance of each planet from the sun.

Planet	Date of encounter	Distance from the sun (in millions of miles)
Earth	8/20/77	93
Jupiter	7/9/79	484
Saturn	8/25/81	887
Uranus	1/24/86	1,784
Neptune	8/24/89	2,795

Write an expression for the distance in millions of miles *Voyager* had traveled as it passed each planet.

Distance of planet from sun → $d - 93$ ← Distance of Earth from sun

Since *Voyager 2* started at Earth, the total distance *Voyager* traveled as it passed each planet is 93 million miles less than the planet's distance from the sun.

B. During the launch and ascent of a space shuttle, about 59,000 gallons of fuel are burned per minute. Write an expression for the gallons of fuel burned by a space shuttle during launch and ascent.

Gallons burned in 1 minute → $59{,}000n$ ← Minutes

C. Use the table to write an expression for finding the area of an object with a length of k.

Length	Area
2	1
4	2
6	3
8	4

Each area is half the length, so the expression is $\frac{k}{2}$.

Write About Math The phrase *45 more than q* can be represented by the expression $q + 45$. Write two other phrases that could be represented by $q + 45$.

Check Understanding

For another example, see Set C, pages 66–67.

Write an expression for each phrase.

1. 16 less than w

2. c divided by 12

3. q more than 10

Practice

For More Practice, see Set C, pages 68–69.

Write an expression for each phrase.

4. 17 added to x **5.** y subtracted from 4 **6.** 30 divided by w

7. 7 more than u **8.** b times 2.8 **9.** 14 less than e

10. Sum of 40 and a **11.** Product of r and 13.5 **12.** p divided by 21

Use the information in each box to write the expression.

13. After *Voyager 2* passed Neptune, it kept going at 58,000 miles per hour.

An expression for the spacecraft's distance from Neptune x hours after passing it

14. An airplane has a cruising speed of about 580 miles per hour.

An expression for the distance traveled by the plane after t hours of flight

Use each table to write an expression for the given data.

15. Charge for x days

Days	Charge (in dollars)
1	5
2	6
3	7
4	8

16. Distance at speed b

Speed	Distance
1	4
2	8
3	12
4	16

17. Dinners for n days

Days	Dinners
1	0
2	1
3	2
4	3

Problem Solving

All the drinking water for a space shuttle is produced as a by-product of its energy system. People consume about 2 quarts of water per day.

18. Write an expression for the amount of water consumed by 1 astronaut on a flight d days long.

19. Write an expression for the amount of water consumed by 5 astronauts on a flight a days long.

Critical Thinking Write two different phrases that could be represented by each expression.

20. $h + 19$ **21.** $m - 8$ **22.** $560x$ **23.** $16r$

24. $\frac{13}{a}$ **25.** $25 - k$ **26.** $64 + y$ **27.** $\frac{36}{t}$

Solving Addition and Subtraction Equations

Build Understanding

After takeoff, a pilot tells the passengers whether the flight will be arriving on time or not. The scheduled time of arrival often needs to be revised because of bad weather or heavy air traffic.

A. On a typical airplane flight, about 30 minutes of the time scheduled for the flight is "ground time." The rest of the time is "air time." Find the air time of a flight from Atlanta to Boston if the flight is scheduled for 136 minutes.

To solve an equation, add or subtract the same number from both sides of the equation.

To find the air time for this flight, write the equation *air time* + *ground time* = *total time*.

$a + g = t$	Name the variables.
$a + 30 = 136$	Substitute 30 for the ground time and 136 for the total time.
$a + 30 - 30 = 136 - 30$	Because 30 has been added to a, subtract 30 from each side to find a.
$a = 106$	
$106 + 30 \stackrel{?}{=} 136$	Check your answer.
$136 = 136$	

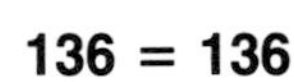

The air time for the flight from Atlanta to Boston is 106 minutes.

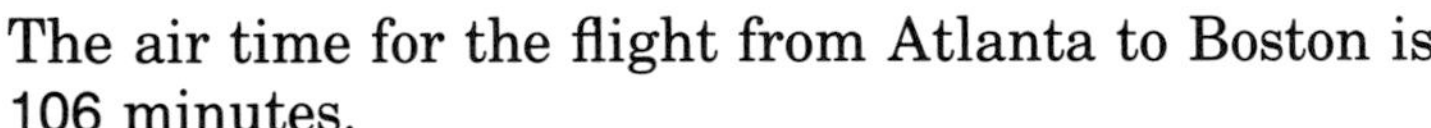

B. Solve $g - 13 = 55$.

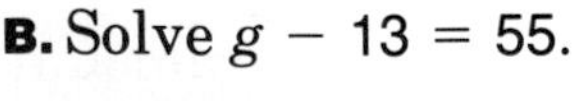

$g - 13 = 55$	13 has been subtracted from g.
$g - 13 + 13 = 55 + 13$	To find g, add 13 to each side.
$g = 68$	

C. Solve $5.1 = 2.3 + m$

$5.1 = 2.3 + m$	2.3 has been added to m.
$5.1 - 2.3 = 2.3 + m - 2.3$	To find m, subtract 2.3 from both sides.
$2.8 = m$	

■ **Talk About Math** How is adding or subtracting the same number from both sides of an equation like placing or removing the same weight from both sides of a balance scale?

Check Understanding

For another example, see Set D, pages 66–67.

Complete each statement with *added to* or *subtracted from*.

1. To solve $k + 245 = 1{,}045$, 245 is $\underline{\quad ? \quad}$ each side of the equation.

2. To solve $0.4 = y - 5.4$, 5.4 is $\underline{\quad ? \quad}$ each side of the equation.

Fill in the missing numbers to solve each equation.

3.
$$x + 20 = 100$$
$$x + 20 - \blacksquare = 100 - \blacksquare$$
$$x = \blacksquare$$

4.
$$135 = z - 86$$
$$135 + \blacksquare = z - 86 + \blacksquare$$
$$\blacksquare = z$$

Practice

For More Practice, see Set D, pages 68–69.

Tell whether you would use mental math or paper and pencil. Then solve each equation. **Remember** to look at the operation sign.

5. $a - 12 = 60$ **6.** $b + 19 = 57$ **7.** $d + 3 = 1{,}002$ **8.** $c - 145 = 987$

9. $8 + e = 29$ **10.** $23 = f - 11$ **11.** $54 = 19 + g$ **12.** $n + 2.2 = 5.7$

13. $r - 13 = 18$ **14.** $h + 33 = 41$ **15.** $19 = b - 7$ **16.** $22 = k + 12$

17. $q - 3 = 57$ **18.** $b + 32 = 57$ **19.** $81 = y - 32$ **20.** $99 = h - 27$

21. $56 = 8 + a$ **22.** $k - 11 = 7$ **23.** $x + 2.4 = 9$ **24.** $w - 3.2 = 2.3$

25. $7.3 = y + 2.5$ **26.** $p - 2.4 = 15.6$ **27.** $5.1 + c = 34.1$ **28.** $7.3 = d - 15.8$

29. $32.1 = x - 4.5$ **30.** $9 = k - 4.6$ **31.** $3.9 = 1.01 + m$ **32.** $2.4 = l - 8.6$

33. $2.9 + v = 9.7$ **34.** $87 - 19 = h - 4$ **35.** $99 - p = 34$ **36.** $2 = 2.4 - z$

Problem Solving

Write and solve an equation. Refer to Example A for Problems 37–40.

37. A flight from Dallas to Houston is scheduled for 73 minutes. What is the actual air time of the flight?

38. **Estimation** Estimate the air time of a flight leaving Buffalo at 8:58 A.M. and arriving in Boston at 10:40 A.M.

39. An airplane with a seating capacity of 212 was carrying 150 passengers from Salt Lake City to Denver. How many empty seats were there?

40. Of 258 passengers, 123 ordered chicken and 107 ordered pasta. The rest requested special meals. How many special meals were served?

ALGEBRA

Solving Multiplication and Division Equations

Build Understanding

A. Doris and Brian are driving from San Francisco to Los Angeles. The distance between the cities is 378 miles. What must their average driving speed be to complete the trip in 7 hours?

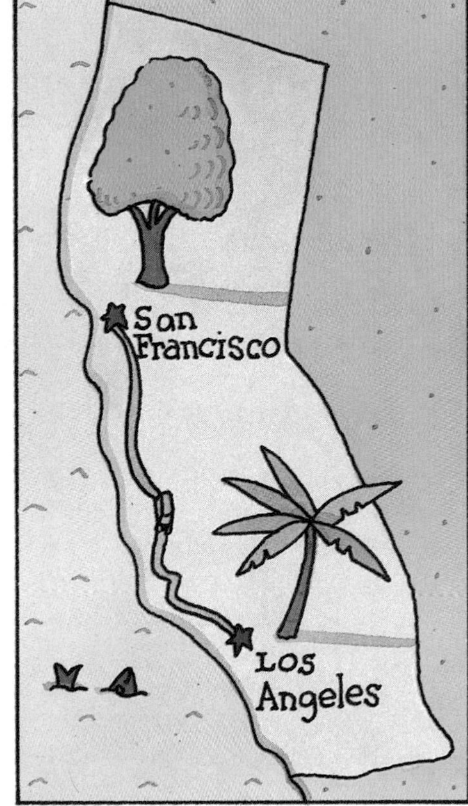

To solve an equation, you can multiply or divide both sides by the same nonzero number.

To find the average driving speed, use the equation *speed* × *time* = *distance.*

$rt = d$	Name the variables.
$7r = 378$	Substitute 7 for the time and 378 for the distance.
$\frac{7r}{7} = \frac{378}{7}$	Because r has been multiplied by 7, divide both sides by 7 to find r.
$r = 54$	
$(54)\,7 \stackrel{?}{=} 378$	Check your answer.
$378 = 378$	

Doris and Brian must average 54 miles per hour to complete the trip in 7 hours.

B. Solve $\frac{f}{9} = 12$.

$\frac{f}{9} = 12$	f has been divided by 9.
$9 \times \frac{f}{9} = 12 \times 9$	To find f, multiply both sides of the equation by 9.
$f = 108$	
$\frac{108}{9} = 12$	Check.

■ **Talk About Math** Can you always multiply to solve division equations and divide to solve multiplication equations? Explain.

Check Understanding

For another example, see Set E, pages 66–67.

Answer each question.

1. By what number would you divide to solve the equation $6y = 30$?
2. By what number would you multiply to solve the equation $24 = \frac{z}{2}$?

Practice

For More Practice, see Set E, pages 68–69.

Tell if you would use mental math or paper and pencil. Then solve each equation.

3. $2n = 20$ **4.** $\frac{b}{6} = 16$ **5.** $132 = \frac{k}{2}$ **6.** $23w = 230$

7. $5a = 50$ **8.** $\frac{y}{23} = 5$ **9.** $2x = 40$ **10.** $\frac{z}{78} = 5$

11. $55r = 5{,}500$ **12.** $\frac{t}{47} = 6$ **13.** $\frac{x}{6 + 4} = 8$ **14.** $9y = 8(3)$

Mixed Practice Solve each equation.

15. $x - 12 = 20$ **16.** $2c = 14$ **17.** $y + 15 = 17$ **18.** $9m = 81$

19. $\frac{x}{20} = 40$ **20.** $24 + d = 80$ **21.** $w - 44 = 7$ **22.** $\frac{a}{7} = 30$

Problem Solving

Write and solve an equation to find the time needed to drive between the two cities at an average speed of 50 miles per hour.

23. Birmingham and Memphis

24. Atlanta and Nashville

	Atlanta, GA	Birmingham, AL	Memphis, TN	Nashville, TN
Atlanta, GA	•	148	414	250
Birmingham, AL	148	•	230	190
Memphis, TN	414	230	•	206
Nashville, TN	250	190	206	•

Solve.

25. **Critical Thinking** Jackson, Tennessee, is 80 miles from Memphis on the road from Memphis to Nashville. Write and solve an equation to find the distance from Jackson to Nashville.

Midchapter Checkup

The table shows the distances Inés plans to cover on a 6-day bike trip.

Number of days	1	2	3	4	5	6
Total number of miles	25	50	75	100	125	150

1. On what day will Inés have traveled 95 miles?

2. Write an expression for the distance traveled by Inés in n days.

Evaluate the expression $z + 18$ for the following values.

3. $z = 8$ **4.** $z = 15$

Solve each equation.

5. $\frac{n}{15} = 3$ **6.** $6z = 42$

Problem-Solving Workshop

Real-Life Decision Making

You plan to take a little over 200 outdoor photos for a special project. You left your regular camera at home. You need to decide whether to buy another regular camera or disposable cameras.

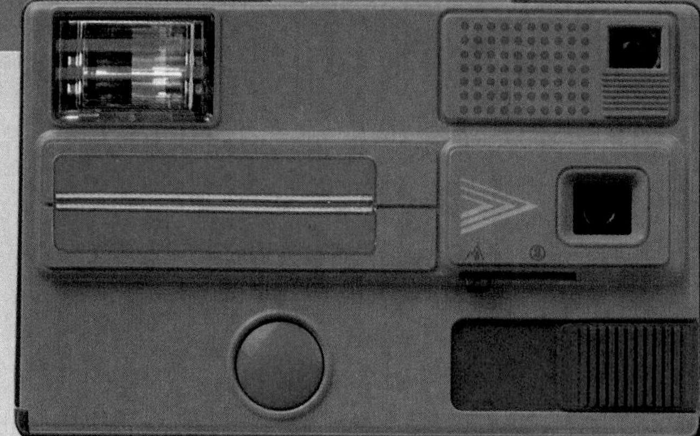

$15.00

$4.75

$3.89

$5.95

With a disposable camera you take 24 photos and hand the camera to the film processor. The processor removes the film and throws the camera away. To take more photos you need to buy another camera.

1. Decide how many rolls of 24 exposures and how many rolls of 36 exposures you will buy.

2. What would the film plus the regular camera cost?

3. What will the disposable cameras cost?

4. What will your total film processing expenses be for a regular camera? for disposable cameras?

5. Decide whether you will buy the disposable cameras or a regular camera.

Film Processing Costs
24 prints for $4.75
36 prints for $5.45

Number-Sense Project

Look back at pages 36-37.

The vertical distance between two lines of latitude 1° apart is about 70 miles. In each exercise, the two cities are almost directly north and south of each other. Use their latitudes to estimate the air distance between them.

1. Chicago (41.5° N) and Mobile (30.4° N)

2. Spokane (47.4° N) and San Diego (32.4° N)

3. Toronto (43.4° N) and Miami (25.5° N)

4. Kansas City (39.0° N) and Houston (29.4° N)

5. Why must the cities be directly north and south of each other to use this method to find distances?

Math-at-Home Activity

Use the chart below to find the value of each person's name in your family. (For example, ERIC has a value of 73¢ (22 + 9 + 18 + 24.) Note which person has the most valuable name.

Z	Y	X	W	V	U	T
1¢	2¢	3¢	4¢	5¢	6¢	7¢

S	R	Q	P	O	N	M
8¢	9¢	10¢	11¢	12¢	13¢	14¢

L	K	J	I	H	G	F
15¢	16¢	17¢	18¢	19¢	20¢	21¢

E	D	C	B	A
22¢	23¢	24¢	25¢	26¢

Explore with a Computer

Use the *Spreadsheet Workshop Project* for this activity.

Mr. MacKenzie took his wife and three teenage children to the movies on bargain night. Tickets were half price of the regular night admission. For a snack they bought two large popcorns at $2.50 each. They spent a total of $21.25 for the evening.

1. At the computer, study the equation set up in the spreadsheet. Change the equation to find how much money the MacKenzies paid per person to see the movie. What is the full price admission?

2. The Valentino family of 5 went to a different theater. They spent $7.50 on snacks and still only spent $21.25 for the evening. What was the price of a ticket at this theater?

ALGEBRA

Write an Equation

Understand
QUESTION
FACTS
KEY IDEA

Plan and Solve
STRATEGY
ANSWER

Look Back
SENSIBLE ANSWER
ALTERNATE APPROACH

Build Understanding

On many word processors you can select different sizes of type. The *point size* measures the height of a line needed to accommodate the letters. There are 72 points in 1 inch.

What is the largest type that can be used so that 28 characters will fit in 4 inches?

Understand QUESTION What is the largest type size that can be used?

FACTS You know the number of characters per inch for each type size; 28 characters must fit in 4 inches.

KEY IDEA The number of characters is the number of inches times the number of characters per inch.

Plan and Solve STRATEGY Write an equation that describes the key idea and solve it.

Total number of characters		Number of inches		Characters per inch
28	=	4	×	c

$$28 = 4c$$

$$\frac{28}{4} = \frac{4c}{4} \quad \text{Divide both sides by 4.}$$

$$7 = c$$

ANSWER Since 24-point type will allow only 6 characters per inch, it is too large. Eighteen point type, which allows 8 characters per inch, is the largest type that can be used.

Look Back SENSIBLE ANSWER Eighteen-point type allows 8 × 4 = 32 characters in 4 inches. Twenty-four point type would allow only 6 × 4 = 24 characters. So, the answer, 18-point type, is sensible.

10 point
Math is fun!
xxxxxxxxxxxxx
(13 characters per inch)

12 point
Math is fun!
xxxxxxxxxxx
(11 characters per inch)

14 point
Math is fun!
xxxxxxxxx
(9 characters per inch)

18 point
Math is fun!
xxxxxxxx
(8 characters per inch)

24 point
Math is fun!
xxxxxx
(6 characters per inch)

Different letters have different widths. The average number of *characters* per inch is given for each point size. Characters are letters, numbers, or spaces.

Talk About Math Would the letters of your first name fit in 1 inch of 24-point type? Explain your answer.

Check Understanding

An 11.5-inch-long page has a total of 3.5 inches of empty space allowed for top and bottom margins. How many inches are left for text?

1. What is the question?
2. What facts are given?
3. Choose a letter to represent the amount of empty space.
4. Write an equation.
5. Solve the equation.
6. Answer the question.
7. Marie got an answer of 15 inches. How do you think she got it?
8. Is Marie's answer sensible? Explain.

Practice

Write an equation that fits the given information about a number of pages, *p*. Then solve the equation.

9. If there were 12 more pages, there would be 400 pages.
10. If there were 17 fewer pages, there would be 400 pages.
11. Half the number of pages is 22.
12. Three times as many pages would be 237 pages.

Choose a ______ Strategy

Sum Savings! Sharon saves her nickels, dimes, and quarters. When she has $10, she deposits the money in her savings account. When she made her last deposit, she noticed that the number of nickels, the number of dimes, and the number of quarters were all the same.

13. How many of each coin did she have?

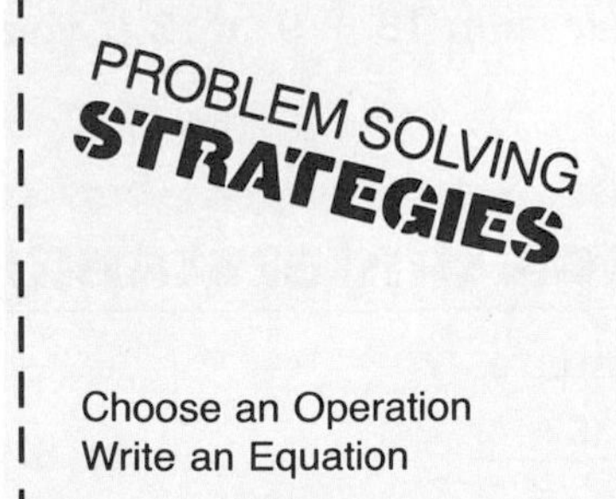

ALGEBRA

Order of Operations

Build Understanding

John Sullivan is a general building contractor. He schedules the order of the work performed by carpenters, plumbers, electricians, and others.

How would the results differ if the painters did their work before the plumbers?
Why is the order in which the jobs are performed important?

A. When there is more than one operation in an expression, the order in which you do the operations is important.

Evaluate $18 + 9 \times 13$.

Do you multiply the sum of 18 and 9 by 13, or do you add 18 to the product of 9 and 13? Is the answer 351 or 135?

To avoid any confusion, mathematicians have agreed on a ***standard order of operations***.

Following the steps, you can see that $18 + 9 \times 13 = 135$.

If there are no parentheses in the expression:

- First multiply and divide in order from left to right. Then add and subtract in order from left to right.

When parentheses and/or division bars are involved in an expression:

- First do all operations within the parentheses.
- Then do all operations above and below the division bars using standard order.
- Finally do all remaining operations using standard order.

B. Evaluate $(8 + 9) \times (7 - 2)$.

$(8 + 9) \times (7 - 2)$ First do all operations within parentheses.

$17 \times 5 = 85$

C. Evaluate $\frac{6 + 3 \times 9}{3}$.

$\frac{6 + 3 \times 9}{3}$ First do all operations above the division bar.

$\frac{6 + 27}{3} = \frac{33}{3} = 11$

■ **Write About Math** How could you write the expression $18 + 9 \times 13$ if you wanted to add first?

Check Understanding

For another example, see Set F, pages 66–67.

Evaluate.

1. $\frac{(8 + 4)}{2}$
2. $8 + \left(\frac{4}{2}\right)$
3. $8 + \frac{4}{2}$
4. $7 + 3 \times 4 - 1$
5. $5 \times 3 + 8 \times 8$
6. $\frac{12}{2} \times 3$
7. $\frac{8 \times 4 + 6}{2}$
8. $\frac{8 \times (4 + 6)}{2}$

Practice

For More Practice, see Set F, pages 68–69.

Evaluate each expression. **Remember** to use the standard order of operations.

9. $(12 - 6) \div 2$ **10.** $12 - (6 \div 2)$ **11.** $5 + 8 \times 7 + 1$ **12.** $4 \times 8 - 2 \times 3$

13. $4 \times (8 - 2) \times 3$ **14.** $\frac{6}{2} + 1$ **15.** $\frac{4 \times 8}{4} - \frac{2 \times 4}{2}$ **16.** $(3.3 - 1.2) \times 1.5$

17. $3.3 - 1.2 \times 1.5$ **18.** $\frac{13 + 8 \times 4}{3 + 2}$ **19.** $\frac{66 + 12}{11 + 2}$ **20.** $\frac{4(2 + 6)}{2(9 - 5)}$

21. $\frac{11 \times 7 + 13}{29 - 4}$ **22.** $75 \div 15 + 6 \times 4$ **23.** $\frac{2 + 5 \times 16 - 12}{2 \times 8 - 2}$ **24.** $\frac{6 \times 4}{4 - 2} + \frac{32 \div 4}{2}$

Mental Math Use mental math to evaluate Exercises 25–36.

25. $7 + 3 \times 0$ **26.** $(7 - 6) \times 896$ **27.** $\frac{17 + 1}{6 \times 3}$ **28.** $(17 - 17) \times 89$

29. $\frac{12 - 12}{164}$ **30.** $280 \times (9 - 8)$ **31.** $\frac{12 + 9}{4 + 3}$ **32.** $26 + 0 \times 14$

33. $\frac{5(7 + 3)}{2(8 - 3)}$ **34.** $88 \div (2 \times 3 + 2)$ **35.** $\frac{23 + 3 \times 4}{9 - 4}$ **36.** $\frac{24 - 3 \times (5 + 3)}{111 + 7 \times 2}$

37. **Calculator** Use this key sequence to compute Exercise 19.

11 [+] 2 [=] [M+] 66 [+] 12 [=] [÷] [MRC] [=]

Write a key sequence to compute Exercise 20.

Problem Solving

Critical Thinking Use the numbers 3, 4, 5, and 6 once in each exercise to make a true statement.

38. $\square + \square(\square - \square) = 17$ **39.** $\frac{\square \times \square}{\square} + \square = 7$

Critical Thinking Insert parentheses to make each statement true. You may need more than one set of parentheses.

40. $5.6 - 4.1 \times 2.8 + 1.2 = 6$

41. $10 \times 15 + 20 \times 2 = 550$

42. $40 - 15 \times 3 + 25 = 100$

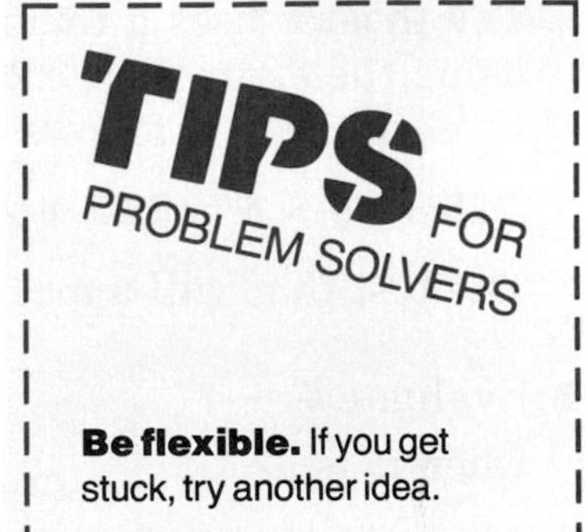

TIPS FOR PROBLEM SOLVERS
Be flexible. If you get stuck, try another idea.

ALGEBRA

Evaluating Expressions: Multiple Operations

Build Understanding

These Scottish dancers, dressed in traditional costume, are shown dancing during a day of Highland games in Chicago.

A. This season the Festival Theater will present four different concerts featuring music and dance groups from the Caribbean, Scotland, India, and France. A season subscription costs \$48. A \$2.25 service charge is added to each order, regardless of the number of subscriptions. The table shows three orders. Column G gives the number of subscriptions ordered and column H gives the total cost of each order.

Season Subscription Sales

F	G	H
Last Name	Subscriptions	Cost
Robinson	1	\$50.25
Chang	2	\$98.25
Washington	3	\$146.25
James	2	\$98.25

What total cost will appear in column H when 5 is entered in Column G?

The theater uses a computer to calculate column H by using the expression $2.25 + 48g$ where g is the number of subscriptions. It follows the standard order of operations.

$$2.25 + 48 \times 5 = 2.25 + 240 = 242.25$$

The cost that will appear in column H is \$242.25.

B. Evaluate $\frac{w}{2} - 11$ when w is 52.

$\frac{w}{2} - 11$ Substitute 52 for w.

$\frac{52}{2} - 11 = 26 - 11$

$= 15$

C. Evaluate $3z + 5$ for the given values of z.

z	$3z + 5$
1	$3 \times 1 + 5 = 3 + 5 = 8$
2	$3 \times 2 + 5 = 6 + 5 = 11$
3	$3 \times 3 + 5 = 9 + 5 = 14$

■ **Talk About Math** In Example C, how much does $3z + 5$ change each time z changes by 1?

Check Understanding

For another example, see Set G, pages 66–67.

Next season, subscriptions to the Festival Theater will cost \$50 and the service charge will be \$2.50 per order. Find the cost of each of the orders below by evaluating the expression $2.50 + 50g$ where g is the number of subscriptions.

1. 1 subscription **2.** 2 subscriptions **3.** 3 subscriptions

Practice

For More Practice, see Set G, pages 68–69.

Evaluate each expression when x is 12.

4. $60 + 5x$ **5.** $6 + \frac{x}{2}$ **6.** $\frac{x + 6}{2}$ **7.** $30 - 2x$

Evaluate each expression when a is 10.

8. $3a - 5$ **9.** $5a - 3$ **10.** $\frac{a + 8}{6}$ **11.** $\frac{a}{2} + 6$

Complete each table.

b	$10b - 1$
1	9
2	**12.**
3	**13.**
4	**14.**
10	**15.**

c	$1.2 + 2c$
1	3.2
2	**16.**
3	**17.**
4	**18.**
10	**19.**

d	$\frac{d}{2} - 11$
22	**20.**
50	**21.**
74	**22.**
100	**23.**
110	**24.**

e	f	$\frac{24}{e} + f$
1	2	26
2	1	**25.**
3	2	**26.**
4	3	**27.**
6	6	**28.**

Problem Solving

Individual tickets to the Festival Theater cost \$15.75.

29. How much is saved by buying one subscription, as given in Example A, instead of 4 individual tickets?

30. Mental Math *Bharata Natyam,* a Hindu dance, will be performed at the theater. What will be the income from the sale of 100 individual tickets?

31. African-American dancers developed tap dancing by combining African dances, the Irish jig, and the English clog. Tap shoes cost \$39.75 plus \$3.20 sales tax. Find the change from \$50.00.

32. Write a problem that could be solved by using the expression in Example C.

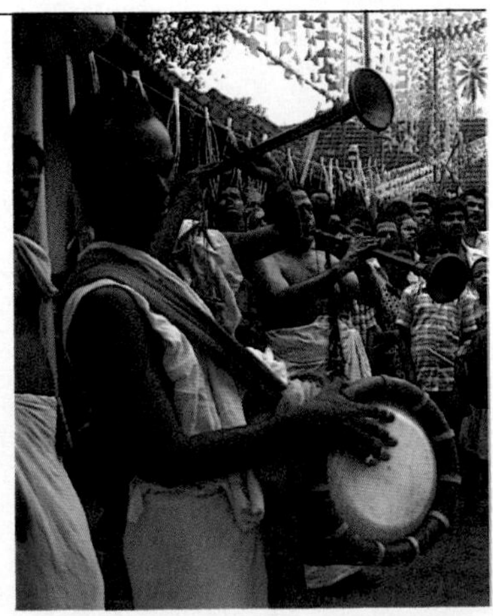

Indian musicians will play the *tabla,* small drums, at one of the theater's concerts.

ALGEBRA

Writing Expressions: Multiple Operations

Build Understanding

A. Maria made signs showing her charges for odd jobs. What expressions did Maria use to determine the charges for more than 1 hour?

Hedge cutting	
Hours	Charge
1	\$3
2	\$6
3	\$9
4	\$12

Lawn mowing	
Hours	Charge
1	\$7
2	\$10
3	\$13
4	\$16

Maria used this expression for the charges for hedge cutting.

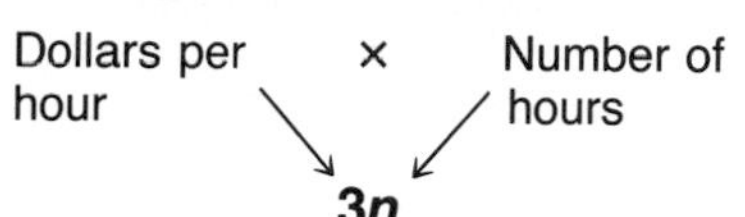

She used this expression for the charges for lawn mowing.

$4 + 3n$

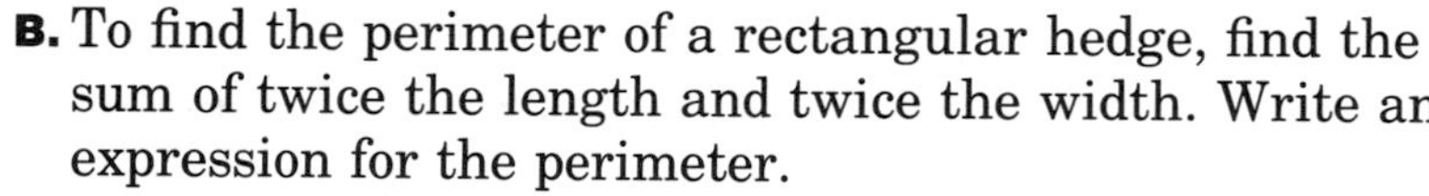

B. To find the perimeter of a rectangular hedge, find the sum of twice the length and twice the width. Write an expression for the perimeter.

First name the variables. Use ℓ for length and w for width.

Twice the length Twice the width

$2\ell + 2w$

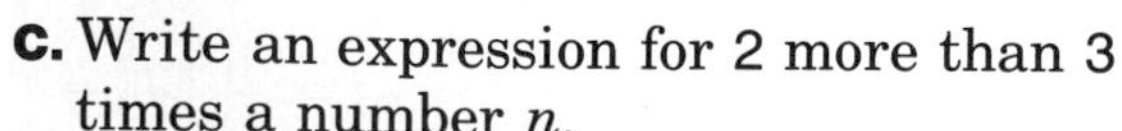

C. Write an expression for 2 more than 3 times a number n.

$3n$ 3 times a number n

$3n + 2$ 2 more than $3n$

D. Write an expression for triple the quotient n divided by 6.

$\frac{n}{6}$ Write the quotient.

$\frac{n}{6} \times 3$, or $\frac{3n}{6}$ Triple the quotient.

Talk About Math In Example B, will you get the same result if you take twice the sum of the length and the width? Explain your answer.

Check Understanding

For another example, see Set H, pages 66–67.

Use the table showing the amounts Errol and Justin charge for house painting for Exercises 1–3.

Hourly Painting Charges

Hours	1	2	3	4	5
Errol	\$5	\$10	\$15	\$20	\$25
Justin	\$6	\$10	\$14	\$18	\$22

1. For each painter, by how much does the charge increase each hour after the first hour?

2. Write an expression for the amount Errol charges for n hours.

3. Write an expression for the amount Justin charges for n hours.

Practice

For More Practice, see Set H, pages 68–69.

Write an expression for each phrase.

4. 2 less than x

5. 5 times x

6. The sum of r and s

7. The product of z and 3

8. x divided by 6

9. 6 divided by x

10. 2 less than the product of x and 6

11. The quotient of 2 more than x divided by 6

12. 10 added to the product of 7 and y.

13. k plus 5 divided by 8.

14. The quotient of v divided by 2 added to the quotient of v divided by 6

15. The product of p and 4 added to the quotient of p divided by 10

Write an expression for each of the following. Use ℓ for length and w for width.

16. Length times width

17. Length added to width

18. Length divided by width

19. Twice the sum of length and width

Problem Solving

Write an expression.

20. Elizabeth charges \$3.50 per hour for babysitting. What does she charge for h hours?

21. For cleaning garages Hank charges \$4 per hour plus a \$5 equipment fee. What does he charge for h hours?

22. Tonya and Luis weed gardens for \$5 per hour plus a \$6 service charge. If they divide their earnings equally, what does each receive for h hours?

23. Brad charges \$1.50 per hour more for dog care than for cat care. Let c be the cost per hour for cat care. What does 8 hours of dog care cost?

ALGEBRA

Solving Two-Step Equations

Build Understanding

A. Lisa plays basketball for the Jets. In a recent game, she scored 23 points. If she made 9 free throws (worth 1 point each), how many field goals (worth 2 points each) did she make?

Let g be the number of field goals Lisa scored. Since each field goal is worth 2 points, the number of points Lisa made on field goals is $2g$. Write an equation showing that Lisa's total number of free throws and field goals is equal to 23 points. Then solve.

$$2g + 9 = 23$$

$$2g + 9 - 9 = 23 - 9$$ Subtract 9 from each side of the equation.

$$2g = 14$$

$$\frac{2g}{2} = \frac{14}{2}$$ Divide each side of the equation by 2.

$$g = 7$$

Lisa made 7 field goals.

B. Solve $10y - 8 = 32$.

$$10y - 8 = 32$$

$$10y - 8 + 8 = 32 + 8$$ Add 8 to each side.

$$10y = 40$$

$$\frac{10y}{10} = \frac{40}{10}$$ Divide each side by 10.

$$y = 4$$

C. Solve $\frac{x}{4} + 2 = 22$.

$$\frac{x}{4} + 2 = 22$$

$$\frac{x}{4} + 2 - 2 = 22 - 2$$ Subtract 2 from each side.

$$\frac{x}{4} = 20$$

$$\frac{x}{4} \times 4 = 20 \times 4$$ Multipy each side by 4.

$$x = 80$$

Write About Math Describe the two steps in solving a two-step equation.

Check Understanding

For another example, see Set I, pages 66–67.

Complete each statement.

1. To solve the equation $3x - 9 = 24$, first add 9 and then ___?___.

2. To solve $\frac{x}{3} + 9 = 24$, first ___?___ and then multiply by 3.

Practice

For More Practice, see Set I, pages 68–69.

Solve each of the following. **Remember** to check your answer.

3. $x + 15 = 36$

4. $11 + 3x = 44$

5. $\frac{c}{8} + 6 = 32$

6. $17 = \frac{r}{2} - 13$

7. $3n - 1.2 = 4.8$

8. $7.7 = 2.7 + 5p$

9. $75 = 11 + 16k$

10. $4 + \frac{n}{4} = 10$

11. $\frac{m}{9} + 18 = 18$

12. $0.8 = 10z - 9.2$

13. $100 + 2h = 700$

14. $3d - 1.8 = 3.9$

15. $5k - 7 = 43$

16. $3 + \frac{m}{7} = 6$

17. $7.1 = 4x + 5.1$

18. $9 + 11d = 20$

19. $14h = 154$

20. $9b + 5 = 86$

21. $0 = \frac{n}{6} - 2$

22. $8r - 7.1 = 4.9$

Problem Solving

Write an equation and then solve it. Check your answers.

23. In professional basketball, certain field goals are worth 3 points. If 7 of 25 points Charles scored came from free throws and 2-point field goals, how many 3-point field goals did he make?

24. **Critical Thinking** Terry said he scored 20 points with three free throws, three 2-point field goals, and the rest 3-pointers. Why must Terry be wrong?

Explore ______ Math

To solve $2x - 8 = 32$, you might first add 8 to each side of the equation. If you first divide each side of the equation by 2, your result would be $\frac{2x}{2} - \frac{8}{2} = \frac{32}{2}$.

25. Do you think you will get the same answer solving either way?

26. Now solve $2x - 8 = 32$ both ways. Are the answers the same?

27. Solve the equation in Example B by dividing each side by 10. Did you find that $y = 4$?

28. Which do you prefer, dividing first or adding first?

ALGEBRA

Use a Formula

Understand
QUESTION
FACTS
KEY IDEA

Plan and Solve
STRATEGY
ANSWER

Look Back
SENSIBLE ANSWER
ALTERNATE APPROACH

Build Understanding

You know one meaning of the word *atmosphere:* the air around the Earth. Because the air pressure at sea level is the weight of a column of air in the atmosphere, that unit of pressure is called 1 *atmosphere.*

Underwater pressure increases very rapidly with increasing depth because water weighs more than air. A scuba diver must plan on 1 additional atmosphere of pressure for every 33 feet of depth.

The pressure can be found by the formula $P = \frac{d}{33} + 1$, where P is the pressure in atmospheres and d is the depth in feet. At what depth is the pressure equal to 3 atmospheres?

Understand QUESTION At what depth is the pressure equal to 3 atmospheres?

FACT The pressure on a diver increases 1 additional atmosphere for every 33 feet of depth.

KEY IDEA The pressure is given by the formula $P = \frac{d}{33} + 1$.

Plan and Solve STRATEGY Use a formula.

$$3 = \frac{d}{33} + 1$$ Substitute 3 for P and solve for d.

$$3 - 1 = \frac{d}{33} + 1 - 1$$ Subtract 1 from each side of the equation.

$$2 = \frac{d}{33}$$

$$2 \times 33 = \frac{d}{33} \times 33$$ Multiply each side of the equation by 33 to find d.

$$66 = d$$

ANSWER At a depth of 66 feet, the pressure equals 3 atmospheres.

Look Back SENSIBLE ANSWER The pressure increases 1 atmosphere for each 33 feet. At 66 ft underwater, it has increased by 2 atmospheres. Added to 1 atmosphere of pressure at the surface, the total is 3 atmospheres of pressure.

Talk About Math One atmosphere of pressure is about 14.7 pounds per square inch. How would you find the pressure of 3 atmospheres?

Check Understanding

Use the formula $P = \frac{d}{33} + 1$ to complete Exercises 1–4.

1. In the formula, *P* stands for ___?___.
2. In the formula, *d* stands for ___?___.
3. The number of atmospheres of pressure at 33 feet is ▒.
4. If $d = 165$ feet, then $P =$ ▒.

Practice

Use the formula $P = \frac{d}{33} + 1$. Tell how many atmospheres of pressure there would be at each depth.

5. 99 feet
6. 3,300 feet
7. Find *d* if *P* is 5 atmospheres.
8. Find *P* if *d* is 198 feet.

A buoy has a volume of 6 cubic feet at the surface. Its volume in cubic feet at a depth of *d* feet is given by the formula $V = \frac{198}{d + 33}$. Solve. **Remember** to check your answers.

9. Use the formula to show that the volume at the surface is 6 cubic feet.
10. Find the volume in cubic feet when *d* is 66 feet.
11. Find the depth in feet if the volume is 4 cubic feet.
12. **Critical Thinking** At what depth is the volume 1 cubic foot?

Use Data Use the chart on page 52 to solve.

13. How many inches do 90 characters of 14-point type require?
14. What is the largest type that can be used so 80 characters fit in 8 inches?

Skills Review

Evaluate each expression when $r = 5$.

1. $15 - r$
2. $6r$
3. $r + 10$
4. $3 - \frac{r}{5}$
5. $9r - 3$
6. $14 + 2r$

Write an expression for each of the following.

7. 12 divided by m
8. t plus 9
9. 16 less than y
10. 7 times i
11. 5 times the sum of n and 15
12. The quotient of 12 less v divided by 3
13. 4 more than the product of 10 and x
14. 7 minus the quotient of r divided by 2

Evaluate each expression.

15. $8 + 6 \times 2$
16. $3 \times 4 \div 2 - 5$
17. $10(4 + 6) \div 2$
18. $7(9 - 7) \times 7$
19. $29 - \frac{56}{8}$
20. $(4 + 3) \times (9 + 1)$

Solve each equation.

21. $t + 15 = 30$
22. $45 = 19 + m$
23. $31 - p = 7$
24. $25 = n - 11$
25. $20 + h = 55$
26. $\frac{q}{12} = 3$
27. $175 = 25v$
28. $\frac{n}{7} = 14$
29. $5r = 35$
30. $81 = 9x$
31. $\frac{t}{5} = 10$
32. $2x + 9 = 43$
33. $100 = 19 + 9c$
34. $\frac{r}{4} - 1 = 6$
35. $\frac{w}{2} - 6 = 0$
36. $3t + 4 = 13$

Problem-Solving Review

Solve each problem.

37. In October, Valley Orchard sold 21 pecks of apples at its roadside stand. Total sales for October and November were 258 pecks. How many pecks were sold in November?
38. Which costs less, 3 videotapes at \$3.79 each or 3 videotapes for \$10.49? How much less?
39. Ann drives 271 miles each week (5 work days) to and from work. How many miles does she drive each day?
40. Lewis is 6 years younger than his brother, Alex. Write an expression for Lewis's age. If Alex is 17 years old, how old is Lewis?
41. The expression $\frac{n}{12}$ gives the number of feet for n inches. How many feet are in 48 inches? In 84 inches?
42. Five less than one eighth of a number is 16. What is the number?
43. **Data File** Use the data on pages 108–109. Write an equation for the weight of the African Bull Elephant as it is related to the Pirarucu.
44. **Make a Data File** Consult an atlas or other reference book to find the distances between your town and the following cities: Boston, MA; New York, NY; Washington, D.C.; Miami, FL; Atlanta, GA; Pittsburgh, PA; Chicago, IL; St. Louis, MO; Houston, TX; Wichita, KS; Denver, CO; Los Angeles, CA; and Seattle, WA. Find the distances between each city to every other city. Make a table to display the data you collect.

Cumulative Skills Review • Chapters 1 and 2

Estimate each answer.

1. 12×88 **2.** 26% of 81 **3.** $671.23 - 68$ **4.** \$456.09 − \$261.75

5. $875 + 932 + 888 + 891 + 907$ **6.** $78{,}682 - 65{,}199$

Multiply.

7. 9×2.3 **8.** 4.5×5.4 **9.** 18.09×1.2 **10.** 0.004×3

11. 0.08×0.02 **12.** 202×3.4 **13.** 7.86×0.9 **14.** 0.7×0.9

Divide.

15. $8\overline{)254}$ **16.** $85 \div 5$ **17.** $12{,}300 \div 6$ **18.** $\frac{1{,}289}{7}$

19. $6{,}939 \div 9$ **20.** $7\overline{)573}$ **21.** $\frac{72}{2}$ **22.** $50{,}000 \div 4$

23. $726 \div 3$ **24.** $6\overline{)503}$ **25.** $4{,}370 \div 5$ **26.** $16{,}008 \div 8$

Evaluate $12m$ for each value of m.

27. $m = 3$ **28.** $m = 9$ **29.** $m = 10$ **30.** $m = 12$

Evaluate $5 + 2t$ for each value of t.

31. $t = 1$ **32.** $t = 4$ **33.** $t = 8$ **34.** $t = 10$

Write an expression for each of the following.

35. 8 minus n **36.** y divided by 3 **37.** h times 18 **38.** 12 plus n

39. 9 less than the product of 8 and f **40.** The quotient of m plus 5 divided by 4

41. 2 times the sum of b and 7 **42.** 9 minus t plus 8

Evaluate each expression.

43. $\frac{5 \times 3 - 3}{4}$ **44.** $\frac{2(8 - 3)}{5}$ **45.** $\frac{56}{8} + 9$ **46.** $30 - 20 \div 5$

47. $6(9 - 4) + 1$ **48.** $72 \div 8 + 1$ **49.** $3 \times (2 + 6 \div 3)$ **50.** $15 + 20 - 5$

Solve.

51. $t + 14 = 20$ **52.** $39 = m - 1$ **53.** $65 - v = 12$ **54.** $7k = 42$

55. $\frac{w}{18} = 3$ **56.** $10p + 3 = 23$ **57.** $89 = 19 + 7r$ **58.** $\frac{a}{2} + 16 = 36$

59. $4u - 3 = 21$ **60.** $4z = 96$ **61.** $77 + b = 101$ **62.** $\frac{x}{7} + 15 = 20$

Reteaching

Set A pages 38–41

This table shows the number of students a counselor at Lakeview Junior High plans to interview by the end of the first week of classes.

Day	1	2	3	4	5
Students	6	12	18	24	30

Remember, tables often help you spot patterns.

1. How many students does the counselor plan to interview each day?
2. About when does the counselor plan to have interviewed 25 students?
3. Assuming the interviews continue at the same rate, about how many days will it take the counselor to interview 75 students?

Set B pages 42–43

Evaluate $63 - d$ when d is 19.

$\mathbf{63 - d}$

$\mathbf{63 - 19}$ Substitute 19 for d.

44 Subtract.

Remember, the value of an expression changes as the value of the variable changes.

Evaluate each expression when $p = 7$.

1. $4p$
2. $\frac{49}{p}$
3. $8 + p$
4. $p - 7$

Set C pages 44–45

Write an expression for the phrase *the sum of 21* and *y*.

$$21 + y$$

Remember, there are many different word phrases for each expression.

Write an expression for each phrase.

1. The quotient n divided by 19
2. The result of multiplying x and 15
3. 2 more than v
4. 8 less than u

Set D pages 46–47

Solve the equation $m + 19 = 35$.

$\mathbf{m + 19 = 35}$ 19 has been added to m.

$\mathbf{m + 19 - 19 = 35 - 19}$ To find m, subtract 19 from both sides.

$\mathbf{m = 16}$

Remember, to solve an equation, you can add or subtract the same number from both sides of the equation.

Solve each equation.

1. $y + 32 = 47$
2. $k + 123 = 456$
3. $r - 146 = 11$
4. $p - 73 = 236$

Set E pages 48–49

Solve $13a = 78$.

$\mathbf{13a = 78}$ 13 and a have been multiplied.

$\mathbf{\frac{13a}{13} = \frac{78}{13}}$ To find a, divide both sides by 13.

$\mathbf{a = 6}$

Remember, to solve an equation, you can divide or multiply both sides by the same nonzero number.

Solve each equation.

1. $17x = 68$
2. $\frac{n}{56} = 8$

Set F pages 54–55

Standard Order of Operations
Always work from left to right.

1. First do the operations within the parentheses or above and below the division bar.
2. Next, multiply and divide.
3. Then, add and subtract.

Remember, watch for parentheses and division bars.

Evaluate each expression.

1. $8 - (2 \times 4)$
2. $63 + 18 \div 3$
3. $44 - 6 \times 7$
4. $\frac{6(3 + 4)}{2(15 - 14)}$

Set G pages 56–57

Evaluate $3x - 11$ when x is 7.

$3x - 11$

$3(7) - 11$ Since x is 7, substitute 7 for x.

$21 - 11 = 10$

Remember, use Standard Order of Operations.

Evaluate $37 + 6t$ for each value of t.

1. $t = 3$
2. $t = 6$

Evaluate each expression when b is 21.

3. $\frac{b + 6}{3} - 5$
4. $\frac{b}{7} + 27$

Set H pages 58–59

Write an expression for the phrase *the sum of twice a number and 14.*

$2x$ 2 times x

$2x + 14$ The sum of $2x$ and 14

Remember, look for word clues such as "less than," "product," and "sum."

1. 6 less than x times 2
2. The quotient 4 divided by t
3. 30 decreased by n
4. The product of 33 and s divided by 17
5. The sum of 8 and three times b

Set I pages 60–61

Solve $4c - 11 = 17$.

$4c - 11 = 17$

$4c - 11 + 11 = 17 + 11$ Add 11 to both sides.

$4c = 28$

$\frac{4c}{4} = \frac{28}{4}$ To find c, divide both sides by 4.

$c = 7$

Remember, add or subtract and then multiply or divide when solving a two-step equation.

Solve each equation.

1. $11w + 34 = 78$
2. $\frac{a}{3} + 4 = 16$
3. $2f - 26 = 20$
4. $\frac{g}{7} - 3 = 4$

More Practice

Set A pages 38–41

Copy and complete each table.

People	3	6	9	12	**1.**
Cars	1	2	**2.**	**3.**	5

Days	Miles
1	200
2	400
3	**4.**
5.	800
7	**6.**

Set B pages 42–43

Copy and complete the table.

i	$7 + i$
0	**1.**
2	**2.**
3.	11
6	**4.**
10	**5.**

Evaluate $11k$ for each value of k.

6. $k = 6$ **7.** $k = 1$ **8.** $k = 3$ **9.** $k = 9$

Evaluate each expression when $z = 3$.

10. $5z$ **11.** $9 + z$ **12.** $24 - z$ **13.** $\frac{54}{z}$

Evaluate each expression when $r = 2$.

14. $r + 2$ **15.** $14 \div r$ **16.** $8r$ **17.** $12 - r$

Set C pages 44–45

Write an expression for each of the following.

1. 22 added to x

2. 45 less than a

3 g divided by 3

4. w times 12

5. The sum of 29.5 and q

6. r plus 9

7. The quotient 6 divided by p

8. v more than 92

9. The result of subtracting j from 72

Set D pages 46–47

Solve each equation.

1. $m + 14 = 29$

2. $y - 52 = 47$

3. $9 + f = 71$

4. $82 = g + 36$

5. $37 = r - 10$

6. $q - 96 = 24$

Set E pages 48–49

Solve each equation.

1. $4y = 88$ **2.** $\frac{q}{10} = 9$ **3.** $132 = 33t$ **4.** $\frac{r}{64} = 3$

5. $35b = 175$ **6.** $\frac{z}{13} = 7$ **7.** $36w = 3{,}600$ **8.** $\frac{k}{97} = 6$

Set F pages 54–55

Evaluate each expression.

1. $10 + 4 \times 7$
2. $52 - 2(3 + 4)$
3. $32 + 22 \div 11$
4. $53 - \frac{49}{7}$
5. $5(6 - 2) + 71$
6. $4 \times 9 + 7 \times 6$
7. $\frac{32}{4} + 10$
8. $7(6 - 4) - 23(3 - 3)$
9. $\frac{7 \times 3 - 6}{3}$
10. $99 - 9 \times 9$
11. $\frac{6(7 + 2)}{3(11 - 2)}$
12. $(10 \times 3) \div (2 \times 3)$
13. $12 \times 3 + 6 \div 2$
14. $12(3 + 6) \div 2$
15. $(12 \times 3 + 6) \div 2$
16. $12 \times (3 + 6 \div 2)$
17. $20 - 5 \times 3 + 8$
18. $(20 - 5) \times 3 + 8$
19. $(20 - 5) \times (3 + 8)$
20. $20 + 8 - 5 \times 3$

Set G pages 56–57

Evaluate $6 + 4r$ for each value of r.

1. $r = 1$
2. $r = 2$
3. $r = 4$
4. $r = 10$
5. $r = 3$

Evaluate each expression when b is 9.

6. $4b - 3$
7. $\frac{b - 7}{6}$
8. $52 + 3b$
9. $\frac{54}{b}$
10. $31 - b$

Evaluate each expression when $x = 6$.

11. $32 + 4x$
12. $\frac{72}{x}$
13. $\frac{x - 2}{16}$
14. $71 - x$
15. $10x + 14$

Set H pages 58–59

Write an expression for each of the following.

1. 2 more than the product of x and 17
2. The quotient 16 less than q divided by 10
3. The result of adding t and 92 and then dividing by 4
4. 37 divided by p minus 4
5. 13 times the sum of 2 and n
6. 9 less than the product of h and 7
7. The product of s and 5 divided by 3
8. The sum of n and 6 times 10
9. 10 times the sum of n and 6
10. 48 divided by the sum of 5 and t

Set I pages 60–61

Solve.

1. $3p + 8 = 29$
2. $\frac{n}{6} - 10 = 2$
3. $121 = 10m + 1$
4. $4d - 3.5 = 7.3$
5. $\frac{f}{7} + 32 = 39$
6. $32c + 47 = 48$
7. $12a - 82 = 2$
8. $\frac{g}{9} + 10 = 17$
9. $15b + 6 = 51$
10. $\frac{a}{3} + 8 = 10$
11. $18n - 24 = 66$
12. $\frac{s}{8} - 44 = 10$

Enrichment

Solving Equations with Variables on Both Sides

Randy told Marcie that if he multiplied his age by 5 and added 3, the result was the same as if he multiplied his age by 3 and added 25. He challenged her to find his age.

Marcie decided to write an equation.

Let n be Randy's age.

$$5n + 3 = 3n + 25$$

Marcie saw that the variable n appeared on both the left and right sides of the equation. Since she wanted it on one side only, she decided to subtract $3n$ from both sides of the equation.

$$5n - 3n + 3 = 3n - 3n + 25$$
$$2n + 3 = 25$$

Now she had an equation she knew how to solve.

$$2n + 3 = 25$$
$$2n + 3 - 3 = 25 - 3$$
$$2n = 22$$
$$\frac{2n}{2} = \frac{22}{2}$$
$$n = 11$$

Randy is 11 years old.

Solve these equations.

1. $4x + 9 = 2x + 19$
2. $7n + 3 = 4n + 27$
3. $14p - 11 = 11p - 8$
4. $m + 7 = 4m - 20$
5. $2k - 5 = 3k - 15$
6. $3y + 23 = 5y + 1$
7. Marcie said to Randy "Four times my age minus 12 is equal to 3 times my age plus 3." How old is Marcie?
8. Alf, Bart, and Curlie are triplets. Alf said, "Twice my age plus 4 times Bart's age minus 47 is the same as 3 times Curlie's age plus 22." How old are Alf, Bart, and Curlie?

Chapter 2 Review/Test

Evaluate each expression when $f = 9$.

1. $43 - f$ **2.** $6f$ **3.** $\frac{f + 9}{3}$

Evaluate $29 - 4w$ for each value of w.

4. $w = 6$ **5.** $w = 2$ **6.** $w = 0$

Bath towels	3	6	9	12
Hotel rooms	1	2	3	4

7. Use the table above to write an expression for the number of bath towels for h hotel rooms.

Solve each equation.

8. $z + 18 = 27$ **9.** $11.3 = m - 7.1$

10. $15b = 120$ **11.** $\frac{a}{6} + 17 = 33$

Write an equation. Then solve the equation.

12. If we had invited 22 more people, we would have invited 200 people.

13. Half as many boxes is 17.

A video store rents tapes for $3. A $2 late fee is charged for each day the tape is not returned by midnight.

14. Write an expression for the total amount owed for a tape that is returned d days late.

15. Evaluate the expression you wrote in Exercise 14 when d is 3.

16. Use the formula $P = \frac{d}{33} + 1$ to determine the number of atmospheres of pressure at a depth (d) of 1,155 feet.

Evaluate each expression.

17. $8 \times 5 - 12 \div 6$

18. $\frac{4(3 + 2)}{5(7 - 6)}$

19. $\frac{17 + 9 \times 5}{8 - 6}$

20. $9 \times (4 + 5) \times 2$

For overseas calls, Optica Telephone Co. charges $2 plus 45¢ for each minute. For the same calls, Zippy Telephone Co. charges $1 plus 75¢ for each minute.

21. Write the expression you would use to figure Optica's rate for m minutes.

22. Write the expression you would use to figure Zippy's rate for m minutes.

Minutes	1	2	3	4	5
Optica's rate					
Zippy's rate					

23. Complete the table above to determine how many minutes long an overseas call has to be for Optica's rate to be cheaper.

a. 1 minute **b.** 5 minutes
c. 3 minutes **d.** 4 minutes

24. **Write About Math** Explain why parentheses are needed to make the statement below true.

$6 \times (12 - 5) + 19 = 61$

Dividing Whole Numbers and Decimals

Did You Know: The Youghiogheny River in Pennsylvania is an exciting river for experienced rafters because it drops 460 feet in 6 miles. This is a drop of 76.7 feet per mile.

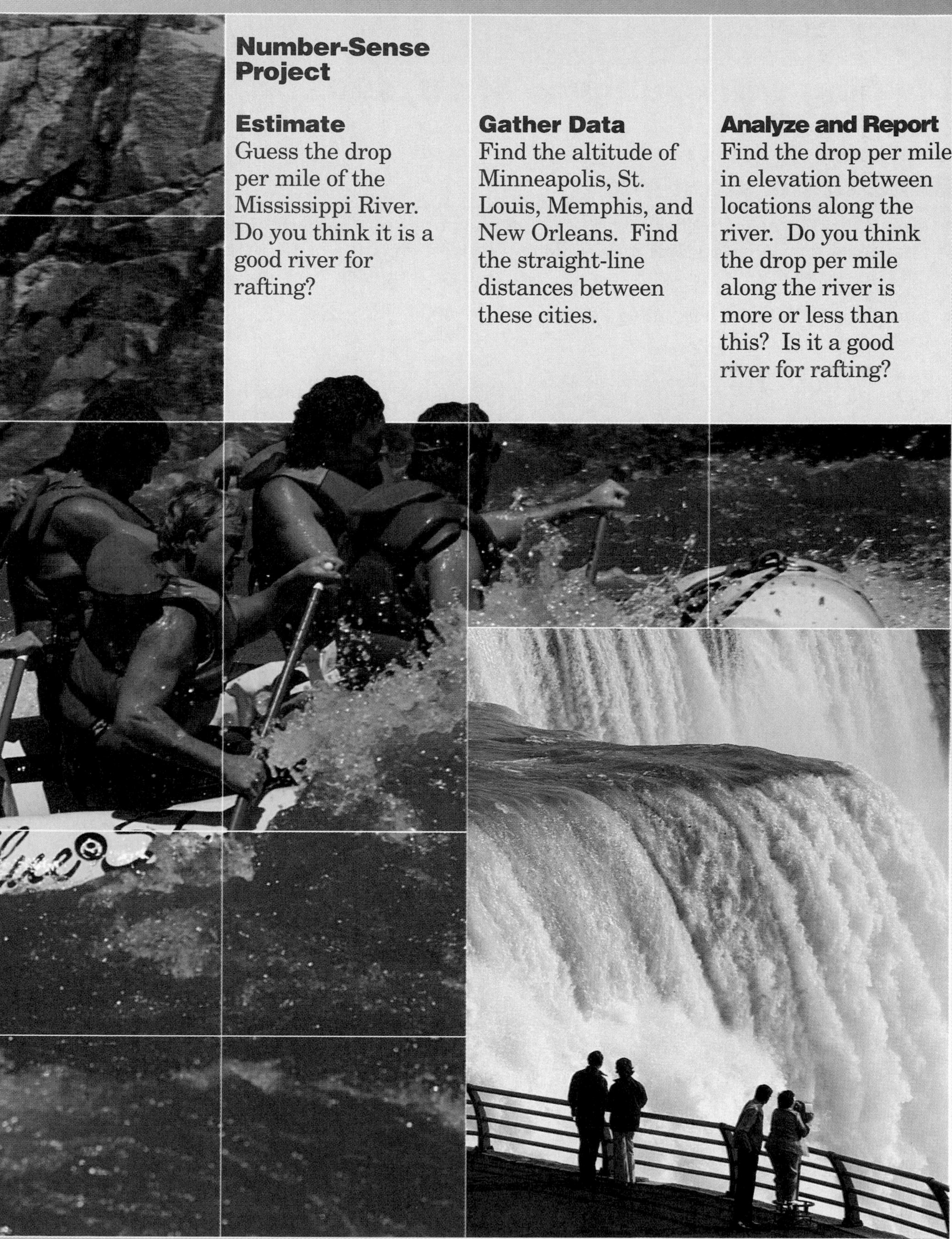

Number-Sense Project

Estimate
Guess the drop per mile of the Mississippi River. Do you think it is a good river for rafting?

Gather Data
Find the altitude of Minneapolis, St. Louis, Memphis, and New Orleans. Find the straight-line distances between these cities.

Analyze and Report
Find the drop per mile in elevation between locations along the river. Do you think the drop per mile along the river is more or less than this? Is it a good river for rafting?

Dividing with Multiples of 10, 100, and 1,000

Build Understanding

A. Mrs. Sullivan cashed a check for \$180. She asked for \$20 bills. How many bills did she receive?

You want to find out how many 20s there are in 180.

$180 \div 20 = 18 \div 2$ (÷ 10 on both)

$= 9$

Mentally divide the dividend and divisor by the same power of 10.

Mrs. Sullivan received 9 twenty-dollar bills.

B. Suppose that the bank packages \$50 bills in amounts of \$2,000. How many bills are in each package?

$2{,}000 \div 50 = 200 \div 5$

$= 40$

Divide the dividend and divisor by 10.

There are 40 fifty-dollar bills in each package.

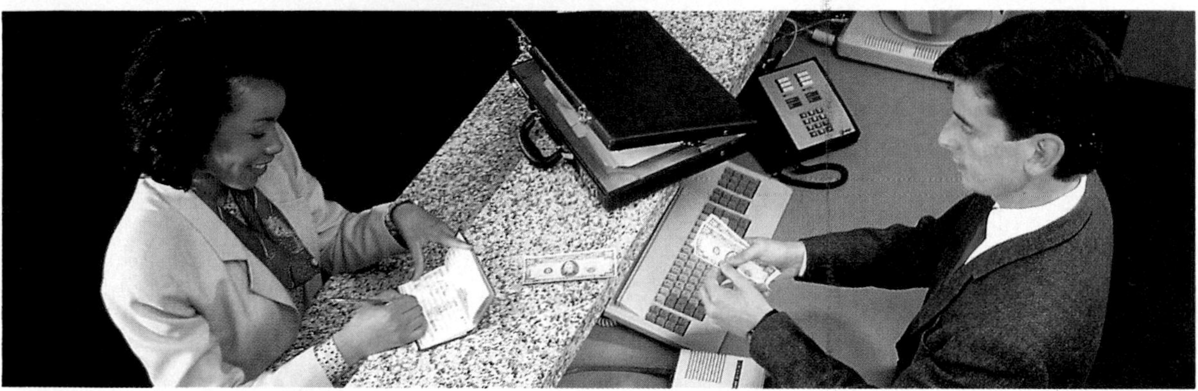

C. Find the quotient $\frac{36{,}000}{900}$.

$\frac{36{,}000}{900} = \frac{360}{9}$ Divide the dividend and divisor by 100.

$= 40$

Talk About Math How do you choose the power of ten to divide by?

Check Understanding

For another example, see Set A, pages 102–103.

Tell what power of ten you would first divide by to find each quotient. Then find each quotient mentally.

1. 200 ÷ 20
2. 3,600 ÷ 60
3. 200,000 ÷ 500
4. 63,000 ÷ 7,000

Number Sense Choose the correct quotient.

5. 400,000 ÷ 800
   a. 500 b. 5,000 c. 50,000
6. 100,000 ÷ 20
   a. 500 b. 5,000 c. 50,000

Practice

For More Practice, see Set A pages 104–105.

Mental Math Divide using mental math.

7. 3,200 ÷ 80 **8.** 100 ÷ 50 **9.** 6,300 ÷ 90 **10.** 12,000 ÷ 400

11. 450 ÷ 90 **12.** 40,000 ÷ 800 **13.** 560,000 ÷ 700 **14.** 4,000 ÷ 500

15. 2,400 ÷ 60 **16.** 9,000 ÷ 100 **17.** 72,000 ÷ 9,000 **18.** 1,000 ÷ 200

19. $\frac{6,400}{800}$ **20.** $\frac{48,000}{6,000}$ **21.** $\frac{210,000}{300}$ **22.** $\frac{42,000}{1,000}$

23. $\frac{280,000}{400}$ **24.** $\frac{720,000}{8,000}$ **25.** $\frac{8,100}{90}$ **26.** $\frac{540,000}{60,000}$

27. $\frac{3,000}{500}$ **28.** $\frac{120,000}{40,000}$ **29.** $\frac{630,000}{700}$ **30.** $\frac{20,000}{5,000}$

Mixed Practice Multiply or divide using mental math.

31. 15 × 100 **32.** 3,000 ÷ 60 **33.** 300 × 200 **34.** 1,500 ÷ 300

35. 5,500 ÷ 110 **36.** 4 × 200 **37.** 30 × 40 **38.** 35,000 ÷ 500

Problem Solving

Solve each problem.

39. Mrs. Sullivan cashed a check for $250 and asked for $50 bills. How many did she receive?

40. Mr. Ing received *d* dollars in $100 bills. Write an expression for the number of $100 bills in *d* dollars.

41. The bank has $20 bills in packs of 50. How much money is in a pack?

42. A roll of dimes is worth $5.00. How many dimes are in it?

Explore ________ Math

Solve each problem.

43. For Exercises 23–26, make a table showing how many zeros are in the dividend, in the divisor, and in the quotient.

44. For each exercise, how does the number of zeros in the quotient relate to the number of zeros in the dividend and in the divisor?

45. Does the same pattern hold true in Exercises 8, 12, 14, 18, and 27? Explain.

46. Write a rule using the results in Exercises 43 and 45 for dividing with multiples of ten.

Number Sense: Using Compatible Numbers

Build Understanding

A. Mr. Vasquez is a landscape contractor. He is going to plant seedlings on land that has an area of 3,750 square feet. Each seedling requires 18 square feet of area. Estimate the number of seedlings needed.

Estimate $3{,}750 \div 18$.

You can estimate a quotient using **compatible numbers.** Compatible numbers are close to the original numbers, and you can compute with them using mental math. Two estimates are shown below.

$$\frac{3{,}750}{18} \rightarrow \frac{3{,}600}{18}, \text{ or about } 200$$

$$\frac{3{,}750}{18} \rightarrow \frac{4{,}000}{20}, \text{ or about } 200$$

About 200 seedlings are needed.

Different sets of compatible numbers may give different estimates.

B. Estimate $31\overline{)2{,}580}$.

$$31\overline{)2{,}580} \rightarrow \overset{80}{30\overline{)2{,}400}}$$

$$31\overline{)2{,}580} \rightarrow \overset{90}{30\overline{)2{,}700}}$$

$$31\overline{)2{,}580} \rightarrow \overset{100}{30\overline{)3{,}000}}$$

C. Estimate $37{,}491 \div 127$.

$$\frac{37{,}491}{127} \rightarrow \frac{37{,}000}{100}, \text{ or } 370$$

$$\frac{37{,}491}{127} \rightarrow \frac{40{,}000}{100}, \text{ or } 400$$

$$\frac{37{,}491}{127} \rightarrow \frac{39{,}000}{130}, \text{ or } 300$$

Talk About Math Which is the better estimate for $43{,}164 \div 62$: $42{,}000 \div 60$ or $48{,}000 \div 60$? Explain.

Check Understanding

For another example, see Set B, pages 102–103.

Estimation Tell which estimate is more reasonable.

1. 3,381 ÷ 53
a. 70 **b.** 600

2. 82,284 ÷ 44
a. 200 **b.** 2,000

3. 45,897 ÷ 111
a. 45 **b.** 400

Practice

For More Practice, see Set B, pages 104–105.

Estimation Write a pair of compatible numbers. Then estimate each quotient.

4. 462 ÷ 12
5. 984 ÷ 19
6. 1,943 ÷ 18
7. 6,976 ÷ 98
8. 161 ÷ 38
9. 493 ÷ 21
10. 3,720 ÷ 13
11. 4,167 ÷ 38
12. 2,478 ÷ 64
13. 31,689 ÷ 772
14. 1,209 ÷ 29
15. 546 ÷ 82
16. $77\overline{)15{,}800}$
17. $46\overline{)19{,}655}$
18. $15\overline{)573}$
19. $93\overline{)15{,}653}$
20. $57\overline{)24{,}808}$
21. $33\overline{)26{,}226}$
22. $73\overline{)50{,}061}$
23. $22\overline{)21{,}600}$
24. $82\overline{)49{,}024}$
25. $511\overline{)34{,}387}$
26. $11\overline{)1{,}010}$
27. $68\overline{)6{,}423}$
28. $\frac{71{,}466}{869}$
29. $\frac{36{,}225}{729}$
30. $\frac{40{,}169}{634}$
31. $\frac{69{,}687}{208}$
32. $\frac{2{,}712}{29}$
33. $\frac{25{,}885}{13}$
34. $\frac{47{,}619}{15}$
35. $\frac{37{,}003}{41}$

Problem Solving

Estimation Estimate to solve each problem.

36. Mr. Vasquez planted bushes along a road 12,560 feet long. Each 14 feet of road, he planted one bush. About how many bushes were needed?

37. **Critical Thinking** Can you tell whether your estimate of a quotient is less than or greater than the actual quotient? Explain.

Reading ___ **Math**

ALGEBRA

Numbers and Symbols Tell if each statement is *true* or *false*.

1. If x is 10, the value of $x + 2$ is 12.

2. $4 \times 7 - 6 \div 2 = 11$

3. When $a = 12$, the expression $24 - 2a$ has the value 1.

4. In the equation, $6m = 9$, m is called a variable.

Applications of Whole Number Division

Build Understanding

Michael Jordan was the scoring leader for the National Basketball Association in 1988. Find the average number of points he scored per game that year.

National Basketball Association Scoring Leaders			
Year	Player	Points	Games
1962	Chamberlain	4,029	80
1985	King	1,809	55
1986	Wilkins	2,366	78
1987	Jordan	3,041	82
1988	Jordan	2,868	82
1989	Jordan	2,633	81

Since we want to find the average points per game, we divide the total points by the number of games.

Find 2,868 ÷ 82.

Paper and Pencil

$$\begin{array}{r} 34 \text{ R80} \\ 82\overline{)2{,}868} \\ \underline{2\,46} \\ 408 \\ \underline{328} \\ 80 \end{array}$$

Calculator

Press: 2,868 [÷] 82 [=]

Display: 34.975609

The answer can be written as 34 R80, $34\frac{40}{41}$, or 34.975609. Rounded to the nearest whole number, Michael Jordan scored about 35 points per game in 1988.

Talk About Math How can you tell the year, by just a quick estimate, in which the all-time scoring record was set?

Check Understanding

For another example, see Set C, pages 102–103.

Estimation Use compatible numbers to estimate each player's average points per game.

1. King in 1985
2. Jordan in 1987

Number Sense Is the digit in each quotient below correct, too large, or too small?

3. $\begin{array}{r} 4 \\ 43\overline{)1{,}613} \end{array}$
4. $\begin{array}{r} 6 \\ 279\overline{)19{,}563} \end{array}$

Divide using paper and pencil or calculator. Round decimal answers to the nearest hundredth.

5. $6\overline{)560}$
6. 806 ÷ 25
7. $\frac{29{,}466}{48}$
8. $32\overline{)67{,}208}$

Practice

For More Practice, see Set C, pages 104–105.

Use the table on page 78. Find each player's average number of points per game. Use paper and pencil or calculator. Round answers to the nearest whole number.

9. Jordan in 1987 **10.** Wilkins in 1986 **11.** King in 1985 **12.** Jordan in 1989

Divide using paper and pencil or calculator. Round decimal answers to the nearest hundredth.

13. 4,483 ÷ 61 **14.** 1,789 ÷ 53 **15.** $47\overline{)4{,}939}$ **16.** $24\overline{)5{,}217}$

17. 8,942 ÷ 18 **18.** 11,766 ÷ 30 **19.** 32,008 ÷ 38 **20.** $82\overline{)71{,}438}$

21. $\frac{24{,}445}{38}$ **22.** $\frac{125{,}842}{425}$ **23.** $\frac{322{,}809}{610}$ **24.** $\frac{716{,}716}{520}$

Divide using paper and pencil, calculator, or mental math. Round decimal answers to the nearest hundredth.

25. 9,849 ÷ 43 **26.** 440 ÷ 11 **27.** $47\overline{)66{,}881}$ **28.** 36,000 ÷ 600

29. $871\overline{)71{,}000}$ **30.** $200\overline{)804{,}000}$ **31.** 78,558 ÷ 367 **32.** $84\overline{)473{,}673}$

Mixed Practice Evaluate each expression using paper and pencil, calculator, or mental math. Round decimal answers to the nearest hundredth.

33. $(228 + 472) \times 40 \div 700$ **34.** $(162 + 273 - 22) \div 45$ **35.** $44 \div 4 + 387 \div 9$

36. $\frac{1{,}242 - 333}{12 \times 3}$ **37.** $\frac{72 \times 1{,}000}{20 \times 30}$ **38.** $\frac{31 + 485 - 17}{49}$

Problem Solving

Solve each problem.

Top 3 College Teams in the Big League Conference

Team	Games	Total number of free throws	2-point shots	3-point shots
The College of Pythagoras	12	180	288	72
Basketmath University	14	252	308	70
Percentage State University	13	156	325	52

39. Find the average number of free throws per game for the College of Pythagoras.

40. Find the average number of 3-point shots per game for Basketmath U.

41. Find the average total points per game for Percentage State.

42. Critical Thinking List all the combinations of shots a player could make to earn 8 points.

43. Critical Thinking Suppose a dividend is 760. The quotient is 25 with a remainder of 10. What is the divisor?

Interpret the Remainder

PROBLEM SOLVING GUIDE

Understand
QUESTION
FACTS
KEY IDEA

Plan and Solve
STRATEGY
ANSWER

Look Back
SENSIBLE ANSWER
ALTERNATE APPROACH

Build Understanding

A. If 218 students and chaperones are going on a ski trip and they plan to travel on buses that can hold 48 people, how many buses are needed?

Understand QUESTION How many buses do they need?

FACTS There are 218 people and each bus can carry up to 48 persons.

KEY IDEA Since you need to find the number of buses, divide the total number of people into groups of 48.

Plan and Solve Divide 218 by 48: $48\overline{)218}$ = **4 R26**

STRATEGY To answer the question, how many buses are needed, you must *interpret the remainder* correctly.

The remainder is 26 when you divide by 48, so 4 buses are not enough. Use the next higher whole number.

ANSWER They should order 5 buses.

Look Back SENSIBLE ANSWER Since 4 buses with 48 people each is less than the total, and 5 buses with 48 people each is more than the total, the answer is reasonable.

B. One night 29 inches of snow fell at the ski resort. How many feet of snow is this?

Divide 29 by 12: $12\overline{)29}$ = **2 R5**

The quotient 2 R5 can be expressed as $2\frac{5}{12}$. In this case, it is sensible to use a mixed number as the answer. So $2\frac{5}{12}$ feet of snow fell.

C. A bakery provides rolls to a ski lodge in packages of 12. If 2,500 rolls are baked, how many packages can be filled? How many rolls will be left over?

Divide 2,500 by 12: $12\overline{)2,500}$ = **208 R4**

So 208 packages can be filled, and 4 rolls will be left over.

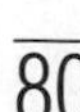

Write About Math Use the exercise shown. Write a problem for which the answer is 7, remainder 3. Write another problem for which the answer is 8.

$$\begin{array}{r} 7 \text{ R3} \\ 4\overline{)31} \\ \underline{28} \\ 3 \end{array}$$

Check Understanding

There are 75 people waiting for a chair lift at Mountain Valley Ski Resort. Each chair holds a maximum of 4 people.

1. How many chairs are needed to carry all of the people?
2. How many chairs will be completely filled?
3. How many people will be in the chair that is not completely filled?
4. The chair lift travels 400 feet per minute. How many minutes does it take to travel 3,900 feet?

Practice

Solve each problem. **Remember** to label the units in your answer.

5. **Calculator** On sale, 12 pairs of ski socks cost $54. Find the cost per pair.
6. A group of 55 skiers separated into groups of 12 each. How many skiers were left over?
7. How many 56-passenger buses are needed to transport 862 skiers?
8. A 2-mile cross-country ski trail is divided into 5 sections. How long is each section?

Choose a Strategy

Fund Raising The members of the ski team are selling jacket patches and bumper stickers to raise money. The jacket patches sell for $1.50 each and the bumper stickers cost $0.99.

9. How much money will Ron collect if he sells 10 patches and 10 stickers?
10. One Saturday Ron started out with 20 patches and 20 stickers. At the end of the day he had collected $23.37. How many of each had he sold?

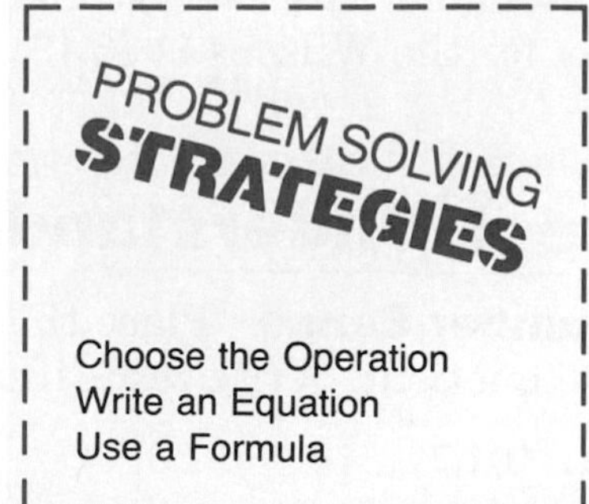

CONSUMER CONNECTION

Dividing Decimals by Whole Numbers

Build Understanding

The Wilsons' electric bill for March was \$98.70. What was the average electricity cost per day for the Wilsons?

Since you want to find an average cost, divide the total cost \$98.70 by 31, the number of days in March.

Find 98.70 ÷ 31. First, estimate using compatible numbers: 90 ÷ 30 = 3

Paper and Pencil
Place the decimal point in the quotient above the decimal point in the dividend.

```
     3.183
31)98.700
   93
    5 7
    3 1
    2 60
    2 48
      120
       93
       27
```

Write zeros as needed.

Calculator

Press: 98.70 [÷] 31 [=]

Display: *3.1838709*

The total residential consumption of electricity in 1988 in the U.S. was 2.48 quadrillion British Thermal Units.

Since the answer is in dollars and cents, round the quotient to the nearest hundredth: \$3.18. The estimate was \$3, so the answer is reasonable. The average electricity cost per day for the Wilsons is \$3.18.

Talk About Math Why can you write an extra zero in the dividend when you divide 98.70 by 31?

Check Understanding

For another example, see Set D, pages 102–103.

Number Sense Place the decimal point correctly in the quotient. Write zeros if needed.

1. 101.7 ÷ 15 $\stackrel{?}{=}$ 6 7 8 **2.** 33.405 ÷ 393 $\stackrel{?}{=}$ 8 5 **3.** 0.00744 ÷ 8 $\stackrel{?}{=}$ 9 3

Divide using paper and pencil or calculator. If necessary, round to the nearest hundredth.

4. 97.62 ÷ 31 **5.** 3.425 ÷ 16 **6.** 0.238 ÷ 5 **7.** 5.297 ÷ 77

Practice

For More Practice, see Set D, pages 104–105.

Divide. Use paper and pencil or calculator. If necessary, round decimal answers to the nearest hundredth.

8. $32\overline{)179.84}$ **9.** $5\overline{)163.8}$ **10.** $7\overline{)2.8567}$ **11.** $21\overline{)1.512}$

12. $14\overline{)162.7}$ **13.** $9\overline{)192.6}$ **14.** $62\overline{)138.88}$ **15.** $55\overline{)4.92}$

16. $0.844 \div 30$ **17.** $0.396 \div 18$ **18.** $323.08 \div 28$ **19.** $4.111 \div 75$

20. $0.928 \div 72$ **21.** $0.455 \div 13$ **22.** $175.95 \div 46$ **23.** $2.008 \div 58$

Number Sense Tell if each quotient is reasonable. Explain your answer.

24. $18.36 \div 6 = 3.06$ **25.** $863.6 \div 68 = 127$ **26.** $0.5944 \div 8 = 0.0743$

27. $22.88 \div 22 = 1.04$ **28.** $0.2601 \div 3 = 0.0867$ **29.** $18.06 \div 14 = 0.129$

ALGEBRA **Mixed Practice** Evaluate each expression when $b = 17$.

30. $b + 9.65$ **31.** $b - 3.8$ **32.** $0.34 \times b$ **33.** $1{,}062.5 \div b$

34. $44.32 - b$ **35.** $b \times 2.15$ **36.** $192.95 \div b$ **37.** $43.905 + b$

38. $b - 1.27$ **39.** $4.32 \times b$ **40.** $b + 7.842$ **41.** $34.68 \div b$

Problem Solving

Solve each problem.

42. **Calculator** On this electric bill, what was the energy charge for one kilowatt-hour? What was the fuel charge per kilowatt-hour?

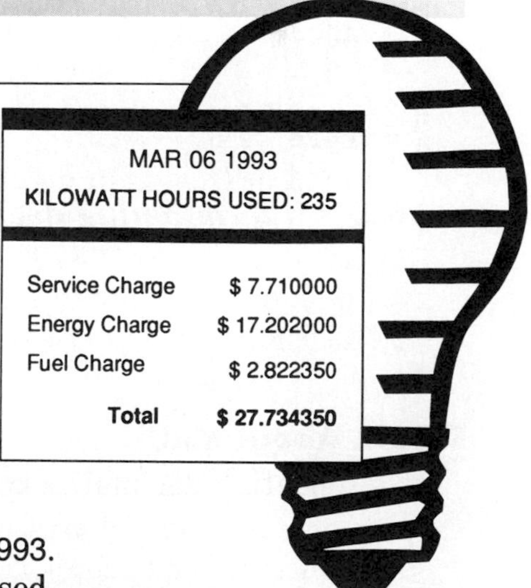

MAR 06 1993

KILOWATT HOURS USED: 235

Service Charge	$ 7.710000
Energy Charge	$ 17.202000
Fuel Charge	$ 2.822350
Total	**$ 27.734350**

43. December's meter reading showed 321 kilowatt-hours were used. What was the average number of kilowatt-hours used each day in December?

44. A family used 225 kilowatt-hours in February of 1993. What was the average number of kilowatt-hours used per week in February?

45. **Critical Thinking** If a customer used 8.4 kilowatt-hours one day, what was the average number of kilowatt-hours used per hour? Was this amount actually used each hour? Explain.

Expressing Fractions as Decimals

Build Understanding

A. The DeSoto High School Pop Band has played six out of ten concerts. You can write this as a fraction or as a decimal.

$\frac{6}{10} = 0.6$

B. Divide to write $\frac{5}{8}$ as a decimal.

```
  0.625
8)5.000
  4 8
    20
    16
     40
     40
      0
```

Write zeros in the dividend and divide.

$\frac{5}{8} = 0.625$

0.625 is a ***terminating decimal.***

C. Write $\frac{16}{33}$ as a decimal.

```
    0.4848 . . .
33)16.0000
   13 2
    2 80
    2 64
      160
      132
       280
       264
        16
```

The digits 4 and 8 repeat in the quotient.

No matter how long you divide, the remainders 28 and 16 will repeat.

0.4848 . . . is a ***repeating*** decimal. To write a repeating decimal, put a bar over the digits that repeat.

$\frac{16}{33} = 0.\overline{48}$

Talk About Math Do you think $\frac{1}{25}$ is a terminating or a repeating decimal? Explain.

Check Understanding

For another example, see Set E, pages 102–103.

Write each fraction as a decimal. Write repeating decimals with a bar.

1. $\frac{4}{100}$ **2.** $\frac{2}{1,000}$ **3.** $\frac{1}{20}$ **4.** $\frac{4}{9} = 0.444\ldots$ **5.** $\frac{4}{27} = 0.148148\ldots$

Practice

For More Practice, see Set E, pages 104–105.

Write each fraction as a decimal. Use a bar to indicate repeating digits.

6. $\frac{1}{2}$ **7.** $\frac{7}{8}$ **8.** $\frac{3}{4}$ **9.** $\frac{6}{25}$ **10.** $\frac{9}{16}$ **11.** $\frac{7}{200}$

12. $\frac{7}{16}$ **13.** $\frac{7}{11}$ **14.** $\frac{33}{100}$ **15.** $\frac{5}{32}$ **16.** $\frac{9}{25}$ **17.** $\frac{1}{3}$

18. $\frac{5}{11}$ **19.** $\frac{1}{4}$ **20.** $\frac{10}{33}$ **21.** $\frac{22}{27}$ **22.** $\frac{7}{9}$ **23.** $\frac{3}{11}$

24. $\frac{2}{9}$ **25.** $\frac{5}{6}$ **26.** $\frac{1}{12}$ **27.** $\frac{7}{15}$ **28.** $\frac{7}{40}$ **29.** $\frac{1}{18}$

Calculator Write each fraction as a decimal. Use a bar to indicate repeating decimals.

30. $\frac{2}{3}$ **31.** $\frac{7}{90}$ **32.** $\frac{11}{60}$ **33.** $\frac{4}{15}$ **34.** $\frac{7}{30}$ **35.** $\frac{11}{12}$

36. $\frac{1}{7}$ **37.** $\frac{5}{22}$ **38.** $\frac{7}{18}$ **39.** $\frac{7}{24}$ **40.** $\frac{9}{40}$ **41.** $\frac{15}{16}$

Problem Solving

Solve each problem.

42. On a standard piano, 36 of the 88 keys are black. Write a fraction and a decimal for the fraction of the keys that are black.

43. Write a fraction and a decimal for the fraction of the piano keys that are white.

Make up a problem using the information given. Then solve.

44. Tom's Music Store at the mall has 6 guitars to sell. Five of them are electric guitars.

45. The DeSoto High Marching Band has 25 members. Of these, 12 play woodwinds.

Midchapter Checkup

Compute using mental math.

1. 320 ÷ 40 **2.** 640,000 ÷ 8,000

Estimate using compatible numbers.

3. $12\overline{)3,400}$ **4.** $591\overline{)49.807}$

Find each quotient. If necessary, round to the nearest hundredth.

5. $\frac{1,976}{59}$ **6.** $\frac{395.6}{92}$ **7.** $\frac{0.261}{9}$

8. Write $\frac{43}{60}$ as a decimal.

9. How many 12-egg cartons are needed for 345 eggs?

Problem Solving WORKSHOP

Explore as a Team

1. Discuss why farmers or construction workers sometimes "pace off" distances instead of measuring more exactly.

2. Estimate the length of your pace.

3. Measure and mark off a distance of 10 to 50 meters in or near your classroom.

TIPS FOR WORKING TOGETHER

To make sure your group understands the task or solution have each group member say it in his/her own words, summarize the steps, or give an example.

4. Pace the distance, counting the number of steps it takes. Do this four times and average the results. (Have another person check that your paces are about the same length.)

5. Find the length of your pace to the nearest tenth.

$$\text{Pace length} = \frac{\text{Distance}}{\text{Number of paces}}$$

6. The team should pick a distance to measure. Each person first estimates and then finds the distance by pacing. Compare the results with the estimates.

$$\text{Distance} = \text{pace length} \times \text{number of paces}$$

Number-Sense Project

Look back at pages 72-73.

The Niagara River connects Lake Erie and Lake Ontario. The distance between the two lakes is 27 miles, but the river is 35 miles long. Lake Erie is 570 feet above sea level and Lake Ontario is 245 feet above sea level. The river drops 162 feet at Niagara Falls.

1. What is the drop in elevation between the two lakes?

2. To the nearest tenth, what is the drop per mile in elevation along the 27 miles from Lake Erie to Lake Ontario?

3. What is the drop per mile along the course of the river?

4. Compare the drop along the course of the Niagara River with that of the Youghiogheny River.

5. If Niagara Falls is ignored, what is the drop per mile along the course of the river?

Explore with a Computer

Use the *Spreadsheet Workshop Project* for this activity.

The Smith triplets are saving money to buy their parents a 20th wedding anniversary gift. They want to buy a slide projector that costs \$87.50. Susie, Fred, and George must first decide how much money they each need to save to buy the gift. Then they will use the spreadsheet to figure out how many hours they need to work to earn their share. Each child will be paid to work full hours. They will not be paid for working part of an hour.

	Amount to Save	Salary per hour	Hours
Susie		\$2.50	
Fred		\$2.50	
George		\$2.50	
Goal			

1. First decide how much money Susie, Fred, and George will each contribute to the gift. At the computer, enter these amounts in the table.

2. Determine how many hours each Smith child should work to earn their share of the cost. What is the total number of hours?

Real-Life Decision Making

1. Which is the best buy in terms of price?

2. Which makes the most sense to buy if only one person in the family drinks juice?

3. Which would be the best buy for *your* family?

4. Name a circumstance where it would make sense to buy the other types.

3 for \$1.89

Multiplying and Dividing by Powers of 10

Build Understanding

Powerful Powers
Groups: With a partner

a. With paper and pencil or a calculator, multiply 4.2 by 10, by 100, and by 1,000. Record your answers.

b. Choose three other numbers and multiply them by 10, 100, and 1,000. Record your answers.

c. Divide 4.2 by 10, 100, and 1,000. Record your answers.

d. Choose three other numbers and divide them by 10, 100, and 1,000. Record your answers.

e. Discuss the answers with your partner. When you think you have figured out the rule, do the problems to the right using mental math.

6.3 × 100   5.8 × 1,000
75 ÷ 10   42.8 ÷ 1,000

f. Look at the answers to the multiplication exercises. What do you notice about the position of the decimal point?

g. Look at the answers to the division exercises. What do you notice about the decimal point?

h. Discuss your observations with your partner. Then do the problems to the right using mental math.

3.7 × 10   117 ÷ 100
46.9 × 100   58.2 ÷ 1,000

Talk About Math Is it easier to multiply and divide by powers of ten using mental math or by using a calculator?

Check Understanding

For another example, see Set F, pages 102–103.

Number Sense Place the decimal point in each product or quotient.

1. 4.5 × 1,000 **45**   **2.** 152.7 × 100 **1,527**   **3.** 0.7 × 1,000 **7**

4. 0.0043 ÷ 100 **43**   **5.** 1.67 ÷ 1,000 **167**   **6.** 256 ÷ 10,000 **256**

A L G E B R A

Practice

For More Practice, see Set F, pages 104–105.

Copy and complete the table. **Remember** to move the decimal point to the right or to the left.

n	$n \times 10$	$n \times 100$	$n \times 1{,}000$	$n \div 10$	$n \div 100$	$n \div 1{,}000$
89.25	**7.**	**8.**	**9.**	**10.**	**11.**	**12.**
0.45	**13.**	**14.**	**15.**	**16.**	**17.**	**18.**
0.03	**19.**	**20.**	**21.**	**22.**	**23.**	**24.**
$2.\overline{52}$	**25.**	**26.**	**27.**	**28.**	**29.**	**30.**

Mixed Practice Copy and complete the tables using mental math or paper and pencil. Tell which method you used.

31.

n	$10 - n$
0	
1.5	
3.7	
	0

32.

m	$\frac{m}{10}$
1	
	1
20	
500	

33.

a	$6a + 2$
3.5	
	2.6
10	
50	

34.

b	$4.1b - 3$
1	
5	
	38
20	

Problem Solving

Use the picture to solve these problems.

35. Find the weight of 10 pennies.

36. Find the weight of 100 nickels.

37. Find the weight of 1,000 dimes.

38. Critical Thinking Can you multiply a number by 1,000 and have fewer than 3 zeros in the product? Explain.

There were 11,346,500,443 pennies minted in the United States in 1988.

Skills Review

pages 42–43

A L G E B R A

Find the value of each expression.

If $j = 5$ **1.** $6j + 4$ **2.** $8j - 7$ **3.** $\frac{j+1}{3}$ **4.** $\frac{10}{j} + j$

If $k = 20$ **5.** $\frac{k}{2} - 5$ **6.** $\frac{k+2}{11}$ **7.** $10 + 5k$ **8.** $\frac{2k}{4} + k$

Dividing by a Decimal

Build Understanding

Mr. Keith bought a 17.7-oz box of Very Bran cereal. Use the sale price chart to find the unit cost (cost per ounce) of the cereal he bought.

Since you want to find the unit cost, divide the total sale price by the number of ounces.

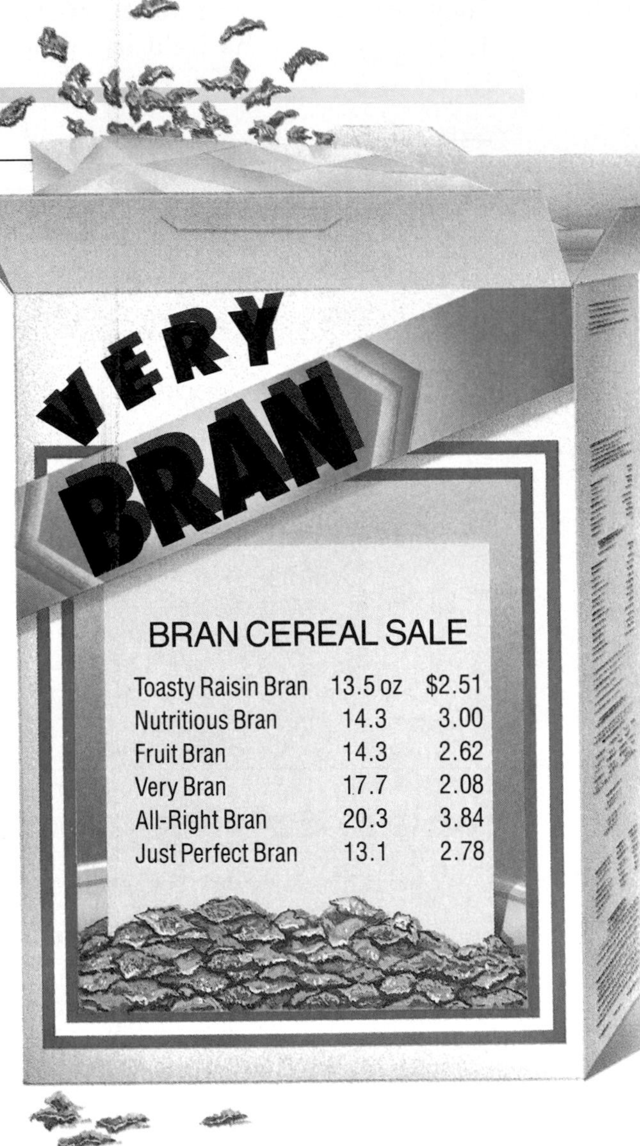

VERY
BRAN
BRAN CEREAL SALE
Toasty Raisin Bran 13.5 oz $2.51
Nutritious Bran 14.3 3.00
Fruit Bran 14.3 2.62
Very Bran 17.7 2.08
All-Right Bran 20.3 3.84
Just Perfect Bran 13.1 2.78

Paper and Pencil

```
        0.117
17.7)2.0800
      1 77
       310
       177
      1330
      1239
        91
```

Calculator

Press: 2.08 ÷ 17.7 =

Display: 0.1175141

Round 0.117 or 0.1175141 to the nearest hundredth. The unit cost is about $0.12 per ounce.

Talk About Math To divide by decimals, multiply both the divisor and dividend by a power of ten to move the decimal. Explain how you decide which power of ten to use.

Check Understanding

For another example, see Set G, pages 102–103.

By what power of 10 would you multiply before dividing?

1. 0.48 ÷ 1.6 **2.** 245 ÷ 3.5 **3.** 0.434 ÷ 0.07

Estimation Estimate to place the decimal point in each quotient. Write zeros if needed.

4. 48,348 ÷ 79 612 **5.** 16.4152 ÷ 136 1207 **6.** 1,481.74 ÷ 4.1 3614

Practice

For More Practice, see Set G, pages 104–105.

Use the chart on page 90. Find the unit cost of each cereal to the nearest cent.

7. Toasty Raisin Bran **8.** Nutritious Bran **9.** All-Right Bran

Use paper and pencil or a calculator to divide. Round decimal answers to the nearest thousandth.
Remember to place the decimal point in the quotient.

10. $0.5\overline{)4.5}$ **11.** $0.25\overline{)0.125}$ **12.** $6\overline{)19.8}$

13. $0.2\overline{)44.68}$ **14.** $3.1\overline{)39.06}$ **15.** $1.04\overline{)2.496}$

16. 28.8 ÷ 1.2 **17.** 0.8 ÷ 0.003 **18.** 12.465 ÷ 0.3

19. 0.03 ÷ 2.75 **20.** 10.40 ÷ 6.12 **21.** 7.105 ÷ 2.9

Mixed Practice Choose mental math, paper and pencil, or calculator to find each quotient. Tell which method you used. Round decimal answers to the nearest thousandth.

22. 28 ÷ 2 **23.** 35 ÷ 0.8 **24.** 0.027 ÷ 10 **25.** 8.36 ÷ 2.75

26. 12.5 ÷ 0.85 **27.** 15.8 ÷ 100 **28.** 0.006 ÷ 0.02 **29.** 803.4 ÷ 7.5

Problem Solving

Calculator Use paper and pencil or a calculator to solve each problem.

30. Which granola bar has the lowest unit cost (cost per ounce)?

31. Which granola bar has the highest unit cost?

32. Kookie granola bars are on sale at two for $3.00. What is the unit cost per ounce?

33. Break 'em Up! bars also come in bite-size (0.3 oz) sample bars for $0.29 each. What is the unit cost for one bar?

Use Data Use the table on page 8 to solve each problem.

34. How many pounds of mangoes can you buy with $2.50?

35. A bag of jicama costs $1.10. How much does it weigh?

Deciding When an Estimate Is Enough

Understand
QUESTION
FACTS
KEY IDEA

Plan and Solve
STRATEGY
ANSWER

Look Back
SENSIBLE ANSWER
ALTERNATE APPROACH

Build Understanding

Doug Harper is the reporter for a weekly TV news feature entitled *The Wise Consumer*. This week's segment is on estimation. He tells viewers: Estimate whenever you do not need an exact answer, or if you just want to be sure that you have enough time, money, or materials. Suppose that Raquel wants to buy apples for herself and 3 friends. Apples cost \$0.37 each, and Raquel has \$1.50. Does she have enough money?

Understand QUESTION Does Raquel have enough money?

FACTS Apples cost \$0.37 each. Raquel has \$1.50.

KEY IDEAS An exact answer does not seem to be needed. Use estimation.

Plan and Solve STRATEGY Round the cost of each apple to \$0.40.

4 × \$0.40 = \$1.60

This estimate is close to the \$1.50 that Raquel has. Sometimes you do not know whether an estimate is enough until you find the estimate. In this case, because an estimate is so close, a wise consumer will find an exact answer.

ANSWER **4 × \$0.37 = \$1.48**

Raquel does have enough money.

Look Back SENSIBLE ANSWER In this case an estimate was not enough, but we could not determine that without trying an estimate.

■ **Talk About Math** Give an example in which you would want to be sure to overestimate a quantity. Give an example in which you would want to underestimate.

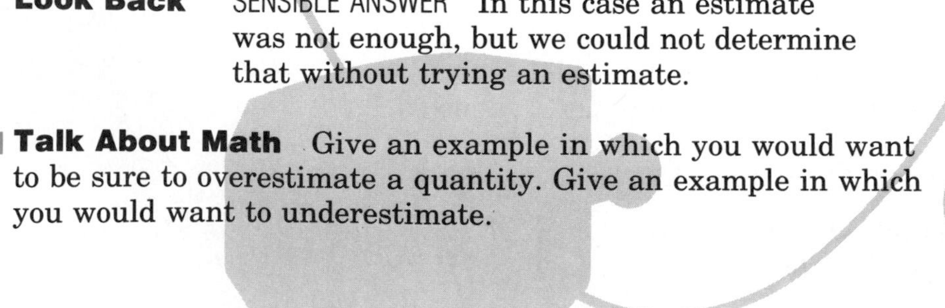

Check Understanding

In each situation, decide whether a wise consumer needs an estimated answer or an exact answer. Explain why.

1. A homeowner is deciding how much paint to buy to paint the garage.
2. A clerk is figuring the sales tax on a customer's purchase.
3. An airline passenger needs to know the departure time for a particular flight.
4. Viewers are interested in the size of the crowd at the President's inauguration.

Practice

Did the consumer in each case make the wise and correct decision?

Organize your work to help you think clearly.

5. Getting ready for her brother's birthday party, Patty estimates that each of the 26 guests will drink 1.5 cups of juice. She estimates $30 \times 2 = 60$ and decides that 60 cups of juice will be enough.
6. Norm had $64 in his checking account and wanted to buy items priced at $21.95, $32.50, and $12.49. He estimated the total cost of the items at $20 + $30 + $10 = $60 and decided to pay by check.
7. Cliff had an important job interview at 9:30 A.M. He knew he could walk 1 block in 1.25 minutes and that he had to walk 13 blocks to his appointment. At 9:15 A.M. he decided he did not need to phone to say he would be late for the appointment.
8. A deep-sea diver will be under water for 45 minutes. She estimates that her air tank is 0.8 full and that a full tank holds 55 minutes of air. She estimates that she has $0.8 \times 50 = 40$ minutes of air and changes to a full tank.

ALGEBRA

Writing Expressions with Decimals

Build Understanding

A museum gift shop sells jewelry and artwork inspired by the world's ancient civilizations.

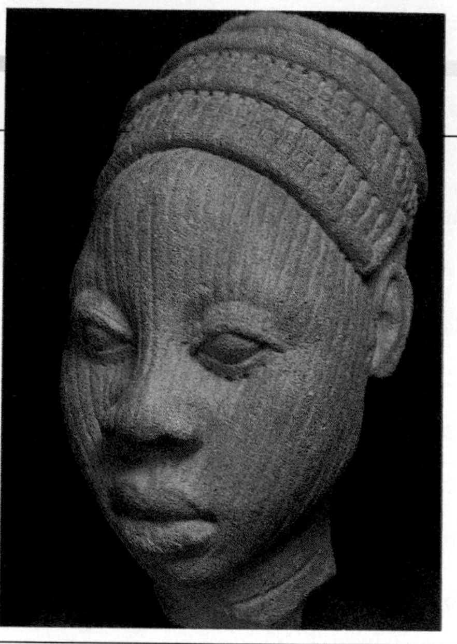

This terracotta head, from the Ife civilization of Nigeria, Africa, is about 800 years old.

A. The shop received m dollars from the sale of terracotta figurines priced at \$16.75 a piece. Write an expression for the number of figurines sold.

$\frac{m}{16.75}$ $\frac{\text{total amount}}{\text{cost per figurine}}$

The expression $\frac{m}{16.75}$ can be used for each of these phrases:

m divided by 16.75
the quotient m divided by 16.75
the result of dividing m by 16.75

B. Write an expression for the total cost of n figurines.

16.75n cost per figurine $\times$ number of figurines

The expression 16.75n can be used for each of these phrases:

16.75 times n n times 16.75
16.75 multiplied by n
the product of 16.75 and n

C. Write an expression for the total cost of a terracotta figurine and a Greek vase priced at x dollars.

16.75 + x cost of figurine + cost of vase

The expression 16.75 + x can be used for each of these phrases:

16.75 plus x 16.75 added to x
x more than 16.75 the sum of 16.75 and x
x increased by 16.75

D. A portrait of Confucius is priced at \$35.50 per print. Write an expression for the change received from d dollars when a print is purchased.

d − 35.50 money given − money spent

The expression d − 35.50 can be used for each of these phrases:

d minus 35.50 35.50 less than d 35.50 subtracted from d
the difference d minus 35.50 d decreased by 35.50

Confucius, one of China's most influential philosophers, lived from 551 to 479 B.C.

Talk About Math Explain how Examples B and C demonstrate the commutative property.

Check Understanding

Write an expression for each phrase.

1. 2.3 times a number
2. A number divided by 2.3
3. The sum of a number and 2.3
4. A number decreased by 2.3

Practice

Number Sense Tell whether the expressions are equal.

5. $2.5 + a$ and $a + 2.5$
6. $9.4 - b$ and $b - 9.4$
7. $0.9 \times c$ and $c \times 0.9$
8. $6.55 \div d$ and $d \div 6.55$

Write an expression for each problem.

9. 3.5 times k
10. m divided by 3
11. The sum of x and 0.45
12. The difference y minus 3.75
13. The quotient 3.4 divided by t
14. The product of x and 6.52
15. 5.4 decreased by a
16. 1.43 more than b
17. 5.6 less than z
18. n multiplied by 6.95
19. x less than 0.42
20. n increased by 9.5
21. 4.5 divided by c
22. h decreased by 0.4
23. 66.4 minus r

Problem Solving

In Ancient Egypt, the cat was a respected animal. The dog was honored in Ancient Persia. This museum shop carries an Egyptian cat pin for $12.50 and a Persian dog pin for $14.75. Write an expression for each problem.

24. The total cost of c cat pins
25. The cost of c cat pins and one dog pin
26. The cost of x dozen cat pins
27. The total income from the sale of d dog pins
28. The number of cat pins sold for a total of n dollars
29. The cost of m cat pins and n dog pins

The cat was revered by the ancient Egyptians. This bronze cat was made in the Late Period, 713–332 B.C.

For each given expression, write a problem.

30. $n + 1.25$
31. $\frac{n}{1.25}$
32. $1.25n$
33. $1.25 - n$

ALGEBRA

Solving Equations Involving Decimals

Build Understanding

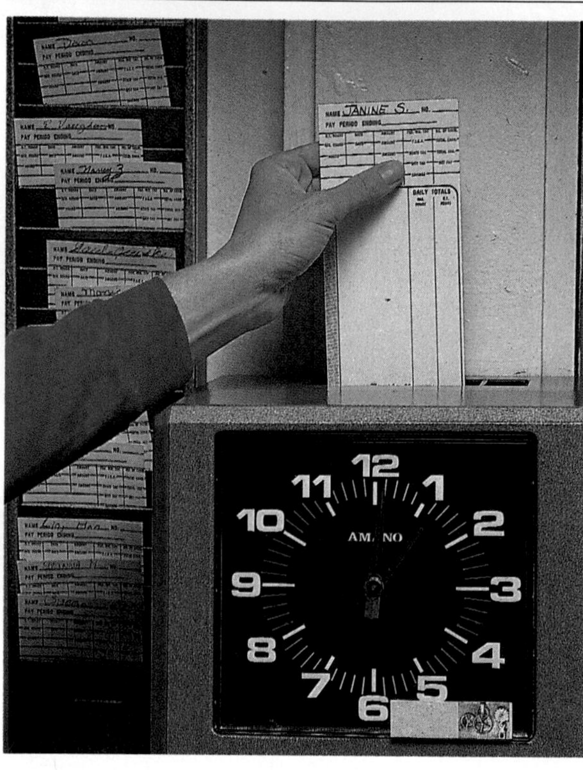

A. Janine earns \$6.50 per hour at her part-time job. Last week her pay before deductions was \$81.25. How many hours did she work last week?

Use a variable, n, to represent the number of hours.

$$6.50n = 81.25$$

Solve the equation for n by dividing both sides of the equation by 6.5.

$$\frac{6.5n}{6.5} = \frac{81.25}{6.5}$$

$$n = 12.5$$

Janine worked 12.5 hours last week.

B. Solve $9.5 = \frac{x}{1.4}$.

Multiply both sides of the equation by 1.4.

$$(1.4)(9.5) = (1.4)\frac{x}{1.4}$$

$$13.3 = x$$

Check the answer by substituting 13.3 for x in the original equation.

$$9.5 \stackrel{?}{=} \frac{13.3}{1.4}$$

$$9.5 = 9.5$$

C. Solve $\frac{m}{3.25} = 14.4$.

Multiply both sides of the equation by 3.25.

$$(3.25)\frac{m}{3.25} = (3.25)(14.4)$$

$$m = (3.25)(14.4)$$

$$m = 46.8$$

Calculator

Press: 46.8 [÷] 3.25 [=]
Display: 14.4

■ **Talk About Math** Look at the equation in Example B. Would you expect the answer to be less than or greater than 9.5? Explain.

Check Understanding

For another example, see Set H, pages 102–103.

Tell which operation you would use to solve for x.

1. $14.3x = 28.6$ **2.** $x - 16.8 = 19.7$ **3.** $6.43 = \frac{x}{8.3}$

Number Sense Tell whether the number given is a solution to the equation. If not, solve the equation.

4. $13x = 7.8 \quad x = 6$ **5.** $\frac{x}{3.6} = 5.7 \quad x = 2.052$ **6.** $13.2 = \frac{y}{0.55} \quad y = 24$

Practice

For More Practice, see Set H, pages 104–105.

Solve each equation. Round decimal answers to the nearest thousandth. **Remember** to line up the decimal points when adding or subtracting.

7. $x + 1.75 = 3.60$ **8.** $t - 11.4 = 1.63$ **9.** $19.03 = z - 1.043$

10. $3.7m = 8.5$ **11.** $0.72 = 14.3b$ **12.** $\frac{a}{14.3} = 17.0$

13. $8.04 = \frac{n}{1.8}$ **14.** $14.8 = 7.4y$ **15.** $\frac{r}{0.01} = 16.4$

16. $500 = \frac{a}{2.5}$ **17.** $6.3 - y = 4.67$ **18.** $\frac{16.8}{x} = 8.4$

19. $\frac{d}{14} = 6.2$ **20.** $1.6m = 14.4$ **21.** $22 = c - 13.45$

22. $55.06 + h = 70$ **23.** $\frac{e}{0.3} = 7.8$ **24.** $16.4 = 0.27w$

25. $\frac{x}{1.7} = 9.8$ **26.** $y + 16.8 = 19.35$ **27.** $8.4 = 3.5m$

Problem Solving

Solve each problem.

28. Keno earned \$105.40 last week. If he worked 15.5 hours, how much did he earn per hour? ($15.5h = \$105.40$)

29. Kim worked 29.25 hours last month. She earned \$5.40 per hour. How much did she earn last month? ($m = 29.25 \times \$5.40$)

30. Janine earned \$58.50 last week. This is half of what she earned during spring vacation. Find her vacation earnings. ($\frac{y}{2} = \$58.50$)

31. **Critical Thinking** What happens when you check your answer to Exercise 10? Explain why this happens.

ALGEBRA

Write an Equation

Understand
QUESTION
FACTS
KEY IDEA

Plan and Solve
STRATEGY
ANSWER

Look Back
SENSIBLE ANSWER
ALTERNATE APPROACH

Build Understanding

The winner of the 1988 Indianapolis 500 mile race averaged 212.86 feet per second. Find the speed in miles per hour. The number of feet per second is about 1.47 times the number of miles per hour.

Understand QUESTION How many miles per hour did the car average?

FACTS The average in feet per second is 212.86. The number of feet per second is about 1.47 times the number of miles per hour.

KEY IDEA Write and solve an equation for the unknown quantity. The answer should be in miles per hour.

Plan and Solve STRATEGY Let n represent the number of miles per hour.

$$212.86 = 1.47n$$

Solve the equation by dividing both sides of the equation by 1.47.

$$\frac{212.86}{1.47} = \frac{1.47n}{1.47}$$

$$144.8 \approx n$$

When you divide 212.86 by 1.47, the quotient is not exact. Round to the nearest tenth. Remember that $\approx$ means "is approximately equal to."

ANSWER The car averaged about 144.8 miles per hour.

Look Back SENSIBLE ANSWER To check, substitute the value back into the equation.

$$212.86 \stackrel{?}{=} (1.47)(144.8)$$

$$212.86 \approx 212.856$$

Talk About Math In the Look Back section, you found that n was not exactly 144.8. Explain what you think caused this.

Check Understanding

Tell which equation you would use to solve each problem.

1. Amy works at the Indy Gift Shop. Her wages of $4.80 per hour are 1.2 times her last year's wages. Find last year's rate of pay.

   a. $1.2w = 4.80$
   b. $\frac{w}{1.2} = 4.80$
   c. $w - 1.2 = 4.80$

2. Geno works at Andy's Garage. His employer deducts about one fourth of Geno's weekly earnings for taxes. If this week's deductions are $28.63, find his earnings for this week.

   a. $s + \frac{1}{4} = 28.63$
   b. $4s = 28.63$
   c. $\frac{s}{4} = 28.63$

Practice

Write and solve an equation for each problem. **Remember** to check your work.

3. The winner of the 1988 Daytona 500-mile race averaged 137.3 miles per hour. Find the average speed in feet per second.

4. How long did it take the winner to complete the 1988 Daytona 500-mile race? **Remember,** distance = rate × time.

5. One year the winner of the Indianapolis 500 averaged 162.175 miles per hour. The winner of the Daytona 500 averaged 176.263 miles per hour. What was the difference in average speed?

6. In 1906, a one-mile speed record of 127.659 miles per hour was set. In 1965, the one-mile speed record was 600.601 miles per hour. How much faster was the 1965 record?

Choose a Strategy

Dabbling in Dates When Holly wrote the date for March 30, 1990, she wrote 3/30/90. She noticed that the product of the month, 3, and the day, 30, equaled the year, 90. She wondered how often that happens.

7. Find the other dates in 1990 for which this is true.
   Hint: What are the prime factors of 90?

8. Find a year for which this is true exactly once.

9. For which years from 1980–1990 will this never be true?

Chapter 3 REVIEW

Skills Review

Multiply or divide. Use mental math.

1. 900 ÷ 30 **2.** 280,000 ÷ 2,000

3. 480,000 ÷ 600 **4.** 6.98 × 1,000

5. 500.43 ÷ 100 **6.** 0.8765 × 10,000

Estimate each quotient by using compatible numbers.

7. 4,601 ÷ 92 **8.** 41,760 ÷ 615

9. 21,865 ÷ 212 **10.** 78,693 ÷ 39

Divide. Round decimal answers to the nearest hundredth.

11. 785 ÷ 14 **12.** 9,300 ÷ 115

13. 24,811 ÷ 67 **14.** 24.18 ÷ 40

15. 75.001 ÷ 33 **16.** 0.45 ÷ 21

Write each fraction as a decimal. Use a bar to indicate repeating digits.

17. $\frac{5}{6}$ **18.** $\frac{21}{25}$ **19.** $\frac{7}{11}$

Use paper and pencil or a calculator to divide. Round decimal answers to the nearest thousandth.

20. 879 ÷ 0.9 **21.** 0.066 ÷ 1.4

22. 42.19 ÷ 2.17 **23.** 590.1 ÷ 16.6

Write an expression for each problem.

24. 3.4 more than x **25.** 2.5 divided by n

Solve each equation.

26. $1.16p = 4.64$ **27.** $\frac{m}{2.3} = 5.75$

28. $r + 8.44 = 12.2$ **29.** $z - 0.05 = 3.02$

Problem-Solving Review

Solve each problem.

30. How many 3-digit numbers have a digital sum of 9?

31. A football stadium seats 60,000 people. All 7 games in a season were sold out. How many tickets were sold?

32. The time it will take the Wagners to reach the campground if they stop 1 hour for lunch is given by the formula $t = \frac{d}{r} + 1$, where t = time in hours, d = distance in miles and r = rate in miles per hour. How many hours will this trip take if the Wagners drive 150 miles at 50 miles per hour?

33. Brad has $40. He wants to buy a pair of jeans for $20.95, a shirt for $15.75, and a belt for $6.25. Does he have enough to buy this outfit?

34. Jan has $2 in quarters. She has an equal number of nickels, dimes, and quarters. How much change does she have in all?

35. **Data File** Use the data on pages 108–109. About what part of the students participating in Junior Achievement were junior-high students?

36. **Make a Data File** Use an almanac or sports reference book. Find a listing of the all-time National Hockey League (NHL) scoring leaders. Make a table with these columns: player's name, games played, goals scored, and average goals scored per game (rounded to the nearest hundredth).

Cumulative Skills Review · Chapters 1–3

Name the form of the number you would use in each situation. Give an example.

1. length of an auto race

2. weight of a dog

3. grade on a math test

4. odometer reading on a car

Use mental math to find each answer.

5. $785 - 271$ **6.** 22×4 **7.** $2 \times 19 \times 5$ **8.** $12 + 48 + 17$

9. $450{,}000 \div 900$ **10.** $800 \div 40$ **11.** $62.4 \div 100$ **12.** $0.035 \times 10{,}000$

Evaluate each expression when $t = 8$.

13. $3t$ **14.** $\frac{t}{2}$ **15.** $t - 5$ **16.** $t + 20$

17. $4t - 1$ **18.** $6 + 2t$ **19.** $40 \div 2t$ **20.** $5(t + 2)$

21. $10t + 20$ **22.** $3(t - 3)$ **23.** $\frac{7}{t + 2}$ **24.** $36 - 4t$

Write an expression for each of the following.

25. k times 16 **26.** m plus 11 **27.** 1.5 times r **28.** 2.7 more than p

29. 9 less than the product of m times 3

30. 12 minus the quotient of 4 divided by k

Estimate each quotient by using compatible numbers.

31. $84{,}125 \div 208$ **32.** $40{,}022 \div 229$ **33.** $1{,}429 \div 69$ **34.** $5{,}630 \div 71$

Divide. Round decimal answers to the nearest hundredth.

35. $365 \div 15$ **36.** $4{,}920 \div 46$ **37.** $14{,}306 \div 71$ **38.** $12.3 \div 12$

39. $926.88 \div 22$ **40.** $0.78 \div 17$ **41.** $19.19 \div 84$ **42.** $2.871 \div 98$

Divide. Round decimal answers to the nearest thousandth.

43. $65.2 \div 1.5$ **44.** $825 \div 0.13$ **45.** $68.86 \div 11.1$ **46.** $0.074 \div 3.8$

Solve each equation.

47. $r + 34 = 70$ **48.** $90 - y = 43$ **49.** $8m = 888$ **50.** $\frac{m}{16} = 9$

51. $245 = 3k + 5$ **52.** $\frac{x}{7} + 1 = 10$ **53.** $2.5w = 50$ **54.** $\frac{h}{4.3} = 12$

55. $42 - t = 11$ **56.** $c - 1.1 = 3.9$ **57.** $6z = 19.5$ **58.** $\frac{v}{9} = 8.5$

Reteaching

Set A pages 74–75

Place value helps you divide with multiples of 10.

270 ÷ 30 tens
270 is 27 tens.
30 is 3 tens.
27 tens ÷ 3 tens = 9

42,**000** ÷ 6**00** = 420 ÷ 6 = 70
39,**000** ÷ 3,**000** = 39 ÷ 3 = 13

Remember, 100 and 1,000 are multiples of 10.

Divide using mental math.

1. 250 ÷ 50 **2.** 5,400 ÷ 90

3. 1,600 ÷ 20 **4.** 4,000 ÷ 50

5. 8,000 ÷ 400 **6.** 20,000 ÷ 400

7. 21,000 ÷ 700 **8.** 480,000 ÷ 6,000

Set B pages 76–77

To estimate a quotient using compatible numbers, look for a dividend that is a multiple of the divisor.

55,983 ÷ 8
55,983 is close to 56,000.
56,000 is a multiple of 8.
Use 56,000 ÷ 8.

Remember, you may change the original divisor, dividend, or both.

Estimate.

1. 22,321 ÷ 44 **2.** 869 ÷ 3

3. 89,999 ÷ 31 **4.** 790 ÷ 18

5. 2,063 ÷ 19 **6.** 1,801 ÷ 295

7. 19,803 ÷ 423 **8.** 1,129 ÷ 374

Set C pages 78–79

Use multiplication facts and estimation to help you divide. Find 372 ÷ 16. Estimate: 320 ÷ 16 = 20.

```
   23R4
16)372     Think:  16 × 2 = 32
   32
   --
    52     Think:  16 × 3 = 48
    48
    --
     4
```

The answer is 23 R4, or 23.25, or $23\frac{1}{4}$.

The answer is close to the estimate of 20.

Remember, a fraction remainder should be in lowest terms.

Divide. Express each quotient as a mixed number.

1. 952 ÷ 48 **2.** 616 ÷ 46

3. 202 ÷ 12 **4.** 777 ÷ 36

5. 15,397 ÷ 4 **6.** 2,910 ÷ 45

Set D pages 82–83

Estimating a product can help you check a decimal quotient with zeros in it.

```
   0.037     2.8 ÷ 70 = 0.04
73)2.701     2.8 is close to 2.701.
```

Remember, try placing the decimal point in the quotient before dividing.

Divide. Check by estimating the product.

1. 72)5.76 **2.** 78)2.886

3. 6)18.36 **4.** 8)0.5944

5. 24)0.1632 **6.** 9)2.061

Set E pages 84–85

To write a fraction as a decimal, divide the numerator by the denominator.

$$\frac{2}{15} = 15\overline{)2.00}\quad 0.1\overline{3}$$

$$\begin{array}{r} 0.1\overline{3} \\ 15\overline{)2.00} \\ \underline{1\,5} \\ 50 \\ \underline{45} \\ 5 \end{array}$$

Remember, place a bar over the digits that repeat.

Write each fraction as a decimal.

1. $\frac{2}{9}$
2. $\frac{3}{5}$
3. $\frac{10}{11}$
4. $\frac{7}{20}$
5. $\frac{16}{27}$
6. $\frac{23}{44}$

Set F pages 88–89

Moving the decimal point right increases a number:

$$1.5 \times 10 = 1.5 = 15.$$

Moving the decimal point left decreases a number:

$$1.5 \div 100 = 0.01.5 = 0.015$$

Remember, the number of zeros in the power of 10 is the number of places you move the decimal point.

Multiply or divide using mental math.

1. 10×9.09
2. $55.7 \div 100$
3. $0.62 \div 10$
4. $8.1 \div 1{,}000$
5. $1{,}000 \times 4.3$
6. $16 \times 10{,}000$

Set G pages 90–91

When dividing by decimals, multiply both the divisor and dividend by the same power of 10 so that you can divide by a whole number divisor.

$0.9\overline{)16.74}$ To get a whole number divisor, multiply 0.9 by 10: $0.9 \times 10 = 9$

Remember, place the decimal point in the quotient after moving decimal points in the dividend and divisor.

Divide.

1. $0.7\overline{)448}$
2. $0.6\overline{)0.009}$
3. $5.9\overline{)72.57}$
4. $2.41\overline{)12.05}$
5. $0.13\overline{)75.959}$
6. $4.08\overline{)2.448}$

Set H pages 96–97

To solve an equation, use the inverse operation. (Addition and subtraction, multiplication and division are inverse operations.)

$1.5x = 9.3$ x has been multiplied by 1.5, so divide by 1.5.

$$\frac{1.5x}{1.5} = \frac{9.3}{1.5}$$

$$x = 6.2$$

Remember, perform the same operation on *both* sides of the equation.

Solve each equation.

1. $0.5d = 4.6$
2. $34.8 = 8.7d$
3. $\frac{a}{4.2} = 7.6$
4. $\frac{s}{0.03} = 3.1$
5. $b + 1.35 = 9.04$

More Practice

Set A pages 74–75

Divide using mental math.

1. 640 ÷ 20 **2.** 3,500 ÷ 50 **3.** 490 ÷ 70 **4.** 24,000 ÷ 60

5. 54,000 ÷ 90 **6.** 7,200 ÷ 80 **7.** 120,000 ÷ 20 **8.** 210,000 ÷ 700

9. 1,600 ÷ 200 **10.** 280,000 ÷ 4 **11.** 22,000 ÷ 1,100 **12.** 450 ÷ 90

13. 630 ÷ 70 **14.** 5,400 ÷ 90 **15.** 16,000 ÷ 800 **16.** 250,000 ÷ 500

17. 8,100 ÷ 900 **18.** 35,000 ÷ 7 **19.** 28,000 ÷ 400 **20.** 200,000 ÷ 500

Set B pages 76–77

Write a pair of compatible numbers for each exercise. Then estimate each quotient.

1. $91\overline{)687}$ **2.** $73\overline{)2,701}$ **3.** $82\overline{)4,430}$ **4.** $224\overline{)11,804}$

5. 2,488 ÷ 892 **6.** 62,008 ÷ 59 **7.** 47,859 ÷ 13 **8.** 95,666 ÷ 285

9. 6,187 ÷ 30 **10.** 75,287 ÷ 251 **11.** 35,998 ÷ 93 **12.** 52,005 ÷ 120

13. 5,710 ÷ 68 **14.** 11,691 ÷ 284 **15.** 23,472 ÷ 58 **16.** 43,811 ÷ 391

Set C pages 78–79

Divide. Round decimal answers to the nearest hundredth.

1. 814 ÷ 29 **2.** 897 ÷ 387 **3.** 1,795 ÷ 342 **4.** 6,700 ÷ 827

5. 2,488 ÷ 34 **6.** 1,272 ÷ 173 **7.** 2,992 ÷ 74 **8.** 316,333 ÷ 398

9. $\frac{8,563}{84}$ **10.** $\frac{89,517}{46}$ **11.** $\frac{82,280}{44}$ **12.** $\frac{84,168}{28}$

13. 3,218 ÷ 28 **14.** 8,064 ÷ 175 **15.** 1,927 ÷ 33 **16.** 30,513 ÷ 16

17. 19,510 ÷ 43 **18.** 10,616 ÷ 56 **19.** 2,439 ÷ 615 **20.** 9,472 ÷ 565

Set D pages 82–83

Find each quotient. Round decimal answers to the nearest hundredth.

1. 16.836 ÷ 46 **2.** 1.476 ÷ 36 **3.** 2.208 ÷ 24 **4.** 0.865 ÷ 5

5. $12\overline{)28.092}$ **6.** $58\overline{)298.106}$ **7.** $15\overline{)1,682.2}$ **8.** $23\overline{)369.15}$

9. $21\overline{)6.854}$ **10.** $56\overline{)290.685}$ **11.** $19\overline{)75.0001}$ **12.** $83\overline{)22.6543}$

13. $18\overline{)53.602}$ **14.** $28\overline{)16.241}$ **15.** $56\overline{)1,064.3}$ **16.** $35\overline{)651.6}$

Set E pages 84–85

Write each fraction as a decimal. Use a bar to indicate repeating digits.

1. $\frac{2}{15}$ **2.** $\frac{1}{9}$ **3.** $\frac{15}{66}$ **4.** $\frac{7}{45}$ **5.** $\frac{11}{37}$ **6.** $\frac{10}{55}$

7. $\frac{16}{45}$ **8.** $\frac{4}{125}$ **9.** $\frac{8}{23}$ **10.** $\frac{3}{8}$ **11.** $\frac{6}{11}$ **12.** $\frac{33}{54}$

13. $\frac{5}{16}$ **14.** $\frac{3}{500}$ **15.** $\frac{8}{55}$ **16.** $\frac{12}{125}$ **17.** $\frac{10}{11}$ **18.** $\frac{9}{20}$

Set F pages 88–89

Multiply or divide.

1. $1{,}000 \times 2.6$ **2.** 5.732×100 **3.** $447.2 \div 100$

4. 10×236.7 **5.** $300.2 \div 10$ **6.** $0.8342 \times 10{,}000$

7. $895.6 \div 1{,}000$ **8.** $9.3 \div 100$ **9.** $0.56 \div 100$

10. $12.85 \div 100$ **11.** $81.3 \times 1{,}000$ **12.** $0.019 \div 1{,}000$

13. 0.109×100 **14.** $3.7 \div 10{,}000$ **15.** $0.4 \times 10{,}000$

Set G pages 90–91

Divide using paper and pencil or a calculator. Tell which method you used. Round decimal answers to the nearest thousandth.

1. $\frac{536}{0.8}$ **2.** $\frac{0.296}{3.7}$ **3.** $\frac{0.324}{5.4}$ **4.** $\frac{2.5}{0.625}$

5. $\frac{7.105}{2.03}$ **6.** $\frac{10.404}{61.2}$ **7.** $\frac{20.712}{86.3}$ **8.** $\frac{0.01458}{0.243}$

9. $8.6\overline{)304.2}$ **10.** $1.2\overline{)144.12}$ **11.** $19.6\overline{)384.16}$ **12.** $73.9\overline{)184.75}$

Set H pages 96–97

Solve each equation.

1. $4.68m = 23.4$ **2.** $\frac{n}{5.5} = 1.1$ **3.** $10.25 = 4.95 + t$

4. $1.8 + a = 3.2$ **5.** $0.001d = 0.0283$ **6.** $b - 99.3 = 1.1$

7. $\frac{c}{2.8} = 4.48$ **8.** $3.75s = 1.875$ **9.** $r - 13.39 = 2.05$

10. $8.3c = 2.49$ **11.** $t + 1.06 = 8.131$ **12.** $x - 5.9 = 10.25$

13. $2.8d = 7.84$ **14.** $\frac{b}{0.04} = 300$ **15.** $7.1 + d = 20$

16. $z - 0.19 = 4.3$ **17.** $0.98 + f = 4$ **18.** $\frac{x}{0.8} = 15$

Enrichment

Expressing Repeating Decimals as Fractions

Before math class, someone wrote a fraction on the chalkboard and beside it wrote the repeating decimal equivalent of the fraction. Unfortunately, someone else rubbed against the board and accidentally erased the fraction.

Anthony claimed that he could find the erased fraction using an equation. He wrote:

Let n be the erased fraction.

$n = 0.272727\ldots$

He multiplied both sides of the equation by 100. $100n = 27.272727\ldots$

He subtracted n from both sides. (**Remember,** $n = 0.272727\ldots$) $-\ n = -0.272727\ldots$

$99n = 27$

Then he solved the equation for n. $\frac{99n}{99} = \frac{27}{99}$

$n = \frac{27}{99}$, or $\frac{3}{11}$

The erased fraction was $\frac{3}{11}$

1. Why did Anthony multiply n by 100 rather than by 10, 1,000, or some other number?

2. What would Anthony have multiplied n by if the repeating decimal had been $0.\overline{4}$? if it had been $0.\overline{235}$?

Express each repeating decimal as a fraction.

3. $0.\overline{7}$ 4. $0.\overline{21}$ 5. $0.\overline{45}$ 6. $0.\overline{86}$

7. $0.\overline{432}$ 8. $0.\overline{603}$ 9. $0.\overline{416}$ 10. $2.\overline{15}$

11. **Calculator** Use your calculator to express $\frac{23}{99}$, $\frac{16}{99}$, $\frac{58}{99}$ as decimals. Then tell an easy way to find a fraction that is equivalent to a decimal that has two repeating digits.

Chapter 3 Review/Test

Multiply or divide.

1. 2,000 ÷ 40 **2.** 90,000 ÷ 300

3. 3.25 × 1,000 **4.** 57 ÷ 100

Choose which estimate is most reasonable.

5. 58,328 ÷ 28

a. 200 **b.** 2,000 **c.** 20,000

6. 91,232 ÷ 105

a. 900 **b.** 9,000 **c.** 90,000

7. Ms. Ferraro has 23,560 bolts to put into bags with 12 bolts in each bag. About how many bags can she fill?

Divide. Round your answers to the nearest hundredth.

8. $61\overline{)3{,}272}$ **9.** 9,462 ÷ 31

10. $8\overline{)5.5}$ **11.** 36.39 ÷ 0.3

12. Juan's club bought 150 hamburger patties for a picnic. Hamburger buns come in packages of 8 buns each. How many bags of buns should the club buy?

Estimate to choose the correct quotient.

13. $42\overline{)2.94}$

a. 0.07 **b.** 0.71 **c.** 7.07

14. $0.25\overline{)373.36}$

a. 14.93 **b.** 149.34 **c.** 1,493.44

15. Tasty Yogurt costs $1.59 for a 9-ounce container. To the nearest cent, how much does the yogurt cost per ounce?

Write each fraction as a terminating or repeating decimal. Use a bar to indicate repeating decimals.

16. $\frac{13}{15}$ **17.** $\frac{9}{20}$

Write an expression for each problem.

18. 8.2 times b **19.** 1.9 less than n

Solve each equation.

20. $x + 1.3 = 6.42$ **21.** $\frac{x}{0.6} = 2.4$

22. Tell which equation could be used to solve the problem.

Mr. Matthews gives one-fifteenth of his weekly earnings to charity. Last week he gave $35 to charity. How much did he earn last week?

a. $\frac{x}{15} = 35$

b. $15x = 35$

c. $35x = \frac{1}{15}$

23. Write About Math Katy wants to buy 18 yards of ribbon. The ribbon costs 48¢ per yard. She has $9.00. She makes the following estimate of how much the ribbon will cost: 20 × 0.50 = 10.00. Can Katy tell from this estimate whether she has enough money? Why or why not?

Data File

1. Season Ticket Prices

	Thursday A-B-C Series 10 Concerts	Friday A-B Series 7 Concerts	Saturday A-B Series 10 Concerts	Friday C-D-E Series Saturday C Series 5 Concerts
Main Floor				
Rows A	$ 50	$ 35	$ 50	$ 25
B	125	87.50	135	67.50
C-D	200	140	220	110
E-O	390	273	440	220
P-X	315	220.50	350	175
Balcony				
Rows A-L	390	273	440	220
J-K-L (Center)	315	220.50	350	175
M-S	250	175	280	140
Gallery				
Rows A-I	125	87.50	135	67.50
J (Partial View)	60	42	60	30
Box Seats				
Side	700	490	700	350
Center	800	560	800	400

1. Chart:
The chart shows the prices for season tickets.

2. Chart:
The chart shows various ways to transport cargo.

3. Graph:
The circle graph shows the number of students that participated in Junior Achievement during a recent school year.

4. Table:
The table shows lengths and weights of the largest animals.

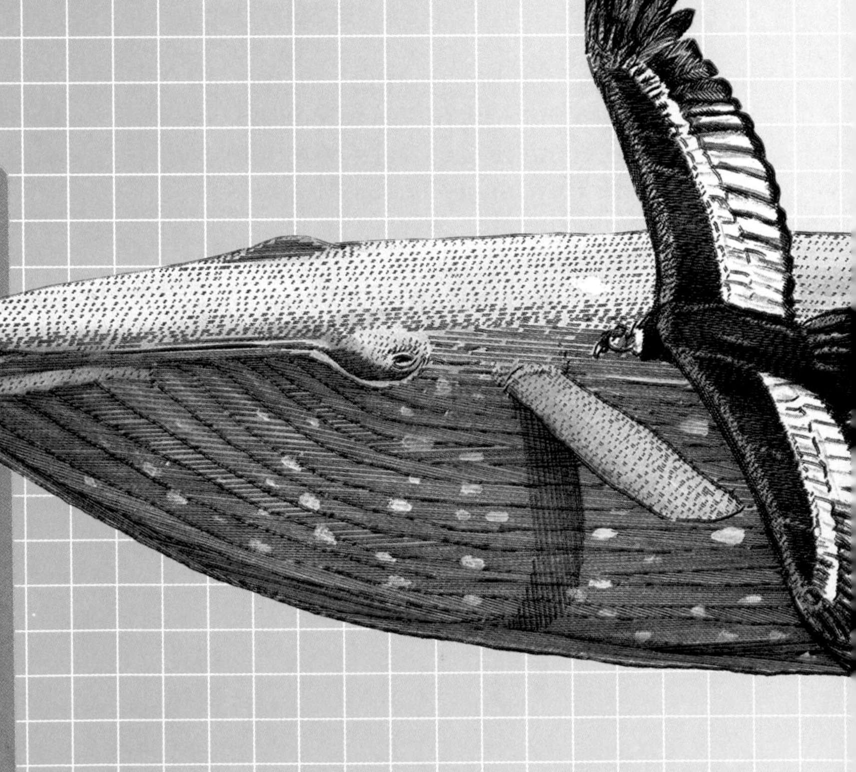

2. Characteristics of Cargo Carriers

	Speed Miles per day	Volume Carried Ton-miles per day	Cost Per ton-mile
RAILROAD TRAIN	480	3,450,000	$0.014
MOTOR TRUCK	700	14,000	$0.05
EXPRESSWAY MOTOR TRUCK	1,000	40,000	$0.05
AIRPLANE (DC-3)	3,600	10,800	$0.22
JET AIRPLANE (707 and DC-8)	11,500	245,000	$0.10 (maximum)
JUMBO JET AIRPLANE (747)	12,000	1,200,000	$0.10 (maximum)
CARGO SHIP	550	6,820,000	$0.01 to $0.05
CONTAINER SHIP	600	17,400,000	$0.01 to $0.05
BARGE TOW	120 (upstream)	4,800,000	$0.01 to $0.02

3. Circle Graph

4. Animal Champions

Largest Animal (living or extinct)

Mammal	Blue Whale	100 ft long	150 tons
Fish	Whale Shark	45 ft long	13 tons
Land animal	African Bull Elephant	10 ft tall	6 tons
Reptile	Salt-water Crocodile	16 ft long	1,150 pounds
Fresh-water fish	Pirarucu	15 ft long	500 pounds
African cat	Lion	10 ft long	500 pounds
Bird	Ostrich	8 ft tall	300 pounds
Lizard	Komodo Dragon	10 ft long	200 pounds
Rodent	Waterhog (Capybara)	4 ft long	150 pounds
Amphibian	Giant Salamander	5 ft long	100 pounds
Flying Bird	Condor	15 ft (wingspan)	25 pounds
Frog	Goliath	1 ft long	10 pounds

Cumulative Review/Test Chapters 1–3

Give the letter for the correct answer.

1. Divide.

$6\overline{)765}$

a. 1.275
b. 12.75
c. 127.5
d. not given

2. Solve $\frac{d}{3} + 10 = 13$.

a. $d = 1$ b. $d = 9$
c. $d = 7\frac{2}{3}$ d. $d = 69$

3. Bill needs 40 ounces of canned tomatoes for spaghetti sauce. Each can of tomatoes contains 12 ounces. How many cans should he buy?

a. 4 cans b. 3 cans c. 5 cans

4. Estimate the sum.

213 + 1,083 + 462

a. 700 b. 1,800
c. 1,600 d. 7,000

5. Evaluate $2t - 3$ when $t = 5$.

a. 2 b. 13 c. 10 d. 7

6. Estimate.

84,982 ÷ 19

a. 40 b. 400
c. 4,000 d. 40,000

7. If potatoes are selling for $0.89 a pound, what will 5.3 pounds of potatoes cost?

a. $4.72 b. $0.47
c. $0.48 d. $47.17

8. Solve mentally.

593 − 480

a. 93
b. 513
c. 213
d. not given

9. Multiply.

0.7×0.9

a. 6.3
b. 0.63
c. 0.063
d. not given

10. Which calculation would be easiest to do by mental math?

a. 137×24 b. $13 \times 7 \times 8$
c. $4 \times 7 \times 25$ d. 36×243

11. Choose the operation that should be used to solve this problem. Then solve the problem.

There are 144 rubber bands in a package. How many rubber bands are in 72 packages?

a. addition; 216 rubber bands
b. multiplication; 10,368 rubber bands
c. subtraction; 72 rubber bands
d. division; 2 rubber bands

12. What is the missing number?

cars	0	1	2	3	4	5
people	0	5	10	15	20	?

a. 20 b. 17 c. 15 d. 25

13. Solve this equation.

$t + 15 = 30$

a. $t = 2$
b. $t = 15$
c. $t = \frac{1}{2}$

14. Which is an expression for the phrase 3 less than v?

a. $v + 3$ b. $v - 3$ c. $3 - v$

15. Solve.

$n + 4 = 12$

a. $n = 3$
b. $n = 8$
c. $n = 16$
d. $n = 48$

16. Choose the equation that should be used to solve the problem. Then solve the problem.

Christine is 6 inches shorter than Ron. Christine is 66 inches tall. How tall is Ron?

a. $h + 6 = 66; h = 60$
b. $6h = 66; h = 11$
c. $h - 6 = 66; h = 72$
d. $h + 66 = 66; h = 0$

17. Evaluate $3 + 5 \times 8 - 2$ using the standard order of operations.

a. 41 **b.** 48
c. 62 **d.** not given

18. What is 63,000 divided by 700?

a. 9 **b.** 90
c. 900 **d.** not given

19. Michael's bowling scores for 4 games were 183, 169, 190, and 186. What is his average?

a. 163 **b.** 174 **c.** 195 **d.** 182

20. A 14-mile trail is divided into 4 equal sections. How long is each section?

a. 3 mi **b.** 3 R2 mi
c. $3\frac{1}{2}$ mi **d.** 4 mi

21. Write $\frac{5}{8}$ as a decimal.

a. 0.625 **b.** $0.62\overline{5}$
c. $0.6\overline{25}$ **d.** $0.\overline{625}$

22. Multiply.

0.308×100

a. 3.08
b. 0.00308
c. 30.8
d. 0.0308

23. Divide.

$0.7\overline{)1.05}$

a. 0.015
b. 0.15
c. 1.5
d. not given

24. Looking at an electronics catalog, Susie decided to buy items that cost $10.98, $25.39, and $9.97. Which is the best estimate of how much money she should take to the store?

a. $30 **b.** $60
c. $50 **d.** $40

25. Which is an expression for the total distance traveled in 2.35 hours at a rate r.

a. $\frac{2.35}{r}$ **b.** $2.35r$
c. $2.35 + r$ **d.** $\frac{r}{2.35}$

26. Solve.

$\frac{x}{0.5} = 1.2$

a. $x = 0.6$
b. $x = 1.7$
c. $x = 0.7$
d. $x = 2.4$

27. Choose the equation that should be used to solve the problem.

How many sheets of paper 24.4 centimeters long can you cut from a roll of paper 146.4 centimeters long?

a. $146.4 - n = 24.4$
b. $n - 24.4 = 146.4$
c. $146.4n = 24.4$
d. $24.4n = 146.4$

28. Solve.

$9v = 27$

a. $v = 3$
b. $v = 243$
c. $v = 30$
d. $v = 24$

Geometry

Did You Know: A magnetic compass points to the magnetic north pole, not the true north pole. To correct for this, use the declination of your location. If the declination is 11°E, the compass points 11° east of true north. True north lies 11° to the left of the magnetic needle.

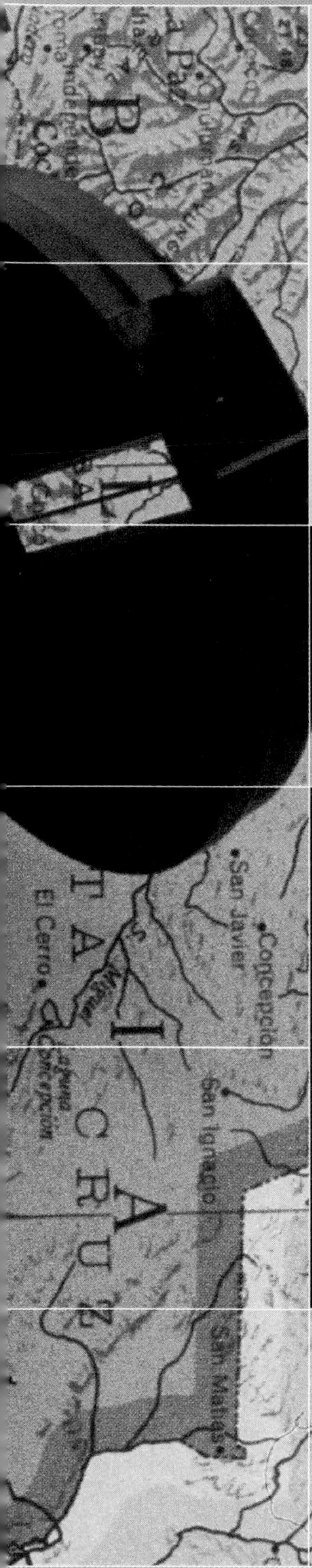

Number-Sense Project

Estimate

Some approximate declinations are:

Cincinnati	0°
Philadelphia	10° W
Bangor, ME	20° W
San Antonio	10° E
Los Angeles	15° E
Helena, MT	20° E

Estimate your area's declination.

Gather Data

Where in the United States are the declinations about 0? East of true north? West of true north? What is the declination where you live?

Analyze and Report

Explain how you would use a compass to find true north where you live.

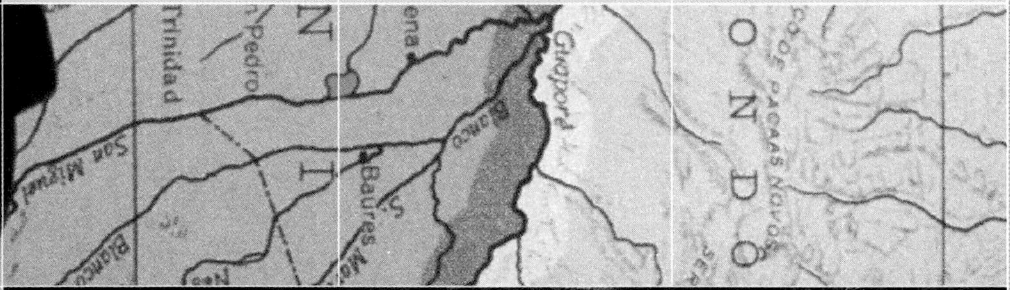

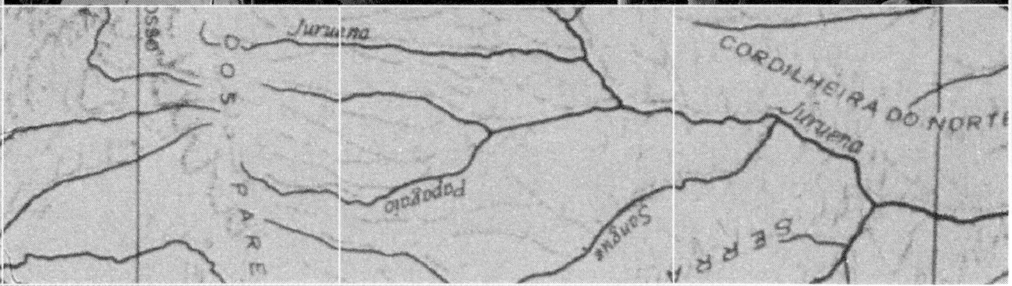

Points, Lines, and Planes

Build Understanding

Mr. Gonzales and his crew use a laser to make sure that they are laying each section of pipe straight. A round disk is placed on the end of each new section of pipe. When a laser beam aimed down the center of the pipe passes through a small hole in the disk, the pipe is in the right position.

Laser technology works in the construction trades to align and check for level assembly.

A. The light from a laser appears as a beam because it strikes and reflects off particles in the air. Each speck of dust in the air suggests a ***point.*** In geometry, a point has a precise location but no size or shape. A point is represented by a dot and named with a capital letter.

When connected, the sections of pipe will form a straight line. In geometry, a ***line*** extends without end in opposite directions. Two points on the line are used to name the line.

If the new section of pipe is not lined up correctly, the laser's light will be blocked, producing a small bright spot on the disk. The path of the beam from the laser to this spot suggests a ***segment.*** A segment contains two points on a line, called ***endpoints,*** and the points between them.

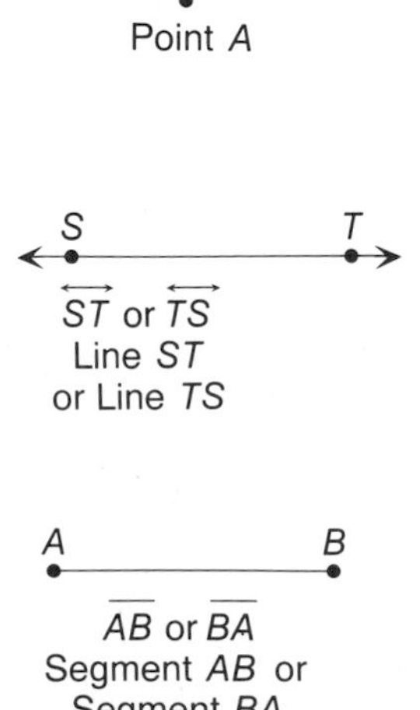

The path of the laser beam suggests a ***ray*** when sections of the pipe are properly aligned. A ray is part of a line with one endpoint. A ray extends without end in one direction. The endpoint of the ray is always named first. Ray *AB* and ray *BA* are not the same ray.

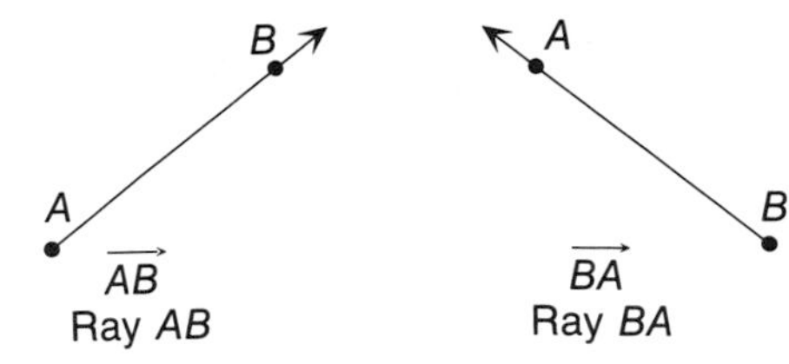

B. A ***plane*** is a flat surface that extends without end in all directions. Lines in the same plane that never intersect, or meet, are called ***parallel lines. Intersecting lines*** are lines in a plane that meet. Intersecting lines share a common point called the ***point of intersection.***

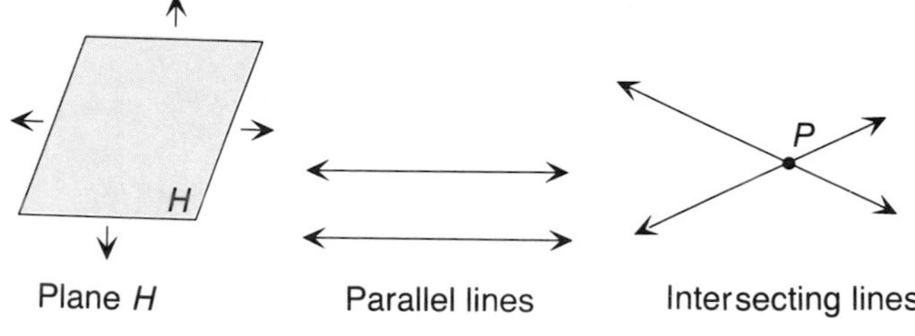

C. ***Skew lines*** are lines that are not in the same plane.

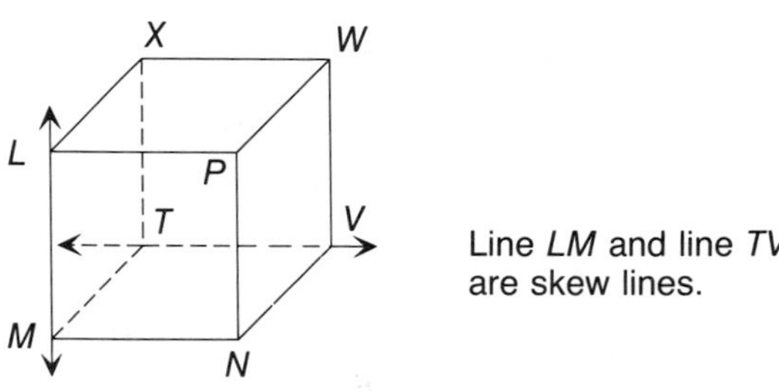

Talk About Math Can skew lines be parallel?

Check Understanding

For another example, see Set A, pages 148–149.

During slide presentations at business meetings, Linda Wong uses a light pointer to point to things on the projection screen.

For Exercises 1–3, tell which geometric idea is suggested.

1. The small spot on the screen made by the pointer

2. The flat surface of the projection screen

3. The path of the beam from the pointer to the spot on the screen

Tell whether each statement is *true* or *false*.

4. A line has 2 endpoints.

5. Another name for segment *XY* is segment *YX*.

6. Another name for $\overrightarrow{VU}$ is $\overrightarrow{UV}$.

Practice

For More Practice, see Set A, pages 150–151.

For Exercises 7–16, use the diagram at the right.

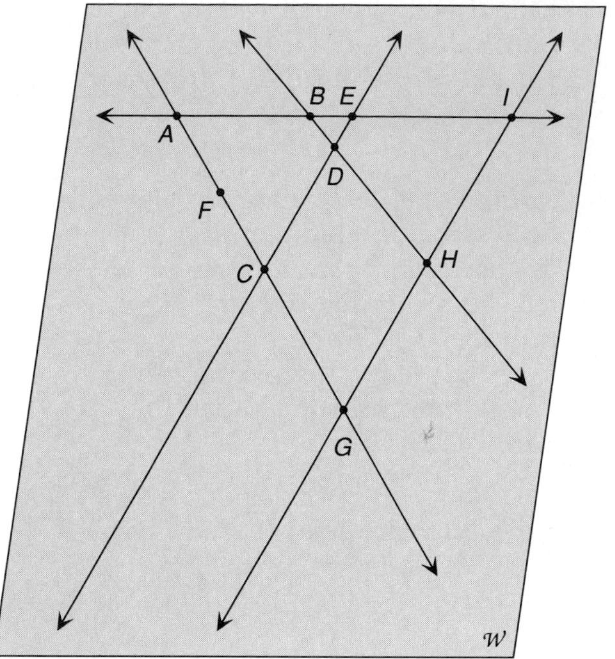

7. Name three segments.

8. Name three lines.

9. Name two pairs of intersecting lines.

10. Name three rays.

11. Name the intersection of $\overleftrightarrow{CG}$ and $\overleftrightarrow{BE}$.

12. Name a plane.

13. Name a pair of lines that appear to be parallel.

14. Give another name for $\overline{GC}$.

15. Give another name for $\overrightarrow{GC}$.

16. Give three other names for $\overleftrightarrow{GC}$.

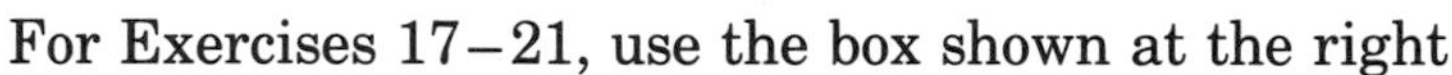

For Exercises 17–21, use the box shown at the right.

17. Name three pairs of intersecting lines.

18. Name the intersection of $\overleftrightarrow{JK}$ and $\overleftrightarrow{KL}$.

19. Name three pairs of parallel lines.

20. Name two lines parallel to $\overleftrightarrow{JK}$.

21. Name two skew lines.

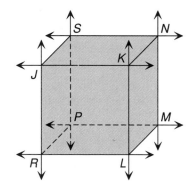

Draw and label each figure described below.

22. Point P

23. $\overline{AB}$

24. $\overrightarrow{CD}$

25. $\overleftrightarrow{EF}$

26. Plane S

27. Parallel lines $\overleftrightarrow{GH}$ and $\overleftrightarrow{JK}$

28. $\overleftrightarrow{MN}$ and $\overleftrightarrow{QR}$ intersecting at T

29. Skew lines $\overleftrightarrow{UV}$ and $\overleftrightarrow{WX}$

Problem Solving

What is the greatest number of points of intersection of the given lines?

30. 2 lines **31.** 3 lines **32.** 4 lines **33.** 5 lines

Jason uses four lasers for special lighting effects for concerts. Draw 4 lines with the given number of points of intersection to indicate a pattern he can make.

34. Three **35.** Four **36.** Six

Solve each problem.

37. Draw two points. How many different lines will contain both points?

38. Use Data Refer to the table on page 89. A roll of quarters is valued at $10. Find its weight.

39. How many segments can you draw using two of the points below at a time?

• • •
• • •
• • •

40. Critical Thinking A farmer has 9 trees that he wants to plant in 10 rows with 3 trees per row. Draw a diagram to show how the farmer can do this. (Hint: Think of the trees as points and the rows as segments.)

Skills Review

pages 78–79, Review, 567

Round each number to the place specified.

1. Tens: 98.2 **2.** Hundreds: 169 **3.** Thousands: 4,490

4. Hundred thousands: 238,409 **5.** Millions: 8,560,085 **6.** Hundreds: 238.427

Divide. If necessary, round to the nearest hundredth.

7. 198 ÷ 12 **8.** 676 ÷ 4 **9.** 375 ÷ 100

10. 75 ÷ 4 **11.** 33 ÷ 15 **12.** 6,494 ÷ 8

13. 8,213 ÷ 215 **14.** 9,999 ÷ 11 **15.** 11,786 ÷ 8

16. 56,088 ÷ 456 **17.** 14,520 ÷ 121 **18.** 21,347 ÷ 50

Mental Math Use mental math to divide.

19. 825 ÷ 5 **20.** 2,000 ÷ 5 **21.** 1,800 ÷ 90

Classifying Angles

Build Understanding

Wright Angles
Ever since her marriage rite, Mrs. Wright exercised her right to fish on the Indian reservation. She did it right, fishing to the right of the upright pole, and caught enough fish to write home about.

What do you notice about the newspaper article? One meaning of the word "angle" is "to fish." In geometry, an ***angle*** is a figure formed by two rays with the same endpoint, which is called the ***vertex*** of the angle. Angles can be classified according to their measures.

A. An ***acute angle*** is an angle with a measure of less than 90°.

A ***right angle*** is an angle with a measure of 90°. The sides of a right angle are ***perpendicular***.

An ***obtuse angle*** has a measure between 90° and 180°.

A B C

$\angle ABC$ (or $\angle CBA$) can also be called $\angle B$.

Acute angle

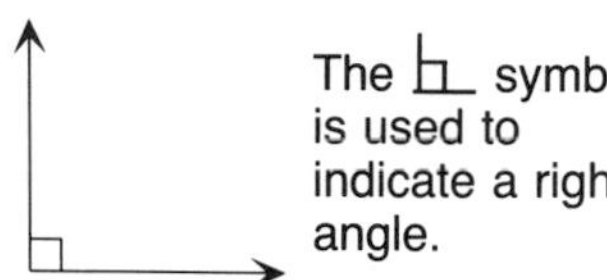

The ⊾ symbol is used to indicate a right angle.

Right angle

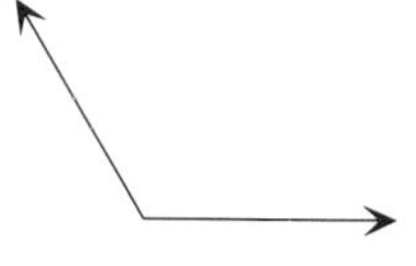

Obtuse angle

B. If the sum of the measures of two angles is 90°, the angles are ***complementary.*** If the sum of the measures of two angles is 180°, the angles are ***supplementary.***

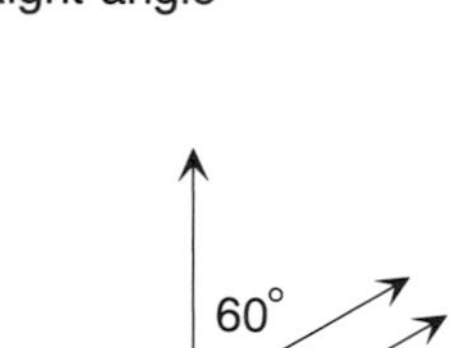
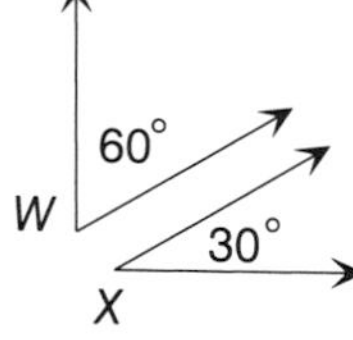

$\angle W$ and $\angle X$ are complementary angles.

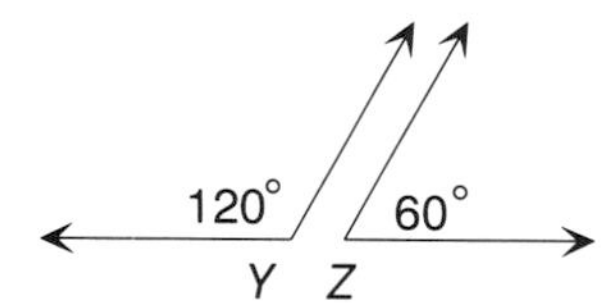

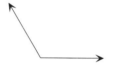

$\angle Y$ and $\angle Z$ are supplementary angles.

C. ***Vertical angles*** are formed by two intersecting lines. ***Adjacent angles*** share a common side and do not overlap.

M N Q P O

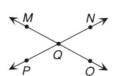

$\angle MQN$ and $\angle PQO$ are vertical angles. $\angle MQP$ and $\angle NQO$ are also vertical angles.

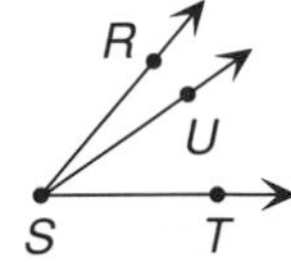

$\angle RSU$ and $\angle UST$ are adjacent angles.

■ **Talk About Math** Must supplementary and complementary angles have adjacent sides? Explain.

Check Understanding

Use the picture of Mrs. Wright for Exercises 1 and 2.

1. What type of angle is formed by the vertical pole and the ground?

2. What type of angle is formed by the fishing pole and the line?

3. Name the vertex of $\angle QRS$.

4. Give two other names for $\angle QRS$.

Practice

Use the diagram to name two of the given angles.

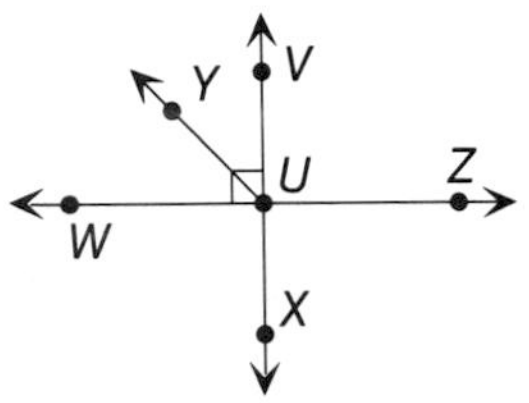

5. Acute angles

6. Vertical angles

7. Supplementary angles

8. Right angles

9. Adjacent angles

10. Angles with $\overrightarrow{UY}$ for one side

11. Obtuse angles

12. Complementary angles

Tell whether these statements are *true* or *false*.

13. Two intersecting lines form only one pair of vertical angles.

14. One of two supplementary angles is always acute.

15. If an angle has a measure of 90°, its sides are perpendicular.

16. Adjacent angles have the same vertex.

17. A 40-degree angle and a 50-degree angle are complementary.

18. A right angle and an 80-degree angle are supplementary.

Problem Solving

Solve.

19. **Estimation** Without using a protractor, try to draw an angle with a measure of 50°. Then measure the angle with a protractor.

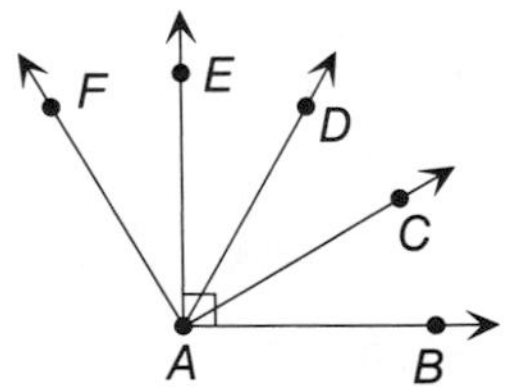

Use the diagram for Problems 20–22. Give the number of

20. different angles.

21. pairs of complementary angles.

22. different obtuse angles.

23. **Critical Thinking** Each angle in a pair of complementary angles is a complement of the other. Does every angle have a complement? Explain.

Classifying Triangles

Build Understanding

A. Triangles can be classified according to the measures of their angles.

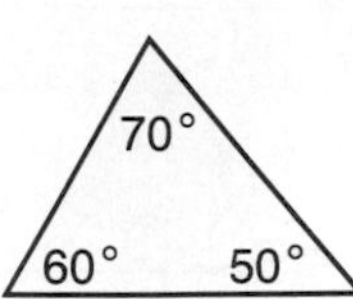

Acute triangle
Three acute angles
70 + 60 + 50 = 180

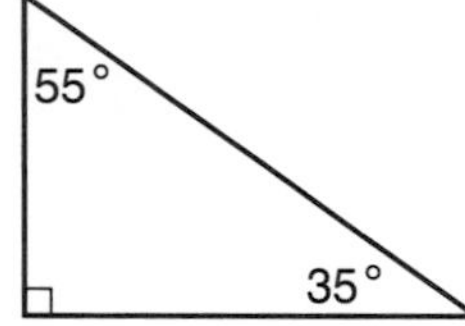

Right triangle
One right angle
90 + 55 + 35 = 180

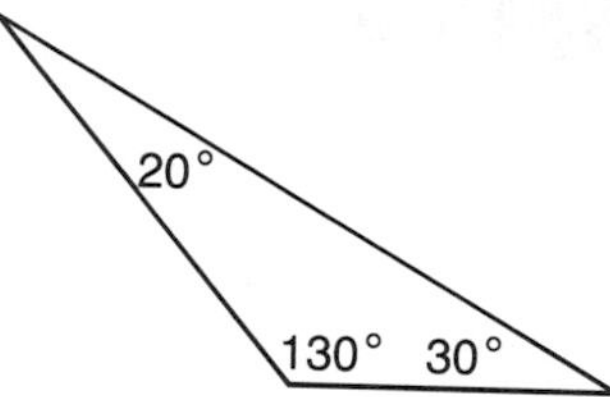

Obtuse triangle
One obtuse angle
130 + 30 + 20 = 180

Notice that in each triangle the sum of the measures of the angles is 180°. This is true for all triangles.

B. Triangles can be classified according to the lengths of their sides.

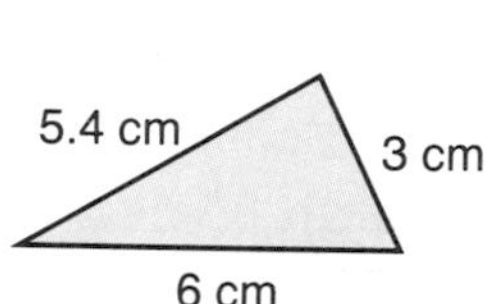

Scalene triangle
No sides of equal length

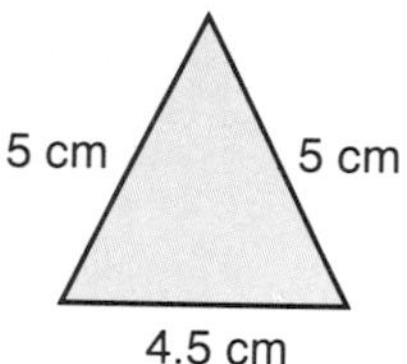

Isosceles triangle
At least two sides of equal length

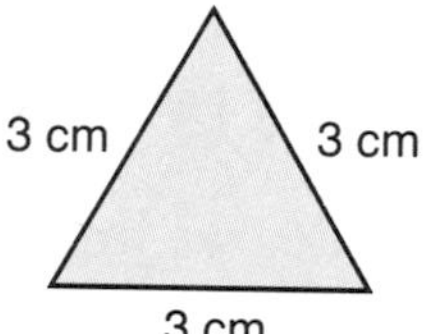

Equilateral triangle
Three sides of equal length

C. Find the measure of angle B.

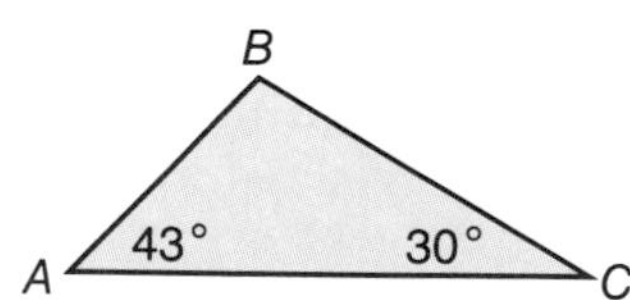

You know that the sum of the measures of the angles in $\triangle ABC$ is 180°.

43 + 30 = 73 Add the measures given. Then subtract the sum from 180°.

180 − 73 = 107

The measure of angle B is 107°, that is, $m\angle B = 107$.

■ **Talk About Math** Can a triangle have two right angles? Can a triangle have two obtuse angles? Explain your answers.

Check Understanding

For another example, see Set B, pages 148–149.

Use $\triangle RST$ for Exercises 1–3.

1. Find $m\angle S$.

2. Is $\triangle RST$ acute, right, or obtuse?

3. Is $\triangle RST$ scalene, isosceles, or equilateral?

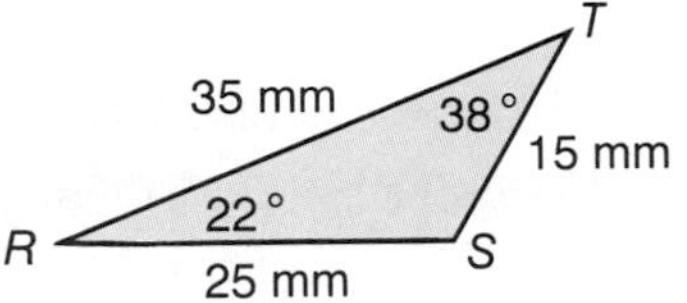

Practice

For More Practice, see Set B, pages 150–151.

Tell whether you would use mental math, paper and pencil, or calculator. Then find the missing angle measure in each triangle.

4. $\angle A$

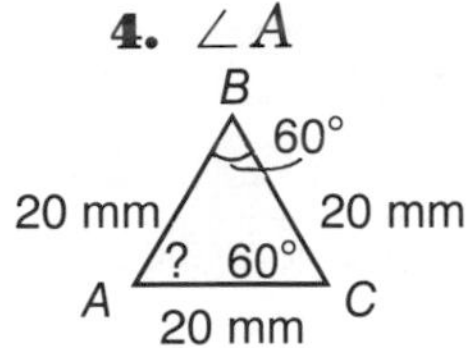

5. $\angle Y$

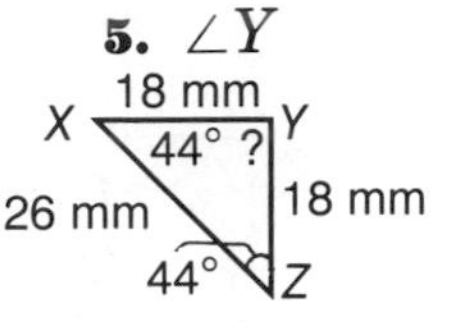

6. $\angle P$

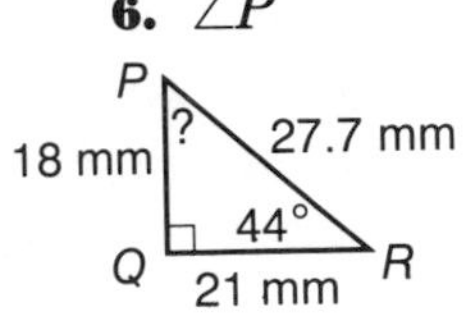

7. $\angle E$

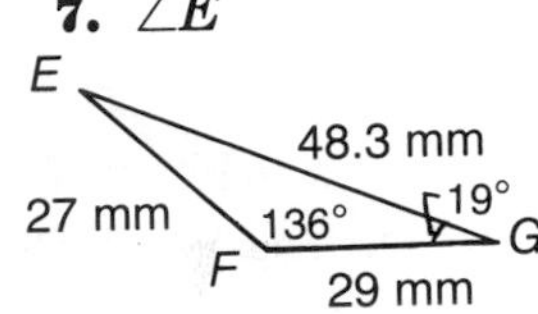

8. $\angle J$

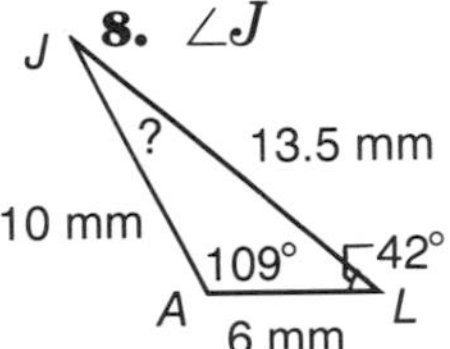

9. $\angle T$

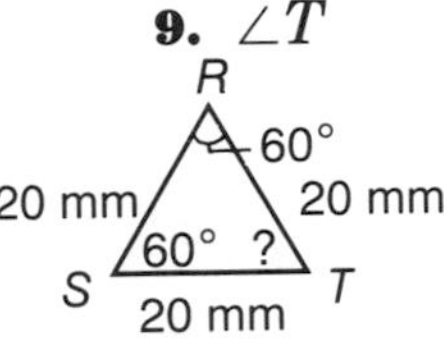

10. $\angle M$

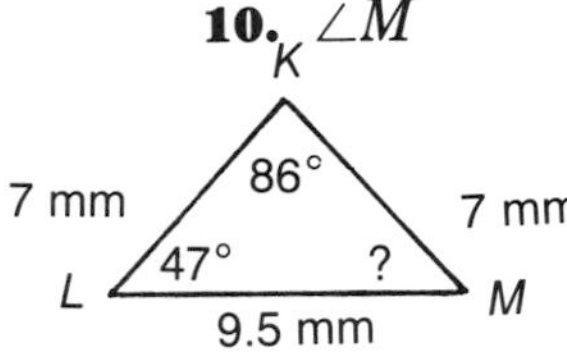

11. $\angle W$

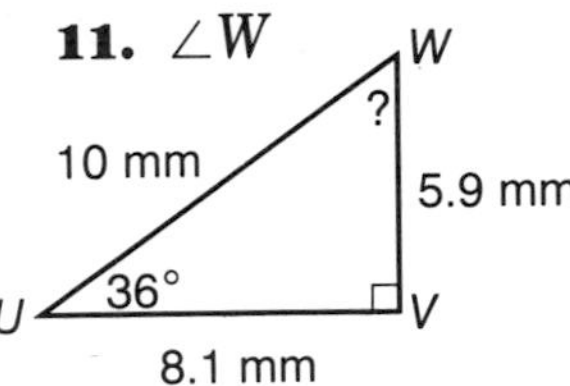

Describe each triangle above using the names *acute, right, obtuse, scalene, isosceles,* or *equilateral*. More than one name may apply.

12. $\triangle ABC$ **13.** $\triangle XYZ$ **14.** $\triangle PQR$ **15.** $\triangle EFG$

16. $\triangle JAL$ **17.** $\triangle RST$ **18.** $\triangle KLM$ **19.** $\triangle UWV$

Problem Solving

Critical Thinking Tell whether each statement is *always true, sometimes true,* or *never true.*

20. A right triangle is also an isosceles triangle.

21. An obtuse triangle is also a right triangle.

22. An acute triangle is also a scalene triangle.

23. An isosceles triangle is also an equilateral triangle.

Solve.

24. The walking path in City Park is in the shape of an equilateral triangle. One side of the path is 350 yards long. How long is the entire path?

Classifying Polygons

Build Understanding

Quilting is a centuries-old art done the world over. In Japan and China quilting is used in coats and kimonos. In Egypt cushion covers and wall hangings are quilted.

In America and many other countries quilts are used as blankets. Many quilt patterns are based on designs from other cultures. The quilt square shown at the right is based on an old Arabic design. The individual pieces of fabric suggest ***polygons.***

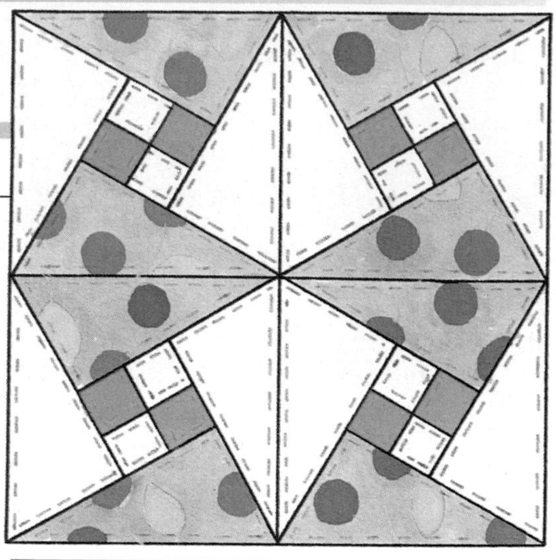

This quilt pattern is called Arabic Lattice.

A. A polygon is a closed figure formed by three or more segments joined at their endpoints. Polygons are classified according to the number of sides they have.

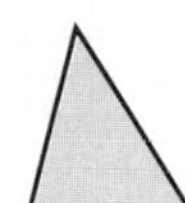

Triangle
3 sides

Quadrilateral
4 sides

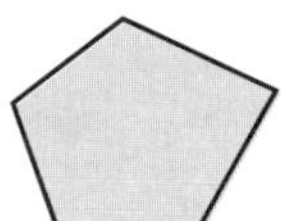

Pentagon
5 sides

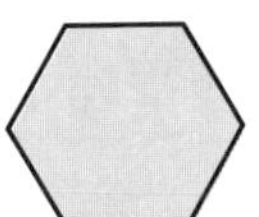

Hexagon
6 sides

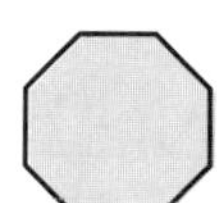

Octagon
8 sides

A polygon with n sides is called an ***n*-gon**. For example, a polygon with 11 sides is called an 11-gon. A polygon is named by giving its vertices in order. The polygon at the right is pentagon $ABCDE$. A ***regular polygon*** is a polygon with all sides of equal length and all angles of equal measure.

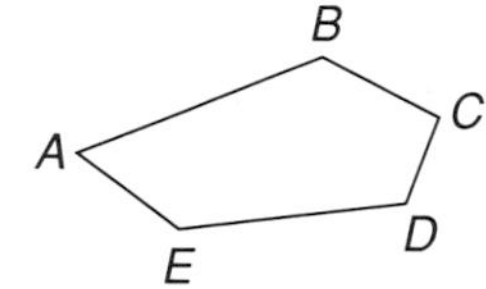

B. These are special quadrilaterals.

Trapezoid
Exactly 2 parallel sides

Parallelogram
Opposite sides parallel and equal in length

C. These are special parallelograms.

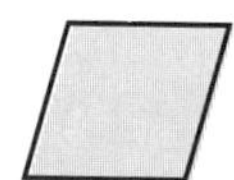

Rhombus
4 sides equal in length

Rectangle
4 right angles

Square
4 sides equal in length and 4 right angles

■ **Write About Math** Which of the figures in Example A are regular?

Check Understanding

For another example, see Set C, pages 148–149.

In the quilt square on page 122, what polygon is suggested by these pieces of fabric?

1. blue pieces

2. large white pieces

3. small white pieces

4. pink pieces

Practice

For More Practice, see Set C, pages 150–151.

Tell whether each statement is *true* or *false*.

5. All squares are rectangles.

6. All squares are rhombuses.

7. All rectangles are squares.

8. All parallelograms are rectangles.

9. All squares are regular polygons.

10. All rhombuses are regular polygons.

Draw the figure described. If it is impossible to draw, explain why.

11. A regular hexagon

12. A 13-gon

13. A rectangle that is not a square

14. A square that is not a rectangle

15. A parallelogram with a right angle

16. A rectangle that is a rhombus

17. A pentagon with sides equal in length but with angles unequal in measure

18. A parallelogram with four sides of different lengths

Problem Solving

Mikhail made quilts with designs influenced by the cultures of Mexico, North America, and Japan. Name the polygons suggested by the pieces of fabric in each quilted square.

19.

Pattern: Mexican Star

20.

Pattern: Arrowheads

21.

Pattern: Japanese Vase

22. **Critical Thinking** Design your own quilt square using at least three different types of polygons. Draw the pattern and identify the various polygons.

Make a Table

Understand
QUESTION
FACTS
KEY IDEA

Plan and Solve
STRATEGY
ANSWER

Look Back
SENSIBLE ANSWER
ALTERNATE APPROACH

Build Understanding

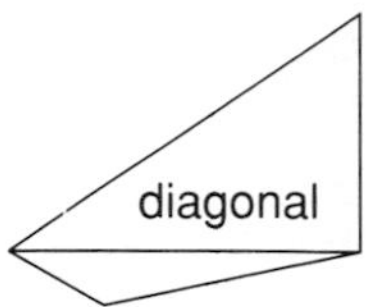

A ***diagonal*** of a polygon is a segment that joins one vertex to another, but is not a side of the polygon. How many diagonals can be drawn from one vertex of a polygon with n sides?

Understand QUESTION How many diagonals can be drawn from one vertex?

FACTS The polygon has n sides.

KEY IDEA A diagonal joins one vertex to another, but is not a side of the polygon.

Plan and Solve STRATEGY Find the number of diagonals that can be drawn from one vertex of a polygon with a given number of sides by drawing a diagram. Repeat the procedure for other polygons. Make a table and look for a pattern.

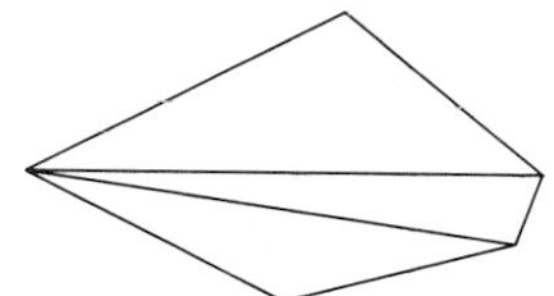

Number of sides	4	5	6	7	8	9	10	11	12
Number of diagonals from one vertex	1	2	3	4	5	6	7	8	9

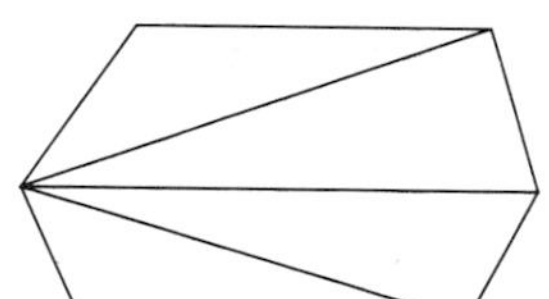

ANSWER In each case, the number of diagonals from one vertex is three less than the number of sides in the polygon. So the number of diagonals from one vertex of a polygon with n sides is three less than n, or $n - 3$.

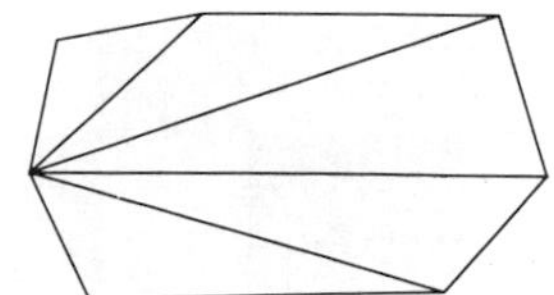

Look Back SENSIBLE ANSWER A polygon with n sides has n vertices. The two vertices adjacent to the one you are using cannot be endpoints of a diagonal, so the answer $n - 3$ is correct.

Talk About Math How many diagonals can be drawn from one vertex of a polygon with 100 sides?

Check Understanding

Tell whether you would use pencil and paper or a calculator. Then find the sum of the angle measures in an n-gon.

1. Copy the table on page 124 and add two rows to the bottom. Label the rows "Number of triangles formed by diagonals from one vertex" and "Sum of the angles of the polygon."

2. Count the number of triangles formed by diagonals from one vertex of each polygon. Enter the information into the table.

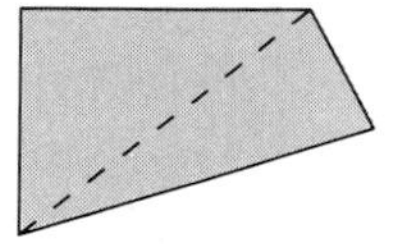
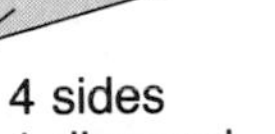

4 sides
1 diagonal
2 triangles

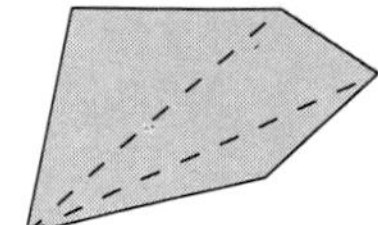

5 sides
2 diagonals
3 triangles

3. Remember, the sum of the angle measures of a triangle is 180°. Complete the fourth row of the table.

ALGEBRA **4.** Look for a pattern that will help you write an equation for the sum of the angle measures in an n-gon. Write the equation.

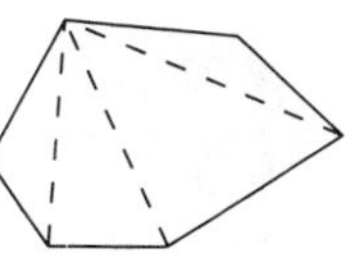

6 sides
▒ diagonals
▒ triangles

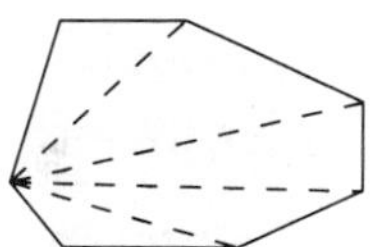

7 sides
▒ diagonals
▒ triangles

Practice

The diagrams show the number of diagonals that can be drawn from all vertices in a quadrilateral or in a pentagon. Copy the table below and use pictures to help you find the total number of diagonals that can be drawn in the polygons.

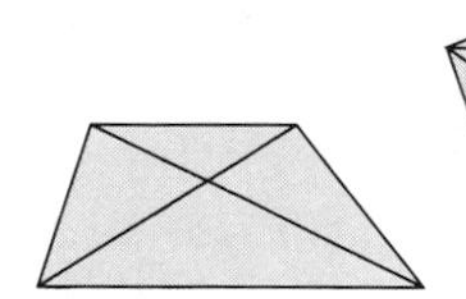

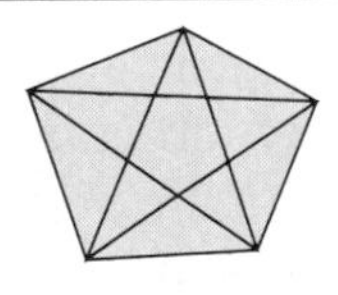

Number of sides in polygon	3	4	5	6	7	8	9	10
Number of diagonals from all vertices	0	2	5	9	**5.**	**6.**	**7.**	**8.**
Increase in number of diagonals		$2 - 0 = 2$	$5 - 2 = 3$	4	**9.**	**10.**	**11.**	**12.**

13. Notice how the number of diagonals increases as the number of sides increases. Use the pattern you see to extend the table for polygons with 11 through 16 sides.

14. **Critical Thinking** Is the total number of diagonals in a 12-sided polygon simply equal to 12 times the number of diagonals from *one* vertex? Explain your answer.

ALGEBRA **15.** The results of Exercises 5–13 show a pattern that can help you find an expression for the number of diagonals in an n-gon. Write the expression.

Circles

Build Understanding

Since the beams these horses are harnessed to keep them a fixed distance from the post, the path is a circle.

In the early 1800s, horses were used to power farm equipment. Today, horsepower is a unit of measure: a one-horsepower machine can lift 550 pounds one foot in one second.

A. A ***circle*** is the set of all points in a plane at a given distance from a point called the ***center***.

A segment that has the center of a circle and a point on the circle as its endpoints is a ***radius***.

A ***chord*** is a segment with endpoints on the circle. A chord passing through the center is a ***diameter***. A diameter of a circle is twice as long as a radius.

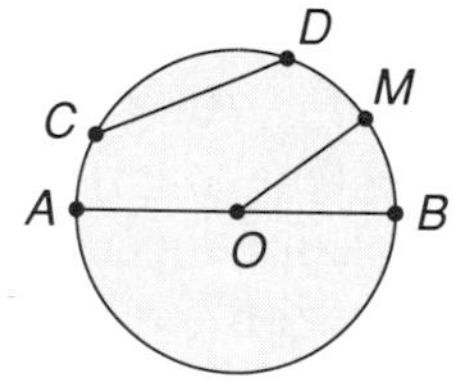

Point O is the center of circle O. $\overline{OM}$ is a radius of circle O. $\overline{OA}$ and $\overline{OB}$ are also radii. $\overline{CD}$ is a chord. $\overline{AB}$ is a diameter.

B. A ***central angle*** is an angle with the vertex at the center of a circle. An ***arc*** is part of a circle. Arc EG, which can be written $\overset{\frown}{EG}$, contains points E and G and the shorter part of the circle between them. $\overset{\frown}{EFG}$ contains points E, G, and the larger part of the circle between them, including point F.

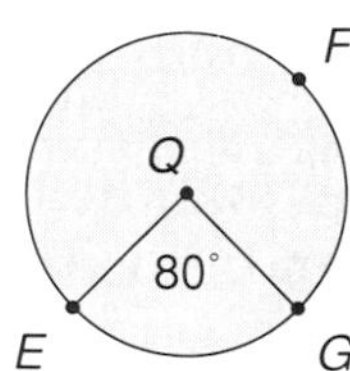

$\angle EQG$ is a central angle, and $\overset{\frown}{EG}$ and $\overset{\frown}{EFG}$ are arcs of circle Q. In circle Q, $m\angle EQG = 80$, so $m\overset{\frown}{EG} = 80$.

C. We say that central angle EQG intercepts $\overset{\frown}{EG}$. The measure of the arc that a central angle intercepts is equal to the measure of the central angle.

Talk About Math How many diameters can be drawn in one circle? Are they of equal length?

Check Understanding

For another example, see Set D, pages 148–149.

Choose the best answer. Use the drawing at the top of the page.

1. The wooden crossbeam is most like the __?__ of a circle.
   a. diameter **b.** radius **c.** arc

2. The vertical post passes through the __?__ of the circle.
   a. center **b.** radius **c.** chord

Practice

For More Practice, see Set D, pages 150–151.

Use circle N.

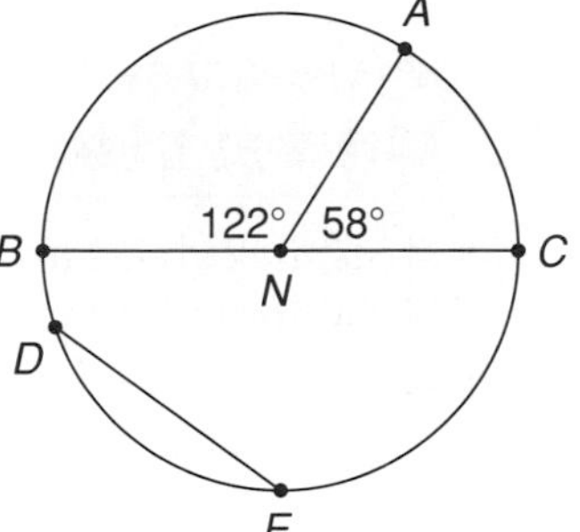

3. Name the center.

4. Name a diameter.

5. Name an arc.

6. Name three radii.

7. Name two central angles.

8. Name two chords.

9. Find the measure of $\overset{\frown}{BA}$.

10. Find the measure of $\overset{\frown}{AC}$.

11. Name the arc that contains points A and D and the shorter part of the circle between them. Name another point on this arc.

12. Name the arc that contains points A and D and the larger part of the circle between them. Name another point on this arc.

13. Name the central angle that intercepts $\overset{\frown}{AB}$.

Draw circle G. Then draw and label each figure in circle G.

14. $\overline{GH}$, a radius

15. $\overline{HJ}$, a diameter

16. $\overline{JK}$, a chord

17. $\angle MGO$, a central angle

Problem Solving

Solve each problem.

18. A radius of a circle is 2 inches long. What is the diameter of the circle?

19. A diameter of a circle is 10 cm. Find the radius of the circle.

Draw circle C showing two perpendicular diameters.

20. What is the measure of each of the four central angles?

21. What is the number of degrees around the center of the circle?

Explore ______ Math

Solve each problem.

22. Draw regular polygons with the following numbers of sides: 3, 4, 6, 8, 10.

23. Describe what seems to happen to the polygons as the number of sides increases.

CAREER CONNECTION

Translations

Build Understanding

Magda designs video games. She is writing a computer program that will display this figure in different locations on the screen. When the different locations of the figure are displayed one after another very quickly, the original figure will appear to "fly" across the screen. Sliding, or translating, a figure from one location to another without turning it is called a ***translation.***

A. Show the results when the figure is translated 5 units to the right.

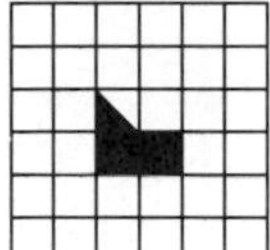

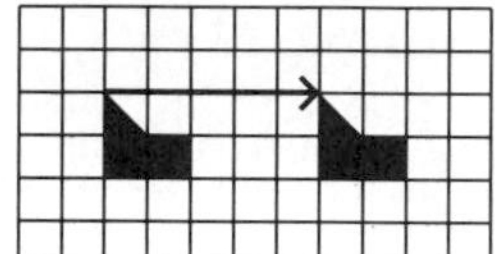

Move the point at the top of the figure 5 units to the right. Do the same for the other points and shade the figure. The two figures have the same size and shape. Two geometric figures with the same size and shape are said to be ***congruent.*** You can think of congruent figures as the same figure moved to a different position.

B. Describe the translation used to move the blue figure to the red one.

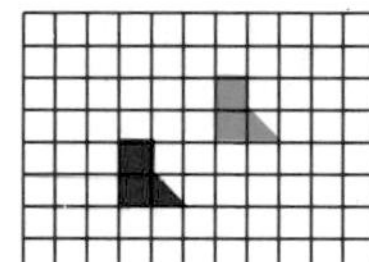

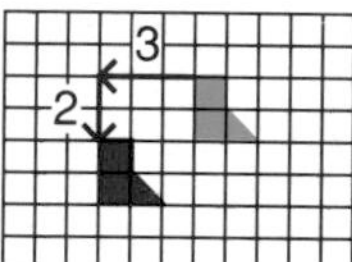

The upper left-hand point of the figure is moved 3 units to the left and 2 units down. All the other points do the same, so the translation is 3 units to the left and 2 units down.

■ **Talk About Math** In Example B, would you get a different translation of the figure if you moved the lower right-hand point of the figure 2 units down and 3 units to the left? Explain your answer.

Check Understanding

Complete each of the following.

1. Figures that have the same size and shape are ___?___.

2. A ___?___ is the slide of a figure from one location to another without turning it.

Practice

Describe the translations used to get the blue figure from the red one.

3.

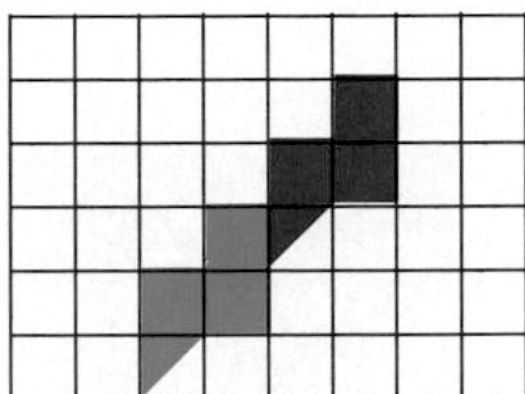

4.

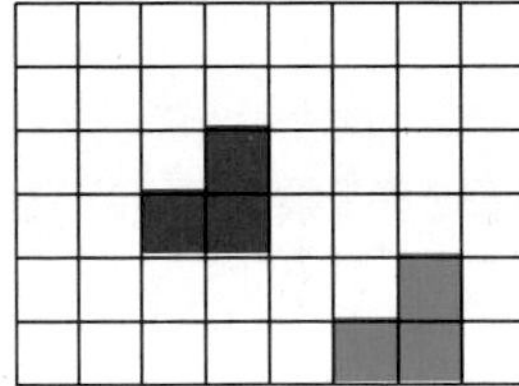

Copy each figure onto grid paper. Then draw the result of the given translation. **Remember** to move each point on the figure the same distance.

5. Up 5 units

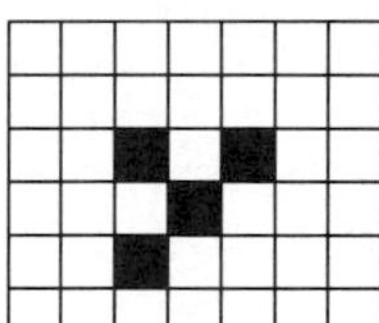

6. 3 units to the right

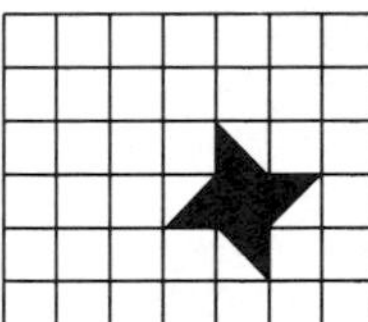

7. Down 2 units, 8 units to the left

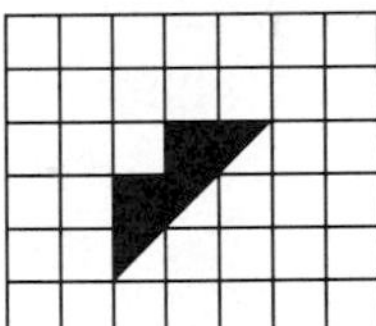

8. Down 2 units, 2 units to the right

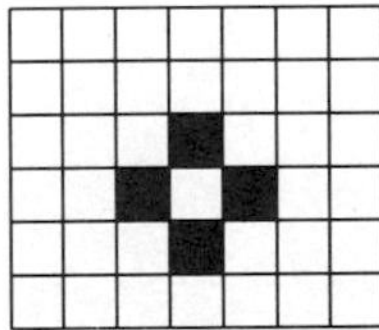

9. Down 3 units, 3 units to the left

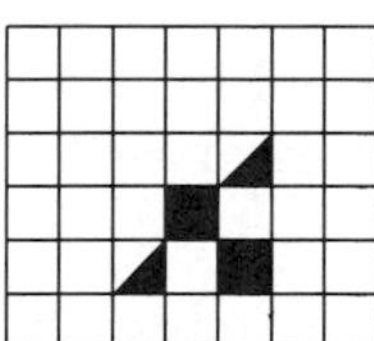

10. Up 1 unit, 1 unit to the right

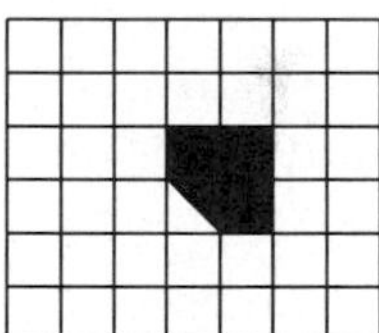

Problem Solving

Describe each translation.

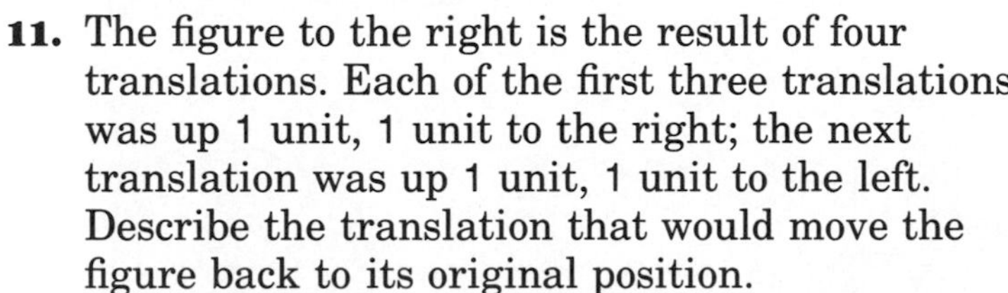

11. The figure to the right is the result of four translations. Each of the first three translations was up 1 unit, 1 unit to the right; the next translation was up 1 unit, 1 unit to the left. Describe the translation that would move the figure back to its original position.

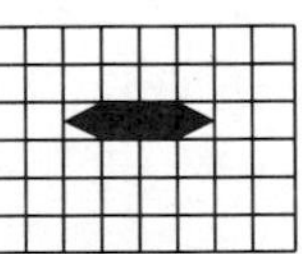

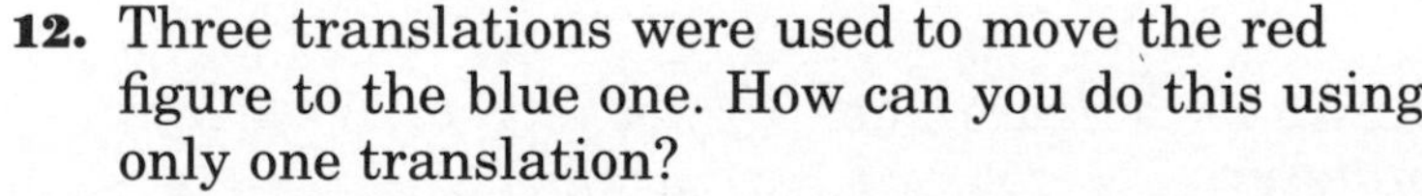

12. Three translations were used to move the red figure to the blue one. How can you do this using only one translation?

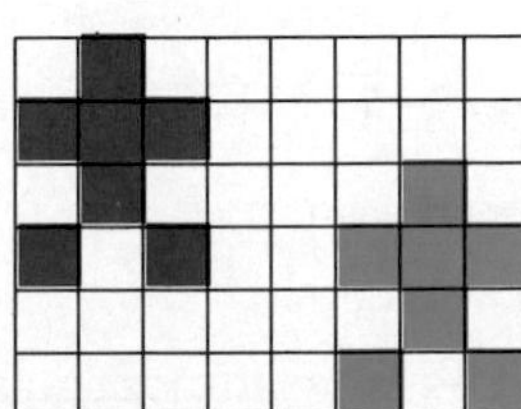

Reflections and Rotations

Build Understanding

Archaeologists can tell a lot about a group of people by studying the patterns on their baskets, cloth, and pottery. Archaeologists can group tribes or bands of people together based on similarities in their designs. By studying changes in such patterns, archaeologists can also determine when a group was introduced to new ideas.

A. The pottery of San Ildefonso Pueblo in New Mexico contains several interesting border patterns. What do you notice about this pattern?

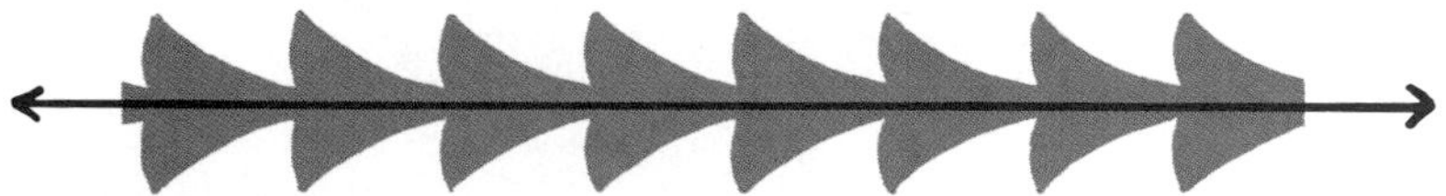

If you flip the top half of this pattern onto the bottom half by folding it, you will find that the two halves are identical. Each half of each figure in the pattern is a ***reflection*** of the other over the fold line. A reflection "flips" a figure over some line or point.

B. When folding a figure results in two matching halves, the fold line is a ***line of symmetry.***

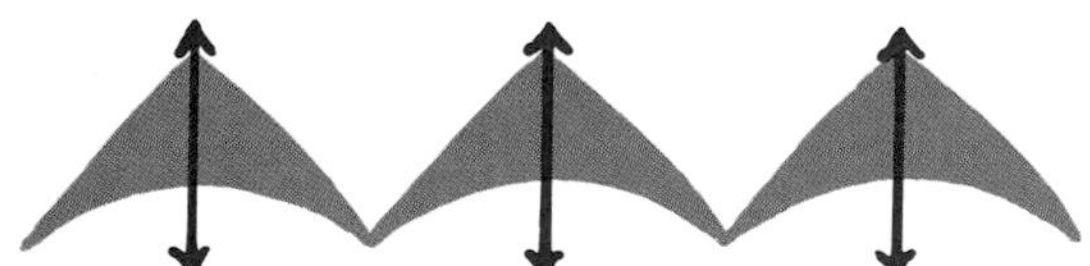

Each figure in this border pattern has one line of symmetry.

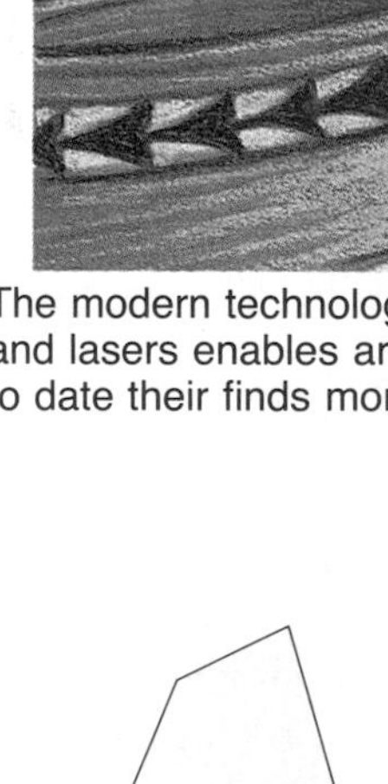

The modern technology of X-rays and lasers enables archaeologists to date their finds more precisely.

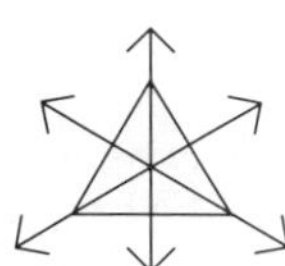

Three lines of symmetry

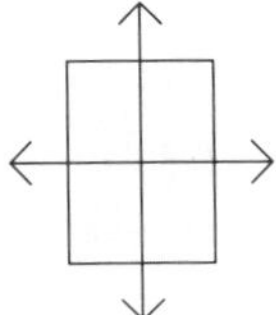
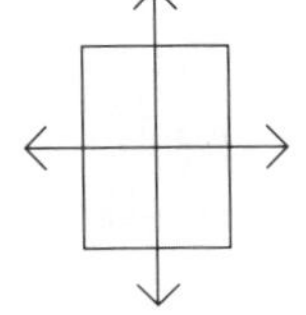

Two lines of symmetry

No lines of symmetry

If a line of symmetry can be drawn for a figure, the figure is said to have ***line symmetry.***

C. The diagram shows two ***rotations.*** A rotation turns a figure around a given point. A 90° clockwise turn of the black triangle around point A gives the red triangle. A 90° clockwise turn of the red triangle gives the blue triangle. A 180° clockwise rotation of the black triangle gives the blue triangle.

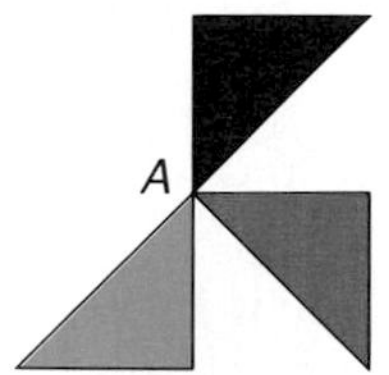

D. This figure taken from a border pattern has ***point symmetry.*** A figure has point symmetry if it looks exactly the same after a rotation of 180° about a point in its center.

Talk About Math How many lines of symmetry does a circle have? Describe them.

Check Understanding

For another example, see Set E, pages 148–149.

Choose the best answer.

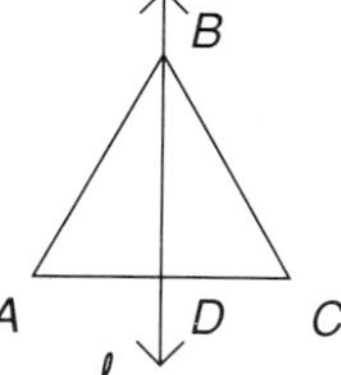

1. $\triangle ABD$ is a ___?___ of $\triangle CBD$ over line ℓ.
a. reflection **b.** translation **c.** 90° rotation

2. Line ℓ is a ___?___ of $\triangle ABC$.
a. reflection **b.** line of symmetry **c.** rotation

Practice

For More Practice, see Set E, pages 150–151.

Tell whether each pattern is formed by a rotation or a reflection of a white figure.

3. 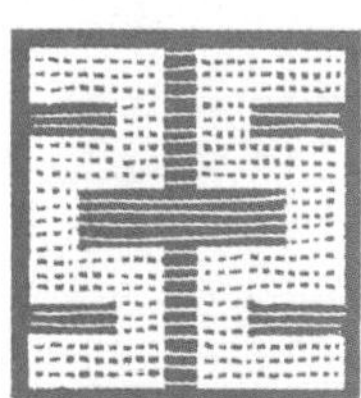

4. 

5. 

6. 

7. 

8. 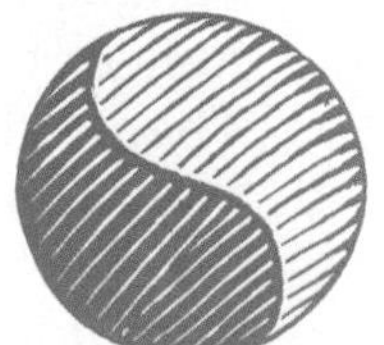

9. 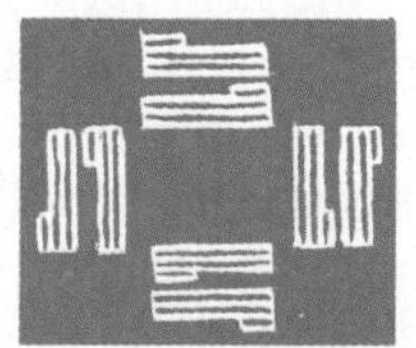

10. 

Trace each letter. Draw all lines of symmetry.

11. B **12.** C **13.** D **14.** S **15.** X **16.** Y **17.** Z

Copy each figure onto grid paper. Draw the rotation or reflection described.

18. Rotate 90° clockwise about Q.

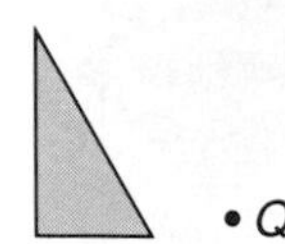

19. Reflect over the line.

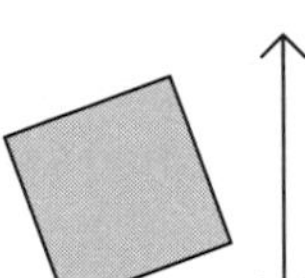

20. Rotate 180° about R.

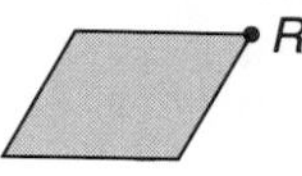

21. Rotate 180° about P.

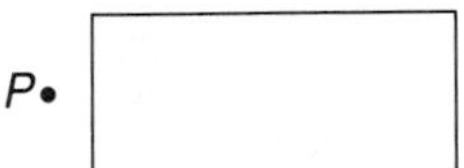

22. Rotate 90° about O.

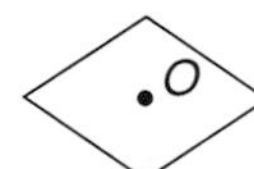

23. Reflect over the line.

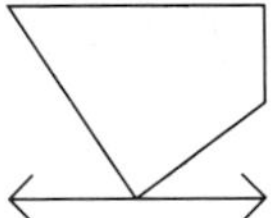

Mixed Practice Copy the figure on grid paper. Draw the reflection, rotation, or translation described.

24. Translate down 5 units and left 3 units.

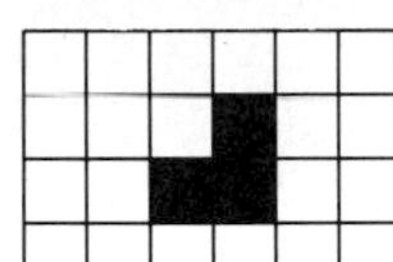

25. Rotate 180° about point B.

26. Reflect over the line.

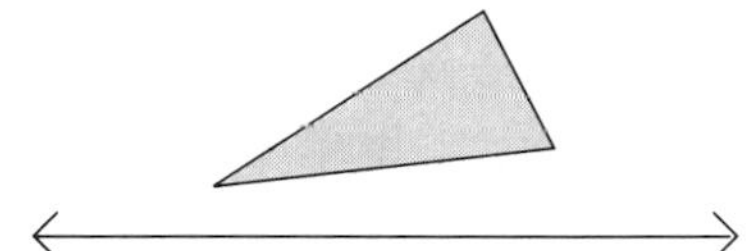

Problem Solving

Solve each problem.

27. Describe how you could get the red figure from the blue one using a rotation and a reflection.

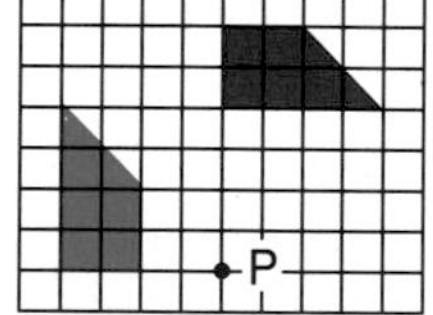

28. Draw a figure for which either a reflection or a rotation will give the same result.

29. Critical Thinking Draw a scalene triangle on grid paper. Reflect the triangle over a grid line. Then reflect the new triangle over another grid line *parallel* to the first. Could you get from the original triangle to the final triangle without using reflections? Explain.

30. Critical Thinking Draw a scalene triangle on grid paper. Reflect the triangle over a grid line. Then reflect the new triangle over another grid line *perpendicular* to the first. Could you get from the original triangle to the final triangle without using reflections? Explain.

Midchapter ______ Checkup

Use the diagram for Exercises 1–7.

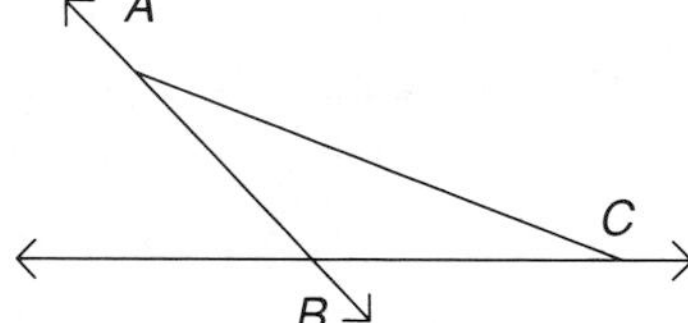

1. Name a ray.
2. Name a segment.
3. Name 2 lines.
4. $\angle ABC$ is a(n) __?__ angle.
5. $\angle BAC$ is a(n) __?__ angle.
6. $\triangle ABC$ is a(n) __?__ triangle.
7. The sum of the angle measures in $\triangle ABC$ is __?__.

Name the polygon with the given number of sides.

8. 5 sides
9. 3 sides
10. 8 sides

Use circle O for Exercises 11–14.

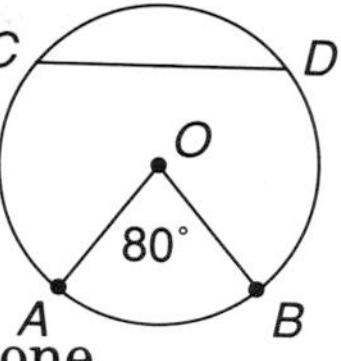

11. Name a radius.
12. Name a chord.
13. Name an arc.
14. Name the center.

Describe the translation used to get the blue figure from the red one.

15.

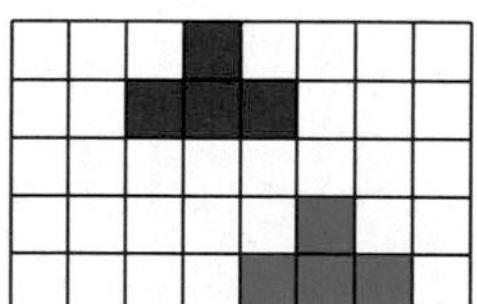

16.

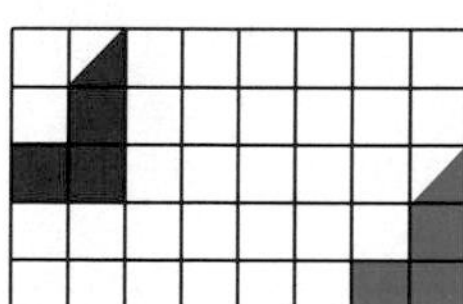

Tell how many lines of symmetry each figure has.

17.

18.

Tell whether the blue figure was reflected or rotated to give the red figure.

19.

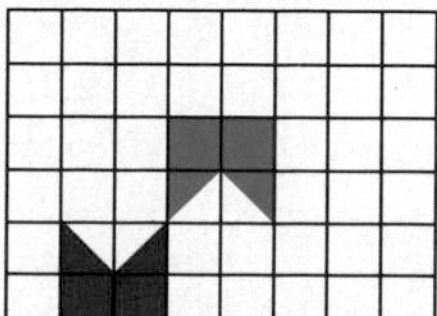

20.

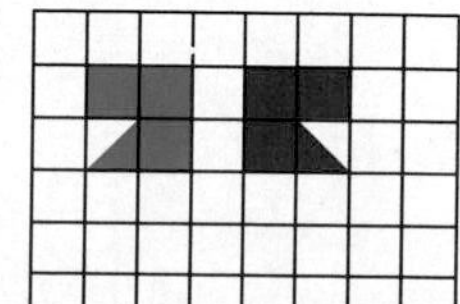

Explore as a Team

An ancient Chinese puzzle called a **tangram** consists of seven pieces. These pieces can be arranged to form many shapes.

With your team, you can make a set of tangram pieces by using a square sheet of paper and folding it according to the following instructions:

1. Fold along the diagonal and cut the square into two pieces. Then fold one triangle in half and cut to make two small triangles. Label these pieces 1 and 2.

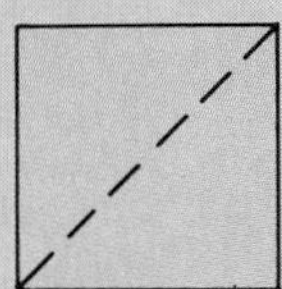
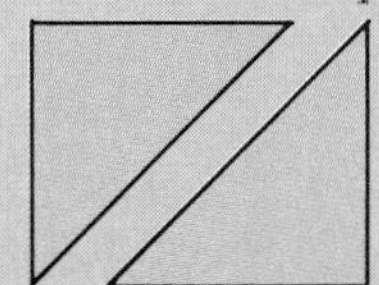
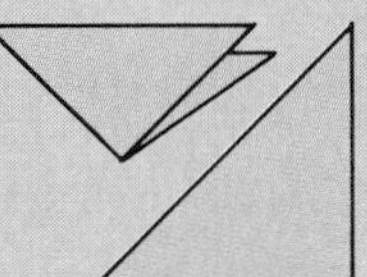
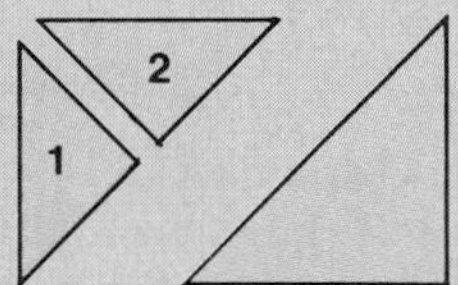

2. Fold the other large triangle. Then fold the square corner to the middle of the opposite side. Cut along this fold. Label this piece 3.

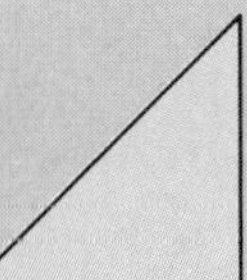
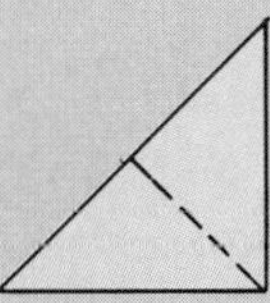
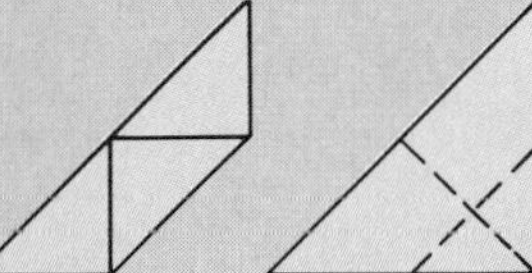
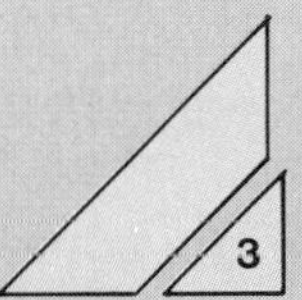

3. Hold the trapezoid piece with the longest side toward you. Fold the lower left corner to the middle of the bottom side. Cut along the two folded lines. Label these pieces 4 and 5.

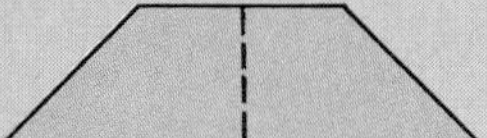
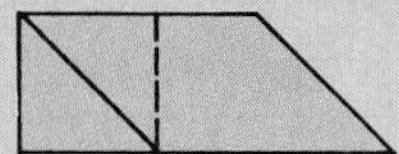
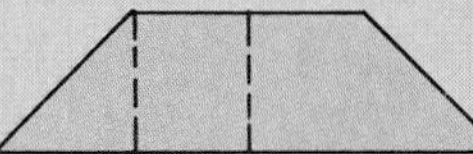
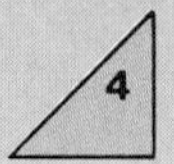

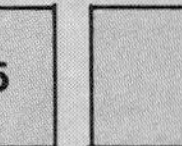

4. Hold the right trapezoid with the right angles to the left and the longest side toward you. Fold the bottom left corner so that the left side and top side coincide. Cut along the fold. Label these pieces 6 and 7.

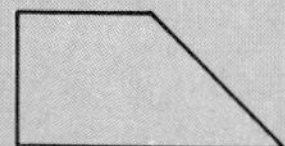
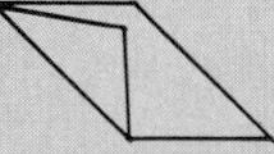
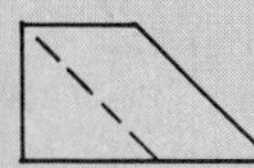
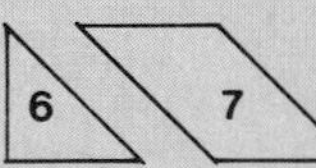

5. Put the pieces back into the square. Then use all seven pieces to make a geometric shape such as a triangle, rectangle, parallelogram, or trapezoid. Also, try to make some of the other shapes shown on this page.

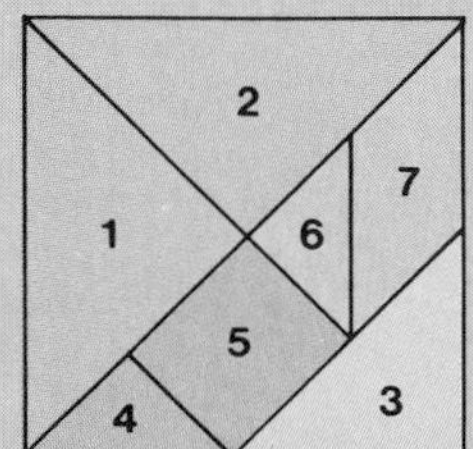

TIPS FOR WORKING TOGETHER

Remember, you can disagree without being disagreeable.

Problem Solving WORKSHOP

Explore with A Computer

Use the *Geometry Workshop Project* for this activity.

When planting a tree in her backyard, Kim dug a hole and discovered four wooden shapes. She found they could fit together to make letters.

1. At the computer, you will see the shapes Kim found. *Rotate, Reflect,* and *Slide* the shapes to rearrange them to make the letters Kim made.

2. Can you make any other letters with the same shapes?

Number-Sense Project

Look back at pages 112-113.

For each exercise, use a circle for a compass and indicate the location of true north when the compass is pointing to magnetic north.

1. Allagash Wilderness, Maine; Declination: 20° W

2. Mt. Rainier, Washington; Declination: 20° E

3. Apostle Islands, Wisconsin; Declination: 0

4. Mt. McKinley, Alaska; Declination: 30° E

5. Melville Bay, Greenland; Declination: 70° W

6. Which of these locations is on a line from the true North Pole to the magnetic North Pole?

Visual-Thinking Activity

Copy the pattern of dots at the right. Without lifting your pencil or retracing, draw a continuous path of four straight line segments, passing through each dot exactly once.

• • •

• • •

• • •

Constructing Segments, Angles, and Bisectors

Build Understanding

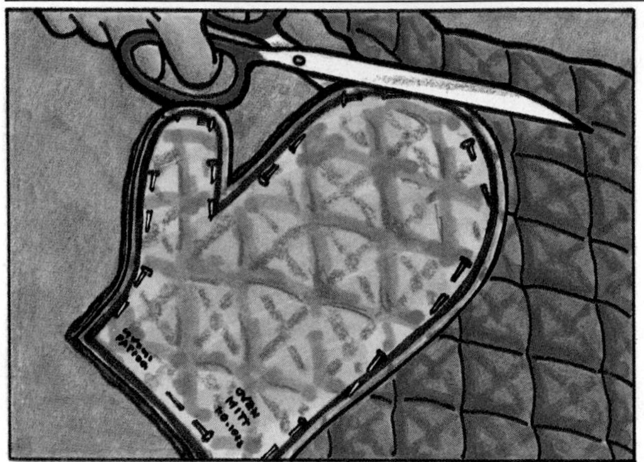

A pattern is used to cut pieces of fabric that are the same size and shape. Figures that are the same size and shape are said to be congruent.

In geometric ***constructions,*** a compass is used to obtain congruent figures. A figure is constructed without measuring the length of line segments or the degrees of angles. Only a compass and a straightedge are used.

A. Construct a segment congruent to $\overline{AB}$.

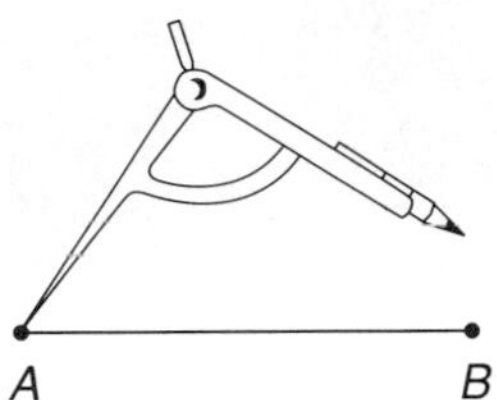

Step 1 Open your compass to the length of $\overline{AB}$.

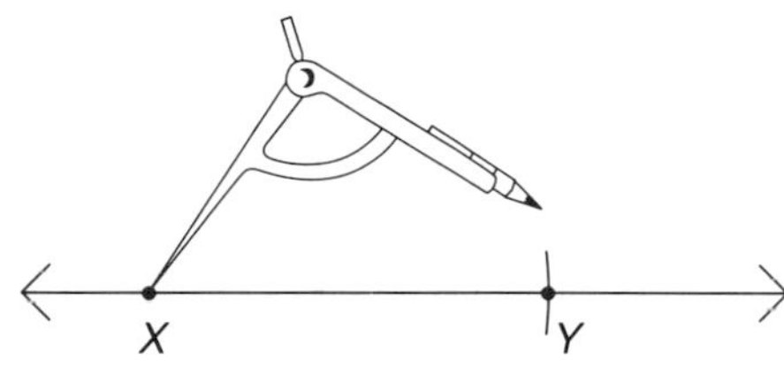

Step 2 Draw a line and label point X. With point X as center, draw an arc that intersects the line. Label the point of intersection Y. $\overline{AB} \cong \overline{XY}$. The symbol $\cong$ means "is congruent to."

B. A ***bisector*** of a segment divides the segment into two congruent segments. Construct a bisector of $\overline{CD}$.

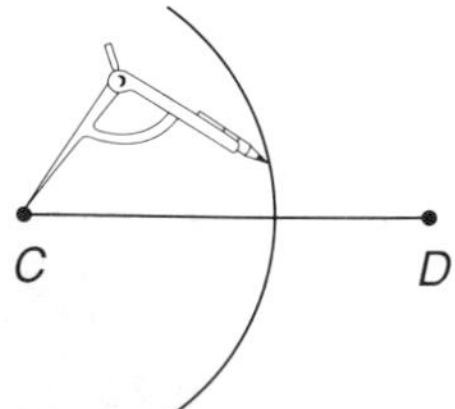

Step 1 With point C as center, open your compass more than halfway to point D. Then draw an arc that intersects $\overline{CD}$.

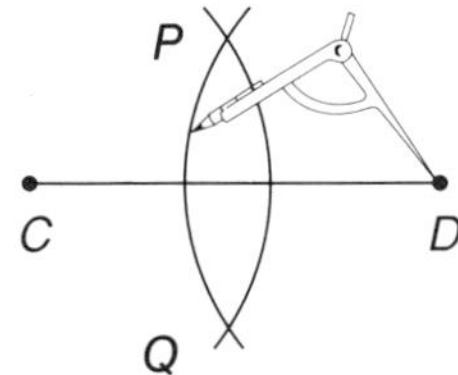

Step 2 Using the same opening and point D as center, draw an arc that intersects the first arc at 2 points. Label the points of intersection P and Q.

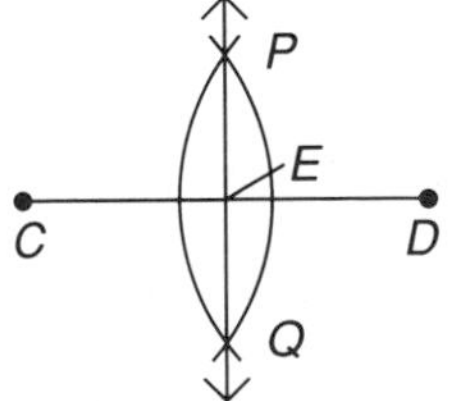

Step 3 Draw $\overleftrightarrow{PQ}$. $\overleftrightarrow{PQ}$ is a bisector of $\overline{CD}$. Point E is the ***midpoint*** of $\overline{CD}$. $\overline{CE} \cong \overline{ED}$

C. Construct an angle congruent to $\angle K$.

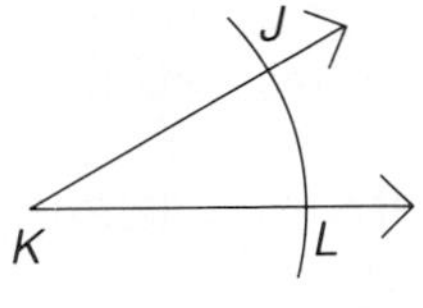

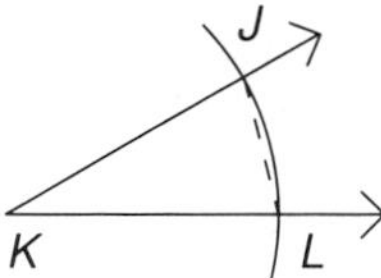

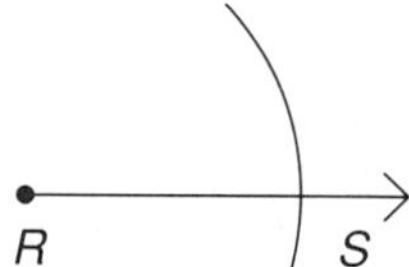

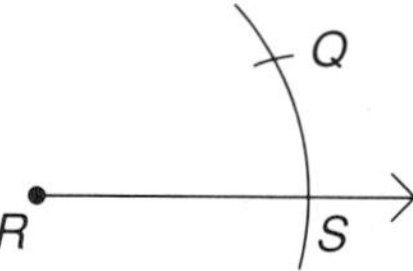

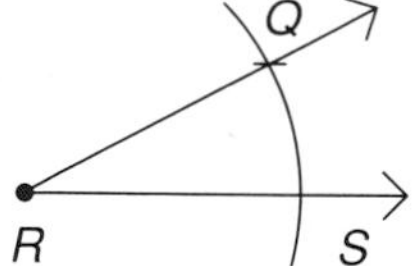

Step 1 Draw a ray with endpoint *R*. With point *K* as center, draw an arc that intersects both sides of $\angle K$. Label the points of intersection *J* and *L*. With the same opening, draw an arc intersecting the ray at point *S*.

Step 2 Open your compass to the length of $\overline{JL}$. With point *S* as center, draw an intersecting arc. Label point *Q*.

Step 3 Draw $\overrightarrow{RQ}$. $\angle K \cong \angle R$

D. A ***bisector*** of an angle divides the angle into two congruent angles. Construct the bisector of $\angle N$.

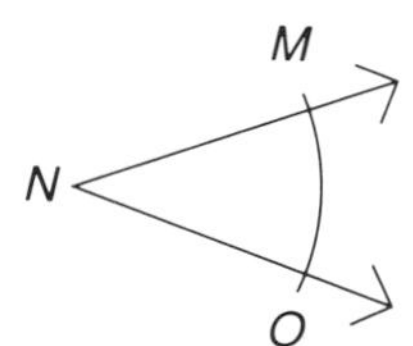

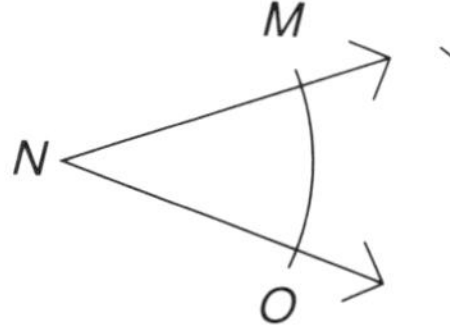

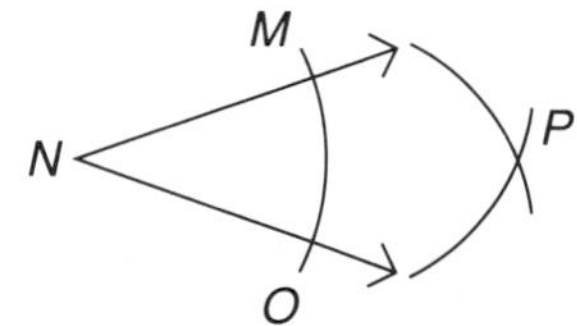

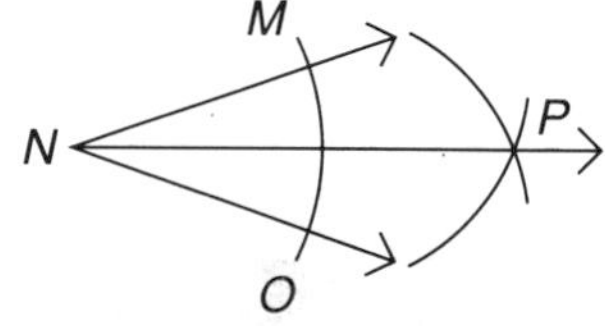

Step 1 With point *N* as center, draw an arc that intersects both sides of $\angle N$. Label the points of intersection *M* and *O*.

Step 2 Using the same opening and point *O* as center, draw an arc as shown.

Step 3 Using the same opening and point *M* as center, draw an intersecting arc. Label the point of intersection *P*.

Step 4 Draw $\overrightarrow{NP}$. $\overrightarrow{NP}$ bisects $\angle N$. $\angle MNP \cong \angle PNO$

■ **Talk About Math** How many bisectors does $\angle N$ in Example D have?

Check Understanding

Complete each sentence.

1. In a geometric ___?___, only a compass and a straightedge are used to draw a figure.

2. The symbol ___?___ means "is congruent to."

3. A ___?___ of an angle divides the angle into two congruent angles.

4. If point *P* is the midpoint of $\overline{MN}$, then ___?___ $\cong$ ___?___.

Practice

Trace each figure. Then use a compass and straightedge to do each construction.

5. Construct a segment congruent to $\overline{EF}$.

6. Construct an angle congruent to $\angle Z$.

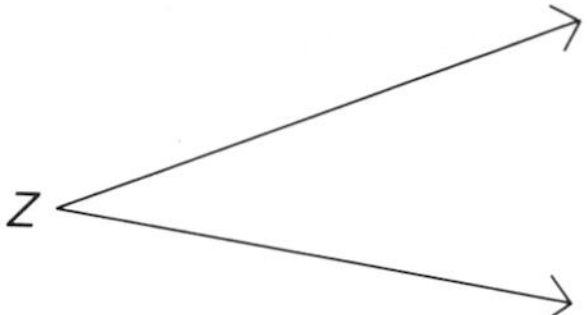

7. Construct a segment congruent to $\overline{MN}$.

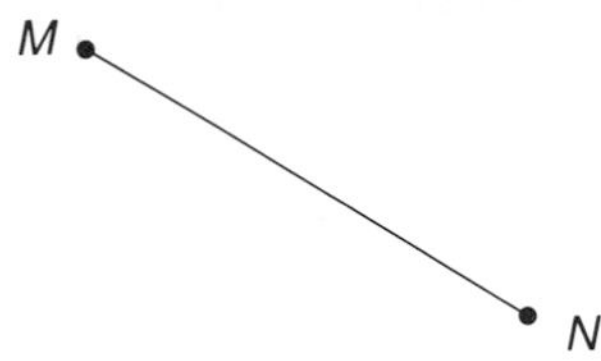

8. Construct an angle congruent to $\angle B$.

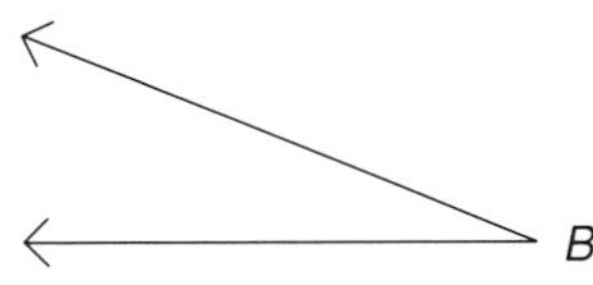

9. Bisect $\angle D$.

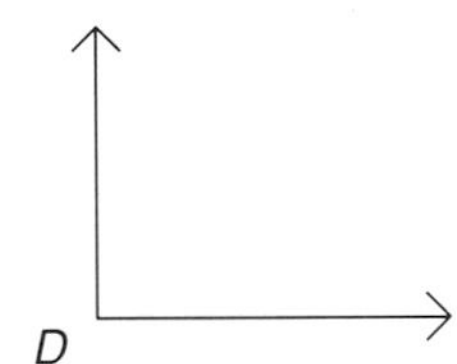

10. Bisect $\overline{PQ}$.

11. Bisect $\angle P$.

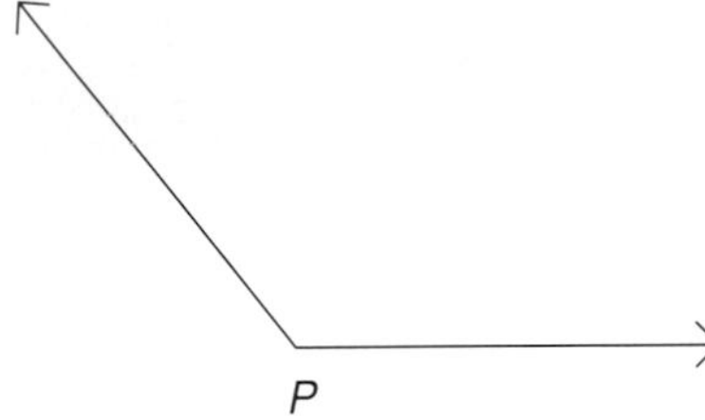

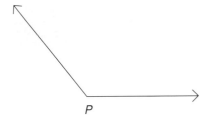

12. Bisect $\overline{RS}$.

13. Construct an angle congruent to $\angle J$.

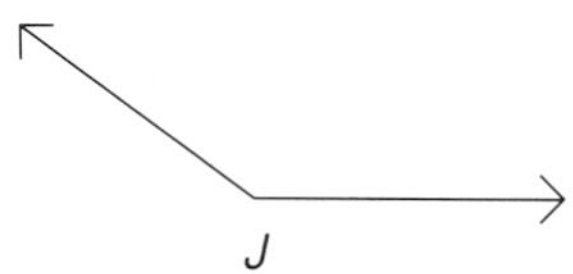

14. Bisect $\overline{GH}$.

15. Bisect $\angle W$.

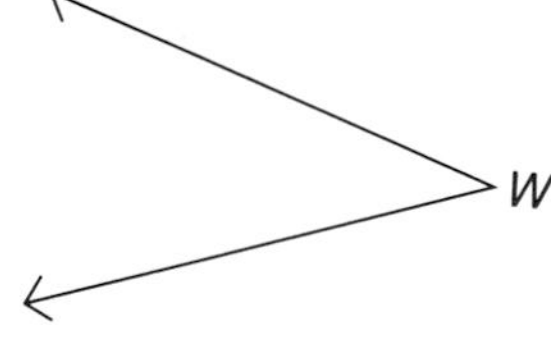

16. Construct an angle congruent to $\angle Y$.

17. Construct a segment congruent to $\overline{TU}$.

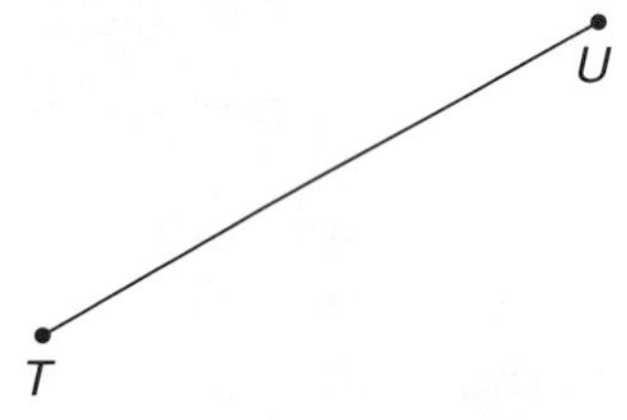

18. Construct an angle congruent to $\angle A$.

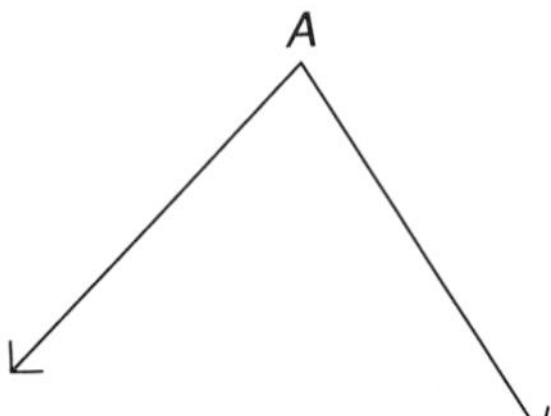

19. Bisect $\angle X$.

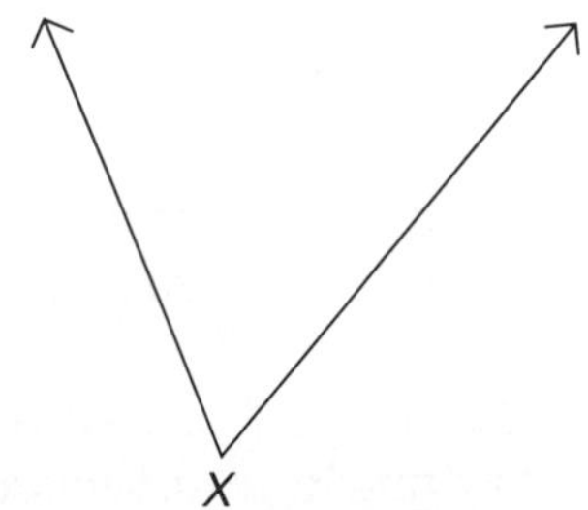

Problem Solving

Number Sense Trace each figure. Then use a compass and a straightedge to do each construction.

20. Construct a segment with length equal to the sum of the lengths of $\overline{CD}$ and $\overline{YZ}$.

21. Construct an angle with measure equal to the sum of the measures of $\angle M$ and $\angle R$.

22. Construct a segment with a length twice that of $\overline{AB}$.

23. Construct an angle with a measure twice that of $\angle Q$.

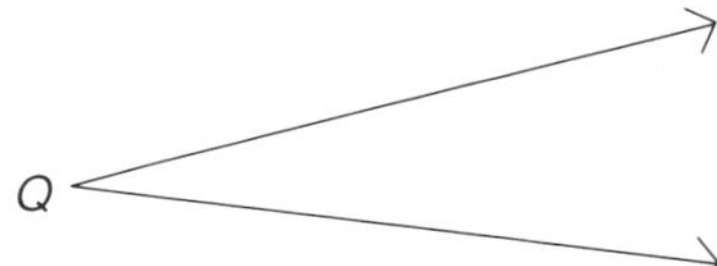

Trace the segment in Problem 22.

24. Construct a bisector of $\overline{AB}$. Label the midpoint M. Name two congruent segments.

25. What do you notice about the measure of each angle with a vertex at M?

26. Use the construction from Problem 24 to construct an angle of 45°.

TIPS FOR PROBLEM SOLVERS
Visualize the problem in your mind to help you understand it better.

Explore Math

Answer the questions about the triangle shown here.

27. Trace $\triangle GHJ$. Construct the bisectors of the three angles of the triangle.

J

G H

28. What do you notice about the angle bisectors?

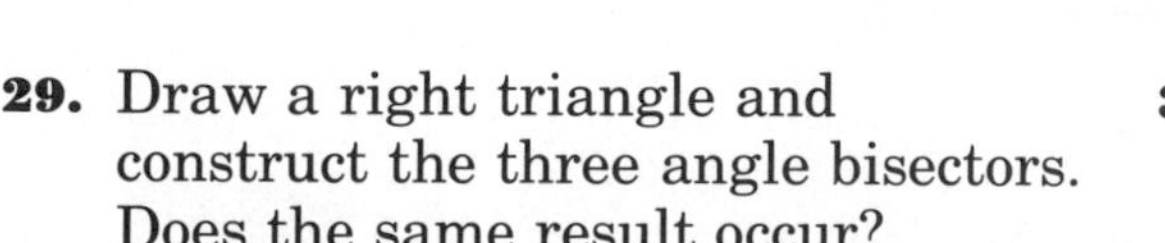

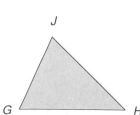

29. Draw a right triangle and construct the three angle bisectors. Does the same result occur?

30. Draw an obtuse triangle and construct the three angle bisectors. Does the same result occur?

Constructing Perpendicular and Parallel Lines

Build Understanding

A. Construct a line perpendicular to $\overleftrightarrow{AB}$ at point X.

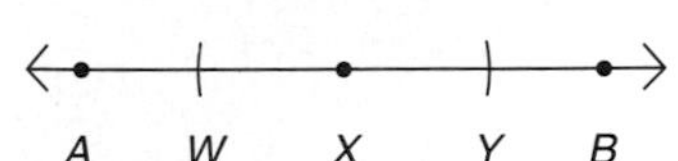

Step 1 Using point X as center, draw two arcs that intersect $\overleftrightarrow{AB}$ on either side of point X. Label the points W and Y.

Step 2 Open the compass wider. Using points W and Y as centers, draw arcs that intersect. Label that point Z.

Step 3 Draw $\overleftrightarrow{ZX}$. $\overleftrightarrow{ZX} \perp \overleftrightarrow{AB}$

$\perp$ means "is perpendicular to."

B. Construct a line perpendicular to $\overleftrightarrow{FG}$ from point H not on $\overleftrightarrow{FG}$.

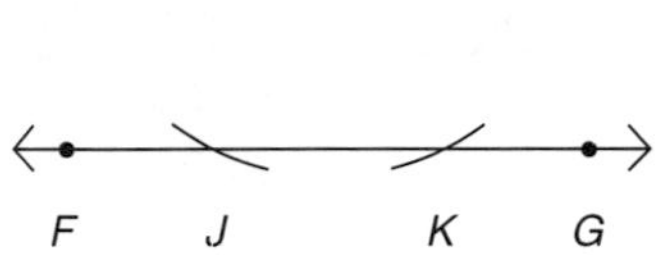

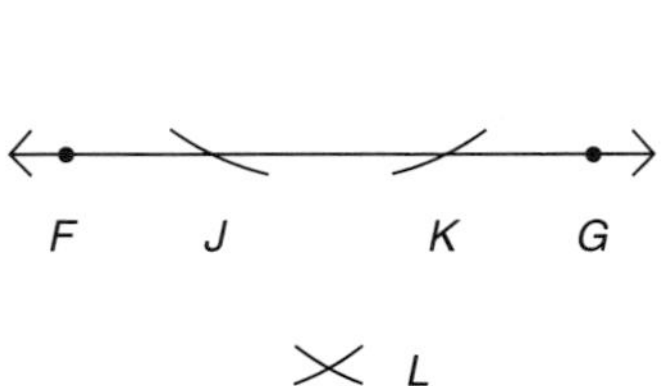

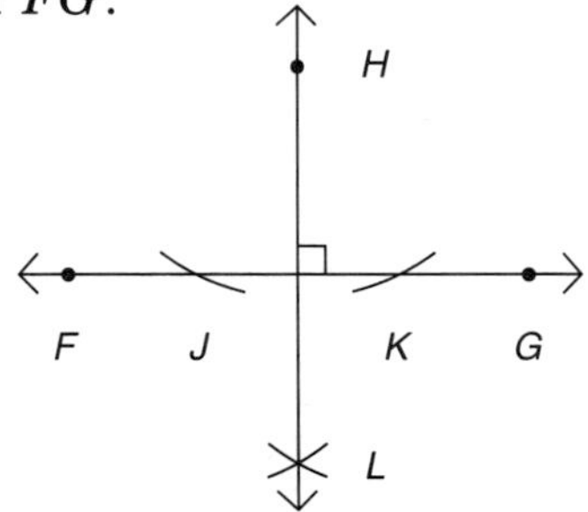

Step 1 Using point H as center, draw an arc that intersects $\overleftrightarrow{FG}$ at two points. Label the points J and K.

Step 2 Using points J and K as centers, draw intersecting arcs below $\overleftrightarrow{FG}$. Label that point L.

Step 3 Draw $\overleftrightarrow{HL}$. $\overleftrightarrow{HL} \perp \overleftrightarrow{FG}$

C. Construct a line parallel to $\overleftrightarrow{MN}$ through point O.

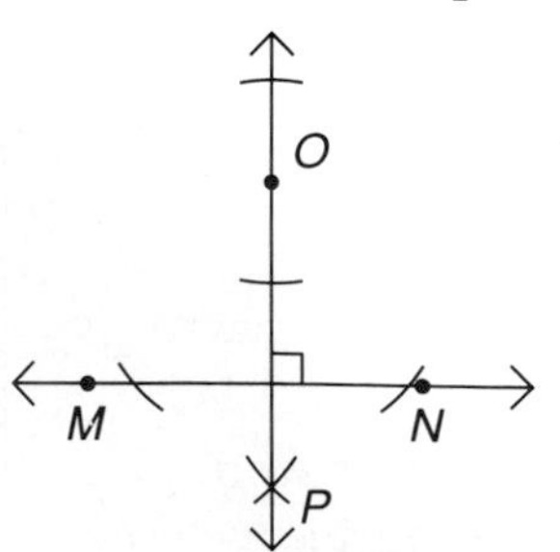

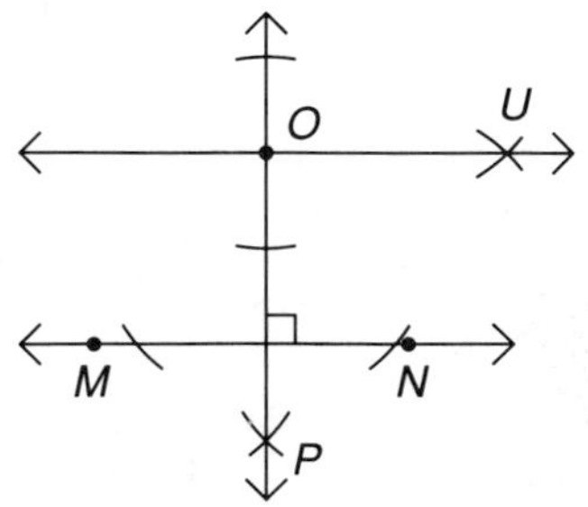

Step 1 Construct $\overleftrightarrow{OP} \perp \overleftrightarrow{MN}$ using the technique in Example B.

Step 2 Construct $\overleftrightarrow{OU} \perp \overleftrightarrow{OP}$ using the technique in Example A. $\overleftrightarrow{OU} \parallel \overleftrightarrow{MN}$. $\parallel$ means "is parallel to."

Write About Math

Describe how you would construct one of the following: a square, a rectangle, a parallelogram, or a trapezoid.

Check Understanding

Use the diagram for Exercises 1–2. $\overleftrightarrow{XY} \perp \overline{AB}$.

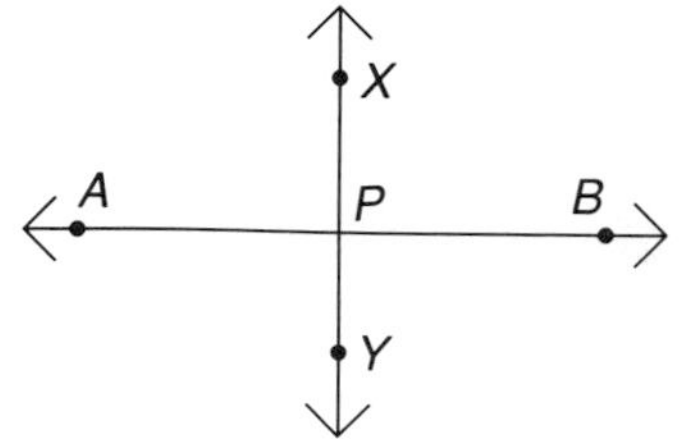

1. Find $m\angle BPY$.

2. Could you use $\overleftrightarrow{XY}$ to construct a line parallel to $\overline{AB}$? Explain your answer.

Practice

Draw the figures described in Exercises 3–8. Then do the constructions.

3. Use your straightedge to draw any line $\overleftrightarrow{XY}$. Construct the line perpendicular to $\overleftrightarrow{XY}$ at point Y.

4. Draw any line $\overleftrightarrow{BC}$ and point A not on $\overleftrightarrow{BC}$. Construct the line from point A perpendicular to $\overleftrightarrow{BC}$.

5. Draw any line $\overleftrightarrow{DE}$ and point F not on $\overleftrightarrow{DE}$. Construct the line through point F parallel to $\overleftrightarrow{DE}$.

6. Draw any line $\overleftrightarrow{JK}$. Construct two lines perpendicular to $\overleftrightarrow{JK}$, one at point J and the other at point K. What is true of the two lines you constructed?

7. Draw any line $\overleftrightarrow{MN}$ and point P not on $\overleftrightarrow{MN}$. Construct the line from point P perpendicular to $\overleftrightarrow{MN}$. Then construct the line perpendicular to $\overleftrightarrow{MN}$ at M. What is true about the two lines you constructed?

8. Draw any line $\overleftrightarrow{AB}$ and two points C and D not on $\overleftrightarrow{AB}$. Construct the line from C perpendicular to $\overleftrightarrow{AB}$. Then construct the line through D parallel to $\overleftrightarrow{AB}$. What is true about the two lines you constructed?

Problem Solving

Use the diagram for Problems 9–11. Tell how many of the given lines you could draw.

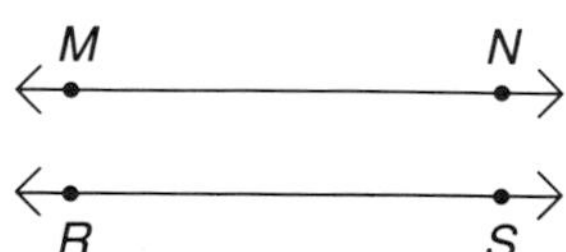

9. Parallel to $\overleftrightarrow{MN}$

10. Perpendicular to $\overleftrightarrow{MN}$

11. **Critical Thinking** Trace $\overleftrightarrow{MN}$ and $\overleftrightarrow{RS}$. Through any point G construct $\overleftrightarrow{GH} \parallel \overleftrightarrow{MN}$. If $\overleftrightarrow{MN} \parallel \overleftrightarrow{RS}$, what is the relationship between $\overleftrightarrow{RS}$ and $\overleftrightarrow{GH}$?

12. Construct a square using side $\overline{AX}$.

A X

Constructing Triangles

Build Understanding

A triangle has three sides that are segments and three angles.

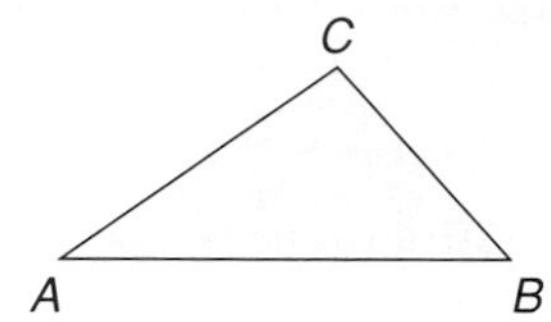

A. Congruent triangles have the same size and shape. You can construct a triangle congruent to $\triangle ABC$ using the sides of $\triangle ABC$.

Step 1 Draw a line and label point *D* on the line. Construct $\overline{DE} \cong \overline{AB}$.

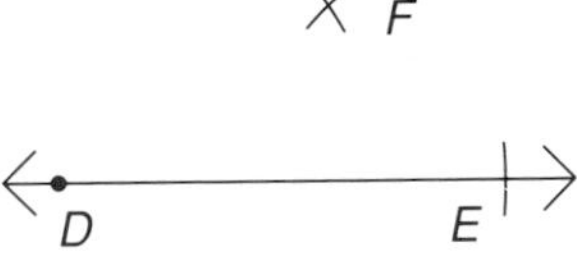

Step 2 With point *D* as center and the compass open to the length of $\overline{AC}$, draw an arc. With point *E* as center and the compass open to the length of $\overline{BC}$, draw an arc that intersects the other arc. Label the point of intersection *F*.

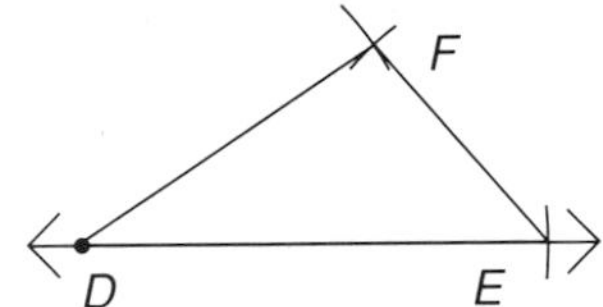

Step 3 Draw $\overline{DF}$ and $\overline{EF}$.
$\overline{DE} \cong \overline{AB}$, $\overline{DF} \cong \overline{AC}$, $\overline{EF} \cong \overline{BC}$
$\triangle DEF \cong \triangle ABC$

B. Construct a triangle congruent to $\triangle XYZ$ using sides $\overline{XZ}$ and $\overline{XY}$ and $\angle X$.

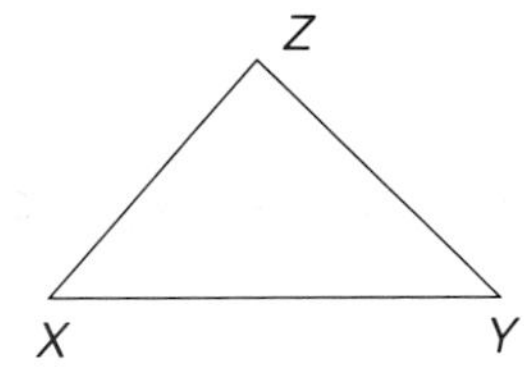

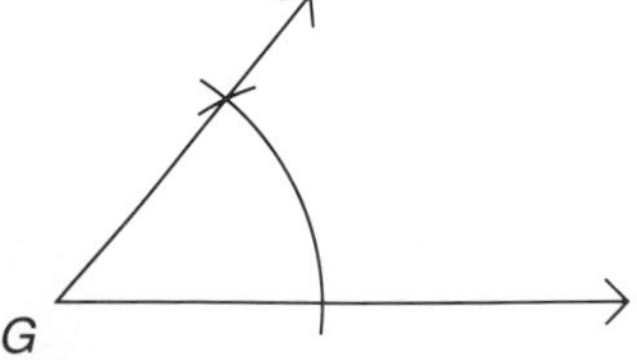

Step 1 Construct $\angle G \cong \angle X$.

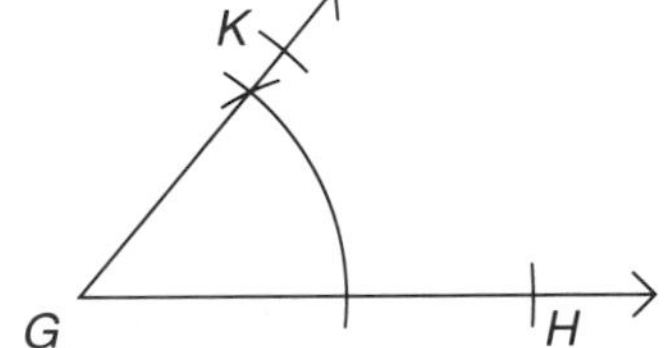

Step 2 On one side of $\angle G$, construct $\overline{GH} \cong \overline{XY}$. On the other side of $\angle G$, construct $\overline{GK} \cong \overline{XZ}$.

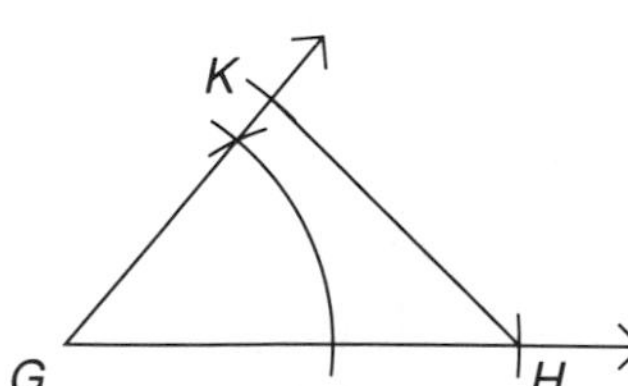

Step 3 Draw $\overline{HK}$.
$\angle G \cong \angle X$, $\overline{GH} \cong \overline{XY}$, $\overline{GK} \cong \overline{XZ}$
$\triangle GHK \cong \triangle XYZ$

■ **Write About Math** In Example B, could you have constructed a triangle congruent to $\triangle XYZ$ using sides $\overline{XZ}$ and $\overline{XY}$ and $\angle Y$? side $\overline{XY}$, $\angle X$, and $\angle Y$? Explain.

Check Understanding

For another example, see Set F, pages 148–149.

Name the third part of $\triangle PQR$ you would use along with the given parts to construct a congruent triangle. Then do each construction.

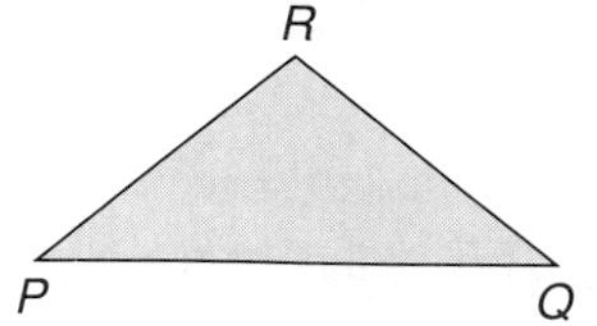

1. $\angle P$, $\overline{PQ}$ **2.** $\angle Q$, $\overline{QR}$ **3.** $\overline{PQ}$, $\overline{PR}$

Practice

For More Practice, see Set F, pages 150–151.

Use $\triangle XYZ$ for Exercises 4 and 5.

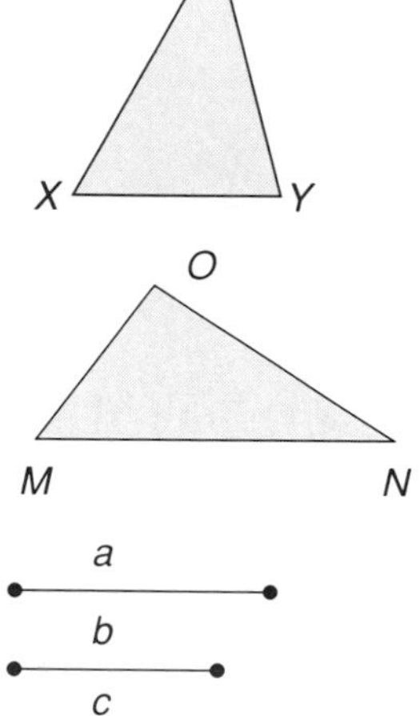

4. Construct a triangle congruent to $\triangle XYZ$ using the sides of $\triangle XYZ$.

5. Construct a triangle congruent to $\triangle XYZ$ using sides $\overline{XY}$ and $\overline{YZ}$ and $\angle Y$.

Use $\triangle MNO$ for Exercises 6–9. Construct a congruent triangle using only the given parts.

6. $\overline{MN}$, $\overline{NO}$, $\overline{MO}$ **7.** $\overline{MN}$, $\overline{MO}$, $\angle M$

8. $\overline{MN}$, $\angle M$, $\angle N$ **9.** $\overline{MN}$, $\overline{NO}$, $\angle N$

For Exercises 10–13, use the given parts to construct a triangle. If you cannot construct the triangle, write *impossible*.

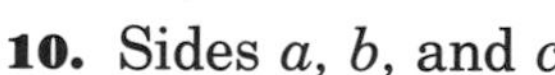

10. Sides a, b, and c **11.** $\angle Q$ between a and b

12. $\angle R$ between b and c **13.** $\angle Q$ between a and c

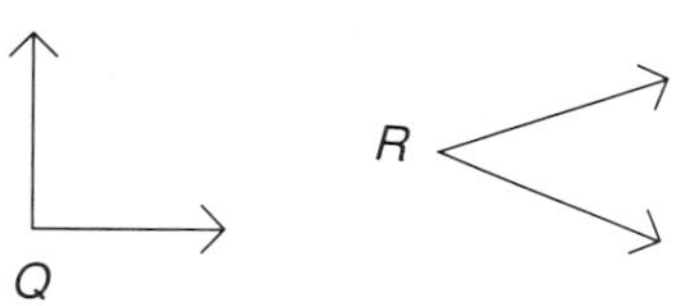

Problem Solving

Use $\triangle MNO$ in Exercises 6–9 to construct the triangle described.

14. $\triangle XYZ$ such that each side has the same length as $\overline{MO}$

15. $\triangle RST$ such that $\overline{RS} \cong \overline{MN}$, $\overline{ST} \cong \overline{NO}$, and $\overline{RT} \cong \overline{MO}$

Visual Thinking Tell whether you could construct a triangle using the given parts. Answer *yes* or *no*.

16.

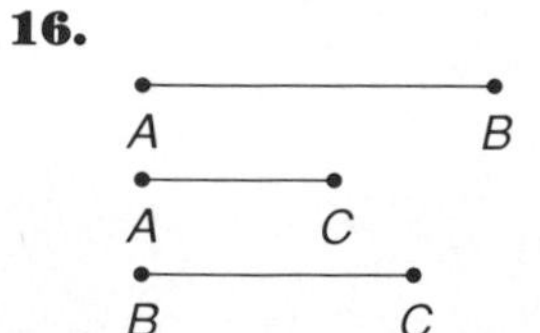

17.

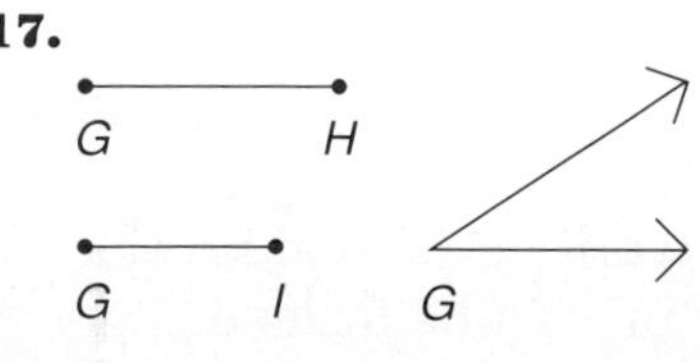

18.

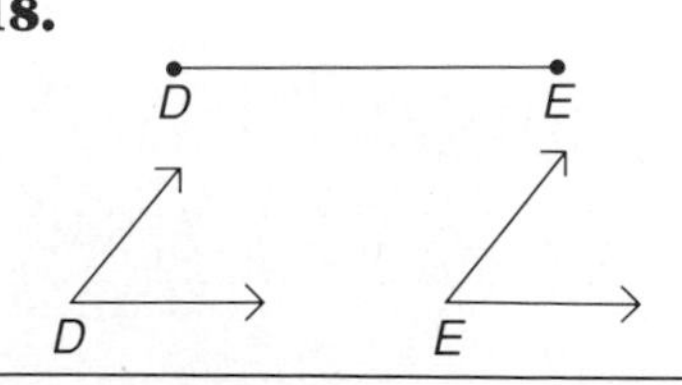

Try and Check

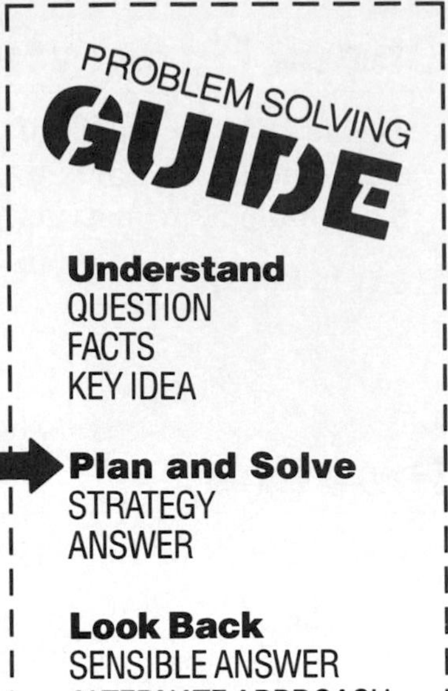

Build Understanding

ACTIVITY

A. Piece It Together
Materials: Drinking straws cut in 1-, 2-, 3-, 4-, and 5-inch lengths
Groups: With a partner

a. Choose any three straws.

b. Try to arrange the straws to form a triangle.

c. Repeat steps a and b 10 times.

d. How many times were you able to form a triangle? What do you notice about a triangle and the lengths of its sides?

B. If the first straw is 3 inches long, what other two lengths are needed to form a scalene triangle?

Understand QUESTION How long are the other two sides of a scalene triangle with one side 3 inches in length?

FACTS Each side of a scalene triangle has a different length. The sides must be 1, 2, 3, 4, or 5 in. long. One side is 3 in.

KEY IDEA Not every combination of three lengths results in a triangle.

Plan and Solve STRATEGY Try each combination of lengths for the two remaining sides.

Draw $\overline{AB}$ with length 3 in. Try to construct a triangle with sides 1 in. and 2 in.

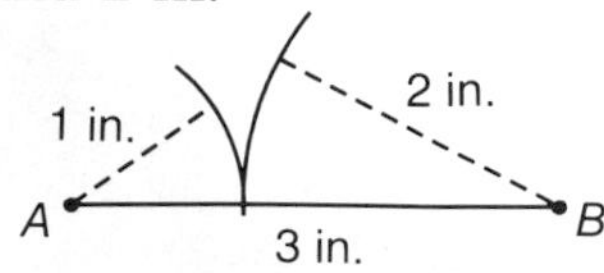

The arcs intersect on $\overline{AB}$.

Try 1 in. and 4 in. and repeat.

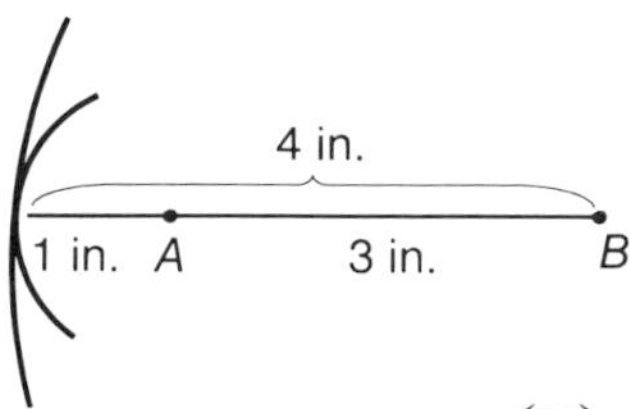

The arcs intersect on $\overleftrightarrow{AB}$.

Try 2 in. and 4 in. and repeat.

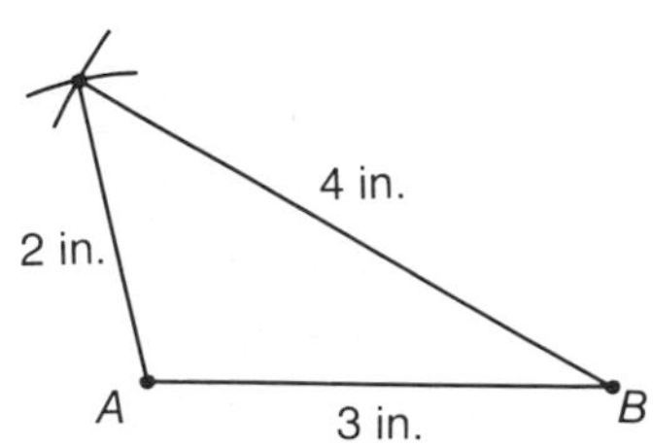

ANSWER A triangle with sides that measure 2 in., 3 in., and 4 in. can be formed.

Look Back ALTERNATE APPROACH You could have used the straws to find that a scalene triangle with sides of 2, 3, and 4 in. is possible.

■ **Talk About Math** What seems to be true about the lengths of the sides of a triangle?

Check Understanding

Refer to Example B for Exercises 1–2.

1. Is there another scalene triangle that could be formed? Explain.
2. If a 6-inch straw is added, what new scalene triangles can be formed?

Practice

Solve each problem. The lengths of all sides must be whole numbers.

3. The lengths of two sides of a triangle are 4 cm and 6 cm. What is the least possible length for the third side?
4. What is the greatest possible length for the third side of the triangle described in Exercise 3?
5. The lengths of two sides of a triangle are 15 mm and 35 mm. What is the least possible length for the third side?
6. What is the greatest possible length for the third side of the triangle described in Exercise 5?
7. Two sides of a triangle have lengths 3 cm and 7 cm. List all possible lengths of the third side.
8. The longest side of a triangle is 6 cm long. List all possible pairs of lengths for the other two sides.

Choose a ______ Strategy

Do the Impossible There are many possible isosceles triangles you could construct from the five different lengths of straws in Example A.

9. Make a list of all the sets of three lengths that would be *impossible* to construct. Can you do it without actually constructing any triangles?

PROBLEM SOLVING
STRATEGIES

Choose an Operation
Write an Equation
Use a Formula
Make a Table
Try and Check

Skills Review

Use the diagram to name each item.

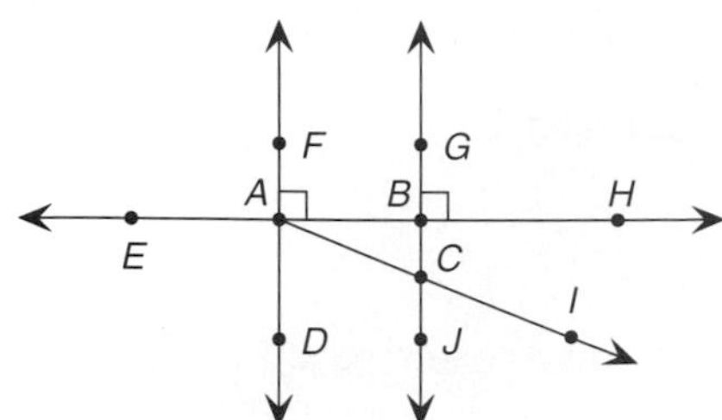

1. Three lines
2. Three rays
3. Two pairs of intersecting lines
4. A pair of parallel lines
5. A pair of perpendicular lines
6. Two right angles
7. Two acute angles
8. An obtuse angle
9. A pair of supplementary angles
10. A pair of complementary angles

Name each polygon.

11. **12.** **13.**

Use the circle to name each item.

14. An arc
15. A radius
16. A chord
17. A central angle

Trace each figure and draw all lines of symmetry.

18. 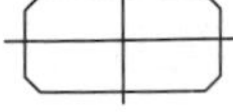 **19.** 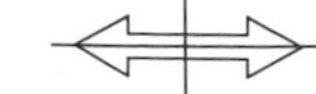

Problem-Solving Review

Solve each problem.

20. In 1980, the population in the United States was about 240 million. In 1860, the population was about one third of that figure. What was the population in 1860? Tell which operation you would use, and then solve.

21. Seven of Carlos's 21 baseball cards are American League players. What part of his collection is American League players? Express your answer as a fraction and as a decimal.

22. Name the acute angles in polygon *ABCD*. Name the supplementary angles.

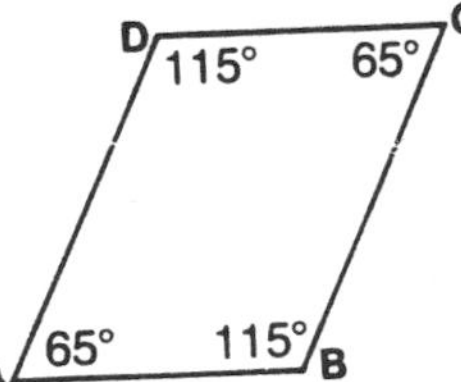

23. One angle of a triangle has a measure of 52°. Another has a measure of 66°. What is the measure of the third angle?

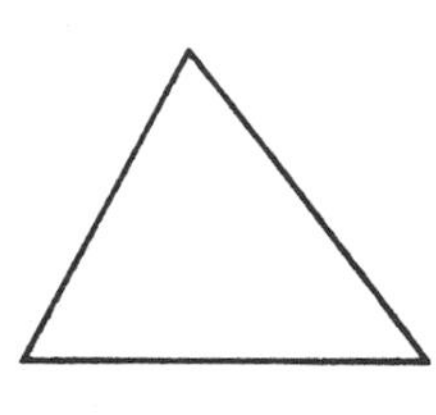

24. **Data File** Use the data on pages 264–265. In the geometric pattern name pairs of polygons that appear to be congruent.

25. **Make a Data File** Take a walk. Observe buildings, windows, trees, cars, signs—any items that suggest geometric shapes. Make a chart showing the geometric shapes and the items you observed with each shape.

Cumulative Skills Review • Chapters 1–4

Choose mental math, paper and pencil, or calculator to compute.

1. $209 + 250.6$ **2.** $7{,}312 - 456.78$ **3.** $16 \times 29 \times 15$ **4.** $6{,}055 \div 5$

5. $2 \times 5 \times 89$ **6.** $11.34 \div 9$ **7.** $68 + 56 + 44$ **8.** $4{,}500 - 199.5$

Evaluate each expression when $m = 6$.

9. $3m$ **10.** $m + 12$ **11.** $27 - m$ **12.** $m \div 2$

Evaluate each expression when $d = 9$.

13. $d \times 7$ **14.** $\frac{d}{1}$ **15.** $d + d + d$ **16.** $d - 3$

Evaluate each expression.

17. $\frac{7(5 + 3)}{24 \div 3}$ **18.** $\frac{5 \times 3 \times 2}{12 - 7}$ **19.** $\frac{72}{8} + 11$ **20.** $28 \div 4 - 2$

21. $18 \div 3 + 4 \times 4$ **22.** $(6 + 3)5 + 1$
46 **23.** $(40 - 20) \div 4$ **24.** $2 + 5 \times 5 - 2$

Multiply or divide.

25. $45{,}000 \div 90$ **26.** $4{,}200 \div 70$ **27.** $16{,}000 \div 400$ **28.** $300{,}000 \div 500$

29. $5.7 \times 1{,}000$ **30.** $0.0786 \times 10{,}000$ **31.** $3.5 \div 100$ **32.** $0.8 \times 1{,}000$

Divide. Round answers to the nearest thousandth.

33. $693 \div 0.9$ **34.** $145.6 \div 1.2$ **35.** $0.0058 \div 0.8$ **36.** $579.59 \div 2.55$

Copy each figure onto grid paper. Then draw the result of the translation, rotation, or reflection given.

37. Rotate 180° about point *p*.

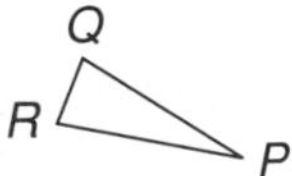

38. Translate right 6 units.

39. Reflect over the line.

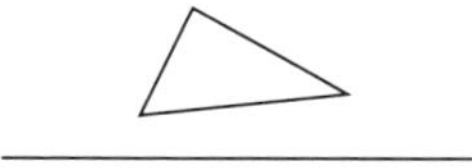

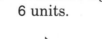

Do each construction.

40. Construct a segment congruent to ST. Then bisect the segment.

41. Construct an angle congruent to $\angle M$. Then bisect the angle.

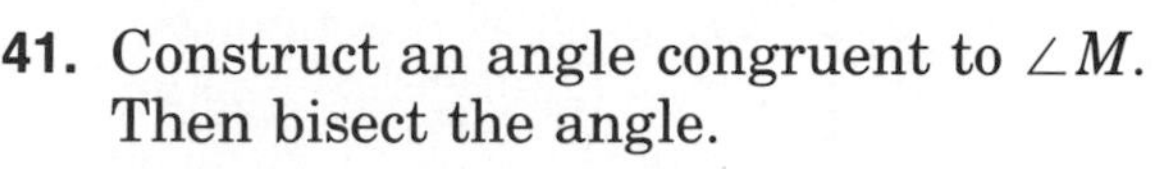

42. Use side, angle, side to construct a triangle congruent to $\triangle ABC$.

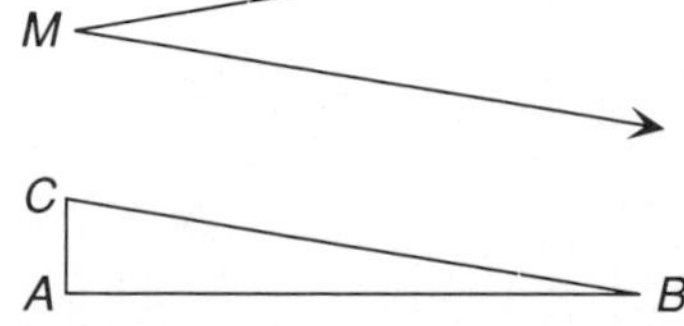

Reteaching

Set A pages 114–117

In the figure below,

(1) the lines AC and BE intersect in a single point, point D;
(2) E is the endpoint of ray EB; and
(3) lines AB and CE are parallel lines.

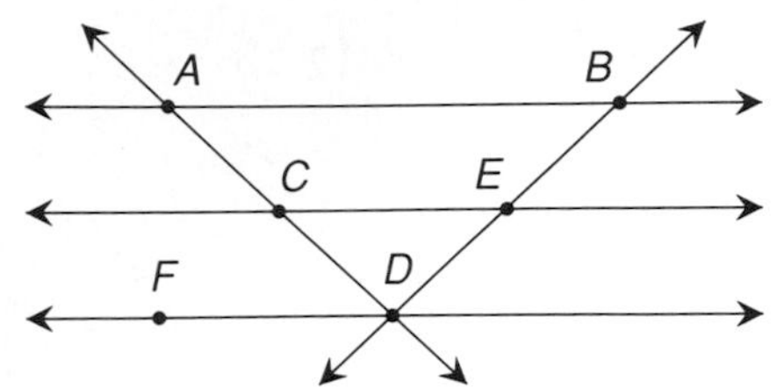

Remember, the symbols for lines, segments, and rays: line AB or $\overleftrightarrow{AB}$; segment XY or $\overline{XY}$; ray FG or $\overrightarrow{FG}$.

Use the figure at the left to name

1. three rays.

2. three segments.

3. two parallel lines.

4. two pairs of intersecting lines.

Set B pages 120–121

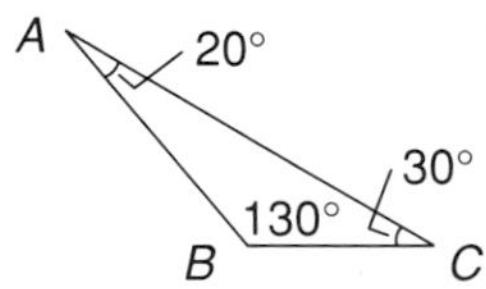

$\triangle ABC$ is an obtuse triangle; the measure of one of its angles, $\angle ABC$, is greater than 90°.

An acute triangle has three acute angles.

A right triangle has one right angle.

$\triangle ABC$ is also scalene; it has no sides of equal length. An isosceles triangle has 2 sides of equal length. An equilateral triangle has 3 sides of equal length.

Remember, the sum of the measures of the angles of a triangle is 180°.

Find the measure of each missing angle. Then classify the triangle by its angles and sides.

1. 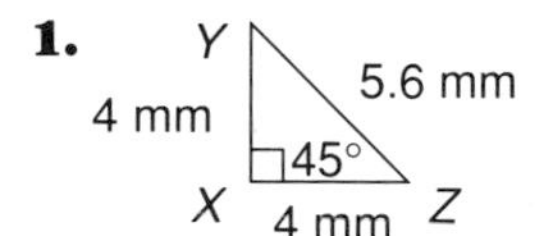

2. 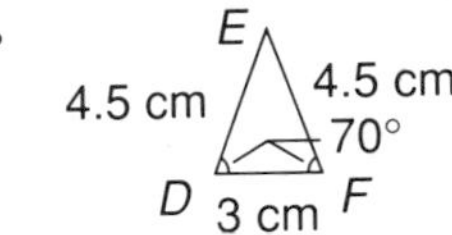

3. 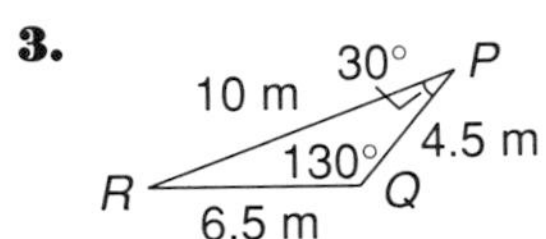

Set C pages 122–123

A polygon can be named according to the number of sides it has.

Polygon	Number of sides
Triangle	3
Quadrilateral	4
Pentagon	5
Hexagon	6
Octagon	8

Remember, a regular polygon has sides of equal length and angles equal in measure.

Identify each figure. Tell which polygons are regular.

1. 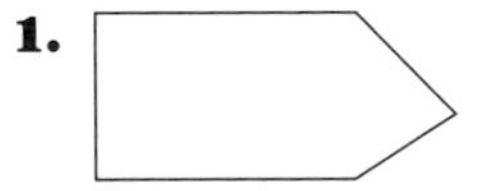

2. 

3. 

4. 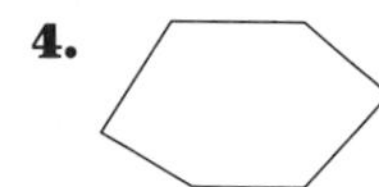

Set D pages 126–127

On circle A,
(1) $\overline{AB}$ is a radius;
(2) $\overline{CD}$ is a diameter;
(3) $\overline{EF}$ is a chord;
(4) $\angle BAD$ is a central angle; and
(5) $\overset{\frown}{BD}$ is an arc.

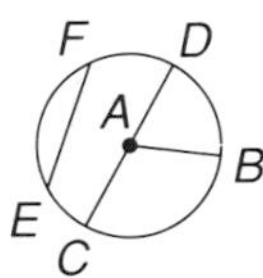

Remember, every point on a circle is located the same distance from the center.

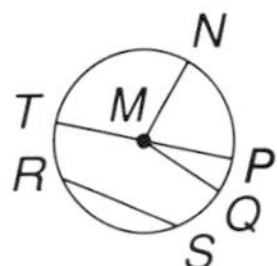

Using circle M above, name

1. three radii.

2. a diameter.

3. a chord.

4. an arc.

5. two central angles.

Set E pages 130–133

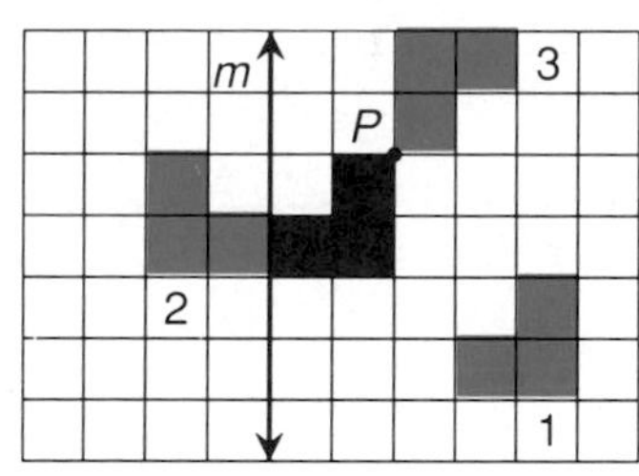

Above, figure 1 results from a translation of the black figure down 2 units and 3 units to the right. Figure 2 results from a reflection of the figure over line m. Figure 3 results from a rotation of the figure of 180° about point P.

Remember, a reflection flips a figure and a rotation turns a figure.

Describe the translation used to get the black figure from the blue figure.

1.

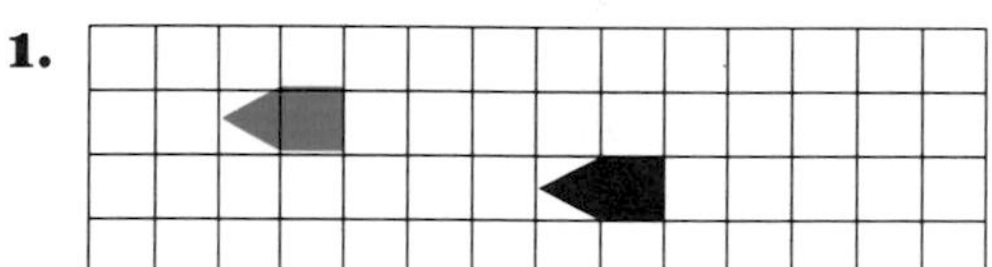

Tell whether a rotation or a reflection of the black figure resulted in the blue figure.

2.

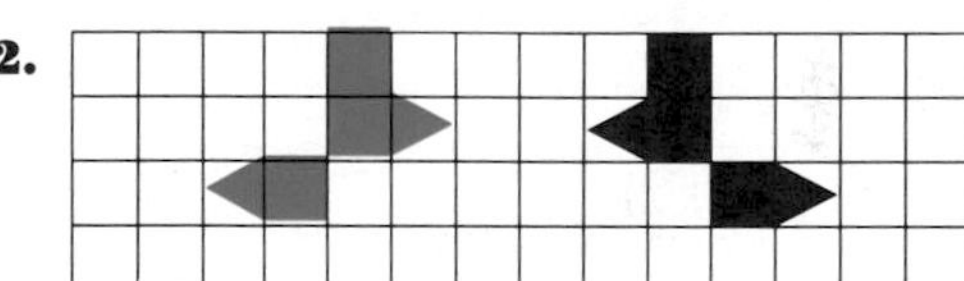

Set F pages 142–143

Using $\overline{DE}$, $\overline{DF}$, and $\angle D$ in Set B, construct $\triangle MNO \cong \triangle DEF$.

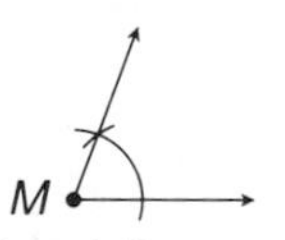

Step 1 Construct $\angle M \cong \angle D$.

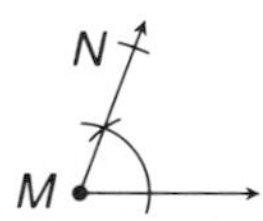

Step 2 On one side of $\angle M$, construct $\overline{MN} \cong \overline{DE}$.

N
M
O

Step 3 On the other side of $\angle M$, construct $\overline{MO} \cong \overline{DF}$.

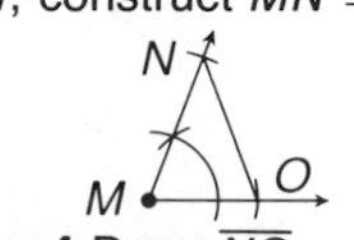

Step 4 Draw $\overline{NO}$.

Remember, only a compass and an unmarked straightedge are used in constructions.

Do each construction.

1. Construct a segment congruent to $\overline{BD}$ in Set A.

2. Construct an angle congruent to $\angle ADF$ in Set A.

3. Construct a triangle congruent to $\triangle PQR$ in Set B.

More Practice

Set A pages 114–117

Use the diagram at the right to name

1. three lines.

2. three line segments.

3. two pairs of intersecting lines.

4. three rays.

5. a pair of parallel lines.

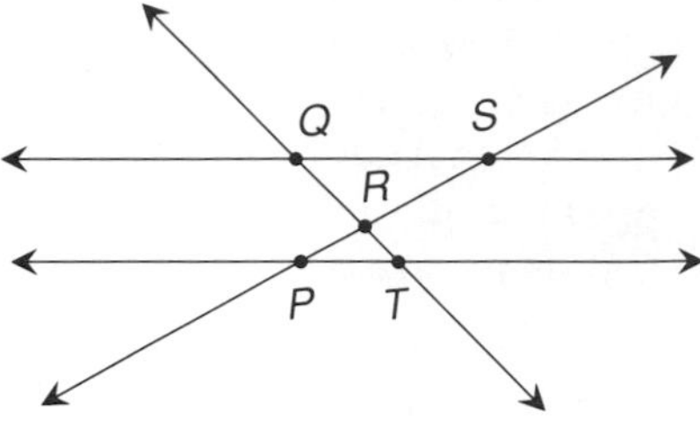

Set B pages 120–121

Use the diagram at the right to name

1. two acute angles.

2. two right angles.

3. two obtuse angles.

4. a pair of complementary angles.

5. a pair of supplementary angles.

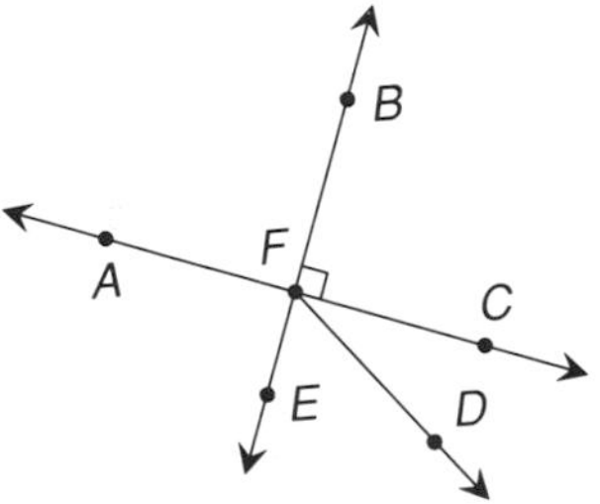

Find the missing angle measure in each triangle. Then classify each triangle as *acute, right, obtuse, scalene, isosceles, equilateral.*

6.

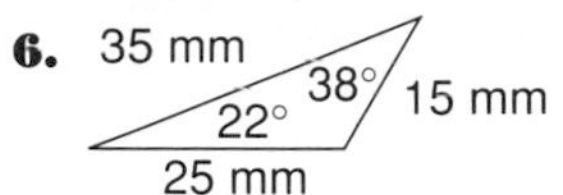

7.

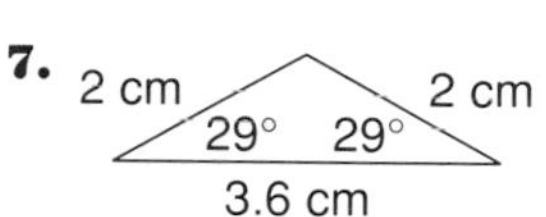

8.

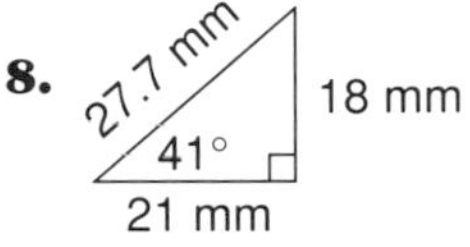

9.

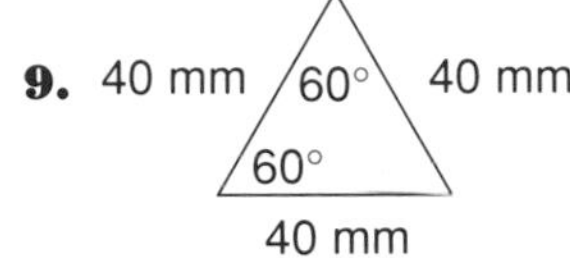

Set C pages 122–123

Name the polygon.

1.

2.

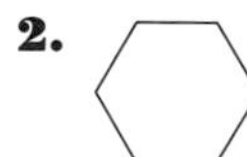

3.

4.

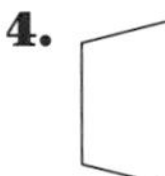

Set D pages 126–127

Using the circle at the right, name

1. the center of the circle.

2. an arc.

3. the diameter.

4. a radius.

5. two chords.

6. a central angle.

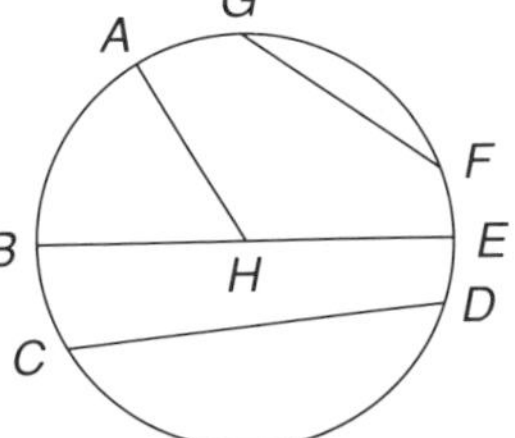

Set E pages 130–133

Copy each figure onto grid paper. Then draw the result of the given translation.

1. Left 4 units

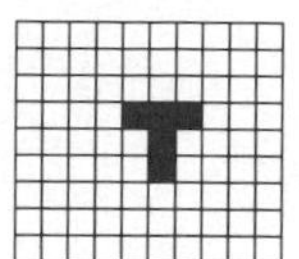

2. Down 3 units

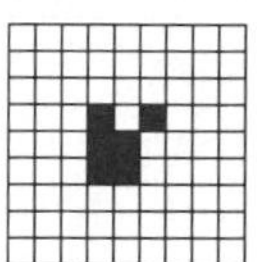

3. Up 2 units, 5 units to the right

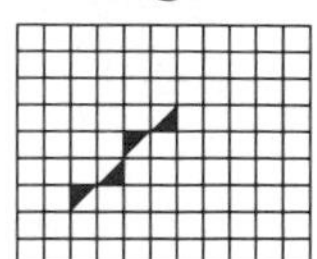

Trace each letter. Draw all lines of symmetry.

4. H **5.** K **6.** F **7.** O **8.** M **9.** N

Copy each figure onto grid paper. Draw its reflection or rotation as described.

10. Rotate 180° about point Q.

11. Reflect over the line.

12. Rotate 90° about point T.

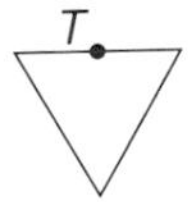

Set F pages 142–143

Do each construction.

1. Construct a segment congruent to $\overline{UV}$.

2. Construct an angle congruent to $\angle B$.

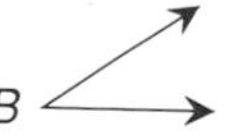

3. Bisect $\overline{MN}$.

4. Bisect $\angle R$.

5. Construct a triangle congruent to $\triangle ABC$. (Use side, angle, side.)

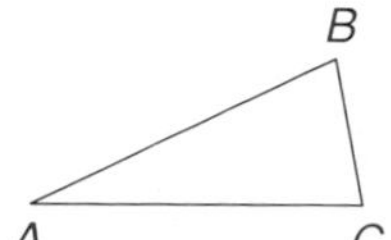

6. Construct a square congruent to $\square DEFG$.

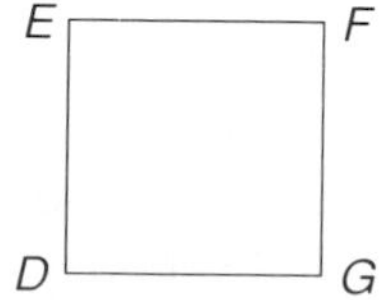

Enrichment

Using Construction

Archaeologists are scientists who analyze objects, such as tools, weapons, and pottery, left by early people. By examining these artifacts, many of which are only fragments of objects, archaeologists can draw conclusions about the lives of the people who made them. Archaeologists use construction to determine the size of whole plates from fragments such as the one shown here.

Using the fragment's rounded edge, draw a chord and label the endpoints A and B. Construct a perpendicular bisector of the chord as shown below.

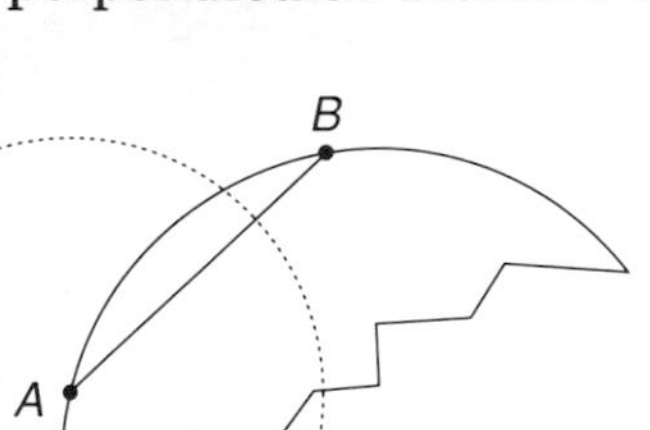

Step 1 Using A as center, draw an arc with a radius slightly greater than $\frac{1}{2}\overline{AB}$.

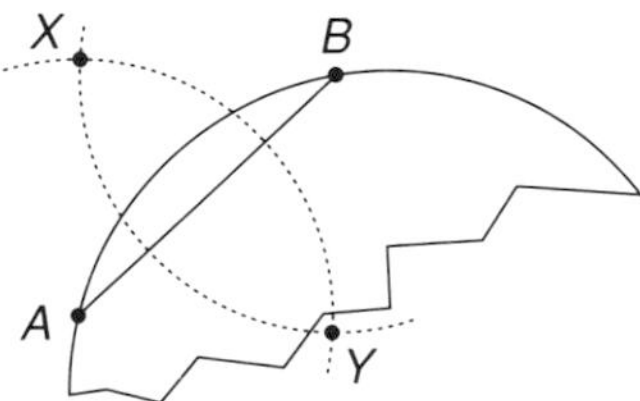

Step 2 Using the same radius but with B as center, draw another arc. Label the points of intersection X and Y.

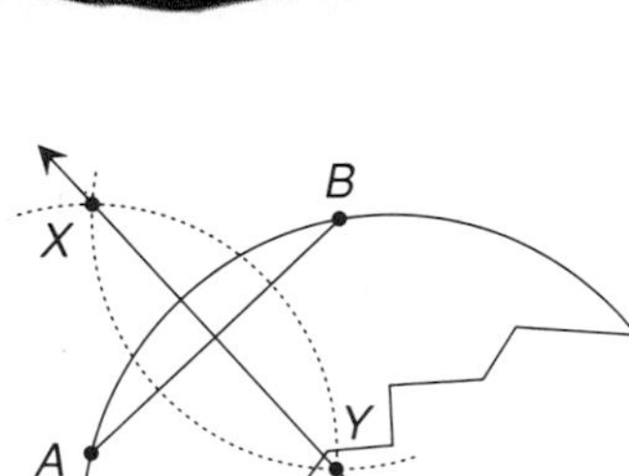

Step 3 Draw $\overleftrightarrow{XY}$. $\overleftrightarrow{XY}$ is the perpendicular bisector of $\overline{AB}$.

Draw another chord, $\overline{CD}$, and construct its perpendicular bisector. Label the point of intersection of the two perpendicular bisectors point P. Point P is the center of the plate.

Use center P to draw a circle with radius $\overline{PA}$. The circle you draw represents the whole plate.

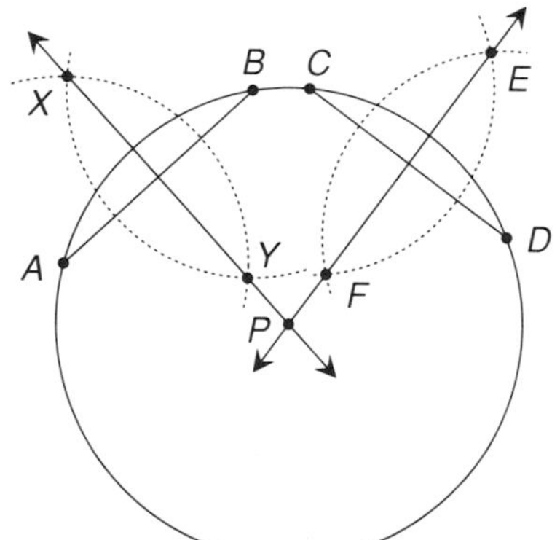

1. Could you use the above method and the fragment to the right to find the center of the plate? Explain your answer.

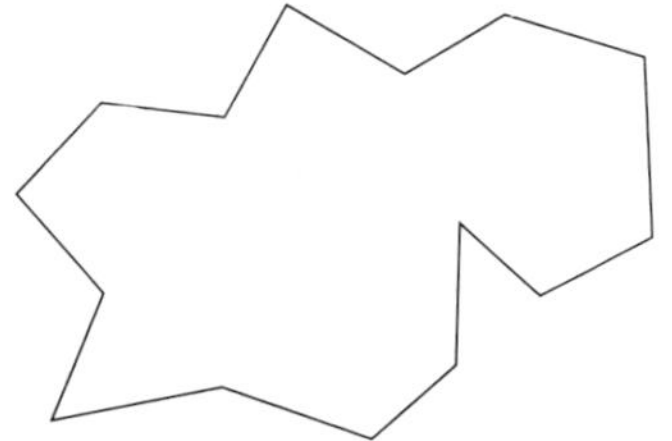

2. Outline a portion of a paper plate. Use the method above to determine the size of the whole plate. Check to see if the plate is actually the size you determined.

Chapter 4 Review/Test

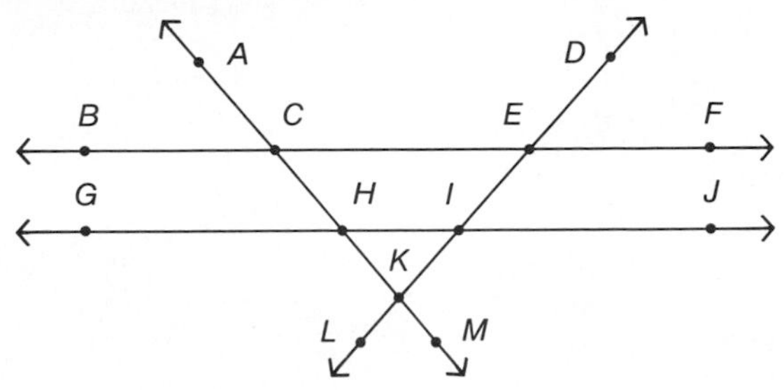

Using the diagram above, name

1. three segments.
2. two rays.
3. a pair of parallel lines.
4. a pair of vertical angles.
5. a pair of adjacent angles.
6. Make a table to find the number of triangles formed from one vertex of a 14-sided polygon.

Using the diagram at the right, name

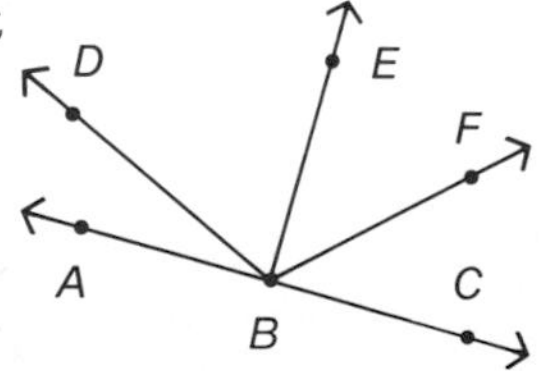

7. a pair of supplementary angles.

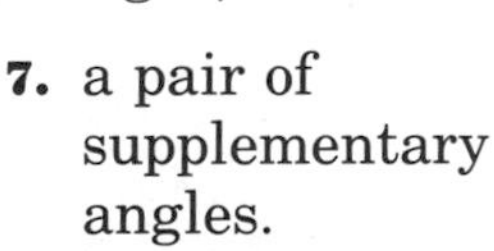

8. an obtuse angle.

Draw each figure.

9. A parallelogram with a right angle
10. A pentagon
11. Describe the translation that moved the red figure to the blue figure.

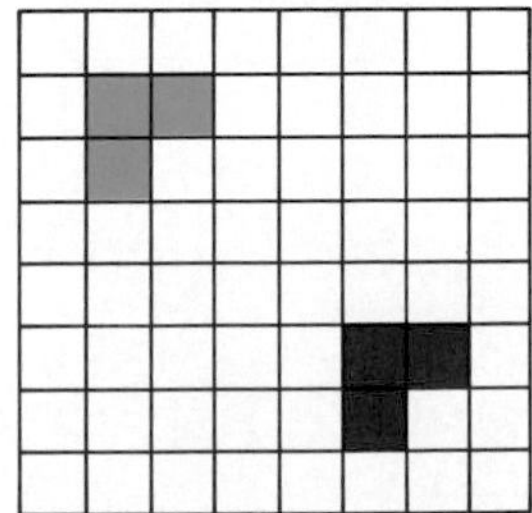

For circle S, name

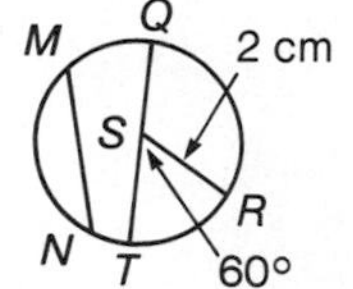

12. two radii.

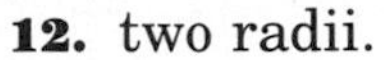

13. two central angles.
14. a diameter.
15. Find $m\overset{\frown}{RT}$.

Tell whether the blue figure resulted from a rotation or a reflection of the red figure.

16. 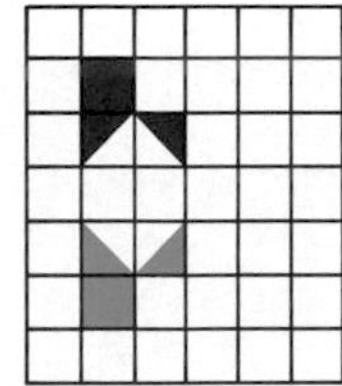

17. 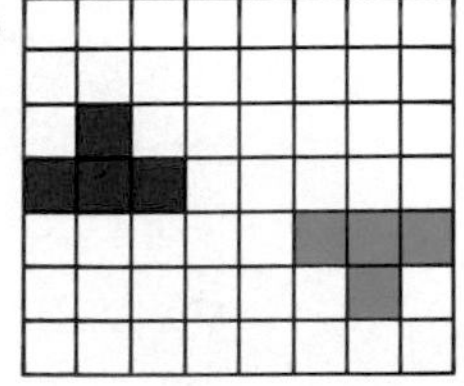

Find the measure of $\angle Y$ and $\angle L$. Classify each triangle by angle and side length.

18. 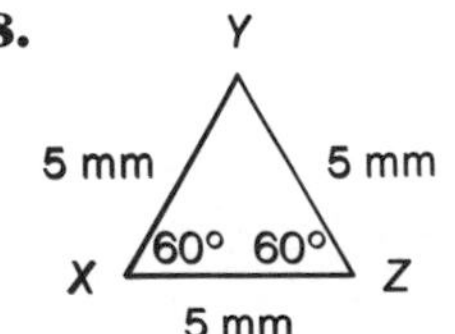

19. 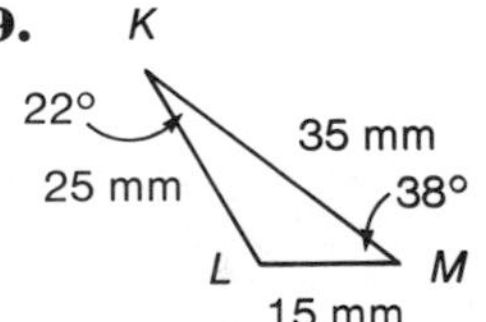

Trace and bisect.

20. $\angle KLM$
21. $\overline{XZ}$
22. Show how you can tell whether or not it is possible to construct a triangle with sides of 3 cm, 4 cm, and 6 cm.
23. Draw $\overleftrightarrow{AB}$. Construct a line perpendicular to $\overleftrightarrow{AB}$ from any point P not on $\overleftrightarrow{AB}$.
24. **Write About Math** Describe another method you could have used to find the answer to Item 22.

Number Theory 5

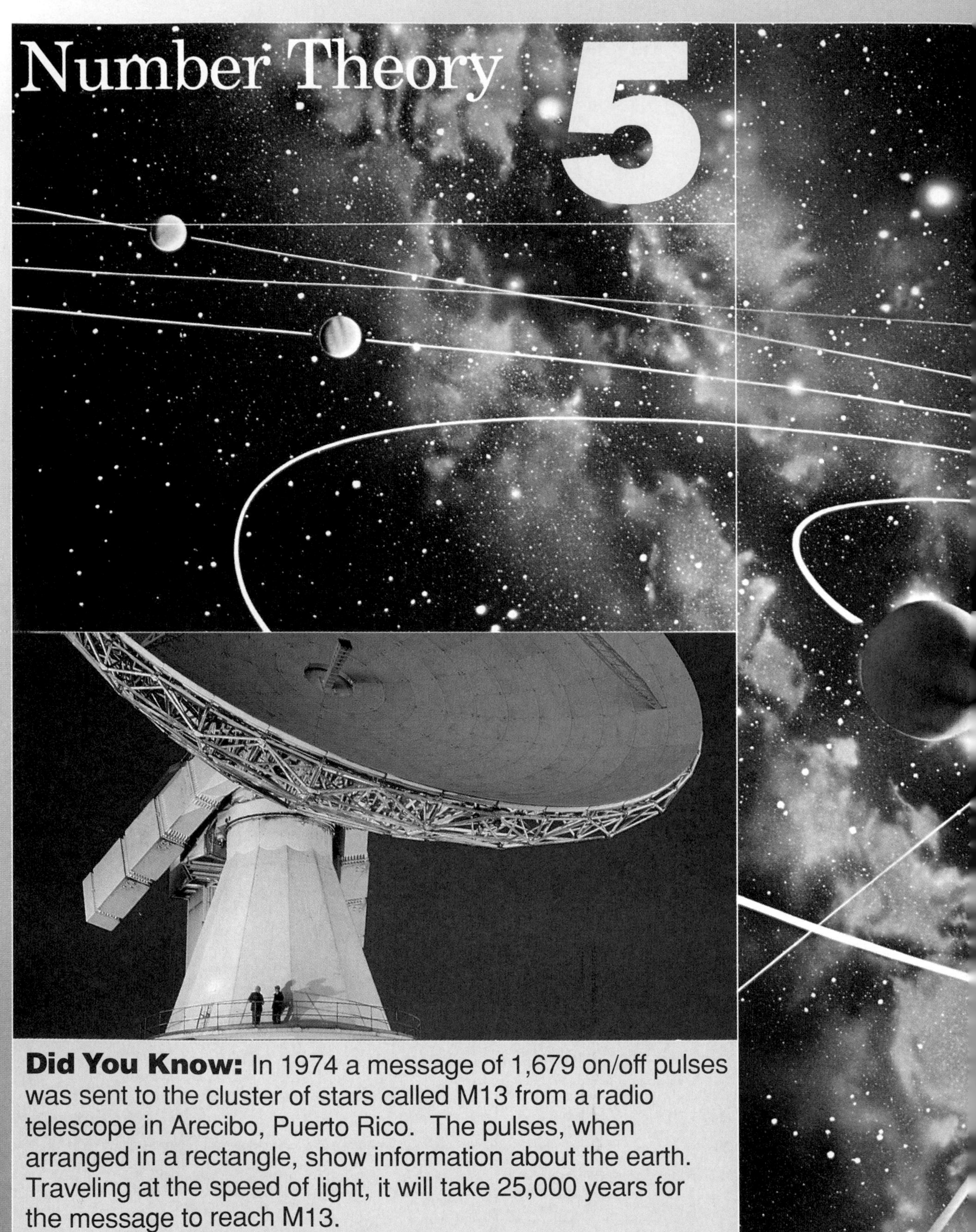

Did You Know: In 1974 a message of 1,679 on/off pulses was sent to the cluster of stars called M13 from a radio telescope in Arecibo, Puerto Rico. The pulses, when arranged in a rectangle, show information about the earth. Traveling at the speed of light, it will take 25,000 years for the message to reach M13.

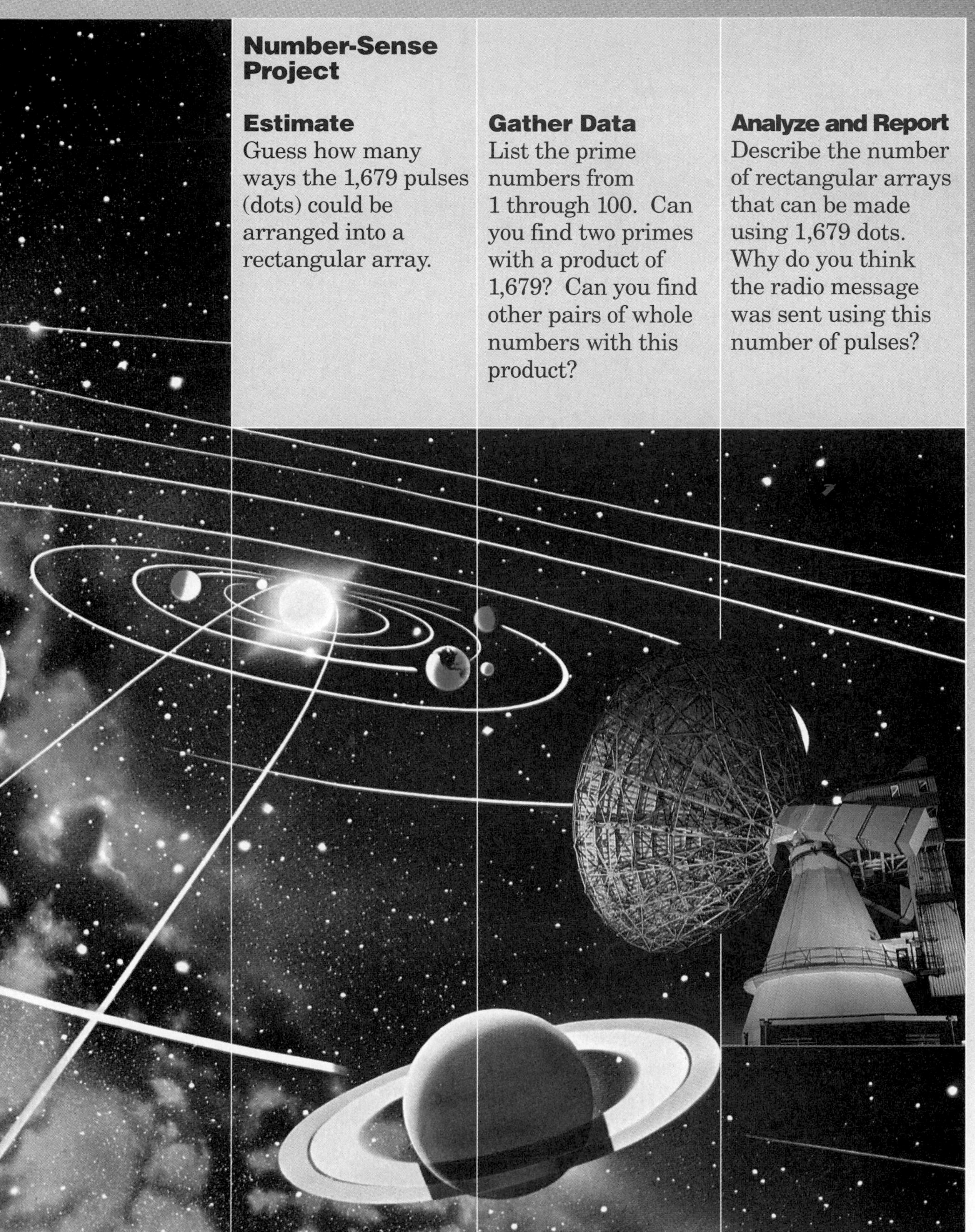

Number-Sense Project

Estimate
Guess how many ways the 1,679 pulses (dots) could be arranged into a rectangular array.

Gather Data
List the prime numbers from 1 through 100. Can you find two primes with a product of 1,679? Can you find other pairs of whole numbers with this product?

Analyze and Report
Describe the number of rectangular arrays that can be made using 1,679 dots. Why do you think the radio message was sent using this number of pulses?

Divisibility

Build Understanding

If the remainder is zero when a whole number is divided by another whole number, the first number is ***divisible*** by the second number.

The numbers that are multiplied to give a product are called ***factors*** of that product.

Divisibility Rules

A number is divisible by 2 if its ones digit is 0, 2, 4, 6, or 8.
A number is divisible by 3 if the sum of its digits is divisible by 3.
A number is divisible by 5 if its ones digit is 0 or 5.
A number is divisible by 9 if the sum of its digits is divisible by 9.
A number is divisible by 10 if its ones digit is 0.

All whole numbers that are divisible by 2 are ***even*** numbers. Whole numbers that are not divisible by 2 are ***odd*** numbers.

Winston has 225 muffins to package for the bake sale. He wants to put the same number of muffins in each bag and have none left over. What can he do?

Winston can use the divisibility rules to see if 225 is divisible by 2, 3, 5, 9, or 10.

225 is not divisible by 2 because its ones digit is not 0, 2, 4, 6, or 8.

225 is divisible by 3 because the sum 2 + 2 + 5 is divisible by 3.

225 is divisible by 5 because its ones digit is 5.

225 is divisible by 9 because the sum 2 + 2 + 5 is divisible by 9.

225 is not divisible by 10 because its ones digit is not 0.

Winston can package 225 muffins in bags of 3, 5, or 9.

■ **Talk About Math** Give an example of a 4-digit number that is divisible by 2, 3, and 5.

225 ÷ 3 = 75

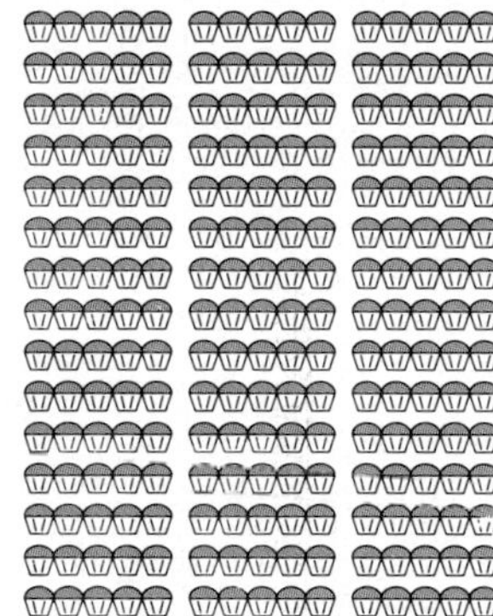

225 ÷ 5 = 45

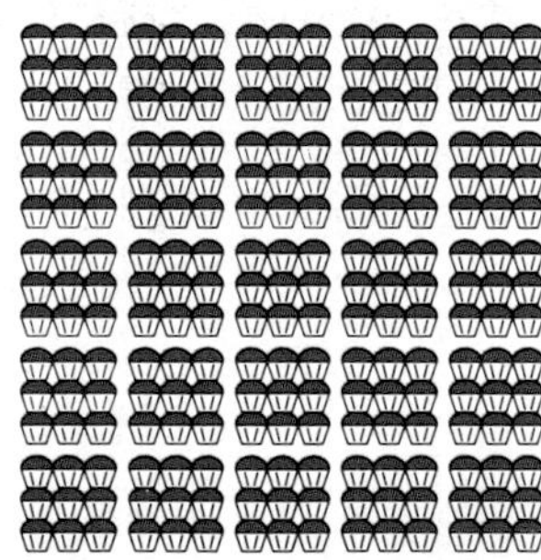

225 ÷ 9 = 25

Check Understanding

For another example, see Set A, pages 180–181.

1. Is 51 divisible by 3? by 5?

2. Is 657 divisible by 5? by 9?

3. Is 198 divisible by 2 *and* 3?

4. If a number is divisible by 10, is it also divisible by 2? Explain your answer.

Practice

For More Practice, see Set A, pages 182–183.

Tell if each number is divisible by 2, 3, 5, 9, or 10. List all possibilities.

5. 465	**6.** 86	**7.** 342	**8.** 357	**9.** 1,140
10. 1,692	**11.** 1,020	**12.** 297	**13.** 1,935	**14.** 360
15. 523	**16.** 4,095	**17.** 600	**18.** 72	**19.** 11,001
20. 16,302	**21.** 7,275	**22.** 1,854	**23.** 4,025	**24.** 67,990
25. 212,310	**26.** 302,175	**27.** 8,003,520	**28.** 606,030	**29.** 41,677
30. 627,300	**31.** 718,466	**32.** 4,000,000	**33.** 19,046,919	**34.** 6,799,830
35. 52,832	**36.** 621,790	**37.** 5,742	**38.** 224	**39.** 13,542

Problem Solving

Solve each problem.

40. Margo has a carton of crackers that contains 9 boxes. The total number of crackers is written on the carton shown at right but is not clear. How many crackers does Margo have?

41. Use the digits 5, 6, and 7 to write the greatest 3-digit number that is divisible by 5 *and* 9.

42. **Use Data** Look at the table on page 78. Which point totals are divisible by 2? 3? 5? 9? or 10?

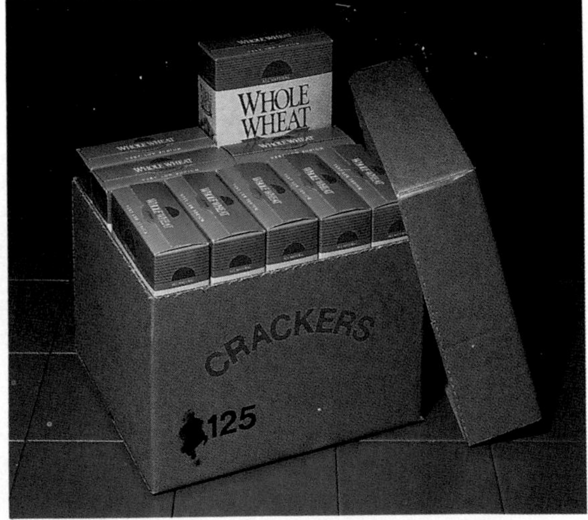

Explore ______ Math

Mental Math Solve.

43. Make a list of the numbers in Exercises 5–39 that are divisible by 3. Underline the numbers that are also divisible by 6.

44. By what 3 numbers are the underlined numbers divisible? How can you tell if a number is divisible by 6 without actually dividing by 6?

Exponents

Build Understanding

A. A certain cell doubles every hour. If you begin with one cell, at the end of 1 hour there are 2 cells, 4 cells at the end of 2 hours, and so on. After 5 hours, how many cells will there be?

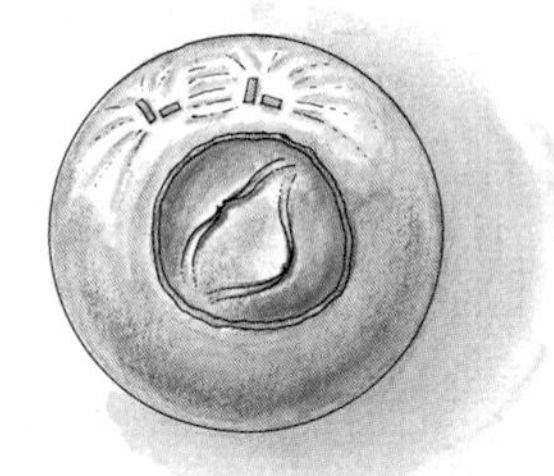

You can write the expression $2 \times 2 \times 2 \times 2 \times 2$ as 2^5 or "2 to the fifth power." In the expression 2^5, 2 is the ***base*** and 5 is the ***exponent***. The exponent tells how many times the base is used as a factor. The product is called the ***standard form*** of the power.

exponent →
$2^5 = 2 \times 2 \times 2 \times 2 \times 2 = 32$ ← **standard form**
base →

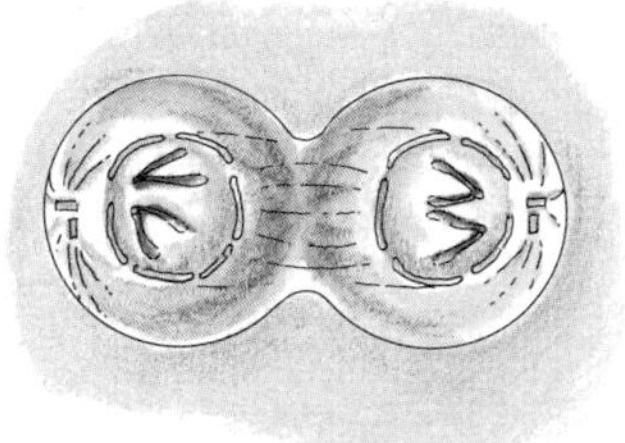

B. Find 10^0.

In the decimal number system, each place represents a power of 10.

Power of 10	10^4	10^3	10^2	10^1	10^0
Standard Form	10,000	1,000	100	10	1
Place Value	ten-thousands	thousands	hundreds	tens	ones

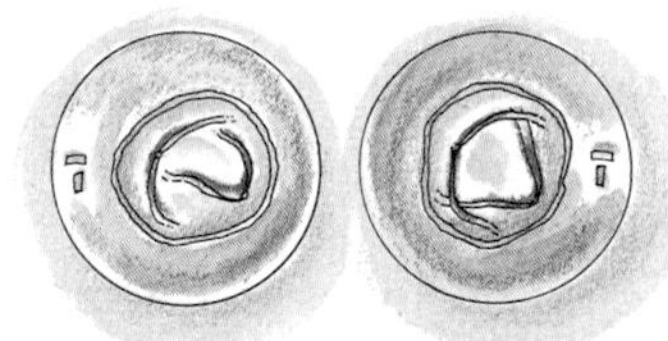

When some cells reach a certain size, they divide and form two new cells, each an exact duplicate of the parent cell. This process is called mitosis.

For each power of 10, the exponent is the same as the number of zeros in the standard form. Notice that $10^1 = 10$ and $10^0 = 1$. The zero power of 10 is 1. The zero power of any nonzero number is one.

C. Write each number using exponents.

$9 \times 9 = 9^2$ — 9^2 is read "9 to the second power" or "9 squared."

$6 \times 6 \times 6 = 6^3$ — 6^3 is read "6 to the third power" or "6 cubed."

$4 \times 4 \times 3 \times 3 \times 3 \times 3 = 4^2 \times 3^4$

$3 \times 3 \times 3 \times 3 \times 2 = 3^4 \times 2^1$

D. Give the standard form of each number.

$12^2 = 12 \times 12 = 144$

$3^3 = 3 \times 3 \times 3 = 27$

$2^2 \times 6^3 = 2 \times 2 \times 6 \times 6 \times 6 = 864$

$5^3 \times 4^2 = 5 \times 5 \times 5 \times 4 \times 4 = 2{,}000$

Write About Math How many ways can you write 64, using exponents?

Check Understanding

For another example, see Set B, pages 180–181.

Rewrite, using exponents.

1. $8 \times 8 \times 8$ **2.** $6 \times 6 \times 6 \times 6 \times 6$ **3.** $15 \times 15 \times 15 \times 15 \times 15 \times 15$

Rewrite each power with factors. Then multiply and write in standard form.

4. 3^2 **5.** 5^3 **6.** 6^4 **7.** 4^1 **8.** 8^2

Practice

For More Practice, see Set B, pages 182–183.

Write each power in standard form. Use mental math or paper and pencil. Tell which method you used.

9. 4^2 **10.** 2^3 **11.** 3^4 **12.** 6^3 **13.** 8^1

14. 5^0 **15.** 7^2 **16.** 2^5 **17.** 5^4 **18.** 7^3

19. 4^3 **20.** 6^2 **21.** 11^2 **22.** 2^7 **23.** 16^0

24. 10^3 **25.** 22^1 **26.** 14^2 **27.** 8^3 **28.** 1^5

29. 15^1 **30.** $30^2 \times 3^2$ **31.** $3^2 \times 2^3$ **32.** $4^3 \times 3^1$ **33.** $2^5 \times 5^2$

34. $2^3 \times 8^2$ **35.** $6^3 \times 4^2$ **36.** $2^4 \times 5^3$ **37.** $8^1 \times 9^3$ **38.** $7^2 \times 4^3$

Calculator Use a calculator to find each of the following.

39. 5^7 **40.** 4^5 **41.** 7^4 **42.** 6^5 **43.** 8^6 **44.** 11^4 **45.** 3^8 **46.** 9^7

Problem Solving

Critical Thinking b^3 means $b \times b \times b$. In Problems 47–49, write an expression without exponents. In Problems 50–51, write an expression with exponents.

47. y^2 **48.** t^4 **49.** a^5 **50.** $m \times m \times m$ **51.** $r \times r \times r \times r$

Explore Math

To simplify $3^3 \times 3^2$, you write $(3 \times 3 \times 3) \times (3 \times 3)$ or 3^5. So, $3^3 \times 3^2 = 3^5$.

52. Simplify $2^2 \times 2^5$. **53.** Simplify $10^2 \times 10^4$.

54. When multiplying powers with the same base, what is true about the exponents?

Prime and Composite Numbers

Build Understanding

A. Can a Square Be a Rectangle?
Materials: Small squares, one size
Groups: 3 or 4 students

a. Use 12 squares and form all possible rectangles. Copy the following table. Record the dimensions of each rectangle and the number of unique rectangles.

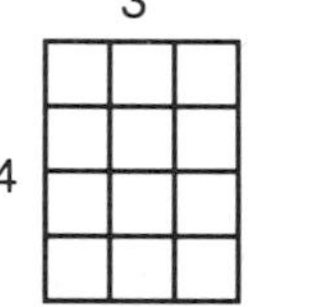

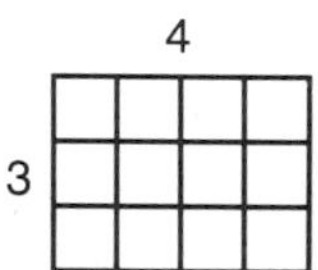

Dimensions 3 × 4 and 4 × 3 have the same shape, so they are counted as one rectangle.

Number of Squares	Dimensions of Rectangles	Number of Unique Rectangles
12	1 × 12, 12 × 1 2 × 6, 6 × 2 3 × 4, 4 × 3	3
13	1 × 13, 13 × 1	1
14	1 × 14, 14 × 1 2 × 7, 7 × 2	2

b. Repeat this activity with 14, 15, 16, 17, 18, and 19 squares. Record your results.

c. With which numbers of squares can you form only one unique rectangle?

d. With which numbers of squares can you form 2 or more unique rectangles?

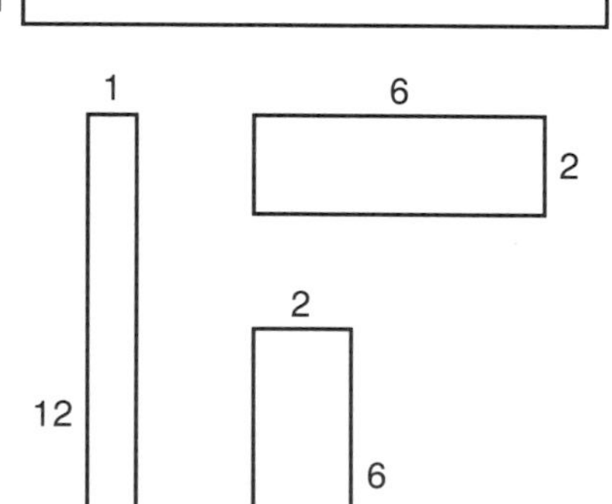

B. Any whole number greater than 1 with exactly 2 factors is a ***prime number***. Any whole number greater than 1 with more than 2 factors is a ***composite number***. The numbers 0 and 1 are neither prime nor composite.

Is 351 a prime number?

Two factors of 351 are 1 and 351. By the divisibility rules, you know that 2, 5, and 10 are not factors of 351. Since 3 + 5 + 1 = 9, the number 351 is divisible by 3 and by 9. So 351 is not a prime number.

C. Is 79 a prime number?

By divisibility rules you know that 79 is not divisible by 2, 3, 5, 9, or 10.

Next, divide 79 by other possible factors. A table of squares can help you decide on the numbers to try. A table of squares can be used to find the greatest number whose square is less than or equal to 79.

$8^2 = 64$, $9^2 = 81$

Try numbers through 8. Since 79 is not divisible by 4, 6, 7, or 8, the number 79 is prime.

Table of Squares
$1^2 = 1$
$2^2 = 4$
$3^2 = 9$
$4^2 = 16$
$5^2 = 25$
$6^2 = 36$
$7^2 = 49$
$8^2 = 64$
$9^2 = 81$
$10^2 = 100$
$11^2 = 121$
$12^2 = 144$
$13^2 = 169$
$14^2 = 196$
$15^2 = 225$

D. Can 119 members of a marching band march in rows of equal numbers? How?

The number of rows times the number of people in each row must equal 119.

Use divisibility rules to test for divisibility by 2, 3, 5, 9, and 10. You will find that 119 is not divisible by 2, 3, 5, 9, or 10.

Use the table of squares to find the greatest square number that is less than or equal to 119.

$10^2 = 100$, $11^2 = 121$

Use division to test for other factors through 10. You'll find that 119 is divisible by 7.

$119 \div 7 = 17$ 119 is not prime; it is composite.

The band members can march in 17 rows with 7 people in each row.

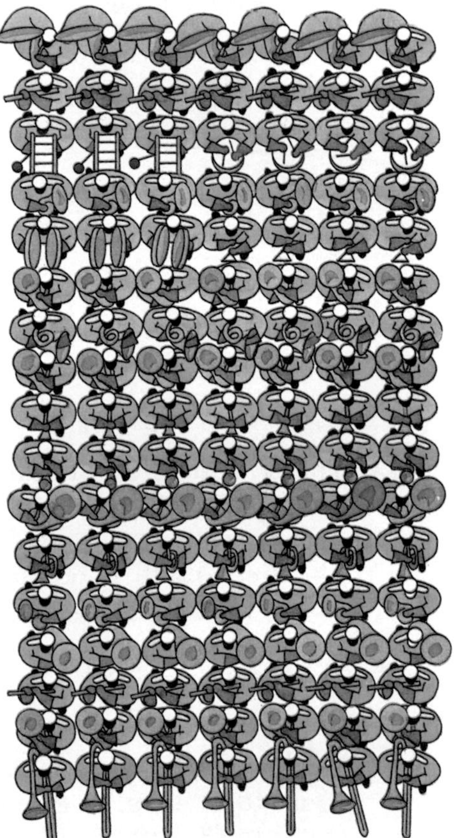

■ **Talk About Math** In Example C, explain why 9 and 10 are too large to be considered factors of 79 after checking through 8.

Check Understanding

For another example, see Set C, pages 180–181.

1. List the prime numbers less than 30.

2. List the first 10 composite numbers.

Use the table of squares to find the greatest number you need to check to find any factors for these numbers.

3. 157 **4.** 201 **5.** 97 **6.** 173

Practice

For More Practice, see Set C, pages 182–183.

Write prime (P) or composite (C).

7. 23	**8.** 39	**9.** 41	**10.** 49	**11.** 91	**12.** 53
13. 43	**14.** 51	**15.** 35	**16.** 59	**17.** 63	**18.** 57
19. 47	**20.** 61	**21.** 38	**22.** 70	**23.** 81	**24.** 87
25. 55	**26.** 67	**27.** 98	**28.** 73	**29.** 25	**30.** 37
31. 97	**32.** 58	**33.** 77	**34.** 101	**35.** 200	**36.** 105

Answer each question.

37. Express 30 as the product of three prime numbers. Is there another solution?

38. Express 30 as the sum of two prime numbers. Is there another pair?

39. Find two prime numbers whose product is an even number. Is there another pair?

40. Find two prime numbers whose difference is one. Is there another pair?

41. Find two prime numbers whose sum is odd. Is there another pair?

42. Find a prime number that is 2 less than a square of a number. Is there another solution?

43. There is one prime number between 2,001 and 2,010 inclusive. What is it?

44. Are there more prime numbers between 10 and 20 inclusive or between 110 and 120 inclusive?

ALGEBRA In 45–48, x stands for a whole number. Answer each question.

45. If x is a prime number, is x^3 prime?

46. **Number Sense** Why is 2 the only even prime number?

47. Is $x^2 + x + 11$ a prime number for x equal to 1? equal to 2? equal to 3? equal to 5? equal to 9?

48. Is $x^2 + x + 11$ always a prime number? If not, give a value for x for which $x^2 + x + 11$ is not prime.

Mixed Practice Write prime (P) or composite (C). If the number is composite, tell if it is divisible by 2, 3, 5, 9 or 10. List all possibilities.

49. 114	**50.** 151	**51.** 113	**52.** 345	**53.** 122	**54.** 131
55. 185	**56.** 106	**57.** 147	**58.** 201	**59.** 157	**60.** 183
61. 109	**62.** 321	**63.** 187	**64.** 243	**65.** 191	**66.** 153

Problem Solving

Solve each problem.

67. Is there a 3-digit prime number that uses each of the digits 6, 7, and 8? Why or why not?

68. In the 18th century, Christian Goldbach theorized that every even number greater than 2 can be expressed as the sum of two prime numbers. Some examples are shown. Write each even number from 12 to 30 as the sum of two primes.

4 = 2 + 2
6 = 3 + 3
8 = 5 + 3
10 = 7 + 3

Calculator Use a calculator to evaluate each expression. Then tell whether each number is prime. Answer *yes* or *no*.

Expression	Number	Prime
2 + 1	**69.**	**70.**
2 × 3 + 1	**71.**	**72.**
2 × 3 × 5 + 1	**73.**	**74.**
2 × 3 × 5 × 7 + 1	**75.**	**76.**
2 × 3 × 5 × 7 × 11 + 1	**77.**	**78.**
2 × 3 × 5 × 7 × 11 × 13 + 1	**79.**	**80.**

81. Create a list of prime numbers from 1 to 100 using the following method devised by the Greek mathematician Eratosthenes.

a. Write all the numbers from 1 to 100.
b. Cross out the number 1; it is not prime.
c. Circle 2 and cross out all other multiples of 2.
d. Circle 3 and cross out all other multiples of 3.
e. Circle 5, the next number that is not crossed out. Cross out other multiples of 5.
f. Continue in the same way. When you have finished, the circled numbers are prime.

Skills Review pages 90–91

Divide. **Remember** to place the decimal point in the quotient.

1. 53.7 ÷ 0.2 **2.** 17.43 ÷ 0.83 **3.** 11.9 ÷ 0.007 **4.** 0.52 ÷ 0.4

Estimation Estimate to place the decimal point in each quotient.

5. 0.05)0.065 13 **6.** 0.02)0.048 24 **7.** 0.46)0.0138 3

Prime Factorization

Build Understanding

A. Any composite number can be written as the product of prime numbers. This product is the ***prime factorization*** of the number.

You can use a factor tree to find the prime factorization of 108.

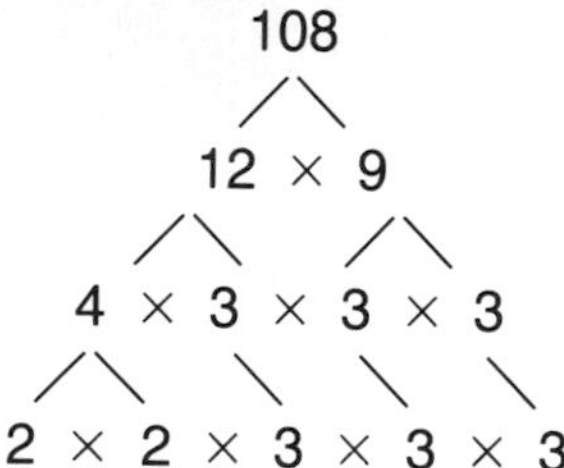

Start with any 2 factors whose product is 108.

Continue to write products. Check for prime factors: 2, 3, 5, 7, and so on.

The last row will contain only prime factors. This is the prime factorization.

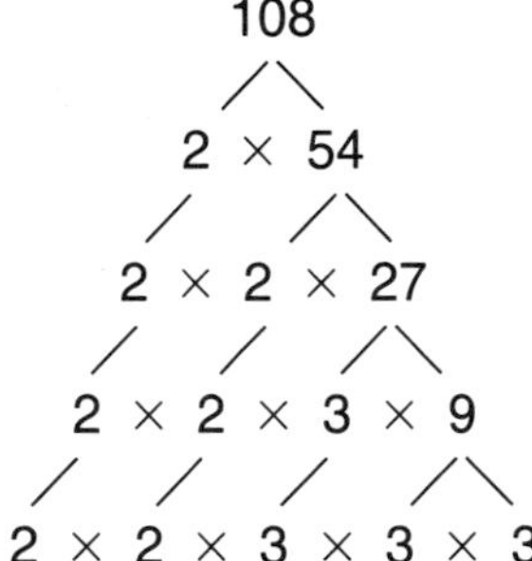

The prime factorization of 108 is 2 × 2 × 3 × 3 × 3. The same prime factorization is obtained from both factor trees.

B. Write the prime factorization of 96, using exponents.

List the prime factors from least to greatest. When a prime factor appears more than once, use exponents in the prime factorization.

The prime factorization of 96 is $2^5 \times 3$.

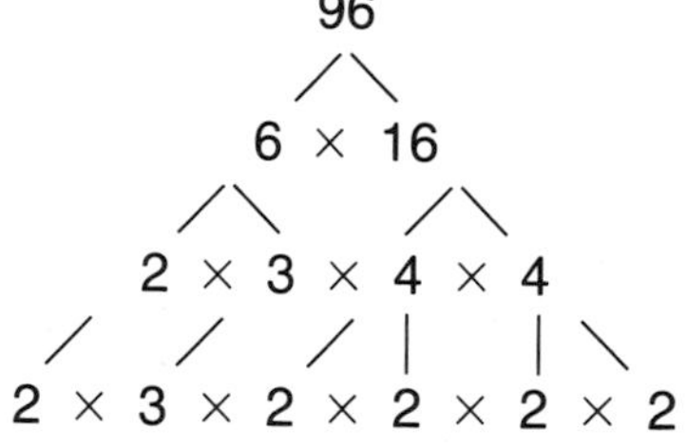

■ **Talk About Math** Why is the prime factorization of a composite number unique to that number?

Check Understanding

For another example, see Set D, pages 180–181.

Copy and complete each factor tree.

1.

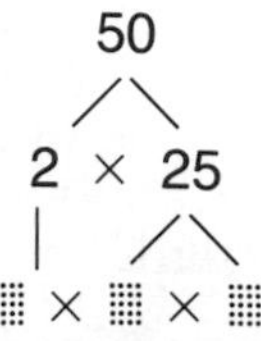

2.

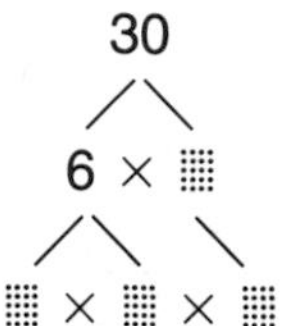

3.

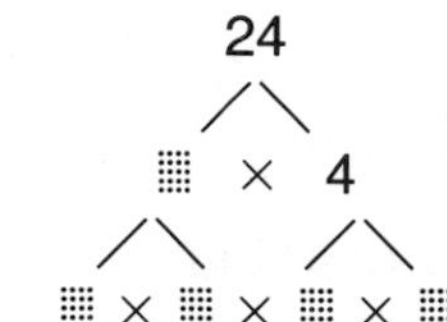

4. Write the prime factorization of 54 using exponents.

Practice

For More Practice, see Set D, pages 182–183.

For each number, choose the letter of the prime factorization.

5. 36 **a.** $2 \times 3 \times 3$ **b.** $2 \times 2 \times 3$ **c.** $2 \times 2 \times 3 \times 3$ **d.** 4×9

6. 63 **a.** 9×7 **b.** $3 \times 3 \times 7$ **c.** $3 \times 7 \times 7$ **d.** $3 \times 3 \times 7 \times 7$

For each number, make a factor tree and write the prime factorization.

7. 32 **8.** 65 **9.** 84 **10.** 126 **11.** 100 **12.** 156

13. 92 **14.** 36 **15.** 63 **16.** 44 **17.** 112 **18.** 124

Write the prime factorization of each number using exponents.

19. 56 **20.** 81 **21.** 93 **22.** 104 **23.** 256 **24.** 450

25. 121 **26.** 144 **27.** 370 **28.** 625 **29.** 220 **30.** 640

31. 515 **32.** 624 **33.** 168 **34.** 725 **35.** 6,776 **36.** 5,439

Problem Solving

Solve.

37. Draw two different factor trees for the number 60. What do you notice about the prime factorization on each factor tree?

38. Find the prime factorization for 24 and for 40. Which prime factors are the same?

39. Write the prime factorization of 36, 49, and 400, using exponents. Use your answers to describe the prime factorization of any square.

40. **Critical Thinking** What do you think will be true about the prime factorization of a cube?

Midchapter Checkup

Tell if each number is divisible by 2, 3, 5, 9, or 10. List all possibilities.

1. 828 **2.** 3,000 **3.** 51,077

Write each power in standard form.

4. 5^5 **5.** 8^3 **6.** $20^1 \times 4^4$

Write prime (P) or composite (C).

7. 56 **8.** 307 **9.** 115

Make a factor tree. Write the prime factorization using exponents.

10. 48 **11.** 90 **12.** 220

Explore as a Team

Work with the members of your team to complete the following steps:

1. Draw a circle. Mark off <u>ten</u> equally spaced points and label them from <u>0 to 9</u>.

2. Choose a number and find some multiples of it. Circle the units digit in each multiple. Continue until you see a pattern. For example:

6: (6) 1(2) 1(8) 2(4) 3(0) 3(6) 4(2) 4(8)

3. On the circle, connect in order the digits you circled.

4. Try other numbers. What other "multiple designs" can you generate?

5. Draw a circle. Mark off <u>nine</u> equally spaced points. Label them from <u>1 to 9</u>.

6. Choose a number and find some multiples of it. For each multiple, find the sum of the digits. If the sum is a 2-digit number, add those digits. Circle the final sum. Continue until you see a pattern. For example:

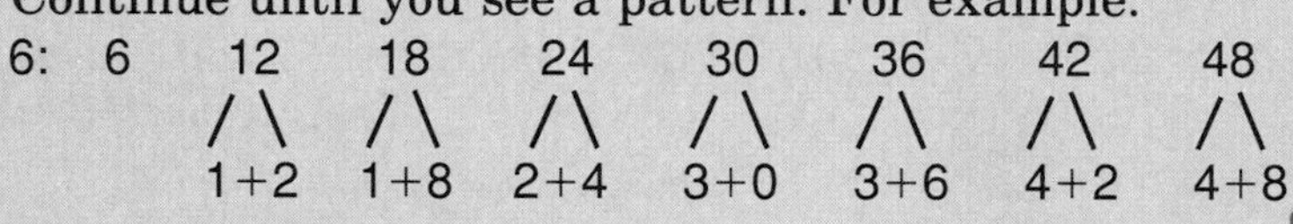

(3) (9) (6) (3) (9) (6) 12

1+2

(3)

7. On the circle, connect in order the digits you circled.

8. Try other numbers. Discuss your designs.

WORKING TOGETHER

WHEN YOU ARE UNSURE, ASK SOMEONE IN YOUR GROUP FOR HELP OR SAY YOU DON'T UNDERSTAND.

Explore with a Computer

Use the *Spreadsheet Workshop Project* for this activity.

1. At the computer, you can type a number from 2—20 in the *Prime Finder* and some numbers will be erased. Try to figure out what the spreadsheet is erasing. What happens to the chart?

2. Reset the chart by typing 1. Type another number less than 20. What happens this time?

3. Reset the table, and type 2. Without resetting the table, enter the next available number. Continue to do this until no more numbers are erased. What was the last number you entered? Describe the numbers that remain.

Number-Sense Project

Look back at pages 154-155. Suppose the 145 dots below are a string of on/off pulses with the dot at the beginning of one line following the dot at the end of the previous line. Arrange the dots in a rectangle so that you can read the message.

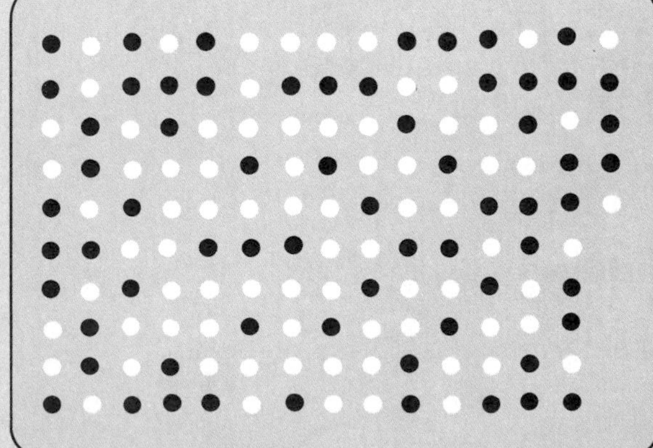

1. In what ways can the 145 dots be arranged in rectangular arrays?

2. Which array do you think was used for this message? Put the dots in this array. What is the message?

3. Make up a dot message of words or pictures and have a classmate try to decode it.

Greatest Common Factor

Build Understanding

A. Since much of Sweden is forested, woodcrafts are widely produced. The airport gift shop wants to arrange a display of 84 Swedish wooden horses in a rectangular array. To find all the possible row and column combinations, find all the factors of 84.

To find all the factors of a number, use the divisibility rules and divide systematically.

1 × 84
2 × 42
3 × 28
4 × 21
6 × 14
7 × 12

Test the different factors 1, 2, 3, and so on. 84 is not divisible by 5, 8, 9, 10, or 11. The next factor is 12. Remember that when factors are equal or the divisor becomes greater than the quotient, there are no more unique factors.

The factors of 84 are 1, 2, 3, 4, 6, 7, 12, 14, 21, 28, 42, and 84.

These brightly painted wooden *Dalarna horses* are made in the province of Dalarna, Sweden.

The horses can be arranged in any of these rectangular arrays.
1 by 84 2 by 42 3 by 28 4 by 21 6 by 14 7 by 12

B. When you write a fraction in lowest terms, you need to find the ***greatest common factor (GCF)*** of the numerator and the denominator. Find the greatest common factor (GCF) of 36 and 48.

Factors of 36: 1, 2, 3, 4, 6, 9, 12, 18, 36
Factors of 48: 1, 2, 3, 4, 6, 8, 12, 16, 24, 48

The common factors of 36 and 48 are 1, 2, 3, 4, 6, and 12.
The greatest common factor is 12.

C. Find the GCF of 72 and 84. You can use prime factorization to find the GCF without listing all the factors.

Write the prime factorization of each number.

Without exponents:	With exponents:
$72 = 2 \times 2 \times 2 \times 3 \times 3$	$72 = 2^3 \times 3^2$
$84 = 2 \times 2 \times 3 \times 7$	$84 = 2^2 \times 3 \times 7$

Multiply the common prime factors. When working with exponents, use the lesser powers of the common prime factors. The product is the GCF.

Without exponents:	With exponents:
$2 \times 2 \times 3 = 12$	$2^2 \times 3 = 12$

The GCF of 72 and 84 is 12.

Talk About Math Use prime factorization to find the GCF in Example B. Do you find prime factorization or listing factors more efficient? Why?

Check Understanding

For another example, see Set E, pages 180–181.

List all the factors of each number.

1. 18 **2.** 27 **3.** 24

Find the GCF of each pair of numbers.

4. 18 and 27 **5.** 36 and 60

Practice

For More Practice, see Set E, pages 182–183.

Find the GCF for each exercise. Use lists if necessary.

6. 9 and 12 **7.** 12 and 15 **8.** 22 and 33 **9.** 63 and 45

10. 25 and 35 **11.** 18 and 81 **12.** 20 and 24 **13.** 7 and 12

14. 36 and 45 **15.** 14 and 28 **16.** 24 and 42 **17.** 16 and 56

18. 5, 10, and 25 **19.** 12, 15, and 24 **20.** 3, 6, and 9 **21.** 16, 24, and 20

Find the GCF for each exercise. Use the prime factorization method.

22. 40 and 16 **23.** 30 and 75 **24.** 42 and 70 **25.** 45 and 150

26. 56 and 84 **27.** 36 and 100 **28.** 35 and 77 **29.** 16 and 72

30. 20 and 100 **31.** 16 and 35 **32.** 56, 84, and 49 **33.** 36, 90, and 126

Problem Solving

Solve. **Remember** to label the units in your answer.

34. Since prehistoric times, baskets have been made by people of all countries. American Indians make baskets for storing and carrying food. Find all the possible row and column combinations for a rectangular display of 64 baskets made by the Pomo Indians of California.

35. Macramé, the art of knotting rope in patterns, has been done by Turks for centuries. A macramé artist needs pieces of rope that are the same length for a design he is making. How long can each piece be if he has three pieces of rope 18, 24, and 42 feet long and there is no waste?

36. **Critical Thinking** In Problem 35, suppose the artist has a fourth piece of rope 15 feet long. Now how long will each piece be?

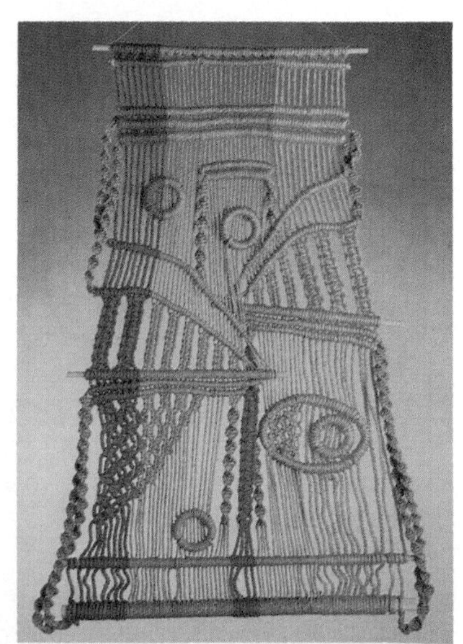

The word *macramé* comes from the Turkish word for *fringed napkin*.

Least Common Multiple

Build Understanding

A single marigold flower can produce up to 175 seeds in a season.

A. Lisa wants to plant three rows of flowers with the same number in each row. Asters come 3 plants per pack, marigolds come 4 plants per pack, and alyssums come 6 plants per pack. What is the least number of plants she can buy to have the same number of each kind of plant?

To have the same number of asters, marigolds, and alyssums, she needs a multiple of 3, 4, and 6. You can find ***multiples*** of a number by multiplying the number by 1, 2, 3, 4, and so on.

Multiples of 3: 3, 6, 9, 12, 15, 18, 21, 24, . . .
Multiples of 4: 4, 8, 12, 16, 20, 24, 28, . . .
Multiples of 6: 6, 12, 18, 24, 30, 36, 42, . . .

Common multiples of 3, 4, and 6 are 12, 24, . . .
The ***least common multiple (LCM)*** of 3, 4, and 6 is 12.

Lisa should buy 12 plants of each kind to have the same number of plants.

B. Find the LCM of 45 and 60 using prime factorization.

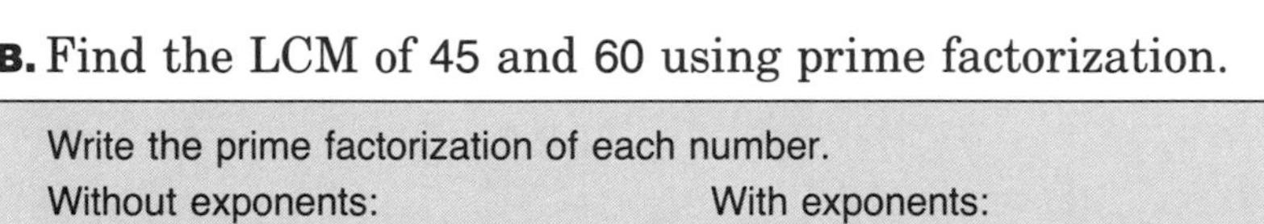

Write the prime factorization of each number.	
Without exponents:	With exponents:
$45 = 3 \times 3 \times 5$ $60 = 2 \times 2 \times 3 \times 5$	$45 = 3^2 \times 5$ $60 = 2^2 \times 3 \times 5$
Choose the greater number of times a factor appears. With exponents, use the greater power of every prime factor. Multiply to find the LCM.	
Without exponents:	With exponents:
$2 \times 2 \times 3 \times 3 \times 5 = 180$	$2^2 \times 3^2 \times 5 = 180$

The LCM of 45 and 60 is 180.

Talk About Math Compare the method of finding the LCM with the method of finding the GCF. How are the methods alike? How are they different?

Check Understanding

For another example, see Set F, pages 180–181.

Use a list of multiples to find the LCM of each pair of numbers.

1. 7 and 9 **2.** 15 and 25 **3.** 10 and 14

The prime factorization of each pair of numbers is given. Find the LCM.

4. $12 = 2 \times 2 \times 3$ $20 = 2 \times 2 \times 5$ **5.** $40 = 2^3 \times 5$ $60 = 2^2 \times 3 \times 5$

Practice

For More Practice, see Set F, pages 182–183.

Find the LCM. Use a list of multiples.

6. 8 and 10 **7.** 10 and 15 **8.** 6 and 9 **9.** 12 and 16

10. 18 and 30 **11.** 5 and 11 **12.** 15 and 45 **13.** 7 and 28

14. 4 and 14 **15.** 12 and 10 **16.** 36 and 60 **17.** 5 and 15

Find the LCM using prime factorization.

18. 14 and 49 **19.** 44 and 55 **20.** 24 and 96 **21.** 25 and 30

22. 35 and 42 **23.** 24 and 25 **24.** 100 and 24 **25.** 36 and 40

26. 21 and 42 **27.** 12 and 15 **28.** 9 and 24 **29.** 60 and 75

Mixed Practice Find the GCF then the LCM of each pair of numbers.

30. 3 and 5 **31.** 7 and 14 **32.** 21 and 27 **33.** 25 and 35

34. 30 and 45 **35.** 15 and 18 **36.** 18 and 54 **37.** 24 and 30

38. 12 and 20 **39.** 49 and 7 **40.** 6 and 7 **41.** 32 and 48

Problem Solving

Solve each problem.

42. In Example A on page 170, suppose alyssums also come 2 plants per pack. The price of a 2-plant pack is $0.49, and the price of a 6-plant pack is $1.39. How should Lisa buy the alyssums for the least cost? Explain.

TIPS FOR
PROBLEM SOLVERS
Share your thinking with others. Explaining your ideas helps you think better.

43. Suppose variables a and b are whole numbers. If the GCF of a and b is 1, what is the LCM of a and b?

Critical Thinking Solve each riddle.

44. Our LCM is 360. Our GCF is 12. What numbers are we?

45. Our LCM is 120. Our GCF is 6. What numbers are we?

46. Our LCM is 80. Our GCF is 8. Neither of us is 80 or 8. What numbers are we?

Make a Table

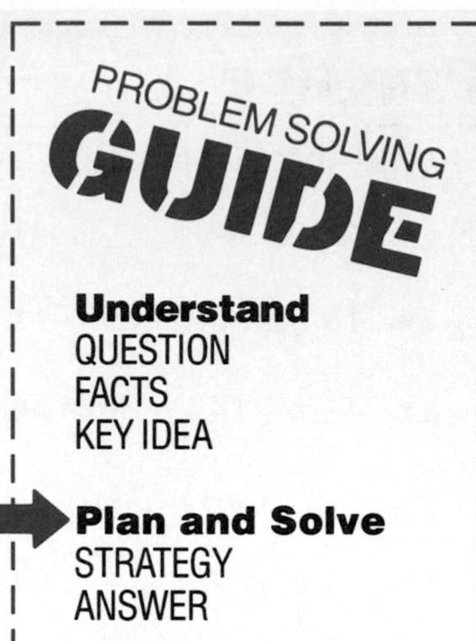

Build Understanding

In a school cafeteria, small tables seat exactly 6 people and large tables seat exactly 9 people. If 129 students can be seated at 18 tables with no empty seats, how many tables of each size are filled?

Understand QUESTION How many tables of each size are filled?

FACTS There are tables for 6 and tables for 9. There are 129 students seated at 18 tables with no empty seats.

KEY IDEA Find a combination of tables that will seat exactly 129 people.

Plan and Solve Try different combinations of tables.

STRATEGY Organize your work by making a table. Start with the combination of cafeteria tables that would seat the least number of students. Then extend the table.

Number of tables seating 6	18	17	16	15	14	13	12	11
Number of tables seating 9	0	1	2	3	4	5	6	7
Number of students seated	108	111	114	117	120	123	126	129

ANSWER There are 11 tables of 6 students each and 7 tables of 9 students each.

Look Back ALTERNATE APPROACH You could start the table with the greatest number of students. Or, you could start with 18 tables of 9 students and 0 tables of 6 students.

Talk About Math Study the table in the example. Describe how the total number of students changes as the combination of tables changes.

Check Understanding

The school library has 16 work tables. One size table seats 6 students. The other size table seats 10 students. There are more tables for 6 than for 10. Answer these questions to find the number of students who can sit in the library.

1. What is the greatest possible number of tables that seat 10?
2. What is the least possible number of tables that seat 10?
3. Make a table of the possible combinations of 16 work tables. Calculate the total number of students for each combination.
4. Which combination of tables allows for the greatest number of seats? the least number of seats?

Practice

Solve each problem. Make a table to find all the possible answers.

5. Tony spent $8.00 on lunch for 7 days. Lunches cost $1.10 without milk and $1.25 with milk. How many lunches with milk did he buy?
6. Fumi has $0.75 in nickels, dimes, and quarters. What combinations of coins might she have?
7. If the science class is divided into groups of 2, 3, or 5, there is 1 extra student each time. There are at least 20 students. What is the least number of students in the science class?
8. In the lunch line there were 10 more girls than boys. Two girls paid and left as 2 more boys got in line. Now there are twice as many girls as boys. How many girls are in line?

Choose a Strategy

ABC Friends Solve.

9. Ann, Caryn, and Bob are friends. One is an artist, one is a baker, and one is a computer programmer, but not necessarily in that order. The artist, who lives next door to Bob, took Caryn to lunch yesterday. As they were entering the restaurant, they saw the computer programmer getting into a taxi. Who is the baker?

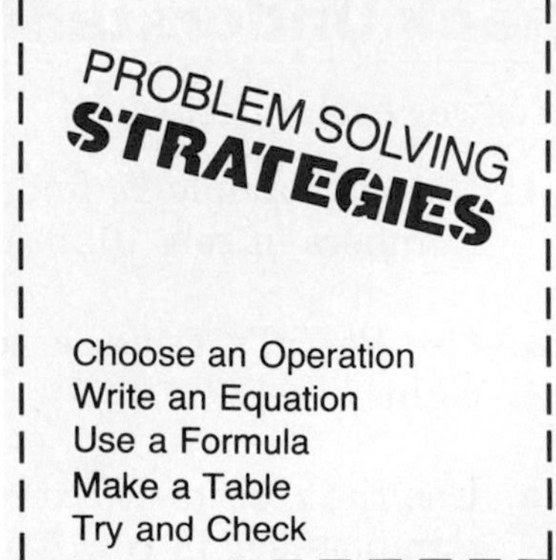

Choose an Operation
Write an Equation
Use a Formula
Make a Table
Try and Check

Patterns in Pascal's Triangle

Build Understanding

The triangular pattern of numbers at the right is known as ***Pascal's Triangle.*** It is named for the seventeenth-century French mathematician, Blaise Pascal. Each number is the sum of the two numbers above and closest to it.

ROW 0	1
ROW 1	1 1
ROW 2	1 2 1
ROW 3	1 3 3 1
ROW 4	1 4 6 4 1
ROW 5	1 5

A. Copy the triangle onto your paper. Complete row 5 and extend the triangle two more rows.

ROW 5	1 5 10 10 5 1
ROW 6	1 6 15 20 15 6 1
ROW 7	1 7 21 35 35 21 7 1

B. The sums of the first two numbers in each row form a pattern. Putting this information in a table makes it easier to identify and to extend the pattern.

Row number	Sum of first two numbers
1	2
2	3
3	4
4	5

The sum of the first two numbers in each row is one greater than the row number.

■ **Write About Math** How many numbers are in row 3? row 4? Write a sentence to describe the relationship between the row number and the number of numbers in that row.

Check Understanding

For another example, see Set G, pages 180–181.

Answer each question.

1. Using Example B, find the sum of the first two numbers in row 10; in row 23.

2. Use Pascal's Triangle to complete the table at the right.

3. Use the results of Exercise 2 to find how many numbers are in row 8 of the triangle? in row 20?

Row number	Number of numbers in the row
0	
1	
2	
3	
4	

Practice

For More Practice, see Set G, pages 182–183.

Find the sum of the numbers in each row of Pascal's Triangle.

Row	Sum of the numbers
0	1
1	2
2	**4.**
3	**5.**
4	**6.**
7.	**8.**
9.	**10.**

Find the number of numbers in a series of rows of Pascal's Triangle.

Row Numbers	Number of numbers
0	1
0–1	3
0–2	6
0–3	**11.**
0–4	**12.**
13.	**14.**
15.	**16.**

Find the sum of the first three numbers in each row of Pascal's Triangle.

Row	Sum of the first three numbers
2	4
3	**17.**
4	**18.**
19.	**20.**
21.	**22.**

Use Pascal's Triangle to find the standard form for powers of 11.

Powers of 11	Standard form
11^0	1
11^1	11
11^2	**23.**
11^3	**24.**
11^4	**25.**

Problem Solving

Solve. Refer to Exercises 4–25.

26. What is the sum of the numbers in row 10 of Pascal's Triangle?

27. How many numbers will appear in the first 12 rows?

28. What is the sum of the first three numbers in row 8 of the triangle?

29. **Calculator** What do you think 11^5 is? Check, using a calculator. What happens after row 4? Why?

Explore ______ Math

Copy and extend Pascal's Triangle to include rows 0 through 14. Follow these steps to find patterns in the triangle.

30. Circle multiples of 2.

31. Describe the patterns that occur.

32. Repeat with multiples of 3 and then multiples of 5, using different colors.

33. Describe these patterns.

Use Logical Reasoning

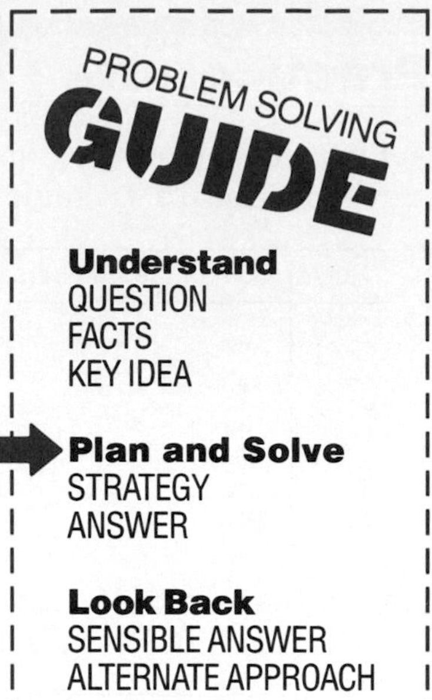

Build Understanding

A grocery distribution center received a shipment of 1,500 cartons containing bran cereal or granola cereal. Bran cereal is packed in 8-box cartons, and granola is packed in 20-box cartons. The invoice was for a total of 15,000 boxes of cereal. The manager said that could not be correct. Was he right?

Understand QUESTION Is there a combination of cartons that totals 15,000 boxes?

FACTS The total number of cartons received was 1,500.

KEY IDEA There are 8-box cartons and 20-box cartons.

Plan and Solve STRATEGY Use logical reasoning to try different combinations, such as 500 and 1,000 or 50 and 1,450. Make a table of the numbers.

20-box cartons of granola	8-box cartons of bran	Boxes of granola	Boxes of bran	Total boxes
500	1,000	10,000	8,000	18,000
400	1,100	8,000	8,800	16,800
300	1,200	6,000	9,600	15,600
200	1,300	4,000	10,400	14,400

Notice that 300 of the 20-box cartons gives too large a total, and 200 of the 20-box cartons gives too small a total. Logical reasoning suggests that you try a number between 300 and 200—for example, 250.

250	1,250	5,000	10,000	15,000

In this case, the total is exactly 15,000 boxes.

ANSWER The manager was incorrect. It is possible to have a total of 15,000 boxes.

Look Back SENSIBLE ANSWER Check that 250 cartons of 20 boxes and 1,250 cartons of 8 boxes give a total of 15,000 boxes.

■ **Talk About Math** After calculating a number of boxes of granola cereal, can you subtract it from 15,000 to determine the number of boxes of bran cereal? Explain why or why not.

Check Understanding

Suppose the bran cereal was packed in cartons of 6 boxes each and the granola in cartons of 24 boxes each. Also, suppose that a shipment of 1,000 cartons contained a total of 14,838 boxes. Answer these questions to find the number of cartons of each type of cereal there would be.

1. If there are four hundred 24-box cartons, how many 6-box cartons are there?
2. How many boxes of each kind of cereal are there? How many boxes of cereal are there altogether?
3. Try five hundred 24-box cartons of granola. How many 6-box cartons of bran are there? How many boxes are there altogether?
4. Is the number of 24-box cartons greater than or less than 400? Greater than or less than 500?
5. What if you try 490 for the number of 24-box cartons? Is the total close to 14,838? Name another number you might try.
6. How many cartons of granola cereal are there? How many cartons of bran cereal are there?

Practice

SuperStore sells shirts as well as groceries. A recent inventory shows 186 T-shirts in stock. The manager thinks that the inventory count is incorrect.

Number of 4 T-shirt packages	Number of 5 T-shirt packages
1	36
2	35
3	34
4	34
5	33
6	32
7	31
8	30
9	30
10	29

Use logical reasoning to help you solve each problem by referring to the table.

7. List any combinations from the table that give a total of 186 T-shirts.
8. Are there other combinations not shown that give a total of 186 T-shirts? If so, list the combinations.

Skills Review

Tell if each number is divisible by 2, 3, 5, 9, or 10. List all possibilities.

1. 250 **2.** 5,231 **3.** 700

4. 3,420 **5.** 1,005 **6.** 5,603,400

Write each power in standard form.

7. 7^2 **8.** 4^3 **9.** 10^0

10. 2^4 **11.** $5^2 \times 2^3$ **12.** $4^2 \times 4^2$

Write prime (P) or composite (C).

13. 31 **14.** 51 **15.** 27

16. 123 **17.** 97 **18.** 83

Write the prime factorization of each number using exponents.

19. 54 **20.** 60 **21.** 100

22. 32 **23.** 64 **24.** 144

Find the greatest common factor (GCF) for each set of numbers.

25. 12 and 16 **26.** 15 and 18

27. 40 and 24 **28.** 24, 36, and 42

Find the least common multiple (LCM) for each set of numbers.

29. 6 and 9 **30.** 8 and 12

31. 24 and 18 **32.** 15 and 20

Use Pascal's triangle to solve each problem.

33. What is the sum of each of the first 6 rows of Pascal's triangle?

34. How many numbers are in row 12?

Problem-Solving Review

Solve each problem.

35. A 3-pound bag of apples costs $1.99. What is the price per pound to the nearest cent?

36. Kim, Dave, and Tammy are in a band. One plays a flute, one plays a trumpet, and one plays a drum. No one plays an instrument that starts with the same letter as his or her first name. Dave and Tammy must blow into their instruments. What instrument does each person play?

37. A group of 33 students and 5 chaperons are planning a rafting trip down Rapid River. The sporting goods store rents 8-person and 6-person rubber rafts. What is the least number of rafts that the group will need?

38. A cook is making 0.3 pound hamburgers from 4.8 pounds of meat. Write and solve an equation to find how many hamburgers he can make.

39. Write the number 100 as the sum of two prime numbers. Then write it as the sum of three prime numbers.

40. **Data File** Use the data on pages 264–265. A 6.0 earthquake is how many times as great as a 3.0 earthquake? Write your answer using exponents.

41. **Make a Data File** Consult a physics or chemistry book to gather data about the half-lives of some common elements. Make a table of half-lives for about ten elements, listing them in increasing order of half-life.

Cumulative Skills Review • Chapters 1–5

Choose paper and pencil or a calculator to multiply or divide.

1. 83 × 1.2 **2.** 4.6 × 464 **3.** 0.05 × 9.4 **4.** 6.003 × 25

5. 78 ÷ 5 **6.** 1,568 ÷ 8 **7.** 56,340 ÷ 9 **8.** 30,621 ÷ 3

Write an expression for each of the following.

9. The sum of 56.7 and n

10. The result of subtracting v from 60

11. The product of r and 9.5

12. 20 times the sum of c and 6

13. 92 divided by the sum of t and 9

14. 8 less than the product of q and 5

Find each quotient. Round decimal answers to the nearest hundredth.

15. 456 ÷ 22 **16.** 5,672 ÷ 41 **17.** 8,912 ÷ 312 **18.** 24,790 ÷ 25

19. 420 ÷ 0.4 **20.** 0.86 ÷ 4.3 **21.** 58.96 ÷ 0.625 **22.** 230.51 ÷ 19.3

Find the missing angle measure in each triangle. Classify each triangle as *acute, right, obtuse, scalene, isosceles,* or *equilateral.*

23.

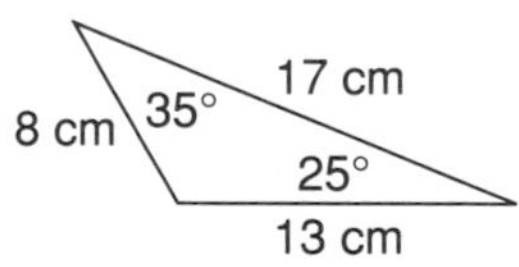

24.

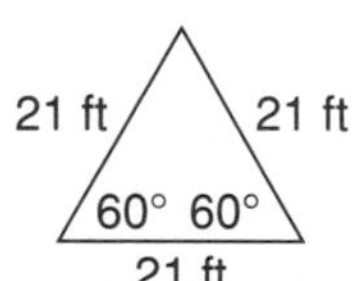

25.

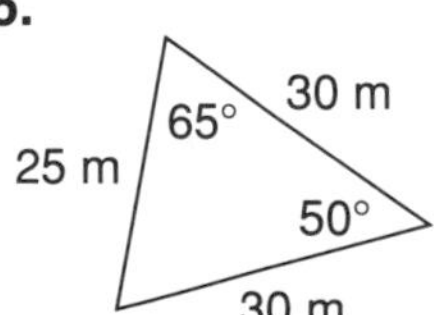

26.

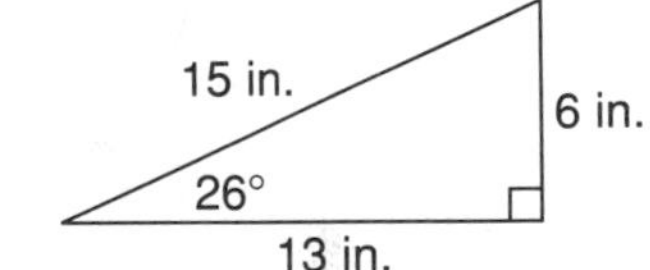

Draw the figures. Then do the constructions.

27. Use your straightedge to draw any line AB. Construct the line perpendicular to $\overleftrightarrow{AB}$ at point B.

28. Draw any line $\overleftrightarrow{LM}$ and point N not on $\overleftrightarrow{LM}$. Construct the line through point N parallel to $\overleftrightarrow{LM}$.

Rewrite each number using exponents.

29. 8 × 8 × 8 × 8 **30.** 6 × 6 × 6 × 6 × 6 × 6 **31.** 7 × 7 × 7 × 5 × 5 × 5

32. 4 × 4 × 4 **33.** 10 × 10 × 10 × 10 × 2 × 2 **34.** 9 × 9 × 3 × 3 × 3

Find the greatest common factor (GCF) and the least common multiple (LCM) of each set of numbers.

35. 9 and 12 **36.** 8 and 10 **37.** 20 and 4 **38.** 6, 8, and 12

39. 3, 10, 9 **40.** 7, 21 **41.** 18, 2, 9 **42.** 50, 60

Independent Study RETEACHING

Reteaching

Set A pages 156–157

A number can be divided evenly with no remainder according to these rules:

Divisor	*Conditions*
2	Ones digit in number is 0, 2, 4, 6, or 8.
3	Sum of digits in number is divisible by 3.
5	Ones digit in number is 0 or 5.
9	Sum of digits in number is divisible by 9.
10	Ones digit is 0.

Remember, whole numbers divisible by 2 are even numbers; whole numbers not divisible by 2 are odd numbers.

1. Which numbers are divisible by 3: 174, 305, 619, 1,923?

2. Which numbers are divisible by 2 and 5: 70, 45, 150, 245?

3. Which numbers are divisible by 9: 49, 711, 225, 1,008?

Set B pages 158–159

A short way of expressing repeated factors is to write the base with an exponent.

$3 \times 3 \times 3 \times 3 = 3^4$

The repeated factor 3 is the base. 3 is used as a factor 4 times, so 4 is the exponent.

Remember, the exponent tells how many times the base is used as a factor.

1. Express $5 \times 5 \times 5$ using an exponent.

2. Rewrite 7^6 with factors.

3. Multiply the factors of 2^5.

Set C pages 160–163

A prime number has exactly 2 factors; it is a whole number greater than 1.

A composite number has more than 2 factors; it is a whole number greater than 1.

0 and 1 are neither prime nor composite numbers.

Remember, you can use the rules for divisibility to test for factors.

Write prime or composite.

1. 22	**2.** 7	**3.** 55
4. 189	**5.** 97	**6.** 19
7. 6	**8.** 173	**9.** 470

Set D pages 164–165

To find the prime factorization of a composite number, work with factor pairs.

$72 = 36 \times 2$ (circled: $\times 2$)	Start with any pair; 2 is prime.
$36 = 9 \times 4$	Factor 36.
$9 = 3 \times 3$ (circled)	Factor 9; 3 is prime.
$4 = 2 \times 2$ (circled)	Factor 4; 2 is prime.

The prime factorization of 72 is $2^3 \times 3^2$.

Remember, you can use exponents in the prime factorization when a prime factor appears more than once.

1. Write factor pairs for 328 to find the factors that are prime numbers.

2. Write the prime factorization of 328.

Set E pages 168–169

To find the greatest common factor (GCF) of two numbers, follow these steps:

1. First write the factors of the smaller number.
2. Arrange the factors in order from least to greatest.
3. Then write the factors from this list that are factors of the second number.
4. Find the greatest of these factors (GCF).

Remember, a systematic approach to listing factor pairs helps you to know that you have found all factors.

What is the greatest common factor of

1. 48 and 96? **2.** 75 and 18?

3. 16 and 80? **4.** 99 and 44?

5. 216 and 144? **6.** 192 and 168?

7. 28 and 112? **8.** 48 and 112?

Set F pages 170–171

To find the least common multiple of two or more numbers, start by writing some multiples of each number.

Then compare the numbers to find common multiples.

Find the lowest number, or least common multiple.

Remember, listing the multiples of each number in order from least to greatest makes it easier to compare the lists.

What is the least common multiple of

1. 4 and 10? **2.** 8 and 14?

3. 16 and 28? **4.** 35 and 20?

5. 100 and 12? **6.** 50 and 6?

7. 16 and 24? **8.** 15 and 40?

9. 50 and 8? **10.** 100 and 6?

Set G pages 174–175

To find the patterns in Pascal's Triangle, look for triangular connections.

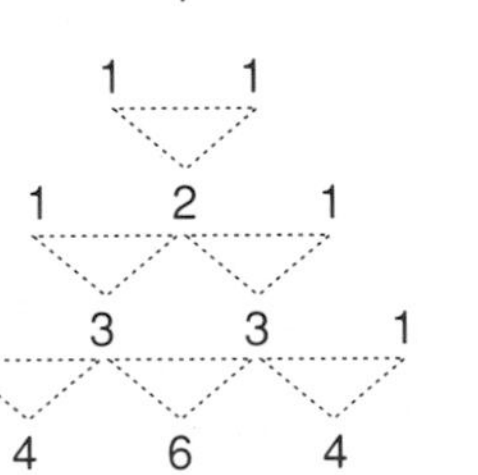

Remember, there is one more number in each row of Pascal's triangle from the top row downward.

1. Which row of Pascal's Triangle has the numbers 1, 6, 15, 20, 15, 6, 1?

2. What are the numbers in row 7 of Pascal's Triangle?

3. What is the sum of the numbers in row 8 of Pascal's Triangle?

4. How many numbers are in row 9 of Pascal's Triangle?

Independent Study MORE PRACTICE

More Practice

Set A pages 156–157

Tell if each number is divisible by 2, 3, 5, 9, or 10. List all possibilities.

1. 257 **2.** 810 **3.** 2,700 **4.** 1,536

5. 771 **6.** 14,399 **7.** 5,648 **8.** 37,177

9. 534,101 **10.** 755,222 **11.** 1,100,002 **12.** 682,486

Set B pages 158–159

Write each in standard form. Use mental math or pencil and paper. Tell which method you used.

1. 8^3 **2.** 2^6 **3.** 9^2 **4.** 3^5

5. 12^1 **6.** 4^4 **7.** 5^5 **8.** 6^3

9. 7^0 **10.** $11^2 \times 5^3$ **11.** $4^4 \times 7^3$ **12.** $9^0 \times 2^3 \times 6^1$

Use a calculator to find each of the following.

13. 2^8 **14.** 8^5 **15.** 3^9 **16.** 9^6

Set C pages 160–163

Write prime or composite.

1. 67 **2.** 15 **3.** 33 **4.** 21 **5.** 45 **6.** 89

7. 17 **8.** 28 **9.** 71 **10.** 93 **11.** 56 **12.** 83

13. 149 **14.** 213 **15.** 724 **16.** 361 **17.** 523 **18.** 901

19. List the composite numbers between 50 and 60.

20. List the prime numbers between 40 and 50.

21. Express 105 as the product of three prime numbers. Is there another solution?

22. Express 106 as the sum of two prime numbers. Is there another pair?

Set D pages 164–165

Make a factor tree for each number. Write the prime factorization for each number.

1. 42 **2.** 72 **3.** 69 **4.** 106 **5.** 180 **6.** 315

Write the prime factorization of each number using exponents.

7. 42 **8.** 76 **9.** 88 **10.** 102 **11.** 288 **12.** 1,575

Set E pages 168–169

Find the GCF for each of the following. Use lists of factors if you need to.

1. 8 and 24 **2.** 27 and 30 **3.** 76 and 56 **4.** 14 and 63

5. 39 and 26 **6.** 84 and 21 **7.** 4, 12, and 24 **8.** 32, 64, and 80

Find the GCF. Use the prime factorization method.

9. 35 and 77 **10.** 55 and 65 **11.** 24 and 96 **12.** 75 and 105

13. 63 and 42 **14.** 27 and 81 **15.** 63, 42, and 84 **16.** 54, 81, and 126

Set F pages 170–171

Find the LCM. Use a list of multiples.

1. 4 and 5 **2.** 3 and 11 **3.** 5 and 6 **4.** 4 and 7

5. 5 and 9 **6.** 8 and 12 **7.** 10 and 25 **8.** 12 and 18

Find the LCM. Use the prime factorization method.

9. 12 and 48 **10.** 15 and 90 **11.** 13 and 65 **12.** 21 and 28

13. 24 and 32 **14.** 18 and 20 **15.** 54 and 108 **16.** 49 and 56

Set G pages 174–175

1. Copy Pascal's Triangle on page 181 and extend it through row 8.

Use Pascal's Triangle from Exercise 1 to complete each table.

Addends	Sum
1	1
1 + 2	3
1 + 2 + 3	6
2.	**3.**
4.	**5.**

Addends	Sum
1 + 3	4
3 + 6	9
6 + 10	16
6.	**7.**
8.	**9.**

Triangle	Number of dots in the triangle
•	1
∴	3
(6-dot triangle)	6
10.	**11.**
12.	**13.**

Independent Study MORE PRACTICE

Enrichment

Perfect, Abundant, and Deficient Numbers

The oldest book of mathematics still in use today is the *Elements*, written more than 2,200 years ago by the Greek mathematician Euclid. In this work, Euclid wrote this definition of ***perfect numbers***:

> A perfect number is a whole number that is equal to the sum of all of its divisors except itself.

The smallest perfect number is 6 because the sum of its divisors except itself, 3 + 2 + 1, is 6.

1. Which of the following numbers is the second smallest perfect number?

a. 8 **b.** 14 **c.** 22 **d.** 28 **e.** 32

2. The third smallest perfect number is either 496 or 500. The divisors of each are listed. Which number is perfect?

496		
1	2	4
8	16	31
62	124	248

500			
1	2	4	5
10	20	25	50
100	125	250	

Euclid knew of only one more perfect number: 8,128. The fifth perfect number was discovered 1,500 years later. It is 33,550,336. Today, 30 perfect numbers are known. The largest perfect number known has 130,100 digits.

3. The numbers 4, 8, 16, 32, and 64 are powers of 2. Find the sum of the divisors other than the number itself for each number. What pattern do you notice?

4. Do you think that any power of 2 is a perfect number? Why or why not?

Two other types of numbers are ***abundant*** and ***deficient***.

> An abundant number is a whole number in which the sum of the divisors except itself is greater than the number itself.

> A deficient number is a whole number in which the sum of all its divisors except itself is less than the number itself.

Tell if each number is abundant or deficient.

5. 16 **6.** 18 **7.** 100 **8.** 132 **9.** 256

Chapter 5 Review/Test

1. Is 2,115 divisible by 2? by 3? by 5? by 9? by 10?

2. Is 38,270 divisible by 2? by 3? by 5? by 9? by 10?

Write each power in standard form.

3. 4^3

4. $2^4 \times 3^2$

5. List the 6 pairs of prime numbers less than 50 whose difference is 2.

6. The recycling box is picked up every 6 days. Waste that is not recycled is picked up every 10 days. On October 1, both are picked up. When will this happen next?

7. When a marching band marches in 4 or 5 columns, there is one marcher left over. What is the least number of band members possible?

The following number pattern is similar to Pascal's Triangle. Use it to answer Exercises 8–10.

2 4 6 3
2 6 10 9 3
2 8 16 19 12 3

8. What is the next row?

9. What is always true of the sum of the numbers in each row in the number pattern?

10. How is the sum of the numbers in one row related to the sum of the numbers in the row before it?

Write the prime factorization of each number using exponents.

11. 48

12. 54

Find the GCF.

13. 16 and 24

14. 52 and 65

Find the LCM.

15. 7 and 11

16. 12 and 48

17. 8 and 10

18. 4 and 22

One company ships paperback books packed 21 to a box and hardcover books packed 12 to a box. Use this information for Exercises 19–21.

19. What combination of paperback book boxes and hardcover book boxes could contain exactly 87 books in full boxes?

20. Choose the method that can be used to tell what combination of boxes could hold 120 books.

    a. Multiply 21 by 12 and compare the product with 120.
    b. Subtract 21 repeatedly from 120 and see if the difference is a multiple of 12.
    c. Compare the LCM of 12 and 21 with 120.
    d. Find out if the GCF of 12 and 21 divides 120 exactly.

21. Which total number of books can be packed exactly in full boxes?

    a. 125 b. 117 c. 119

22. **Write About Math** *A* and *B* are two different whole numbers. Their GCF is *A*. Their LCM is *B*. Which one is greater? Why?

Fraction Computation

6

Did You Know: A fully grown Etruscan shrew, which lives in Africa, is about 3 inches long (including the tail) and weighs about one-sixteenth of an ounce. The shrew eats up to three times its weight every day.

Number-Sense Project

Estimate
How long do you think it would take you to eat an amount of food equal to your weight?

Gather Data
Keep a record of the approximate weight of each item of food you eat for three days.

Analyze and Report
What is the weight of the food you eat each day? Estimate how long it would take you to eat an amount equal to your weight. Estimate how many pounds of food you eat per year.

Equal Fractions

Build Understanding

A. The clock face shows three ***equal fractions***: $\frac{1}{4}$, $\frac{3}{12}$, and $\frac{15}{60}$. You can multiply or divide the numerator and the denominator of a fraction by the same nonzero number to find an equal fraction.

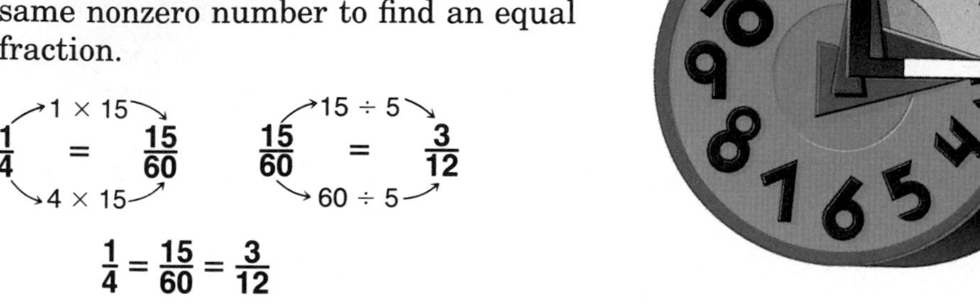

$$\frac{1}{4} = \frac{15}{60} \quad (1 \times 15,\ 4 \times 15) \qquad \frac{15}{60} = \frac{3}{12} \quad (15 \div 5,\ 60 \div 5)$$

$$\frac{1}{4} = \frac{15}{60} = \frac{3}{12}$$

B. Find the missing number. $\frac{2}{3} = \frac{\square}{24}$

$\frac{2}{3} = \frac{\square}{24}$ (3×8) 3 is multiplied by 8 to get 24.

$\frac{2}{3} = \frac{16}{24}$ (2×8) So multiply 2 by 8.

A fraction is in ***lowest terms*** when 1 is the only common factor of the numerator and the denominator.

C. Find the missing number. $\frac{12}{20} = \frac{3}{\square}$

$\frac{12}{20} = \frac{3}{\square}$ ($12 \div 4$) 12 is divided by 4 to get 3.

$\frac{12}{20} = \frac{3}{5}$ ($20 \div 4$) So divide 20 by 4.

$\frac{1}{4}$, $\frac{2}{3}$, and $\frac{3}{5}$ are fractions in lowest terms.

Here are two methods to rename a fraction in lowest terms.

D. Divide the numerator and the denominator by common factors until the only common factor is 1.

$$\frac{12}{30} = \frac{4}{10} = \frac{2}{5} \quad (12 \div 3,\ 30 \div 3;\ 4 \div 2,\ 10 \div 2)$$

E. Find the GCF of the numerator and the denominator. Then divide both by their GCF.

$\frac{12}{30} = \frac{2}{5}$ ($12 \div 6$, $30 \div 6$) 6 is the GCF of 12 and 30.

■ **Talk About Math** How many fractions could you find that are equal to $\frac{4}{5}$? How many fractions equal to $\frac{4}{5}$ are in lowest terms?

Check Understanding

For another example, see Set A, pages 224–225.

Give each missing number.

1. $\frac{2}{5} = \frac{2 \times 4}{5 \times 4} = \frac{\square}{\square}$ **2.** $\frac{12}{16} = \frac{12 \div 4}{16 \div 4} = \frac{\square}{\square}$ **3.** $\frac{3}{8} = \frac{\square}{16}$ **4.** $\frac{10}{20} = \frac{1}{\square}$

Find the GCF of the numerator and denominator.
Then tell if the fraction is in lowest terms. Write *yes* or *no*.

5. $\frac{6}{8}$ **6.** $\frac{10}{15}$ **7.** $\frac{21}{28}$ **8.** $\frac{25}{50}$ **9.** $\frac{11}{20}$

Practice

For More Practice, see Set A, pages 226–227.

Give each missing number.

10. $\frac{1}{4} = \frac{\square}{16}$ **11.** $\frac{1}{16} = \frac{\square}{48}$ **12.** $\frac{6}{9} = \frac{\square}{3}$ **13.** $\frac{5}{10} = \frac{1}{\square}$ **14.** $\frac{3}{8} = \frac{18}{\square}$

15. $\frac{15}{40} = \frac{\square}{8}$ **16.** $\frac{5}{12} = \frac{\square}{36}$ **17.** $\frac{3}{10} = \frac{\square}{30}$ **18.** $\frac{24}{32} = \frac{3}{\square}$ **19.** $\frac{21}{30} = \frac{7}{\square}$

20. $\frac{3}{5} = \frac{\square}{15}$ **21.** $\frac{30}{36} = \frac{\square}{6}$ **22.** $\frac{12}{\square} = \frac{3}{10}$ **23.** $\frac{48}{54} = \frac{\square}{9}$ **24.** $\frac{14}{21} = \frac{2}{\square}$

25. $\frac{2}{3} = \frac{\square}{9} = \frac{8}{\square} = \frac{10}{\square}$ **26.** $\frac{3}{8} = \frac{6}{\square} = \frac{\square}{24} = \frac{\square}{32}$ **27.** $\frac{9}{10} = \frac{18}{\square} = \frac{27}{\square} = \frac{\square}{40}$

Write each fraction in lowest terms.

28. $\frac{11}{12}$ **29.** $\frac{16}{20}$ **30.** $\frac{9}{12}$ **31.** $\frac{7}{10}$ **32.** $\frac{9}{24}$ **33.** $\frac{6}{16}$

34. $\frac{4}{18}$ **35.** $\frac{7}{16}$ **36.** $\frac{6}{24}$ **37.** $\frac{14}{28}$ **38.** $\frac{12}{21}$ **39.** $\frac{27}{56}$

Problem Solving

Use the clock in Example A to answer Problems 40–41.

40. Write three equal fractions for one half hour.

41. Write three equal fractions for three-quarters of an hour.

Visual Thinking Write a fraction in lowest terms for the shaded part in each figure.

42.

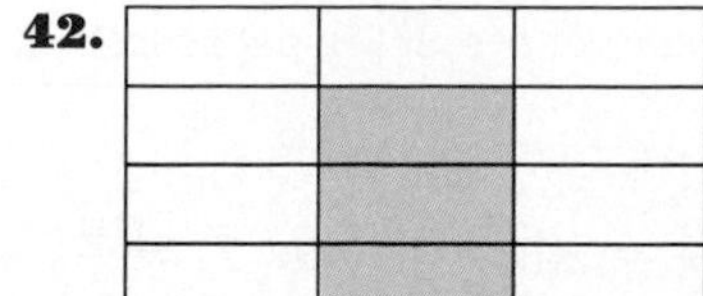

43.

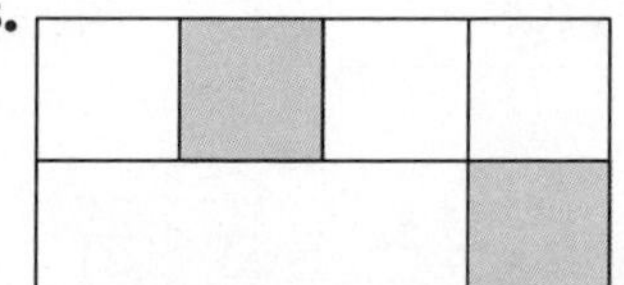

44.

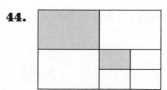

Mixed Numbers and Improper Fractions

Build Understanding

You can see that the bolt is $2\frac{1}{4}$ inches long.

A number such as $2\frac{1}{4}$, which has a whole-number part and a fraction part, is called a ***mixed number***. Every mixed number and whole number greater than zero can be written as an ***improper fraction***. In an improper fraction, the numerator is greater than or equal to the denominator.

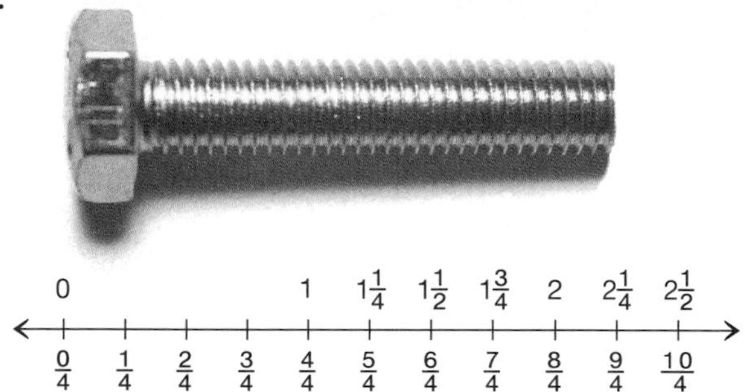

A. Write $2\frac{1}{4}$ as a fraction.

You can see from the number line that $2\frac{1}{4}$ is $\frac{9}{4}$.

Or you can multiply and add as shown below.

$2\frac{1}{4}$ (+, ×)

$4 \times 2 = 8$ Multiply the denominator by the whole number.

$8 + 1 = 9$ Add the numerator to the product.

$2\frac{1}{4} = \frac{9}{4}$ Write the sum over the denominator.

B. Write 3 as a fraction with a denominator of 5.

First write 3 as a fraction: $\frac{3}{1}$.

Then write an equal fraction with a denominator of 5.

$\frac{3}{1} = \frac{\square}{5}$

$\frac{3}{1} = \frac{15}{5}$ (3×5, 1×5) Multiply both numerator and denominator by 5.

$3 = \frac{15}{5}$

C. Write $\frac{37}{4}$ as a mixed number.

$\frac{37}{4} = 37 \div 4$

$4\overline{)37}$ = $9\frac{1}{4}$ ←remainder ←divisor

$\frac{37}{4} = 9\frac{1}{4}$

Talk About Math What is true about the numerator and the denominator of a fraction greater than one? a fraction equal to zero? a fraction equal to one?

Check Understanding

For another example, see Set B, pages 224–225.

Give each missing number.

1. $2\frac{3}{4} = \frac{\square}{4}$ **2.** $3\frac{1}{5} = \frac{16}{\square}$ **3.** $\square\frac{\square}{20} = \frac{31}{20}$ **4.** $\frac{29}{10} = \square\frac{\square}{10}$ **5.** $7 = \frac{\square}{2}$

Practice

For More Practice, see Set B, pages 226–227.

Write each improper fraction as a whole number or as a mixed number. **Remember** to write the fraction in the mixed number in lowest terms.

6. $\frac{9}{6}$ **7.** $\frac{5}{2}$ **8.** $\frac{21}{5}$ **9.** $\frac{9}{3}$ **10.** $\frac{27}{4}$ **11.** $\frac{8}{6}$

12. $\frac{11}{2}$ **13.** $\frac{19}{5}$ **14.** $\frac{16}{5}$ **15.** $\frac{32}{8}$ **16.** $\frac{23}{12}$ **17.** $\frac{27}{6}$

Write each number as an improper fraction.

18. $5\frac{5}{6}$ **19.** $8\frac{1}{4}$ **20.** $9\frac{5}{8}$ **21.** $1\frac{3}{16}$ **22.** $6\frac{2}{3}$ **23.** $10\frac{7}{12}$

24. $4\frac{1}{9}$ **25.** $7\frac{4}{5}$ **26.** $2\frac{3}{11}$ **27.** $5\frac{3}{4}$ **28.** $3\frac{7}{8}$ **29.** $6\frac{2}{10}$

Mixed Practice Write each fraction as either a fraction in lowest terms, a whole number, or a mixed number whose fraction part is in lowest terms.

30. $\frac{8}{3}$ **31.** $\frac{14}{21}$ **32.** $\frac{7}{42}$ **33.** $\frac{7}{5}$ **34.** $\frac{20}{6}$ **35.** $\frac{29}{3}$

36. $\frac{45}{5}$ **37.** $\frac{5}{40}$ **38.** $\frac{25}{10}$ **39.** $\frac{23}{8}$ **40.** $\frac{60}{12}$ **41.** $\frac{33}{11}$

42. $\frac{80}{10}$ **43.** $\frac{4}{12}$ **44.** $\frac{13}{39}$ **45.** $\frac{43}{7}$ **46.** $\frac{24}{40}$ **47.** $\frac{16}{20}$

48. $\frac{22}{55}$ **49.** $\frac{26}{4}$ **50.** $\frac{54}{9}$ **51.** $\frac{15}{32}$ **52.** $\frac{18}{60}$ **53.** $\frac{64}{8}$

Problem Solving

Solve each problem.

54. The length of a nail is $1\frac{3}{8}$ inches. Express the length as an improper fraction.

55. A paintbrush is 16 inches long. Express the length as a mixed number of feet.

Skills Review

pages 168–171

Give the least common multiple of each pair.

1. 4, 8 **2.** 6, 3 **3.** 6, 8 **4.** 9, 12 **5.** 5, 9

Give the greatest common factor of each pair.

6. 12, 15 **7.** 36, 72 **8.** 9, 12 **9.** 15, 45 **10.** 12, 10

CAREER CONNECTION

ALGEBRA

Comparing and Ordering Fractions and Mixed Numbers

Build Understanding

A. Rosa Berrios, an artist, designed two stamps, one $\frac{7}{8}$ of an inch wide and the other $\frac{5}{8}$ of an inch wide. Which stamp is wider?

Compare $\frac{5}{8}$ and $\frac{7}{8}$.

$5 < 7$, so $\frac{5}{8} < \frac{7}{8}$. **$7 > 5$, so $\frac{7}{8} > \frac{5}{8}$.**

If two fractions have a common denominator, you can compare them by comparing their numerators.

The $\frac{7}{8}$-inch stamp is wider.

B. Compare $\frac{5}{8}$ and $\frac{2}{3}$.

To compare $\frac{5}{8}$ and $\frac{2}{3}$, you need a common denominator. The least common denominator of $\frac{5}{8}$ and $\frac{2}{3}$ is the least common multiple of 8 and 3, which is 24.

$\frac{5}{8} \;\square\; \frac{2}{3}$ Write the fractions with a denominator of 24.

$\downarrow \quad \downarrow$

$\frac{15}{24} \;\square\; \frac{16}{24}$ Compare the numerators.

$15 < 16$, so $\frac{15}{24} < \frac{16}{24}$.

$\frac{5}{8} < \frac{2}{3}$

C. List $\frac{2}{5}$, $\frac{1}{3}$, and $\frac{3}{10}$ in order from least to greatest.

$\frac{2}{5} \quad \frac{1}{3} \quad \frac{3}{10}$ Write the fractions with a common denominator.

$\downarrow \quad \downarrow \quad \downarrow$

$\frac{12}{30} \quad \frac{10}{30} \quad \frac{9}{30}$ 30 is the least common denominator.

$\frac{9}{30} \quad \frac{10}{30} \quad \frac{12}{30}$ Order the numerators.

$\downarrow \quad \downarrow \quad \downarrow$

$\frac{3}{10} \quad \frac{1}{3} \quad \frac{2}{5}$

The fractions in order from least to greatest are $\frac{3}{10}$, $\frac{1}{3}$, and $\frac{2}{5}$.

D. Compare $3\frac{2}{3}$ and $3\frac{3}{4}$.

$3\frac{2}{3} \;\square\; 3\frac{3}{4}$ Write the fractions with a common denominator.

$\downarrow \quad \downarrow$

$3\frac{8}{12} \;\square\; 3\frac{9}{12}$ The whole numbers are the same.

$3\frac{8}{12} < 3\frac{9}{12}$ Compare the fractions.

$\downarrow \quad \downarrow$

$3\frac{2}{3} < 3\frac{3}{4}$

E. **Calculator** Compare $\frac{5}{8}$ and $\frac{2}{3}$ by changing each fraction to a decimal.

Press: 5 [÷] 8 [=] **Display:** *0.625*

Press: 2 [÷] 3 [=] **Display:** *0.6666666*

$0.625 < 0.6666666$, so $\frac{5}{8} < \frac{2}{3}$.

■ **Talk About Math** In Example C, can you use 15 as a common denominator? 60? 45? 90? Explain.

Check Understanding

For another example, see Set C, pages 224–225.

Solve each problem.

1. Name the whole-number parts of $3\frac{1}{2}$ and $2\frac{3}{4}$. Must you compare $\frac{1}{2}$ and $\frac{3}{4}$ in order to compare $3\frac{1}{2}$ and $2\frac{3}{4}$? Explain.

2. Compare $1\frac{1}{2}$ and $\frac{5}{6}$. How do you know that $1\frac{1}{2}$ is greater than $\frac{5}{6}$ without comparing the fractions?

Write the fractions with their least common denominator.

3. $\frac{2}{3}, \frac{7}{10}$ **4.** $\frac{2}{9}, \frac{1}{2}$ **5.** $1\frac{1}{7}, \frac{1}{3}$ **6.** $\frac{1}{6}, \frac{8}{15}$ **7.** $\frac{1}{4}, \frac{5}{6}, \frac{2}{3}$ **8.** $\frac{3}{10}, \frac{3}{7}, 1\frac{1}{5}$

Practice

For More Practice, see Set C, pages 226–227.

Compare the numbers. Use <, >, or =.

9. $\frac{5}{8} \ \square \ \frac{7}{8}$ **10.** $\frac{5}{6} \ \square \ \frac{2}{3}$ **11.** $\frac{2}{5} \ \square \ \frac{1}{2}$ **12.** $2\frac{4}{25} \ \square \ 3\frac{1}{3}$

13. $8\frac{11}{12} \ \square \ 6\frac{9}{16}$ **14.** $2\frac{1}{3} \ \square \ 2\frac{1}{4}$ **15.** $2\frac{2}{3} \ \square \ 1\frac{11}{12}$ **16.** $4\frac{13}{16} \ \square \ 4\frac{17}{20}$

17. $1\frac{5}{6} \ \square \ 1\frac{7}{10}$ **18.** $\frac{1}{6} \ \square \ \frac{8}{48}$ **19.** $\frac{8}{5} \ \square \ 1\frac{1}{2}$ **20.** $2\frac{9}{10} \ \square \ 3\frac{9}{10}$

21. $3\frac{3}{4} \ \square \ 3\frac{9}{12}$ **22.** $5\frac{1}{4} \ \square \ 5\frac{2}{5}$ **23.** $6\frac{5}{8} \ \square \ 6\frac{2}{3}$ **24.** $5\frac{5}{6} \ \square \ \frac{35}{6}$

List the numbers from least to greatest.

25. $\frac{3}{4}, \frac{5}{6}, \frac{1}{2}$ **26.** $\frac{5}{6}, \frac{13}{16}, \frac{11}{12}$ **27.** $2, 1\frac{7}{8}, \frac{5}{3}$ **28.** $3\frac{2}{3}, \frac{17}{6}, 3\frac{1}{2}$

29. $\frac{7}{8}, \frac{12}{16}, \frac{2}{4}$ **30.** $2\frac{3}{5}, \frac{17}{8}, \frac{9}{4}$ **31.** $4\frac{7}{10}, 4\frac{9}{12}, \frac{36}{8}$ **32.** $\frac{5}{6}, \frac{3}{4}, \frac{7}{9}$

Calculator Compare the numbers by first changing each fraction to a decimal. Use a calculator.

33. $3\frac{5}{8} \ \square \ 3\frac{17}{30}$ **34.** $7\frac{7}{16} \ \square \ 7\frac{11}{25}$ **35.** $1\frac{13}{20} \ \square \ 1\frac{2}{3}$ **36.** $10\frac{1}{32} \ \square \ 10\frac{7}{200}$

Problem Solving

Solve each problem.

37. Which is longer, an address label $2\frac{5}{8}$ in. long or one $2\frac{3}{4}$ in. long?

38. Which is larger, a file-folder label $3\frac{1}{2}$ in. × $\frac{21}{32}$ in. or one $3\frac{1}{2}$ in. × $\frac{9}{16}$ in.?

Critical Thinking Solve each problem.

39. Which is longer, 10 months or 3 quarters of a year?

40. Which is longer, $\frac{1}{3}$ of a day or 9 hours?

Estimating Sums and Differences

Build Understanding

A fraction is equal to $\frac{1}{2}$ if twice the numerator is equal to the denominator. $\frac{5}{10} = \frac{1}{2}$ $2 \times 5 = 10$	A fraction is less than $\frac{1}{2}$ if twice the numerator is less than the denominator. $\frac{2}{5} < \frac{1}{2}$ $2 \times 2 < 5$	A fraction is greater than $\frac{1}{2}$ if twice the numerator is greater than the denominator. $\frac{3}{4} > \frac{1}{2}$ $2 \times 3 > 4$

One way to estimate sums of fractions is to compare the fractions with $\frac{1}{2}$.

A. Estimate $\frac{3}{10} + \frac{1}{3}$.

$\frac{3}{10} < \frac{1}{2}$, since $2 \times 3 < 10$.

$\frac{1}{3} < \frac{1}{2}$, since $2 \times 1 < 3$.

The sum is less than 1 since each addend is less than $\frac{1}{2}$.

B. Estimate $\frac{5}{8} + \frac{3}{5}$.

$\frac{5}{8} > \frac{1}{2}$, since $2 \times 5 > 8$.

$\frac{3}{5} > \frac{1}{2}$, since $2 \times 3 > 5$.

The sum is greater than 1 since each addend is greater than $\frac{1}{2}$.

C. Estimate $\frac{2}{5} + \frac{2}{3}$.

$\frac{2}{5} < \frac{1}{2}$, since $2 \times 2 < 5$.

$\frac{2}{3} > \frac{1}{2}$, since $2 \times 2 > 3$.

You cannot tell if the sum is greater than 1 or less than 1. You do know the sum is greater than $\frac{2}{3}$, the larger fraction.

D. You can estimate the sum of mixed numbers by rounding each mixed number to the nearest whole number.

Estimate $7\frac{2}{3} + 4\frac{1}{4}$.

Round $7\frac{2}{3}$ to 8. Since the fraction is greater than $\frac{1}{2}$, round up.

Round $4\frac{1}{4}$ to 4. Since the fraction is less than $\frac{1}{2}$, round down.

The sum is about 8 + 4, or 12.

E. You can estimate the difference of mixed numbers by using only the whole-number parts.

Estimate $9\frac{3}{4} - 5\frac{3}{8}$.

The difference is about 9 − 5, or 4.

■ **Write About Math** Estimate the sum in Example D by using only the whole-number parts. Did you get the same estimate? Will this always happen?

Check Understanding

For another example, see Set D, pages 224–225.

Classify each fraction as greater than $\frac{1}{2}$, less than $\frac{1}{2}$, or equal to $\frac{1}{2}$.

1. $\frac{3}{5}$ **2.** $\frac{8}{16}$ **3.** $\frac{5}{12}$ **4.** $\frac{9}{16}$ **5.** $\frac{11}{20}$

Estimate by using only the whole-number parts.

6. $5\frac{3}{4} + 4\frac{1}{8}$ **7.** $2\frac{1}{2} + 6\frac{7}{8}$ **8.** $2\frac{1}{4} - 1\frac{1}{16}$ **9.** $11\frac{1}{8} - 9\frac{2}{4}$

Practice

For More Practice, see Set D, pages 226–227.

Estimate by using the methods shown in Examples A–C.
Is the sum: (a) less than 1, (b) greater than 1,
or (c) greater than the larger fraction in the exercise?

10. $\frac{1}{8} + \frac{2}{5}$ **11.** $\frac{1}{3} + \frac{1}{6}$ **12.** $\frac{4}{5} + \frac{2}{3}$ **13.** $\frac{3}{4} + \frac{3}{8}$ **14.** $\frac{3}{10} + \frac{5}{8}$

15. $\frac{4}{6} + \frac{3}{5}$ **16.** $\frac{1}{4} + \frac{1}{3}$ **17.** $\frac{4}{7} + \frac{2}{5}$ **18.** $\frac{3}{10} + \frac{4}{9}$ **19.** $\frac{2}{9} + \frac{3}{7}$

20. $\frac{7}{10} + \frac{1}{3}$ **21.** $\frac{7}{8} + \frac{7}{12}$ **22.** $\frac{2}{3} + \frac{9}{16}$ **23.** $\frac{1}{4} + \frac{11}{15}$ **24.** $\frac{3}{8} + \frac{3}{10}$

Estimate. Explain how you estimated.

25. $\frac{1}{6} + \frac{2}{5}$ **26.** $\frac{7}{10} + \frac{3}{4}$ **27.** $\frac{5}{6} + \frac{2}{3}$ **28.** $\frac{1}{5} + \frac{3}{4}$ **29.** $1\frac{2}{3} + 2\frac{2}{3}$

30. $9\frac{1}{3} - 1\frac{1}{4}$ **31.** $8\frac{1}{4} + 2\frac{5}{6}$ **32.** $3\frac{7}{8} + 2\frac{2}{3}$ **33.** $8\frac{5}{8} - 3\frac{1}{4}$ **34.** $21\frac{3}{5} - 15\frac{1}{6}$

35. $11\frac{4}{5} - 9\frac{3}{4}$ **36.** $7\frac{1}{3} + 3\frac{3}{8}$ **37.** $15\frac{5}{6} - 6\frac{4}{5}$ **38.** $22\frac{1}{2} + 7\frac{2}{3}$ **39.** $8\frac{7}{9} + 10\frac{10}{14}$

40. $6\frac{1}{4} + 6\frac{1}{5}$ **41.** $29\frac{5}{8} - 1\frac{3}{8}$ **42.** $4\frac{5}{8} - 2\frac{1}{4}$ **43.** $\frac{1}{6} + \frac{3}{4}$ **44.** $7\frac{2}{3} + 7\frac{2}{3}$

Problem Solving

Estimate to solve each problem.

45. A recipe calls for $2\frac{1}{2}$ cups of rye flour and $3\frac{3}{4}$ cups of white flour. Can you use a $1\frac{1}{2}$-quart (6-cup) mixing bowl? Explain your answer.

46. A recipe for herb bread calls for $\frac{3}{4}$ cup of scalded milk. Will 1 cup of milk be enough to make 2 loaves? Explain your answer.

47. Kasumi made 50 bran muffins for the bake sale. She sold her muffins for 59¢ each. If she sold all the muffins she brought, about how much money did she make from the bake sale?

Adding Fractions and Mixed Numbers

Build Understanding

A. Caitlin is a commercial artist. She is assembling two pieces to be framed as a collage. One piece is $4\frac{13}{16}$ inches high, and the other piece is $3\frac{5}{16}$ inches high. What height is the collage?

Since you want to find the total height, you add. Find $4\frac{13}{16} + 3\frac{5}{16}$.

Estimate by rounding each number to the nearest whole number: 5 + 3 = 8.

$$\begin{array}{r} 4\frac{13}{16} \\ +\ 3\frac{5}{16} \\ \hline \frac{18}{16} \end{array}$$

Since the denominators are the same, add the numerators.

$$\begin{array}{r} 4\frac{13}{16} \\ +\ 3\frac{5}{16} \\ \hline 7\frac{18}{16} \end{array} = 7 + \frac{18}{16} = 7 + 1\frac{2}{16} = 8\frac{2}{16} = 8\frac{1}{8}$$

Add the whole numbers. Then rename the answer.

The exact answer is close to the estimate. The collage is $8\frac{1}{8}$ inches high.

B. Find $\frac{4}{5} + \frac{5}{8}$.

Estimate by comparing each fraction to $\frac{1}{2}$: $\frac{4}{5} > \frac{1}{2}$ and $\frac{5}{8} > \frac{1}{2}$, so the sum is greater than 1.

$\frac{4}{5} = \frac{32}{40}$ Write the fractions with the least common denominator, 40.

$+\frac{5}{8} = \frac{25}{40}$ Add the numerators.

$\frac{57}{40} = 1\frac{17}{40}$ Rename as a mixed number.

The exact answer is reasonable because the sum is greater than 1.

C. Find $3\frac{1}{3} + 12\frac{1}{6} + 2\frac{2}{3}$.

Estimate using whole-number parts: 3 + 12 + 2 = 17.

$$\begin{array}{rcl} 3\frac{1}{3} &=& 3\frac{2}{6} \\ 12\frac{1}{6} &=& 12\frac{1}{6} \\ +\ 2\frac{2}{3} &=& 2\frac{4}{6} \\ \hline && 17\frac{7}{6} = 17 + \frac{7}{6} \end{array}$$

Write the fractions with the least common denominator, 6. Add the whole numbers. Add the fractions. Rename.

$$17 + \frac{7}{6} = 17 + 1\frac{1}{6} = 18\frac{1}{6}$$

The exact answer is close to the estimate.

D. Mental Math Find $4\frac{1}{3} + 6\frac{1}{4} + 3\frac{2}{3}$. To make the addition easier, look for special numbers that have a sum of 1.

$$4\frac{1}{3} + 6\frac{1}{4} + 3\frac{2}{3} = \left(4\frac{1}{3} + 3\frac{2}{3}\right) + 6\frac{1}{4} = 8 + 6\frac{1}{4} = 14\frac{1}{4}$$

■ **Talk About Math** Is a fraction always in lowest terms if the numerator is a prime number? if the denominator is a prime number? Use Example B to explain.

Check Understanding

For another example, see Set E, pages 224–225.

Give the missing numbers.

1. $\begin{array}{r} \frac{5}{12} \\ +\frac{5}{12} \\ \hline \frac{\square}{12} = \frac{\square}{6} \end{array}$

2. $\begin{array}{r} \frac{11}{16} \\ +\frac{9}{16} \\ \hline \frac{\square}{16} = 1\frac{\square}{16} = 1\frac{1}{4} \end{array}$

3. $\begin{array}{r} \frac{2}{5} = \frac{\square}{20} \\ +\frac{1}{4} = \frac{\square}{20} \\ \hline \frac{\square}{20} \end{array}$

4. $\begin{array}{r} 5\frac{9}{16} = 5\frac{9}{16} \\ +3\frac{3}{4} = 3\frac{\square}{16} \\ \hline 8\frac{\square}{16} = 9\frac{\square}{16} \end{array}$

5. $1\frac{7}{5} = 2\frac{\square}{5}$

6. $\frac{12}{9} = 1\frac{\square}{9} = 1\frac{\square}{3}$

7. $8\frac{17}{12} = 9\frac{\square}{12}$

8. $10\frac{19}{10} = 11\frac{\square}{10}$

9. When you add zero to any fraction, what is the result?

Practice

For More Practice, see Set E, pages 226–227.

Add.

10. $\begin{array}{r} 3\frac{1}{5} \\ +2\frac{3}{5} \\ \hline \end{array}$

11. $\begin{array}{r} 1\frac{5}{6} \\ +5\frac{1}{6} \\ \hline \end{array}$

12. $\begin{array}{r} 6\frac{3}{4} \\ +3\frac{3}{4} \\ \hline \end{array}$

13. $\begin{array}{r} 9\frac{4}{9} \\ +2\frac{4}{9} \\ \hline \end{array}$

14. $6\frac{3}{8} + 3\frac{7}{8}$

15. $5\frac{1}{8} + 2\frac{6}{8}$

16. $1\frac{2}{3} + 2\frac{2}{3}$

17. $5\frac{4}{15} + 10\frac{10}{15}$

18. $\begin{array}{r} 1\frac{15}{16} \\ +\frac{9}{16} \\ \hline \end{array}$

19. $\begin{array}{r} \frac{1}{2} \\ +\frac{1}{6} \\ \hline \end{array}$

20. $\begin{array}{r} \frac{1}{4} \\ +\frac{5}{12} \\ \hline \end{array}$

21. $\begin{array}{r} \frac{4}{5} \\ +\frac{7}{10} \\ \hline \end{array}$

22. $\frac{3}{4} + \frac{5}{8}$

23. $\frac{2}{3} + \frac{3}{5}$

24. $\frac{1}{3} + \frac{1}{4}$

25. $\frac{3}{10} + \frac{1}{6}$

26. $\frac{5}{8} + \frac{7}{12}$

27. $\frac{1}{6} + \frac{4}{9}$

28. $\frac{3}{8} + \frac{11}{12}$

29. $\frac{4}{5} + \frac{4}{9}$

In Exercises 30–37, tell whether you would use mental math or paper and pencil. Then find each sum. **Remember** to look for fractions that have a sum of 1.

30. $\frac{1}{5} + \frac{4}{5}$

31. $\frac{5}{9} + \frac{4}{9}$

32. $2\frac{11}{13} + 1\frac{6}{13}$

33. $5\frac{6}{15} + 7\frac{9}{15}$

34. $11\frac{11}{22} + 12\frac{9}{22}$

35. $6\frac{2}{3} + 3\frac{1}{4} + 2\frac{1}{3}$

36. $\frac{1}{3} + 6\frac{1}{6} + 1\frac{2}{3}$

37. $4\frac{3}{10} + 1\frac{2}{3} + \frac{7}{10} + 4\frac{1}{3}$

38. **Calculator** The memory keys on a calculator can be used to add fractions. To find $\frac{5}{8} + \frac{11}{20}$, use these keys.

5 [÷] 8 [=] *0.625* [M+] 11 [÷] 20 [=] *0.55* [+] [MRC] [=] *1.175*

Find $\frac{3}{5} + \frac{15}{16}$ using a calculator. Write which keys you pressed.

Evaluate each expression when $n = \frac{1}{3}$.

39. $n + 1\frac{1}{3}$

40. $n + \frac{1}{6}$

41. $n + \frac{7}{8}$

42. $n + \frac{4}{5}$

43. $\frac{1}{3} + 8\frac{1}{2} + n$

44. $2\frac{5}{6} + n + 1\frac{1}{8}$

45. $3n + \frac{1}{18} + \frac{2}{5}$

Problem Solving

Solve each problem.

46. Caitlin decides she wants to make a border for the collage shown in the picture on page 196. The top and bottom borders are $1\frac{1}{16}$ inches each. What is the total height of the collage and the border?

47. **Estimation** Caitlin's collage is 5 inches wide. She wants to make equal left and right borders of $\frac{5}{8}$ inch each. Will a frame 6 inches wide be wide enough?

48. If Caitlin increased her left and right borders to $\frac{7}{8}$ inch each (instead of $\frac{5}{8}$), would the 6-inch frame width have to increase by more or less than $1\frac{1}{2}$ inches? Explain your answer.

Caitlin often paints with acrylics. Acrylics come in tubes $1\frac{1}{8}$ inches wide by 5 inches. Sometimes the tubes are packed vertically in carrying cases.

49. Critical Thinking How many tubes will fit vertically in a case 7 inches wide? Explain your thinking.

50. How wide must a case be in order to hold 8 tubes? How can you solve the problem without multiplying?

51. Acrylics are available in a smaller size, $\frac{3}{4}$ inch by 4 inches. How many smaller tubes would fit in a case designed for two larger tubes?

52. If the larger tubes were packed horizontally, how many tubes would fit in a case 5 inches high and 11 inches long?

Midchapter Checkup

Write three equal fractions for each fraction.

1. $\frac{2}{5}$ **2.** $\frac{5}{8}$ **3.** $\frac{1}{12}$ **4.** $\frac{6}{25}$ **5.** $\frac{7}{100}$

Give each missing number.

6. $7\frac{3}{8} = \frac{\blacksquare}{8}$ **7.** $8 = \frac{\blacksquare}{5}$ **8.** $19 = \frac{\blacksquare}{1}$ **9.** $10\frac{6}{10} = \frac{\blacksquare}{\blacksquare}$

10. $\frac{7}{2} = \blacksquare\frac{1}{2}$ **11.** $\frac{49}{6} = 8\frac{\blacksquare}{\blacksquare}$ **12.** $\frac{100}{20} = \blacksquare$ **13.** $1\frac{11}{16} = \frac{\blacksquare}{\blacksquare}$

List the numbers from greatest to least.

14. $\frac{1}{4}, \frac{4}{5}, \frac{2}{10}$ **15.** $\frac{12}{12}, \frac{19}{20}, \frac{1}{8}$ **16.** $\frac{49}{8}, 5, 6\frac{3}{4}$ **17.** $4\frac{5}{6}, 4\frac{1}{2}, 2\frac{5}{16}$

Estimate each sum or difference. Explain how you estimated.

18. $\frac{1}{5} + \frac{5}{16}$ **19.** $\frac{9}{10} + \frac{7}{8}$ **20.** $2\frac{3}{4} + 6\frac{1}{6}$ **21.** $25\frac{7}{12} - 11\frac{3}{16}$

In Exercises 22–25, tell whether you would use mental math, paper and pencil, or a calculator. Then find each sum.

22. $3\frac{3}{5} + 2\frac{1}{10} + 4\frac{2}{5}$ **23.** $\frac{9}{16} + \frac{11}{12}$ **24.** $\frac{7}{10} + \frac{3}{4}$ **25.** $9\frac{1}{8} + 8\frac{5}{8} + 2\frac{1}{16}$

Explore as a Team

Magazine publishers make money by selling advertising space on the pages of their magazines. The advertiser can choose the size of the ad. Usually the ads are either a full page, $\frac{1}{2}$ page, $\frac{1}{3}$ page, or $\frac{2}{3}$ page. In this activity, you will work as a team to discover what fraction of a magazine is devoted to advertising.

1. Choose a magazine. Look through it and discuss whether you think it has too much, too little, or the right amount of advertising. Estimate what fraction of the magazine is made up of advertising. Each person should write down his or her estimate.

2. Mark each page with a fraction to represent the part that is devoted to advertising.

3. Make a chart to show the results.

Find the total amount of advertising space by adding all the fractional parts together.

Advertising Space	Full pages	$\frac{1}{2}$ page	$\frac{1}{3}$ page	$\frac{2}{3}$ page
Number of pages	//	𝍸 //	𝍸 ///	////

4. Find what part of the magazine is actually devoted to advertising.

$$\text{Fraction of magazine devoted to advertising} = \frac{\text{Total number of pages of advertising space}}{\text{Total number of pages in magazine}}$$

5. Compare your results with your estimate. Compare your team's results with other teams in the class.

TIPS FOR WORKING TOGETHER

Involve your whole group. Help everyone to participate.

If you cut a piece of pie that was $\frac{1}{20}$ of $\frac{1}{2}$ of it, how much would you have?

ANSWER: I don't know exactly, but it can't be very much!

Explore with a Computer

Use the *Fraction Workshop Project* for this activity.

1. At the computer, shade parts of the unit to match this problem:

$$\frac{6}{8} \times \frac{2}{6}$$

2. Find the product by counting how much of the figure is shaded by overlapping shaded areas. Write this amount in lowest terms.

3. Display another unit to show the following problem, and count the overlapping shaded areas:

$$\frac{3}{4} \times \frac{1}{3}$$

4. Compare the results of the two problems. Explain the results you found.

Number-Sense Project

Look back at pages 186-187.

1. How much food does a full-grown Etruscan shrew eat
a. per day? **b.** per year?

It is estimated that the average American eats 100,000 pounds of food in his or her lifetime (in about 70 years). Use this data for Problems 2-4.

2. Estimate the number of pounds of food the average American eats
a. per year. **b.** per day.

3. What fraction of his or her weight does a 120-pound person eat per day?

4. At this rate, how long would it take a 120-pound person to eat 120 pounds of food?

Math-at-Home Activity

Take a survey of at least 8 people who live with or near you. Ask them to name their favorite food.

What fraction liked chicken the best?
Did more or less than $\frac{1}{2}$ like pizza?
What fraction did not name hamburgers?

Subtracting Fractions and Mixed Numbers

Build Understanding

A. George filled the bird feeder in his backyard. The bag of seeds weighed $8\frac{3}{4}$ pounds before he filled the feeder. Afterwards, the bag of seeds weighed $7\frac{1}{4}$ pounds. How many pounds of seed did he use?

To find the amount used, you subtract. Find $8\frac{3}{4} - 7\frac{1}{4}$.

Estimate using the whole-number parts.
$8 - 7 = 1$

$$\begin{array}{r} 8\frac{3}{4} \\ -7\frac{1}{4} \\ \hline \frac{2}{4} \end{array}$$

Since the denominators are the same, subtract the numerators.

$$\begin{array}{r} 8\frac{3}{4} \\ -7\frac{1}{4} \\ \hline 1\frac{2}{4} = 1\frac{1}{2} \end{array}$$

Subtract the whole numbers.

Then rename.

The answer is close to the estimate.

George used $1\frac{1}{2}$ pounds of birdseed.

B. Find $8\frac{7}{8} - 2\frac{3}{16}$.

Estimate using rounding.
$9 - 2 = 7$

Write the fractions with the least common denominator, 16.

$$\begin{array}{rcl} 8\frac{7}{8} & = & 8\frac{14}{16} \\ -2\frac{3}{16} & = & 2\frac{3}{16} \\ \hline & & 6\frac{11}{16} \end{array}$$

Subtract the numerators.

Subtract the whole numbers.

The answer is close to the estimate.

C. Find $\frac{5}{6} - \frac{1}{4}$.

Write the fractions with the least common denominator, 12.

$$\begin{array}{rcl} \frac{5}{6} & = & \frac{10}{12} \\ -\frac{1}{4} & = & \frac{3}{12} \\ \hline & & \frac{7}{12} \end{array}$$

Subtract the numerators.

■ **Write About Math** Find each sum. What conclusion can you make? Can you draw the same conclusion for subtraction problems?

$\frac{1}{2} + \frac{1}{4}$ $\quad \frac{1}{4} + \frac{1}{2}$ $\quad \frac{1}{5} + \frac{2}{5}$ $\quad \frac{2}{5} + \frac{1}{5}$

Check Understanding

For another example, see Set F, pages 224–225.

Give the missing numbers.

1. $\begin{array}{r} 2\frac{1}{2} = 2\frac{\square}{16} \\ -1\frac{7}{16} = 1\frac{7}{16} \\ \hline 1\frac{\square}{16} \end{array}$

2. $\begin{array}{r} 4\frac{5}{6} = 4\frac{\square}{30} \\ -2\frac{7}{10} = 2\frac{\square}{30} \\ \hline 2\frac{\square}{30} = 2\frac{\square}{15} \end{array}$

3. $\begin{array}{r} \frac{5}{8} = \frac{5}{8} \\ -\frac{1}{2} = \frac{\square}{8} \\ \hline \frac{\square}{8} \end{array}$

4. $\begin{array}{r} \frac{2}{3} = \frac{8}{\square} \\ -\frac{1}{4} = \frac{3}{\square} \\ \hline \frac{5}{\square} \end{array}$

5. Number Sense What is true about the difference of equal fractions?

Practice

For More Practice, see Set F, pages 226–227.

Subtract.

6. $\frac{3}{4} - \frac{2}{5}$ **7.** $\frac{7}{8} - \frac{1}{4}$ **8.** $\frac{2}{3} - \frac{3}{8}$ **9.** $6\frac{3}{4} - \frac{2}{3}$ **10.** $4\frac{5}{6} - 2\frac{3}{10}$

11. $16\frac{7}{8} - 6\frac{5}{12}$ **12.** $9\frac{3}{4} - 3\frac{2}{5}$ **13.** $9\frac{7}{10} - \frac{1}{4}$ **14.** $\frac{13}{16} - \frac{2}{5}$ **15.** $5\frac{1}{6} - 3\frac{1}{10}$

16. $1\frac{15}{16} - 1\frac{6}{8}$ **17.** $22\frac{1}{2} - \frac{1}{5}$ **18.** $\frac{6}{8} - \frac{3}{4}$ **19.** $43\frac{2}{3} - 42\frac{1}{2}$ **20.** $\frac{2}{5} - \frac{1}{15}$

Mixed Practice Add or subtract.

21. $8\frac{2}{3} - 6\frac{5}{9}$ **22.** $16\frac{9}{10} + 5\frac{3}{10}$ **23.** $6\frac{3}{9} - 4\frac{1}{3}$ **24.** $14\frac{11}{12} - \frac{3}{8}$ **25.** $\frac{9}{16} + \frac{1}{5}$

26. $\frac{7}{10} + \frac{2}{3}$ **27.** $\frac{8}{9} - \frac{5}{12}$ **28.** $6\frac{2}{3} + 5\frac{7}{8}$ **29.** $9\frac{1}{4} + 7\frac{6}{8}$ **30.** $4\frac{7}{9} - \frac{7}{16}$

Problem Solving

Solve each problem. **Remember** to include units in your answers.

31. George is making a mixture to feed the birds. He uses $\frac{1}{2}$ lb of sunflower seeds and $\frac{3}{8}$ lb of corn. How much more sunflower seed does he have than corn?

32. An empty bird feeder will hold $2\frac{1}{2}$ lb of seed. George has $1\frac{1}{2}$ lb of sunflower seeds and $\frac{3}{4}$ lb of wild bird mix. How much more or less than $2\frac{1}{2}$ lb does he have?

33. On one day $\frac{3}{16}$ of the birds at the feeder were robins, $\frac{1}{8}$ were cardinals, and $\frac{1}{16}$ were blue jays. What fraction of the birds were other kinds of birds?

Subtracting Mixed Numbers with Renaming

Build Understanding

A. For her science project Mu Lan is growing bean seedlings under normal conditions as a control group. She records their growth each week in the graph shown here. How much did her plants grow between week 4 and week 5?

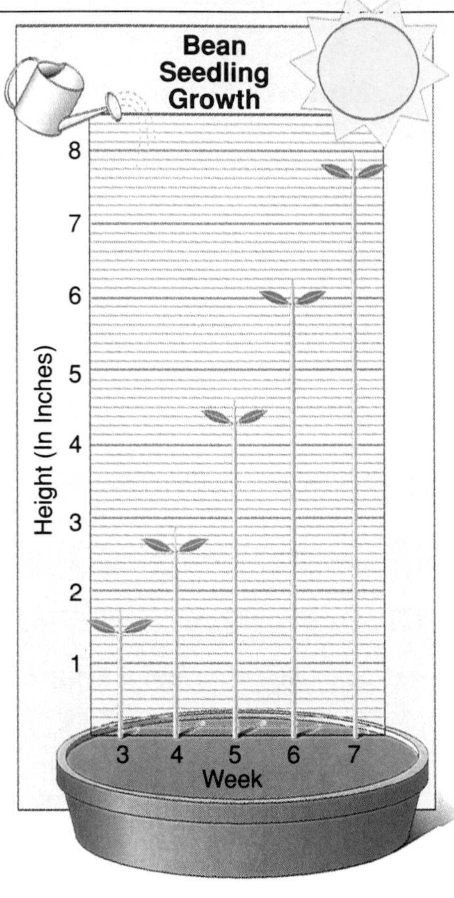

You need to find the difference in height between week 5 and week 4.

Find $4\frac{5}{8} - 2\frac{7}{8}$.

Estimate by using the whole-number parts.
$4 - 2 = 2$

$$\begin{array}{r} 4\frac{5}{8} = 3\frac{13}{8} \\ -\,2\frac{7}{8} = 2\frac{7}{8} \\ \hline 1\frac{6}{8} = 1\frac{3}{4} \end{array}$$

Since $\frac{5}{8} < \frac{7}{8}$, you need to rename.
$4\frac{5}{8} = 4 + \frac{5}{8} = 3\frac{8}{8} + \frac{5}{8} = 3\frac{13}{8}$

Write $\frac{6}{8}$ in lowest terms.

The answer is close to the estimate. Mu Lan's bean seedlings grew $1\frac{3}{4}$ inches between week 4 and week 5.

B. Find $9 - 1\frac{5}{12}$.

$$\begin{array}{r} 9 = 8\frac{12}{12} \\ -1\frac{5}{12} = 1\frac{5}{12} \\ \hline 7\frac{7}{12} \end{array}$$

Rename 9 as $8\frac{12}{12}$.

C. Find $3\frac{1}{6} - 1\frac{3}{4}$.

$$\begin{array}{r} 3\frac{1}{6} = 3\frac{2}{12} = 2\frac{14}{12} \\ -\,1\frac{3}{4} = 1\frac{9}{12} = 1\frac{9}{12} \\ \hline 1\frac{5}{12} \end{array}$$

Write the fractions with a common denominator so you can subtract. Then rename $3\frac{2}{12}$.

■ **Talk About Math** Is it always sufficient just to compare numerators before subtracting mixed numbers? Explain your answer.

Check Understanding

For another example, see Set G, pages 224–225.

Write each missing number.

1. $2\frac{1}{3} = 1\frac{▩}{3}$ **2.** $9 = 8\frac{▩}{6}$ **3.** $8\frac{5}{6} = 8\frac{▩}{12} = 7\frac{▩}{12}$ **4.** $10\frac{1}{4} - 5\frac{4}{5} = 10\frac{▩}{20} - 5\frac{▩}{20} = ▩$

Practice

For More Practice, see Set G, pages 226–227.

Subtract. **Remember** to write answers in lowest terms.

5. $6\frac{1}{4} - 5\frac{3}{4}$ **6.** $4\frac{3}{16} - 2\frac{7}{16}$ **7.** $9 - 2\frac{3}{10}$ **8.** $3\frac{1}{3} - 2\frac{1}{2}$ **9.** $4\frac{1}{5} - 2\frac{2}{3}$ **10.** $66 - 33\frac{1}{3}$

11. $7 - 1\frac{3}{4}$ **12.** $7\frac{3}{8} - 2\frac{5}{6}$ **13.** $12\frac{3}{10} - 9\frac{5}{6}$ **14.** $17\frac{1}{3} - 11\frac{3}{8}$ **15.** $8\frac{2}{3} - 3\frac{3}{4}$

16. $9 - 2\frac{5}{8}$ **17.** $30\frac{1}{3} - 9\frac{2}{3}$ **18.** $16\frac{3}{8} - 15\frac{7}{8}$ **19.** $9\frac{1}{2} - 4\frac{3}{4}$ **20.** $11 - 9\frac{5}{6}$

21. $4\frac{3}{16} - 3\frac{6}{8}$ **22.** $19\frac{1}{6} - 5\frac{2}{3}$ **23.** $12\frac{4}{15} - 9\frac{3}{5}$ **24.** $20 - 8\frac{11}{12}$ **25.** $8\frac{3}{10} - 2\frac{7}{8}$

26. $6\frac{2}{3} - 4\frac{3}{4}$ **27.** $5 - 3\frac{2}{15}$ **28.** $10\frac{1}{5} - 9\frac{2}{3}$ **29.** $9\frac{1}{6} - 8\frac{3}{4}$ **30.** $10\frac{3}{10} - 9\frac{4}{5}$

31. $18\frac{1}{2} - 4\frac{3}{5}$ **32.** $5\frac{1}{4} - 4\frac{4}{9}$ **33.** $15 - 10\frac{7}{8}$ **34.** $8\frac{3}{8} - 1\frac{7}{12}$ **35.** $5\frac{1}{5} - 2\frac{3}{8}$

Problem Solving

Use Mu Lan's graph on page 204 to answer these questions.
How much did Mu Lan's plants grow during these time periods?

36. Between week 3 and week 6

37. Between week 6 and week 7

38. By the end of week 7

Choose a Strategy

Does Green Mean Grow? Mark studied the effects of light on plant growth. He used only one color light on each plant. One-third of the plants received red light and $\frac{1}{2}$ of this number received blue light. Of the plants that received neither red nor blue light, $\frac{1}{3}$ received violet light and $\frac{1}{4}$ received green light. The rest of the plants received yellow light. What fraction of the plants received yellow light?

39. What fraction of the plants received blue light?

40. What fraction received red or blue light? neither red nor blue light?

41. What fraction received violet light? green light?

42. What fraction of the plants received yellow light?

ALGEBRA

Write an Equation

Understand
QUESTION
FACTS
KEY IDEA

Plan and Solve
STRATEGY
ANSWER

Look Back
SENSIBLE ANSWER
ALTERNATE APPROACH

Build Understanding

Mr. Patrick built a cabinet for a cassette deck. He trimmed $1\frac{5}{16}$ inches from a piece of wood so that he would have a piece of wood $5\frac{1}{2}$ inches long. How long was the original piece of wood?

Understand QUESTION How long was the original piece of wood?

FACTS He trimmed $1\frac{5}{16}$ inches. The final piece was $5\frac{1}{2}$ inches long.

Plan and Solve STRATEGY Write an equation to show how the facts are related. Use ℓ for the original length of the board.

original length		amount trimmed off		final length
↓		↓		↓

$$\ell - 1\frac{5}{16} = 5\frac{1}{2}$$ Solve the equation for ℓ.

$$\ell - 1\frac{5}{16} + 1\frac{5}{16} = 5\frac{1}{2} + 1\frac{5}{16}$$ Add $1\frac{5}{16}$ to both sides of the equation.

$$\ell = 6\frac{13}{16}$$

ANSWER The original length of the piece was $6\frac{13}{16}$ inches.

Look Back SENSIBLE ANSWER Since $1\frac{5}{16}$ is about $1\frac{1}{2}$, the original length was about $5\frac{1}{2} + 1\frac{1}{2}$, or 7 inches. The answer, $6\frac{13}{16}$, is reasonable because it is close to the estimate.

■ **Write About Math** Write another equation you could use to solve this problem. What operation did you use?

Check Understanding

Use the following information to answer Exercises 1–8. Mr. Patrick made the opening for the cassette deck in the cabinet $6\frac{5}{8}$ inches high. The cassette deck is $5\frac{13}{16}$ inches high. How much open space is left above the cassette deck?

1. What is the question?

2. In what units will your answer be?

3. What is the height of the cassette deck?

4. What is the height of the cabinet opening?

5. What operation will you use to solve the problem?

6. Write an equation.

7. Solve the equation.

8. Is your answer reasonable?

Practice

Solve each problem. For Problems 9–12 write and solve an equation. For Problems 10 and 11 refer to the information in Problems 1–9.

9. Over the cassette deck, Mr. Patrick built a space for a stereo receiver that is $6\frac{3}{4}$ inches high. The difference between the height of the receiver and the height of its enclosure is $\frac{5}{8}$ inch. What is the height of the enclosure?

10. What is the total height of the space for the two components in the cabinet Mr. Patrick made?

11. What is the total height of the cabinet? The 3 boards of the shelves are each $\frac{3}{4}$ inch high.

12. Mr. Patrick made the cabinet in $8\frac{1}{4}$ hours. It took him $2\frac{1}{4}$ hours more to build it than to varnish it. How long did he spend doing each of these two jobs?

13. Mr. Patrick organized his 86 cassette tapes in stacks having 8 or 9 tapes per stack. How many stacks does he have?

14. Mr. Patrick has $71 to spend on a pair of headphones and new cassettes. If the headphones cost $44 and one cassette costs $7.79, how many cassettes can he buy?

Multiplying Fractions and Mixed Numbers

Build Understanding

Wei Ch'I is an ancient game of strategy that originated in China about 2300 B.C. It is very popular in Japan, where it is called *Go,* and also in Korea, where it is called *Pa-Tok*.

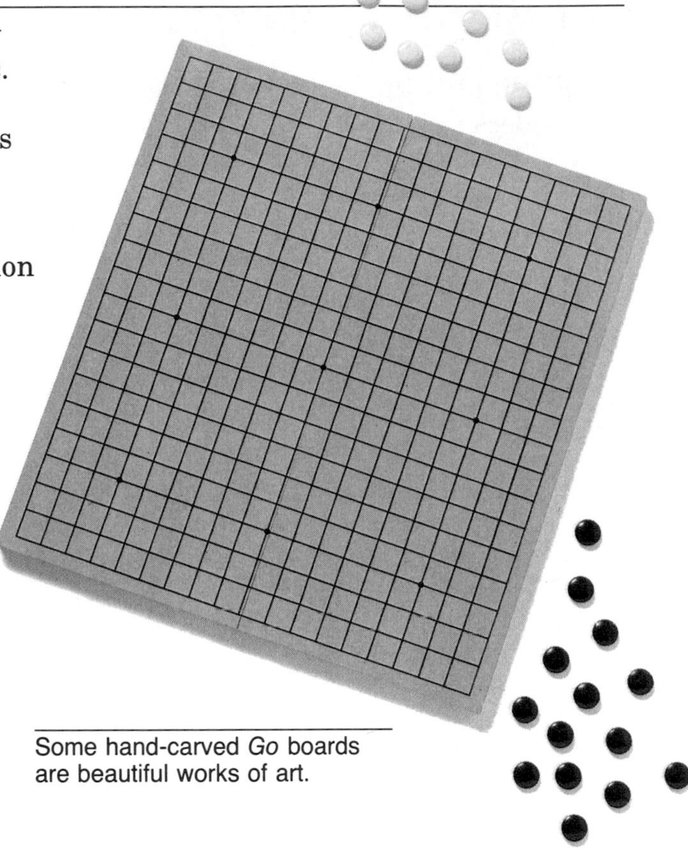

Some hand-carved *Go* boards are beautiful works of art.

A. Pang made a simple *Go* board. He used $\frac{3}{4}$ of $\frac{1}{2}$ of a sheet of plywood. What fraction of the whole sheet did he use?

To find $\frac{3}{4}$ of $\frac{1}{2}$, you can multiply. "Of" means multiply.

The picture can be used to find $\frac{3}{4} \times \frac{1}{2}$.

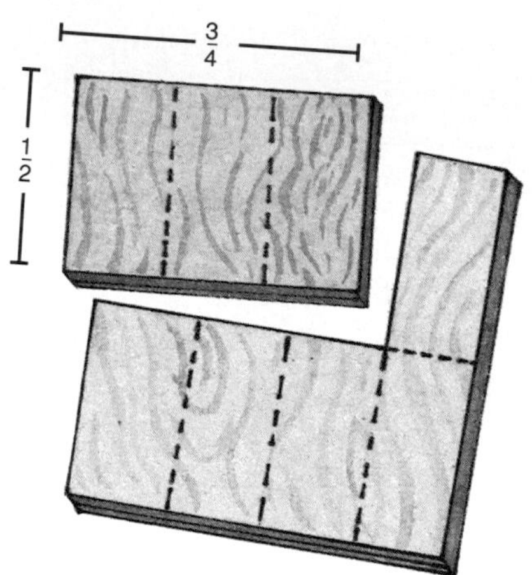

The sheet is divided in half. Each half is divided into fourths. The shaded section represents $\frac{3}{4}$ of $\frac{1}{2}$. It also represents $\frac{3}{8}$ of the sheet.

So, $\frac{3}{4} \times \frac{1}{2} = \frac{3}{8}$.

You can also find the product by multiplying the numerators and then multiplying the denominators.

$$\frac{3}{4} \times \frac{1}{2} = \frac{3 \times 1}{4 \times 2} = \frac{3}{8}$$

The *Go* board will be made from $\frac{3}{8}$ of a sheet of plywood.

B. Pang is making *Go* boards as gifts. If it takes him $2\frac{3}{4}$ hours to cut and sand each board, how long will it take him to cut and sand 12 boards? Find $12 \times 2\frac{3}{4}$.

$$12 \times 2\frac{3}{4}$$

Write 12 and $2\frac{3}{4}$ as fractions.

$$\frac{12}{1} \times \frac{11}{4} = \frac{\overset{3}{\cancel{12}} \times 11}{1 \times \underset{1}{\cancel{4}}} = \frac{33}{1} = 33$$

You can use a shortcut to multiply. Divide the numerator and the denominator by any common factors. The number 4 is a common factor of 4 and 12.

It will take Pang 33 hours to cut and sand 12 boards.

C. Find a ***range*** for $7\frac{1}{2} \times 3\frac{2}{3}$. Then find the exact answer.

Round both numbers up; multiply.
$8 \times 4 = 32$
Round both numbers down; multiply.
$7 \times 3 = 21$
The product is between 21 and 32.

$$7\frac{1}{2} \times 3\frac{2}{3} = \frac{15}{2} \times \frac{11}{3}$$
$$= \frac{\overset{5}{\cancel{15}} \times 11}{2 \times \underset{1}{\cancel{3}}}$$
$$= \frac{55}{2} = 27\frac{1}{2}$$

The answer $27\frac{1}{2}$ is reasonable, since it is between 21 and 32.

D. Mental Math Two numbers are ***reciprocals*** if their product is 1. Sometimes you can multiply by finding reciprocals.

Find $\frac{2}{3} \times \frac{3}{5} \times \frac{3}{2}$.

$$\frac{2}{3} \times \frac{3}{5} \times \frac{3}{2} = \left(\frac{2}{3} \times \frac{3}{2}\right) \times \frac{3}{5}$$
$$= 1 \times \frac{3}{5}$$
$$= \frac{3}{5}$$

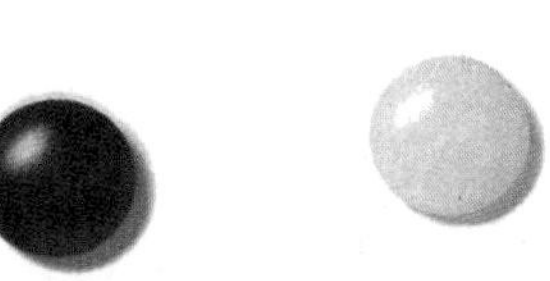

■ **Talk About Math** Describe how you would multiply $\frac{1}{8} \times 16$ mentally.

Check Understanding

For another example, see Set H, pages 224–225.

Copy each rectangle and shade to find the product. Write the product. **Remember** to write each product in lowest terms.

1. $\frac{1}{4} \times \frac{1}{3}$

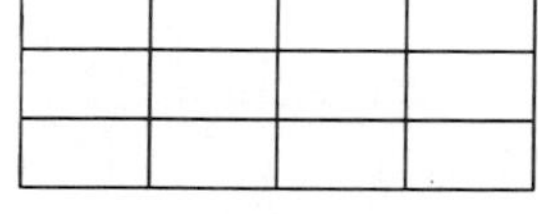

2. $\frac{1}{2} \times \frac{1}{3}$

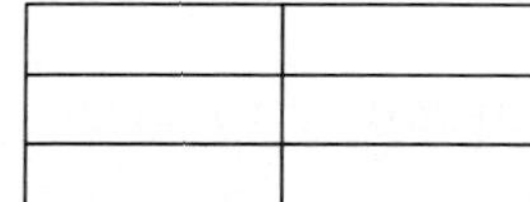

3. $\frac{5}{6} \times \frac{3}{4}$

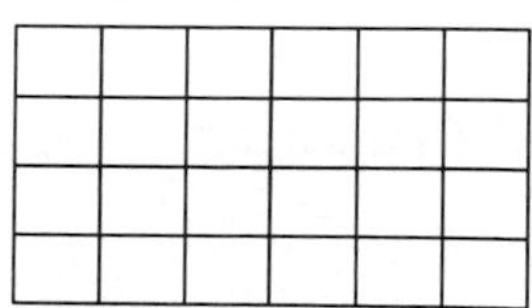

Write each number as a fraction. Then, give the reciprocal of each number.

4. 9 **5.** $6\frac{1}{2}$ **6.** $2\frac{2}{3}$ **7.** 6 **8.** $\frac{2}{3}$ **9.** $3\frac{5}{8}$

Give the missing numbers.

10. $\frac{7}{12} \times \frac{3}{4} = \frac{\square \times \square}{\square \times \square} = \frac{21}{48} = \frac{\square}{\square}$

11. $1\frac{2}{3} \times \frac{9}{10} = \frac{\square \times \square}{\square \times \square} = \frac{\square}{\square} = \square\frac{\square}{\square}$

Practice

For More Practice, see Set H, pages 226–227.

Multiply. Use the shortcut method when possible.

12. $\frac{3}{5} \times \frac{1}{3}$ **13.** $\frac{3}{20} \times \frac{3}{8}$ **14.** $\frac{1}{4} \times \frac{1}{2}$ **15.** $\frac{5}{6} \times \frac{4}{5} \times \frac{1}{2}$

16. $\frac{1}{16} \times 0$ **17.** $\frac{1}{4} \times 1\frac{2}{5}$ **18.** $12 \times \frac{2}{3}$ **19.** $2\frac{1}{3} \times 4\frac{5}{6}$

20. $2\frac{1}{8} \times 4\frac{2}{5}$ **21.** $4\frac{1}{2} \times 1\frac{1}{3}$ **22.** $6\frac{2}{3} \times 1\frac{1}{8}$ **23.** $\frac{3}{8} \times \frac{4}{5}$

24. $12 \times 5\frac{1}{8}$ **25.** $9\frac{2}{5} \times 1$ **26.** $\frac{7}{8} \times \frac{2}{5} \times \frac{3}{10}$ **27.** $2\frac{5}{6} \times 4\frac{1}{2}$

28. What can you say about any fraction or mixed number multiplied by 1? by 0?

Multiply. Tell whether you would use paper and pencil or mental math.

29. $0 \times \frac{13}{15}$ **30.** $1 \times \frac{16}{17}$ **31.** $\frac{7}{9} \times \frac{3}{5}$ **32.** $\frac{2}{7} \times \frac{1}{4} \times \frac{7}{8}$

33. $32 \times \frac{1}{4}$ **34.** $\frac{8}{3} \times \frac{3}{8}$ **35.** $6 \times \frac{7}{12}$ **36.** $\frac{2}{9} \times 18$

37. $\frac{3}{4} \times \frac{4}{3}$ **38.** $\frac{3}{4} \times 20$ **39.** $\frac{6}{5} \times \frac{7}{10} \times \frac{5}{6}$ **40.** $9 \times 1\frac{3}{4}$

41. $4 \times 2\frac{1}{3}$ **42.** $15 \times \frac{1}{15}$ **43.** $6\frac{5}{8} \times \frac{4}{5}$ **44.** $24 \times \frac{5}{6}$

45. Number Sense Look at your answers in Exercises 1–3. Are the products less than or greater than 1? What can you conclude about the product of two fractions less than 1?

Estimate each product by finding a range. Then multiply.

46. $4\frac{1}{2} \times 6$ **47.** $8 \times 5\frac{1}{4}$ **48.** $2\frac{1}{6} \times 4$ **49.** $3\frac{1}{5} \times 1\frac{3}{4}$

50. $4\frac{1}{3} \times 1\frac{1}{3}$ **51.** $2\frac{2}{3} \times 1\frac{1}{8}$ **52.** $\left(2\frac{1}{3}\right)\left(2\frac{2}{3}\right)$ **53.** $\left(6\frac{1}{2}\right)\left(\frac{2}{13}\right)$

Mixed Practice Compute. **Remember** to follow the order of operations.

54. $\frac{1}{2} + \frac{3}{4} \times \frac{5}{8}$ **55.** $\left(\frac{3}{8} - \frac{1}{16}\right) \times \frac{3}{5}$ **56.** $\frac{1}{2} + \frac{3}{4} \times \frac{1}{3}$

57. $3\frac{1}{5} \times \frac{1}{2} + \frac{5}{12}$ **58.** $3 \times \frac{2}{9} + 4\frac{3}{5}$ **59.** $\frac{3}{10} \times \left(5 - 4\frac{1}{2}\right)$

60. $8 \times \left(\frac{7}{8} + \frac{2}{3}\right)$ **61.** $6\frac{1}{4} - \frac{2}{3} \times \frac{3}{4}$ **62.** $4\frac{5}{8} + 1\frac{4}{5} - 3\frac{7}{10}$

Problem Solving

Chess was first played in Asia centuries ago. Later variations were played in Persia (Iran), Arabia, Spain, Europe, and the rest of the world. Today, chess masters from all countries compete in international tournaments.

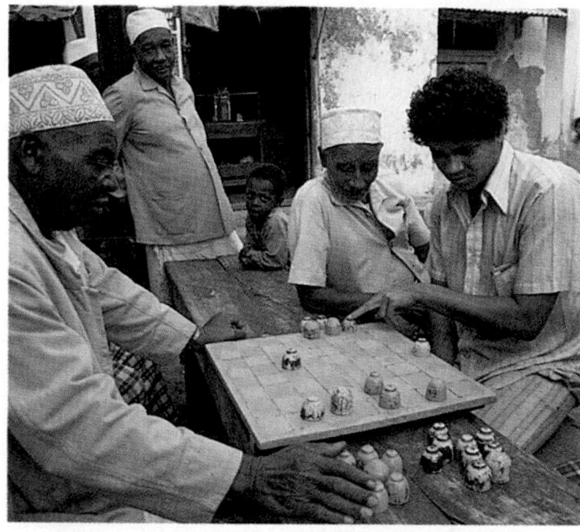
In Kenya, a traditional Swahili game very similar to chess is still played.

Solve each problem.

63. Pang used $\frac{1}{2}$ of $\frac{1}{4}$ of a sheet of plywood to make a chessboard. What fraction of a whole sheet did he use?

64. How many additional sheets of plywood would Pang need to make another 10 chessboards of equal size?

65. Pang spent $3\frac{1}{2}$ hours making a chessboard and $2\frac{1}{2}$ times as long making a *Go* board. How long did it take to make the *Go* board?

66. Would a project that takes $1\frac{1}{2}$ times as long as making a chessboard take more or less time than making a *Go* board? How much more or less? (Refer to Problem 65.)

Choose a Strategy

Don't Lose Your Marbles The game of marbles was played thousands of years ago in Egypt and Rome. Today, it is enjoyed by children the world over.

There is a box of marbles in the game room at Park Junior High. When two people share the marbles equally, one marble is left over. When three people share the marbles equally, one marble is left over. Similarly, when four, five, or six people share the marbles, one marble is left over. But when seven people share the marbles, no marbles are left. What is the least number of marbles that could be in the box?

67. Is the number of marbles even? How do you know?

68. Is the number of marbles a multiple of 3? 4? 5? 6? 7?

69. What is the least number of marbles that could be in the box?

Work Backward

Build Understanding

Alicia, Barry, and Carol hung posters around town to advertise their school's Winter Carnival. Alicia took $\frac{1}{4}$ of the posters, Barry took $\frac{1}{3}$ of what remained, and Carol took the 48 posters that were left. How many posters did they start with?

Understand FACTS Alicia took $\frac{1}{4}$ of the total number of posters. Barry took $\frac{1}{3}$ of those that Alicia left, and Carol took 48. All the posters were taken.

Plan and Solve STRATEGY Work backward. There were 48 posters left for Carol. Since Barry's share was $\frac{1}{3}$ of what Alicia left, Carol's share must have been $\frac{2}{3}$ of what Alicia left.

If $\frac{2}{3}$ of what was left is 48, then $\frac{1}{3}$ of what was left is 24. So $\frac{3}{3}$, or the number of posters left after Alicia took hers, is 72.

Alicia's share was $\frac{1}{4}$. Therefore, the 72 posters that remained after she took her share must have been $\frac{3}{4}$ of the total.

If $\frac{3}{4}$ of the total number of posters is 72, $\frac{1}{4}$ of the total number of posters is 24.

So $\frac{4}{4}$, or the total number of posters, is 96.

ANSWER They started with 96 posters.

Look Back SENSIBLE ANSWER Check your answer. Alicia took $\frac{1}{4}$ of the posters ($\frac{1}{4} \times 96 = 24$ and $96 - 24 = 72$). Barry took $\frac{1}{3}$ of the remaining posters ($\frac{1}{3} \times 72 = 24$, $72 - 24 = 48$). The number of posters remaining after Alicia and Barry took theirs, 48, is correct. So the answer is sensible.

Understand
QUESTION
FACTS
KEY IDEA

Plan and Solve
STRATEGY
ANSWER

Look Back
SENSIBLE ANSWER
ALTERNATE APPROACH

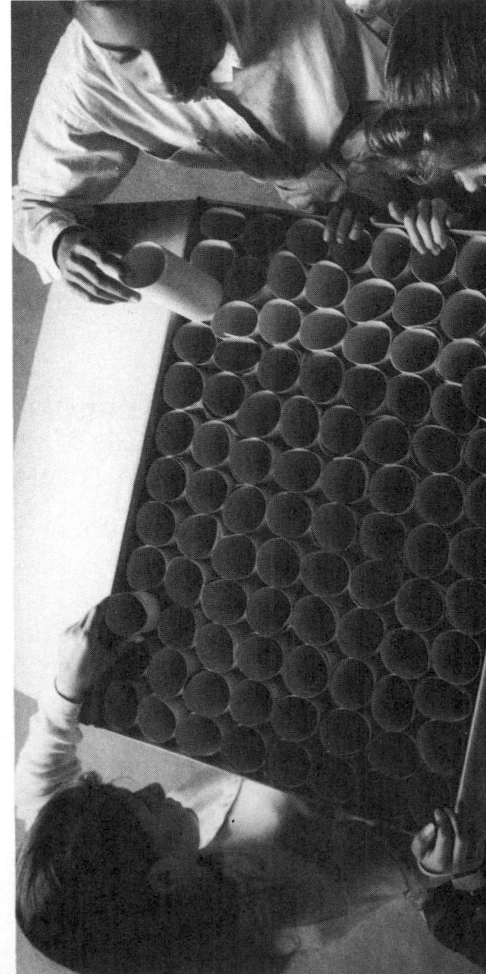

ALGEBRA

■ **Talk About Math** If n represents the number of posters to begin with, did Alicia take $\frac{1}{4}n$? Did Barry take $\frac{1}{3}n$? Explain.

Check Understanding

One fifth of the Winter Carnival tickets were sold the first week, leaving 800 tickets still to sell. How many tickets were originally available?

1. How many tickets were left at the end of the first week?
2. What fraction of the starting number is that?
3. Use your answers to Exercises 1 and 2 to find the original number of tickets.

Practice

Solve each problem.

4. In 1988, carnival ticket prices were twice the 1980 prices. They fell \$2.50 in 1989, and then rose \$3.75 to \$8.25 in 1990. How much were tickets in 1980?
5. Marnie is skiing in a 10-km race. When she has skied 3 times as far as she has skied already, she will be 2 km from the finish line. How far has she skied?
6. Hal's skating time for the 1,000-meter race was 2 minutes. If he skated the first 500 meters of the race in 1 minute 12.25 seconds, how long did it take him to skate the second 500 meters?
7. On the ski team, $\frac{2}{3}$ of the spots are taken by high school students. Half the remaining places are taken by eighth graders, and $\frac{2}{3}$ of the rest are taken by seventh graders. That leaves 4 places for sixth graders. How many skiers are on the team?

Reading ______ Math

Looking for Main Ideas Reread the *Strategy* portion of the example on page 212. Answer the following questions.

1. How do you know that Carol's posters were $\frac{2}{3}$ of the posters left by Alicia?
2. How do you know that 72 posters were $\frac{3}{4}$ of all of the posters?
3. List 3 main ideas of the lesson on page 212.

Dividing Fractions and Mixed Numbers

Build Understanding

A. Divide and Conquer
Materials: Grid paper, ruler
Groups: With a partner

Gregory exercises by running three miles a day. Each city block he runs is $\frac{1}{8}$ mile long. How many blocks does he run each day?

Since you need to find the number of equal parts, you can divide.

Find $3 \div \frac{1}{8}$.

a. Make a model of this problem by drawing a diagram.

$\frac{1}{8}$ mile = 1 block

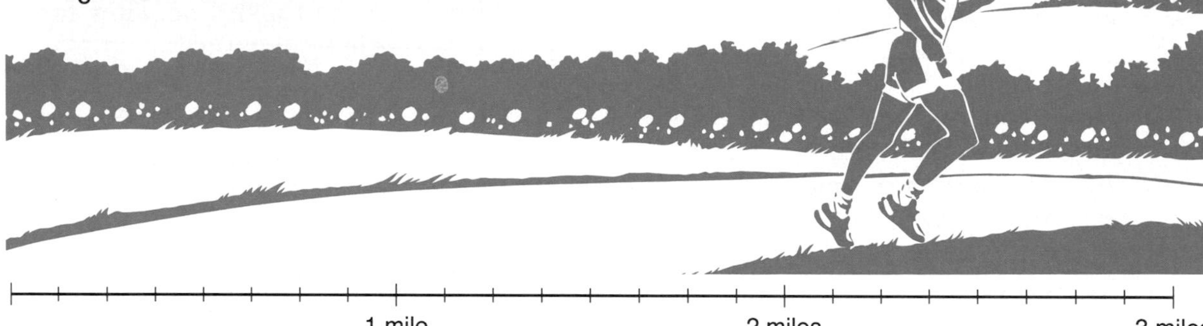

1 mile 2 miles 3 miles

How many $\frac{1}{8}$s are there in 1? in 2? in 3? What is $3 \div \frac{1}{8}$?

How many blocks does Gregory run each day?

b. Look at your answer for $3 \div \frac{1}{8}$. Compare it with the product of 3 and 8. What do you notice?

c. How are $\frac{1}{8}$ and 8 related?

d. Find $6 \div \frac{3}{4}$ by drawing a diagram. Compare your answer with the product of $6 \times \frac{4}{3}$. What do you notice?

How are $\frac{3}{4}$ and $\frac{4}{3}$ related?

e. Give a multiplication problem that you could solve to find the answer to each of these division problems.

$5 \div \frac{2}{3}$ $7 \div \frac{5}{4}$ $8 \div \frac{1}{10}$

B. Find $2\frac{1}{2} \div \frac{2}{3}$.

Dividing by any number gives the same result as multiplying by its reciprocal.

$2\frac{1}{2} \div \frac{2}{3}$

$\frac{5}{2} \div \frac{2}{3}$ Write $2\frac{1}{2}$ as an improper fraction.

$\frac{5}{2} \times \frac{3}{2}$ To divide $\frac{5}{2}$ by a fraction, multiply by the reciprocal of the divisor. The divisor is $\frac{2}{3}$. The reciprocal of $\frac{2}{3}$ is $\frac{3}{2}$.

$\frac{5}{2} \times \frac{3}{2} = \frac{15}{4} = 3\frac{3}{4}$ Write $\frac{15}{4}$ as a mixed number.

C. Find $9 \div 6\frac{3}{4}$.

$9 \div 6\frac{3}{4}$

$\frac{9}{1} \div \frac{27}{4}$ Write 9 and $6\frac{3}{4}$ as improper fractions.

$\frac{9}{1} \times \frac{4}{27} = \frac{\overset{1}{\cancel{9}}}{1} \times \frac{4}{\underset{3}{\cancel{27}}}$ Multiply $\frac{9}{1}$ by the reciprocal of $\frac{27}{4}$.

$= \frac{4}{3} = 1\frac{1}{3}$

D. Find $\frac{\frac{1}{2}}{5}$. Remember: $\frac{\frac{1}{2}}{5}$ means $\frac{1}{2} \div 5$.

$\frac{1}{2} \div 5$

$\frac{1}{2} \div \frac{5}{1}$ Write 5 as an improper fraction.

$\frac{1}{2} \times \frac{1}{5} = \frac{1}{10}$ Multiply $\frac{1}{2}$ by the reciprocal of $\frac{5}{1}$.

■ **Talk About Math** What number is its own reciprocal? Is there any number that does not have a reciprocal?

Check Understanding

For another example, see Set I, pages 224–225.

Draw pictures to answer Exercises 1–3.

1. How many $\frac{3}{5}$s are there in 3?

2. How many $\frac{1}{8}$s are there in $\frac{3}{4}$?

3. $3\frac{3}{4} \div \frac{3}{4}$

Find each missing number.

4. $8 \div \frac{2}{3} = \frac{8}{1} \times \frac{\square}{\square}$

5. $\frac{3}{8} \div 4 = \frac{3}{8} \times \frac{\square}{\square}$

6. $\frac{1}{2} \div \frac{3}{5} = \frac{1}{2} \times \frac{\square}{\square} = \frac{\square}{\square}$

7. $9\frac{1}{2} \div \frac{3}{4} = \frac{\square}{2} \div \frac{3}{4} = \frac{\square}{\square} \times \frac{\square}{3} = \square$

8. $12 \div 5\frac{2}{5} = \frac{\square}{1} \div \frac{\square}{5} = \frac{\square}{\square} \times \frac{\square}{\square} = \square$

9. $1\frac{7}{8} \div 1\frac{2}{3} = \frac{\square}{8} \div \frac{\square}{3} = \frac{\square}{\square} \times \frac{\square}{\square} = \square$

Divide.

10. $\frac{5}{8} \div 8$

11. $39 \div 3\frac{1}{4}$

12. $2\frac{4}{5} \div 1\frac{3}{10}$

13. $\frac{2}{3} \div 5\frac{5}{6}$

Practice

For More Practice, see Set I, pages 226–227.

Divide. **Remember** to multiply by the reciprocal of the divisor.

14. $7 \div \frac{7}{8}$ **15.** $3 \div \frac{7}{10}$ **16.** $\frac{5}{8} \div \frac{1}{6}$ **17.** $\frac{1}{10} \div 1\frac{3}{5}$ **18.** $6\frac{1}{2} \div 4$

19. $2\frac{3}{4} \div 6$ **20.** $1\frac{3}{4} \div 2\frac{1}{2}$ **21.** $4\frac{2}{3} \div 1\frac{1}{3}$ **22.** $5 \div 3\frac{1}{2}$ **23.** $10 \div 4\frac{3}{8}$

24. $\frac{2}{3} \div 4$ **25.** $\frac{3}{5} \div 6$ **26.** $3\frac{1}{3} \div \frac{2}{3}$ **27.** $1\frac{4}{5} \div \frac{7}{12}$ **28.** $\frac{1}{5} \div 1\frac{1}{2}$

29. $\dfrac{\frac{2}{3}}{\frac{3}{4}}$ **30.** $\dfrac{\frac{9}{16}}{\frac{3}{8}}$ **31.** $\dfrac{\frac{1}{3}}{8}$ **32.** $\dfrac{3}{1\frac{1}{4}}$ **33.** $\dfrac{2}{3\frac{3}{4}}$

Mixed Practice Multiply or divide.

34. $\frac{7}{8} \times \frac{1}{2}$ **35.** $\frac{7}{8} \div \frac{1}{2}$ **36.** $4\frac{1}{3} \div \frac{7}{9}$ **37.** $16 \div \frac{1}{6}$ **38.** $5\frac{1}{2} \times 20$

39. $\frac{5}{8} \div \frac{5}{9}$ **40.** $3\frac{3}{4} \times 2\frac{1}{4}$ **41.** $5\frac{3}{4} \div \frac{1}{9}$ **42.** $16 \times \frac{1}{4}$ **43.** $\frac{5}{6} \times \frac{1}{2} \times \frac{2}{3}$

Problem Solving

One way to compute your safe exercise heart rate (in beats per minute) is to subtract your age from 220 and take $\frac{3}{4}$ of the difference, rounded to the nearest whole number.

44. Compute your safe exercise heart rate.

45. Compute the safe exercise heart rate for a 40-year-old person.

46. After running, Chris found her heart rate to be 160. She is 20 years old. Is that a safe rate?

47. Nils, who is 32, took his heart rate after he worked out. It was 180. Is that a safe rate?

Organize your work to help you think clearly.

Solve each problem.

48. Juanita walks at the rate of $\frac{1}{16}$ mile per minute. How long would it take her to walk 3 miles?

49. If a person's step length is $2\frac{1}{5}$ feet, how many steps would make a mile? **Remember** 1 mi = 5,280 ft.

In Problems 50–53, the numbers shown near each bicycle give the circumference, or the distance around each wheel.

50. If the Ordinary is ridden 1,260 feet, the number of turns of the small wheel is how many times that of the large wheel?

51. Your great-great grandfather might have ridden the Ordinary. How many times did its large wheel turn in 660 feet?

The Ordinary bicycle became popular in the United States in the 1860s.

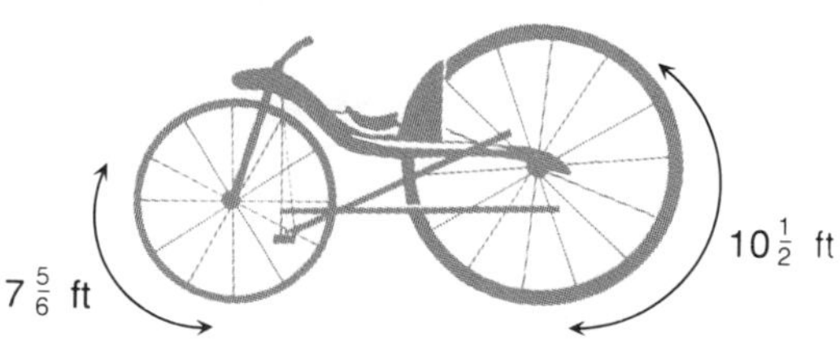

Macmillan's Hobbyhorse of 1839 was the first 2-wheeled vehicle to resemble the modern bicycle.

52. How many times the circumference of the Ordinary's small wheel was that of the large wheel?

53. Your great-great-great grandmother might have ridden Macmillan's Hobbyhorse. How many times did its large wheel turn in a distance of 660 feet (about 1 city block)?

Explore ______ Math

54. Look at your answers to Exercises 14–33 and tell which have quotients greater than 1, equal to 1, or less than 1.

Now look at the following exercises. Predict whether each quotient will be greater than 1, equal to 1, or less than 1.

55. $\frac{3}{5} \div \frac{4}{5}$ **56.** $\frac{3}{8} \div 2$ **57.** $5 \div \frac{3}{4}$ **58.** $\frac{7}{8} \div \frac{1}{3}$ **59.** $1\frac{1}{2} \div \frac{3}{2}$ **60.** $1\frac{3}{4} \div 2\frac{1}{2}$

61. In Exercises 55–60, were your predictions correct?

62. Write three division problems, one each in which the quotient is greater than 1, equal to 1, and less than 1.

63. Write a rule stating how you can determine if a quotient will be greater than 1, equal to 1, or less than 1.

ALGEBRA

Solving Multiplication and Division Equations

Build Understanding

A. Manny is planting green beans in a community garden. He uses $\frac{3}{5}$ of a packet for each row. If Manny has 3 packets of beans, how many rows of beans can he plant?

Total number of packets = Fraction of packet for 1 row × Number of rows

$$3 = \frac{3}{5}r$$

$$\left(\frac{5}{3}\right) 3 = \left(\frac{5}{3}\right) \frac{3}{5} r$$ Multiply both sides of the equation by the reciprocal of $\frac{3}{5}$, which is $\frac{5}{3}$.

$$5 = 1r$$

$$5 = r$$ $1r = r$

Manny can plant 5 rows of green beans.

B. Solve $3m = \frac{1}{2}$.

$$3m = \frac{1}{2}$$

$$\frac{3}{1}m = \frac{1}{2}$$ Write 3 as a fraction.

$$\left(\frac{1}{3}\right)\frac{3}{1}m = \left(\frac{1}{3}\right)\frac{1}{2}$$ Multiply both sides of the equation by the reciprocal of $\frac{3}{1}$, which is $\frac{1}{3}$.

$$m = \frac{1}{6}$$

C. Solve $5\frac{1}{2}n = 3$.

$$5\frac{1}{2}n = 3$$

$$\frac{11}{2}n = \frac{3}{1}$$ Write the numbers as fractions.

$$\left(\frac{2}{11}\right)\frac{11}{2}n = \left(\frac{2}{11}\right)\frac{3}{1}$$ Multiply both sides of the equation by the reciprocal of $\frac{11}{2}$.

$$n = \frac{6}{11}$$

Talk About Math Study the examples. What is the purpose of multiplying by the reciprocal in solving an equation?

Check Understanding

For another example, see Set J, pages 224–225.

Write the reciprocal for each of these numbers.

1. $\frac{4}{5}$ **2.** $\frac{1}{6}$ **3.** $2\frac{5}{7}$ **4.** 8

By what reciprocal will you multiply to solve each equation?

5. $16 = \frac{2}{5}m$ **6.** $\frac{7}{1}x = \frac{7}{2}$ **7.** $\frac{a}{5} = \frac{1}{2}$

8. Solve the equations in Exercises 5–7.

Practice

For More Practice, see Set J, pages 226–227.

Solve each equation.

9. $\frac{1}{3}b = 8$ **10.** $5 = 1\frac{1}{7}p$ **11.** $3k = 4\frac{3}{4}$ **12.** $\frac{m}{3} = 1\frac{1}{6}$

13. $\frac{3}{4}m = 6$ **14.** $\frac{1}{2}a = \frac{5}{7}$ **15.** $7 = \frac{1}{3}n$ **16.** $4s = \frac{1}{5}$

17. $4\frac{3}{4}t = 19$ **18.** $\frac{1}{2}z = \frac{7}{8}$ **19.** $1\frac{1}{4}x = \frac{5}{12}$ **20.** $4\frac{1}{3}d = 5\frac{4}{7}$

21. $6m = \frac{1}{2}$ **22.** $\frac{2}{9}c = 8$ **23.** $1\frac{1}{4}h = 6\frac{1}{4}$ **24.** $11 = \frac{1}{5}a$

25. $9w = \frac{3}{4}$ **26.** $57 = 3\frac{1}{6}m$ **27.** $\frac{2}{3}a = 0$ **28.** $3 = \frac{b}{7}$

Mixed Practice Solve each equation.

29. $a + \frac{2}{5} = \frac{4}{5}$ **30.** $m - \frac{3}{7} = \frac{6}{7}$ **31.** $\frac{1}{2}x = 7$ **32.** $7b = \frac{7}{9}$

33. $1\frac{5}{8} + x = 5$ **34.** $8a = \frac{4}{5}$ **35.** $x - \frac{5}{8} = \frac{3}{4}$ **36.** $20s = \frac{3}{5}$

37. $4\frac{1}{8} = 5d$ **38.** $\frac{2}{7} = \frac{x}{2}$ **39.** $b + \frac{2}{3} = \frac{5}{6}$ **40.** $\frac{1}{4}e = 9$

Problem Solving

Solve each problem.

41. Two-thirds of a packet of corn will sow 1 row in the garden. Manny has 4 packets of corn seed. How many rows of corn can he plant?

42. Manny used $2\frac{1}{4}$ packets of seeds to plant 3 rows of beets. What fraction of a packet did he use in each row?

43. Manny plants $7\frac{1}{2}$ rows of flowers with $3\frac{3}{4}$ packets of seed. How many rows does each packet plant?

44. **Critical Thinking** Manny planted onions during the first week of April. The onions will be ready to harvest in 14 weeks. Tomatoes are ready to harvest 8 weeks after planting. When should Manny plant his tomatoes so that his onions and tomatoes are ready to harvest at the same time?

Find a Pattern

Understand
QUESTION
FACTS
KEY IDEA

Plan and Solve
STRATEGY
ANSWER

Look Back
SENSIBLE ANSWER
ALTERNATE APPROACH

Build Understanding

All living things contain radioactive carbon 14 (C-14). After death, the amount of C-14 decreases as shown in the table. If the pattern continues, how much C-14 will remain in a fossil 22,800 years old?

Decrease in C-14

Years after death	Amount of C-14 remaining
0	1
5,700	$\frac{1}{2}$
11,400	$\frac{1}{4}$
17,100	▦
22,800	▦

Understand QUESTION How much C-14 will remain after 22,800 years if the pattern continues?

FACT The amount of C-14 decreases with time.

Plan and Solve STRATEGY Look at the terms in the table for the amount of C-14 remaining. Find a pattern to determine how the amount of C-14 decreases.

Can you find each term by subtracting one half from the preceding term?

No. $1 - \frac{1}{2} = \frac{1}{2}$ $\quad \frac{1}{2} - \frac{1}{2} = 0$

Can you find each term by multiplying the preceding term by one half?

Yes. $\frac{1}{2} \times 1 = \frac{1}{2}$ $\quad \frac{1}{2} \times \frac{1}{2} = \frac{1}{4}$

Now use this pattern to find the missing terms.

$\frac{1}{2} \times \frac{1}{4} = \frac{1}{8}$ $\quad \frac{1}{2} \times \frac{1}{8} = \frac{1}{16}$

ANSWER One sixteenth of the C-14 will remain after 22,800 years.

Look Back ALTERNATE APPROACH You can also solve this problem by drawing a picture. Divide a square in half. Divide one of the halves in half, one of the quarters in half, and one of the eighths in half.

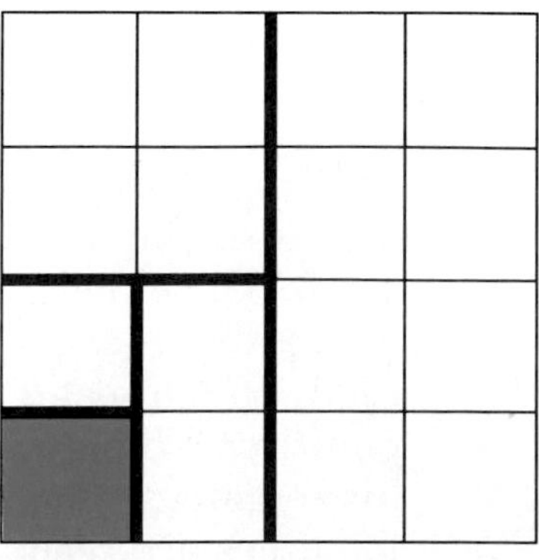

Talk About Math Will the amount of C-14 in a fossil ever totally disappear? Explain your answer.

Check Understanding

Use the table for C-14 in the example.

1. In the table on page 220, what pattern can you find in the column labeled years after death? What are the next two entries after 22,800 years?

2. Write the next three terms.
$2\frac{1}{3}$ 3 $3\frac{2}{3}$ ▒ ▒ ▒

Practice

Explain how the terms are related. Then write the next three terms.

3. 1 $\frac{1}{3}$ $\frac{1}{9}$ ▒ ▒ ▒

4. $\frac{1}{5}$ $1\frac{2}{5}$ $2\frac{3}{5}$ ▒ ▒ ▒

5. $\frac{1}{3}$ $\frac{7}{6}$ 2 ▒ ▒ ▒

6. $\frac{3}{4}$ $\frac{9}{16}$ $\frac{27}{64}$ ▒ ▒ ▒

7. Write the next two entries in the table for the decrease in radioactive cobalt 60.

Years	0	$5\frac{1}{4}$	$10\frac{1}{2}$		
Amount left	1	$\frac{1}{2}$	$\frac{1}{4}$		

8. If a fossil contains $\frac{1}{64}$ of the original amount of C-14, about how old is the fossil?

The "half-life" of a substance is the amount of time it takes for the substance to decrease by $\frac{1}{2}$. The half-life of C-14 is 5,700 years.

9. The half-life of fluoride-18 is 2 hours. After how many hours would $\frac{1}{256}$ of flouride-18 remain in a substance?

10. What is the half-life of carbon-11 if $\frac{1}{64}$ of the substance remains after two hours?

Baltic amber preserved this dragonfly 40,000,000 years ago.

Chapter 6 REVIEW

Skills Review

Write each fraction as a whole number or as a mixed number.

1. $\frac{17}{7}$ **2.** $\frac{24}{4}$ **3.** $\frac{11}{5}$

Write each number as a fraction.

4. $3\frac{2}{5}$ **5.** $7\frac{4}{11}$ **6.** $1\frac{5}{9}$

Compare the numbers. Use $<$, $>$, or $=$.

7. $\frac{15}{18} \;\blacksquare\; \frac{5}{6}$ **8.** $\frac{7}{9} \;\blacksquare\; \frac{3}{5}$

9. $5\frac{1}{2} \;\blacksquare\; 4\frac{7}{8}$ **10.** $3\frac{3}{9} \;\blacksquare\; 3\frac{1}{3}$

Add or subtract.

11. $\frac{1}{3} + \frac{1}{2}$ **12.** $\frac{5}{6} + \frac{2}{3}$

13. $1\frac{4}{9} + 2\frac{4}{9}$ **14.** $3\frac{2}{5} + 4\frac{1}{4}$

15. $\frac{11}{12} - \frac{1}{3}$ **16.** $2\frac{1}{2} - 1\frac{1}{6}$

17. $10 - 3\frac{7}{8}$ **18.** $5\frac{3}{5} - 1\frac{9}{10}$

Multiply or divide.

19. $\frac{1}{5} \times \frac{3}{4}$ **20.** $12 \times \frac{2}{3}$

21. $\frac{5}{6} \times \frac{3}{10}$ **22.** $\frac{15}{16} \times 1\frac{3}{5}$

23. $0 \times \frac{12}{19}$ **24.** $4 \div \frac{1}{4}$

25. $\frac{4}{5} \div 4$ **26.** $\frac{9}{10} \div \frac{3}{5}$

27. $1\frac{7}{8} \div \frac{3}{4}$ **28.** $14 \div 1\frac{3}{7}$

Solve each equation.

29. $\frac{4}{5}n = 20$ **30.** $\frac{1}{2}r = \frac{3}{8}$

31. $\frac{v}{15} = \frac{2}{3}$ **32.** $5m = 1\frac{1}{4}$

33. $\frac{2}{3}k = \frac{4}{7}$ **34.** $2\frac{1}{2}h = 7\frac{1}{2}$

35. $20 = \frac{7}{8}m$ **36.** $\frac{7}{8}m = \frac{7}{10}$

Problem-Solving Review

Solve each problem.

37. Jason and Rafe are planning a hike of 7.9 km. They plan to hike 2.8 km, stop for lunch, and then hike the rest of the distance in 3 hours. How many kilometers will they need to hike each hour after lunch?

38. The school bookstore sells pens for \$0.25, tablets for \$0.40, and pencils for \$0.10. One day, only pens and tablets were sold. If the amount collected was \$6.55, how many of each were sold?

39. An isosceles triangle has one angle that measures 40°. Name all possible measures of the other two angles.

40. Toya has saved \$120. She estimates that she has enough money for a \$94.95 bike, a \$11.50 helmet, and a \$8.25 bicycle light. Is she correct?

41. A mixture of nuts contains $1\frac{1}{3}$ pounds cashews and $1\frac{3}{8}$ pounds peanuts. What is the total weight of this mixture?

42. **Data File** Use the data on pages 264–265. Suppose you have 20 feet of $\frac{1}{2}$-inch conduit. How much will you have left over if you make a large xylophone? Assume that each cut uses $\frac{1}{8}$-inch of conduit.

43. **Make a Data File** Visit a hardware or building supply store and obtain a chart for nail sizes. Make a table of some common sizes, with one column for the size numbers and one column for lengths.

Cumulative Skills Review • Chapters 1–6

Estimate each answer.

1. $25.96 + 24.02 + 26.1$ **2.** $89.3 - 71.998$ **3.** $4 \times 55 \times 24$

4. 0.48×29.88 **5.** $94{,}512 - 15{,}677$ **6.** $45.009 + 2.3 + 17.19$

7. $4\frac{11}{21} + 3\frac{2}{5}$ **8.** $12\frac{3}{4} - 4\frac{5}{8}$ **9.** $\frac{2}{9} + \frac{7}{11}$

10. $6{,}342 \div 78$ **11.** $13{,}029 \div 629$ **12.** $54{,}933 \div 1{,}098$

Solve each equation.

13. $n + 45 = 77$ **14.** $80 = n - 12$ **15.** $32 - p = 15$

16. $20t = 140$ **17.** $\frac{n}{25} = 10$ **18.** $3{,}500 = 70g$

19. $4m + 19 = 35$ **20.** $\frac{v}{9} + 50 = 55$ **21.** $5.6 = \frac{y}{8} - 10.4$

22. $\frac{5}{9}k = 25$ **23.** $\frac{7}{8} = \frac{1}{2}n$ **24.** $\frac{3}{5}c = 9$

25. $7.5n = 18.75$ **26.** $\frac{c}{0.05} = 1.2$ **27.** $e + 0.009 = 1.245$

Use the diagram to name two of the given angles.

28. Acute angles **29.** Obtuse angles

30. Complementary angles **31.** Right angles

32. Supplementary angles **33.** Vertical angles

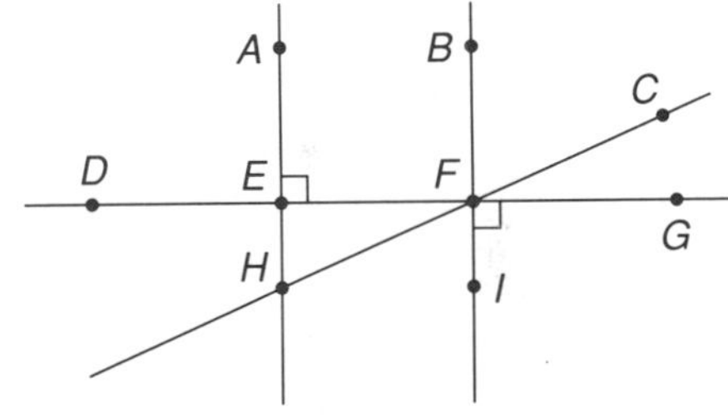

Tell if each number is divisible by 2, 3, 5, 9, or 10. List all possibilities.

34. 435 **35.** 450 **36.** 72,270 **37.** 198,522 **38.** 8,422 **39.** 400,500

Write *prime* or *composite*.

40. 85 **41.** 93 **42.** 74 **43.** 103 **44.** 213 **45.** 531

Write each fraction in lowest terms.

46. $\frac{21}{28}$ **47.** $\frac{45}{54}$ **48.** $\frac{12}{36}$ **49.** $\frac{20}{45}$ **50.** $\frac{27}{33}$ **51.** $\frac{92}{138}$

Write each fraction as a whole number or as a mixed number.

52. $\frac{47}{9}$ **53.** $\frac{27}{6}$ **54.** $\frac{48}{8}$ **55.** $\frac{39}{3}$ **56.** $\frac{52}{5}$ **57.** $\frac{43}{7}$

Reteaching

Set A pages 188–189

To find an equal fraction, multiply.

$\frac{2}{5} = \frac{?}{15}$ Think: What number × 5 = 15? (3) That number (3) × 2 = 6. So $\frac{2}{5} = \frac{6}{15}$.

Remember, multiply the numerator and the denominator by the same nonzero number.

Give each missing number.

1. $\frac{2}{5} = \frac{\square}{10}$ 2. $\frac{7}{8} = \frac{\square}{24}$ 3. $\frac{5}{6} = \frac{\square}{54}$

4. $\frac{3}{4} = \frac{15}{\square}$ 5. $\frac{10}{12} = \frac{40}{\square}$ 6. $\frac{1}{9} = \frac{7}{\square}$

Set B pages 190–191

To write an improper fraction as a mixed number, divide the numerator by the denominator.

$$\frac{55}{2} = 55 \text{ divided by } 2 = 2\overline{)55} \quad 27 \text{ R1} = 27\tfrac{1}{2}$$

$$\begin{array}{r} 27 \text{ R1} \\ 2\overline{)55} \\ \underline{4} \\ 15 \\ \underline{14} \\ 1 \end{array}$$

Remember, the remainder and the divisor form the fraction part of the mixed number.

Give each missing number.

1. $\frac{26}{3} = \square\frac{\square}{\square}$ 2. $\frac{7}{4} = \square\frac{\square}{\square}$

3. $\frac{82}{11} = \square\frac{\square}{\square}$ 4. $\frac{131}{10} = \square\frac{\square}{\square}$

Set C pages 192–193

To compare fractions, first find a common denominator. Then compare numerators.

$\frac{5}{8}\ \frac{3}{4}\ \frac{1}{2}$ The least common denominator is 8. (**8** × 1, **4** × 2, **2** × 4)

↓ ↓ ↓

$\frac{5}{8}\ \frac{6}{8}\ \frac{4}{8}$ The numerators in order from least to greatest are 4, 5, 6.

So $\frac{1}{2} < \frac{5}{8} < \frac{3}{4}$.

Remember, compare the numerators when the fractions have common denominators.

1. Write $\frac{1}{5}$, $\frac{3}{4}$, $\frac{7}{10}$ with a common denominator.

2. Write the original fractions in order from least to greatest.

Set D pages 194–195

Round to estimate the sum of mixed numbers.

$$4\tfrac{5}{6} + 9\tfrac{1}{7} = 5 + 9 = 14$$

Remember, round up if the fraction is greater than $\frac{1}{2}$ and down if less than $\frac{1}{2}$.

Estimate by rounding.

1. $5\frac{5}{12} + 2\frac{2}{3}$ 2. $1\frac{4}{5} + \frac{1}{2}$ 3. $6\frac{4}{9} + 3\frac{3}{8}$

Set E pages 196–199

To add mixed numbers (1) write the fractions with the least common denominator, (2) add the whole numbers, (3) add the fractions.

Remember, rename your answer.

Add.

1. $7\frac{3}{4} + 4\frac{1}{2} + 8\frac{7}{8}$ 2. $10\frac{7}{9} + 9\frac{1}{3} + 1\frac{2}{9}$

Set F pages 202–203

When subtracting, make sure fractions have the same denominator.

$\frac{8}{9} - \frac{5}{9} = \frac{3}{9} = \frac{1}{3}$ $\quad \frac{7}{12} - \frac{1}{2} = \frac{7}{12} - \frac{6}{12} = \frac{1}{12}$

Remember, write your answer in lowest terms.

Subtract.

1. $\frac{2}{5} - \frac{1}{15}$ **2.** $\frac{9}{20} - \frac{7}{20}$ **3.** $\frac{2}{25} - \frac{1}{15}$

Set G pages 204–205

Rename mixed numbers in order to subtract. Rename the whole-number part as a mixed number.

$6\frac{1}{4} - 3\frac{1}{3} = 6\frac{3}{12} - 3\frac{4}{12}$ Rename $6\frac{3}{12}$. $6 = 5\frac{12}{12}$.

$6\frac{3}{12} = 5\frac{12}{12} + \frac{3}{12} = 5\frac{15}{12}$ $\quad 5\frac{15}{12} - 3\frac{4}{12} = 2\frac{11}{12}$

Remember, write the fractions with common denominators; then rename.

Subtract.

1. $19\frac{3}{8} - 1\frac{2}{3}$ **2.** $22\frac{1}{6} - 10\frac{5}{9}$

3. $9\frac{3}{5} - 8\frac{3}{4}$ **4.** $1\frac{5}{6} - \frac{7}{8}$

Set H pages 208–211

Finding a common factor in a numerator and denominator makes multiplying fractions faster.

$7\frac{1}{9} \times \frac{1}{8} = \frac{64}{9} \times \frac{1}{8}$ 8 is a common factor of 64 and 8. So divide 64 and 8 by 8.

$\frac{\overset{8}{\cancel{64}}}{9} \times \frac{1}{\underset{1}{\cancel{8}}} = \frac{8}{9} \times \frac{1}{1} = \frac{8}{9}$

Remember, write a mixed number as an improper fraction.

Multiply.

1. $4\frac{2}{5} \times \frac{9}{11}$ **2.** $5\frac{1}{7} \times 1\frac{1}{6}$ **3.** $\frac{1}{14} \times 3\frac{1}{2}$

Set I pages 214–217

To divide fractions and mixed numbers, multiply by the divisor's reciprocal.

$3\frac{1}{3} \div \frac{2}{9} = \frac{10}{3} \times \frac{9}{2}$ The reciprocal of $\frac{2}{9}$ is $\frac{9}{2}$.

$\frac{\overset{5}{\cancel{10}}}{\underset{1}{\cancel{3}}} \times \frac{\overset{3}{\cancel{9}}}{\underset{1}{\cancel{2}}} = \frac{15}{1} = 15$

Remember, write a mixed number as an improper fraction before dividing.

Divide.

1. $2\frac{2}{5} \div \frac{4}{7}$ **2.** $6\frac{1}{3} \div 2\frac{2}{3}$ **3.** $10 \div 6\frac{5}{6}$

Set J pages 218–219

To solve for the variable, find the reciprocal of the number with the variable. Then multiply by the reciprocal.

$8 = \frac{2}{5}n$ Use the reciprocal of $\frac{2}{5}$: $\frac{5}{2}$.

Multiply both sides by $\frac{5}{2}$:

$\frac{5}{\underset{1}{\cancel{2}}} \times \overset{4}{\cancel{8}} = \frac{\overset{1}{\cancel{2}}}{\underset{1}{\cancel{5}}}n \times \frac{\overset{1}{\cancel{5}}}{\underset{1}{\cancel{2}}}$

$20 = n$

Remember, two numbers are reciprocals if their product is 1.

Solve each equation.

1. $\frac{7}{8}r = 14$ **2.** $5s = \frac{7}{12}$ **3.** $4\frac{1}{6}t = 2$

4. $\frac{1}{24} = \frac{3}{4}p$ **5.** $7 = 5\frac{3}{5}y$ **6.** $3x = \frac{3}{20}$

Independent Study RETEACHING

More Practice

Set A pages 188–189

Give each missing number.

1. $\frac{4}{5} = \frac{\square}{15}$ **2.** $\frac{6}{7} = \frac{18}{\square}$ **3.** $\frac{42}{48} = \frac{7}{\square}$ **4.** $\frac{5}{6} = \frac{\square}{12} = \frac{\square}{18} = \frac{20}{\square}$

Set B pages 190–191

Write each fraction as a whole number or as a mixed number.

1. $\frac{13}{8}$ **2.** $\frac{18}{4}$ **3.** $\frac{21}{2}$ **4.** $\frac{20}{5}$ **5.** $\frac{11}{6}$ **6.** $\frac{16}{7}$

Write each number as a fraction.

7. $4\frac{3}{8}$ **8.** $7\frac{1}{2}$ **9.** $1\frac{4}{5}$ **10.** $2\frac{6}{11}$ **11.** $10\frac{6}{7}$ **12.** $3\frac{7}{9}$

Set C pages 192–193

Compare the numbers. Use >, <, or =.

1. $\frac{7}{9} \square \frac{5}{9}$ **2.** $\frac{3}{8} \square \frac{3}{4}$ **3.** $2\frac{4}{9} \square 2\frac{2}{3}$ **4.** $4\frac{5}{13} \square 5\frac{1}{6}$

List the numbers from greatest to least.

5. $\frac{2}{3}, 1\frac{1}{2}, \frac{3}{4}$ **6.** $\frac{5}{8}, \frac{3}{5}, \frac{5}{6}$ **7.** $\frac{23}{11}, 2\frac{1}{9}, \frac{19}{10}$ **8.** $5\frac{3}{4}, 5\frac{2}{5}, \frac{42}{8}$

Set D pages 194–195

Estimate. Explain how you estimated.

1. $\frac{7}{8} + \frac{5}{6}$ **2.** $\frac{2}{7} + \frac{1}{4}$ **3.** $\frac{3}{10} + \frac{2}{5}$ **4.** $3\frac{5}{6} + 2\frac{5}{6}$

5. $4\frac{2}{11} + 2\frac{2}{9}$ **6.** $7\frac{4}{5} - 3\frac{3}{4}$ **7.** $10\frac{7}{10} + 10\frac{10}{13}$ **8.** $24\frac{11}{12} - 15\frac{2}{9}$

Set E pages 196–199

Add.

1. $\frac{4}{7} + \frac{5}{14}$ **2.** $\frac{3}{8} + \frac{2}{3}$ **3.** $\frac{3}{4} + \frac{7}{10}$ **4.** $\frac{13}{18} + \frac{1}{6}$ **5.** $\frac{2}{9} + \frac{4}{15}$ **6.** $\frac{3}{4} + \frac{6}{7}$

7. $4\frac{4}{9} + 4\frac{7}{9}$ **8.** $3\frac{2}{7} + 2\frac{5}{7}$ **9.** $8\frac{5}{6} + 3\frac{1}{2}$ **10.** $12\frac{5}{8} + 9\frac{3}{16}$ **11.** $15\frac{2}{3} + 5\frac{3}{5}$

12. $4\frac{2}{11} + 4\frac{4}{11}$ **13.** $6\frac{1}{6} + 8\frac{7}{10}$ **14.** $11\frac{3}{4} + 8\frac{7}{9}$ **15.** $24\frac{7}{12} + 57\frac{7}{8}$

16. $5\frac{1}{6} + 2\frac{2}{3}$ **17.** $4\frac{2}{5} + 8\frac{3}{10}$ **18.** $7\frac{5}{18} + 11\frac{1}{2}$ **19.** $15\frac{3}{8} + 6\frac{3}{16}$

Set F pages 202–203

Subtract.

1. $\frac{7}{9} - \frac{2}{9}$
2. $\frac{11}{12} - \frac{6}{15}$
3. $\frac{15}{18} - \frac{4}{9}$
4. $\frac{5}{8} - \frac{1}{6}$
5. $\frac{12}{15} - \frac{1}{4}$
6. $6\frac{5}{7} - 3\frac{5}{7}$
7. $3\frac{9}{10} - 2\frac{3}{10}$
8. $8\frac{10}{13} - 4\frac{4}{13}$
9. $7\frac{11}{16} - 4\frac{3}{16}$
10. $66\frac{17}{20} - 30\frac{3}{8}$

Set G pages 204–205

Subtract.

1. $8\frac{1}{9} - 3\frac{7}{9}$
2. $10 - 5\frac{6}{11}$
3. $14\frac{1}{6} - 13\frac{1}{2}$
4. $9\frac{3}{4} - 6\frac{9}{10}$
5. $21\frac{1}{4} - 18\frac{4}{7}$
6. $7\frac{3}{16} - 2\frac{3}{4}$
7. $11 - 2\frac{2}{5}$
8. $4\frac{3}{10} - 1\frac{12}{25}$
9. $10\frac{3}{8} - 6\frac{7}{12}$
10. $16\frac{2}{15} - 10\frac{2}{3}$

Set H pages 208–211

Multiply.

1. $\frac{1}{7} \times \frac{3}{4}$
2. $\frac{4}{9} \times \frac{4}{9}$
3. $\frac{3}{7} \times \frac{1}{4}$
4. $\frac{7}{12} \times \frac{4}{5} \times \frac{5}{7}$
5. $0 \times \frac{1}{11}$
6. $1\frac{1}{3} \times \frac{9}{10}$
7. $16 \times \frac{3}{4}$
8. $3\frac{9}{15} \times 1\frac{3}{10}$
9. $\frac{9}{23} \times 1$
10. $\frac{16}{25} \times \frac{5}{8}$
11. $9 \times 3\frac{5}{9}$
12. $\frac{4}{5} \times \frac{3}{4} \times \frac{5}{6}$
13. $3\frac{2}{7} \times 3\frac{4}{5}$
14. $8\frac{1}{8} \times 5\frac{1}{10}$
15. $\left(1\frac{7}{8}\right)\left(7\frac{1}{9}\right)$
16. $\left(6\frac{2}{3}\right)\left(6\frac{2}{3}\right)$

Set I pages 214–217

Divide.

1. $6 \div \frac{2}{3}$
2. $9 \div \frac{9}{13}$
3. $\frac{5}{8} \div \frac{1}{4}$
4. $\frac{4}{7} \div \frac{4}{7}$
5. $4\frac{3}{8} \div 2$
6. $10 \div 1\frac{1}{4}$
7. $\frac{5}{6} \div 3$
8. $5\frac{3}{5} \div 2\frac{4}{5}$
9. $1\frac{5}{7} \div 1\frac{11}{12}$
10. $17 \div 2\frac{3}{7}$

Set J pages 218–219

Solve each equation.

1. $\frac{4}{7}a = 28$
2. $12 = \frac{4}{5}t$
3. $18s = \frac{3}{10}$
4. $\frac{1}{4} = \frac{7}{8}x$
5. $\frac{6}{7}b = 24$
6. $\frac{8}{17} = 4k$
7. $9\frac{2}{3}d = 29$
8. $7\frac{3}{5} = \frac{2}{5}m$
9. $\frac{3}{5}a = 30$
10. $\frac{7}{12} = 14c$
11. $\frac{3}{8} = \frac{3}{4}x$
12. $3\frac{3}{8} = 3s$

Enrichment

Harmonic Sequences

Sylvia designs musical instruments. She cuts musical strings of the same thickness into different lengths so that the strings produce different musical tones. Sylvia cuts four strings in the following lengths:

$6\frac{1}{4}$ in. $8\frac{1}{2}$ in. $10\frac{3}{4}$ in. 13 in.

These four numbers form an ***arithmetic sequence*** because the difference between each pair of consecutive terms is the same. In this arithmetic sequence, there is a difference of $2\frac{1}{4}$ in. between any two consecutive terms.

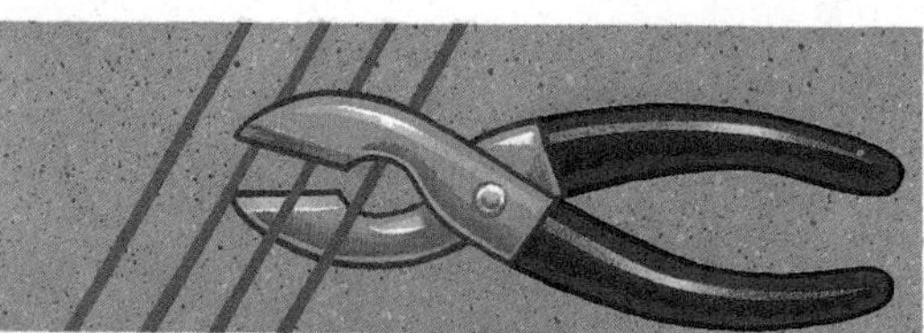

Strings of the above lengths do not produce musical harmony. Sylvia cut four other strings in the following lengths;

$6\frac{1}{4}$ in. $8\frac{1}{3}$ in. $12\frac{1}{2}$ in. 25 in.

These strings do produce musical harmony. These four numbers form a ***harmonic sequence***. The reciprocals of the terms in a harmonic sequence form an arithmetic sequence. To find the reciprocals of these four numbers, first write the mixed numbers as improper fractions.

$\frac{25}{4}$ $\frac{25}{3}$ $\frac{25}{2}$ $\frac{25}{1}$

Then find the reciprocals.

$\frac{4}{25}$ $\frac{3}{25}$ $\frac{2}{25}$ $\frac{1}{25}$

The reciprocals form an arithmetic sequence, since there is a difference of $\frac{1}{25}$ between any two consecutive terms.

Determine if each of the following sequences is an arithmetic sequence, a harmonic sequence, or neither.

1. 1 2 3 4

2. $\frac{1}{2}$ $\frac{1}{4}$ $\frac{1}{6}$ $\frac{1}{8}$

3. 1 2 3 5

4. $4\frac{5}{8}$ $4\frac{7}{8}$ $5\frac{1}{8}$ $5\frac{3}{8}$

5. $\frac{2}{25}$ $\frac{2}{17}$ $\frac{2}{9}$ 2

6. $\frac{2}{3}$ $\frac{8}{9}$ $1\frac{1}{3}$ $2\frac{2}{3}$

7. $\frac{3}{40}$ $\frac{3}{20}$ $\frac{3}{10}$ $\frac{3}{5}$

8. $\frac{3}{40}$ $\frac{1}{10}$ $\frac{3}{20}$ $\frac{3}{10}$

9. $\frac{5}{8}$ $1\frac{3}{8}$ $2\frac{1}{8}$ $2\frac{7}{8}$

10. $\frac{3}{7}$ $\frac{3}{4}$ $\frac{3}{2}$ 3

11. $2\frac{1}{2}$ $3\frac{1}{6}$ $3\frac{5}{6}$ $4\frac{1}{2}$

12. $\frac{5}{6}$ 1 $1\frac{1}{4}$ $1\frac{2}{3}$

Chapter 6 Review/Test

Is each fraction in lowest terms? Write *yes* or *no*. If a fraction is not in lowest terms, write it that way.

1. $\frac{7}{8}$ **2.** $\frac{8}{10}$

Write each fraction as a whole number or mixed number.

3. $\frac{24}{8}$ **4.** $\frac{19}{10}$

Write each mixed number as a fraction.

5. $2\frac{4}{5}$ **6.** $9\frac{1}{2}$

7. List from least to greatest.

$1\frac{2}{3}, 1\frac{3}{4}, \frac{19}{12}$

8. Choose the *best* estimate for the following sum by comparing each fraction to $\frac{1}{2}$.

$$\frac{1}{4} + \frac{1}{3}$$

a. greater than 1
b. less than 1
c. greater than the larger fraction

Add or subtract.

9. $2\frac{1}{8} + 4\frac{5}{8}$ **10.** $10\frac{1}{2} - 6\frac{3}{4}$

11. $\frac{5}{6} + \frac{1}{2}$ **12.** $5\frac{3}{4} - 2\frac{5}{8}$

Multiply or divide.

13. $\frac{2}{3} \times \frac{1}{2}$ **14.** $2\frac{4}{5} \times 1\frac{3}{8}$

15. $15 \div \frac{2}{3}$ **16.** $2\frac{1}{2} \div \frac{1}{8}$

17. Beth is $67\frac{3}{4}$ inches tall. Amy is $63\frac{5}{8}$ inches tall. How much taller is Beth than Amy?

18. Write an equation. Then solve the problem.

Tony bought a bookshelf for his new encyclopedia. Each of the volumes is $11\frac{1}{4}$ inches tall. The shelves are $11\frac{7}{8}$ inches apart. How much space will there be above each volume?

19. Gregg sold $\frac{1}{4}$ of his quota of tickets on the first day. After that he could sell only 10 more tickets, so he missed his quota by 5 tickets. What was his quota?

Solve each equation.

20. $\frac{2}{3}t = 10$ **21.** $\frac{1}{3}x = \frac{7}{8}$

22. Write the next three terms of

$6\frac{2}{3}, 3\frac{1}{3}, 1\frac{2}{3}, \ldots$

23. Write About Math Which of the numbers in this problem are needed to solve the problem? Explain your answer.

Zania has three slabs of rock to build a short path. Each slab is $2\frac{2}{3}$ feet by $3\frac{1}{4}$ feet. If she leaves $\frac{1}{2}$ foot between each slab, what is the longest path she can make?

Measurement 7

Did You Know: The average person walks 70,000 miles in a lifetime. When walking, a person's foot hits the ground about 1,000 times in each mile.

Number-Sense Project

Estimate
About how many miles do you think you walk each day?

Gather Data
Keep a record of how many miles you walk each day for a week.

Analyze and Report
Use your data to find the average number of miles you walk per day. At this rate, how many miles would you walk per year? in a lifetime of 70 years?

Equal Customary Units of Length, Area, and Volume

Build Understanding

Ancient Egyptians, Greeks, and Romans used units of measure based on the human body. The ***cubit*** is the distance from the tip of the middle finger to the elbow. It was the basic unit of measure used to build the pyramids of Egypt. The ***foot*** was the length of an adult foot, and the ***yard*** was the length from the chin to the fingertips of an outstretched arm.

This wall painting from 1500 B.C. shows Egyptian workers measuring land using a 12-cubit rope.

As time went on, the use of these and other units of measure spread throughout Europe, Africa, and the rest of the world. Some units were finally standardized only a few centuries ago. Today, the customary system of measurement used in the United States includes the ***mile***, the ***yard***, the ***foot***, and the ***inch***.

Length	
12 inches = 1 foot	5,280 feet = 1 mile
3 feet = 1 yard	1,760 yards = 1 mile

A. Express 100 inches as feet and inches.

100 ÷ 12 = 8 R4

100 in. = 8 ft 4 in.

There are 12 inches in 1 foot. Since a foot is longer than an inch, there will be *fewer than* 100 feet, so *divide* 100 by 12.

B. Change 120 yards to feet.

3 × 120 = 360

120 yards = 360 feet

There are 3 feet in 1 yard. Since feet are shorter than yards, there will be *more than* 120 feet, so *multiply* 120 by 3.

C. To measure length, see how many units fit in the given length. To measure area, see how many *square* units fit in the given area.

How many square feet are in a square yard?

A square yard measures 3 feet on each side.

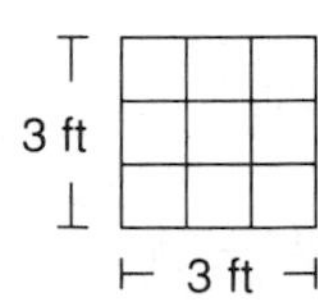

3 × 3 = 9

1 sq yd = 9 sq ft

Area
144 square inches (sq in.) = 1 square foot (sq ft)
9 sq ft = 1 sq yd
43,560 sq ft = 1 acre
640 acres = 1 sq mi

D. Give low and high estimates of the area of this leaf print (not counting the stem). Then give a reasonable estimate of the area.

In the print, 13 squares are entirely shaded and 35 squares are partially or entirely shaded. A reasonable estimate is the average of these low and high estimates.

$\frac{13 + 35}{2} = \frac{48}{2} = 24$

The print is about 24 square units.

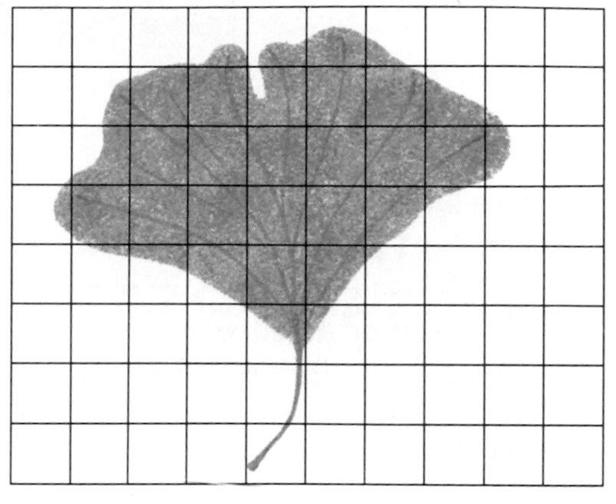

This is a print of a leaf from a ginkgo tree. The ginkgo tree is native to China and Japan.

E. A truck can haul 9.4 cubic yards of soil. How many cubic feet can it haul?

Since a cubic foot is a smaller unit, multiply the number of cubic yards by 27.

27 × 9.4 = 253.8

The truck can carry 253.8 cu ft of soil.

Volume
1,728 cubic inches (cu in.) = 1 cubic foot (cu ft)
27 cu ft = 1 cubic yard (cu yd)

■ **Talk About Math** Explain why you think it was necessary to standardize units of measure based on the human body. What problems might be created if the units were not standardized?

Check Understanding

For another example, see Set A, pages 258–259.

Tell whether you would multiply or divide to change

1. inches to yards.

2. yards to feet.

3. miles to yards.

4. square feet to square yards.

5. cubic feet to cubic inches.

Find each missing number.

6. 120 ft = ▒ yd

7. $\frac{1}{2}$ mi = ▒ yd

8. 100 ft = ▒ yd ▒ ft

9. What customary unit would you use to measure the length of your classroom?

10. Estimate and then measure the length and width of your classroom.

11. How many cubic feet are in a cubic yard?

12. What customary unit would you use to describe how much carpeting is needed to cover a living room floor?

Practice

For More Practice, see Set A, pages 260–261.

Choose the best measure.

13. The length of a book
1 ft 1 sq ft 1 yd

14. The width of a house
40 ft 40 yd 40 sq ft

15. The area of a bedroom
120 sq ft 120 sq yd 120 ft

16. The volume of a lunch box
56 cu in. 366 cu in. 1 cu ft

Find each missing number. Use the tables on pages 232–233.

17. 7.5 ft = ▒ in.

18. 2.5 mi = ▒ yd

19. 15 yd = ▒ ft

20. 80 in. = ▒ ft ▒ in.

21. 936 sq in. = ▒ sq ft

22. 54 sq ft = ▒ sq yd

23. 2,592 cu in. = ▒ cu ft

24. 9.2 cu yd = ▒ cu ft

25. 1,664 acres = ▒ sq mi

Estimation Using a ruler, estimate the length.

26. Find a low estimate for the length of this curve by measuring the segments inside the curve.

27. Find a high estimate for the length of this curve by measuring the segments outside the curve.

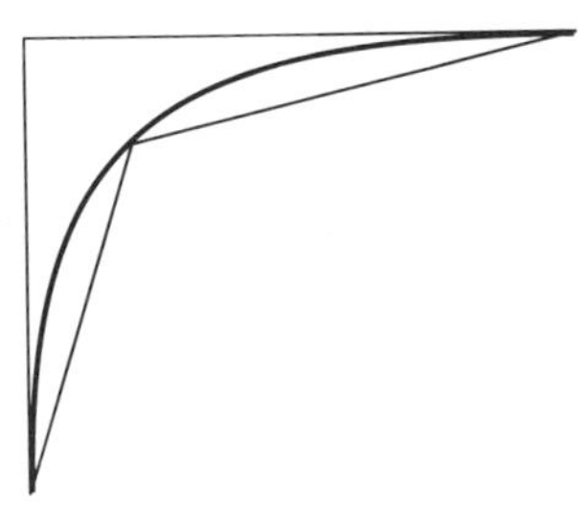

Find the area.

28.

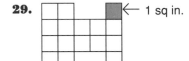

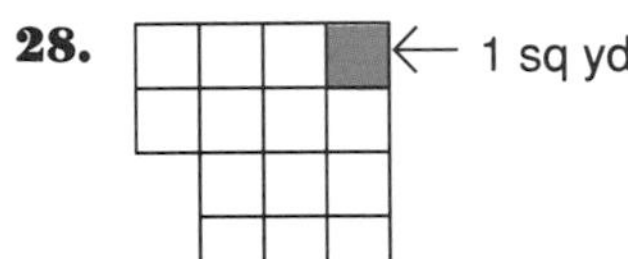

29. ← 1 sq in.

30.

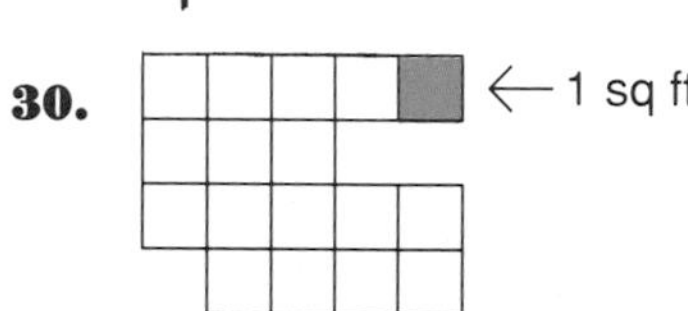

Estimation Estimate the area of each figure by averaging a low estimate and a high estimate. Each square represents 1 square inch.

31.

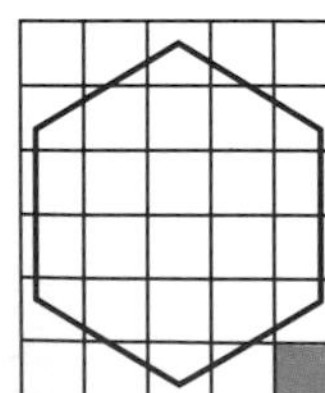

32.

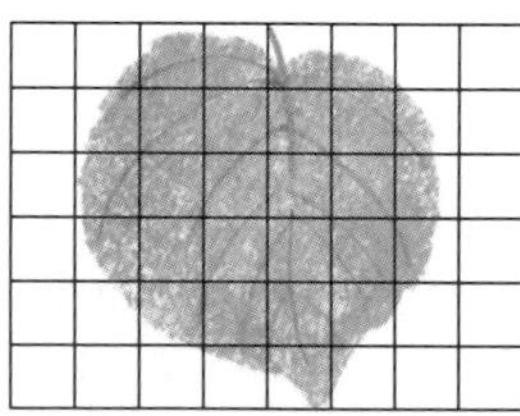

The Italian alder tree is native to Italy.

33.

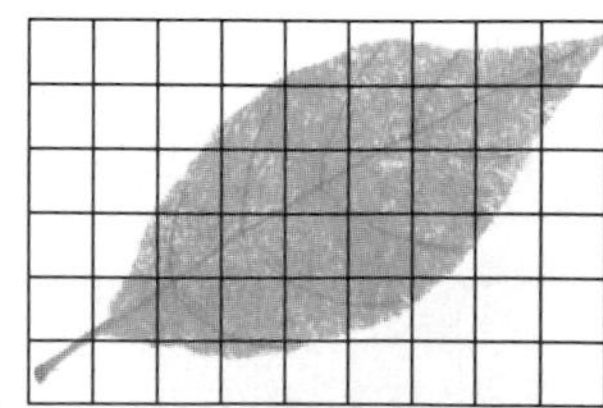

The Portugal laurel tree is native to Portugal and Spain.

Find the volume. Each cube represents 1 cubic inch.

34.

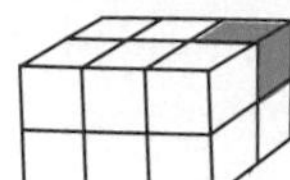

35.

36.

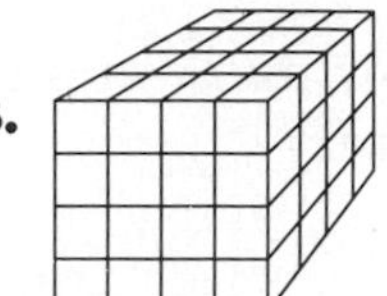

Problem Solving

Number Sense Is it better to underestimate or overestimate the size of each item described? Explain why.

The umbrella sedge, a popular houseplant, is native to the swamps of Africa.

37. The height of a houseplant that will fit on a bookshelf

38. The length of a table needed for a microcomputer

39. The volume of a container needed to hold a pile of sand

Solve each problem. **Remember** to label the units in your answer.

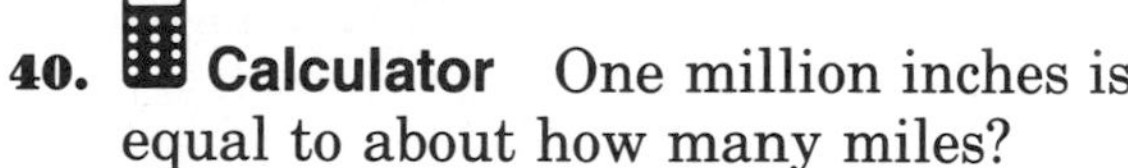

40. **Calculator** One million inches is equal to about how many miles?

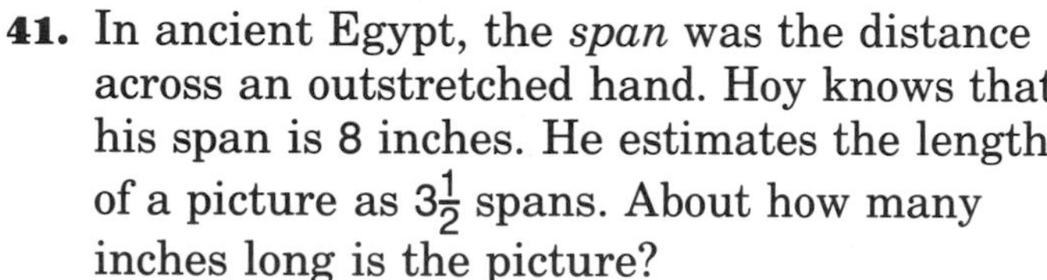

41. In ancient Egypt, the *span* was the distance across an outstretched hand. Hoy knows that his span is 8 inches. He estimates the length of a picture as $3\frac{1}{2}$ spans. About how many inches long is the picture?

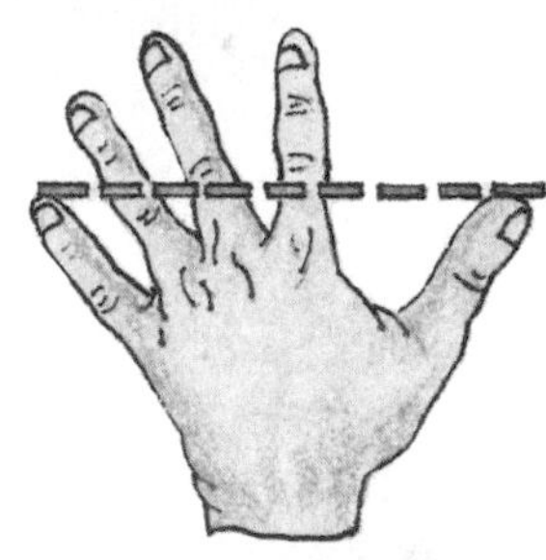

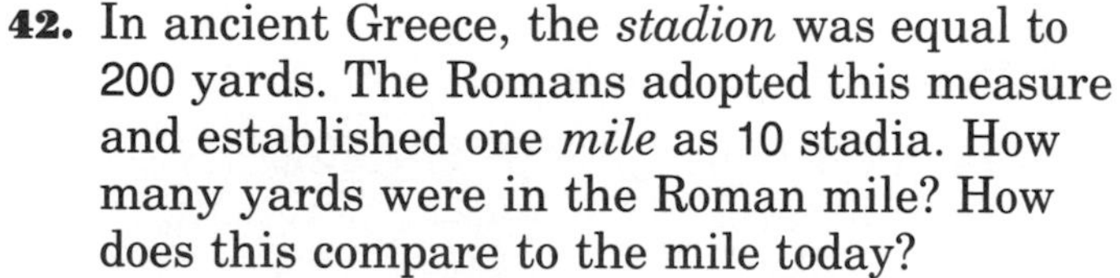

42. In ancient Greece, the *stadion* was equal to 200 yards. The Romans adopted this measure and established one *mile* as 10 stadia. How many yards were in the Roman mile? How does this compare to the mile today?

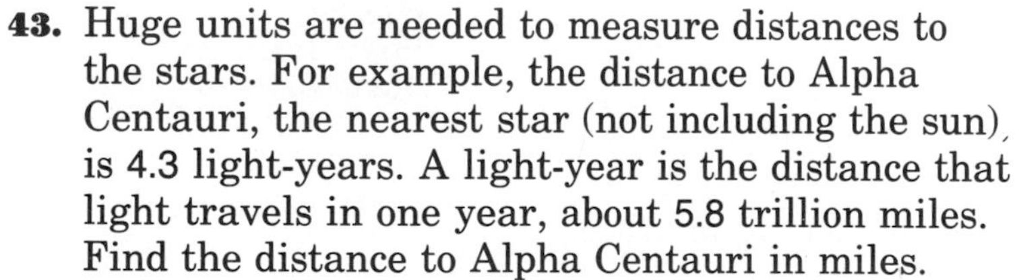

43. Huge units are needed to measure distances to the stars. For example, the distance to Alpha Centauri, the nearest star (not including the sun), is 4.3 light-years. A light-year is the distance that light travels in one year, about 5.8 trillion miles. Find the distance to Alpha Centauri in miles.

TIPS FOR PROBLEM SOLVERS
Be flexible. If you get stuck, try another idea.

Skills Review pages 196–199

Add.

1. $\frac{3}{8} + \frac{1}{4}$ **2.** $5\frac{1}{4} + 3\frac{1}{3}$ **3.** $156\frac{7}{8} + 17\frac{3}{10}$ **4.** $2\frac{4}{9} + 3\frac{1}{3}$ **5.** $6\frac{3}{7} + 2\frac{2}{3}$

Equal Customary Units of Weight and Capacity

Build Understanding

A. A sign on a bridge lists a load limit of 4 tons. Can a truck with a loaded weight of 12,500 pounds safely cross the bridge?

4 T = ▒ lb

4 × 2,000 = 8,000

4 T = 8,000 lb

There are 2,000 pounds in 1 ton. Since a pound is a smaller unit than a ton, there will be more than 4 pounds, so multiply 4 by 2,000.

The truck cannot cross the bridge safely.

Weight
16 ounces (oz) = 1 pound (lb) 2,000 lb = 1 ton (T)

Capacity
8 fluid ounces (fl oz) = 1 cup (c) 2 c = 1 pint (pt) 2 pt = 1 quart (qt) 4 qt = 1 gallon (gal)

B. An automobile has the capacities shown in the table at the right. How many gallons of cooling mixture would you have to buy to fill the cooling system?

13.4 qt = ▒ gal

13.4 ÷ 4 = 3.35

13.4 qt = 3.35 gal

There are 4 quarts in 1 gallon. Since a gallon has a greater capacity than a quart, there will be fewer than 13.4 gallons, so divide 13.4 by 4.

You would have to buy 4 gallons of cooling mixture.

Refill Capacities	
Cooling system	13.4 qt
Oil crankcase	5.0 qt
Fuel tank	19.5 gal
Power steering	2.5 pt
Transmission	12.0 qt

C. 38 fl oz = ▒ c ▒ oz

Divide 38 by 8, because there are 8 fluid ounces in a cup.

38 ÷ 8 = 4 R6

38 oz = 4 c 6 oz

■ **Talk About Math** If a dictionary weighs 4.5 pounds, is its weight in ounces more or less than 4.5? Explain.

Check Understanding

For another example, see Set B, pages 258–259.

Choose the better unit.

1. A person
pound ounce

2. A box of cereal
ounce ton

3. A glass of juice
gallon cup

Find each missing number.

4. 18 gal = ▒▒ qt

5. 12 yd 2 ft = ▒▒ ft

6. 72 oz = ▒▒ lb ▒▒ oz

Practice

For More Practice, see Set B, pages 260–261.

Estimation Choose the best measure.

7. Weight of a marble
1 oz 10 oz 1 lb

8. Weight of a bar of soap
4 oz 4 lb 4 T

9. Capacity of an aquarium
2 c 2 pt 20 qt

10. Capacity of an auto fuel tank
20 c 20 qt 20 gal

Find each missing number. Use paper and pencil or calculator.

11. 9 qt = ▒▒ pt

12. 9 gal = ▒▒ qt

13. 25 pt = ▒▒ qt ▒▒ pt

14. 5 T = ▒▒ lb

15. 144 oz = ▒▒ lb

16. 5,200 lb = ▒▒ T ▒▒ lb

17. 4.25 gal = ▒▒ qt

18. 2 qt = ▒▒ fl oz

19. 8 lb 6 oz = ▒▒ oz

20. 1 qt = ▒▒ fl oz

21. 25 c = ▒▒ qt ▒▒ c

22. 9.8 qt = ▒▒ gal

23. 2.5 T = ▒▒ lb

24. 48 pt = ▒▒ gal

25. 5.6 lb = ▒▒ oz

Problem Solving

Solve each problem. Use the chart on page 236.

26. Find the capacity, in ounces, of the automobile power steering unit.

27. Find the capacity, in quarts, of the automobile fuel tank.

28. Find the capacity, in gallons, of the automobile transmission unit.

29. Find the capacity, in gallons, of the automobile oil crankcase.

30. How many more pints of fluid does the oil crankcase hold than the power steering unit?

31. The fuel tank is $\frac{1}{4}$ full. How many gallons will it take to fill the tank?

Too Much, Too Little Information

Understand
QUESTION
FACTS
KEY IDEA

Plan and Solve
STRATEGY
ANSWER

Look Back
SENSIBLE ANSWER
ALTERNATE APPROACH

Build Understanding

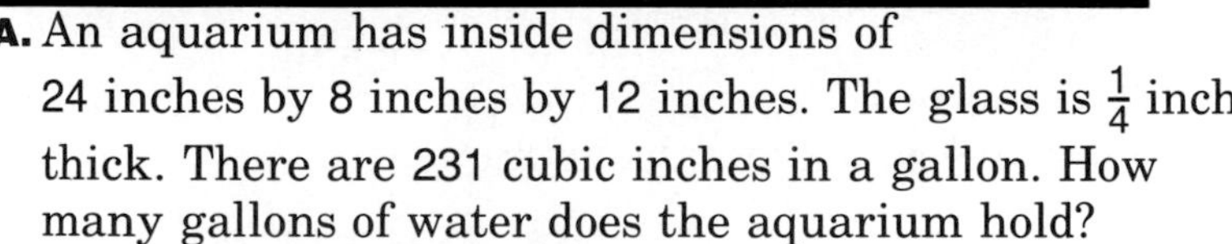

A. An aquarium has inside dimensions of 24 inches by 8 inches by 12 inches. The glass is $\frac{1}{4}$ inch thick. There are 231 cubic inches in a gallon. How many gallons of water does the aquarium hold?

Understand QUESTION How many gallons of water does the aquarium hold?

FACTS Dimensions: 24 in. by 8 in. by 12 in. Glass: $\frac{1}{4}$ in. thick. 1 gallon equals 231 cu in.

KEY IDEA Too much information is given; the thickness of the glass is not needed.

Plan and Solve STRATEGY Find the volume in cubic inches, then change to gallons.

$V = 24 \times 8 \times 12$ or 2,304 cu in.

2,304 = 2,304 $\div$ 231 $\approx$ 9.97 gallons

ANSWER The aquarium holds about 10 gallons.

Look Back SENSIBLE ANSWER It seems reasonable that about 10 one-gallon containers of water could be poured into the aquarium.

B. A larger aquarium is 36 inches by 12 inches. How many gallons of water does it hold?

There is too little information to solve the problem.

Write About Math
What information do you need to solve Example B? Rewrite Example B so that it can be solved.

Check Understanding

In each problem state any information that is *not* needed to solve the problem. Do not solve.

1. The estimated weights of several historic ships are given in the table. How many times as much as the *Santa Maria* did the *Queen Mary* weigh?

Santa Maria	150 tons
Mayflower	180 tons
Titanic	46,000 tons
Queen Mary	81,000 tons

2. A blue whale weighs about 4,000 pounds at birth and gains an average of 200 pounds a day until it reaches 300,000 pounds. How many tons does it weigh at birth?

Practice

If there is not enough information given, write *too little information.* Otherwise, solve each problem. Use information from Check Understanding or the Fact Sheet.

Fact Sheet
1 cu in. of water weighs 0.554 oz
1 cu ft of water weighs 62.4 lb
1 acre = 43,560 sq ft
1 gal = 231 cu in.

3. The *Mayflower* weighed how much more than the *Santa Maria*?

4. In one year, earthworms can turn over about 18 tons of earth in an acre. How many pounds is this?

5. A bald eagle can build a nest 12 feet deep with walls over a foot thick. What is the radius of the nest?

6. About how many pounds does a gallon of water weigh?

Choose a Strategy

Atlantic Adventure A supersonic jet with 70 passengers on board begins its four-hour flight from London to Washington at the same time that a subsonic jet begins its eight-hour flight from Washington to London. There are 267 passengers on the subsonic jet.

7. After how many hours will the two planes pass?

PROBLEM SOLVING
STRATEGIES

- Choose an Operation
- Write an Equation
- Use a Formula
- Make a Table
- Try and Check
- Use Logical Reasoning
- Work Backward
- Find a Pattern

Overview of the Metric System

Build Understanding

In France, Marie measures a flag using a meter stick.

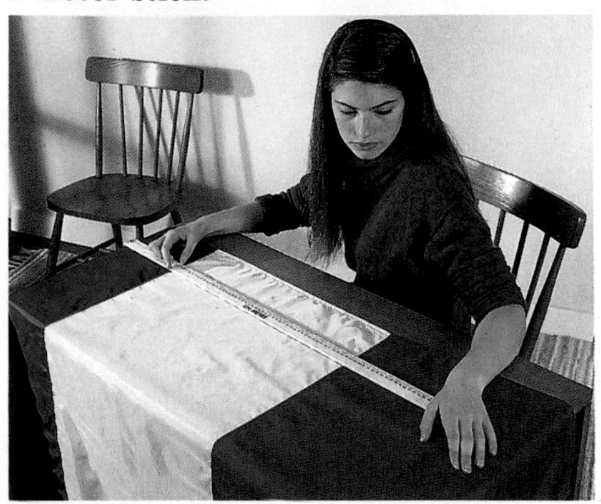

In the United States, Mary measures a flag using a yardstick.

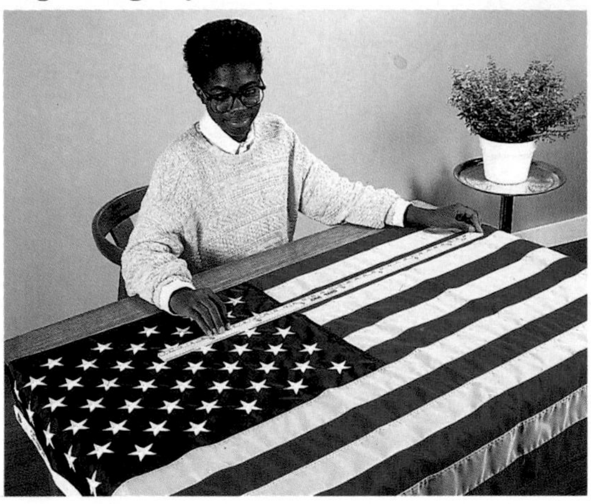

In 1777, the American flag had only 13 stars, one for each state. By 1960, there were 50 stars.

A. Most countries of the world use the system Marie is using, called the ***metric system.*** It is easy to use, like dollars and cents.

The chart at the right shows some examples to help you remember the important units of the metric system.

Unit	Example
1 meter (m)	The width of a typical classroom door
1 centimeter (cm)	The width of the fingernail on your index finger
1 kilometer (km)	The distance a person might walk in about 12 minutes
1 liter (L)	The amount of lemonade in a small pitcher
1 gram (g)	The weight of a paper clip
1 kilogram (kg)	The weight of a large package of hamburger

B. The chart below shows some prefixes that are used with ***meter, gram,*** and ***liter.*** For example, 1 *kilo*liter (kL) is the same capacity as 1,000 liters (L), and 1 *centi*meter is the same as 0.01 meters.

Prefix	kilo-	hecto-	deka-	—	deci-	centi-	milli-
Meaning	1,000	100	10	1	0.1	0.01	0.001

■ **Talk About Math** Vitamins are measured using milligrams. Name some other things in the U.S. that are commonly measured using metric units.

Check Understanding

For another example, see Set C, pages 258–259.

Choose the best measure.

1. Thickness of a coin
cm mm L

2. Weight of a notebook
mg kL kg

3. Length of a river
L km m

Practice

For More Practice, see Set C, pages 260–261.

Give an appropriate unit for measuring each of the following. Complete each unit of measure with either *gram, liter,* or *meter.*

4. Weight of a dash of salt: milli ?

5. Length of a tennis racket: centi ?

6. weight of a horse: kilo ?

7. Width of a finger: milli ?

8. Distance between cities: kilo ?

9. Volume of a pitcher: centi ?

Use the table on page 240 to find each missing number.

10. 1 cm = ▒ m

11. 1 cm = ▒ mm

12. 1 g = ▒ mg

13. 1 mg = ▒ g

14. 1 L = ▒ mL

15. 1 kL = ▒ L

16. 1 mm = ▒ cm

17. 1 hL = ▒ dL

18. 1 mg = ▒ cg

19. 1 cL = ▒ L

20. 1 kg = ▒ g

21. 1 m = ▒ cm

22. 1 mL = ▒ cL

23. 1 m = ▒ mm

24. 1 L = ▒ kL

Write the units of measure in order from smallest to largest.

25. mL kL L

26. g kg mg

27. cm mm km m

Problem Solving

Under certain conditions, one milliliter of water weighs one gram and has a volume of one cubic centimeter. Use this fact to find each measure.

28. The volume of 40 mL of water

29. The weight of 40 mL of water

30. The weight of 3 L of water

31. The volume of 1 kg of water

32. **Critical Thinking** If the metric prefixes were used with the dollar as the unit, what would be another name for $0.01? for $0.10? for $10? for $100? for $1,000?

33. A math book is 0.215 meter wide. What do you think would be a more appropriate measure of its width?

Metric Units of Length, Area, and Volume

Build Understanding

Olga Gonzales, a building contractor, is adding a room to a house. She needs 6 meters of weather stripping around the door. The wall she is painting has an area of 12 square meters. For heating and cooling purposes, the room has a volume of 60 cubic meters.

To change to a smaller unit of length, multiply by 10, 100, 1,000, and so on.

To change to a larger unit of length, multiply by 0.1, 0.01, 0.001, and so on.

× 10 × 10 × 0.1 × 0.1

thousands	hundreds	tens	ones	tenths	hundredths	thousandths
kilometer km	hectometer hm	dekameter dam	meter m	decimeter dm	centimeter cm	millimeter mm

A. A shelf over the fireplace in the room is 15 centimeters wide. Is the shelf wide enough for a flower pot with a base 137 millimeters wide?

Look at the chart. To change centimeters to millimeters, multiply by 10.

15 × 10 = 150

15 cm = 150 mm

The shelf is wide enough.

B. The shelf is 365 centimeters long. What is its length in meters?

Look at the chart. To change centimeters to meters, multiply by 0.01.

Think: cm dm m Multiply by 0.1 twice.

× 0.1 × 0.1→× 0.01

365 × 0.01 = 3.65

365 cm = 3.65 m

Metric units of area are shown in the table below.

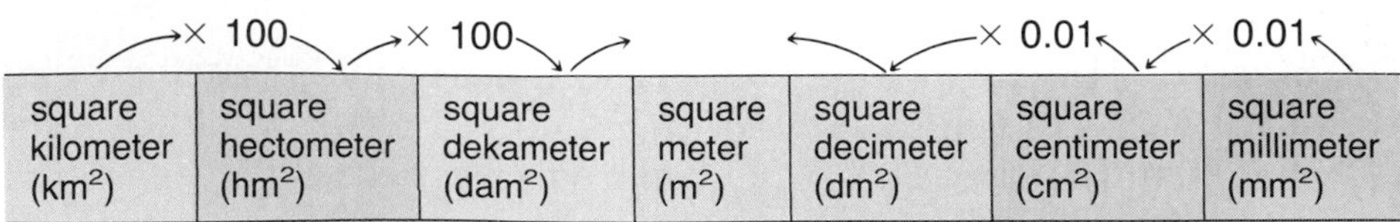
× 100 × 100 × 0.01 × 0.01

square kilometer (km^2)	square hectometer (hm^2)	square dekameter (dam^2)	square meter (m^2)	square decimeter (dm^2)	square centimeter (cm^2)	square millimeter (mm^2)

C. You can also solve Example B by dividing. Dividing by 10 is the same as multiplying by 0.1.

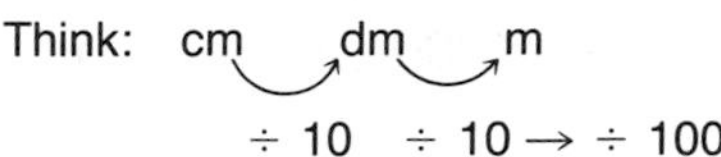

$\div$ 10 $\div$ 10 $\rightarrow$ $\div$ 100

Divide by 100.

365 ÷ 100 = 3.65

365 cm = 3.65 m

D. The area of the shelf is 5,475 cm^2. Find the area in square meters.

Think: cm^2 dm^2 m^2

$\times$ 0.01 $\times$ 0.01 $\rightarrow$ $\times$ 0.0001

Multiply by 0.0001.

5,475 × 0.0001 = 0.5475

5,475 cm^2 = 0.5475 m^2

1 cm^2

Metric units of volume are shown in the table below.

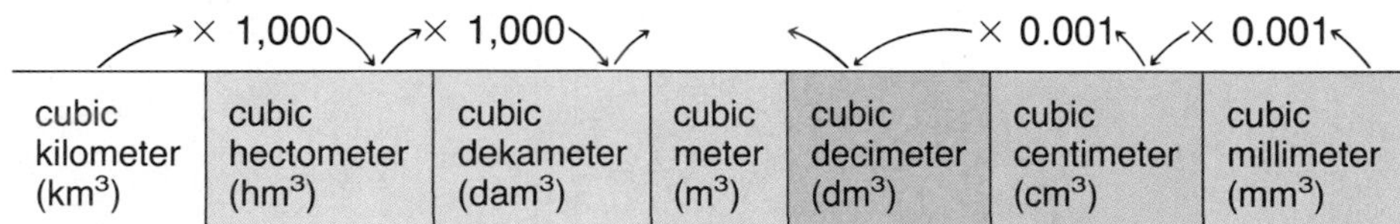

cubic kilometer (km^3)	cubic hectometer (hm^3)	cubic dekameter (dam^3)	cubic meter (m^3)	cubic decimeter (dm^3)	cubic centimeter (cm^3)	cubic millimeter (mm^3)

E. 60 m^3 = ▒ cm^3

Think: m^3 dm^3 cm^3

$\times$ 1,000 $\times$ 1,000 $\rightarrow$ $\times$ 1,000,000

Multiply by 1,000,000.

60 × 1,000,000 = 60,000,000

60 m^3 = 60,000,000 cm^3

F. 60 cm^3 = ▒ dm^3

Multiply by 0.001.

60 × 0.001 = 0.06

or

Divide by 1,000.

60 ÷ 1,000 = 0.06

60 cm^3 = 0.06 dm^3

1 cm^3

Write About Math Show another way to solve Example D.

Check Understanding

For another example, see Set D, pages 258–259.

Choose the best unit of measure.

1. Length of a room
m m^2 m^3

2. Your height
mm m km

3. Area of a book cover
cm^2 cm cm^3

4. Area of your state
km^2 cm^2 m^2

5. Volume of a water storage tank
m^3 m^2 m

6. Volume of a moving van
m^3 cm^3 mm^3

Practice

For More Practice, see Set D, pages 260–261.

Find each missing number.

7. 0.25 m = ▦ cm **8.** 7 m = ▦ mm **9.** 3,000 cm^2 = ▦ m^2

10. 892 m^2 = ▦ mm^2 **11.** 7 m^3 = ▦ mm^3 **12.** 6,000,000 m^3 = ▦ km^3

13. ▦ cm = 2,365 mm **14.** 125 dm^2 = ▦ m^2 **15.** ▦ cm^3 = 20 m^3

16. 23 hm^2 = ▦ cm^2 **17.** ▦ dm = 5,450 mm **18.** 140,000 m^3 = ▦ dam^3

19. 33 hm^2 = ▦ m^2 **20.** ▦ mm = 12 dam **21.** ▦ m^3 = 245 hm^3

Find each area.

22.
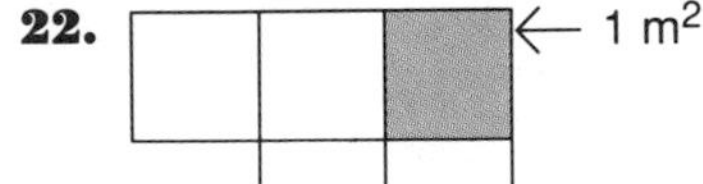

23.
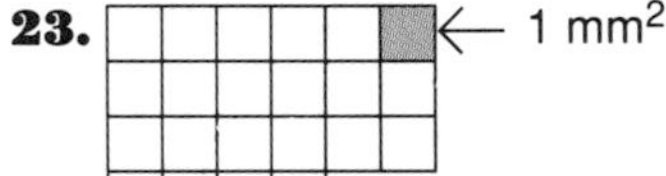

24.
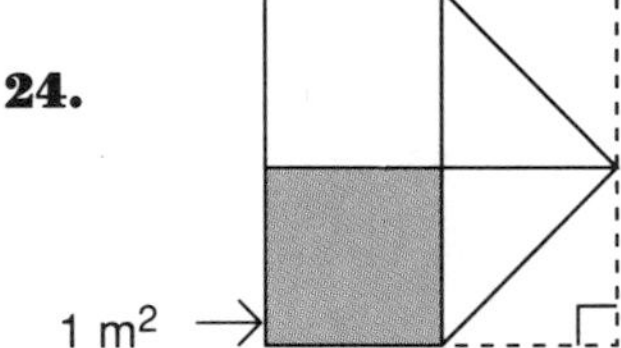

25.
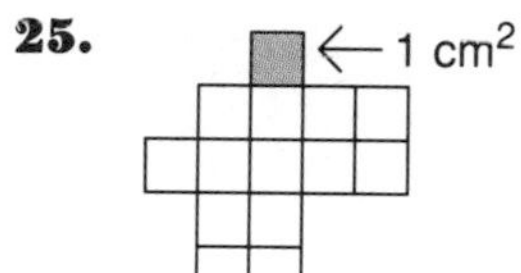

26.
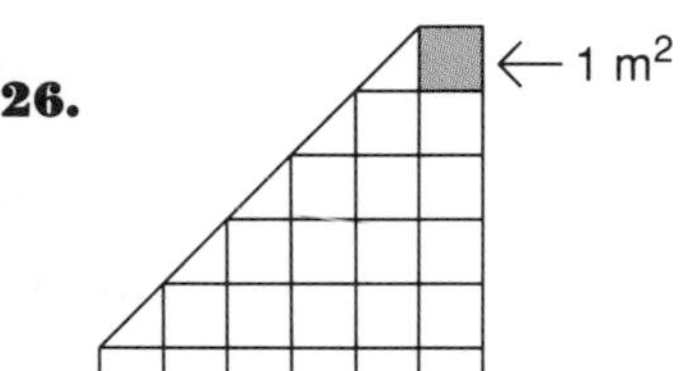

27.
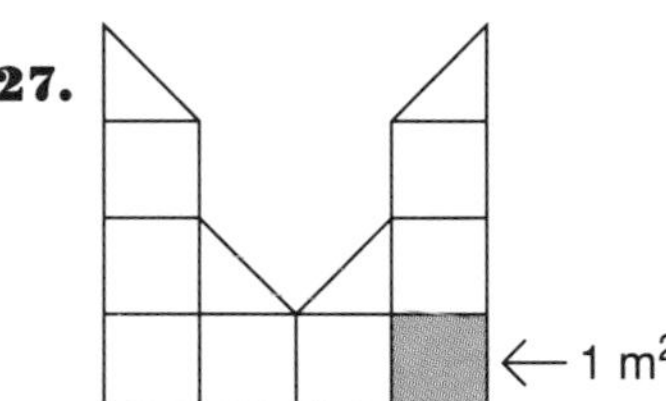

Find each volume.

28.
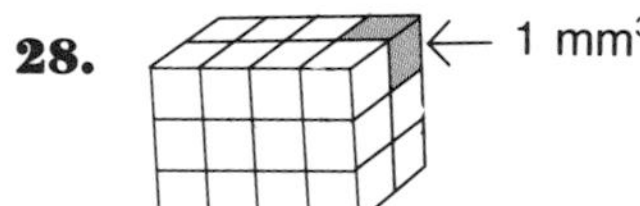

29.
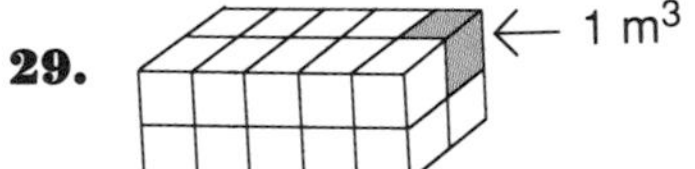

30.
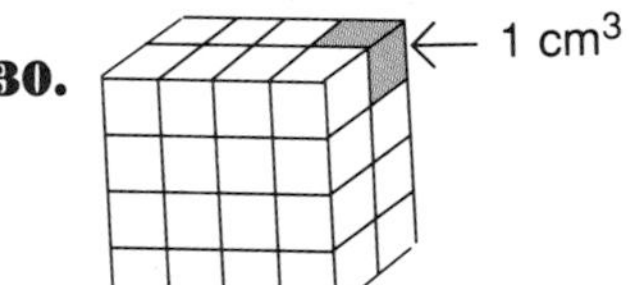

Problem Solving

Solve each problem.

31. Give possible dimensions for the door so that Olga needs 6 meters of weather stripping to go around the sides and top.

32. Give possible dimensions for the wall Olga is painting so that it has an area of 12 square meters.

33. Give possible dimensions for the room so that it has a volume of 60 cubic meters and so that one wall has an area of 12 square meters.

Explore Math

Using 12 centimeter cubes make a figure that is 6 cubes wide, 1 cube deep, and 2 cubes high. Answer the following questions.

34. What is the volume of the solid?

35. Use the cubes to form a figure with a different shape. What is the volume of the new figure?

36. Can other figures be formed using the 12 cubes?

37. Can figures with different shapes have the same volume?

Midchapter Checkup

1. Find the volume.

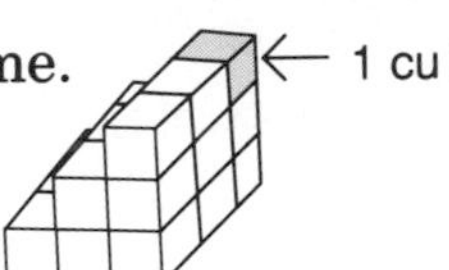

2. Choose the best measure for the volume of a soup can.
50 sq ft   30 cu in.   6 cu in.

Find each measure.

3. A car weighs 1.4 tons. Find the weight in pounds.

4. How many ounces are there in $2\frac{3}{4}$ c milk?

Imagine that a survey was taken of all the seventh graders in your school. Use appropriate metric units to give reasonable averages for the following.

5. Height

6. Weight

7. Water a person would drink on a hot day

8. Distance a teenager could run in 20 minutes

Complete the following.

9. 1 L = ▒ mL

10. 100 g = ▒ kg

11. 1 cm = ▒ mm

12. 1 dL = ▒ L

13. 0.8 m = ▒ cm

14. 1,600 mg = ▒ g

15. Find the area.

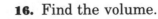

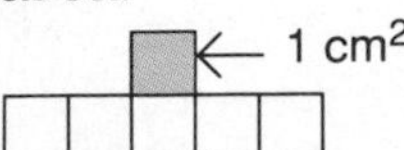

16. Find the volume.

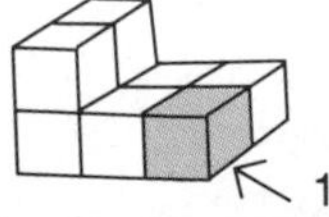

Problem-Solving Workshop

Real-Life Decision Making

You want to buy one or two goldfish and a fish bowl to put them in. Fish bowls are available in four sizes: 1 gallon, $1\frac{1}{2}$ gallon, 2 gallon, and $2\frac{1}{2}$ gallon.

A fish bowl should only be filled to the widest part so the fish can get the most possible oxygen. These fish bowls should only be filled $\frac{2}{3}$ full.

The rule to decide how much water to allow for each fish is as follows:

Minimum number of gallons of water	=	Fish length in inches (not counting the tail)

This fish measures $\frac{3}{4}$ inch (the tail doesn't count). So he needs $\frac{3}{4}$ gallon of water.

1. How much water would you use to fill each fish bowl available?
2. Measure each fish. How much water does each need?
3. Into which fish bowls can you put a $\frac{3}{4}$-inch fish? Give reasons.
4. Into which fish bowls could you put two fish, each measuring $\frac{3}{4}$-inch?
5. Decide which two fish and which fish bowl you would buy.

Problem Solving WORKSHOP

Explore with a Computer

Use the *Spreadsheet Workshop Project* for this activity.

1. Sam is trying to fold a square sheet of cardboard into a box. In the diagram Sam drew, he found that he would need to cut four small squares from the corners of the sheet of cardboard to form the box. How large should he cut these squares so the resulting box will have the greatest possible volume?

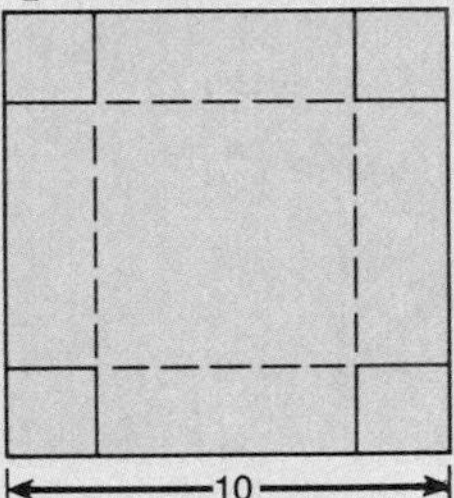

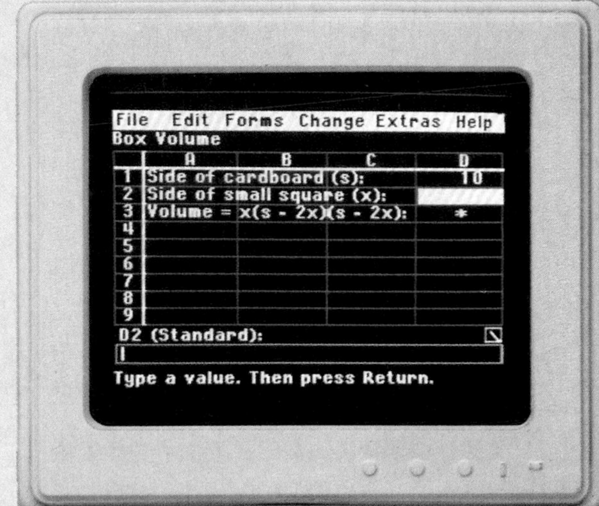

2. At the computer, type the size of the small square to find the greatest possible volume.

Number-Sense Project

Look back at pages 230-231.

About how many times would your feet hit the ground if you walked

1. $\frac{1}{4}$ mile? **2.** 3 miles?

About how far have you walked if your feet have hit the ground

3. 300 times? **4.** 4,000 times?

A jogger's feet hit the ground about 2,000 times per mile. About how many times would your feet hit the ground if you jogged

5. 0.1 mile? **6.** $\frac{3}{4}$ mile?

About how far have you jogged if your feet have hit the ground

7. 10,000 times? **8.** 500 times?

Tell if you have been walking or jogging

9. if your feet have hit the ground 900 times in 0.9 mile.

10. if your feet have hit the ground 1,500 times in $\frac{3}{4}$ miles.

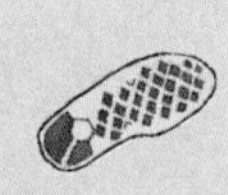
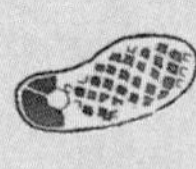
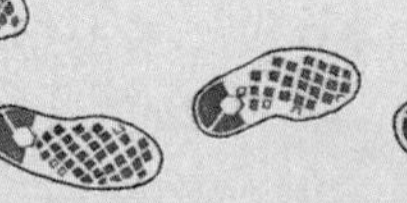
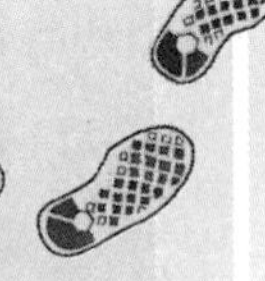

Metric Units of Capacity and Mass

Build Understanding

A. A camper went to fill up a 4-liter water jug. He had to carry the water quite far and wondered how much it weighed.

A liter of water weighs about 1 kilogram. So 4 liters of water would weigh about 4 kilograms.

B. Capacity and mass are also related to volume.

Capacity	Mass	Volume
1 L of water	1 kg of water	1,000 cm^3 of water

C.

The capacity of the eyedropper is about 1 milliliter.

A paper clip weighs about a gram.

To change to a smaller unit, multiply by 10, 100, 1,000, and so on.

To change to a larger unit, multiply by 0.1, 0.01, 0.001, and so on.

→ × 10 → × 10 → (toward smaller units) ← × 0.1 ← × 0.1 ← (toward larger units)

kiloliter (kL)	hectoliter (hL)	dekaliter (daL)	liter (L)	deciliter (dL)	centiliter (cL)	milliliter (mL)
kilogram (kg)	hectogram (hg)	dekagram (dag)	gram (g)	decigram (dg)	centigram (cg)	milligram (mg)

D. A container of oil holds 2,000 mL. Find its capacity in liters.

Think: mL ×0.1 cL ×0.1 dL ×0.1 L

Multiply by 0.001.

2,000 × 0.001 = 2

2,000 mL = 2 L

E. Joyce weighs about 50 kilograms. Find her weight in grams.

Think: kg ×10 hg ×10 dag ×10 g

Multiply by 1,000.

50 × 1,000 = 50,000

50 kg = 50,000 g

■ **Talk About Math** Example B states that 1 L of water has a volume of 1,000 cm^3 and weighs 1 kg. What are the capacity and volume of 1 g of water?

Check Understanding

For another example, see Set E, pages 258–259.

Estimation Choose the more sensible measure of capacity.

1. Pot of soup
700 mL 700 L

2. Glass of juice
250 mL 250 L

3. Spoonful of vanilla
5 mL 500 mL

4. Mental Math Find how many paper clips weigh 2 kilograms.

Practice

For More Practice, see Set E, pages 260–261.

Find each missing number. **Remember** to check your work.

5. 4,325 mg = ▒ g

6. 2.3 L = ▒ mL

7. 7,350 mL = ▒ L

8. 44 kg = ▒ g

9. 4,781 mL = ▒ dL

10. 1.2 kg = ▒ dag

11. 5,600 mg = ▒ dg

12. 0.023 kL = ▒ daL

13. 152 dg = ▒ cg

14. 536 mg = ▒ dg

15. 5.7 hL = ▒ L

16. 23 kg = ▒ mg

17. 6.7 kL = ▒ hL

18. 82.5 cg = ▒ dg

19. 4,090 g = ▒ hg

Mixed Practice Find each missing number.

20. 6 km = ▒ m

21. 32 mg = ▒ g

22. 0.9 hL = ▒ L

23. 674 mm = ▒ m

24. 440 m^2 = ▒ cm^2

25. 2.8 kg = ▒ g

26. 4 km^3 = ▒ m^3

27. 5 L = ▒ kL

28. 78 dm = ▒ cm

Problem Solving

Solve each problem.

29. A swimming pool has a volume of 6,500 cubic meters. What is its capacity in liters?

30. A 120-milliliter bottle of cough syrup contains how many 5-milliliter doses?

31. A box of cereal weighs 570 grams and costs $1.89. What is the cost per serving to the nearest cent if each serving contains 30 grams?

32. If an egg weighs about 50 grams, do a dozen eggs weigh more or less than a kilogram? How many grams more or less?

Give Sensible Answers

Understand
QUESTION
FACTS
KEY IDEA

Plan and Solve
STRATEGY
ANSWER

Look Back
SENSIBLE ANSWER
ALTERNATE APPROACH

Build Understanding

A. Holly heard about a 5K (kilometers) run. One kilometer is about 0.6 mile. She can run one mile in eight minutes. She wondered how long it would take her to run the 5 kilometers.

Understand QUESTION How long would it take Holly to run the 5 kilometers?

FACTS 1 kilometer is about 0.6 mile. Holly can run 1 mile every 8 minutes.

KEY IDEA Since you need to find the total time it takes to run a given distance, change kilometers to miles and use the rate of 8 minutes per mile.

Plan and Solve STRATEGY Change 5 kilometers to miles. Then multiply to find the time.

$5 \times 0.6 = 3$ **1 km $\approx$ 0.6 mi**

5 kilometers $\approx$ 3 miles

$8 \times 3 = 24$

ANSWER Holly can run 3 miles, or 5 kilometers, in about 24 minutes.

Look Back SENSIBLE ANSWER Holly can run 5 miles in 40 minutes. Since a kilometer is a little more than half a mile, it should take her a little more than half the time. So 24 minutes sounds sensible.

B. In the United States both metric and customary units are used. It is helpful to know a few approximate equivalents.

Distance	Capacity	Mass/Weight
1 kilometer $\approx$ 0.6 mile 1 meter $\approx$ 1 yard 1 inch $\approx$ 2.5 centimeters	1 liter $\approx$ 1 quart	1 kilogram $\approx$ 2.2 lb

About how many gallons are 28 liters? One liter is a little more than a quart. There are 4 quarts in a gallon, so divide 28 by 4. Twenty-eight liters are a little more than 7 gallons.

Talk About Math If she can keep up the pace, how long would it take Holly to run 10 kilometers?

Check Understanding

Tell which customary unit you would use to measure each quantity.

1. 150 mg **2.** 16 L

Tell which metric unit you would use to measure each quantity.

3. 3.6 lb **4.** 10 yd

Number Sense Tell which is more.

5. A mile or a kilometer **6.** A kilogram or a pound

Practice

Estimation Estimate each measure in the appropriate customary unit.

7. 12 m **8.** 9 kg **9.** 6 L **10.** 850 g

Estimate each measure in the appropriate metric unit.

11. 3 qt **12.** 5 ft **13.** 6 fl oz **14.** 16 lb

Solve each problem.

15. Holly feels she should never run in an event for more than an hour. What is the maximum number of kilometers she can run?

16. Holly takes a gallon thermos to the event. Juice comes in liter bottles. About how many liters of juice can she pour into the thermos?

Reading ______ Math

Classifying Measurements Classify each of the following units as measures of either *length, time,* or *weight.*

1. second **2.** millimeter **3.** inch **4.** minute

5. ton **6.** pound **7.** gram **8.** mile

9. month **10.** kilometer **11.** year **12.** ounce

Precision in Measurement

Build Understanding

Is an error of one half inch a big error? If you are giving the distance from Los Angeles to Chicago, an error of one half inch doesn't matter. If you are a cabinetmaker, this error could result in lopsided furniture.

If you correctly measure to the nearest inch, then one inch is called the ***precision*** of the measurement, and one half inch is the ***greatest possible error (GPE)***. The precision of a measurement is always the same as the unit used to measure, and the greatest possible error is always half the unit.

A. Little Room for Error
Materials: Math Sketcher
Groups: With a partner

a. Measure the coin's diameter to the nearest centimeter. Then measure the coin to the nearest millimeter. Record your measurements.

b. Which measurement is the more precise?

c. When the coin is measured to the nearest centimeter, what are the precision and the greatest possible error?

d. When it is measured to the nearest millimeter, what are the precision and the GPE?

B. Find 6.35 cm + 4.2 cm + 8 cm. Round the answer to the least precise measurement.

6.35 cm (precise to 0.01 cm)
4.2 cm (precise to 0.1 cm)
+ 8 cm (precise to 1 cm)
18.55 cm → 19 cm

When you add or subtract measurements, the answer is only as precise as the least precise measurement.

Talk About Math If something is correctly measured as 4 inches to the nearest inch, what is the smallest it could be? How much shorter than 4 inches could it be? Explain why.

Check Understanding

For another example, see Set F, pages 258–259.

Tell which measurement is more precise.

1. 3.4 L or 385 mL **2.** 11 yd or 3 ft **3.** 8 g or 8 kg

Which is the greatest possible error?

4. For 13 in.
$\frac{1}{2}$ in. 1 in.

5. For 13 cm
0.5 cm 0.5 mm

6. For $13\frac{1}{2}$ in.
$\frac{1}{2}$ in. $\frac{1}{4}$ in.

Practice

For More Practice, see Set F, pages 260–261.

Give the unit of measure and the greatest possible error.

7. 51 cm **8.** $8\frac{1}{2}$ in. **9.** 5.65 km **10.** $3\frac{1}{4}$ in. **11.** 736 mm **12.** $5\frac{1}{2}$ ft

13. 9.341 m **14.** 16.2 g **15.** 74 L **16.** 3.0 cm **17.** $3\frac{5}{8}$ yd **18.** 0.04 kg

Add. Give the sum to the less precise unit of measure.

19. 4.2 cm + 8 cm **20.** 6.35 cm + 4.2 cm **21.** $4\frac{7}{8}$ in. + $1\frac{3}{4}$ in.

22. 0.6 cm + 7 cm + 8.64 cm **23.** $14\frac{3}{4}$ ft + $22\frac{1}{2}$ ft + 11 ft

Mixed Practice Compute. Round to the less precise unit of measure.

24. $3\frac{1}{8}$ in. + 8 in. **25.** 35 cm + 8.4 cm **26.** 3.6 m − 1.62 m

27. 54.09 km − 19.6 km **28.** 0.89 g + 3.8 g **29.** 4.82 cm − 2.366 cm

30. $8\frac{1}{2}$ in. − $3\frac{3}{4}$ in. **31.** 8.5 L + 1.3 L + 9.44 L **32.** 18.3 kg − 11.57 kg

33. 5 ft − $2\frac{1}{4}$ ft **34.** 22.0 m + 45.89 m **35.** 7.146 mL − 4.03 mL

Problem Solving

Solve each problem.

36. The winning time in the 1992 Olympics men's 400-meter relay race was 37.40 seconds. How much less was this than the 1912 winning time of 42.4 seconds?

37. The winning height in the 1992 Olympic pole vault event was 19 ft $\frac{1}{4}$ in. How much higher was this than the winning height of 10 ft 10 in. in 1896?

38. **Critical Thinking** Fred's 200-meter dash was timed to the nearest tenth at 45.7 seconds. Luis was timed to the nearest hundredth at 45.68 seconds. Was Fred faster? Explain.

Use Data from a Table

Understand
QUESTION
FACTS
KEY IDEA

Plan and Solve
STRATEGY
ANSWER

Look Back
SENSIBLE ANSWER
ALTERNATE APPROACH

Build Understanding

Part of a Pittsburgh flight schedule is shown. How long will Flight 176 to Miami take? How long will Flight 25 to Los Angeles take?

Understand QUESTION What is the elapsed time for each flight?

FACTS Flight 176 leaves at 10:35 A.M. and arrives at 1:15 P.M. Flight 25 leaves at 9:55 A.M. and arrives at 12:02 P.M.

KEY IDEA You can use a number line to represent the 24 hours in a day.

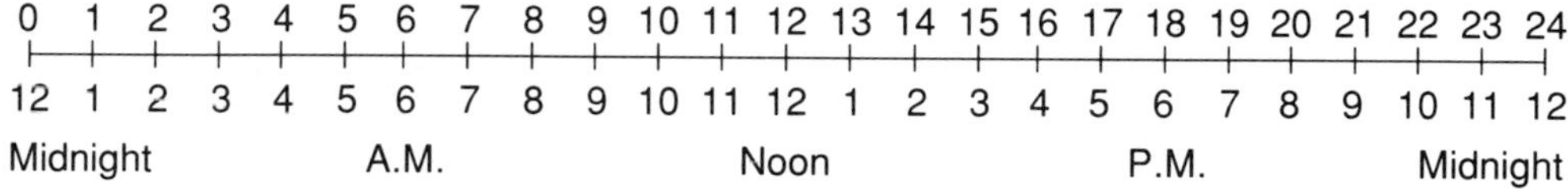

Plan and Solve STRATEGY Change time to 24-hour time and subtract. (Pittsburgh to Miami)

$$\begin{array}{rcrcr} 1{:}15 \text{ P.M.} & = & 13 \text{ h } 15 \text{ min} & = & 12 \text{ h } 75 \text{ min} \\ -10{:}35 \text{ A.M.} & = & -10 \text{ h } 35 \text{ min} & = & -10 \text{ h } 35 \text{ min} \\ \hline & & & & 2 \text{ h } 40 \text{ min} \end{array}$$

Since Los Angeles is in a different time zone, change 12:02 (Pacific time) to 12:02 + 3 h = 15:02 (Eastern time).

$$\begin{array}{rcr} 15 \text{ h } \ 2 \text{ min} & = & 14 \text{ h } 62 \text{ min} \\ -\ 9 \text{ h } 55 \text{ min} & = & -\ 9 \text{ h } 55 \text{ min} \\ \hline & & 5 \text{ h } \ 7 \text{ min} \end{array}$$

ANSWER The trip to Miami takes 2 hr, 40 min. The Los Angeles trip takes 5 hr, 7 min.

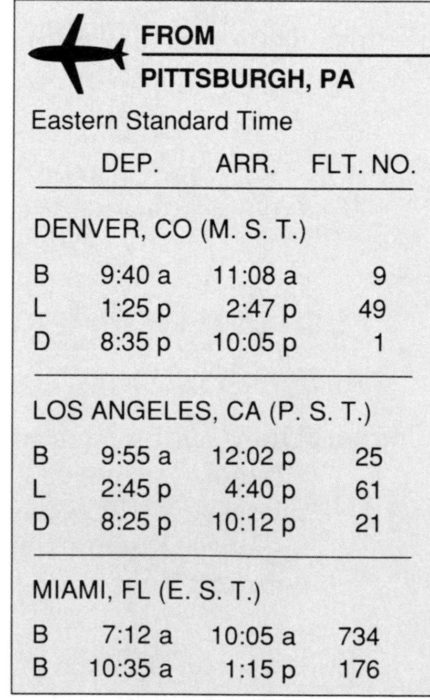

FROM PITTSBURGH, PA

Eastern Standard Time

	DEP.	ARR.	FLT. NO.
DENVER, CO (M. S. T.)			
B	9:40 a	11:08 a	9
L	1:25 p	2:47 p	49
D	8:35 p	10:05 p	1
LOS ANGELES, CA (P. S. T.)			
B	9:55 a	12:02 p	25
L	2:45 p	4:40 p	61
D	8:25 p	10:12 p	21
MIAMI, FL (E. S. T.)			
B	7:12 a	10:05 a	734
B	10:35 a	1:15 p	176

About 1 billion people fly every year.

Look Back ALTERNATE APPROACH Could you answer the second question by changing the departure time to Pacific time and then subtracting the times?

■ **Talk About Math** How could you use mental math to solve Example A? Explain.

Check Understanding

Use the number line on page 254 to write each time as a given hour in the 24-hour day. For example, 1:00 P.M. is the thirteenth hour in the day.

1. 6:15 P.M.

2. 9:30 A.M.

3. Noon

4. 2:30 P.M.

5. 3:35 P.M.

6. 10:42 P.M.

Find the missing numbers.

7. 3 h 15 min = 2 h ▒ min

8. 6 h 5 min = 5 h ▒ min

9. 7 h 75 min = 8 h ▒ min

10. 12 h 85 min = 13 h ▒ min

Practice

Add or subtract. **Remember** to rename minutes as hours in your answer where possible.

11.
```
  4 h 18 min
+8 h 50 min
```

12.
```
  16 h  5 min
 − 4 h 10 min
```

13.
```
  15 h
−12 h 10 min
```

Find the elapsed time.

14. From 3:45 A.M. to 9:15 A.M.

15. From 4:45 A.M. to 1:30 P.M.

16. From 9:05 A.M. to 4:20 P.M.

17. From 11:35 A.M. to 2:35 P.M.

Solve each problem. Use the schedule on page 254.

18. How long will a trip take from Pittsburgh to Denver on Flight 9? (The time difference between the cities is 2 hours.)

19. How long will a trip take from Pittsburgh to Los Angeles on Flight 21?

Solve.

20. Some mortgage schedules require monthly payments for 20 years. With this schedule, how many payments are required?

21. **Critical Thinking** If Valentine's Day is on a Wednesday this year, on what day will it be next year if this year is not a leap year? if this year is a leap year?

Chapter 7 REVIEW

Skills Review

Find each missing number.

1. 3.5 ft = ▩ in.
2. 10 yd = ▩ ft
3. 360 sq in. = ▩ sq ft
4. 162 cu ft = ▩ cu yd
5. 7 qt = ▩ pt
6. 128 oz = ▩ lb
7. 4,500 lb = ▩ T
8. 5 gal = ▩ qt
9. 1 g = ▩ mg
10. 1 hL = ▩ dL
11. 1 mm = ▩ cm
12. 1 mg = ▩ cg
13. 0.1 m = ▩ cm
14. 4 m^3 = ▩ mm^3
15. 25 kg = ▩ g
16. 5,600 mL = ▩ dL
17. 3.5 kg = ▩ dag
18. 6.9 L = ▩ mL

Find each area.

19. 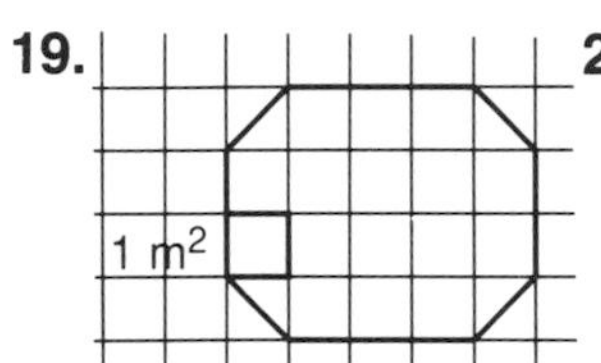

20. 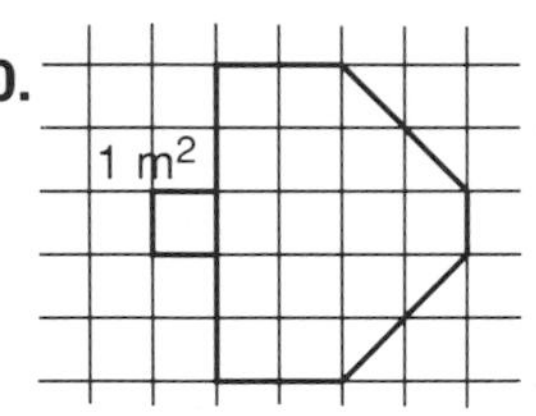

Give the precision of each measurement and the greatest possible error.

21. 79 g
22. 9 ft 5 in.
23. $12\frac{1}{2}$ in.
24. 7.92 km

Add. Give the sum to the less precise unit of measure.

25. 2.4 mL + 8 mL
26. $1\frac{2}{3}$ yd + 7 yd
27. $3\frac{1}{2}$ in. + $2\frac{3}{4}$ in.
28. 41.235 km + 10.2 km

Problem-Solving Review

Solve each problem.

29. One side of a square garden measures 3 ft 4 in. How much fencing is needed to enclose the entire garden?

30. Ginny practices the piano for 40 minutes each day. Write and solve an equation to find the number of hours she practices each week.

31. The price of turkey is $0.89 per pound. To the nearest cent, what is the cost of a turkey that weighs 10.64 lb?

32. A spool of ribbon contains 20 feet. How many $1\frac{1}{2}$-foot pieces of ribbon can be cut from this spool?

33. Mr. O'Brien has fewer than 40 students in his class. If he tries to seat them in equal rows of 4 or 6, two students are left over. If he tries to seat them in rows of 5, one student is left over. How many students are in his class?

34. **Data File** Use the data on pages 264–265. About how much does 1 cubic foot of $1 bills weigh? About how much is 1 cubic foot of $1 bills worth?

35. **Make a Data File** Visit your local supermarket and find the cereal section. List 8 different kinds (such as corn flakes and shredded wheat), the weight (in ounces and in grams), and the price of each kind. Make a table listing the type of cereal, the price, the weight in ounces, and the weight in grams.

Cumulative Skills Review • Chapters 1–7

Compute mentally to find each answer.

1. $9 \times 3 \times 5 \times 2$ **2.** $47 + 32 + 53 + 17$ **3.** $780 - 331$ **4.** 5×398

5. $16{,}000 \div 400$ **6.** $4{,}200 \div 60$ **7.** $480{,}000 \div 800$ **8.** $72{,}000 \div 9{,}000$

9. $5{,}588 \div 100$ **10.** $0.76 \times 1{,}000$ **11.** $1.08 \div 10{,}000$ **12.** $0.009 \times 10{,}000$

Evaluate each expression when $p = 8$.

13. $8 + p$ **14.** $p \div 2$ **15.** $9p$ **16.** $17 - p$

17. $3p - 5$ **18.** $\frac{p}{4} + 1$ **19.** $12 + 5p$ **20.** $50 - (24 \div p)$

Use a compass and straightedge to do each construction.

21. Construct an angle congruent to LMN. Then bisect the angle.

22. Draw any line PT and point R not on PT. Construct the line through point R parallel to PT.

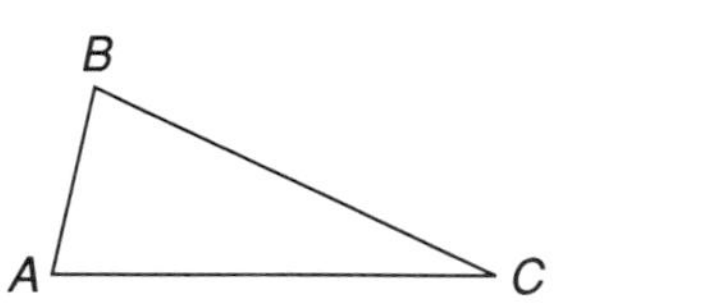

23. Construct a triangle congruent to $\triangle ABC$.

Use exponents to write the prime factorization for each number.

24. 36 **25.** 90 **26.** 200 **27.** 144 **28.** 1,000 **29.** 539

Add or subtract.

30. $\frac{5}{9} + \frac{1}{3}$ **31.** $\frac{7}{8} + \frac{3}{4}$ **32.** $2\frac{4}{5} + 3\frac{1}{2}$ **33.** $\frac{9}{10} - \frac{7}{10}$

34. $\frac{11}{12} - \frac{5}{8}$ **35.** $3\frac{1}{2} - 2\frac{1}{6}$ **36.** $8 - 4\frac{11}{12}$ **37.** $5\frac{1}{4} - 2\frac{1}{2}$

Choose the best measure.

38. Weight of a baseball cap
a. 2 oz **b.** 2 lb **c.** 2 T

39. Height of a basketball hoop
a. 10 in. **b.** 10 ft **c.** 10 yd

Find each volume.

40.

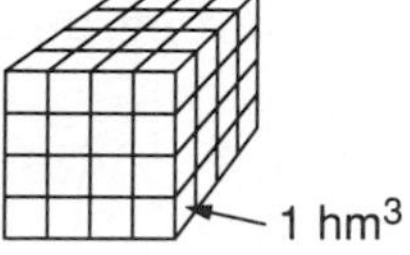

41.

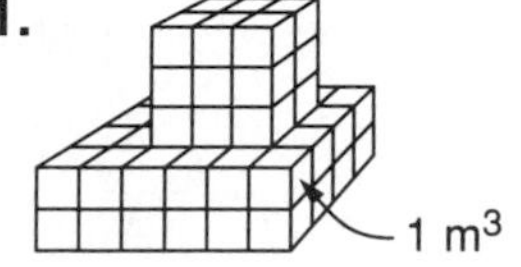

42.

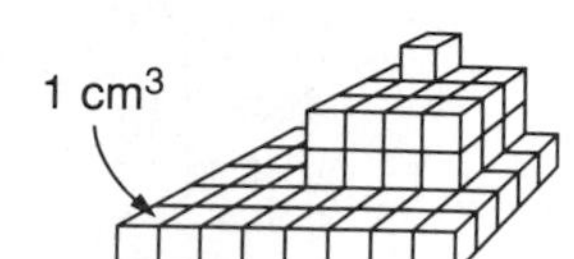

Reteaching

Set A pages 232–235

When finding equal units of measure, first determine whether to multiply or divide. Multiplication increases. Division decreases.

24 ft = ? yd
3 ft = 1 yd Number of yd < number of ft. Number decreases, so divide.

24 ÷ 3 = 8
24 ft = 8 yd

2 mi = ? ft
1 mi = 5,280 ft Number of ft > number of mi. Number increases, so multiply.

2 × 5,280 = 10,560
2 mi = 10,560 ft

Remember, converting from a *smaller unit to a larger unit* of measure results in a *smaller* number. Changing from a *larger unit to a smaller unit* results in a *larger* number. Find each missing number.

1. 108 in. = ▦ ft
2. 21,120 ft = ▦ mi
3. 17.5 yd = ▦ ft
4. 6.2 ft = ▦ in.

Set B pages 236–237

There are $8\frac{1}{2}$ (or 8.5) pints of chicken soup in a cooking pot. To find the number of 1-cup servings, multiply. To find the number of quarts, divide.

2 c = 1 pt (more c; × to increase)
2 × 8.5 = 17
There are 17 cups in the pot.

1 qt = 2 pt (fewer qt; ÷ to decrease)
$8.5 \div 2 = 4.25 = 4\frac{1}{4}$
There are $4\frac{1}{4}$ quarts in the pot.

Remember, 8 fluid ounces and 1 cup are equal measures of capacity. Find each measure.

1. How many ounces are 3 pounds of cheese?
2. How many ounces are 5 cups of tomato sauce?
3. How many cups are 4 ounces of oil?
4. How many pounds are 64 ounces of sausage?

Set C pages 240–241

The chart shows the meanings of some metric prefixes.

Prefix	Meaning
kilo-	1,000
hecto-	100
deka-	10
deci-	$\frac{1}{10}$
centi-	$\frac{1}{100}$
milli-	$\frac{1}{1,000}$

Remember, a paper clip weighs about 1 gram.

Find each measure.

1. Which weight is the appropriate weight of 20 paper clips, 2 decigrams or 2 dekagrams?
2. Which weight is greater than 300 paper clips, 1 kilogram or 2 hectograms?
3. How many milligrams do 4 paper clips weigh?
4. A box of paper clips that weighs 1.75 kg contains how many paper clips?

Set D pages 242–245

To change to a larger unit, divide.
Divide metric units of area by 100.
Divide metric units of volume by 1,000.

Metric Units—Largest to Smallest

km | hm | dam | m | dm | cm | mm

75 dm^2 = ? dam^2
Change dm^2 to m^2: 75 ÷ 100 = 0.75
Change m^2 to dam^2: 0.75 ÷ 100 = 0.0075
75 dm^2 = 0.0075 dam^2

Remember, dividing by 100 or 1,000 is the same as multiplying by 0.01 or 0.001. Find each missing number.

1. 113 mm^2 = ▒ cm^2
2. 46 m^2 = ▒ hm^2
3. 46 m^3 = ▒ dam^3
4. 9 dam^3 = ▒ km^3
5. 64 cm^2 = ▒ m^2

Set E pages 248–249

To change to a smaller unit, multiply.
Multiply metric units of capacity or mass by 10.

5 liters = ? centiliters
Change liters to deciliters:
5 × 10 = 50
Change deciliters to centiliters:
50 × 10 = 500
5 liters = 500 centiliters

Remember, you can use the meanings of metric prefixes to determine which metric unit is smaller.

Use the list in Set C to check size order of metric units. Find each missing number.

1. 16.5 liters = ▒ milliliters
2. 8 dekagrams = ▒ grams
3. 25 kilograms = ▒ decigrams
4. 2,950 milliliters = ▒ liters
5. 18,650 grams = ▒ kilograms

Set F pages 252–253

To determine the precision of a measurement, identify the smallest unit used.

17.25 kilograms
The smallest unit is 0.01 kilogram.
The precision of measurement is 0.01 kilogram.

$8\frac{2}{3}$ ft
The smallest unit is $\frac{1}{3}$ ft.
The precision of measurement is $\frac{1}{3}$ ft.

Remember, the greatest possible error (GPE) is always half the precision of a measurement. Give the greatest possible error.

	Measurement	GPE
1.	1.7 mm	▒
2.	263 m	▒
3.	84 ft	▒
4.	9 mi	▒
5.	8.1 cm	▒
6.	$5\frac{1}{3}$ ft	▒

More Practice

Set A pages 232–235

Choose the best measure.

1. The length of a driveway
a. 50 in. **b.** 50 mi **c.** 50 ft

2. The width of a garden
a. 20 sq ft **b.** 20 ft **c.** 200 yd

3. The area of a TV screen
a. 300 sq in. **b.** 300 sq ft **c.** 30 sq yd

4. The volume of a cereal box
a. 20 cu in. **b.** 200 cu in. **c.** 200 cu ft

Find each missing number. Use the tables on page 232.

5. 34 ft = ▒ yd ▒ ft

6. 10 ft = ▒ in.

7. 100 yd = ▒ ft

8. 110 in. = ▒ ft ▒ in.

9. 82 sq ft = ▒ sq in.

10. $7\frac{1}{3}$ sq yd = ▒ sq ft

11. Find the area.

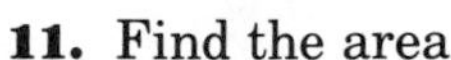

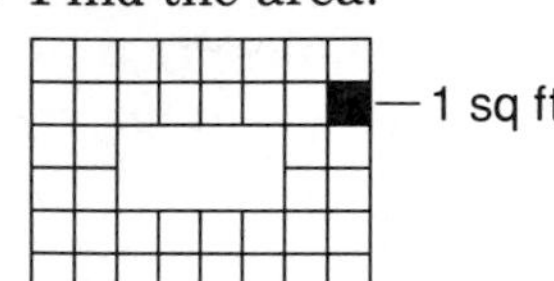

12. Find the volume.

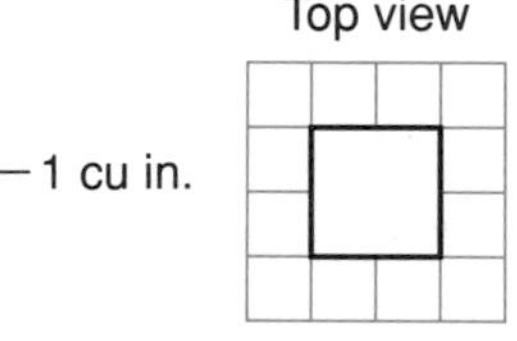

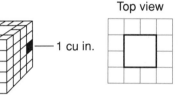

Set B pages 236–237

Choose the best measure.

1. Weight of a rose
a. $\frac{1}{2}$ oz **b.** 20 oz **c.** $\frac{1}{2}$ lb

2. Capacity of a sprinkling can
a. 2 fl oz **b.** 2 gal **c.** 2 c

Find each missing number.

3. 6 pt = ▒ qt

4. 14 qt = ▒ gal ▒ qt

5. 10 lb = ▒ oz

6. 20 c = ▒ qt

7. 96 fl oz = ▒ qt

8. 92 oz = ▒ lb ▒ oz

Set C pages 240–241

Choose the best measure.

1. Weight of an apple
a. kg **b.** kL **c.** g

2. Distance between two houses
a. m **b.** km **c.** mm

Complete each unit of measure with either *gram, liter,* or *meter.*

3. Thickness of a magazine: centi___?___

4. Weight of a book: kilo___?___

5. Height of a drinking glass: deci___?___

6. Volume of a thimble: milli___?___

Use the table on page 240 to find each missing number.

7. 1 m = ▒ cm

8. 10 mm = ▒ cm

9. 1 kg = ▒ g

10. 1,000 mg = ▒ g

11. 500 mL = ▒ L

12. 100 m = ▒ hm

Set D pages 242–245

Find each missing number.

1. 10 cm ▒ m **2.** 142 mm = ▒ m **3.** 500 mm^2 = ▒ cm^2

4. 20 m^2 = ▒ cm^2 **5.** 16,000 mm^3 = ▒ cm^3 **6.** 500 m^2 = ▒ dm^2

Find each area.

7.

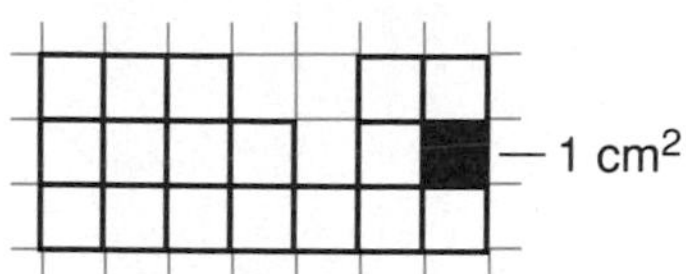

8.

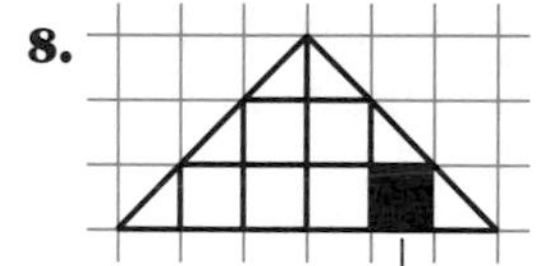

9.

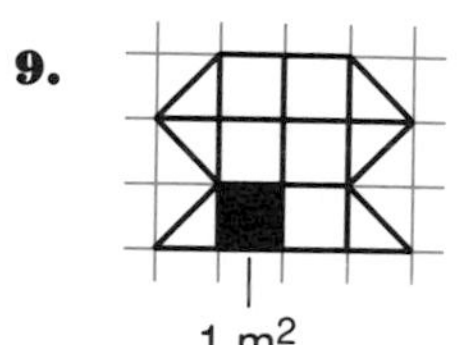

Find each volume.

10.

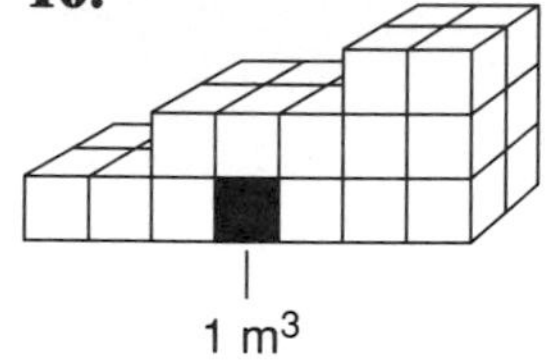

11.

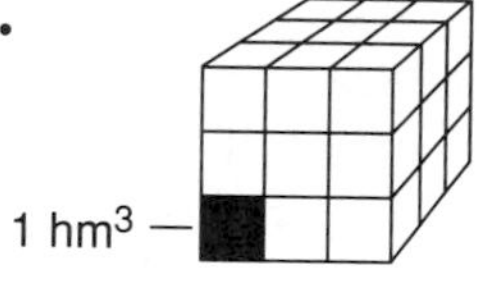

12.

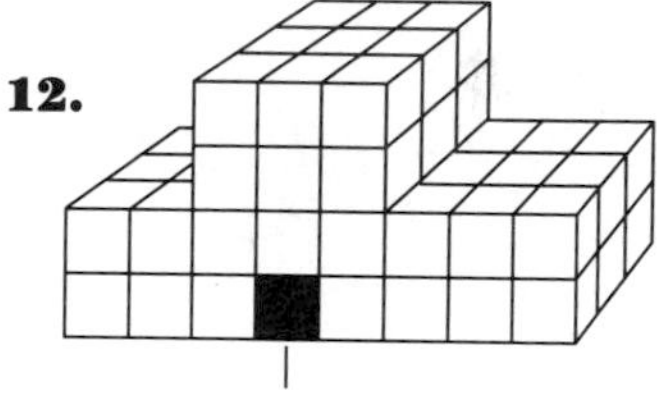

Set E pages 248–249

Find each missing number.

1. 7 kg = ▒ g **2.** 24 g = ▒ mg **3.** 0.17 L = ▒ mL

4. 243 hL = ▒ L **5.** 76 dL = ▒ L **6.** 11,590 mg = ▒ kg

7. 62 mL = ▒ L **8.** 0.04 g = ▒ cg **9.** 3.5 hg = ▒ dg

10. 85 g = ▒ mg **11.** 210 mL = ▒ L **12.** 3.5 kg ▒ g

13. 10,500 mg = ▒ kg **14.** 2.6 L = ▒ mL **15.** 16,000 mg = ▒ g

Set F pages 252–253

Give the precision of the measurement and the greatest possible error.

1. 16 ft **2.** 4.8 m **3.** 341 g **4.** $11\frac{5}{8}$ in.

5. 3 L **6.** 14 cm **7.** 10 yd **8.** 5.9 kg

Add. Give the sum to the less precise unit of measure.

9. 7.16 g + 2.4 g **10.** 8 in. + $4\frac{1}{2}$ in. **11.** 22.6 m + 13.08 m

12. 0.3 mm + 1.37 mm **13.** 5 L + 7.3 L **14.** 11 in. + $9\frac{7}{8}$ in.

Enrichment

Relative Error

All measurements are subject to error; none is truly exact. One way to define and calculate the accuracy of a measurement is to find its ***relative error***.

Ms. Johanssen said her property is 200 meters by 2,000 meters. What is the relative error of each of these two measurements? Which is the more accurate measurement?

Recall that the greatest possible error (GPE) for any measurement is $\frac{1}{2}$ the unit being used. The relative error of a measurement is the ratio of the GPE to the measurement.

The GPE in each of Ms. Johanssen's measurements is 0.5 meter. Divide to find the relative error of the measurements. Write each quotient as a percent.

0.5 [÷] 200 [=]	0.5 [÷] 2000 [=]
0.0025 = 0.25%	0.00025 = 0.025%
The relative error is 0.25%.	The relative error is 0.025%.

The smaller the relative error, the more accurate the measurement. The measurement of 2,000 meters is more accurate.

Use paper and pencil or a calculator to find the relative error for each measurement. Give your answer to the nearest 0.1 percent.

1. 30 m **2.** 275 m **3.** 335 km **4.** 62 cm **5.** 24.7 m **6.** 84.5 cm

7. 32.8 km **8.** 1,500 m **9.** 45 m **10.** 116.8 mm **11.** 12.5 m **12.** 100 m

Compare the relative error of each measurement. Tell which measurement in the pair is more accurate.

13. 120 km or 1,200 m

14. 11.7 kg or 122.6 kg

15. 87.6 m or 876 cm

16. 25.55 kg or 2.55 g

17. 4 or 4.0

18. 4.0 or 4.00

19. The relative error for 32 inches is 1.6%. Find another measurement that has the same relative error.

Chapter 7 Review/Test

Choose the best measure.

1. The area of a book cover

a. 70 in. **b.** 70 sq in. **c.** 70 sq ft

2. Weight of a quart of milk

a. 6 oz **b.** 20 lb **c.** 2 lb

3. Volume of a drinking glass

a. 200 cm^3 **b.** 200 m^3 **c.** 200 mm^3

4. Mass of a teaspoon

a. 50 kg **b.** 5 kg **c.** 50 g

Find each missing number.

5. 3.5 ft = ▒ in. **6.** 28 qt = ▒ gal

7. 1 m = ▒ cm **8.** 143 cm = ▒ m

9. 1 g = ▒ mg **10.** 4.5 L = ▒ mL

11. 3 sq yd = ▒ sq ft

12. 3 cm^2 = ▒ mm^2

13. 1,200 g = ▒ kg

Find the area or volume.

14. 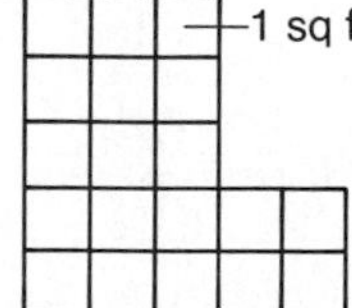

15. 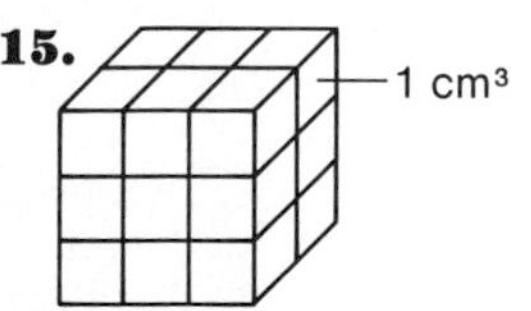

16. Choose the answer using estimation.

An object on the moon weighs about $\frac{1}{6}$ of what it does on Earth. What does a 75-kg astronaut wearing his 20-kg spacesuit weigh in pounds on the moon?

a. 95 lb **b.** 16 lb **c.** 35 lb

Add or subtract. Give answers to the less precise unit.

17. $3\frac{1}{3}$ in. + 2 in.

18. 34.34 kg − 14.5 kg

19. What is the greatest possible error in 13.5 cm?

20. Mr. Gonzales bought 3.65 pounds of meat. What is the precision of this measurement?

Use this table for Items 21 and 22.

Squares and Square Roots

No.	Square	Square Root
81	6,561	9.000
82	6,724	9.055
83	6,889	9.110
84	7,056	9.165
85	7,225	9.220

21. How much greater is the square of 84 than the square of 81?

22. For this table, does the increase in the size of the square or the square root remain the same between consecutive numbers in the table? What is the increase?

23. Write About Math Is there enough information in the problem to solve it? Write *yes* or *no*. If there is not enough information, rewrite the problem so it can be solved.

There are 330 breeds of cats. The record weight is held by an Australian cat named "Himmy" who weighed 46 pounds 15 ounces. How much heavier was "Himmy" than Natalie's cat, "Cinnamon"?

Data File

A Cool Million

One million $1 bills would weigh more than a ton and could be packed into a 42-cubic-foot space — about the capacity of two average refrigerators.

1. Report

1. Report:
The report gives the weight and volume of one million $1 bills.

2. Pattern:
The pattern on the patchwork quilt shows the repeat of the Texas Star block.

3. List:
The list shows the lengths of conduit pipe needed to make a xylophone.

4. Chart:
The chart shows the size measurements for boys' and teen boys' clothes.

5. Chart:
The chart shows the Richter Scale which was devised by Charles Richter for measuring the magnitude of earthquakes.

2. Patchwork Quilt And Pattern

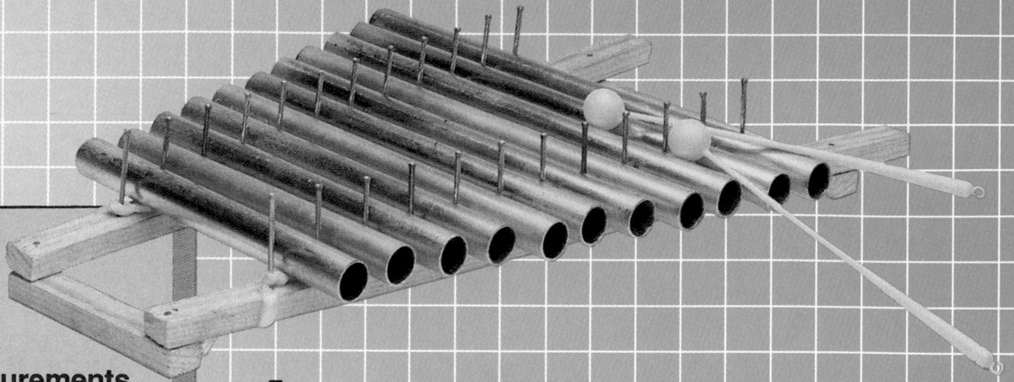

3. Chart

Conduit Pipe Xylophone
($\frac{1}{2}$ in. conduit)

	Measurements large	small
low so	$22\frac{7}{16}$"	$11\frac{7}{32}$"
low la	$21\frac{1}{4}$"	$10\frac{5}{8}$"
low ti	20"	10"
do	$19\frac{1}{2}$"	$9\frac{3}{4}$"
re	$18\frac{1}{4}$"	$9\frac{1}{8}$"
mi	$17\frac{1}{8}$"	$8\frac{9}{16}$"
fa	$16\frac{5}{8}$"	$8\frac{5}{16}$"
so	$15\frac{5}{8}$"	$7\frac{13}{16}$"
la	$14\frac{3}{4}$"	$7\frac{3}{8}$"
ti	$13\frac{3}{4}$"	$6\frac{7}{8}$"
high do	$13\frac{7}{16}$"	$6\frac{23}{32}$"

4. Pattern Measurements

Size	7	8	10	12	14	16	18	20
Chest	26	27	28	30	32	$33\frac{1}{2}$	35	$36\frac{1}{2}$
Waist	23	24	25	26	27	28	29	30
Hip (Seat)	27	28	$29\frac{1}{2}$	31	$32\frac{1}{2}$	34	$35\frac{1}{2}$	37
Neck	$11\frac{3}{4}$	12	$12\frac{1}{2}$	13	$13\frac{1}{2}$	14	$14\frac{1}{2}$	15
Height	48	50	54	58	61	64	66	68

5. Richter Scale

Richter Number	Increase in Magnitude of an Earthquake
8	10,000,000
7	1,000,000
6	100,000
5	10,000
4	1,000
3	100
2	10
1	1

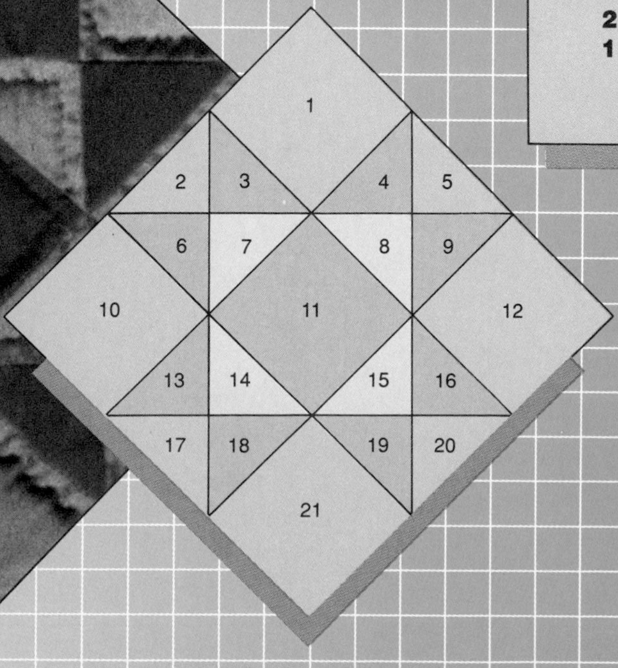

Cumulative Review/Test Chapters 1–7

Give the letter for the correct answer.

1. If beef costs \$2.49 a pound, how much is 3.4 pounds?

a. \$6.17 **b.** \$20.37
c. \$8.47 **d.** not given

2. Which is the easiest way to find the answer to 137×100?

a. mental math
b. paper and pencil
c. calculator
d. look it up

3. Choose the best operation for solving this problem.

Jeremy has traveled 217 miles. His trip is 438 miles. How far does he still have to go?

a. addition **b.** subtraction
c. multiplication **d.** division

4. Solve $s + 14 = 23$.

a. $s = 9$ **b.** $s = 19$
c. $s = 27$ **d.** $s = 37$

5. The sport store is having a sale. Sweatshirts cost \$10 and sweatpants cost \$8. Choose the expression that tells how to find the cost of s sweatshirts and n sweatpants.

a. $n + (10 + 8)\,s$
b. $(10 + 8)\,s + n$
c. $8s + 10n$
d. $10s + 8n$

6. Which means the same as $\frac{2}{11}$?

a. 0.18 **b.** $0.\overline{18}$
c. $0.1\overline{8}$ **d.** not given

7. Evaluate $3 \times 8 - (4 \times 2)$.

a. 0 **b.** 16 **c.** 24 **d.** 40

8. Which equation could be used to solve this problem?

Sally has lost $\frac{1}{10}$ of her weight on her new diet. She lost 13 pounds. How much did Sally weigh before the loss?

a. $\frac{w}{10} = 13$ **b.** $w - \frac{1}{10} = 13$
c. $w + 13 = \frac{1}{10}$ **d.** $13w = \frac{1}{10}$

9. Choose the name for this figure.

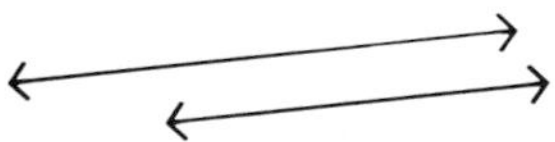

a. intersecting lines
b. parallel lines
c. an angle
d. perpendicular lines

10. Which two angles are supplementary?

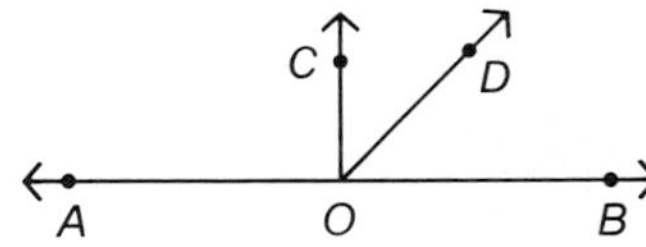

a. $\angle DOB$ and $\angle DOC$
b. $\angle DOB$ and $\angle AOC$
c. $\angle COB$ and $\angle DOB$
d. $\angle DOB$ and $\angle DOA$

11. In triangle ABC, $\angle A$ measures 37° and $\angle B$ measures 24°. What is the measure of $\angle C$?

a. 61° **b.** 29° **c.** 143° **d.** 119°

12. Which quadrilateral has all four sides equal in length?

a. trapezoid **b.** parallelogram
c. rhombus **d.** rectangle

13. Which means 3.4 less than h?

a. $3.4h$ **b.** $h - 3.4$
c. $3.4 + h$ **d.** $3.4 - h$

14. Which divides 2,841 evenly?

a. 2 **b.** 3 **c.** 5 **d.** 9

15. Which number is prime?

a. 21 **b.** 39 **c.** 43 **d.** 51

16. Starting today, Jennifer plans to eat beef every 12th day and baked potato every 15th day. In how many days can she have steak and baked potato at the same meal?

a. 3 days **b.** 60 days
c. 120 days **d.** 180 days

17. Which is a row from Pascal's Triangle?

a. 2 6 10 9 3
b. 1 2 3 2 1
c. 1 2 3 5 8
d. 1 4 6 4 1

18. Which fraction is the same as $3\frac{5}{8}$?

a. $\frac{7}{8}$ **b.** $\frac{23}{8}$ **c.** $\frac{29}{8}$ **d.** $\frac{39}{8}$

19. Find $2\frac{1}{6} - \frac{7}{10}$.

a. $\frac{7}{15}$ **b.** $2\frac{7}{15}$
c. $1\frac{7}{15}$ **d.** not given

20. Which equation could be used to solve this problem?

Jeremy is 6 ft $\frac{1}{2}$ inches tall, while Claude is 6 ft $1\frac{3}{4}$ inches tall. How much taller is Claude than Jeremy?

a. $x + 1\frac{3}{4} = \frac{1}{2}$
b. $\frac{1}{2} - x = 1\frac{3}{4}$
c. $\frac{1}{2}x = 1\frac{3}{4}$
d. $x + \frac{1}{2} = 1\frac{3}{4}$

21. Solve the equation $\frac{3}{4}r = \frac{5}{6}$.

a. $r = \frac{1}{12}$ **b.** $r = 1\frac{1}{9}$
c. $r = \frac{15}{24}$ **d.** $r = 1\frac{7}{12}$

22. Choose the best measure for the length of a guitar.

a. 4 in. **b.** 4 sq in.
c. 4 ft **d.** 4 sq ft

23. What is the missing number?

$2 \text{ m}^2 = ▒ \text{ cm}^2$

a. 200 **b.** 20,000
c. 2,000 **d.** 2,000,000

24. What information do you need to solve this problem?

Georgianne made muffins for the school bake sale. She sold them at 12¢ each. How much money did she make for the school?

a. cost of muffin ingredients
b. number of muffins made
c. number of muffins sold
d. number of students at sale

Relating Ratio, Proportion, and Percent

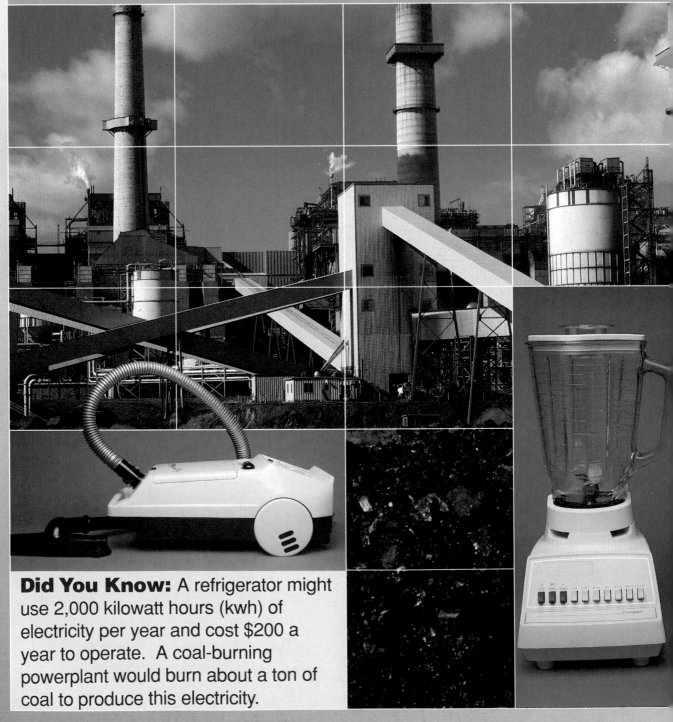

Did You Know: A refrigerator might use 2,000 kilowatt hours (kwh) of electricity per year and cost $200 a year to operate. A coal-burning powerplant would burn about a ton of coal to produce this electricity.

Number-Sense Project

Estimate

Select a light in your home. Guess how many hours it burns each day. How much do you think it costs to burn this light for a year?

Gather Data

Keep track of the number of hours the light burns in one week and the wattage of each bulb in the light. You might also find the cost of a kwh of electricity in your area.

Analyze and Report

How many kwh were used to burn the light for one week? How much does this much electricity cost? At this rate, what is the cost for one year?

Ratio

Build Understanding

A. From this picture of Rob's music collection, can you write the ratio of compact discs to tapes?

A ***ratio*** is a *number pair* that compares two quantities. The ratio of compact discs to tapes is three to five. You can write this as:

$\frac{3}{5}$ or 3:5. Read both as "3 to 5."

The ***first term*** in the ratio is 3 because compact discs are mentioned before tapes. Since tapes are mentioned second, 5 is the ***second term*** in the ratio. Notice that the ratio of tapes to compact discs is $\frac{5}{3}$.

$\frac{3}{5}$ and $\frac{5}{3}$ are *not* the same ratio.

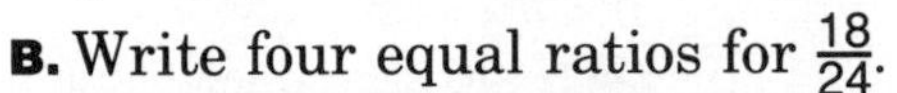

B. Write four equal ratios for $\frac{18}{24}$.

You can write ***equal ratios*** by multiplying or dividing both terms of the ratio by the same nonzero number.

$$\frac{18}{24} = \frac{18 \div 2}{24 \div 2} = \frac{9}{12} \qquad \frac{18}{24} = \frac{18 \div 3}{24 \div 3} = \frac{6}{8} \qquad \frac{18}{24} = \frac{18 \div 6}{24 \div 6} = \frac{3}{4}$$

$$\frac{18}{24} = \frac{3}{4} = \frac{3 \times 4}{4 \times 4} = \frac{12}{16}$$

Since $\frac{3}{4}$ is an equal ratio to $\frac{18}{24}$, you can multiply 3 and 4 by the same nonzero number to get a ratio equal to $\frac{18}{24}$.

$\frac{3}{4}$, $\frac{6}{8}$, $\frac{9}{12}$, and $\frac{12}{16}$ are equal ratios for $\frac{18}{24}$.

■ **Talk About Math** How many ratios are equal to 2:3? Explain your answer.

Check Understanding

For another example, see Set A, pages 294–295.

Rob's sister Luann has 7 compact discs and 12 tapes. Write the ratio of

1. Luann's compact discs to tapes.

2. Luann's tapes to compact discs.

3. compact discs to the total number of Luann's compact discs and tapes.

4. compact discs in Luann's collection to compact discs in Rob's collection.

Practice

For More Practice, see Set A, pages 296–297.

Copy and complete.

5. $\frac{2}{3} = \frac{4}{\square} = \frac{\square}{9} = \frac{\square}{12} = \frac{10}{\square}$

6. $\frac{1}{2} = \frac{3}{\square} = \frac{5}{\square} = \frac{\square}{8} = \frac{\square}{4}$

7. $\frac{12}{36} = \frac{\square}{18} = \frac{\square}{12} = \frac{3}{\square} = \frac{24}{\square}$

Write three equal ratios for each situation.

8. 3 guitars to 2 keyboards

9. 40 country tapes to 30 classical tapes

10. 8 Mozart compact discs to 4 Beethoven compact discs

11. 18 jazz tapes to 24 country tapes

12. 4 tapes for 12 dollars

13. 32 tapes to 20 compact discs

Write four equal ratios.

14. $\frac{1}{3}$

15. $\frac{10}{9}$

16. $\frac{6}{7}$

17. $\frac{12}{3}$

18. $\frac{36}{24}$

19. $\frac{30}{100}$

20. $\frac{12}{21}$

21. $\frac{64}{40}$

22. $\frac{25}{21}$

23. $\frac{15}{45}$

24. $\frac{4}{5}$

25. $\frac{6}{16}$

26. $\frac{15}{30}$

27. $\frac{12}{8}$

28. $\frac{20}{50}$

29. $\frac{18}{27}$

30. $\frac{1}{8}$

31. $\frac{2}{9}$

32. $\frac{6}{11}$

33. $\frac{30}{36}$

Problem Solving

Solve each problem.

34. Dean has 27 compact discs and 36 tapes. What is the ratio of the number of his compact discs to the total number of his compact discs and tapes?

35. Juanita bought a box of records at a garage sale. There were 26 records in all, of which 15 were jazz records. What is the ratio of jazz records to all the records? What is the ratio of jazz records to records that were not jazz?

Critical Thinking Which ratio is NOT equal to the others?

36. $\frac{12}{18}, \frac{15}{20}, \frac{16}{24}, \frac{24}{36}$

37. $\frac{6}{10}, \frac{15}{25}, \frac{20}{35}, \frac{24}{40}$

38. $\frac{1}{4}, \frac{1.5}{4.5}, \frac{3}{9}, \frac{5}{15}$

ALGEBRA

Proportions

Build Understanding

A. Shells, beads, feathers, tobacco, salt, and copper rings all have been used as money. Today, dollars are the official currency of many countries. There are Australian, Jamaican, Canadian, Solomon Island, as well as United States dollars.

Malcolm exchanged 20 U.S. dollars for 386.20 Jamaican dollars. Later, he exchanged 30 U.S. dollars for 579.30 Jamaican dollars. Was the same exchange rate used each time?

$$\frac{\text{U.S. Dollars}}{\text{Jamaican Dollars}} \quad \frac{20}{386.20} = \frac{1}{19.31} \text{ and } \frac{30}{579.30} = \frac{1}{19.31}$$

($\div 20$ on the first ratio; $\div 30$ on the second ratio)

Since both $\frac{20}{386.20}$ and $\frac{30}{579.30}$ are equal to $\frac{1}{19.31}$, they are equal to each other. Two equal ratios form a ***proportion.***

The same exchange rate was used each time.

Cowrie shells have been used as money in China, India, Thailand, and Africa.

B. Solve $\frac{8}{20} = \frac{6}{y}$.

$$\frac{8}{20} = \frac{8 \div 4}{20 \div 4} = \frac{2}{5}$$

You can replace $\frac{8}{20}$ with any ratio equal to it.

$$\frac{2}{5} = \frac{6}{y}$$

($\times 3$ on numerator and denominator)

Since $2 \times 3 = 6$, multiply 5×3 to find y.

$y = 15$

■ **Talk About Math** Explain why the solution to $\frac{20}{8} = \frac{y}{6}$ is the same as the solution to $\frac{8}{20} = \frac{6}{y}$.

Check Understanding

For another example, see Set B, pages 294–295.

Complete each sentence.

1. A ratio is a number pair that compares two ___?___.

2. In a proportion, the ratios are ___?___.

Do the ratios form a proportion? Write *yes* or *no*.

3. $\frac{2}{5} \stackrel{?}{=} \frac{6}{15}$

4. $\frac{10}{25} \stackrel{?}{=} \frac{2}{5}$

5. $\frac{3}{11} \stackrel{?}{=} \frac{6}{33}$

6. $\frac{14}{35} \stackrel{?}{=} \frac{16}{40}$

Practice

For More Practice, see Set B, pages 296–297.

State whether you would (a) multiply or divide or (b) first find an equal ratio and then multiply to solve Exercises 7–14. Then solve.

7. $\frac{3}{5} = \frac{n}{20}$ **8.** $\frac{7}{9} = \frac{21}{y}$ **9.** $\frac{2.5}{9} = \frac{x}{18}$ **10.** $\frac{6}{30} = \frac{x}{25}$

11. $\frac{16}{28} = \frac{4}{n}$ **12.** $\frac{8}{20} = \frac{12}{n}$ **13.** $\frac{1}{4} = \frac{x}{24}$ **14.** $\frac{6}{15} = \frac{t}{35}$

Solve each proportion.

15. $\frac{1}{6} = \frac{5}{n}$ **16.** $\frac{4}{7} = \frac{c}{35}$ **17.** $\frac{24}{32} = \frac{3}{x}$ **18.** $\frac{60}{48} = \frac{s}{4}$

19. $\frac{0.7}{2} = \frac{x}{18}$ **20.** $\frac{30}{20} = \frac{a}{8}$ **21.** $\frac{15}{18} = \frac{n}{24}$ **22.** $\frac{49}{28} = \frac{21}{y}$

23. $\frac{9}{10} = \frac{45}{n}$ **24.** $\frac{12}{40} = \frac{9}{y}$ **25.** $\frac{4}{0.3} = \frac{12}{n}$ **26.** $\frac{16}{36} = \frac{4}{n}$

27. $\frac{12}{8} = \frac{m}{20}$ **28.** $\frac{0.4}{10} = \frac{y}{5}$ **29.** $\frac{6}{42} = \frac{n}{35}$ **30.** $\frac{8}{6} = \frac{x}{15}$

31. $\frac{2.5}{5} = \frac{x}{4}$ **32.** $\frac{27}{45} = \frac{m}{55}$ **33.** $\frac{9}{n} = \frac{1}{12}$ **34.** $\frac{15}{25} = \frac{6}{t}$

35. $\frac{3}{1.2} = \frac{2.5}{s}$ **36.** $\frac{v}{3.9} = \frac{2}{13}$ **37.** $\frac{4}{7} = \frac{d}{2.1}$ **38.** $\frac{6}{g} = \frac{10}{7}$

Problem Solving

Write a proportion, and then solve. **Remember** to place first and second terms in the same order.

39. If 100 Japanese yen (¥100) are worth 1.48 Solomon Island dollars, find the value of 2,000 Japanese yen in Solomon Island dollars.

40. If eight Australian dollars could be exchanged for three Irish pounds, how many Australian dollars would be needed to get 72 Irish pounds?

41. Critical Thinking Use the numbers 1, 2, 4, 8, and 16 to write four proportions. Use each number only once in each proportion.

42. Number Sense Without computing, how might you know $\frac{33}{44} \stackrel{?}{=} \frac{16}{12}$ is not a proportion?

Prior to 1966, Australia used a money system of pounds, shillings, and pence.

ALGEBRA

Solving Proportions

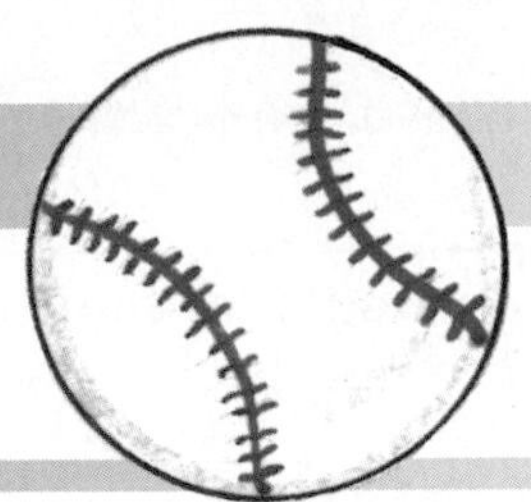

Build Understanding

BATTING RECORD		MAY
PLAYER	AB	H
JUAN	18	6
AMY	12	4
PETE	21	8
LISA	13	5
TOM	15	7
JOYCE	20	9

A. Coach Wong is comparing the batting records of his players. The ratio of Juan's hits to times at bat is 6 to 18. The ratio of Amy's hits to times at bat is 4 to 12. Since 6 to 18 and 4 to 12 are equal ratios, they form a proportion.

$$\frac{6}{18} = \frac{4}{12}$$ 6 × 12 and 18 × 4 are the ***cross-products.***

$$6 \times 12 = 72$$
$$18 \times 4 = 72$$ The cross-products are equal.

In a proportion, the cross-products are equal. If the cross-products are equal, the ratios form a proportion.

B. Use the table to write ratios of hits to times at bat for Pete and Lisa. Are the ratios equal?

$$\frac{\text{hits}}{\text{times at bat}} \rightarrow \overset{\text{Pete}}{\frac{8}{21}} \stackrel{?}{=} \overset{\text{Lisa}}{\frac{5}{13}} \leftarrow \frac{\text{hits}}{\text{times at bat}}$$

$8 \times 13 \stackrel{?}{=} 21 \times 5$ Find the cross-products.

$104 \neq 105$ ≠ means "is not equal to."

Since the cross-products are not equal, the ratios are not equal.

C. If Pete bats 84 times, how many hits must he make to have the same ratio of hits to times at bat as he had in May?

Use n for the number of hits. Write a proportion.

$$\frac{\text{hits}}{\text{times at bat}} \rightarrow \frac{8}{21} = \frac{n}{84} \leftarrow \frac{\text{hits}}{\text{times at bat}}$$

$8 \times 84 = 21 \times n$ Find cross-products.

$672 = 21n$ Multiply.

$\frac{672}{21} = \frac{21n}{21}$ Divide both sides by 21 to find n.

$32 = n$

Pete must make 32 hits.

■ **Talk About Math** Maria used the key sequence 15 [×] 40 [÷] 24 [=] to solve the proportion $\frac{15}{24} = \frac{n}{40}$. Did Maria's method work? Explain.

Check Understanding

For another example, see Set C, pages 294–295.

Do the ratios form a proportion? Write *yes* or *no*. State each cross-product.

1. $\frac{7}{3} \stackrel{?}{=} \frac{9}{4}$

2. $\frac{3}{0.9} \stackrel{?}{=} \frac{2}{0.6}$

Solve each proportion using cross-products.

3. $\frac{a}{4} = \frac{15}{20}$

4. $\frac{2.1}{c} = \frac{7}{2}$

Practice

For More Practice, see Set C, pages 296–297.

Solve each proportion.

5. $\frac{9}{t} = \frac{3}{8}$ **6.** $\frac{8}{6} = \frac{b}{27}$ **7.** $\frac{r}{9} = \frac{70}{30}$ **8.** $\frac{2}{0.2} = \frac{10}{a}$ **9.** $\frac{3}{1.5} = \frac{2}{x}$

10. $\frac{a}{18} = \frac{40}{90}$ **11.** $\frac{16}{14} = \frac{m}{35}$ **12.** $\frac{c}{15} = \frac{8}{6}$ **13.** $\frac{21}{28} = \frac{x}{24}$ **14.** $\frac{x}{5} = \frac{21}{15}$

15. $\frac{2.1}{x} = \frac{0.7}{2}$ **16.** $\frac{10}{45} = \frac{4}{a}$ **17.** $\frac{21}{n} = \frac{70}{20}$ **18.** $\frac{15}{t} = \frac{12}{4}$ **19.** $\frac{1}{9} = \frac{x}{36}$

20. $\frac{t}{1.8} = \frac{3}{0.2}$ **21.** $\frac{t}{18} = \frac{40}{45}$ **22.** $\frac{3}{1.8} = \frac{2}{n}$ **23.** $\frac{3}{n} = \frac{9}{15}$ **24.** $\frac{1.6}{4} = \frac{n}{10}$

Choose mental math, paper and pencil, or a calculator to solve each proportion. Tell which method you chose.

25. $\frac{14}{36} = \frac{n}{18}$ **26.** $\frac{21}{27} = \frac{28}{p}$ **27.** $\frac{10}{24} = \frac{z}{84}$ **28.** $\frac{0.6}{s} = \frac{1.2}{8}$ **29.** $\frac{1.5}{36} = \frac{2.5}{y}$

30. $\frac{21}{28} = \frac{27}{m}$ **31.** $\frac{2}{3} = \frac{8}{m}$ **32.** $\frac{5}{18} = \frac{x}{36}$ **33.** $\frac{t}{12} = \frac{6}{18}$ **34.** $\frac{0.6}{3} = \frac{1}{n}$

35. $\frac{0.6}{2.4} = \frac{d}{7.2}$ **36.** $\frac{18}{42} = \frac{33}{n}$ **37.** $\frac{1}{3} = \frac{n}{18}$ **38.** $\frac{16}{12.8} = \frac{r}{19.2}$ **39.** $\frac{3}{4} = \frac{12}{a}$

40. $\frac{24}{n} = \frac{10}{5}$ **41.** $\frac{5}{7} = \frac{10}{t}$ **42.** $\frac{32}{36} = \frac{24}{x}$ **43.** $\frac{7}{x} = \frac{42}{24}$ **44.** $\frac{24}{x} = \frac{56}{49}$

Problem Solving

Write a proportion. Then solve.

45. Juan got 35 hits during the season. His ratio of hits to times at bat during the season was the same as Lisa's during May. (See table on page 274.) How many times was he at bat during the season?

46. During the season, Tom batted 96 times and got 36 hits. Maria batted 72 times and had the same ratio of hits to times at bat as Tom. How many hits did Maria get?

47. In problems 45 and 46, do the ratios of Juan and Tom form a proportion?

48. During the season, Joyce batted 80 times and got 36 hits. Do Joyce's ratio of hits to times at bat during the season form a proportion with her ratio from May? (See table on page 274.)

Don't give up. Some problems take longer than others.

ALGEBRA

Write an Equation

Understand
QUESTION
FACTS
KEY IDEA

Plan and Solve
STRATEGY
ANSWER

Look Back
SENSIBLE ANSWER
ALTERNATE APPROACH

Build Understanding

Mrs. Jones drove 156 miles and used 6 gallons of gasoline. At this rate, can she drive the 561 miles from Memphis to Houston on a full tank of 21 gallons of gasoline?

A **rate** is a ratio that compares one quantity to a different kind of quantity: feet to seconds; people to square miles. The ratio of the number of miles to the number of gallons of gasoline is a rate.

Understand QUESTION Is the number of miles Mrs. Jones can drive on a full tank of gasoline greater or less than 561 miles?

FACTS The car uses 6 gallons of gasoline to travel 156 miles. The gasoline tank holds 21 gallons of gasoline.

KEY IDEA Find the number of miles Mrs. Jones can drive on a full tank and compare it to 561 miles.

Plan and Solve STRATEGY Write a proportion. Let n be the number of miles traveled on a full tank.

$$\frac{156}{6} = \frac{n}{21} \begin{matrix} \leftarrow \text{miles} \\ \leftarrow \text{gallons} \end{matrix}$$

Note that a proportion is an equation.

Solve the proportion.

$$156 \times 21 = 6 \times n$$ Write the cross-products.

$$3{,}276 = 6n$$

$$\frac{3{,}276}{6} = \frac{6n}{6}$$ Solve for n.

$$546 = n$$

ANSWER Since Mrs. Jones can travel 546 miles on a full tank of gasoline, she cannot drive 561 miles from Memphis to Houston on a full tank.

An odometer records a car's mileage, which is necessary when calculating gas mileage.

Look Back SENSIBLE ANSWER To check the solution for n, substitute for n in the proportion.

$$\frac{156}{6} \stackrel{?}{=} \frac{546}{21}$$

$$156 \times 21 \stackrel{?}{=} 6 \times 546$$

$$3{,}276 = 3{,}276$$

Talk About Math If $n = 592$, could Mrs. Jones complete the trip? Explain.

Check Understanding

Solve each problem by writing and solving a proportion. Mrs. Jones's car uses gas at the same rate as in the example.

1. Mrs. Jones drove 234 miles. How much gasoline did her car use?
2. **Estimation** Estimate how far Mrs. Jones can drive her car on 11 gallons of gasoline.

Practice

Solve each problem by writing and solving a proportion.

3. If gasoline costs $0.96 a gallon, how much will it cost Mrs. Jones to buy 18.5 gallons?
4. Yoko rides her bike 2.25 kilometers in 9 minutes. How far can she travel in 1 hour?
5. While in Japan the Osbornes exchanged $1,500 U.S. dollars to Japanese yen. How many yen did they receive? The exchange rate is 133 yen for 1 dollar.

Choose a ______ Strategy

Chess, Anyone? If Rob Robot wins a chess game, he scores 3 points, but if he loses, his opponent scores 5 points. If Ms. Sanapaw plays 128 games, how many games must each win to have equal scores?

6. Will they tie if Ms. Sanapaw wins 3 games out of 16? How many games out of 16 must she win to score the same as Rob?
7. How many games must she win if they play 8 games? 32 games? 64 games? 128 games?

Choose an Operation
Write an Equation
Use a Formula
Make a Table
Try and Check
Use Logical Reasoning
Work Backward
Find a Pattern

Similar Figures

Build Understanding

A. Find the Similar Pairs
Materials: Math Sketcher
Groups: Small groups of 3–6 students each

a. Figures that have the same shape but not necessarily the same size are ***similar figures***. Which of the figures below are similar?

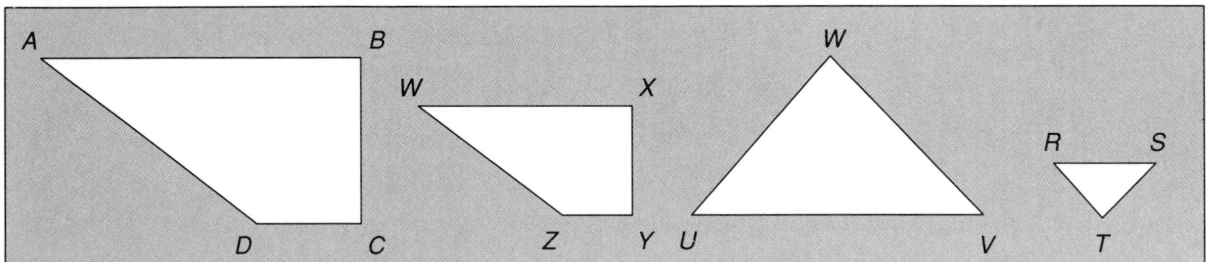

Trace the shapes.

b. Measure the matching or ***corresponding*** angles. What do you notice?

c. Formulate a rule about the corresponding angles.

d. Measure the corresponding sides. Write the ratios comparing the lengths of corresponding sides.

e. Do the pairs of ratios form proportions? Use a calculator or paper and pencil to find out.

B. If $\triangle MCL \sim \triangle TAP$, find the length of $\overline{CL}$.

$\sim$ means "is similar to."

If two polygons are similar, the ratios of the lengths of corresponding sides are equal and the corresponding angles are congruent.

$$\begin{array}{l} \text{Length of } \overline{MC} \rightarrow \\ \text{Length of } \overline{TA} \rightarrow \end{array} \frac{4}{5} = \frac{n}{8} \begin{array}{l} \leftarrow \text{Length of } \overline{CL} \\ \leftarrow \text{Length of } \overline{AP} \end{array}$$

$$\mathbf{4 \times 8 = 5 \times \mathit{n}}$$ Use cross-products.

$$\mathbf{32 = 5\mathit{n}}$$

$$\mathbf{\frac{32}{5} = \frac{5\mathit{n}}{5}}$$

$$\mathbf{6.4 = \mathit{n}}$$

The length of $\overline{CL}$ is 6.4 units.

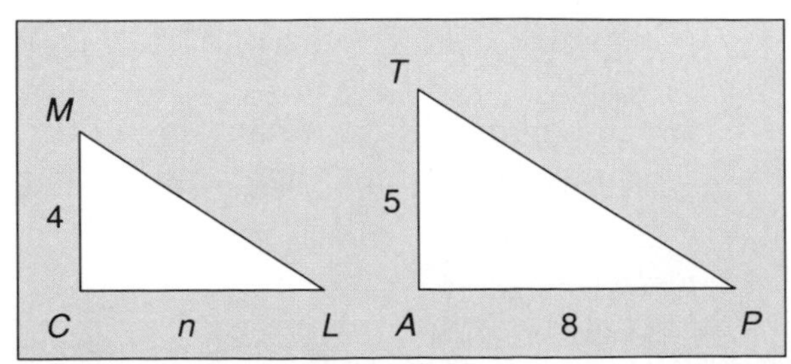

c. A tree 6 meters tall casts a shadow 9 meters long. A meter stick placed near the tree has a shadow 1.5 meters long. Find out if similar triangles are formed.

$$\begin{array}{rcl} \text{Tree shadow} \rightarrow \frac{9}{1.5} & = & \frac{6}{1} \leftarrow \text{Tree height} \\ \text{Stick shadow} \rightarrow & & \leftarrow \text{Stick height} \end{array}$$

$$9 \times 1 \stackrel{?}{=} 1.5 \times 6$$

$$9 = 9$$

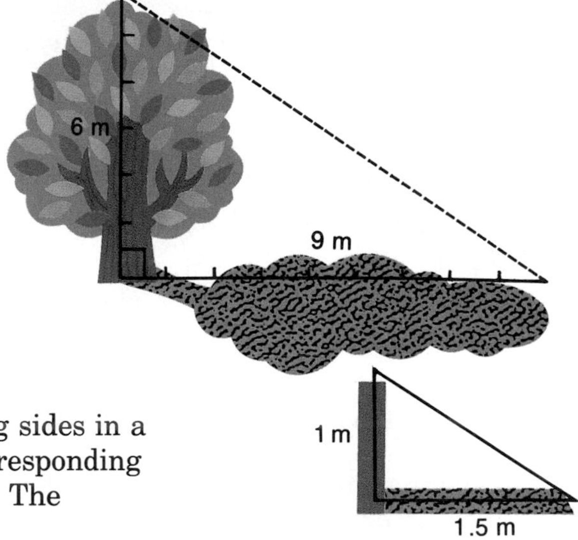

In the right triangles that are formed, the ratios of the lengths of the corresponding sides are equal. The right triangles are similar.

If the ratios of the lengths of corresponding sides in a polygon are equal and the measures of corresponding angles are equal, the polygons are similar. The triangles that are formed are similar.

Write About Math On grid paper draw rectangle *ABCD*. Draw a similar rectangle with corresponding sides in the ratio of 2:3. What do you notice about rectangle *A'B'C'D'*?

Check Understanding

For another example, see Set D, pages 294–295.

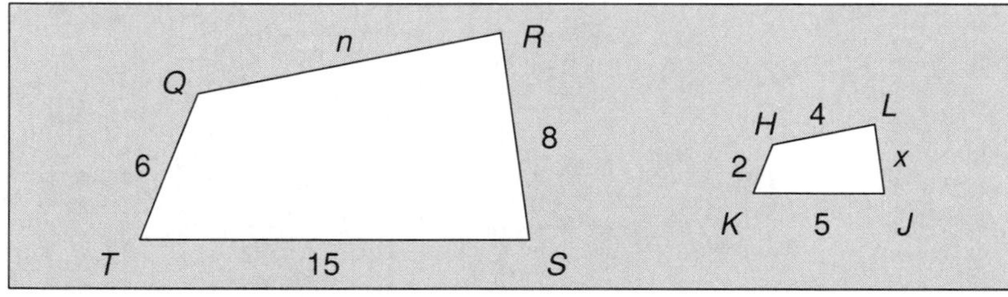

Use the similar figures above. Name the corresponding angle or side.

1. $\angle S$ **2.** $\angle Q$ **3.** $\angle K$ **4.** $\overline{QT}$ **5.** $\overline{QR}$ **6.** $\overline{LJ}$

Write the letter of the correct answer.

7. Which proportion would you solve to find the length of $\overline{LJ}$?

a. $\frac{6}{2} = \frac{x}{8}$ **b.** $\frac{2}{6} = \frac{x}{8}$ **c.** $\frac{6}{8} = \frac{x}{2}$ **d.** $\frac{n}{4} = \frac{x}{8}$

8. Which proportion would you solve to find the length of $\overline{QR}$?

a. $\frac{5}{15} = \frac{n}{4}$ **b.** $\frac{15}{n} = \frac{4}{5}$ **c.** $\frac{5}{15} = \frac{4}{n}$ **d.** $\frac{15}{5} = \frac{4}{n}$

Practice

For More Practice, see Set D, pages 296–297.

Is each pair of figures similar? Write *yes* or *no*.

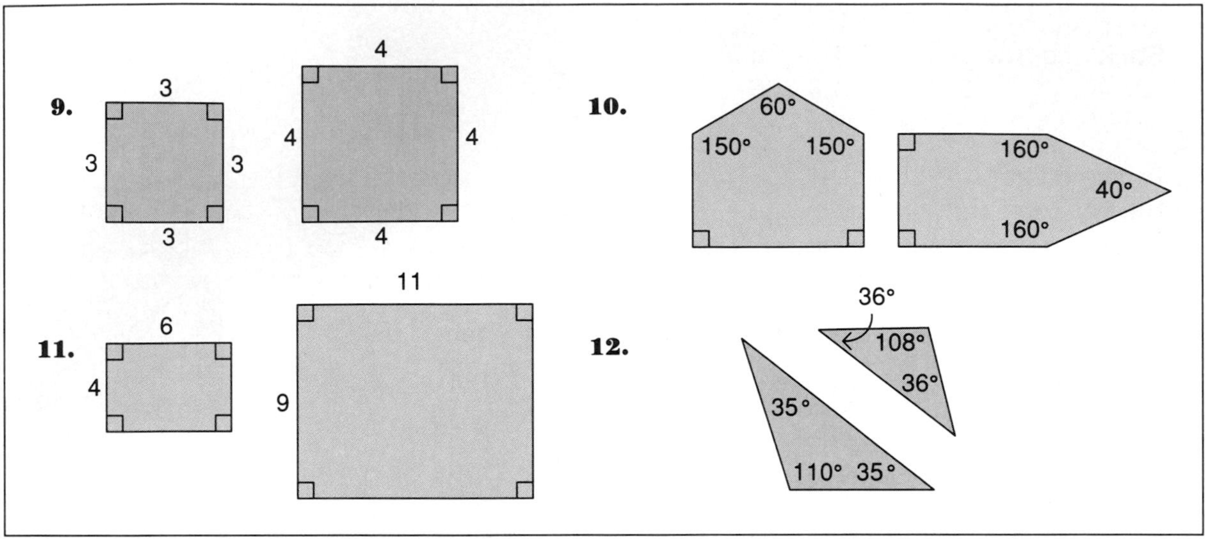

Each pair of polygons below is similar. Find each missing length.

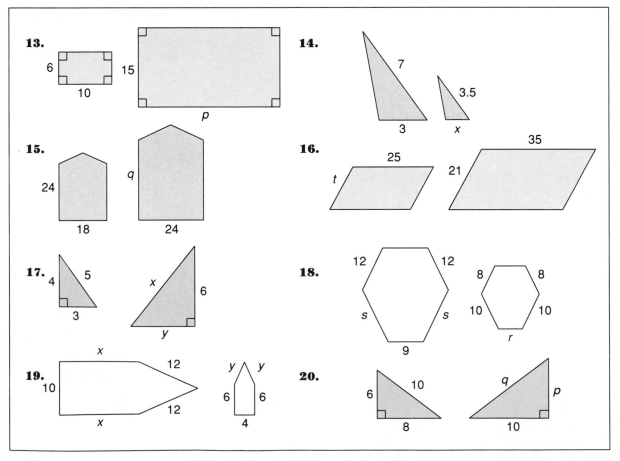

13. 6, 10; 15, p

14. 7, 3; 3.5, x

15. 24, 18; q, 24

16. t, 25; 21, 35

17. 4, 5, 3; x, 6, y

18. 12, 12, s, s, 9; 8, 8, 10, 10, r

19. x, 12, 10, 12, x; y, y, 6, 6, 4

20. 6, 10, 8; q, p, 10

Problem Solving

Solve each problem.

21. The shadow of a flagpole is 9.6 meters long. The shadow of a meter stick placed next to the flagpole is 1.2 meters long. Find the height of the flagpole.

22. The mast of a sailboat casts a shadow 32 feet long. A 5-foot-tall woman standing next to the mast casts a shadow 4 feet long. How tall is the mast of the sailboat?

23. Elena wants to enlarge some of the photographs from her trip to China. The original photographs are 4 in. wide and 6 in. long. The length of the enlargements will be 15 in. How wide will the enlargements be?

24. A rectangular painting is 50 cm long and 40 cm wide. A copy of the painting has been made into a greeting card. The width of the card is 12 centimeters. What is the length of the card?

25. **Critical Thinking** Two squares are always similar. Find other examples of polygons that are always similar. What do these polygons have in common?

Midchapter Checkup

Write four equal ratios for each situation.

1. 4 chairs to 1 table

2. 3 seniors to 4 freshmen

3. 62 students to 3 teachers

Do the ratios form a proportion? Answer *yes* or *no*.

4. $\frac{6}{9} \stackrel{?}{=} \frac{3}{4}$

5. $\frac{7}{10} \stackrel{?}{=} \frac{3.5}{5}$

6. $\frac{8}{12} \stackrel{?}{=} \frac{24}{36}$

7. $\frac{9}{5} \stackrel{?}{=} \frac{7.2}{4}$

Solve each proportion. Choose mental math, paper and pencil, or a calculator. Tell which method you chose.

8. $\frac{10}{25} = \frac{x}{5}$

9. $\frac{56}{z} = \frac{8}{5}$

10. $\frac{5}{7.5} = \frac{2}{u}$

11. $\frac{15}{9} = \frac{n}{24}$

Solve.

12. On Donna's bike, the rear wheel turns 770 times per mile. If the ratio of pedal turns to rear-wheel turns in fifth gear is 5 to 14, how many times will she have to turn the pedals to ride one mile?

Problem-Solving Workshop

Explore as a Team

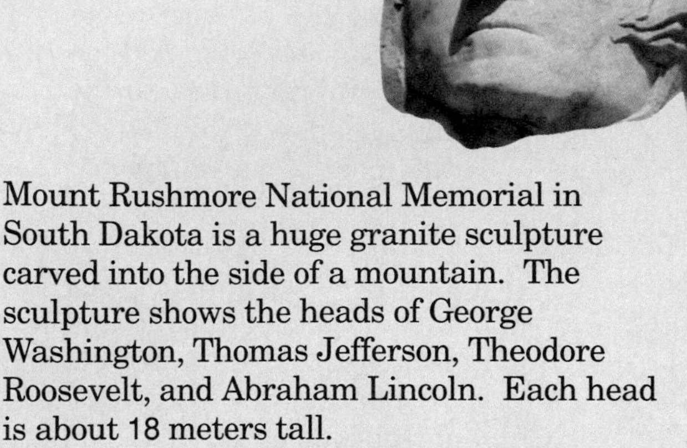

Mount Rushmore National Memorial in South Dakota is a huge granite sculpture carved into the side of a mountain. The sculpture shows the heads of George Washington, Thomas Jefferson, Theodore Roosevelt, and Abraham Lincoln. Each head is about 18 meters tall.

1. Work as a team to discover the approximate length of each nose on the sculpture. In order to do this, each team member should measure his or her own head height and nose length. Then use the following proportion to find the nose length on the sculpture.

$$\frac{\text{Your nose length}}{\text{Your head height}} = \frac{\text{President's nose length}}{\text{President's head height}}$$

2. Average the answers you obtain in Exercise 1 for all the members of your team.

3. Complete a table similar to the one below for each member of your team. Discuss the proportion you will use to find each length.

Measurements	Yours	Sculpture
head height		18 meters
nose length		
arm length		
total height		

4. Average the lengths you obtain in Exercise 3 for all the members of your team.

5. Suppose you knew the exact dimensions of the sculpture. Discuss why they might be different from the answers you obtain.

Don't decide by voting. Try to understand which might be the best solution and why.

Explore with a Computer

Use the *Spreadsheet Workshop Project* for this activity.

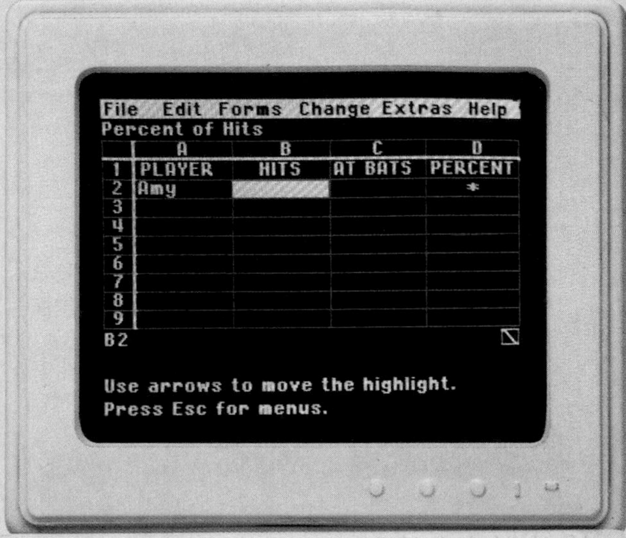

1. If a baseball player had 8 hits in 25 at bats, the percent of hits would be 32 hits out of 100 or 32%. Enter 8 and 32 in the chart. The percent will be calculated for you.

2. What if a player had 12 hits in 40 at bats? At the computer, enter this data in the chart. What is the percent of hits?

3. Choose one of the players below. Estimate their percent of hits before entering the data into the computer.

Player	Hits	At Bats	Year
Ty Cobb	248	591	1911
Joe DiMaggio	193	588	1950
Kirk Gibson	95	290	1981

Number-Sense Project

Look back at pages 268-269. Find the cost per month for operating each appliance. Use a rate of $0.10 per kwh for the cost of electricity or use the rate in your area.

Appliance	Watts	Hours per month
Hair dryer	1,000	5
Color TV	140	60
Microwave	1,450	6

Math-at-Home Activity

The next time your family takes a car trip, calculate the miles per gallon. Note the odometer reading when the gas tank is full. The next time you stop for gas, use the new odometer reading to determine the miles traveled.

$$\text{Miles per gallon} = \frac{\text{Miles traveled}}{\text{Gallons to fill tank}}$$

Scale Drawings

Build Understanding

The dinosaur exhibit at the Science Center includes a model of a stegosaurus. The scale of the model is 20 centimeters to 2.5 meters. The actual height of a stegosaurus was about 3.5 meters. How tall is the model?

Scale:
20 cm → 2.5 m

The stegosaurus was a vegetarian whose length ranged from 6 to 7.5 meters. Its brain was about the size of a golf ball.

Write a proportion. Use n for the height (in centimeters) of the model.

$$\frac{n}{3.5} = \frac{20}{2.5} \begin{array}{l} \leftarrow \textbf{centimeters} \\ \leftarrow \textbf{meters} \end{array}$$

$$n \times 2.5 = 3.5 \times 20$$

$$2.5n = 70$$

$$\frac{2.5n}{2.5} = \frac{70}{2.5}$$

$$n = 28$$

Check:

$$\frac{28}{3.5} \stackrel{?}{=} \frac{20}{2.5}$$

$$28 \times 2.5 \stackrel{?}{=} 3.5 \times 20$$

$$70 = 70$$

The height of the model is 28 centimeters.

Talk About Math Suppose you want to make a model of a brontosaurus. Discuss the steps you would need to follow.

Check Understanding

For another example, see Set E, pages 294–295.

Measure the scale drawing of the rooms at the Center that contain the "Reptiles of Today" exhibit.

Write a proportion to find the actual length of each room.

1. Turtles
2. Lizards

Write a proportion to find the actual width of each room.

3. Alligators
4. Snakes

ALLIGATOR

LIZARD

SNAKE

TURTLE

w

ℓ

Scale:
1 cm → 1.5 m

Practice

For More Practice, see Set E, pages 296–297.

Find the actual length or width of the rooms in Exercises 1–4 by solving each proportion.

5. Exercise 1 **6.** Exercise 2 **7.** Exercise 3 **8.** Exercise 4

The length and width on a scale drawing of some rooms at the Science Center are listed below. Find the actual length and width of each room. Use the scale 1 cm → 1.5 m.

9. Auditorium: ℓ = 14 cm, w = 16 cm

10. Office: ℓ = 3.2 cm, w = 2.8 cm

11. Cafeteria: ℓ = 25 cm, w = 32 cm

12. Gift Shop: ℓ = 4 cm, w = 6.5 cm

13. Science Lab: ℓ = 8 cm, w = 10.5 cm

14. Library: ℓ = 14.5 cm, w = 9 cm

ALGEBRA **Mixed Practice** Solve each equation.

15. $\frac{1}{2}x = 9$ **16.** $3.8 + x = 12.2$ **17.** $\frac{3}{4}x = 18$ **18.** $x - \frac{3}{4} = 1\frac{1}{2}$

19. $x + 1\frac{1}{3} = 6$ **20.** $\frac{1}{4}x = 15$ **21.** $\frac{2}{3}x = 16$ **22.** $x - 6.4 = 1.7$

Problem Solving

Solve each problem.

23. At the whale exhibit at the Science Center, six inches on the model represents 10 feet of the whale's actual size. The model of the blue whale is 6 feet long. About how long is a blue whale?

24. Felipe is preparing a salt solution for a demonstration at the Center. He needs to use 15 grams of salt for every 0.75 liter of water. How much salt must he use for 4.5 liters of water?

Explore ______ Math

Work in a small group to make a scale drawing of your classroom. Include the furniture.

25. How will you get actual measurements? What type of measuring device will be most useful?

26. What scale will you use? Why?

ALGEBRA

Use Data from a Diagram

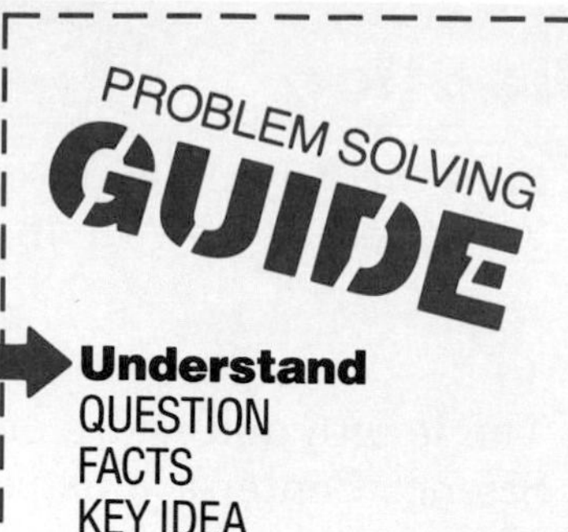

Build Understanding

The Archer family is planning a backpacking trip in the Big Oak Wilderness. The first day they intend to hike from the parking lot to Desolation Camp by way of Zeta Pass. On the map the total length measures about 3.2 cm. Find the actual distance.

Understand QUESTION How far is it from the parking lot to Desolation Camp?

FACTS The map length is about 3.2 cm. The scale is 2.4 cm to 9 km.

KEY IDEA The scale on the map is a ratio comparing map length to actual distance.

Plan and Solve STRATEGY Write a proportion using the scale ratio and the ratio comparing map length with actual distance.

Map Scale **Trail Distance**

$$\frac{2.4}{9} = \frac{3.2}{n} \begin{array}{l}\leftarrow \text{centimeters} \\ \leftarrow \text{kilometers}\end{array}$$

$$2.4 \times n = 9 \times 3.2$$

$$2.4n = 28.8$$

$$\frac{2.4n}{2.4} = \frac{28.8}{2.4}$$

$$n = 12$$

ANSWER The distance is about 12 km.

Look Back SENSIBLE ANSWER Check to see that the proportion is set up correctly. Estimate the actual distance to Desolation Camp. If the scale is 2.4 cm to 9 km, it is reasonable that 3.2 cm on the map represents an actual distance of 12 km.

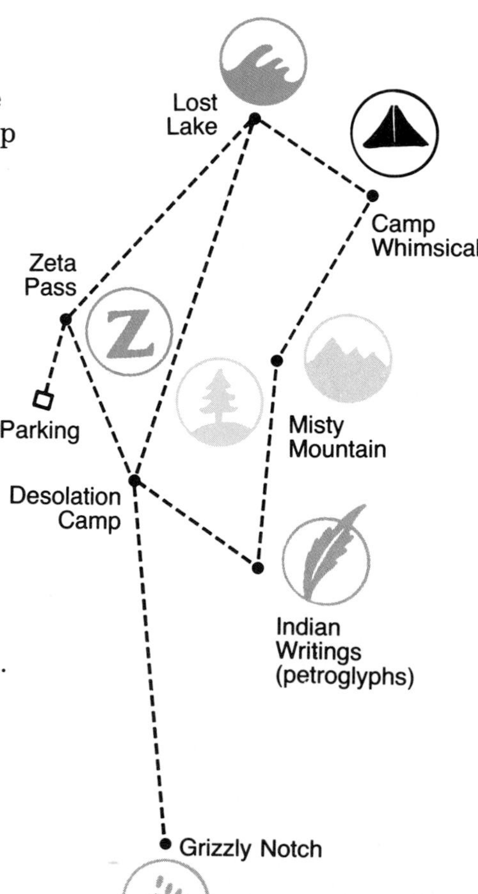

■ **Talk About Math** The Archers make Desolation Camp their base. They can walk up to 15 km per day. Can they hike to Grizzly Notch and back to base in one day? Explain.

Check Understanding

On the second and third days, the Archers hike from Desolation Camp to Camp Whimsical via the petroglyphs and Misty Mountain. Find the total hiking distance.

1. Use the map to compare the distance hiked the second and third days to the distance hiked the first day. Is this distance about (a) 5 times as long, (b) 2 times as long, or (c) half as long as the distance hiked the first day?

2. Measure the map length from Desolation Camp to Camp Whimsical by the route described.

3. Write and solve a proportion to find the distance hiked the second and third days.

4. Which seems more efficient: (a) to add the map lengths and then convert to a distance; or (b) to convert each map length to a distance and then add? Explain.

Practice

Solve each problem. Use the map on page 286.

5. On the fourth day, the Archers will hike from Camp Whimsical to Lost Lake. Measure the map length and then find the actual distance.

6. From Lost Lake, Mike and Sue Archer will hike to Zeta Pass by way of Desolation Camp. The others will hike directly to Zeta Pass. Measure both routes. How much farther must Mike and Sue hike?

Choose a ________ Strategy

Who's hungry? On the last day, the Archers wanted to reach their car by 4 P.M. They stopped for lunch at 1 P.M. with 7 km of hiking ahead of them. If they plan to hike at a rate of 3 km per hour, how long can they stop for lunch?

7. How long will it take the Archers to hike 7 km?
8. How much time do they have until 4 P.M.?
9. How much time is left for the lunch stop?

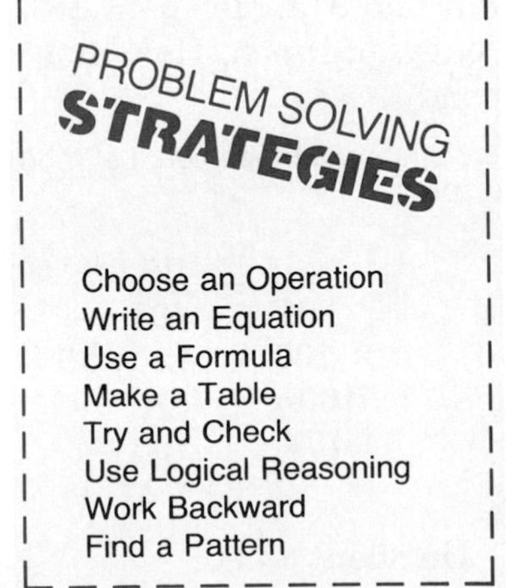

PROBLEM SOLVING
STRATEGIES
Choose an Operation
Write an Equation
Use a Formula
Make a Table
Try and Check
Use Logical Reasoning
Work Backward
Find a Pattern

Solving Percent Problems Using Proportions

Build Understanding

Recall that ***percent*** means "out of 100."

A. On a Wednesday night Emilio's Restaurant served 100 dinners. The four main courses served were:

Chicken	38	Beef	26
Fish	30	Pasta	6

The hundreds square shows how many chicken dinners were sold. The ratio $\frac{38}{100}$ is one way to write "38 out of 100." The ratio $\frac{38}{100}$ can also be written as 38%.

$$\frac{38}{100} = 38\% \qquad 38\% = \frac{38}{100}$$

B. Write each ratio as a percent.

$$\frac{32}{100} = 32\%$$

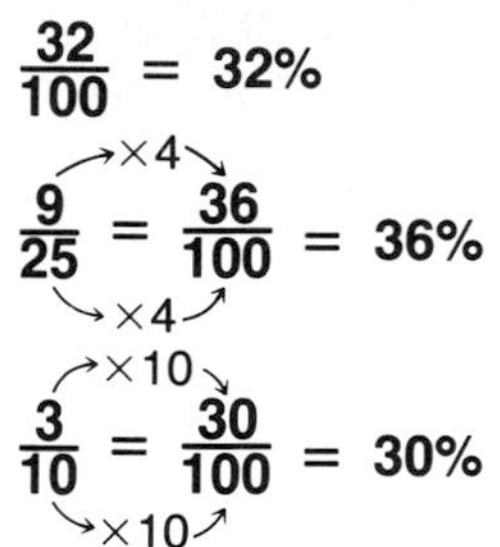

$$\frac{9}{25} = \frac{36}{100} = 36\% \quad (\times 4)$$

$$\frac{3}{10} = \frac{30}{100} = 30\% \quad (\times 10)$$

C. Write each percent as a ratio with a second term of 100.

$$3\% = \frac{3}{100}$$

$$82\% = \frac{82}{100}$$

$$40\% = \frac{40}{100}$$

D. Neil had $12. He spent 35% of his money on lunch. How much did he spend?

You can use a proportion. Let n be the amount he spent.

$$\frac{n}{12} = \frac{35}{100} \begin{array}{l} \leftarrow \textbf{Cost of lunch} \\ \leftarrow \textbf{Total money} \end{array}$$

$$n \times 100 = 12 \times 35$$

$$\frac{100n}{100} = \frac{420}{100}$$

$$n = 4.2$$

He spent $4.20.

E. Mental Math Diego left 15% of his family's lunch bill for a tip. If he left a tip of $3.00, what was the amount of the bill?

Let b be the amount of the bill.

$$\frac{3}{b} = \frac{15}{100} \quad (\times 5)$$

$$5b = 100$$

$$b = 20$$

The bill was $20.

F. **Calculator** Suppose the tax on an \$18 dinner is \$1.26. What percent is the tax rate?

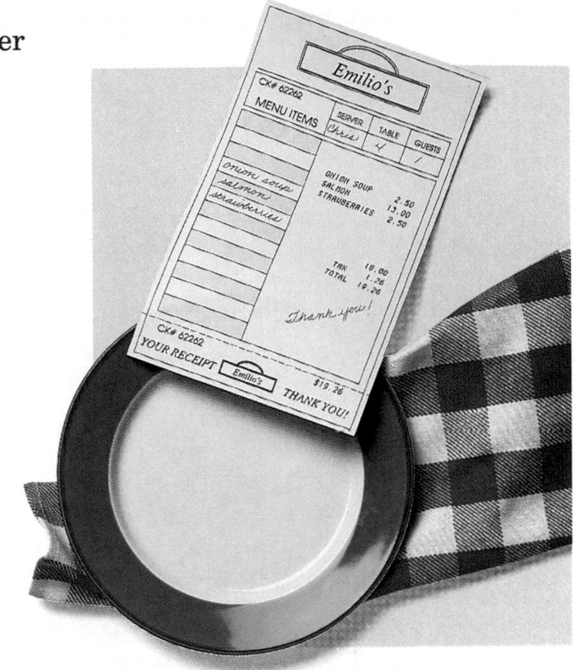

Let t be the tax rate.

$$\frac{t}{100} = \frac{1.26}{18}$$

$$18t = 100 \times 1.26$$

Press: 100 [×] 1.26 [÷] 18 [=]
Display: 7

The tax rate is 7%. Since you are looking for a percent, remember to include % in your answer.

■ **Talk About Math** In Example E, could you use division to figure the amount of the bill? Explain.

Check Understanding

For another example, see Set F, pages 294–295.

Write a ratio and a percent for the shaded part of each figure.

1. 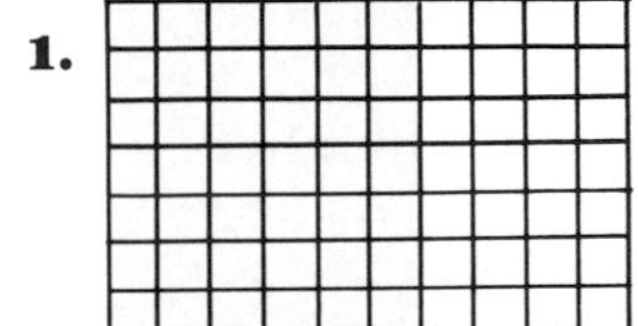

2. 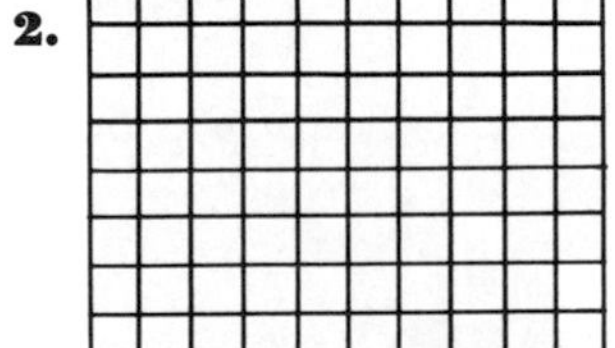

3. 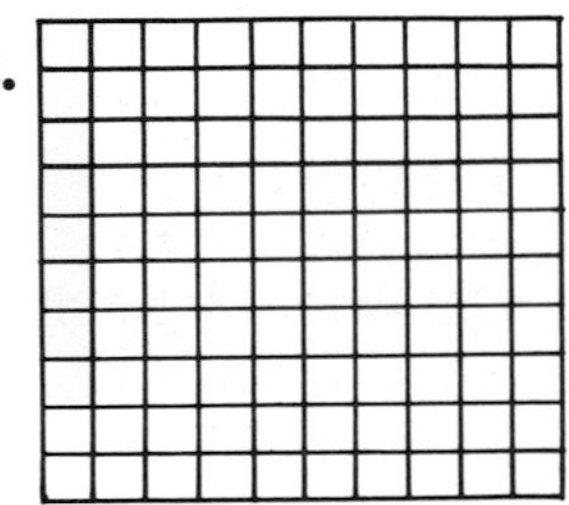

Write each percent as a ratio with a second term of 100.

4. 33% **5.** 90% **6.** 9% **7.** 1%

Write each ratio as a percent.

8. $\frac{47}{100}$ **9.** $\frac{1}{10}$ **10.** $\frac{4}{25}$ **11.** $\frac{9}{50}$

Which proportion would you use to solve these problems?

12. Find 45% of 20.

a. $\frac{n}{100} = \frac{45}{20}$ **b.** $\frac{45}{100} = \frac{n}{20}$ **c.** $\frac{20}{100} = \frac{45}{n}$ **d.** $\frac{n}{45} = \frac{100}{20}$

13. 15 is 60% of what number?

a. $\frac{60}{100} = \frac{15}{n}$ **b.** $\frac{15}{100} = \frac{n}{60}$ **c.** $\frac{n}{100} = \frac{60}{15}$ **d.** $\frac{n}{15} = \frac{60}{100}$

Practice

For More Practice, see Set F, pages 296–297.

Write each percent as a ratio.

14. 83% **15.** 19% **16.** 7% **17.** 15%

18. 5% **19.** 50% **20.** 35% **21.** 100%

Write each ratio as a percent.

22. $\frac{37}{100}$ **23.** $\frac{73}{100}$ **24.** $\frac{9}{100}$ **25.** $\frac{40}{100}$

26. $\frac{7}{10}$ **27.** $\frac{19}{20}$ **28.** $\frac{1}{2}$ **29.** $\frac{1}{5}$

30. $\frac{3}{4}$ **31.** $\frac{13}{25}$ **32.** $\frac{10}{40}$ **33.** $\frac{21}{35}$

Write and solve a proportion for each.

34. 21 is what percent of 84?

35. What is 15% of 20?

36. Find 90% of 40.

37. 30 is what percent of 150?

38. 30% of what number is 6?

39. 15 is what percent of 20?

40. Find 75% of 48.

41. 5 is 10% of what number?

42. 40% of what number is 22?

43. 63 is 70% of what number?

44. 60 is what percent of 125?

45. What is 35% of 80?

Choose mental math, paper and pencil, or a calculator to find each answer. Tell which method you chose.

46. Find 40% of 40.

47. 50% of what number is 14?

48. 33 is 6% of what number?

49. What percent of 350 is 28?

50. 12 is what percent of 48?

51. 39 is what percent of 52?

52. What is 25% of 60?

53. 90% of what number is 90?

Problem Solving

Solve each problem.

54. What percent of the dinners served by Emilio's Restaurant in Example A were fish dinners?

55. What percent of the dinners served by Emilio's Restaurant were not beef dinners?

56. A juice drink is made with 30% cranberry juice and 70% grapefruit juice. Write a ratio to describe the amount of cranberry juice to grapefruit juice.

57. On Saturday night, 85% of Emilio's customers ordered a pasta dish. On Sunday night, 16 out of 20 customers ordered pasta. Which night had the larger percent of pasta orders?

58. Diane's dessert cost $3. If that was 20% of the total cost of her dinner, how much did the dinner cost?

59. In a survey, 60 of 150 students selected Emilio's as their favorite restaurant. What percent of the students chose Emilio's?

60. **Use Data** Joyce's parents took her to Emilio's to celebrate her baseball team's winning season. Use the table on page 274 to compute Joyce's batting average.

61. Emilio bought a $120 blender for 20% off the regular price. Margo bought the same blender for $100. Who had the better buy?

Skills Review

pages 168–171

Find the greatest common factor of each pair of numbers.

1. 4, 8 **2.** 12, 6 **3.** 9, 36 **4.** 10, 15

5. 21, 14 **6.** 60, 90 **7.** 11, 21 **8.** 9, 5

Find the greatest common factor of each set of numbers.

9. 4, 6, 8 **10.** 12, 15, 9 **11.** 5, 6, 7 **12.** 3, 12, 9

Find the least common multiple of each pair of numbers

13. 3, 6 **14.** 5, 15 **15.** 45, 60 **16.** 10, 8

17. 9, 4 **18.** 3, 11 **19.** 15, 4 **20.** 6, 9

Find the least common multiple of each set of numbers.

21. 3, 6, 12 **22.** 3, 4, 5 **23.** 6, 8, 10 **24.** 16, 8, 12

Chapter 8 REVIEW

Skills Review

Write three equal ratios.

1. $\frac{5}{6}$ **2.** $\frac{9}{10}$ **3.** $\frac{42}{36}$

Do the ratios form a proportion? Write *yes* or *no*.

4. $\frac{4}{5} \stackrel{?}{=} \frac{14}{15}$ **5.** $\frac{14}{21} \stackrel{?}{=} \frac{2}{3}$

6. $\frac{3}{4} \stackrel{?}{=} \frac{16}{24}$ **7.** $\frac{1}{4} \stackrel{?}{=} \frac{12}{48}$

Use cross products to solve each proportion.

8. $\frac{n}{5} = \frac{12}{15}$ **9.** $\frac{c}{14} = \frac{14}{28}$

10. $\frac{42}{m} = \frac{7}{8}$ **11.** $\frac{12}{32} = \frac{3}{a}$

12. $\frac{t}{4} = \frac{2.4}{3.2}$ **13.** $\frac{4}{2.5} = \frac{b}{7.5}$

Is each pair of figures similar? Write *yes* or *no*.

14. 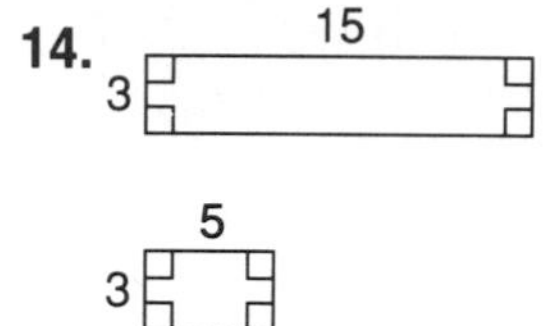

15. 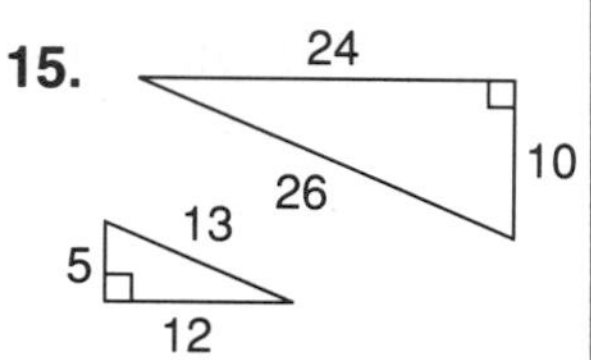

A drawing of a garden uses the scale 3 cm to 5 m. The scale drawing of the garden is 15 cm long and 12.3 cm wide.

16. Write proportions to find the actual length and width of the garden.

17. Find the actual dimensions of the garden.

Write each percent as a ratio.

18. 78% **19.** 4% **20.** 99%

Write and solve a proportion for each.

21. 34 is what percent of 85?

22. 80% of what number is 76?

Problem-Solving Review

Solve each problem.

23. Vincent earns $4.25 an hour at Pat's Pizza Parlor. Last week he earned $68. Write and solve an equation to find how many hours he worked last week.

24. A scout troop is going to the skating rink. Four scouts can ride in each car, and 7 can ride in each van. If all seats are filled in each car and van, describe the least number of vehicles needed to take 33 scouts to the rink.

25. A box contains 3 packets of fruit drink mix. Each packet makes 2 quarts of fruit drink. How many 8-oz servings can be made from each box of mix?

26. Mrs. Smith dismissed $\frac{1}{3}$ of the class. Then she dismissed $\frac{1}{2}$ of the students remaining. Finally, she dismissed the last 7 students. How many students are in Mrs. Smith's class?

27. On a map 2.5 cm = 8 km. The distance on the map from Four Corners to Redbud is 5.8 cm. What is the actual distance between the two towns?

28. **Data File** Use the data on pages 414–415. The cost of which cookware has been reduced by 50%?

29. **Make a Data File** Choose some packaged food item that is available in different brands and in different-sized containers. For example, you might choose peanut butter or jam. Make a table of the information and calculate each unit price.

Cumulative Skills Review • Chapters 1–8

Choose mental math, paper and pencil, or calculator to compute.

1. $54 + 3.67$ **2.** $24{,}884 \div 4$ **3.** 345×209 **4.** $5000 - 3{,}450$

Solve each equation.

5. $v + 24 = 46$ **6.** $52 - k = 41$ **7.** $25t = 550$ **8.** $\frac{y}{12} = 12$

9. $7p + 5 = 40$ **10.** $\frac{h}{9} - 2 = 6$ **11.** $3.14 + w = 6.22$ **12.** $5.9a = 7.08$

Use the circle at the right to name each.

13. The center **14.** A radius

15. A diameter **16.** An arc

17. A central angle **18.** A chord

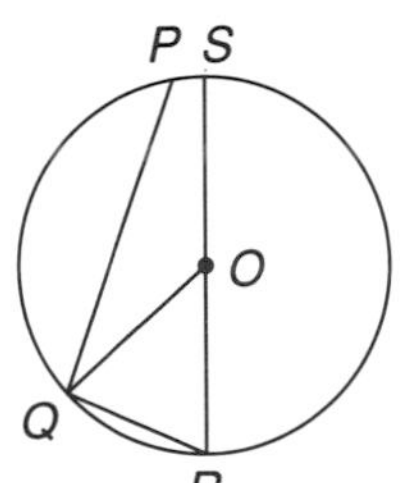

Write each number in standard form.

19. 4^4 **20.** 13^0 **21.** 2^5 **22.** 15^1 **23.** $10^2 \times 3^2$ **24.** $2^3 \times 5^3$

Write each fraction as a whole number or as a mixed number.

25. $\frac{29}{3}$ **26.** $\frac{67}{9}$ **27.** $\frac{84}{4}$ **28.** $\frac{56}{14}$ **29.** $\frac{75}{8}$ **30.** $\frac{56}{7}$

Find each missing number.

31. 95 in. = ▒ ft ▒ in. **32.** 89 ft = ▒ yd ▒ ft **33.** 504 sq in. = ▒ sq ft

34. 15 pt = ▒ qt ▒ pt **35.** 128 fl oz = ▒ qt **36.** 1,000 cm = ▒ m

37. 900 mm^2 = ▒ cm^2 **38.** 15 g = ▒ mg **39.** 6,000 mL = ▒ L

Each pair of polygons is similar. Find each missing length.

40.

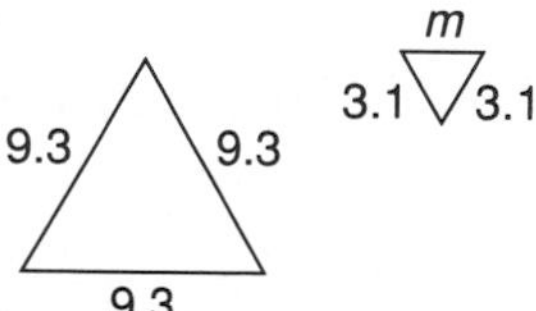

41.

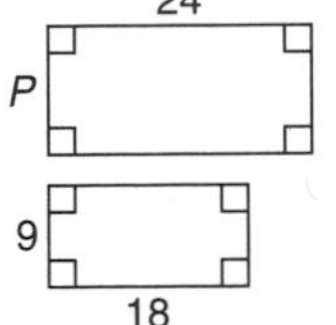

42.

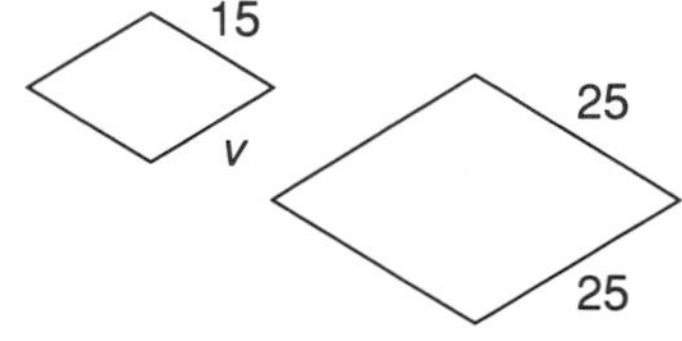

Write each ratio as a percent.

43. $\frac{7}{100}$ **44.** $\frac{7}{10}$ **45.** $\frac{3}{4}$ **46.** $\frac{19}{20}$ **47.** $\frac{7}{25}$ **48.** $\frac{7}{50}$

Write and solve a proportion for each.

49. 23 is what percent of 92? **50.** 12 is 6% of what number?

Reteaching

Set A pages 270–271

In Tanya's neighborhood, there are 6 dogs for every 7 cats. The ratio of dogs to cats is $\frac{6}{7}$. Write equal ratios for $\frac{6}{7}$.

$$\frac{6}{7} = \frac{12}{14} = \frac{18}{21} = \frac{24}{28} = \frac{60}{70}$$

(numerator and denominator each ×2, ×3, ×4, ×10)

Remember, you multiply or divide both terms of a ratio by the same number to find an equal ratio.

Write the following ratios.

1. Cats to dogs
2. Dogs to the total number of pets
3. Cats to the total number of pets

Write three equal ratios for each situation.

4. 5 canaries to 6 goldfish
5. 11 hamsters to 8 guinea pigs

Set B pages 272–273

In Bert's neighborhood, the ratio of dogs to cats is $\frac{3}{4}$. There are 27 dogs. Use a proportion to find the number of cats.

$\frac{3}{4} = \frac{27}{c}$ Since $3 \times 9 = 27$, then $4 \times 9 = c$.

So $c = 36$. There are 36 cats in Bert's neighborhood.

Remember, a proportion consists of two equal ratios.

Are the ratios proportions? Write *yes* or *no.*

1. $\frac{5}{6} \stackrel{?}{=} \frac{25}{30}$
2. $\frac{7}{8} \stackrel{?}{=} \frac{49}{64}$
3. $\frac{8}{18} \stackrel{?}{=} \frac{24}{54}$
4. $\frac{12}{7} \stackrel{?}{=} \frac{60}{35}$

Write a proportion.

5. 9 to 10 is the same as 27 to 30.
6. 4 is to 5 as 32 is to 40.

Set C pages 274–275

You can use cross products to solve a proportion. In a proportion, cross products are equal.

Solve $\frac{y}{9} = \frac{32}{36}$.

$\frac{y}{9} = \frac{32}{36}$ Cross products: $y \times 36$ 9×32

$y \times 36 = 9 \times 32$

$y \times 36 = 288$

$y = \frac{288}{36}$

$y = 8$

Remember, cross products are terms diagonally opposite each other in a proportion.

Do these ratios form proportions? Write *yes* or *no*. Use cross products.

1. $\frac{5}{7} \stackrel{?}{=} \frac{65}{91}$
2. $\frac{16}{10} \stackrel{?}{=} \frac{68}{40}$

Write the cross products.

3. $\frac{92}{46} = \frac{120}{60}$
4. $\frac{29}{87} = \frac{51}{153}$

Solve the proportions by using cross products.

5. $\frac{1.5}{6} = \frac{4.5}{s}$
6. $\frac{18}{t} = \frac{81}{63}$
7. $\frac{p}{11} = \frac{49}{77}$
8. $\frac{40}{48} = \frac{r}{72}$
9. $\frac{5}{d} = \frac{10}{7}$
10. $\frac{29}{203} = \frac{f}{35}$

Set D pages 278–281

These polygons are similar. Corresponding angles are congruent. The ratios of the lengths of corresponding sides are equal.

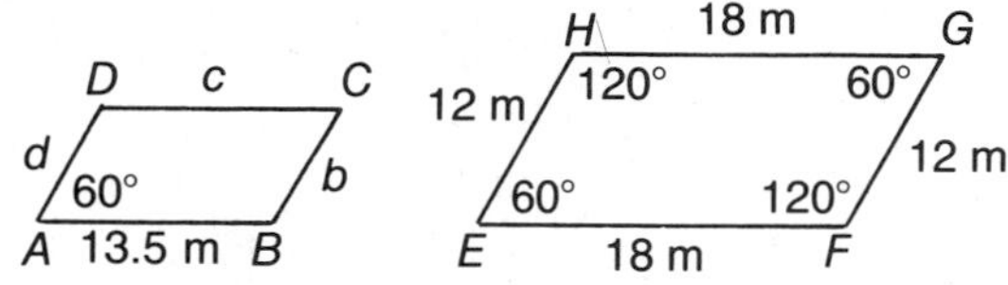

Find the length of side $\overline{BC}$ by using proportions.

$$\frac{13.5}{18} = \frac{b}{12} \qquad \frac{\text{length of } \overline{AB}}{\text{length of } \overline{EF}} = \frac{\text{length of } \overline{BC}}{\text{length of } \overline{FG}}$$

$18b = 13.5 \times 12$

$18b = 162$

$b = \frac{162}{18}$

$b = 9$ Side $\overline{BC}$ is 9 m long.

Remember, similar figures have the same shape, but not necessarily the same size, with corresponding sides and angles.

Name the corresponding angle or side.

1. $\angle D$ **2.** $\overline{DC}$ **3.** $\angle C$

4. $\overline{EH}$ **5.** $\overline{AD}$ **6.** $\angle G$

Write the letter of the correct answer.

7. Which proportion would you solve to find the length of $\overline{DC}$?

a. $\frac{12}{9} = \frac{c}{18}$ **b.** $\frac{9}{12} = \frac{c}{18}$ **c.** $\frac{9}{12} = \frac{18}{c}$

8. Find the length of side $\overline{DC}$.

9. Find the measure of $\angle C$.

10. Find the length of side $\overline{AD}$.

Set E pages 284–285

A doll house is similar to a family's house. The scale of the doll house is 4 in. to 5 ft. The actual length of the house is 30 ft. Find the length of the doll house.

$\frac{d}{30} = \frac{4}{5}$ inches / feet

$5d = 30 \times 4$

$5d = 120$

$d = \frac{120}{5}$

$d = 24$ The doll house is 24 in. long.

Remember, label units in your proportion so that your answer is in the correct units.

1. The house is 24 ft wide. Write a proportion to find the width of the dollhouse.

2. The house is 20 ft high. Write a proportion to find the height of the dollhouse.

3. Find the width of the doll house.

4. Find the height of the doll house.

Set F pages 288–291

A percent can be written as a ratio, with a second term of 100.

$$18\% = \frac{18}{100}$$

Similarly, a ratio can be written as a percent. If you need to, write an equal ratio with a second term of 100.

$$\frac{4}{5} = \frac{80}{100} = 80\%$$

Remember, percent means "out of 100." So the second term in the ratio must be 100.

Write each percent as a ratio with a second term of 100.

1. 5% **2.** 98% **3.** 29% **4.** 77%

Write each ratio as a percent.

5. $\frac{65}{100}$ **6.** $\frac{8}{10}$ **7.** $\frac{19}{25}$ **8.** $\frac{13}{20}$

Independent Study MORE PRACTICE

More Practice

Set A pages 270–271

Write four equal ratios for each situation.

1. 9 soft rock tapes to 16 new age tapes

2. 50 digital tapes to 30 compact discs

3. 7 Vivaldi tapes to 12 Bach tapes

Write three equal ratios.

4. $\frac{3}{4}$ **5.** $\frac{11}{5}$ **6.** $\frac{20}{28}$ **7.** $\frac{7}{9}$ **8.** $\frac{35}{25}$

9. $\frac{17}{21}$ **10.** $\frac{60}{45}$ **11.** $\frac{18}{72}$ **12.** $\frac{33}{88}$ **13.** $\frac{4}{13}$

14. $\frac{7}{8}$ **15.** $\frac{5}{6}$ **16.** $\frac{12}{16}$ **17.** $\frac{28}{40}$ **18.** $\frac{32}{20}$

19. $\frac{40}{12}$ **20.** $\frac{12}{64}$ **21.** $\frac{10}{25}$ **22.** $\frac{15}{100}$ **23.** $\frac{50}{35}$

Set B pages 272–273

Solve each proportion.

1. $\frac{1}{2} = \frac{a}{16}$ **2.** $\frac{5}{9} = \frac{25}{b}$ **3.** $\frac{36}{42} = \frac{c}{14}$

4. $\frac{77}{22} = \frac{21}{d}$ **5.** $\frac{14}{20} = \frac{56}{e}$ **6.** $\frac{5}{1.6} = \frac{f}{4.8}$

7. $\frac{18}{27} = \frac{40}{g}$ **8.** $\frac{12}{39} = \frac{60}{h}$ **9.** $\frac{n}{33} = \frac{1.5}{5.5}$

10. $\frac{2}{5} = \frac{a}{15}$ **11.** $\frac{8}{14} = \frac{4}{c}$ **12.** $\frac{45}{20} = \frac{s}{4}$

13. $\frac{4.8}{0.8} = \frac{96}{t}$ **14.** $\frac{n}{2.4} = \frac{4}{0.6}$ **15.** $\frac{36}{9} = \frac{r}{3}$

16. $\frac{5}{12} = \frac{75}{p}$ **17.** $\frac{20}{m} = \frac{220}{121}$ **18.** $\frac{x}{8} = \frac{70}{560}$

19. $\frac{18}{20} = \frac{v}{60}$ **20.** $\frac{c}{12} = \frac{12}{6}$ **21.** $\frac{6}{a} = \frac{42}{63}$

Set C pages 274–275

Solve each proportion by using cross products.

1. $\frac{m}{52} = \frac{3}{4}$ **2.** $\frac{6}{21} = \frac{2}{n}$ **3.** $\frac{14}{p} = \frac{42}{54}$

4. $\frac{5}{1.2} = \frac{r}{8.4}$ **5.** $\frac{6}{11} = \frac{48}{s}$ **6.** $\frac{69}{t} = \frac{23}{8}$

7. $\frac{27}{w} = \frac{9}{7.2}$ **8.** $\frac{y}{20} = \frac{21}{105}$ **9.** $\frac{9}{0.25} = \frac{108}{z}$

10. $\frac{80}{20} = \frac{x}{0.9}$ **11.** $\frac{54}{189} = \frac{18}{p}$ **12.** $\frac{x}{5.4} = \frac{2.2}{12}$

13. $\frac{s}{35} = \frac{96}{28}$ **14.** $\frac{0.56}{0.77} = \frac{8}{w}$ **15.** $\frac{16}{128} = \frac{3}{c}$

16. $\frac{2.8}{3.6} = \frac{x}{18}$ **17.** $\frac{2}{0.7} = \frac{2.8}{r}$ **18.** $\frac{0.4}{6} = \frac{d}{51}$

19. $\frac{a}{16} = \frac{12.5}{40}$ **20.** $\frac{2}{0.8} = \frac{e}{2.4}$ **21.** $\frac{48}{p} = \frac{14}{7}$

Set D pages 278–281

Is each pair of figures similar? Write *yes* or *no*.

1. 15 cm, 32°, 18°, 130°, 6 cm, 9 cm — 2 cm, 32°, 130°, 5 cm, 3 cm, 18°

2. 6 in., 10 in. — 40 in., 15 in.

Each pair of polygons is similar. Find each missing length.

3. **4.** **5.**

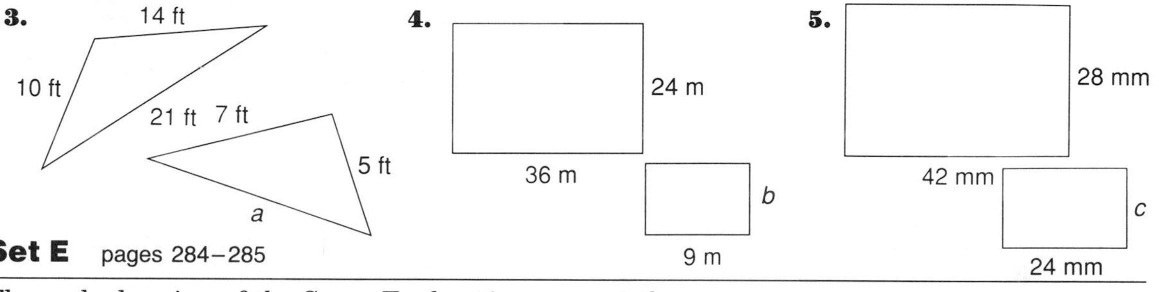

Set E pages 284–285

The scale drawing of the Space Exploration room at the Science Center is 2 cm to 3 m. The scale drawing is 4.6 cm long and 3.2 cm wide.

1. Write a proportion to find the actual length of the room.

2. Write a proportion to find the actual width of the room.

3. Find the actual length of the room.

4. Find the actual width of the room.

The scale drawing of the Explore Your Universe room at the Center is 2 cm to 3 m. The scale drawing is 3.8 cm long and 3.4 cm wide.

5. Write a proportion to find the actual length of the room.

6. Write a proportion to find the actual width of the room.

7. Find the actual length of the room.

8. Find the actual width of the room.

Set F pages 288–291

Write each percent as a ratio.

1. 62% **2.** 8% **3.** 27% **4.** 95%

Write each ratio as a percent.

5. $\frac{71}{100}$ **6.** $\frac{9}{10}$ **7.** $\frac{2}{5}$ **8.** $\frac{1}{4}$

Write and solve a proportion for each.

9. 26 is what percent of 65?

10. What is 60% of 90?

11. 75% of what number is 27?

12. 42 is what percent of 105?

Independent Study ENRICHMENT

Enrichment

The Golden Ratio

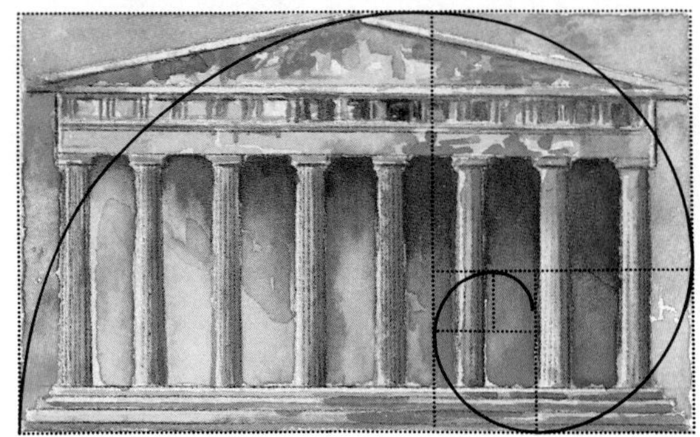

When Greek architects designed the Parthenon in Athens in 447 B.C., they used the ***golden ratio*** (ϕ) (read "phi") to determine its proportions. In the years since, artists have often employed the same proportions in their work because they produce shapes that are pleasing to the eye.

Golden ratio (ϕ) $= \frac{\text{Length}}{\text{Width}} = \frac{1 + \sqrt{5}}{2} \approx 1.618$

Use $\phi \approx 1.618$ to find the missing dimension of each rectangle with golden ratio proportions.

1. Length = 3.8832 cm
   Width = ?
2. Width = 28.5 m
   Length = ?
3. Length = 158.7258 dm
   Width = ?
4. Width = 27.5 in.
   Length = ?
5. Length = 14 ft
   Width = ?
6. Width = 64 mi
   Length = ?
7. To the nearest foot, the Parthenon is 101 feet long. To the nearest foot, how high is it?

Use your calculator to evaluate the following. Use $\phi = 1.6180339$.

8. ϕ^2
9. $\phi^2(\phi - 1)$
10. What do you notice about your answers to Exercises 8 and 9?

ϕ appears in connection with the Fibonacci Sequence. Each number in the Fibonacci Sequence is obtained by adding the two previous numbers:

1, 1, 2, 3, 5, 8, 13, 21, 34, 55, 89, . . .

11. Find the next 3 numbers in the sequence.
12. **Calculator** Divide each number you found in Exercise 11 by the number that precedes it in the Fibonacci Sequence. What do you notice about the quotients?

Chapter 8 Review/Test

1. Which contains three equal ratios for 3 pencils to 2 students?

a. $\frac{2}{3}, \frac{8}{12}, \frac{10}{15}$

b. $\frac{3}{2}, \frac{8}{6}, \frac{16}{12}$

c. $\frac{6}{4}, \frac{9}{6}, \frac{12}{8}$

Solve each proportion.

2. $\frac{3}{5} = \frac{s}{25}$

3. $\frac{13}{4} = \frac{52}{b}$

4. $\frac{12}{w} = \frac{8}{14}$

5. $\frac{x}{40} = \frac{15}{24}$

Write a proportion. Then solve.

6. Gloria wants to make a stew for 12 people. The recipe serves 8 and calls for 4 pounds of meat. How much meat should Gloria use?

7. Derek's motorboat travels 7 miles in 2 hours when trolling for fish. How far can Derek troll in 5 hours?

Use the similar triangles below in Exercises 8 and 9.

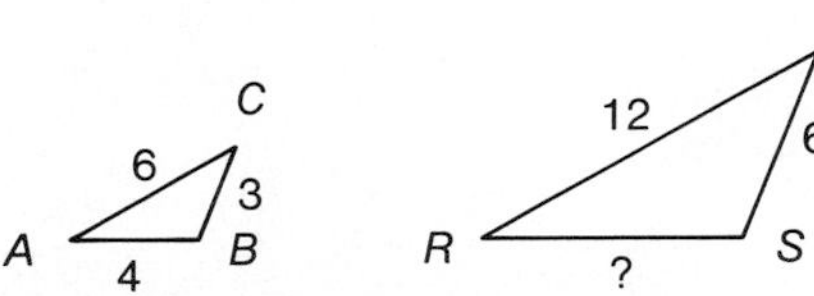

8. Which side of $\triangle ABC$ corresponds to $\overline{ST}$ in $\triangle RST$?

9. Write a proportion to find the length of $\overline{RS}$. Solve the proportion.

10. On an archaeological drawing, the distance from the entrance to where the mummy was found is 13 cm. If the scale is 1 cm = 0.5 m, what is the actual distance?

11. On this map, Amy measured the distance along the pathway from the main temple to Pyramid A to be about 6 cm.

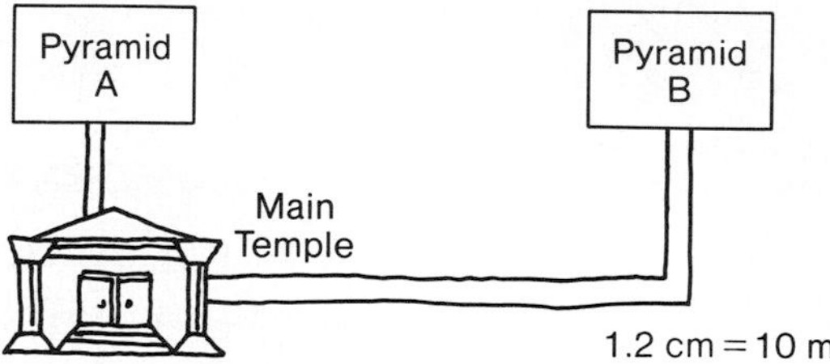

How long is the walkway from the main temple to Pyramid A?

Write each ratio as a percent.

12. $\frac{27}{100}$

13. $\frac{2}{5}$

14. Write and solve a proportion to find 25% of 36.

15. Write and solve a proportion to find what percent 12 is of 60.

16. After 2 weeks the architect told Mr. Rautu that 20% of the house was complete. At that rate, how long would it take to build the whole house?

17. Bob can make 20 wooden windmills in 3 weeks. Choose the equation that will help predict how long it will take to fill an order of 50 windmills.

a. $\frac{3}{20} = \frac{n}{50}$

b. $(50 - 20) \times 3 = n$

c. $\frac{50}{3} = \frac{n}{20}$

d. $20 \times 3 - 50 = n$

18. Write About Math Suppose you want to make a scale drawing of the first floor of a house whose outside dimensions are 40 ft by 50 ft. Your sheet of paper is $8\frac{1}{2}$ in. by 11 in. What scale would you choose? Why?

Percent

9

Did You Know: A large percentage of the food we eat is made up of water. Apples are 85% water and watermelon is 97% water. Pineapples are about 87% water.

Number-Sense Project

Estimate

What percent of a grape do you think is water?

Gather Data

A raisin is a sun-dried grape. Weigh some grapes and an equal number of raisins. Repeat two more times.

Analyze and Report

Assume the difference in the weight of the raisins and grapes is the weight of the water in the grapes. Find the percent of water in grapes.

Percents and Decimals

Build Understanding

A. Mr. Hill's social studies class surveyed 100 people at the mall to see how many people intended to vote in the next election.

61 said they would vote.
34 said they were undecided.
5 said they would not vote.

Since 61 out of 100 people intend to vote, you can think of 61 out of 100 as 61 hundredths, or 61 percent.

0.61 = 61%

B. Write as a decimal and as a percent the number of people who are undecided about voting.

34 out of 100 = 0.34 = 34%

To write a percent for a decimal, move the decimal point 2 places to the right and write a percent sign. Insert zeros if necessary.

0.45 = 45% **0.7 = 70%**

0.125 = 12.5% **0.006 = 0.6%**

1.35 = 135% **2 = 200%**

C. Of the people surveyed, 5 out of 100, or 5%, said they would not vote. Write 5% as a decimal.

5% = 5 hundredths = 0.05

To write a decimal for a percent, move the decimal point 2 places to the left and omit the percent sign. Insert zeros if necessary.

93% = 0.93 **62.5% = 0.625**

0.5% = 0.005 **100% = 1.00 = 1**

1% = 0.01 **150% = 1.50 = 1.5**

Talk About Math In Example A, the goal of the class was to survey 100 voters. What percent of their goal would the class achieve if they surveyed 150 voters?

Check Understanding

For another example, see Set A, pages 328–329.

Write a decimal and a percent describing each of the following.

1. 18 out of 100 **2.** 90 out of 100 **3.** 50 out of 100 **4.** 1 out of 100

Copy and fill in the missing numbers.

5. 0.5 out of 100 is ▒%. **6.** ▒ out of 100 is 22%. **7.** 65% is 65 out of ▒.

Practice

For More Practice, see Set A, pages 330–331.

Write each decimal as a percent. **Remember** to insert zeros if necessary.

8. 0.38 **9.** 0.77 **10.** 0.05 **11.** 0.08 **12.** 0.4

13. 0.9 **14.** 2.38 **15.** 1.42 **16.** 0.006 **17.** 0.875

18. 0.034 **19.** 0.998 **20.** 5.3 **21.** 1.0 **22.** 5

23. 0.409 **24.** 0 **25.** 0.42 **26.** 0.002 **27.** 3

28. 4.88 **29.** 0.0025 **30.** 0.375 **31.** 0.03 **32.** 0.045

Write each percent as a decimal.

33. 42% **34.** 87% **35.** 6% **36.** 3% **37.** 18%

38. 13% **39.** 30% **40.** 70% **41.** 125% **42.** 275%

43. 0.8% **44.** 0.1% **45.** 100% **46.** 0.38% **47.** 16.8%

48. 0.6% **49.** 31% **50.** 400% **51.** 0.83% **52.** 350%

53. 0.27% **54.** 52.9% **55.** 0% **56.** 2% **57.** 13.84%

Write the numbers in order from least to greatest.

58. 0.3% 30% 3% **59.** 0.72 7.2% 0.72% **60.** 52% 0.6 68%

61. 5 450% 510% **62.** 0.08 7.2% 0.066 **63.** 0.1% 0.1 1 1%

Problem Solving

Solve each problem.

64. If 12 out of the 100 people surveyed by Mr. Hill's class were under 21 years old, what percent were under 21?

65. If 23 out of 100 people surveyed were 30 years old or younger, what percent were 30 or younger?

66. What percent of the people were over 30?

67. **Critical Thinking** What percent of the people in the survey were from 21 years old through 30 years old?

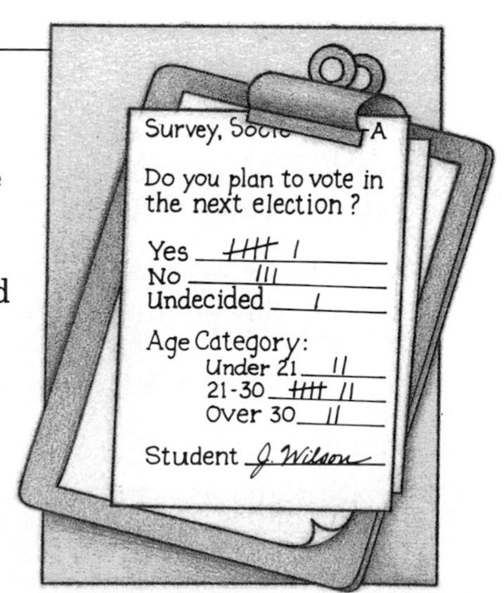

Percents and Fractions

Build Understanding

A mosaic is a picture or design made by cutting and gluing together small pieces, such as stones, seeds, or tiles. In ancient times, mosaics were used to decorate buildings in Asia Minor, Egypt, Greece, and Rome. In the western hemisphere, the Incas, Mayans, and Aztecs used mosaics to decorate jewelry and small objects. Today, artists in all countries produce beautiful mosaics.

This double-headed serpent shows how skillfully Aztec craftsmen decorated with mosaics.

ACTIVITY

A. Mosaic Madness

Materials: Grid paper, colored pens or marking pencils in blue, red, and yellow

In art class, Sonia is making a mosaic design by using four colors of square tiles. The design is shown at the right. What part of the design is red? What part is blue? What part is yellow? What part is white?

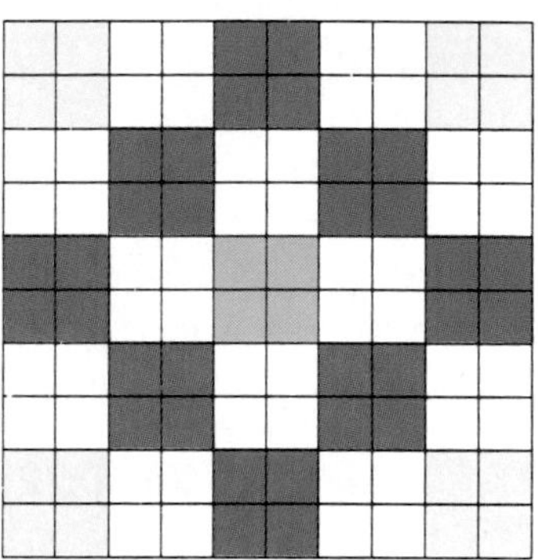

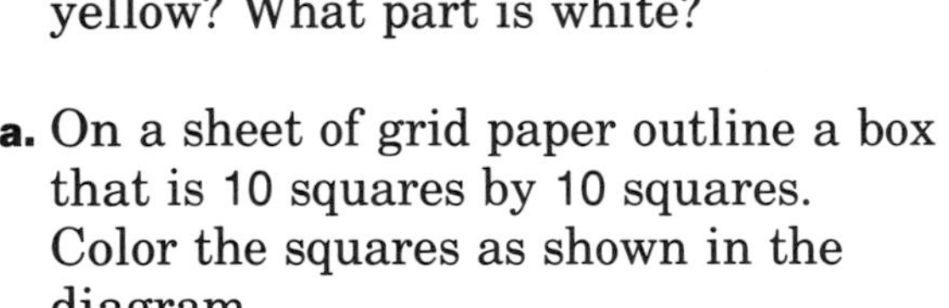

a. On a sheet of grid paper outline a box that is 10 squares by 10 squares. Color the squares as shown in the diagram.

b. How many squares out of 100 are red? Express the answer as a percent. Then express the percent as a fraction in lowest terms.

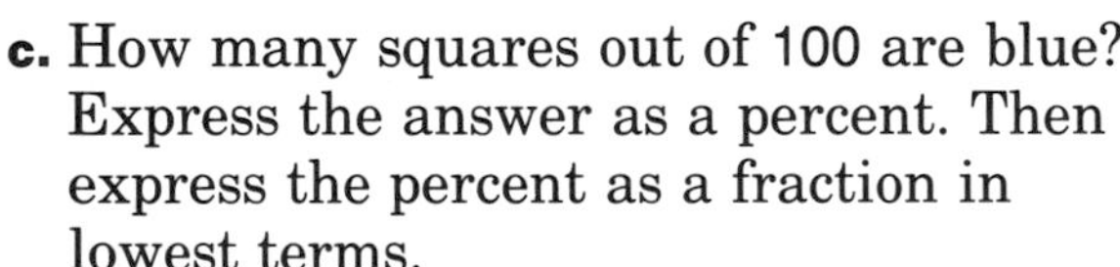

c. How many squares out of 100 are blue? Express the answer as a percent. Then express the percent as a fraction in lowest terms.

d. How many squares out of 100 are yellow? Express the answer as a percent. Then express the percent as a fraction in lowest terms.

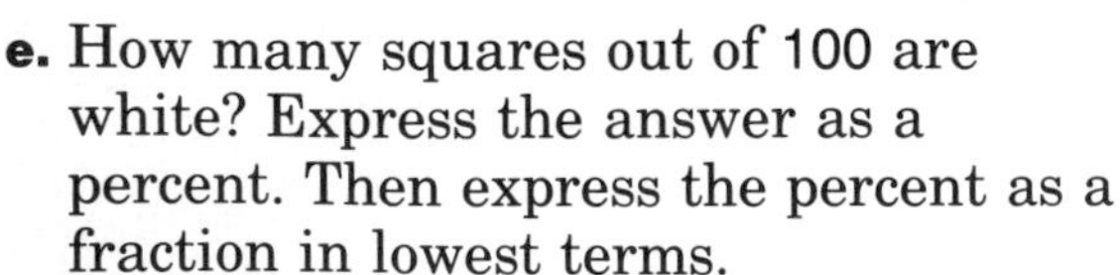

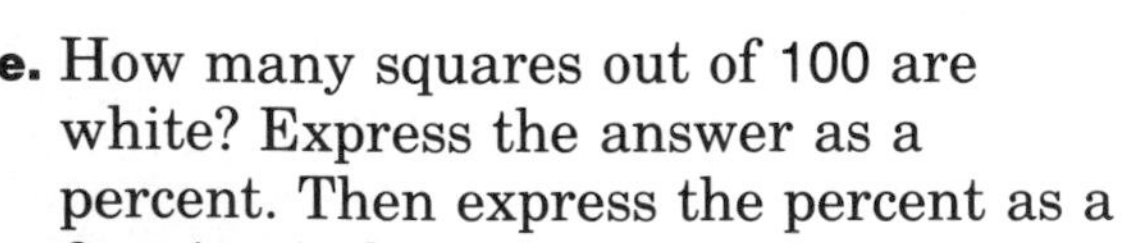

e. How many squares out of 100 are white? Express the answer as a percent. Then express the percent as a fraction in lowest terms.

f. Make your own design using a 10-by-10 grid. Show 40% of the design in one color. Then express 40% as a fraction in lowest terms.

B. Write 120% as a mixed number.

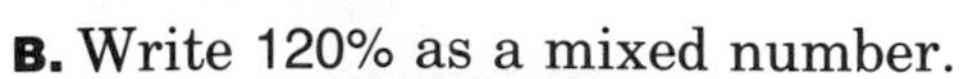

$$120\% = \frac{120}{100} = 1\frac{20}{100} = 1\frac{1}{5}$$

C. Write $1\frac{1}{2}$ as a percent.

$$1\frac{1}{2} = \frac{3}{2} = \frac{150}{100} = 150\%$$

This section of a mosaic floor is in a Roman villa in Spain. The villa was built during the Roman period in Spain, 200 B.C. to 400 A.D.

D. Sonia is designing an Italian-style mosaic. About $\frac{5}{8}$ of the tiles she has are needed for the background. Write $\frac{5}{8}$ as a percent.

Since $\frac{5}{8}$ means 5 ÷ 8, you can find the answer by dividing.

$$0.62\frac{4}{8} = 0.62\frac{1}{2} = 62\frac{1}{2}\% = 62.5\%$$

$$\begin{array}{r} 8\overline{)5.00} \\ \underline{4\,8} \\ 20 \\ \underline{16} \\ 4 \end{array}$$

E. Write $16\frac{2}{3}\%$ as a fraction in lowest terms.

$$16\frac{2}{3}\% = \frac{16\frac{2}{3}}{100}$$

$16\frac{2}{3} \div 100$ — $\frac{16\frac{2}{3}}{100}$ means $16\frac{2}{3} \div 100$.

$$\frac{50}{3} \div \frac{100}{1} = \frac{50}{3} \times \frac{1}{100} = \frac{50 \times 1}{3 \times 100} = \frac{1}{6}$$

Talk About Math In Example A, could more than 100% of the mosaic be red?

Check Understanding

For another example, see Set B, pages 328–329.

Find each missing number.

1. $12\% = \frac{▦}{100} = \frac{▦}{25}$

2. $\frac{4}{5} = \frac{▦}{100} = ▦\%$

3. $\frac{20}{20} = \frac{▦}{100} = ▦\%$

4. $20\% = \frac{20}{100} = \frac{1}{▦}$

5. $150\% = \frac{150}{100} = 1\frac{▦}{100} = 1\frac{1}{2}$

6. $2\frac{1}{5} = \frac{11}{5} = \frac{▦}{100} = ▦\%$

7. Which division expression would you use to write $\frac{5}{8}$ as a decimal, $8\overline{)5}$ or $5\overline{)8}$?

8. Which division expression would you use to write $66\frac{2}{3}\%$ as a fraction, $66\frac{2}{3} \div 100$ or $100 \div 66\frac{2}{3}$?

Practice

For More Practice, see Set B, pages 330–331.

Write each fraction as a percent.

9. $\frac{9}{100}$ **10.** $\frac{15}{25}$ **11.** $\frac{1}{10}$ **12.** $\frac{7}{20}$ **13.** $\frac{8}{16}$ **14.** $\frac{6}{10}$ **15.** $\frac{1}{4}$

16. $\frac{4}{5}$ **17.** $\frac{112}{100}$ **18.** $\frac{3}{8}$ **19.** $\frac{0.7}{100}$ **20.** $\frac{1}{3}$ **21.** $\frac{5}{2}$ **22.** $\frac{6.7}{100}$

23. $\frac{1}{40}$ **24.** $\frac{2}{5}$ **25.** $\frac{180}{100}$ **26.** $\frac{3}{4}$ **27.** $\frac{9}{4}$ **28.** $\frac{7}{8}$ **29.** $\frac{42.5}{100}$

Write each percent as a fraction or a mixed number.
Remember to write the answer in lowest terms.

30. 10% **31.** 40% **32.** 75% **33.** 7% **34.** 88% **35.** 12.3% **36.** 1%

37. 31% **38.** 0.1% **39.** 52% **40.** 24% **41.** 95% **42.** 150% **43.** 67.5%

44. $33\frac{1}{3}\%$ **45.** 425% **46.** 90% **47.** $83\frac{2}{3}\%$ **48.** 3% **49.** 87.5% **50.** 9.4%

Copy and complete the table. The first row is done for you. Save the table to use for reference.

Fraction	Decimal	Percent
$\frac{1}{2}$	0.5	50%
51.	**52.**	75%
$\frac{1}{4}$	**53.**	**54.**
55.	$0.33\frac{1}{3}$	**56.**
57.	**58.**	$66\frac{2}{3}\%$
59.	0.2	**60.**
$\frac{1}{8}$	**61.**	**62.**
63.	**64.**	$37\frac{1}{2}\%$
65.	0.625	**66.**
$\frac{7}{8}$	**67.**	**68.**

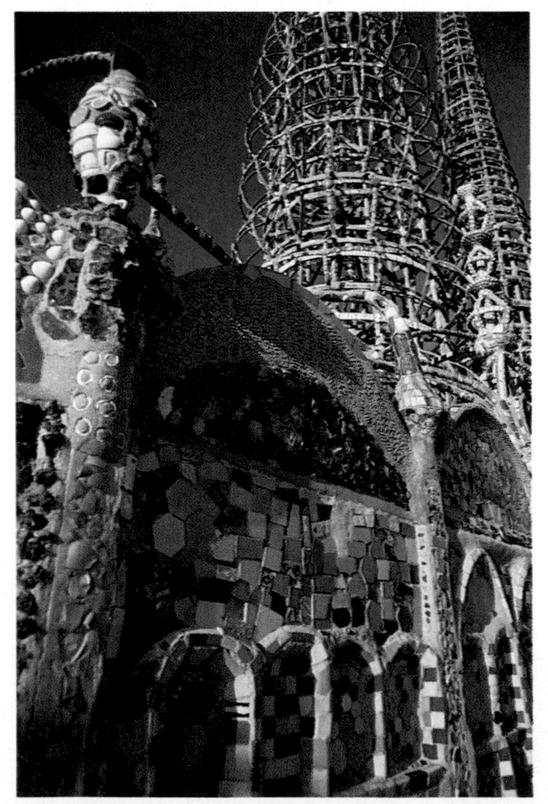

It took tile setter Simon Rodia 33 years to construct these steel towers decorated in mosaics. The towers are located in the Watts district of Los Angeles.

Problem Solving

Solve. **Remember** to use lowest terms in your answer.

69. Japanese people often pave their garden paths in mosaics of pebbles and clay tiles. Kenji used clay tiles for 55% of his garden path. Write 55% as a fraction in lowest terms.

70. The Village Art Gallery exhibits 20 mosaics. Three of the mosaics feature Persian (Iranian) designs. What percent of the mosaics show these designs?

71. Borders made from geometric patterns are popular in mosaics. Jack is using about $\frac{1}{8}$ of the tiles he has for a geometric border. What percent is this?

72. At the city museum, 0.6% of the Native American artifacts are mosaics. Write 0.6% as a fraction in lowest terms.

The pattern of this mosaic was adapted from a Persian carpet design.

Explore ______ Math

Solve each problem.

73. Look at Exercises 9–29. Which answers are greater than 50%? less than 50%? equal to 50%?

74. Pick one exercise where the answer is greater than 50%. Multiply the numerator of the fraction by 2. Is the product greater or less than the denominator?

75. Pick another exercise where the answer is less than 50%. Multiply the numerator by 2. Is the product greater or less than the denominator?

76. Pick another exercise where the answer is equal to 50%. Multiply the numerator by 2. Is the product equal to the denominator?

Determine if the fractions are greater than, less than, or equal to 50%.

77. $\frac{11}{25}$ **78.** $\frac{9}{16}$ **79.** $\frac{12}{25}$ **80.** $\frac{14}{28}$ **81.** $\frac{26}{50}$

82. Change each fraction in Exercises 77–81 to a percent. Were your predictions correct?

83. Write a rule for determining if a fraction is greater than 50%, less than 50%, or equal to 50%.

ALGEBRA

Finding a Percent of a Number

Build Understanding

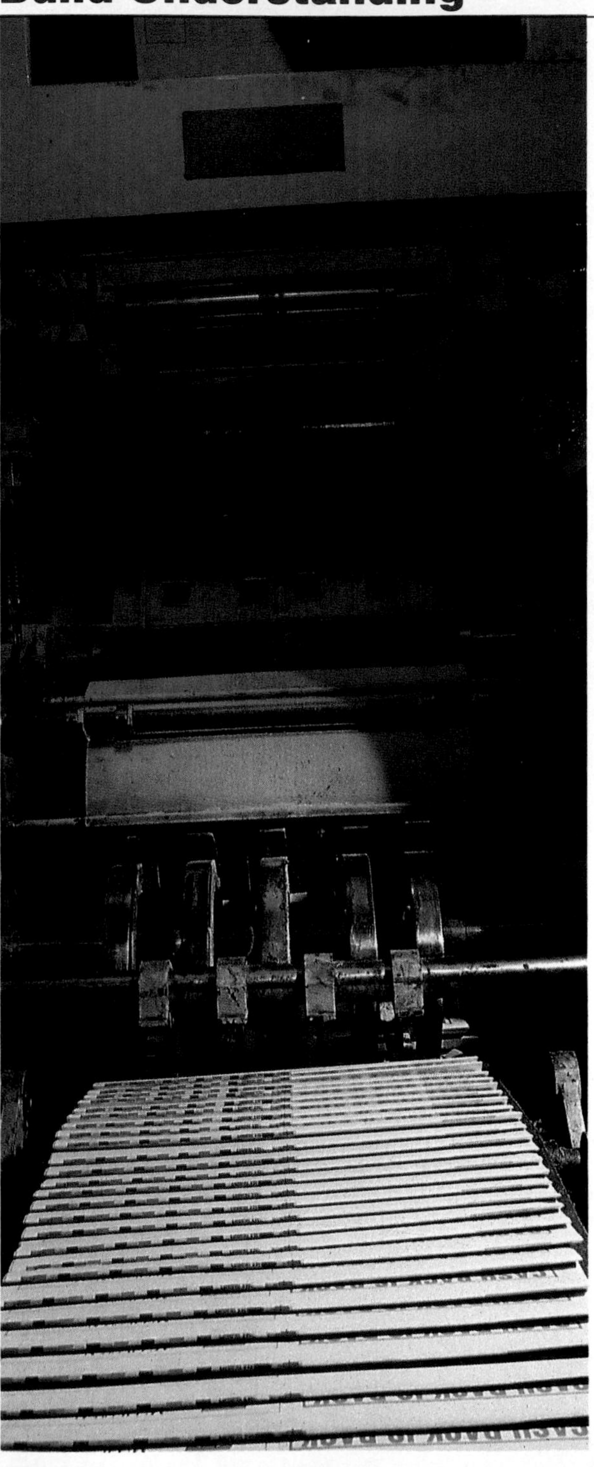

A. On Saturdays, the *Times-Star* reduces the number of pages in the newspaper by 15%. The daily newspaper has an average of 40 pages. How many pages shorter is the Saturday newspaper?

You can use a proportion.

What is 15% of 40?

$$\frac{15}{100} = \frac{n}{40}$$

Another method is to write and solve an equation.

What is 15% of 40?

$$n = 0.15 \times 40$$

$$n = 6$$

The newspaper is 6 pages shorter.

B. On Thursdays, the *Times-Star* has a 20% increase in orders for ads. Normally, there are 150 ad orders. What is the increase in orders on Thursdays?

What is 20% of 150?

20% is $\frac{1}{5}$. Sometimes it's easier to use a fraction for the percent.

$$n = \frac{1}{5} \times 150$$

$$n = 30$$

On Thursdays, the orders for ads increase by 30.

More than 60 million newspapers are delivered every weekday in the U.S.

C. Calculator Use a calculator to find 20% of 150. There are two ways to do this.

Press: 20 [×] 150 [%] **Display:** *30*

Press: [.] 20 [×] 150 [=] **Display:** *30*

Can you find a third way by using the fact that 20% is $\frac{1}{5}$?

D. Mental Math Find 75% of 80. Sometimes you can use a fraction to do the computation mentally.

75% is $\frac{3}{4}$.

$c = \frac{3}{4} \times 80$ $\quad 80 \div 4 = 20$

$\quad 20 \times 3 = 60$

$c = 60$

■ **Talk About Math** If a certain percent of 36 is 54, what can you say about the percent? If a certain percent of 36 is 34, what about the percent?

Check Understanding

For another example, see Set C, pages 328–329.

Which numbers would you multiply to find each answer?

1. 39% of 65 **a.** 39 × 65 **b.** 0.39 × 65 **c.** 0.39 × 0.65
2. $33\frac{1}{3}$% of 15 **a.** $33\frac{1}{3} \times 15$ **b.** $\frac{1}{3} \times 0.15$ **c.** $\frac{1}{3} \times 15$
3. 50% of 8 **a.** $\frac{1}{2} \times 8$ **b.** $\frac{1}{2} \times \frac{1}{8}$ **c.** 50 × 8

Find the answers to Exercises 4–6.

4. What is 0% of 180?
5. What is 100% of 125?
6. **Number Sense** If the *Times-Star* allows 40% of a page for news copy, 20% for photos, and 40% for advertisements, can the page include any other material? Explain.

Practice

For More Practice, see Set C, pages 330–331.

Find each answer. Tell whether you wrote the percent as a fraction or a decimal. **Remember** to move the decimal point when you use a decimal.

7. 25% of 36
8. 50% of 20
9. 28% of 62
10. 10% of 120
11. 75% of 60
12. $33\frac{1}{3}$% of 600
13. 50% of 12
14. 25% of 16
15. 100% of 8
16. 27% of 500
17. 32% of 25
18. 40% of 260
19. $87\frac{1}{2}$% of 200
20. 0.7% of 200
21. 62.5% of 40

Mental Math Use mental math to solve Exercises 22–27.

22. 10% of 60
23. 25% of 120
24. $33\frac{1}{3}$% of 45
25. 50% of 60
26. 75% of 48
27. $66\frac{2}{3}$% of 90

Tell whether you would use mental math, paper and pencil, or a calculator. Then find each answer.

28. 50% of 62 = ▒
29. 40% of 180 = ▒
30. What is 25% of 84?
31. $17\frac{1}{2}$% of 200 = ▒
32. What is $33\frac{1}{3}$% of 75?
33. Find $66\frac{2}{3}$% of 78.
34. Find 22% of 62.5.
35. What is 62.5% of 80?
36. Find 0.2% of 300.
37. $37\frac{1}{2}$% of 104 is what number?
38. 75% of 44 is what number?
39. 9.5% of 60 is what number?
40. 18.9% of 20 is what number?
41. 250% of 560 is what number?
42. 125% of 400 is what number?

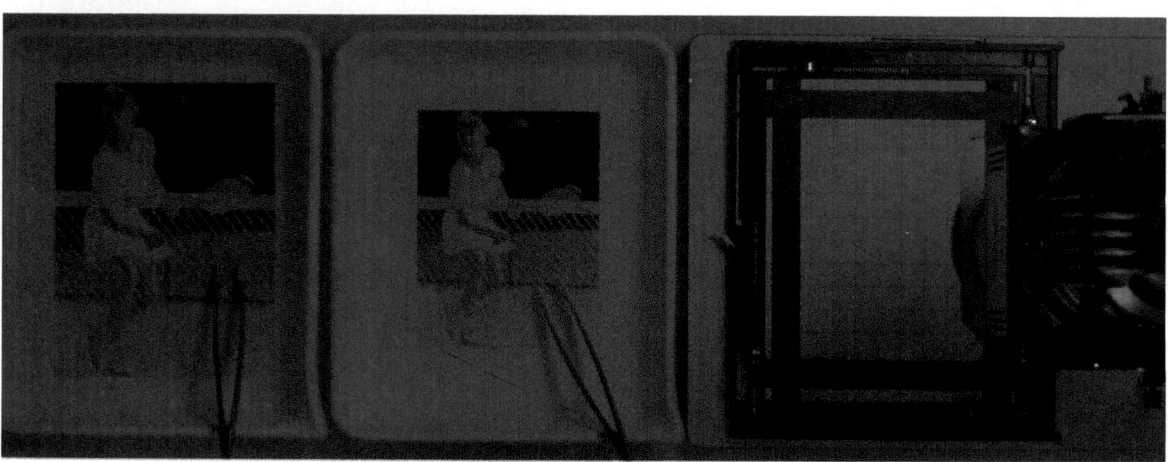

Problem Solving

The photo lab at the *Times-Star* reduces each side of a sports picture by 20%. The original size of the photo is 10 inches by 15 inches. Solve each problem.

43. By how many inches is the 10-inch side reduced?
44. By how many inches is the 15-inch side reduced?
45. What are the dimensions of the reduced picture?

Solve each problem.

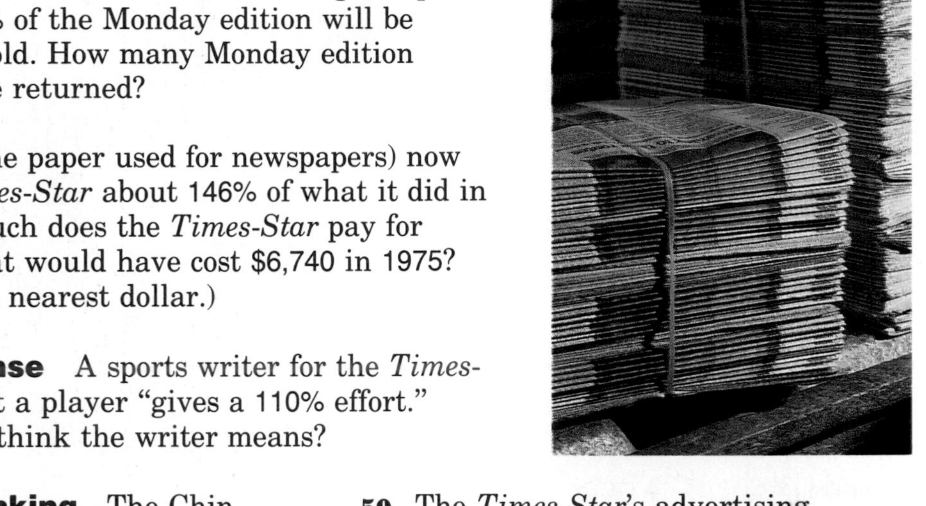

46. The *Times-Star* prints 50,000 newspapers for its Monday edition. The circulation manager expects that about 3% of the Monday edition will be returned unsold. How many Monday edition papers will be returned?

47. Newsprint (the paper used for newspapers) now costs the *Times-Star* about 146% of what it did in 1975. How much does the *Times-Star* pay for newsprint that would have cost $6,740 in 1975? (Round to the nearest dollar.)

48. **Number Sense** A sports writer for the *Times-Star* says that a player "gives a 110% effort." What do you think the writer means?

49. **Critical Thinking** The Chin family advertised their garage sale in the *Times-Star* and earned $224 from the sale. They set aside 75% of that money for their vacation. How much did they set aside? How much vacation money would they have had if they had set aside 80.5%?

50. The *Times-Star*'s advertising department bought a computer system that cost $2,375 plus sales tax. If the tax rate was $5\frac{1}{2}$%, how much was the tax? What was the total cost of the computer system? Round your answers to the nearest cent.

Midchapter Checkup

Write each decimal as a percent and write each percent as a decimal.

1. 0.61 **2.** 1.75 **3.** 0.095 **4.** 84% **5.** 125% **6.** 10.5%

Write each fraction as a percent and write each percent as a fraction or a mixed number.

7. $\frac{3}{5}$ **8.** $\frac{1}{3}$ **9.** $\frac{5}{4}$ **10.** 64% **11.** 110% **12.** $66\frac{2}{3}$%

Tell whether you would use mental math, paper and pencil, or a calculator. Then find each answer.

13. What is 28% of 140?

14. Find 125% of 360.

15. 32% of 18 = ▒

16. Find $33\frac{1}{3}$% of 186.

17. What is 9.5% of 12,000?

18. 56.4% of 195 = ▒

Problem-Solving Workshop

Explore as a Team

In this activity, you will be choosing a gift for each member of your team. You have $100 to spend altogether. Come as close as you can to $100 without going over that amount.

You will need a collection of catalogs, advertisement fliers, and newspaper ads.

1. Discuss among yourselves the kinds of gifts you would like to receive. Talk about the kind of clothes you like, the hobbies you have, the music you prefer, the books you like to read, and so on.

2. Look through catalogs, fliers, and ads. Then choose one or more items for each person.

3. For each person, make a "gift sheet" with the person's name at the top. Cut out pictures of the gifts for each person and paste the pictures on each person's gift sheet. On a separate sheet, itemize the gifts, their cost, and the total amount spent. Remember that the total amount you spend cannot be more than $100.

TIPS FOR WORKING TOGETHER

Tell someone when he or she does or says something that helps you.

First pirate: "How much did you pay for your earrings?"

Second pirate: "$2.00"

First pirate: "Not bad for a buccaneer!"

Explore with a Computer

Use the *Spreadsheet Workshop Project* for this activity.

1. At the computer, study the spreadsheet chart. Predict what will happen if you change the denominator of the fraction to 3. to 5. Try these numbers.

2. Change the denominator back to 2. Predict what will happen if you change the numerator in the first column to 2. to 3. Try these numbers.

3. Explain what happens to the decimal and percent value with different numerators and denominators.

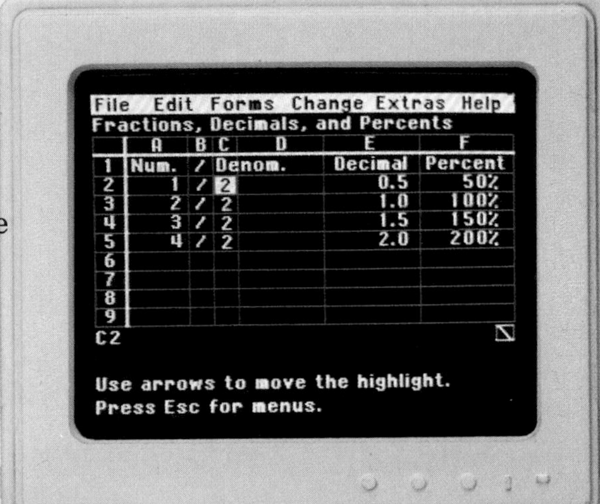

File Edit Forms Change Extras Help
Fractions, Decimals, and Percents
A B C D E F
1 Num. / Denom. Decimal Percent
2 1 / 2 0.5 50%
3 2 / 2 1.0 100%
4 3 / 2 1.5 150%
5 4 / 2 2.0 200%
6
7
8
9
C2
Use arrows to move the highlight.
Press Esc for menus.

Number-Sense Project

Look back at pages 300-301.
About how much water is in

a. 5 pounds of apples?

b. a 10-pound watermelon?

c. a 3-pound pineapple?

d. 4 pounds of grapes?

Math-at-Home Activity

The next time you and your family are at a restaurant, offer to check the bill and calculate the tip.

a. Check the bill to see if the items and prices listed are correct. Check the total.

b. Calculate the tip by using the "tipping guide" shown below.

Service	Tip
Excellent	20%
Good	15%
Fair	10%
Poor	5%

ALGEBRA

Finding What Percent One Number Is of Another

Build Understanding

A. The seventh-grade class is having a book fair. Their order included 300 novels. So far, 180 novels have been sold. What percent of the novels have been sold?

You can write and solve an equation.

180 is what percent of 300?

$$180 = n \times 300$$

$$\frac{180}{300} = \frac{n \times 300}{300}$$

$$n = 0.6 = 60\%$$

60% of the novels have been sold.

B. Last year the class ordered and sold 300 science fiction books. This year they ordered 330. What percent of last year's science fiction order is this year's?

330 is what percent of 300?

$$330 = n \times 300$$

$$\frac{330}{300} \quad \frac{n \times 300}{300}$$

$$n = \frac{110}{100} = 110\%$$

330 books are 110% of 300 books.

C. **Calculator** Use a calculator to solve Example A.

Press: 180 [÷] 300 [%]

Display: *60*

Talk About Math When you find what percent one number is of another, how can you tell whether the answer will be less than 100% or greater than 100%?

Check Understanding

For another example, see Set D, pages 328–329.

Which equation could you use to answer each question?

1. 18 is what percent of 25?
   a. $18 \times 25 = n$ b. $18 = n \times 25$
2. 100 is what percent of 80?
   a. $100 = n \times 80$ b. $80 = 100 \times n$
3. What percent of 200 is 150?
   a. $n = 200 \times 150$ b. $n \times 200 = 150$
4. What percent of 75 is 25?
   a. $n \times 25 = 75$ b. $n \times 75 = 25$

Mental Math Use mental math to solve Exercises 5–6.

5. 3 is what percent of 4?
6. What percent of 1 is 3?

Practice

For More Practice, see Set D, pages 330–331.

Find each answer. **Remember** to write an equation.

7. What percent of 5 is 3?

8. What percent of 9 is 6?

9. What percent of 40 is 16?

10. 9 is what percent of 15?

11. 250 is what percent of 500?

12. 12 is what percent of 4?

13. 84 is what percent of 200?

14. What percent of 350 is 140?

15. What percent of 20 is 15?

16. 60 is what percent of 160?

17. 70 is what percent of 35?

18. 5 is what percent of 1,000?

19. What percent of 12.5 is 5?

20. What percent of 480 is 80?

21. 45 is what percent of 20?

22. What percent of 25 is 12.5?

Mixed Practice Copy and complete the table.

Fraction	Decimal	Percent
23.	0.09	**24.**
25.	**26.**	8.4%
$\frac{13}{20}$	**27.**	**28.**

Answer each question.

29. What is 300% of 2?

30. What percent of 78 is 26?

31. What is 18% of $2,000?

32. What percent of $32 is $2.40?

Problem Solving

Solve each problem.

33. Francisco sold 24 adventure books last year. This year he sold 27 adventure books. What percent of last year's sales is this year's sales?

34. **Estimation** The seventh-grade class ordered 1,000 books. If they sell 952 books, about what percent of their order is this?

35. Melissa sold 24 books. Her mother bought $33\frac{1}{3}$% of the books she sold. How many books did her mother buy?

36. By Thursday the seventh-grade class sold 600 books. Yuri sold 15 of them. What percent of the class's books did Yuri sell?

ALGEBRA

Finding a Number When a Percent of It Is Known

Build Understanding

A. Amy earned \$1,897 in commissions last month by selling personal computers. This was 28% of her total monthly sales amount. What was the amount of Amy's total sales for the month?

You can write and solve an equation to find the total sales for the month.

1,897 is 28% of what number?

$1{,}897 = 0.28 \times n$

$\frac{1{,}897}{0.28} = \frac{0.28 \times n}{0.28}$

$\frac{1{,}897}{0.28} = n$

$n = 6{,}775$

Check by putting 6,775 in for n in the original equation.

$1{,}897 \stackrel{?}{=} 0.28 \times 6{,}775$

$1{,}897 = 1{,}897$

The answer checks. Amy's total sales for the month amounted to \$6,775.

B. Shing sold 13 computer programs this week. This was $6\frac{1}{2}\%$ of all the programs in stock in the store. How many programs were in stock?

13 is $6\frac{1}{2}\%$ of n.

$13 = 0.065 \times n$

$\frac{13}{0.065} = \frac{0.065 \times n}{0.065}$

$\frac{13}{0.065} = n$

$n = 200$

There were 200 programs in stock.

Write About Math Write proportions that you could use to solve Examples A and B. Solve your proportions. Do you get the same answer in each case?

Check Understanding

For another example, see Set E, pages 328–329.

Which equation could you use to answer Exercises 1–2?

1. 250 is 5% of what number? **a.** $250 = 0.05 \times n$ **b.** $250 \times n = 0.05$

2. 120% of what number is 6? **a.** $1.2 \times n = 6$ **b.** $6 \times 1.2 = n$

Number Sense Find each answer.

3. 79 is 100% of what number?

4. 25% of what number is 25?

Practice

For More Practice, see Set E, pages 330–331.

Use an equation to find each number in Exercises 5–20. Tell whether you used mental math, paper and pencil, or calculator.

5. 25% of what number is 300?

6. 12% of what number is 9?

7. 55 is 10% of what number?

8. 40 is $12\frac{1}{2}$% of what number?

9. 40% of what number is 12.5?

10. 150 is 75% of what number?

11. 20% of what number is $6\frac{1}{2}$?

12. $\frac{1}{4}$% of what number is 4.9?

13. 8% of what number is 5.2?

14. 180 is 150% of what number?

15. 3.5% of what number is 7?

16. 53% of what number is 63.6?

17. 0.8% of what number is 24?

18. 50% of what number is 44?

19. $\frac{3}{8}$ is 50% of what number?

20. $33\frac{1}{3}$% of what number is 37?

Number Sense In Exercises 21 and 22, complete sentence B so that it means the same as sentence A.

21. A: Attendance this year is $1\frac{1}{2}$ times last year's attendance.
B: Attendance this year is __?__% greater than it was last year.

22. A: Total rainfall last year was 2% less than for the previous year.
B: Total rainfall last year was __?__% of the rainfall the previous year.

Problem Solving

Solve each problem.

23. Mr. Akai earned $273 in commissions last week by selling home computer programs. This was 26% of his total weekly sales. Find his total sales for the week.

24. A 20% down payment for a snowmobile is $550. How much does the snowmobile cost?

25. On her first day in the store, Mrs. Rohas sold a refrigerator. Her commission was 16% and she earned $84 on the sale. What was the price of the refrigerator?

26. **Critical Thinking** A salesman says, "I'll take $\frac{1}{4}$ off the ticketed price and then 25% off that price, so you'll actually pay half price." Do you agree? Why or why not?

ALGEBRA

Use a Formula

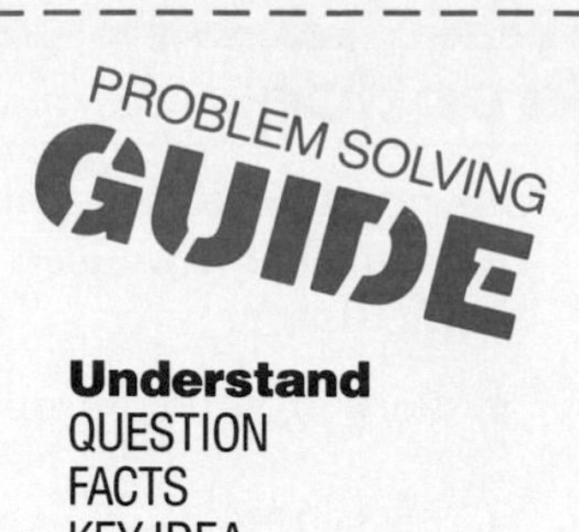

Understand
QUESTION
FACTS
KEY IDEA

Plan and Solve
STRATEGY
ANSWER

Look Back
SENSIBLE ANSWER
ALTERNATE APPROACH

Build Understanding

The Math Club deposited $288 in a savings account for 6 months. If the bank pays simple interest at the rate of 6%, how much interest will the Math Club receive?

Understand QUESTION How much simple interest will the Math Club receive after 6 months? *Interest* is the amount paid for the use of money.

FACTS *Principal* is the amount borrowed or invested. You know the principal is $288.
Rate is the percent of the principal paid for using money for a year. The interest rate is 6%.
Time is always expressed in years:
6 months = 0.5 year.

Plan and Solve STRATEGY Use the formula for simple interest:

Interest = Principal × Rate × Time (in years)

$I = P \times R \times T$

$I = (288)(6\%)(0.5)$

$I = (288)(0.06)(0.5)$

$I = 8.64$

Calculator

Press: 288 [×] 6 [%] [×] 0.5 [=]

Display: 8.64

ANSWER The Math Club received $8.64 in interest.

Look Back ALTERNATE APPROACH You can also use logical reasoning to solve this problem. If the rate is 6% for 1 year, then the rate is 3% for $\frac{1}{2}$ year. Write a proportion to find the interest. Then solve.

■ **Write About Math** The Math Club receives $8.64 in interest as well as the principal of $288, for a total of $296.64. If A represents the total amount of money received, write a formula for finding A in terms of I and P.

Check Understanding

The seventh grade made $410 from a rummage sale. They deposited it in a 6-month savings certificate that pays 7% simple interest per year. How much interest will the club earn on the certificate?

1. What principal did the club deposit?

2. What is the interest rate?

3. What is the time period?

4. What formula will you use? How much interest will the club earn?

Practice

For Problems 5–8, tell whether you would use paper and pencil or a calculator. Then solve each problem.

5. Angie invested $500 at 5.75% simple interest for 2 years. How much interest did she earn?

6. Phil borrowed $300 at 11.5% simple interest. How much interest did he pay for 1 year?

7. Faye invested $750 at $6\frac{1}{2}$% simple interest 3 years ago. How much interest has she earned?

8. Nara loaned Don $500 at 10% simple interest for 1 year. What is the total amount Don must repay?

Choose a ______ Strategy

Delicate Decisions Suppose you are a baseball player negotiating your salary for the next two years. You are offered three choices:

A. A 10% raise in Year 1 and a 15% raise in Year 2

B. A 15% raise in Year 1 and a 10% raise in Year 2

C. A 25% raise in Year 1 and no raise in Year 2

9. Which of the plans would you choose? Explain.

Choose an Operation
Write an Equation
Use a Formula
Make a Table
Try and Check
Use Logical Reasoning
Work Backward
Find a Pattern

CAREER CONNECTION

ALGEBRA

Estimating with Percents

Build Understanding

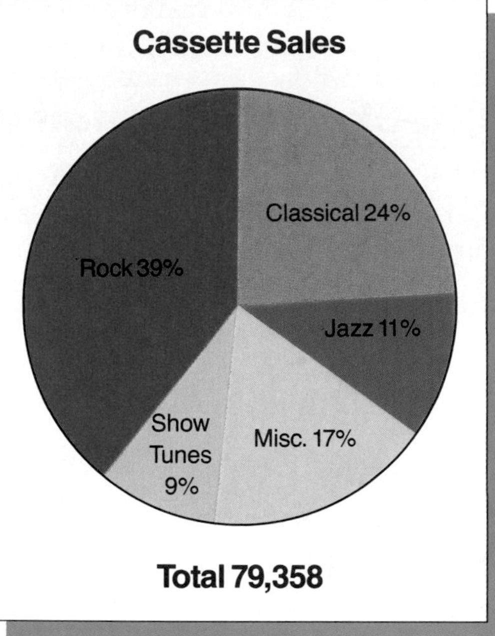

Ida Long owns a record shop. Last year, the total sales from cassettes was $79,358. The circle graph shows the percent of sales at Ida's store for each category of cassettes.

A. Estimate the sales amount, in dollars, for classical cassettes sold last year.

Estimate 24% of $79,358. 24% is close to 25%. 79,358 is close to 80,000.

Think: **25% of 80,000**

$25\% = \frac{1}{4}$

$\frac{1}{4} \times 80{,}000 = 20{,}000$

24% of $79,358 ≈ $20,000

The sales amount for classical cassettes was about $20,000.

B. Estimate. What percent of 124 is 60?

Think: $60 = n \times 124$

$n \approx \frac{60}{120} = \frac{1}{2} = 50\%$

60 ≈ 50% of 124

C. Estimate. 36% of what number is 153?

Think: $36\% \approx \frac{1}{3}$

If $\frac{1}{3}$ of a number is 153, then the whole number is 3 × 153.

Think: $153 \approx 150$
$3 \times 150 = 450$

36% of 450 ≈ 153

Talk About Math In Example A, what two categories combined have more sales—rock and show tunes, or classical and jazz? How do you know?

Check Understanding

For another example, see Set F, pages 328–329.

Estimate to choose the most reasonable answer.

1. 52% of 418
a. 150 **b.** 200 **c.** 21

2. 75% of x is 14.
a. 20 **b.** 140 **c.** 70

3. What percent could you use to estimate 12% of a number?

4. How can you estimate what percent 4 is of 49?

Practice

For More Practice, see Set F, pages 330–331.

Estimate. **Remember** to think of a number close to the given number.

5. What percent of 75 is 21?

6. 24% of what number is 200?

7. What percent of 80 is 21?

8. 45% of 10,618

9. 67% of 90,025

10. What percent of 699 is 349?

11. 48% of n is 5,147.

12. 11% of 1,497

13. 49% of 1,197

14. What percent of 125 is 60?

15. 21% of n is 198.

16. 27% of n is 1.5.

17. 204% of what number is 610?

18. 35% of 3,100

19. 53% of n is 7.1.

20. What number is 1.2% of 504?

21. What percent of 896 is 91?

22. 19% of what number is 30?

23. 91 is what percent of 30?

24. 13% of 796 is what number?

25. 35% of 27,713

26. What percent of 58.6 is 30.1?

27. 0.6 is 9% of what number?

28. 23% of 2

Problem Solving

Use the graph in Example A to estimate the sales amounts, in dollars, for each cassette category.

29. Rock

30. Miscellaneous

31. Jazz

Estimate to solve each problem. Describe your estimation strategy.

32. Out of 128 cassette tapes sold in one day, 42 were rock cassettes. Estimate what percent of the tapes were rock cassettes.

33. The state where Ida's store is located charges a 5% sales tax. If Ida collected $22 in sales tax for one day, estimate the total sales for the day.

34. On Monday, Ida sold 11 rock cassette tapes and 9 classical tapes. What percent of the tapes sold on Monday were rock tapes?

35. A cassette tape costs $8.49. Ida makes 25% of the selling price as income. What does Ida earn as income by selling one cassette?

ALGEBRA

Solving Percent Problems Using Equations

Build Understanding

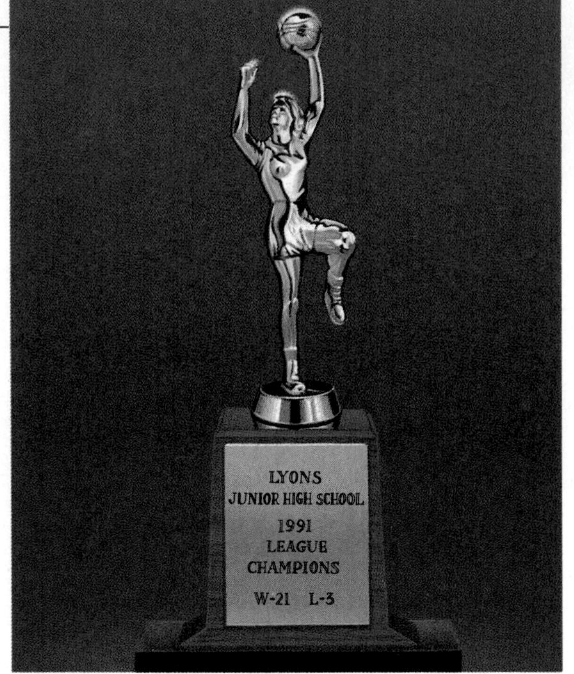

A. The girls' basketball team won the league championship. During the regular season, they won 21 out of their 24 games. What percent of the games did they win?

You can solve this problem by writing an equation.

What percent of 24 is 21?

$$n \times 24 = 21$$

$$24 \times n = 21$$

$$\frac{24 \times n}{24} = \frac{21}{24}$$

$$n = \frac{7}{8}, \text{ or } 87\frac{1}{2}\%$$

The girls' basketball team won $87\frac{1}{2}\%$ of the regular season games.

B. 27 is 75% of what number?

$$27 = 0.75 \times n$$

$$\frac{27}{0.75} = \frac{0.75 \times n}{0.75}$$

$$\frac{27}{0.75} = n$$

$$n = 36$$

C. 55% of what number is 11?

$$0.55 \times n = 11$$

$$\frac{0.55 \times n}{0.55} = \frac{11}{0.55}$$

$$n = \frac{11}{0.55}$$

$$n = 20$$

Write About Math In Example A, what other percent could you find? Write an equation for this problem.

Check Understanding

For another example, see Set G, pages 328–329.

Choose the equation you could use to answer Exercises 1–3.

1. 175 is 20% of what number? **a.** $175 \times 0.20 = x$ **b.** $175 = 0.20 \times x$
2. What percent of 48 is 30? **a.** $48 \times m = 30$ **b.** $48 = 30 \times m$
3. 56% of what number is 14? **a.** $0.56 \times 14 = t$ **b.** $0.56 \times t = 14$

Practice

For More Practice, see Set G, pages 330–331.

Estimate. Tell whether you would use paper and pencil, mental math, or a calculator. Write and solve an equation for each exercise.

4. 20% of what number is 6?

5. 36 is $37\frac{1}{2}$% of what number?

6. What percent of 25 is 15?

7. 65% of what number is 39?

8. 12 is 15% of what number?

9. What percent of 42 is 7?

10. 80% of 40 is what number?

11. 46 is 40% of what number?

12. 125% of what number is 15?

13. 174 is 75% of what number?

14. 0.9% of 200 is what number?

15. What percent of 225 is 117?

16. 51 is $33\frac{1}{3}$% of what number?

17. 6.6 is 11% of what number?

18. 195% of 80 is what number?

19. What percent of 2,000 is 510?

20. 63 is 21% of what number?

21. What percent of 600 is 402?

22. 38 is what percent of 380?

23. 48% of what number is 288?

Problem Solving

Write and solve an equation to answer Problems 24–27. Round to the nearest whole number.

24. Marilee scored 15 points in the final game. This was 20% of the team's score. How many points did the team score?

25. In the final game, 18 girls played. If 90% of the team played in that game, how many girls are on that team?

26. As goalie on the soccer team, Gordie allowed only 7 goals in 198 attempts. What percent of the attempts were goals?

27. Susan's team won 60% of their field hockey games. They played 45 games during the season. How many games did they win?

Skills Review

pages 202–205

Subtract.

1. $\frac{3}{4} - \frac{1}{2}$

2. $\frac{7}{8} - \frac{2}{3}$

3. $6\frac{7}{8} - 3\frac{1}{4}$

4. $13\frac{2}{3} - 9\frac{7}{8}$

Multiple-Step Problems

Understand
QUESTION
FACTS
KEY IDEA

Plan and Solve
STRATEGY
ANSWER

Look Back
SENSIBLE ANSWER
ALTERNATE APPROACH

Build Understanding

Ace Sporting Goods is having a sale. The regular price of athletic shoes is $51.60. The store is offering a 20% discount. What is the sale price?

Understand QUESTION What is the price after a 20% discount?

FACTS You know the regular price is $51.60 and the discount is 20%.

KEY IDEA How are the regular price and the sale price related? After finding the discount, you will need to subtract.

Plan and Solve STRATEGY First, find 20% of $51.60. Then subtract the amount of the discount from the regular price.

$n = 0.20 \times 51.60$
$n = 10.32$ discount

Regular price − Discount = Sale price

$$51.60 - 10.32 = 41.28$$

ANSWER The sale price is $41.28.

Look Back SENSIBLE ANSWER Think: 20% is $\frac{1}{5}$, and $\frac{1}{5}$ of 50 is 10. So a discount of $10.32 on $51.60 is reasonable.

Write About Math Write two equations for finding the answer to the example. Use P for price, R for discount percent, D for discount amount, and S for sale price. Can you write one equation that combines these two equations?

Over 70 million pairs of athletic shoes were sold in the U.S. in 1989.

Check Understanding

The regular price of a surfboard is $178. Ace Sporting Goods is offering a 30% discount.

1. What is the regular price of the surfboard?
2. What percent is the surfboard marked down?
3. How much is the reduction?
4. How much is the sale price?

Practice

For Problems 5–14, tell whether you would use pencil and paper or a calculator. Then solve each problem. **Remember** to look back at your answer to see if it is reasonable.

5. A ski outfit is selling for 25% off the regular price. How much does the outfit cost if the regular price is $265?
6. Steve bought a snowmobile priced at $3,745. What was the total price he paid if the sales tax was 4%?
7. Over a twenty-year period, the price of a mid-sized fishing boat increased to 300% of the original. If the boat cost $2,250 twenty years ago, what is the cost of a comparable boat today?
8. During the past ten years, the price of skis increased to 200% of the original. If skis cost $49.95 ten years ago, what do they cost today?
9. A pair of running shoes is on sale for $36. The original cost was $60. What is the percent of discount?
10. A tennis book regularly sells for $49.50. If the book is selling at a $33\frac{1}{3}$% discount, what is the sale price of the book?
11. A ski sweater was marked up 25% and then marked down 20% of the new price. What percent was the final price of the original price?
12. **Use Data** From the bar graph on page 22, compute the expected percent change in population between 1960 and 2010.
13. Curt bought a set of golf clubs and other golf equipment at Ace Sporting Goods. His total bill is $840. If he pays by June 15, he receives a 2% discount. If he pays after July 15, he must pay a 5% late fee. How much is Curt's bill if he pays before June 15? After July 15?
14. Ace Sporting Goods gives a 4% discount to customers who pay monthly. If a bill is $42.71, how much will the customer owe if the bill is paid within a month?

Skills Review

Write each decimal as a percent.

1. 0.45 **2.** 0.09 **3.** 0.005

4. 2.3 **5.** 1.67 **6.** 0.253

Write each fraction as a percent.

7. $\frac{83}{100}$ **8.** $\frac{13}{20}$ **9.** $\frac{33}{50}$

10. $\frac{1}{10}$ **11.** $\frac{2}{5}$ **12.** $\frac{9}{18}$

Find each answer.

13. 20% of 20 **14.** $66\frac{2}{3}$% of 99

15. 0.8% of 400 **16.** 87.5% of 48

17. 90% of 150 **18.** 120% of 60

19. What percent of 12 is 4?

20. 15 is what percent of 75?

21. What percent of 400 is 84?

22. 75% of what number is 33?

23. 60 is $33\frac{1}{3}$% of what number?

24. 2 is $\frac{1}{2}$% of what number?

Estimate.

25. 32% of 180 **26.** 9% of 48

27. What percent of 72 is 35?

Write and solve an equation

28. 15% of what number is 45?

29. What percent of 30 is 33?

30. 18 is 15% of what number?

Problem-Solving Review

Solve each problem.

31. Mr. Simmons wants to show the 153 students in his class a video about Rome. Sean and Teddy set up chairs so there are an equal number in each row. How many rows did they set up? How many chairs were in each row? List all possibilities.

32. A cargo plane can carry 30 tons of cargo. It currently has 18 tons on board. Write and solve an equation to find how many tons of cargo can still be loaded on the plane.

33. Betty slept $\frac{5}{12}$ of a day and Dolores slept $\frac{3}{8}$ of a day. Which girl slept longer?

34. The Martinez family had dinner at Patty's Pantry. The bill was $32 plus $1.92 tax. What percent is the tax rate?

35. Yvonne wants to enlarge a $1\frac{1}{2}$ in. by $3\frac{1}{4}$ in. picture of a rabbit by 30% on each side. What will be the dimensions of the enlargement?

36. **Data File** Use the data on pages 414–415. How many more people chose white sneakers than chose red sneakers?

37. **Make a Data File** Find a newspaper or magazine the lists the budget for a family, a charitable organization, a business, or local, state, or national government. Change dollar amounts to percents of the total. Make a chart listing each budget item and the percent of the total spent on that item.

Cumulative Skills Review · Chapters 1–9

Multiply or divide.

1. 7.5×304 **2.** 0.45×6.004 **3.** $8{,}442 \div 9$ **4.** $13{,}510 \div 5$

5. $4{,}368 \div 56$ **6.** $20{,}240 \div 230$ **7.** $2.61 \div 29$ **8.** $18.936 \div 3.6$

Evaluate $7 + 3w$ for each value of w.

9. $w = 2$ **10.** $w = 10$ **11.** $w = 6$ **12.** $w = 5$

Use the diagram to name each.

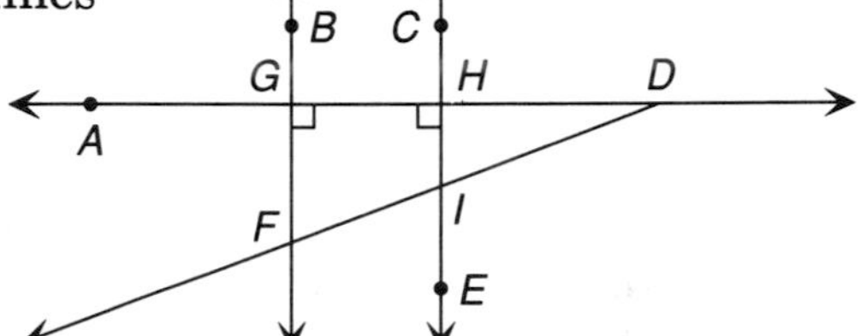

13. 2 lines

14. A pair of intersecting lines

15. 2 rays

16. 2 right angles

17. An acute angle

18. A pair of parallel lines

19. A pair of supplementary angles

Find the greatest common factor and the least common multiple.

20. 12 and 14 **21.** 20 and 36 **22.** 15 and 21 **23.** 27 and 45

Compare the numbers. Use >, <, or =.

24. $\frac{11}{15} \;\square\; \frac{2}{3}$ **25.** $\frac{5}{8} \;\square\; \frac{7}{16}$ **26.** $4\frac{5}{6} \;\square\; 4\frac{15}{18}$ **27.** $2\frac{7}{9} \;\square\; 2\frac{2}{3}$

Give the precision of the measurement and the greatest possible error.

28. 13 g **29.** $13\frac{3}{4}$ in. **30.** 2.8 cm **31.** 1.05 m

Solve each proportion.

32. $\frac{2}{3} = \frac{m}{27}$ **33.** $\frac{n}{7} = \frac{18}{42}$ **34.** $\frac{10}{r} = \frac{40}{88}$ **35.** $\frac{25}{15} = \frac{n}{3}$

36. $\frac{c}{20} = \frac{12}{15}$ **37.** $\frac{0.6}{p} = \frac{0.3}{10}$ **38.** $\frac{7}{16} = \frac{y}{48}$ **39.** $\frac{9}{0.25} = \frac{36}{v}$

Find each answer.

40. 60% of 45 **41.** 0.8% of 500 **42.** 300% of 39 **43.** $37\frac{1}{2}$% of 80

44. What percent of 80 is 22?

45. 75 is what percent of 90?

46. 45 is 37.5% of what number?

47. 35% of what number is 49?

48. 26 is what percent of 78?

49. 55 is 27.5% of what number?

50. 22% of what number is 33?

51. What percent of 30 is 12?

Reteaching

Set A pages 302–303

Percent means "per hundred." So,

45% = 45 hundredths
= 0.45

To write a decimal for a percent, move the decimal point two places to the left and omit the percent sign.

0.33 = 33 hundredths
= 33%

To write a percent for a decimal, move the decimal point two places to the right and write a percent sign.

Remember, insert zeros if necessary.

Write each percent as a decimal.

1. 23% **2.** 56% **3.** 69% **4.** 92%

5. 100% **6.** 155% **7.** 200% **8.** 8%

9. 3% **10.** 80% **11.** 0.7% **12.** 4.3%

Write each decimal as a percent.

13. 0.35 **14.** 0.87 **15.** 0.73 **16.** 0.99

17. 0.02 **18.** 0.08 **19.** 1.25 **20.** 3.62

Set B pages 304–307

To write a fraction as a percent, divide the numerator by the denominator. To write $\frac{5}{8}$ as a decimal, divide 5 by 8.

$$0.62\frac{4}{8} = 0.62\frac{1}{2} = 62\frac{1}{2}\% = 62.5\%$$

$$\begin{array}{r} 0.62\frac{4}{8} \\ 8\overline{)5.00} \\ \underline{4\,8} \\ 20 \\ \underline{16} \\ 4 \end{array}$$

To write a percent as a fraction or mixed number, write the percent with a denominator of 100 and omit the percent sign.

$$45\% = \frac{45}{100} = \frac{9}{20}$$

Remember, write fractions in lowest terms.

Write each fraction as a percent.

1. $\frac{5}{100}$ **2.** $\frac{6}{10}$ **3.** $\frac{13}{25}$ **4.** $\frac{11}{20}$

5. $\frac{3}{4}$ **6.** $\frac{3}{5}$ **7.** $\frac{7.2}{100}$ **8.** $\frac{7}{8}$

9. $\frac{115}{100}$ **10.** $\frac{13}{8}$ **11.** $\frac{3}{2}$ **12.** $\frac{7}{3}$

Write each percent as a fraction or mixed number.

13. 25% **14.** 50% **15.** 30% **16.** $33\frac{1}{3}\%$

17. $12\frac{1}{2}\%$ **18.** $83\frac{1}{3}\%$ **19.** 4% **20.** 2%

21. 175% **22.** 210% **23.** 190% **24.** 360%

Set C pages 308–311

To find a percent of a number, write an equation.

What is 48% of 200?

↓ ↓ ↓ ↓ ↓

n **= 0.48 × 200** *is* means "equals"
of means "times"

n **= 96**

Remember, write the percent as a fraction or decimal before multiplying.

1. Find 60% of 325. **2.** Find 8% of 70.

3. Find 21% of 34. **4.** Find 50% of 20.

5. Find 25% of 24. **6.** Find $33\frac{1}{3}\%$ of 75.

7. Find 100% of 47. **8.** Find 21.4% of 150.

Set D pages 314–315

To find what percent one number is of another, write and solve an equation.

75 is what percent of 300?

$75 = n \times 300$ — *is* means "equals", *of* means "times"

$n = \frac{75}{300} = \frac{1}{4}$

$n = 25\%$

Remember, write your answer as a percent.

1. 21 is what percent of 42?
2. 85 is what percent of 850?
3. 18 is what percent of 9?
4. 53 is what percent of 159?

Set E pages 316–317

To find a number when a percent of it is known, write an equation.

248 is 16% of what number?

$248 = 0.16 \times n$ — *is* means "equals", *of* means "times"

$n = \frac{248}{0.16}$

$n = 1{,}550$

Remember, write the percent as a decimal or fraction before dividing.

1. 18 is 9% of what number?
2. 34% of what number is 17?
3. 85 is 10% of what number?
4. 0.2% of what number is 30?

Set F pages 320–321

To estimate using percents, round or use compatible numbers.

What percent of 215 is 48?

$n \times 215 = 48$ ← 48 close to 50; 215 close to 200

$n \times 200 = 50$

$n = \frac{50}{200} = \frac{1}{4} = 25\%$

48 is about 25% of 215.

Remember, choose numbers that make computations easy.

Estimate.

1. 18 is what percent of 98?
2. What is 53% of 309?
3. What is 37% of 88?
4. 48% of what number is 788?

Set G pages 322–323

Here's how different percent problems look as equations.

What percent of 20 is 10?

$n \times 20 = 10$

10 is 50% of what number?

$10 = 0.5 \times n$

50% of what number is 10?

$0.5 \times n = 10$

Remember, you can use estimation to check whether you have a sensible answer.

Write and solve an equation.

1. What percent of 16 is 4?
2. 62.5% of what number is 50?
3. 12 is 12% of what number?
4. 23% of what number is $5\frac{3}{4}$?

More Practice

Set A pages 302–303

Write each decimal as a percent.

1. 0.21 **2.** 0.68 **3.** 0.06 **4.** 3.81 **5.** 0.008

6. $0.33\frac{1}{3}$ **7.** 1.16 **8.** 10 **9.** 0.52 **10.** 0.625

11. 0.28 **12.** 0.6 **13.** 2.09 **14.** 0.105 **15.** 0.077

Write each percent as a decimal.

16. 5% **17.** 79% **18.** 0.02% **19.** 130% **20.** $24\frac{1}{2}$%

21. 40% **22.** 0.37% **23.** 650% **24.** 0.5% **25.** 19%

26. 81% **27.** 7% **28.** 120% **29.** 16.5% **30.** $4\frac{1}{2}$%

Set B pages 304–307

Write each fraction as a percent.

1. $\frac{8}{25}$ **2.** $\frac{4}{20}$ **3.** $\frac{5}{4}$ **4.** $\frac{18}{36}$ **5.** $\frac{0.3}{100}$

6. $\frac{21}{14}$ **7.** $\frac{9}{36}$ **8.** $\frac{48}{36}$ **9.** $\frac{0.9}{100}$ **10.** $\frac{7}{4}$

11. $\frac{72}{1200}$ **12.** $\frac{12}{96}$ **13.** $\frac{25}{150}$ **14.** $\frac{0.8}{120}$ **15.** $\frac{15}{40}$

Write each percent as a mixed number or fraction in lowest terms.

16. 12% **17.** 60% **18.** 27% **19.** 55% **20.** 250%

21. $6\frac{2}{3}$% **22.** 64% **23.** $5\frac{1}{2}$% **24.** 0.2% **25.** 12.5%

26. 118% **27.** 5.4% **28.** 15.1% **29.** $42\frac{1}{2}$% **30.** 6.8%

Set C pages 308–311

Find each answer.

1. 30% of 20 **2.** 31% of 53 **3.** 5% of 140 **4.** $66\frac{2}{3}$% of 210

5. 0.5% of 100 **6.** $12\frac{1}{2}$% of 144 **7.** 75% of 340 **8.** 110% of 16

9. 40% of 150 **10.** 120% of 65 **11.** 68% of 250 **12.** 150% of 260

13. 71% of 500 **14.** $5\frac{1}{2}$% of 200 **15.** 10.4% of 350 **16.** 15% of 172

17. 12% of 310 **18.** 18% of 50 **19.** 120% of 80 **20.** 7% of 150

21. 72% of 84 **22.** 200% of 45 **23.** 20.5% of 62 **24.** 0.3% of 16

25. 42% of 64 **26.** 8% of 125 **27.** $6\frac{1}{2}$% of 250 **28.** 140% of 15

Set D pages 314–315

Find each answer.

1. What percent of 92 is 23?

2. 33 is what percent of 55?

3. 117 is what percent of 300?

4. What percent of 250 is 5?

5. What percent of 12 is 18?

6. 63 is what percent of 72?

7. 62 is what percent of 93?

8. 60 is what percent of 12,000?

9. What percent of 900 is 990?

10. What percent of 822 is 548?

Set E pages 316–317

Find each answer by using an equation.

1. 20% of what number is 14.4?

2. 45 is 75% of what number?

3. 7 is $12\frac{1}{2}$% of what number?

4. 9% of what number is 27?

5. 25% of what number is 75?

6. 0.9 is 72% of what number?

7. $33\frac{1}{3}$% of what number is 80?

8. 15% of what number is 120?

9. 120% of what number is 360?

10. 45 is 90% of what number?

Set F pages 320–321

Estimate.

1. 25% of 49

2. 22% of 80

3. What percent of 91 is 33?

4. 69% of n is 3,517.

5. 73% of 120

6. 452 is 91% of what number?

7. 110% of 203

8. $33\frac{1}{3}$% of 599

9. 22% of what number is 55?

10. $12\frac{1}{2}$% of 64

11. 9% of 510

12. What percent of 900 is 29?

Set G pages 322–323

Write and solve an equation.

1. 56% of what number is 56?

2. What percent of 75 is 25?

3. 48 is 15% of what number?

4. 99% of what number is 495?

5. What percent of 31 is 62?

6. 0.1% of what number is 0.012?

7. Find 64% of 95.

8. 110% of what number is 121?

9. $33\frac{1}{3}$% of what number is 74?

10. What is 12.5% of 168?

Enrichment

Percent of Increase or Decrease

At Optical Supply Company, the price of a pair of binoculars decreased from \$240 to \$204. The price of a telescope increased from \$550 to \$595.

Binoculars		*Telescope*	
\$240		\$595	
− 204		− 550	
\$ 36	decrease	\$ 45	increase

To find the percent of increase or decrease, divide the amount of increase or decrease by the original cost of the item. Express the change as a percent. Round to the nearest whole percent.

$$\frac{\text{decrease} \rightarrow 36}{\text{original price} \rightarrow 240} = 0.15 = 15\%$$

$$\frac{\text{increase} \rightarrow 45}{\text{original price} \rightarrow 550} = 0.08 = 8\%$$

The percent of decrease in the price of binoculars was 15%.

The percent of increase in the price of a telescope was 8%.

Find the percent of increase or decrease.

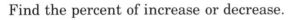

1. From 5 to 8
2. From 30 to 9
3. From 44 to 66
4. From 25 to 45
5. From 10 to 11
6. From 100 to 87
7. From 90 to 27
8. From 17 to 34
9. From 170 to 195.5
10. From 300 to 369
11. From 2 to $2\frac{1}{2}$
12. From 52 to 0

13. From 1970 to 1980, the population of the United States increased from 203.3 million to 226.5 million. To the nearest tenth of a percent, what was the percent of increase of population?

14. The world's fastest growing plant is the Pacific giant kelp. A kelp plant grew from 75 feet in length to 76 feet 6 inches in one day. Find the percent of increase in the length.

15. Workers agreed to take a cut in pay from \$7.50 per hour to \$7.05 per hour. What was the percent of decrease in the hourly rate?

Chapter 9 Review/Test

Write each decimal or fraction as a percent.

1. 0.375

2. 0.3

3. $\frac{9}{20}$

4. $\frac{7}{8}$

Write each percent as a decimal.

5. 4%

6. 150%

7. Find $66\frac{2}{3}$% of 60.

8. Find 27% of 20.

9. 175% of 400 is what number?

10. Gus estimates that 60% of his mail is "junk mail." If he receives 30 pieces of mail a week, about how many pieces are "junk"?

11. 3 is what percent of 12?

12. 240 is what percent of 160?

13. Of the 180 students who tried out for the glee club, only 144 were able to get in. What percent were not able to join the glee club?

14. 25% of what number is 200?

15. 30 is 75% of what number?

16. Ken spent 25% of his first paycheck on a $43.75 uniform he needed for work. What was the amount of his first paycheck?

17. Michelle invested $300 at 6% simple interest for 3 years. How much interest did she earn?

Estimate.

18. 26% of what number is 40?

19. What percent of 75 is 19?

20. What is 48% of 88?

21. Write an equation that could be used to solve this problem.

A seed company guarantees that 80% of its seeds will sprout. If you want 20 plants, how many seeds should you buy?

22. Choose the first step to be done in solving this problem.

Jon saw a sweater that had been marked down from $89 to $75. A sign said that every sweater was marked down an additional 20% from the price on the sticker. What percent would Jon save from the original price of $89?

a. Subtract $75 from $89.
b. Find 20% of $75.
c. Find what percent $75 is of $89.

23. **Write About Math** A calculator was marked up 40% from cost by the dealer. During a sale, the dealer marked the price down 40%. Did the dealer make money, lose money, or break even? Why?

Geometry and Measurement 10

Did You Know: Your heart is a busy machine linked to 100,000 miles of arteries, veins, and blood vessels. It's about as big as your fist and weighs 10 ounces. Each day it beats more than 100,000 times and pumps more than 1,800 gallons of blood. In one hour, it generates enough muscle power to lift a small car 2 feet off the ground.

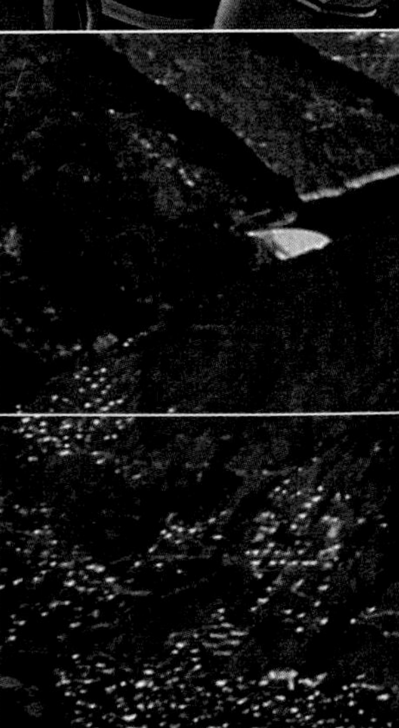

Number-Sense Project

Estimate
How much do you think vigorous activity, like running for 3 minutes, will increase your heartbeat per minute?

Gather Data
Take your pulse while you are sitting at your desk. Also take it after mild activity, moderate activity, and vigorous activity.

Analyze and Report
Make a graph to show how your pulse rate increases as your level of activity increases.

Three-Dimensional Figures

Build Understanding

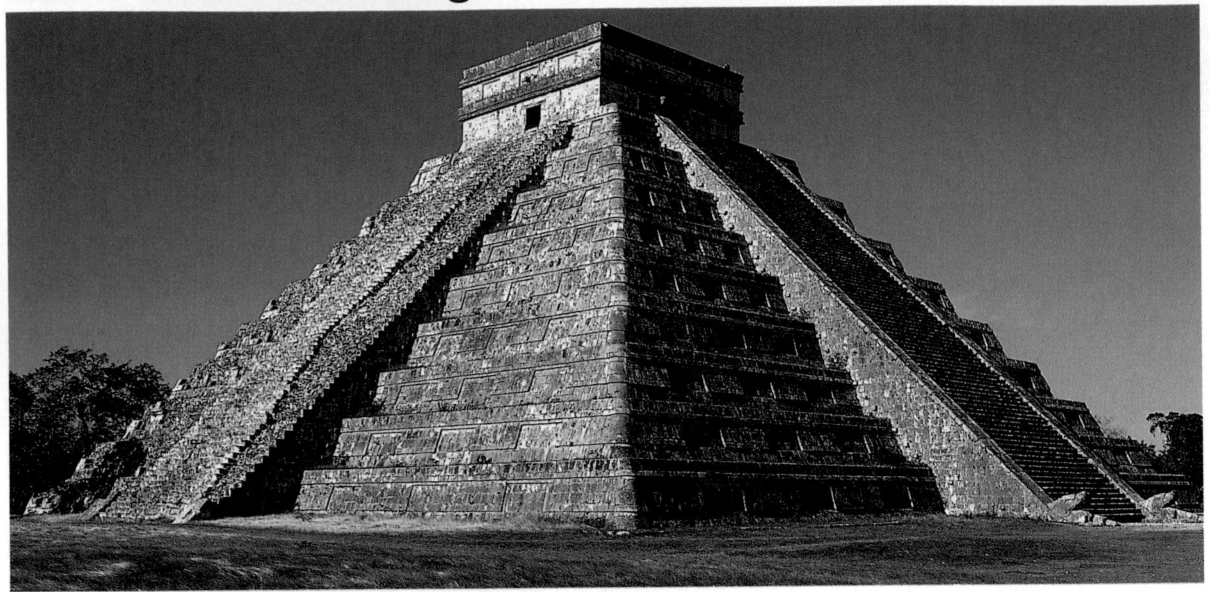

Many ancient civilizations used polyhedrons in the design of their buildings. El Castillo, a Mayan temple, is as tall as a 7-story building.

A. A ***polyhedron*** is a three-dimensional figure with flat surfaces, or ***faces.*** Each face is a polygon.

A ***prism*** is a polyhedron with two parallel and congruent bases. All other faces are parallelograms.

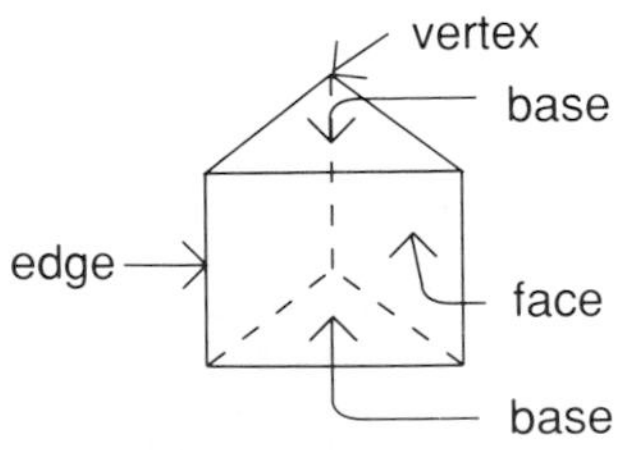

Triangular prism

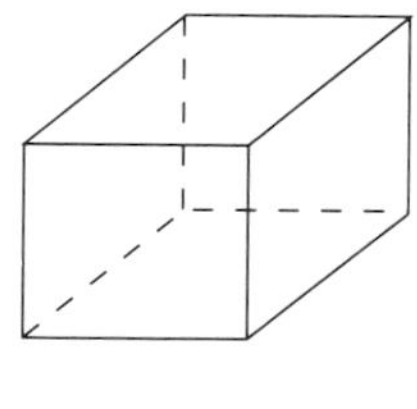

Rectangular prism

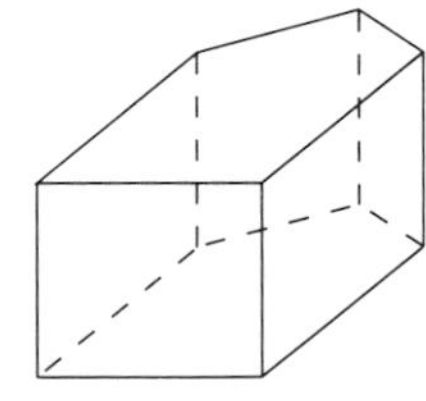

Pentagonal prism

A ***pyramid*** has one base. The other faces are triangular regions.

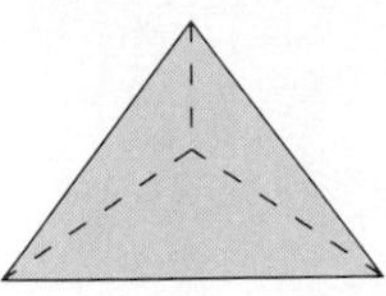

Triangular pyramid

Rectangular pyramid

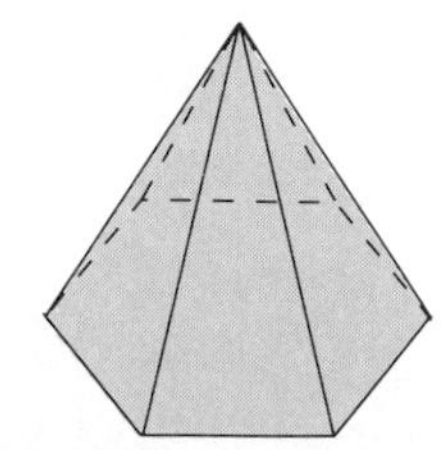

Hexagonal pyramid

**B.** Three-dimensional figures with curved surfaces are not polyhedrons. Which of these figures are not polyhedrons?

a.

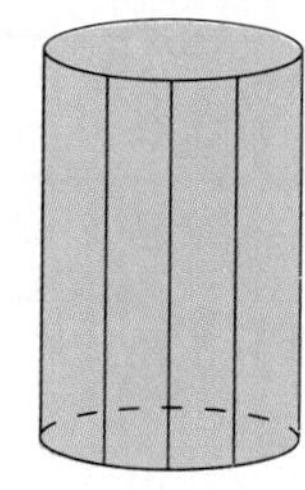

b.

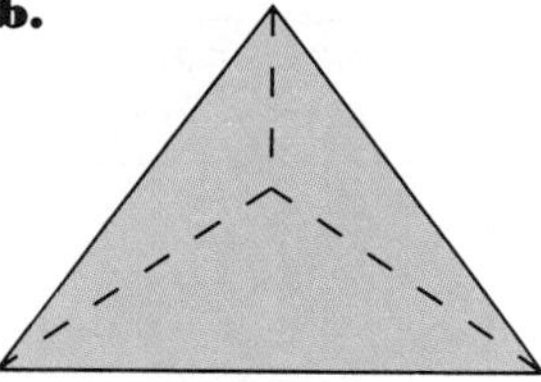

c.

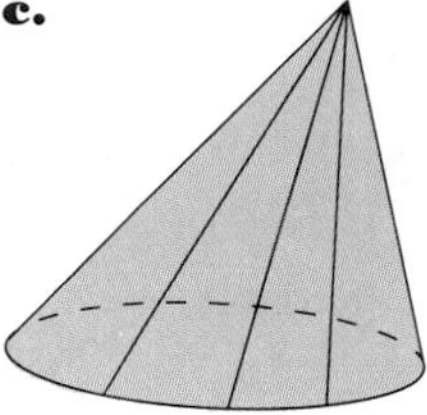

d.

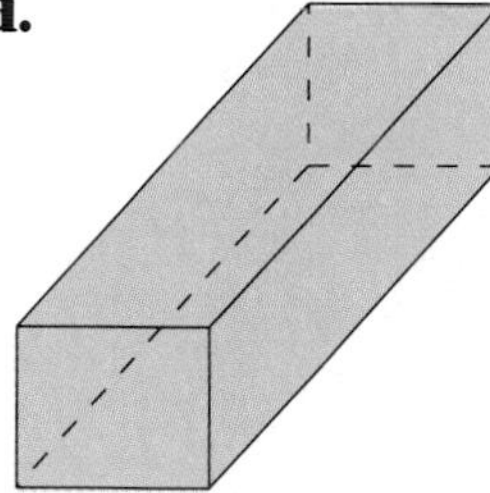

e.

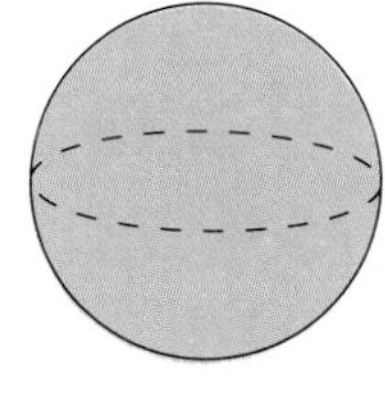

f.

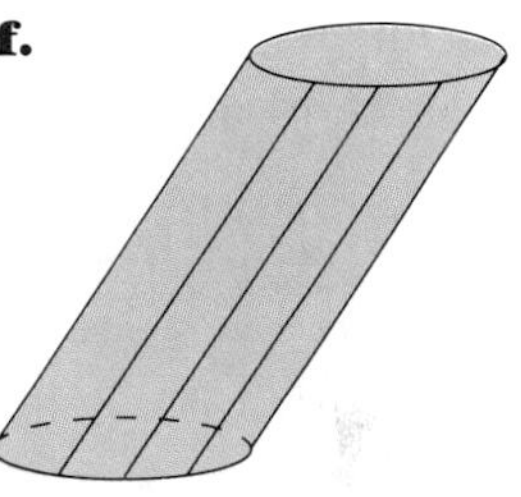

The figures in a, c, e, and f are not polyhedrons.

Talk About Math Is every prism a polyhedron? Is every polyhedron a prism? Explain.

Check Understanding

Tell whether the figure is a prism. Explain your answer.

1.

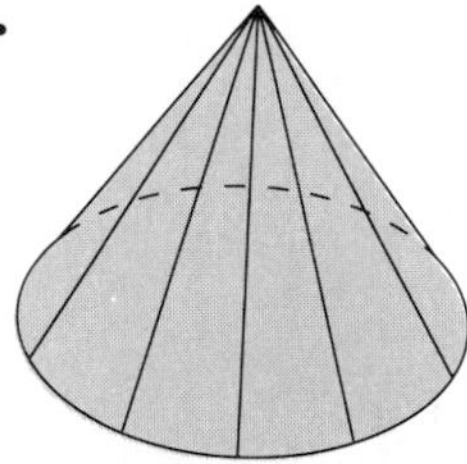

2.

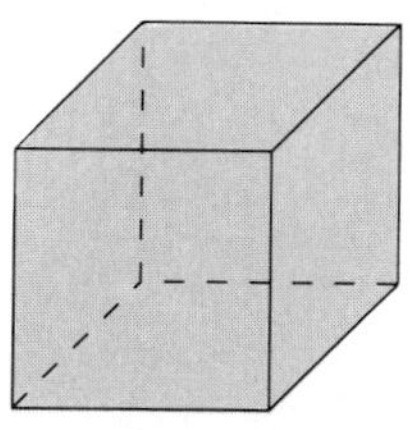

3.

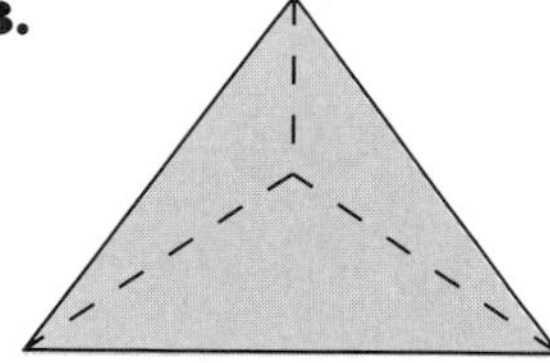

Name the blue part of each polyhedron.

4.

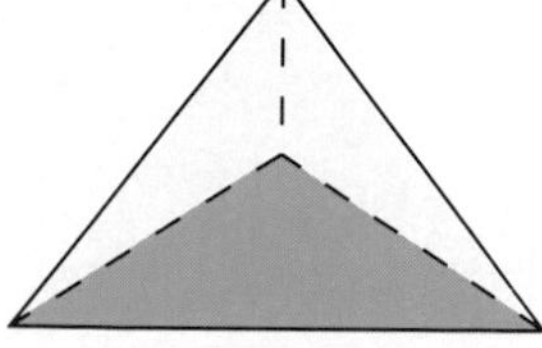

5.

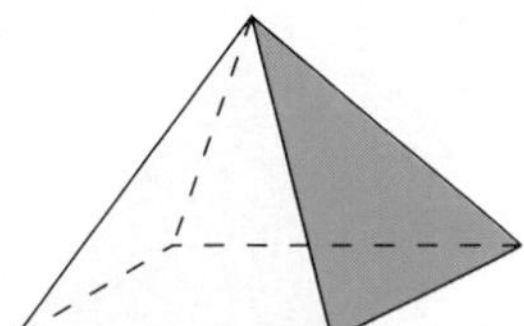

6.

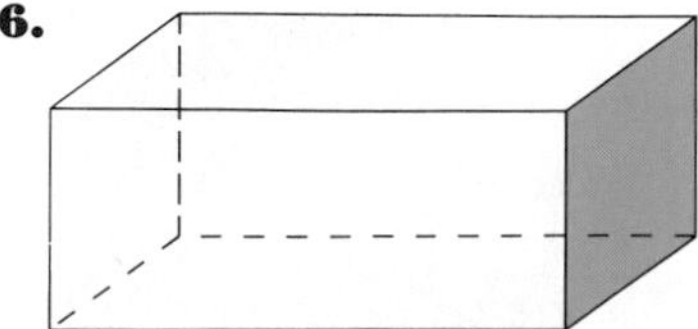

Practice

Copy and complete the table. **Remember** to count the base in your answer.

Polyhedron	Number of faces	Number of vertices	Number of edges
Triangular Pyramid	**7.**	**8.**	**9.**
Rectangular Prism	**10.**	**11.**	**12.**
Square Pyramid	**13.**	**14.**	**15.**
Triangular Prism	**16.**	**17.**	**18.**

Match each three-dimensional figure with its pattern.

19. 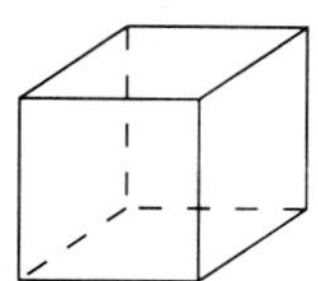

20. 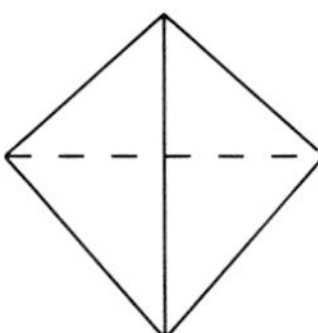

21. 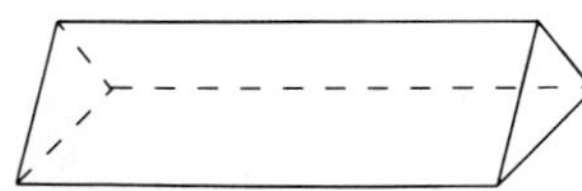

22. 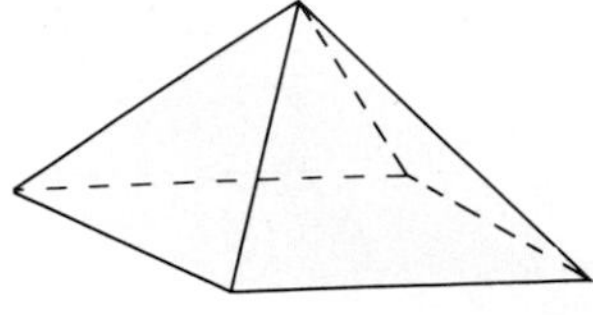

a. 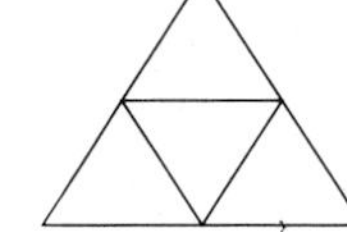

b. 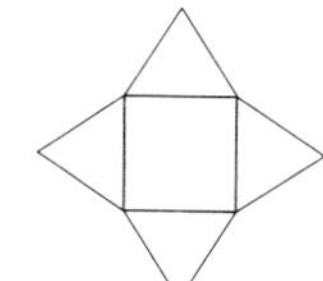

c. 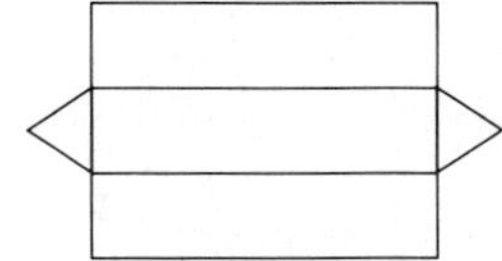

d. 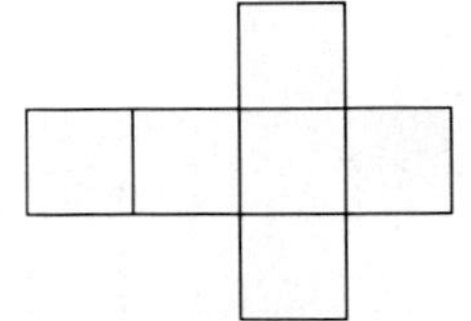

Problem Solving

Solve.

23. A decagon is a ten-sided polygon. How many faces, edges, and vertices will a pyramid with a decagonal base have?

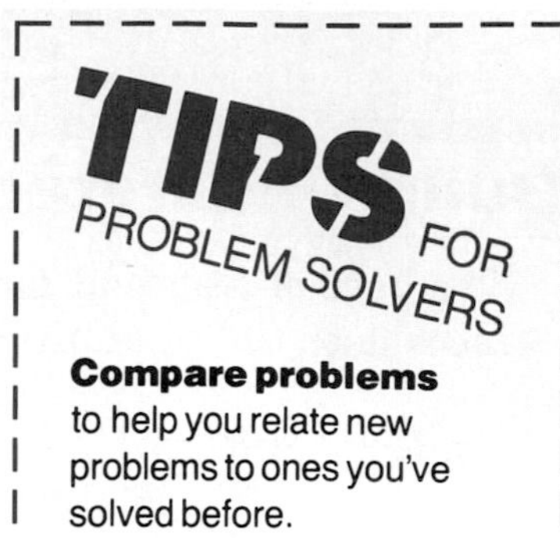

TIPS FOR PROBLEM SOLVERS
Compare problems to help you relate new problems to ones you've solved before.

24. A square pyramid is atop a square prism. Their bases are congruent. How many faces does the resulting polyhedron have? how many vertices? how many edges?

25. **Critical Thinking** A prism has seven faces. Describe its bases.

ALGEBRA ▶ Look at the table of faces, edges, and vertices that you completed (Exercises 7–18). Solve each problem.

26. For each polyhedron, give the sum of the number of faces (F) and the number of vertices (V).

27. Write a formula that relates the sum of F and V to the number of edges (E).

Visual Thinking Suppose that each solid is cut on the edges, unfolded, and laid flat. Describe the figure that results by stating the number of rectangles, circles, and triangles.

28.

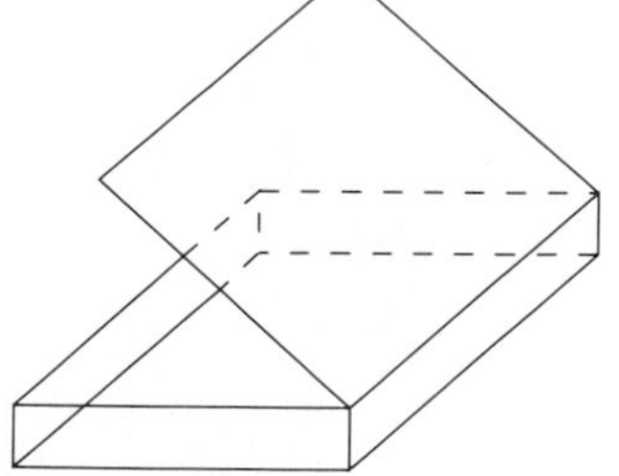

29.

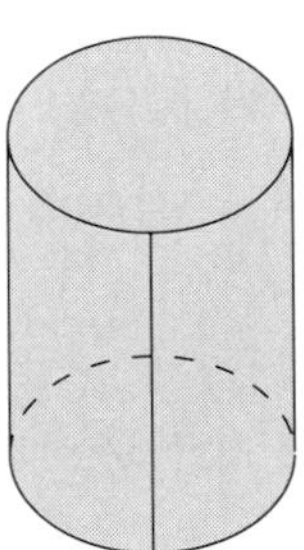

30.

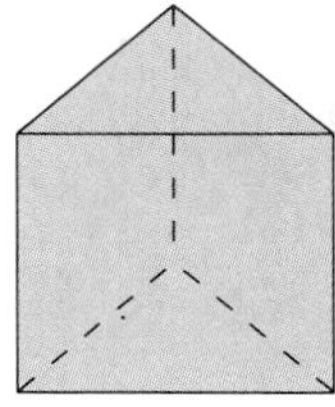

Skills Review pages 208–211, 214–218

Multiply.

1. $\frac{2}{3} \times \frac{4}{5}$ **2.** $\frac{1}{5} \times 1\frac{2}{4}$ **3.** $\frac{1}{6} \times 8$ **4.** $3\frac{5}{6} \times 1\frac{2}{3}$

Divide.

5. $\frac{5}{6} \div \frac{2}{3}$ **6.** $\frac{4}{5} \div 1\frac{1}{10}$ **7.** $\frac{\frac{3}{4}}{\frac{9}{16}}$ **8.** $\frac{5}{2\frac{2}{3}}$

Solve a Simpler Problem

Understand
QUESTION
FACTS
KEY IDEA

Plan and Solve
STRATEGY
ANSWER

Look Back
SENSIBLE ANSWER
ALTERNATE APPROACH

Build Understanding

The base of a special pyramid has 16 sides. How many faces does the pyramid have?

Understand QUESTION How many faces does a 16-sided pyramid have?

FACTS The base of the pyramid has 16 sides. A pyramid has 1 base. A base is also a face.

KEY IDEA It would be difficult to draw this pyramid. Try simpler pyramids and look for a pattern.

Plan and Solve STRATEGY Solve a simpler problem. Try a triangular pyramid.

If a pyramid has a base with 3 sides, there are 4 faces.

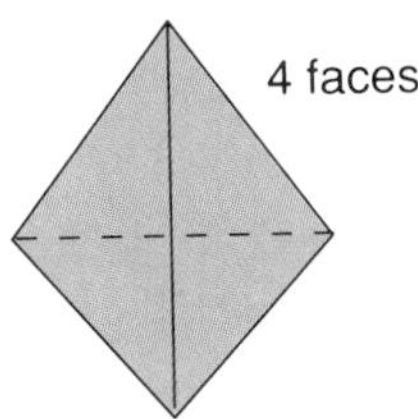

If a pyramid has a base with 4 sides, there are 5 faces.

If a pyramid has a base with 8 sides, there are 9 faces.

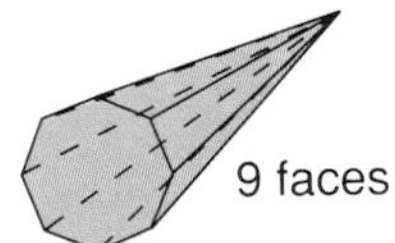

The pattern seems to be that the number of faces is 1 more than the number of sides of the base.

ANSWER A pyramid with a 16-sided base has 17 faces.

Look Back SENSIBLE ANSWER Each side of the base meets a different face, so the answer makes sense. The total number of faces of a pyramid is 1 more than the number of sides of the base.

Talk About Math How many edges does a 16-sided pyramid have? What strategy can you use to find the answer?

Check Understanding

Answer each question.

1. How many bases does a prism have?
2. Are the bases also faces?
3. How many faces does a prism with a 50-sided base have?

Practice

Copy and complete the table below. Use the diagrams to complete Exercises 4–6 and 11–13. Then find a pattern and use it to complete Exercises 7–10 and 14–17.

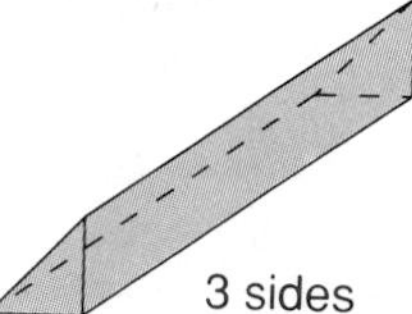
3 sides

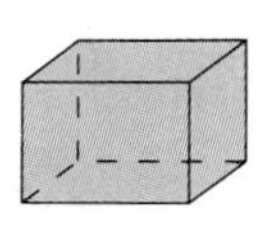
4 sides

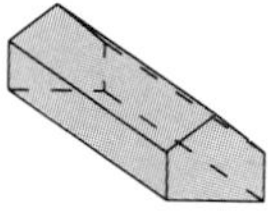
5 sides

Number of sides in the base of the prism	3	4	5	7	10	30	50
Number of faces in the prism	**4.**	**5.**	**6.**	**7.**	**8.**	**9.**	**10.**
Number of edges in the prism	**11.**	**12.**	**13.**	**14.**	**15.**	**16.**	**17.**

Choose a ______ Strategy

Squares Squared Find the number of squares in the square.

18. How many 1×1 squares are in the figure?
19. How many 2×2 squares are there?
20. Continue to find the number of $n \times n$ squares. Organize your results in a table. What is the largest $n \times n$ square?
21. How many squares are in the figure?

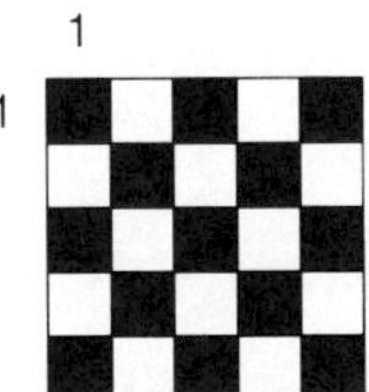

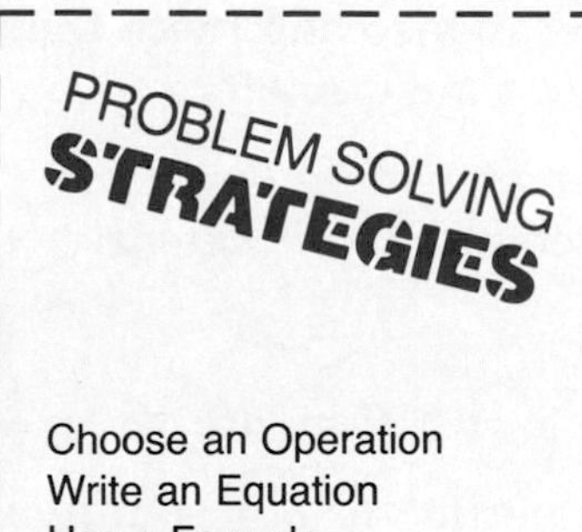

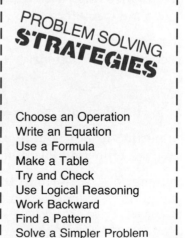

Choose an Operation
Write an Equation
Use a Formula
Make a Table
Try and Check
Use Logical Reasoning
Work Backward
Find a Pattern
Solve a Simpler Problem

ALGEBRA

Perimeter and Area of Rectangles

Build Understanding

A. Tony Mason is the head of maintenance at the Seaside Inn. He wants to caulk the windows of the inn before winter. Each window measures 5 ft by 3.5 ft. He finds the perimeter to determine the amount of caulking needed.

The ***perimeter*** of a figure is the measure of the distance around it. You can find the perimeter by adding the lengths of the sides.

$$P = 3.5 \text{ ft} + 5 \text{ ft} + 3.5 \text{ ft} + 5 \text{ ft} = 17 \text{ ft}$$

You can also add twice the width to twice the length to get the perimeter.

Perimeter of a rectangle	=	Twice the length	+	Twice the width

$$P = 2\ell + 2w$$

$$P = 2(5) + 2(3.5) = 10 + 7 = 17$$

The perimeter of a square window can be found by using the following formula.

Perimeter of a square	=	4 times the length of a side

$$P = 4s$$

$$P = 4(5) = 20 \text{ ft}$$

The perimeter of the square is 20 ft.

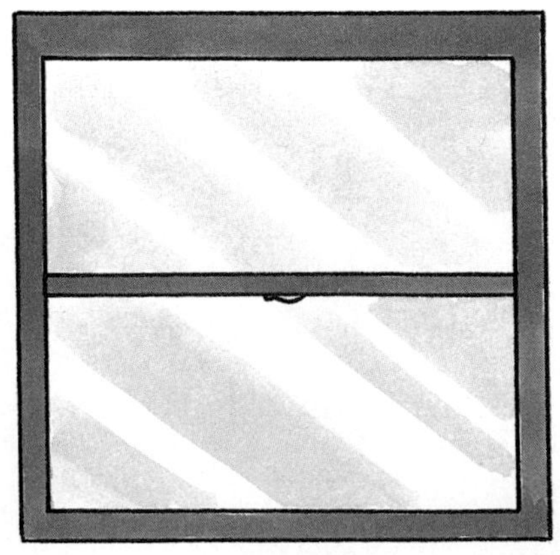

B. Tony must paint the walls and put in wall-to-wall carpeting in the room shown in Figure B. To do this, Tony must find the area of the walls and floor. The number of square units enclosed by a figure is the ***area.*** For example, the area of Figure A is 20 square units. Notice that there are 4 rows with 5 squares in each. To find the area of a rectangle use the following formula.

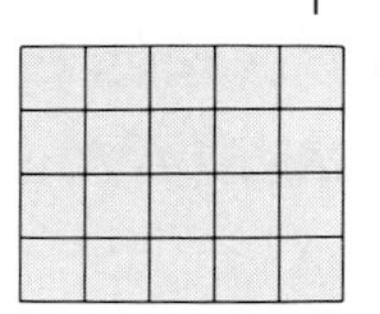

Figure A

Area of a rectangle = length × width

$A = \ell \times w$

A = 5 × 4, or 20 square feet

Find the area of the floor in Figure B.

$A = \ell \times w$

A = 20 × 30, or 600 square feet

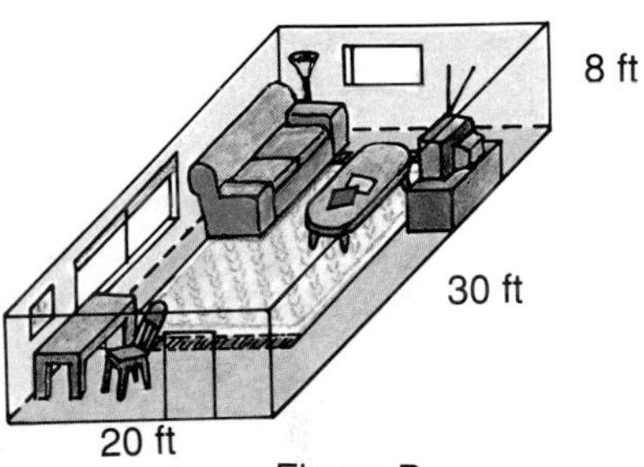

Figure B

Find the area of the shorter wall.

A = 20 × 8, or 160 square feet

Find the area of the longer wall.

A = 30 × 8, or 240 square feet

Now find the area of all four walls.

160 + 240 + 160 + 240 = 800 square feet

C. The area of a square is found by the following formula.

Area of a square = side × side

$A = s \times s$

$A = s^2$

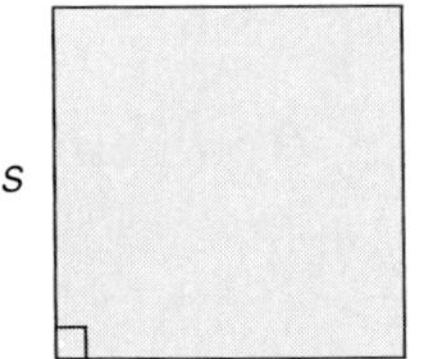

Talk About Math
A square is always a rectangle. Is a rectangle always a square? Explain.

Check Understanding

For another example, see Set A, pages 372–373.

Tell whether area or perimeter is involved.

1. Amount of grass seed to buy
2. Amount of lawn to be mowed
3. Number of bags of soil
4. Amount of fencing needed

Tell the meaning of the underlined symbol in each formula.

5. $\underline{A} = \ell \times w$
6. $\underline{\ell} \times w = A$
7. $\ell \times \underline{w} = A$
8. $4\underline{s} = P$
9. $\underline{P} = 2\ell + 2w$

Practice

For More Practice, see Set A, pages 374–375.

Mental Math Compute the area and perimeter of each figure.

10. 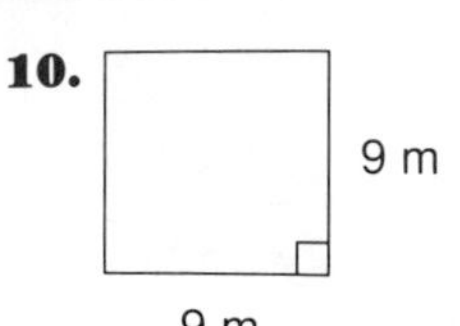

11. **12.** 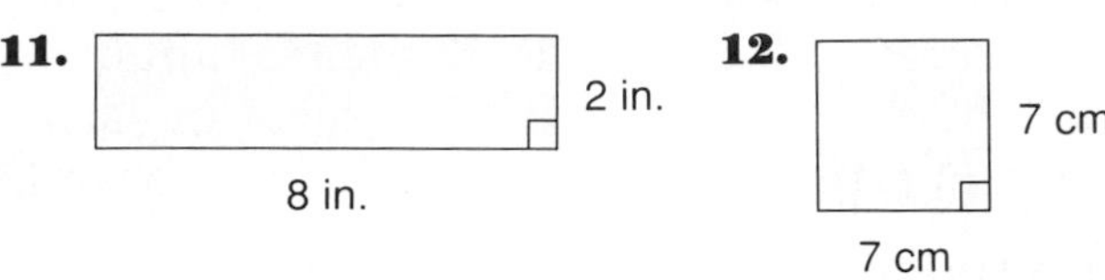

13. 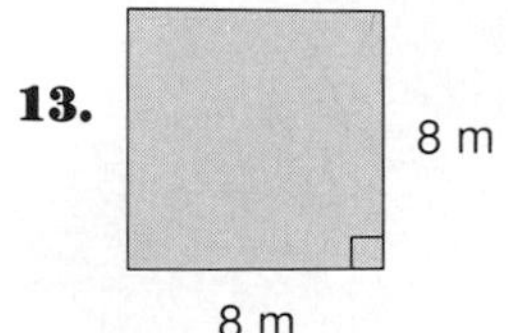

14. **15.** 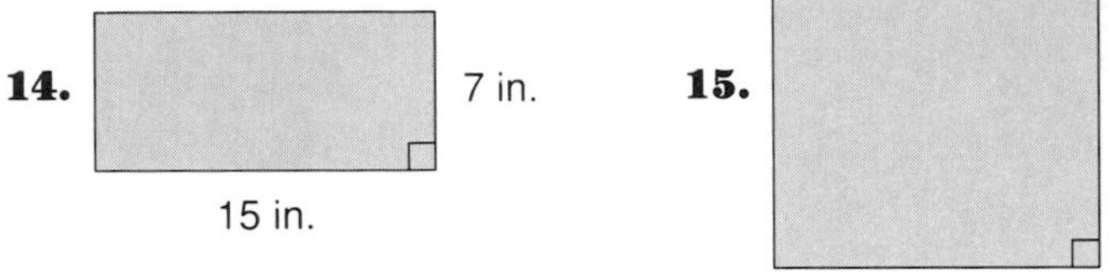

Find the area and perimeter. Tell whether you use mental math or paper and pencil. **Remember** to label units in your answers.

16. A rectangle 7.5 cm by 2.5 cm

17. A square 22 in. on each side

18. A square $4\frac{1}{2}$ in. by $4\frac{1}{2}$ in.

19. A rectangle $7\frac{1}{2}$ in. by 10 in.

20. A square 12 ft on each side

21. A rectangle 10 in. by 9 in.

22. A rectangle $4\frac{1}{4}$ ft by 7 ft

23. A square 1.6 m by 1.6 m

24. A rectangle 135 yd by 47 yd

25. A rectangle $2\frac{1}{2}$ ft by $2\frac{2}{3}$ ft

Find the length of each rectangle. **Remember** that $A = \ell \times w$, so $\ell = \frac{A}{w}$.

26. Area = 12 sq ft; width = $2\frac{1}{2}$ ft

27. Area = 26 cm^2; width = 5.2 cm

28. Area = 6.4 m^2; width = 0.8 m

29. Area = 24 sq in.; width = $3\frac{3}{4}$ in.

30. Area = 52 cm^2; width = 8 cm

31. Area = 45.1 cm^2; width = 8.2 cm

Problem Solving

Tony is designing a garden at a state historical site. Use Tony's plan to solve each problem. **Remember** to label units in your answer.

32. What is the area of the lily garden? If Tony plans to use 1 lily plant per square foot, how many lily plants will he need?

33. Tony wants to edge the lily garden with a low picket fence. How many feet of fencing will he need?

34. How many square feet of sod will Tony need for the lawn area? If sod is sold in 1-ft by 3-ft strips, how many strips of sod will he need?

35. Tony will center each dahlia on an 8-inch square. If dahlias are sold 12 to a box, how many boxes will he need?

Explore Math

For Exercises 36 and 37, draw the figure on grid paper and use whole numbers for the dimensions. Then answer the questions.

36. Draw five different rectangles each with a perimeter of 20 centimeters.

37. What is the area of each rectangle in Exercise 36? Record each length, width, and area.

38. As the difference in the dimensions increases, what happens to the area?

39. As the difference in the dimensions decreases, what happens to the area?

40. What is the difference in the dimensions when the rectangle has the greatest area?

41. What is the greatest area for the given perimeter?

ALGEBRA

Perimeter and Area of Parallelograms and Triangles

Build Understanding

A. Moving Triangles
Materials: Grid paper, scissors
Groups: With a partner

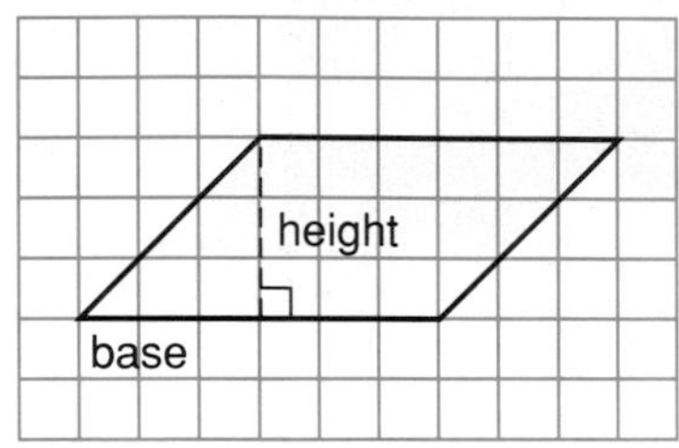

a. On grid paper, draw a parallelogram like the one shown.

b. What is the base of the parallelogram? the height? the area? (Count squares.)

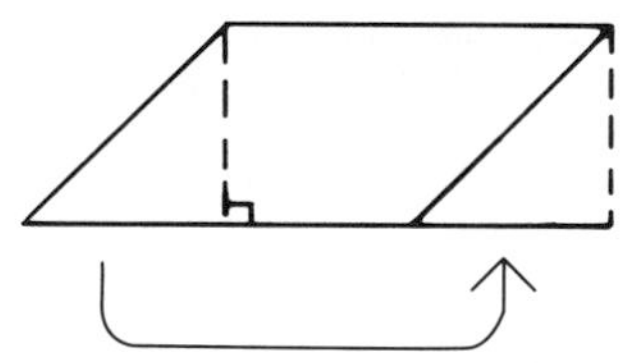

c. Now cut out the parallelogram. Cut off the triangle on the left, and move it to the right.

d. What is the name of the new figure? What is the area of the new figure?

e. Repeat the activity twice, using parallelograms with a base and height different from the one shown.

f. Compare the areas of the parallelograms and the new figures. Write a formula for each.

B. You can think of any triangle as half a parallelogram that has the same base and height.

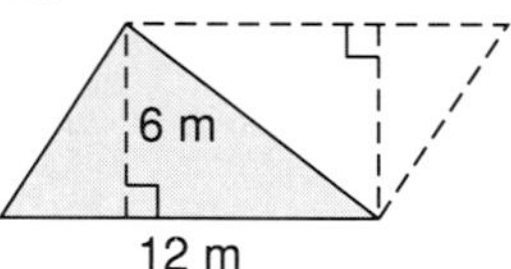

The area of the parallelogram is 72 m^2, so the area of the triangle is 36 m^2.

$A = \frac{1}{2}bh$ The area of a triangle is equal to one half the base times the height.

Talk About Math When is the height of a triangle equal to one of the sides? Can the height of a parallelogram ever be equal to one of the sides?

C. Find the perimeter and the area of the parallelogram and the triangle. (Use 0.5 for $\frac{1}{2}$.)

$P = 8 + 6 + 8 + 6$

$P = 28$ m

$P = 7 + 8 + 6$

$P = 21$ m

$A = bh$	$A = \frac{1}{2}bh$
$A = 8 \times 5$	$A = 0.5 \times 8 \times 5$
$A = 40$ m^2	$A = 20$ m^2

Check Understanding

For another example, see Set B, pages 372–373.

In each diagram, name the line segment that is the height for the given base. Find the perimeter and area of each figure.

1. **2.**

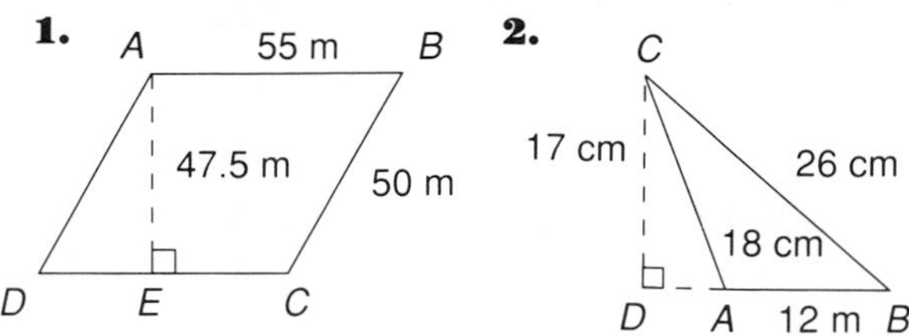

Practice

For More Practice, see Set B, pages 374–375.

Find the perimeter and the area. **Remember** that the height is perpendicular to the base.

3.

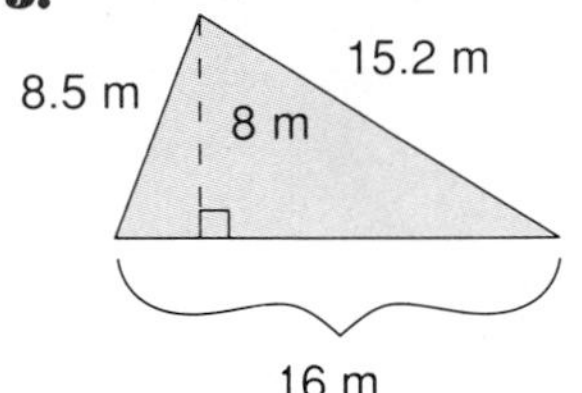

4.

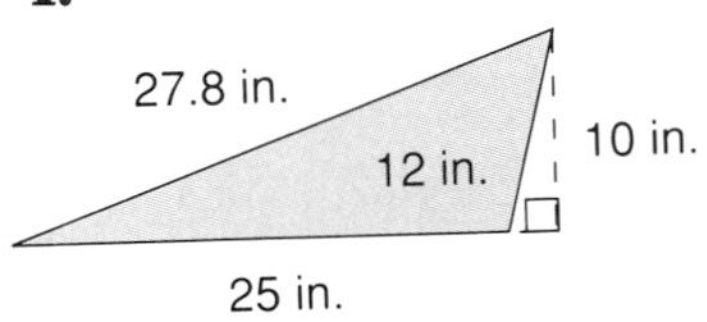

5.

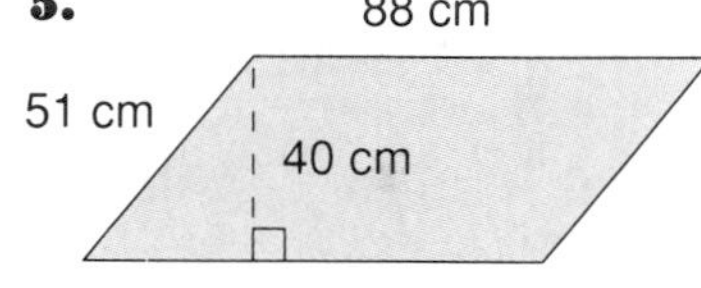

You can make a sketch to help answer these exercises. Find the area of a

6. triangle with base of $1\frac{1}{4}$ ft and height of 4 ft.

7. parallelogram with base of 9.8 cm and height of 4.2 cm.

8. parallelogram with base of 20 in. and height of $12\frac{1}{4}$ in.

9. triangle with base of 8 in. and height of $6\frac{3}{8}$ in.

10. square that is 4.6 in. on a side.

11. triangle with a base of 7.2 cm and a height of 7.2 cm.

Problem Solving

Critical Thinking Solve each problem.

12. Find the area of a triangle with base of 4 in. and height of 3 in.; with base of 8 in. and height of 3 in.; with base of 4 in. and height of 6 in.

13. Find the area of a triangle with base of 5 in. and height of 3 in.; with base of 10 in. and height of 6 in.; with base of 15 in. and height of 9 in.

14. What happens to the area of a triangle when either its base or its height is multiplied by a number?

15. What happens to the area of a triangle when both its base and its height are multiplied by the same number?

Perimeter and Area of Other Polygons

Build Understanding

A. The Taj Mahal in Agra, India was built by the Indian ruler Shah Jahan in memory of his wife Mumtaz Mahal. The building is octagonal with four sides each about 44.5 meters long and four sides each about 8.5 meters long. Find its perimeter.

Since four sides are each 44.5 m long, and the remaining four sides are each 8.5 m long, multiply each length by 4 and then add to find the perimeter.

$P = (4 \times 44.5) + (4 \times 8.5)$
$P = 178 + 34$
$P = 212$

The perimeter of the Taj Mahal is 212 meters.

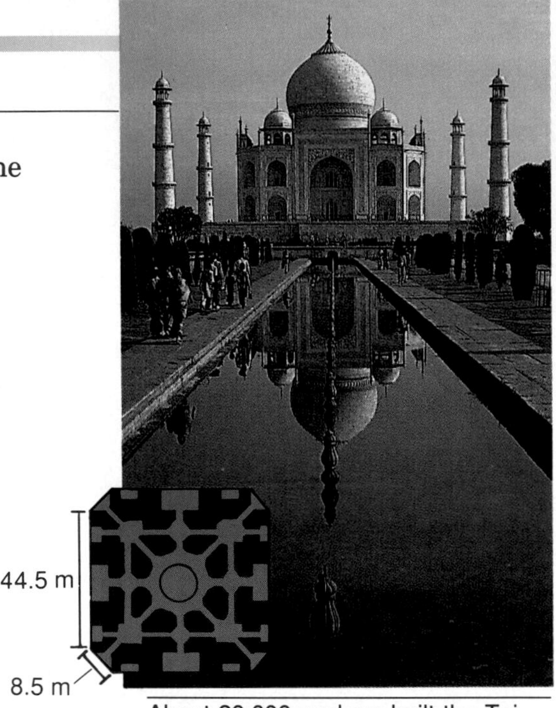

About 20,000 workers built the Taj Mahal between 1632 and 1653.

B. Find the area of the polygon shown.

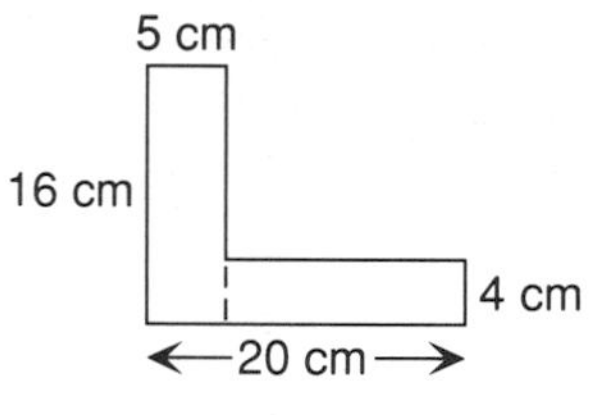

Divide the polygon into two rectangles. Find the area of each. Then add the areas. Recall that the formula for the area of a rectangle is $A = \ell \times w$.

Area of vertical rectangle = 5×16, or 80 cm^2
Area of horizontal rectangle = 15×4, or 60 cm^2

The polygon's area is 80 cm^2 + 60 cm^2, or 140 cm^2.

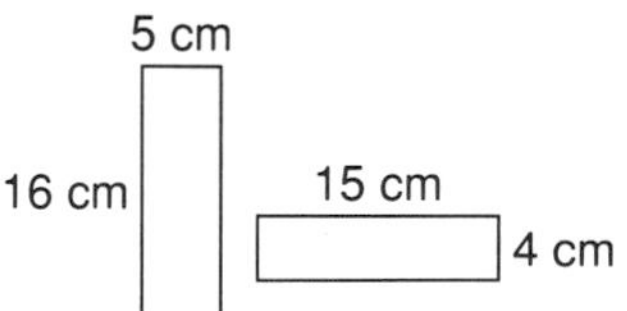

Talk About Math Divide the polygon in Example B in another way to find its area. Explain.

Check Understanding

For another example, see Set C, pages 372–373.

Copy each polygon. Find the perimeter and area of each polygon.

1.

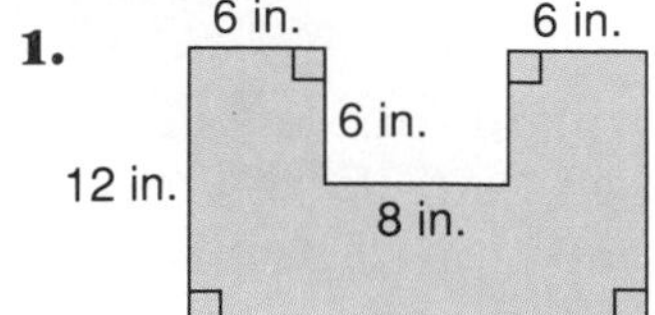

2.

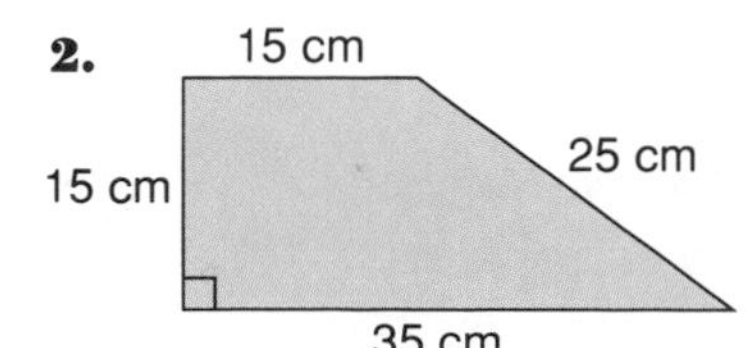

3.

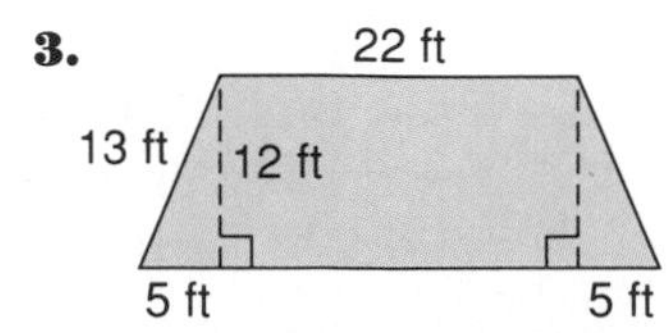

Practice

For More Practice, see Set C, pages 374–375.

Find the perimeter and the area of each polygon. Tell whether you use paper and pencil or calculator. **Remember** to label units in your answers.

4.

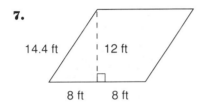

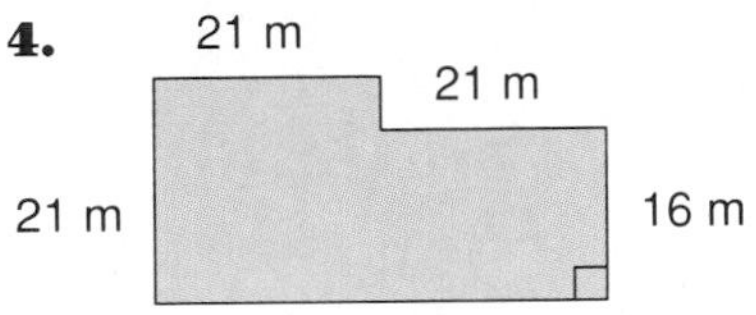

5.

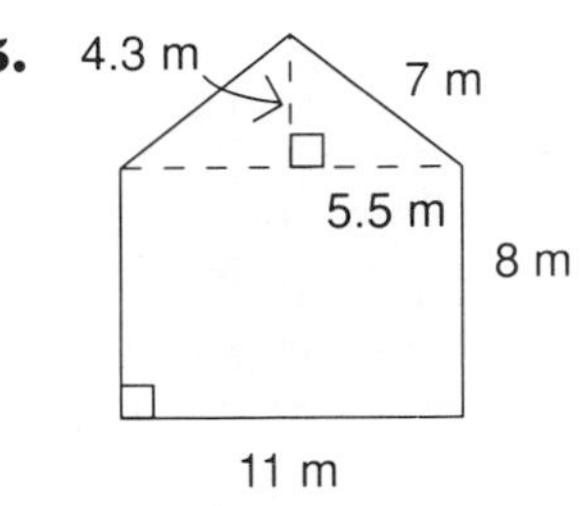

6.

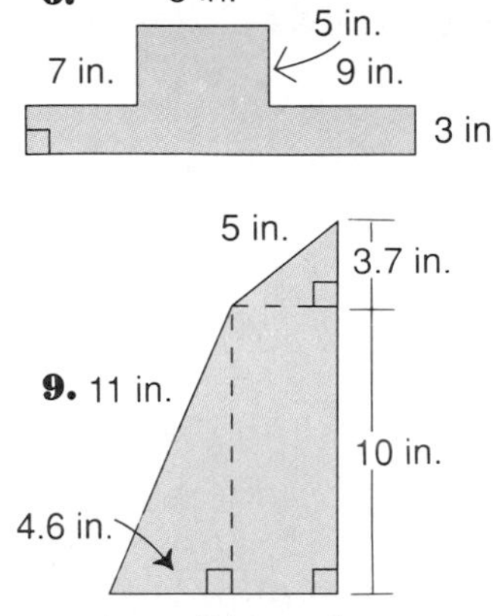

7.

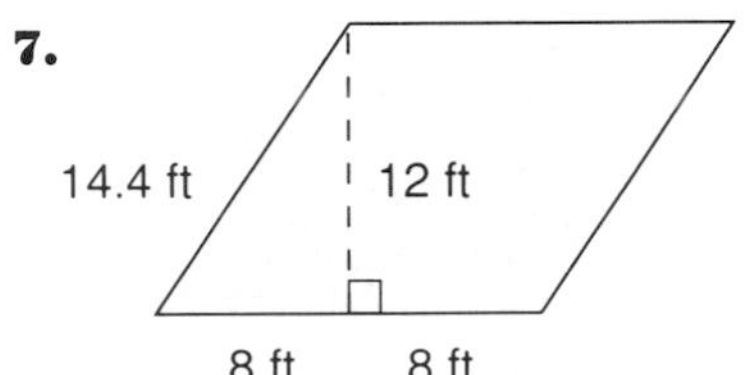

8.

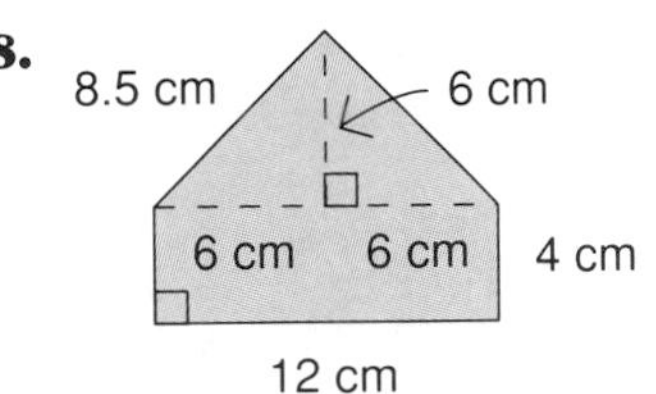

9.

Problem Solving

Solve.

10. The Palace of the Governors in Uxmal, Mexico was built in about 900 A.D. It is rectangular, with a length of 98 m and a width of 11.9 m. Find the perimeter and area of the floor.

11. The famous Leaning Tower of Pisa is the bell tower, or *campanile,* for the Pisa Cathedral. The base of the cathedral itself is ✝-shaped with the dimensions shown. Find the perimeter and area of the base.

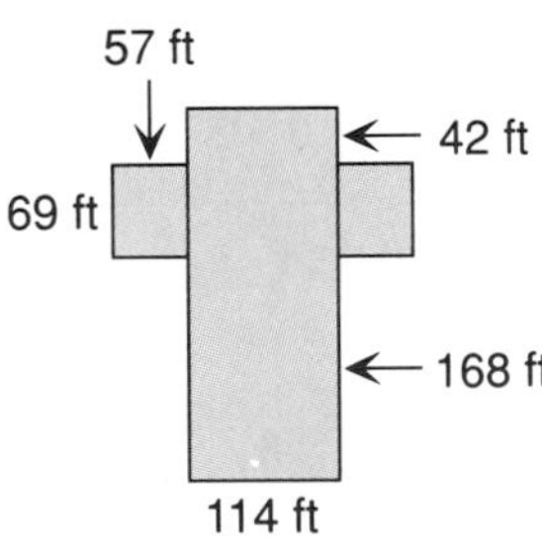

12. The base of the Great Pyramid in Egypt is square. Its perimeter is about 922.4 m. Find the length of each side and the area of the base.

13. The Pentagon building in Washington, D.C. is a regular pentagon about 300 m on each side. Find its perimeter.

Octagonal windows were used in the Moorish Baths in Granada, Spain, built in the eleventh century.

ALGEBRA

Circumference of a Circle

Build Understanding

The distance around a circle is called the ***circumference.*** The ratio of the circumference, C, of a circle to the diameter, d, is always the same. It is a number named by the Greek letter π (pi). It is a decimal that never ends or repeats. To 9 decimal places, $\pi = 3.141592653$. Two approximations for π are 3.14 and $\frac{22}{7}$. Use $C = \pi d$ as a formula for finding the circumference of a circle.

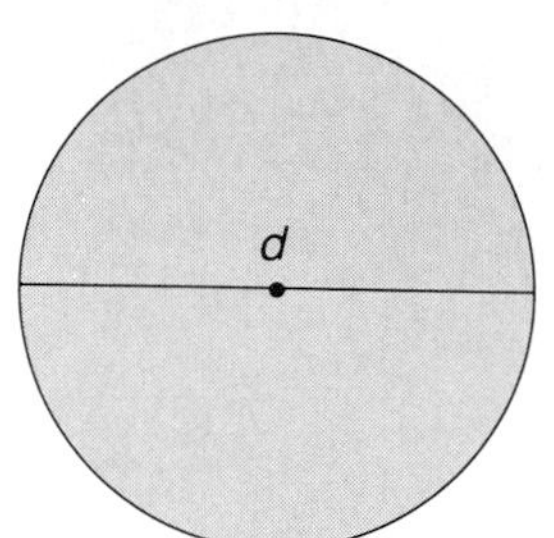

A. Sandy Lehto runs an amusement park. She wants to string lights around the carousel's circular top with a diameter of 30 ft. How many feet of lights will she need?

30 ft

Carousel

Find the circumference of the carousel's circular top. Use the formula $C = \pi d$.

$\boldsymbol{C = \pi d \approx 3.14 \times 30 \approx 94.2}$ **ft**

Sandy will need about 94.2 ft of lights.

B. Sandy also wants to enclose the carousel area with a circular wooden railing. The radius of the railing will be 21 ft. How many feet of rail will she need?

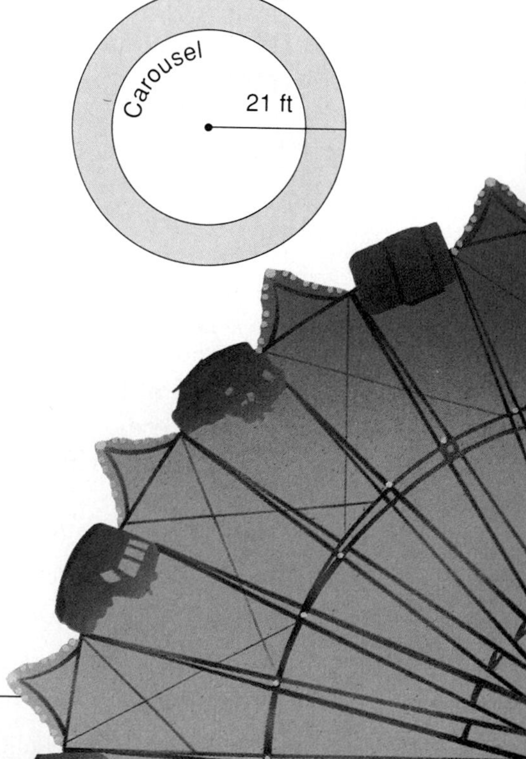

To find the amount of railing, you can find the circumference of the circular area. Since the radius, r, is half the diameter, another formula for circumference is $C = 2\pi r$.

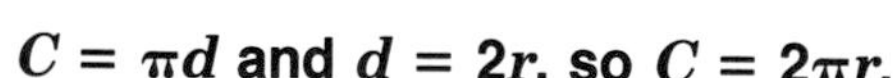

$\boldsymbol{C = \pi d}$ **and** $\boldsymbol{d = 2r}$**, so** $\boldsymbol{C = 2\pi r}$**.**

Use this formula to find the circumference.

$\boldsymbol{C = 2\pi r \approx 2 \times \frac{22}{7} \times 21 \approx 132}$ **ft**

Sandy will need about 132 ft of wooden railing.

■ **Write About Math** Could you use 3 for π when you want to estimate the circumference of a circle? Suggest a situation calling for an estimate.

The Ferris wheel at Tsukuba, Japan, has a height of 278 ft 10 in. It has 46 cars and holds 384 riders.

Check Understanding

For another example, see Set D, pages 372–373.

Answer each question. Round to the nearest tenth. Use 3.14 for π.

1. The diameter of a circle is 7.68 m. What is the circumference?

2. The radius of a circle is 9.7 cm. What is the circumference?

Practice

For More Practice, see Set D, pages 374–375.

Find the circumference. Tell whether you use paper and pencil or calculator. Round to the nearest tenth. Use 3.14 for π.

3. 

$r = 12$ mm

4. 

$d = 17$ mm

5. 

$d = 15$ ft

Find the circumference of the circle whose radius or diameter is given. Round to the nearest tenth. Use 3.14 for π.

6. Diameter: 1 ft

7. Radius: 6 cm

8. Diameter: 28 in.

9. Radius: 16 in.

10. Diameter: 5 in.

11. Diameter: 3.4 cm

12. Radius: 50 cm

13. Diameter: 24 in.

14. Radius: 0.6 cm

15. Radius: $4\frac{1}{2}$ ft

16. Diameter: $6\frac{1}{5}$ in.

17. Radius: $9\frac{1}{4}$ in.

Problem Solving

Solve each problem. **Remember** to draw a figure to help you solve the problem. Use $\pi \approx \frac{22}{7}$.

18. A Ferris wheel has a diameter of 42 ft. If Sandy wants to string lights around both rims of the Ferris wheel, how many feet of lights will she need?

19. Sandy wants to install new seats on the Ferris wheel. If 22 seats are to be equally spaced around the wheel, how far apart will the seats be?

20. **Critical Thinking** What is the radius of the largest circle that can be cut from a 6-in. square?

Area of a Circle

Build Understanding

A. The weather radar station at Freedom College covers a circular region 10 miles in diameter. What area does the weather station cover?

Study the diagram to estimate the area of the weather station.

The area of the square is equal to the area within the circle plus the area outside the circle. So, the area of a circle 10 miles wide is less than 100 square miles. To estimate the area of the circle, estimate the area outside the circle and subtract.

Area of square	−	Area outside circle	=	Area of circle
100	**−**	**22**	**=**	**78**

The area of the circle is about 78 square miles.

Use the formula for the area of a circle to get a better estimate. The formula for the area of a circle is $A = \pi r^2$. The radius is 5 miles.

$$A \approx (3.14)(5)^2 \approx 3.14 \times 25 \approx 78.5 \text{ square miles}$$

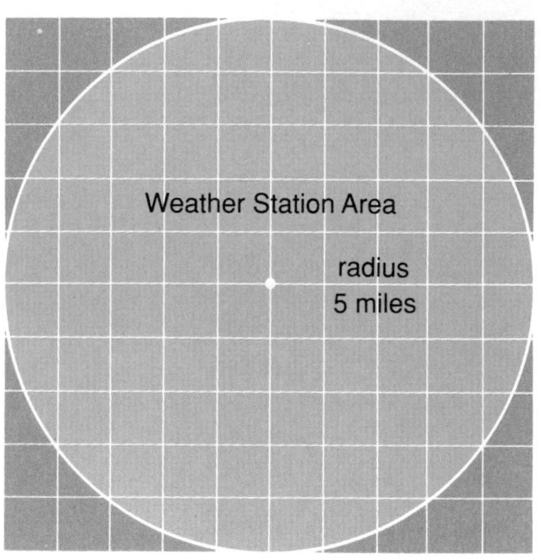

There are 12 squares entirely outside the circle. There are 32 squares entirely or partially outside the circle. A reasonable estimate for the area outside the circle is $\frac{12 + 32}{2} = 22$ square miles.

B. To find the area of this figure, break it up into a rectangle and a semicircle.

The area of the circle is

$A = \pi r^2 \approx 3.14 \times (6)^2 \approx 113$ **sq in.**

So the area of a semicircle is $\frac{1}{2}$ the area of the circle, or about 56.5 sq in.

The area of the rectangle is

$A = \ell \times w = 15 \times 12 = 180$ **sq in.**

Finally, combine the two areas.

56.5 sq in. + 180 sq in. = 236.5 sq in.

The area of the figure is about 236.5 sq in.

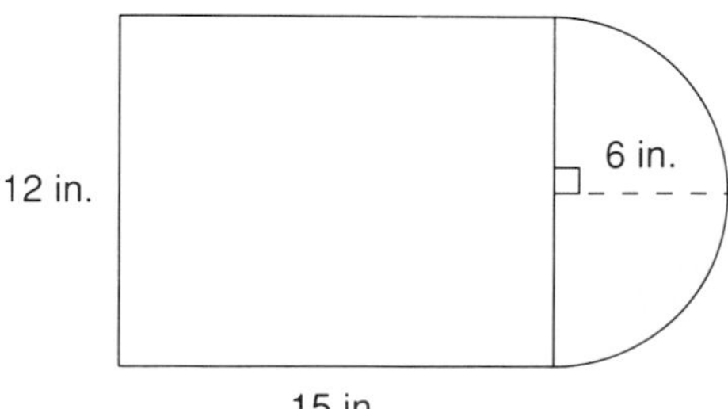

Write About Math
Write a formula for the area of a circle in terms of the diameter d.

Check Understanding

For another example, see Set E, pages 372–373.

Find the area of each figure. Round to the nearest tenth. Use 3.14 for π.

1.

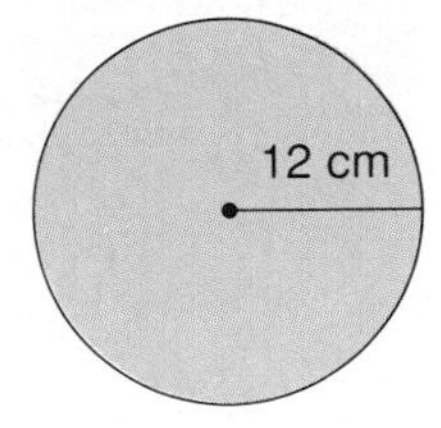

2.

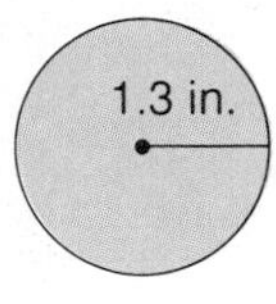

3.

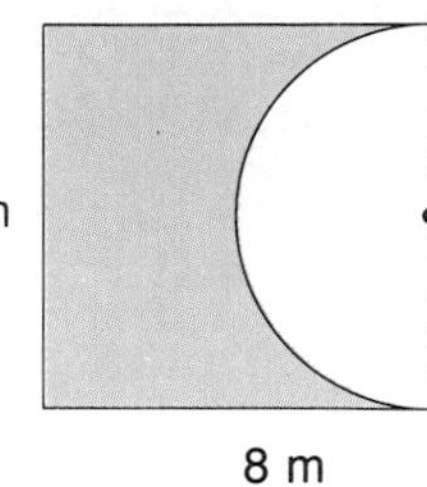

Practice

For More Practice, see Set E, pages 374–375.

Find the area of each circle. Round to the nearest tenth. Use 3.14 for π. Tell whether you use paper and pencil or a calculator. **Remember** to label units in your answer.

4. Diameter: 11 mm
5. Radius: 21.8 cm
6. Diameter: 16.5 cm

7. Radius: 92 mm
8. Diameter: 6.9 m
9. Radius: 1.6 m

10. Radius: 1.3 cm
11. Radius: 0.7 cm
12. Diameter: 7.5 cm

13. Diameter: 1.6 m
14. Radius: 8 m
15. Diameter: 4.6 m

Find the area of each circle. Use $\frac{22}{7}$ for π.

16. Radius: $52\frac{1}{5}$ ft
17. Diameter: $16\frac{1}{3}$ ft
18. Radius: $16\frac{5}{8}$ in.

19. Diameter: $\frac{7}{22}$ in.
20. Radius: $14\frac{1}{4}$ yd
21. Diameter: $1\frac{2}{3}$ yd

22. Diameter: $10\frac{1}{2}$ in.
23. Diameter: 56 in.
24. Radius: $4\frac{1}{5}$ in.

25. Radius: $1\frac{3}{4}$ in.
26. Diameter: 70 in.
27. Radius: $8\frac{1}{6}$ in.

Estimation Estimate the area of each circle as (a) less than 100 sq in., (b) between 100 and 200 sq in., or (c) greater than 200 sq in.

28. Radius: 6 in.
29. Diameter: 8 in.
30. Diameter: 14 in.

31. Diameter: 10 in.
32. Diameter: $30\frac{1}{3}$ in.
33. Radius: 11 in.

Mixed Practice Find the area of each shaded region. Round to the nearest tenth. Use 3.14 for π. **Remember** to look for simpler figures whose area you can find.

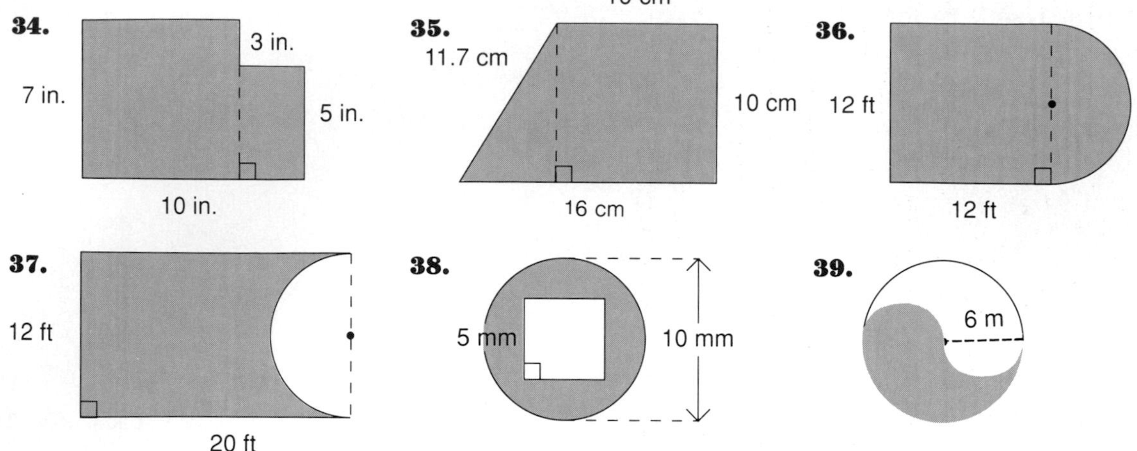

Problem Solving

Solve each problem. Round to the nearest tenth. Use 3.14 for π. **Remember** that you can use addition and subtraction to find areas.

40. The weather radar station in Clark County covers the area shown in the figure. Find the area *not* covered by the weather station.

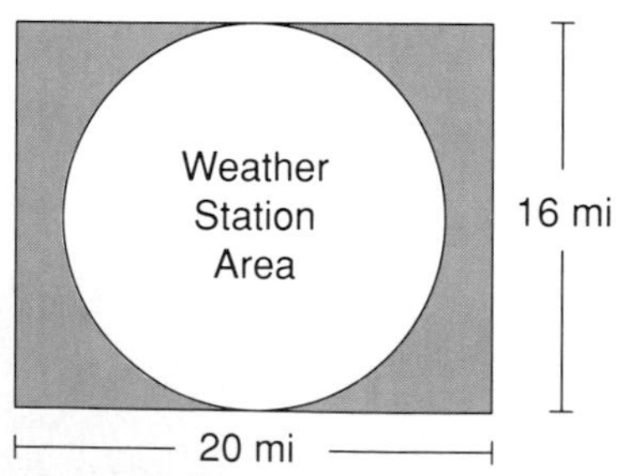

41. The area covered by the weather radar station in Vienna County extends into neighboring Rome County, as the figure shows. Find the area in Rome County *not* covered by the weather station.

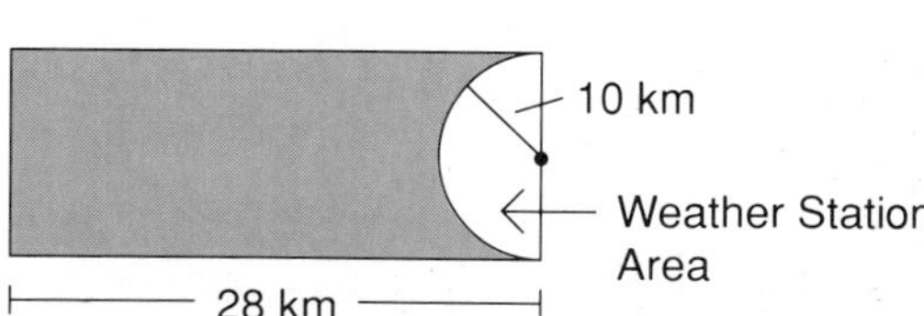

Critical Thinking Find the radius and diameter of each circle.

42. $A = 64\pi \text{ mm}^2$

43. $A = 81\pi \text{ mm}^2$

44. $A = 625\pi$ sq ft

45. **Use Data** Use the information on page 350. Sandy wants to plant grass seed between the carousel and the wooden railing. A box of seed covers 200 sq ft. How many boxes will Sandy need?

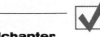

Midchapter Checkup

Name each figure below.

1. 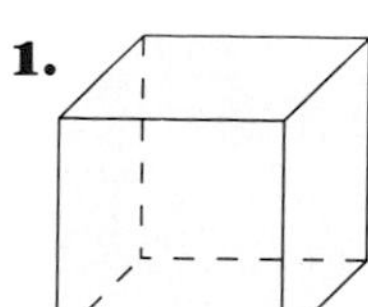

2. 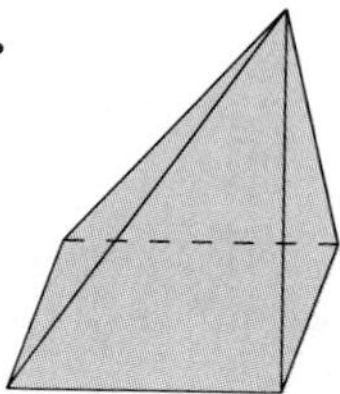

3. 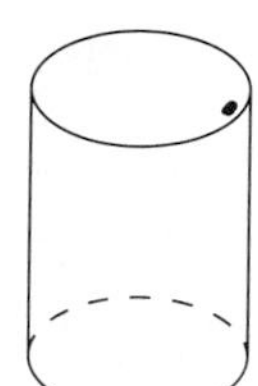

4. 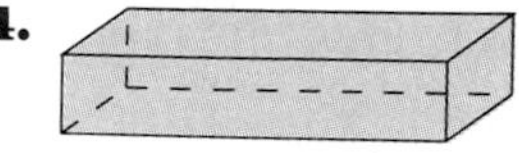

Find the perimeter and area of each rectangle.

5. 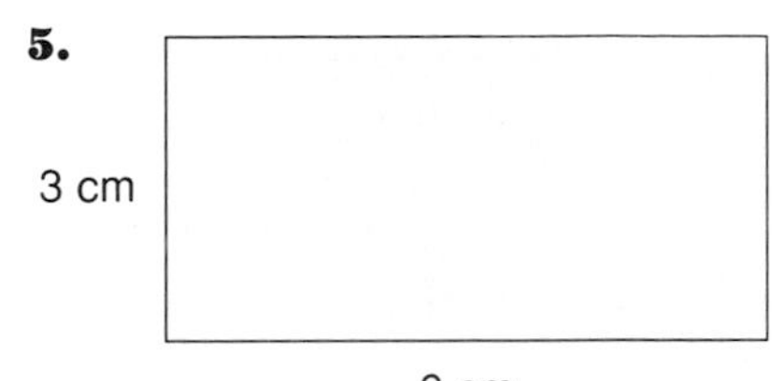

6. 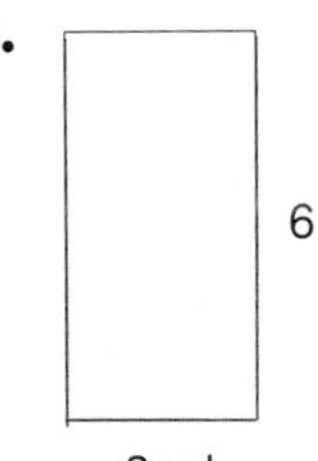

7. 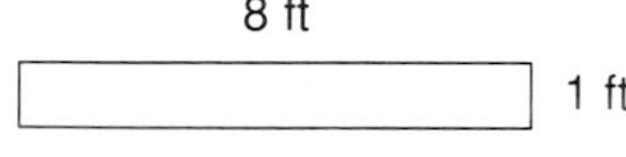

Find the perimeter and area of each figure. All measurements are in inches.

8. 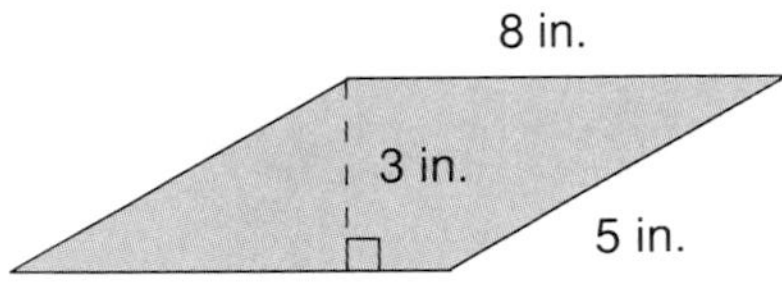

9. 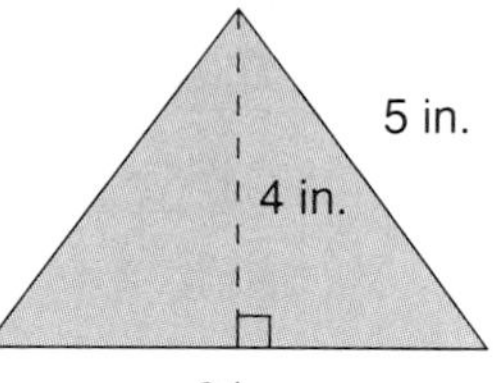

10. 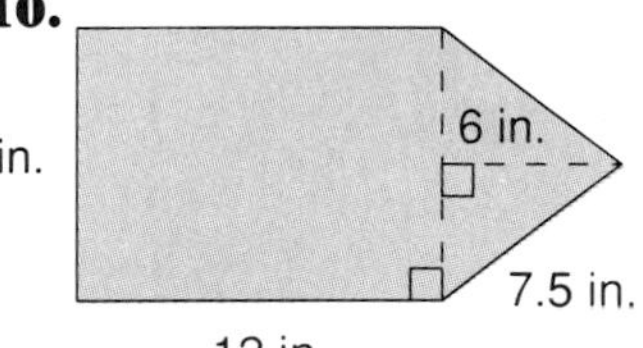

Find the circumference of each circle. Use $\pi = 3.14$.

11. 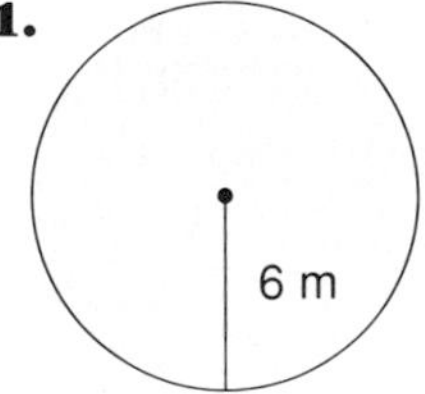

12. 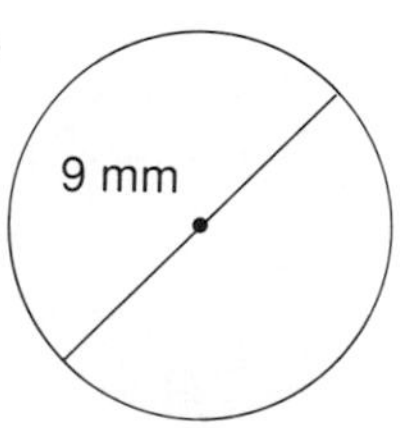

13. 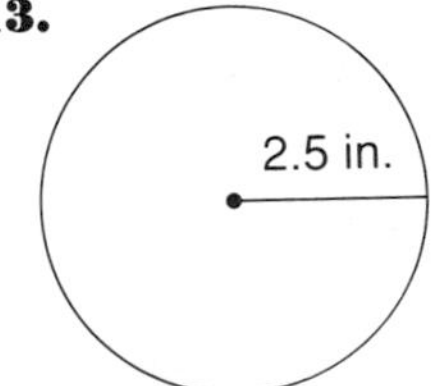

Find the area of each shaded region. Use $\pi = 3.14$.

14. 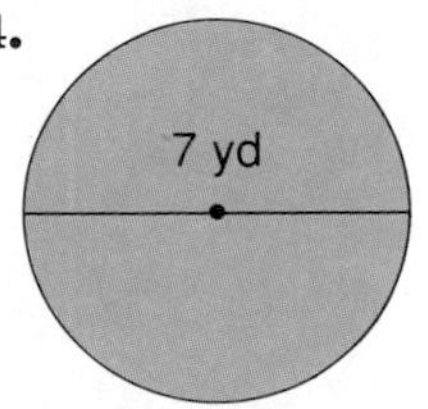

15. 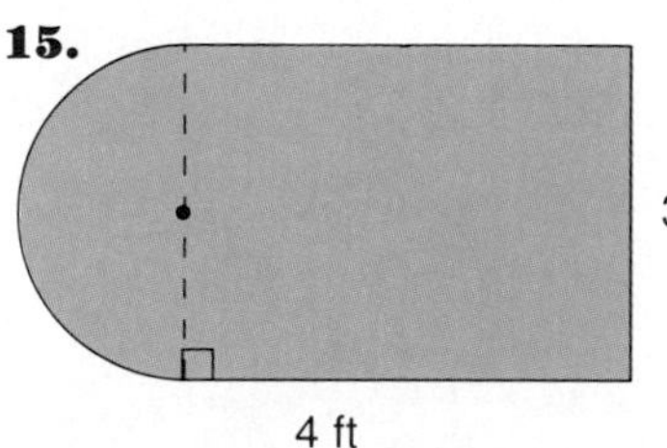

16. 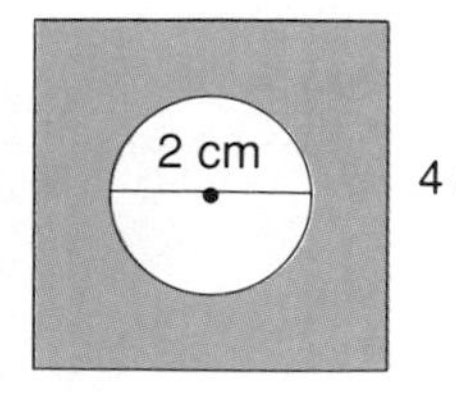

Problem-Solving Workshop

Explore as a Team

In this activity, you will write math riddles and jokes.

1. Make a list of math vocabulary terms. Expand the list by writing noun and verb forms of words. For example, multiplication can also be listed as multiply, multiplier, multiples, and multiplicand.

2. Use your list of math words to write "inside" riddles and jokes. To do this, you change or replace syllables "inside" words to make new words or phrases.

Example 1 Change a syllable to a different meaning.

What tools are used in arithmetic?
Multi*pliers*!

Example 2 Change a syllable to a word that sounds the same but is spelled differently.

What's the best angle to approach a problem from?
A *try*-angle!

Example 3 What do you call happy-go-lucky triangles and squares? *Jolly*gons!

TIPS FOR WORKING TOGETHER

Involve your whole group. Help everyone to participate.

Math-at-Home Activity

Ask a family member to help you make these five regular polyhedron models using drinking straws and string.

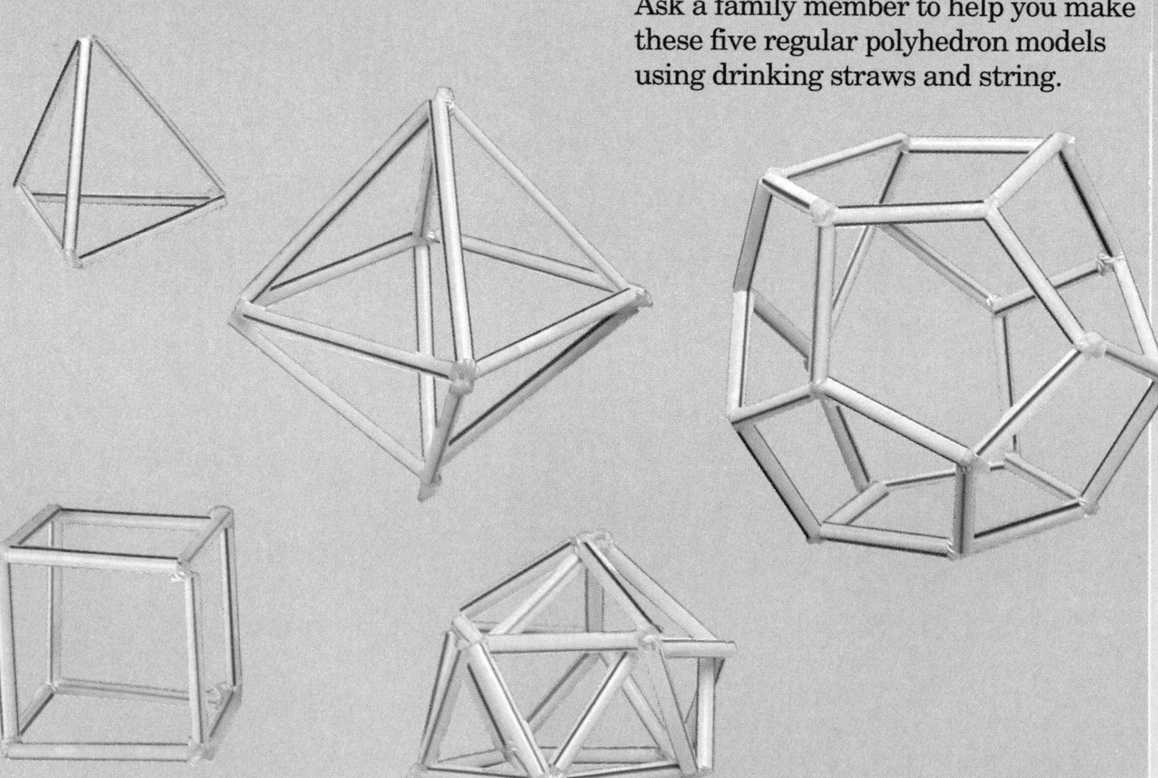

Explore with a Computer

Use the *Geometry Workshop Project* for this activity.

Mrs. Chen wants to install a new red and white checkerboard tile floor in her kitchen. The kitchen is 10 feet wide and 12 feet long. To make a checkerboard pattern, she will need an equal number of red and white tiles. Each floor tile is one square foot.

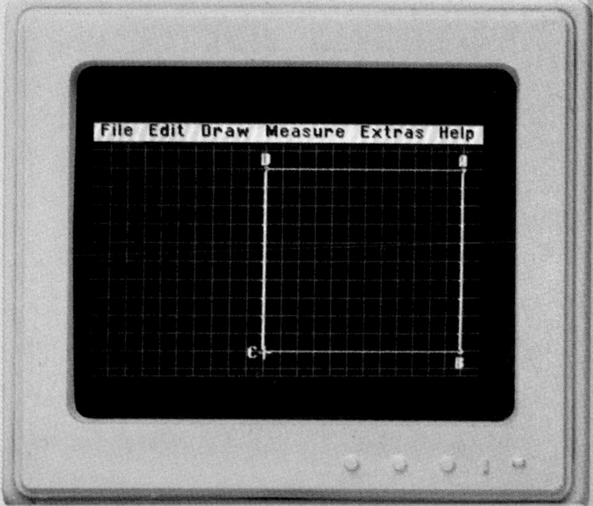

1. At the computer, use the *Measure Polygon option* to find the area and the perimeter of the floor.

2. How many tiles of each color will Mrs. Chen need to cover her kitchen floor?

3. Without changing the perimeter of the room, how many different rectangular shaped rooms can you design? Which room has the greatest area? Which room has the smallest area? How many tiles would you need for each room?

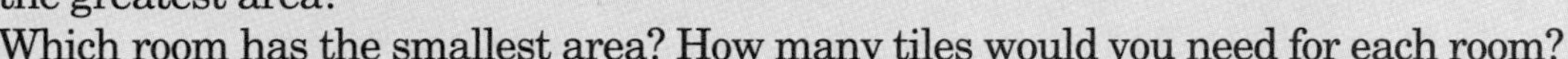

Number-Sense Project

Look back at pages 334-335.

1. At the rate given, how long would it take your heart to pump the capacity of the gasoline tank on a small car (about 10 gallons)?

2. At the rate given, how long would it take for your heart to generate enough muscle power to lift a small car 10 feet?

3. The length of your veins, arteries, and blood vessels is equal to how many round trips between New York and Los Angeles (5,000 miles)?

4. How many times does your heart beat in one day? In one year? In a lifetime of 70 years?

Visual Thinking Activity

Each square is divided into two parts. In which cases are the two parts congruent?

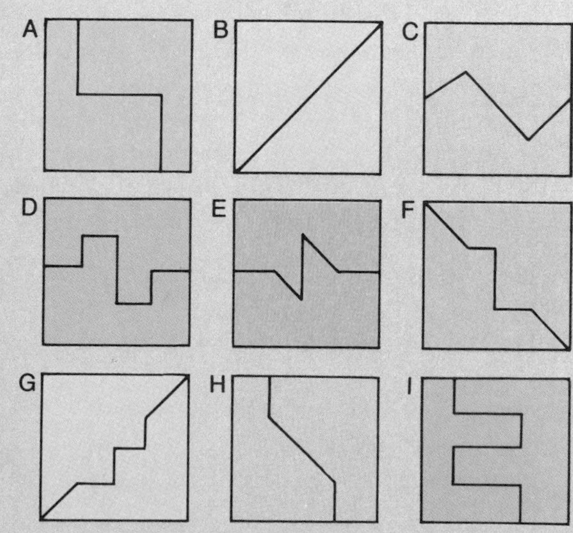

ALGEBRA

Surface Area of a Polyhedron

Build Understanding

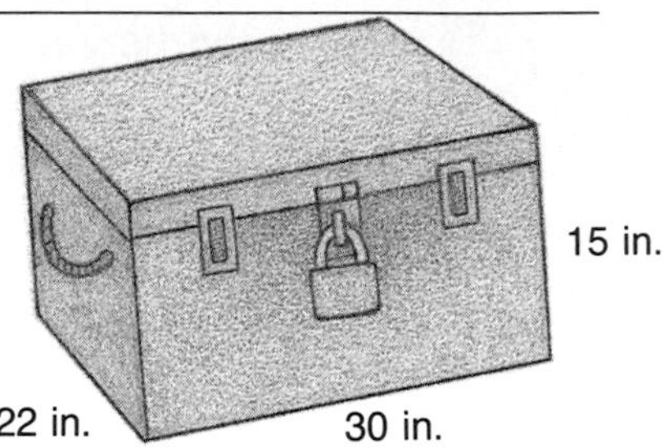

Several students are going camping. They want to line an equipment box which has the dimensions shown. How much plastic sheeting will they need to line the box?

Since the box is a rectangular prism, it has 6 faces. The box's ***surface area*** is the sum of the area of all the faces.

Make a list of the faces. Use the formula $A = \ell \times w$ to find the area of each face.

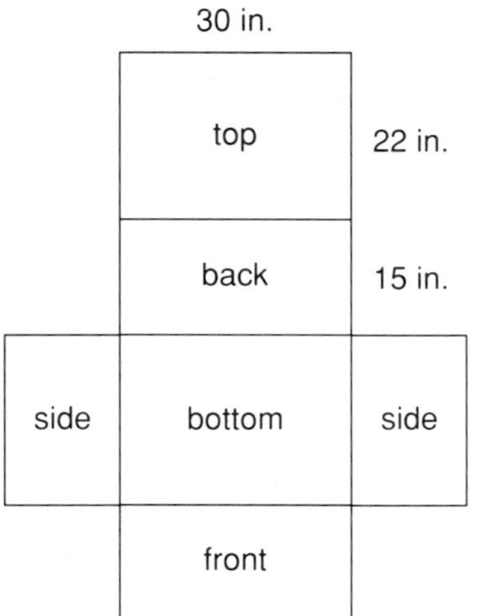

Face	Dimensions	Area
Top	22 in. × 30 in.	660 sq in.
Back	15 in. × 30 in.	450 sq in.
Bottom	22 in. × 30 in.	660 sq in.
Front	15 in. × 30 in.	450 sq in.
Left side	22 in. × 15 in.	330 sq in.
Right side	22 in. × 15 in.	330 sq in.
Total		2,880 sq in.

They will need 2,880 sq in. of plastic sheeting.

Talk About Math Use the list of faces above to describe a shortcut for computing the surface area of a rectangular prism.

Check Understanding

For another example, see Set F, pages 372–373.

The students use water repellant on a tent that is a square pyramid with the dimensions shown in the figure. How much surface must they cover?

1. How many faces are there?

2. Do any of them have the same area?

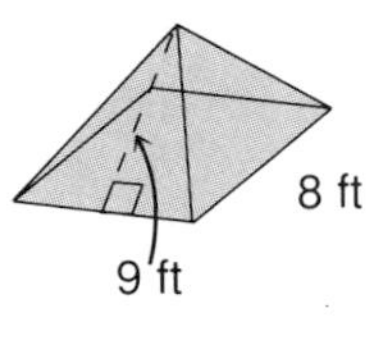

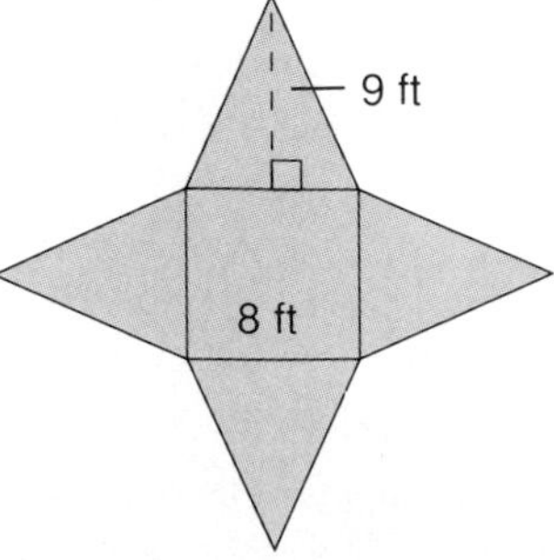

3. Make a table of all the faces.

4. Find the surface area of the square pyramid tent.

Practice

For More Practice, see Set F, pages 374–375.

Find the surface area of each figure, and then name it. **Remember** to include all surfaces in your calculations.

5. 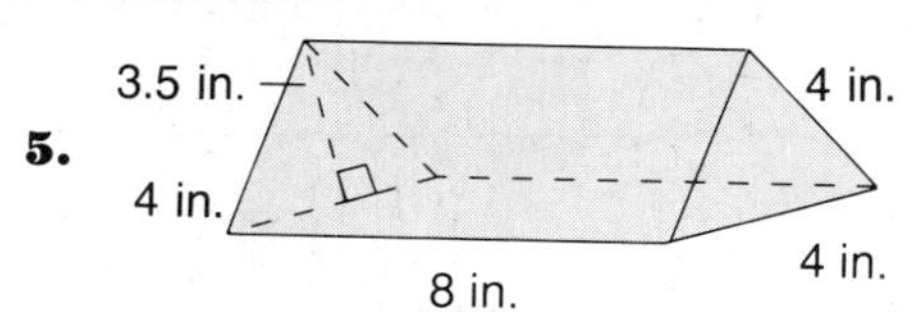

6. 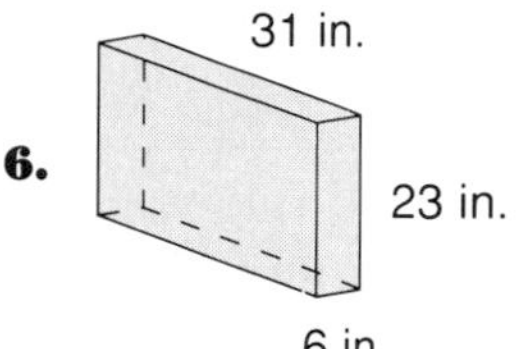

7. 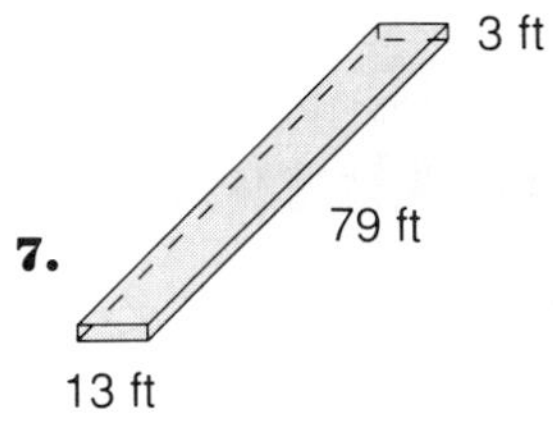

8. 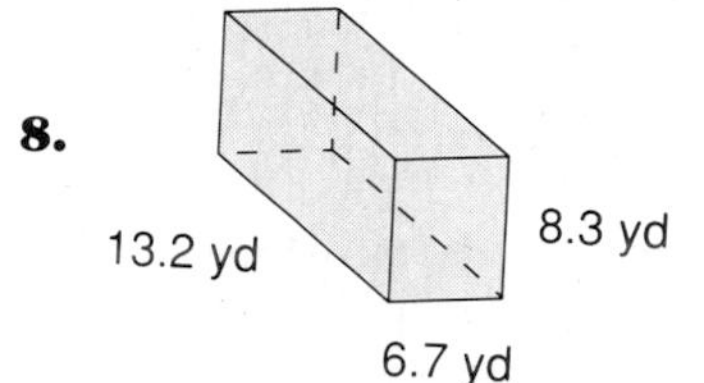

9. 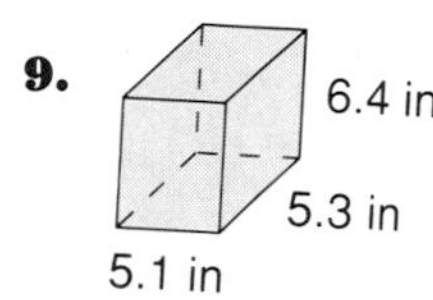

10. 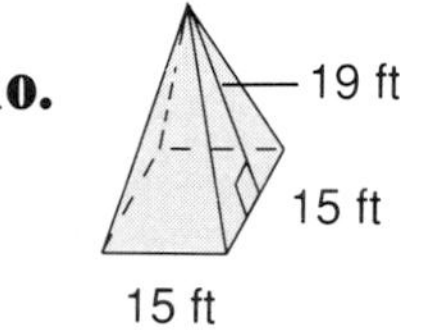

11. 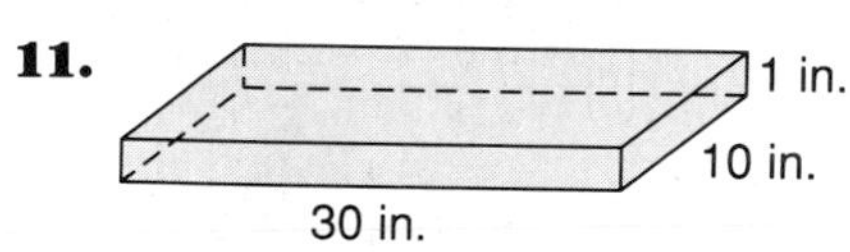

12. 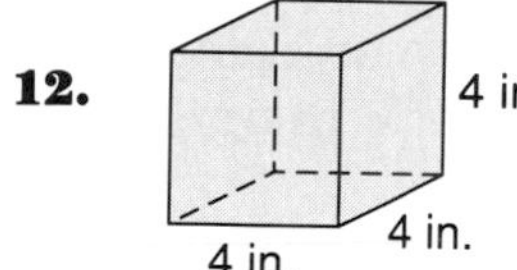

13. 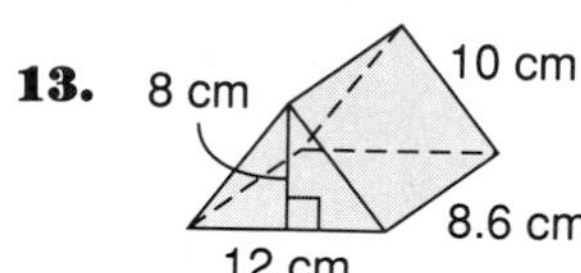

14. 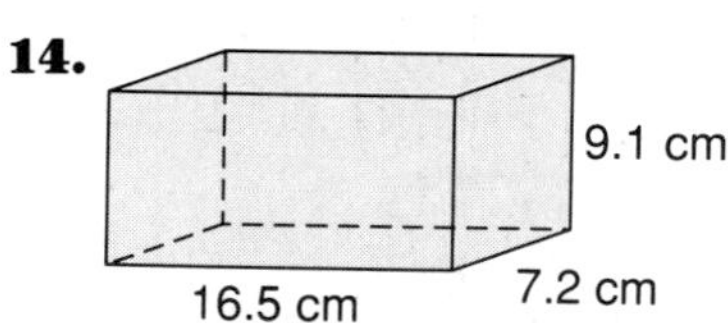

15. 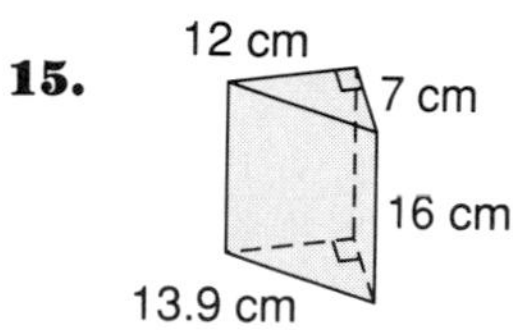

16. 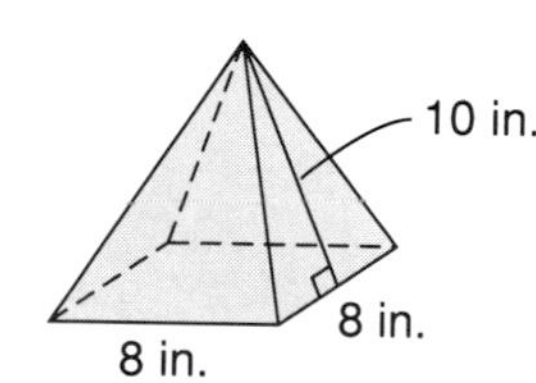

Problem Solving

Solve. **Remember** to label the units in your answers.

A shop class is making a reflector oven to take on a camping trip. The students want their oven to be in the shape of a rectangular prism 24 in. long by 14 in. wide by 10 in. high.

17. How much stainless steel will they need to line the reflector oven?

18. If stainless steel comes in 2 ft by 3 ft sheets, how many sheets do they need?

19. **Calculator** What happens to the surface area of a rectangular prism when each dimension is doubled? Make a table to explain.

20. **Calculator** What happens to the surface area of a rectangular prism when each dimension is halved? Make a table to explain.

ALGEBRA

Surface Area of a Cylinder

Build Understanding

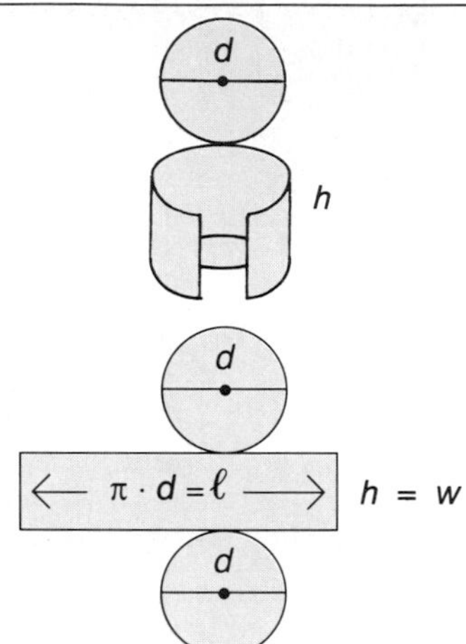

Joe Hernandez is a structural engineer. He plans to build a gas storage tank like the one shown here. How much sheet steel will Joe need?

If the tank were cut apart, you would see that the bases (the top and the bottom) are circles and the curved surface is a rectangle. Notice that the length of the rectangle is the circumference of the base, and the width is the height of the tank.

Use formulas to find the surface area of a cylindrical storage tank with a diameter of 6 m and a height of 9 m.

Area of Base	**Area of Curved Surface**	
$A = \pi r^2$	$A = \ell w$	ℓ is the circumference of the base, or πd; w is the height, h.
$A \approx 3.14\ (3)^2$	$A = (\pi d)h$	
$A \approx 28.26\ \text{m}^2$	$A \approx 3.14\ (6)(9)$	
	$A \approx 169.56\ \text{m}^2$	

The total surface area is $28.26 + 28.26 + 169.56 = 226.08\ \text{m}^2$.

Joe will need about 226.1 m^2 of steel.

Calculator

Press: 3.14 [×] 3 [×] 3 [×] 2 [=] [M+] 3.14 [×] 6 [×] 9 [+] [MRC] [=]

Display: 226.08

Write About Math Write the formula for the area of the curved surface of a cylinder in terms of the radius, r.

Check Understanding

For another example, see Set G, pages 372–373.

Another storage tank Joe plans to build is a cylinder 10 m high and 15 m in diameter. Answer each exercise. Round to the nearest tenth. Use 3.14 for π.

1. Draw a diagram of the flattened cylinder.
2. What formula would you use to find the area of the top of the cylinder?
3. What formula would you use to find the area of the curved part of the cylinder?
4. Find the surface area of the cylinder.

Practice

For More Practice, see Set G, pages 374–375.

Find the surface area of each cylinder. Round to the nearest tenth. Use 3.14 as π. **Remember** to include both bases in your calculations.

5.

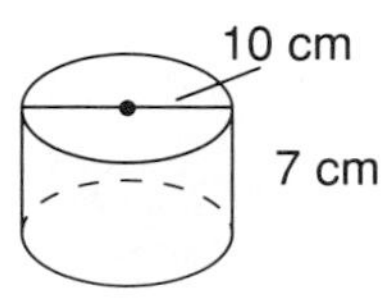

6.

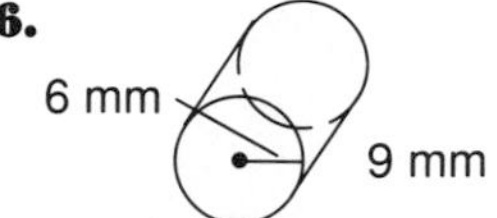

7.

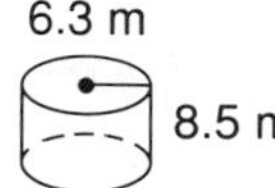

8. radius: 17 mm
height: 21 mm

9. diameter: 36 m
height: 15 m

10. radius: 6.9 cm
height: 8.5 cm

11. diameter: 3.13 m
height: 17.4 m

12. diameter: 4.5 cm
height: 8.5 cm

13. radius: 2 m
height: 15 m

14. radius: 10 cm
height: 5 cm

15. radius: 3.3 cm
height: 10 cm

16. diameter: 10 cm
height: 14 cm

Mixed Practice Find the surface area. Tell whether you use paper and pencil or calculator. Use $\frac{22}{7}$ for π.

17.

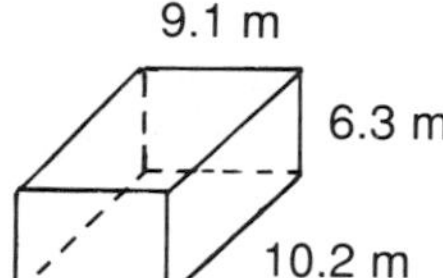

18.

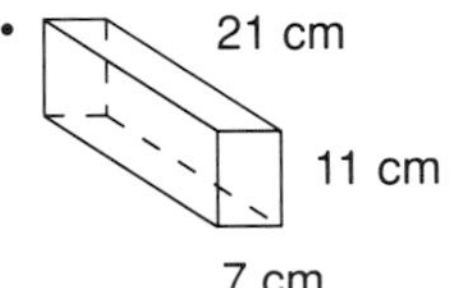

19.

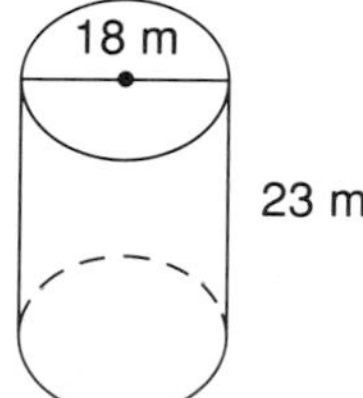

Problem Solving

Solve each problem. Use 3.14 for π. For Problems 21–22, round to the nearest tenth.

20. Three cylindrical gas storage tanks that Joe built need to be painted. Which of the 3 tanks require the most paint? (Note: the bottom is not painted.)

a.

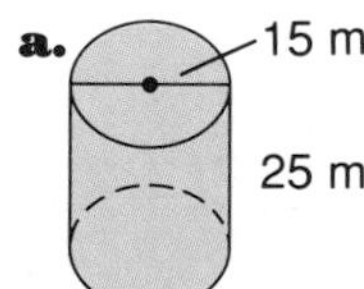

b.

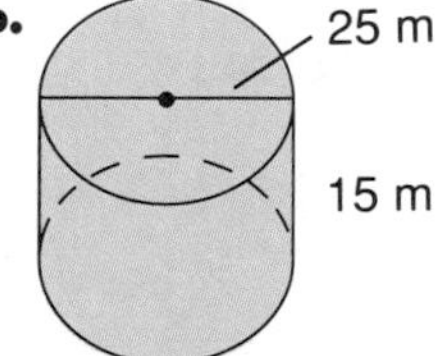

c. 11 m, 20 m

21. **Calculator** How does the surface area of the curved surface of a cylinder change if the radius is doubled? Make a table and explain what happens.

22. **Calculator** What is the change in the surface area of the curved surface of a cylinder if the radius is halved? Make a table and explain what happens.

ALGEBRA

Volume of Prisms and Cylinders

Build Understanding

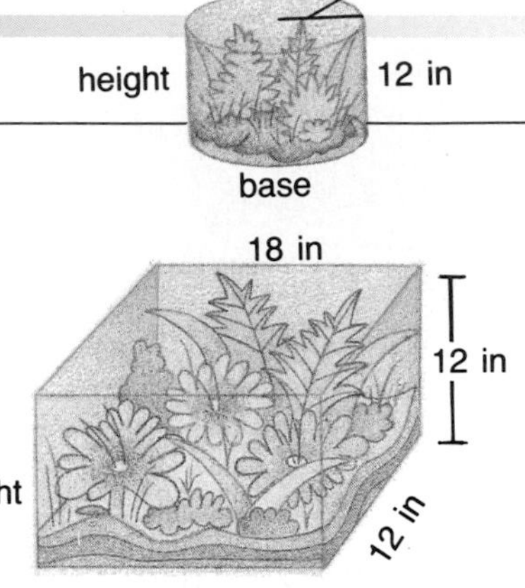

The volume of any prism or cylinder is $V = Bh$, where B is the area of the base and h is the height of the prism or cylinder. The formula for B varies according to the shape of the base.

Annalisa's Flower Shop sells two types of terrariums, a rectangular prism tank and a cylindrical tank. What is the volume of each tank?

A. The base of the rectangular prism tank is a rectangle. The area of the rectangular base is $B = \ell w$. So the volume of the rectangular prism is $V = \ell wh$.

You can use this formula to find the volume of the rectangular prism tank.

$V = \ell wh$

$V = (18)(12)(12)$

$V = 2{,}592$

The volume of the rectangular prism tank is 2,592 cubic inches, or 1.5 cu ft.

B. The base of the cylindrical tank is a circle. The area of the circular base is $B = \pi r^2$. So the volume of the cylinder is $V = \pi r^2 h$.

You can use this formula to find the volume of the cylindrical terrarium. Use 3.14 for π.

$V = \pi r^2 h$

$V \approx (3.14)(9)^2(12)$

$V \approx 3{,}052.08$

The volume of the cylindrical terrarium is about 3,052 cubic inches, or 1.77 cu ft.

C. Find the volume of the triangular prism shown. Notice that the base of the prism is a triangle. So its area is $\frac{1}{2}$ times the base of the triangle times the height of the triangle. Use 0.5 for $\frac{1}{2}$. The volume of the triangular prism, then, is $V = Bh$.

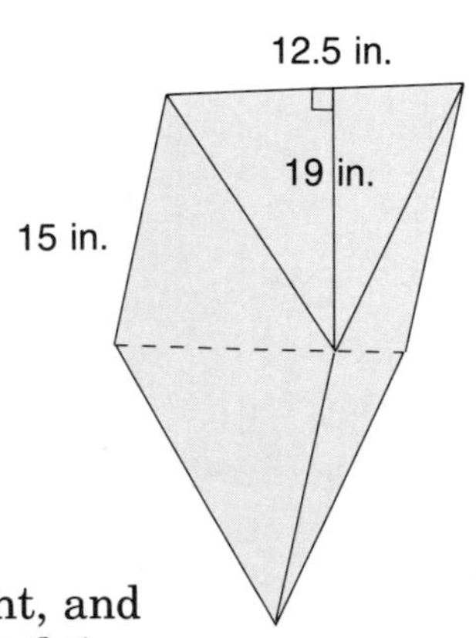

$V = Bh$

$V = (0.5)(12.5)(19)(15)$

$V = 1{,}781.25$

The volume of the triangular prism is 1,781.25 cubic inches.

■ **Talk About Math** If a prism and a cylinder are equal in height, and if the areas of their bases are equal, are their volumes equal? Explain.

Check Understanding

For another example, see Set H, pages 372–373.

Find the volume of each prism or cylinder.
Round to the nearest tenth.

1. 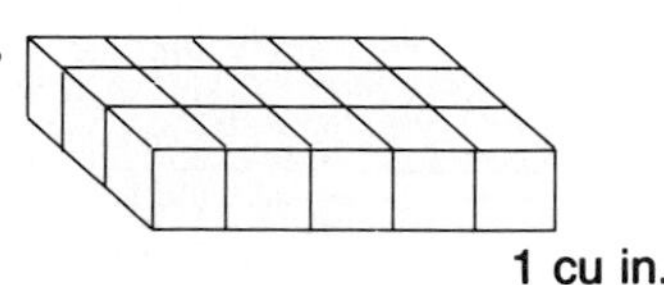

2. 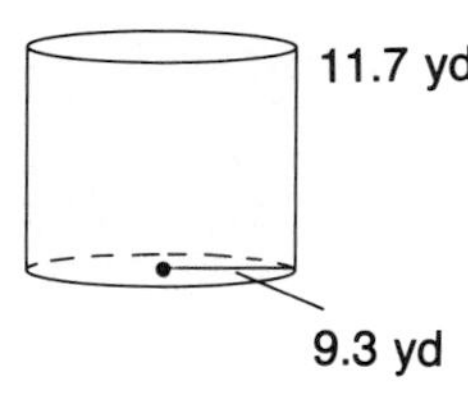

3. 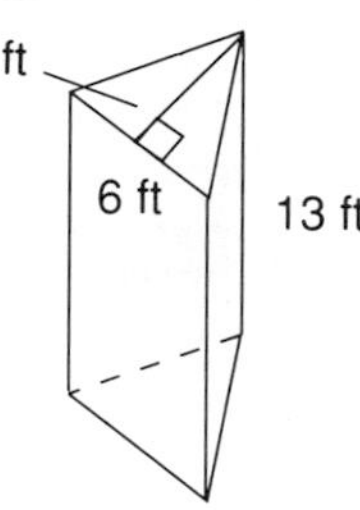

Practice

For More Practice, see Set H, pages 374–375.

Find each volume. Tell whether you use paper and pencil or calculator. Round to the nearest tenth. Use 3.14 for π. **Remember** to multiply the area of the base times the height of the prism or cylinder.

4. 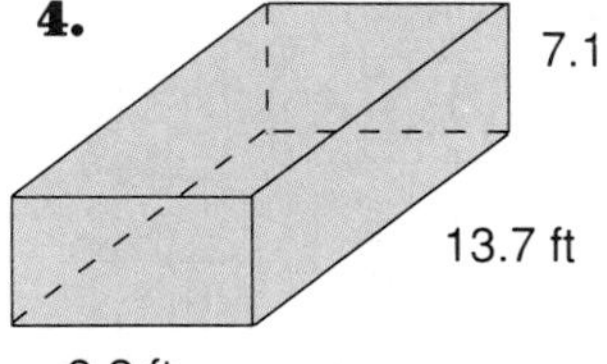

5. 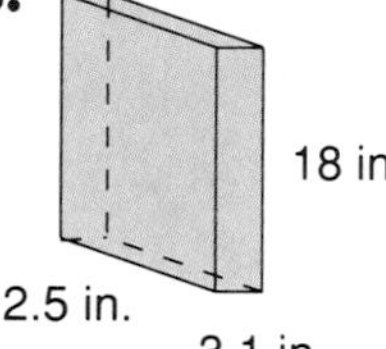

6. 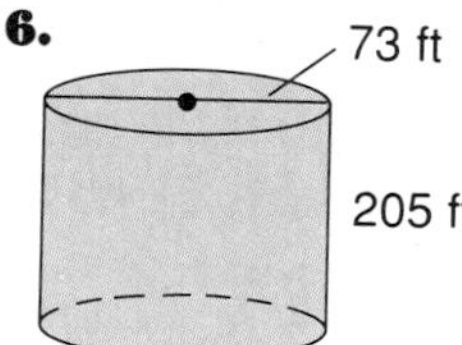

7. 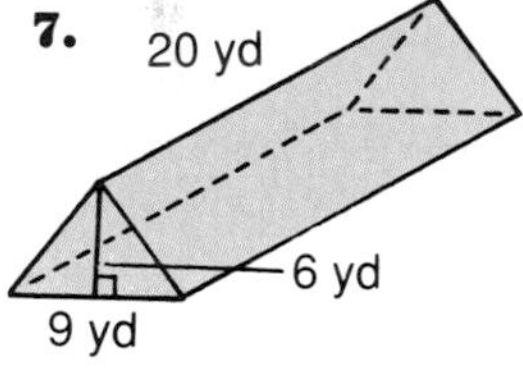

Find the volume of each rectangular prism.

8. length: 7.1 cm
width: 6.4 cm
height: 5 cm

9. length: 10.5 m
width: 10.5 m
height: 15 m

10. length: 26 ft
width: 18 ft
height: 80 ft

Find the volume of each cylinder. Use 3.14 for π.

11. radius: 4 cm
height: 0.8 cm

12. radius: 7.5 in.
height: 12 in.

13. radius: 2.8 cm
height: 8 cm

Find the volume of each triangular prism.

14. height of base: 13 cm
length of base: 6 cm
height of prism: 14 cm

15. height of base: 3.2 m
length of base: 6.4 m
height of prism: 8.9 m

16. height of base: 26 cm
length of base: 20 cm
height of prism: 30 cm

Problem Solving

Solve each problem.

17. An aquarium measures 3 ft long, 2.5 ft wide, and 2.5 ft high. What is its volume?

18. One cubic foot of water is about 7.5 gallons. How many gallons of water will the aquarium in Problem 17 hold?

ALGEBRA

Volume of Pyramids and Cones

Build Understanding

The volume of a pyramid or cone is $V = \frac{1}{3}Bh$, where B is the area of the base and h is the height. The formula for B varies according to the shape of the base.

A. Find the volume of the rectangular pyramid.

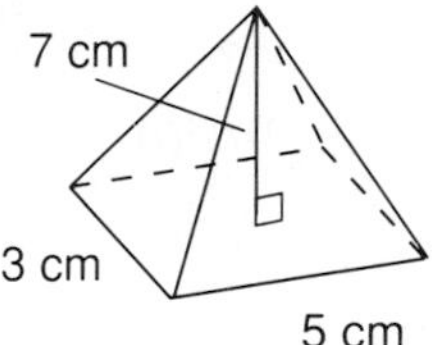

The base of the rectangular pyramid is a rectangle. The area of the base, then, is $B = \ell w$. So the volume of a rectangular pyramid is $V = \frac{1}{3}\ell wh$.

Use this formula to find the volume of the rectangular pyramid.

$V = \frac{1}{3}\ell wh$

$V = \frac{1}{3}(5)(3)(7)$

$V = 35$

The volume is 35 cm^3.

B. Find the volume of the cone.

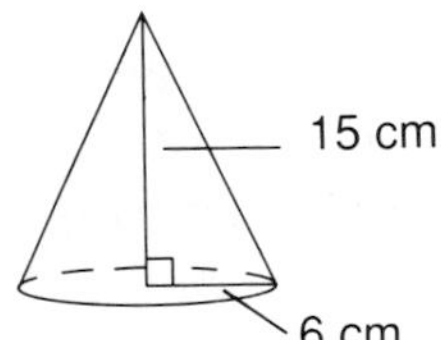

The base of the cone is a circle. The area of the base, then, is $B = \pi r^2$. So the volume of a cone is $V = \frac{1}{3}\pi r^2 h$.

Use this formula to find the volume of the cone. (Use 3.14 for π.)

$V = \frac{1}{3}\pi r^2 h$

$V \approx \frac{1}{3}(3.14)(6)^2(15)$

$V \approx 565.2$

The volume is about 565.2 cm^3.

Talk About Math If a pyramid and a cone have equal heights, when would their volumes be equal?

Check Understanding

For another example, see Set I, pages 372–373.

What shape is the base in each?

1.

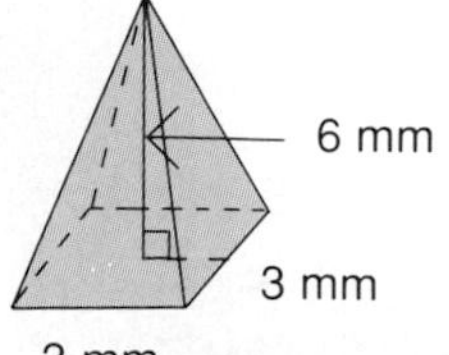

2.

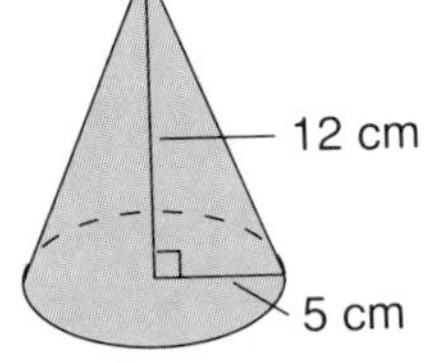

3.

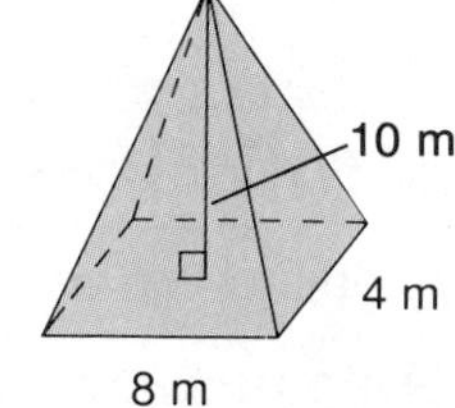

4. Find the volume of each pyramid or cone in Exercises 1–3.

Practice

For More Practice, see Set I, pages 374–375.

Find each volume to the nearest tenth. Use 3.14 for π. **Remember** to use the area of the base and the height in your calculations.

5.

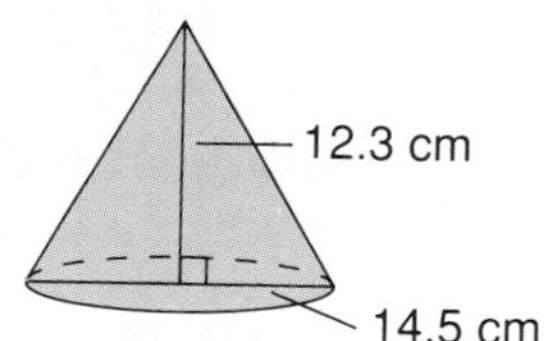

6.

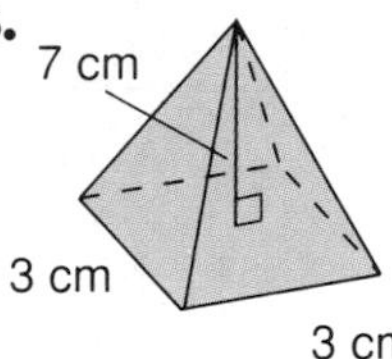

7.

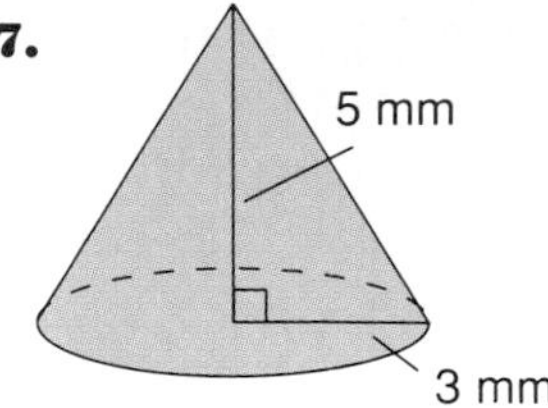

8. length: 6.3 cm
width: 4 cm
height: 5.2 cm

9. radius: 7 m
height: 4.2 m

10. length: 18.3 in.
width: 4.5 in.
height: 16 in.

11. radius: 20 cm
height: 10.2 cm

12. radius: 15 in.
height: 25 in.

13. length: 9 cm
width: 12.5 cm
height: 22 cm

14. radius: 10 in.
height: 12 in.

15. length: 3.8 cm
width: 1.6 cm
height: 8.1 cm

16. radius: 8 m
height: 9.7 m

Problem Solving

Solve each problem. **Remember** to draw a figure to show the given information.

17. A package of popcorn is shaped like a cone. The height of the cone is 12 cm, and its radius is 8 cm. How much popcorn does it hold?

18. A silver paperweight has the shape of a square pyramid. The height of the pyramid is 8 cm, and each side of the base is 3 cm. What is its weight if a cubic centimeter of silver weighs 10.5 grams?

Explore Math

Answer each question. Use paper and pencil or a calculator for finding volumes.

19. Find the volumes of a square prism and a square pyramid when $s = 1$, $h = 2$; $s = 2$, $h = 2$; $s = 10$, $h = 10$; $s = 10$, $h = 20$.

20. How are the volumes of a square prism and a square pyramid having the same dimensions related?

21. Find the volumes of a cone and a cylinder when $r = 1$, $h = 2$; $r = 2$, $h = 2$; $r = 10$, $h = 10$; $r = 10$, $h = 20$.

22. How are the volumes of a cone and a cylinder having the same dimensions related?

ALGEBRA

Geometric Relationships

Build Understanding

A. Suppose you want to make a box holding twice as much as this box.

$V = \ell wh$
$= 4 \times 3 \times 2$
$= 24$

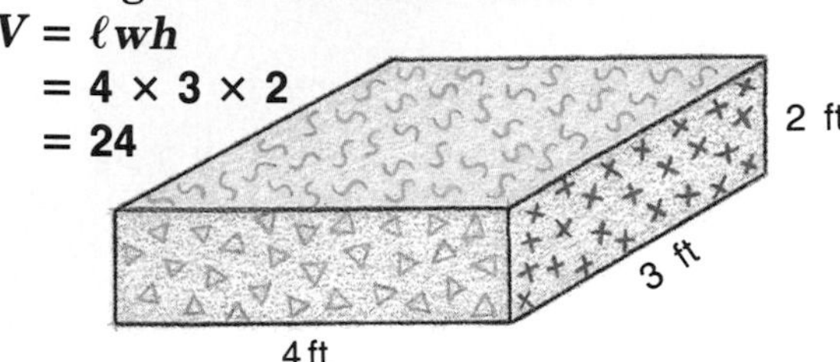

The volume of the box is 24 cu ft.

Double the length: $V = 8 \times 3 \times 2$
$V = 48$ cu ft

Double the width: $V = 4 \times 6 \times 2$
$V = 48$ cu ft

Double the height: $V = 4 \times 3 \times 4$
$V = 48$ cu ft

To make a box with twice the volume, double only one of its dimensions.

B. What happens to the volume of a box when you double all of its dimensions?

The volume of the small box is

$V = \ell wh$
$= 3 \times 2 \times 1$
$= 6$ cu in.

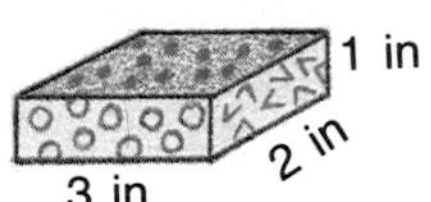

When you double its dimensions, its volume is

$V = 6 \times 4 \times 2$
$= 48$ cu in.

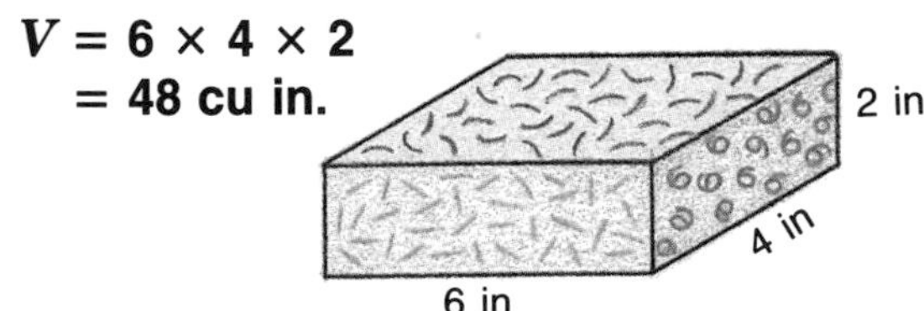

Since $48 \div 6 = 8$, the volume of the larger box is 8 times the volume of the smaller box.

Talk About Math What happens to the volume of a cube if its dimensions are halved?

Check Understanding

Answer each question. **Remember** the area of a rectangle is given by $A = \ell w$.

1. Compute the perimeter of rectangle A and of rectangle B.

2. Compare the perimeters. How many times as great is the perimeter of the larger rectangle?

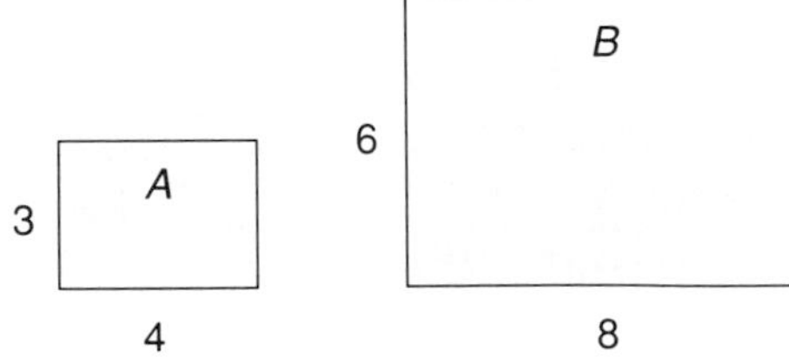

3. Compute the areas of the two rectangles.

4. Compare the areas. How many times as great is the area of the larger rectangle?

Practice

Answer each question.

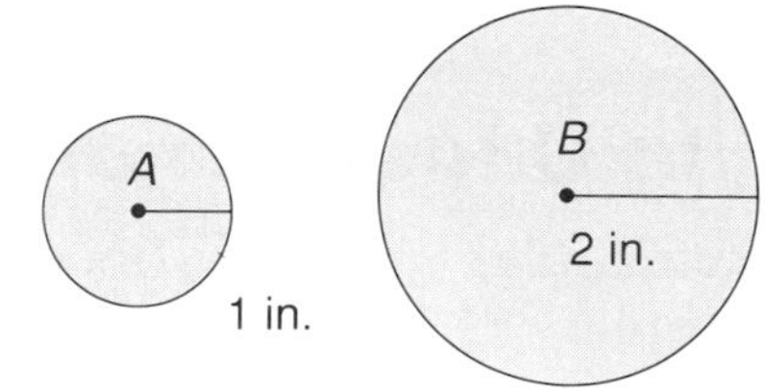

5. Find the circumference and area of the two circles at the right.

6. Compare the areas and circumferences. How many times as great is the area of circle B? How many times as great is the circumference of circle B?

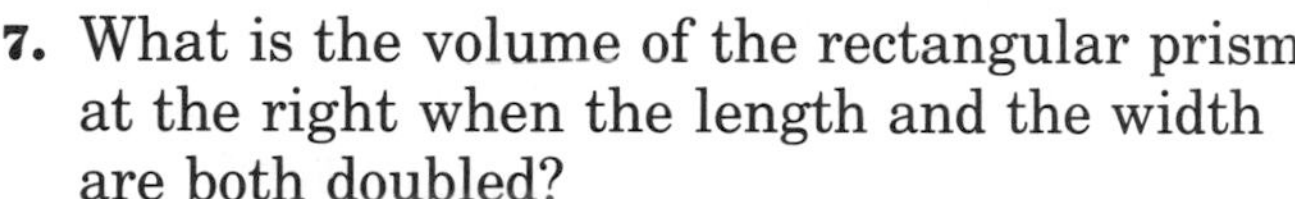

7. What is the volume of the rectangular prism at the right when the length and the width are both doubled?

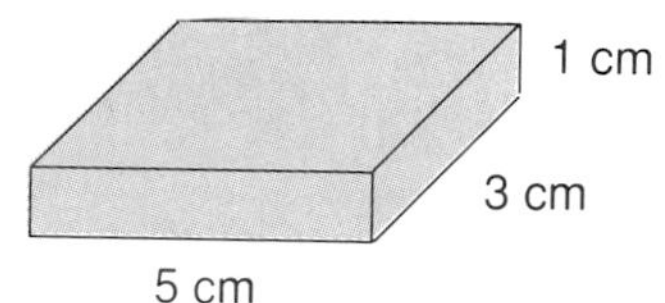

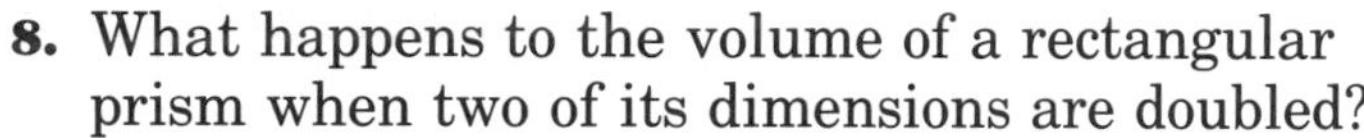

8. What happens to the volume of a rectangular prism when two of its dimensions are doubled?

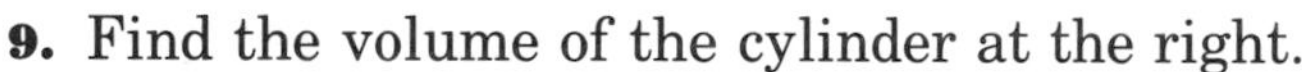

9. Find the volume of the cylinder at the right.

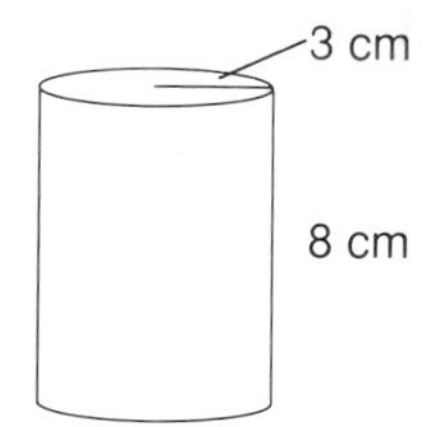

10. If you double each dimension of the cylinder, what is the volume?

11. How many times as great as the volume of the cylinder in Exercise 9 is the volume of the cylinder in Exercise 10?

12. How does the increase in the volume of the cylinder in Exercise 10 compare with the increase in the volume of the rectangular prism in Example B?

Problem Solving

Solve.

13. **Critical Thinking** Explain why the volume of a rectangular prism is 8 times as great as that of the original prism when each dimension is doubled.

14. What happens to the volume of a rectangular prism if each dimension is multiplied by 3? by 10? by n?

15. A rectangular box has a height of 6 cm, a length of 4 cm, and a width of 5 cm. Give the dimensions of a box that has twice the volume of this box.

16. A cylinder has a radius of 3 in. and a height of 10 in. Give the dimensions of a cylinder with eight times the volume.

ALGEBRA

Use a Formula

Understand
QUESTION
FACTS
KEY IDEA

Plan and Solve
STRATEGY
ANSWER

Look Back
SENSIBLE ANSWER
ALTERNATE APPROACH

Build Understanding

Rectangular Pyramid

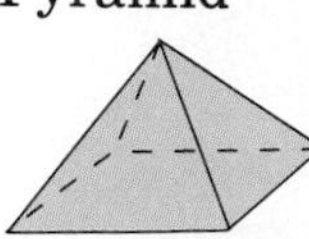

$V = \frac{1}{3}\ell wh$

Cylinder

$V = \pi r^2 h$

Cone

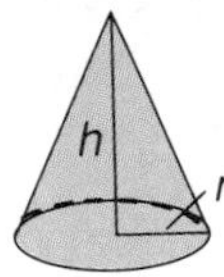

$V = \frac{1}{3}\pi r^2 h$

Sphere

$V = \frac{4}{3}\pi r^3$

Circle

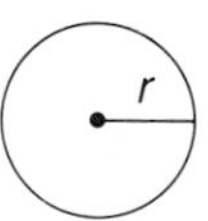

$A = \pi r^2$

Ellipse

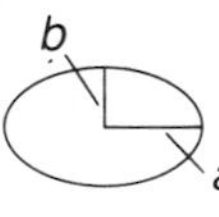

$A = \pi ab$

What is the glass area of the elliptical mirror shown?

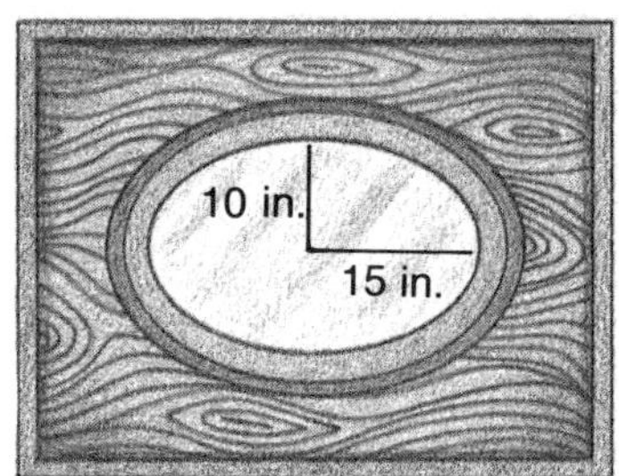

Understand

QUESTION What is the area of the ellipse?

FACTS a is 15 in. and b is 10 in.

KEY IDEA The answer will be a number of square inches.

Plan and Solve

STRATEGY Use the formula for the area of an ellipse: $A = \pi ab$. Find the area of the mirror. Let $a = 15$ in. and $b = 10$ in.

$A = 3.14 \times 15 \times 10$
$A = 471$ sq in.

ANSWER The area of the mirror is 471 sq in.

Look Back

SENSIBLE ANSWER If the mirror were circular with a radius of 10 in., the area would be 3.14×10^2, or 314. If the mirror were circular with a radius of 15 in., the area would be $3.14 \times (15)^2$, or 706.5. The answer, 471, is between 314 and 706.5, so it is reasonable.

Talk About Math In an ellipse if a is equal to b, what figure results?

Check Understanding

Masumi is curious about the difference in volume of an orange and a grapefruit. The radius of the grapefruit is 4.7 cm, and the radius of the orange is 3.6 cm.

1. What are you asked to find?
2. What facts do you know?
3. What formula can you use?
4. Solve the problem.
5. **Calculator** Write the key sequence you would use to solve the problem on a calculator. Use the memory.

Practice

Solve each problem. Use 3.14 for π, and round answers to the nearest whole number. Tell whether you use paper and pencil or a calculator.

6. What is the volume of the tent?

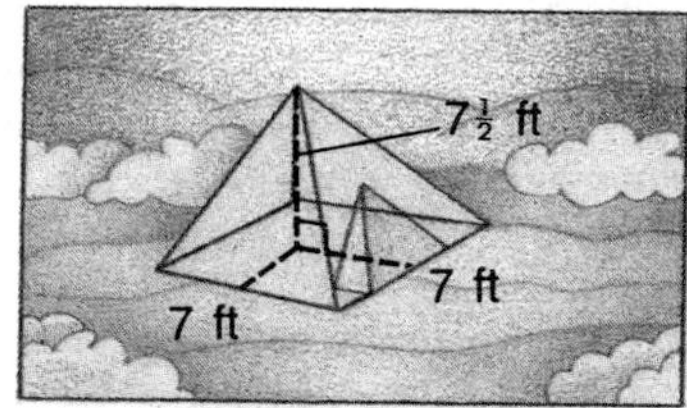

7. How much frozen yogurt does this cone hold?

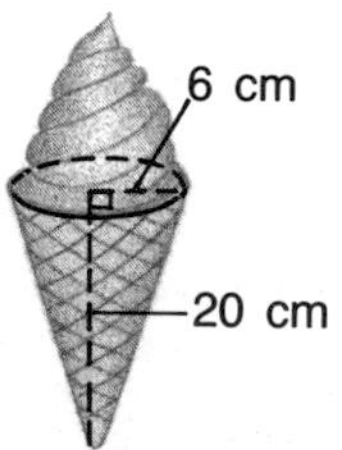

8. What is the volume of this toy chest?

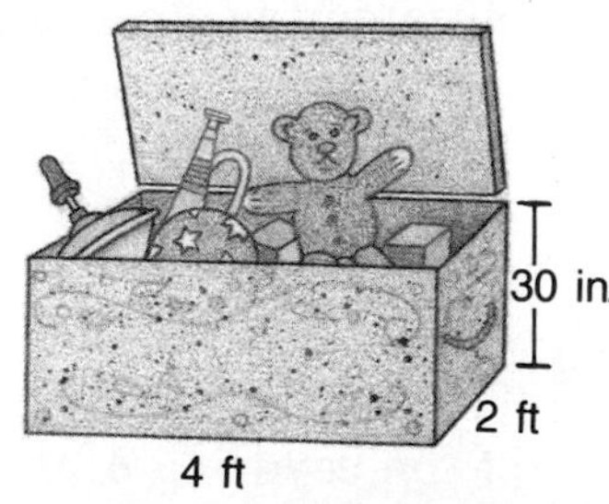

9. Find the area of the elliptical garden.

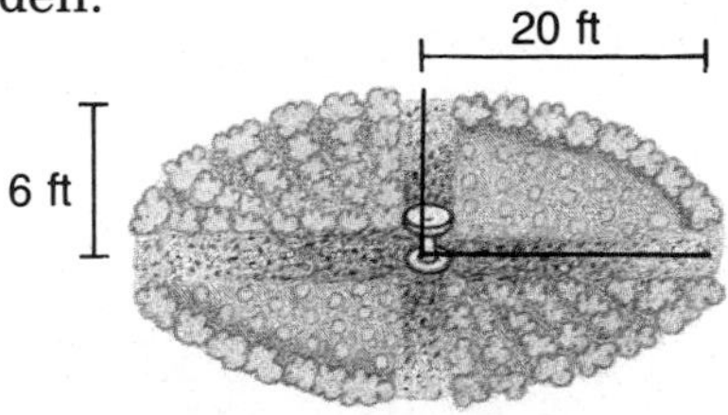

10. Find the volume of this storage bin.

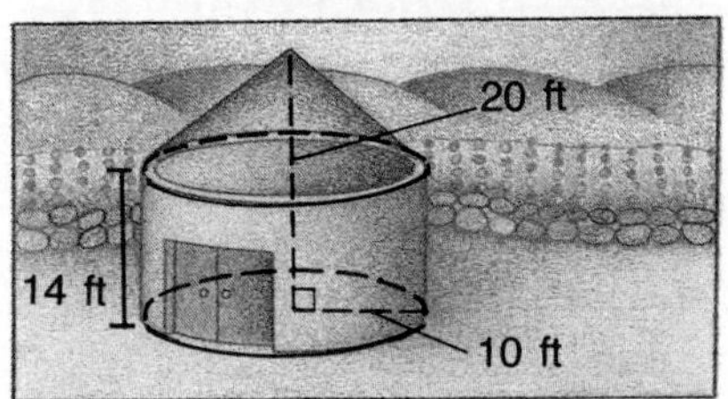

11. The circumference of a round table is 4.7 ft. What is its radius?

12. **Calculator** If 1 gallon of water occupies 230 cu in., how many gallons does the storage bin in Exercise 10 hold?

Skills Review

Name each figure.

1. 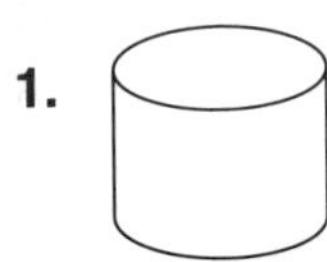

2. 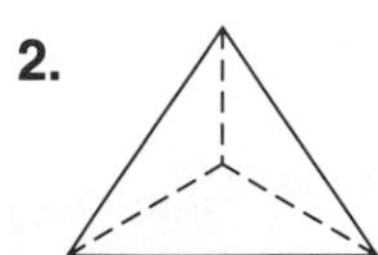

3. 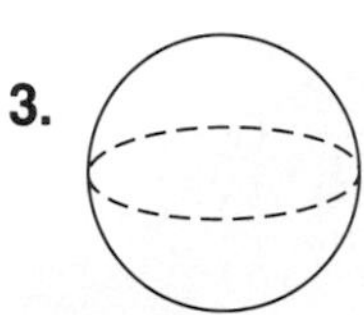

4. 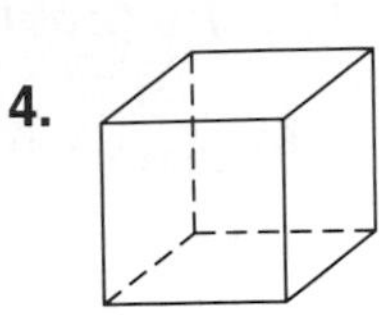

Find the area and perimeter.

5. 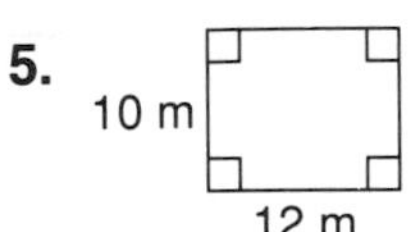

6. 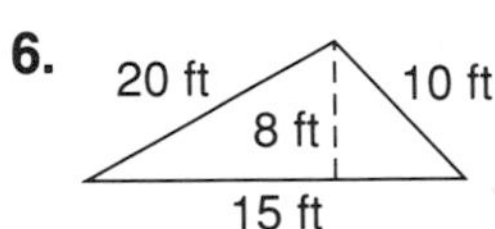

7. 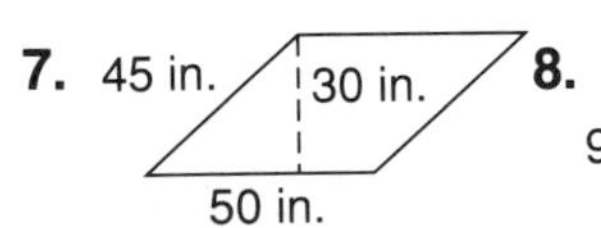

8. 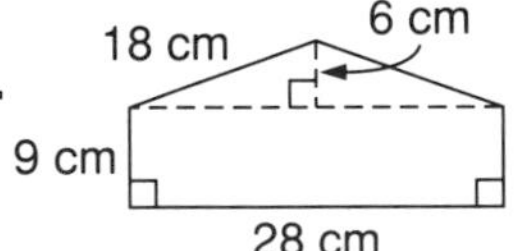

Find the circumference and the area.
Use 3.14 for π.

9.  

10. 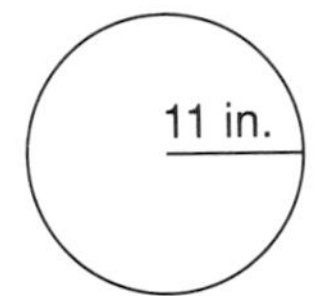

Find the surface area.

11. 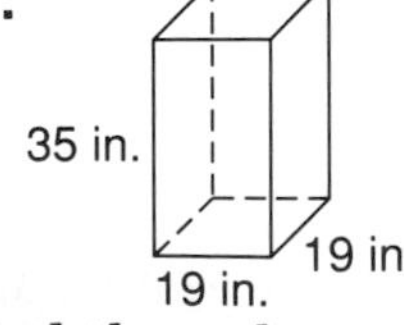

12. 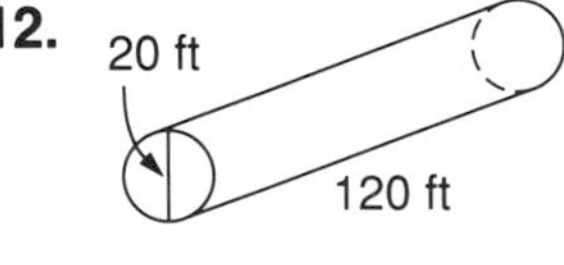

Find the volume.

13. 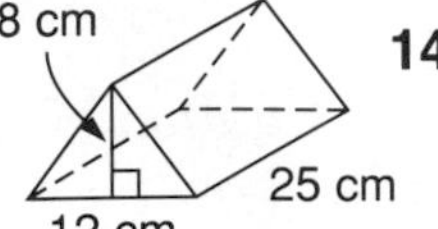

14. 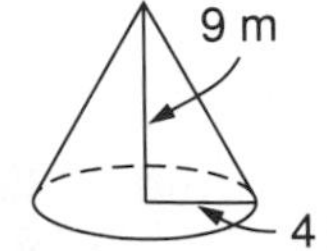

Problem-Solving Review

Solve each problem.

15. An 18-oz jar of peanut butter sells for $1.79. A 48-oz jar sells for $4.99. Which size jar is the better buy?

16. In a bookstore, narrow shelves hold 12 books and wide shelves hold 16 books. Josey stocked the racks with 164 books. She filled 12 shelves. How many shelves of each size did she use? Make a table of all possibilities.

17. In a Taft School survey, 225 of 500 students said they enjoyed science fiction. What percent of the students surveyed enjoy science fiction?

18. Leroy sells magazine subscriptions. He gets 16% commission on his sales. Last month, he earned $388.64. What was the amount of his sales?

19. A toy chest has the shape of a rectangular prism. How many faces does it have? How many edges?

20. A class is making a rainbow streamer as a ceiling border around the homeroom. The room is 20 ft by 22 ft. What length should they make the streamer?

21. **Data File** Use the data on pages 414–415. What is the surface area of the covering of the kite?

22. **Make a Data File** Consult a craft book for making toys, holiday decorations, or other crafts. Select a project. Draw a diagram that shows how the piece is constructed. Label the dimensions, list materials, and give all directions.

Cumulative Skills Review • Chapters 1–10

Evaluate each expression

1. $6(3 + 4) \div 2$ **2.** $7 + 3 \times 5 - 10$ **3.** $(12 \times 4) \div (12 \times 2)$ **4.** $67 - 15 \times 4 + 1$

Divide. Round decimal answers to the nearest thousandth.

5. $786 \div 0.8$ **6.** $0.889 \div 6.3$ **7.** $14.002 \div 10.2$ **8.** $256.98 \div 56.05$

Name the polygon.

9. 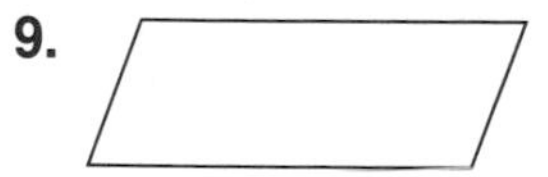

10.

11. 

12.

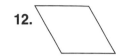

Multiply or divide.

13. $\frac{7}{9} \times \frac{3}{5}$ **14.** $2\frac{5}{8} \times 1\frac{1}{3}$ **15.** $\frac{16}{27} \times 0$ **16.** $3\frac{3}{8} \times \frac{4}{9}$

17. $9 \div \frac{5}{6}$ **18.** $\frac{7}{8} \div \frac{7}{16}$ **19.** $4\frac{1}{2} \div \frac{3}{4}$ **20.** $24 \div 1\frac{1}{2}$

Find each missing number.

21. 12 c ▒ qt **22.** 12 lb = ▒ oz **23.** 5 cm = ▒ mm **24.** 500 mg = ▒ g

25. 10 m^2 = ▒ cm^2 **26.** 50 mm^2 = ▒ cm^2 **27.** 75 g = ▒ mg **28.** 5.7 L = ▒ mL

Write three equal ratios.

29. $\frac{15}{18}$ **30.** $\frac{5}{16}$ **31.** $\frac{9}{10}$ **32.** $\frac{8}{16}$ **33.** $\frac{18}{27}$ **34.** $\frac{1}{2}$

Write each percent as a decimal and as a fraction or mixed number.

35. 5% **36.** 25% **37.** 80% **38.** 52% **39.** 7.5% **40.** 410%

Find the volume of each figure.

41. 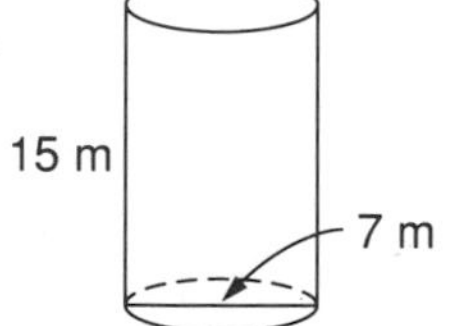

42. 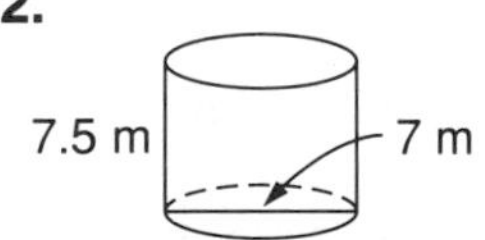

43. 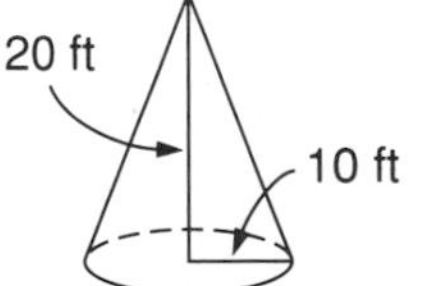

44. 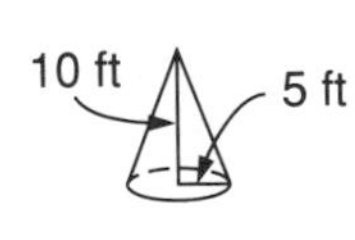

Use the volumes of the above figures to answer these questions.

45. What happens to the volume of a cylinder when the height is doubled?

46. What happens to the volume of a cone when the dimensions are doubled?

Reteaching

Set A pages 342–345 Error prevention

The perimeter of a rectangle is found by using the formula $P = 2\ell + 2w$. The area of a rectangle is found by using the formula $A = \ell w$.

Remember, the length and width are the same in a square.

Find the perimeter and area of each rectangle.

1. $\ell = 8$ in., $w = 4$ in.

2. $s = 2.8$ m

3. $\ell = 58$ yd, $w = 10$ yd

4. 10 cm, 4 cm

Set B pages 346–347

The area of a triangle is found using the formula $A = \frac{1}{2}bh$. The area of a parallelogram is found using the formula $A = bh$.

Remember, you can use 0.5 for $\frac{1}{2}$ in the formula for the area of a triangle.

Find the perimeter and area of each figure.

1.

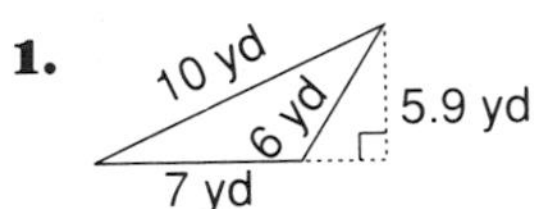

2.

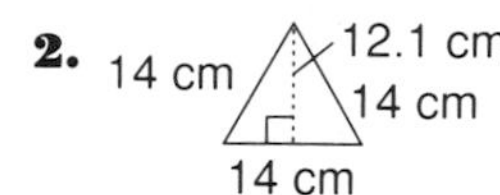

3.

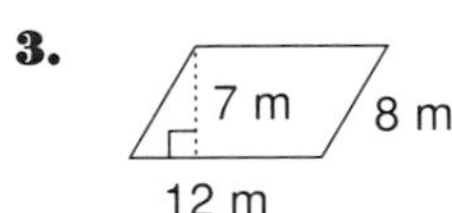

4.

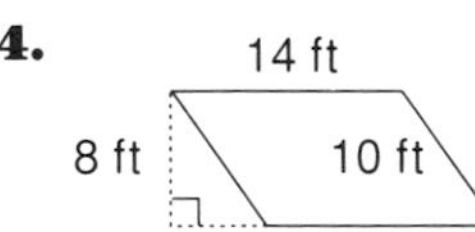

Set C pages 348–349

To find the area of a polygon, you can break it into simpler shapes.

Remember, area is measured in square units.

Find the perimeter and area of each polygon.

1.

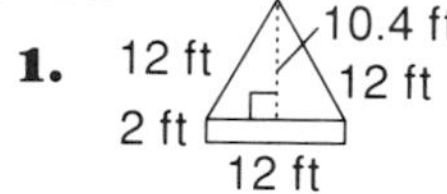

2.

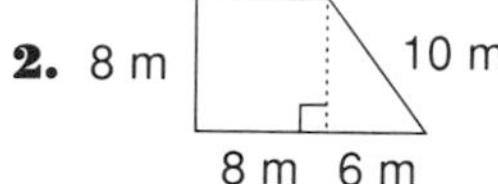

Set D pages 350–351

To find the circumference of a circle, use the formula $C = \pi d$.

Remember, the diameter of a circle is twice the radius.

Find the circumference of each circle. Round to the nearest whole number. Use $\pi = 3.14$.

1. Diameter: 12 ft

2. Radius: 1.8 m

3. Diameter: 8.3 cm

4. Radius: 10 in.

Set E pages 352–355

To find the area of a circle, use the formula $A = \pi r^2$.

Remember, the radius of a circle is one half the diameter.

Find the area of each circle. Round to the nearest whole number. Use $\pi = 3.14$.

1. Diameter: 24 mm

2. Radius: 8.3 ft

3. Diameter: 2 ft

4. Radius: 12 cm

Set F pages 358–359

To find the surface area of a polyhedron, make a table listing all the faces. Find the area of each and then add.

Remember, label the units in your answers.

Find the surface area of each polyhedron.

1.

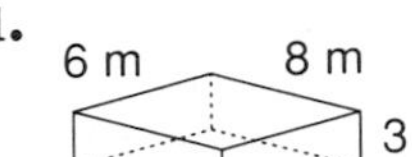

2.

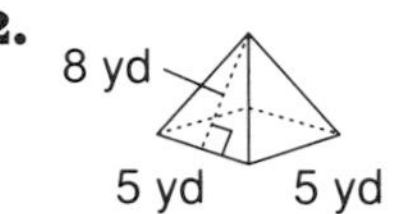

Set G pages 360–361

To find the surface area of a cylinder, find the area of the bases. Use the formula $A = \pi r^2$. Then find the area of the curved surface using the formula $A = (\pi d)h$. Add the three numbers.

Remember, a cylinder has two bases.

Find the surface area of each cylinder. Round to the nearest whole number. Use 3.14 for π.

1.

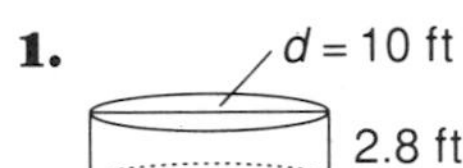

2.

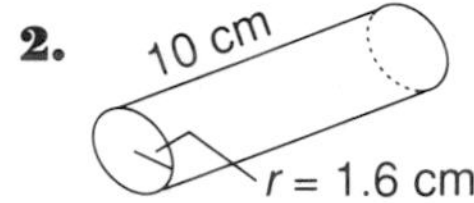

3. $r = 16$ ft
$h = 8$ ft

4. $d = 12$ cm
$h = 20.5$ cm

Set H pages 362–363

To find the volume of a rectangular prism, use $V = \ell wh$. To find the volume of a cylinder, use the formula $V = \pi r^2 h$. To find the volume of a triangular prism, use the formula $V = Bh$.

Remember, volume is measured in cubic units.

Find the volume of each solid. Round to the nearest whole number.

1.

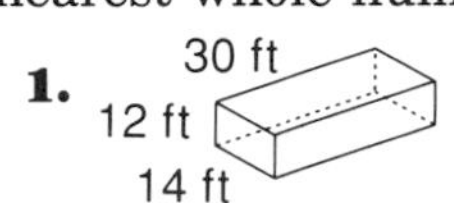

2.

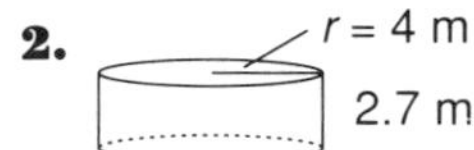

3. 5 cm, 6 cm, 4 cm

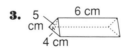

4. 18 in., 18 in., 18 in.

Set I pages 364–365

The general formula for the volume of a pyramid or cone is $V = \frac{1}{3}Bh$. So, the volume of a rectangular pyramid is $V = \frac{1}{3}\ell wh$ and that of a cone is $V = \frac{1}{3}\pi r^2 h$.

Remember, multiply the product of the area of the base and the height by $\frac{1}{3}$.

Find the volume of each figure to the nearest whole number. Use 3.14 for π.

1.

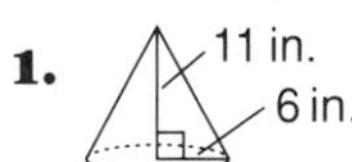

2.

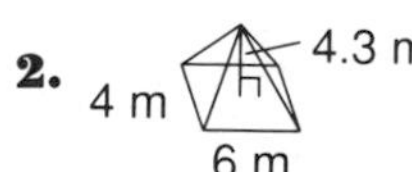

3. Cone:
$r = 2.8$ cm
$h = 3$ cm

4. Rectangular pyramid:
$\ell = 12$ ft, $w = 8$ ft
$h = 16\frac{1}{2}$ ft

More Practice

Set A pages 342–345

Find the perimeter and the area of each rectangle.

1. 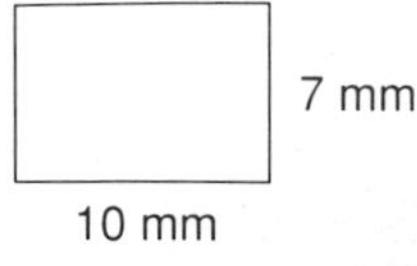

2. 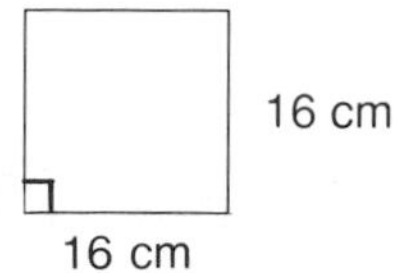

3. 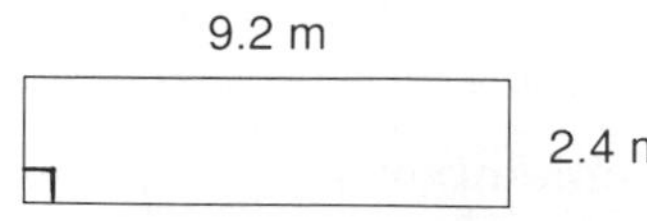

4. $\ell = 20$ m
$w = 5$ m

5. $s = 101$ mm

6. $\ell = 27$ cm
$w = 51.5$ cm

Set B pages 346–347

Find the perimeter and the area of each figure.

1. 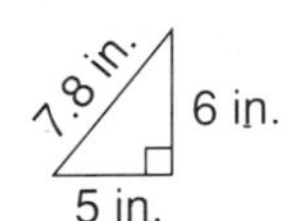

2. 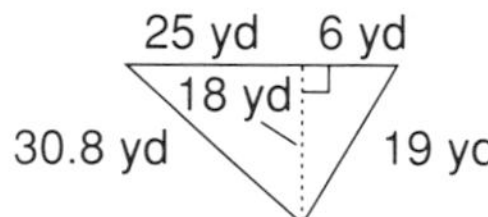

3. 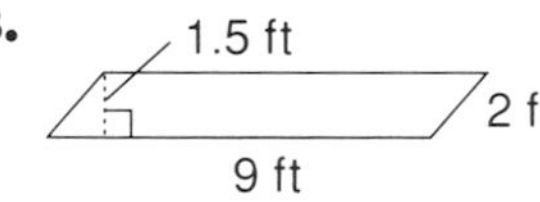

4. 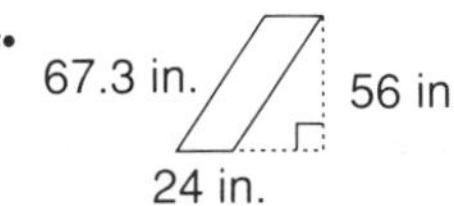

5. 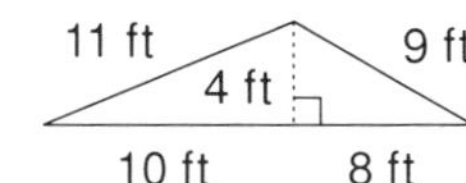

6. 91 yd, 88 yd, 88 yd

Set C pages 348–349

Find the perimeter and the area of each polygon.

1. 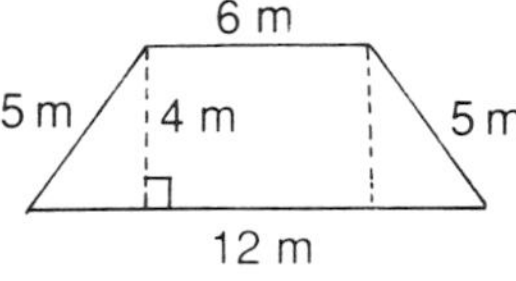

2. 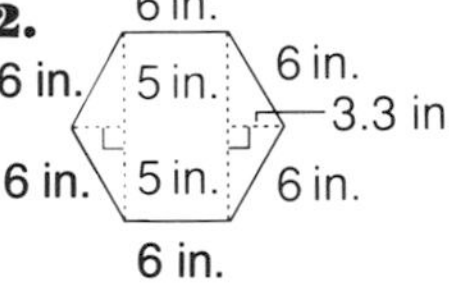

3. 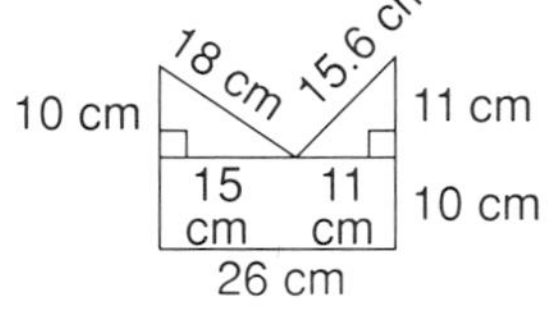

Set D pages 350–351

Find the circumference of each circle. Round to the nearest whole number. Use 3.14 for π.

1. Radius: 14.8 ft
2. Diameter: 29 yd
3. Radius: 1.02 in.
4. Diameter: 34 yd
5. Radius: 89 in.
6. Radius: 112 ft

Set E pages 352–355

Find the area of each circle. Round to the nearest whole number. Use $\frac{22}{7}$ for π.

1. Diameter: $8\frac{3}{4}$ m
2. Radius: $10\frac{1}{2}$ cm
3. Diameter: $23\frac{1}{3}$ mm
4. Radius: $5\frac{1}{11}$ cm
5. Radius: 28 m
6. Diameter: $8\frac{2}{5}$ cm

Set F pages 358–359

Find the surface area of each polyhedron. Round to the nearest whole number.

1. 8 cm, 8 cm, 19 cm, 7 cm, 8 cm

2. 28.4 m, 26 m, 10 m, 25 m

3. 12 mm, 10.3 mm, 26 mm, 12 mm, 12 mm

Set G pages 360–361

Find the surface area of each cylinder. Round to the nearest whole number. Use 3.14 for π.

1.
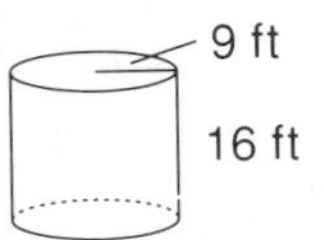

2.
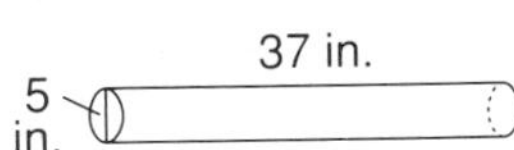

3.
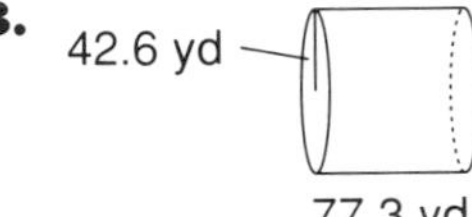

Set H pages 362–363

Find each volume. Round to the nearest whole number. Use 3.14 for π.

1.
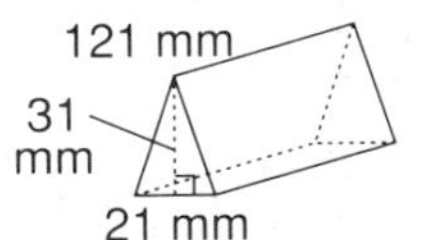

2.
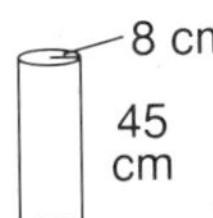

3.
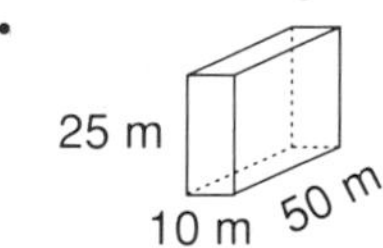

4. Rectangular prism
$\ell = 4$ m
$w = 12$ m
$h = 6$ m

Set I pages 364–365

Find each volume. Round to the nearest whole number. Use 3.14 for π.

1.
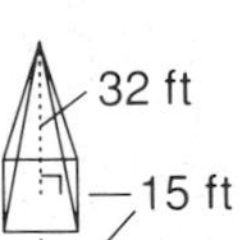

2.
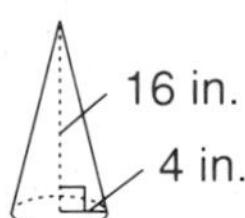

3.
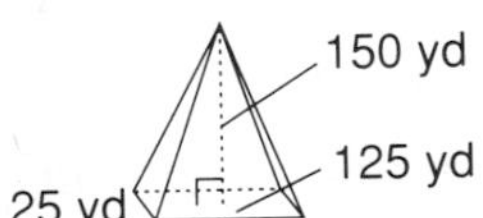

4.
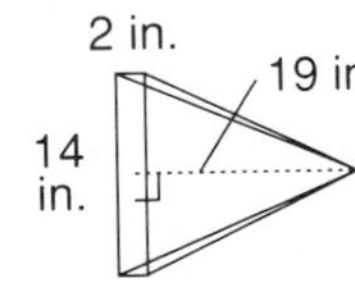

Enrichment

Dimensions Related to Surface Area

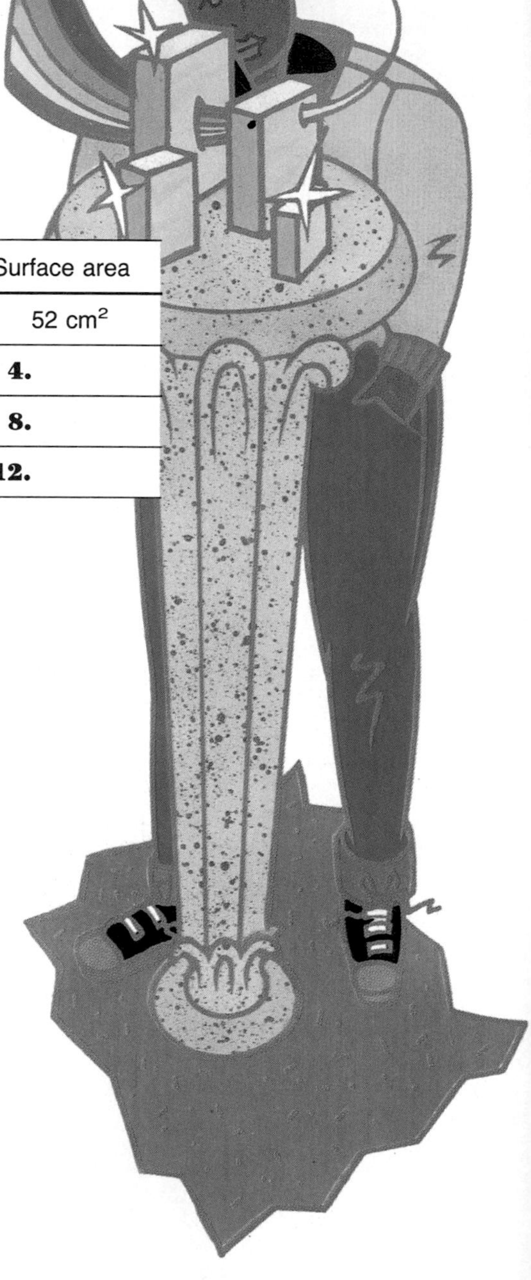

Donald is working on a sculpture for the Rembrandt School art exhibit. His sculpture consists of an arrangement of several rectangular prisms. Each prism has the same shape, but there are a number of sizes. The dimensions of the smallest prisms are 2 cm by 3 cm by 4 cm. He wants the largest prisms to have a surface area that is 16 times as great. How will the dimensions of the largest prisms compare with those of the smallest prisms?

Complete the table to find the surface area of the prisms.

	Width	Length	Height	Surface area
Smallest prisms	2 cm	3 cm	4 cm	52 cm^2
Dimensions doubled	**1.**	**2.**	**3.**	**4.**
Dimensions tripled	**5.**	**6.**	**7.**	**8.**
Dimensions quadrupled	**9.**	**10.**	**11.**	**12.**

13. What happens to the surface area of a prism when the dimensions are doubled? tripled?

14. What are the dimensions of the largest prisms in Donald's sculpture?

15. Suppose Donald decided he wanted to use prisms that were even smaller than those he had. How do you think halving the dimensions of a prism affects its surface area?

Kim is also submitting a sculpture for exhibit. Her sculpture is a collection of cylinders.

16. Each of the smallest cylinders has a height of 10 cm and a radius of 8 cm. What is the surface area of the cylinders in her sculpture that have dimensions that are double those of the smallest cylinder? Triple? Write answers in terms of π.

17. Do you think doubling the height or doubling the radius of the base would cause a greater change in the surface area of a cylinder? Explain your answer.

Chapter 10 Review/Test

1. How many edges does an octagonal pyramid have?

2. The following is a pattern for a polyhedron. Name the polyhedron.

In Exercises 3–6, find the area and perimeter of each figure.

3. A rectangle that is 1.6 m by 3.4 m

4. A parallelogram with a base of 40 cm, the other side of 30 cm, and a height of 25 cm

5. A triangle with a base of 12 in., other sides of 5 in. and 8.5 in., and a height of 3 in.

6.

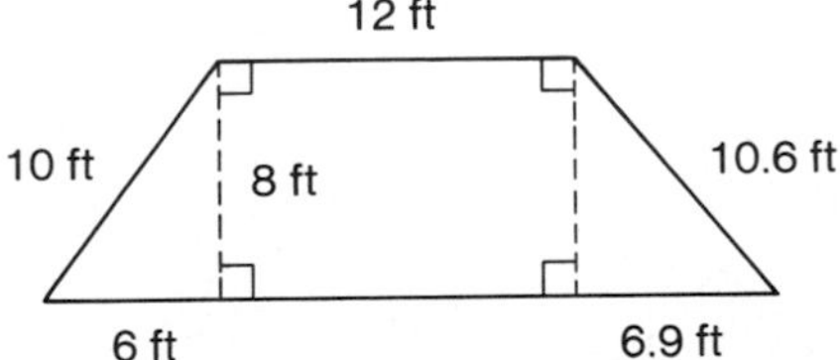

7. Etta wants to plant 1 pepper plant for each 2 square feet. If her pepper plot is 4 feet by 8 feet, how many plants should she buy?

8. Roger is planning to buy fencing to enclose a circular garden with a radius of 7 feet. Which is the best estimate of how much fencing he will need?

   a. 22 ft   b. 44 ft   c. 154 ft

9. Find the circumference of a circle whose diameter is 8 cm. (Use 3.14 for π.)

10. Find the area of a circle whose radius is 14 m. (Use $\frac{22}{7}$ for π.)

What is the total surface area of each figure? (Use 3.14 for π.)

11. Triangular prism

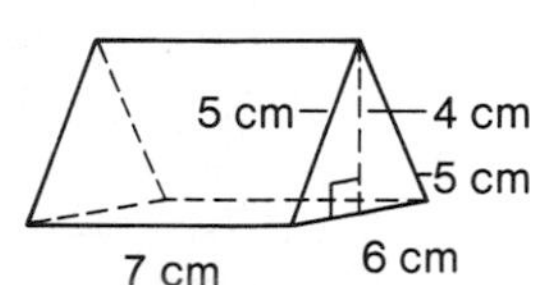

12. Cylinder

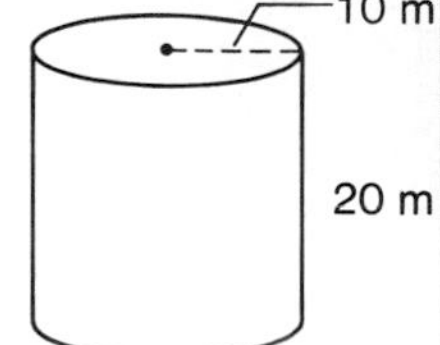

13. Georgia has a block of wood that is 4 inches by 6 inches by 8 inches. She wants to cover the entire surface with felt. What is the least amount of felt she will need? (Do not allow for scrap.)

What is the volume of each figure?

14. Rectangular prism

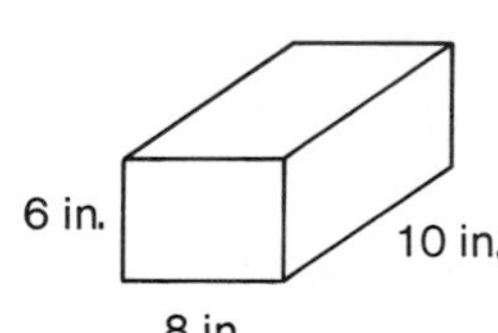

15. Square pyramid

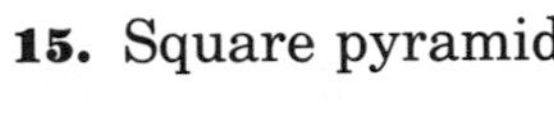

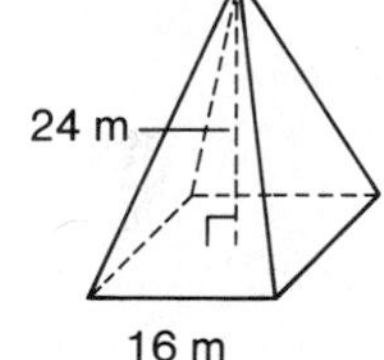

16. Find the volume of a cylinder that has a radius of 5 cm and a height of 10 cm. Use the formula $V = \pi r^2h$ and 3.14 for π.

17. What information do you need to find the volume of a cone 6 in. high?

18. **Write About Math** If you double the height of a rectangular prism, does either its volume or the surface area double? If one does not double, explain why it does not.

CHAPTER REVIEW/TEST

Statistics 11

Did You Know: Each of the twelve United States federal banks that issue paper money has a letter designation.

A	Boston	G	Chicago
B	New York	H	St. Louis
C	Philadelphia	I	Minneapolis
D	Cleveland	J	Kansas City
E	Richmond	K	Dallas
F	Atlanta	L	San Francisco

Number-Sense Project

Estimate

Which city on the list is closest to you? If you looked at ten bills, guess how many will be from this city.

Gather Data

Find the letter designation on a bill. Then look at ten bills and give the bank at which each was issued.

Analyze and Report

How close was your guess? Combine your results with those of the other students. Are all the banks represented?

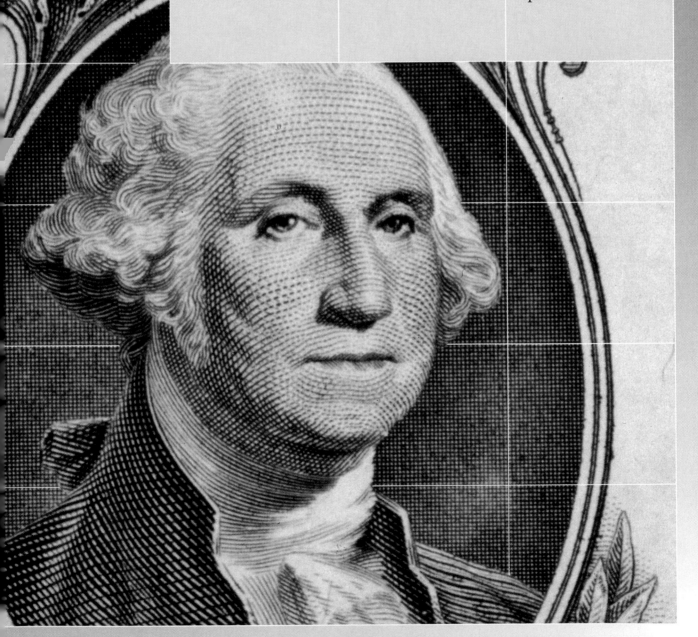

Interpreting the Mean, Median, and Mode

Build Understanding

This advertisement appeared in the *Greene Hills Gazette*.

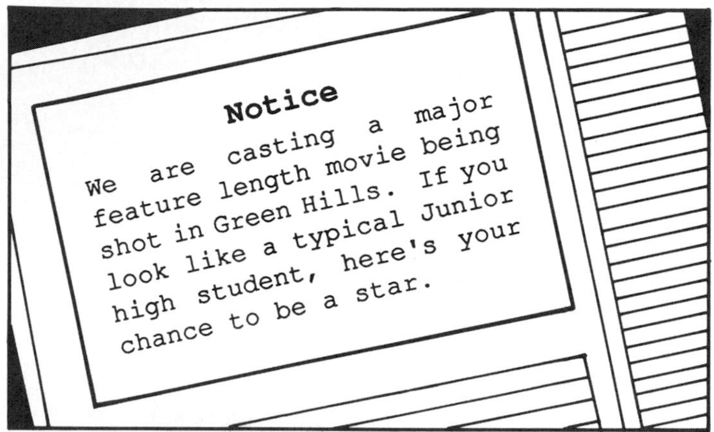

Which of the Greene Hills citizens below should answer the ad?

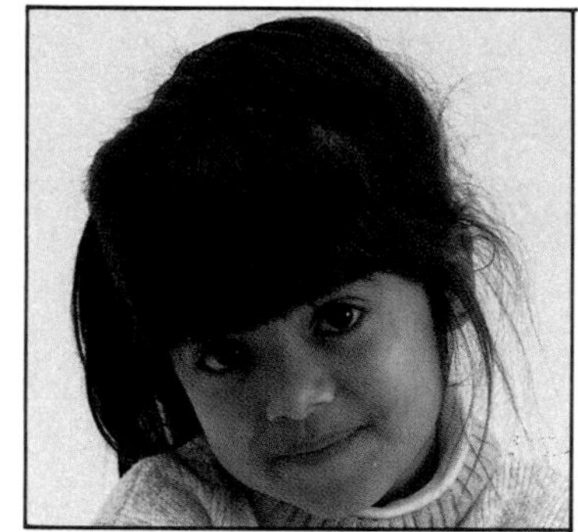
Maria Valenzuela

Art Mann

Todd Arnold

Maria Valenzuela is too young and Art Mann is too old to portray a typical junior high school student. Todd Arnold has many of the characteristics of the larger group of all junior high school students, so he should answer the ad.

A. Sometimes we talk about ***data***, or pieces of information, in terms of one number that is typical of the data. The studio recorded the number of calls received about the ad shown above for each of 5 days.

Monday	Tuesday	Wednesday	Thursday	Friday
7	93	70	64	66

The number of calls on Monday was not typical for the week. Neither was the number of calls on Tuesday. The ***mean***, or average, of the number of calls for all 5 days would give you a "typical" number for the week. The mean is the sum of the items in the data divided by the number of items in the data.

$$\frac{7 + 93 + 70 + 64 + 66}{5} = \frac{300}{5} = 60$$

The mean number of calls was 60.

B. Another number that is typical of the data is the ***median***. The median is the middle number in the set of data when the numbers are put in increasing order.

Find the median of the number of telephone calls in Example A.

Put the data in increasing order. The median is the middle number.

7 64 [66] 70 93

The median is 66.

If the number of calls were recorded for 6 days, there would be an even number of items in the data set. The median in a data set with an even number of items is the average of the two middle numbers.

7 12 [64] [66] 70 93

64 + 66 = 130   130 ÷ 2 = 65

The median is 65.

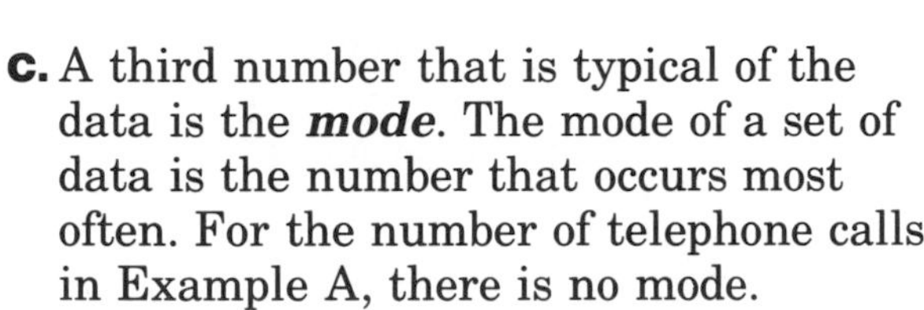

C. A third number that is typical of the data is the ***mode***. The mode of a set of data is the number that occurs most often. For the number of telephone calls in Example A, there is no mode.

Find the mode of this set of data.

15 38 21 38 38 15 63

The number 38 occurs more than any other number in the set, so 38 is the mode.

D. The ***range*** of the data will tell you how far apart the items are spread. The range is the difference between the greatest and least numbers in the data.

What is the range of the number of telephone calls in Example A?

Subtract the least number from the greatest number of calls.

93 − 7 = 86

The range of the calls received is 86.

Talk About Math Do you have to arrange data in increasing order to find the median? the mode? the mean?

Check Understanding

For another example, see Set A, pages 408–409.

Using the set of data at the right, find

8 9 2 9 3 0 4

1. the mean.
2. the median.
3. the mode.

Using the set of data at the right, find

32 16 17 8 32 15

4. the mode.
5. the mean.
6. the median.

Practice

For More Practice, see Set A, pages 410–411.

Tell whether you would use mental math, paper and pencil or a calculator to find the mean of each set of data. Then find the mean. Round to the nearest tenth.

7. 11 4 9 7

8. 48 13 36 13

9. 9 8 7 2 4

10. 5 9 8 1 8 17

11. 758 941 555 839
104 926 839 835

12. 476 473 478 461 476
475 466 461 478 476
474 469 478 450 478

Find the mode for the set of data in the given exercise.

13. Exercise 7

14. Exercise 8

15. Exercise 9

16. Exercise 10

17. Exercise 11

18. Exercise 12

Find the median for each set of data in the given exercise.

19. Exercise 7

20. Exercise 8

21. Exercise 9

22. Exercise 10

23. Exercise 11

24. Exercise 12

Find the range for the set of data in the given exercise.

25. Exercise 7

26. Exercise 8

27. Exercise 9

28. Exercise 10

29. Exercise 11

30. Exercise 12

The chart at the right lists the height and weight of each player on the Grove Junior High girls' basketball team. Use this data to find

31. the mean height.

32. the mode of the heights.

33. the range of the heights.

34. the mean weight.

35. the median weight.

36. the range of the weights.

37. the mode of the weights.

Player	Height (inches)	Weight (pounds)
Gina	60	91
Shauna	53	80
Riko	53	83
Julia	53	76
Lisa	55	78
Sarah	56	86
Denise	61	96
Shanika	62	95
Maria	63	93
Nancy	58	87
Elizabeth	62	94
Luann	61	93

Problem Solving

Use the set of data in Example A for Problems 38–40.

38. Can you think of a reason only seven people responded to the ad on Monday?

39. Which number, the median or the mean, is the better "typical" number in the set of data? Explain.

40. **Number Sense** If the number of calls on Monday were really 70, how would the median be affected? the mode? the mean? the range?

41. **Mental Math** The mean of a set of numbers is 12. The sum of this set of numbers is 72. How many numbers are in the set?

Critical Thinking For Problems 42–47, write a set of data containing at least five items with the given median, mean, mode, or range.

42. Median of 74

43. Mode of 20

44. Mean of 13

45. Range of 16

46. Mean of 38, median of 41, mode of 29 and 41

47. Mean of 28, median of 28, mode of 24, and range of 10

Don't give up. Some problems take longer than others.

Explore ______ Math

Sometimes one number describes a set of data better than another. The range shows how spread out the set of data is. The mode, the median, and the mean show the size of the numbers in a set of data.

The Moys own a bicycle shop. Explain whether the range, the mode, the median, or the mean would be the best measure to find the given information.

48. The most popular brand of bicycles

49. The spread in age of people who buy bicycles

50. The average monthly profit for the past 6 months

51. The typical selling price of a boy's bicycle

Gathering and Organizing Data

Build Understanding

ACTIVITY

A. Surveying Minute Masters
Materials: Watch or clock with a second hand
Groups: With a partner

How well do you think seventh graders can estimate how long a minute is? You cannot survey all seventh graders, so you will use a ***sample***, or some of the people from the total group.

a. Decide with your partner who will be the timer and who will be the experimenter. The experimenter closes his or her eyes, and the timer says “start.” The experimenter raises a hand when he or she estimates that a minute has passed. The timer measures the actual length of time and writes it in seconds.

b. Switch roles and repeat the experiment.

c. You can compile the results for the entire class in a ***frequency table*** like the one shown. A frequency table shows how often a particular outcome occurs. Make a mark in the tally column for each experimenter's time. Add all the tallies to find the frequency of each outcome.

d. Were most of the seventh graders in your sample able to estimate a minute within 10 seconds?

e. Do you think your sample tells you how well seventh graders can estimate when a minute of time has passed? Explain.

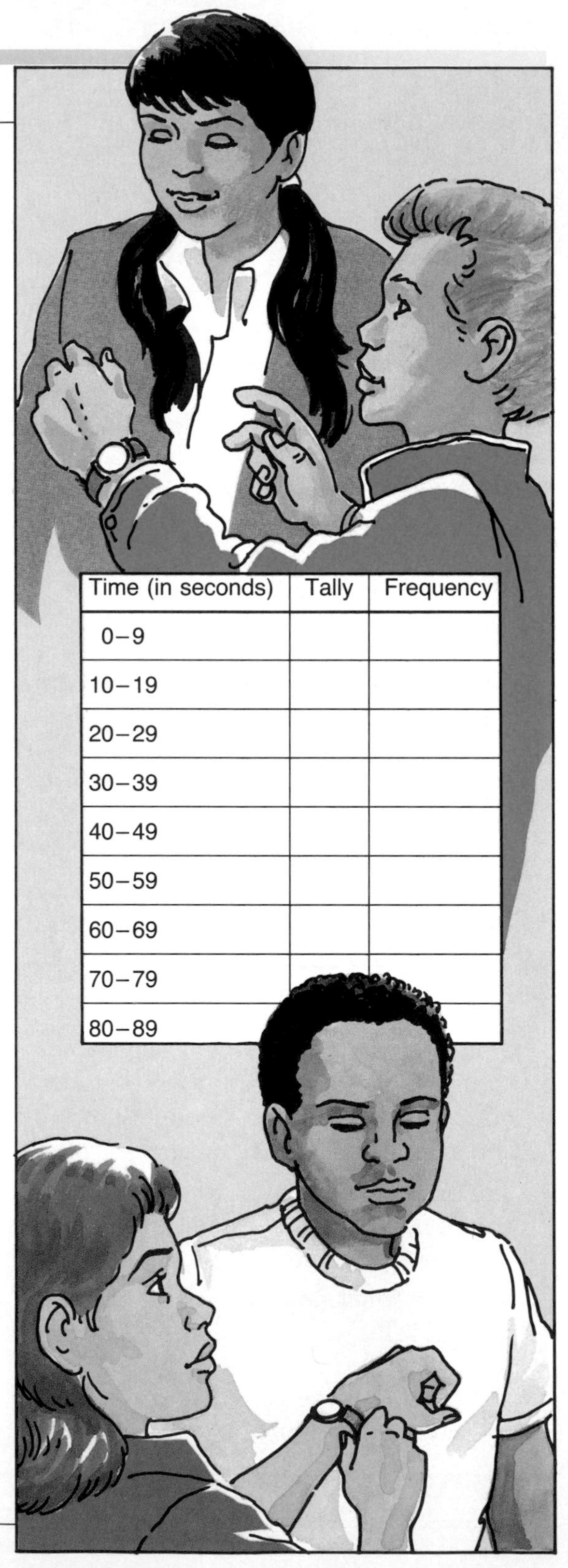

Time (in seconds)	Tally	Frequency
0–9		
10–19		
20–29		
30–39		
40–49		
50–59		
60–69		
70–79		
80–89		

B. Instead of a frequency table, you could show the data your class collected in a ***line plot***. A line plot gives you a "picture" of the data. Heather made this line plot of the data her class collected for the activity in Example A.

The height of each column of Xs shows how often the outcome occurred. Most of the estimates in Carolina's class were between 50 and 59 seconds.

Time (in seconds)	Tally	Frequency
0–9		0
10–19		0
20–29	|	1
30–39	|	1
40–49	|||	3
50–59	~~||||~~ |||	8
60–69	~~||||~~ |	6
70–79	||	2
80–89		0

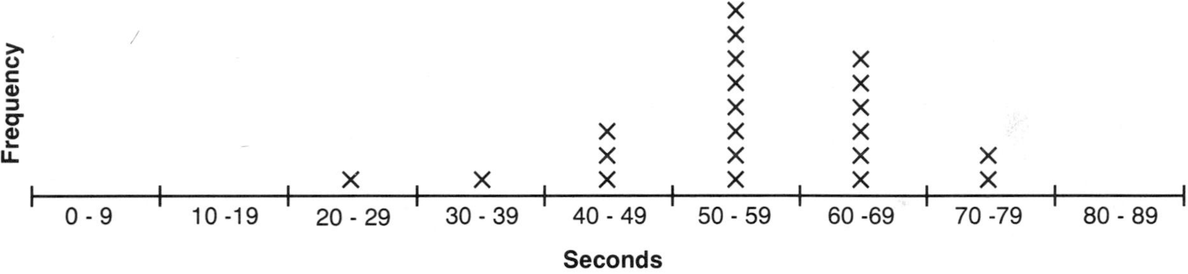

Talk About Math A frequency table and a line plot show the same information. What is the advantage of using a line plot?

Check Understanding

For another example, see Set B, pages 408–409.

Use the information in Examples A and B to complete each sentence.

1. A part of the total group to be surveyed is called a __?__.
2. A __?__ table is used to show how often a particular outcome occurs.
3. On a __?__, columns of Xs give a "picture" of a set of data.
4. In Example B, most students estimated the length of a minute to be __?__ seconds.
5. What entries include times within 10 seconds of one minute?
6. In Example B, can you tell how many students were within 10 seconds of the actual minute? Explain.
7. Make a line plot of the data you collected in Example A.

Practice

For More Practice, see Set B, pages 410–411.

Tina asked 20 seventh-grade students how many brothers and sisters they have. Use the results of her survey to answer Exercises 8 and 9.

3 2 0 1 2 5 0 4 1 2

2 3 1 6 2 0 2 1 3 2

Brothers and sisters	Tally	Frequency
0		
1		
2		
3		
4		
5		
6		

8. Copy and complete the frequency table.

9. Make a line plot of the data.

The following data shows the number of sporting events 30 seventh-grade students watched in one week. Use the data to answer Exercises 10 and 11.

0 5 3 0 8 4 2 3 2 6 1 0 0 2 0

1 7 3 2 5 3 1 8 3 5 0 1 4 3 0

Sporting events watched	Tally	Frequency
0		
1		
2		
3		
4		
5		
6		
7		
8		

10. Copy and complete the frequency table.

11. Make a line plot of the data.

Heather asked 25 seventh-grade students how many video movies they rent in one month. Use the results of her survey to answer Exercises 12 and 13.

4 6 4 3 3 2 2 0 2 3 1 6

3 3 0 4 0 1 2 0 4 6 1 1 2

Video movies rented	Tally	Frequency
0		
1		
2		
3		
4		
5		
6		

12. Copy and complete the frequency table.

13. Make a line plot of the data.

Mixed Practice Find the mean, the median, and the mode for each set of data.

14. 23, 5, 19, 23, 5, 9, 0, 23, 2, 13, 16, 24

15. Data for Exercises 8 and 9

16. Data for Exercises 10 and 11

17. Data for Exercises 12 and 13

18. 3 6 8 4 8 12 9 2

19. 100, 250, 360, 92, 140

Problem Solving

On the frequency table and the line plot in Examples A and B, the numbers 0–9, 10–19, 20–29, and so on, are ***intervals***. The interval 0–9 contains the numbers 0, 1, 2, 3, 4, 5, 6, 7, 8, and 9, for a total of ten possibilities.

20. Does each interval contain the same number of possibilities?

21. **Critical Thinking** Is it better to use a smaller interval for the data? Why?

Use the data from Exercises 8–11 for Problems 22 and 23.

22. Can you tell from Tina's sample how many brothers and sisters the seventh graders have? Explain.

23. Can you tell from a sample how many sporting events the seventh graders watched? Would it matter if all the students surveyed were girls? boys?

The line plot at the right shows how many sweatshirts of each size were sold in one week during a school fund-raiser. Use the line plot to answer Problems 24 and 25.

Frequency	Extra Small	Small	Medium	Large	Extra Large
	X X X X	X X X X X X	X X X X X X X X X	X X X X X X X X X X X	X X X X X X X

24. How many sweatshirts were sold for the week?

25. Find the median and the mode of the sizes sold for the week.

Choose a ______ Strategy

It's a Shoe-In What are the shoe sizes of your classmates?

26. Take a survey to find the shoe sizes of your classmates. Record each student's size, separating the girls' sizes from the boys' sizes.

27. Organize the data in two frequency tables. Did you use the same interval in each table?

28. Show the data in one line plot. Use one color for Xs for girls and another color for Xs for boys.

29. What is the median shoe size of the girls? the boys? the class?

30. What is the mode shoe size of the girls? the boys? the class?

31. What is the range of shoe sizes for the girls? the boys? the class?

32. Would it have been easier to compare the data if you had made one line plot for the girls, another for the boys, and a third for the class? Explain.

ALGEBRA

Solve a Simpler Problem

Understand
QUESTION
FACTS
KEY IDEA

Plan and Solve
STRATEGY
ANSWER

Look Back
SENSIBLE ANSWER
ALTERNATE APPROACH

Build Understanding

To find the red fox population in Riverside Forest, naturalists caught 200 foxes, tagged them, and released them. Later they caught 50 foxes and found 30 of them tagged. How many red foxes are there?

Understand QUESTION How many red foxes are in the forest?

FACTS A group of 200 foxes was captured, tagged, and released. Then another group, or sample, was recaptured. In this sample, 30 out of 50 foxes were tagged.

KEY IDEA Since it would be difficult to count every fox, the naturalists can estimate the number by solving a simpler problem.

Plan and Solve STRATEGY Use ratios to form a proportion.

Total tagged foxes→ / Total foxes in park→ $\frac{200}{n} = \frac{30}{50}$ ←Tagged foxes in sample / ←Total foxes in sample

$30n = 10{,}000$ Round to the nearest
$n = 333.333$ whole number.

ANSWER There are about 333 red foxes in Riverside Forest.

Look Back ALTERNATE APPROACH Of the foxes captured in the second sample, $\frac{30}{50}$, or 60%, were tagged. Assume that 60% of the total red fox population was tagged in the first sample. Sixty percent of what number is 200?

$0.60 \times n = 200$

$n = \frac{200}{0.60}; n = 333.3$

The answer obtained, 333, is a reasonable answer.

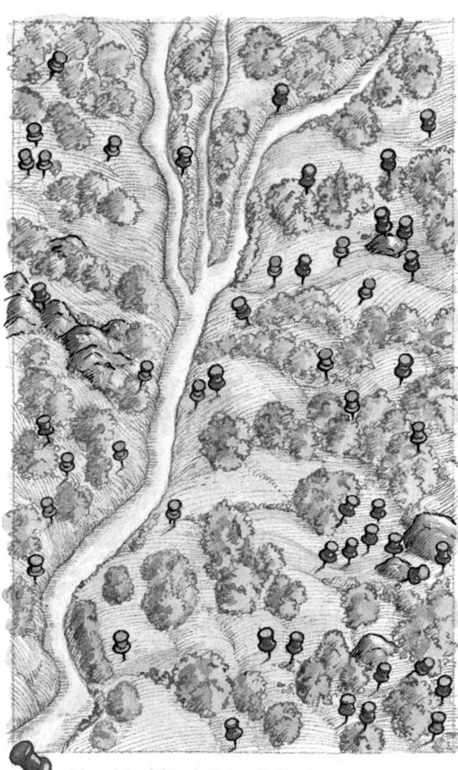

Tagged foxes in sample

Untagged foxes in sample

Naturalists not only like to know the number of animals in an area but also where they have been captured.

■ **Talk About Math** If another sample of 100 red foxes were captured, do you think the estimate of the total number of red foxes would be the same? Explain.

Check Understanding

The naturalists at Riverside Forest decide to take one more sample of the red fox population. How can they use the results of both samples to find the number of red foxes?

	1st sample	2nd sample
Tagged foxes	30	45
Foxes in sample	50	100

1. Write the sum of the tagged foxes and the sum of the captured foxes as a ratio.

2. Write the ratio you got in Exercise 1 and the ratio of the total number of tagged foxes to the total number of foxes as a proportion.

3. Solve the proportion you wrote in Exercise 2.

4. How does the answer you got in Exercise 3 for 2 samples compare to the estimate for one sample?

5. Which estimate do you think is more accurate? Why?

Practice

Answer each question.

6. Naturalists stocked a lake with 300 trout, a species that was new to the lake. Of the 100 fish that were captured, 40 of them were trout. What was the fish population of the lake?

7. **Critical Thinking** Naturalists captured one sample of foxes in a $24\frac{1}{2}$ square mile rectangular area that was twice as long as it was wide. What were the dimensions of the area?

8. A total of 400 penguins were captured and tagged. Use the chart at the right that shows the results of four samples to find the total number of penguins.

9. A fifth sample of the penguins gave the results of 20 tagged in a sample of 55. Using this new information, what is the total number of penguins?

	1st sample	2nd sample	3rd sample	4th sample
Tagged penguins	50	35	17	40
Penguins in sample	200	100	100	100

Stem-and-Leaf Plots

Build Understanding

Lupe, a sports statistician provides sportscasters with the information they read on the air.

Receptions made by NFC leaders

Year	Catches	Year	Catches	Year	Catches
1970	71	1976	58	1982	60
1971	58	1977	51	1983	78
1972	62	1978	88	1984	106
1973	67	1979	80	1985	92
1974	63	1980	83	1986	86
1975	73	1981	85	1987	91

Lupe might use a ***stem-and-leaf plot*** to organize and to provide a "picture" of the data for leading pass receivers in the National Football Conference, 1970–1987.

Stem	Leaf
5	1 8 8
6	0 2 3 7
7	1 3 8
8	0 3 5 6 8
9	1 2
10	6

First, find the smallest and the largest numbers, 51 and 106. This information will help you know where to begin and end the stem part of the stem-and-leaf plot. The stems are the tens and hundreds digits. The leaves are the ones digits, arranged in order.

From the stem-and-leaf plot you can find the range, median, and mode. The range is 55. The median is between 73 and 78, or 75.5. In this case, the mode is 58.

■ **Talk About Math** When using the stem-and-leaf plot, when do you have to take an average of two numbers to find the median?

Check Understanding

For another example, see Set C, pages 408–409.

On your own paper, use the data to complete the stem-and-leaf plot at right.

Receptions made by AFC leaders

1970	57	1973	57	1976	64	1979	82	1982	54	1985	86
1971	61	1974	72	1977	71	1980	89	1983	92	1986	95
1972	58	1975	60	1978	71	1981	88	1984	89	1987	66

Stem	Leaf
1. 5	▒ 7 7 8
2. ▒	0 1 ▒ 6
3. 7	▒ 1 2
4. 8	2 ▒ 8 9 ▒
5. ▒	2 ▒

6. Find the highest and lowest values.

7. Find the range.

Practice

For More Practice, see Set C, pages 410–411.

Make a stem-and-leaf plot for each set of data.

8. 23 35 49 42 37 21 22
19 33 37 34 23 45 30

9. 6 12 15 15 8 20 17
25 32 27 13 12 19 21

10. 75 54 46 60 61
58 42 63 51 53

11. 92 143 156 120 137
111 144 155 119 144

12. 72 83 81 83 74 95
91 92 84 72 80 77

13. 36 12 16 27 30 11
23 24 23 12 19 31

14. 52 37 43 38 65 58
30 46 35 42 62 66

15. 164 171 174 153 182
158 152 167 189 150

16. 306 321 310 324 317
334 316 338 325 335

17. 48 36 49 41 54 53
34 46 41 38 52 39

18. 203 216 222 211 209
204 229 215 205 228

19. 986 982 963 971 984
961 988 975 975 986

Mixed Practice Using the stem-and-leaf plot find the range and the mode for each.

20. Exercise 8

21. Exercise 15

22. Exercise 19

Problem Solving

Refer to the stem-and-leaf plot in Exercises 1–5 for Problems 23–25.

23. Make a line plot from the stem-and-leaf plot.

24. In how many years did the AFC leaders catch more than 70 passes?

25. Using the stem-and-leaf plot, find the median for receptions made by the AFC leaders.

26. **Use Data** Make a stem-and-leaf plot for all the numbers found in Problems 6–21 on page 169.

Midchapter Checkup

Use the following data for Exercises 1 and 2.
15 27 9 14 31 27 25

1. Find the mean, median, and mode.

2. Make a stem-and-leaf plot.

The data below shows the number of books read in three months by 20 different seventh graders. Use this data to answer Exercises 3–5.
6 8 1 3 9 4 6 7 1 5 2 8 7 9 1 5 1 8 0 4

3. Make a frequency table of the data.

4. Make a line plot of the data.

5. Find the range, mean, median, and mode.

Problem-Solving Workshop

Real-Life Decision Making

1. Your neighbors want you to babysit for their children. They say they will pay you the "going rate."

You take a survey and ask other junior high students if they babysit, and if so, how much they charge per hour. The results are shown below.

a. Three students babysat for children in their family and didn't get paid for it ($0). Would you include this in your survey results? Why or why not?

b. Find the mode, median, and mean of the data. Would you tell all three to the neighbor? Which one would you emphasize?

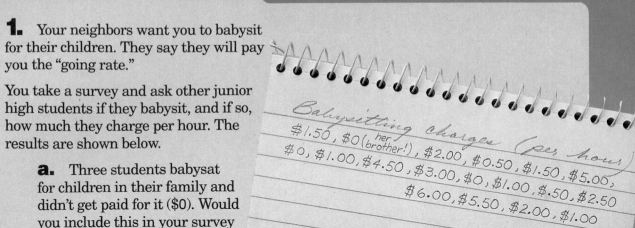

Babysitting charges (per hour)
$1.50, $0 (her brother!), $2.00, $0.50, $1.50, $5.00,
$0, $1.00, $4.50, $3.00, $0, $1.00, $.50, $2.50
$6.00, $5.50, $2.00, $1.00

Visual-Thinking Activity

The faces on each block are identical. Tell which symbols are opposite each other.

Explore with a Computer

Use the *Graphing and Probability Workshop Project* for this activity.

Day	Amount
Monday	$48.00
Tuesday	$72.00
Wednesday	$96.00
Thursday	$24.00
Friday	$72.00
Saturday	$168.00

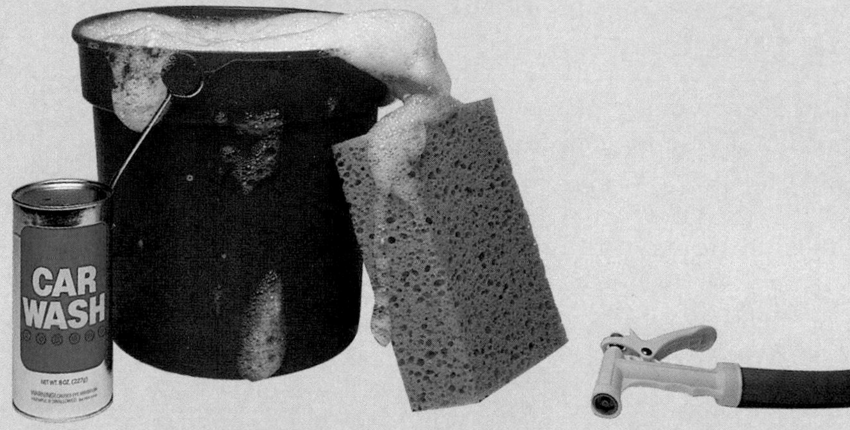

The 7th grade organized a Neighborhood Help Week. For one week, students worked to earn money for sports uniforms. They raked leaves, painted mailboxes, and washed cars. Students collected $480.00 in all.

1. At the computer, view the data as a Bar Graph. Which day did the students collect the most money?

2. Use the *Statistics option* to view the mean, median, mode, and range. What was the average amount of money earned per day? If the students worked on Sunday, would the range change? If on Friday they had earned only $70.00, would the mode change? Explain.

Number-Sense Project

Look back at pages 378–379.

1. Notice the letter following the serial number on a bill. The first time currency is printed at one of the banks (the first run), the letter A is added at the end of the serial number until all the 8-digit numbers are used. The second run uses B, the third C, and so on. All letters except the O are used.

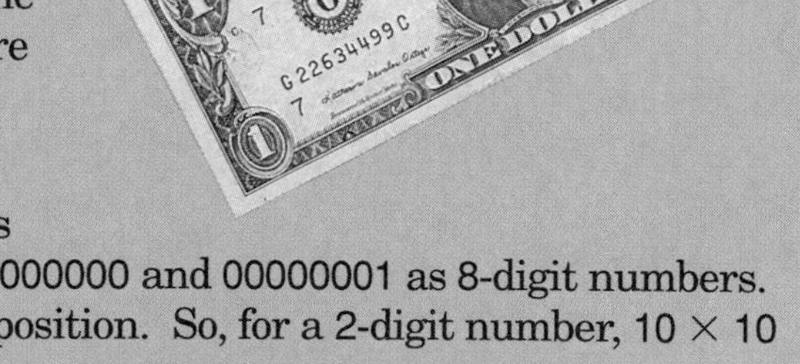

a. How many different 8-digit serial numbers can be written using the digits 0 through 9? Consider numbers like 00000000 and 00000001 as 8-digit numbers. HINT: Ten digits are possible for each position. So, for a 2-digit number, 10×10 numbers are possible, and so on.

b. How many bills are there in a run?

c. Which run is indicated by D? By M?

Bar Graphs and Histograms

Build Understanding

A. Julian drew a double bar graph to help him visualize how well different items had sold at one of his stores. First he drew and labeled the vertical axis to show the number sold, keeping each interval the same. Next he drew and labeled a horizontal axis to show what items were sold. Then he drew bars for each year to show the number of each item sold. Finally he wrote a title for the graph.

Items Sold (in Thousands)	1980	1985	1990
Records	6.0	3.9	2
Cassettes	5.6	3	3
T-shirts	1.7	.8	.4
CDs	0	1	2.6
Videos	0	1.7	3.5

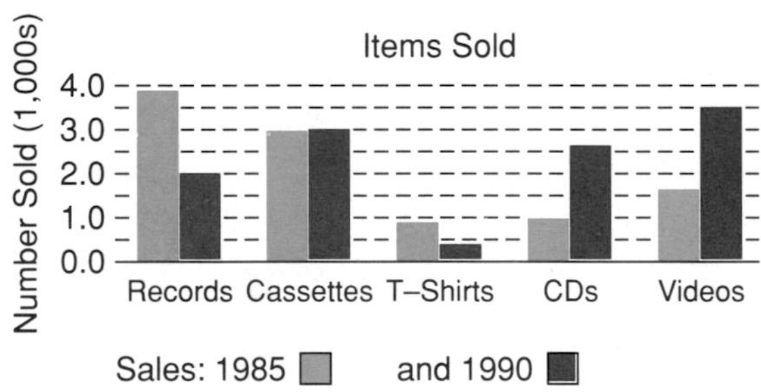

B. Julian also collected data on the number of years his male and female employees had worked for him. To help him visualize this data he drew a histogram of his male employees.

He drew the histogram in the same way he drew his bar graph, except there is no space between the bars and equal intervals are shown on the horizontal axis.

Employees' Years of Experience					
Years	0–4	5–9	10–14	15–19	20–24
Male	34	14	7	12	24
Female	17	9	23	18	10

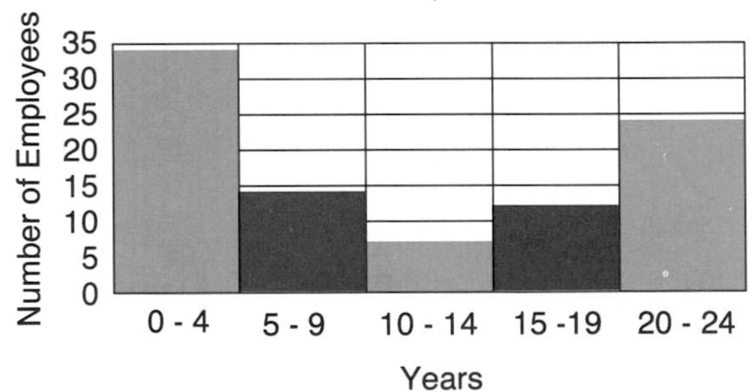

Talk About Math Discuss the differences and similarities between a bar graph, double bar graph, and a histogram.

Check Understanding

For another example, see Set D, pages 408–409.

1. **Estimation** In Example A, about how many cassette tapes did Julian's store sell in 1990? 1985?

2. In Example B, which two intervals have about the same number of employees?

Practice

For More Practice, see Set D, Pages 410–411.

Use the graphs in Examples A and B for Exercises 3–4.

3. In Example A, which category showed the biggest change between 1985 and 1990?

4. In Example B, what is another possible interval Julian could have used when gathering his data?

Draw the graphs asked for. **Remember** to use equal intervals on the axes, label the axes and title the graph.

5. Using the data in Example A, draw a double bar graph comparing 1980 with 1990.

6. Using the data in Example A, draw a double bar graph comparing 1980 and 1985.

7. Using the data in Example B, draw a histogram showing the years of employment for female employees.

8. Using the data in Example B, draw a histogram showing the years of employment for all employees.

Use the graphs of Exercises 5–8 to answer these questions.

9. Which item had the greatest sales increase between 1980 and 1990?

10. Which item had the smallest sales change between 1980 and 1985?

11. Were there more men or women among the employees with over 10 years of experience?

12. Which interval had the least number of total employees?

Problem Solving

Draw the following graphs.

13. Julian surveyed 51 customers in several age groups. He wanted to know how many liked jazz. His data is shown in the table below. Draw a histogram of the data.

Age group	Likes Jazz
10–19	5
20–29	12
30–39	9
40–49	7
50–59	18

14. Julian wanted to know how many types of records were sold in January 1989 and 1990. Make a double bar graph using the data below.

Sales for January	1989	1990
Easy Listening	89	59
Country	37	45
Jazz	55	37
Classical	25	20
Rock	97	67

Circle Graphs

The Basque language is spoken by only about 500,000 to 750,000 people in Northern Spain and Southern France. Basque is not a member of any of the major language families; linguists do not know its origin.

Build Understanding

The graphs on this page show the major language families of the world. Each language family is made up of languages that developed from a "parent" language. English, Spanish, Russian, and Hindi are some of the languages in the Indo-European language family. The bar graph lets you compare the different language families. The ***circle graph*** shows the share each language family has of the languages spoken around the world.

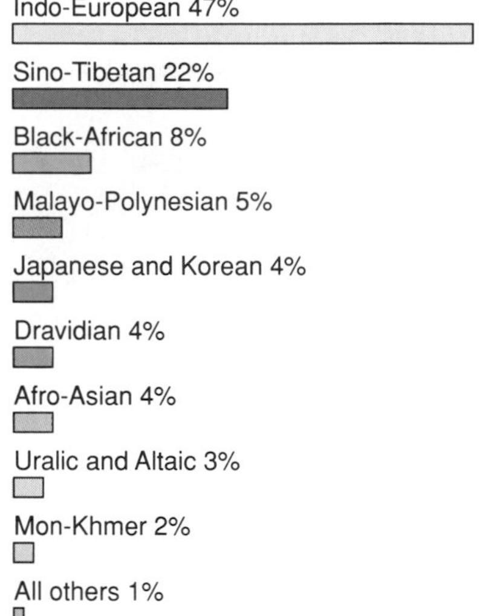

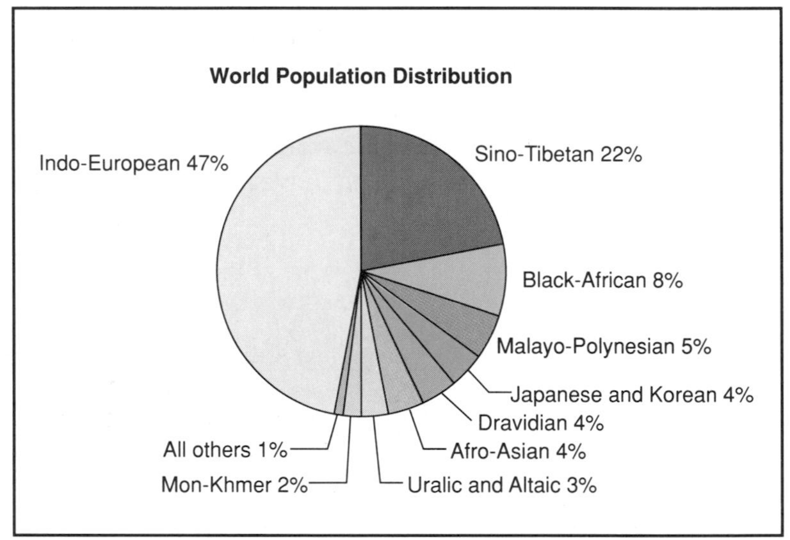

A. The population of the world in 1990 was about 5.4 billion people. About how many people in the world speak a language that is part of the Indo-European language family?

Find 47% of 5.4 billion.

$n = 0.47 \times 5.4$
$n = 2.538$ billion

About 2,538,000,000 people speak an Indo-European language.

B. About 4% of the world speaks an Afro-Asian language. What is the measure of the central angle needed to represent the Afro-Asian language family on a circle graph?

Write the percent as a decimal. Multiply by 360°. Round to the nearest degree.

$4\% \text{ of } 360° = 0.04 \times 360$
$= 14.40$

An angle of about 14° would represent the Afro-Asian language family.

Talk About Math About 32% of the population of Belgium speaks French. About 17% of the population of Canada speaks French. Can you conclude that there are more French-speaking Belgians than French-speaking Canadians?

Check Understanding

For another example, see Set E, pages 408–409.

Use the circle graph on page 396 to answer Exercises 1 and 2.

1. Which three language families are spoken by the same percentage of the world's population?

2. Write the percent of people speaking a language belonging to the Black African language family as a decimal.

Practice

For More Practice, see Set E, pages 410–411.

Use the information in Example A to find the number of people who speak languages belonging to each of the following language families.

3. Sino-Tibetan
4. Japanese and Korean
5. Mon-Khmer
6. Black African
7. Malayo-Polynesian
8. All others
9. Dravidian
10. Uralic and Altaic
11. Afro-Asian

Find the measure of the central angle needed to represent each percent on a circle graph. Round each answer to the nearest degree.

12. 47%
13. 2%
14. 8%
15. 22%
16. 5%
17. 3%

Problem Solving

Solve each problem.

18. China has a population of about 1.1 billion people. About 70% of the people speak Mandarin, a Chinese dialect. How many people speak Mandarin?

19. Today, there are about 7,000,000 speakers of Quechua, a South American Indian language. What percent of the world population does this represent? What would be the measure of the central angle to represent Quechua? Round to the nearest tenth of a degree.

Sino-Tibetan languages, such as Chinese, consist of one-syllable words.

Broken-Line Graphs

Build Understanding

A. Every ten years since 1790 the U.S. has taken a census of the population. Data from each census often is organized in a ***broken-line graph*** to indicate upward or downward trends, or to show changes over time.

This broken-line graph shows the population of Texas from 1900 to 1990. What other information does it give you?

You can find the population of Texas for each census year from 1900 to 1990. You can also see that the population was greater each time the census was taken. The steepness of each line segment shows the rate of increase.

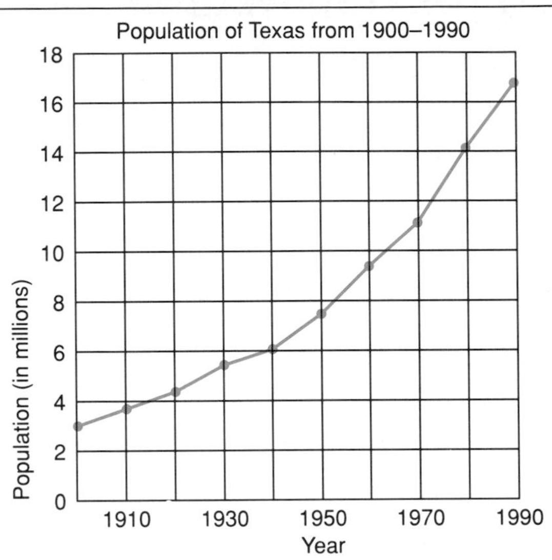

B. A ***double broken-line graph*** shows two sets of data on the same axes. This one shows the population of Texas and Illinois from 1900 to 1990.

With this graph you can find the population of each state for each census year from 1900 and 1990. You can also see that Texas grew faster than Illinois.

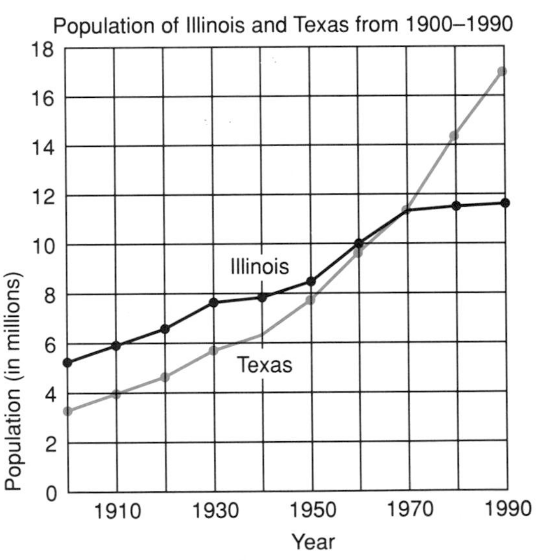

Talk About Math For what 10-year period did the population of Texas increase the most?

Check Understanding

For another example, see Set F, pages 408–409.

Use the broken-line graphs in Examples A and B for Exercises 1–4.

1. What was the approximate population of Texas in 1930?
2. What was the approximate population of Illinois in 1940?
3. In what year was the population of Illinois approximately 7.8 million?
4. In what year were the populations of Illinois and Texas about the same?

Practice

For More Practice, see Set F, pages 410–411.

Use the table for Exercises 5–10.

Population (in millions)

	1900	1910	1920	1930	1940	1950	1960	1970	1980	1990
Florida	0.5	0.8	1.0	1.5	1.9	2.8	5.0	6.8	9.7	12.9
New Jersey	1.9	2.5	3.2	4.0	4.2	4.8	6.1	7.2	7.4	7.7
Ohio	4.2	4.8	5.8	6.6	6.9	7.9	9.7	10.7	10.8	10.8
Tennessee	2.0	2.2	2.3	2.6	2.9	3.3	3.6	3.9	4.6	4.9

5. Draw a broken-line graph for the population of Florida. Graph the data for New Jersey on the same grid.

6. Draw a double broken-line graph for the populations of Ohio and Tennessee.

7. Between what two census years did the population of Florida increase the most? the population of New Jersey?

8. Between what two census years did the population of Ohio increase the least? the population of Tennessee?

9. In what year were the populations of Florida and New Jersey about the same?

10. In what year was there the greatest difference in population in Ohio and Tennessee?

Problem Solving

Use the table above and the graph in Example B for Problems 11–13.

11. Compare the data. Which of the six states had the greatest change in population between 1900 and 1990? Which had the least?

12. Which state had the greatest increase in population from one census year to the next? In what decade did it occur?

13. **Critical Thinking** Compare your graph of New Jersey and Florida to the graph of Illinois and Texas. What trend do you notice in the population of the two southern states? the two northern states? Explain.

Skills Review pages 274–275

ALGEBRA

Solve each proportion.

1. $\frac{27}{x} = \frac{15}{20}$ **2.** $\frac{3}{9} = \frac{x}{21}$ **3.** $\frac{0.04}{5} = \frac{0.02}{x}$ **4.** $\frac{x}{155} = \frac{0.002}{0.05}$

Make a Graph

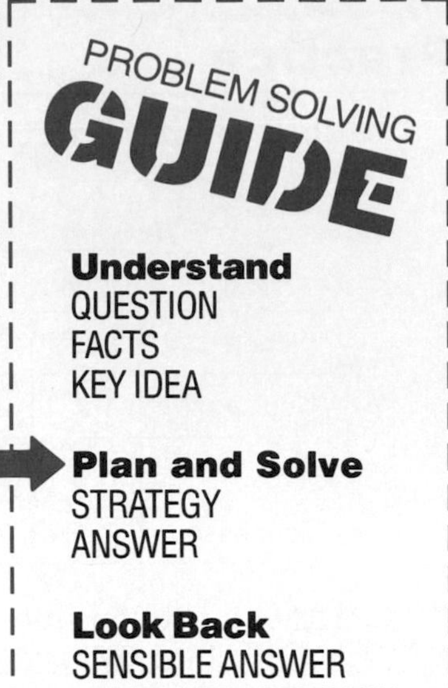

Build Understanding

In which league, American or National, does the home-run leader tend to hit more home runs?

Most Home Runs Hit by a Player 1978–1988		
Year	National League	American League
1978	40	46
1979	48	45
1980	48	41
1981	31	22
1982	37	39
1983	40	39
1984	36	43
1985	37	40
1986	37	40
1987	49	49
1988	39	42

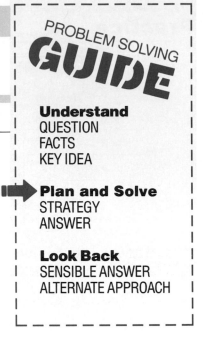

Understand QUESTION Which league has the hitter who tends to hit more home runs?

FACTS The table shows the home-run records. Make a graph using the data.

KEY IDEA A double broken-line graph best shows change over time in two sets of data.

Plan and Solve STRATEGY Make a double broken-line graph to compare home runs for the two leagues.

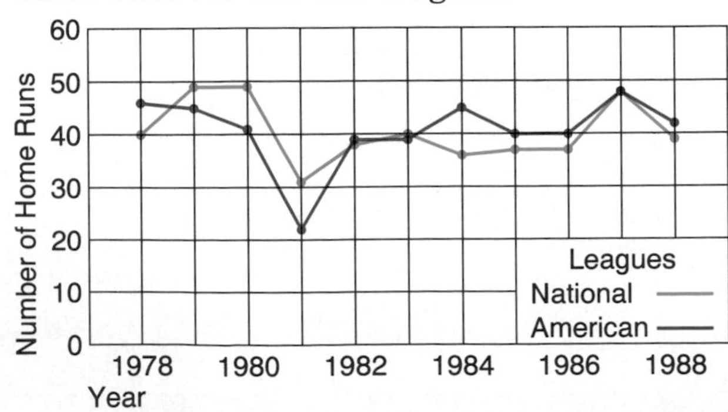

ANSWER The graph shows that the leading National League home-run hitter had more home runs in 4 of the 11 years shown and that the leading American League home-run hitter had more home runs in 6 of the 11 years shown.

Look Back SENSIBLE ANSWER All the data was used and plotted correctly. The double broken-line graph displayed the data so comparisons were easy to make.

Talk About Math Could you have shown the data on page 400 as well using a bar graph? a circle graph? Explain.

Check Understanding

Use the double broken-line graph on page 400 for Exercises 1–4.

1. In what years did the American League's leading home-run hitter have more home runs than the National League's?
2. How many home runs did the leading home-run hitter of the American League have in 1981?
3. In what year was the difference in the number of home runs hit by each league's leading home-run hitter the greatest? What was the difference?
4. In what year was the difference in the number of home runs the least? What was the difference?

Practice

The table shows the runs-batted-in leaders of the National League and the American League.

5. Would you make a double bar graph or a double broken-line graph to show the data for 1978–1988? Explain.
6. Graph the data. **Remember** to use equal intervals.
7. Which league had the better runs-batted-in leader for 5 consecutive years?
8. In what year did both leagues have the lowest number of runs-batted-in for the period shown?

League RBI leaders			
National		American	
Year	RBI	Year	RBI
1978	120	1978	139
1979	118	1979	139
1980	121	1980	122
1981	91	1981	78
1982	109	1982	136
1983	121	1983	126
1984	106	1984	123
1985	125	1985	145
1986	119	1986	121
1987	137	1987	134
1988	109	1988	124

CONSUMER CONNECTION

Misuse of Statistics

Build Understanding

The yearly circulation of the *Daily Bugle* newspaper is shown below for 1985 to 1990.

Year	1985	1986	1987	1988	1989	1990
Circulation	100,000	100,060	100,120	100,210	100,300	100,410

A. What do you notice about these two graphs?

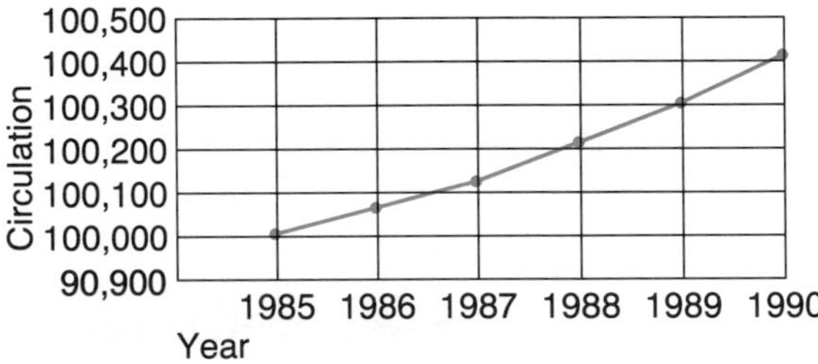

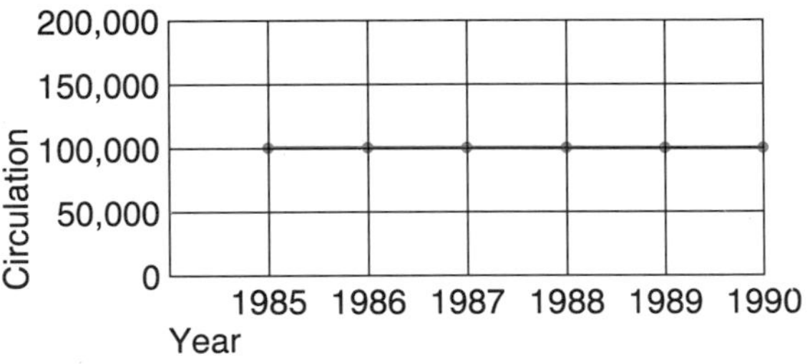

The marketing department of the *Daily Bugle* prepared this graph to show how the circulation of the newspaper had increased dramatically from 1985 to 1990.

The marketing department of a competitor newspaper prepared a graph showing that circulation of the *Daily Bugle* had increased only slightly.

Both graphs show the same data. The vertical axis of the first graph uses smaller intervals. This causes the line segments to rise more sharply and seems to show a more dramatic increase in circulation.

B. In a brochure the *Daily Bugle* gives to potential new employees, it lists its average weekly salary as $600. How might this figure be misleading?

If eight employees make $150 a week and two of the employees make $2,400 a week, the mean salary would be raised by the two high salaries. A new employee would be more likely to make about $150 a week.

■ **Talk About Math** How could the line on the first graph of Example A be made to rise even more sharply?

Check Understanding

For another example, see Set G, pages 408–409.

Refer to Example A for Exercises 1–4.

1. How many newspapers does each unit on the vertical axis stand for in the first graph? in the second graph?

2. By what percent did the *Daily Bugle's* circulation increase from 1985–1990?

3. Which graph shows that the paper's circulation increased rapidly?

4. Why is the first graph misleading?

Practice

For More Practice, see Set G, pages 410–411.

An editor found these statements in various articles. Explain how each statement is a misuse of statistics.

5. Since most accidents occur in the home, it is safer to stay away from home as much as possible.

6. Recent surveys show that 60% of the people think George Flowers will be the next president. He is sure to win.

Compare each headline with the graph below it. Then tell if the headline is accurate or misleading.

7. Fourth Quarter Revenues Sky Rocket in 1992!

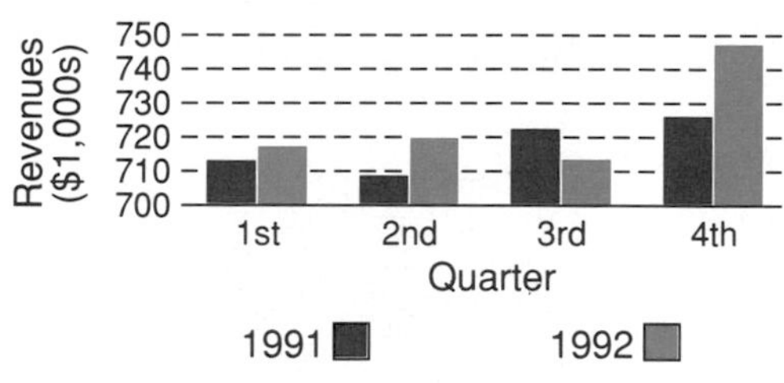

8. Twice as Many Books Donated This Year as Last Year!

Problem Solving

A sports writer for the *Daily Bugle* gathered the data in the table.

Visiting team	Attendance
Pirates	50,000
Dodgers	50,020
Cardinals	50,025
Cubs	50,050
Mets	50,600

9. Graph the data so it appears that attendance soared for the Mets' game.

10. Graph the data so it appears there was only a slight rise in attendance for the Mets' game.

11. Write a headline for each graph.

Make a Graph

Understand
QUESTION
FACTS
KEY IDEA

Plan and Solve
STRATEGY
ANSWER

Look Back
SENSIBLE ANSWER
ALTERNATE APPROACH

Build Understanding

In golf, par is the number of strokes it *should* take a skillful golfer to get the ball in the hole. If your score is around par for every hole, you'll probably be happy with your score.

The City Golf Course was redesigned recently. Many of the golfers think that the new Number 5 hole is the most difficult on the course. Other players think the Number 12 hole is the most difficult. How can Ana, the manager of the course, use the players' scorecards to decide who is right?

Understand QUESTION Do more golfers score over par on the Number 5 hole or the Number 12 hole?

FACT The players' scorecards have their scores for each hole.

KEY IDEA A graph would provide the course manager with a "picture" of the players' scores on each hole.

Plan and Solve STRATEGY The manager can make a frequency table from the scorecards, then make a bar graph of the data.

ANSWER The bar graph shows that more golfers score over par on the Number 12 hole than on any other hole. Number 12 is the most difficult.

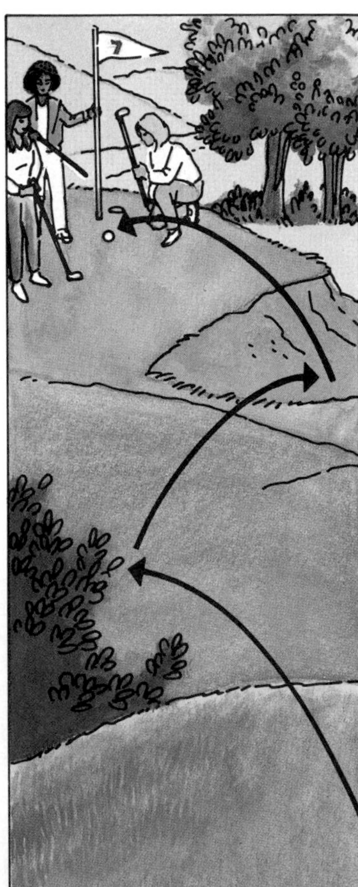

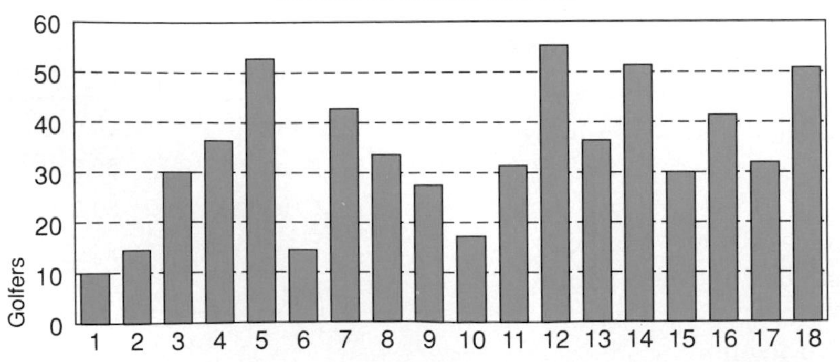

Look Back SENSIBLE ANSWER A bar graph lets you compare different categories. Not every hole has the same difficulty. The manager can see from the bar graph that more golfers score over par on the Number 12 hole.

Spaniard Severiano Ballesteros plays professional golf in Europe and in the United States. Through 1992, he had won five major championships.

Write About Math Are the first nine holes of the City Golf Course more or less difficult than the last nine holes? Explain your answer.

Check Understanding

Use the bar graph on page 404 to tell about how many golfers scored over par on hole Number

1. 1. **2.** 3. **3.** 5. **4.** 6. **5.** 12. **6.** 18.

Practice

Here are Sumi's scores for 18 holes of golf.

Hole	1	2	3	4	5	6	7	8	9	10	11	12	13	14	15	16	17	18	Total
Sumi	4	4	6	3	4	3	5	3	4	4	6	5	3	4	4	3	5	4	74
Par	4	4	5	3	4	4	4	3	4	4	4	4	3	4	4	3	5	4	70

7. Make a double broken-line graph to compare Sumi's score with the par on each hole.

8. On how many holes did Sumi shoot par?

9. On which hole did Sumi shoot under par?

The table shows the number of medals won by countries in the 1992 Winter Olympics.

10. Would you make a bar graph or a circle graph to show what percent of the medals was won by each country? Explain.

11. What percent of the medals was won by each country? by all other countries?

12. Draw the appropriate graph to show the percent of medals won by each country.

Number of medals won 1992 Winter Olympics	
Country	Medals
Germany	26
Unified Team	23
Austria	21
Norway	20
Italy	14
All other countries	67

Chapter 11 REVIEW

Skills Review

Find the range, mean, median and mode for each set of data.

1. 14, 25, 46, 11, 23, 24, 66, 12, 10

2. 436, 475, 523, 574, 878, 354, 235, 475

The data shows the number of pets owned by 20 students: 0, 3, 5, 1, 1, 7, 0, 3, 4, 2, 2, 2, 2, 5, 1, 2, 1, 0, 0, 4.

3. Make a frequency table for the data.

4. Plot the data on a line plot.

The data shows the height in inches of the members of Mr. Clark's class: 60, 58, 65, 66, 57, 64, 72, 68, 70, 66, 59, 60, 65, 70, 67, 71.

5. Make a stem-and-leaf plot for the heights.

Draw a double bar graph to show the data.

6. Items sold (in Thousands)

	1990	1992
Computers	5.4	6.1
Printers	4.9	5.4
Modems	1.2	2.5
Scanners	0.6	1.3

Use the data in the circle graph. If Roger's home cost $120,000, how much was spent on each item?

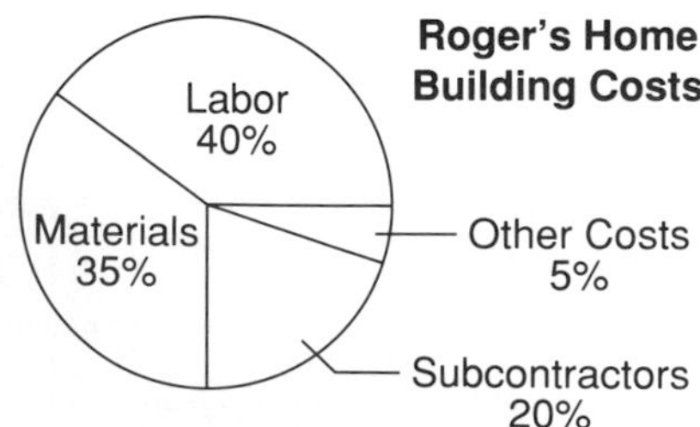

7. Labor
8. Materials
9. Subcontractors
10. Other costs

Problem-Solving Review

Solve each problem.

11. Lupe is $4\frac{1}{2}$ feet tall. Her brother is $1\frac{1}{3}$ times as tall as she is. How tall is her brother?

12. Grady is helping his Dad make bran muffins for the Grange Breakfast. He gets to keep 2 muffins for every 48 muffins they make. If they make 144 muffins, how many can Grady keep?

13. Find the area of the figure at the right. Use 3.14 for π.

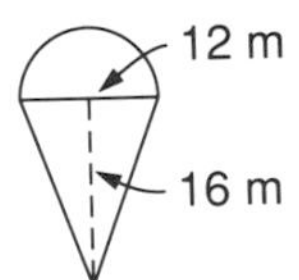

14. Mr. Slavinski harvested 10 pumpkins. He recorded their weights, in pounds, as 3, 10, 6, 5, 6, 7, 10, 8, 6, 5. What is the mean weight of the pumpkins? What is the range of the weights?

15. The Maine Wildlife Commission wanted to know how many bald eagles nest in Maine. Scientists visited 50 nesting sites and tagged the pair of adult eagles in each nest, a total of 100 eagles. Two years later, they visited 50 sites and counted 58 tagged eagles of the 100 adults at the nests. About how many bald eagles nest in Maine?

16. **Data File** Use the data on pages 414–415. Make a graph to compare a baseball fan's costs at five major-league ballparks.

17. **Make a Data File** Use the data you gathered for Problem 37 on page 326. Make a circle graph showing the percent of total income spent on the budget items in your chart.

Cumulative Skills Review • Chapters 1–11

Estimate each answer.

1. \$254.89 − \$170.32 **2.** 498 + 514 + 489 **3.** 888×54 **4.** 78.4 − 27.1

5. $6{,}376 \div 79$ **6.** $36{,}572 \div 605$ **7.** $78{,}023 \div 1{,}154$ **8.** $24{,}699 \div 48$

9. $\frac{1}{5} + \frac{2}{13}$ **10.** $\frac{7}{9} + \frac{9}{10}$ **11.** $2\frac{3}{4} - \frac{7}{8}$ **12.** $5\frac{5}{9} - 3\frac{1}{2}$

Copy each figure on grid paper.
Draw the reflection, rotation, or translation described.

13. Translate down 3 units and left 3 units.

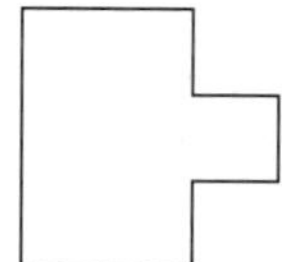

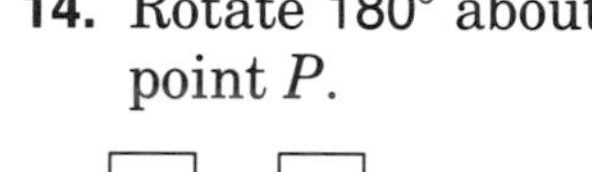

14. Rotate 180° about point *P*.

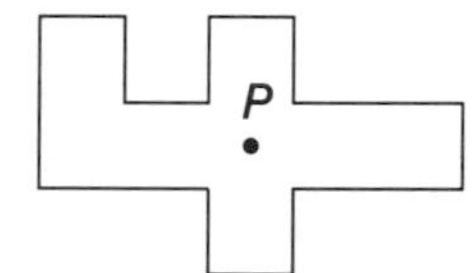

15. Reflect over the line.

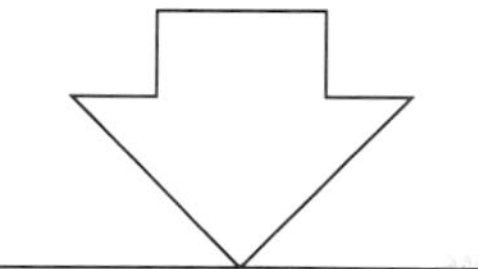

A drawing of a building uses the scale 2 cm to 5 m.
The drawing is 6.4 cm wide and 9 cm long.

16. Write a proportion to find the actual width of the building.

17. Write a proportion to find the actual length of the building.

18. Find the actual width of the building.

19. Find the actual length of the building.

Write and solve an equation for each exercise.

20. 98% of what number is 588?

21. 360 is 80% of what number?

22. What percent of 148 is 37?

23. $66\frac{2}{3}$% of what number is 72?

Find the circumference and area of each circle.
Round to the nearest whole number. Use 3.14 for π.

24. Radius: 25 ft **25.** Diameter: 34.8 m **26.** Radius: 120 cm **27.** Diameter: 28 yd

Use the line graph to answer the questions.

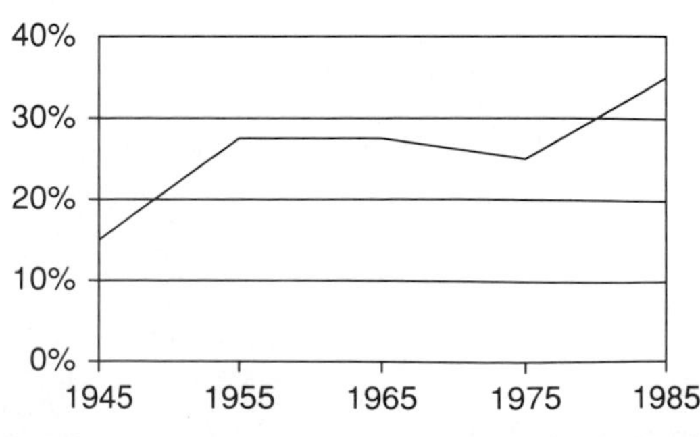

28. In 1945, about what percent of the mail was third class?

29. In what year was 37% of the mail third class?

30. Over what 10-year period did the percentage of third-class mail stay the same?

Reteaching

Set A pages 380–383

Look at this set of data.

12 29 18 9 53 35 12

$$\text{Mean} = \frac{\text{Sum of numbers}}{\text{Number of numbers}}$$

$$\text{Mean} = \frac{168}{7} = 24$$

Median: middle number when numbers are written in increasing order

9 12 12 [18] 29 35 53

Median

Mode: most frequently occurring number

The mode is 12.

Remember, divide the sum of the two middle numbers by 2 to find the median of a data set with an even number of items.

8 6 11 8 3 0 9

Using the set of data above, find

1. the mean. **2.** the median.

3. the mode.

17 55 72 34 21 55 40 22 67 55

Using the data above, find

4. the mean. **5.** the median.

6. the mode.

Set B pages 384–387

5 3 7 5 4 3 2 6 6 5 7 7

The data above could be compiled in a frequency table or plotted on a line plot.

Response	Tally	Frequency
2	|	1
3	||	2
4	|	1
5	|||	3
6	||	2
7	|||	3

```
Frequency
                     X           X
        X            X     X     X
  X     X     X      X     X     X
  2     3     4      5     6     7
            Response
```

Remember, you can use a frequency table or a line plot to show how often a particular outcome occurs.

Twenty-five families were asked to tell how many newspaper or magazine subscriptions they currently have. The results of the survey are shown.

0 1 0 3 4 1 2 2 2 7 9 0 0

1 2 1 1 6 5 1 2 3 4 3 0

1. Make a frequency table for the data.

2. Make a line plot for the data.

Set C pages 390–391

The leaves 4, 9, 1, and 7 on the stem 2 represent the numbers 24, 29, 21, and 27. This stem-and-leaf plot shows that numbers in the 20s occurred more often than single-digit numbers or numbers in the teens or 30s.

Stem	Leaves
0	2 3 7
1	0
2	1 4 7 9
3	1 3

Remember, leaves represent digits in the ones place and stems represent digits in the tens or hundreds place.

Make a stem-and-leaf plot for each set of data.

1.
7 12 29 13
1 8 14 22
30 2 19 20

2.
122 96 113 81
87 96 121 127
73 134 101 133

Set D pages 394–395

The histogram shows that the most common range for round-trip airline flights was 0–2.

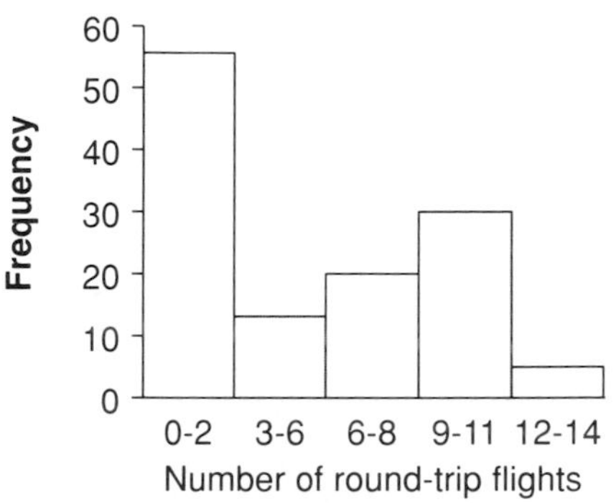

Remember, a histogram is a bar graph that shows frequency.

1. Use the data below to make a histogram.

Average Length of Stay in Pleasanton

Days	Frequency
1–2	22
3–4	16
5–6	8
7–8	3

Set E pages 396–397

Bow 'n Meow Pet Shop Profits from Sales

Cats	43%	Fish	17%
Dogs	32%	Birds	8%

Find the measure of the central angle that represents the profit from the sale of cats.

$0.43 \times 360° = 154.8° \approx 155°$

Remember, a percent can be written as a decimal.

1. Make a circle graph for the data in the example.
2. If the total profits from sales are $150,000, what is the profit from the sale of dogs?

Set F pages 398–399

This broken-line graph shows the attendance at Blasters home games this season.

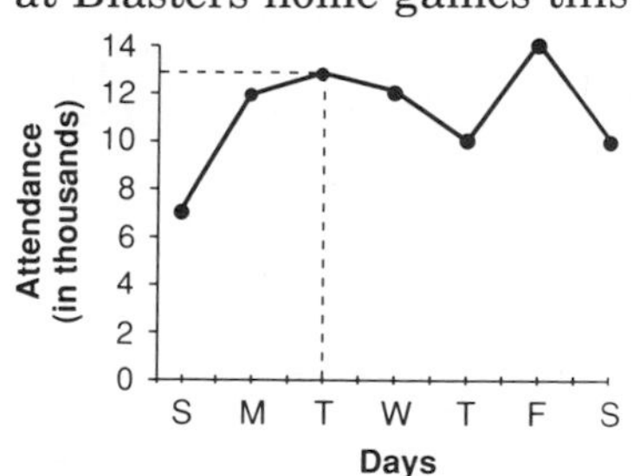

The dotted line shows how to read the graph for Tuesday when the attendance was 13,000.

Remember, the lines on a broken-line graph simply connect the dots and do not represent any value.

Use the graph at the left to find the attendance for

1. Sunday.
2. Monday.
3. Friday.
4. Saturday.

Set G pages 402–403

Adjusting the vertical scale changes the impression given by each graph below.

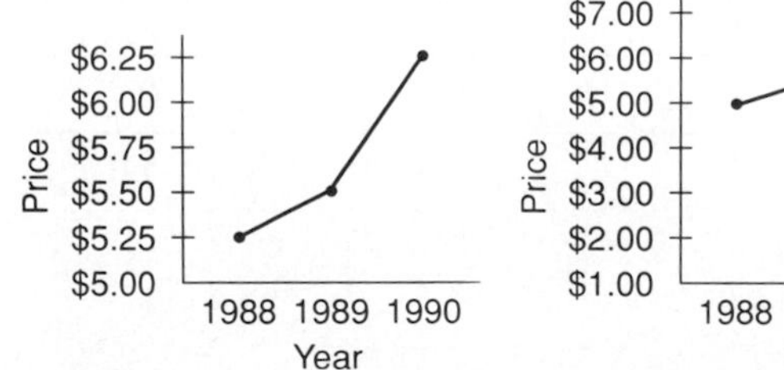

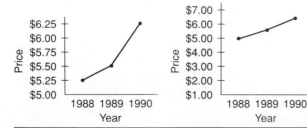

Remember, the steepness of the line in a broken-line graph does not necessarily indicate a rapid rise or fall.

Year	1986	1987	1988	1989
Number of teachers	435	441	444	450

1. Draw two graphs, one showing the number of teachers increasing rapidly, the other staying the same.

More Practice

Set A pages 380–383

Find the mean, median, and mode for each set of data.

1. 17, 9, 11, 15, 10, 16, 17, 12, 14, 9, 17, 13, 12, 11

2. 198, 190, 185, 200, 192, 188, 186, 180, 181, 200, 199, 193, 182, 180, 183, 181

Set B pages 384–387

Sensors placed by a traffic engineer showed the following number of cars passed through the intersection of Grove and Elm during 20 three-minute intervals.

0	3	2	7	1	2	2	4	0	3
5	1	1	2	4	2	6	7	8	7

1. Make a frequency table for the data.

2. Plot the data on a line plot.

Set C pages 390–391

City	High	Low	City	High	Low
Atlanta	85	60	Miami	88	76
Bismarck	70	39	Nashville	85	56
Boston	74	51	New Orleans	80	70
Cleveland	76	50	New York	73	55
Dallas	89	64	Philadelphia	78	54
Denver	83	50	Portland, OR	62	46
Detroit	72	50	San Francisco	67	50
Houston	91	58	Seattle	58	45
Kansas City	84	58	St. Louis	83	59
Los Angeles	75	59	Washington, D.C.	78	55

The high and low temperatures for an October day in 20 U.S. cities are shown at the left.

1. Make a stem-and-leaf plot for the high temperatures.

2. Make a stem-and-leaf plot for the low temperatures.

Set D pages 394–395

Monthly Utility Costs

Month	Utility	Cost
Sept.	Gas Electric	\$15 \$60
Jan.	Gas Electric	\$75 \$70
April	Gas Electric	\$30 \$58

Number of Times Someone in Your Family Made a Trip to the Grocery Store in the Last Week

Days	Tally	Frequency
0	||	2
1	~~||||~~ ~~||||~~ ~~||||~~ ||	17
2	~~||||~~ ~~||||~~ ||||	14
3	~~||||~~ |||	8
4	~~||||~~	5
5	||||	4
6	||	2
7	|	1

1. For the set of data that would best be shown in a double-bar graph, make a double-bar graph.

2. For the set of data that would best be shown in a histogram, make a histogram.

Set E pages 396–397

The circle graph shows the breakdown of the costs to manufacture a personal computer.

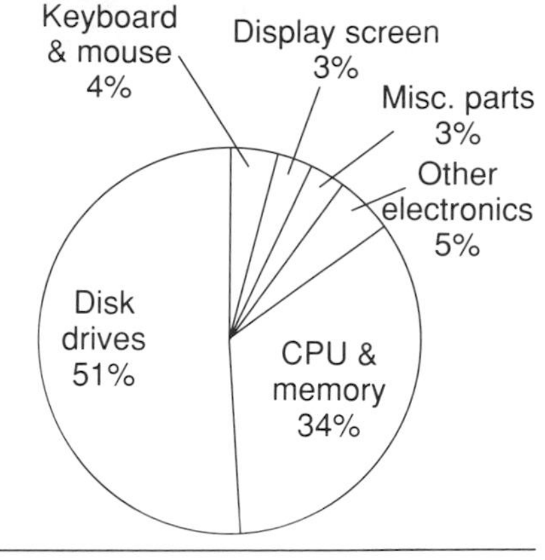

If the total cost to manufacture the computer is approximately $590, about how much is spent on each part?

1. Keyboard & mouse
2. CPU
3. Disk drives
4. Display screen
5. Other electronics
6. Miscellaneous parts

Set F pages 398–399

Using the broken-line graph at the right, find the attendance in

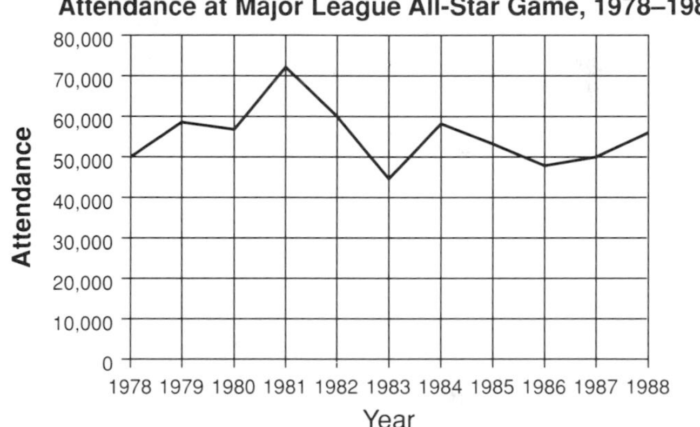

1. 1978.
2. 1982.
3. 1987.
4. 1988.
5. In what year was attendance the lowest?
6. In what year was attendance the highest?

Set G pages 402–403

Tell whether the headline above each graph is accurate or misleading.

1. October Sales of *Greater Bridgeton* Magazine Soar!

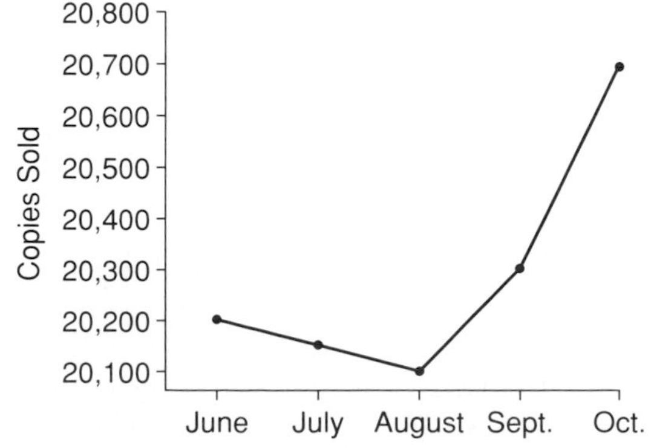

2. More than ever, people prefer Brackers over Plaza brand crackers!

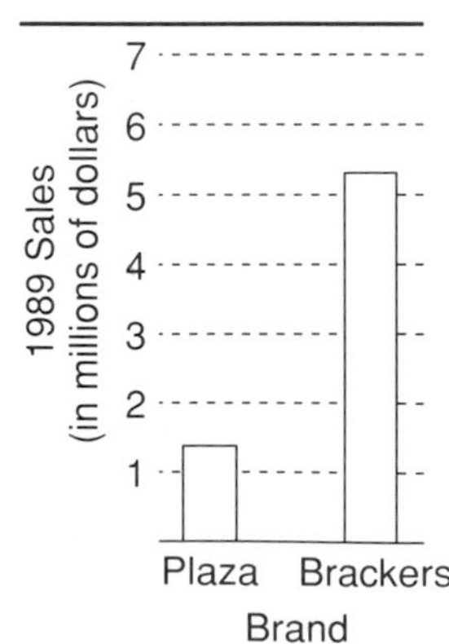

Enrichment

Box-and-Whisker Plots

A ***box-and-whisker plot*** is a way of displaying data to show the median values of a set of scores. The plot below shows the winning times for men's Olympic 100-meter dash from 1896 to 1988.

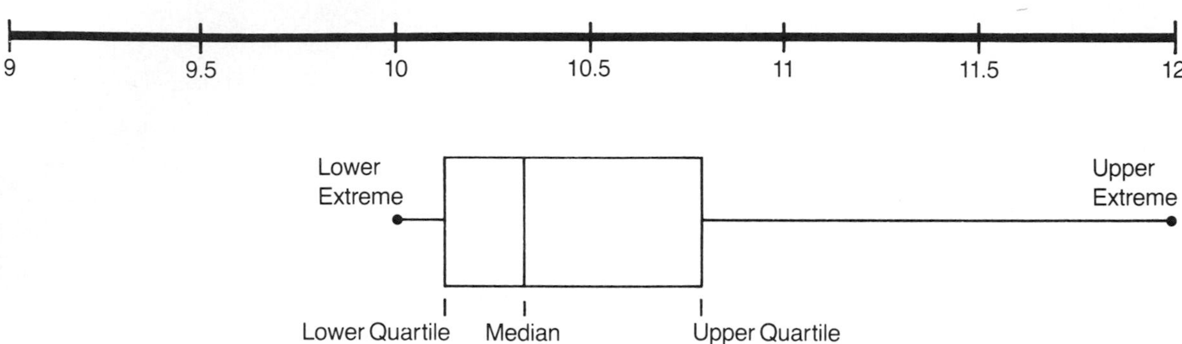

The ***lower quartile***, 10.14, is the median of the lower half of the set of winning times when the times are put in increasing order. The ***upper quartile***, 10.8, is the median of the upper half of the winning times. A box is drawn between the upper and lower quartiles. The median, 10.3, is marked by a vertical line across the box. The ***extremes***, 12 and 9.92, are the highest and lowest winning times. Lines, called ***whiskers***, are drawn from the box to both extremes.

The following scores show how 30 students rated their football team, using a scale from 0 to 100.

38, 46, 71, 42, 67, 55, 62, 33, 68, 76, 66, 54, 82, 73, 47,
39, 58, 78, 55, 85, 80, 70, 32, 65, 44, 57, 70, 38, 69, 51

1. Place the scores in order from least to greatest.
2. Find the median rating.
3. Find the lower and upper quartiles.
4. Find the lower extreme and the upper extreme.
5. Draw a number line. Mark points along it for each of the scores.
6. Draw a box between the upper and lower quartiles.
7. Draw whiskers from the upper and lower quartiles to the extremes.
8. Describe how the students rated the football team.

Chapter 11 Review/Test

1. Park rangers captured and tagged 150 deer. Later, they recaptured 50 deer and found that 30 were tagged. Estimate the park's deer population.

9 10 12 29 20 33 27 14
8 17 8 31 25 21 25

For the set of data above,

2. make a frequency table. Begin with interval 1–5.

3. make a line plot, using the same intervals.

4. make a stem-and-leaf plot.

5. find the mean.

6. find the median.

7. find the mode.

8. A truck manufacturer made 185,000 X-600 pick-up trucks last year. Use the circle graph to tell how many X-600s were silver.

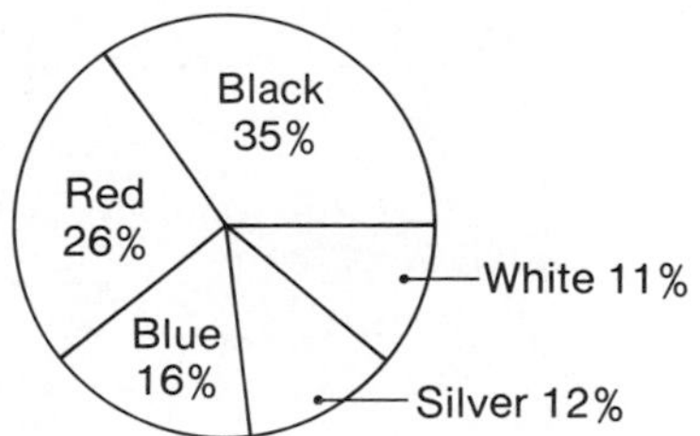

9. Tell whether the following headline and graph are accurate or misleading. Explain your answer.

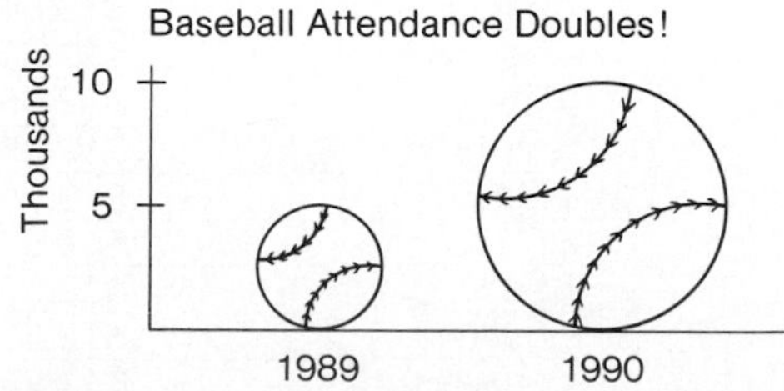

10. Tell which is the appropriate *first step* in making a circle graph.

a. Calculate the measure of the central angle for each category.
b. Change each value to a percent.
c. Measure the angles with a protractor.

Use the double broken-line graph for Item 11.

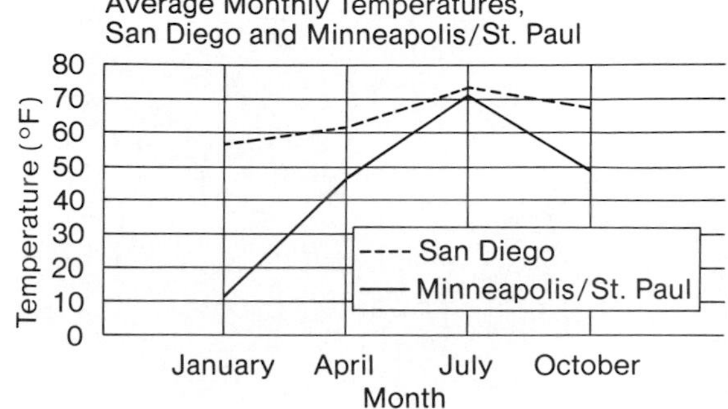

11. For which city is the range of temperatures greater?

12. Make a double broken-line graph to show the number of student absences during two weeks: Week 1–26, 18, 9, 20, 35; Week 2–13, 9, 18, 10, 35.

Days Absent	0–4	5–9	10–14	15–19	20–24
Girls	5	12	19	12	2
Boys	7	15	18	11	0

For the set of data above,

13. make a histogram showing the absences of all students.

14. make a double bar graph comparing absences of girls and boys.

15. **Write About Math** Explain why a circle graph best displays the data given in Item 8.

Data File

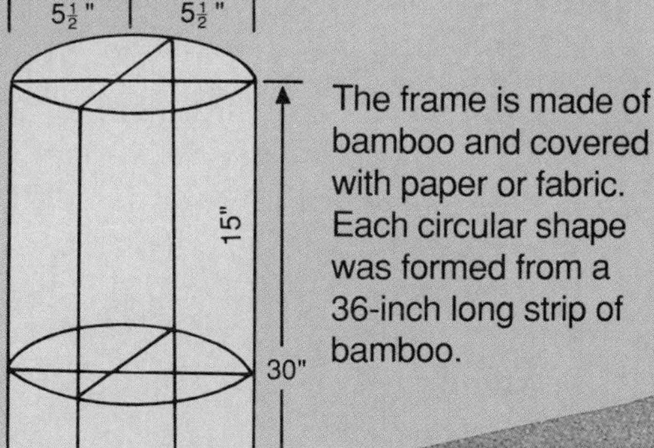

The frame is made of bamboo and covered with paper or fabric. Each circular shape was formed from a 36-inch long strip of bamboo.

1. Construction Instruction

1. Diagram
The diagram shows a lantern kite, a traditional Chinese kite.

2. Table
The table shows the average cost for a ticket, parking, and food at major-league baseball parks.

3. Chart
The chart gives the regular and the sale prices for cookware

4. Scale Drawing
The furniture cutouts can be used to determine furniture arrangement.

5. Graph
The graph shows the color of sneakers purchased by 1,000 people.

2. Table

Fan's costs for baseball	
Chicago (NL)	$22.00
Toronto	$18.12
Boston	$17.25
New York (NL)	$17.10
New York (AL)	$16.75
Detroit	$15.65
Chicago (AL)	$15.50
Philadelphia	$14.50
Oakland	$14.25
California	$13.75
Pittsburgh	$13.75
Seattle	$13.75
Cleveland	$13.60
Minnesota	$13.35
Baltimore	$13.25
Montreal	$13.12
Atlanta	$13.00
Los Angeles	$13.00
Milwaukee	$12.85
San Francisco	$12.85
Texas	$12.75
St. Louis	$12.65
San Diego	$12.50
Houston	$12.25
Kansas City	$11.90
Cincinnati	$11.75

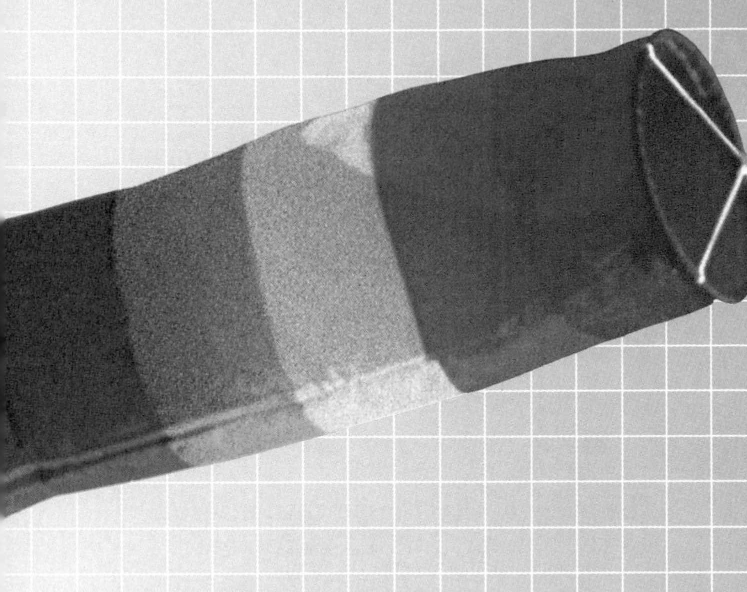

4. Scale Drawing

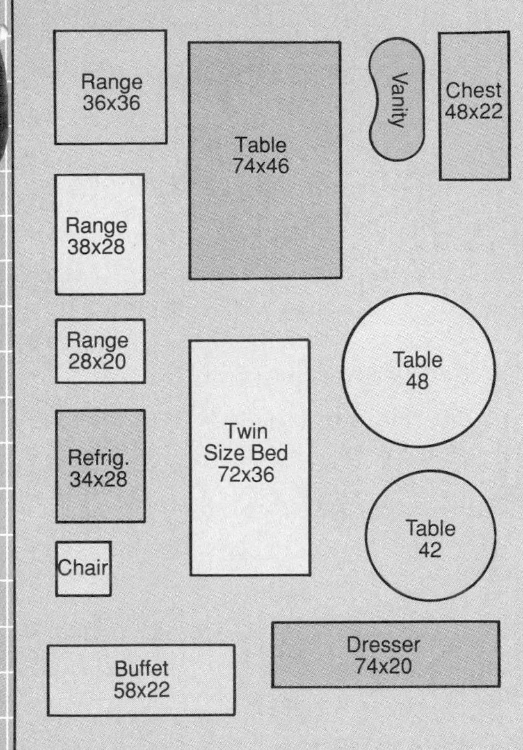

3. Sale Prices

25% to 50% off Cookware
Porcelain/enamel exterior with scratch-resistant non-stick interior. Saucepans have stainless lids with steam vents.

	Reg.	**Sale**
1-qt. saucepan	23.99	**11.99**
2-qt. saucepan	29.99	**22.49**
3-qt. saucepan	32.99	**24.49**
8-qt. stockpot	52.99	**38.99**
7-in. frying pan	12.99	**6.49**
8-in frying pan	16.99	**11.99**
10-in. frying pan	23.99	**17.99**
11-in. frying pan	27.99	**20.99**
Wok frying pan	43.99	**32.99**
Chicken frying pan	46.99	**34.99**
Teakettle	34.99	**25.99**

5. Graph

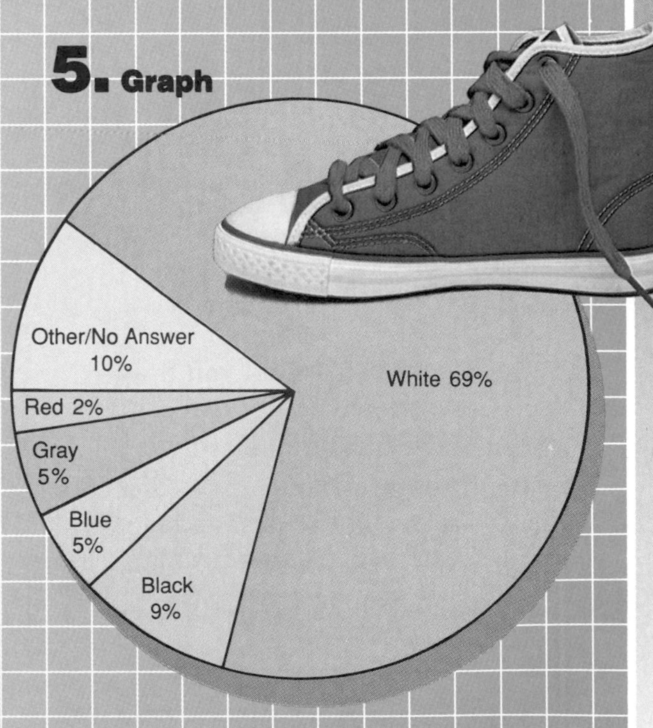

Cumulative Review/Test Chapters 1–11

Choose the letter for the correct answer.

1. Which operation would you use to solve the problem?

How much longer is a distance of 492 miles than a distance of 379 miles?

a. addition **b.** multiplication
c. subtraction **d.** division

2. Which is an expression for the product of $\frac{1}{2}$ of the base b and the height h?

a. $\frac{1}{2} + b + h$ **b.** $b - h - \frac{1}{2}$
c. $\frac{1}{2}bh$ **d.** $\frac{bh}{\frac{1}{2}}$

3. In $\triangle ABC$, $\angle A$ measures 43° and $\angle B$ measures 29°. What is the measure of $\angle C$?

a. 18° **b.** 47° **c.** 72° **d.** 108°

4. Which is the least common multiple of 24 and 18?

a. 6 **b.** 36 **c.** 72 **d.** 432

5. Shana can stack all her quarters in piles of 2, 3, 4, 5, 6, 10, and 12 with none left over. What is the least amount that she could have?

a. \$6 **b.** \$12.50
c. \$15 **d.** \$60

6. Which equation would you use to solve the problem?
A butterfly's antennae are $\frac{3}{4}$ inch long. The entire butterfly is 2 inches long, including the antennae. How long is the body of the butterfly?

a. $b + 2 = \frac{3}{4}$ **b.** $b + \frac{3}{4} = 2$
c. $b - 2 = \frac{3}{4}$ **d.** $b - \frac{3}{4} = 2$

7. Divide.

$38\overline{)3.04}$

a. 0.08
b. 0.82
c. 9.19
d. not given

8. Find the missing number in 3.8 kg = ▦ g.

a. 0.0038 **b.** 380
c. 38 **d.** 3,800

9. The area of a rectangle with sides of 3.7 centimeters and 2.1 centimeters is

a. 3.885 cm^2. **b.** 11.6 cm^2.
c. 7.77 cm^2. **d.** not given.

10. Subtract mentally to find 365 − 198.

a. 63 **b.** 167 **c.** 263 **d.** 267

11. Which are vertical angles?

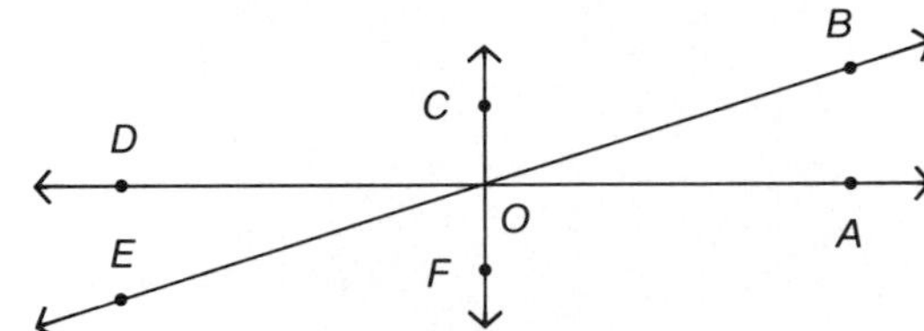

a. $\angle AOB$, $\angle BOD$
b. $\angle AOB$, $\angle BOC$
c. $\angle AOF$, $\angle FOD$
d. $\angle BOC$, $\angle FOE$

12. What is 75% of 60?

a. 45 **b.** 80
c. 125 **d.** not given

13. 40 is 80% of what number?

a. 20 **b.** 32
c. 50 **d.** not given

14. 350 is what percent of 250?

a. 71% **b.** 140%
c. 875% **d.** not given

Choose the proportion you could use to solve the problems in Items 15–17.

15. Kevin is mixing concrete. He uses 5 cups of water for each bag of mix. For a quarter bag of mix, how much water should he use?

a. $\frac{1}{5} = \frac{w}{0.25}$ **b.** $\frac{1}{0.25} = \frac{w}{5}$
c. $\frac{1}{w} = \frac{5}{0.25}$ **d.** $\frac{1}{5} = \frac{0.25}{w}$

16. What percent is 15 of 105?

a. $\frac{15}{105} = \frac{x}{100}$ **b.** $\frac{15}{100} = \frac{x}{105}$
c. $\frac{100}{105} = \frac{15}{x}$ **d.** $\frac{100}{15} = \frac{x}{105}$

17. Triangles *ABC* and *NPQ* are similar. Find the length of $\overline{NP}$.

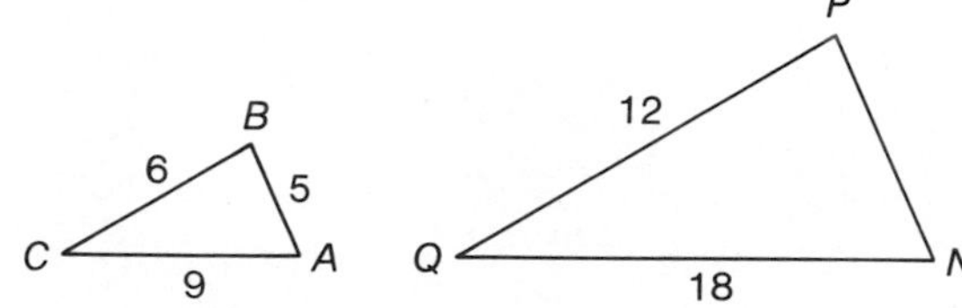

a. $\frac{12}{18} = \frac{x}{9}$ **b.** $\frac{12}{5} = \frac{x}{6}$
c. $\frac{6}{5} = \frac{12}{x}$ **d.** $\frac{9}{18} = \frac{6}{x}$

18. In Item 17, find the length of $\overline{NP}$.

a. 2 **b.** 4 **c.** 8 **d.** not given

19. Which expression means 3.5 less than *x*?

a. $3.5 - x$ **b.** $3.5 + x$
c. $x - 3.5$ **d.** $x + 3.5$

20. Use the formula $a = 5b - 2$ to find a when $b = 7$.

a. 5 **b.** 10 **c.** 21 **d.** 33

21. What is the perimeter of a rectangle with sides of 8 feet and 12 feet?

a. 20 ft **b.** 40 ft
c. 96 ft **d.** not given

22. John's cat spends 12 hours each day sleeping, 3 hours hunting, 1 hour eating, 4 hours playing, and 4 hours wandering around. In a circle graph, what central angle should be used for the time spent hunting?

a. 3° **b.** 12.5°
c. 45° **d.** not given

23. What is the greatest possible error in a measurement of $27\frac{1}{8}$ inches?

a. 1 in. **b.** $\frac{1}{8}$ in.
c. $\frac{1}{4}$ in. **d.** $\frac{1}{16}$ in.

24. Which pair of ratios forms a proportion?

a. $\frac{4}{9} \stackrel{?}{=} \frac{27}{12}$ **b.** $\frac{4}{27} \stackrel{?}{=} \frac{9}{12}$
c. $\frac{4}{9} \stackrel{?}{=} \frac{12}{27}$ **d.** $\frac{12}{9} \stackrel{?}{=} \frac{4}{27}$

25. What is the volume of a square pyramid with a base that is 10 meters on a side and a height of 15 meters?

a. 50 m^3 **b.** 500 m^3
c. 150 m^3 **d.** 1,500 m^3

26. For the set of data 3, 5, 6, 7, 10, the number 6 is the

a. mean. **b.** median.
c. mode. **d.** range.

27. A machine that makes light bulbs produces 250 bulbs each hour, or 2,000 in an 8-hour shift. If an inspector tests 100 bulbs during the shift and finds that 20 of them are defective, about how many defective bulbs did the machine make that shift?

a. 20 **b.** 200 **c.** 400 **d.** 1,980

Probability 12

Did You Know: The most frequently sung songs in English are "Happy Birthday," "For He's a Jolly Good Fellow," and "Auld Lang Syne." The first six notes of "Happy Birthday" are sol, sol, la, sol, do, ti.

Number-Sense Project

Estimate

Guess how many "tunes" you can write using the seven notes do, re, mi, fa, sol, la, ti. A note can be repeated one or more times.

Gather Data

Use the seven notes. Write all the possible one-note "tunes." Then write all the possible two-note "tunes" by adding a second note to each one-note "tune."

Analyze and Report

As the number of notes increases by 1, how does the number of possible "tunes" you can write increase? How many three-note "tunes" can you write? how many seven-note "tunes?"

Experimental Probability

Build Understanding

A. A Pile of Money
Materials: Play money in different denominations
Groups: Small groups of two or more students

a. Make a frequency table like the one shown.

Value	Tally	Frequency
$1		
$5		
$10		
$20		

b. Draw one bill from the pile. What is the value of the bill? Tally the outcome in the table. Then put the bill back in the pile.

c. Repeat step b of this experiment 50 times.

d. How many times did you draw a $1 bill? Count your tallies and write the number in the frequency column of the table. Complete the frequency column for $5, $10, and $20 bills.

e. Use your frequency table to estimate the ***experimental probability***, or chances of drawing a $1 bill from the stack.

Use this formula to estimate an experimental probability.

$$\text{Probability of an event} = \frac{\text{Number of successes}}{\text{Number of trials}}$$

For your experiment, the number of ***trials*** is 50, which is the number of times you drew a bill from the stack. The number of ***successes*** is the frequency with which you drew a $1 bill from the stack.

The probability of the event occurring, that is the probability of drawing a $1 bill, is written $P(\$1)$.

$$P(\$1) = \frac{\blacksquare}{50}$$

Write the experimental probability of drawing a $1 bill as a fraction in lowest terms.

B. The table gives the outcomes of Mike Smith's last 100 plate appearances. What is the probability that he will get a double his next plate appearance?

Use the table to find the number of times Mike Smith hit a double during his 100 plate appearances.

$P(\text{double}) = P(D) = \frac{7}{100}$, or 0.07

You can also write the probability as a percent. The probability that Mike will hit a double on his next plate appearance is 7%.

TIGERS

Mike Smith • Catcher

TOTALS

Home runs	4
Triples	0
Doubles	7
Singles	19
Walks	8
Sacrifices	2
Outs	60
Total	100

C. Is Mike certain, unlikely, or likely to get an out on his next plate appearance? a home run?

Certain events are events that will always occur. They are given a probability of 1 or 100%. ***Impossible events*** will never occur; they are given a probability of 0 or 0%. The probability that an event will happen is 0, 1, or between 0 and 1.

Because he made an out (*O*) 60 times out of his last 100 plate appearances, it is ***likely*** that Mark will make an out $\left(\frac{60}{100} = 0.60 = 60\%\right)$. It is ***unlikely*** that he will hit a home run (*H*) $\left(\frac{4}{100} = 0.04 = 4\%\right)$.

The probability scale below shows how close the probability of an event is to 0 (impossible) or 1 (certain).

Impossible — H — O — Certain

0 0.25 0.50 0.75 1

■ **Talk About Math** What event might be considered the least likely for Mike? Explain.

Check Understanding

For another example, see Set A, pages 444–445.

The table shows the number of T-shirts of each color given away in the first 2 minutes after the gates opened on Tigers T-Shirt Night.

Color	Tally	Frequency
Red	𝍸 𝍸 |||| 𝍸 𝍸	
Blue	𝍸 𝍸 𝍸 𝍸 𝍸 |||	
Green	𝍸 𝍸 𝍸 𝍸 𝍸 ||||	

1. What is the frequency for a green shirt?

2. What is the number of trials?

3. What does *P*(green) mean?

4. Find the probability that a green shirt will be given away.

Practice

For More Practice, see Set A, pages 446–447.

Draw a probability scale like the one in Example C. Then use the table in Example B to show Mike Smith's chances of making the following plays on his next plate appearance. On the scale write the letter corresponding to each play.

5. A sacrifice (*C*) **6.** A walk (*W*) **7.** A triple (*T*) **8.** A single (*S*)

Refer to the table in Example B. Tell whether you would use paper and pencil, mental math, or a calculator to estimate the probability that on his next plate appearance Mike Smith will

9. get a walk or a sacrifice.

10. not get a hit.

11. get a double or a triple.

12. get a sacrifice or a walk.

13. get a walk or a single.

14. get a hit.

The table at the right gives the outcomes of Mark Wade's last 200 plate appearances. What is the probability that on his next plate appearance Mark will

15. get a double?

16. get an out?

17. get a triple?

18. get a walk?

19. get a single?

20. get a sacrifice?

21. get a home run?

22. get a walk or hit?

23. get a home run, double, or triple?

24. get a walk, hit, out, or sacrifice?

TOTALS	
Home runs	6
Triples	2
Doubles	9
Singles	20
Walks	10
Sacrifices	5
Outs	148
Total	200

Use the frequency table from Exercises 1–4 to find the probability that the next person would get a T-shirt of the color indicated. **Remember** to write your answer as a fraction in lowest terms.

25. Blue **26.** Red **27.** Red or Blue

28. Draw a probability scale for the events in Exercises 25–27.

Number Sense Write your answers to Exercises 25–27 as

29. decimals. **30.** percents.

Problem Solving

Refer to the table in Example B.

31. **Calculator** This formula shows how to calculate a baseball player's average.

$$\text{Batting average} = \frac{\text{Number of hits}}{\text{Number of times at bat}}$$

What is Mike Smith's batting average if walks and sacrifices are not counted in the times at bat? Round your answer to the nearest thousandth.

Greg Sekula keeps track of his batting records against right-handed and left-handed pitchers. He compiled this data in a table.

Find the probability that Greg will do the following on his next time at bat.

	Right-handed pitchers	Left-handed pitchers
Hits	35	10
Outs	65	40
Total	100	50

32. get a hit against a left-handed pitcher

33. not get a hit against a left-handed pitcher

34. **Estimation** If he gets a hit, estimate the probability that it will be against a right-handed pitcher.

ALGEBRA ▶ **35.** If the experimental probability of an event is $\frac{x}{y}$, how are x and y related?

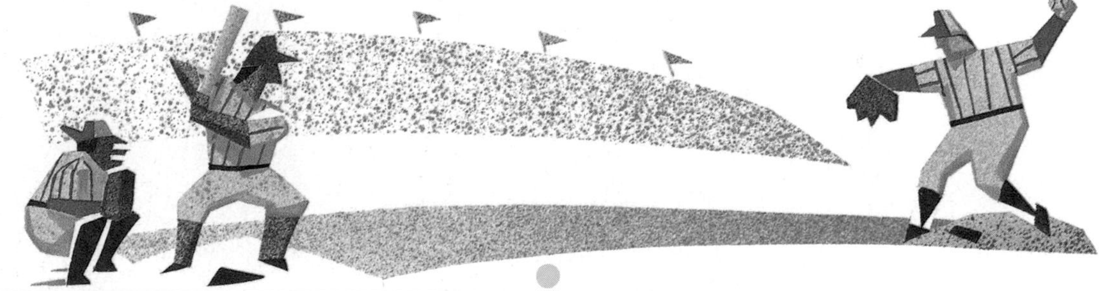

Reading ______ Math

Symbols In a coin-tossing experiment, the symbol P(tail, head) means the probability of getting a tail and then a head in this order. Write the phrase represented by the symbols.

1. P(head)

2. P(head, tail)

3. P(tail, head)

4. P(head, head)

5. P(tail, tail)

6. P(tail, head, tail)

Collecting Data

Understand
QUESTION
FACTS
KEY IDEA

Plan and Solve
STRATEGY
ANSWER

Look Back
SENSIBLE ANSWER
ALTERNATE APPROACH

Build Understanding

The Star Tire Company wants to find out how long each of its 250,000 Van Winkle tires will last. If the company tests all the tires, it will not have any left to sell. So Star will test a ***sample***, a small number of tires, to find how many will last less than 20,000 miles.

Understand QUESTION How many of the tires will last less than 20,000 miles?

FACT Test results for 500 tires are available.

KEY IDEA The data from the sample group of 500 tires can be used to estimate results for 250,000 tires.

Plan and Solve STRATEGY Use the test data in the table to find the probability that a tire will last less than 20,000 miles. Five tires wore out before 15,000 miles and 10 wore out between 15,000 and 19,999 miles.

P(less than 20,000 miles) =

$$\frac{5 + 10}{500} = \frac{15}{500} = \frac{3}{100}$$

Of the tires tested, $\frac{3}{100}$ did not last 20,000 miles. If 3 out of 100 tires probably will not last, how many of the 250,000 tires produced will not last? Write and solve a proportion.

$$\frac{3}{100} = \frac{n}{250{,}000}$$

$$3 \times 250{,}000 = 100 \times n$$

$$750{,}000 = 100n$$

$$\frac{750{,}000}{100} = \frac{100n}{100}$$

$$7{,}500 = n$$

Test Results for 500 Van Winkle Tires	
Mileage until worn out	Number of tires
10,000–14,999	5
15,000–19,999	10
20,000–24,999	42
25,000–29,999	107
30,000–34,999	218
35,000–39,999	95
40,000 or more	23

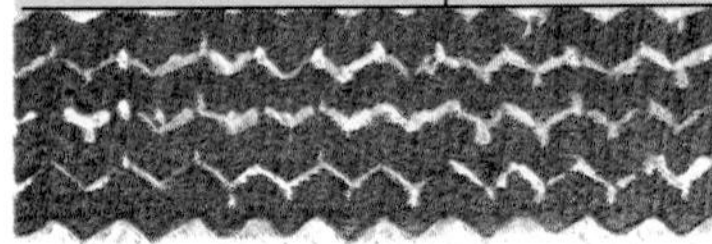

The pneumatic tire was invented in 1845. It was not perfected and in general use until 1895, 50 years later!

ANSWER The company should expect that 7,500 tires will not last 20,000 miles.

Look Back ALTERNATE APPROACH Use a calculator. Write *P*(less than 20,000 miles) as a decimal. Then multiply it by the 250,000 tires produced.

$P(\text{less than 20,000 miles}) = \frac{3}{100} = 0.03$

$0.03 \times 250{,}000 = 7{,}500$

■ **Talk About Math** Do you think exactly 7,500 of the 250,000 tires will last less than 20,000 miles? Explain.

Check Understanding

How many of the 250,000 tires produced will last 30,000–39,999 miles? Refer to the table on page 424.

1. List the facts you need from the table.

2. Fill in the missing numbers of this proportion. $\frac{\square + \square}{500} = \frac{n}{\square}$

3. Solve the proportion in Exercise 2 to find how many of the 250,000 tires produced will last 30,000–39,999 miles.

4. **Calculator** Do you get the same answer when you solve the problem using decimals and a calculator?

Practice

Star Tire Company sent out 800 questionnaires to see whether the 375,000 people who bought the company's products last year are satisfied with them. The table shows the data collected from the 640 questionnaires returned to Star. Use the data in the table to predict the total number of Star customers in each category.

Star Tire Questionnaire Results

Response	Number
Completely satisfied	347
Satisfied	198
Somewhat dissatisfied	28
Dissatisfied	56
Will never buy Star product again	11

5. Completely satisfied

6. Satisfied

7. Somewhat dissatisfied

8. Will never buy Star product again

9. Less than satisfied

10. Dissatisfied

11. **Critical Thinking** What percent of the questionnaires that were sent out were returned to Star?

12. **Critical Thinking** What type of graph would you make to show the data in the table on page 424? Explain. Then, draw the graph.

Theoretical Probability

Build Understanding

A. A Lovely Complement
Materials: 10 index cards
Groups: Small groups of 2–3 students

a. Write each letter of the word *statistics* on one of the ten cards. Copy the frequency table at the right.

Letter	Tally
Consonant	
Vowel	

b. Shuffle the cards and spread them face down on a desk. Draw one card. Is the letter a consonant or a vowel? Tally the result in the frequency table. Replace the card and reshuffle.

When a card is replaced before the next draw, the experiment is *with replacement.* If you did not replace the card, it is *without replacement.*

c. Repeat step b 50 times. Tally the results. What is the experimental probability of drawing a consonant? What is the experimental probability of drawing a vowel?

d. The ***theoretical probability*** tells you what *should* happen in an experiment.

$$\text{Theoretical Probability} = \frac{\text{Number of favorable outcomes}}{\text{Number of equally likely outcomes}}$$

The theoretical probability of drawing a vowel is $\frac{3}{10}$, or 0.3. Is this close to the frequency with which you drew a vowel in the experiment? Find the theoretical probability of drawing a consonant.

e. Add the theoretical probability of drawing a vowel to the theoretical probability of drawing a consonant. What number do you get? Drawing a vowel and drawing a consonant are ***complementary events*** because one or the other event always occurs. The probabilities of complementary events add up to 1.

$P(\text{consonant}) + P(\text{vowel}) = 0.7 + 0.3 = 1$

B. What is the theoretical probability of getting a sum that is divisible by 3 if you toss 2 number cubes?

First find all possible outcomes. The list of possible outcomes, or ***sample space***, for rolling 2 number cubes may be presented in a chart.

	1	2	3	4	5	6
1	2	3	4	5	6	7
2	3	4	5	6	7	8
3	4	5	6	7	8	9
4	5	6	7	8	9	10
5	6	7	8	9	10	11
6	7	8	9	10	11	12

There are 36 equally likely outcomes. Of those outcomes, 12 are divisible by 3.

$P(\text{sum divisible by 3}) = \frac{12}{36} = \frac{1}{3}$

Talk About Math In Example A, is your theoretical probability the same as your experimental probability? Explain any differences.

Check Understanding

For another example, see Set B, pages 444–445.

Mental Math Find the theoretical probability of drawing the following letters from the word *statistics*.

1. $P(\text{S})$ **2.** $P(\text{T})$ **3.** $P(\text{C})$ **4.** $P(\text{Y})$ **5.** $P(\text{S or T})$

Practice

For More Practice, see Set B, pages 446–447.

For Exercises 6–8, tell whether you would use mental math or paper and pencil. Then use the information in Example B to find the theoretical probability.

6. $P(\text{sum is 7})$ **7.** $P(\text{sum not 7})$ **8.** $P(\text{sum is 2 or 12})$

A number is selected from numbers 1 through 20. Find the probability for each event and the complementary event.

9. $P(\text{prime})$ **10.** $P(\text{multiple of 5})$ **11.** $P(\text{multiple of 3})$

12. $P(\text{odd})$ **13.** $P(\text{multiple of 10})$ **14.** $P(\text{multiple of 4})$

15. Answer Exercises 9–14 using the set of factors for 36.

Find the theoretical probability of drawing the following letters from the word *probability*.

16. $P(\text{vowel})$ **17.** $P(\text{consonant})$ **18.** $P(\text{B or P})$

Problem Solving

Write a 6-letter word with the given property.

19. $P(\text{vowel}) = \frac{1}{3}$ **20.** $P(\text{vowel}) = \frac{1}{2}$

21. $P(\text{T}) = \frac{1}{3}$ **22.** $P(\text{T}) = \frac{1}{2}$

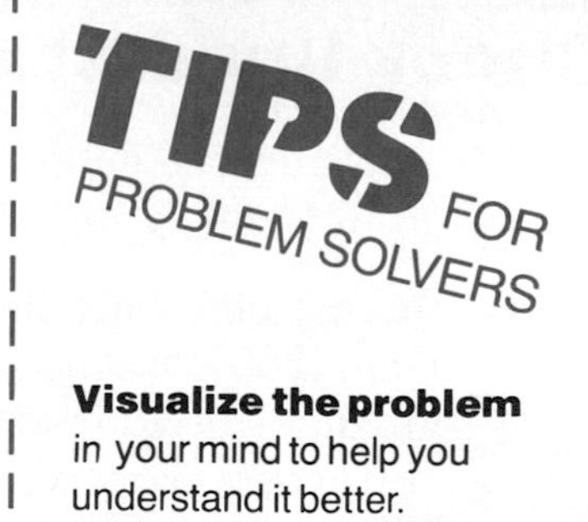
TIPS
PROBLEM SOLVERS FOR
Visualize the problem
in your mind to help you understand it better.

Visual Thinking A 3 × 3 × 3-unit cube is painted green and then cut into 27 identical smaller cubes. These cubes are put into a bag and mixed thoroughly. What is the probability that a cube chosen from the bag has the given number of green faces?

23. 0 **24.** 1 **25.** 2 **26.** 3 **27.** 4

Probability Games

Build Understanding

ACTIVITY

A. Fair Play?
Materials: A spinner divided into thirds labeled with 1, 2, and 3
Groups: With a partner

a. Spin the spinner twice.

b. Multiply the two numbers.

c. You earn a point if the product is even. Your partner earns a point if the product is odd. Tally your score.

d. Play the game 20 times. The winner has the greater number of points.

e. Play the game again and determine who the winner is.

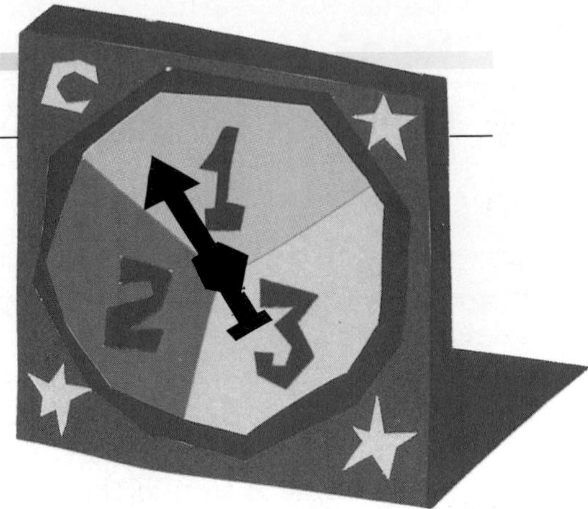

Each year the Parker Brothers Company prints more play money for their Monopoly game than the U.S. Mint prints real money.

B. Is Activity A a fair game?

A game of chance is ***fair*** when either player is equally likely to win. The table at the right shows all possible outcomes (sample space), the products, and the winning player. Even products are more likely than odd products, so the game is not fair.

All possible outcomes	Product	Winning player
1,1	1	partner
1,2	2	you
1,3	3	partner
2,1	2	you
2,2	4	you
2,3	6	you
3,1	3	partner
3,2	6	you
3,3	9	partner

■ **Talk About Math** Is it possible to change the scoring in Activity A to make the game fair? Explain.

Check Understanding

For another example, see Set C, pages 444–445.

Toss two number cubes and find their product. You earn a point if the product is even. Your partner earns a point if the product is odd.

1. Make a chart similar to the one on page 426 showing the possible outcomes of your experiment.

2. What is the theoretical probability of an odd product? an even product?

3. What is the experimental probability of an odd product? an even product?

4. Is this game fair? If not, how might you change the scoring to make it fair?

Practice

For More Practice, see Set C, pages 446–447.

Tell whether a game with these instructions is fair. Spin the spinner twice. If the spinner lands on the same color twice, you get a point. If the spinner lands on different colors, your partner gets a point.

5. 

6. 

7. 

Determine if each game is fair. **Remember** to make a table similar to the one in Example B.

8. Roll two number cubes numbered 1–6. Add the two numbers. You get a point if the sum is even; your partner gets a point if the sum is odd.

9. Roll two number cubes numbered 1–6. Multiply the sum of the two numbers by five. You get a point if the product is even; your partner gets a point if the product is odd.

10. Use the spinner in Exercise 5. Spin the spinner three times. You get a point if the same color is spun all three times; your partner gets a point if the spinner lands on different colors.

11. Use the spinner in Exercise 7. Spin the spinner once. You get a point if the spinner lands on red; your partner gets a point if the spinner lands on blue.

Problem Solving

Critical Thinking Design your own game.

12. A fair game for two players that uses two number cubes

13. An unfair game for two players that uses two number cubes

Midchapter Checkup

Find the theoretical probability of drawing the following letters from the word *mathematics*.

1. P(M) **2.** P(C) **3.** P(E or T) **4.** P(vowel)

5. If Player 1 scores a point whenever the pointer lands on pink, and Player 2 scores a point whenever the pointer lands on blue, is a game using the spinner at the right fair?

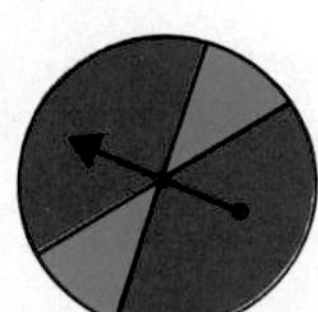

Fundamental Counting Principle

Build Understanding

Students at Canton Junior High will participate in a Community Cultural Festival by presenting a program. Each homeroom will choose from 4 cultures, 3 aspects of that culture, and 2 methods of presentation. How many choices does each homeroom have?

Use the ***fundamental counting principle*** to find the number of choices, or possible outcomes. Multiply the number of choices for each category.

Number of choices for a culture		Number of choices for an aspect		Number of methods of presentation		Number of possible outcomes
4	×	**3**	×	**2**	=	**24**

There are 24 possible outcomes, so each homeroom has 24 choices.

■ **Talk About Math** If the number of choices for each category in the Example were doubled, would the total number of choices also double? Explain your answer.

Check Understanding

For another example, see Set D, pages 444–445.

Refer to the example above for Exercises 1 and 2.

These Hispanic dancers in traditional costume are an important part of this Cinco de Mayo festival.

1. Next year, traditional costumes, such as the Japanese kimono, and arts and crafts will be added to the list of aspects. How many choices will each homeroom have then?

2. In addition to the changes made in Exercise 1, two new methods of presentation may also be added. If so, then how many choices will each homeroom have?

Practice

For More Practice, see Set D, pages 446–447.

Answer each question.

3. Yumiko's homeroom will present a program featuring a Hispanic dance, song, and traditional instrument. They can choose from 6 types of dances, 4 songs, and 5 instruments. How many choices do they have?

4. Yumiko's class chose the marimba, a percussion instrument similar to a xylophone, as the instrument they would present. How many choices do they have for the remaining features?

Nettie's homeroom chose to present the foods of India. She found recipes for 4 types of chutney, a spicy relish; 3 types of masala, a spice mixture; 6 types of aloo, a potato dish; 5 types of paratha, a layered bread; and 8 types of meat kabobs. How many choices does her homeroom have if it decides to prepare one recipe of

5. chutney, aloo, and paratha?

6. masala, kabobs, paratha, and chutney?

7. each type of food?

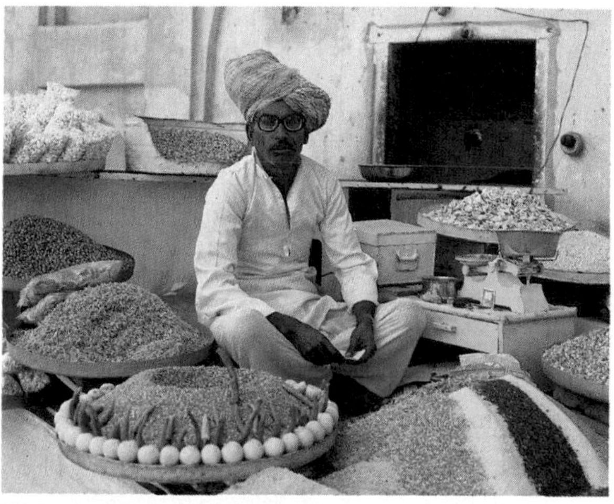

Combinations of spices are an important part of many Indian dishes.

Problem Solving

Solve each problem.

8. A Canadian television station featured the festival on its evening newscast. Sarah found that call letters for television stations in Canada begin with a C and are followed by three more letters. How many different TV station call letters are possible?

9. Three local radio stations are broadcasting live from the festival. Radio station call letters in the U.S. must start with K or W and are 3 or 4 letters long. KYW and WSCR are two radio stations. How many radio station call letters are possible?

Skills Review

pages 308–311

Solve.

1. Find 2.5% of 100.

2. What is 64% of 64?

3. 150% of what number is 105?

Explore as a Team

TIPS FOR WORKING TOGETHER

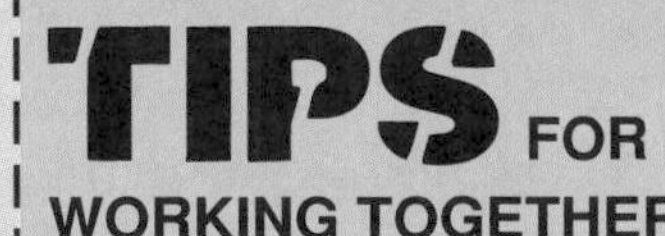

Work as a group. If you understand, help another group member. Don't work ahead of the others.

1. Draw the geometric design shown below. Hold a slightly bent paper clip at least 12 inches above the design. Drop the clip. What color did the tip point to? Do you think it will point to the same color if you drop it again?

2. Predict what will happen if you drop the clip 100 times.

3. Drop the clip 100 times. (Members of the team should take turns dropping it.) Make a chart to show the results.

4. Discuss your findings. What color occurred most often? Least often? What fraction of the outcomes were blue? green? yellow? purple? What would you guess is true of the geometric design?

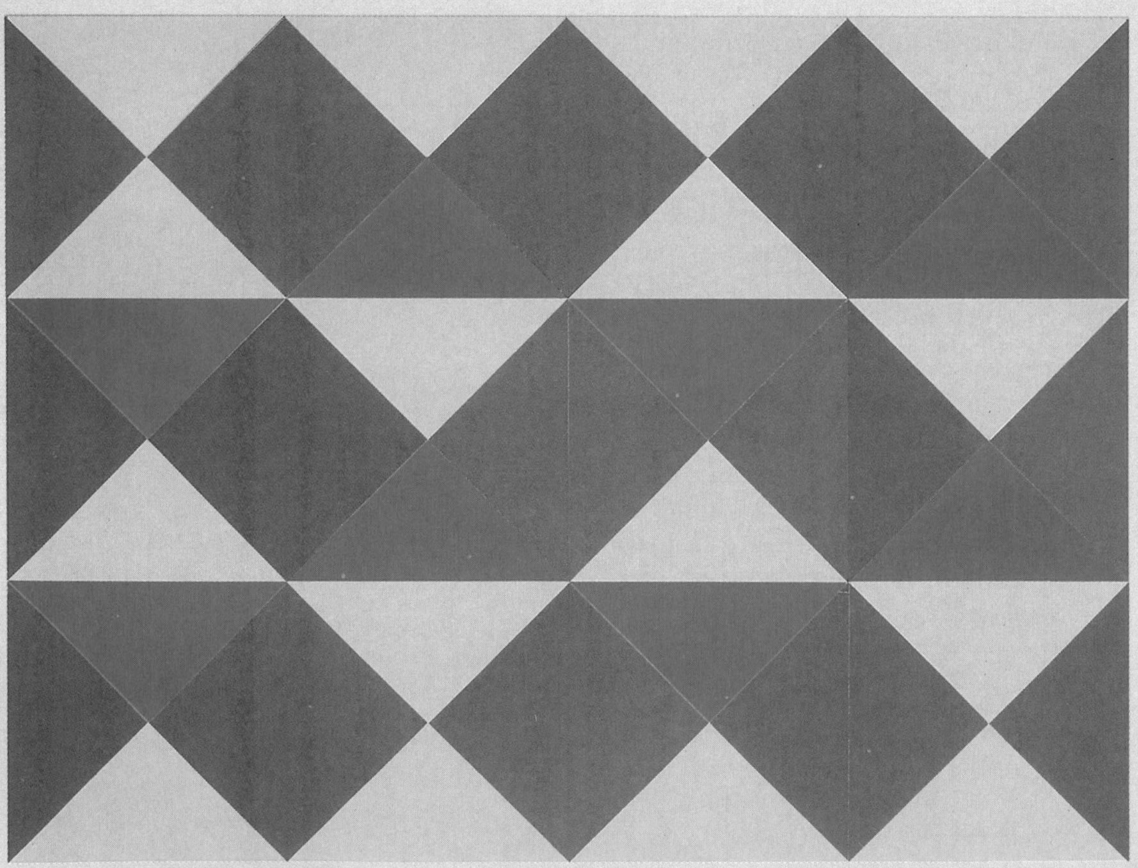

Explore with a Computer

Use the *Graphing and Probability Workshop Project* for this activity.

1. At the computer, make your own spinner. Record on paper the theoretical probability of each outcome.

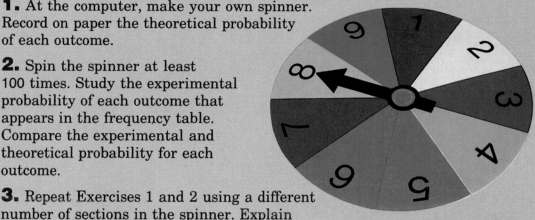

2. Spin the spinner at least 100 times. Study the experimental probability of each outcome that appears in the frequency table. Compare the experimental and theoretical probability for each outcome.

3. Repeat Exercises 1 and 2 using a different number of sections in the spinner. Explain how the fraction for the probability of an outcome is related to the design of the spinner.

Number-Sense Project

Look back at pages 418–419.

1. A full piano keyboard has 52 white keys and 36 black keys. The white keys are divided into 8 octaves, each consisting of the notes A, B, C, D, E, F, and G. If you randomly played any white key what is the probability you would play the following?

a. Middle C **b.** Any C **c.** Any G

Real-Life Decision Making

1. This chart shows how one seventh grader spends the 24 hours in a school day.

a. What fraction of the day does this person spend on each activity?

b. Make a chart to plan *your* school day.

Activity	Number of hours
Sleep	8
Eat	2
School	6
Homework	2
Television	1
Recreation	2
Other	3

Independent Events

Build Understanding

Each day Mr. Jordan chooses a Scientist of the Day in his class. This week he will choose the students from this list: Pablo, Ellen, Ted, Jane, Zack, Bill.

A. Mr. Jordan wrote each name on a slip of paper. To select Monday's Scientist of the Day, he drew one of the slips of paper. What is the probability (P) that he drew a boy's name?

$$P(\text{boy}) = \frac{4}{6} \begin{array}{l} \leftarrow \text{Monday's favorable outcomes} \\ \leftarrow \text{Monday's equally likely outcomes} \end{array}$$

The probability that Mr. Jordan drew a boy is $\frac{4}{6}$, or $\frac{2}{3}$.

B. When he chose Monday's Scientist of the Day, Mr. Jordan replaced the first slip. What is the probability that he selected a boy on Tuesday?

Any of the 6 students on the list could be chosen on both Monday and Tuesday. What happened on Monday does not affect what happens on Tuesday, so the draws are ***independent events***.

With replacement, there are 6 × 6, or 36 possible pairs of names (possible outcomes) that could be selected for Monday and Tuesday, as shown in the table at the right. In 16 of the 36 pairs, both names are boys. The probability of selecting two boys, one on Monday and one on Tuesday, is $\frac{16}{36} = \frac{4}{9}$, or about 44%.

(Pablo, Ellen)	(Ellen, Pablo)
(Pablo, Ted)	(Ellen, Ted)
(Pablo, Jane)	(Ellen, Jane)
(Pablo, Zack)	(Ellen, Zack)
(Pablo, Bill)	(Ellen, Bill)
(Pablo, Pablo)	(Ellen, Ellen)
(Jane, Pablo)	(Zack, Pablo)
(Jane, Ellen)	(Zack, Ellen)
(Jane, Ted)	(Zack, Ted)
(Jane, Zack)	(Zack, Jane)
(Jane, Bill)	(Zack, Bill)
(Jane, Jane)	(Zack, Zack)
(Bill, Pablo)	(Ted, Pablo)
(Bill, Ellen)	(Ted, Ellen)
(Bill, Ted)	(Ted, Jane)
(Bill, Jane)	(Ted, Zack)
(Bill, Zack)	(Ted, Bill)
(Bill, Bill)	(Ted, Ted)

C. Another way of finding the probability of a series of events is to multiply the probability (P) of each event by the probability of the next event.

Monday P(boy)		Tuesday P(boy)		Monday and Tuesday P(boy, boy)
$\frac{4}{6}$	×	$\frac{4}{6}$	=	$\frac{16}{36} = \frac{4}{9}$

The probability of choosing a boy on both days with replacement of the slips is $P(\text{boy, boy}) = \frac{4}{9}$.

■ **Write About Math** In Example C how would you calculate with decimals?

Check Understanding

For another example, see Set E, pages 444–445.

Tell whether the events are independent. Give a reason for your answer.

1. a. Ahmed plays soccer after school.
b. Ahmed goes to a movie on Saturday.

2. a. You can get an A, B, C, D, or F on your next quiz in math.
b. You can pass or fail a music audition.

Practice

For More Practice, see Set E, pages 446–447.

What is the probability that Mr. Jordan will choose the following students on Monday and Tuesday if he replaces the name drawn on Monday?

3. Ted, then Jane
4. Jane, then Ted
5. Two girls
6. A girl, then a boy
7. Ted or Bill, then Pablo
8. Ellen or Jane, then Ted or Zack
9. A boy, then Ellen

Mr. Jordan brought to class a box containing 5 red, 3 yellow, and 2 blue cubes. He asked Pablo to draw a cube, record its color, and put it back in the box. Pablo drew another cube and noted its color. Find each probability.

10. P(R,Y)
11. P(Y,B)
12. P(R,R)
13. P(no red)
14. P(two of same color)

Problem Solving

Mr. Jordan's science class is studying blood types. The table shows the probability that someone living in the United States has a given blood type. What is the probability that two people selected from your class will have the blood type(s) listed in Exercises 15–19?

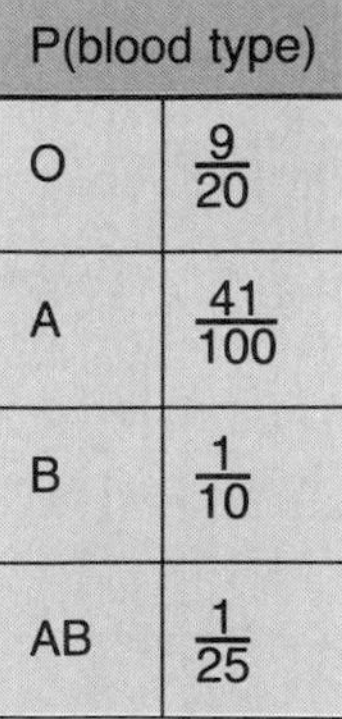

P(blood type)	
O	$\frac{9}{20}$
A	$\frac{41}{100}$
B	$\frac{1}{10}$
AB	$\frac{1}{25}$

15. P(A,A)
16. P(B,B)
17. P(A,O)
18. P(AB,AB)
19. P(A,AB)

Use Data Refer to the table on page 421. Suppose Mike went to bat 4 times in 1 game. Find the probability that he made each of the following plays.

20. P(S,S,S,S)
S means a single

21. 4 outs

22. 2 singles followed by 2 outs

Dependent Events

Build Understanding

A. Audrey manages a video store. The 15 most-popular tapes this week include 7 action, 3 comedies, 2 dramas, 1 family, and 2 instructional.

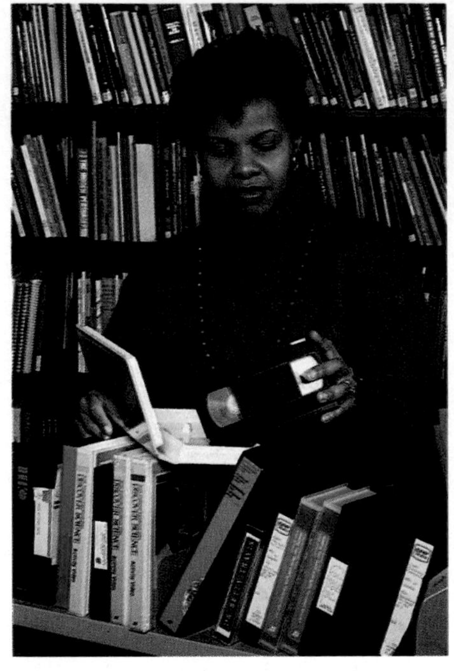

Before placing the tapes on the shelves, she randomly chooses 2 to show at the store. What is the probability that both of them will be comedies? This probability experiment is *without replacement.*

The probability that the first movie is a comedy is $\frac{3}{15}$. If a comedy is chosen, 14 movies remain, of which 2 are comedies. The probability that the second movie is a comedy is $\frac{2}{14}$.

The outcome of the second selection is influenced by the outcome of the first selection. The selections are ***dependent*** events.

To find the probability of a series of events, multiply the probability of each event by the probability of the next event.

Probability first is comedy		Probability second is comedy		Probability both are comedies
$\frac{3}{15}$	$\times$	$\frac{2}{14}$	$=$	$\frac{6}{210} = \frac{1}{35}$

The probability that a comedy will be chosen both times is $\frac{6}{210}$, or $\frac{1}{35}$.

B. If Audrey decides to show 3 movies one day, what is the probability that she will select 1 movie from each of these categories: action, comedy, and instructional, and show them in that order?

Probability first is action		Probability second is comedy		Probability third is instructional	
$\frac{7}{15}$	$\times$	$\frac{3}{14}$	$\times$	$\frac{2}{13}$	$= \frac{7 \times 3 \times 2}{15 \times 14 \times 13} = \frac{42}{2730} = \frac{1}{65}$

The probability that a movie from each category is selected is $\frac{1}{65}$.

Talk About Math

In Example B, if Audrey first showed a comedy, then an action, is the answer still $\frac{1}{65}$? Explain.

Check Understanding

For another example, see Set F, pages 444–445.

Refer to Example A for Exercises 1–2. Find each probability.

1. The first tape is instructional. The second tape is a drama.
2. Both tapes are dramas.

Practice

For More Practice, see Set F, pages 446–447.

A customer randomly selects two tapes from the list of 15 most-rented movies. On the list are 5 action, 4 comedy, 1 classic, 2 drama, 1 family, and 2 instructional. Find each probability.

3. Both tapes are instructional.
4. Both tapes are comedies.
5. The first tape will be a classic and the second will be an action tape.
6. The first tape is an action tape, the second tape is a comedy.
7. The first tape is a comedy and the second tape is a drama.
8. The first tape is a family tape, and the second tape is a comedy.
9. Both tapes are action tapes.
10. Both tapes are dramas.
11. The first tape is a drama, the second tape is an action tape.
12. The first tape is a classic and the second tape is also a classic.

Problem Solving

Refer to Example A for Problems 13–14.

13. On Monday, Audrey selected an instructional film and a drama. What is the probability that she will choose 2 action movies on Tuesday from the tapes that remain?
14. Audrey decided to move 2 of the action movies into the drama category. Recalculate the probability you found in Problem 13.

Choose a ______ Strategy

Go Fish Suppose you get dressed in the dark. You reach into your sock drawer and pull out one sock and then another.

15. Find the different ways that 2 socks can be selected from 2 green socks and 1 red sock.
16. What is the probability that you selected 1 red sock and 1 green sock?
17. Your drawer has 2 red socks, 2 blue socks, and 1 green sock. What is the probability you selected 2 blue socks?

Probability Tree Diagrams

Build Understanding

A. Tina placed a green circle on 4 cards and a blue square on 2 cards. She wondered what the probability would be of drawing a green circle and then a blue square if she replaced the first card before drawing the second card (with replacement).

She found the theoretical probability of this experiment by making a ***probability tree diagram.*** In a tree diagram, each path shows a possible outcome. Each branch of the tree shows the probability of the event.

The probability of drawing a green circle and then a blue square is $\frac{2}{9}$.

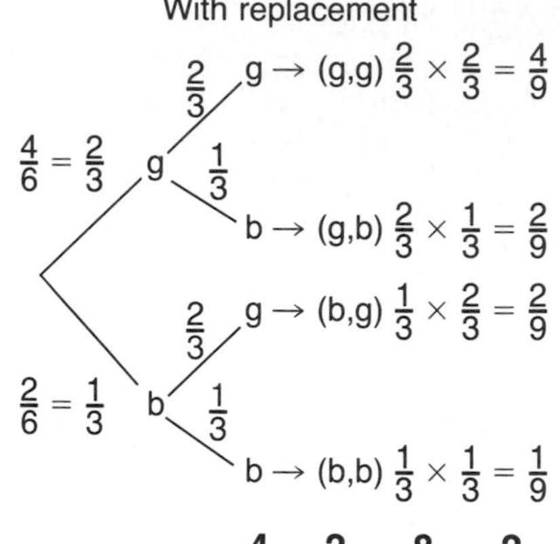

$$P(g,b) = \frac{4}{6} \times \frac{2}{6} = \frac{8}{36} = \frac{2}{9}$$

B. What is the probability of drawing a green circle and then a blue square without replacement?

Since the second draw is made with 5 cards, not 6, the probability for each second draw is different from that with replacement.

The probability of drawing a green circle and then a blue square without replacement is $\frac{4}{15}$.

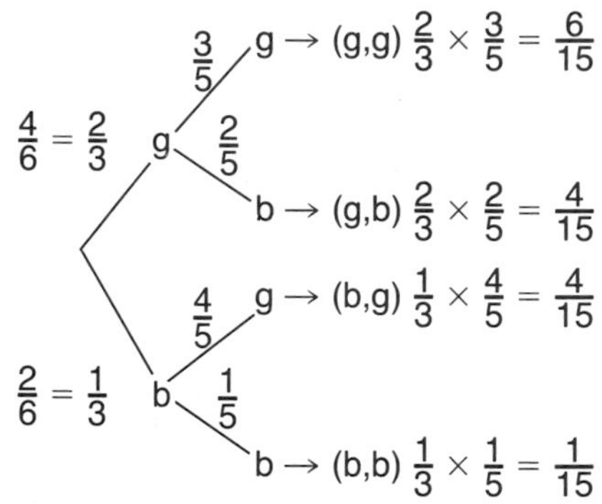

$$P(g,b) = \frac{4}{6} \times \frac{2}{5} = \frac{8}{30} = \frac{4}{15}$$

■ **Talk About Math** Are the experiments in Examples A and B composed of independent or dependent events? How do you know?

Check Understanding

For another example, see Set G, pages 444–445.

A small deck of cards has "1" on 5 cards and "2" on 5 cards. A card is drawn at random. Then, without replacing the first card, a second card is drawn. Make a tree diagram and find the probabilities.

1. $P(1,1) =$ $\frac{5}{10} \times \frac{4}{9} =$ ▦

2. $P(1,2) =$ $\frac{5}{10} \times$ ▦ $=$ ▦

3. $P(2,1) =$ ▦ $\times$ ▦ $=$ ▦

4. $P(2,2) =$ ▦ $\times$ ▦ $=$ ▦

Practice

For More Practice, see Set G, pages 446–447.

A bag contains 5 red marbles, 3 yellow marbles, and 2 blue marbles. One marble is removed from the bag, its color is recorded, and the marble is placed back in the bag. A second marble is removed. Use a probability tree diagram to find each probability.

5. P(R,Y) **6.** P(Y,B) **7.** P(R,R) **8.** P(B,R)

Find the probability of each exercise when the first marble is *not* placed back in the bag.

9. Exercise 5 **10.** Exercise 6 **11.** Exercise 7 **12.** Exercise 8

The cubes shown at the right are placed in a box. A cube is removed from the box, its color is recorded, and the cube is placed back in the box. A second cube is removed. Use a probability tree to find each probability.

13. P(Y,G) **14.** P(G,G)

15. P(G,P) **16.** P(O,O)

Find the probability of each exercise when the first cube is *not* placed back in the bag.

17. Exercise 13 **18.** Exercise 14 **19.** Exercise 15 **20.** Exercise 16

Mixed Practice Find the complement for each exercise.

21. Exercise 5 **22.** Exercise 6 **23.** Exercise 15 **24.** Exercise 16

Problem Solving

Every day Tina Froemel meets Joe Cruz at his house, and they go to the library. There is a $\frac{3}{7}$ chance that Tina will walk to Joe's house and a $\frac{4}{7}$ chance that she will ride her bike. Then she and Joe are equally likely to walk, ride their bikes, or get a ride from Joe's mother. Draw a probability tree to solve Problems 25–27.

25. What is the probability that Tina will walk to Joe's house and then to the library?

26. What is the probability that Tina will walk to Joe's house and then get a ride to the library?

27. **Critical Thinking** How would the probabilities for Problems 25 and 26 change if the chance that Tina would ride her bike to Joe's house were twice as great as the chance that she would walk?

Use Data from a Table

PROBLEM SOLVING GUIDE

Understand
QUESTION
FACTS
KEY IDEA

Plan and Solve
STRATEGY
ANSWER

Look Back
SENSIBLE ANSWER
ALTERNATE APPROACH

Build Understanding

At a football game, a referee tosses a coin to determine which team will kick off first. If a referee tosses a coin in 100 games, how many times will it be heads? tails?

Understand QUESTION Of 100 coin tosses, how many are heads? How many are tails?

FACTS There are 2 possible outcomes for each coin toss: heads and tails.

KEY IDEA It is time-consuming to toss a coin 100 times. The *random number table* below can be used to *simulate*, or imitate, 100 tosses of a coin.

A random number table consists of many strings of digits. Each digit in a string had an equal probability of being selected and was selected randomly. This table allows you to find probabilities without having to toss coins or mix and draw items.

10480	15014	01536	02011
22368	46573	25595	85393
24130	48360	22527	97265
42167	93093	06423	61680
81647	91646	69719	14194
30995	89198	27982	53402
76393	64809	15179	24830
17856	16376	39440	53537
62590	36207	49340	32081
93965	34095	71341	57004

Plan and Solve STRATEGY Use 100 consecutive digits from the table. For this experiment, begin with the numbers in row one. Let even numbers and zero equal heads. Let odd numbers equal tails.

1 0 4 8 0 1 5 0 1 4 0 1 5 3 6 0 2 0 1 1 . . .
↓ ↓ ↓ ↓ ↓ ↓ ↓ ↓ ↓ ↓ ↓ ↓ ↓ ↓ ↓ ↓ ↓ ↓ ↓ ↓
T H H H H T T H T H H T T T H H H H T T

ANSWER There were 52 heads and 48 tails.

Look Back SENSIBLE ANSWER What is the theoretical probability of the outcome heads? $\frac{5}{10}$, or 50%. tails? $\frac{5}{10}$, or 50%. The experimental outcome is close to the theoretical outcome.

■ **Talk About Math** How would you use the random number table to answer this problem: In 25 tosses of a number cube, how often will you get the number 3?

Check Understanding

Use the random number table to simulate tossing 2 coins 100 times.

1. If you let even numbers and zero equal heads, what will odd numbers equal?

2. Letting pairs of numbers represent two coins, what must be true about a pair of numbers that represent 2 heads? 2 tails?

Use the random number table to simulate spinning a spinner divided into thirds numbered 1, 2, and 3.

3. Ignore any 0 on the table. Let 1, 2, or 3 represent number "1" on the spinner, and let 4, 5, or 6 represent "2." What number(s) will represent the "3" on the spinner?

4. Out of 100 trials, how many times did you get the "2" on the spinner?

5. What is the theoretical probability of getting the number "2" on the spinner?

6. Compare the theoretical probability found in Exercise 5 with the simulation probability found in Exercise 4.

Practice

Use thc table on page 440 to simulate the following. Tell what the digits will represent in each.

7. Imagine spinning a spinner divided into tenths, and labeled with the letters A, B, C, D, E, F, G, H, I, and J 25 times.

8. Five pencils (white, black, blue, red, and green) are in a cloth bag. Without looking in the bag, remove one pencil. Record the color, and then replace the pencil. Perform the simulation 20 times.

Explore Math

Make a fair spinner with each section equal. Use the spinner to create a random number table.

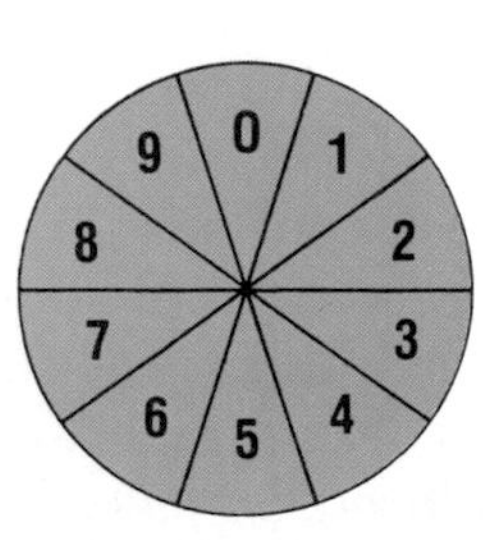

9. Spin the spinner 50 times. Write the result of each spin, and form groups of 5 numbers.

10. Compare your table to 50 entries on page 440. Did you get the same number of odd and even numbers?

Chapter 12 REVIEW

Skills Review

The table shows Julie's basketball record so far this season. Find each probability.

	Shots	Free Throws
Made	72	22
Missed	88	33
Total	160	55

1. Julie will make her next shot.

2. Julie will miss her next free throw.

Find the theoretical probability of drawing each letter from the word *complementary*.

3. P(C)   4. P(E)   5. P(P or T)

If the spinner lands on a letter, you get a point. If it lands on a number, your partner gets a point. Tell whether this game is fair for each spinner.

6. 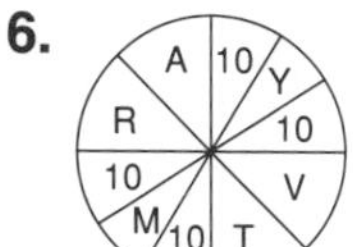

7. 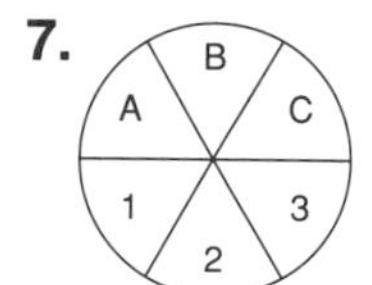

8. 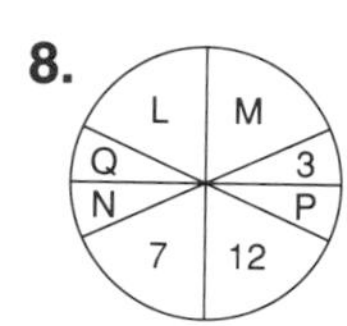

Computer Connection makes computers with 4 hard drive choices, 5 monitor choices, 3 case choices and 3 keyboard choices. With the following options, how many choices are there?

9. Hard drive, case, keyboard

10. Hard drive, monitor, case

A box contains 20 balls: 8 red, 4 blue, 6 green and 2 yellow. Find each probability if each ball is replaced after it is drawn and if each ball is not replaced.

11. P(R, B)   12. P(G, Y, B)

Problem-Solving Review

Solve each problem.

13. The Grand Canyon is about 280 miles long. The Longs took $7\frac{1}{2}$ days to ride it on horseback. About how many miles did they ride each day?

14. Belinda wants to buy a tape deck that is 45.5 cm wide. Will the tape deck fit on a shelf 0.48 m wide?

15. The regular price of a tape deck is $269. It is on sale for 30% off. What is the sale price?

16. The table lists the approximate speeds, in miles per hour, of some animals. Use the data to make a stem-and-leaf plot of animal speeds.

Cheetah	70
Pronghorn	61
Lion	50
Elk	45
Coyote	43
Gray fox	42
Zebra	40
Rabbit	35
Reindeer	32
Giraffe	32
Grizzly Bear	30
Deer	30
Qurarter horse	48
Greyhound	39

17. Sam tossed a coin 100 times. It landed heads 44 times and tails 56 times. What is P(heads)? P(tails)?

18. If Sam tosses the coin 2,500 times, how many heads can he expect?

19. **Data File** Use the data on pages 558–559. Suppose you turn the set of dominoes over, mix them up, and pick two dominoes. What is P(two doubles)?

20. **Make a Data File** Survey about 50 students about a TV show, a book or a product. Use the categories very good, good, fair, poor, didn't see (or didn't read or don't use). Tally the responses and use the data to predict the responses for your entire school.

Cumulative Skills Review • Chapters 1–12

Solve each equation.

1. $t + 87 = 100$ **2.** $78 - v = 61$ **3.** $7m = 147$ **4.** $\frac{r}{15} = 5$

5. $8y + 4 = 84$ **6.** $\frac{w}{6} + 3 = 11$ **7.** $6.5c = 52$ **8.** $7.9 + h = 12.4$

Find each answer.

9. What percent of 150 is 225? **10.** 45 is what percent of 75?

11. 95 is 19% of what number? **12.** 125% of what number is 50?

Find the perimeter and area of each figure.

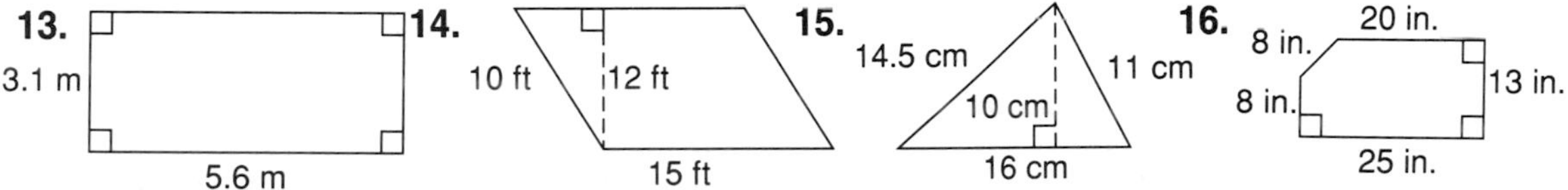

The data shows the cost of thirteen calculators rounded to the nearest dollar.
\$24, \$49, \$67, \$38, \$29, \$48, \$39, \$57, \$55, \$64, \$33, \$54, \$67

17. What is the range of the calculator prices? **18.** Find the mean price.

19. What is the mode of the prices? **20.** What is the median calculator price?

21. Make a stem-and-leaf plot to show the data.

Give reasons why each of the following statements used by advertisers is a misuse of statistics.

22. Pearly White Toothpaste is recommended by 19 out of 20 dentists.

23. Soapier Laundry soap gets your clothes 90% cleaner.

24. 9 out of 10 people surveyed preferred Jeanne's Jams.

There are 10 sandwiches in a basket: 5 are cheese, 3 are tomato, and 2 are ham.

25. Draw a probability tree diagram for selecting two sandwiches if there is no replacement.

Use your probability tree diagram to find each probability.

26. *P*(cheese, cheese) **27.** *P*(cheese, tomato) **28.** *P*(ham, cheese) **29.** *P*(ham, ham)

Reteaching

Set A pages 420–423

The results for 50 spins of this spinner are shown.

Letter	Tally	Frequency
A	𝍸 𝍸 II	12
B	𝍸 𝍸 𝍸 II	17
C	𝍸 𝍸	10
D	𝍸 𝍸 I	11

Remember the formula for estimating probability.

$$\textbf{Probability} = \frac{\textbf{Number of successes}}{\textbf{Number of trials}}$$

Use the frequency table at the left to write the probability that the spinner will point to the given letter as a fraction in lowest terms. Then write each probability as a decimal.

1. A **2.** B

3. C **4.** D

Set B pages 426–427

Find the theoretical probability of drawing the letter A from the word PROBABILITY.

$P(\mathbf{A}) = \frac{\mathbf{1}}{\mathbf{11}}$ ←Number of favorable outcomes / ←Number of equally likely outcomes

The probability of drawing the letter A is $\frac{1}{11}$, or 0.091.

Remember that to calculate theoretical probability, you need to count the total number of possible outcomes.

Find the theoretical probability of drawing each of the following letters from the word PROBABILITY.

1. P(Y) **2.** P(B) **3.** P(I) **4.** P(K)

Set C 428–429

Tell whether this game is fair.

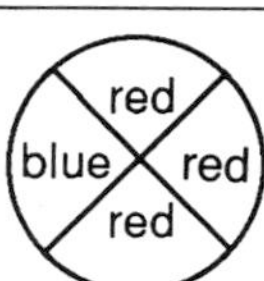

You earn a point if the spinner points to red. Your partner earns a point if the spinner points to blue.

The game is not fair because the probability that the spinner will point to red is greater than the probability that it will point to blue.

Remember that in a fair game the outcomes are equally likely.

Tell whether each game is fair. Explain your answers.

1. You and your partner take turns tossing two number cubes. If the product of the two top numbers is a two-digit number, you earn a point. If the product is a single-digit number, your partner earns a point.

Complete the table below to help you answer the problem.

	1	2	3	4	5	6
1	1	2	3			
2	2	4	6			
3	3	6				
4	4					
5						
6						

Set D 430–431

Customers can choose from 9 flavors, 3 sizes, and either a cone or a cup of yogurt. How many choices does a customer have?

Use the Fundamental Counting Principle.

9	×	3	×	2	=	54
Number of choices for flavor		Number of choices for size		Number of choices for serving		Total number of choices

Customers have 54 choices.

Remember, the product of the choices gives the total number of choices.

1. Find the total number of choices if 3 new flavors are added.
2. Find the total number of choices if only 4 different flavors are available.
3. Find the total number of choices if a second kind of cone is added.

Set E pages 434–435

Tell whether the following events are independent.

A. You come down with laryngitis.
B. The evening news is broadcast.

The events are independent. Though you might be inconvenienced by the loss of your voice, the evening news will be broadcast as usual.

Remember, when two events are independent, the outcome of the first does not affect the outcome of the second.

Tell whether each pair of events is independent. Explain your answers.

1. A. You select a book from a shelf.
   B. Without replacing the first book, you select another one from the shelf.
2. A. While fishing in a pond stocked with several varieties of fish, you catch a small bass. You then return the fish to the water.
   B. You catch another small bass.

Set F pages 436–437

The cards below are mixed thoroughly and placed facedown on a table.

1	1	1	2
3	4	5	5
6	7	7	8

Remember, to find the probabilities of a series of events, multiply each of the probabilities.

Find each probability when the cards at the left are selected one after the other.

1. P(1, 1)
2. P(2, 3)
3. P(1, 5)
4. P(3, 6)
5. P(2, 8)
6. P(5, 7)

Set G pages 438–439

The probability tree diagram to the right shows the probability of selecting letters from a box, with replacement.

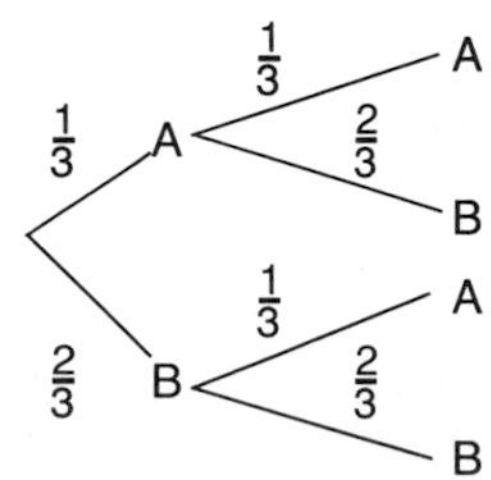

Remember, each branch of a probability tree diagram shows the probability of the event.

Use the probability tree diagram at the left to find each probability.

1. P(A,A)
2. P(B,B)

More Practice

Set A pages 420–423

Refer to the table on page 421.

Draw a probability scale showing the probability that each of the following events will occur. On the scale, write the letter corresponding to each event.

1. The next person through the gate will get a red T-shirt. (R)
2. The next person through the gate will get a blue T-shirt. (E)
3. The next person through the gate will get a yellow T-shirt. (Y)
4. The next person through the gate will get a T-shirt. (T)
5. The next person through the gate will get a red or blue T-shirt. (G)
6. The next person through the gate will get a green or blue T-shirt. (B)

Set B pages 426–427

A number is selected from the set of two-digit whole numbers. Find each probability.

1. *P*(multiple of 5)
2. *P*(sum of the digits is 10)
3. *P*(divisible by 7)

A number is selected from the set of factors of 48. Find each probability.

4. *P*(multiple of 6)
5. *P*(even)
6. *P*(multiple of 7)

From these letters, CALCULUS, find each probability.

7. *P*(vowel)
8. *P*(consonant)
9. *P*(C)

Set C pages 428–429

Tell whether each game is fair. Explain your answers.

1. Your partner rolls a pair of number cubes. If the product of the top numbers is divisible by 3, your partner gets a point. If the product is not divisible by 3, you get a point.
2. You and your partner take turns spinning this spinner. If it lands on an even number, you get a point, and if it lands on an odd number, your partner gets a point.

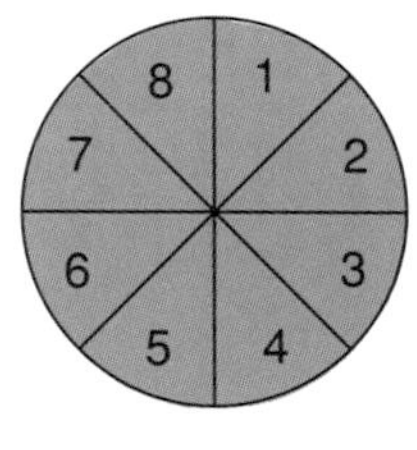

3. You select a card from the six cards shown at the right. Your partner tries to guess the letter on the card. Your partner earns a point for a correct guess, and you earn a point for an incorrect guess.

Set D pages 430–431

A tent manufacturer makes 1- and 2-door, warm-weather and cold-weather tents that come in 3 sizes, 2 colors, and 2 styles. With the following options, how many choices are there?

1. Size, color, doors, weather
2. Size, style, doors
3. How many different choices are there altogether?

Set E pages 434–435

A box contains 10 cubes: 4 white, 2 blue, 3 yellow, and 1 orange. Find the probability for each series of draws if each cube is replaced after it is drawn.

1. *P*(Y, O)
2. *P*(B, B)
3. *P*(O, W, B)
4. *P*(Y, Y, Y)
5. *P*(O, O)
6. *P*(W, B, Y)

Set F pages 436–437

A single-serving package contains the following flavors of fruit snacks: 15 raspberry, 11 strawberry, 7 orange, and 4 grape. Find each probability.

1. The first flavor selected is raspberry, and the second flavor is grape.
2. The first two flavors are orange.
3. The first flavor selected is strawberry, and the second flavor is orange.
4. The first two flavors are both raspberry.
5. The first flavor selected is raspberry, the second flavor is orange, and the third flavor is grape.
6. The first flavor selected is grape, the second flavor is grape, and the third flavor is orange.
7. *P*(raspberry, raspberry)
8. *P*(strawberry, strawberry)

Set G pages 438–439

The following colors come in a box of 10 pens: 4 black, 4 green, and 2 red.

1. Draw a probability tree diagram for the problem if there is no replacement.

Use your probability tree diagram to find each probability.

2. *P*(black, black)
3. *P*(green, red)
4. *P*(red, red)

Enrichment

Permutations and Combinations

Juan, Maria, Caryl, and Frank are finalists in their school's trivia contest. How many ways can first, second, and third place be awarded?

First place can be awarded to any of the four students. Second place can be awarded to any of the three remaining students, and third place can be awarded to either of the two remaining students. Each possible way the students can finish in order from first to third place is called a ***permutation***.

1st place choices		2nd place choices		3rd place choices	
4	×	3	×	2	= 24

There are 24 different ways that first, second, and third place can be awarded.

How many 3-member teams can be selected from the four finalists?

The order in which the 3 members of the team are arranged does not matter. The team of Juan, Maria, and Caryl is the same as the team of Maria, Caryl, and Juan. For any team of 3 students there are 6 possible arrangements that contain the same members.

First member		Second member		Third member	
3	×	2	×	1	= 6

To find the number of different teams, or ***combinations***, divide the number of possible teams, 24, by the number of ways to get the same team.

$$\frac{4 \times 3 \times 2}{3 \times 2 \times 1} = \frac{24}{6} = 4$$

There are four possible 3-member teams.

1. How many different 3-member teams can be made from a group of five students?

2. If no digits are repeated, how many 4-digit numbers can be formed using the digits 1–7?

3. How many different triangles can be drawn using three of the points P, Q, R, S, T as vertices?

Chapter 12 Review/Test

Life of Bulbs in Hours	Number of Bulbs
600–699	105
700–799	97
800–899	144
900–999	98
1,000–1,099	56

Use the table above for Items 1 and 2.

1. Find the probability that a light bulb will last less than 800 hours.

2. Predict the number of light bulbs out of 700,000 that will last longer than 899 hours.

3. Use the probability scale below to tell whether event A or event B is more likely to occur.

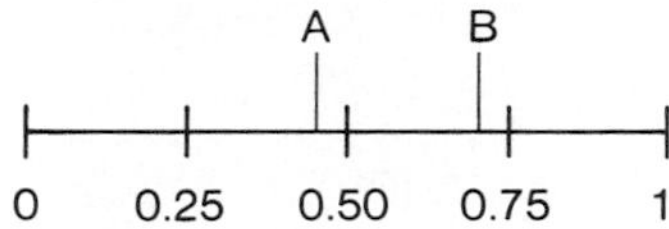

4. A catalog offers shirts in 4 colors, 3 styles, and 6 sizes. How many choices for shirts are there?

A number is selected from 1–25. Find the probability for each event.

5. *P*(multiple of 5)

6. *P*(even number)

Determine if the following game is fair. Explain your answer.

7. You select a card from eight cards numbered 1–8. Your partner tries to guess the number on the card. Your partner earns a point for a correct guess and you earn a point for an incorrect guess.

On Mrs. Vale's desk was a box that held 6 red pens, 4 blue pens, and 5 black pens. She asked Laura to pick a pen, put it back in the container, and then pick another pen. What is the probability that Laura will pick

8. a red pen and a black pen?

9. two black pens?

10. a blue pen and a red pen?

An organization is considering 12 cities as sites for its next two meetings. Two of the cities are located in the Northeast, two are located in the Midwest, five are located in the South, and three are located in the West. <u>The site of the first meeting cannot also be the site of the second meeting.</u>

11. Which statement best describes what the underlined sentence tells you about this problem?

    a. The events are independent.
    b. The events are dependent.
    c. The events are complementary.
    d. The events are impossible.

Find the probability that the meetings will be held in a

12. Southern and a Midwestern city.

13. two Southern cities.

14. Draw a probability tree diagram for two spins of this spinner.

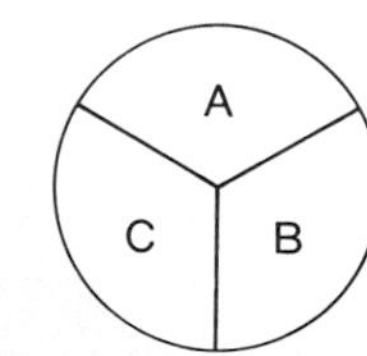

15. **Write About Math** Explain why random number tables are used to find experimental probabilities.

CHAPTER REVIEW/TEST

Integers and Rational Numbers 13

Did You Know: The eroded remains of many old volcanos in the ocean form "pinnacles," "rocks," and "banks" with elevations from about −650 feet to about +1,000 feet. Banks have negative elevations, while pinnacles and rocks often form needle-like spires rising vertically from the sea.

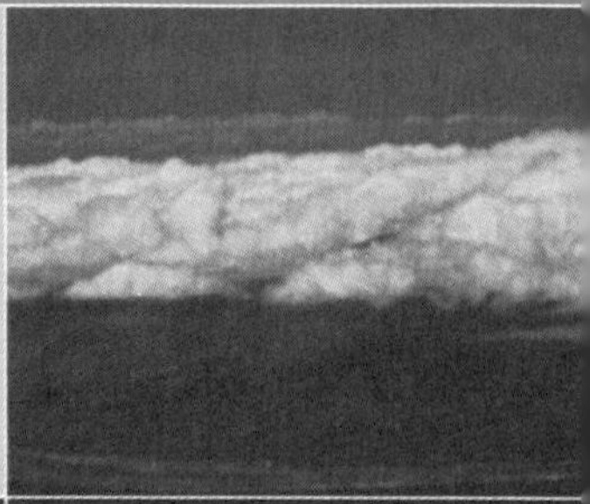

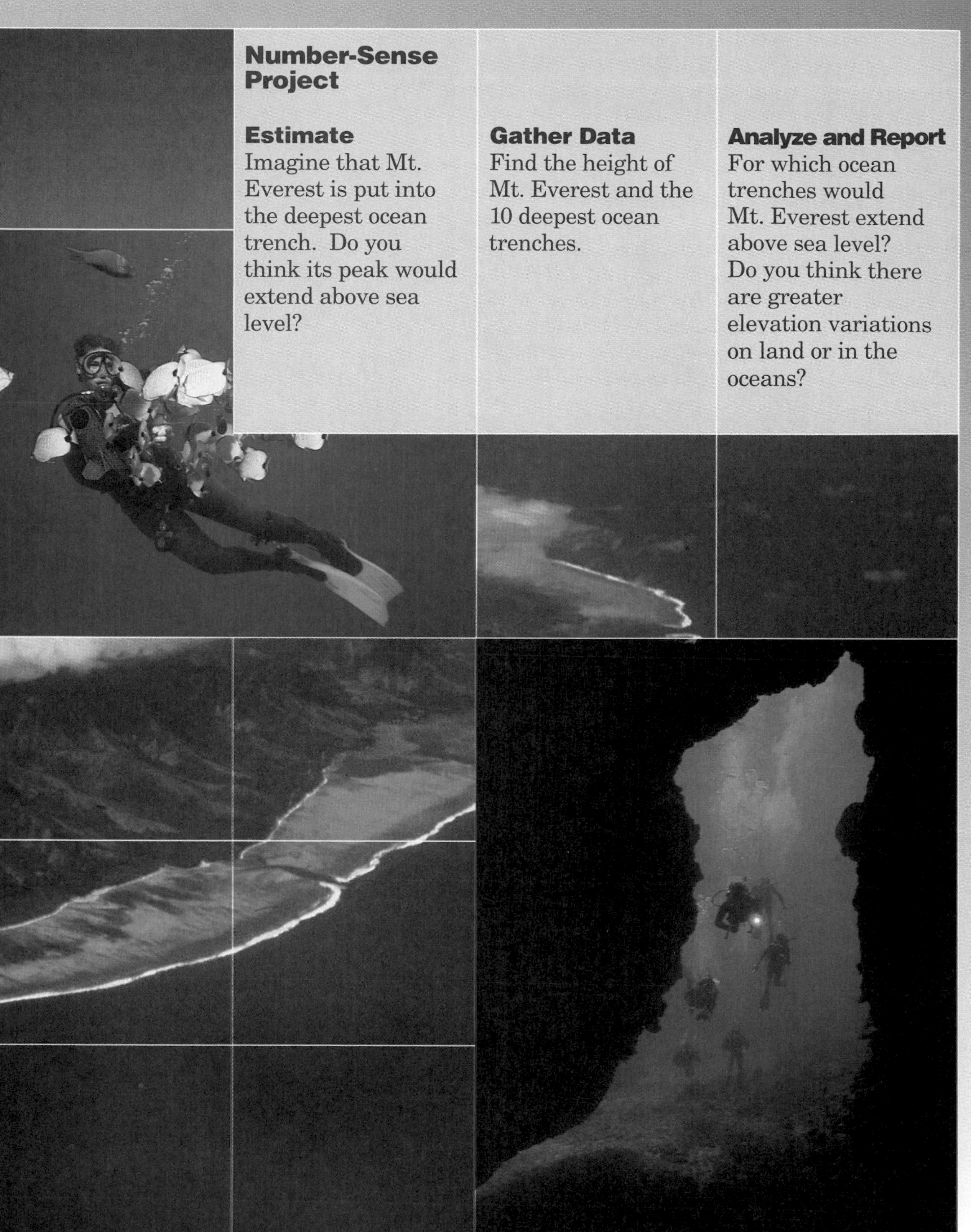

Number-Sense Project

Estimate

Imagine that Mt. Everest is put into the deepest ocean trench. Do you think its peak would extend above sea level?

Gather Data

Find the height of Mt. Everest and the 10 deepest ocean trenches.

Analyze and Report

For which ocean trenches would Mt. Everest extend above sea level? Do you think there are greater elevation variations on land or in the oceans?

SCIENCE CONNECTION

ALGEBRA

Meaning of Integers

Build Understanding

A. The boat is at sea level. Use the ***integer*** 0 to show this.

The General Sherman Tree in Sequoia National Park is about 275 ft high. Use the ***positive integer*** +275 to show the top of the tree is 275 ft above sea level.

The anchor of the boat is about 25 ft below sea level. Use the ***negative integer*** −25 to show this.

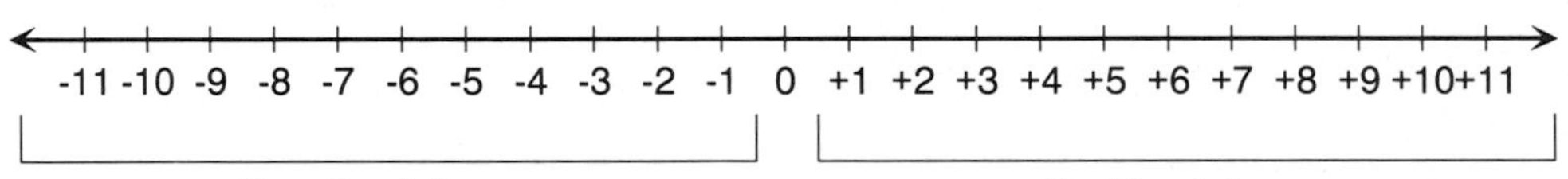

B. On a horizontal number line, positive integers are shown to the right of zero and negative integers are shown to the left.

For any two numbers on the number line, the one farther to the right is the greater.

$-3 > -10 \quad -8 < -2 \quad -6 < 0 \quad +1 > -6$

Positive integers are usually written without signs. So, +17 is written as 17.

C. The ***absolute value*** of an integer is its distance from zero on the number line. Notice that −8 is 8 units from zero. The absolute value of −8 is 8. This is written $|-8| = 8$.

Pairs of integers with the same absolute value are called ***opposites.*** Positive 17 is the opposite of −17, and −258 is the opposite of +258.

■ **Talk About Math** What is the absolute value of 0? What is the opposite of 0?

Check Understanding

For another example, see Set A, pages 482–483.

Answer each exercise.

1. Give an example of a quantity that can be represented by the integer −20.

2. Name an integer that is neither positive nor negative.

3. **Number Sense** Which number is greater, −1,000 or 1?

4. What is the absolute value of −12?

Practice

For More Practice, see Set A, pages 484–485.

Express each quantity as an integer.

5. A height of 75 ft
6. A depth of 53 meters
7. 45 degrees below zero
8. 28 degrees above zero
9. A profit of $475
10. A loss of $110
11. An increase of 18
12. A decrease of 42
13. 80 ft below sea level
14. 36 ft above sea level
15. A gain of 9 lb
16. A loss of 6 lb

Complete each exercise. Use $>$ or $<$.

17. 35 ▒ −2
18. −6 ▒ 12
19. −7 ▒ −15

Number Sense Which is greater?

20. −2,000 or 2
21. −500 or 500
22. −1,000 or 100

Write the absolute value and opposite of each integer.

23. −11
24. −43
25. 2
26. −45
27. 59
28. −456
29. 18
30. 20
31. −46
32. −23
33. −126
34. 302

Problem Solving

Write the solution to each problem using integers.

35. Bluefin tuna swim in the upper waters, between 0 ft and 600 ft below sea level. Write the maximum depth using an integer.

36. Lantern fish swim at depths between 180 m and 910 m below sea level. Using integers, write the range of depths at which they swim.

37. The branches of a redwood are 150 ft above the ground. Write the distance using an integer.

38. **Critical Thinking** What is the opposite of the opposite of 8? of −31? In general, what is the opposite of the opposite of *n*? of −*n*?

Skills Review

pages 308–311, 314–315

Copy and solve each problem.

1. 12% of 85 = ▒
2. 35 = ▒% of 70
3. 110% of 400 = ▒
4. 40% of ▒ = 32
5. 11 = ▒% of 20
6. 82% of 50 = ▒
7. 28 = ▒% of 20
8. 12.5% of 8 = ▒

CAREER CONNECTION

ALGEBRA

Adding Integers

Build Understanding

A. Reba kept track of her golf scores during one tournament by recording the number of strokes she was above or below par on each day. If −4 represents four strokes below par, how much above or below par was she by the second day?

Day	Score compared to par
Mon	−4
Tues	−5
Wed	6
Thurs	−2
Fri	8

Find $-4 + (-5)$.

Use a number line. Starting at 0, move 4 units to the left to represent −4. Then move 5 more units left to represent −5: $-4 + (-5) = -9$. Reba was 9 strokes below par by the second day.

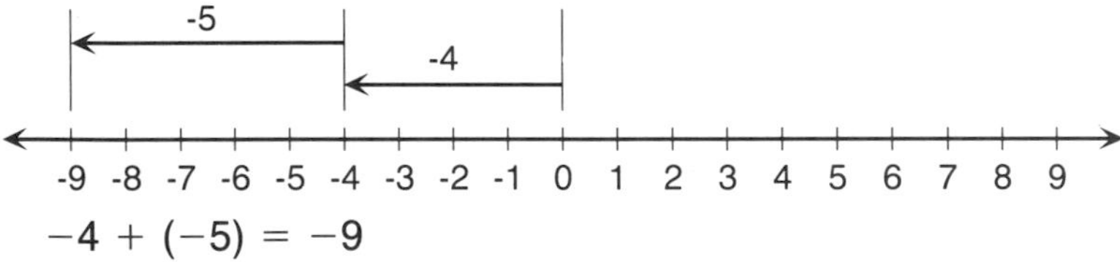

$-4 + (-5) = -9$

To add two integers with the same sign, add without regard to the sign and then use the sign of both integers in the answer.

In 1978, Nancy Lopez became the first woman to be named both Rookie of the year and LPGA Player of the year in the same season.

B. How many strokes above or below par was she by Wednesday?

Find $-9 + 6$.

On the number line, start at 0 and move 9 units to the left. Then move 6 units to the right: $-9 + 6 = -3$. Her score on Wednesday was 3 strokes below par.

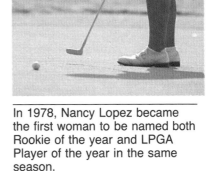

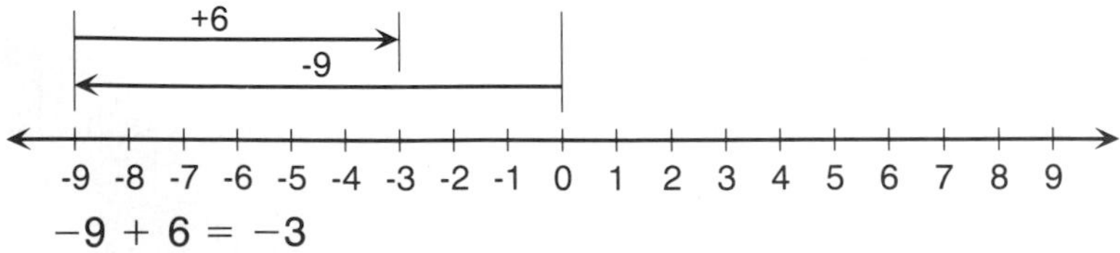

$-9 + 6 = -3$

To add two integers with opposite signs, first find the absolute value of each integer. Subtract the lesser absolute value from the greater, and use the sign of the greater in the answer.

Talk About Math

How much above or below par were Reba's combined scores for the week?

Check Understanding

For another example, see Set B, pages 482–483.

Tell whether each sum will be positive, negative, or zero. Explain why.

1. $-7 + 4$ **2.** $89 + 54$ **3.** $67 + (-67)$ **4.** $11 + (-16)$

5. $-15 + (-15)$ **6.** $-6 + 12$ **7.** $-21 + (-21)$ **8.** $27 + (-26)$

Practice

For more practice, see Set B, pages 484–485.

Add. Use a number line if necessary.

9. $8 + 23$ **10.** $-17 + (-9)$ **11.** $-4 + (-6)$ **12.** $25 + 14$

13. $-7 + 2$ **14.** $-5 + (-1)$ **15.** $-13 + 10$ **16.** $19 + (-22)$

17. $-4 + 8$ **18.** $-7 + 7$ **19.** $0 + (-8)$ **20.** $15 + (-11)$

21. $-7 + (-9)$ **22.** $-15 + 8$ **23.** $16 + 22$ **24.** $9 + (-18)$

25. $-35 + 0$ **26.** $-12 + (-5)$ **27.** $-7 + (-19)$ **28.** $-20 + 10$

29. $-11 + (-6)$ **30.** $-10 + 14$ **31.** $-10 + 20$ **32.** $-14 + 32$

33. $-16 + 19 + 12$ **34.** $18 + (-11) + (-10)$ **35.** $4 + (-2) + (-8) + 3$

36. $29 + 3 + (-30)$ **37.** $-4 + (-10) + 26$ **38.** $87 + (-43) + (-87)$

39. $-15 + 41 + (-10)$ **40.** $1 + (-8) + (-13)$ **41.** $-22 + (-10) + (-2)$

42. $-3 + (-11) + (-12)$ **43.** $-16 + 91 + (-16)$ **44.** $24 + 26 + (-26)$

Problem Solving

The table at the right shows how much above or below par 5 golfers were at the end of a 4-day tournament. Use the information from the table.

Player	Above (+) or below (−) par
Sun Li	−12
Julio	8
Nikki	9
Patrick	−15
Rosanna	−10

45. Who had the best score; that is, who had the lowest score?

46. Nikki and Rosanna were partners. How much above or below par were their combined scores?

47. Julio and Patrick were partners. Describe their combined performance.

48. How much above or below par were all 5 players together?

ALGEBRA

Subtracting Integers

Build Understanding

A. Look for a Pattern

Groups: With a partner

a. Study these equations. Then give the next three equations that continue the pattern.

$$10 - 2 = 8$$
$$10 - 1 = 9$$
$$10 - 0 = 10$$
$$10 - (-1) = 11$$
$$10 - (-2) = 12$$
$$10 - (-3) = 13$$

b. Give the numbers that complete the equations that match the subtraction equations in part a.

$10 - 2 = 8$ $10 + (-2) = 8$	$10 - 1 = 9$ $10 + ▒ = 9$
$10 - 0 = 10$ $10 + ▒ = 10$	$10 - (-1) = 11$ $10 + ▒ = 11$
$10 - (-2) = 12$ $10 + ▒ = 12$	$10 - (-3) = 13$ $10 + ▒ = 13$

c. Study the pattern in part b and describe a way for using addition to subtract two integers.

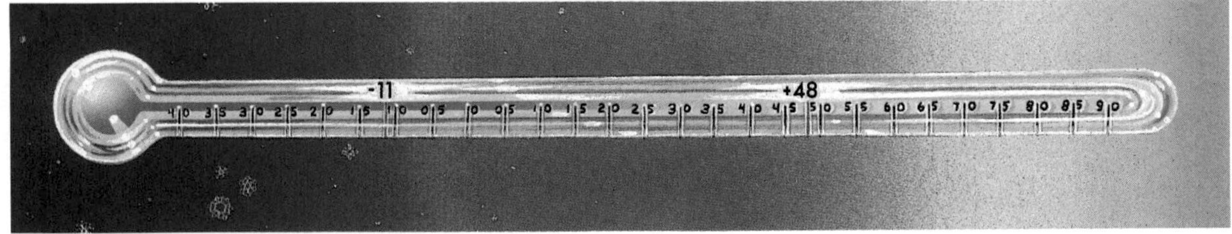

B. One day the high temperature was 48°; the low was −11°. How many degrees did it fall? Compare your rule to the computation shown. Does your rule give the same answer?

$$48 - (-11)$$
$$48 + 11 = +59$$

The temperature had dropped 59°.

■ **Talk About Math** If you subtract a positive number from a negative number, will the answer be positive or negative? Explain.

Check Understanding

For another example, see Set C, pages 482–483.

Find the missing numbers.

1. $5 - (-2) = 5 + ▒ = ▒$

2. $-8 - 3 = -8 + ▒ = ▒$

3. $-6 - (-1) = -6 + ▒ = ▒$

4. $9 - 17 = 9 + ▒ = ▒$

Practice

For More Practice, see Set C, pages 484–485.

Write each subtraction exercise as addition. Then compute.

5. $-6 - 2$ **6.** $-7 - 6$ **7.** $3 - 8$ **8.** $6 - 5$

9. $-5 - (-3)$ **10.** $-8 - 4$ **11.** $10 - 3$ **12.** $2 - 8$

Subtract.

13. $-7 - (-7)$ **14.** $24 - (-19)$ **15.** $28 - (-10)$ **16.** $16 - (-16)$

17. $0 - 22$ **18.** $0 - (-34)$ **19.** $-29 - 29$ **20.** $-13 - 17$

21. $-24 - 6$ **22.** $-14 - (-22)$ **23.** $20 - 90$ **24.** $59 - 44$

25. $-34 - 78$ **26.** $-27 - (-4)$ **27.** $75 - (-25)$ **28.** $-16 - 26$

29. $32 - (-7)$ **30.** $-25 - (-25)$ **31.** $-16 - (-9)$ **32.** $-35 - (-46)$

Mixed Practice Add or subtract.

33. $-23 - 14$ **34.** $-23 + 14$ **35.** $19 - (-15)$ **36.** $19 + (-15)$

37. $0 - (-25)$ **38.** $-14 + 28$ **39.** $7 - 11$ **40.** $-47 - (-23)$

41. $-8 - 26$ **42.** $20 + (-10)$ **43.** $-13 + (-25)$ **44.** $-24 - (-26)$

45. $12 + (-12)$ **46.** $-8 + 92$ **47.** $-18 + (-17)$ **48.** $-32 - (-8)$

Problem Solving

Critical Thinking Solve each problem.

49. Is there a greatest integer? Explain.

50. If a and b are integers, then $a - b = a + \boxed{}$.

51. The high temperature in Minneapolis on a summer day was 89°F. The high temperature on a winter day was −27°F. How much lower was the winter temperature?

52. **Use Data** Use the table on page 455 to find out how many strokes separated Sun Li and Julio in the golf tournament.

53. The hottest recorded temperature in the world was 136°F at Azizia, Libya, in 1922. The coldest recorded temperature was −129°F at Vostok, Antarctica, in 1983. Find the difference.

ALGEBRA

Multiplying Integers

Build Understanding

A. Multiplying positive integers is like multiplying whole numbers.

Multiply $(+6) \times (+3)$.

Since $6 \times 3 = 18$,
$(+6) \times (+3) = +18$.

The product of two positive integers is positive.

B. You can use addition to help find the product of a positive integer and a negative integer.

Multiply: $6 \times (-3)$.

$$6 \times (-3) = (-3) + (-3) + (-3) + (-3) + (-3) + (-3) = -18$$

The product of a positive integer and a negative integer is negative.

C. You can use patterns to find the product of two negative integers.

Multiply: $(-6) \times (-3)$.

Note that the product $-6 \times (-3)$ can be written $(-6)(-3)$.

$(-6)(+3) = -18$
+ 6
$(-6)(+2) = -12$
+ 6
$(-6)(+1) = -6$
+ 6
$(-6)\ 0 = 0$
+ 6
$(-6)(-1) = +6$
+ 6
$(-6)(-2) = +12$
+ 6
$(-6)(-3) = +18$

Each product increases by 6.

+ × + = +
+ × − = −
− × + = −
− × − = +

The product of two negative integers is positive.

If two integers have the same sign, their product is positive. If two integers have opposite signs, their product is negative.

■ **Talk About Math** When multiplying three nonzero numbers, name all the possibilities that will give you a negative answer.

Check Understanding

For another example, see Set D, pages 482–483.

Tell whether each product will be positive, negative, or zero.

1. $(-84)(-39)$ **2.** $(12)(-9)$ **3.** $57(-3)(-2)$ **4.** $(-32)(-64)(-53)$ **5.** $-7(0)$

Mental Math Find each product.

6. $9(-3)$ **7.** $(-4)(-8)$ **8.** $(-6)(5)$ **9.** $(-7)(-6)$ **10.** $(-8)(4)$

Practice

For More Practice, see Set D, pages 484–485.

Multiply.

11. 12×20 **12.** $100(15)$ **13.** $13 \times (-14)$ **14.** -8×20 **15.** $(-11)(8)$

16. $(17)(-5)$ **17.** $(-9)(-4)$ **18.** $(12)(30)$ **19.** $(-50)(4)$ **20.** $(-7)(-14)$

21. $60(-5)$ **22.** $4 \times (-40)$ **23.** -16×6 **24.** $(-23)(-5)$ **25.** $8 \times (-25)$

26. -9×18 **27.** $(-4)(-8)(-3)$ **28.** $5(7)(-6)$ **29.** $(-4)(-4)(-4)$ **30.** $(-8)(-10)(8)$

31. $(41)(3)$ **32.** $(-7)(-24)$ **33.** -6×4 **34.** $(4)(-3)(6)$ **35.** $(8)(-9)$

36. $(56)(-10)$ **37.** $(-25)(-4)$ **38.** -12×9 **39.** $(-4)(31)(-5)$ **40.** $(13)(50)$

41. $2(-4)(-90)$ **42.** -40×9 **43.** $(-16)(100)$ **44.** $(-6)(5)(-3)$ **45.** $(17)(-18)(0)$

Find each product. **Remember** that 4^2 means 4×4. So, $(-3)^2$ means $(-3) \times (-3)$.

46. $(-3)^2$ **47.** $(-2)^4$ **48.** $(-2)^5$ **49.** $(-1)^5$ **50.** $(-3)^4$

51. 3^4 **52.** $(-4)^3$ **53.** $(-5)^2$ **54.** $(-5)^3$ **55.** $(-1)^{100}$

Problem Solving

Answer the following questions.

56. Suppose you wanted to find the product of a set of 23 numbers. If 12 of the numbers were positive and the rest were negative, would the product be positive or negative?

57. **Calculator** Investigate, using Exercises 11–45, how your calculator can be used to multiply with negative integers. Explain.

Critical Thinking Suppose that b represents a negative integer and that x represents a positive integer.

58. When will b^x be positive?

59. When will b^x be negative?

ALGEBRA

Dividing Integers

Build Understanding

To discover the rules for dividing integers, remember that multiplication and division are inverse operations.

$24 \div 3 = 8$ because $8 \times 3 = 24$

A. Find the quotient $-21 \div (-3)$. Use inverse operations. If $-21 \div (-3) = n$, then $n \times (-3) = (-21)$.
Since $7 \times (-3) = -21$, the answer is 7.
So, $-21 \div (-3) = 7$.

If a negative integer is divided by a negative integer, the quotient is positive.

$+ \div + = +$

$+ \div - = -$

$- \div + = -$

$- \div - = +$

B. Find the quotient $45 \div (-9)$. Use inverse operations. If $45 \div (-9) = n$, then $n \times (-9) = 45$.
Since $(-5) \times (-9) = 45$, the answer is -5.
So, $45 \div (-9) = -5$.

If a positive integer is divided by a negative integer, the quotient is negative.

To divide integers, divide as if they were whole numbers. Then use the rules of signs for multiplication.
If two integers have the same sign, their quotient is positive.
If two integers have opposite signs, their quotient is negative.

C. The quotient of 0 divided by any nonzero number is 0.

$0 \div a = \frac{0}{a} = 0$ because $0 \times a = 0$.

However, 0 cannot be used as a divisor. The expressions $a \div 0$ and $0 \div 0$ have no meaning in mathematics.

■ **Talk About Math** Discuss why dividing by zero has no meaning.

Check Understanding

For another example, see set E, pages 482–483.

Mental Math Find each quotient.

1. $20 \div (-5)$ **2.** $-36 \div 6$ **3.** $-48 \div (-8)$ **4.** $-100 \div 10$ **5.** $-45 \div (-9)$

Practice

For More Practice, see Set E, pages 484–485.

Write the missing number.

6. $(-3)(\square) = 12$ **7.** $(-5)(\square) = 15$ **8.** $42 = 6\,(\square)$ **9.** $9(\square) = -27$

10. $4(\square) = -20$ **11.** $25 = (\square)(-5)$ **12.** $-63 = (-7)(\square)$ **13.** $(-8)(\square) = -48$

Divide. **Remember** to check the sign in the answer.

14. $-20 \div (-4)$ **15.** $25 \div (-5)$ **16.** $-63 \div 9$ **17.** $-48 \div 6$

18. $-49 \div (-7)$ **19.** $-40 \div (-8)$ **20.** $54 \div (-6)$ **21.** $36 \div (-4)$

22. $56 \div (-2)$ **23.** $-48 \div (-8)$ **24.** $72 \div (-9)$ **25.** $-35 \div (-7)$

26. $-28 \div 4$ **27.** $-90 \div (-9)$ **28.** $27 \div (-3)$ **29.** $-64 \div (-8)$

30. $44 \div (-2)$ **31.** $-36 \div 3$ **32.** $-1 \div (-1)$ **33.** $0 \div (-7)$

34. $-52 \div (-4)$ **35.** $77 \div (-7)$ **36.** $-48 \div 4$ **37.** $-95 \div (-5)$

38. $\frac{-81}{-9}$ **39.** $\frac{56}{-7}$ **40.** $\frac{-57}{3}$ **41.** $\frac{84}{-7}$ **42.** $\frac{-51}{17}$ **43.** $\frac{-18}{-3}$

44. $\frac{-40}{8}$ **45.** $\frac{-42}{14}$ **46.** $\frac{99}{-11}$ **47.** $\frac{-75}{-15}$ **48.** $\frac{-60}{5}$ **49.** $\frac{-16}{-16}$

Problem Solving

Complete the following.

50. Critical Thinking The sum, difference, and product of any two integers is always an integer. However, the quotient of any two integers is not always an integer. Give three examples.

51. $(-24) \div 3 = 24 \div (-3) = -8$

Give three more examples to illustrate the principle that

$(-a) \div b = a \div (-b)$.

Midchapter Checkup

Add, subtract, multiply, or divide.

1. $-8 + 2$ **2.** $-3 \times (-12)$ **3.** $-125 \div 5$ **4.** $8 - (-8)$ **5.** $12 + (-18)$

6. $5 \times (-14)$ **7.** $220 \div (-11)$ **8.** 45×6 **9.** $-3 - 14$ **10.** -7×15

11. $-2 + 16$ **12.** $35 \div (-7)$ **13.** $15 - 29$ **14.** $15 + 78$ **15.** $-200 \div 25$

Problem-Solving Workshop

Real-Life Decision Making

1. Which is the best buy in terms of price?

2. Which box of cereal would make the most sense to buy if you were the only one in your family who liked that kind?

3. Which would be the best buy for *your* family?

4. For each of the three boxes of cereal, name a circumstance where it would make sense to buy it.

Visual-Thinking Activity

How many boxes are in the stack at the right?

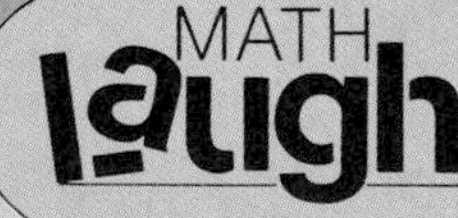

I want you to lend me $10 but only give me five.

Why only five?

Because I'll owe you $5 and then you'll owe me $5... and that will make us even!

Explore with a Computer

Use the *Spreadsheet Workshop Project* for this activity.

Find the pattern or rule for the sign of the product of three integers.

1. At the computer, type three integers into the spreadsheet. Then change their signs, noticing whether the product is positive or negative.

2. Record the results for several sets of integers. Write the rule for the sign of the product of three integers.

3. Repeat Exercises 1 and 2 with four integers.

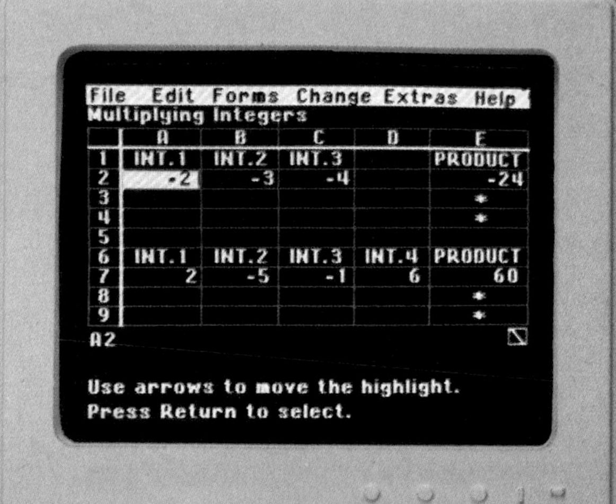

File Edit Forms Change Extras Help
Multiplying Integers
A B C D E
1 INT.1 INT.2 INT.3 PRODUCT
2 -2 -3 -4 -24
3 *
4 *
5
6 INT.1 INT.2 INT.3 INT.4 PRODUCT
7 2 -5 -1 6 60
8 *
9 *
A2
Use arrows to move the highlight.
Press Return to select.

Number-Sense Project

Look back at pages 450–451.

1. In 1960 the bathyscaph **Trieste** descended 35,820 feet to the bottom of the Marianas Trench in 4.8 hours. The ascent took about 3.3 hours.

a. Describe the **Trieste's** descent in feet per minute.

b. Describe the **Trieste's** ascent in feet per minute.

c. In a record breath-held dive, a diver averaged –3.3 feet per second for 104 seconds. How many feet did this diver descend?

ALGEBRA

Use Data from a Table

PROBLEM SOLVING GUIDE

Understand
QUESTION
FACTS
KEY IDEA

Plan and Solve
STRATEGY
ANSWER

Look Back
SENSIBLE ANSWER
ALTERNATE APPROACH

Build Understanding

Many people believe that high tide is the best time to fish. Harry Alvarez uses tide tables to know when the tide will be at its highest and how high it will be. Parts of his tide table for Boston with correction tables for other areas are shown.

Harry plans to go fishing near Atlantic City, New Jersey, on the morning of June 2. When will the high tide occur there, and how high will it be?

Tide Correction Table

Location	Time Difference	Height Difference
Maine		
Bar Harbor	−34 min	27 cm
Portland	−12 min	−18 cm
New York		
Coney Island	−213 min	−149 cm
Oyster Bay	4 min	−55 cm
New Jersey		
Atlantic City	−236 min	−168 cm
Cape May	−208 min	−162 cm
Maryland		
Havre de Grace	681 min	−235 cm
Annapolis	265 min	−229 cm

Tide Table for Boston

	Time of high tide		Tide height in centimeters	
Day	Morning	Evening	Morning	Evening
June 1	5:00	5:45	270	262
2	6:00	6:30	262	265
3	6:45	7:25	256	268
4	7:45	8:15	253	274
5	8:30	9:00	256	265

Understand QUESTION When will the morning high tide occur in Atlantic City and how high will it be?

FACTS The morning high tide in Boston on June 2 occurs at 6:00 A.M. The correction for Atlantic City is −236 min.

The height of the morning high tide for Boston on June 2 is 262 cm. The correction for Atlantic City is −168 cm.

KEY IDEA Harry must add −236 minutes to 6 A.M. to find the time of the morning high tide. He must add −168 cm to 262 cm to find the height of the morning high tide.

Plan and Solve

236 min = 3 h 56 min

$$\begin{array}{rcr} 6\text{ h }0\text{ min} & = & 5\text{ h }60\text{ min} \\ +(-3\text{ h }56\text{ min}) & = & -3\text{ h }56\text{ min} \\ \hline & & 2\text{ h }\ 4\text{ min, or 2:04 A.M.} \end{array}$$

$$\begin{array}{r} 262\text{ cm} \\ +(-168\text{ cm}) \\ \hline 94\text{ cm} \end{array}$$

ANSWER In Atlantic City on the morning of June 2, the high tide will occur at 2:04 A.M. and the height of the tide will be 94 cm.

Look Back

SENSIBLE ANSWER Check your work.

$$\begin{array}{r} 2\text{ h }\ 4\text{ min} \\ +3\text{ h }56\text{ min} \\ \hline 5\text{ h }60\text{ min} = 6\text{ h, or 6 A.M.} \end{array} \qquad \begin{array}{r} 94\text{ cm} \\ +168\text{ cm} \\ \hline 262\text{ cm} \end{array}$$

Talk About Math Why doesn't each city have its own tide table as Boston does?

Check Understanding

Use the tables on page 464 to compare the tides at Annapolis and Boston.

1. Does the high tide at Annapolis happen earlier or later than the high tide in Boston? By how many minutes?
2. Where is the height of high tide greater? How much greater?

Practice

Find the time and height of each high tide on the given date in the given city.

3. Portland, Maine, June 1, morning tide
4. Coney Island, New York, June 5, evening tide
5. Cape May, New Jersey, June 3, morning tide
6. Havre de Grace, Maryland, June 2, evening tide
7. Annapolis, Maryland, June 2, morning tide
8. Bar Harbor, Maine, June 5, evening tide
9. Which city on the chart has the highest high tide? Which has the lowest? What is the difference?
10. Which city on the chart has the earliest high tide? Which has the latest? What is the difference?

ALGEBRA

Rational Numbers

Build Understanding

A. Positive and negative fractions and mixed numbers, as well as integers, can be located on the number line. On the number line shown below, several such numbers are shown.

All the numbers shown on the number line can be written as a ratio of two integers:

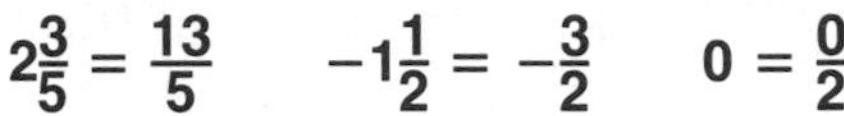

$2\frac{3}{5} = \frac{13}{5}$ $\quad -1\frac{1}{2} = -\frac{3}{2}$ $\quad 0 = \frac{0}{2}$

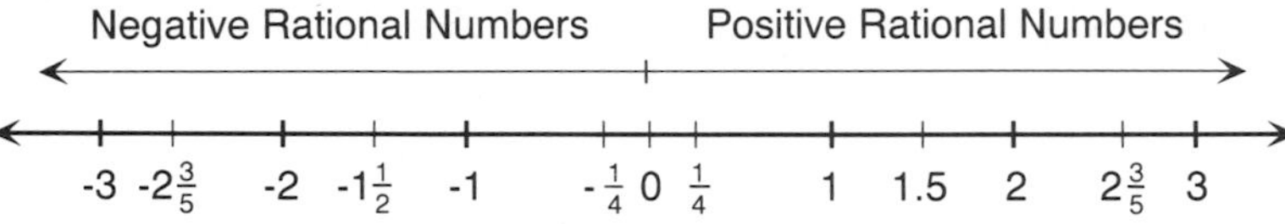

These numbers are called ***rational numbers.*** A ***rational number*** is a number that can be written as a ratio of two integers. All the numbers shown on the number line above are rational numbers.

B. Every rational number has an opposite. The opposite of $-2\frac{3}{5}$ is $2\frac{3}{5}$. The opposite of $-1\frac{1}{2}$ is $1\frac{1}{2}$, or 1.5.

Numbers that are opposites are at equal distances from 0 on the number line.

C. Compare $-\frac{2}{3}$ and $-1\frac{3}{8}$. Use <, >, or =.

Rational numbers are ordered on the number line in increasing order from left to right. Since $-\frac{2}{3}$ is to the right of $-1\frac{3}{8}$, $-\frac{2}{3} > -1\frac{3}{8}$.

D. Operations with rational numbers follow the same rules as operations with integers. Study these two examples.

$2\frac{3}{5} - \left(-1\frac{4}{5}\right) =$

$2\frac{3}{5} + 1\frac{4}{5} =$

$3\frac{7}{5} = 4\frac{2}{5}$

$(-4.5)(6.3) =$

-28.35

■ **Write About Math** Are all integers rational numbers? Are all rational numbers integers? Use examples to explain.

Check Understanding

For another example, see Set F, pages 482–483.

Mental Math Compute.

1. $(-3.8)(-1)$ **2.** $4\frac{1}{2} + \left(-3\frac{1}{2}\right)$ **3.** $3\frac{3}{5} - \left(-6\frac{2}{5}\right)$ **4.** $-4.5 \div (-9)$

Practice

For More Practice, see Set F, pages 484–485.

Show that each number is rational by writing it as a ratio of two integers.

5. 6 **6.** 0 **7.** −2 **8.** $\frac{2}{3}$ **9.** −5.4 **10.** $-3\frac{2}{3}$

Compare. Use <, >, or =.

11. $-\frac{1}{6}$ ▒ $-\frac{1}{4}$ **12.** $-\frac{1}{9}$ ▒ (−1.9) **13.** $-\frac{2}{3}$ ▒ $-\frac{4}{6}$ **14.** 0 ▒ $-\frac{1}{8}$

15. $-3\frac{2}{5}$ ▒ −4 **16.** $\frac{3}{2}$ ▒ −2 **17.** −0.8 ▒ −0.7 **18.** −5.1 ▒ −2.1

List the numbers in order from least to greatest.

19. 0, $-\frac{1}{2}$, $\frac{3}{4}$ **20.** $-\frac{1}{3}$, $-\frac{1}{10}$, $-\frac{1}{5}$ **21.** $2\frac{4}{5}$, −1, $\frac{3}{2}$ **22.** 0.6, −0.6, −1.6

Compute.

23. $-\frac{2}{3} + \left(-2\frac{3}{4}\right)$ **24.** $-1\frac{1}{5} - 2\frac{1}{2}$ **25.** 4 + (−7.82) **26.** 3.2 − 3.85

27. $-3\left(\frac{1}{2}\right)$ **28.** $3\frac{1}{2}\left(-\frac{7}{8}\right)$ **29.** −4(1.5) **30.** −4.9 ÷ 0.49

31. $(-6) \div -1\frac{1}{2}$ **32.** $\frac{5}{8} + \left(-4\frac{1}{4}\right)$ **33.** −7.38 − (−9.06) **34.** −8.4 ÷ (−0.7)

35. $\left(-2\frac{2}{3}\right)\left(-5\frac{3}{8}\right)$ **36.** $3\frac{3}{4} - \left(-6\frac{1}{2}\right)$ **37.** −3.2 + 5.8 **38.** 6.2(−1.1)

Problem Solving

Solve.

39. Mrs. Smith owns 500 shares of the Tri-X Company. One day the stock lost $\frac{5}{8}$ of a point per share. By how much did the value of her shares decline? (1 point = $1.00)

40. During the 5 trading days last week, a stock gained $\frac{1}{2}$, lost $\frac{5}{8}$, lost 1, gained $\frac{1}{8}$, and gained 1. What was the overall change for the week?

Explore ______ Math

41. The rational number $\frac{1}{2}$ is between $\frac{1}{4}$ and $\frac{3}{4}$. Find a rational number between $\frac{1}{4}$ and $\frac{1}{2}$, and a rational number between $\frac{1}{2}$ and $\frac{3}{4}$.

42. Find a second rational number between $\frac{1}{4}$ and $\frac{1}{2}$. How many rational numbers are there between $\frac{1}{4}$ and $\frac{1}{2}$? Explain.

ALGEBRA

Square Roots

Build Understanding

A. What number times itself is 64?

$8 \times 8 = 64$ 64 is the ***square*** of 8.

$\sqrt{64} = 8$ 8 is the positive ***square root*** of 64.

Numbers such as 64, 25, and 169 are called ***perfect squares*** because their square roots are integers.

B. Estimate $\sqrt{18}$.

$\sqrt{16} = 4$ and $\sqrt{25} = 5$. So,

$\sqrt{18}$ must be between 4 and 5.

$\sqrt{18}$ cannot be written as the ratio of two integers. Therefore, it is an ***irrational number***. Many square roots are irrational numbers.

C. Find $\sqrt{40}$ to the nearest tenth. A calculator gives this approximate value for $\sqrt{40}$:

6.3245553

So, to the nearest tenth, $\sqrt{40} = 6.3$

D. You may use the table on page 587, like the one shown here, to find the square root of an integer.

n	n^2	$\sqrt{n}$
46	2,116	6.782
47	2,209	6.858
48	2,304	6.928
49	2,401	7.000
50	2,500	7.071

Find $\sqrt{50}$ to the nearest tenth.

Find 50 in the column headed by n. Move across to the $\sqrt{n}$ column. Read: $\sqrt{50} = 7.071$, to the nearest tenth, $\sqrt{50} = 7.1$.

The table on page 587 gives squares and square roots for numbers from 1 to 50. The squares are all exact. However, most of the square roots are approximations.

■ **Talk About Math** In Example B, will $\sqrt{18}$ be closer to 4 or 5? Explain.

Check Understanding

For another example, see Set G, pages 482–483.

1. Is 7 a perfect square? Explain. How about 144? 78?

2. Which integers are the square roots of 9? Explain.

3. Between which two positive integers is $\sqrt{60}$?

4. **Calculator** Use your calculator to find $\sqrt{500}$ to the nearest tenth.

Practice

For More Practice, see Set G, pages 484–485.

Between which two consecutive integers is each of the following?

5. $\sqrt{29}$ **6.** $\sqrt{50}$ **7.** $\sqrt{72}$ **8.** $\sqrt{89}$ **9.** $\sqrt{112}$

Find the two square roots of each of these perfect squares.

10. 49 **11.** 225 **12.** 81 **13.** 36 **14.** 196

Estimation Estimate the positive square root of each number to the nearest integer.

15. 11 **16.** 75 **17.** 150 **18.** 200 **19.** 57

Use your calculator or the table on page 587 to find each square root. Round each answer to the nearest tenth.

20. $\sqrt{81}$ **21.** $\sqrt{36}$ **22.** $\sqrt{100}$ **23.** $\sqrt{64}$ **24.** $\sqrt{49}$

25. $\sqrt{29}$ **26.** $\sqrt{30}$ **27.** $\sqrt{15}$ **28.** $\sqrt{21}$ **29.** $\sqrt{42}$

30. $\sqrt{31}$ **31.** $\sqrt{45}$ **32.** $\sqrt{35}$ **33.** $\sqrt{12^2}$ **34.** $\sqrt{(36)^2}$

Problem Solving

Solve these problems. If necessary, round answers to the nearest tenth.

35. Integers like 81, 36, and 100 are perfect squares. Their square roots are integers. Name three other perfect squares.

36. Name two more integers greater than 1,000 that are perfect squares.

37. If an integer is not a perfect square, its square root is not a rational number. For example, 24 is not a perfect square, so $\sqrt{24}$ is an irrational number. Name three other irrational numbers.

Take risks. Try your hunches. They often work.

38. How many integers are perfect squares? How many are not? How many irrational numbers must there be?

39. Find the length of a side of a square with area 40 cm^2.

40. The box shown has a square base. Its volume is 120 cm^3. Find the dimensions of the base.

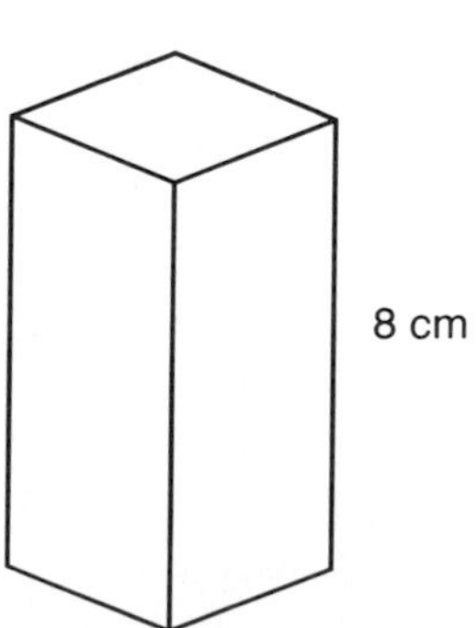

ALGEBRA

Pythagorean Theorem

Build Understanding

ACTIVITY

A. Area Discovery
Materials: Paper, ruler, scissors
Groups: With a partner

About 2,500 years ago, a Greek mathematician named Pythagoras proved that a pattern exists in all right triangles. This pattern had been used by the ancient Egyptians and Babylonians 4,000 years ago.

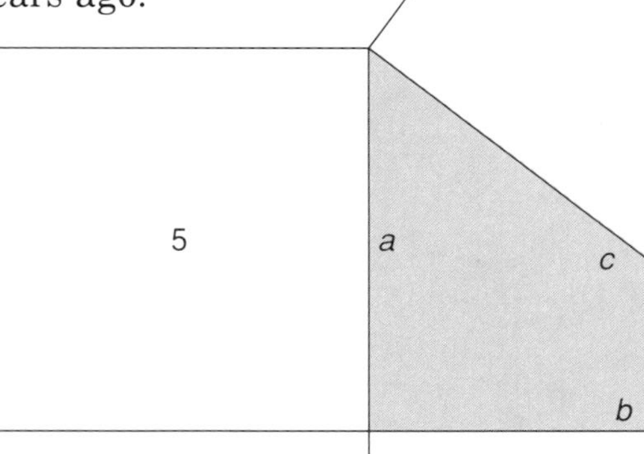

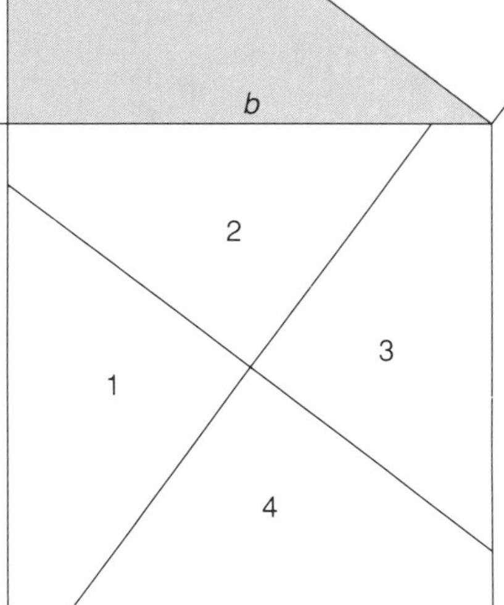

a. What kind of triangle is the colored triangle?

b. Trace the three squares at the right.

c. Cut apart pieces 1, 2, 3, 4, and 5 in the two smaller squares.

d. Fit the pieces into the large square.

e. Area of the square drawn on side a = ▦ units.
Area of the square drawn on side b = ▦ units.
Area of the square drawn on side c = ▦ units.

f. How does the area of the large square compare with the sum of the areas of the two smaller squares?

B. In a right triangle, the side opposite the right angle is the ***hypotenuse***. It is always the longest side. The other two sides are called the ***legs*** of the right triangle.

In a right triangle, the area of the square on the hypotenuse is equal to the sum of the areas of the squares on the legs. Remember you can write the area of a square as $a \times a$ or a^2. In Example A, you would write $a^2 + b^2 = c^2$.

Find the hypotenuse in the figure below.

$$a^2 + b^2 = c^2$$
$$6^2 + 8^2 = c^2$$
$$36 + 64 = c^2$$
$$100 = c^2$$
$$10 = c$$

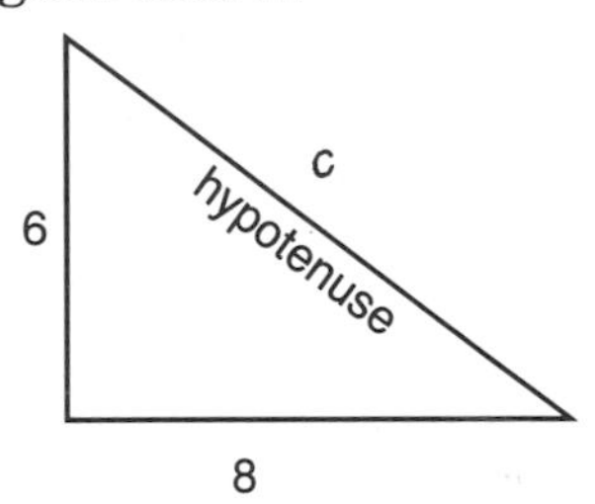

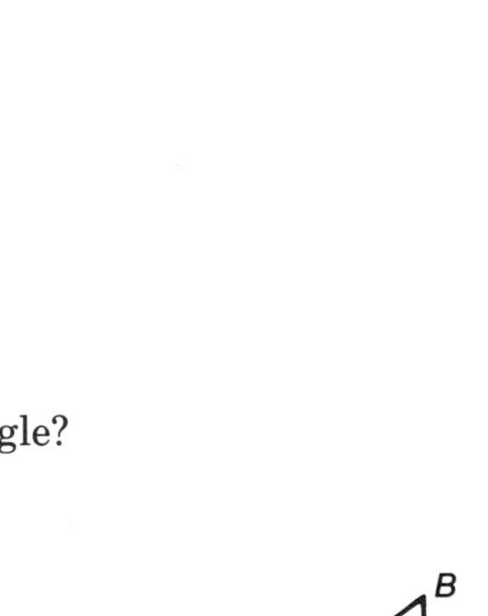

This page from a 2,000 year-old mathematics book shows that Chinese mathematicians knew that $c^2 = a^2 + b^2$ for all right triangles.

C. Find the length of side a.

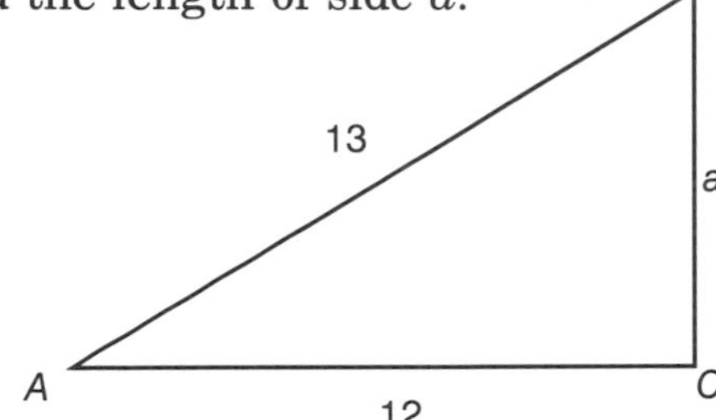

$$a^2 + b^2 = c^2$$
$$a^2 + 12^2 = 13^2$$
$$a^2 + 144 = 169$$
$$a^2 = 25$$
$$a = \sqrt{25}$$
$$a = 5$$

The third side of the triangle is 5 units long.

D. A triangle has sides 3, 3, and 5 units long. Is it a right triangle?

$5^2 = 25$, and $3^2 + 3^2 = 18$

Since $25 \neq 18$, the triangle is not a right triangle.

Write About Math In triangle ABC, angles A and B are acute and angle C is a right angle. The Pythagorean Theorem states that in any right triangle, $a^2 + b^2 = c^2$. What similar statements can be written if $m\angle C < 90°$? if $m\angle C > 90°$?

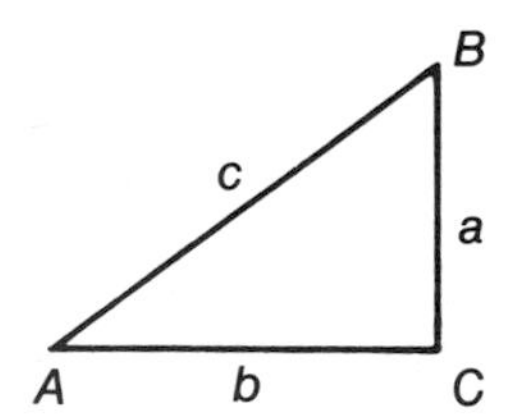

Check Understanding

For another example, see Set H, pages 482–483.

Find the missing numbers.

1. $a^2 + b^2 = c^2$
$9^2 + 12^2 = c^2$
▒ + ▒ $= c^2$
▒ $= c^2$
▒ $= c$

2. $a^2 + b^2 = c^2$
$a^2 + 8^2 = 10^2$
a^2 + ▒ = ▒
a^2 = ▒
a = ▒

3. $a^2 + b^2 = c^2$
$8^2 + b^2 = 17^2$
▒ + b^2 = ▒
b^2 = ▒
b = ▒

Practice

For More Practice, see Set H, pages 484–485.

Two side lengths of a right triangle are given. Find the third length.

4.

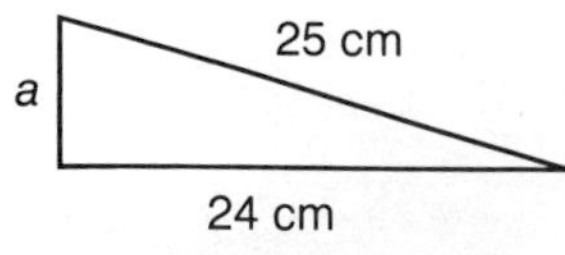

5.

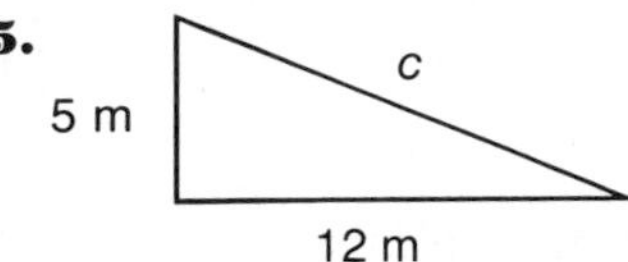

6.

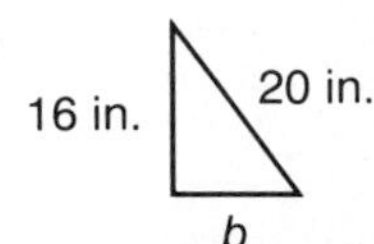

In Exercises 7–22, a, b, and c are lengths of sides in a right triangle. Find the third length. Round decimal answers to the nearest tenth.

7. $a = 12$, $b = 16$, $c = $ ■

8. $a = 6$, $b = 3$, $c = $ ■

9. $a = 2$, $b = 1$, $c = $ ■

10. $a = 21$, $b = $ ■, $c = 29$

11. $a = 24$, $b = $ ■, $c = 25$

12. $a = $ ■, $b = 15$, $c = 39$

13. $a = $ ■, $b = 12$, $c = 20$

14. $a = 5$, $b = $ ■, $c = 19$

15. $a = 17$, $b = 17$, $c = $ ■

16. $a = $ ■, $b = 25$, $c = 60$

17. $a = 45$, $b = 60$, $c = $ ■

18. $a = 18$, $b = $ ■, $c = 27$

19. $a = 5$, $b = $ ■, $c = 14$

20. $a = 7$, $b = 11$, $c = $ ■

21. $a = 9$, $b = 9$, $c = $ ■

22. $a = 1$, $b = $ ■, $c = 5$

Tell whether or not each of the following is a right triangle.

23. $a = 3, b = 2, c = 4$

24. $a = 20, b = 21, c = 29$

25. $a = 15, b = 36, c = 39$

26. $a = 8, b = 7, c = 15$

27. $a = 24, b = 32, c = 40$

28. $a = 42, b = 40, c = 58$

Problem Solving

Solve each problem. If necessary, round answers to the nearest tenth.

29. In ancient Egypt, surveyors used ropes with knots placed at equal intervals to measure distances. If Egyptian surveyors used knotted ropes to form the triangle shown at the right, is angle C a right angle?

30. Central Park in New York is 0.5 mi wide by 2.5 mi long. Find the length of a diagonal path across the park.

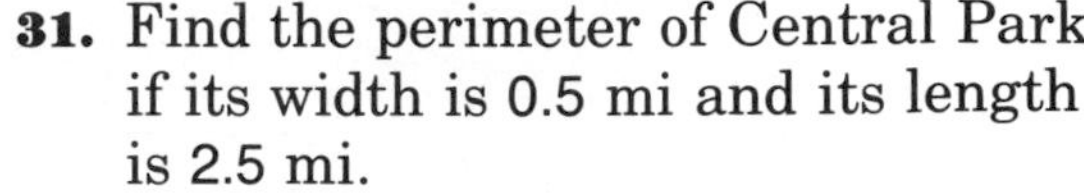

31. Find the perimeter of Central Park if its width is 0.5 mi and its length is 2.5 mi.

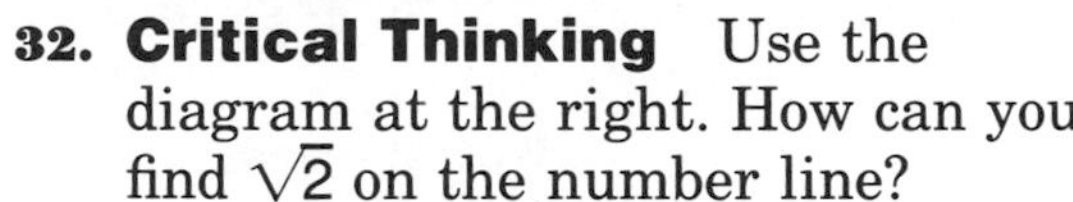

32. Critical Thinking Use the diagram at the right. How can you find $\sqrt{2}$ on the number line?

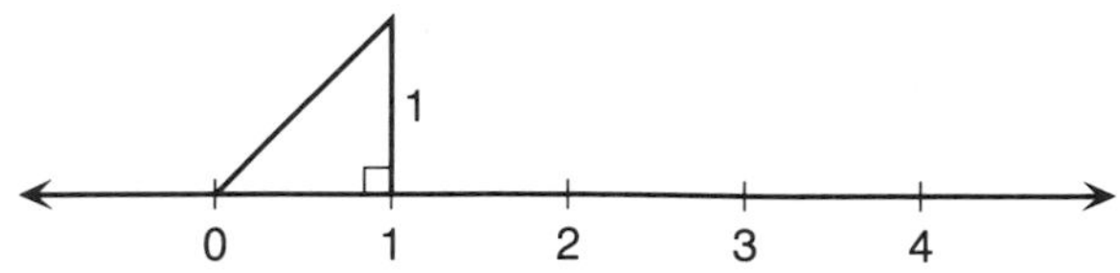

33. Use the result of Problem 32 to find $\sqrt{3}$ on the number line.

Pythagorean triples are sets of three numbers, a, b, c, such that $a^2 + b^2 = c^2$. For example, since $3^2 + 4^2 = 5^2$, the numbers 3, 4, and 5 form a Pythagorean triple.

Pythagorean Triples

a	b	c
3	4	5
6	8	10
9	12	15

34. In the list of the Pythagorean triples at the right, find a pattern and write the next two lines.

35. Test the triples you wrote in Exercise 34 to see if $a^2 + b^2 = c^2$.

36. Examine the results of Exercises 1–28 to find other Pythagorean triples.

37. Use a pattern similar to that of Exercise 34 to make a list of other sets of three numbers. Test the sets of numbers in your list to see if $a^2 + b^2 = c^2$.

38. Critical Thinking Write a statement about how you might find even more Pythagorean triples when you know one.

39. How many Pythagorean triples are there?

Pythagoras conducted extensive mathematical investigations, including studies of odd and even numbers and prime and square numbers.

Choose a Strategy

Pythagorean Search The perimeter of a right triangle is less than 25 inches. The length of each side in inches is a whole number. What is the greatest possible area?

40. Study the results of Problems 34–37. How can you use these results to solve the problem?

41. What strategy will you use?

42. How can you be sure that you have identified the greatest possible area?

ALGEBRA

Use a Formula

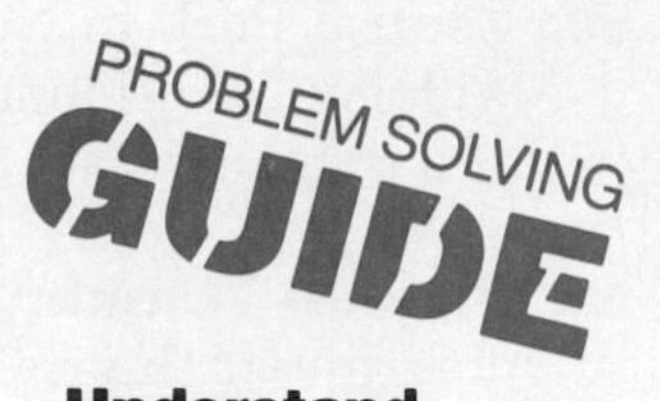

Understand
QUESTION
FACTS
KEY IDEA

Plan and Solve
STRATEGY
ANSWER

Look Back
SENSIBLE ANSWER
ALTERNATE APPROACH

Build Understanding

Sometimes when solving a problem it is helpful to use a formula. One of the formulas that can be used to solve problems is the Pythagorean Theorem, $a^2 + b^2 = c^2$

Romeo needs a ladder to reach Juliet's window, which is 12 feet above the ground. His ladder is 15 feet long. How far away from the wall can the base of the ladder be placed and still reach the window?

Understand QUESTION How far away from the wall can the ladder be placed?

FACTS The hypotenuse is 15 ft long. One side is 12 ft long.

Plan and Solve STRATEGY You can use a formula, the Pythagorean Theorem, to find the length of the third side of the triangle. This will tell you how far from the side of the wall the ladder should be placed.

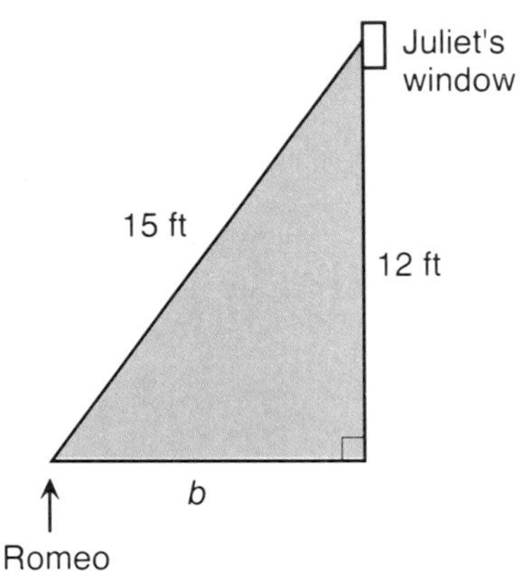

$$a^2 + b^2 = c^2$$

$$12^2 + b^2 = 15^2$$

$$144 + b^2 = 225$$

$$b^2 = 81$$

$$b = 9$$

ANSWER Romeo can place the foot of the ladder 9 feet away from the wall and still reach Juliet's window.

Look Back SENSIBLE ANSWER Check your work.

$$9^2 + 12^2 \stackrel{?}{=} 15^2$$

$$81 + 144 \stackrel{?}{=} 225$$

$$225 = 225$$

Talk About Math
What would happen if Romeo put the base of the ladder 15 ft away from the foot of the wall?

Check Understanding

1. Complete these versions of the formula for the Pythagorean Theorem and use one to solve Exercise 2.

$a^2 = c^2$ ▒ b^2

$b^2 = c^2$ ▒ a^2

2. Romeo needed to reach a 15-ft height with a 17-ft ladder. How far from the wall should he put the base of the ladder? Complete.

$b^2 = c^2 -$ ▒^{2}

$b^2 = 17^2 -$ ▒$^2 =$ ▒

$b =$ ▒

Practice

Solve each problem.

3. As Romeo and Juliet were leaving her house, they had to cross the town square. Each side of the square is about 40 meters long. How much shorter would it be for them to cut across the square rather than go along the perimeter? Give your answer to the nearest meter.

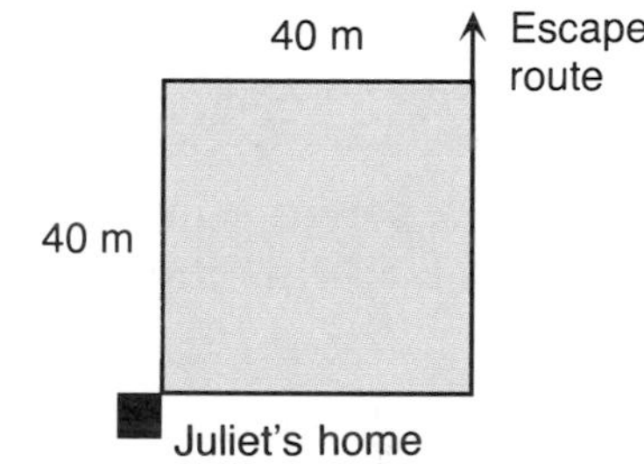

4. **Calculator** When he was flying his kite, Romeo noticed that he had let out 75 feet of string and that the kite was directly over a spot 48 feet away. About how high above the ground was the kite? Give your answer to the nearest foot.

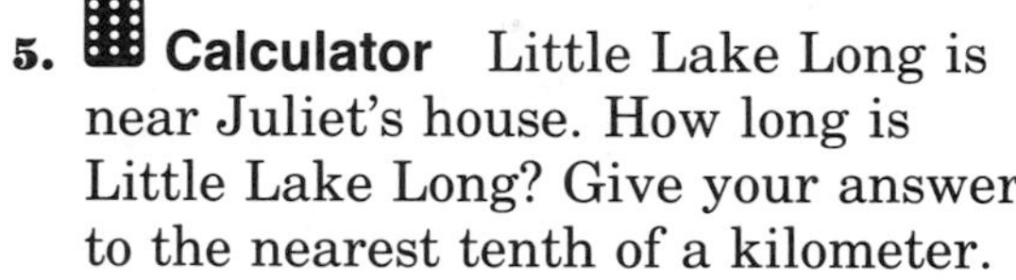

5. **Calculator** Little Lake Long is near Juliet's house. How long is Little Lake Long? Give your answer to the nearest tenth of a kilometer.

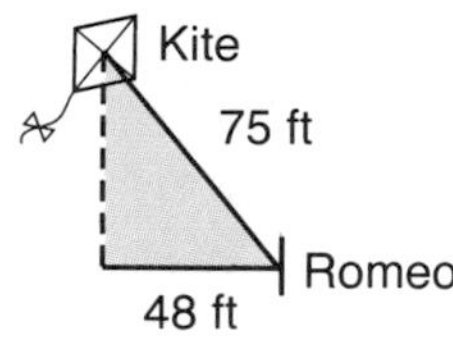

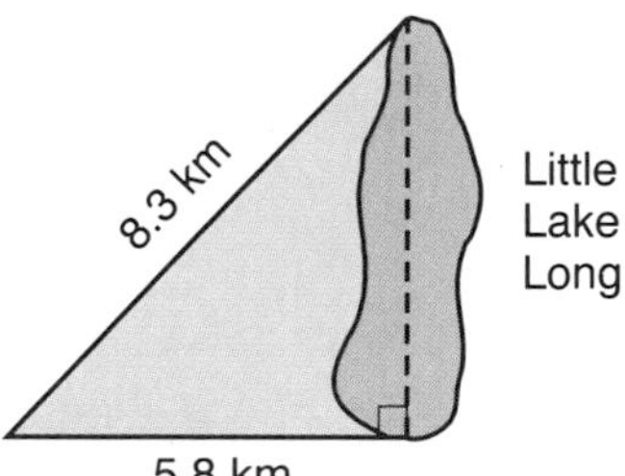

Reading ______ Math

Using a Glossary Use the Glossary to find the definition of each underlined word. Use the definition to complete each statement.

1. In the expression 2^3, the exponent is ▒.

2. In the expression 4^2, the base is ▒.

3. The fifth power of 2 is ▒.

4. Five raised to the 3rd power is ▒.

ALGEBRA

Exponents and Powers of 10

Build Understanding

A. In a science fiction book, *Lightyears in Space*, Aaron read that a spacecraft was capable of flying at the speed of light. At that speed, in 5 seconds it would travel almost 1,000,000 miles. One mile is 0.000001 of that distance.

$1{,}000{,}000 = 10 \times 10 \times 10 \times 10 \times 10 \times 10 = 10^6$

$0.000001 = \frac{1}{1{,}000{,}000} = \frac{1}{10^6} = 10^{-6}$

If n is a positive integer, 10^n means that 10 is a factor n times and 10^{-n} is equal to $\frac{1}{10^n}$.

B. What pattern do you notice?

$10^4 = 10{,}000 \qquad 10^{-4} = \frac{1}{10{,}000} = 0.0001$

$10^3 = 1{,}000 \qquad 10^{-3} = \frac{1}{1{,}000} = 0.001$

$10^2 = 100 \qquad 10^{-2} = \frac{1}{100} = 0.01$

$10^1 = 10 \qquad 10^{-1} = \frac{1}{10} = 0.1$

$10^0 = 1 \qquad 10^0 = 1 = 1$

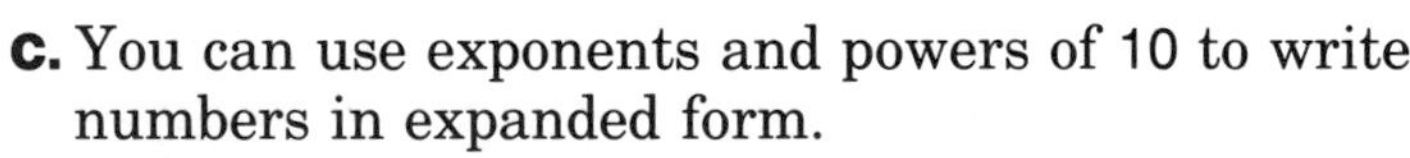

C. You can use exponents and powers of 10 to write numbers in expanded form.

$9{,}356 = (9 \times 10^3) + (3 \times 10^2) + (5 \times 10^1) + (6 \times 10^0)$

$67.045 = 60 + 7 + \frac{0}{10} + \frac{4}{100} + \frac{5}{1{,}000}$

$= 6(10^1) + 7(10^0) + 0(10^{-1}) + 4(10^{-2}) + 5(10^{-3})$

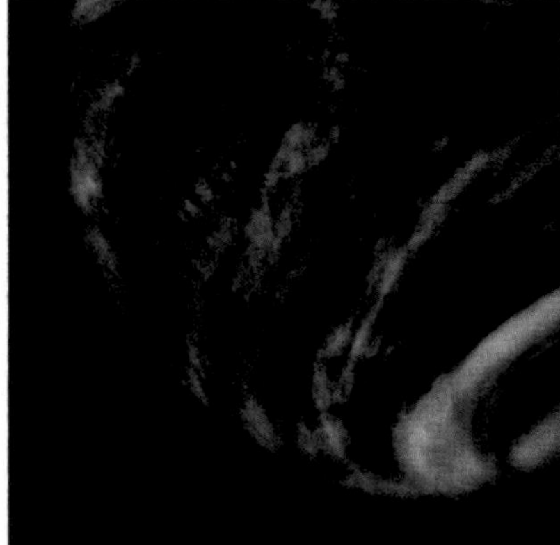

■ **Talk About Math** If n is a negative integer, is 10^n greater or less than 1? Explain. What about 10^{-n} if n is a negative integer?

Check Understanding

For another example, see Set I, pages 482–483.

Write in expanded form.

1. 0.342 **2.** 4.033 **3.** 12.902 **4.** 40,322 **5.** 25.9

Write in standard form.

6. $3(10^4) + 2(10^3) + 5(10^2) + 8(10) + 3 + 7(10^{-1}) + 5(10^{-2})$

7. $6(10^{-2}) + 8(10^{-3})$

8. $3(10^3) + 9 + 4(10^{-2}) + 5\,(10^{-3}) + 9(10^{-4})$

Practice

For More Practice, see Set I, pages 484—485.

Write each number with an exponent.

9. 1,000 **10.** 100,000 **11.** $\frac{1}{1{,}000}$ **12.** $\frac{1}{100{,}000}$

13. 1 **14.** 10,000,000 **15.** 0.0000001 **16.** 0.0001

Write in standard form.

17. 10^7 **18.** 10^3 **19.** 10^{-5} **20.** 10^0

21. 10^{-10} **22.** $4(10^5)$ **23.** 10^{-7} **24.** $7(10^{-2})$

Write in expanded form.

25. 792 **26.** 23,789 **27.** 1,229,756 **28.** 0.876

29. 0.156 **30.** 0.2759 **31.** 0.0452 **32.** 20.506

33. 45.2 **34.** 7.257 **35.** 50.23 **36.** 456.003

Write in standard form.

37. $4(10)^5 + 3(10)^4 + 8(10)^3 + 3(10)^2 + 8(10) + 7$

38. $3(10^{-1}) + 5(10^{-2}) + 8(10^{-3})$ **39.** $4(10^2) + 5 + 6(10^{-1}) + 5\ (10^{-3})$

Problem Solving

Solve.

40. **Critical Thinking** Write 10^5, 10^8, and 10^{12} without exponents. Write a rule about the number of zeros in 10^n when written without exponents.

41. **Critical Thinking** Write 10^{-2}, 10^{-3}, and 10^{-4} without exponents. Write a rule about the number of zeros in 10^{-n} when it is written without exponents.

42. In *Lightyears in Space*, one distance described is 10^{100}. This number is called a *googol*. How many zeros are in the standard form of 1 googol?

43. In *Lightyears in Space,* Marta read about a computer that has a *gigabyte* of memory. The number of bytes in a gigabyte is 1 followed by 9 zeros. Write this number with an exponent.

44. Computer time is measured in *nanoseconds*. A nanosecond is 0.000000001 second. Write this number with an exponent.

45. How many nanoseconds are there in a second? in a minute?

ALGEBRA

Scientific Notation

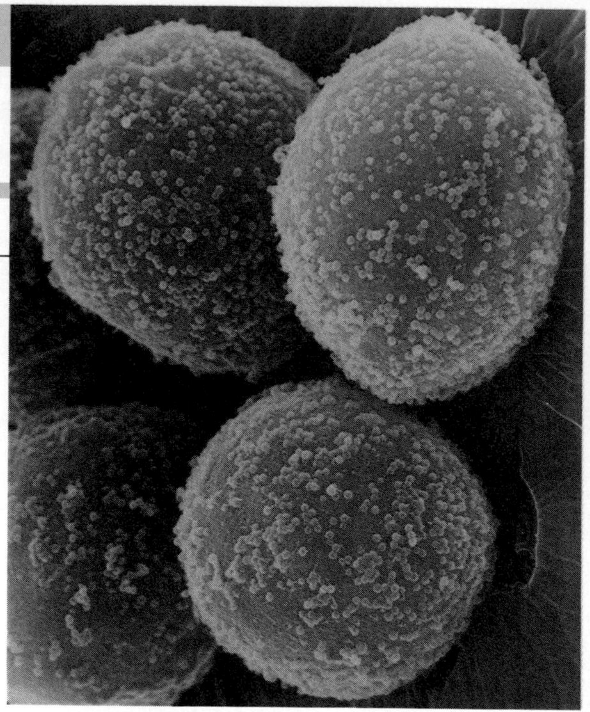

A grain of pollen ranges in size from 15 to 200 micrometers long. One micrometer is equal to 10^{-6} meter or one millionth of a meter.

Build Understanding

Scientists must often work with numbers that are very large or very small. ***Scientific notation*** is a convenient way to write such numbers. For example, $32{,}000{,}000 = 3.2 \times 10^7$ and $0.0000017 = 1.7 \times 10^{-6}$.

To write a number in scientific notation, write it as a product in which the first factor is a number greater than or equal to 1 and less than 10 and the second factor is a power of 10.

A. Hanna is a laboratory scientist. She writes 87,000 in scientific notation.

The decimal point must be moved 4 places to the left.

8.7000. 4 places to the left

The number of places the decimal point is moved to the left gives the positive exponent, or power, of 10.

$\mathbf{87{,}000 = 8.7 \times 10^4}$

B. Hanna writes the very small number 0.000004 in scientific notation.

The decimal point must be moved 6 places to the right.

0.000004. 6 places to the right

The number of places the decimal point is moved to the right gives the negative exponent, or power, of 10.

$\mathbf{0.000004 = 4.0 \times 10^{-6}}$

C. She can write 1.4×10^5 in ***standard form***. She knows that 10^5 is 1 followed by 5 zeros. Thus we move the decimal point 5 places to the right.

$\mathbf{1.4 \times 10^5 \rightarrow 140000.}$

$\mathbf{= 140{,}000}$

D. She converts the small number 6.57×10^{-3} into standard form. She knows 10^{-3} means 0.001. Thus we move the decimal point 3 places to the left.

$\mathbf{6.57 \times 10^{-3} \rightarrow .00657}$

$\mathbf{= 0.00657}$

Write About Math When a number is written in scientific notation, how can you quickly tell if it is a large number or a small number?

Check Understanding

For another example, see Set J, pages 482–483.

Find the value of n in each number.

1. $3{,}579 = 3.579 \times 10^n$ **2.** $89{,}300 = n \times 10^4$ **3.** $0.145 = 1.45 \times 10^n$

4. $0.00593 = n \times 10^{-3}$ **5.** $n = 2.4 \times 10^5$ **6.** $n = 6.75 \times 10^{-4}$

Practice

For More Practice, see Set J, pages 484–485.

Write each number in scientific notation.

7. 275 **8.** 5,725,000 **9.** 98.5 **10.** 937.56

11. 0.471 **12.** 0.011 **13.** 0.000201 **14.** 0.00007

15. 0.0602 **16.** 125.6 **17.** 0.0008 **18.** 0.0052

Write each number in standard form.

19. 8.12×10^5 **20.** 4.698×10^2 **21.** 1.03×10^7 **22.** 5.2×10^{10}

23. 3.7×10^{-1} **24.** 5.7234×10^{-4} **25.** 7.964×10^{-3} **26.** 4.7×10^{-8}

27. 6.04×10^{-2} **28.** 9.25×10^6 **29.** 2.4×10^{-5} **30.** 6.093×10^4

Problem Solving

Solve.

31. The amount of energy released by splitting an atom is 4×10^{-11} joules. Write that number in standard form.

32. The estimated surface area of Jupiter is 64,017,000,000 km^2. Write that number in scientific notation.

33. Carol read that a snail moves 0.03 miles per hour and a turtle moves 0.18 miles per hour. Write each rate in scientific notation.

34. Hanna read that there were 2.45×10^8 people in the United States. Write that number in standard form.

35. **Critical Thinking** List these numbers in order from least to greatest: 1.23×10^{-2}, 3.44×10^{-3}, 1.02×10^4, 7.8×10^{-5}. Do not rewrite the numbers in standard form.

Skills Review

Express each quantity as an integer.

1. A loss of 20 points
2. 5 degrees below zero
3. A profit of \$27

Add or subtract.

4. $-7 + 9$
5. $9 + (-3)$
6. $-12 + (-10) + 2$
7. $15 - (-2)$
8. $-14 - (-5)$
9. $-13 - 8$

Multiply or divide.

10. $12 \times (-5)$
11. -8×10
12. $(-4)(-4)(-4)$
13. $56 \div (-7)$
14. $-72 \div (-8)$
15. $-32 \div 4$

Compare. Use $<$, $>$, or $=$.

16. $-\frac{1}{3}$ ▒ $-\frac{1}{2}$
17. 0 ▒ $-\frac{1}{4}$
18. $-5\frac{3}{4}$ ▒ $-5\frac{6}{8}$
19. $\frac{4}{2}$ ▒ -2

Estimate the positive square root of each number to the nearest integer.

20. $\sqrt{80}$
21. $\sqrt{51}$
22. $\sqrt{140}$

In each exercise, a, b and c are lengths of sides in a right triangle. Find the missing length. Round answers to the nearest tenth.

23. $a = 36$, $b = 15$, $c =$ ▒
24. $a = 7$, $b =$ ▒, $c = 25$
25. $a =$ ▒, $b = 20$, $c = 25$

Write in standard form.

26. 10^{-4}
27. 7.8×10^{-2}
28. 9×10^{5}

Problem-Solving Review

Solve each problem.

29. The pitcher's mound on a baseball field is about 60 ft from home plate. A pitcher's fastball travels about 120 ft per second. How long does it take the ball to reach home plate? Use the formula $d = rt$.

30. A baseball infield has the shape shown. What shape is the polygon?

31. In June, Diego got 18 hits out of 54 times at bat. If he bats 81 times in July, how many hits must he get to keep his June ratio of hits to times at bat?

32. Death Valley, California is the lowest spot in North America. It is about 282 ft, or 85 m, below sea level. Write the depth below sea level as integers.

33. Jubilee Pass, south of Death Valley, has an elevation of 1,280 ft. What is the difference between the lowest point in Death Valley and the elevation of Jubilee Pass?

34. **Data File** Use the data on pages 558–559. How many different combinations of settings are possible for the drum pads? Write your answer using exponential notation.

35. **Make a Data File** Consult a world almanac or other reference. Find the record high and low temperatures for your state and for 6 neighboring states. Make a bar graph showing the data.

Cumulative Skills Review • Chapters 1–13

Write prime or composite.

1. 83 **2.** 93 **3.** 77 **4.** 245 **5.** 181 **6.** 459

Choose the best measure.

7. The length of a boat
a. 8 yd **b.** 8 in.
c. 8 mi

8. The capacity of a bowl
a. 4 oz **b.** 4 c
c. 4 gal

9. The weight of a grapefruit
a. $\frac{1}{4}$ mg **b.** $\frac{1}{4}$ g
c. $\frac{1}{4}$ kg

Solve each proportion.

10. $\frac{9}{27} = \frac{n}{3}$ **11.** $\frac{8}{m} = \frac{40}{50}$ **12.** $\frac{6}{0.2} = \frac{v}{0.8}$ **13.** $\frac{t}{15} = \frac{7.5}{5}$

Identify each figure.

14. 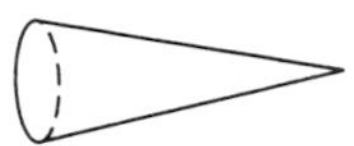

15. 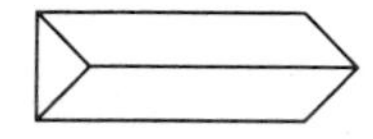

16. 

17. 

The table shows attendance at a school play.

18. Make a bar graph to display the data.

Week 1		Week 2		Week 3		Week 4	
Adult	Student	Adult	Student	Adult	Student	Adult	Student
356	206	298	225	410	176	203	251

A person selects markers from a drawer without replacing them. The drawer contains 20 markers: 5 are red, 4 are blue, 6 are green, 3 are yellow and 2 are orange. Find each probability.

19. *P*(red, red) **20.** *P*(blue, orange) **21.** *P*(green, blue)

22. *P*(red, blue) **23.** *P*(red, red, blue) **24.** *P*(red, red, red)

Write the absolute value and opposite of each integer.

25. −5 **26.** 27 **27.** −99 **28.** 256

Write each number in expanded form.

29. 730 **30.** 60,900 **31.** 586.03 **32.** 0.00062

Write each number in scientific notation.

33. 5,000,000 **34.** 0.00034 **35.** 0.00000018 **36.** 860

Reteaching

Set A pages 452–453

The absolute value of a number is its distance from 0 on the number line.

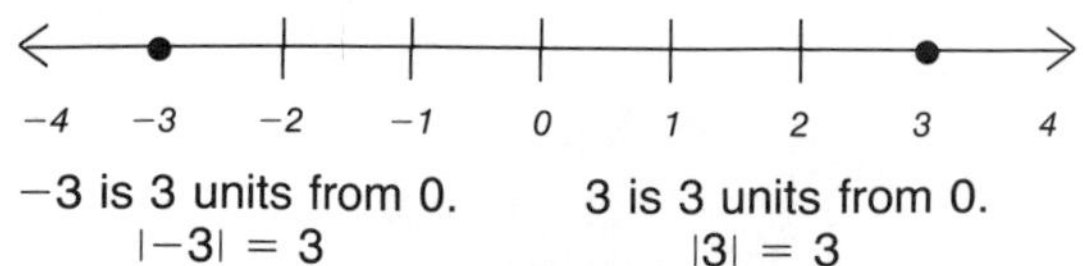

−3 is 3 units from 0. |−3| = 3

3 is 3 units from 0. |3| = 3

Remember, the absolute value of a nonzero number is always positive.

Write the absolute value.

1. −12 **2.** 8 **3.** 0

4. −45 **5.** 20 **6.** −200

Set B pages 454–455

You can use a number line to add two integers.

Find −6 + 4.

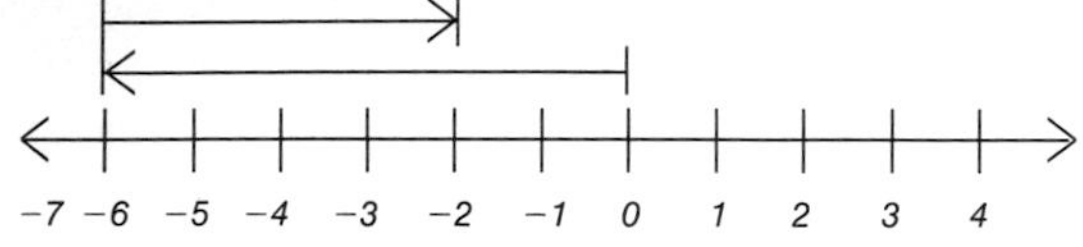

Move 6 units left. Then move 4 units right.

−6 + 4 = −2

Remember, the sum of two integers with opposite signs has the same sign as the sign of the integer with the greater absolute value.

Add. Use a number line if necessary.

1. −3 + 4 **2.** −12 + (−3)

3. 14 + (−6) **4.** −23 + 15

Set C pages 456–457

Find −5 − (−12).

−5 − (−12) = −5 + 12
= 7

To subtract −12, add the opposite.

Remember, to subtract an integer, add its opposite.

1. −7 − (−2) **2.** −11 − (−16)

3. 8 − (−2) **4.** 9 − 15

5. −4 − (−8) **6.** 12 − 5

7. 16 − 29 **8.** −14 − (−9)

Set D pages 458–459

Find −2 × 5.

−2 × 5 = (−2) + (−2) + (−2) + (−2) + (−2)
= −10

Multiply −2 × 5. The product is negative.

Remember, the product of two negative integers is positive.

1. −3 × 7 **2.** −5 × (−4)

3. 12 × (−7) **4.** 9 × 6

5. −5 × (−2) × (−3) **6.** 2 × 7 × (−5)

Set E pages 460–461

Find −36 ÷ 9.

36 ÷ 9 = 4 Divide as if the numbers were whole numbers.

−36 ÷ 9 = −4 The quotient is negative because the numbers have opposite signs.

Remember, the quotient of two integers with the same sign is positive.

1. 12 ÷ (−6) **2.** −36 ÷ 4

3. −100 ÷ (−10) **4.** 35 ÷ (−7)

5. 120 ÷ 12 **6.** −39 ÷ 3

Set F pages 466–467

Find $-3\frac{1}{2} - 2\frac{1}{4}$.

$$-3\frac{1}{2} - 2\frac{1}{4} = -3\frac{1}{2} + \left(-2\frac{1}{4}\right)$$
$$= -\frac{7}{2} + \left(-\frac{9}{4}\right)$$
$$= -\frac{14}{4} + \left(-\frac{9}{4}\right)$$
$$= -\frac{23}{4}, \text{ or } -5\frac{3}{4}$$

To subtract, add the opposite. Write the numbers as ratios of two integers.

Remember, the rules for operating with integers apply to rational numbers.

Compute.

1. $-15\frac{2}{3} + 9\frac{5}{6}$ **2.** $3\frac{2}{5} - 4\frac{4}{5}$

3. $1\frac{3}{7} \times \left(-4\frac{1}{5}\right)$ **4.** $-1\frac{5}{8} \div 1\frac{7}{32}$

5. $-13\frac{7}{16} - \left(-7\frac{5}{12}\right)$ **6.** $11\frac{1}{4} \div \left(-2\frac{1}{2}\right)$

Set G pages 468–469

You may use a table or a calculator to find the square root of a number if it is not a perfect square.

$\sqrt{60} = 7.74597 \approx 7.7$

Remember, the square root of a number multiplied by itself equals the number.

Find the positive square root of each number. Round to the nearest tenth if necessary.

1. 36 **2.** 100 **3.** 144 **4.** 225

5. 15 **6.** 84 **7.** 110 **8.** 300

Set H pages 470–473

You can use the Pythagorean Theorem to find the missing side of a right triangle.

$b = 4$, c, $a = 3$

$$c^2 = a^2 + b^2$$
$$c^2 = 3^2 + 4^2$$
$$= 9 + 16 = 25$$
$$c = \sqrt{25} = 5$$

Remember, the hypotenuse is the longest side.

Find the missing length.

1. 7, 25, a **2.** 20, b, 16 **3.** 10, c, 24

Set I pages 476–477

Exponents can be used to write a number in expanded form.

$$386 = (3 \times 100) + (8 \times 10) + (6 \times 1)$$
$$= (3 \times 10^2) + (8 \times 10^1) + (6 \times 10^0)$$

Remember, use negative exponents for decimal numbers.

Write in exponential form.

1. 63,000 **2.** 3,825 **3.** 0.07

Set J pages 478–479

Write 127,000 in scientific notation.

$127{,}000 = 1.27 \times 10^5$ 5 places to the left

Remember, if you move the decimal point to the right, you need to use a negative exponent.

Write in scientific notation.

1. 35 **2.** 8,000 **3.** 0.002

4. 452,000 **5.** 0.0003 **6.** 0.2365

7. 3,809,000,000 **8.** 0.0000034

More Practice

Set A pages 452–453

Complete each exercise. Use > or <.

1. -8 ▦ 12 **2.** -11 ▦ 3 **3.** -12 ▦ -24 **4.** 21 ▦ -4

Write the absolute value.

5. -3 **6.** 7 **7.** 8 **8.** 0 **9.** -9 **10.** -21

Set B pages 454–455

Add. Use a number line if necessary.

1. $-2 + 13$ **2.** $11 + (-8)$ **3.** $-9 + (-4)$ **4.** $-12 + 9$

5. $23 + (-18)$ **6.** $-12 + (-14)$ **7.** $12 + 14$ **8.** $-9 + (-4)$

9. $-8 + 16$ **10.** $14 + (-13)$ **11.** $8 + (-8)$ **12.** $7 + (-18)$

Set C pages 456–457

Write the opposite of each number.

1. -14 **2.** 0 **3.** 12 **4.** -5 **5.** -9 **6.** 8

Find the difference.

7. $-4 - 8$ **8.** $15 - 20$ **9.** $8 - (-4)$ **10.** $23 - 15$

11. $-9 - (-15)$ **12.** $-8 - (-3)$ **13.** $21 - (-3)$ **14.** $0 - (-6)$

Set D pages 458–459

Tell whether each product will be positive, negative, or zero.

1. $2(-7)$ **2.** $(-3)(-4)$ **3.** $(0)(6)$ **4.** $(-5)(3)$

Find each product.

5. $-3 \times (-5)$ **6.** 2×8 **7.** $(-4) \times 6$ **8.** $(-12)(-6)$

9. $4 \times (-9)$ **10.** -3×7 **11.** $(-6)(5)$ **12.** $14(-10)$

Set E pages 460–461

Find each quotient.

1. $24 \div (-8)$ **2.** $18 \div 6$ **3.** $(-33) \div (-11)$ **4.** $-25 \div 5$

5. $0 \div (-6)$ **6.** $20 \div (-5)$ **7.** $-100 \div (-20)$ **8.** $-55 \div 5$

9. $84 \div 4$ **10.** $0 \div 9$ **11.** $121 \div (-11)$ **12.** $-300 \div 50$

13. $45 \div (-9)$ **14.** $-66 \div (-11)$ **15.** $-72 \div 9$ **16.** $54 \div 6$

Set F pages 466–467

Compare. Use <, >, or =.

1. $-2\frac{1}{2}$ ▒ $3\frac{1}{4}$ **2.** $6\frac{1}{2}$ ▒ $6\frac{1}{3}$ **3.** $-7\frac{2}{3}$ ▒ $-7\frac{3}{4}$ **4.** $-10\frac{5}{8}$ ▒ $-10\frac{5}{6}$

Write the opposite of each rational number.

5. $-2\frac{3}{4}$ **6.** $6\frac{1}{2}$ **7.** $-12\frac{3}{5}$ **8.** $18\frac{1}{7}$ **9.** $11\frac{6}{11}$ **10.** $-21\frac{3}{5}$

Compute.

11. $\frac{2}{3} \times \left(-6\frac{3}{5}\right)$ **12.** $4\frac{1}{2} - \left(-3\frac{5}{6}\right)$ **13.** $12\frac{5}{8} + \left(-16\frac{1}{4}\right)$ **14.** $-5\frac{1}{2} \div \left(-1\frac{3}{4}\right)$

Set G pages 468–469

Find the positive square root of each number.

1. 25 **2.** 100 **3.** 144 **4.** 256

Use your calculator or the table on page 587 to help find the square root of each number. Round each answer to the nearest tenth.

5. 82 **6.** 21 **7.** 115 **8.** 250

Set H pages 470–473

In each exercise, a, b, and c are the lengths of the sides in a right triangle. The hypotenuse is c. Find the missing length.

1. $a = 10$, $b =$ ▒, $c = 26$

2. $a = 15$, $b = 20$, $c =$ ▒

3. $a =$ ▒, $b = 30$, $c = 34$

4. $a = 4$, $b = 8$, $c =$ ▒

Set I pages 476–477

Write in standard form.

1. 10^3 **2.** 10^{-2} **3.** $(4 \times 10^2) + (3 \times 10) + (0 \times 10^0) + (2 \times 10^{-1})$

Write in expanded form.

4. 286 **5.** 40,200 **6.** 0.0035 **7.** 0.00806 **8.** 826.0231

Set J pages 478–479

Write in scientific notation.

1. 3,089 **2.** 0.92 **3.** 45,000,000 **4.** 0.00023

Write in standard form.

5. 1.2×10^7 **6.** 1.88×10^{-4} **7.** 8×10^9 **8.** 2.8×10^{-7}

Enrichment

Computing with Scientific Notation

To multiply two numbers written in scientific notation, multiply the decimal parts separately and the powers of ten separately. To multiply powers of ten, add the exponents.

$(3 \times 10^8) \times (2 \times 10^5)$

$= (3 \times 2) \times (10^8 \times 10^5)$

$= (3 \times 2) \times 10^{13}$

$= 6 \times 10^{13}$

To divide two numbers written in scientific notation, divide the decimal parts separately and the powers of ten separately. To divide powers of ten, subtract the exponents.

$(8 \times 10^{15}) \div (2 \times 10^9)$

$= (8 \div 2) \times (10^{15} \div 10^9)$

$= (8 \div 2) \times (10^6)$

$= 4 \times 10^6$

Some answers will need to be rewritten in scientific notation. For example, $(8 \times 10^4) \times (6 \times 10^3) = 48 \times 10^7$. To write 48×10^7 in scientific notation, divide the decimal part of the number by 10, and multiply the power of 10 by 10. Multiplying by 10 and then dividing it by 10 does not change the value of the product.

$$48 \times 10^7 = 4.8 \times 10^8$$

I just have to get organized!

Find each product or quotient.

1. $(2 \times 10^6) \times (4 \times 10^8)$
2. $(9 \times 10^{11}) \div (3 \times 10^4)$
3. $(6 \times 10^{18}) \div (1.5 \times 10^{12})$
4. $(2.3 \times 10^4) \times (3.5 \times 10^7)$
5. $(5.89 \times 10^{13}) \div (1.9 \times 10^6)$
6. $(6.04 \times 10^5) \times (1.23 \times 10^{19})$

Write each number in scientific notation.

7. 26×10^3
8. 98×10^{10}
9. 38.37×10^6
10. 10.8842×10^{26}

Multiply. Write each answer in scientific notation.

11. $(7.5 \times 10^8) \times (8.9 \times 10^7)$
12. $(8.8 \times 10^{18}) \times (9.4 \times 10^{13})$
13. $(6.4 \times 10^5) \times (8.9 \times 10^8) \times (7.5 \times 10^{11})$

Chapter 13 Review/Test

Express the following as integers.

1. 72° above zero

2. A loss of $987

Add or subtract.

3. $13 + (-7)$

4. $(-12) + (-8)$

5. $-8 - 3$

6. $9 - (-5)$

7. $-\frac{1}{4} + 5\frac{1}{3}$

8. $4.3 - 5.2$

9. The first year Bryan owned stock in the Acme Corporation, it gained 8 points. The next year, it lost 15 points. Write an integer to tell how much it changed in the two years.

10. What is the absolute value of -15?

Multiply or divide.

11. $8 \times (-4)$

12. $-12 \times (-5)$

13. $-45 \div 9$

14. $\frac{-52}{-13}$

15. $4\frac{1}{2}(-\frac{5}{9})$

16. $-3.3 \div 33$

17. Show that -3.2 is a rational number by writing it as a ratio of two integers.

18. List the numbers in order from least to greatest: $\frac{1}{3}$, $-2\frac{1}{4}$, $-\frac{5}{7}$

19. Between what two consecutive whole numbers is $\sqrt{10}$?

20. Here is a table of eclipses for one year:

Eclipse	Date	Time (E.S.T.)
Moon	2/20	9:56 A.M.
Sun	3/7	1:08 P.M.
Moon	8/16	9:20 P.M.
Sun	8/31	12:31 A.M.

The time is given as Eastern Standard Time (E.S.T.). The correction for Pacific Standard Time is -3 hours. When should you look for the moon's eclipse on February 20 if you live in Pacific Standard Time?

21. Estimate the positive square root of 53 to the nearest integer.

22. The sides of a right triangle are 3 and 4 units long. How long is the hypotenuse?

23. Jeremy set his 26-foot ladder against a third-floor window sill, which is 24 feet above the ground. How far is the bottom of Jeremy's ladder from the building?

24. Write 523.904 in expanded form.

Write in scientific notation.

25. 150,000,000

26. 0.000035

27. **Write About Math** Suppose that a is a positive number and b is a negative number. Can you be sure that $a - b$ is positive? Explain your answer.

Expressions and Equations with Rational Numbers 14

Did You Know: The word "taxicab" comes from taximeter (a machine to keep track of the fare due) and cabriolet (a kind of one-horse carriage). The Jinrikisha, a two-wheeled cart pulled by a runner, and the pedicab, a three-wheeled vehicle similar to a bicycle, were once widely used as taxicabs in Japan and China. The first motorized taxicabs were used in Paris, France. Today, Mexico City has the largest taxicab fleet with over 60,000 vehicles.

Number-Sense Project

Estimate

Assume you had to pay for transportation to the nearest airport. How much do you think the trip would cost?

Gather Data

Find the cost of taxicab service in your area or in some area you would like to visit. Include the cost for the first mile, for each additional mile, and extra charges that might apply.

Analyze and Report

Compute the actual cost of a ride to the airport, or make up an imaginary ride and compute the cost.

ALGEBRA

Order and Properties of Operations

Build Understanding

You know that the order in which operations are carried out may change the value of the expression.

To compute with rational numbers, use the same standard order of operations that you use with whole numbers and integers.

When there is more than one operation in an expression, first multiply and divide from left to right. Then add and subtract from left to right.

When parentheses or division bars are involved, follow the rules at the right.

First do operations within parentheses.
Next do operations above and below division bars.
Then do remaining operations, using standard order.

Operations with rational numbers have the same properties as operations with whole numbers and integers. These properties can be used together with the standard order of operations to simplify computations.

Commutative properties of addition and multiplication	$(-1.4) + 3 = 3 + (-1.4)$ $\frac{1}{3} \times \frac{3}{4} = \frac{3}{4} \times \frac{1}{3}$
Associative properties of addition and multiplication	$2\frac{1}{2} + \left[\left(-\frac{1}{2}\right) + \frac{2}{3}\right] = \left[2\frac{1}{2} + \left(-\frac{1}{2}\right)\right] + \frac{2}{3}$ $0.4 \times (1.2 \times 5) = (0.4 \times 1.2) \times 5$
Properties of one and zero	$0 + \frac{12}{5} = \frac{12}{5}$ $0 \times (-5.39) = 0$ $1 \times 3\frac{1}{6} = 3\frac{1}{6}$
Distributive property	$6 \times \left(\frac{2}{3} + 4\right) = \left(6 \times \frac{2}{3}\right) + (6 \times 4)$
Closure property If a and b are rational numbers, $a + b$ is a unique rational number, and $a \times b$ is a unique rational number.	$8.7 + 3.2 = 11.9$ $\frac{1}{5} \times \frac{3}{4} = \frac{3}{20}$

A. Compute $\frac{1}{2} \times [(-2) \times 6]$ first by using just the standard order of operations and then by using the associative property.

Standard order of operations

$$\frac{1}{2} \times [(-2) \times 6] = \frac{1}{2} \times (-12)$$
$$= -6$$

Associative property

$$\frac{1}{2} \times [(-2) \times 6] = \left[\frac{1}{2} \times (-2)\right] \times 6$$
$$= -1 \times 6$$
$$= -6$$

B. Compute $8.5 \times 14 + 8.5 \times (-4)$ first by using just the standard order of operations and then by using the distributive property.

Standard order of operations

$$8.5 \times 14 + 8.5 \times (-4) =$$
$$(8.5 \times 14) + [8.5 \times (-4)] =$$
$$119 + (-34) = 85$$

Distributive property

$$8.5 \times 14 + 8.5 \times (-4) =$$
$$8.5 \times [14 + (-4)] =$$
$$8.5 \times (10) = 85$$

C. A fraction or a division bar represents both a division symbol and a grouping symbol. Expressions above or below the bar must be simplified before finding the quotient.

Compute $5.1^2 - \frac{4(6.7 + 2.3)}{18}$.

$$5.1^2 - \frac{4(6.7 + 2.3)}{18} = 5.1^2 - \frac{4(9)}{18}$$ First, do operations inside parentheses.

$$= 5.1^2 - \frac{36}{18}$$ Then do operations above the division bar.

$$= 26.01 - 2 = 24.01$$

■ **Talk About Math** Do you think subtraction of rational numbers is associative? Give examples to show why or why not.

Check Understanding

For another example, see Set A, pages 512–513.

Use the standard order of operations to compute each answer.

1. $12 + 18 \times (-2)$
2. $2^3 \times 5 - \frac{24}{6}$
3. $\frac{6\frac{1}{2} - 2}{2} + 4\frac{3}{4}$

Find each missing number. Name the property you used.

4. ▒ $\times (-54.8) = -54.8$
5. $(3 \times$ ▒$) + (3 \times 12) = 3(9 + 12)$
6. $5 + [6.2 + (-4.1)] =$ (▒ $+ 6.2) + (-4.1)$
7. $3\frac{1}{2} \times$ ▒ $= 0$

Practice

For More Practice, see Set A, pages 514–515.

Compute each answer. State which property or properties you used.

8. $138.2 \times 79.23 \times 0 \times (-41)$

9. $(4)\left(\frac{7}{2} + \frac{3}{4}\right)$

10. $(23.5 \times 1) + (1.45 \times 0) + 6.5$

11. $-2.8 \times 7 + (-2.8) \times 3$

12. $\left(\frac{5}{16}\right)(8 - 8)$

13. $(17.4)(6) + (17.4)(-5)$

14. $(-15)\left(\frac{2}{3} + \frac{4}{5}\right)$

15. $\left(2\frac{3}{4} + -2\frac{3}{4}\right)(6 + -11)$

Find the value of the variable that makes the statement true. Name the property or properties you used.

16. $(-7)(64.8) = 64.8x$

17. $\frac{7}{8}b = \frac{7}{8}$

18. $27.6 \times (g + 45) = 27.6 \times 15 + 27.6 \times 45$

19. $-6 + n = -6$

20. $3w = 0$

21. $8(9 - 4) = 72 - r$

22. $7\frac{1}{3} + x = 1\frac{3}{4} + 7\frac{1}{3}$

23. $(3.2 \times 6.4) \times 1.8 = 3.2 \times (6.4 \times b)$

24. $3.5(16 + 1) = n + 3.5$

25. $9.17 = 9.17x$

Compute each answer using the standard order of operations.

26. $5 + (-8)[21 + (-17)] + 2.75$

27. $-21 + \dfrac{\frac{7}{2} + (-4)}{6} \times 24$

28. $\dfrac{17 - 5(-3 + 4)}{3 - 3^2} + \dfrac{2}{5}$

29. $\frac{3}{4}[5 + 4 \times 2 + (-13)] \div 10$

30. $\left(\dfrac{6^2 + 8^2}{40 - 30}\right)\left(\dfrac{7^2 + 1}{2^2 + 6}\right)$

31. $17.5 + (-12) \div 0.75 + 6 + (-7.5)$

32. $\dfrac{6(-7 + 5) - (3 + -15)}{2(3^2 + 9^2)}$

33. $15 \times \dfrac{\frac{4}{5} + 1}{3} + (-4)$

Insert grouping symbols to make the equations true.

34. $4 + 3 \times 4 \div 4 + 2 = 9$

35. $4 + 3 \times 4 \div 4 + 2 = \frac{16}{6}$

36. $9 + 4 \times 6 \div 3 - 2 = 9$

37. Insert grouping symbols in a different arrangement that still makes Exercise 36 true.

Problem Solving

Number Sense The diagram below shows all of the kinds of numbers you have studied. Classify each number by listing all the names that apply.

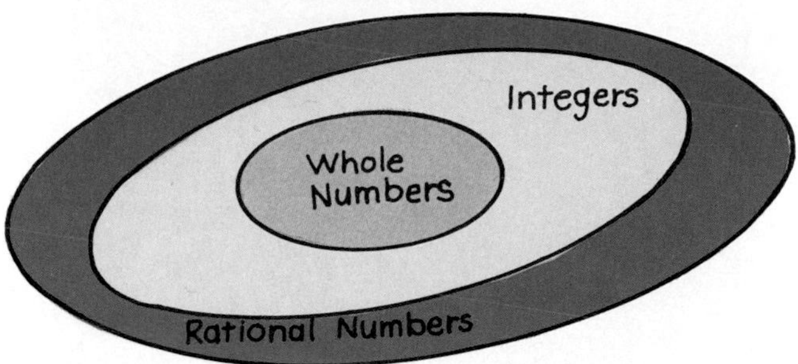

38. $-\frac{2}{3}$

39. 0

40. −12.3

41. $6\frac{3}{4}$

42. −9

43. 2.6×10^8

44. Critical Thinking Write an expression involving four rational numbers, excluding zero, such that the answer is the same if you work it from left to right or right to left.

45. Critical Thinking Use the four rational numbers you used in Problem 44 to write an expression such that the answers are different if you work it in each direction.

46. Tom said "$6 \times 4 + 2 + 8 \div 2$ is equal to $2 + 3 \times 3 + 3 + 20 \div 2$." Sam said that they are not equal. Insert grouping symbols to make Tom's statement true.

47. Add grouping symbols to the number expressions in Problem 46 to make Sam's claim true.

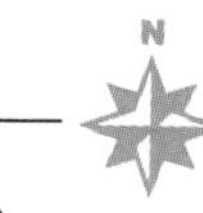

Explore ________ Math

Using each of the digits 1, 2, 3, and 4 once; the operations +, −, ×, ÷; exponents; and grouping symbols, it is possible to write expressions that equal many different numbers. For example: $(4 - 3) \times (2 - 1) = 1$.

48. Using the digits listed above, write expressions that are equal to each of the whole numbers from 1 to 10.

49. Using each of the digits 3, 5, 7, and 9 once; the operations +, −, ×, ÷; exponents; and grouping symbols, write expressions that are equal to each of the whole numbers from 1 to 10.

ALGEBRA

Evaluating and Writing Addition and Subtraction Expressions

Build Understanding

Mr. Brown runs a newsstand. He computes his monthly profit by subtracting expenses, E, from sales, S. His profit is expressed $S - E$.

A. Mr. Brown's sales were $37,678.40, his expenses $33,424.80. Evaluate $S - E$ to find his profit.

$S - E = 37{,}678.40 - 33{,}424.80 = 4{,}253.60$

His monthly profit was $4,253.60.

B. Mr. Brown pays $1,950 per month for a sales permit. Write a new expression to show his profit.

The expression $S - E - 1{,}950$ gives Mr. Brown's profit.

C. Word phrases can be translated into mathematical expressions. Numerical expressions contain only numbers and can be evaluated. Algebraic expressions contain at least one variable and cannot be evaluated until numbers are substituted for the variables.

There are over 10,000 different newspapers currently published in the United States.

Word Phrase	Mathematical Expression
$4.95 increased by $0.35	$4.95 + 0.35$
17 books fewer than y books	$y - 17$
The number of customers, c, decreased by 291	$c - 291$
The sum of the number of books, b, and the number of newspapers, n	$b + n$

D. Write an expression for *x pounds lighter than 24.5 pounds*. Evaluate the expression when $x = 0.25$.

$24.5 - x$

$24.5 - 0.25$

24.25

E. Evaluate $8b + 3c - 18$ when $b = \frac{3}{4}$ and $c = -2$.

$8b + 3c - 18$

$8\left(\frac{3}{4}\right) + 3(-2) - 18$

$6 + (-6) - 18$

-18

Substitute $\frac{3}{4}$ for b and -2 for c. Then follow the standard order of operations.

■ **Write About Math** Write an expression for Example A to find Mr. Brown's sales.

Check Understanding

For another example, see Set B, pages 512–513.

Write an expression for each phrase.

1. p dollars decreased by \$0.40

2. \$2 more than the original price, n

Evaluate each expression when $n = -6$.

3. $2n - 15$

4. $45 + n$

5. $\frac{7n}{-3} - 12$

Practice

For More Practice, see Set B, pages 514–515.

Write an expression for each phrase.

6.

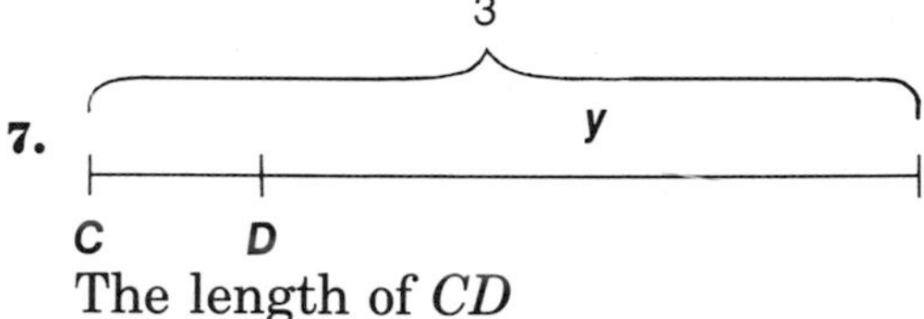

The length of AB

7.

The length of CD

8. The cost of a \$29 item with x dollars off after an increase of y dollars

9. The opposite of the sum of p and q

Use the figure at the right to write an expression.

10. The distance from X to Z, going through Y

11. The distance saved by going directly from X to Z (instead of through Y)

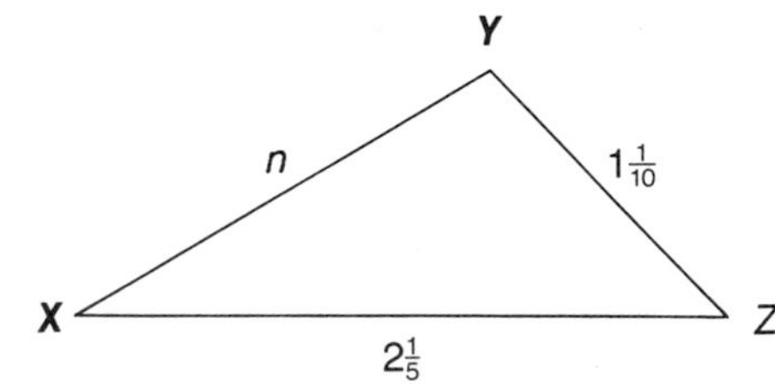

Evaluate each expression when $x = -3$ and $y = 0.5$.

12. $15 - y + 2x$

13. $\frac{18y}{-3x} - 2$

14. $\frac{2y - 10}{x}$

15. $\frac{y^2 - 25}{x}$

Number Sense Answer each question. Then explain your answer.

16. Which is greater, m or $-m$?

17. Which is less, $n - 2$ or $n - 3$?

Problem Solving

Solve.

18. If Mr. Brown's profit in April was \$4,253.60, what was his average *daily* profit?

19. If Mr. Brown's expenses in May were \$71,902 and his sales were \$77,496, how much was his profit? **Remember** to use the expression in Example B to compute his profit.

ALGEBRA

Solving Addition and Subtraction Equations

Build Understanding

A. In June, Mr. Brown's newsstand made a profit of $1,384.32. If his expenses were $24,592.64, how much were his sales?

Remember that Sales − Expenses = Profit, or $S - E = P$.

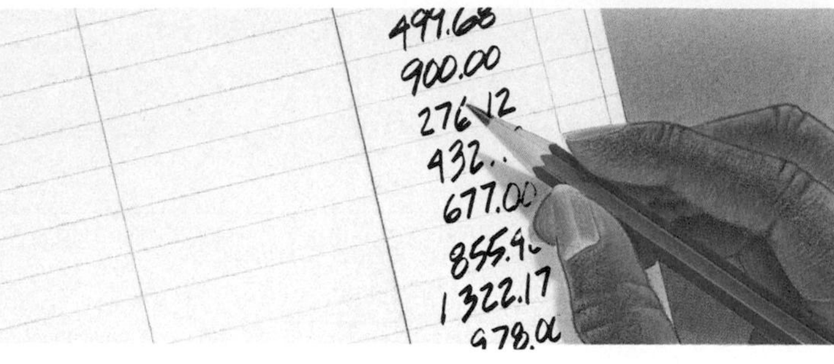

$$S - 24{,}592.64 = 1{,}384.32$$
$$S - 24{,}592.64 + 24{,}592.64 = 1{,}384.32 + 24{,}592.64$$
$$S = 25{,}976.96$$

Substitute values for P and E. To find S, add 24,592.64 to both sides of the equation.

Mr. Brown's sales were $25,976.96.

B. Solve $x + \frac{2}{3} = -\frac{1}{4}$.

$$x + \frac{2}{3} = -\frac{1}{4}$$
$$x + \frac{2}{3} - \frac{2}{3} = -\frac{1}{4} - \frac{2}{3}$$
$$x = \frac{-3}{12} - \frac{8}{12}$$
$$x = -\frac{11}{12}$$

Subtract $\frac{2}{3}$ from each side of the equation.

Check: $x + \frac{2}{3} = -\frac{1}{4}$

$$-\frac{11}{12} + \frac{2}{3} = -\frac{1}{4}$$
$$-\frac{3}{12} = -\frac{1}{4}$$
$$-\frac{1}{4} = -\frac{1}{4}$$

Substitute $-\frac{11}{12}$ for x. Does $-\frac{11}{12} + \frac{2}{3} = -\frac{1}{4}$? The answer checks.

Talk About Math When would Mr. Brown's profit be negative?

Check Understanding

For another example, see Set C, pages 512–513.

Write an equation, then solve.

1. A customer at the newsstand spent a total of $12.65. If she spent $9.90 on books and the rest on magazines, how much did she spend on magazines?

2. Mr. Brown had a loss last Tuesday of $211.65. If his expenses for the day were $482.45, how much were his sales?

3. If a number is decreased by $18\frac{7}{10}$, the answer is $4\frac{1}{2}$. What is the number?

4. The sum of 4.5 and what number is 27.8?

Practice

For More Practice, see Set C, pages 514–515.

Solve each equation. Check your answer.

5. $a - 3.6 = -13.4$

6. $\frac{3}{2} + x = \frac{4}{5}$

7. $a - 1.3 = 7.1$

8. $-13.5 + r = 13.5$

9. $5.15 + r = -9.95$

10. $\frac{2}{3} + q = 0$

11. $a + \frac{3}{5} = \frac{2}{5}$

12. $23\frac{1}{2} = m + 16\frac{2}{3}$

13. $c - 12\frac{9}{10} = 4\frac{1}{5}$

14. $4.06 + x = 2.33$

15. $-1.6 + c = -7.2$

16. $6 = t - (-8.34)$

17. $-14.4 + n = 12.1$

18. $b - 11.4 = -1.5$

19. $q + (-7.34) = -18$

20. $n - 3.9 = -1$

21. $x - \frac{5}{8} = \frac{5}{8}$

22. $0 = -3\frac{1}{4} + b$

23. $-30 = m - 25$

24. $t - 16\frac{5}{6} = 3\frac{2}{3}$

25. $4\frac{1}{8} = x + (-7)$

Problem Solving

Solve.

26. The cost of a book sold in Mr. Brown's stand increased by $0.90. If the new cost is $4.35, find the original cost.

27. Estimation Use the information in Example A to estimate Mr. Brown's yearly profit.

Visualize the problem in your mind to help you understand it better.

28. Mr. Brown sold 843 newspapers one morning. If 137 newspapers remained, how many newspapers did Mr. Brown have at the beginning of the day?

29. Jose makes at *most* $250 per month. If he made $58 during each of the first 3 weeks of the month, could he have earned $20 during the rest of the month? $80? $100? Explain.

Skills Review pages 308–311, 314–317

Find each answer.

1. What is 50% of 42?

2. 75% of 88 is what number?

3. 48% of what number is 60?

4. What percent of 18 is 4?

ALGEBRA

Evaluating and Writing Multiplication and Division Expressions

Build Understanding

ACTIVITY

A. Park Here
Groups: With a partner

Mrs. Gull owns a parking garage. She made a table showing the rates.

a. Do you think Mrs. Gull added, subtracted, multiplied, or divided to compute the parking fees for each hour?

b. Continue the table for the next 5 hours.

c. Write an expression you could use to determine the parking fees for t hours.

d. If the rate remains the same, how much would Mrs. Gull charge for 24 hours?

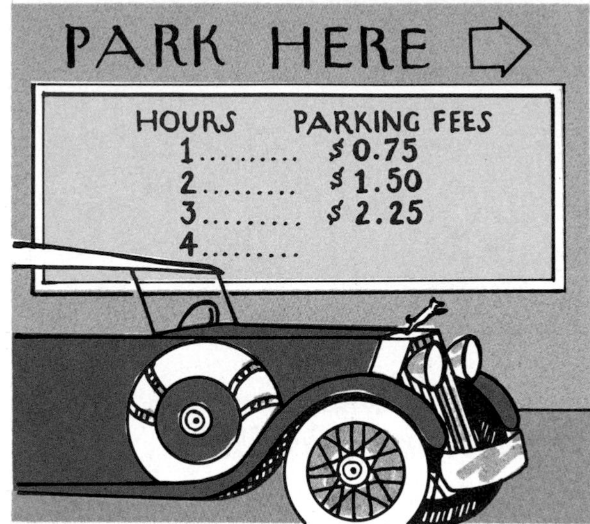

The largest parking lot in the world is located at the West Edmonton Mall in Edmonton, Alberta, Canada, with covered garaging for 20,000 cars and an overflow facility for 10,000 more.

B. Evaluate $\frac{3a}{4} - \frac{6b}{-3}$ when $a = -12$ and $b = -\frac{1}{2}$.

$\frac{3a}{4} - \frac{6b}{-3}$ Substitute -12 for a and $-\frac{1}{2}$ for b.

$$\frac{3(-12)}{4} - \frac{6\left(-\frac{1}{2}\right)}{-3} = \frac{-36}{4} - \frac{-3}{-3}$$

$$= -9 - 1 = -10$$

■ **Talk About Math** How would the evaluation of the expression in Example B be different if b were positive?

Check Understanding

For another example, see Set D, pages 512–513.

Write an expression for each phrase.

1. 12 cars in each of 6 sections
2. p monthly passes costing $125.50 each
3. Paid a total of $5.25 for t hours
4. $\frac{1}{5}$ of the price, p

Practice

For More Practice, see Set D, pages 514–515.

Mental Math Use mental math to evaluate each expression when $y = 9$.

5. $\frac{2}{3}y$ **6.** $\frac{y}{4.5}$ **7.** $-0.6y$ **8.** $\frac{1}{3}y - 5$

Evaluate each expression when $n = 0.5$.

9. $8n + 7$ **10.** $5n^2$ **11.** $\frac{4-n}{n}$ **12.** $(2n)^2 + (-9n) - 1$

Evaluate each expression when $b = \frac{5}{6}$ and $c = -18$.

13. $\frac{12b}{5} - \frac{1}{2}c$ **14.** $b(6 - c)$ **15.** $\frac{-24\left(b - \frac{3}{4}\right)}{c}$ **16.** $\frac{b(c + 15)}{5}$

Evaluate each expression when $r = 1.4$ and $s = -3.5$.

17. $\frac{s(2r + 6.2)}{3}$ **18.** $\frac{s}{5} + \frac{14}{r}$ **19.** $\frac{-2(-3.4 + r)}{s + 7.5}$ **20.** $5r^2 + 4s + 0.2$

Mixed Practice Evaluate each expression when $a = 4$.

21. $\frac{6a}{3} - 2$ **22.** $\frac{7a + 8}{4}$ **23.** $-10 + a$ **24.** $\frac{-4}{a} - 1$

Problem Solving

Mrs. Gull has determined that her profit per day on each parking space in her garage is $0.95.

25. Write an expression to determine Mrs. Gull's daily profit on x spaces.

26. Evaluate the expression you wrote in Problem 25 for $x = 285$.

Midchapter Checkup

Evaluate each expression. **Remember** to use the standard order of operations.

1. $3\frac{1}{2} \times [4 - (10 + 1)]$ **2.** $\frac{15 - 32}{2} + 4.1$

Write an expression for each phrase.

3. n increased by $\frac{2}{3}$ **4.** 4.5 times the sum of 5 and p

Solve each equation.

5. $4\frac{1}{3} + t = 4\frac{5}{6}$ **6.** $24\frac{1}{2} = c - 16\frac{2}{3}$ **7.** $10\frac{1}{8} + w = 11\frac{3}{4}$

Problem-Solving Workshop

Real-Life Decision Making

1. You and your friends are producing 30 tapes that you have presold for $6.00 each. You need to decide which blank tapes to buy and which songs to tape.

a. You need to find the total time the songs will take. (Remember, 60 seconds equals 1 minute.)

b. Decide if you are going to tape all of the songs or if you should leave some out.

c. Decide which blank tapes you will buy.

d. What will your recording costs be? Will you make a profit?

The recording studio charges $4 for each recorded minute. These are the songs you would like to record:

SONG	TIME (Minutes: Seconds)
My Dog, Sam	3:55
First Day of School	4:38
What a Silly Game	3:47
Too Much to Do	6:29
Over the Weekend	7:34
The Rain is Gone	5:26

What goes up but never comes down?

Your age.

Explore with a Computer

Use the *Spreadsheet Workshop Project* for this activity.

1. Sally works as a computer aide at the Tech Art Lab on Saturday afternoons. In 4.5 hours she earns $15.75. How much money does Sally earn per hour?

2. In one month, Sally earned $62.50, including a bonus of $10.00 for making a bulletin board of printouts. At the computer, use the equation to find how many hours Sally worked.

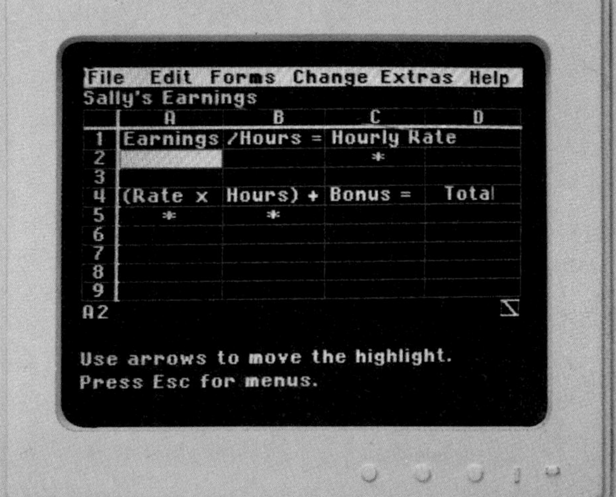

Number-Sense Project

Look back at pages 488–489.

1. Compute the costs of the following taxicab rides using the rates shown.

First mile or fraction thereof:	$1.50
Each additional $\frac{1}{10}$ mile:	$0.12
Each additional mile:	$1.20
Waiting time, per minute:	$0.50
Each additional person:	$1.00

	Distance in miles	Waiting in minutes	Extra passengers
a.	4	0	0
b.	7	0	3
c.	9	3	0
d.	8.2	0	2
e.	14.9	2.5	1

Math-at-Home Activity

Choose the birth year of one person in your family. Use the operations of +, −, ×, ÷ and the four digits from the birth year to make phrases which equal 0, 1, 2, 3, and so on. See how far you can go. For example, if the birth year is 1942, you might have the following:

1 9 4 2

$(4 \times 2) + 1 - 9 = 0$

$9 - (1 \times 2 \times 4) = 1$

$9 - (1 + 2 + 4) = 2$

$(1 \times 9) - 4 - 2 = 3$

$1 + 9 - 4 - 2 = 4$

ALGEBRA

Solving Multiplication and Division Equations

Build Understanding

A. Students in Mrs. Ivy's art class designed a poster. They paid a printer $199.50 for 950 copies. What was the cost per copy?

Let c represent the cost of 1 copy.

Number of copies → 950; Cost per copy → c; Total cost → 199.5

$$950 \times c = 199.5$$ Write an equation.

$$\frac{950c}{950} = \frac{199.5}{950}$$ Divide each side of the equation by 950.

$$c = 0.21$$

The cost per copy was $0.21.

B. Solve $\frac{n}{-35} = 24$.

$$\frac{n}{-35} = 24$$

$$\frac{(-35)n}{-35} = 24\,(-35)$$ Multiply each side of the equation by −35.

$$n = -840$$

C. Solve $\left(-\frac{3}{4}\right)x = \frac{1}{2}$.

$$\left(-\frac{3}{4}\right)x = \frac{1}{2}$$

$$\left(-\frac{4}{3}\right)\left(-\frac{3}{4}\right)x = \frac{1}{2}\left(-\frac{4}{3}\right)$$

$$x = -\frac{2}{3}$$

Multiply each side of the equation by the reciprocal of $-\frac{3}{4}$ which is $-\frac{4}{3}$.

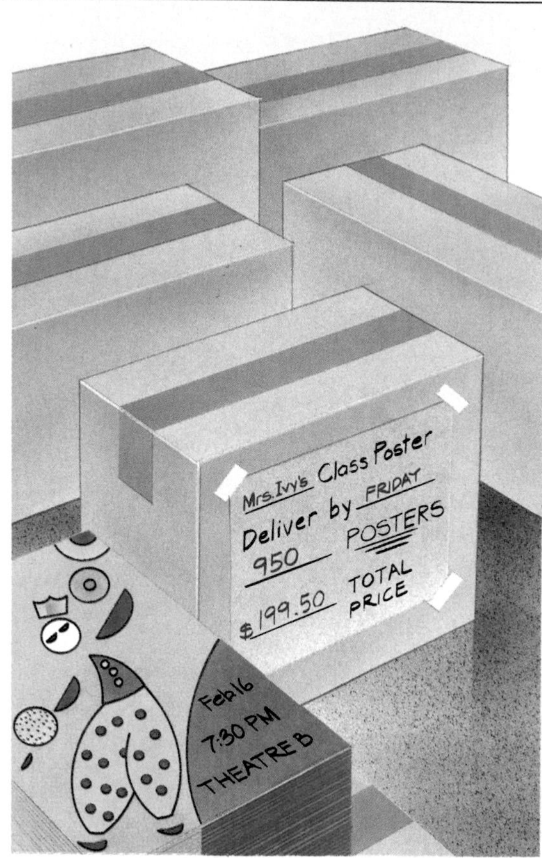

Talk About Math Look at the solutions to Examples A, B, and C. What general statement can you make about solving multiplication and division equations?

Check Understanding

For another example, see Set E, pages 512–513.

Choose the equation you would use to solve each problem. Then solve.

1. The printer bundled the 950 copies into 10 equal stacks. How many copies were in each stack?

a. $s \times 10 = 950$ **b.** $\frac{s}{10} = 950$

2. The printer charges $21.25 for 125 additional copies. What is the price for each additional copy?

a. $125 \times p = 21.25$ **b.** $\frac{p}{125} = 21.25$

Practice

For More Practice, see Set E, pages 514–515.

Solve.

3. $-6t = 84$ **4.** $1.4y = -70$ **5.** $\frac{1}{2}t = \frac{5}{6}$ **6.** $2n = 5.3$

7. $\frac{-2}{3}n = \frac{5}{12}$ **8.** $\frac{3}{4} = \frac{-5}{8}w$ **9.** $\frac{3}{5}x = \frac{9}{10}$ **10.** $4x = -12$

11. $-2.5x = 10$ **12.** $\frac{x}{-16} = 16$ **13.** $\frac{3}{4}s = 32$ **14.** $7.1x = 78.1$

15. $\frac{1}{3} = \frac{5}{6}n$ **16.** $4n = -216$ **17.** $\frac{n}{-6} = 2\frac{1}{3}$ **18.** $-3.2x = -25.6$

Solve. Tell whether you used mental math, paper and pencil, or a calculator to solve each equation.

19. $-15u = 4.5$ **20.** $-3x = 1\frac{2}{3}$ **21.** $\frac{x}{-18} = -3$ **22.** $5 = \frac{-40}{r}$

23. $\frac{n}{10} = -31$ **24.** $-18 = 3t$ **25.** $4y = 1\frac{3}{4}$ **26.** $\frac{75}{r} = -3$

For Exercises 27–32, write an equation. Then solve each equation.

27. Twice a number divided by 3 is 24. Find the number.

28. What number multiplied by $-\frac{2}{3}$ is $-\frac{4}{9}$?

29. What number divided by -6 is equal to $2\frac{1}{2}$?

30. Three times a number is equal to 10.5. Find the number.

31. Four times a number divided by 5 is equal to 20. Find the number.

32. What number multiplied by 7 is equal to 6.3?

Problem Solving

Use the information in Example A to solve each problem. The students used $\frac{4}{5}$ of the posters.

33. How many posters did they display?

34. The remaining posters were sold as souvenirs for $2.50 each. How much money was collected?

35. Calculate the profit made by the art students after deducting the printing cost for 950 posters.

36. The printer made a profit of $0.04 per poster. What was the printer's profit on the entire order?

ALGEBRA

Write an Equation

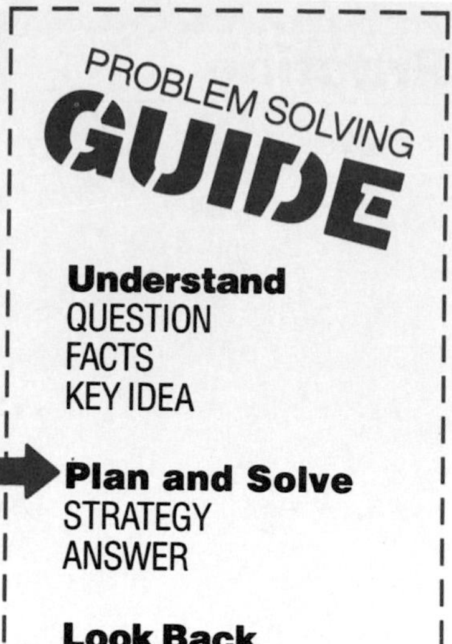

Build Understanding

An airplane flies from London to Chicago in $8\frac{1}{4}$ hours. If the speed of the plane is 480 miles per hour, how far is London from Chicago?

Understand QUESTION How far is London from Chicago?

FACTS For every hour in the air, the plane travels a distance of 480 miles. The plane is in the air for $8\frac{1}{4}$ hours.

KEY IDEA To find the total distance, you can multiply the speed of the plane by the number of hours in the air.

Plan and Solve STRATEGY Write an equation that shows the total distance equals the distance the plane travels in one hour multiplied by the total time in hours.

Total distance		Distance in one hour		Hours in air
d	=	480	×	$8\frac{1}{4}$
d	=	480	×	8.25
d	=	3,960		

ANSWER The total distance from London to Chicago is 3,960 miles.

Look Back ALTERNATE APPROACH You can make a table and compute the distance.

Hours	1	2	3	4	5	6	7	8
Distance	480	960	1,440	1,920	2,400	2,880	3,360	3,840

From the table you can see that the distance after 8 hours is 3,840 miles. An additional $\frac{1}{4}$ hour is proportional to $\frac{1}{4}$ the distance in one hour, or, 120. Then 3,840 + 120 is 3,960 miles.

Write About Math Show how you would calculate the travel time if you knew the distance and the speed.

Check Understanding

An airplane can fly 450.5 miles per hour. With a tailwind of 40 miles per hour, it can fly more quickly.

1. What is the speed of the plane with no wind? What is the speed of the wind?
2. Write and solve an equation that answers the question, "What is the speed of the plane with the tailwind?"

Practice

Solve each problem.

3. The air distance between Chicago and Los Angeles is 1,745 miles. The air distance between Los Angeles and Honolulu is 2,557 miles. Find the total air distance between Chicago and Honolulu.
4. **Number Sense** The distance between Chicago and Mexico City is about $\frac{1}{5}$ the distance between Chicago and Cape Town, which is 8,491 miles. About how far is it from Chicago to Mexico City?
5. The speed of a plane is 345 miles per hour. The speed of a plane with a tailwind is 358.2 miles per hour. What is the wind speed?
6. **Use Data** Create and solve your own equation using any of the mathematical expressions found on page 494.

Choose a ________ Strategy

All Aboard A train left at noon traveling 40 mi/h. Another train left at 1:00 P.M. going in the opposite direction at 60 mi/h.

7. What distance will each train have traveled by 3:00 P.M.?
8. What fraction of that distance did each train travel by 1:00 P.M.? by 2:00 P.M.?
9. If both trains reach their destinations at 4:00 P.M., what distance will each have traveled?

PROBLEM SOLVING
STRATEGIES

- Choose an Operation
- Write an Equation
- Use a Formula
- Make a Table
- Try and Check
- Use Logical Reasoning
- Work Backward
- Find a Pattern
- Solve a Simpler Problem
- Make a Graph

Solving Two-Step Equations

Build Understanding

A. Students in Mr. Jackson's English class can earn up to 2 points for each book report they write. Also, if students compare 2 books written by the same author, they can earn an additional 0.75 points.

Emma wrote 3 book reports. She earned the same number of points for each book report and the additional 0.75 points. She earned a total of 5.25 points. How many points did Emma earn for one book report?

Let b equal the number of points Emma earned for one book report.

$$3b + 0.75 = 5.25$$ Write an equation.

$$3b + 0.75 - 0.75 = 5.25 - 0.75$$ Subtract 0.75 from each side of the equation.

$$3b = 4.5$$

$$\frac{3b}{3} = \frac{4.5}{3}$$ Divide each side of the equation by 3.

$$b = 1.5$$

Emma earned 1.5 points for each book report.

B. Solve $-8t + 2 = 17$.

$$-8t + 2 = 17$$

$$-8t + 2 - 2 = 17 - 2$$ Subtract 2 from each side of the equation.

$$-8t = 15$$

$$\frac{-8t}{-8} = \frac{15}{-8}$$ Divide each side of the equation by -8.

$$t = -1\frac{7}{8}$$

Check:

$$-8\left(-1\frac{7}{8}\right) + 2 \stackrel{?}{=} 17$$

$$-8\left(-\frac{15}{8}\right) + 2 \stackrel{?}{=} 17$$

$$-(-15) + 2 \stackrel{?}{=} 17$$

$$17 = 17$$

■ **Talk About Math** Explain why the equations in Examples A and B are two-step equations. What are the two steps in each equation?

Check Understanding

For another example, see Set F, pages 512–513.

Describe the two steps you would use to solve the equation, then solve.

1. $10d - 4 = 8$ **2.** $\frac{x}{8} - 6 = 2$ **3.** $27 = \frac{x}{4} + 13$

Practice

For More Practice, see Set F, pages 514–515.

Solve each equation.

4. $4a - 2 = 14$ **5.** $3a - 12 = 45$ **6.** $5a + 3 = 8$ **7.** $12x + 41 = 89$

8. $10a - 15 = 85$ **9.** $\frac{x}{3} + 8 = 15$ **10.** $12w + 8 = -16$ **11.** $\frac{y}{5} - 8 = 2$

12. $3s - 14 = 16$ **13.** $45 = 13m - 20$ **14.** $6x + 4 = 22$ **15.** $\frac{s}{3} + 2 = 6$

16. $\frac{a}{4} + 6 = 17$ **17.** $\frac{x}{5} - 9 = 11$ **18.** $\frac{t}{7} + 9 = 10$ **19.** $24 = \frac{c}{4} + 11$

20. $2c + 12 = 12$ **21.** $20 = 5z - 20$ **22.** $\frac{a}{12} - 12 = 1$ **23.** $41 = 8x - 15$

24. $\frac{n}{5} + 5 = 65$ **25.** $7x + 3 = 38$ **26.** $10s - 21 = 79$ **27.** $\frac{n}{8} - 4 = 4$

28. $12t + 5 = 89$ **29.** $2x - 8 = 16$ **30.** $\frac{x}{3} + 7 = 4$ **31.** $9x - 18 = 0$

32. $\frac{a}{6} + 4 = 5$ **33.** $5x + 6 = -34$ **34.** $\frac{n}{2} - 7 = 0$ **35.** $25t - 35 = 90$

36. $6x + 8 = 8$ **37.** $\frac{n}{3} - 7 = 22$ **38.** $-7t + 132 = 15t$ **39.** $8x + 3\frac{1}{3} = 5x$

Problem Solving

Mr. Jackson gives additional points for book reports on biographies. He will also add 1.5 points if the student gives the report orally. Write an equation, then solve each problem using this information.

40. Shawn earned 6.5 additional points for 5 book reports on biographies. One was an oral report. How many additional points does Mr. Jackson give for a book report on a biography?

41. Juan wrote 2 book reports, receiving the same number of points for each. He also received additional points because one book report was on a biography which he presented orally. If Juan received a total of 6.3 points, how many points did he receive for each book report?

ALGEBRA

Use a Formula

Understand
QUESTION
FACTS
KEY IDEA

Plan and Solve
STRATEGY
ANSWER

Look Back
SENSIBLE ANSWER
ALTERNATE APPROACH

Build Understanding

Formulas are equations describing relationships. In a formula, one variable is expressed in terms of other quantities or algebraic expressions.

In science class, Megan learned this formula for changing temperature in degrees Fahrenheit to degrees Celsius.

$$C = \frac{5(F - 32)}{9}$$

What is 48°F in degrees Celsius?

Understand QUESTION How do you change 48°F to degrees Celsius?

FACT The formula is $C = \frac{5(F - 32)}{9}$

Plan and Solve STRATEGY Substitute 48 for F in the formula.

$$C = \frac{5(48 - 32)}{9}$$

$$C = \frac{5(16)}{9}$$

$$C = \frac{80}{9}$$

$$C \approx 8.9$$

ANSWER Rounded to the nearest whole number, 48°F is 9°Celsius.

Look Back SENSIBLE ANSWER The Celsius scale measures freezing at 0° C and boiling at 100° C while the Fahrenheit scale measures freezing at 32° F and boiling at 212° F. A temperature of 48° F is about 10 degrees above freezing on the Fahrenheit scale, so a similar temperature on the Celsius scale would be a few degrees above 0. Therefore 48° F = 9° C is a sensible answer.

■ **Talk About Math** Explain how you can use mental math to find 32°F in degrees Celsius.

Check Understanding

$F = \frac{9C}{5} + 32$ expresses degrees Celsius in degrees Fahrenheit (°*F*).

1. To find 100°C in °*F* what number do you substitute for C?
2. Which operation would you perform first? second? third?
3. Find the value of *F*.
4. Show −15°C in degrees Fahrenheit.

Practice

The amount of gold in jewelry is measured in karats. You can find the percent of gold in a piece of jewelry, g, with the formula $g = \frac{25k}{6}$, where k is the number of karats.

Find the percent of gold in a ring with the given number of karats.

5. 14
6. 18
7. 24

When doing strenuous exercise, a person n years old can safely attain b heartbeats per minute. Use the formula at the right for Exercises 8–10.

$$b = \frac{4(220 - n)}{5}$$

8. Find b for a person who is 13 years old.
9. Find b for a person who is 50 years old.
10. Find b for a person who is 40 years old.
11. How do your answers for Exercises 9 and 10 compare?
12. **Calculator** Find the age of a person for whom 114 heartbeats per minute is the highest safe number. Round to the next whole number.

Reading ——— Math

Following Examples

1. In the example in this lesson, what value was substituted for *F* in the formula?
2. Which operation was performed first? second? third?
3. Why was the answer rounded to the nearest whole number?

Chapter 14 REVIEW

Skills Review

Insert grouping symbols to make the equations true.

1. $7 + 3 \times 5 - 6 \div 2 + 1 = 48$
2. $9 \times 2 + 2 - 8 \times 4 - 1 = 12$
3. $6 - 2 \times 4 + 5 \div 3 \times 2 = 6$

Evaluate each expression when $n = -4$ and $m = 0.2$

4. $m + n$
5. $12 + n - m$
6. $m + n - 0.1$
7. $2n + 8$
8. $30 + 4n + 5m$
9. $n^2 + 8$
10. $\frac{5n + 10}{m}$
11. $\frac{10n - 1}{m}$

Solve each equation.

12. $a + 4.5 = 8.6$
13. $n - \frac{4}{5} = 2\frac{1}{5}$
14. $\frac{7}{8} + y = 0$
15. $-5.2 + v = 3$
16. $\frac{1}{2} - \frac{3}{5} = k$
17. $c - 0.8 = -1.8$
18. $w + 3.6 = -4.2$
19. $\frac{7}{10} - m = -\frac{1}{5}$
20. $-5m = -40$
21. $3r = -15$
22. $1.5k = -6$
23. $\frac{1}{4}c = -2$
24. $\frac{1}{2} = -\frac{3}{8}n$
25. $\frac{t}{-3} = 4$
26. $-8.8 = 4v$
27. $-12 = \frac{c}{-3}$
28. $5t - 3 = 12$
29. $-3p - 4 = 5$
30. $\frac{r}{9} - 7 = -9$
31. $12 + \frac{w}{4} = 4$
32. $8c - 6 = 10$
33. $-8r + 12 = 4r$
34. $-100 = 4h - 20$
35. $10k = 7k + 18$

Problem-Solving Review

Solve each problem.

36. Melanie is buying napkins for a party. Bunny print napkins are $1.79 for 100. Model train print napkins are 85¢ for 50. Which is the better buy?

37. On October 1, Minneapolis has about $11\frac{2}{3}$ hours of daylight. By October 31, it has only $10\frac{1}{4}$ hours. How many more hours of daylight does Minneapolis have on October 1 than it has on October 31?

38. My age times 2, less 5 is 17. How old am I?

39. The number of years it takes to double the money in a savings account is given by the expression $\frac{70}{I}$, where I is the annual rate of interest as a percent. Find the number of years needed to double your money when the annual interest rate is $8\frac{1}{4}\%$. Round your answer to the nearest tenth.

40. **Data File** Use the data on pages 558–559. Write an equation relating the area of each ocean to the size of the United States.

41. **Make a Data File** Consult a reference book to find the lengths of dinosaurs. Make a table listing the name and the length (in feet) of at least 6 dinosaurs. Compare each dinosaur length with the length of a large crocodile by dividing each length by 20. Round your answers to the nearest hundredth. Make a third column in the table to list the comparisons.

Cumulative Skills Review • Chapters 1–14

Find the missing angle measure in each triangle. Then classify each as acute, right, or obtuse, and as scalene, isosceles, or equilateral.

1. 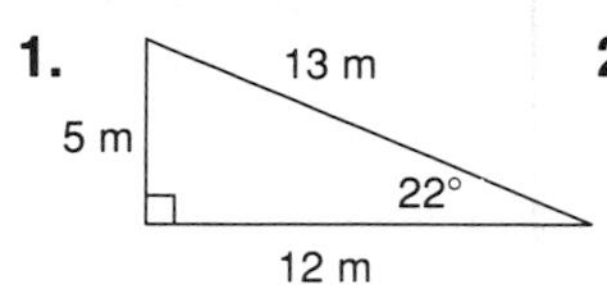

2. 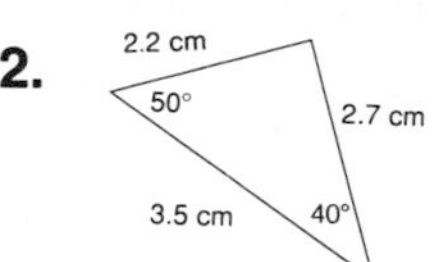

3. 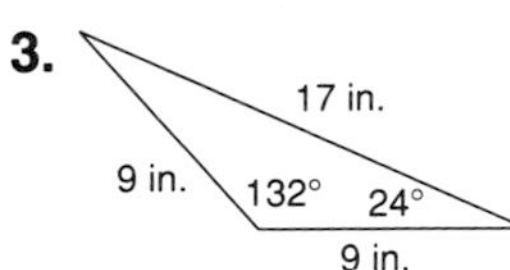

4. 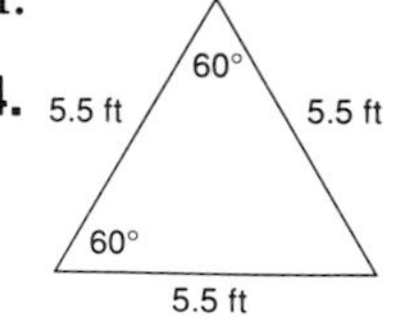

Use the broken line graph.

5. In what month were both stocks the same price?

6. What was the price of MMP stock in June?

7. In what month was the difference in price between the stocks greatest?

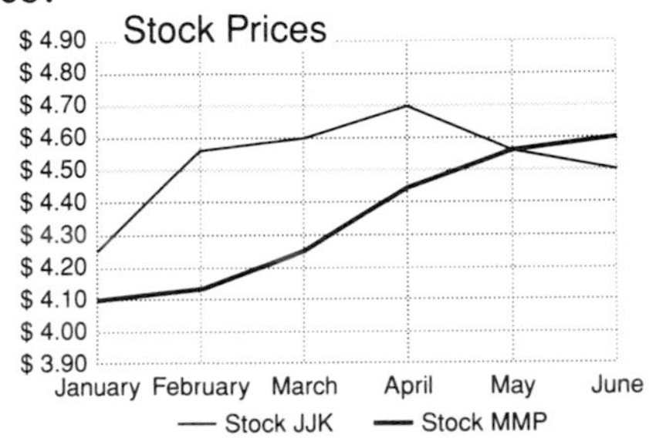

A number is selected from the set of numbers from 1 through 20. Find each probability.

8. P(even) **9.** P(divisible by 6) **10.** P(prime number)

11. P(multiple of 5) **12.** P(greater than 10) **13.** P(greater than 25)

Add or subtract.

14. $\frac{3}{4} + \frac{5}{16}$ **15.** $2\frac{4}{5} + 3\frac{7}{10}$ **16.** $5 - 2\frac{4}{9}$ **17.** $\frac{7}{8} - \frac{1}{4}$

18. $-12 + 3$ **19.** $18 + (-9)$ **20.** $-8 + (-8)$ **21.** $5 + (-7)$

22. $4 - (-3)$ **23.** $-6 - (-9)$ **24.** $10 - (-4)$ **25.** $-3 - (-1)$

Use your calculator or the table on page 587.
Find the square root of each number to the nearest tenth.

26. $\sqrt{34}$ **27.** $\sqrt{17}$ **28.** $\sqrt{27}$ **29.** $\sqrt{43}$

Solve each equation.

30. $74 = r + 20$ **31.** $t - 12 = 71$ **32.** $7w = 91$ **33.** $\frac{v}{10} = 12$

34. $m - 12.2 = 12.2$ **35.** $5\frac{1}{2} + p = 9$ **36.** $-4.9 = z + 2$ **37.** $n - 1.5 = -3.9$

38. $5p = 20.5$ **39.** $\frac{2}{3}m = -22$ **40.** $0.4m = -2$ **41.** $\frac{y}{-6} = 12$

42. $2s + 5 = 6$ **43.** $\frac{m}{3} - 3 = 10$ **44.** $2.4r - 0.6 = 4.2$ **45.** $\frac{t}{9} - \frac{2}{12} = \frac{1}{2}$

Reteaching

Set A pages 490–493

Compute $\left[7\frac{1}{2} + \left(\frac{-2}{3}\right)\right] + 1\frac{2}{3}$.

$\left[7\frac{1}{2} + \left(\frac{-2}{3}\right)\right] + 1\frac{2}{3}$

$7\frac{1}{2} + \left[\left(\frac{-2}{3}\right) + 1\frac{2}{3}\right]$ Use the associative property.

$7\frac{1}{2} + 1$ Do the operation in parentheses first.

$8\frac{1}{2}$

Remember, you use the standard order of operations and the same properties that you use with integers and whole numbers to compute with rational numbers.

Compute. State which property or properties you used.

1. $6\left(\frac{2}{3} + \frac{5}{6}\right)$

2. $2.8 \times 17.3 \times 0$

3. $\dfrac{2\frac{1}{5} \times \left(\frac{2}{11} \times 5\right)}{2}$

4. $\frac{7.2 \times 1}{2}$

Set B pages 494–495

Write an expression for the phrase *12 more than n decreased by m.* Then evaluate the expression when n is 3 and m is 7.

$n + 12$ 12 more than n

$(n + 12) - m$ decreased by m

$(3 + 12) - 7$ Substitute 3 for n and 7 for m.

$15 - 7 = 8$

Remember, look for word clues to help you write expressions.

Write an expression for each phrase.

1. The opposite of the sum of s and r

2. The sum of a less than 2 and b

3. j increased by 9

4. 17 more than y decreased by 2

Evaluate each expression.

5. Exercise 1 when s is -8 and r is 14

6. Exercise 4 when y is 13

Set C 496–497

Solve $b - 16 = 27$.

$b - 16 = 27$

$b - 16 + 16 = 27 + 16$ To find b, add 16 to both sides of the equation.

$b = 43$

Solve $j + 23 = 44$.

$j + 23 = 44$

$j + 23 - 23 = 44 - 23$ To find j, subtract 23 from both sides of the equation.

$j = 21$

Remember, add or subtract the same number from both sides to solve an addition or subtraction equation.

Solve each equation.

1. $a + 4.1 = 5.3$

2. $\frac{2}{5} + q = \frac{1}{3}$

3. $z - 2.7 = 1.9$

4. $43 + m = 7$

5. $17\frac{1}{4} = w - 9\frac{2}{3}$

6. $c + 4.45 = -2.25$

Set D pages 498–499

Write an expression for the phrase *the product of* 6.5 *and m*. Evaluate the expresion when m is 3.

$m \times 6.5$ The product of m and 6.5

3×6.5 Substitute 3 for m.

19.5

Remember, think about standard order of operations when writing or evaluating multiplication or division expressions.

Write an expression for each phrase.

1. Half as long as b
2. The quotient of 4.2 and c

Evaluate each expression.

3. Exercise 1 when b is 19
4. Exercise 2 when c is 0.4
5. $r\left(s - \frac{2}{3}\right)$ when r is -24 and s is $\frac{-3}{4}$

Set E pages 502–503

Solve $-6.2x = 217$.

$$-6.2x = 217$$

$$\frac{-6.2x}{-6.2} = \frac{217}{-6.2}$$ To find x, divide both sides of the equation by -6.2.

$$x = -35$$

Solve $\frac{c}{15} = 4$.

$$\frac{c}{15} = 4$$

$$\frac{c}{15} \times 15 = 4 \times 15$$ To find c, multiply both sides of the equation by 15.

$$c = 60$$

Remember, check your answer by substituting it for the variable in the original equation.

Solve.

1. $\frac{2}{5}y = 16$
2. $\frac{x}{7} = 5.8$
3. $\frac{3}{8} = \frac{-5}{16}b$
4. $-12g = 3.6$
5. $\frac{2}{7}k = 2\frac{2}{3}$
6. $56 = \frac{s}{16}$

Set F pages 506–507

Solve $4r + 8 = 15$.

$$4r + 8 = 15$$

$$4r + 8 - 8 = 15 - 8$$ Subtract 8 from both sides of the equation.

$$\frac{4r}{4} = \frac{7}{4}$$ Divide both sides by 4.

$$r = 1\frac{3}{4}$$

Remember, two steps in a two-step equation: addition or subtraction and multiplication or division.

Solve.

1. $\frac{f}{5} - 5 = 35$
2. $3d + 6 = 33$
3. $63 = \frac{a}{10} + 60$
4. $5q - 0.25 = 4.50$

More Practice

Set A pages 490–493

Compute. Tell what property or properties you used.

1. $6 \times \left(\frac{2}{3} \times \frac{1}{4}\right)$

2. $\frac{17}{32}(12) - \frac{17}{32}(11)$

3. $0.4 \times 3.7 \times 0$

4. $\frac{15}{16}\left(\frac{4}{5} + \frac{1}{15}\right)$

5. $5.8(9 - 9)$

6. $2.1 + (-63 + 0.9)$

Compute using the standard order of operations.

7. $13 - \frac{10[3.6 + (-2.6)]}{5}$

8. $\frac{1}{2}\left[21 + \left(\frac{18}{2} - 29\right) \div 2\right]$

9. $34.6 + 7.2 \times 9.4 - 14$

10. $10 - 4(-19 + 3) + 47\frac{1}{3}$

11. $(9.2 + 8.6 \times 7.4) \div (-4)$

12. $-14.7 \div 0.7 + 6.3 \times 3$

13. $\frac{2}{3}\left[27 - \left(\frac{15}{3} + 4\right) \div 3\right]$

14. $-\frac{3}{4}\left[40 + \left(\frac{16}{2} - 56\right)\right]$

Set B pages 494–495

Write an expression for each phrase.

1.

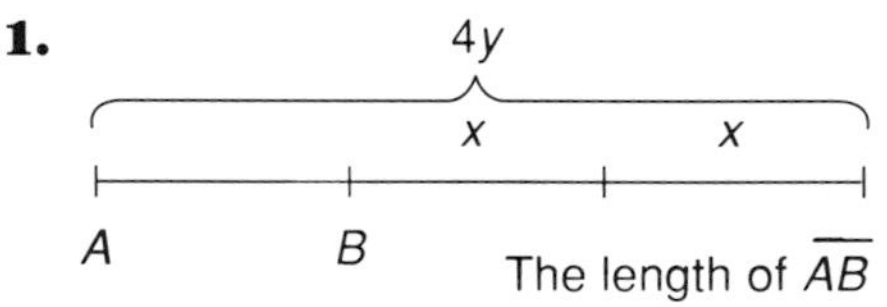

2.

ℓ m m m

C D

$\frac{1}{2}$ the length of $\overline{CD}$

3. The opposite of the sum of r and s

4. Two thirds of the difference of 9 and t

5. The opposite of the product of 5 and y

6. Three fourths of the sum of m and 3

Evaluate each expression when $r = -3$ and $s = 2$.

7. $r - s$

8. $r + 3s$

9. $5r + s$

10. $5 - 3 + r$

Evaluate each expression when $j = 4$ and $k = -2$.

11. $j - 5$

12. $j + 2k + 10$

13. $19 - k + j$

14. $j - k$

Set C pages 496–497

Solve each equation.

1. $d + 3 = 29$

2. $y - 17.9 = 10.1$

3. $\frac{-4}{3} + x = \frac{1}{3}$

4. $21.3 = a - 2.4$

5. $9\frac{1}{9} + q = 12\frac{2}{3}$

6. $2.5 = p + 9.3$

7. $s + 34 = 23.9$

8. $b - \frac{1}{4} = \frac{1}{3}$

9. $-32.3 + r = 7.8$

10. $c - 4 = 21$

11. $x - 13.2 = 1.8$

12. $s + 6.4 = 10.5$

13. $14.3 = b - 7.5$

14. $4\frac{1}{3} + d = 8\frac{1}{2}$

15. $7 = r + 2.31$

16. $f + \frac{3}{10} = \frac{3}{4}$

17. $-12.1 + t = -9$

18. $a - \frac{7}{8} = \frac{1}{2}$

Set D pages 498–499

Write an expression for each phrase.

1. 150 seats in r rows

2. 150 tickets divided among p people

3. The opposite of the product of 9 and t

4. The quotient of 6 and m

5. s dresses costing $27.50 each

6. r cookies evenly shared among 8 people

7. 10 people dividing a profit of x dollars

8. The product of 5 and c plus 7

Evaluate each expression.

9. Exercise 1 when $r = 25$

10. Exercise 2 when $p = 30$

11. Exercise 3 when $t = \frac{3}{5}$

12. Exercise 4 when $m = 1.5$

13. Exercise 7 when $x = \$1,800$

14. Exercise 8 when $c = 8$

Set E pages 502–503

Solve.

1. $48.4 = 4c$ **2.** $\frac{3}{2}f = 1$ **3.** $-3b = 63$ **4.** $\frac{39}{h} = -3$

5. $-13.1i = 52.4$ **6.** $\frac{9}{10}j = 90$ **7.** $5y = 12.5$ **8.** $\frac{v}{4} = -32$

9. $\frac{x}{-15} = -8$ **10.** $24.6 = 6r$ **11.** $\frac{1}{5}s = 17$ **12.** $\frac{5}{16} = \frac{3}{8}z$

13. $-11.3c = -45.2$ **14.** $6x = -10.8$ **15.** $\frac{v}{5} = -7$ **16.** $\frac{3}{8} = \frac{9}{10}b$

17. $\frac{2}{3}t = -24$ **18.** $3.2 = -0.4s$ **19.** $\frac{t}{-9} = -7$ **20.** $\frac{r}{8} = -4$

Set F pages 506–507

Solve.

1. $7c + 29 = 43$ **2.** $57 = 20x - 3$ **3.** $\frac{99}{q} + 7 = 40$ **4.** $\frac{t}{3} - 17 = -8$

5. $8q + 9 = 41$ **6.** $-9b + 13 = -59$ **7.** $\frac{d}{2} + 3\frac{1}{2} = 47\frac{1}{2}$ **8.** $3 = 17f - 49$

9. $26 = \frac{y}{14} + 12$ **10.** $167.5 = 3e + 22$ **11.** $4.9 + 2w = 18.3$ **12.** $\frac{v}{3} - 8 = 11$

13. $10p + 6 = 36$ **14.** $-8a + 12 = 44$ **15.** $\frac{s}{12} + 15 = 20$ **16.** $\frac{c}{3} + 8\frac{2}{3} = 9\frac{1}{3}$

17. $4z - 6.8 = 3.2$ **18.** $1.75 = 7p - 1.75$ **19.** $-33 = \frac{v}{5} - 37$ **20.** $\frac{a}{8} - 6 = 30$

Independent Study ENRICHMENT

Enrichment

Function Notation

A function can be thought of as a rule that explains how to operate on one number in order to produce another number. For example, if the function "multiply by 3" operates on the number 7, it produces the number 21.

(7) → [Function: Multiply by 3] → (21)

The symbol f(x) (read "f of x") is used to write a function.

$f(x) = 4x + 2$ is the algebraic way of writing, "Multiply the number x by 4 and add 2."

To evaluate $f(x) = 4x + 2$ when $x = 9$, substitute 9 in place of x.

$f(9) = 4(9) + 2 = 36 + 2 = 38$

Explain what happens to x in each function.

1. $f(x) = x + 4$ **2.** $f(x) = \frac{1}{2}x - 9$ **3.** $f(x) = x^2 + x$ **4.** $f(x) = \frac{x}{7} + 5$

Evaluate the following functions for the given values of x.

$f(x) = 3x + 5$	**5.** f(8)	**6.** f(1)	**7.** f(−2)	**8.** f(0)
$f(x) = \frac{1}{5}x - 7$	**9.** f(40)	**10.** f(140)	**11.** f(15)	**12.** f(0)
$f(x) = 12 - x$	**13.** f(9)	**14.** f(0)	**15.** f(−15)	**16.** f(30)
$f(x) = x^2 - 3$	**17.** f(5)	**18.** f(9)	**19.** f(1)	**20.** f(−4)

The function $f(x) = 16x^2$ tells the number of feet an object will fall in x seconds. Find the the distance an object will fall in

21. 3 seconds. **22.** 5 seconds. **23.** 10 seconds. **24.** 20 seconds.

Chapter 14 Review/Test

Evaluate each expression when $d = 0.5$ and $e = -10$.

1. $\frac{3(e - 6)}{d}$

2. $27d + 18 - 4e$

The formula $F = \frac{9C}{5} + 32$ is used to express degrees Celsius in degrees Fahrenheit.

3. Express 5°C in degrees Fahrenheit.

4. Express −30°C in degrees Fahrenheit.

Compute.

5. $54.7 \times 0 \times 119.2 \times 63.1$

6. $9\left(\frac{2}{3} + \frac{5}{18}\right)$

7. $\frac{1}{6} + 3\left[\frac{2(3 - 5)}{3}\right]$

8. $(19.2)(-7) + (19.2)(8)$

9. Concert tickets cost $18.50 each, plus a $2.50 service charge for each order. Write an equation to find the number of tickets John bought if his order totaled $113.50.

Solve.

10. $(-19)(47.3) = 47.3x$

11. $20 + \frac{x}{6} = -13$

12. $\frac{2}{3} + y = \frac{4}{5}$

13. $a - 11.7 = 2.2$

14. $\frac{-5}{6}t = 25$

15. $5m = -3\frac{1}{4}$

16. $\frac{c}{7} - 17 = 26$

17. $57 = 9m - 76.2$

18. Show where grouping symbols should be placed to make the following number sentence true.
$10 + 14 \div 2 \times 6 = 2$

19. A manufacturer claims that the cost of running one of its ceiling fans is $0.11 per day. Write an expression for the cost for d days.

20. Evaluate the expression you wrote in Item 19 when $d = 365$.

Write an expression for each phrase.

21. The perimeter of rectangle $ABCD$

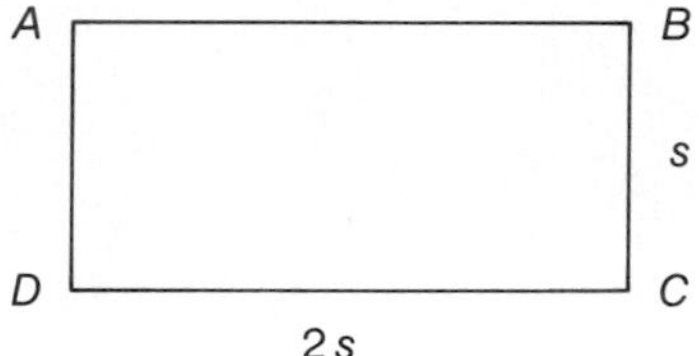

22. The length of $\overline{XY}$

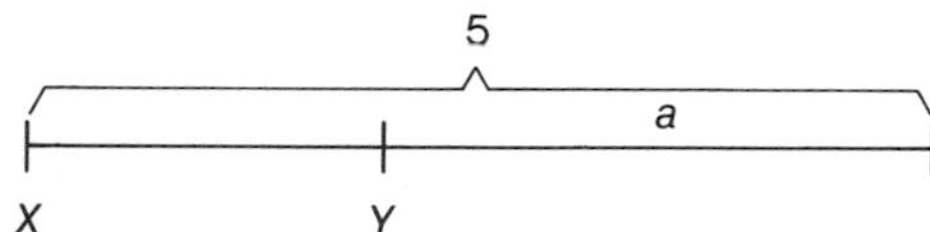

23. The Cheng family's restaurant bill was $19.65. If the Chengs spent $10.75 on a pizza and the rest on salads and drinks, how much did they spend on salads and drinks?

24. **Write About Math** In your own words, explain how you solved Item 16.

Graphing Equations and Inequalities 15

Did You Know: The *timberline* on a mountain is the elevation above which few, if any, trees grow. The timberline ranges from about 13,000 feet in the tropics to 3,000 feet in the far north.

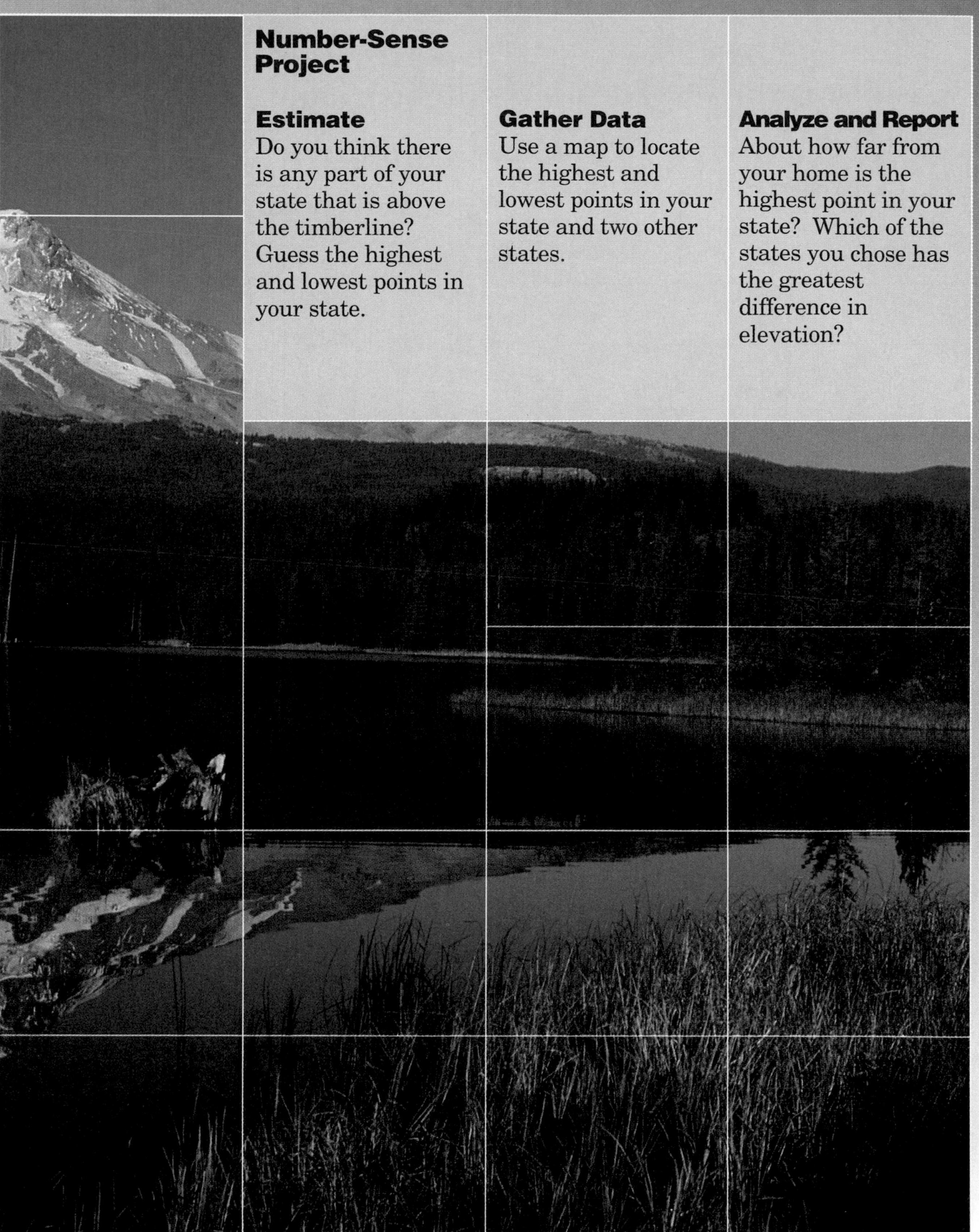

Number-Sense Project

Estimate
Do you think there is any part of your state that is above the timberline? Guess the highest and lowest points in your state.

Gather Data
Use a map to locate the highest and lowest points in your state and two other states.

Analyze and Report
About how far from your home is the highest point in your state? Which of the states you chose has the greatest difference in elevation?

Graphing on the Number Line

Build Understanding

A. The ***graphs*** of three different sets of numbers are shown below. How would you describe them?

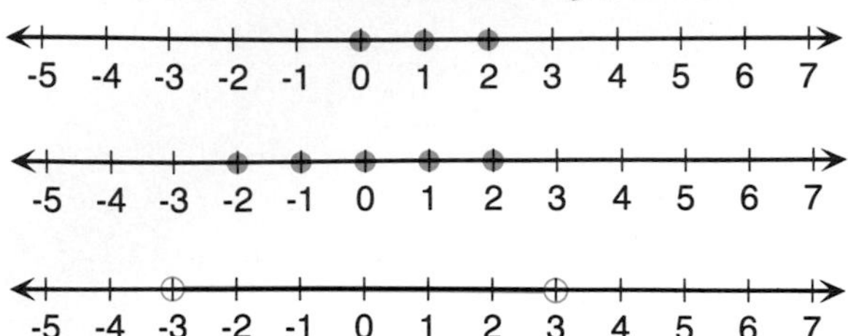

all *whole numbers* less than 3

all *integers* between 3 and -3

all numbers between 3 and -3

B. Graph the solution for $x < 4$. The solutions for an inequality depend on the replacements allowed for the variable.

Using whole numbers as replacements, you get

Using integers as replacements, you get

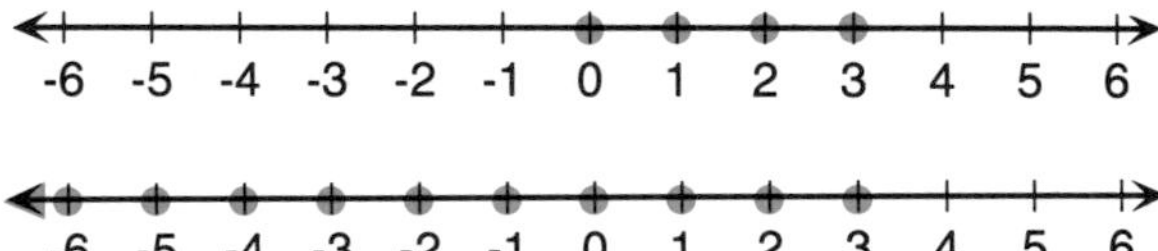

A darkened arrow (←) indicates that all integers less than -6 are also included.

Using all numbers as replacements, you get

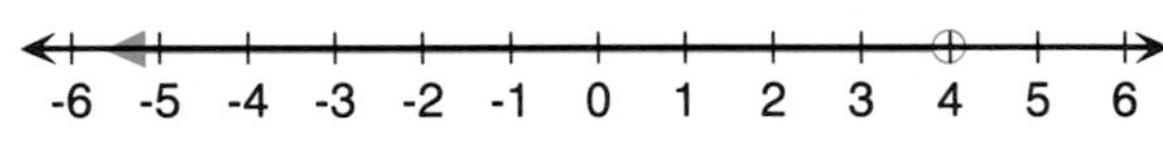

Unless told otherwise, assume all numbers can be used as replacements in an equation or inequality.

C. Graph the solutions for each sentence.

Remember that $|x|$ means all numbers that are x units from 0 on the number line.

$|x| = 3$

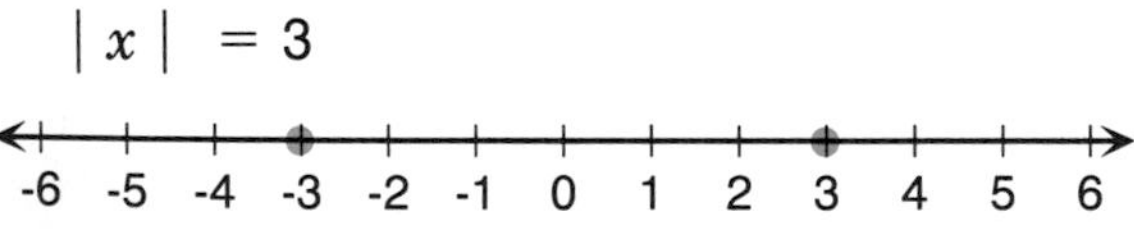

This graph shows all numbers that are 3 units from 0 on the number line.

$|x| > 3$

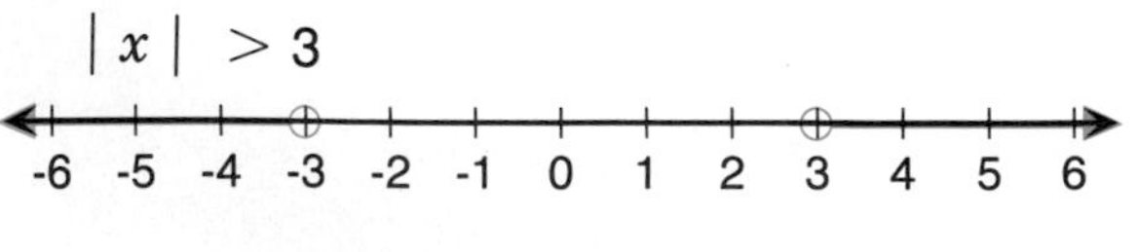

This graph shows all numbers more than 3 units from 0 on the number line. Open circles show that 3 and -3 are not included.

$|x| \leq 3$

-6 -5 -4 -3 -2 -1 0 1 2 3 4 5 6

This graph shows all numbers 3 units or less from 0 on the number line. Closed circles show that 3 and -3 are included.

Talk About Math In Example C, what replacements are allowed for the variable?

Check Understanding

For another example, see Set A, pages 552–553.

Match each equation or inequality with its graph.

1. $y \geq 3$
2. $|x| \leq 5$
3. $|y| > 1$
4. $|x| = 5$

a. -6 -5 -4 -3 -2 -1 0 1 2 3 4 5 6

b. -6 -5 -4 -3 -2 -1 0 1 2 3 4 5 6

c. -6 -5 -4 -3 -2 -1 0 1 2 3 4 5 6

d. -6 -5 -4 -3 -2 -1 0 1 2 3 4 5 6

Practice

For More Practice, see Set A, pages 554–555.

Graph the following sets of numbers.

5. All numbers between 6 and −6
6. Integers between 2 and −2
7. Whole numbers greater than 2
8. All numbers less than 2
9. Whole numbers less than 6
10. Integers greater than −2

Graph the solution of each sentence.

11. $y \geq 5$
12. $y < 5$
13. $|x| = 4$
14. $|x| > 4$
15. $|x| \leq 4$
16. $y \leq -2$
17. $|y| = 6$
18. $x \geq -4$
19. $|y| > 2$
20. $x < 0$
21. $y \geq -1$
22. $|x| < 4$

Problem Solving

Write an inequality or absolute value equation for each solution. Then draw a graph.

23. Yvonne weighs less than 125 pounds.
24. Alma has no more than \$15 in her pocket.
25. The Dodgers will score at least 3 runs.
26. Roberto and Kiko each live 4 miles from school in opposite directions.
27. **Critical Thinking** Graph and label three points between $\frac{3}{4}$ and 1 on a number line. Explain how you found your points.

Graphing Points in the Coordinate Plane

Build Understanding

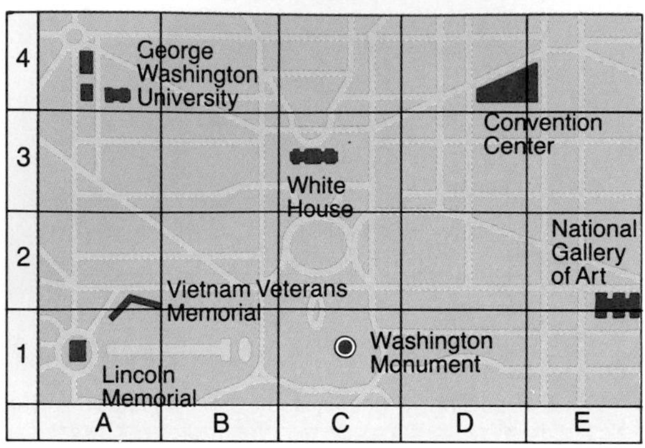

John Adams, second President of the United States, was the first to live in the White House.

Places on a map can be located by a letter and number. On this map, the White House is located in region C3.

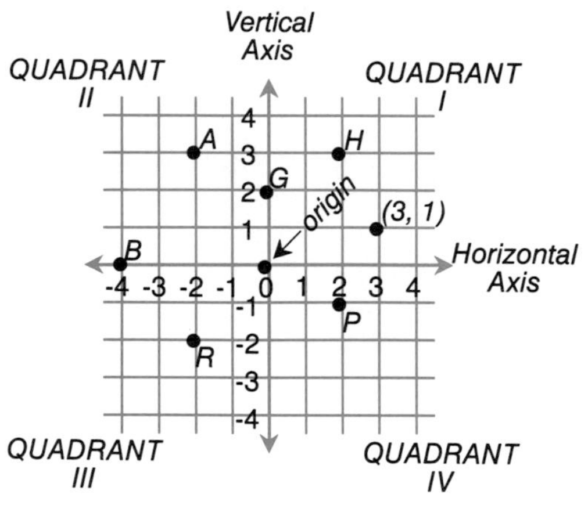

To locate a point in the plane, you need an ordered pair of numbers, which are called the ***coordinates*** of the point. A coordinate plane is formed by placing two number lines perpendicular to each other. The number lines are called ***axes.*** The point of intersection is the ***origin.***

Use the coordinate grid for Examples A–D.

A. An urban planner identifies population concentrations by locating points in a plane. To locate the point with coordinates (3, 1), start at the origin and go 3 units along the horizontal axis in the positive direction. Then go up 1 unit along a vertical line of the grid in the positive direction. This is called plotting a point.

This point lies in one of four sections of the grid called ***quadrants.*** They are labeled counterclockwise I, II, III, and IV. The ordered pair (0, 0) locates the origin.

B. Give the coordinates of point A.

To get to point A, start at the origin and go 2 units to the left (-2) and 3 units up (3). The coordinates are (-2, 3).

C. Name the point located by the ordered pair (2, -1).

The point located by (2, -1) is P.

D. In what quadrant is point B?

Point B lies in no quadrant. It is on the horizontal axis.

Talk About Math Does (3, 2) name the same point as (2, 3)? Explain.

Check Understanding

For another example, see Set B, pages 552–553.

Use the grid at the right for Exercises 1–6.
Name the coordinates for each point.

1. I **2.** C **3.** K

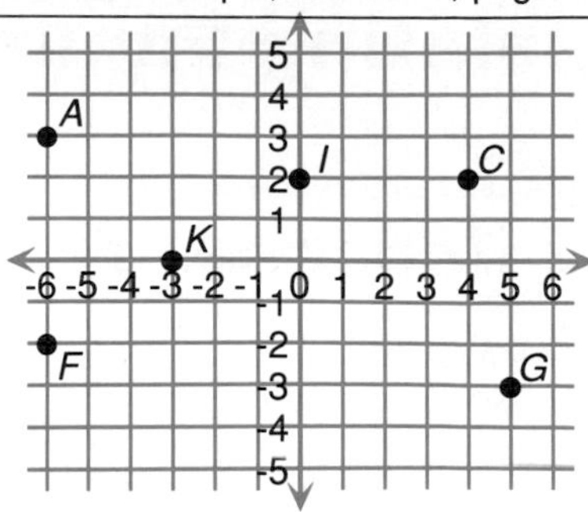

Name the point located by each ordered pair.

4. (−6, 3) **5.** (5, −3) **6.** (−6, −2)

Practice

For More Practice, see Set B, pages 554–555.

In which quadrant or on which axis is each point located?

7. A(2, 5) **8.** B(−2, −5) **9.** C(2, −5) **10.** D(−2, 5) **11.** E(0, −5) **12.** F(−5, 0)

On a grid, plot each point. Connect the points in order and connect the last point with the first. Name the polygon that results.

13. (−2, 3), (−4, 5), (−6, 3), (−4, 1)

14. (−2, 0), (0, −4), (−4, −3)

15. (3, −1), (4, −2), (3, −5), (0, −2)

16. (1, 3), (3, 0), (7, 0), (5, 3)

17. (1, −3), (5, −3), (4, −1), (2, −1)

18. (−2, 3), (2, 3), (3, 0), (0, −3), (−3, 0)

19. (−5, 0), (3, 0), (−5, −3)

20. (−4, 1), (2, 1), (2, −1), (−4, −1)

Problem Solving

Solve each problem.

21. A planner for a school system recommends schools at points A, B, and C on a map. Graph A(1, 4), B(4, 4), C(4, 1) and draw $\triangle ABC$.

22. Multiply each number in the ordered pairs in Problem 21 by two. Graph on the same grid and connect the new points to form $\triangle DEF$.

23. How do the lengths of the sides of the two triangles compare? How do their areas compare?

24. **Critical Thinking** How can you enlarge a figure and keep it similar in shape to the original? How would you get a triangle with sides 3 times the original?

Don't give up. Some problems take longer than others.

ALGEBRA

Translating Figures in the Coordinate Plane

Build Understanding

Slips and Slides
Materials: Grid paper
Groups: With a partner

a. Copy $\triangle ABC$ on your grid paper. Then draw $\triangle A'B'C'$. (Read A prime, B prime, C prime.) $\triangle A'B'C'$ is the ***image*** of $\triangle ABC$ and is the result of sliding $\triangle ABC$ 4 units to the right.

b. Compare the coordinates of both triangles. What do you notice?

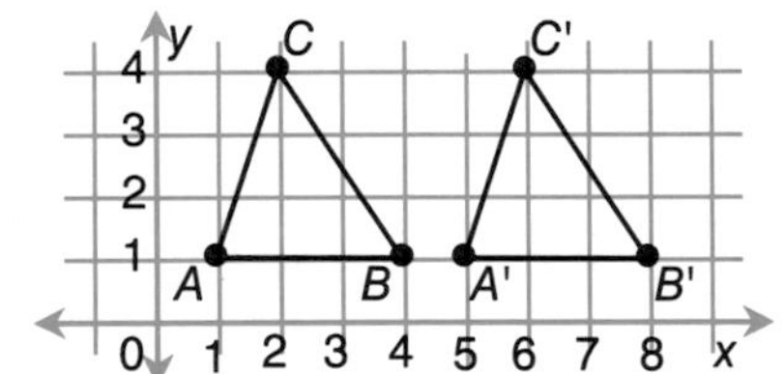

$\triangle ABC$	$\triangle A'B'C'$
A (1, 1)	**A' (5, 1)**
B (4, 1)	**B' (8, 1)**
C (2, 4)	**C' (6, 4)**

c. Adding 4 to the first coordinate for each vertex produces a horizontal slide, or *horizontal translation*, of 4 units to the right. How could you produce a horizontal translation 4 units to the *left*?

d. Copy figure $DEFG$ on your grid paper. Add -5 to the second coordinate of each vertex. What are the coordinates of D', E', F', and G'? Graph $D'E'F'G'$.

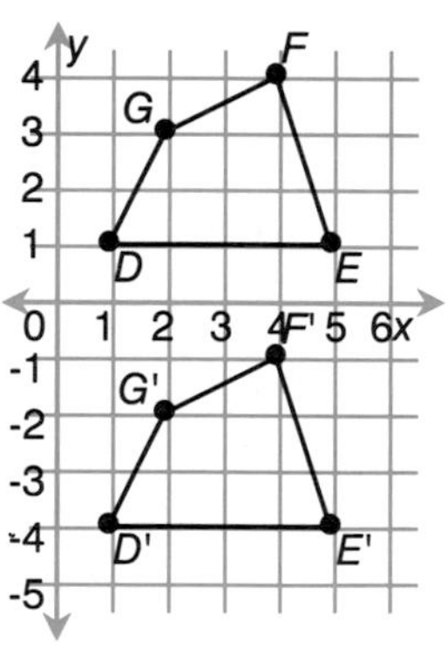

e. Figure $D'E'F'G'$ is a *vertical translation* 5 units downward of figure $DEFG$. What would you do to translate $DEFG$ 5 units *upward*?

f. Cut out figures $DEFG$ and $D'E'F'G'$ and place one on top of the other. What do you notice about their size and shape? A figure and its translation image are *congruent*.

Talk About Math How would you translate a figure 2 units to the right and 3 units downward? a figure 3 units to the left and 2 units up?

Check Understanding

For another example, see Set C, pages 552–553.

Mental Math Find the coordinates of the image of each point.

1. Point $A(3, 5)$ translated 6 units to the right.

2. Point $B(-2, 4)$ translated 3 units downward.

Practice

For More Practice, see Set C, pages 554–555.

Use grid paper to draw $\triangle ABC$ with $A(-5, 5)$, $B(-2, 1)$, and $C(-2, 5)$. On the same set of axes, graph the images of $\triangle ABC$ under the translations described below. Give the coordinates of the vertices.

3. A horizontal translation of +4 units

4. A vertical translation of +5 units

5. A horizontal translation of −2 units

6. A vertical translation of −1 units

7. A horizontal translation of +4 units and a vertical translation of +5 units

8. A horizontal translation of −2 units and a vertical translation of −1 unit

9. A horizontal translation of +4 units and a vertical translation of −1 unit

10. A horizontal translation of −2 units and a vertical translation of +5 units

A square has vertices $A(-2, 1)$, $B(2, 1)$, $C(2, 5)$, and $D(-2, 5)$. Find the coordinates of the vertices for each translation.

11. 2 units to the left

12. 4 units to the right

13. 3 units down

14. 5 units up and 3 units right

15. 5 units down and 3 units left

16. 6 units up and 5 units right

A right triangle has vertices $A(1, 3)$, $B(1, -2)$, and $C(5, -2)$. Find the coordinates of the vertices for each translation.

17. 3 units down

18. 4 units to the left

19. 2 units up

20. 1 unit down and 2 units right

21. 2 units up and 1 unit left

22. 3 units down and 3 units right

Will the following produce a horizontal or vertical translation? Also tell the direction of the slide. Use *up, down, left,* or *right.*

23. Add −3 to the first coordinate of each point.

24. Add 4 to the second coordinate of each point.

Problem Solving

Use grid paper to solve the following problems.

25. Draw rhombus $A(1, 1)$, $B(3, 2)$, $C(4, 4)$, $D(2, 3)$. What integer values are needed so that the image falls completely within quadrant III?

26. Find the area of a parallelogram with coordinates $A(3, -2)$, $B(7, -2)$, $C(5, -4)$, and $D(1, -4)$.

27. $\triangle P'Q'R'$ is a slide image of $\triangle PQR$ with vertices $P(-4, 4)$, $Q(-1, 15)$, and $R(-3, -1)$. R' has coordinates (2, 3). What are the coordinates of P' and Q'?

28. Find the area of the right triangle described in Exercises 17–22 on page 525.

29. **Critical Thinking** If (x, y) represents any point in a coordinate plane, how can you represent an image of a point under a translation of 3 units right and 4 units down?

30. The cross-stitch pattern shown is repeated to make a border for a tablecloth. Copy the pattern onto grid paper and translate it to the right 9 units. Repeat the translation 3 times, writing the coordinates for points A, B, C, and D for each translation. What are the coordinates for the tenth repetition?

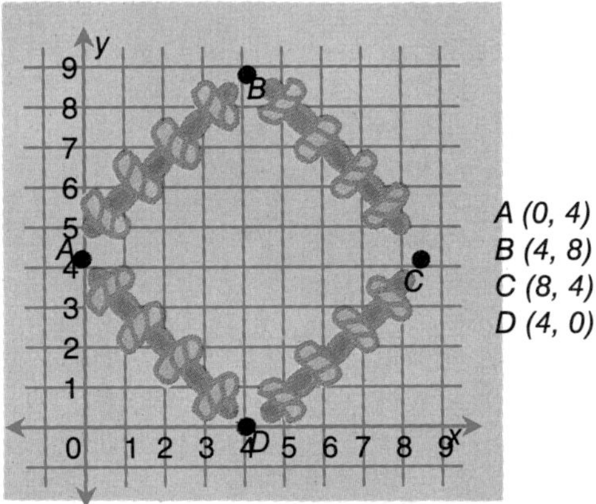

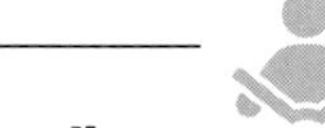

Reading ______ Math

Number Lines and Scales Complete each of the following.

1. If point B has coordinates (30, 20), then point A has coordinates (▒, ▒).

2. If point A has coordinates (100, 0), then point B has coordinates (▒, ▒).

3. If one unit is represented by 12 marks on the axis, what are the coordinates for points A, B, and C?

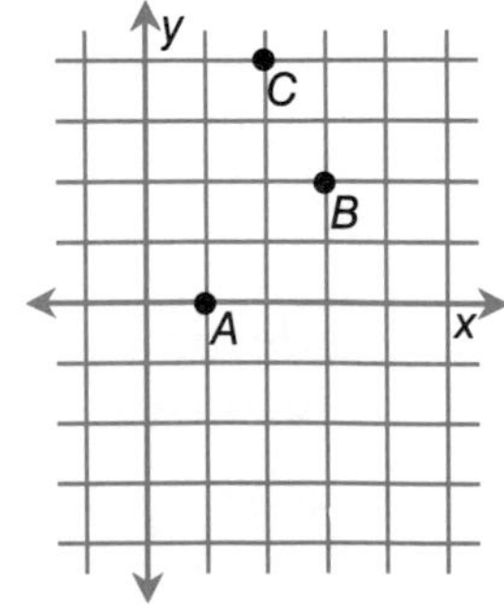

Skills Review

Name the point on the number line that corresponds to each rational number.

1. $1\frac{3}{4}$ **2.** -3 **3.** -0.2 **4.** -1.5 **5.** $-4\frac{1}{2}$ **6.** 4

Compute. Tell whether you use paper and pencil, calculator, or mental math.

7. $-34 \times (-4) \times 62$

8. $83 \times (-52) \times 13$

9. $-34 \times (-62) \times (-27)$

10. $-575 \div (-25)$

11. $840 \div (-15)$

12. $-728 \div (-14)$

13. $-\frac{1}{2} + \left(-\frac{3}{4}\right)$

14. $\frac{7}{8} + \left(-\frac{1}{4}\right)$

15. $\frac{3}{5} - \left(-\frac{1}{5}\right)$

16. $\frac{2}{3} \times \left(-\frac{3}{4}\right) \times \frac{1}{2}$

17. $\left(-\frac{3}{4}\right) \div \frac{3}{8}$

18. $1.3 + (-0.7)$

In Exercises 19–24, first find the answers for parts a, b, and c, and then order a, b, and c from least to greatest.

19. **a)** $-5 \times 3 + 2$
b) $4(-2) - 8$
c) $-8 + 16 - 7$

20. **a)** $21.4 + 63$
b) $-120 + 75$
c) $-57 + 36.8$

21. **a)** $(-2)(-2)$
b) $(-2)(-2)(-2)$
c) $(-2)(-2)(-2)(-2)$

22. **a)** $-\frac{1}{5} + \left(-\frac{3}{4}\right)$
b) $\frac{3}{5} - \frac{1}{4}$
c) $-\frac{3}{4} + \frac{4}{5}$

23. **a)** $-\frac{1}{4} \times \frac{2}{3}$
b) $\frac{5}{8} \times \frac{4}{15}$
c) $\frac{3}{2} \times \left(-\frac{5}{9}\right)$

24. **a)** $-\frac{5}{7} \times \frac{14}{25} + \frac{21}{20}$
b) $\frac{3}{8} + \frac{2}{3} - \frac{13}{24}$
c) $\frac{1}{4}\left[-\frac{2}{3} + \left(-\frac{1}{3}\right)\right]$

25. **a)** $3 \div 6 \times 2$
b) $3 \div 0.6 \times 2$
c) $3 \div 0.6 \times (-2)$

26. **a)** $\frac{1}{2} \div \frac{1}{4} + (-5)$
b) $\left(\frac{1}{4}\right)(2)(-5) + 5$
c) $\left(\frac{1}{2} + \frac{1}{4}\right)5$

27. **a)** $\left(-\frac{3}{7} + \frac{1}{21}\right) \div -4$
b) $\left(-\frac{3}{7} + \frac{1}{21}\right) \div -\frac{1}{4}$
c) $-4 \div \left(-\frac{3}{7} + \frac{1}{21}\right)$

ALGEBRA

Reflections in the Coordinate Plane

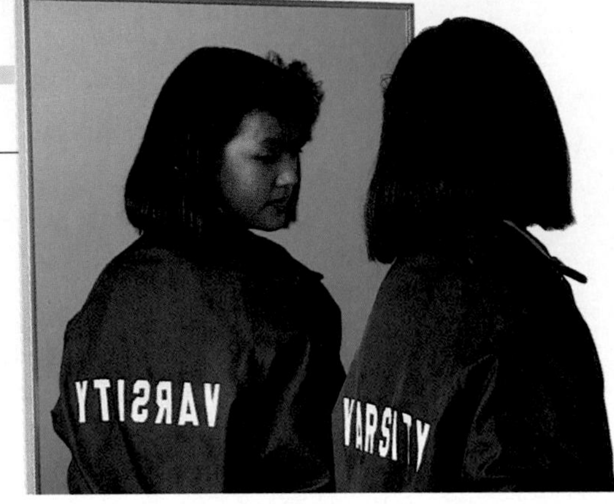

Build Understanding

ACTIVITY

Flipping Out
Materials: Grid paper
Group: With a partner

When you look in a mirror, you see your reflection, or mirror image. It looks just like you although it is reversed or flipped.

Similarly, you can find reflected images of geometric figures in the coordinate plane.

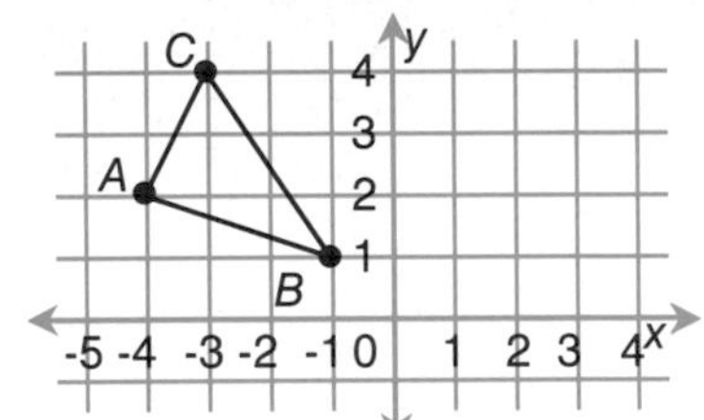

a. Copy $\triangle ABC$ onto grid paper. Then fold the paper along the vertical, or y-axis, so that $\triangle ABC$ is on the outside.

b. Hold your paper to the light, and trace the triangle on the other side of the paper. Opening up the paper you see $\triangle ABC$ and $\triangle A'B'C'$, its image reflected over the y-axis.

In this case, the y-axis is the ***line of reflection.***

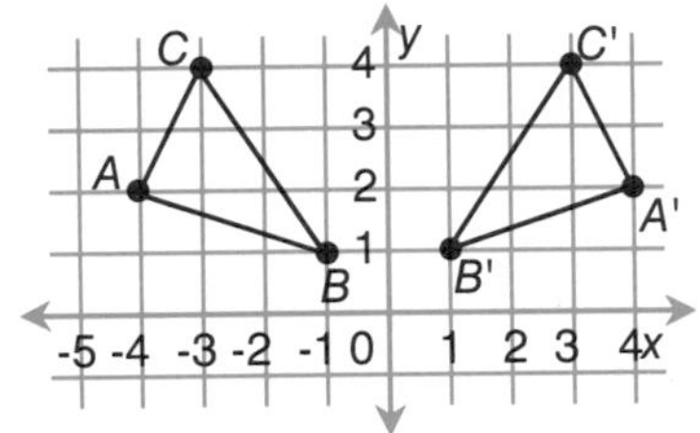

c. List the coordinates of both triangles. What pattern do you see? What is the line of reflection?

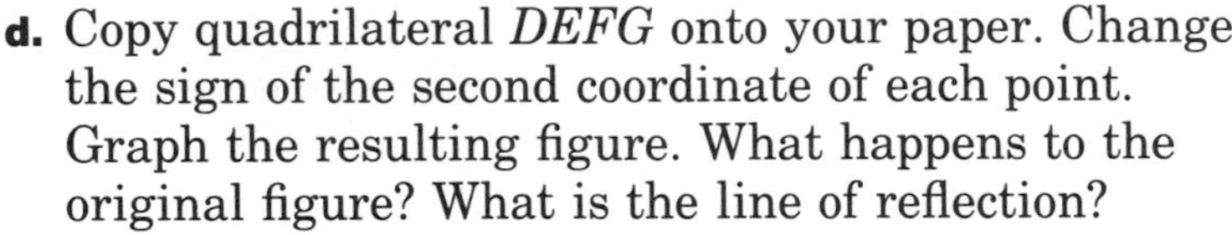

d. Copy quadrilateral $DEFG$ onto your paper. Change the sign of the second coordinate of each point. Graph the resulting figure. What happens to the original figure? What is the line of reflection?

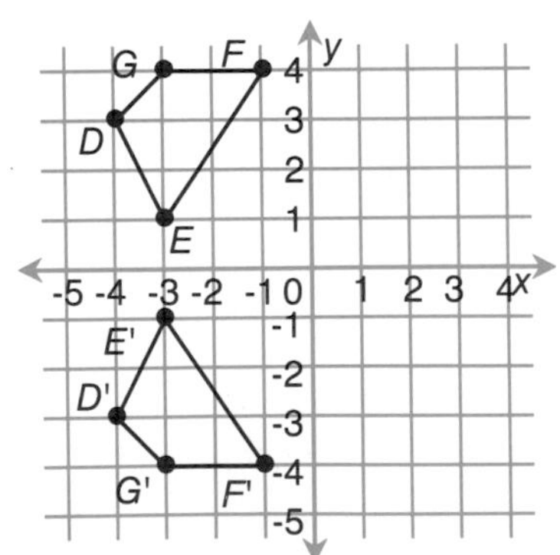

e. Fold your paper along the x-axis and hold the paper up to the light. What do you notice about the two quadrilaterals? Are the figures congruent?

Talk About Math Describe what happens to a figure in the coordinate plane when the sign of the first coordinate for each point is changed; and when only the sign of the second coordinate for each point is changed.

Check Understanding

For another example, see Set D, pages 552–553.

Use the diagram to answer the following questions.

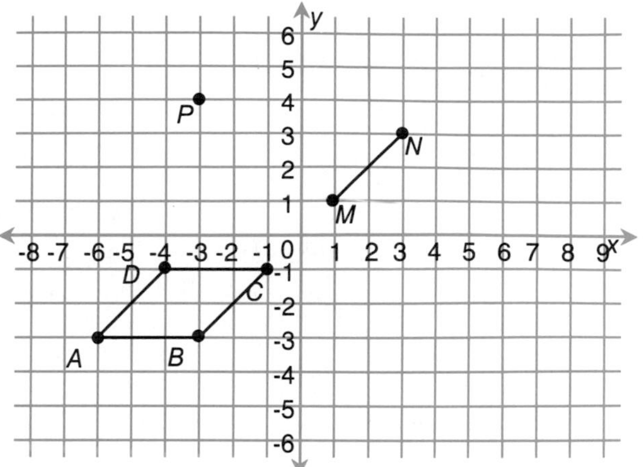

1. If point P is reflected over the y-axis, what are the coordinates of the image?
2. If point P is reflected over the x-axis, what are the coordinates of the image?
3. If $\overline{MN}$ is reflected over the x-axis, what are the coordinates of the endpoints of the image?
4. If $ABCD$ is reflected over the y-axis, what are the coordinates of the vertices of the image?

Practice

For More Practice, see Set D, pages 554–555.

Mental Math What would be the image of (3, 7) under each transformation?

5. a reflection over the x-axis
6. a reflection over the y-axis

Use the figure to answer each question.

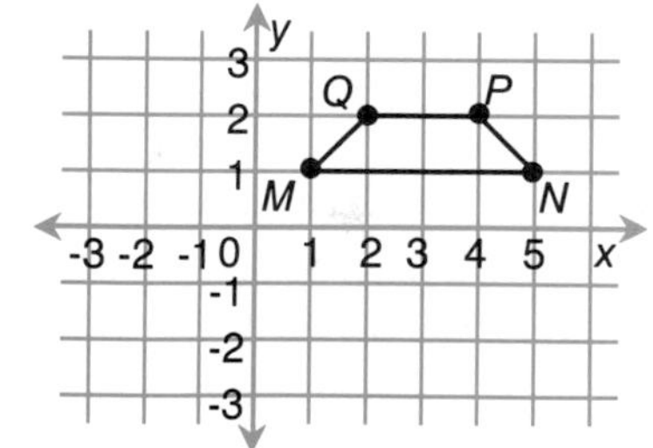

7. If you reflect $MNPQ$ over the x-axis, what are the coordinates of the vertices of the image?
8. If you reflect $MNPQ$ over the y-axis, what are the coordinates of the vertices of the image?
9. If the coordinates of the vertices of a square are D (1, 4), E (3, 1), F (6, 3), and G (4, 6), what are the coordinates of the image produced by a reflection over the y-axis?

Trace each figure, and reflect it over the given line. What do you see?

10. 

11. 

12. 

Mixed Practice Given the figure *ABCD*, match each transformation below with the appropriate graph.

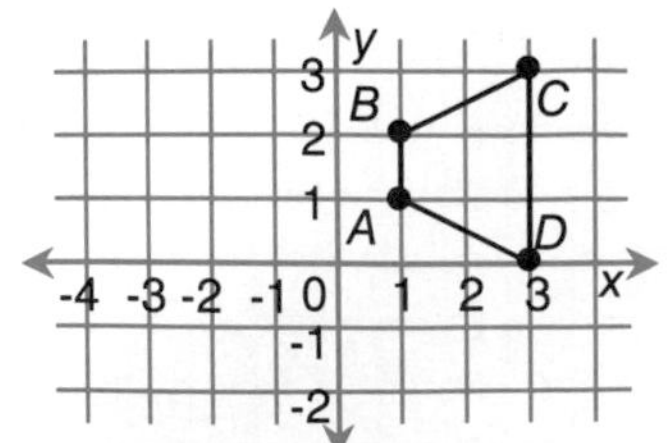

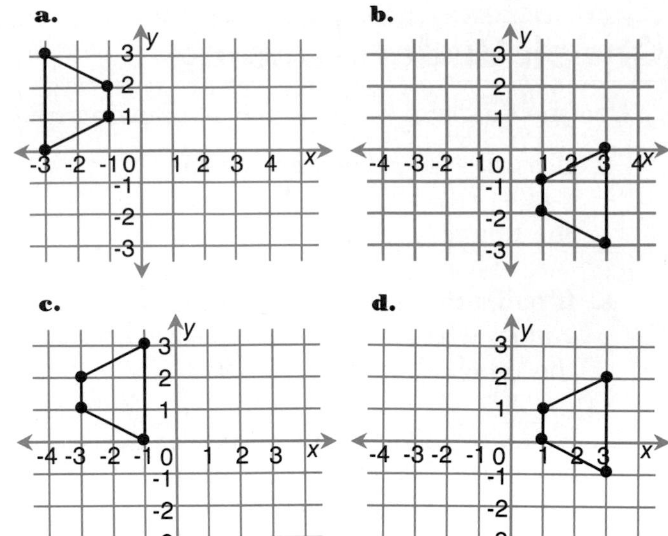

13. Horizontal translation

14. Vertical translation

15. Reflection over the x-axis

16. Reflection over the y-axis

Match the transformations of *EFGH* with the images shown below.

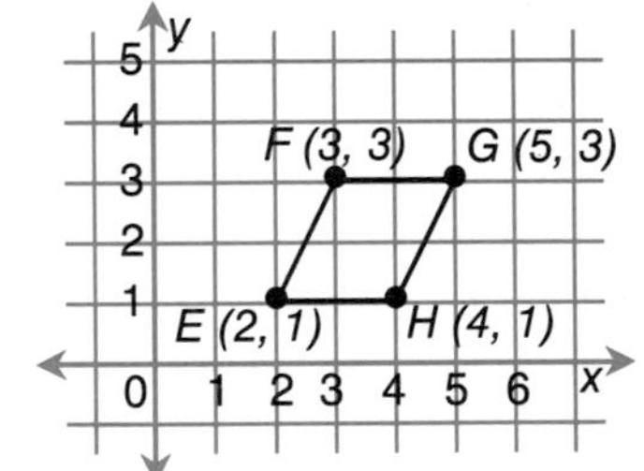

17. Reflection over the y-axis

18. Reflection over the x-axis

19. Horizontal translation

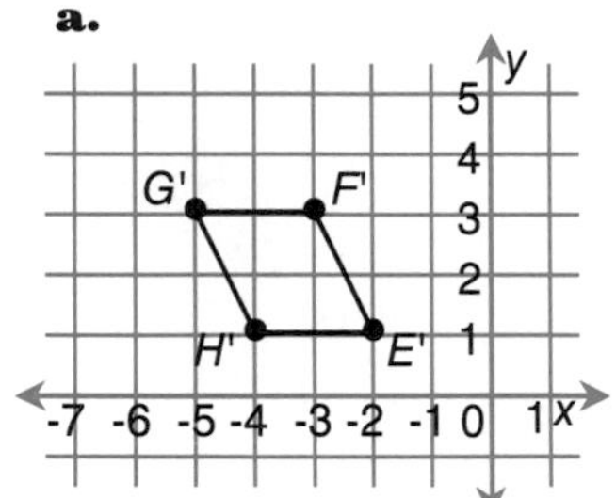

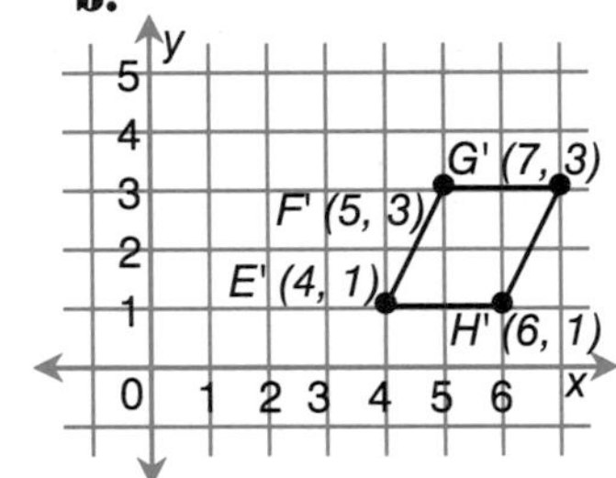

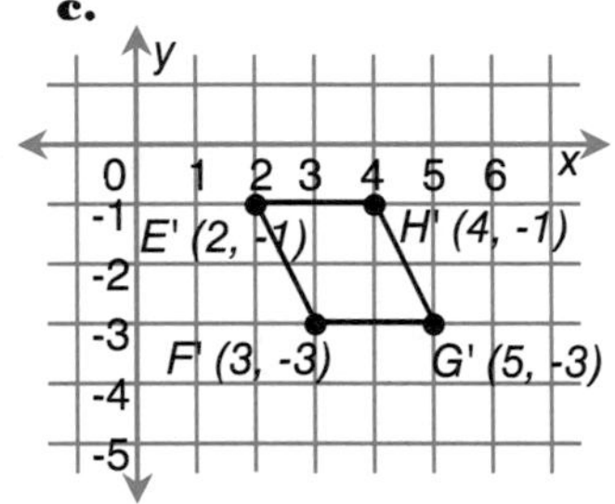

Problem Solving

Complete the following by using grid paper.

20. Draw any triangle *ABC*. Reflect the triangle over the x-axis. Reflect the result over the y-axis. What are the coordinates of the final triangle?

21. Switch the order of the reflections in $\triangle ABC$ (reflect $\triangle ABC$ over the y-axis, then the x-axis). Is the resulting triangle the same as in Problem 20?

22. Draw any quadrilateral *ABCD*. Reflect it over the *x*-axis. Then translate the resulting quadrilateral 6 units to the left. What are the coordinates of the final quadrilateral?

23. Use the same quadrilateral as in Problem 22, but switch the order of the transformations. That is, first translate the quadrilateral 6 units to the left. Then reflect it over the *x*-axis. Is the resulting quadrilateral the same as in Problem 22?

24. Use Data Copy the cross-stitch pattern on page 526 onto grid paper, and create a pattern for the center of a table napkin. First, reflect figure *ABCD* over the *x*-axis, then reflect the resulting figure over the *y*-axis. Finally, reflect this figure over the *x*-axis to form a pattern of four squares. Give the coordinates for points *A, B, C,* and *D* on this final reflection.

Explore Math

Copy these examples onto grid paper.

MOM 1881 1001 WOW

25. The words and numbers above are examples of ***palindromes***. What do you think a palindrome is?

26. Critical Thinking Palindromes are similar to reflections in the coordinate plane, because they read the same around a central letter or point between letters. In the name HANNAH, the central point occurs between the two Ns. In the number 4896984, the central number is 6. Find the central point or letter for these palindromes.

NOON	60488406
391252193	ABLE WAS I ERE I SAW ELBA
STEP ON NO PETS	2002
21123432112	MADAM, I'M ADAM
A MAN, A PLAN, A CANAL, PANAMA	60600606

27. Can you discover at least two other words and numbers that are palindromes?

28. The sentence below is not a palindrome, but it has an unusual property. What is it?

NOW NO SWIMS ON MON

Rotations in the Coordinate Plane

Build Understanding

Fabrics from many cultures contain patterns made by transforming geometric figures. This Korean applique pattern features complex shapes with point symmetry.

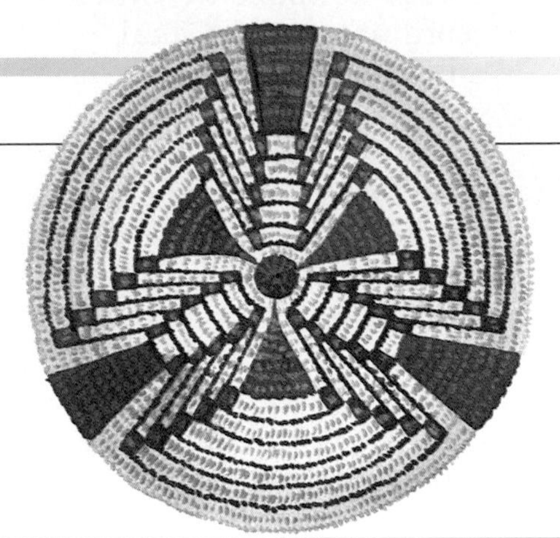

This basket designed by Pima Indians in North America symbolizes a water source in the center and streams radiating from it.

Geometric figures can be moved from one position to another by translations (slides), reflections (flips), or rotations (turns).

In each piece of art above, a single pattern is rotated around the center. Any point on the pattern stays the same distance from the center as it is rotated. Geometric figures can also be rotated in a coordinate plane using the origin as the *center of rotation.*

A. When rectangle $ABCD$ is rotated 90° counterclockwise around (0,0), rectangle $A'B'C'D'$ is the image.

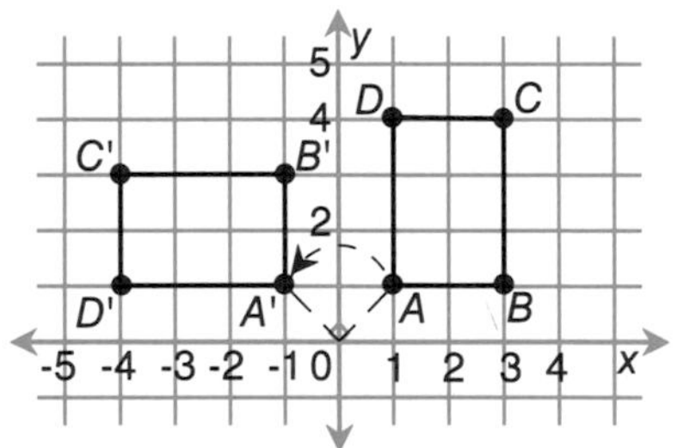

To test this, trace rectangle $ABCD$ on a piece of paper. Then place your pencil point on (0,0) and turn your paper until the figure you traced coincides with rectangle $A'B'C'D'$, the rotated image of the original figure.

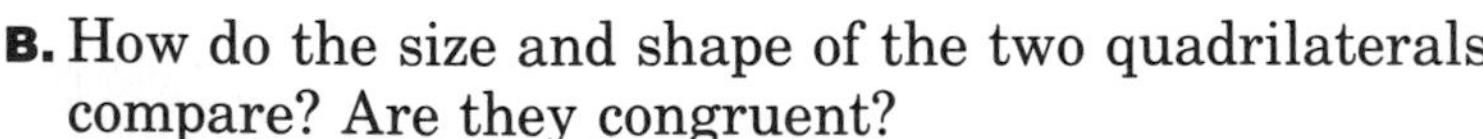

B. How do the size and shape of the two quadrilaterals compare? Are they congruent?

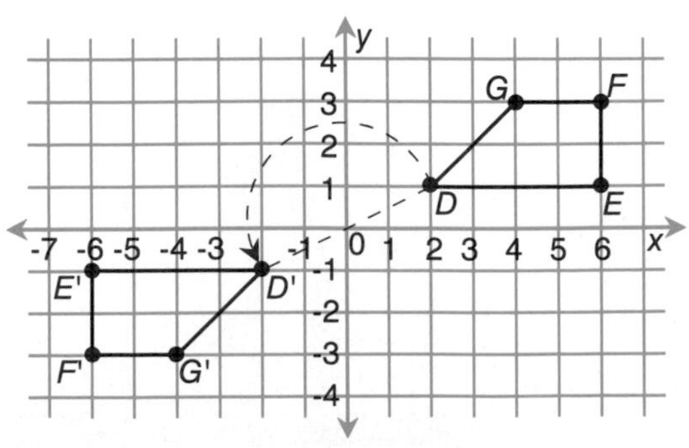

If you place your pencil point at (0,0) and turn the paper 180° clockwise, $D'E'F'G'$ is the image of $DEFG$. $DEFG$ has been rotated 180° clockwise around (0,0).

The two quadrilaterals have the same size and shape and therefore are congruent.

■ **Talk About Math** In Example B, can you get the same image using other transformations? Explain.

Check Understanding

For another example, see Set E, pages 552–553.

Choose the figure that is the image of figure h under a rotation.

1.

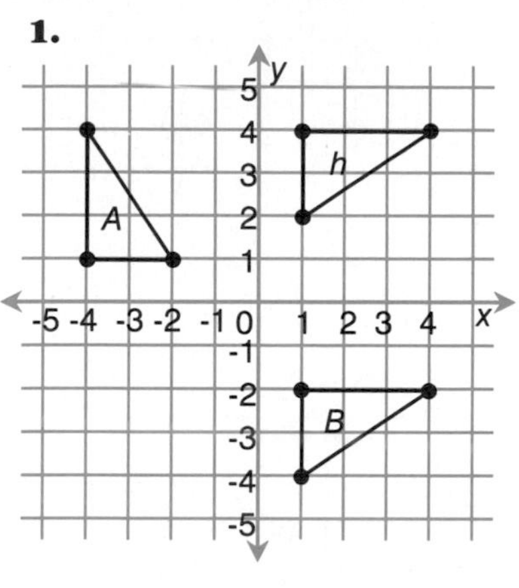

2.

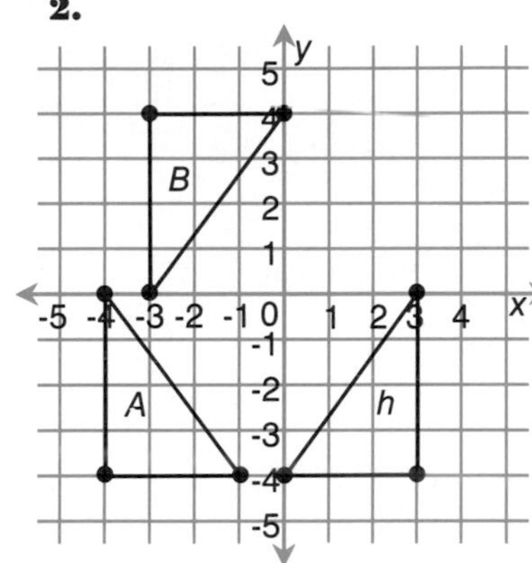

3.

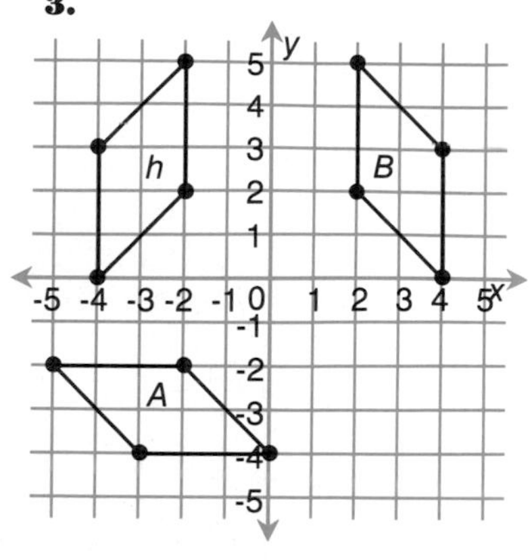

Practice

For More Practice, see Set E, pages 554–555.

Copy each figure on grid paper. Name the coordinates of the vertices of each rotated image.

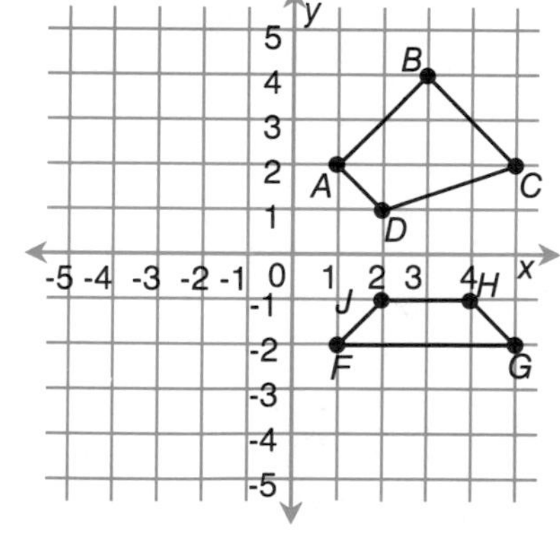

4. A 90° counterclockwise rotation of the figure $ABCD$

5. A 180° clockwise rotation of figure $ABCD$

6. A 90° clockwise rotation of figure $FGHJ$

7. A 180° counterclockwise rotation of figure $FGHJ$

Choose the next figure in the sequence.

8. 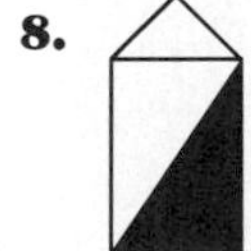 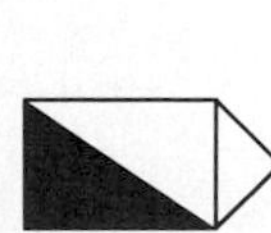 

a. 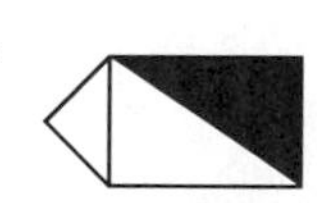 **b.**  **c.** 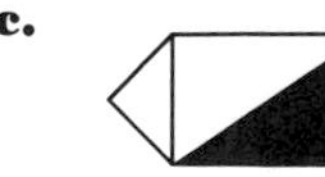

9.   

a.  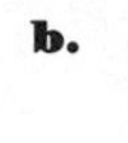 **b.**   **c.** 

Mixed Practice Identify each transformation as a translation, reflection, or rotation.

10.

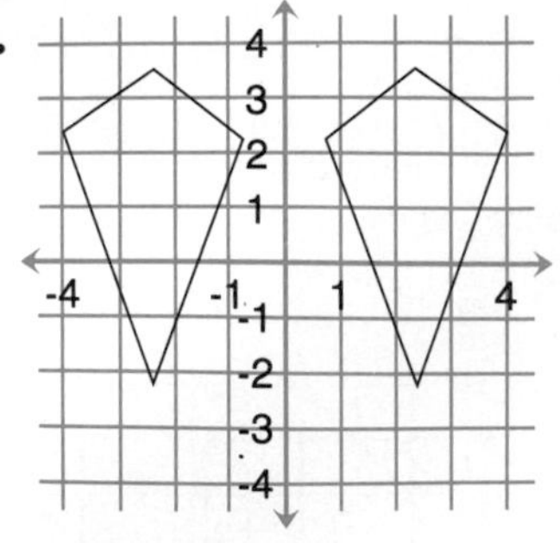

11.

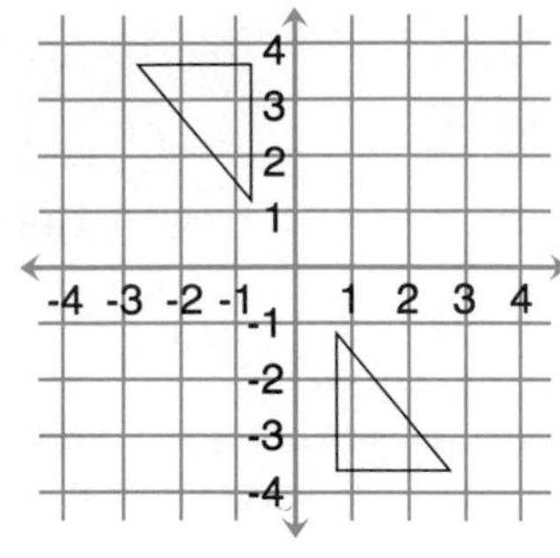

12.

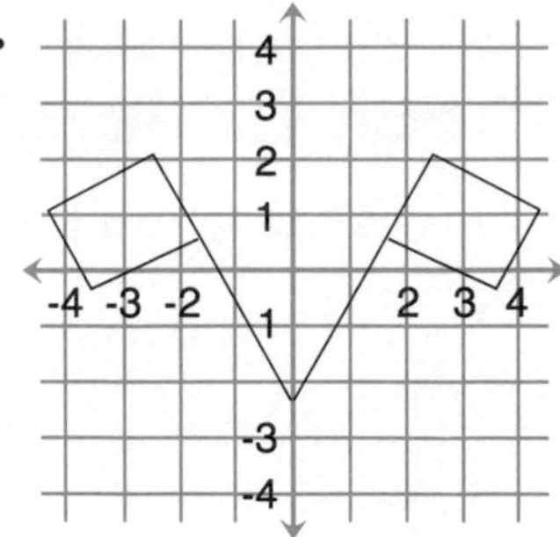

Describe what transformation(s) might have taken place to produce the images.

13.

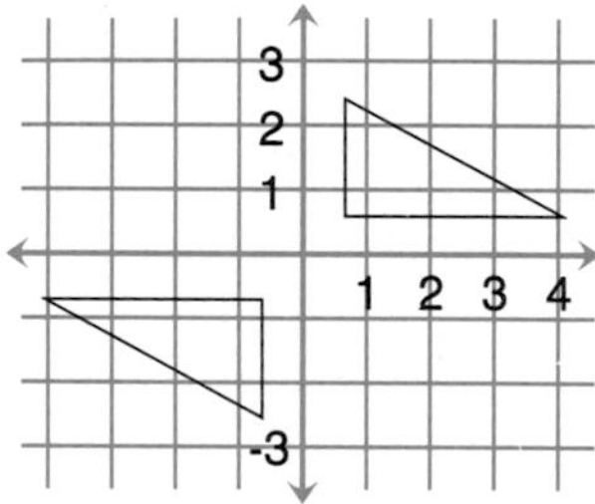

14.

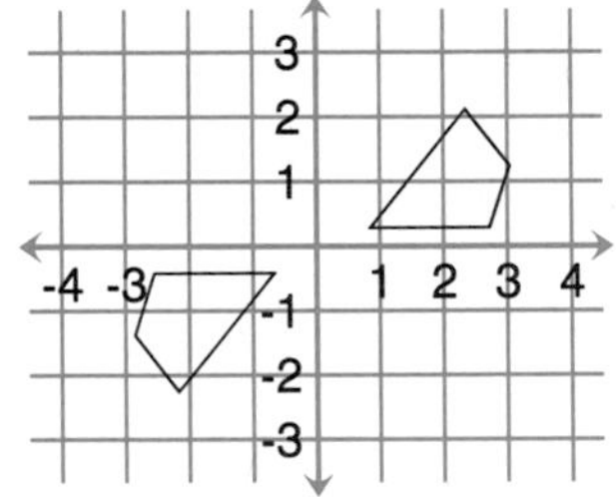

Problem Solving

Visual Thinking Visualize moving these figures. Which figures can be turned or slid (not flipped) to match the first figure?

15. **a.**  **b.**  **c.** **d.**

16. **a.**  **b.** **c.** **d.** 

Remember that a figure has *point symmetry* if it remains unchanged after a rotation of 180° around its center. For each rosemaling design below, tell whether the figure has point symmetry. Answer *yes* or *no*.

17.

18.

Rosemaling is a classic Norwegian art form that was once done on walls or ceilings of homes and historic buildings in Norway.

Midchapter Checkup

Graph the following sets of numbers.

1. $|x| = 3$ **2.** $|x| \leq 2$ **3.** $x = -2$ **4.** $x < -1$ **5.** $x \geq 0$

Use the graph below and name the point located by each ordered pair.

6. (3, 1) **7.** (−1, −1) **8.** (3, 3) **9.** (−2, 2) **10.** (0, −3) **11.** (1, 2)

Copy the trapezoid on grid paper. Give the coordinates of the vertices under the transformations below.

12. horizontal translation of −3 units

13. vertical translation of +2 units

14. translation 4 units right and 3 units down

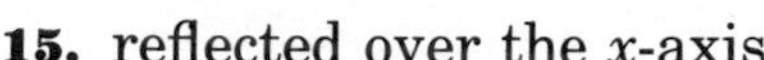

15. reflected over the x-axis

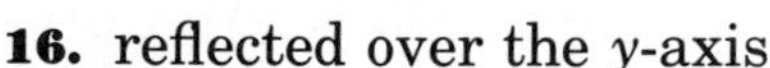

16. reflected over the y-axis

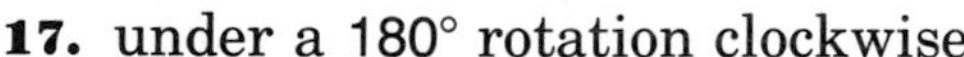

17. under a 180° rotation clockwise

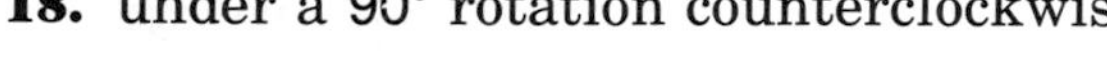

18. under a 90° rotation counterclockwise

Choose the next figure in the sequence.

19.     **a.**  **b.**  **c.** 

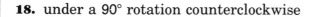

20. 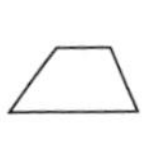 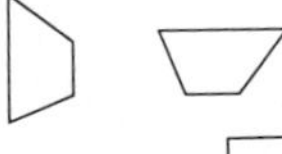 **a.** 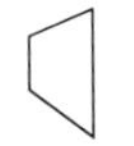 **b.** 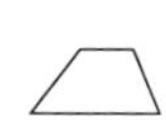 **c.** 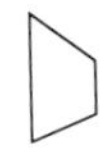

21.  **a.** 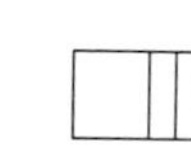 **b.** 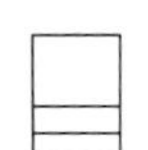 **c.** 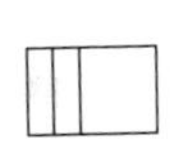

Identify each transformation as a translation, reflection, or rotation.

22.

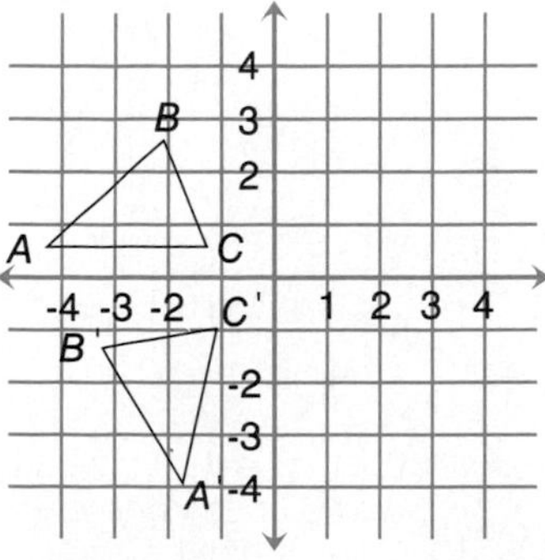

23.

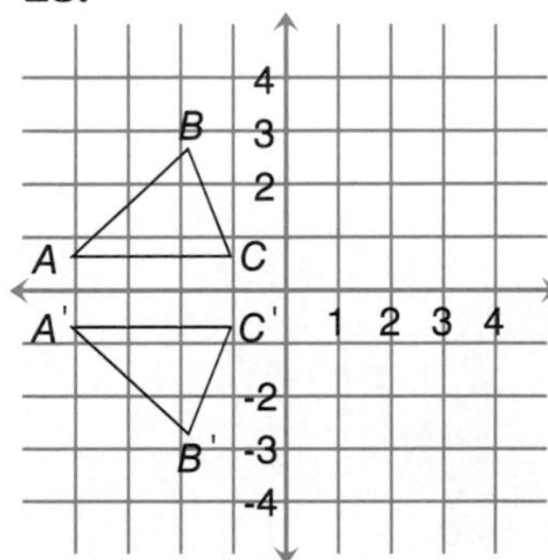

24.

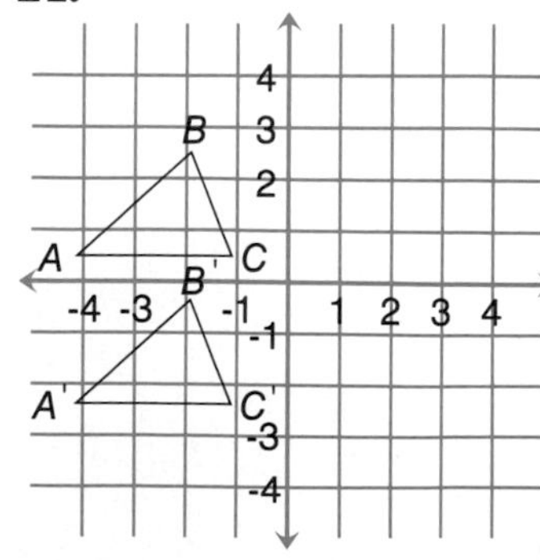

Explore as a Team

1. Play a game of "Hit or Miss" with another person.

a. Each person needs two pieces of graph paper. Decide how large your playing field will be. Then label each horizontal and vertical axis with identical labels.

b. Each player takes one of the graphs and secretly draws a point, a line segment, a triangle, a square, and a rectangle.

c. The first player begins the game by naming an ordered pair. The opponent must say whether it is a *hit* or a *miss*. (On the bottom gameboard at the right, the ordered pair (2, 2) would be a hit and (4, 4) would be a miss.)

Then the first player marks the second piece of graph paper in order to keep track of whether or not the guess "hit" or "missed" the opponent's shapes.

For the game shown, it takes one hit to find the point, two hits to find the line segment, three hits to find the triangle, four hits to find the square, and six hits to find the rectangle.

d. The game continues with players taking turns naming an ordered pair. The winner is the first person to find (hit) the opponent's shapes.

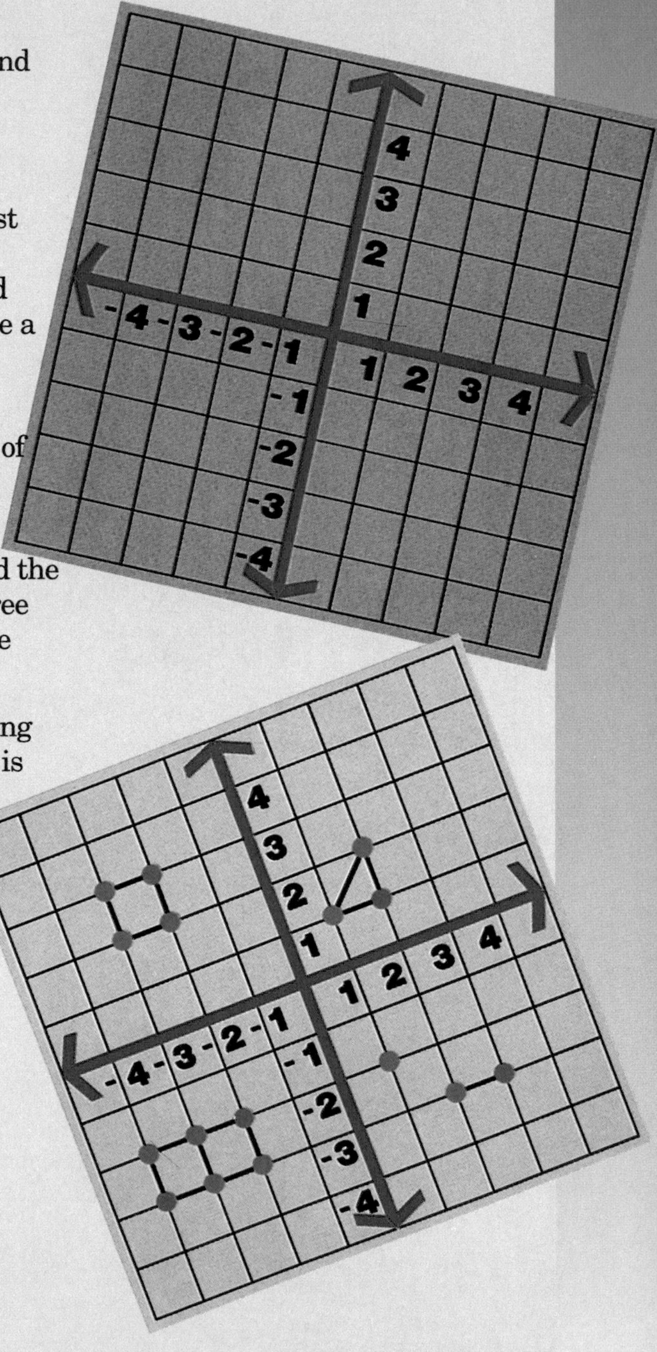

Be a good tutor. Make up similar problems or easier ones to help someone.

Explore With a Computer

Use the *Geometry Workshop Project* for this activity.

Roger created scenery for the school play. He had to design a boat and its mirror image. Roger drew the first design on a grid.

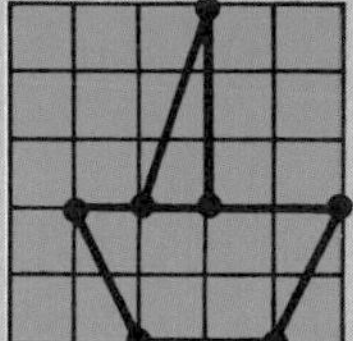

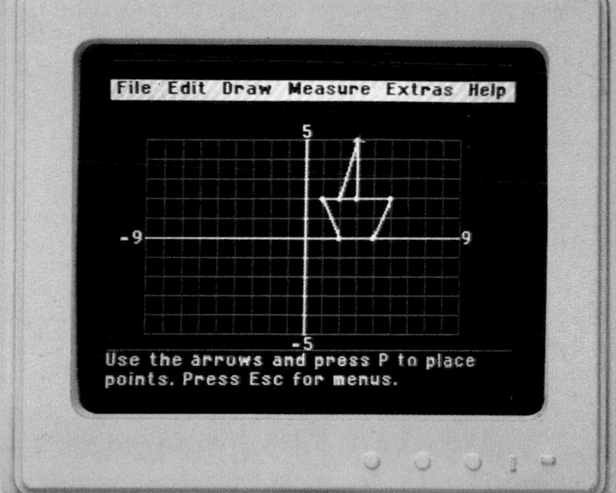

1. Make a reflection of the image. What are the points Roger would use to design the reflection? At the computer, plot these points.

2. Draw segments to connect the points.

Number-Sense Project

Look back at pages 518–519.

1. Mount Hood in Oregon rises from its base at 3,000 feet above sea level to a height of over 11,000 feet above sea level. The timberline is at 6,000 feet above sea level. A scale drawing of Mount Hood is shown at the right. The region between the base and the timberline is shaded.

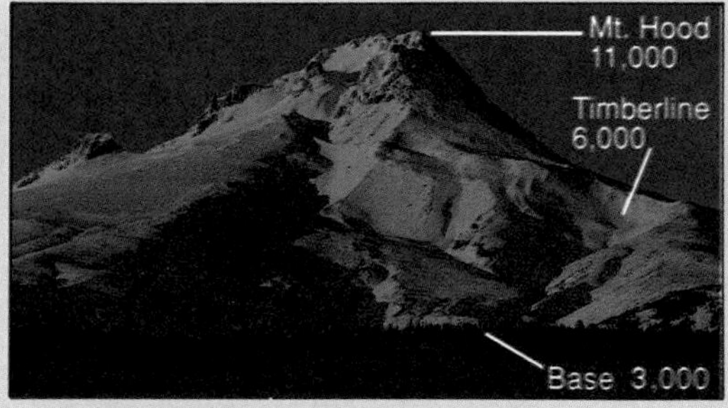

Make a similar drawing for each mountain listed below. Use 1 inch for 4,000 feet. Shade the region, if any, above the base but below the timberline. All elevations given have been rounded.

	Mountain	Elevation	Timberline	Base
a.	Mt. McKinley	20,000	3,000	3,000
b.	Kilimanjaro	19,000	10,000	5,000
c.	Mt. Everest	29,000	12,000	16,000

Draw a Diagram

Understand
QUESTION
FACTS
KEY IDEA

Plan and Solve
STRATEGY
ANSWER

Look Back
SENSIBLE ANSWER
ALTERNATE APPROACH

Build Understanding

As a tile setter, John tiles a floor so that no tiles overlap and there are no gaps. When polygons are arranged in this way, they are said to ***tessellate.*** The arrangement is called a ***tessellation.*** What shapes can John use for his tiles?

One of John's designs uses horizontal and vertical translations of the hexagon. Which other regular polygons will also tessellate and which transformations are needed to make a tessellation?

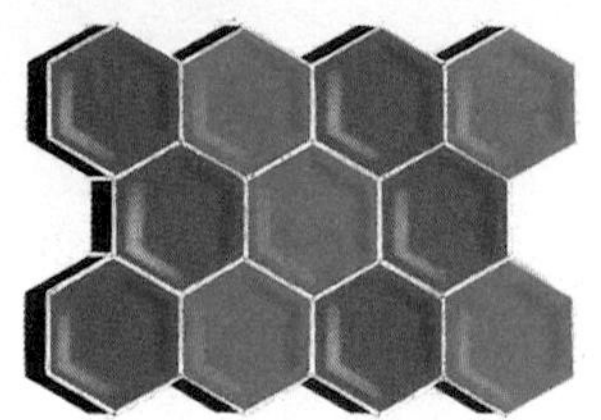

Understand QUESTION Which other regular polygons will tessellate? Which transformations are needed?

FACTS Figures must be joined edge to edge.

KEY IDEA Repeated figures must cover the surface with no gaps and no overlapping.

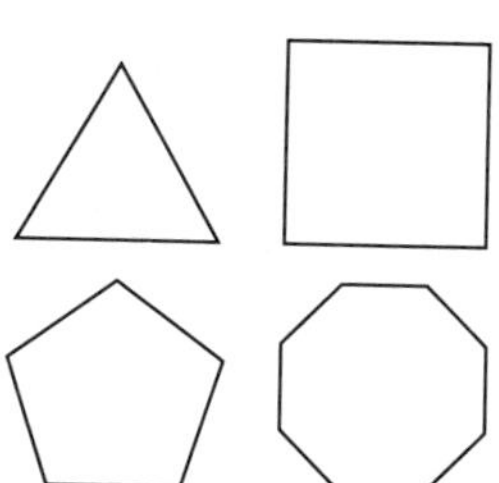

Plan and Solve STRATEGY Trace each figure and try to repeat the tracing so that no gaps or overlapping occurs.

ANSWER The triangle and the square tessellate.

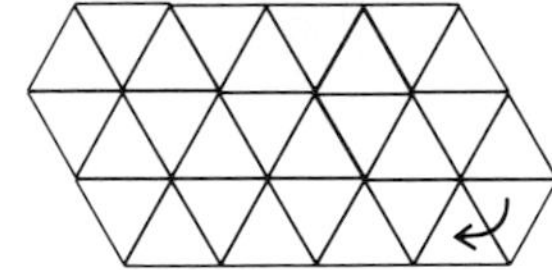

Rotate the equilateral triangle 60°.

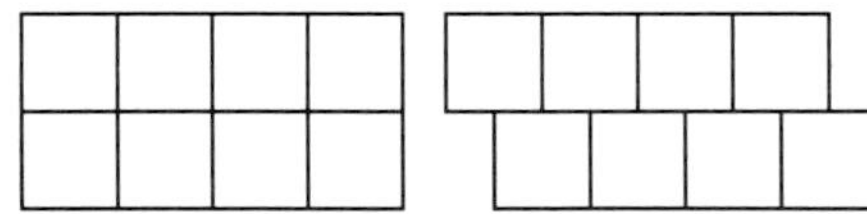

Translate the square horizontally and vertically.

Look Back Both the regular pentagon and the regular octagon leave gaps.

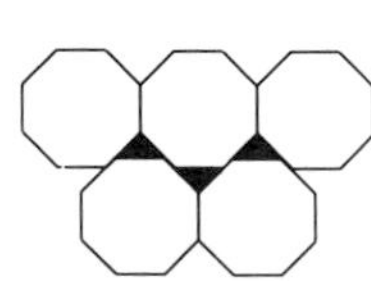

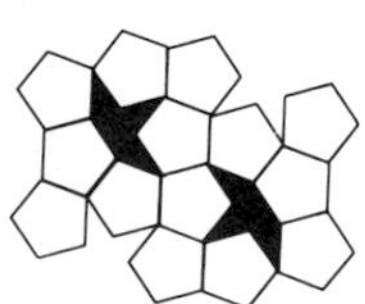

■ **Talk About Math** Two arrangements show how a square tessellates. Are other arrangements possible?

Check Understanding

Refer to the figures to answer the questions.

1. Which figure shows that a right triangle tessellates? Which transformations are used?

2. Which figure shows that a parallelogram tessellates? Which transformations are used?

3. Show at least one other way to tessellate with a right triangle.

a.

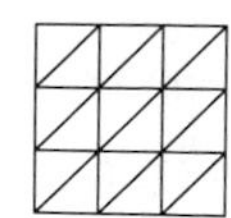

b.

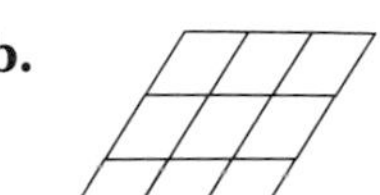

Practice

Determine if each figure tessellates. **Remember,** there can be no gaps or overlaps.

4.

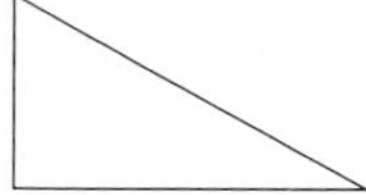

5.

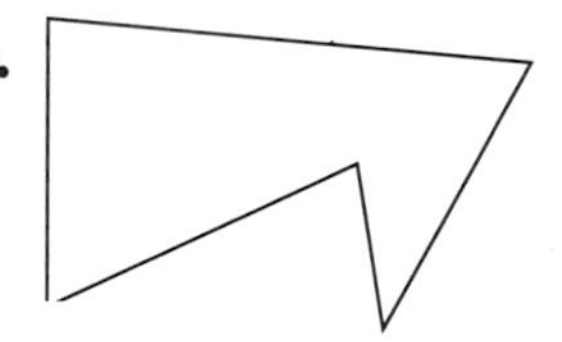

6.

7.

8.

9.

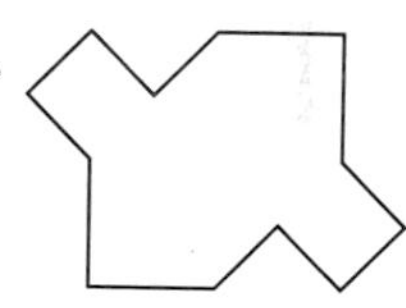

10.

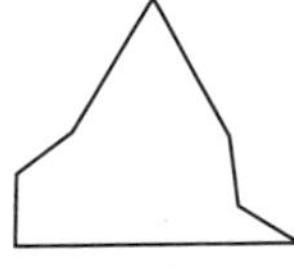

11.

12.

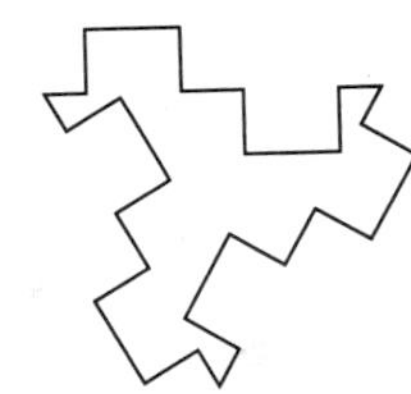

13. Draw a triangle that is not a right triangle or an equilateral triangle. Does it tessellate?

Choose a ________ Strategy

Puzzling Pentominoes A ***pentomino*** is formed when five congruent squares are joined at their edges. There are twelve ways to form pentominoes. Four are shown.

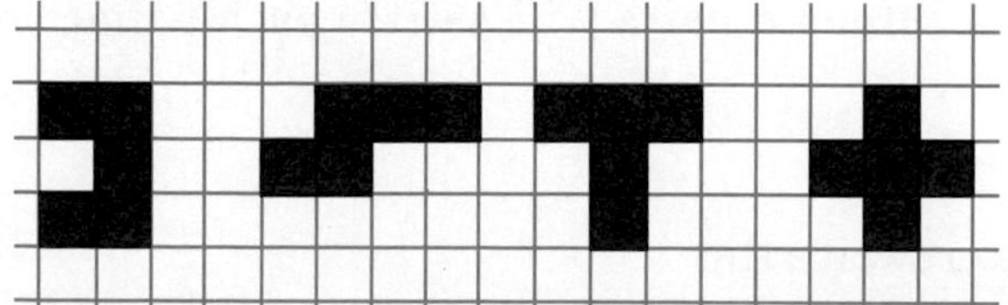

14. Using grid paper, draw the other eight pentominoes.

15. Show one of the pentominoes that will tessellate.

Solving Problems in Two Variables

Build Understanding

Rebecca works part-time after school in a pet shop and earns \$6 an hour.

A. One day Rebecca earned a total of \$15. How many hours did she work? Let x represent the number of hours.

$$6x = 15$$

$$x = 2.5$$

She worked 2.5 hours. This equation has one solution.

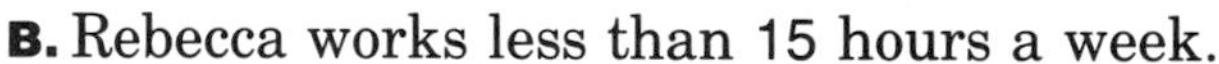

B. Rebecca works less than 15 hours a week.

$$x < 15$$

This inequality has many solutions.
Some possible solutions are 1, 2, 2.5, 3, ...

C. Rebecca describes her earnings using the equation $y = 6x$, where y is her salary and x is the number of hours she works.

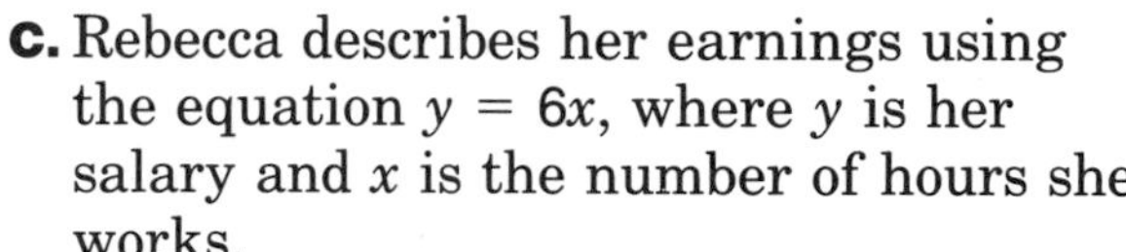

The equation $y = 6x$ has two variables, so two numbers are needed to make it true. Each solution is an ordered pair.

The chart shows her possible earnings.

x	$6x$	y	(x, y)
hours	rate (hours)	earnings	solutions
1	6(1)	6	(1, 6)
2	6(2)	12	(2, 12)
4	6(4)	24	(4, 24)
10	6(10)	60	(10, 60)

These are just some of the many solutions to this equation.

D. Solve $2x + y = 5$ for y in terms of x. Then make a table of ordered pairs.

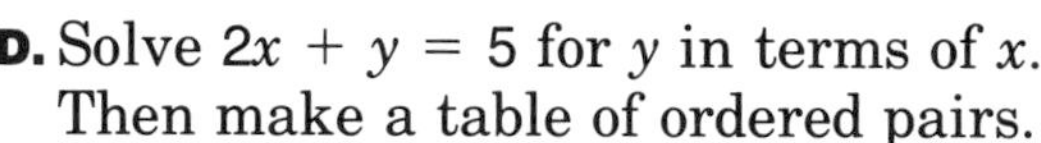

$$2x + y = 5$$

$$y = -2x + 5$$

x	$-2x + 5$	y	(x, y)
−2	−2(−2) + 5	9	(−2, 9)
−1	−2(−1) + 5	7	(−1, 7)
0	−2(0) + 5	5	(0, 5)
1	−2(1) + 5	3	(1, 3)

Again, these ordered pairs are just some of the solutions. Since you can choose any value for x, an infinite number of ordered pairs will satisfy each equation.

■ **Write About Math** Why is it helpful to rewrite the equation in terms of one variable?

Check Understanding

For another example, see Set F, pages 552–553.

Choose the ordered pairs that are solutions of each equation.

1. $y = -3x$ **a.** (1, 3) **b.** (−4, 12) **c.** (3, 9) **d.** (−2, 6)

2. $2x + y = 12$ **a.** (−5, −2) **b.** (1, 10) **c.** (3, 6) **d.** (6, 3)

Practice

For More Practice, see Set F, pages 554–555.

Substitute the given values for x. Find the corresponding values for y.

$y = \frac{x}{4}$

x	y	(x, y)
−8	−2	(−8, −2)
−4	**3.**	**4.**
0	**5.**	**6.**
4	**7.**	**8.**
8	**9.**	**10.**

$y = -3x + 2$

x	y	(x, y)
−2	8	(−2, 8)
−1	**11.**	**12.**
0	**13.**	**14.**
1	**15.**	**16.**
2	**17.**	**18.**

$y = x - 1$

x	y	(x, y)
−3	−4	(−3, −4)
−1	**19.**	**20.**
0	**21.**	**22.**
1	**23.**	**24.**
3	**25.**	**26.**

Set up a table to find ordered pairs to satisfy each equation. Solve for y first, if necessary.

27. $y = -3x - 7$ **28.** $2x + y = -1$ **29.** $x + y = 12$

30. $y = \frac{1}{2}x - 4$ **31.** $3y = x + 9$ **32.** $y - x = 7$

33. $y = 2x + 6$ **34.** $-3x + y = 4$ **35.** $2x + y = 0$

36. $y = 2x + 9$ **37.** $2y = x + 6$ **38.** $4y + 8x = -16$

Problem Solving

Write an equation using two variables to represent each of the following.

39. Samantha ushers at a theater. Adult tickets to a play cost \$3; children's tickets cost \$1.50; the total sales are \$165.

40. A taxi company where Jose works charges \$1.25 plus \$0.50 for each $\frac{1}{4}$ mile or any part thereof.

41. **Calculator** Determine two ordered pairs for Exercise 29 using a decimal for x.

42. Rates at a parking lot where Jill works are \$3 for the first half hour plus \$0.75 for each additional half hour to a maximum of \$9.75.

Graphing Linear Equations

Build Understanding

A. Antonio has already saved \$30 for an electric guitar. He earns \$4.50 per hour. If t represents his total savings and h the hours worked, you can express Antonio's money with the equation $t = 30 + 4.50h$ or with this chart.

h	t	(h, t)
0	30.00	(0, 30.00)
1	34.50	(1, 34.50)
2	39.00	(2, 39.00)

The largest electric guitar is 14 ft $3\frac{1}{4}$ in. tall, weighing 309 lb.

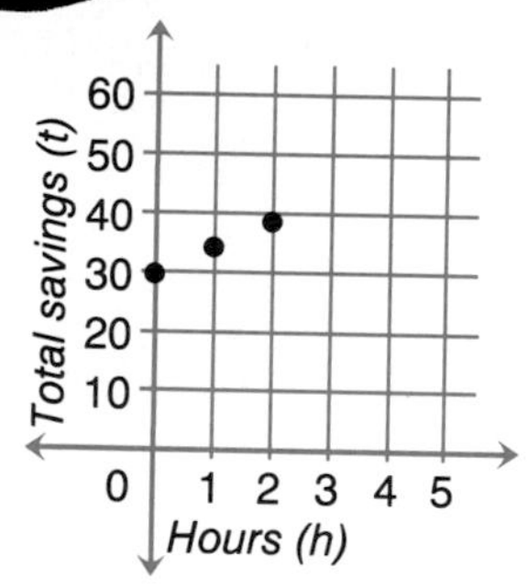

Each ordered pair is a ***solution*** of the equation. For example, (2, 39.00) means that if Antonio works 2 hours he will have \$39 toward his guitar.

B. Only a few points are shown in the first graph. Yet an *infinite* number of ordered pairs satisfy the equation. All the points lie on a straight line as shown in the second graph.

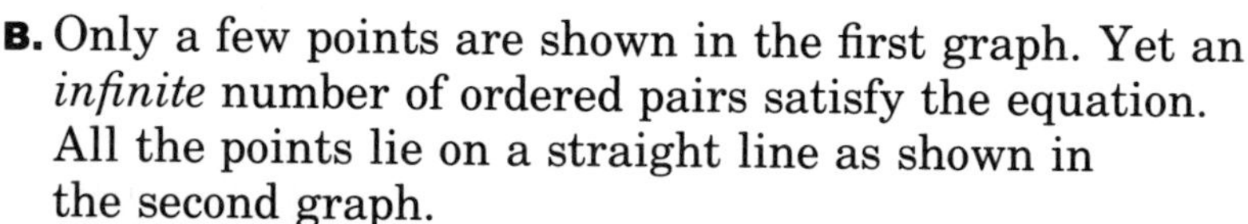

An equation with solutions lying on a straight line is called a ***linear equation.*** Every ordered pair satisfying the equation will correspond to a point on the line. The coordinates of every point on the line will satisfy the equation.

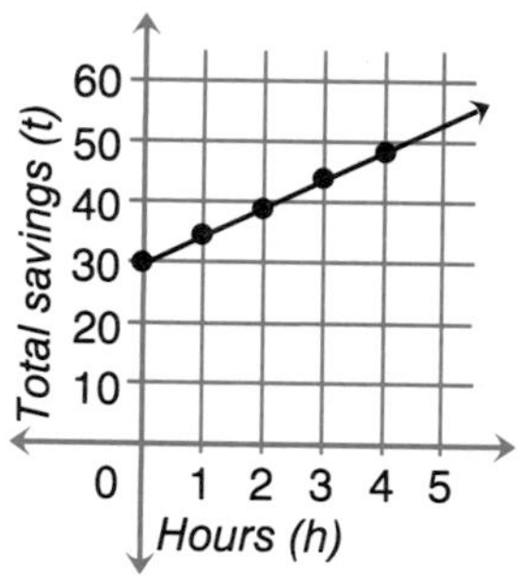

C. Graph $y = 2x + 3$. Make a table. Then graph the ordered pairs and connect the points.

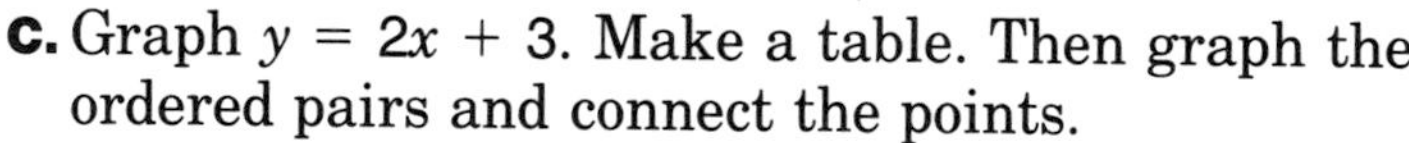

x	−2	0	1
y	−1	3	5

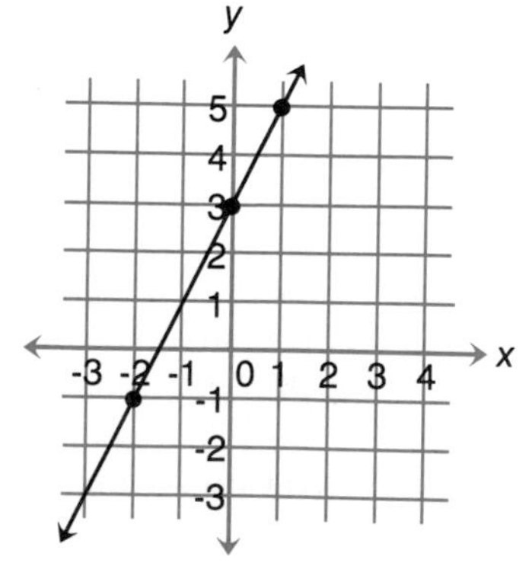

■ **Talk About Math** Is there a way to tell where the graph of a linear equation will cross the y-axis just by looking at the equation?

Check Understanding

For another example, see Set G, pages 552–553.

Copy and complete each table. Graph the ordered pairs. Connect the points.

1. $y = x - 5$

x	−3	0	2	4	6
y	−8				

2. $2x + y = 1$

x	−2	−1	0	1	2
y	5				

3. Number Sense Compare the ordered pairs in Exercises 1 and 2. Does y always increase as x increases?

Practice

For More Practice, see Set G, pages 554–555.

Find the value of y for at least four values of x. Graph the ordered pairs. Connect the points.

4. $y = x + 5$ **5.** $y = -2x$ **6.** $y = -x + 3$ **7.** $y = 3x - 5$

8. $y = -x$ **9.** $y = -\frac{1}{3}x$ **10.** $y = 2x + 1$ **11.** $y = -4x + 1$

12. $y = x - 8$ **13.** $y = x + 2$ **14.** $y = -2x - 2$ **15.** $y = -3x$

16. $y = 2x - 5$ **17.** $y = 2x + 2$ **18.** $y = 1 - \frac{1}{2}x$ **19.** $y = \frac{1}{3}x + 1$

20. $\frac{2}{3}x + y = 0$ **21.** $2x + y = 3$ **22.** $\frac{3}{4}x + y = 1$ **23.** $2x + y = 1$

Problem Solving

Solve.

24. Sales of stereos A, B, and C can be represented by $y = 2x + 3$, $y = 2x + 1$, and $y = 2x - 2$. Describe the relationship between these equations. (Graph them on one coordinate grid.)

Explore Math

Complete the following.

25. Graph $y = 2x + 1$, $y = 3x + 1$, and $y = x + 1$ on the same coordinate grid.

26. How are the graphs in Problem 25 alike? How do they differ?

27. What relationship is there between the equations and their graphs?

Solving Pairs of Linear Equations by Graphing

Build Understanding

A. Pauline likes puzzles. Lin says to her, "I'm thinking of two numbers. Their sum is 24. Their difference is 6. What are the numbers?"

If you let x and y represent the numbers, then $x + y = 24$ and $x - y = 6$.

There are many ordered pairs that satisfy each equation. However, you must find one ordered pair that will satisfy both equations. This ordered pair is a solution of the ***system of equations.***

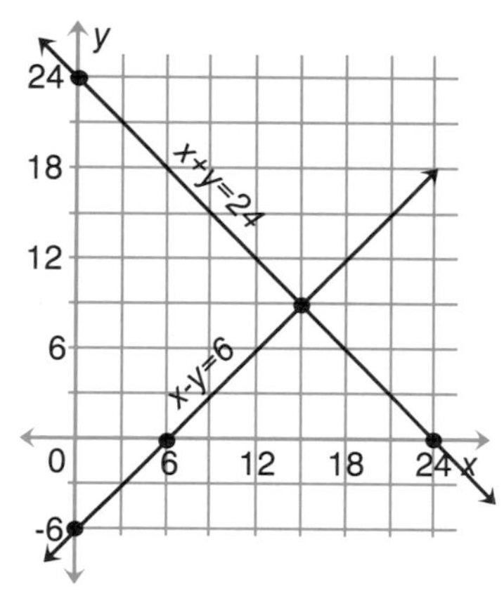

If you graph both equations on the same grid, the two lines intersect at (15, 9). Since this point of intersection is on both lines, its coordinates must satisfy both equations.

You must check the ordered pair in both equations.

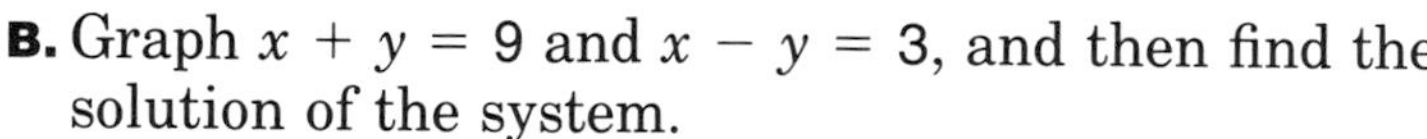

$x + y = 24$	$x - y = 6$
$15 + 9 = 24$	$15 - 9 = 6$
$24 = 24$	$6 = 6$

Therefore, the two numbers are 15 and 9.

B. Graph $x + y = 9$ and $x - y = 3$, and then find the solution of the system.

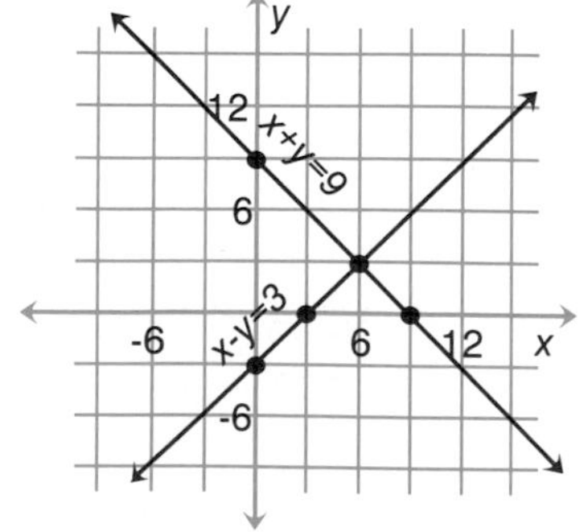

The graphs intersect at (6, 3), which is the solution of the system.

Check:

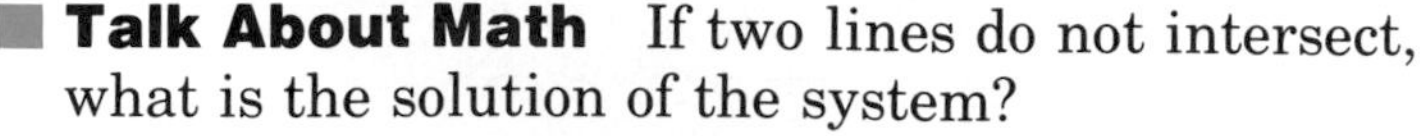

$x + y = 9$	$x - y = 3$
$6 + 3 \stackrel{?}{=} 9$	$6 - 3 \stackrel{?}{=} 3$
$9 = 9$	$3 = 3$

Talk About Math If two lines do not intersect, what is the solution of the system?

Check Understanding

For another Example, see Set H, pages 552–553.

Use the graph below to find the solution for each system of equations.

1. $y = x + 5$
$y = -x - 1$

2. $y = x + 5$
$y = \frac{1}{3}x - 5$

3. $y = -x - 1$
$y = \frac{1}{3}x - 5$

4. $y = -2x + 8$
$y = -x - 1$

5. $y = -2x + 8$
$y = x + 5$

6. $y = 0$
$y = -2x + 8$

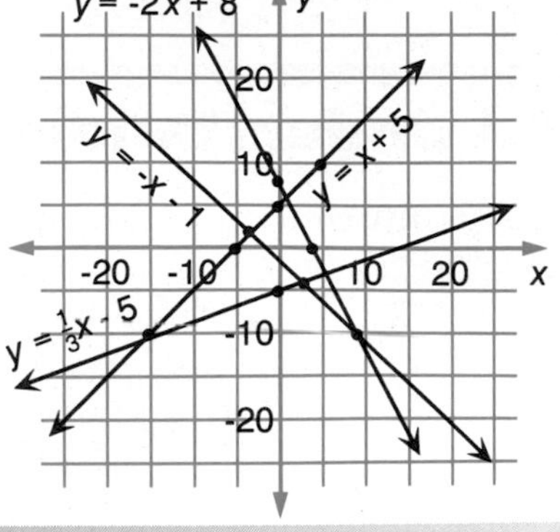

Practice

For More Practice, see Set H, pages 554–555.

Graph each pair of equations on the same grid to find the solution. Check each solution in both equations.

7. $y = -x + 3$
$y = 2x - 3$

8. $y = x + 6$
$y = -3x + 2$

9. $y = x + 5$
$y = x - 2$

10. $y = 2x + 3$
$y = x - 2$

11. $y = x + 5$
$y = 2x + 3$

12. $y = 2x + 1$
$y = -x + 4$

13. $y = x + 4$
$y = -x + 4$

14. $y = 2x - 3$
$y = -2x - 3$

15. $y = x - 1$
$y = x + 2$

16. $y = -x + 7$
$y = 2x + 1$

17. $y = x + 5$
$y = x - 3$

18. $y = 7 - 2x$
$y = -1 - x$

19. $y = 3x + 4$
$2x + y = -1$

20. $y = 1 - 2x$
$x + 2y = 5$

21. $y = 7 - x$
$2x - 3y = 4$

22. **Estimation** Estimate the point of intersection of the graphs of the equations $y = -x + 1$ and $y = x - 2$.

Problem Solving

Solve each problem.

23. Graph $y = 2x + 1$ and $y = 2x - 3$.

24. Graph $x + y = -3$ and $2x + 2y = -6$.

25. What do you notice about the graphs in Problem 23? Can these lines intersect? Why or why not? What is the solution to the system?

26. What do you notice about the graphs in Problem 24? What is the solution to the system?

ALGEBRA

Make a Graph

Understand
QUESTION
FACTS
KEY IDEA

Plan and Solve
STRATEGY
ANSWER

Look Back
SENSIBLE ANSWER
ALTERNATE APPROACH

Build Understanding

The student council wants to hire a disc jockey. Jazzy Jack charges $8 per hour plus a $4 fee to set up. Mellow Mary charges a $10 set-up fee plus $6 per hour. When will it cost less to hire Jazzy Jack? When will it cost less to hire Mellow Mary? When will the cost be the same?

Understand QUESTION When will it cost less to hire Jazzy Jack? to hire Mellow Mary? When will the cost be the same?

FACTS Jazzy Jack charges $8 per hour plus a $4 set-up fee. Mellow Mary charges $6 per hour plus a $10 set-up fee.

KEY IDEA The cost for each disc jockey increases by a constant amount each hour. The cost for Jack increases faster than the cost for Mary.

Plan and Solve STRATEGY Write equations to represent the cost (c) to hire each disc jockey in terms of the number of hours (h) worked. Then graph both equations on the same grid and look for a point of intersection.

	Jazzy Jack	Mellow Mary
h	$c = 8h + 4$	$c = 6h + 10$
1	12	16
2	20	22
3	28	28
4	36	34

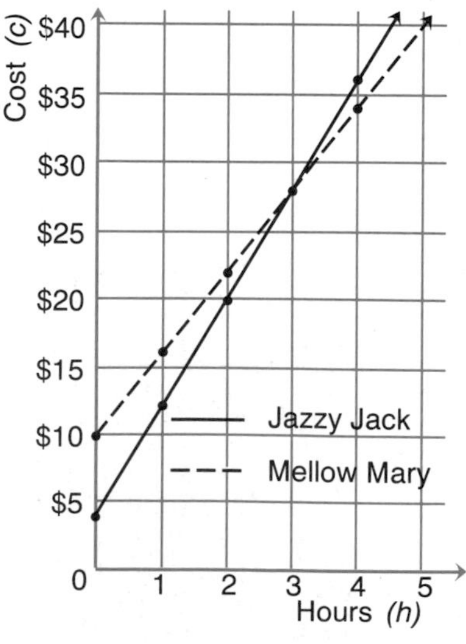

The lines intersect at (3, 28).

ANSWER It costs the same to hire either disc jockey for a 3-hour dance. For a shorter dance, hire Jack. For a longer dance, hire Mary.

Look Back SENSIBLE ANSWER Although Mary charges $6 more to set up, Jack charges $2 more per hour to play. It takes him 3 hours to catch up with Mary's price.

■ **Talk About Math** How would you determine the cost for Musical Matt at $7 per hour and a $7 set-up fee?

Check Understanding

The student council wants to hire a catering service for refreshments. Best Bites charges $10 plus $2 per person. Fine Food charges $3 per person.

1. If x people attend and C stands for the total cost, what equation shows the cost of using Best Bites?

2. What equation shows the cost for Fine Food?

3. Copy and complete the graph. Where do the lines intersect?

4. For what number of people would the cost be the same?

5. If 40 people attend the dance, which catering service would cost less?

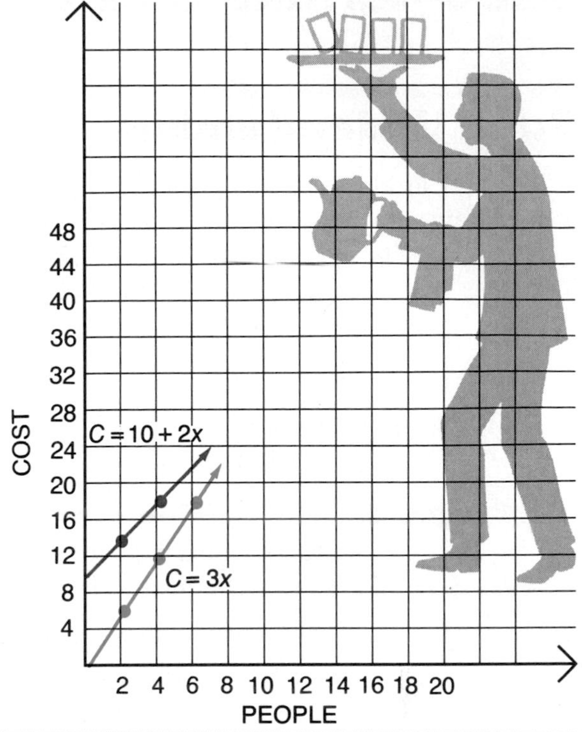

Practice

Jazzy Jack needed to rent a van for one day to carry his equipment to the dance. Cheap Cars charges $15 a day plus $0.30 per mile. Mighty Motors has vans for $10 per day plus $0.40 per mile. Use the information to solve Exercises 6–8.

6. Find the equations for renting from Cheap Cars and from Mighty Motors and draw their graphs on the same grid.

7. At how many miles is the rental cost the same?

8. Jack needs to drive 150 miles. Which company is cheaper? How much will he save?

The council plans to rent a car for a one-day, one-way trip. Reliable Rental charges $0.20 a mile plus a $50 fee. Speedy Rental charges $0.25 a mile plus a $30 fee. Use this information to solve Exercises 9–10.

9. Draw the graphs for Reliable Rentals and Speedy Rentals on the same grid.

10. The trip is 200 miles. Which company is cheaper? How much will be saved?

ALGEBRA

Use Alternate Strategies

Understand
QUESTION
FACTS
KEY IDEA

Plan and Solve
STRATEGY
ANSWER

Look Back
SENSIBLE ANSWER
ALTERNATE APPROACH

Build Understanding

The cost of operating the Pickwick Theater is $1,250 per show, and tickets cost $5 each. The cost of operating the Tivoli Theater is $900 per show, and tickets cost $4 each.

The profit or loss from one show at each theater is the same when a certain number of tickets is sold at each theater. What is the number of tickets, and what is the profit or loss?

Understand

QUESTION How many tickets must be sold at each theater so that the profit or loss is the same? Is it a profit or loss?

FACTS Operating costs at the Pickwick are $1,250 and tickets cost $5. At the Tivoli, the operating costs are $900 and tickets are $4.

KEY IDEA The ticket sales minus the operating cost is either the profit (if the answer is positive), or the loss (if the answer is negative).

Plan and Solve

STRATEGY Make a table before making a double-line graph. The point where the lines intersect will be the answer.

Pickwick

Number of tickets	0	100	200
Profit/loss	−$1,250	−$750	−$250

Tivoli

Number of tickets	0	100	200
Profit/loss	−$900	−$500	−$100

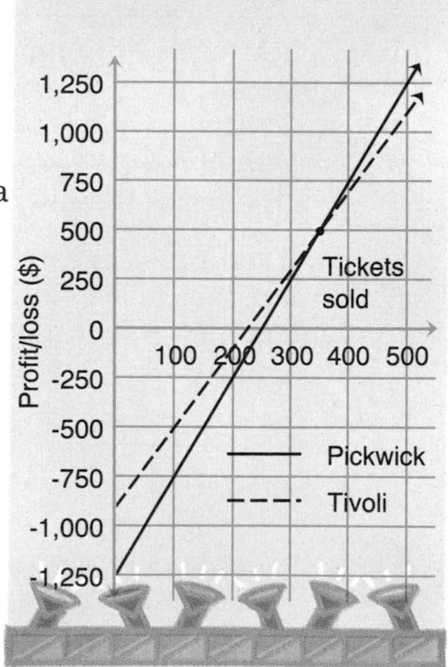

ANSWER The lines intersect at (350, 500). When the theaters sell 350 tickets each, they make a profit of $500 each.

The seating plan of modern theaters comes mainly from 4th-century B.C. Greek amphitheater design.

Look Back ALTERNATE APPROACH Another way to solve this problem is to write an equation:

$$5n - 1{,}250 = 4n - 900$$

$$5n + (-4n) - 1{,}250 = 4n - 900 + (-4n)$$ Add the opposite of $4n$.

$$n - 1{,}250 + 1{,}250 = -900 + 1{,}250$$ Add the opposite of $-1{,}250$.

$$n = 350$$

■ **Talk About Math** Suggest a third strategy you might use to solve this problem. What are the advantages and disadvantages of each of the three strategies?

Check Understanding

Use the graph on page 548 to answer the questions.

1. How many tickets must the Pickwick sell for a showing before there is a profit?
2. How many tickets must the Tivoli sell for a showing before there is a profit?
3. How many tickets must the Pickwick sell for a showing to make a $1,000 profit?
4. How many tickets must the Tivoli sell for a showing to make a $1,000 profit?

Practice

Mr. Kim is going to change the rates at his health club. He checks the competition and finds that the City Health Club charges $25 a month plus $5 per visit, and the Super Health Club charges $5 a month and $10 per visit. Solve Exercises 5–9 using this information. Tell whether you use pencil and paper or calculator to solve.

5. For one month, when do the two clubs cost the same?
6. When is the City Health Club cheaper?
7. When is the Super Health Club cheaper?
8. Mr. Kim decides to charge $15 per month and $7 per visit. When is his club cheaper for a month than the other two?
9. You expect to go to a health club twice a week. Which club is the better buy for you? Are there other factors you should consider?

Skills Review

Graph the solutions of each sentence or inequality.

1. $y \leq 2$ **2.** $y = -4$ **3.** $|y| > 4$

Plot each point on a grid. Connect the points in order and connect the last point with the first. Name the resulting polygon.

4. (−1,1), (2,3), (5,3), (5,−1), (2,−1)

5. (−2,−2), (−2,2), (2,2), (2,−2)

Use grid paper for Exercises 6–9.

6. Draw $\triangle LMN$ with $L(-4,-1)$, $M(-1,-1)$, $N(-1,-3)$

7. Translate $\triangle LMN$ 2 units down and 5 units right.

8. Reflect $\triangle LMN$ over the y-axis. What are the coordinates?

9. Rotate $\triangle LMN$ 180° clockwise. What are the coordinates?

Set up a table to find ordered pairs to satisfy each equation. Solve for y first, if necessary.

10. $y = 2x - 1$ **11.** $y + 3 = x$

12. $2x + y = -2$ **13.** $y = \frac{1}{2}x$

Find the value of y for at least four values of x. Graph the ordered pairs. Connect the points.

14. $y = 3x - 3$ **15.** $y = -\frac{1}{2}x + 2$

Graph each pair of equations on the same grid to find the solutions. Check each solution in both equations.

16. $y = -x + 3$
$y = 2x - 3$
(2,1)

17. $y = -2x - 3$
$y = x + 3$
(−2,1)

Problem-Solving Review

Solve each problem.

18. The area of a square plant table is 90.25 sq in. What is the length of each side? Use a calculator or the table on page 587.

19. Samantha worked at the snack bar 5 days last week. She earned the same amount each day. She also earned $20 babysitting. Her total earnings for the week were $156.50. How much did she earn each day at the snack bar?

20. Martin wants to buy at least $1\frac{1}{2}$ pounds of haddock, but no more than $2\frac{1}{2}$ pounds. Write an inequality for the problem. Then draw a graph.

21. A class wants to rent a pony for rides at a fair. Thoroughbred Stables charges $6 an hour plus $40 for delivery and pickup. Country Trails charges $9 an hour plus $25 for delivery and pickup. Draw graphs for the charges of the two stables. Which stable is less expensive if the pony is rented for 8 hours?

22. **Data File** Use the data on pages 558–559. Graph the equation relating to gills and pints.

23. **Make a Data File** Consult the financial pages of a newspaper or business magazine. Find the current exchange rate between the U.S. dollar and foreign currency, such as the English pound or Japanese yen. Make a table listing the exchange value for $1, $5, $10 and $100. Graph your data as ordered pairs on a coordinate grid.

Cumulative Skills Review • Chapters 1–15

Find each answer. Compute mentally.

1. $792 + 508$ **2.** 72×5 **3.** $6 \times 2 \times 4 \times 5$ **4.** $84 + 91 + 6 + 16$

5. $64{,}000 \div 800$ **6.** $250{,}000 \div 50$ **7.** $0.765 \times 10{,}000$ **8.** $6.7 \div 1{,}000$

Give the precision and the greatest possible error for each measurement.

9. $5\frac{1}{2}$ ft **10.** 21 yards **11.** 12.4 cm **12.** $3\frac{7}{8}$ in.

Write and solve a proportion for each.

13. 80% of what number is 64? **14.** 92 is 200% of what number?

15. What is 45% of 140? **16.** 150 is what percent of 250?

Write each decimal or fraction as a percent.

17. 0.44 **18.** 0.005 **19.** 3.02 **20.** $\frac{7}{20}$ **21.** $\frac{110}{88}$ **22.** $\frac{0.8}{100}$

Jack has 10 baseball caps: 4 are red, 3 are white, 2 are blue and 1 is green. Each day he selects one at random and replaces it at night. What is the probability he will choose each of the following on two consecutive days?

23. P(R,W) **24.** P(B,G) **25.** P(G,W) **26.** P(R,R) **27.** P(W,W) **28.** P(B,B)

Multiply or divide.

29. $-7 \times (-2)$ **30.** $6 \times (-6)$ **31.** 4×4 **32.** -5×6

33. $100 \div (-10)$ **34.** $-55 \div 11$ **35.** $-64 \div (-8)$ **36.** $24 \div 4$

Evaluate each expression when $m = \frac{1}{2}$ and $n = 8$.

37. $n - m$ **38.** $m + n$ **39.** $2m + 5 + n$ **40.** $2n - 4m$

41. $m \div n$ **42.** $\frac{3}{4}n + 6m$ **43.** $2n^2 - \frac{m}{2}$ **44.** $\frac{n}{4} + 10m$

Graph the solutions of each equation or inequality.

45. $x < 3$ **46.** $x \leq -1$ **47.** $|x| > 2$ **48.** $x = -4$

Select four values for x and find the corresponding values of y. Graph the ordered pairs and connect the points.

49. $y = \frac{1}{2}x - 2$ **50.** $y = -x + 4$ **51.** $y = -2x$ **52.** $y = 3x - 2$

53. $y = 1 - x$ **54.** $y = 4x - 3$ **55.** $y = 2 - 2x$ **56.** $y = -3x + 1$

Reteaching

Set A pages 520–521

A graph can be used to show the solutions of an equation or inequality.

Graph the solutions of $x \le 2$.

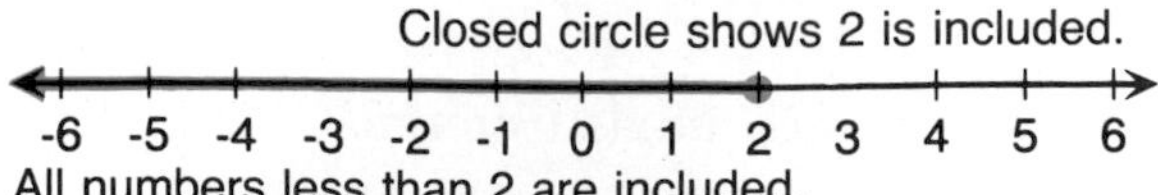

Remember, an open circle shows that a point is not included and that a closed circle shows that it is.

Graph the solution for each sentence.

1. $x > -4$ **2.** $x \le 0$ **3.** $x \ge 1$

4. $|x| = 4$ **5.** $|x| \ge 4$ **6.** $|x| < 4$

Set B pages 522–523

Point *A* is at (4, 3). Point *B* is at (−2, −1).

Remember, the first coordinate is the distance along the *horizontal* axis.

Name the point for each ordered pair.

1. (0, 4) **2.** (5, 2) **3.** (−5, 3)

4. (−2, −4) **5.** (−2, 4) **6.** (2, 0)

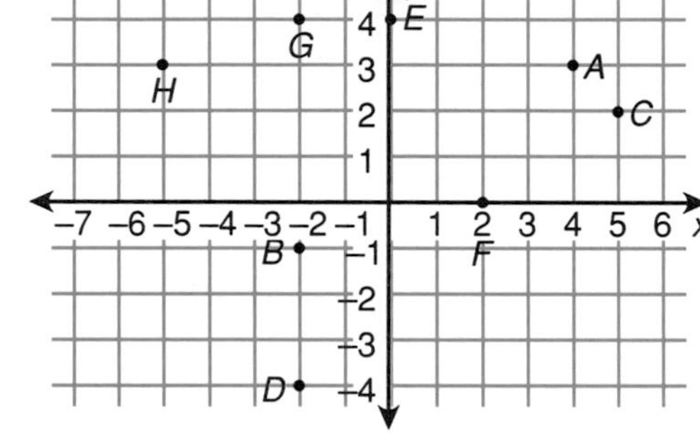

Set C pages 524–527

△*ABC* has been translated 4 units to the left and 5 units down.

Remember, the coordinates change by the same amount in a translation.

Copy △*ABC* on grid paper. On the same set of axes, graph its images under each translation. Give the coordinates of the vertices.

1. A horizontal translation of −6 units

2. A vertical translation of 2 units

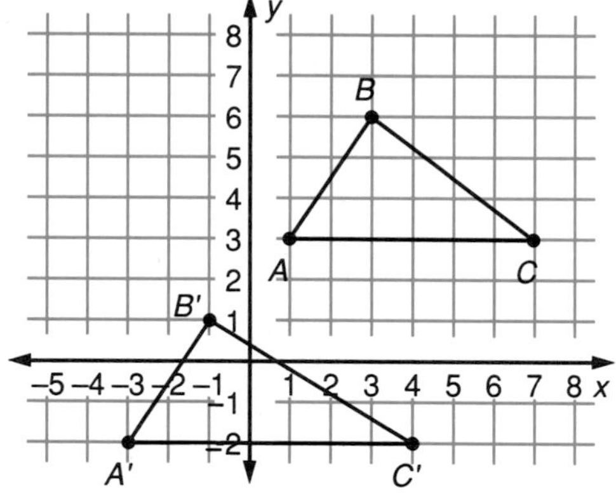

Set D pages 528–531

Figure *ABCD* has been reflected over the *x*-axis. The coordinates of figure *A′B′C′D′* are *A′*(3, −1), *B′*(3, −5), *C′*(9, −5), and *D′*(9, −1).

Remember, the sign of the *x*-coordinate changes if the figure has been reflected over the *y*-axis.

What would be the coordinates of the vertices of the figure *ABCD* under a reflection over the *y*-axis?

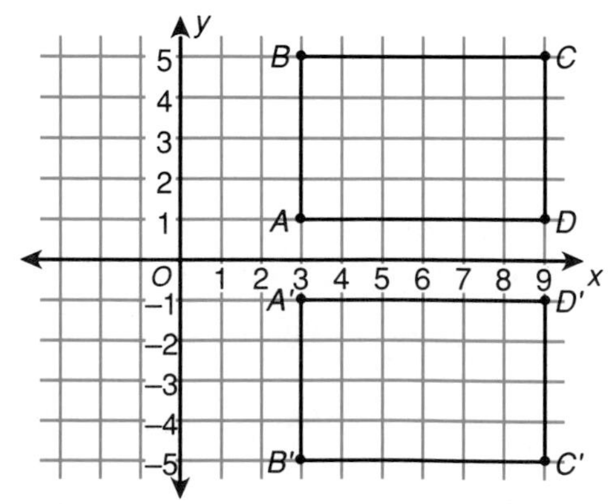

Set E pages 532–535

$\triangle ABC$ has been rotated 90° clockwise around the origin O. The coordinates of $\triangle A'B'C'$ are $A'(2, 1)$, $B'(4, 1)$, $C'(2, 4)$.

Remember, the image under a rotation is congruent to the original figure.

Copy $\triangle ABC$ onto grid paper.

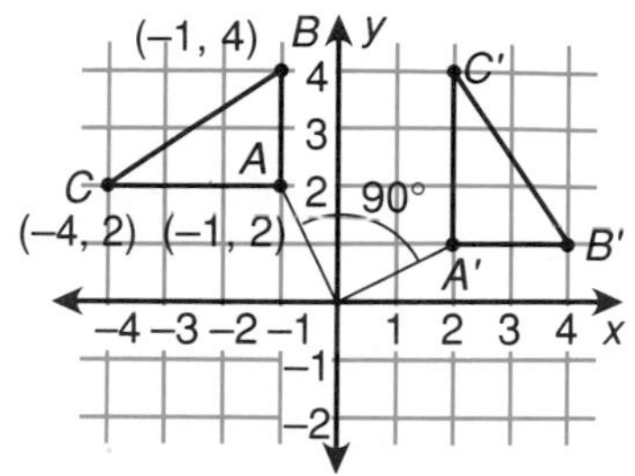

1. Give the coordinates of the vertices of its image under a 90° counterclockwise rotation around the origin O.
2. Give the coordinates of the vertices of its image under a 180° rotation around the origin O.

Set F pages 540–541

The following table shows some solutions of the equation $y - x = 3$.
$y = x + 3$

x	$x + 3$	y	(x, y)
−2	−2 + 3	1	(−2, 1)
−1	−1 + 3	2	(−1, 2)
0	0 + 3	3	(0, 3)
1	1 + 3	4	(1, 4)

Remember, first solve for y. Then choose any values for x.

Make a table of five ordered pairs for each equation.

1. $y = -x - 1$
2. $y = \frac{x}{2}$
3. $x + y = 4$
4. $y - 2x = 5$

Set G pages 542–543

To graph the solutions to an equation, make a table of ordered pairs that satisfy the equation. Then graph the points and connect them with a line.

Remember, choose convenient values for x to make a table.

Make a table of at least five ordered pairs. Then graph the ordered pairs and connect them with a line.

1. $y = 2x$
2. $y = x + 4$
3. $x + y = 2$
4. $y + \frac{1}{2}x = 0$

Set H pages 544–545

To solve a pair of linear equations by graphing, graph each line on the same grid. The point at which the lines intersect is the solution of the system of equations.

Remember, the solution to a pair of linear equations is an *ordered pair*.

Graph each pair of equations on the same grid to find the solution.

1. $x - y = 3$
$x + y = 5$
2. $y = x + 2$
$y = 2x$
3. $y = x + 3$
$y = x$
4. $y = 3x + 4$
$y = 2x - 1$

More Practice

Set A pages 520–521

Graph the following sets of numbers.

1. All numbers greater than -3

2. Whole numbers between 4 and 11

3. Integers between -5 and 5

4. All numbers less than 5

Graph the solution of each equation or inequality.

5. $|y| = 1$

6. $x \geq -3$

7. $x < 1$

8. $y \leq 2$

Set B pages 522–523

Use the grid at the right for Exercises 1–7. Name the coordinates of the following points.

1. C **2.** B **3.** F **4.** D

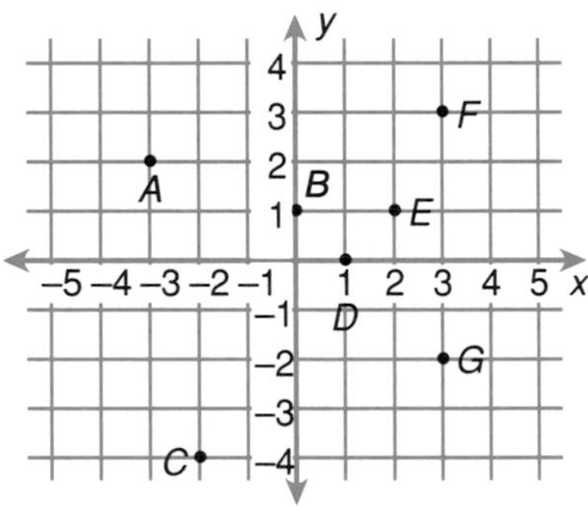

Name the point located by each ordered pair.

5. $(-3, 2)$ **6.** $(3, -2)$ **7.** $(2, 1)$

On a grid, plot each point. Connect the points in order, and connect the last point with the first. Name the polygon that results.

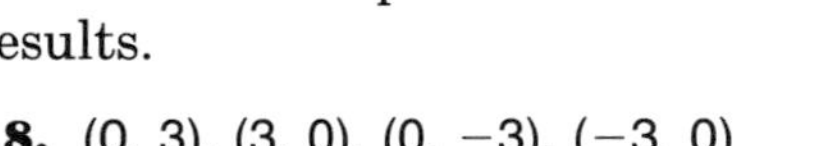

8. $(0, 3)$, $(3, 0)$, $(0, -3)$, $(-3, 0)$

Set C pages 524–527

Copy figure $ABCD$ on grid paper. On the same set of axes, graph its images under the translations described below. Give the coordinates of the vertices.

1. A horizontal translation of -1 unit

2. A vertical translation of 3 units

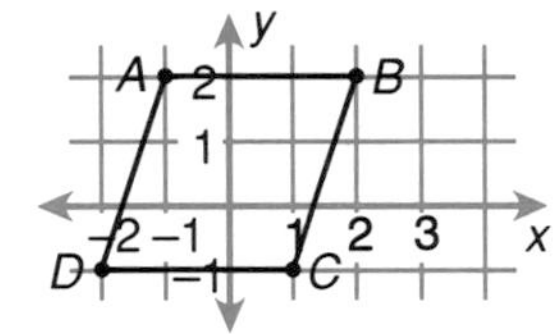

Set D pages 528–531

Give the coordinates of the point $(-2, -5)$ under each transformation.

1. A reflection over the y-axis

2. A reflection over the x-axis

Refer to the figure to answer the questions.

3. If you reflect $ABCD$ over the y-axis, what are the coordinates of the vertices of the image?

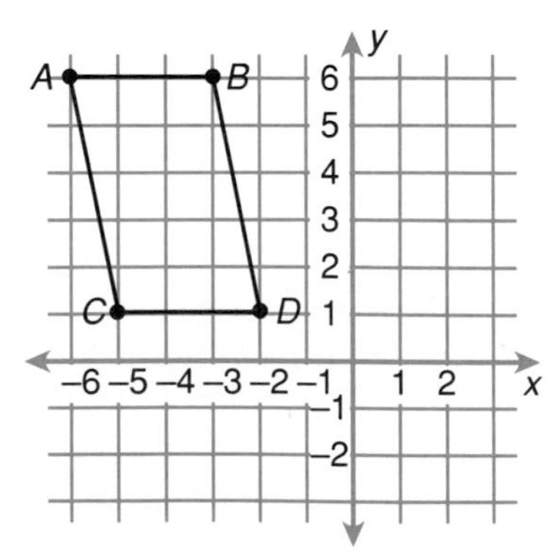

Set E pages 532–535

Use figure *ABCDEF* for Exercises 1–3.

1. Give the coordinates of the vertices of its image under a 90° clockwise rotation around the origin *O*.

2. Give the coordinates of the vertices of its image under a 180° rotation around the origin *O*.

3. Give the coordinates of the vertices of its image under a 90° counterclockwise rotation around the origin *O*.

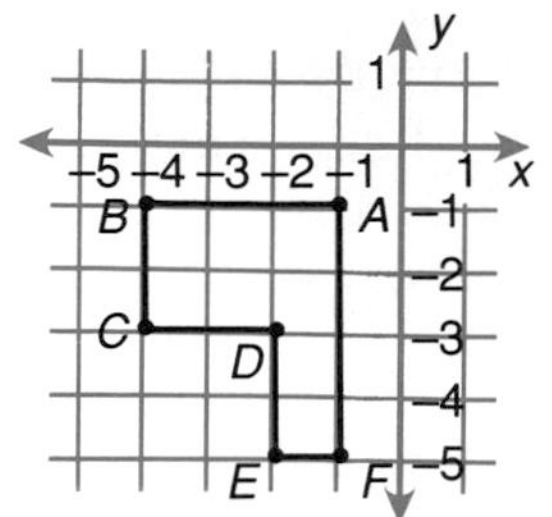

Choose the next figure in the sequence.

4.  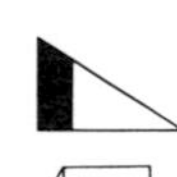  **a.**  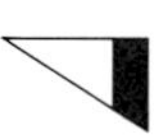 **b.**  **c.**  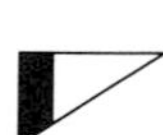

5.   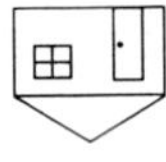 **a.**   **b.**   **c.** 

Set F pages 540–541

Set up a table to find ordered pairs to satisfy each equation. Solve for *y* first, if necessary.

1. $y = 2x - 3$ **2.** $3x + y = 4$ **3.** $x - y = -2$

4. $y = \frac{1}{4}x + 6$ **5.** $2y = x + 18$ **6.** $y - 3x = 5$

Set G pages 542–543

Select four values for *x* and find the corresponding values of *y*. Graph the ordered pairs and connect the points.

1. $y = 6x$ **2.** $y = 2x - 2$ **3.** $y = \frac{1}{5}x + 4$ **4.** $y = 4x + 1$

5. $y = -\frac{1}{2}x$ **6.** $y = \frac{x}{6} - 9$ **7.** $y + 4x = 6$ **8.** $3x - y = 2$

Set H pages 544–545

Graph each pair of equations on the same grid to find the solution. Check each solution in both equations.

1. $y = x + 1$
$y = -2x + 1$

2. $y = \frac{1}{2}x + 4$
$y = 3x - 1$

3. $y = \frac{1}{3}x - 1$
$y = x - 3$

4. $y = 6x - 3$
$y = 6x + 4$

5. $y = -x - 3$
$y = \frac{1}{3}x + 1$

6. $y = 5x - 4$
$y = 2x + 5$

7. Estimate the point of intersection of the graph of these equations.
$y = -4x - 3$
$y = x + 9$

Enrichment

Graphing Nonlinear Equations

The graphs of some equations are not straight lines. Such equations are called ***nonlinear equations***.

The nonlinear equation graphed at the right is called a ***hyperbola***.

1. Write the coordinates of the points labeled *A* through *H*.
2. For each of the points you have listed, multiply the x-coordinate by the y-coordinate. What do you notice about each product?
3. Based on your results, which of the following nonlinear equations is the equation of the hyperbola?

   a. $x^2yx = 12$ **b.** $xy = 4$
   c. $xy = 12$ **d.** $\frac{x}{y} = 12$

The circle below is the graph of a nonlinear equation.

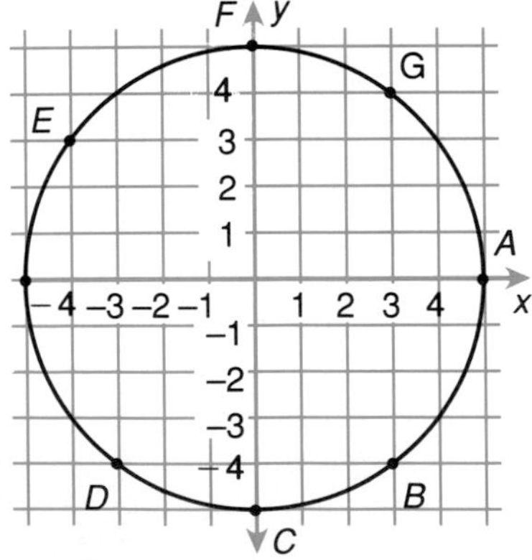

4. Write the coordinates of the points labeled *A* through *G*.
5. For each of the points you have listed, add the square of the x-coordinate to the square of the y-coordinate. What do you notice about each sum?
6. Based on your results, which of these equations is the equation of the circle?

   a. $x + y = 5$ **b.** $(x + y)^2 = 52$
   c. $x^2 + y^2 = 25$ **d.** $x^2 + y^2 = 5$

Chapter 15 Review/Test

Graph the following sets of numbers.

1. All numbers less than 1

2. $|x| \leq 3$

Give the coordinates of each point.

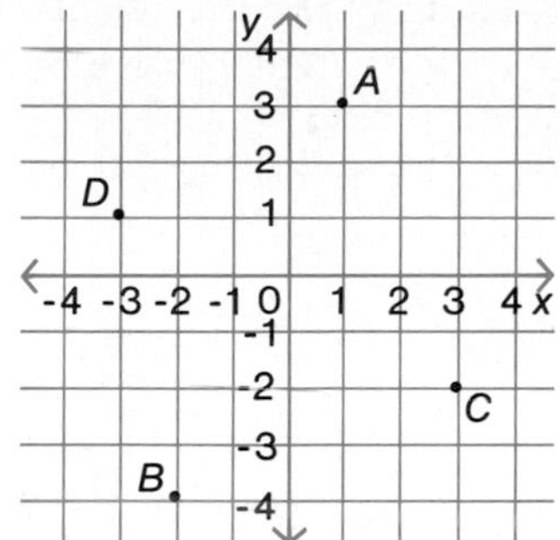

3. *A* 4. *B* 5. *C* 6. *D*

For each of Items 7–9, name the coordinates of the vertices of the image of $\triangle ABC$ under the given transformation.

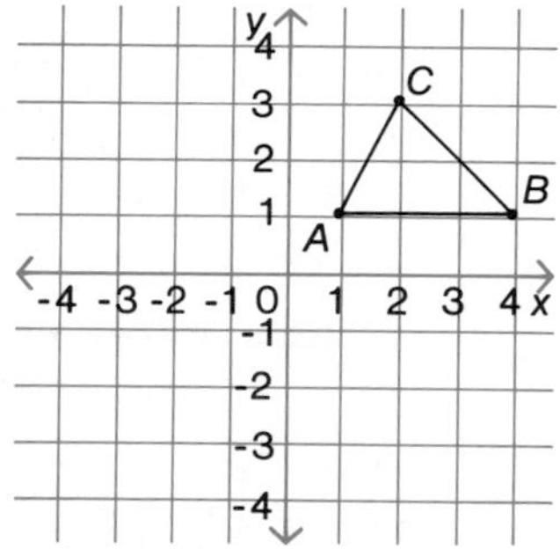

7. Translation 3 units up

8. Reflection over the *y*-axis

9. Reflection over the *x*-axis

10. What is the image of the point (5, 0) after a rotation of 90° counterclockwise?

11. Write an equation in two variables to describe this problem.
Sonja has some dimes and some nickels. The total amount is worth 95¢.

12. Which figure tessellates: a parallelogram or a regular pentagon?

13. List the numbers missing from the table of points for the graph of $y = 2x + 3$.

x	0	1	3	−2
y	▒	▒	▒	▒

14. Graph the equation $y = 2x + 3$. Use the completed table from Item 13.

15. Use the graph to find the solution for $x + y = 4$ and $x - y = 2$.

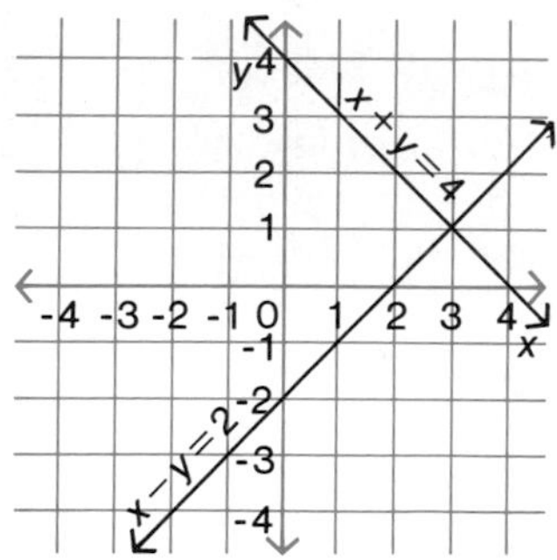

16. Solve $y = 12 - x$ and $y = x - 4$ by graphing.

17. Write the equations that describe this problem.
Rob saves baseball and football cards. If he had twice as many baseball cards, he would have 19 cards. Right now he has 2 more baseball cards than football cards. How many of each does he have?

18. Find the solution to Item 17 without drawing a graph.

19. **Write About Math** When will two equations that describe a problem have no solution?

Data File

1. Ocean Sizes

a. Pacific
64,186,300 square miles, almost 20 times the size of the U.S.

b. Atlantic
33,420,000 square miles, about half the size of the Pacific, or 10 times the size of the U.S.

c. Indian
28,350,500 square miles, about 8 times the size of the U.S.

d. Arctic
5,105,700 square miles, about $1\frac{1}{2}$ times the size of the U.S.

1. Almanac Entry
The Almanac entry compares ocean areas to the size of the United States.

2. Game
The game shows a double-six Domino set.

3. Diagram
The diagram shows a keyboard with an enlargement of the drum pads.

4. Table
The table shows the Official U.S. Measures of Volume for wet and dry measurements.

5. Chart
The chart shows the wind chill factor which occurs when the wind and the air temperature combine to make the air feel colder than the thermometer reading.

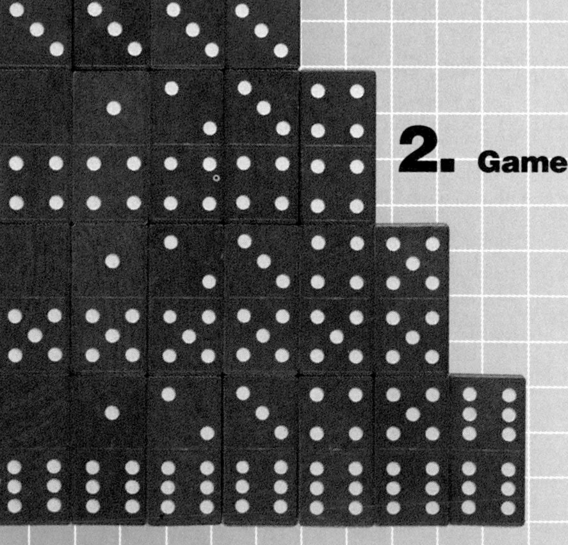

2. Game

3. Diagram

4. U.S. Measures of Volume

Liquid

60 minims = 1 fluid dram
8 fluid drams = 1 fluid ounce
4 fluid ounces = 1 gill
4 gills = 1 pint
2 pints = 1 quart
4 quarts = 1 gallon

Dry

2 pints = 1 quart
8 quarts = 1 peck
4 pecks = 1 bushel

5. Wind Chill Factor

Wind Speed (mph)	Thermometer Reading (degrees Fahrenheit)															
	35	30	25	20	15	10	5	0	-5	-10	-15	-20	-25	-30	-35	-40
5	33	27	21	19	12	7	0	-5	-10	-15	-21	-26	-31	-36	-42	-47
10	22	16	10	3	-3	-9	-15	-22	-27	-34	-40	-46	-52	-58	-64	-71
15	16	9	2	-5	-11	-18	-25	-31	-38	-45	-51	-58	-65	-72	-78	-85
20	12	4	-3	-10	-17	-24	-31	-39	-46	-53	-60	-67	-74	-81	-88	-95
25	8	1	-7	-15	-22	-29	-36	-44	-51	-59	-66	-74	-81	-88	-96	-103
30	6	-2	-10	-18	-25	-33	-41	-49	-56	-64	-71	-79	-86	-93	-101	-109
40	3	-5	-13	-21	-29	-37	-45	-53	-60	-69	-76	-84	-92	-100	-107	-115

Cumulative Review/Test Chapters 1–15

Choose the letter for the correct answer.

1. Which represents 7 parts out of a total of 8 parts?

a. $\frac{7}{8}$ **b.** $\frac{8}{7}$ **c.** 78 **d.** 87

2. Solve the equation $3x = 75$.

a. $x = 25$ **b.** $x = 72$
c. $x = 78$ **d.** $x = 225$

3. Divide. $5\overline{)1.7}$

a. 0.034 **b.** 0.34 **c.** 3.4 **d.** 34

4. Which values of *a*, *b*, and *c* *cannot* be the lengths of the sides of a triangle?

a. $a = 3$ in., $b = 4$ in., $c = 5$ in.
b. $a = 6$ cm, $b = 6$ cm, $c = 6$ cm
c. $a = 5$ in., $b = 8$ in., $c = 5$ in.
d. $a = 2$ cm, $b = 3$ cm, $c = 6$ cm

5. Find the standard form of $2^3 + 3^3$.

a. 15 **b.** 216 **c.** 35 **d.** 18

6. Add. $\frac{2}{3} + \frac{3}{4}$

a. $\frac{5}{12}$ **b.** $\frac{5}{7}$ **c.** $\frac{6}{7}$ **d.** $1\frac{5}{12}$

7. What is a good estimate for the weight of a D battery (the kind used in most flashlights)?

a. 0.4 oz **b.** 4 oz
c. 4 lb **d.** 40 lb

8. Which proportion could be used to solve this problem?
Jon's recipe calls for 2 cups of oatmeal for 6 servings. How many cups of oatmeal should he use for 8 servings?

a. $\frac{2}{6} = \frac{c}{8}$ **b.** $\frac{2}{8} = \frac{c}{6}$
c. $\frac{6}{8} = \frac{c}{2}$ **d.** $\frac{8}{c} = \frac{2}{6}$

9. Which is the best estimate of 48% of 59?

a. 120 **b.** 30 **c.** 33 **d.** 25

10. What is the perimeter of a triangle with sides $a = 5$ m, $b = 12$ m, and $c = 13$ m?

a. 30 m **b.** 96 m
c. 48 m **d.** 38 m

11.

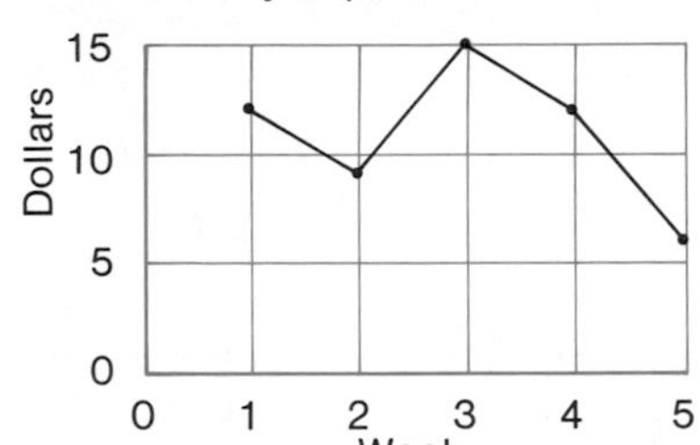

During which pair of weeks were the weekly expenses the same?

a. 1 and 2 **b.** 1 and 3
c. 1 and 4 **d.** 1 and 5

12. What is the probability that a number selected between 1 and 100 (inclusive) is a multiple of 12?

a. 0 **b.** $\frac{1}{10}$ **c.** $\frac{2}{25}$ **d.** $\frac{3}{25}$

13. Beth has 3 blouses, 4 skirts, and 6 scarves that all go together. How many outfits does this make?

a. 13 outfits **b.** 24 outfits
c. 63 outfits **d.** 72 outfits

14. There are 3 red balls and 6 white balls in a bag. If you draw 2 balls, replacing the first before drawing the second, what is the probability that both are red?

a. $\frac{1}{2}$ **b.** $\frac{1}{9}$ **c.** $\frac{3}{16}$ **d.** $\frac{1}{27}$

15. In Exercise 14, if the first ball drawn had not been replaced before the second ball was drawn, what could be said about the events?

a. The events are complementary.
b. The events are independent.
c. The events are dependent.

16. Subtract. $-4 - (-7)$

a. -3 **b.** -11 **c.** 3 **d.** 11

17. Divide. $\frac{-24}{-8}$

a. -1.4 **b.** -3 **c.** $\frac{1}{4}$ **d.** 3

18. Multiply. $-3\left(-2\frac{1}{3}\right)$

a. -5 **b.** -7 **c.** 5 **d.** 7

19. Mike placed a 15-foot ladder against a house. The foot of the ladder was 9 feet away from the house. How high did the ladder reach?

a. 9 ft **b.** 12 ft
c. 15 ft **d.** 24 ft

20. Which placement of grouping symbols makes this sentence true? $3 \times 7 - 8 + 5 = 8$

a. $(3 \times 7) - (8 + 5) = 8$
b. $3 \times (7 - 8) + 5 = 8$
c. $3 \times (7 - 8 + 5) = 8$

21. Evaluate $\frac{4(d - 7)}{t}$ when $d = 5$ and $t = 0.5$.

a. 1.6 **b.** -4 **c.** -16 **d.** -40

22. Solve $15 + \frac{x}{3} = 9$.

a. -18 **b.** -2 **c.** -6 **d.** 72

23. Diskettes cost $0.75 each. Postage and handling for each order is $3.00. Write an equation to find the number of diskettes Carolyn ordered if she paid $18.00.

a. $0.75(d + 3) = 18$
b. $0.75d + 3 = 18$
c. $3d + 0.75 = 18$
d. $3(d + 0.75) = 18$

The vertices of $\triangle XYZ$ are at $X(2, -2)$, $Y(5, 0)$, and $Z(3, 4)$. Use this information for Exercises 24–26.

24. What is the image of point X after a translation of the triangle 3 units to the left?

a. $(5, -1)$ **b.** $(-2, 2)$
c. $(-1, -3)$ **d.** $(-1, -2)$

25. What is the image of point Z after a reflection over the x-axis?

a. $(-3, -4)$ **b.** $(-3, 4)$
c. $(3, -4)$ **d.** $(4, 3)$

26. What is the image of point Y after a rotation of 180° counterclockwise?

a. $(0, 5)$ **b.** $(-5, 0)$
c. $(0, -5)$ **d.** $(5, 0)$

27. Write two equations to describe this problem.

Maxwell had a savings account and a checking account that totaled $350. If he doubled his savings, he would have $600. How much was in each account?

a. $x + y = 350,\ 2x + y = 600$
b. $2x + y = 350,\ x + y = 600$
c. $2(x + y) = 350,\ x + y = 600$
d. $x + 2y = 350,\ 2x + y = 600$

Whole Number Numeration

Review

A. The speed of light can be expressed as 186,000 miles per second, or as 669,600,000 miles per hour. In these two numbers, the digit 6 is used in four different places. The chart shows the meaning of the 6 in each place.

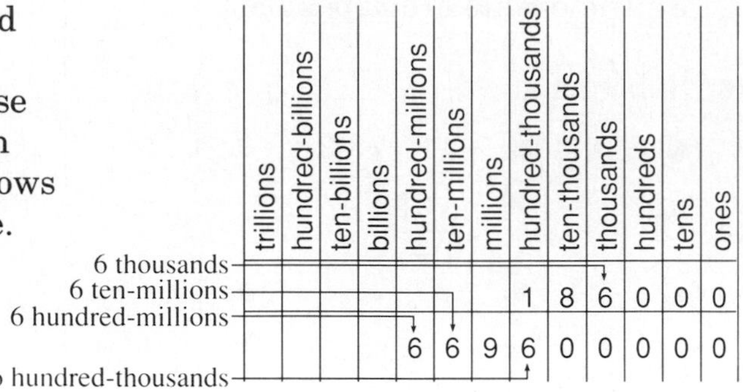

trillions	hundred-billions	ten-billions	billions	hundred-millions	ten-millions	millions	hundred-thousands	ten-thousands	thousands	hundreds	tens	ones
							1	8	6	0	0	0
				6	6	9	6	0	0	0	0	0

6 thousands
6 ten-millions
6 hundred-millions
6 hundred-thousands

B. Write two hundred one million, five thousand in standard form and in expanded form.

Standard form **Expanded form**

201,005,000 = 200,000,000 + 1,000,000 + 5,000

Practice

Tell what the 4 means in each number.

1. 4,356,900 **2.** 423,759,000 **3.** 4,100,000,000 **4.** 143,200,000,000

Write each number in standard form.

5. seventy billion **6.** five hundred-million **7.** two billion

8. 316 million, 217 thousand, ninety **9.** 5 billion, 756 million, 432 thousand

Write each number in words and in expanded form.

10. 350,000 **11.** 73,200,800 **12.** 15,000,000,000 **13.** 356,972,394

For each exercise, tell which number is greater.

14. 3 million or 3 billion **15.** 27 thousand or 20 thousand 7

16. The chart shows the approximate distance of some planets from the sun, in miles. Write the distances in order from least to greatest.

Mars	142,437,500	Earth	93,500,000
Mercury	36,187,500	Neptune	2,810,625,000
Saturn	891,875,000	Uranus	1,793,750,000

Decimal Numeration

Review

A. The number 5.003475 has six decimal places, that is, six digits after the decimal point. Remember, each decimal place has a special place value.

millions	hundred-thousands	ten-thousands	thousands	hundreds	tens	ones	tenths	hundredths	thousandths	ten-thousandths	hundred-thousandths	millionths
						5	0	0	3	4	7	5

five and three thousand four hundred seventy-five millionths

$$5.003475 = 5\frac{3,475}{1,000,000}$$

B. List 0.96, 0.999, and 0.9 in order from least to greatest.

0.960 0.999 0.900 First, write the decimals with the same number of decimal places.

0.900 $<$ 0.960 $<$ 0.999 Then compare the numbers and write them in order.

0.9 0.96 0.999 Rewrite the numbers in their original form.

Practice

Write each number as a decimal.

1. $\frac{56}{100}$ **2.** $\frac{2}{100}$ **3.** $\frac{85}{1,000}$ **4.** $\frac{586}{10,000}$ **5.** $\frac{3}{10}$ **6.** $\frac{7,295}{1,000,000}$

7. Twelve hundredths **8.** Sixty-five and four tenths **9.** Two thousandths

10. Ten ten-thousandths **11.** Five and two thousandths **12.** Six hundred-thousandths

Tell what the 3 means in each number.

13. 35.06 **14.** 0.3426 **15.** 17.136 **16.** 9.62003 **17.** 8.623047

Write each number in words.

18. 50.05 **19.** 210.6 **20.** 8.0001 **21.** 0.00003 **22.** 30.008 **23.** 0.056

24. Write the answers for Exercises 1–6 in order from least to greatest.

Adding and Subtracting Whole Numbers

Review

A. Find 6,329 + 42,398 + 627.

```
    2                              1 2                              1 1 2
  6,329   Add the ones.          6,329   Add the tens.            6,329   Continue adding
 42,398   Rename.               42,398   Rename.                 42,398   and renaming.
+   627   24 ones =            +   627   15 tens =              +   627
 ------   2 tens 4 ones         ------   1 hundred 5 tens        ------
      4                             54                           49,354
```

B. Find 28,904 − 7,627.

```
                                                                 9
   8 10                                                       8 10 14
 28,904   More ones are needed.                     28,904   Then rename to get more ones.
− 7,627   First, rename to get more tens.          − 7,627   10 tens 4 ones = 9 tens 14 ones
 ------   9 hundreds = 8 hundreds 10 tens           ------
                                                    21,277   Subtract.
```

Practice

Add.

1. 56,428 + 7,451 + 5,228

2. 28,321 + 9,048 + 7,556

3. 97,652 + 38,473 + 44,756

4. 648,516 + 93,494 + 65,338

5. 736,338 + 109,379 + 529,891

6. 631 + 42 + 98 + 304 **7.** 7,273 + 53,905 + 93,879 **8.** 8,806 + 98 + 428 + 80

Subtract.

9. 8,039 − 6,895 **10.** 4,605 − 933 **11.** 7,814 − 915 **12.** 84,106 − 10,878 **13.** 66,000 − 45,831

14. 4,731 − 1,492 **15.** 2,351 − 1,761 **16.** 73,001 − 247 **17.** 8,242 − 2,106

18. 44,212 − 98 **19.** 92,003 − 74,009 **20.** 60,407 − 1,986 **21.** 71,357 − 4,009

Add or subtract.

22. 5,964 + 297 **23.** 3,816 − 672 **24.** 9,073 + 689 **25.** 7,191 − 6,834

26. 10,000 − 1,999 **27.** 7,368 + 4,485 **28.** 17,218 − 14,643 **29.** 9,006 + 3,854

SKILLS REVIEW

Multiplying Whole Numbers

Review

A. Find 30 × 156.

```
  156    Remember, 30 = 3 × 10.        1 1
×  30    Write 0 to show that you      156
    0    multiply by 10.             ×  30
                                     4,680   Then multiply by 3.
```

B. Find 27 × 3,165.

```
  3,165
×    27    Think of 27 as 20 + 7.
 22 155    Multiply 7 and 3,165.
 63 300    Multiply 20 and 3,165.
 85,455    Add 22,155 and 63,300.
```

C. Find 607 × 493.

```
    493
  × 607
  3 451    7 × 493 = 3,451
295 800    600 × 493 = 295,800
299,251    Add 3,451 and 295,800.
```

Practice

Multiply.

1. 36 × 50 **2.** 47 × 90 **3.** 76 × 13 **4.** 59 × 41 **5.** 14 × 22 **6.** 56 × 15 **7.** 63 × 46

8. 815 × 70 **9.** 697 × 60 **10.** 703 × 25 **11.** 325 × 17 **12.** 648 × 93 **13.** 873 × 54 **14.** 415 × 80

15. 2,307 × 42 **16.** 1,806 × 71 **17.** 4,552 × 17 **18.** 1,823 × 34 **19.** 493 × 123 **20.** 375 × 604

21. 756 × 300 **22.** 914 × 500 **23.** 256 × 700 **24.** 398 × 200 **25.** 614 × 400 **26.** 1,315 × 600

27. 457 × 309 **28.** 668 × 529 **29.** 826 × 378 **30.** 135 × 407 **31.** 3,215 × 119 **32.** 4,326 × 203

33. 46 × 89 **34.** 3,428 × 35 **35.** 911 × 72 **36.** 1,234 × 98 **37.** 3,008 × 16

38. 37 × 44 **39.** 6,175 × 12 **40.** 305 × 160 **41.** 642 × 385 **42.** 509 × 208

43. 406 × 45 × 39 **44.** 15 × 328 × 83 **45.** 73 × 4 × 604 **46.** 93 × 30 × 422

47. 55 × 146 × 27 **48.** 72 × 421 × 9 **49.** 22 × 843 × 96 **50.** 82 × 22 × 301

SKILLS REVIEW

Adding and Subtracting Decimals

Review

A. Find 8.34 + 9.785.

$$\begin{array}{r} {\scriptstyle 1\,1} \\ 8.340 \\ +\ 9.785 \\ \hline 18.125 \end{array}$$

Since 9.785 has three decimal places, write 8.34 with three decimal places. Then line up the decimal points and add. Remember to write the decimal point in the answer.

B. Find 84 − 16.724.

$$\begin{array}{r} {\scriptstyle 13\ 9\ 9} \\ {\scriptstyle 7\ \not{3}\ \not{10}\not{10}10} \\ \not{8}\,\not{4}.\not{0}\,\not{0}\,\not{0} \\ -\,1\,6.7\,2\,4 \\ \hline 6\,7.2\,7\,6 \end{array}$$

Write 84 with the decimal point and three zeros to show thousandths. Line up the decimal points and subtract. Write the decimal point in the answer.

Practice

Add.

1. 1.032 + 7.938 **2.** 3.94 + 4.06 **3.** 23.738 + 9.006 **4.** 0.95 + 0.37 **5.** 0.62 + 0.89 **6.** 738.2 + 89.8

Subtract.

7. 5.17 − 2.64 **8.** 8.342 − 6.097 **9.** 15.007 − 9.038 **10.** 107.94 − 84.68 **11.** 56.92 − 29.35 **12.** 28.4 − 19.6

Add or subtract. Watch the signs.

13. 9.85 + 2.076 **14.** 17.1 − 3.762 **15.** 77.4 − 9.85 **16.** 43.01 + 4.9001

17. 0.8 + 2.751 + 24.5 **18.** 75 − 38.65 **19.** 4.2 + 6.08 + 13.7 **20.** 110.3 − 76.51

Copy and complete this weekend hotel bill. All tax and tips are included.

Charges	Friday	Saturday	Sunday	Item Totals
Room	$49.95	$49.95		**21.** _____
Restaurant	$15.64	$45	$9.15	**22.** _____
Room Service	$3.95	$5		**23.** _____
Daily Totals	**24.** _____	**25.** _____	**26.** _____	**27.** _____ Total Charges
HOTEL BIJOU				$50 Deposit
				28. _____ Balance Due

Rounding Whole Numbers and Decimals

Review

A. Round each of the numbers listed below so that only one digit is not zero.
356 84 9,630

356 ↓ 400	Since the greatest place value used is the hundreds place, round 356 to the nearest hundred. The digit to the right of the hundreds place is 5, so the digit in the hundreds place increases by 1. To the nearest hundred, 356 rounds to 400.
84 ↓ 80	Round 84 to the nearest ten. The digit to the right of the tens place is less than 5, so the digit in the tens place stays the same. To the nearest ten, 84 rounds to 80.
9,630 ↓ 10,000	Round 9,630 to the nearest thousand. The digit to the right of the thousands place is greater than 5, so the digit in the thousands place increases by 1. Since 1 more than 9 is 10, the ten-thousands place is also affected.

B. Round 14.9536 to the nearest one and to the nearest hundredth.

14.9536 ↓ **15** The digit to the right of the ones place is greater than 5, so the ones digit increases by 1. Drop all digits to the right of the ones place.

14.9536 ↓ **14.95** The digit to the right of the hundredths place is less than 5, so the hundredths digit stays the same.

Practice

Round each number to the nearest thousand, nearest hundred and nearest ten.

1. 3,104 **2.** 7,582 **3.** 9,643 **4.** 4,039 **5.** 42,022 **6.** 37,900 **7.** 35,483

8. 9,015 **9.** 2,128 **10.** 873 **11.** 719 **12.** 49,921 **13.** 23,987 **14.** 10,909

Round each number so that only one digit is not zero.

15. 2,803,200 **16.** 8,077,000 **17.** 9,894,100 **18.** 853,672 **19.** 908,173

Copy the chart and complete it.

Number	Nearest one	Nearest tenth	Nearest hundredth	Nearest thousandth
15.637	**20.**	**21.**	**22.**	
0.00936			**23.**	**24.**
9.8955	**25.**	**26.**	**27.**	**28.**

Two-Digit Divisors: One-Digit Quotients

Review

A. Find 78 ÷ 24.

```
   3 R6
24)78
   72
    6
```

Divide. THINK: 24 rounds to 20. How many 2s in 7? 3
Write 3 above the 8.
Multiply. 3 × 24 = 72
Subtract and compare. 6 < 24
The remainder is 6.

CHECK:

```
   24
 ×  3
   72
 +  6
   78
```

Multiply the divisor by the quotient.
Add the remainder.
The result is the dividend.

B. Find 144 ÷ 48.

```
    2
48)144
    96
    48
```

Divide.
Round 48 to 50.
There are two 5s in 14.
Multiply.
Subtract and compare.
48 = 48, so 2 is too small.

```
    3
48)144
   144
     0
```

Try 3.
Multiply.
Subtract and compare.

C. Find 403 ÷ 84.

```
    5
84)403
   420
```

Divide.
Round 84 to 80.
There are five 8s in 40.
Multiply.
420 > 403, so 5 is too big.

```
    4 R67
84)403
   336
    67
```

Try 4.
Multiply.
Subtract and compare.
The remainder is 67.

Practice

Divide.

1. 23)92 **2.** 19)68 **3.** 47)453 **4.** 62)372 **5.** 91)275 **6.** 34)256

7. 83)412 **8.** 74)283 **9.** 25)117 **10.** 53)309 **11.** 28)226 **12.** 36)234

13. 21)79 **14.** 63)181 **15.** 55)304 **16.** 18)161 **17.** 39)284 **18.** 28)144

19. 431 ÷ 78 **20.** 529 ÷ 88 **21.** 218 ÷ 37 **22.** 129 ÷ 16 **23.** 226 ÷ 68

24. 541 ÷ 62 **25.** 645 ÷ 72 **26.** 484 ÷ 65 **27.** 364 ÷ 79 **28.** 443 ÷ 48

29. 323 ÷ 56 **30.** 136 ÷ 17 **31.** 216 ÷ 27 **32.** 105 ÷ 19 **33.** 136 ÷ 15

34. 140 ÷ 18 **35.** 523 ÷ 62 **36.** 179 ÷ 57 **37.** 495 ÷ 85 **38.** 226 ÷ 68

39. 512 ÷ 52 **40.** 312 ÷ 36 **41.** 150 ÷ 19 **42.** 168 ÷ 25 **43.** 108 ÷ 16

44. 397 ÷ 43 **45.** 536 ÷ 61 **46.** 454 ÷ 87 **47.** 604 ÷ 78 **48.** 653 ÷ 95

Two-Digit Divisors: Multi-Digit Quotients

Review

A. Find 845 ÷ 43.

$$\begin{array}{r} 1 \\ 43\overline{)845} \\ \underline{43} \\ 41 \end{array}$$

Divide.
THINK: There are two 4s in 8, but 2 × 43 is 86, so 2 is too big. Try 1.
Multiply, subtract, and compare.

$$\begin{array}{r} 19 \text{ R28} \\ 43\overline{)845} \\ \underline{43\downarrow} \\ 415 \\ \underline{387} \\ 28 \end{array}$$

Bring down.
THINK: 10 × 43 = 430
Try 9.
Multiply, subtract, and compare.
The remainder is 28.

B. Find 7,715 ÷ 38.

$$\begin{array}{r} 203 \text{ R1} \\ 38\overline{)7{,}715} \\ \underline{76\downarrow} \\ 11 \\ \underline{0\downarrow} \\ 115 \\ \underline{114} \\ 1 \end{array}$$

Divide.
Multiply.
Subtract and compare.
Bring down.
Divide. There are no 38s in 11. Write zero above the 1.
Multiply, subtract, and compare. Bring down.
Divide.
Multiply, subtract, and compare.
The remainder is 1.

C. Find 4,506 ÷ 15.

$$\begin{array}{r} 300 \text{ R6} \\ 15\overline{)4{,}506} \\ \underline{45\downarrow} \\ 00 \\ \underline{0\downarrow} \\ 06 \\ \underline{0} \\ 6 \end{array}$$

Divide. There are three 15s in 45.
Multiply.
Subtract, compare, and bring down.
Divide. There are no 15s in 0.
Write zero above the zero.
Multiply.
Subtract, compare, and bring down.
Divide. There are no 15s in 6.
Write zero above the 6.
Multiply, subtract, and compare.
The remainder is 6.

Practice

Divide.

1. $31\overline{)829}$ **2.** $47\overline{)989}$ **3.** $38\overline{)476}$ **4.** $63\overline{)885}$ **5.** $47\overline{)2{,}178}$ **6.** $71\overline{)3{,}842}$

7. $22\overline{)3{,}850}$ **8.** $38\overline{)837}$ **9.** $42\overline{)697}$ **10.** $28\overline{)941}$ **11.** $60\overline{)8{,}133}$ **12.** $26\overline{)6{,}343}$

13. $78\overline{)2{,}405}$ **14.** $28\overline{)2{,}246}$ **15.** $55\overline{)27{,}885}$ **16.** $81\overline{)34{,}124}$ **17.** $86\overline{)26{,}098}$

18. 856 ÷ 32 **19.** 843 ÷ 79 **20.** 7,823 ÷ 27 **21.** 24,135 ÷ 54 **22.** 18,924 ÷ 63

23. 915 ÷ 13 **24.** 326 ÷ 15 **25.** 1,154 ÷ 81 **26.** 17,621 ÷ 40 **27.** 31,658 ÷ 63

28. 728 ÷ 18 **29.** 739 ÷ 43 **30.** 1,069 ÷ 21 **31.** 15,132 ÷ 66 **32.** 23,410 ÷ 76

Angles

Review

A. Two rays with a common endpoint form an angle. In the angle shown, $\overrightarrow{BA}$ and $\overrightarrow{BC}$ are the sides of $\angle ABC$. Point B is the vertex of this angle. The angle can also be called $\angle CBA$ or $\angle B$.

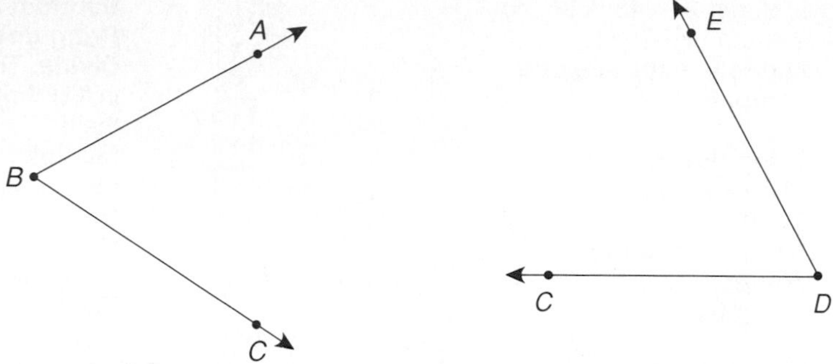

B. Using a protractor, you find the measure of an angle in degrees.
Place the center mark of the protractor on the vertex of the angle.
Place the zero mark of one scale on a side of the angle.
Read the measure where the other side of the angle crosses the scale.
$m\angle CDE = 62°$

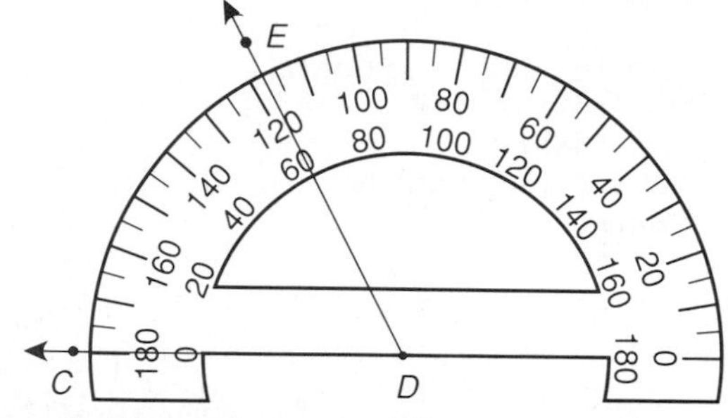

The symbol "m" is read "the measure of."

C. Draw $\angle EFG$ so that $m\angle EFG = 125°$.
Draw $\overrightarrow{FE}$. Place the center of the protractor on point F and a zero mark on $\overrightarrow{FE}$. Use the scale with this zero mark and draw point G at 125°.
Then draw $\overrightarrow{FG}$.

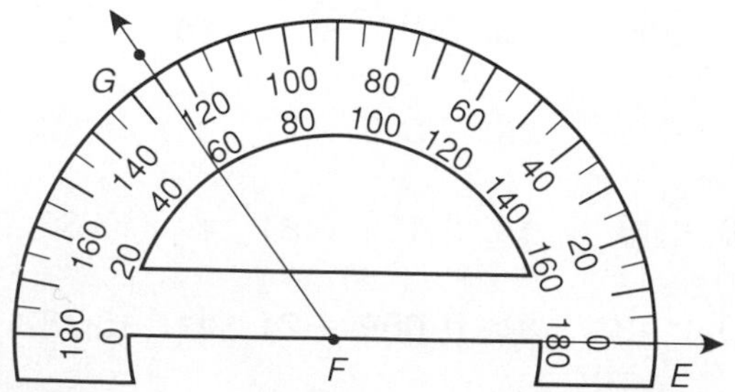

Practice

For each angle, name the sides and the vertex. Then name the angle three different ways.

1.

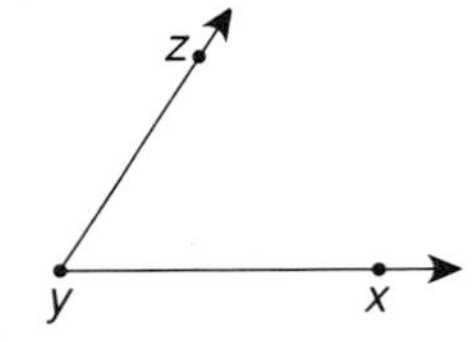

2.

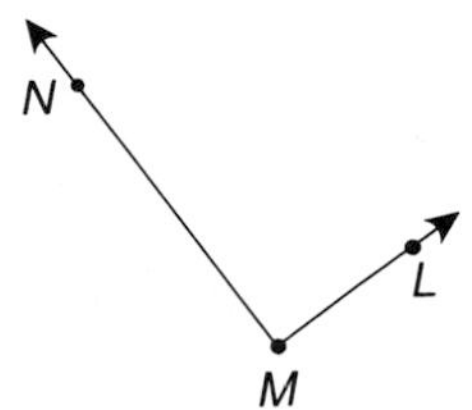

3.

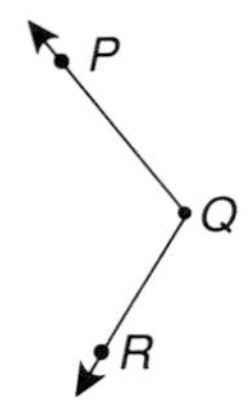

Find the measure of each angle in the figure below.

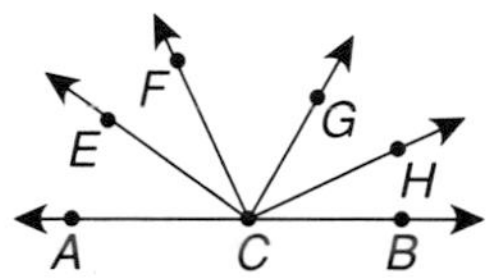

4. $\angle ACE$ **5.** $\angle ECH$ **6.** $\angle FCG$ **7.** $\angle GCH$ **8.** $\angle ECB$

9. $\angle HCB$ **10.** $\angle ACF$ **11.** $\angle ECG$ **12.** $\angle FCH$ **13.** $\angle ACH$

14. $\angle FCB$ **15.** $\angle GCB$ **16.** $\angle ACG$ **17.** $\angle ECF$ **18.** $\angle ACB$

Use a protractor to draw each angle with the given measure. Label each angle according to its name.

19. $m\angle MNO = 65°$ **20.** $m\angle HIJ = 110°$ **21.** $m\angle QRS = 35°$

22. $m\angle STU = 170°$ **23.** $m\angle CDE = 15°$ **24.** $m\angle EFG = 90°$

25. $m\angle JKL = 95°$ **26.** $m\angle XYZ = 80°$ **27.** $m\angle ACE = 73°$

28. $m\angle RTV = 26°$ **29.** $m\angle KGC = 128°$ **30.** $m\angle LSW = 47°$

31. $m\angle XZA = 82°$ **32.** $m\angle MJW = 51°$ **33.** $m\angle MGS = 139°$

34. $m\angle ABC = 5°$ **35.** $m\angle JLM = 45°$ **36.** $m\angle BMD = 180°$

SKILLS REVIEW

Adding Fractions

Review

A. Find $\frac{7}{8} + \frac{3}{8} + \frac{4}{8}$.

$\frac{7}{8} + \frac{3}{8} + \frac{4}{8} = \frac{7 + 3 + 4}{8}$ Since the denominators are the same, add the numerators.

$= \frac{14}{8} = 1\frac{6}{8}$ Write the sum over the common denominator. Rename $\frac{14}{8}$ as a mixed number.

$= 1\frac{3}{4}$ Write $\frac{6}{8}$ in lowest terms.

B. Find $\frac{1}{4} + \frac{5}{6}$.

$\frac{1}{4} = \frac{3}{12}$

$+\frac{5}{6} = \frac{10}{12}$

Before you can add, you need to find a common denominator. Any number that is a multiple of both 4 and 6 can be used. The least common multiple of 4 and 6 is 12, so 12 is the least common denominator for $\frac{1}{4}$ and $\frac{5}{6}$.

$\frac{13}{12} = 1\frac{1}{12}$ Add. Rename $\frac{13}{12}$ as a mixed number.

Practice

Add.

1. $\frac{3}{10} + \frac{3}{10}$ **2.** $\frac{3}{8} + \frac{5}{8}$ **3.** $\frac{3}{4} + \frac{3}{4}$ **4.** $\frac{1}{2} + \frac{1}{2}$ **5.** $\frac{3}{10} + \frac{9}{10}$ **6.** $\frac{4}{5} + \frac{3}{5}$

7. $\frac{5}{12} + \frac{11}{12}$ **8.** $\frac{15}{16} + \frac{9}{16}$ **9.** $\frac{9}{20} + \frac{13}{20}$ **10.** $\frac{4}{5} + \frac{3}{5}$ **11.** $\frac{7}{12} + \frac{5}{12}$ **12.** $\frac{5}{6} + \frac{5}{6}$

13. $\frac{3}{4} + \frac{3}{4} + \frac{3}{4}$ **14.** $\frac{7}{8} + \frac{7}{8} + \frac{5}{8}$ **15.** $\frac{7}{12} + \frac{11}{12} + \frac{5}{12}$ **16.** $\frac{3}{10} + \frac{9}{10} + \frac{9}{10}$ **17.** $\frac{4}{5} + \frac{3}{5} + \frac{3}{5}$

18. $\frac{1}{2} + \frac{2}{5}$ **19.** $\frac{2}{3} + \frac{1}{4}$ **20.** $\frac{1}{3} + \frac{3}{5}$ **21.** $\frac{3}{4} + \frac{1}{8}$ **22.** $\frac{2}{5} + \frac{7}{10}$ **23.** $\frac{5}{12} + \frac{3}{4}$ **24.** $\frac{1}{2} + \frac{5}{6}$

25. $\frac{1}{6} + \frac{3}{5}$ **26.** $\frac{3}{5} + \frac{7}{8}$ **27.** $\frac{3}{8} + \frac{5}{12}$ **28.** $\frac{7}{10} + \frac{1}{6}$ **29.** $\frac{2}{3} + \frac{1}{8} + \frac{5}{6}$ **30.** $\frac{1}{3} + \frac{3}{4} + \frac{1}{2}$ **31.** $\frac{3}{4} + \frac{2}{5} + \frac{7}{10}$

Subtracting Fractions

Review

A. Find $\frac{7}{8} - \frac{5}{8}$.

$\frac{7}{8} - \frac{5}{8} = \frac{7-5}{8}$ The fractions have the same denominator, so subtract the numerators.

$= \frac{2}{8}$ Write the difference over the common denominator, 8.

$= \frac{1}{4}$ Write $\frac{2}{8}$ in lowest terms.

B. Find $\frac{7}{16} - \frac{1}{4}$.

$\frac{7}{16} = \frac{7}{16}$ Since 16 is a multiple of 4, the least common denominator is 16.

$-\frac{1}{4} = \frac{4}{16}$ Write $\frac{1}{4}$ with the denominator 16 and subtract from $\frac{7}{16}$.

$\frac{3}{16}$

Practice

Subtract.

1. $\frac{5}{8} - \frac{1}{8}$ **2.** $\frac{4}{5} - \frac{1}{5}$ **3.** $\frac{11}{12} - \frac{7}{12}$ **4.** $\frac{9}{10} - \frac{7}{10}$ **5.** $\frac{11}{16} - \frac{3}{16}$ **6.** $\frac{5}{6} - \frac{1}{6}$

7. $\frac{3}{4} - \frac{1}{4}$ **8.** $\frac{5}{8} - \frac{3}{8}$ **9.** $\frac{7}{12} - \frac{1}{12}$ **10.** $\frac{7}{16} - \frac{3}{16}$ **11.** $\frac{15}{16} - \frac{9}{16}$ **12.** $\frac{7}{8} - \frac{3}{8}$

13. $\frac{9}{10} - \frac{3}{5}$ **14.** $\frac{5}{6} - \frac{2}{3}$ **15.** $\frac{9}{10} - \frac{1}{2}$ **16.** $\frac{4}{5} - \frac{1}{6}$ **17.** $\frac{2}{3} - \frac{3}{8}$ **18.** $\frac{3}{5} - \frac{1}{3}$ **19.** $\frac{7}{8} - \frac{2}{3}$

20. $\frac{3}{4} - \frac{2}{5}$ **21.** $\frac{5}{6} - \frac{3}{8}$ **22.** $\frac{7}{8} - \frac{3}{10}$ **23.** $\frac{3}{4} - \frac{2}{3}$ **24.** $\frac{2}{5} - \frac{1}{12}$ **25.** $\frac{7}{8} - \frac{5}{12}$ **26.** $\frac{5}{6} - \frac{7}{10}$

27. $\frac{11}{12} - \frac{7}{12}$ **28.** $\frac{7}{8} - \frac{1}{4}$ **29.** $\frac{7}{10} - \frac{2}{3}$ **30.** $\frac{9}{10} - \frac{1}{3}$ **31.** $\frac{1}{2} - \frac{1}{7}$ **32.** $\frac{3}{4} - \frac{3}{10}$ **33.** $\frac{9}{10} - \frac{1}{8}$

Customary Units of Length, Area, and Volume

Review

A. The most common customary units of length are the inch (in.), the foot (ft), the yard (yd), and the mile (mi). The distance from the tip of your thumb to the first knuckle is about 1 inch. From that knuckle to the inside of your elbow is about 1 foot. The width of a door is about 1 yard. A distance of 8 city blocks is about 1 mile.

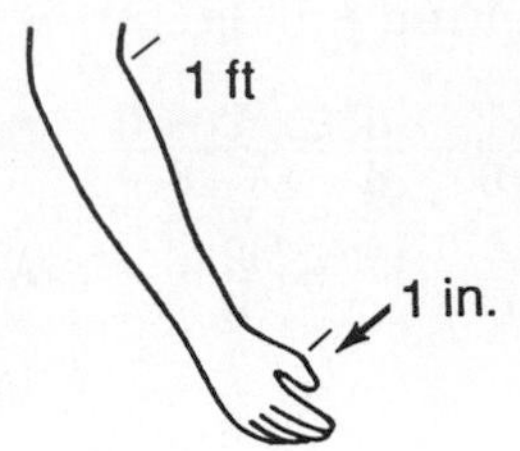

B. Area is measured in square units. One square inch is the area covered by a square that measures 1 inch on each side. One square foot is the area covered by a square that measures 1 foot on each side. One square yard and one square mile are also units of area.

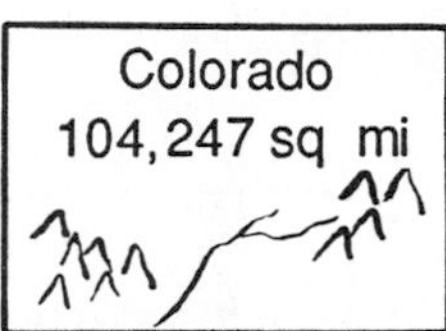

C. One cubic inch is the volume of a cube that measures 1 inch on each side. One cubic foot is the volume of a cube that measures 1 foot on each side. One cubic yard is also a unit of volume.

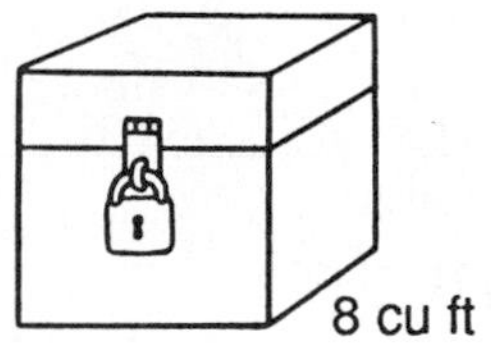

Practice

Choose the most sensible unit to use for each measure.

1. Length of a fishing rod
inches yards miles

2. Width of a street
inches feet miles

3. Floor to ceiling height
inches feet yards

4. Actual distance between two cities
feet yards miles

5. Map distance between two cities
inches feet miles

6. Area of the cover of this book
sq inches sq feet

7. Volume of a microwave oven
cubic inches cubic feet

8. Volume of a refrigerator
cubic inches cubic feet

9. Area of your school's playground
sq inches sq feet

Choose the most sensible length, area, or volume.

10. Length of a race
3 ft 3 yd 3 mi

11. Blueprint area of a room
2 sq in. 2 sq yd 2 sq mi

12. Volume of a pencil box
24 cu in. 24 cu ft 24 cu yd

13. Height of an adult
62 in. 62 ft 62 yd

14. Actual area of a room
90 sq in. 90 sq ft 90 sq mi

15. Volume of a bread box
1 cu in. 1 cu ft 1 cu yd

Customary Units of Weight and Capacity

Review

A. Common customary units of weight are the ounce (oz), the pound (lb), and the ton (T).

A slice of bread weighs about 1 ounce.
A loaf of bread weighs about 1 pound.
A car weighs about 1 ton.

B. Common customary units of capacity are the fluid ounce (fl oz), the cup (c), the pint (pt), the quart (qt), and the gallon (gal).

A melted ice cube produces about 1 fluid ounce of water. A water glass holds about 1 cup. Dairy products are often sold in containers that hold 1 pint, 1 quart, or 1 gallon.

Practice

Choose the most sensible unit to use for each measure of capacity or weight.

1. Capacity of a small mixing bowl
cups pints quarts

2. Capacity of a water heater
pints quarts gallons

3. Capacity of a juice glass
fluid ounces cups pints

4. Weight of a piano
ounces pounds tons

5. Weight of a light bulb
ounces pounds tons

6. Weight of an elephant
ounces pounds tons

Choose the most sensible measure.

7. Full box of cereal
18 oz 18 lb 18 T

8. Full bowl of cereal
1 fl oz 1 c 1 pt

9. Weight of a letter
1 oz 1 lb 1 T

10. Glass of milk
1 fl oz 1 c 1 gal

11. Soup in a can
10 oz 10 lb 10 T

12. Weight of a truck
2 oz 2 lb 2 T

13. Capacity of a bucket
2 fl oz 2 c 2 gal

14. Weight of a bag of flour
5 oz 5 lb 5 T

15. Full tank of gas in a car
18 pt 18 qt 18 gal

16. Weight of a whale
2 oz 2lb 2 T

17. Weight of a goldfish
5 oz 5 lb 5 T

18. Capacity of a fish bowl
4 fl oz 4 c 4 gal

Independent Study Handbook

Contents

How to Use a Calculator

Calculators are used in everyday life at home and at work. They are useful tools when computing with large numbers or when computations involve many numbers. ***Remember:***

- **Do** estimate to check whether you pushed the correct buttons.
- **Don't** use a calculator when paper and pencil or mental math is faster.

Calculator displays

- **Number of digits** How many digits will your calculator display? If you press 99,999 × 99,999 to generate a number with more digits than the display can show, most calculators will show some kind of "error" message.
- **Unnecessary zeros** If you add 2.10 and 3.20, does your display show 5.3 or 5.30? Calculators usually drop unnecessary zeros.
- **Rounding** If you divide 2 by 3, do you see 0.6666666 or 0.6666667? Many calculators drop any digits after 8 digits, rather than round.

Calculator keys

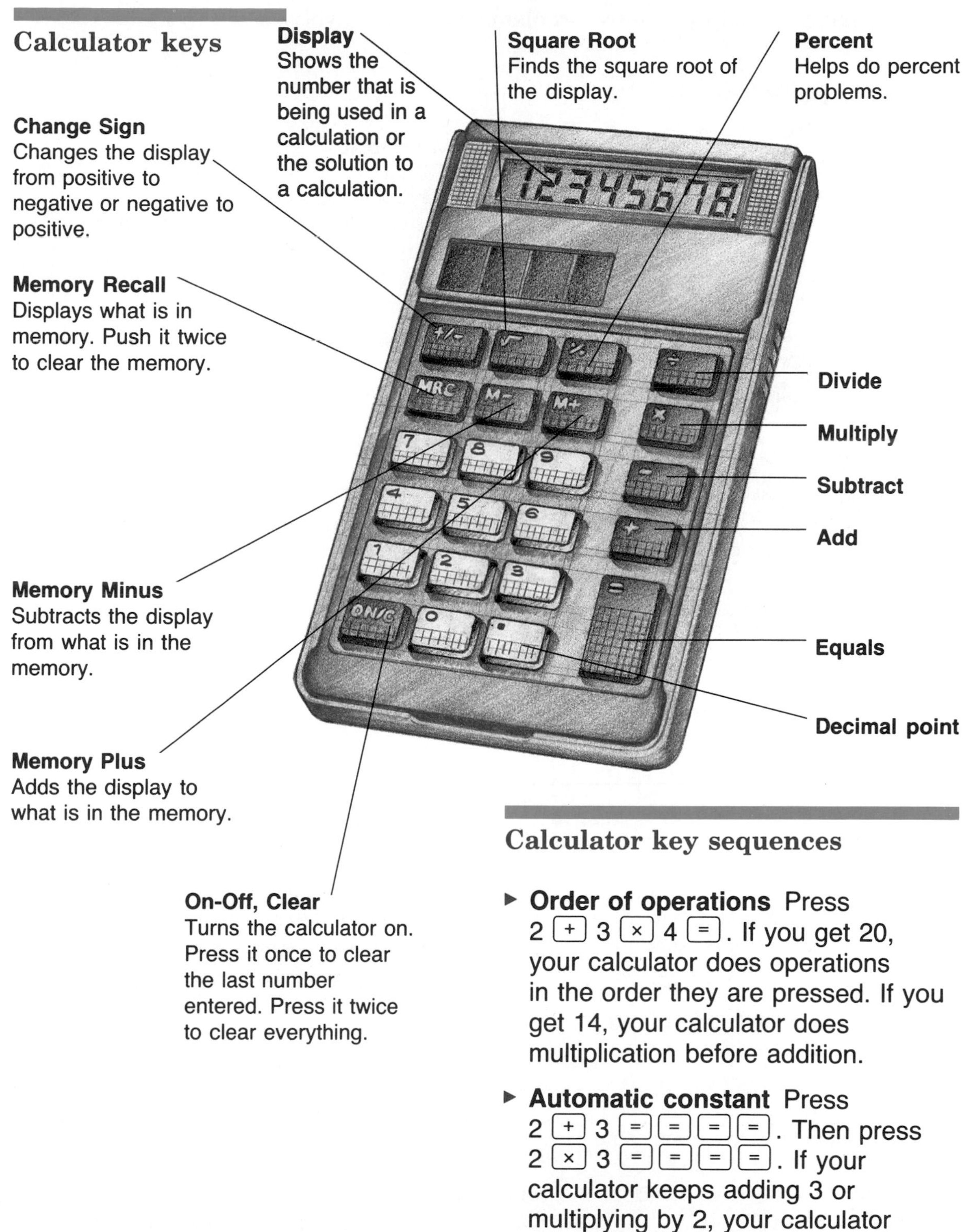
Display
Shows the number that is being used in a calculation or the solution to a calculation.
Square Root
Finds the square root of the display.
Percent
Helps do percent problems.
Change Sign
Changes the display from positive to negative or negative to positive.
Memory Recall
Displays what is in memory. Push it twice to clear the memory.
Divide
Multiply
Subtract
Add
Memory Minus
Subtracts the display from what is in the memory.
Equals
Decimal point
Memory Plus
Adds the display to what is in the memory.
On-Off, Clear
Turns the calculator on. Press it once to clear the last number entered. Press it twice to clear everything.
12345678.
+/-
√
%
÷
MRC
M-
M+
×
7
8
9
−
4
5
6
+
1
2
3
=
ON/C
0
.

Calculator key sequences

- **Order of operations** Press 2 [+] 3 [×] 4 [=]. If you get 20, your calculator does operations in the order they are pressed. If you get 14, your calculator does multiplication before addition.
- **Automatic constant** Press 2 [+] 3 [=] [=] [=] [=]. Then press 2 [×] 3 [=] [=] [=] [=]. If your calculator keeps adding 3 or multiplying by 2, your calculator has an automatic constant.

Problem-Solving Help File

Use these pages to help you solve problems more effectively.

Problem-Solving Guide

There is no recipe or magic formula for solving problems. But keeping a problem-solving guide in mind can help you become a better problem solver.

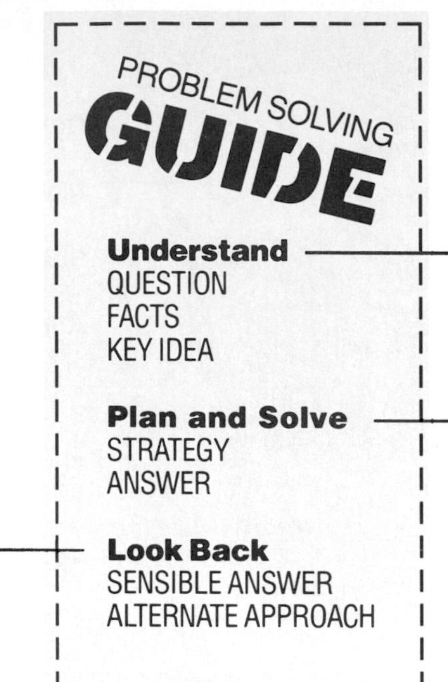

Understand

QUESTION

- What are you asked to find?
- Try to state the question in your own words.
- Is an exact answer needed?

FACTS

- What facts are given?
- Is there too much or too little information?
- Is data needed from a picture, table, or graph?
- Do you need to collect some data?

KEY IDEA

- How are the facts and the question related?
- Are there groups that are part of a whole?
- Are two groups being compared?
- Are there groups that are joining or separating?
- Are there groups of the same size?

Plan and Solve

STRATEGY

- What can you do to solve the problem?
- Can the problem be solved by computing?
- Estimate the answer.
- Choose a strategy. Try another, if needed.

ANSWER

- Give the answer in a sentence.
- Do you need to interpret a remainder?
- Is rounding needed?

Look Back

SENSIBLE ANSWER

- Did you check your work?
- Did you use all the needed data?
- Does your answer have the correct units?
- Is your answer close to the estimate?
- Is your answer reasonable for the situation?

ALTERNATE APPROACH

- Is there another way to get the same answer?
- Could you use the same strategy differently?
- Would another strategy be faster or simpler?

Problem-Solving Strategies

You might think of problem-solving strategies as problem-solving tools that you own and use when needed. One or more strategies might be used for a problem. And if one strategy doesn't work, try another one.

PROBLEM SOLVING
STRATEGIES

Choose an Operation
Write an Equation
Use a Formula
Make a Table
Try and Check
Use Logical Reasoning
Work Backward
Find a Pattern
Solve a Simpler Problem
Make a Graph
Draw a Diagram

Problem-Solving Behaviors and Attitudes

When you solve problems, do you give up quickly or lack confidence? Behaviors and attitudes can affect your work. So, remember these tips. They can help you become a better problem solver.

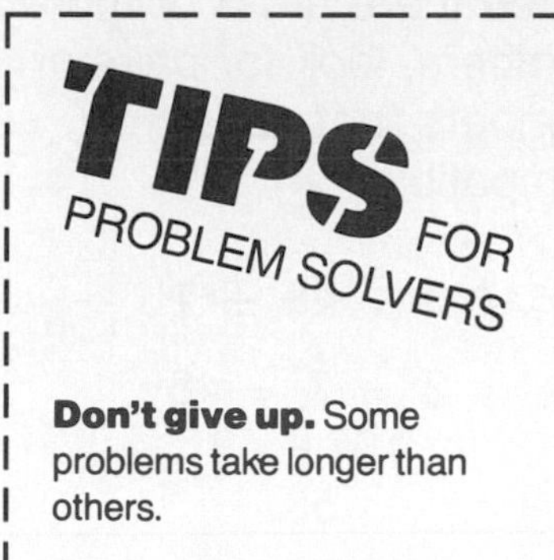
TIPS FOR
PROBLEM SOLVERS
Don't give up. Some problems take longer than others.

Tips for Problem Solvers

- **Don't give up.** Some problems take longer than others.
- **Be flexible.** If you get stuck, try another idea.
- **Be confident** so you can do your best.
- **Take risks.** Try your hunches. They often work.
- **Brainstorm to get started**—one idea will lead to another.
- **Visualize the problem** in your mind to help you understand it better.
- **Compare problems** to help you relate new problems to ones you've solved before.
- **Think about your thinking.** Pause to ask, "How is this going to help me solve the problem?"
- **Share your thinking with others.** Explaining your ideas helps you think better.
- **Organize your work** to help you think clearly.

Mental Math Strategies

For simple calculations, mental math can be a more effective computation method than paper and pencil or a calculator. To sharpen your mental math skills, use the strategies shown on these pages.

Breaking Apart Numbers

Break apart one or more numbers to get numbers that are easier to use.

54 + 23
54 + 20 + 3 — Break apart 23.
74 + 3
77

87 × 2
(80 + 7) × 2 — Break apart 87.
(80 × 2) + (7 × 2) — Use the distributive property.
160 + 14
174

35 + 48
(30 + 5) + (40 + 8) — Break apart 35 and 48.
(30 + 40) + (5 + 8) — Regroup the numbers.
70 + 13
83

60% of 900
6 × 0.10 × 900 — Break apart 60%.
6 × 90 — Find 10% of 900.
540 — Then multiply by 6.

Compatible Numbers

Compatible numbers are pairs of numbers that are easy to use. Look for numbers like 1, 10, 100 or 3, 30, 300 that are easy to use.

40 + 30
70

28 × 10
280

180 ÷ 60
3

When there are 3 or more numbers, look for pairs of numbers that are compatible.

3 + 48 + 7
3 + 7 + 48
10 + 48
58

$\frac{1}{3}$ × 7 × 12
$\frac{1}{3}$ × 12 × 7
4 × 7
28

Using Equivalent Forms

Divide to find "fraction of."

$\frac{1}{3} \times 180$

180 ÷ 3
60

Change decimals or percents to fractions to get a number that is easier to use.

25% of 32

$\frac{1}{4}$ of 32

32 ÷ 4

8

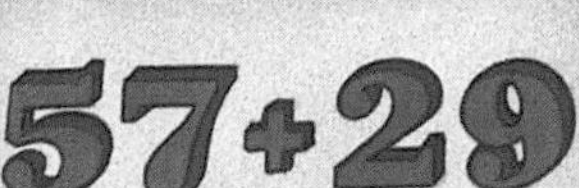

Compensation

Change one number to make it easy to use. Then change the answer to compensate.

57 + 29

57 + 30 = 87 — Add 1 to 29 to get 30.

87 − 1 = 86 — Subtract 1 from the answer.

165 − 97

165 − 100 = 65 — Add 3 to 97 to get 100.

65 + 3 = 68 — Add 3 to the answer.

Change one number to make it easy to use. Then change the other number to compensate.

66 + 19
65 + 20 — Add 1 to 19 and subtract 1 from 66.
85

157 − 98 — Add 2 to 98 and to 157.
159 − 100
59

Estimation Strategies

In everyday life, an exact answer is often unnecessary. For example, you can estimate while shopping to see if you have enough money.

When you do need an exact answer, estimation helps you find possible errors. Estimation is especially important for checking whether you pushed a wrong button on a calculator.

To help you make good estimates, use the estimation strategies shown on these pages.

Front-End Digits

Use just the first digit in each number to help you make an estimate.

$$\begin{array}{r} \mathbf{173} \\ \mathbf{421} \\ \underline{\mathbf{+348}} \end{array} \qquad \begin{array}{r} 100 \\ 400 \\ \underline{+300} \\ 800 \end{array}$$

Since 73 + 21 + 48 is about 100, you can also adjust the estimate by adding 100 to get 900.

Rounding

Round to one nonzero digit.

$$\begin{array}{r} \mathbf{425} \\ \underline{\mathbf{\times 28}} \end{array} \qquad \begin{array}{r} 400 \\ \underline{\times \ \ 30} \\ 12{,}000 \end{array}$$

Round to the same place.

$$\begin{array}{r} \mathbf{28.45} \\ \underline{\mathbf{-\ 3.79}} \end{array} \qquad \begin{array}{r} 28 \\ \underline{-\ 4} \\ 24 \end{array}$$

$$\mathbf{13\tfrac{1}{4} + 8\tfrac{7}{8}}$$
$$13 + 9$$
$$22$$

Round to the nearest half.

$$\mathbf{\tfrac{3}{8} + 2\tfrac{5}{8} + \tfrac{1}{4}}$$
$$\tfrac{1}{2} + 2\tfrac{1}{2} + \tfrac{1}{2}$$
$$3\tfrac{1}{2}$$

Round both numbers up and both numbers down to get a range.

$$\mathbf{57 \times 84} \qquad \begin{array}{l} 60 \times 90 = 5{,}400 \\ 50 \times 80 = 4{,}000 \end{array}$$

57 × 84 is between 4,000 and 5,400.

Substituting Compatible Numbers

Use numbers that are close to the original numbers.

$23\overline{)476}$
$24\overline{)480}$ or $23\overline{)460}$ or $25\overline{)500}$
$23\overline{)476}$ is about 20.

24 × 78 × 4
25 × 78 × 4
100 × 78
24 × 78 × 4 is about 7,800.

$\frac{1}{3}$ × 187

$\frac{1}{3}$ × 180

$\frac{1}{3}$ × 187 is about 60.

26% of 32
25% of 32

$\frac{1}{4}$ × 32

26% of 32 is about 8.

Clustering

Look for groups of numbers that are close to the same number.

6,278 **6,589** **5,893** **+6,134**	Each number is about 6,000, so the sum is about 4 × 6,000 or 24,000.

$4\frac{7}{8} + 5\frac{1}{5} + 4\frac{2}{3}$

Each number is about 5, so the sum is about 3 × 5 or 15.

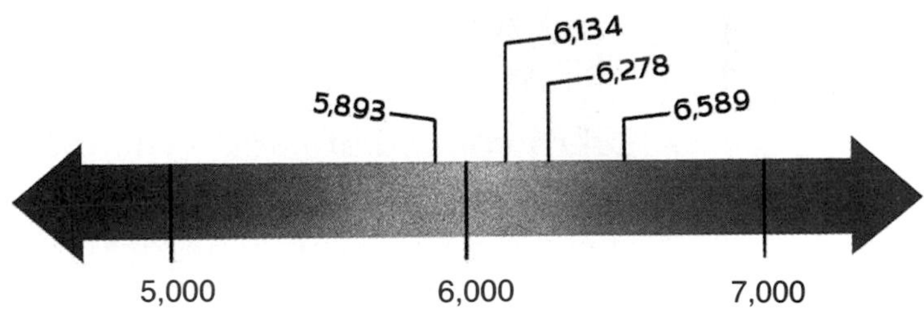

Comparing to a Reference Point

Compare the numbers to numbers you can work with easily.

346 **+438**	Both numbers are less than 500, so the sum is less than 1,000.
$\frac{5}{8} + \frac{3}{5}$	Both numbers are greater than $\frac{1}{2}$, so the sum is greater than 1.

Math Study Skills

Try these math study skills to help you do your best.

Build Understanding
A. A market gets boxes of
24 heads in each box.
heads of lettuce are in
Since each box contai
same number of he

Before a Lesson

- **Preview the lesson.** Look over the lesson to see what it's about.
- **Set a purpose.** Are you about to learn a new topic or revisit a familiar one?
- **Recall what you know.** What have you learned about this topic previously?

Build Understanding

Reading the lesson

- **Read slowly.** Don't try to read a math book as fast as a story book.
- **Learn vocabulary and symbols.** Note new math terms and symbols. Use the glossary and index. Watch for words like "product" that have other meanings outside of math.
- **Read diagrams, tables, graphs.** Use a ruler to help you read rows and columns.
- **Do the examples.** Work the examples yourself as you go through them.

Doing Activities

- **Use materials.** Keep the materials organized. Use them to explore new ideas.
- **Work with others.** When you work with others, use the tips for working together given on page 586.

Check Understanding

Trying on your own

- **Note what you don't understand.** When you try some exercises, be aware of what you don't understand.
- **Reread the lesson.** When you don't understand, reread the "Build Understanding" section.

Preventing errors

- **Find another example.** When you need another example, turn to the "Reteaching" set at the back of the chapter.
- **Try again.** Keep trying until you feel you understand.

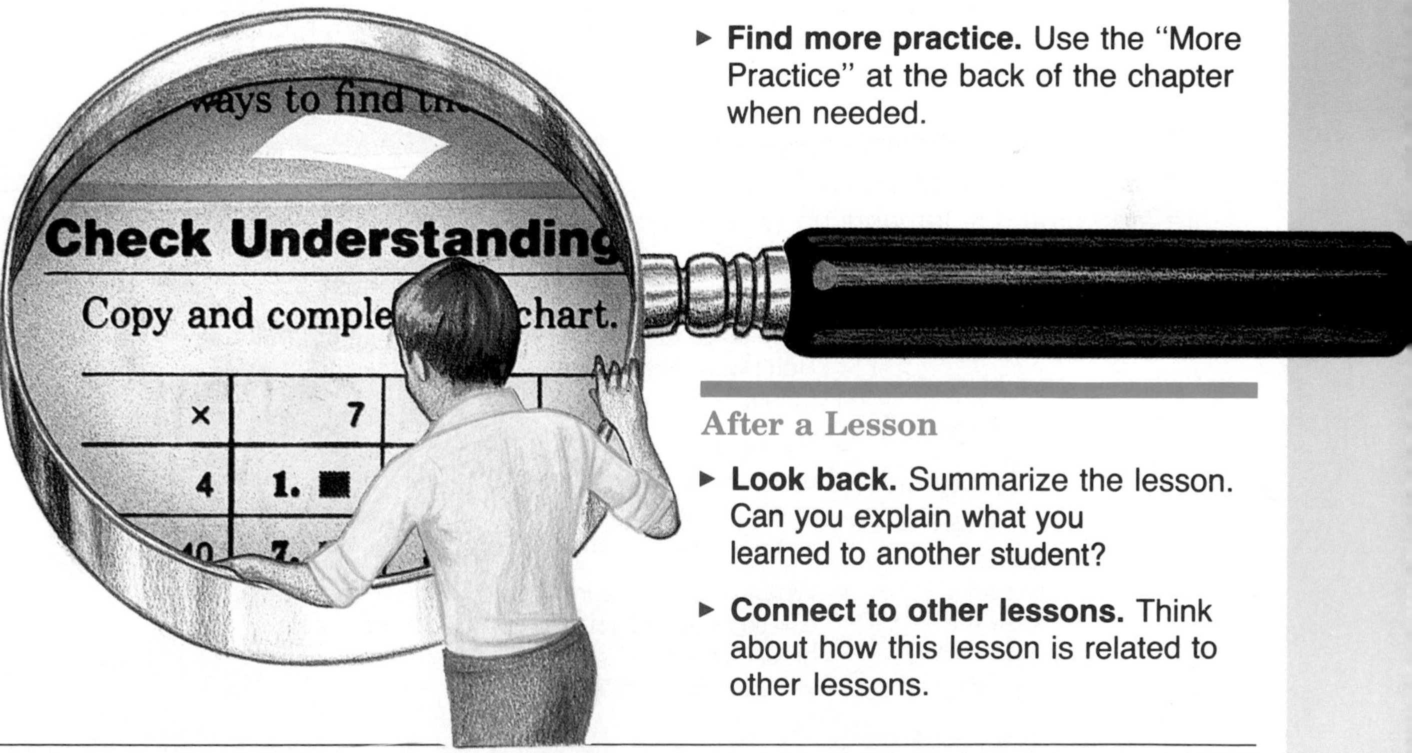

Practice and Problem Solving

Reading the exercises

- **Read directions.** Read carefully.
- **Read word problems.** Read slowly and reread, if needed.

Doing written work

- **Show your work.** Record what you did. Make your paper easy to follow and the answer easy to find.
- **Check your work.** Read what you write.
- **Find more practice.** Use the "More Practice" at the back of the chapter when needed.

After a Lesson

- **Look back.** Summarize the lesson. Can you explain what you learned to another student?
- **Connect to other lessons.** Think about how this lesson is related to other lessons.

Working in Groups

Working in groups during math class will help you learn and enjoy mathematics. You will also learn to work as a member of a team.

TIPS FOR
WORKING TOGETHER
You can disagree without being disagreeable.

Roles for Group Members

When you work in a group, it can be helpful for each person to have a role. Some roles are:

- **Reporter**—This person summarizes the group's thinking.
- **Encourager**—This person encourages group members to take part and to work together well.
- **Recorder**—This person records the group's work.
- **Checker**—This person asks group members to explain their thinking or may ask others if they agree.
- **Materials Manager**—This person gets any materials that are needed and returns them at the end of class.

Tips for Working Together

Here are some tips for working well with others in a group.

- Involve your whole group. Help everyone to participate.
- Help keep your group on task.
- To make sure your group understands the task or solution, have each group member say it in his/her own words, summarize the steps, or give an example.
- Work as a group. If you understand, help another group member. Don't work ahead of the others.
- Be a good tutor. Make up similar problems or easier ones to help someone understand.
- When you are unsure, ask someone in your group for help or say you don't understand.
- Tell someone when he or she does or says something that helps you.
- Don't decide by voting. Try to understand which might be the best solution and why.
- Remember, you can disagree without being disagreeable.

Tables

Metric System

Length	10 millimeters (mm)	=	1 centimeter (cm)
	10 centimeters 100 millimeters	=	1 decimeter (dm)
	10 decimeters 100 centimeters	=	1 meter (m)
	1,000 meters	=	1 kilometer (km)
Area	100 square millimeters (mm^2)	=	1 square centimeter (cm^2)
	10,000 square centimeters	=	1 square meter (m^2)
	100 square meters	=	1 are (a)
	10,000 square meters	=	1 hectare (ha)
Volume	1,000 cubic millimeters (mm^3)	=	1 cubic centimeter (cm^3)
	1,000 cubic centimeters	=	1 cubic decimeter (dm^3)
	1,000,000 cubic centimeters	=	1 cubic meter (m^3)
Mass (weight)	1,000 milligrams (mg)	=	1 gram (g)
	1,000 grams	=	1 kilogram (kg)
	1,000 kilograms	=	1 metric ton (t)
Capacity	1,000 milliliters (mL)	=	1 liter (L)

Customary System

Length	12 inches (in.)	=	1 foot (ft)
	3 feet 36 inches	=	1 yard (yd)
	1,760 yards 5,280 feet	=	1 mile (mi)
	6,076 feet	=	1 nautical mile
Area	144 square inches (sq in.)	=	1 square foot (sq ft)
	9 square feet	=	1 square yard (sq yd)
	4,840 square yards	=	1 acre (A)
Volume	1,728 cubic inches (cu in.)	=	1 cubic foot (cu ft)
	27 cubic feet	=	1 cubic yard (cu yd)
Weight	16 ounces (oz)	=	1 pound (lb)
	2,000 pounds	=	1 ton (T)
Capacity	8 fluid ounces (fl oz)	=	1 cup (c)
	2 cups	=	1 pint (pt)
	2 pints	=	1 quart (qt)
	4 quarts	=	1 gallon (gal)

Squares and Square Roots

n	n^2	$\sqrt{n}$
1	1	1.000
2	4	1.414
3	9	1.732
4	16	2.000
5	25	2.236
6	36	2.449
7	49	2.646
8	64	2.828
9	81	3.000
10	100	3.162
11	121	3.317
12	144	3.464
13	169	3.606
14	196	3.742
15	225	3.873
16	256	4.000
17	289	4.123
18	324	4.243
19	361	4.359
20	400	4.472
21	441	4.583
22	484	4.690
23	529	4.796
24	576	4.899
25	625	5.000
26	676	5.099
27	729	5.196
28	784	5.292
29	841	5.385
30	900	5.477
31	961	5.568
32	1,024	5.657
33	1,089	5.745
34	1,156	5.831
35	1,225	5.916
36	1,296	6.000
37	1,369	6.083
38	1,444	6.164
39	1,521	6.245
40	1,600	6.325
41	1,681	6.403
42	1,764	6.481
43	1,849	6.557
44	1,936	6.633
45	2,025	6.708
46	2,116	6.782
47	2,209	6.856
48	2,304	6.928
49	2,401	7.000
50	2,500	7.071

Glossary

Absolute value The number of units a number is from 0 on a number line.

Acute angle An angle with a measure less than 90°.

Acute triangle Triangle with three acute angles.

Adjacent angles Angles that have a common vertex and a common side between them.

Angle ($\angle$) A figure formed by two rays with the same endpoint.

Arc A part of a circle.

Area A number given in *square units* that indicates the size of the inside of a plane figure.

Associative property The way in which addends (or factors) are grouped does not affect the sum (or product).
$(a + b) + c = a + (b + c)$
$(a \times b) \times c = a \times (b \times c)$

Average A number obtained by dividing the sum of two or more addends by the number of addends.

Axes Two intersecting perpendicular number lines used for graphing ordered pairs.

Base (Of an exponent) A number raised to a power. In 4^3, 4 is the base. (Geometry) A name used for a side of a polygon or surface of a space figure.

Bisect To divide into two congruent parts.

Breaking apart numbers Changing the form of a number so computing with it is easier.

Broken-line graph A drawing that shows how quantities change over time.

Central angle An angle with its vertex at the center of a circle.

Chord A segment with both endpoints on a circle.

Circle A plane figure with all points the same distance from a given point called the *center*.

Circle graph A drawing that compares the parts of a quantity with the whole quantity.

Circumference The distance around a circle.

Closure property If a and b are rational numbers, then $a + b$ and $a \times b$ are unique rational numbers.

Clustering An estimation method used if all the numbers are close to the same number.

Common denominator A common multiple of two or more denominators. A common denominator for $\frac{1}{6}$ and $\frac{3}{8}$ is 48.

Common factor A number that is a factor of two or more numbers. A common factor of 6 and 12 is 3.

Common multiple A number that is a multiple of two or more numbers.

Commutative property The order in which numbers are added (or multiplied) does not affect the sum (or product).
$a + b = b + a$
$a \times b = b \times a$

Compatible number A number close to the number in the problem being solved that is used for mental computation.

Compensation To make computing easier, change a number by adding to it, or subtracting from it, then making the same change to the answer.

Complementary angles Two angles whose measures add up to 90°.

Composite number A whole number, greater than 0, that has more than two factors.

Cone A solid figure formed by connecting a circle to a point not in the plane of the circle.

Congruent figures Two figures with the same size and shape.

Construction The drawing of a figure using only a compass and a straightedge.

Coordinates An ordered pair of numbers used to locate a point in a coordinate plane.

Corresponding parts Matching parts of similar figures.

Cross-products The cross-products of the ratios $\frac{3}{4}$ and $\frac{9}{12}$ are 3×12 and 4×9.

Cube A prism with all square faces.

Customary system of measurement A system for measuring length in *inches, feet, yards, miles;* capacity in *cups, pints, quarts, gallons;* weight in *ounces, pounds, tons;* temperature in *degrees Fahrenheit.*

Cylinder A solid figure with two circular bases that are parallel and congruent.

Data A collection of gathered information that has not been organized.

Decimal A number used to name a whole quantity and/or a fractional part.

Degree (Of an angle) A unit for measuring angles.

Dependent events Events for which one outcome affects another outcome.

Diagonal A segment with two nonadjacent vertices of a polygon as its endpoints.

Diameter In a circle, a segment that passes through the center and that has both endpoints on the circle.

Distributive property When a factor is a sum, multiplying each addend before adding does not change the product.

Divisible One number is divisible by another if the remainder is zero after dividing.

Divisor A number by which another number is divided.

Edge Segment where two faces of a polyhedron meet.

Endpoint The point at the end of a segment or ray.

Equation A mathematical sentence that states the equality of expressions.

Equilateral triangle Triangle with three congruent sides.

Estimate A number that is close to another number. A name used for a calculation not requiring an exact answer.

Event A collection of possible outcomes of an experiment.

Experimental probability Ratio of the number of successes to the number of trials.

Exponent A number that tells how many times the base is to be used as a factor. 4^3 means $4 \times 4 \times 4$, and is read 4 to the third *power*.

Expression A mathematical phrase that uses numbers, variables, and operation symbols to represent a value.

Face Flat surface that is part of a polyhedron.

Factor (1) A number to be multiplied. (2) A number that divides evenly into a given second number is a factor of that number.

Formula An equation that states a general fact or rule by using variables.

Fraction A number that names a part of a whole or of a set.

Frequency table A table that shows the number of times a particular item occurs in a set of data.

Front-end digit The digit in a number that has the greatest place value.

Fundamental Counting Principle If there are m possible outcomes for one event, n possible outcomes for a second event, and p possible outcomes for a third event, then the total number of possible outcomes is $m \times n \times p$.

Graph A drawing used to show information in an organized way.

Greatest common factor (1) The greatest number that is a factor of two or more numbers. (2) The greatest number that divides two or more numbers with no remainder.

Greatest possible error One half of the unit being used to find a measure.

Height The segment from a vertex perpendicular to the line containing the opposite side.

Hexagon A six-sided polygon.

Histogram A bar graph used to show the frequency of items in a set of data.

Hypotenuse In a right triangle, the side opposite the right angle.

Image A figure resulting from a transformation.

Improper fraction A fraction whose numerator is equal to or greater than its denominator.

Independent events Events for which one outcome does not affect another outcome.

Inequality A mathematical sentence with one of the following symbols: $\neq, <, >, \leq, \geq$.

Integers The whole numbers and their opposites. Some integers are +3, −3, 0, +16, −16.

Intersecting lines Lines that meet at a point.

Intervals The constant difference between numbers, such as on the scale of a graph.

Irrational number A number that cannot be written as a fraction. A nonrepeating decimal that goes on endlessly.

Isosceles triangle Triangle with two congruent sides.

Least common multiple (LCM) The smallest number that is a common multiple of two or more given numbers. The least common multiple for 6 and 8 is 24.

Legs of a right triangle The two sides forming the right angle.

Line A set of points continuing without end in both directions.

Line of symmetry A line on which a figure can be folded into two congruent parts.

Linear equation An equation with solutions which lie on a straight line when graphed.

Line plot A graph that uses Xs to show information and compare quantities.

Lowest terms A fraction for which 1 is the greatest common factor of both the numerator and the denominator.

Mean *See* average.

Median The middle number in a group of numbers when the numbers are listed in order.

Metric system The system of measures that uses *meter, liter, gram,* and *degrees Celsius.*

Midpoint A point that divides a segment into two congruent segments.

Mixed number A number that has a whole number part and a fraction part.

Mode Number that occurs most often in a set of data.

Multiple A multiple of a number is the product of that number and a whole number.

N-gon A polygon with n sides.

Negative integer An integer less than 0, such as -5.

Obtuse angle An angle with a measure greater than 90° and less than 180°.

Obtuse triangle Triangle with one obtuse angle.

Octagon An eight-sided polygon.

Opposites Two numbers whose sum is 0.

Origin On a coordinate grid, the point, (0, 0), where the two number lines, or axes, intersect.

Parallel lines Lines in a plane that never meet.

Parallelogram A quadrilateral with opposite sides parallel and congruent.

Pattern A general idea by which things can be arranged or events can happen in an organized way.

Pentagon A five-sided polygon.

Percent (%) A ratio that compares a number to 100. 45% means 45 hundredths.

Perfect squares A number whose square root is an integer.

Perimeter The sum of the lengths of the sides of a polygon.

Permutation An ordered selection of items from a given group.

Perpendicular lines Lines that intersect to form right angles.

Pi (π) The number obtained by dividing the circumference of any circle by its diameter. A common approximation for π is 3.14.

Place value The number each digit represents is determined by the position the digit occupies.

Plane A flat surface that extends without end in all directions.

Point An exact location in space.

Polygon A closed plane figure made by line segments.

Polyhedron A solid figure made up of flat surfaces called *faces.* Each face is a polygon.

Positive integer An integer greater than 0, such as $+35$.

Precision A property of measurement based on the size of the unit of measure. The smaller the unit, the more precise the measurement.

Prime factorization A number written as the product of prime numbers. $30 = 2 \times 3 \times 5$

Prime number A whole number, greater than 1, that has exactly two factors: itself and 1.

Prism A polyhedron with two parallel, congruent faces, called *bases.* All other faces are parallelograms.

Probability A number from 0 to 1 that tells how likely it is that a given event will occur. The closer to 1, the *more likely* the event is to occur. The closer to 0, the *less likely* it is to occur.

Probability tree diagram An organized way to list all possible outcomes of an experiment. Each branch shows the probability of the event.

Proper factors All the factors of a number except the number itself.

Property of one The product of one and a number is that number.

Property of zero The sum of 0 and a number is that number. The product of 0 and a number is 0.

Proportion A statement that two ratios are equal. $\frac{2}{5} = \frac{12}{30}$

Pyramid The solid figure formed by connecting points of a polygon to a point not in the plane of the polygon. The polygon and its interior is the *base.*

Pythagorean Theorem In a right triangle, the sum of the squares of the legs equals the square of the hypotenuse.

Quadrant One of the four parts into which a plane is divided by two perpendicular lines.

Quadrilateral A four-sided polygon.

Quotient The answer after dividing one number by another.

Radius (1) In a circle, a segment that connects the center of the circle with a point on the circle. (2) In a circle, the distance from the center to a point on the circle.

Range The difference between the greatest and the least numbers in a set of data.

Rate A ratio that compares one quantity to a different kind of quantity.

Ratio A pair of numbers that expresses a rate or a comparison.

Rational number Any number that can be written as a fraction. A terminating or repeating decimal.

Ray A set of points that has one endpoint and that extends without end in one direction.

Reciprocals Two numbers whose product is 1. $\frac{3}{4}$ and $\frac{4}{3}$ are reciprocals because $\frac{3}{4} \times \frac{4}{3} = 1$.

Rectangle A parallelogram with four right angles.

Reflection A change in location of a figure by flipping it over a line or point creating a mirror image.

Regular polygon A polygon with all sides congruent and all angles congruent.

Repeating decimal A decimal in which one or more digits keep repeating, such as 0.518181818...

Rhombus A parallelogram with four congruent sides.

Right angle An angle with a measure of 90°.

Right triangle Triangle with one right angle.

Rotation A change in location of a figure by turning it about a point.

Rounded number A number expressed to the nearest 10, 100, 1,000 and so on.

Sample Part of a group upon which an experiment or survey is conducted.

Sample space A list of possible outcomes.

Scale drawing A drawing made so that distances in the drawing are proportional to actual distances.

Scalene triangle Triangle with no congruent sides.

Scientific notation A way to write a number as the product of a power of 10 and a number greater than or equal to 1 and less than 10.

Segment Two points and the straight path between them.

Sequence A set of numbers in a certain order, usually formed by a pattern.

Similar figures Figures with the same shape but not necessarily the same size.

Skew lines Lines that are in two different planes.

Solution A value of a variable that makes an equation true.

Sphere A solid figure with all points the same distance from a given point called the *center*.

Square (Geometry) a rectangle with four congruent sides. (Numeration) To multiply a number by itself.

Square root A number a is the square root of a number b if $a \times a = b$. 3 is the square root of 9.

Standard form The notation for writing numbers using the digits 0–9 and each place represents a power of ten.

Standard order of operations Rules for finding the value of an expression.

Statistics Numerical facts that are collected, organized, and analyzed.

Stem-and-leaf plot A way to display numerical data in which tens digits (stems) appear in a vertical line and ones digits (leaves) appear in horizontal lines.

Success A *favorable outcome* of a probability experiment. An outcome that meets a specific condition.

Supplementary angles Two angles whose measures add up to 180°.

Surface area The sum of the areas of all the surfaces of a space figure.

Terminating decimal A decimal with an exact number of nonzero digits, such as 0.375.

Theoretical probability Ratio of the favorable outcomes to the possible outcomes for an event.

Translation A change in location of a figure by *sliding* it without turning it.

Transformation A flip, slide, or turn that changes the location of a figure on a plane without changing its size or shape.

Trapezoid A quadrilateral with one pair of parallel sides.

Trial An attempt to carry out an event.

Triangle A three-sided polygon.

Variable A letter or symbol used to represent a number.

Vertex (1) The common endpoint of two rays that form an angle. (2) The point of intersection of two sides of a polygon. (3) The point of intersection of the edges of a polyhedron.

Vertical angles Angles formed by two intersecting lines and sharing only a vertex.

Volume A number given in cubic units that indicates the size of the inside of a solid figure.

Whole number One of the numbers 0, 1, 2, 3, and so on.

Answers for Selected Odd-Numbered Exercises

Chapter 1

Pages 4-5
1. 8 minutes past 5 o'clock **3.** 58 cents **5.** 5 parts out of a total of 8 parts **7.** 1.0 **9.** $\frac{4}{4}$ **Exercises 11-17,** answers will vary. **11.** Whole; 32°F **13.** Whole; 5 ft 5 in. **15.** Fraction; whole; $2\frac{1}{2}$c; 3t **17.** Percent; 7% **19.** 60513-1050; 05412; 5-digit whole number or 5-digit whole number followed by dash and 4-digit whole number **21.** 3.2; 5.6 The range of the Richter scale is from 1 to 10 with 2 as the smallest earthquake that can be felt and 8.5 as a devastating earthquake.

Pages 6-7
1. 800 **3.** 2 numbers **5.** 10 **7.** 2 in the 20s; 3 in the 30s; 4 in the 40s **9.** 45 **11.** 252 **13.** 5 **15.** 8 **17.** 20 times

Pages 8-9
1. 68.4 **3.** 420.0 **5.** 50 **7.** 0.00167 **9.** 0.42 **11.** 2.5191 **13.** $2.83 **15.** $5.97 **17.** $0.77 **19.** $4.43 **21.** 0.1 **23.** 1.0379 **25.** 1.053 **27.** 536.9 **29.** 38.925 **31.** 22.0875 **33.** 21.4137 **35.** 3.372 **37.** 3.35775 **39.** 96.03 **41.** $2.38 **43.** Yes

Pages 10-13
1. a. front-end; b. clustering **3.** a. rounding; b. front-end **5.** b; 6 x 4 = 24 **7.** 15 **9.** 48 **11.** 80 **Exercises 13-17,** estimates may vary. **13.** » 550 **15.** » 8,300 **17.** » 55,000 **19.** 500 **21.** 3,600 **23.** 300 **25.** 7,800 **27.** 48 **29.** 400 **31.** 500 **33.** $200.00; $300.00 **35.** 2,000; 3,000 **Exercises 37-45,** methods may vary. **37.** 800; front-end **39.** 24, rounding **41.** 120; clustering **43.** $40; rounding **45.** 20; rounding **Exercises 47-51,** methods may vary. **47.** 400; rounding; 398; P **49.** 1,000; clustering; 1,004; C **51.** 1,000; compatible numbers; 852.0552; C **53.** About $20.00 **55.** No

Pages 16-17
1. 87; commutative **3.** 0; zero property **5.** 583 **7.** 353 **9.** 47 **11.** 2,010 **13.** 800 **15.** 168 **17.** 2,450 **19.** 95 **21.** 650 **23.** 763 **25.** 100 **27.** 60 **29.** $1,716 **Skills Review 1.** 1,026; P **3.** 744,827; C **5.** 30,186; P

Pages 18-21
1. 9 **3.** 17 **5.** 21 **7.** 20 **9.** 440 **11.** 173 hours ÷ 9 girls = $19\frac{2}{9}$ hours **13.** Less; the dividend is less and the divisors are equal. **15.** Addition **17.** Multiplication **19.** 3 h **21.** 5 h **23.** 18 R3; 18.6; $18\frac{3}{5}$ **25.** 240 R1; 240.25; $240\frac{1}{4}$ **27.** 117 R3; 117.5; $117\frac{1}{2}$ **29.** 2,409 R1; 2,409.2; $2{,}409\frac{1}{5}$ **31.** 213 R2; $213.\overline{6}$; $213\frac{2}{3}$ **33.** 3,065 R1; 3,065.2; $3{,}065\frac{1}{5}$ **35.** 170 R4; 170.8; $170\frac{4}{5}$ **37.** 1,208 R5; $1{,}208.\overline{83}$; $1{,}208\frac{5}{6}$ **39.** 50,036; 50,063; 50,066 **41.** 1,014 **43.** 22,599 **45.** 10,230 **47.** 56.02 **49.** 2,485 **51.** $13{,}274\frac{5}{7}$ **53.** About 26 h **55.** About 19 h **57.** Down **59.** Up **61.** Down **Explore Math 63.** 5; 5; 5 **65.** 6; 6; 6 **67.** Both divisor and dividend are multiplied by the same power of 10, but the answers are the same. **69.** 24; 240; 2,400

Pages 22-23
1. Paris; Hamburg; Rome **3.** Yes; addition and multiplication **5.** Multiply by 365. 365(2.4 + 1.9 + 1.5) = 2,117 lb/person/yr **7.** Decreased; increased by 70 million 1960-1983 (3.89 million/yr) and increased by 40 million from 1988-2010 (1.82 million/yr) **9.** 0.1 billion metric tons

Pages 24-25
Exercises 1-33, method choices vary. **1.** 887; M **3.** 19; P **5.** 4,094; C **7.** 58; M **9.** 15; P **11.** 370; C **13.** 10,000; M **15.** 8.375; C **17.** 276; M **19.** 900; C **21.** 1,535 C **23.** 539; C **25.** 5.3076; C **27.** 5; M **29.** 120; M **31.** 99; M **33.** 295.28; C **35.** 267 mi; P **37.** Cleveland is 44 miles closer; M

Pages 26-27
1. Last item **3.** 20 carpenters, 20 electricians, 16 wardrobe, 12 prop, 8 sound people **5.** Addition **7.** Addition; 2 weeks **9.** Multiplication; 9,504 sq ft **Choose a Strategy 11.** 20 bikes **13.** 50 bikes

Chapter 2

Pages 38-41
1. 3 days **3.** 10 miles **5.** 4 **7.** 6 **9.** 6 **11.** 5 **13.** 14 **15.** 4 **17.** 1,200 **19.** 12 **21.** 6 **23.** 28 **25.** 8 **27.** 4 **29.** 17 **31.** 63 **33.** 10 **35.** 7 **37.** $85 **39.** 3; By the relationship in the table you need 20 ÷ 7 = $2\frac{6}{7}$ campfires. Since you cannot build a fraction of a campfire, 3 campfires are needed. **41.** Between 12 noon and 1 P.M.

43.

Hour	Miles Covered
2:15 P.M.	0
3:15	0
4:15	3
5:15	6
6:15	9
7:15	12
8:15	15

They should wait until morning to return. **45.** 6,000 feet **Skills Review 1.** 1.63 **3.** 2.49 **5.** 72.21 **7.** 48.582 **9.** 1,770.796

Pages 42-43
1. 25 **3.** 45 **5.** 37.5 **7.** 5 **9.** 11 **11.** 8 **13.** 20 **15.** 8 **17.** 8 **19.** 16 **21.** 1 **23.** 4 **25.** 28 **27.** 2

29. 23 **31.** 75 **33.** 67 **35.** 300 **37.** 1 **39.** $3\frac{1}{3}$
41. Greater than
43.

n	$\frac{n}{9}$
1	0.1111 . . .
2	0.222 . . .
3	0.333 . . .
4	0.444 . . .
5	0.555 . . .

So, $\frac{6}{9} = 0.666\ldots$

n	$\frac{n}{11}$
1	0.090909 . . .
2	0.181818 . . .
3	0.272727 . . .
4	0.363636 . . .
5	0.454545 . . .

So, $\frac{6}{11} = 0.545454\ldots$

45. $45 **47.** 12 nights **49.** When $x = y$

Pages 44-45
1. $w - 16$ **3.** $10 + q$ **5.** $4 - y$ **7.** $u + 7$ **9.** $e - 14$ **11.** $13.5r$ **13.** $58{,}000x$ **15.** $x + 4$ **17.** $n - 1$ **19.** $5(2a)$ or $10a$ **21.** 8 less than m; 8 subtracted from m **23.** 16 times r; the product of 16 and r **25.** K less than 25; k subtracted from 25 **27.** The quotient of 36 divided by t; 36 divided by t

Pages 46-47
1. Subtracted from **3.** 20; 20; 80 **Exercises 5-35,** methods may vary. **5.** $a = 72$; M **7.** $d = 999$; M **9.** $e = 21$; M **11.** $g = 35$; M **13.** $r = 31$; P **15.** $b = 26$; M **17.** $q = 60$; M **19.** $y = 113$; P **21.** $a = 48$; M **23.** $x = 6.6$; P **25.** $y = 4.8$; P **27.** $c = 29$; P **29.** $x = 36.6$; P **31.** $m = 2.89$; P **33.** $v = 6.8$; P **35.** $p = 65$; P **37.** $a + 30 = 73$; $a = 43$ min **39.** $212 = 150 + s$; 62 empty seats

Pages 48-49
1. 6 **Exercises 3-13,** methods may vary. **3.** $n = 10$; M **5.** $k = 264$; P **7.** $a = 10$; M **9.** $x = 20$; M **11.** $r = 100$; M **13.** $x = 80$; M **15.** $x = 32$ **17.** $y = 2$ **19.** $x = 800$ **21.** $w = 51$ **23.** $50t = 230$; 4.6h **25.** $d = 206 - 80$ or $80 + d = 206$; 126 mi

Pages 52-53
1. How many inches are left for text? **3.** Answers may vary. **5.** $s = 8$ **7.** She added 3.5 instead of subtracting it. **9.** $p + 12 = 400$; $p = 388$ **11.** $\frac{p}{2} = 22$; $p = 44$ **Choose a Strategy** **13.** She had 25 coins of each kind.

Pages 54-55
1. 6 **3.** 10 **5.** 79 **7.** 19 **9.** 3 **11.** 62 **13.** 72 **15.** 4 **17.** 1.5 **19.** 6 **21.** 3.6 **23.** 5 **25.** 7 **27.** 1 **29.** 0 **31.** 3 **33.** 5 **35.** 7 **37.** [9] [−] 5 [=] [x] 2 [=] [M+] 2 [+] 6 [=] [x] 4 [+] [MRC] [=] **39.** $\frac{4 \times 3}{6} + 5$
41. $10 \times (15 + 20 \times 2) = 550$

Pages 56-57
1. 1; 52.50 **3.** 152.50 **5.** 12 **7.** 6 **9.** 47 **11.** 11 **13.** 29 **15.** 99 **17.** 7.2 **19.** 21.2 **21.** 14 **23.** 39 **25.** 13 **27.** 9 **29.** $12.75 **31.** $7.05

Pages 58-59
1. $5; $4 **3.** $4n + 2$ **5.** $5x$ **7.** 3z **9.** $\frac{6}{x}$ **11.** $\frac{x + 2}{6}$ **13.** $\frac{k + 5}{8}$ **15.** $4p + \frac{p}{10}$ **17.** $\ell + w$ **19.** $2(\ell + w)$ **21.** $5 + 4h$ **23.** $8(c + \$1.50)$

Pages 60-61
1. divide by 3 **3.** $x = 21$ **5.** $c = 208$ **7.** $n = 2$ **9.** $k = 4$ **11.** $m = 0$ **13.** $h = 300$ **15.** $K = 10$ **17.** $x = 0.5$ **19.** $h = 11$ **21.** $n = 12$ **23.** $3g + 7 = 25$; $g = 6$ **Explore Math** **25.** Yes **27.** Yes

Pages 62-63
1. Pressure **3.** 2 **5.** 4 atmospheres **7.** 132 feet **9.** $V = \frac{198}{0 + 33} = 6$ **11.** 16.5 feet **13.** 10 in.

Chapter 3

Pages 74-75
1. 10; 10 **3.** 100; 400 **5.** a **7.** 40 **9.** 70 **11.** 5 **13.** 800 **15.** 40 **17.** 8 **19.** 8 **21.** 700 **23.** 700 **25.** 90 **27.** 6 **29.** 900 **31.** 1,500 **33.** 60,000 **35.** 50 **37.** 1,200 **39.** 5 $50 bills **41.** $1,000
Explore Math
43.

Exercise No.	23	24	25	26
Dividend	4	4	2	4
Divisor	2	3	1	4
Quotient	2	1	1	0

45. No. It is one less than the number of zeros in the dividend minus the number of zeros in the divisor.

Pages 76-77
1. b **3.** b **Exercises 5-35,** answers may vary. Sample answers are given. **5.** $1{,}000 \div 20$; 50 **7.** $7{,}000 \div 100$; 70 **9.** $500 \div 20$; 25 **11.** $4{,}000 \div 40$; 100 **13.** $32{,}000 \div 800$; 40 **15.** $560 \div 80$; 7 **17.** $50\overline{)20{,}000}$; 400 **19.** $100\overline{)16{,}000}$; 160 **21.** $30\overline{)27{,}000}$; 900 **23.** $22\overline{)22{,}000}$; 1,000 **25.** $500\overline{)35{,}000}$; 70 **27.** $64\overline{)6{,}400}$; 100 **29.** $\frac{35{,}000}{700}$; 50 **31.** $\frac{70{,}000}{200}$; 350 **33.** $\frac{26{,}000}{13}$; 2,000 **35.** $\frac{37{,}000}{37}$; 1,000 **37.** If the divisor is unchanged, using an approximate dividend that is larger than the actual dividend will result in an estimated quotient that is larger than the actual quotient. The reverse is also true. A dividend approximated smaller than actual yields an estimated quotient smaller than the actual quotient. If the dividend is unchanged, using an approximate divisor that is larger than the actual will result in an estimated quotient that is smaller than the actual. And, a smaller approximated divisor yields an estimated quotient larger than the actual. If both the dividend and the divisor are approximated, one can't tell without further calculation.

Pages 78-79
1. $1{,}800 \div 60$; 30 **3.** Too large **5.** 93.33 **7.** 613.88 **9.** 37 **11.** 33 **13.** 73.49; 73 R30; $73\frac{30}{61}$

Pages 78-79 (continued)
15. 105.09; 105 R4; $105\frac{4}{47}$ **17.** 496.78; 496 R14; $496\frac{7}{9}$ **19.** 842.32; 842 R12; $842\frac{6}{19}$ **21.** 643.29; 643 R11; $643\frac{11}{38}$ **23.** 529.20; 529 R119; $529\frac{119}{610}$ **25.** 229.05; 229 R2; $229\frac{2}{43}$ **27.** 1,423 **29.** 81.52; 81 R449; $81\frac{449}{871}$ **31.** 214.05; 214 R20; $214\frac{20}{367}$ **33.** 40 **35.** 54 **37.** 120 **39.** 15 free throws **41.** 74 points **43.** 30

Pages 80-81
1. 19 chairs **3.** 3 people **5.** $4.50 per pair **7.** 16 buses **Choose a Strategy** **9.** $24.90

Pages 82-83
1. 6.78 **3.** 0.00093 **5.** 0.21 **7.** 0.07 **9.** 32.76 **11.** 0.07 **13.** 21.4 **15.** 0.09 **17.** 0.02 **19.** 0.05 **21.** 0.04 **23.** 0.03 **25.** No, the decimal is off; 12.7 **27.** Yes, it is exact **29.** No, the decimal is off; 1.29 **31.** 13.2 **33.** 62.5 **35.** 36.55 **37.** 60.905 **39.** 73.44 **41.** 2.04 **43.** 10.35 kilowatt hours **45.** 0.35 kilowatt hours; no, because the customer wouldn't be using as much electricity if he/she were sleeping or were at work.

Pages 84-85
1. 0.04 **3.** 0.05 **5.** $0.\overline{148}$ **7.** 0.875 **9.** 0.24 **11.** 0.035 **13.** $0.\overline{63}$ **15.** 0.15625 **17.** $0.\overline{3}$ **19.** 0.25 **21.** $0.\overline{814}$ **23.** $0.\overline{27}$ **25.** $0.8\overline{3}$ **27.** $0.4\overline{6}$ **29.** $0.0\overline{5}$ **31.** $0.0\overline{7}$ **33.** $0.2\overline{6}$ **35.** $0.91\overline{6}$ **37.** $0.22\overline{7}$ **39.** $0.291\overline{6}$ **41.** 0.9375 **45.** $\frac{52}{88}$ or $\frac{13}{22}$; $0.5\overline{90}$

45. What fraction of the band plays woodwinds? $\frac{12}{25}$

Pages 88-89
1. 4,500.0 **3.** 700.0 **5.** 0.00167 **7.** 892.5 **9.** 89,250 **11.** 0.8925 **13.** 4.5 **15.** 450 **17.** 0.0045 **19.** 0.3 **21.** 30 **23.** 0.0003 **25.** $25.\overline{25}$ **27.** $2{,}525.\overline{25}$ **29.** $0.0\overline{25}$ **35.** 31.1 g **37.** 2,270 g **Skills Review** **1.** 34 **3.** 2 **5.** 5 **7.** 110

Pages 90-91
1. 10 **3.** 100 **5.** 0.1207 **7.** $0.19 **9.** $0.19 **11.** 0.5 **13.** 223.4 **15.** 2.4 **17.** 266.667 **19.** 0.011 **21.** 2.45 **Exercises 23-29,** methods may vary. **23.** 43.75; P **25.** 3.04; C **27.** 0.158; M **29.** 107.12; P **31.** Kookie granola bar **33.** $0.97 **35.** 1.39 lb

Pages 92-93
1. Estimate **3.** Exact **5.** Correct **7.** Incorrect

Pages 94-95
1. $2.3n$ **3.** $n + 2.3$ **5.** Yes **7.** Yes **9.** $3.5k$ **11.** $x + 0.45$ **13.** $\frac{3.4}{t}$ **15.** $5.4 - a$ **17.** $z - 5.6$ **19.** $0.42 - x$ **21.** $\frac{4.5}{c}$ **23.** $66.4 - r$ **25.** $12.50c + 14.75$ **27.** $14.75d$ **29.** $12.50m + 14.75n$ **31.** The number of books sold at $1.25 each for a total of n dollars. **33.** The change received from $1.25 for an item costing n dollars.

Pages 96-97
1. Division **3.** Multiplication **5.** No; $x = 20.52$ **7.** $x = 1.85$ **9.** $z = 20.073$ **11.** $b = 0.050$ **13.** $n = 14.472$ **15.** $r = 0.164$ **17.** $y = 1.63$ **19.** $d = 86.8$ **21.** $c = 35.45$ **23.** $e = 2.34$ **25.** $x = 16.66$ **27.** $m = 2.4$ **29.** $157.95 **31.** The answer does not check exactly; the product 3.7 x 2.297 = 8.4989 instead of 8.5 because the answer is rounded.

Pages 98-99
1. a **3.** 201.4 feet per second **5.** 14.088 miles per hour **Choose a Strategy** **7.** 5/18; 6/15; 9/10; 10/9 **9.** 1982; 1983; 1986; 1989

Chapter 4

Pages 114-117
1. Point **3.** Segment **5.** True **Exercises 7-29,** answers may vary. Samples are given.
7. $\overline{AB}$, $\overline{CD}$; $\overline{GH}$ **9.** $\overleftrightarrow{GH}$ and $\overleftrightarrow{AE}$; $\overleftrightarrow{AG}$ and $\overleftrightarrow{CE}$ **11.** A **13.** $\overleftrightarrow{CE}$ and $\overleftrightarrow{GI}$ **15.** $\overleftrightarrow{GF}$ **17.** $\overleftrightarrow{SJ}$ and $\overleftrightarrow{JK}$; $\overleftrightarrow{SN}$ and $\overleftrightarrow{KN}$; $\overleftrightarrow{RL}$ and $\overleftrightarrow{LK}$ **19.** $\overleftrightarrow{SJ}$ and $\overleftrightarrow{NK}$; $\overleftrightarrow{SN}$ and $\overleftrightarrow{JK}$; $\overleftrightarrow{RP}$ and $\overleftrightarrow{LM}$ **21.** $\overleftrightarrow{JR}$ and $\overleftrightarrow{PM}$ **31.** 3 points **33.** 10 points **35.** Four **37.** 1 line **39.** 28 segments **Skills Review** **1.** 100 **3.** 4,000 **5.** 9,000,000 **7.** 16.5 **9.** 3.75 **11.** 2.2 **13.** 38.2 **15.** 1,473.25 **17.** 120 **19.** 165 **21.** 20

Pages 118-119
1. Right angle **3.** Point R **Exercises 5-11,** answers may vary. Samples are given. **5.** $\angle WUY$ and $\angle YUV$ **7.** $\angle WUY$ and $\angle YUZ$ **9.** $\angle YUV$ and $\angle VUZ$ **11.** $\angle YUZ$ and $\angle YUX$ **13.** False **15.** True **17.** True **19.** Answers may vary. **21.** 2 pairs **23.** No. If an angle has a measure less than 90°, it has a complement, and the sum of their measures is 90°. If an angle has a measure greater than 90°, it does not have a complement. The sum of its measure and the measure of any other angle will be greater than 90°.

Pages 120-121
1. 120° **3.** Scalene **Exercises 5-11,** methods may vary. **5.** P; 92° **7.** P or C; 25° **9.** M; 60° **11.** P or C; 54° **13.** Obtuse; isosceles **15.** Obtuse; scalene **17.** Acute; equilateral **19.** Right; scalene **21.** Never true **23.** Sometimes true

Pages 122-123
1. Square **3.** Square **5.** True **7.** False **9.** True **19.** White: rectangle; large orange: square; small orange; triangle; large yellow: square; small yellow: triangle; blue: trapezoid **21.** Tan: triangle and square (some tan pieces are not polygons because of curves); red: parallelogram; orange: parallelogram; yellow: triangle; brown: triangle; blue: trapezoid; green: not polygons (because of curves)

Pages 126-127

1. a **3.** *N* **5.** Answer may vary. Sample: $\widehat{AC}$ **7.** $\angle BNA$; $\angle ANC$ **9.** 122° **11.** $\widehat{AD}$; *B*. **13.** $\angle ANB$ **19.** 5 cm **21.** 360° **Explore Math 23.** They become more circular.

Pages 128-129

1. Congruent **3.** 2 units left, 2 units down **11.** 2 units left, 4 units down

Pages 130-133

1. a **3.** Reflection or rotation **5.** Reflection or rotation **7.** Reflection or rotation **9.** Rotation

Pages 136-139

1. construction **3.** bisector

Pages 140-141

1. 90° **9.** Infinitely many

Pages 142-143

1. $\overline{PR}$ or $\angle Q$ **3.** $\overline{RQ}$ or $\angle P$ **17.** Yes

Pages 144-145

1. Yes; 3 in., 4 in., 5 in. **3.** 3 cm **5.** 21 mm **7.** 5 cm; 6 cm; 7 cm; 8 cm; 9 cm **Choose a Strategy 9.** 1 in., 1 in., 2 in.; 1 in., 1 in.; 3 in., 1 in., 1 in. 4 in.; 1 in., 1 in., 5 in.; 1 in., 2 in., 3 in.; 1 in., 2 in.; 4 in.; 1 in., 2 in., 5 in., 1 in.; 3 in., 4 in.; 3 in., 5 in.; 1 in., 4 in., 5 in.; 2 in., 2 in., 4 in.; 2 in., 2 in., 5 in.; 2 in., 3 in., 5 in.; yes

Chapter 5

Pages 156-157

1. Yes; no **3.** Yes **5.** 3, 5 **7.** 2, 3, 9 **9.** 2, 3, 5, 10 **11.** 2, 3, 5, 10 **13.** 3, 5, 9 **15.** None **17.** 2, 3, 5 10 **19.** 3 **21.** 3, 5 **23.** 5 **25.** 2, 3, 5, 9, 10 **27.** 2, 3, 5, 9, 10 **29.** None **31.** 2 **33.** 3 **35.** 2 **37.** 2, 3, 9 **39.** 2, 3 **41.** 765 **Explore Math 43.** 465; 342; 357; 1,140; 1,692; 1,020; 297; 1,935; 360; 4,095; 600; 72; 11,001; 16,302; 7,275; 1,845; 212,310; 302,175; 8,003,520

Pages 158-159

1. 8^3 **3.** 15^6 **5.** 5 x 5 x 5; 125 **7.** 4; 4 **9.** 16; M **11.** 8; P **13.** 8; M **15.** 49; M **17.** 625; P **19.** 64; P **21.** 121; M **23.** 1; M **25.** 22; M **27.** 512; P **29.** 15; M **31.** 72; M **33.** 800; P **35.** 3,456; P **37.** 5,832; P **39.** 78,125 **41.** 2,401 **43.** 262,144 **45.** 6,561 **47.** $y \times y$ **49.** $a \times a \times a \times a \times a$ **51.** r^4 **Explore Math 53.** (10 x 10) x (10 x 10 x 10 x 10) = 10^6

Pages 160-163

1. 2, 3, 5, 7, 11, 13, 17, 19, 23, 29 **3.** 13 **5.** 10 **7.** P **9.** P **11.** C **13.** P **15.** C **17.** C **19.** P **21.** C **23.** C **25.** C **27.** C **29.** C **31.** P **33.** C **35.** C **37.** 2 × 5 × 3; no **39.** Answers may vary. Sample: 5 × 2; yes; 3 × 2 **41.** Answers may vary. Sample: 3 + 2; yes; 5 + 2 **43.** 2,003 **45.** No **47.** Yes; yes; yes; yes; yes **49.** C; 2, 3 **51.** P **53.** C; 2 **55.** C; 5 **57.** C; 3 **59.** P **61.** P **63.** C **65.** P **67.** No; 6 + 7 + 8 = 21. 21 is divisible by 3. **69.** 3 **71.** 7 **73.** 31 **75.** 211 **77.** 2,311 **79.** 30,031 **81.** The prime numbers from 1-100; 2, 3, 5, 7, 11, 13, 17, 19, 23, 29, 31, 37, 41, 43, 47, 53, 59, 61, 67, 71, 73, 79, 83, 89, 97 **Skills Review 1.** 268.5 **3.** 1,700.0 **5.** 1.3 **7.** 0.03

Pages 164-165

1. 2, 5, 5 **3.** 6, 3, 2, 2, 2 **5.** c **7.** 2^5 **9.** $2^2 \times 3 \times 7$ **11.** $2^2 \times 5^2$ **13.** $2^2 \times 23$ **15.** $3^2 \times 7$ **17.** $2^4 \times 7$ **19.** $2^3 \times 7$ **21.** 3 × 31 **23.** 2^8 **25.** 11^2 **27.** 2 × 5 × 37 **29.** $2^2 \times 5 \times 11$ **31.** 5 × 103 **33.** $2^3 \times 3 \times 7$ **35.** $2^3 \times 7 \times 11^2$ **37.** They are the same factors. **39.** All of the exponents are even numbers. $2^2 \times 3^2$; 7^2; $2^4 \times 5^2$

Pages 168-169

1. 1, 2, 3, 6, 9, 18 **3.** 1, 2, 3, 4, 6, 8, 12, 24 **5.** 12 **7.** 3 **9.** 9 **11.** 9 **13.** 1 **15.** 14 **17.** 8 **19.** 3 **21.** 4 **23.** 15 **25.** 15 **27.** 4 **29.** 8 **31.** 1 **33.** 18 **35.** 6 feet

Pages 170-171

1. 63 **3.** 70 **5.** 120 **7.** 30 **9.** 48 **11.** 55 **13.** 28 **15.** 60 **17.** 15 **19.** 220 **21.** 150 **23.** 600 **25.** 360 **27.** 60 **29.** 300 **31.** 7; 14 **33.** 5; 175 **35.** 3; 90 **37.** 6; 120. **39.** 7; 49 **41.** 16; 96 **43.** *ab* **45.** One solution is 6 and 120.

Pages 172-173

1. 7 tables

3.

Tables for 6	Tables for 10	Students
9	7	124
10	6	120
11	5	116
12	4	112
13	3	108
14	2	104
15	1	100

5. 2 lunches **7.** 31 students **Choose a Strategy 9.** Caryn

Pages 174-175

1. 11; 24 **3.** 9; 21 **5.** 8 **7.** 5 **9.** 6 **11.** 10 **13.** 0-5 **15.** 0-6 **17.** 7 **19.** 5 **21.** 6 **23.** 121 **25.** 14,641 **27.** 78 **29.** 161,051; the entires in the Pascal Triangle (row 5) are 2-digit numbers. If you multiplied the long way, you would have to "carry" and rename. If you "carry" and rename in row 5 you will get 161,051. **Explore Math 31.** They form symmetric and inverted triangular patterns. **33.** They also form symmetric and inverted triangular patterns.

Pages 176-177

1. 600 cartons **3.** 500 cartons; 15,000 boxes **5.** Yes; 491 cartons **7.** 16 + 170; 36 + 150

Chapter 6

Pages 188-189

1. 8; 20 3. 6 5. 2; no 7. 7; no 9. 1; yes 11. 3 13. 2 15. 3 17. 9 19. 10 21. 5 23. 8 25. 6; 12; 15 27. 20; 30; 36 29. $\frac{4}{5}$ 31. $\frac{7}{10}$ 33. $\frac{3}{8}$ 35. $\frac{7}{16}$ 37. $\frac{1}{2}$ 39. $\frac{27}{56}$ 41. $\frac{3}{4} = \frac{9}{12} = \frac{45}{60}$ 43. $\frac{1}{4}$

Pages 190-191

1. 11 3. 1; 11 5. 14 7. $2\frac{1}{2}$ 9. 3 11. $1\frac{1}{3}$ 13. $3\frac{4}{5}$ 15. 4 17. $4\frac{1}{2}$ 19. $\frac{33}{4}$ 21. $\frac{19}{16}$ 23. $\frac{127}{12}$ 25. $\frac{39}{5}$ 27. $\frac{23}{4}$ 29. $\frac{62}{10}$ 31. $\frac{2}{3}$ 33. $1\frac{2}{5}$ 35. $9\frac{2}{3}$ 37. $\frac{1}{8}$ 39. $2\frac{7}{8}$ 41. 3 43. $\frac{1}{3}$ 45. $6\frac{1}{7}$ 47. $\frac{4}{5}$ 49. $6\frac{1}{2}$ 51. $\frac{15}{32}$ 53. 8 55. $1\frac{1}{3}$ feet **Skills Review** 1. 8 3. 24 5. 45 7. 36 9. 15

Pages 192-193

1. 3, 2; no 3. $\frac{20}{30}, \frac{21}{30}$ 5. $1\frac{3}{21}, \frac{7}{21}$ 7. $\frac{3}{12}, \frac{10}{12}, \frac{8}{12}$ 9. < 11. < 13. > 15. > 17. > 19. > 21. = 23. < 25. $\frac{1}{2}, \frac{3}{4}, \frac{5}{6}$ 27. $\frac{5}{5}, 1\frac{7}{8}, 2$ 29. $\frac{2}{4}, \frac{12}{16}, \frac{7}{8}$ 31. $\frac{36}{8}, 4\frac{7}{10}, 4\frac{9}{12}$ 33. $3.625, 3.5\overline{6}$; > 35. $1.65, 1.\overline{6}$; < 37. $2\frac{3}{4}$ in. 39. 10 months

Pages 194-195

1. Greater than $\frac{1}{2}$ 3. Less than $\frac{1}{2}$ 5. Greater than $\frac{1}{2}$ 7. 2 + 6 = 8 9. 11 − 9 = 2 11. *a* 13. *c* 15. *b* 17. *c* 19. *a* 21. *b* 23. *c* **Exercises 25-43,** estimates may vary. 25. <1; C 27. >1; C 29. 2 + 3 = 5; R 31. 8 + 3 = 11; R 33. 8 − 3 = 5; W 35. 12 − 10 = 2; R 37. 16 − 7 = 9; R 39. 9 + 11 = 20: R 41. 30 - 1 = 29; R 43. $>\frac{3}{4}$; C 45. No, estimate for flour is 7 cups. 47. 50 x 0.60 = 30; she made about $30.00.

Pages 196-199

1. 10; 5 3. 8; 5; 13 5. 2 7. 5 9. You get the same fraction. 11. 7 13. $11\frac{8}{9}$ 15. $7\frac{7}{8}$ 17. $15\frac{14}{15}$ 19. $\frac{2}{3}$ 21. $1\frac{1}{2}$ 23. $1\frac{4}{15}$ 25. $\frac{7}{15}$ 27. $\frac{11}{18}$ 29. $1\frac{11}{45}$ **Exercises 31-37,** method may vary. 31. 1; M 33. 13; M 35. $12\frac{1}{4}$; M 37. 11; P 39. $1\frac{2}{3}$ 41. $1\frac{5}{24}$ 43. $9\frac{1}{6}$ 45. $1\frac{41}{90}$ 47. No 49. 6 tubes; add $1\frac{1}{8} + 1\frac{1}{8} \ldots$ (6) 51. 3 tubes

Pages 202-203

1. 8; 1 3. 4; 1 5. The difference of equal fractions equals zero. 7. $\frac{5}{8}$ 9. $6\frac{1}{12}$ 11. $10\frac{11}{24}$ 13. $9\frac{9}{20}$ 15. $2\frac{1}{15}$ 17. $22\frac{3}{10}$ 19. $1\frac{1}{6}$ 21. $2\frac{1}{9}$ 23. 2 25. $\frac{61}{80}$ 27. $\frac{17}{36}$ 29. 17 31. $\frac{1}{8}$ 33. $\frac{5}{8}$

Pages 204-205

1. 4 3. 10; 22 5. $\frac{1}{2}$ 7. $6\frac{7}{10}$ 9. $1\frac{8}{15}$ 11. $5\frac{1}{4}$ 13. $2\frac{7}{15}$ 15. $4\frac{11}{12}$ 17. $20\frac{2}{3}$ 19. $4\frac{3}{4}$ 21. $\frac{7}{16}$ 23. $2\frac{2}{3}$ 25. $5\frac{17}{40}$ 27. $1\frac{13}{15}$ 29. $\frac{5}{12}$ 31. $13\frac{9}{10}$ 33. $4\frac{1}{8}$ 35. $2\frac{33}{40}$ 37. $1\frac{3}{4}$ inches **Choose a Strategy** 39. $\frac{1}{6}$ 41. $\frac{1}{6}, \frac{1}{8}$

Pages 206-207

1. How much open space is left above the cassette deck? 3. $5\frac{13}{16}$ inches 5. Subtraction 7. $n = \frac{13}{16}$ 9. $h - \frac{5}{8} = 6\frac{3}{4}$; $h = 7\frac{3}{8}$ in. 11. $t = 14 + \frac{3}{4} + \frac{3}{4} + \frac{3}{4}$; $t = 16\frac{1}{4}$ in. 13. $s = \frac{86}{8}$; $s = 10\frac{3}{4}$; he has 11 stacks

Pages 208-211

1. $\frac{1}{12}$ 3. $\frac{5}{8}$ 5. $\frac{13}{2}, \frac{2}{13}$ 7. $\frac{6}{1}, \frac{1}{6}$ 9. $\frac{29}{8}, \frac{8}{29}$ 11. $\frac{5}{3} \times \frac{9}{10}, \frac{3}{2}$; $1\frac{1}{2}$ 13. $\frac{9}{160}$ 15. $\frac{1}{3}$ 17. $\frac{7}{20}$ 19. $11\frac{5}{18}$ 21. 6 23. $\frac{3}{10}$ 25. $9\frac{2}{5}$ 27. $12\frac{3}{4}$ **Exercises 29-43,** method choices may vary. 29. 0; M 31. $\frac{7}{15}$; P 33. 8; M 35. $3\frac{1}{2}$; P 37. 1; M 39. $\frac{7}{10}$; M 41. $9\frac{1}{3}$; P 43. $5\frac{3}{10}$; P 45. Less than 1; the product of two fractions less than 1 will also be less than 1. 47. 40 to 48; 42 49. 3 to 8; $5\frac{3}{5}$ 51. 2 to 6; 3 53. 0 to 6; 1 55. $\frac{3}{16}$ 57. $2\frac{1}{60}$ 59. $\frac{3}{20}$ 61. $5\frac{3}{4}$ 63. $\frac{1}{8}$ 65. $8\frac{3}{4}$ **Choose a Strategy** 67. No; it is not divisible by 2. 69. 301 marbles

Pages 212-213

1. 800 tickets 3. 1,000 tickets 5. $2\frac{2}{3}$ km 7. 72 skiers

Pages 214-217

1. 5 3. 5 5. 1; 4 7. 19; 19; 2; 4; $12\frac{2}{3}$ 9. 15; 5; 15; 8; 3; 5; $1\frac{5}{40}$ 11. 12 13. $\frac{4}{35}$ 15. $4\frac{2}{7}$ 17. $\frac{1}{16}$ 19. $\frac{11}{24}$ 21. $3\frac{1}{2}$ 23. $2\frac{2}{7}$ 25. $\frac{1}{10}$ 27. $3\frac{3}{35}$ 29. $\frac{8}{9}$ 31. $\frac{1}{24}$ 33. $\frac{8}{15}$ 35. $1\frac{3}{4}$ 37. 96 39. $1\frac{1}{8}$ 41. $51\frac{3}{4}$ 43. $\frac{5}{18}$ 45. 135 beats/minute 47. No, he is 39 beats over his safe rate of 141. 49. 2,400 steps 51. $41\frac{19}{21}$ times 53. $62\frac{6}{7}$ times **Explore Math** 55. <1; $\frac{3}{4}$ 57. >1; $6\frac{2}{3}$ 59. = 1 63. If the divisor is less than the dividend, the quotient is greater than 1. If the divisor equals the dividend, the quotient is 1. If the divisor is greater than the dividend, the quotient is less than 1.

Pages 218-219

1. $\frac{5}{4}$ 3. $\frac{7}{19}$ 5. $\frac{5}{2}$ 7. $\frac{5}{1}$ 9. $b = 24$ 11. $k = 1\frac{7}{12}$ 13. $m = 8$ 15. $n = 21$ 17. $t = 4$ 19. $x = \frac{1}{3}$ 21. $m = \frac{1}{12}$ 23. $h = 5$ 25. $w = \frac{1}{12}$ 27. $a = 0$ 29. $a = \frac{2}{5}$ 31. $x = 4$

33. $x = 3\frac{3}{8}$ **35.** $x = 1\frac{3}{8}$ **37.** $d = \frac{33}{40}$ **39.** $b = \frac{1}{6}$ **41.** 6 rows **43.** 2 rows

Pages 220-221
1. Each term is found by adding 5,700 to the preceding term. 28,500; 34,200 **3.** Multiply by $\frac{1}{3}$; $\frac{1}{27}$, $\frac{1}{81}$, $\frac{1}{243}$ **5.** Add $\frac{5}{6}$; $\frac{17}{6}$, $\frac{22}{6}$, $\frac{27}{6}$ **7.** Years $15\frac{3}{4}$, 21; amount left $\frac{1}{8}$, $\frac{1}{16}$ **9.** 16 hours

Chapter 7

Pages 232-235
1. Divide **3.** Multiply **5.** Multiply **7.** 880 **9.** Feet (or yards) **11.** 27 cu ft **13.** 1 ft **15.** 120 sq ft **17.** 90 **19.** 45 **21.** 6.5 **23.** 1.5 **25.** 2.6 **27.** Estimate may vary. $2\frac{3}{4}$ in. **29.** 16 sq in. **31.** 13 sq in. **33.** $25\frac{1}{2}$ sq in. **35.** 24 cu in. **37.** Overestimate, or the plant may not fit. It also needs room to grow. **39.** Overestimate, or the sand may not fit **41.** 28 inches **43.** About 24.94 trillion miles **Skills Review 1.** $\frac{5}{8}$ **3.** $174\frac{7}{40}$ **5.** $9\frac{2}{21}$

Pages 236-237
1. Pound **3.** Cup **5.** 38 **7.** 1 oz **9.** 20 qt **11.** 18 **13.** 12; 1 **15.** 9 **17.** 17 **19.** 134 **21.** 6; 1 **23.** 5,000 **25.** 86.6 **27.** 78 qt **29.** 1.25 gal **31.** 14.625 gal

Pages 238-239
1. Weights of *Mayflower* and *Titanic* **3.** 30 tons **5.** Too little information **Choose a Strategy 7.** 2 hr 40 min

Pages 240-241
1. mm **3.** km **5.** Meter **7.** Meter **9.** Liter **11.** 10 **13.** 0.001 **15.** 1,000 **17.** 1,000 **19.** 0.01 **21.** 100 **23.** 1,000 **25.** mL, L, kL **27.** mm, cm, m, km **29** 40 g **31.** 1,000 cm^3 **33.** 21.5 cm

Pages 242-245
1. m **3.** cm^2 **5.** m^3 **7.** 25 **9.** 0.3 **11.** 7,000,000,000 **13.** 236.5 **15.** 20,000,000 **17.** 54.5 **19.** 330,000 **21.** 245,000,000 **23.** 26 mm^2 **25.** 14 cm^2 **27.** 10 m^2 **29.** 20 m^3 **31.** 2.5 m by 1 m **33.** 3 m by 4 m by 5 m **Explore Math 35.** 12 cubic centimeters **37.** Yes

Pages 248-249
1. 700 mL **3.** 5 mL **5.** 4.325 **7.** 7.35 **9.** 47.81 **11.** 56 **13.** 1,520 **15.** 570 **17.** 67 **19.** 40.90 **21.** 0.032 **23.** 0.674 **25.** 2,800 **27.** 0.005 **29.** 6,500,00 L **31.** 10¢ per serving

Pages 250-251
1. Ounce **3.** Kilogram **5.** A mile **7.** 12 yd **9.** 6 qt **11.** 3 L **13.** 200 mL **15.** 12.5 kilometers

Pages 252-253
1. 385 mL **3.** 8 g **5.** 0.5 cm **7.** cm; $\frac{1}{2}$ cm **9.** km; 0.005 km **11.** mm; 0.5 mm **13.** m; 0.0005 m **15.** L; 0.5L **17.** yd; $\frac{5}{16}$ yd **19.** 12 cm **21.** $6\frac{3}{4}$ in. **23.** 48 ft **25.** 43 cm **27.** 34.5 km **29.** 2.45 cm **31.** 19.2 L **33.** 3 ft **35.** 3.12 mL **37.** 8 ft 2 in.

Pages 254-255
1. 18:15 **3.** 12:00 **5.** 15:35 **7.** 75 **9.** 15 **11.** 13 h 8 min **13.** 2 h 50 min **15.** 8 h 45 min **17.** 3 h **19.** 4 h 47 min **21.** Thursday; Friday

Chapter 8

Pages 270-271
1. $\frac{7}{12}$ **3.** $\frac{7}{19}$ **5.** 6; 6; 8; 15 **7.** 6; 4; 9; 72 **Exercises 9-33,** answers may vary. Samples are given. **9.** $\frac{40}{30}$, $\frac{4}{3}$, $\frac{8}{6}$ **11.** $\frac{18}{24}$, $\frac{6}{8}$, $\frac{9}{12}$ **13.** $\frac{32}{20}$, $\frac{16}{10}$, $\frac{8}{5}$ **15.** $\frac{10}{9}$, $\frac{20}{18}$, $\frac{30}{27}$, $\frac{40}{36}$ **17.** $\frac{12}{3}$, $\frac{4}{1}$, $\frac{8}{2}$, $\frac{16}{4}$ **19.** $\frac{30}{100}$, $\frac{3}{10}$, $\frac{6}{20}$, $\frac{9}{30}$ **21.** $\frac{64}{40}$, $\frac{8}{5}$, $\frac{16}{10}$, $\frac{24}{15}$ **23.** $\frac{15}{45}$, $\frac{1}{3}$, $\frac{2}{6}$, $\frac{3}{9}$ **25.** $\frac{6}{16}$, $\frac{3}{8}$, $\frac{9}{24}$, $\frac{12}{32}$ **27.** $\frac{12}{8}$, $\frac{3}{2}$, $\frac{6}{4}$, $\frac{9}{6}$ **29.** $\frac{18}{27}$, $\frac{2}{3}$, $\frac{4}{6}$, $\frac{6}{9}$ **31.** $\frac{2}{9}$, $\frac{4}{8}$, $\frac{6}{27}$, $\frac{8}{36}$ **33.** $\frac{30}{36}$, $\frac{5}{6}$, $\frac{10}{12}$, $\frac{15}{18}$ **35.** $\frac{15}{26}$, $\frac{15}{11}$

Pages 272-273
1. Quantities **3.** Yes **5.** Yes **7.** a; $n = 12$ **9.** a; $x = 4$ **11.** b; $n = 7$ **13.** a; $x = 6$ **15.** $n = 30$ **17.** $x = 4$ **19.** $x = 6.3$ **21.** $n = 20$ **23.** $n = 50$ **25.** $n = 0.9$ **27.** $m = 30$ **29.** $n = 5$ **31.** $x = 2$ **33.** $n = 108$ **35.** $s = 1$ **37.** $d = 1.2$ **39.** $\frac{100}{1.48} = \frac{2,000}{s}$; $s = 29.6$ Solomon Island dollars **41.** $\frac{1}{2} = \frac{4}{8}$, $\frac{2}{4} = \frac{8}{16}$, $\frac{1}{2} = \frac{8}{16}$, $\frac{1}{8} = \frac{2}{16}$

Pages 274-275
1. No; 28, 27 **3.** $20a = 60$; $a = 3$ **5.** $t = 24$ **7.** $r = 21$ **9.** $x = 1$ **11.** $m = 40$ **13.** $x = 18$ **15.** $x = 6$ **17.** $n = 6$ **19.** $x = 4$ **21.** $t = 16$ **23.** $n = 5$ **Exercises 25-43,** method choices may vary. **25.** $n = 7$; M **27.** $z = 35$; C, P **29.** $y = 60$; P, C **31.** $m = 12$; M **33.** $t = 4$; P, C **35.** $d = 1.8$; M **37.** $n = 6$; M **39.** $a = 16$; M **41.** $t = 14$; M **43.** $x = 4$; M **45.** $\frac{35}{a} = \frac{5}{13}$; $a = 91$ times **47.** No

Pages 276-277
1. $\frac{156}{6} = \frac{234}{g}$; $g = 9$ gal **3.** $\frac{0.96}{1} = \frac{x}{18.5}$; \$17.76 **5.** $\frac{133}{1} = \frac{y}{1500}$; 199,500 yen **Choose a Strategy 7.** 3; 12; 24; 48

Pages 278-281
1. $\angle J$ **3.** $\angle T$ **5.** $\overline{HL}$ **7.** b **9.** Yes **11.** No **13.** $p = 25$ **15.** $q = 32$ **17.** $x = 7.5$; $y = 4.5$ **19.** $x = 15$; $y = 4.8$

Pages 278-281 (continued)
21. 8 m **23.** 10 in. **25.** Equilateral triangles; regular polygons of any kind. All angles and sides are equal.

Pages 284-285
1. $\frac{4}{\ell}=\frac{1}{1.5}$ **3.** $\frac{3}{w}=\frac{1}{1.5}$ **5.** $\ell = 6$ m **7.** $w = 4.5$ m **9.** $\ell = 21$ m; $w = 24$ m **11.** $\ell = 37.5$ m; $w = 48$ **13.** $\ell =$ 12 m; $w = 15.75$ m **15.** $x = 18$ **17.** $x = 24$ **19.** $x = 4\frac{2}{3}$ **21.** $x = 24$ **23.** 120 ft **Explore Math 25.** Steel tape measure

Pages 286-287
1. About twice as long (b) **3.** $\frac{7.2}{x} = \frac{2.4}{9}$; $x = 27$ km **5.** 1.8 cm; 6.75 km **Choose a Strategy 7.** 2 h 20 min **9.** 40 min

Pages 288-291
1. $\frac{60}{100}$, 60% **3.** $\frac{8}{100}$; 8% **5.** $\frac{90}{100}$ **7.** $\frac{1}{100}$ **9.** 10% **11.** 18% **13.** a **15.** $\frac{19}{100}$ **17.** $\frac{15}{100}$ **19.** $\frac{50}{100}$ **21.** $\frac{100}{100}$ **23.** 73% **25.** 40% **27.** 95% **29.** 20% **31.** 52% **33.** 60% **35.** $\frac{15}{100}=\frac{x}{20}$; $x = 3$ **37.** $\frac{30}{150}=\frac{n}{100}$; $n = 20$ **39.** $\frac{15}{20}=\frac{n}{100}$; $n = 75$ **41.** $\frac{5}{n}=\frac{10}{100}$; $n = 50$ **43.** $\frac{63}{n}=\frac{70}{100}$; $n = 90$ **45.** $\frac{35}{100}=\frac{x}{80}$; $x = 28$ **Exercises 47-53,** method choices may vary. **47.** 28; M, P **49.** 8%; C, P **51.** 75% **53.** 100; M **55.** 74% **57.** Saturday **59.** 40% **61.** Emilio (paid $96) **Skills Review 1.** 4 **3.** 9 **5.** 7 **7.** 1 **9.** 2 **11.** 1 **13.** 6 **15.** 180 **17.** 36 **19.** 60 **21.** 12 **23.** 120

Chapter 9

Pages 302-303
1. 0.18; 18% **3.** 0.5; 50% **5.** 0.5 or $\frac{1}{2}$ **7.** 100 **9.** 77% **11.** 8% **13.** 90% **15.** 142% **17.** 87.5% **19.** 99.8% **21.** 100% **23.** 40.9% **25.** 42% **27.** 300% **29.** 0.25% **31.** 3% **33.** 0.42 **35.** 0.06 **37.** 0.18 **39.** 0.3 **41.** 1.25 **43.** 0.008 **45.** 1 **47.** 0.168 **49.** 0.31 **51.** 0.0083 **53.** 0.0027 **55.** 0 **57.** 0.1384 **59.** 0.72% 7.2% 0.72 **61.** 450% 5 510% **63.** 0.1% 1% 0.1 1 **65.** 23% **67.** 11%

Pages 304-307
1. 12; 3 **3.** 100; 100 **5.** 50 **7.** $8\overline{)5}$ **9.** 9% **11.** 10% **13.** 50% **15.** 25% **17.** 112% **19.** 0.7% **21.** 250% **23.** 2.5% **25.** 180% **27.** 225% **29.** 42.5% **31.** $\frac{2}{5}$ **33.** $\frac{7}{100}$ **35.** $1\frac{123}{1{,}000}$ **37.** $\frac{31}{100}$ **39.** $\frac{13}{25}$ **41.** $\frac{19}{20}$ **43.** $\frac{27}{40}$ **45.** $4\frac{1}{4}$ **47.** $\frac{251}{300}$ **49.** $\frac{7}{8}$ **51.** $\frac{3}{4}$ **53.** 0.25 **55.** $\frac{1}{3}$ **57.** $\frac{2}{3}$ **59.** $\frac{1}{5}$ **61.** 0.125 **63.** $\frac{3}{8}$ **65.** $\frac{5}{8}$ **67.** 0.875 **69.** $\frac{11}{20}$ **71.** $12\frac{1}{2}$% **Explore Math 73.** greater than 50%: 10, 14, 16, 17, 18, 21; less than 50%: 9, 11, 12, 15, 19, 20, 22; equal to 50%: 13 **75.** Less **77.** Less **79.** Less **81.** Greater **83.** If 2 x numerator < denominator, fraction < 50%; if 2 x numerator = denominator, fraction = 50%; if 2 x numerator > denominator, fraction > 50%.

Pages 308-311
1. b **3.** a **5.** 125 **7.** 9; f **9.** 17.36; d **11.** 45; f **13.** 6; f **15.** 8; f, d **17.** 1.4; d **19.** 135; d **21.** 104; f **23.** 30 **25.** 30 **27.** 60 **Exercises 29-41,** methods may vary. **29.** 72; C, P **31.** 35; C, P **33.** 52; P **35.** 50; C, P **37.** 39; P, C **39.** 5.7; P, C **41.** 1,400; P, C **43.** 2 in. **45.** 8 in. by 12 in. **47.** $9,840 **49.** $168.00; $180.32

Pages 314-315
1. b **3.** b **5.** 75% **7.** 60%; $n \times 5 = 3$ **9.** 40%; $n \times 40 = 16$ **11.** 50%; $n \times 500 = 250$ **13.** 42%; $n \times 200 = 84$ **15.** 75%; $n \times 20 = 15$ **17.** 200%; $n \times 35 = 70$ **19.** 40%; $n \times 12.5 = 5$ **21.** 225%; $n \times 20 = 45$ **23.** $\frac{9}{100}$ **25.** $\frac{21}{250}$ **27.** 0.65 **29.** 6 **31.** $360 **33.** 112.5% **35.** 8

Pages 316-317
1. a **3.** 79 **Exercises 5-19,** methods may vary. **5.** 1,200; $0.25 \times n = 300$; P, M **7.** 550; $55 = 0.10 \times n$; M **9.** 31.25; $0.4 \times n = 12.5$; P, C **11.** 32.5; $0.2 \times n = 6.5$; P, C **13.** 65; $0.08 \times n = 5.2$; P, C **15.** 200; $0.035 \times n = 7$; P, C **17.** 3,000; $0.008 \times n = 24$; P, C **19.** 0.75; $0.50 \times n = \frac{3}{8}$; P, C **21.** 50 **23.** $1,050 **25.** $525

Pages 318-319
1. $410 **3.** $\frac{1}{2}$ year **Exercises 5-7,** methods may vary. **5.** $57.50; P or C **7.** $146.25; P or C **Choose a Strategy 9.** Plan C would pay the most over 2 years.

Pages 320-321
1. b **3.** 10% **Exercises 5-27,** estimate may vary. Sample is given. **5.** 25% **7.** 25% **9.** 60,000 **11.** 10,000 **13.** 600 **15.** 1,000 **17.** 300 **19.** 14 **21.** 10% **23.** 300% **25.** 10,000 **27.** 5 **29.** $32,000 **31.** $8,000 **33.** 400; 5% is $\frac{1}{20}$; if $\frac{1}{20}$ of the sales tax is about 20, then the total sales tax is 20 x 20. **35.** $2.00; $\frac{1}{4} \times 8 = 2$

Pages 322-323
1. b **3.** b **Exercises 5-13,** methods may vary. **5.** 96; P, C; $36 = 0.375n$; $n = 96$ **7.** 60; P, C; $0.65n = 39$; $n = 60$ **9.** $16\frac{2}{3}$%; P, M; $7 = 42n$; $n = 16\frac{2}{3}$% **11.** 115; P, C; $46 = 0.4n$; $n = 115$ **13.** 232; P, C; $174 = \frac{3}{4}n$; $n = 232$ **15.** 52%; P, C; $225n = 117$;

$n = 0.52$ **17.** 60; P, C; $0.11n = 6.6$; $n = 60$ **19.** 25.5%; P, C; $2{,}000n = 510$; $n = 0.255$ **21.** 67%; P, C; $600n = 402$; $n = 0.67$ **23.** 600; P, C; $0.48n = 288$; $n = 600$ **25.** $0.9n = 18$; 20 girls **27.** $0.6(45) = n$; 27 games **Skills Review** **1.** $\frac{1}{4}$ **3.** $3\frac{5}{8}$

Pages 324-325
1. $178.00 **3.** $53.40 **Exercises 5-13,** methods may vary. **5.** $198.75; C, P **7.** $6,750; P, C **9.** 40%; P **11.** 100%; C, P **13.** $823.20; $882.00

Chapter 10

Pages 336-339
1. Not a prism; its base is not a polygon and it has a curved surface. **3.** Not a prism; it has one base and other faces are triangular regions. **5.** Triangular face **7.** 4 **9.** 6 **11.** 8 **13.** 5 **15.** 8 **17.** 6 **19.** d **21.** c **23.** 11 faces; 20 edges; 11 vertices **25.** Its bases are pentagons **27.** $F + V = E + 2$ **29.** 2 circles; 1 rectangles **Skills Review** **1.** $\frac{8}{15}$ **3.** $1\frac{1}{3}$ **5.** $1\frac{1}{4}$ **7.** $1\frac{1}{3}$

Pages 340-341
1. 2 **3.** 52 **5.** 6 **7.** 9 **9.** 32 **11.** 9 **13.** 15 **15.** 30 **17.** 150 **Choose a Strategy** **19.** 16 **21.** 55

Pages 342-345
1. Area **3.** Area **5.** Area **7.** Width **9.** Perimeter **11.** $A = 16$ sq in.; $P = 20$ in. **13.** $A = 64$ m^2; $P = 32$ m; M **15.** $A = 34{,}850$ sq ft; $P = 750$ ft; P **17.** $A = 484$ sq in.; $P = 88$ in.; P **19.** $A = 75$ sq in.; $P = 35$; P **21.** $A = 90$ sq in.; $P = 38$ in.; M **23.** $A = 2.56$ m^2; $P = 6.4$ m; P **25.** $A = 6\frac{2}{3}$ sq ft; $P = 10\frac{1}{3}$ ft; P **27.** $\ell = 5$ cm **29.** $\ell = 6\frac{2}{5}$ in. **31.** $\ell = 5\frac{1}{2}$ cm **33.** 74 ft **35.** 36 boxes **Explore Math** **37.** $A = \ell \times w$, $9 = 9 \times 1$; $16 = 8 \times 2$; $21 = 7 \times 3$; $24 = 6 \times 4$; $25 = 5 \times 5$ **39.** The area increases. **41.** 25 cm^2

Pages 346-347
1. $\overline{AE}$; 210 m; 2,612.5 m^2 **3.** $A = 64$ m^2; $P = 39.7$ m **5.** $A = 3{,}520$ cm^2; $P = 278$ cm **7.** $A = 41.16$ cm^2 **9.** $A = 25\frac{1}{2}$ sq in. **11.** $A = 25.92$ cm^2 **13.** 7.5 sq in.; 30 sq in.; 67.5 sq in. **15.** The area is multiplied by the square of the number,

Pages 348-349
1. $A = 192$ sq in.; $P = 76$ in. **3.** $A = 324$ sq ft; $P = 80$ ft **5.** $A = 111.65$ m^2; $P = 41$ m; C **7.** $A = 192$ sq ft; $P = 60.8$ ft; C **9.** $A = 63.29$ sq in. $P = 37.7$ in.; C **11.** $A = 39{,}672$ sq ft; $P = 1{,}014$ ft **13.** $P = 1{,}500$ m

Pages 350-351
1. 24.1 m **Exercises 3-5,** methods may vary. **3.** 75.4 mm; C **5.** 47.1 ft; P or C **7.** 37.7 cm **9.** 100.5 in. **11.** 10.7 cm **13.** 75.4 in. **15.** 28.3 ft **17.** 58.1 in. **19.** 6 ft apart

Pages 352-355
1. 452.2 cm^2 **3.** 38.9 m^2 **Exercises 5-15,** methods may vary. A samples is given. **5.** 1,492 cm^2; C **7.** 26,577 mm^2; C **9.** 8 m^2; P **11.** 1.5 cm^2; C **13.** 2 m^2; P **15.** 16.6 m^2; C **17.** $209\frac{11}{18}$ sq ft **19.** $\frac{7}{88}$ sq in. **21.** $2\frac{23}{126}$ sq yd **23.** 2,464 sq in. **25.** $9\frac{5}{8}$ sq in. **27.** $209\frac{11}{18}$ sq in. **29.** a **31.** a **33.** c **35.** 130 cm^2 **37.** 183.5 sq ft **39.** 56.5 m^2 **41.** 403 km^2 **43.** $r = 9$ mm; $d = 18$ mm **45.** 4 boxes

Pages 358-359
1. 5 **3.**

Face	Dimensions
front	8 ft base x 9 ft height triangle
back	8 ft base x 9 ft height triangle
right side	8 ft base x 9 ft height triangle
left side	8 ft base x 9 ft height triangle
bottom	8 ft x 8 ft square

5. 110 sq in. prism **7.** 2,606 sq ft prism **9.** 187.18 sq in. prism **11.** 680 sq in.; prism **13.** 371.2 cm^2; prism **15.** 610.4 cm^2; prism **17.** 1,432 sq in. **19.** When each dimension is doubled, the surface area is four times greater.

ℓ	w	h	surface area
1	1	1	6
2	2	2	24
4	4	4	96

Pages 360-361
3. $A = 2\pi rh$ **5.** 376.8 cm^2 **7.** 586.5 m^2 **9.** 3,730.3 m^2 **11.** 186.4 m^2 **13.** 213.5 m^2 **15.** 275.6 cm^2 **Exercises 17-19,** method choices may vary. **17.** 428.82 m^2; C **19.** $1{,}810\frac{2}{7}$ m^2; P **21.** The surface area of the curved surface is halved if the radius is halved.

r	h	Surface area of curved surface
2	10	125.6
4	10	251.2
8	10	502.4

Pages 362-363
1. 15 cu in. **3.** 156 cu ft **Exercises 5-7,** method choices may vary. **5.** 697.5 cu in.; C **7.** 540 cu yd; P **9.** 1,653.8 m^3 **11.** 40.2 cm^3 **13.** 196.9 cm^3 **15.** 91.1 m^3 **17.** 18.75 cu ft

Pages 364-365
1. Square **3.** Rectangle **5.** 676.7 cm^3 **7.** 47.1 mm^3 **9.** 215.4 m^3 **11.** 4,270.4 cm^3 **13.** 825 cm^3 **15.** 16.4 cm^3 **17.** 804 cm^3 of popcorn **Explore Math**
19.

s	h	V of square Prism	V of square Pyramid
1	2	2	$\frac{2}{3}$
2	2	8	$\frac{8}{3}$
10	10	1,000	$\frac{1{,}000}{3}$
10	20	2,000	$\frac{2{,}000}{3}$

Pages 364-365 (continued)

21.

r	h	V of Cone	V of Cylinder
1	2	$\frac{2}{3}\pi$	2π
2	2	$\frac{8}{3}\pi$	8π
10	10	$\frac{1,000}{3}\pi$	$1,000\pi$
10	20	$\frac{2,000}{3}\pi$	$2,000\pi$

Pages 366-367
1. A: 14 ft; B: 28 ft **3.** A: 12 sq ft; B: 48 sq ft **5.** A: 6.28 in., 3.14 sq in.; B: 12.56 in., 12.56 sq in. **7.** 60 cm^3 **9.** 226 cm^3 **11.** Exercises 10's volume is about 8 times Exercise 9's volume **13.** The volume is multiplied by $2 \times 2 \times 2$, or 8. **15.** Answers may vary. Sample answer is given 12, 4, 5

Pages 368-369
1. The difference in volume of 2 spheres **3.** $V = \frac{4}{3}\pi r^3$ **5.** 3.6 [x] 3.6 [x] 3.6 [M-] 4.7 [x] 4.7 [x] 4.7 [M+] [MRC] [=] [x] 4 [÷] 3 [x] 3.14 [=] **7.** 754 cm^3; C **9.** 377 sq ft; C **11.** 0.7 ft; P

Chapter 11

Pages 380-383
1. 5 **3.** 9 **5.** 20 **Exercises 7-11,** method choices may vary. **7.** 7.8; P **9.** 6.0; M **11.** 724.6; C **13.** None **15.** None **17.** 839 **19.** 8 **21.** 7 **23.** 837 **25.** 7 **27.** 7 **29.** 837 **31.** 58 inches **33.** 10 inches **35.** 89 pounds **37.** 93 pounds **39.** The median (66); the mean is lowered by the low number of call s on Monday. **41.** 6 **43.** 198, 20, 18, 6, 20, 91, 20 **45.** 20, 21, 22, 30, 36 **47.** 24, 24, 28, 30, 34 **Explore Math 49.** Range; range is the measurement for any "spread" of data. **51.** Mode; the word typical means "common" or "most likely," mode best measures "most likely."

Pages 384-387
1. Sample **3.** Line plot **5.** 50-59; 60-69 **7.** Answers will vary. **15.** 2.1; 2; 2 **17.** 2.5; 2;.2 and 3 **19.** 188.4; 140; no mode **21.** As long as there is room, it may give a more accurate picture of the data. However, if the intervals are too small, you may not be able to get the feel of any trends. **23.** You could make an estimate from a sample group of 30 students, but a larger group would give a better estimate; a survey of all girls would probably differ from a survey of all boys. **25.** Medium; large **Choose a Strategy Exercises 27-31,** Answers will vary.

Pages 388-389
1. $\frac{75}{150} = \frac{1}{2}$ **3.** $n = 400$ **5.** The second one is probably more accurate; it was found using a larger sample. **7.** 3.5 miles = width, 7 miles = length **9.** 1,370

Pages 390-391
1. 4 **3.** 1 **5.** 9; 5 **7.** 41

9.

Stem	Leaf
0	6 8
1	2 2 3 4 5 5 7 9
2	0 1 5 7
3	2

11.

Stem	Leaf
9	2
10	
11	1 9
12	0
13	7
14	3 4 4
15	5 6

13.

Stem	Leaf
1	1 2 2 6 9
2	3 3 4 7
3	0 1 6

15.

Stem	Leaf
15	0 2 3 8
16	4 7
17	1 4
18	2 9

17.

Stem	Leaf
3	4 6 8 9
4	1 1 6 8 9
5	2 3 4

19.

Stem	Leaf
96	1 3
97	1 5 5
98	2 4 6 6 8

21. 39; no mode 71

Pages 394-395
1. 3,000; 3,000 **3.** Records **9.** Videos **11.** Women

Pages 396-397
1. Japanese and Korean, Dravidian; Afro-Asian **3.** 1.188 billion **5.** 108 million **7.** 270 million **9.** 216 million **11.** 216 million **13.** 7° **15.** 79° **17.** 11° **19.** 36°; 10%

Pages 398-399
1. 6,000,000 **3.** 1930 **7.** 1980 and 1990; 1950 and 1960 **9.** 1970 **11.** Florida; Tennessee **13.** Increasing; leveling off; as people retire, they move to warmer climates. **Skills Review 1.** $x = 36$ **3.** $x = 2.5$

Pages 400-401
1. 1978, 1982, 1984, 1985, 1986, 1988 **3.** 1981; 9 **5.** Double broken-line graph; broken-line graphs show changes over time better. **7.** American League

Pages 402-403
1. 100; 50,000 **3.** First graph **5.** It may be that

most accidents occur in the home because people spend most of their time in the home. **7.** Misleading **11.** Answers will vary.

Pages 404-405
1. 10 **3.** 51 **5.** 55 **9.** 6 **11.** Soviet Union: 21%; East Germany: 18%; Switzerland: 11%; Austria: 7%; West Germany: 6%; all other countries 37%

Chapter 12

Pages 420-423
1. 29 **3.** The probability that a green shirt will be given away in the first 2 minutes after the gates opened. **Exercises 9-13,** methods may vary. **9.** MM; $\frac{8+2}{100}=\frac{1}{10}$ **11.** MM; $\frac{7+0}{100}=\frac{7}{100}$ **13.** P; $\frac{8+19}{100}=\frac{27}{100}$ **15.** $\frac{9}{200}$ **17.** $\frac{2}{200}=\frac{1}{100}$ **19.** $\frac{20}{200}=\frac{1}{10}$ **21.** $\frac{6}{200}=\frac{3}{100}$ **23.** $\frac{6+2+9}{200}$ **25.** $\frac{28}{81}$ **27.** $\frac{52}{81}$ **29.** $0.\overline{34567901}$; $0.\overline{296}$; $0.\overline{641975308}$ **31.** 0.333 **33.** $\frac{40}{50}=80\%$ **35.** x must be less than or equal to y.

Pages 424-425
1. 500 tires were tested; 218 tires tested wore out between 30,000 and 34,999 miles; 95 tires tested wore out between 35,000 and 39,900 miles **3.** 156,500 **5.** 203,320 customers **7.** 16,406 customers **9.** 55,664 customers **11.** 80%

Pages 426-427
1 $\frac{3}{10}=0.3$ **3.** $\frac{1}{10}=0.1$ **5.** $\frac{3}{5}=0.6$ **7.** M; $\frac{30}{36}=\frac{5}{6}$ **9.** $\frac{8}{20}=\frac{2}{5}; \frac{3}{5}$ **11.** $\frac{6}{20}=\frac{3}{10}; \frac{7}{10}$ **13.** $\frac{2}{20}=\frac{1}{10}; \frac{9}{10}$ **15.** $\frac{2}{9}; \frac{7}{9}$; 0, 1; $\frac{2}{3}; \frac{1}{3}$ **Exercises 19-21,** answers may vary. Samples are given. **19.** Number **21.** Traits **23.** $\frac{1}{27}$ **25.** $\frac{12}{27}=\frac{4}{9}$ **27.** $\frac{0}{27}$

Pages 428-429
1.

	1	2	3	4	5	6
1	1	2	3	4	5	6
2	2	4	6	8	10	12
3	3	6	9	12	15	18
4	4	8	12	16	20	24
5	5	10	15	20	25	30
6	6	12	18	24	30	36

3. Answers may vary. **5.** Fair **7.** Fair **9.** The game is fair. **11.** The game is fair. **13.** Answers may vary. Sample given. Roll two number cubes, and find their sum. You score a point if the sum is a multiple of 3; your partner scores a point if the sum is not a multiple of 3.

Pages 430-431
1. 40 choices **3.** 120 choices **5.** 120 choices **7.** 2,880 choices **9.** 36,504 call letters **Skills Review** **1.** 2.5 **3.** 70

Pages 434-435
1. Both pairs of events are independent. The first event does not affect the second. **3.** $\frac{1}{36}$ **5.** $\frac{1}{9}$ **7.** $\frac{1}{18}$ **9.** $\frac{1}{9}$ **11.** $\frac{6}{100}=0.06$ **13.** $\frac{25}{100}=0.25$ **15.** $\frac{1,681}{10,000}$ **17.** $\frac{369}{2,000}$ **19.** $\frac{41}{2,500}$ **21.** $\frac{12,960,000}{100,000,000}$

Pages 436-437
1. $\frac{2}{105}$ **3.** $\frac{1}{105}$ **5.** $\frac{1}{42}$ **7.** $\frac{4}{105}$ **9.** $\frac{4}{42}$ **11.** $\frac{1}{21}$ **13.** Tuesday from the tapes that remain $\frac{7}{26}$ **Choose a Strategy** **15.** Let G_1 and G_2 represent the two green socks and let R represent the red sock. Then the possible ways of picking two socks are G_1G_2, G_2G_1, G_1R, RG_1, G_2R, and RG_2.
17. Probability that first is blue × Probability that second is blue

$$\frac{2}{5} \times \frac{1}{4} = \frac{2}{20} = \frac{1}{10}$$

Students might also list all possible pairings using R_1, R_2, B_1, B_2, and G. Then they would find there are 20 possible pairings, with 2 out of 20 consisting of both blue, that is, B_1B_2 and B_2B_1.

Pages 438-439
1. $\frac{2}{9}$ **3.** $\frac{5}{10}; \frac{5}{9}; \frac{5}{18}$ **5.** $\frac{3}{20}$ **7.** $\frac{1}{4}$ **9.** $\frac{1}{6}$ **11.** $\frac{2}{9}$ **13.** $\frac{1}{8}$ **15.** $\frac{1}{24}$ **17.** $\frac{3}{22}$ **19.** $\frac{1}{22}$ **21.** $\frac{17}{20}$ **23.** $\frac{23}{24}$ **25.** $\frac{1}{7}$ **27.** 25: $\frac{1}{9}$; 26: $\frac{1}{9}$

Pages 440-441
1. Tails **3.** 7, 8, 9 **5.** $\frac{1}{3}$ **7.** Let each letter represent a digit from 0 to 9. **Explore Math** **9.** Answers may vary.

Chapter 13

Pages 452-453
1. Answers may vary. Temperature, depth, debt **3.** 1 **5.** 75 **7.** –45 **9.** 475 **11.** 18 **13.** –80 **15.** 9 **17.** > **19.** > **21.** 500 **23.** 11; 11 **25.** 2; –2 **27.** 59; –59 **29.** 18; –18 **31.** 46; 46 **33.** 126; 126 **35.** –600 ft **37.** 150 ft **Skills Review** **1.** 10.2 **3.** 440 **5.** 55 **7.** 140

Pages 454-455
1. Negative; the sign of the number with the greater absolute value is negative. **3.** Zero; the sum of a number and its opposite is zero. **5.** Negative; both addends are negative. **7.** Negative; both addends are negative. **9.** 31 **11.** –10 **13.** –5 **15.** –3 **17.** 4 **19.** –8 **21.** –16 **23.** 38 **25.** –35 **27.** –26 **29.** –17 **31.** 10 **33.** 15 **35.** –3 **37.** 12 **39.** 16 **41.** –34 **43.** 59 **45.** Patrick **47.** 7 below par

Pages 456-457
1. 2; 7 **3.** 1; –5 **5.** –6 + (–2) = –8 **7.** 3 + (–8) = –5 **9.** –5 + 3 = –2 **11.** 10 + (–3) = 7 **13.** 0 **15.** 38 **17.** –22 **19.** –58 **21.** –30 **23.** –70 **25.** –112 **27.** 100 **29.** 39 **31.** –7 **33.** –37 **35.** 34 **37.** 25 **39.** –4 **41.** –34 **43.** –38 **45.** 0 **47.** –35 **49.** No,

Pages 456-457 (continued)
whatever integer you could "think" of, you can always add one to it. **51.** 116° lower **53.** 265°

Pages 458-459
1. Positive **3.** Positive **5.** Zero **7.** 32 **9.** 42 **11.** 240 **13.** –182 **15.** –88 **17.** 36 **19.** –200 **21.** –300 **23.** –96 **25.** –200 **27.** –96 **29.** –64 **31.** 123 **33.** –24 **35.** –72 **37.** 100 **39.** 620 **41.** 720 **43.** –1,600 **45.** 0 **47.** 16 **49.** –1 **51.** 81 **53.** 25 **55.** 1 **57.** Answers may vary. On some calculators, you can change the sign of a number by using the sign-change key [+/-]. Once the number has the sign you want, use the multiplication key to multiply. **59.** When x is odd

Pages 460-461
1. –4 **3.** 6 **5.** 5 **7.** –3 **9.** –3 **11.** –5 **13.** 6 **15.** –5 **17.** –8 **19.** 5 **21.** –9 **23.** 6 **25.** 5 **27.** 10 **29.** 8 **31.** –12 **33.** 0 **35.** –11 **37.** 19 **39.** –8 **41.** –12 **43.** 6 **45.** –3 **47.** 5 **49.** 1 **51.** Answers may vary. (–21) + 7 = 21 + (–7) = –3; (–12) + 4 = 12 + (–4) = –3; (-16) + 2 = 16 + (–2) = –8

Pages 464-465
1. Later; 265 minutes **3.** 4:48 A.M.; 252 cm **5.** 3:17 A.M.; 94 cm **7.** 10:25 A.M.; 33 cm **9.** Bar Harbor; Havre de Grace; 262 cm

Pages 466-467
1. 3.8 **3.** 10 **5.** $\frac{6}{1}$ **7.** $\frac{-4}{2}$ **9.** $\frac{-27}{5}$ **11.** > **13.** = **15.** > **17.** < **19.** $-\frac{1}{2}, 0, \frac{3}{4}$ **21.** $-1, \frac{3}{2}, 2\frac{4}{5}$ **23.** $-3\frac{5}{12}$ **25.** –3.82 **27.** $-1\frac{1}{2}$ **29.** –6 **31.** 4 **33.** 1.68 **35.** $14\frac{1}{3}$ **37.** 2.6 **39.** $312.50 **Explore Math** **41.** $\frac{3}{8}, \frac{5}{8}$

Pages 468-469
1. No; $\sqrt{7}$ is not an integer; yes; no **3.** 7, 8 **5.** 5, 6 **7.** 8, 9 **9.** 10, 11 **11.** 15, –15 **13.** 6, –6 **15.** 3 **17.** 12 **19.** 8 **21.** 6.0 **23.** 8.0 **25.** 5.4 **27.** 3.9 **29.** 6.5 **31.** 6.7 **33.** 12.0 **Exercises 35-39,** answers may vary. Samples are given. **35.** 16; 49; 64 **37.** $\sqrt{31}$; $\sqrt{8}$; $\sqrt{444}$ **39.** 6.3 cm

Pages 470-473
1. 81; 144; 225; 15 **3.** 64; 289; 225; 15 **5.** c = 13 m **7.** 20 **9.** 2.2 **11.** 7 **13.** 16 **15.** 24.0 **17.** 75 **19.** 13.1 **21.** 12.7 **23.** No **25.** Yes **27.** Yes **29.** Yes **31.** 6 mi **33.** Draw another right triangle having one leg with length $\sqrt{2}$ and another leg with length 1. Measure the length of the hypotenuse with a compass and then mark off that distance from 0 on the number line. **35.** $12^2 + 16^2 = 20^2$; $15^2 + 20^2 = 25^2$ **37.** Answers may vary. **39.** Unlimited number **Choose a Strategy** **41.** Answers may vary. Try and check

Pages 474-475
1. –; – **3.** 23 m shorter **5.** 5.9 km

Pages 476-477
1. $(3 \times 10^{-1}) + (4 \times 10^{-2}) + (2 \times 10^{-3})$ **3.** $(1 \times 10^{1}) + (2 \times 10^{0}) + (9 \times 10^{-1}) + (0 \times 10^{-2}) + (2 \times 10^{-3})$ **5.** $(2 \times 10^{1}) + (5 \times 10^{0}) + (9 \times 10^{-1})$ **7.** 0.068 **9.** 10^3 **11.** 10^{-3} **13.** 10^0 **15.** 10^{-7} **17.** 10,000,000 **19.** 0.00001 **21.** 0.0000000001 **23.** 0.0000001 **25.** $(7 \times 10^{2}) + (9 \times 10^{1}) + (2 \times 10^{0})$ **27.** $(1 \times 10^{6}) + (2 \times 10^{5}) + (2 \times 10^{4}) + (9 \times 10^{3}) + (7 \times 10^{2}) + (5 \times 10^{1}) + (6 \times 10^{0})$ **29.** $(1 \times 10^{-1}) + (5 \times 10^{-2}) + (6 \times 10^{-3})$ **31.** $(4 \times 10^{-2}) + (5 \times 10^{-}) + (2 \times 10^{-4})$ **33.** $(4 \times 10^{1}) + (5 \times 10^{0}) + (2 \times 10^{-1})$ **35.** $(5 \times 10^{1}) + (0 \times 10^{0}) + (2 \times 10^{-1}) + (3 \times 10^{-2})$ **37.** 438,387 **39.** 405.605 **41.** 0.01; 0.001; 0.0001; the number of zeros in 10^{-n} when it is written without exponents is equal to $n - 1$. **43.** 10^9 **45.** 10^9; 60×10^9 or 6×10^{10}

Pages 478-479
1. 3 **3.** –1 **5.** 240,000 **7.** 2.75×10^2 **9.** 9.85×10^1 **11.** 4.71×10^{-1} **13.** 2.01×10^{-4} **15.** 6.02×10^{-2} **17.** 8×10^{-4} **19.** 812,000 **21.** 10,300,000 **23.** 0.37 **25.** 0.007964 **27.** 0.0604 **29.** 0.000024 **31.** 0.00000000004 **33.** 3.0×10^{-2} mph; 1.8×10^{-1} mph **35.** 7.8×10^{-5}, 3.44×10^{-3}, 1.23×10^{-2}, 1.02×10^4

Chapter 14

Pages 490-493
1. –24 **3.** 7 **5.** 9; Distributive **7.** 0; Multiplication of zero **9.** 17; Distributive **11.** –28; Distributive **13.** 17.4; Distributive; Multiplication of one **15.** 0; Multiplication of zero **17.** $b = 1$; Multiplication of one **19.** $n = 0$; Additive of zero **21.** $r = 32$; Distributive **23.** $b = 1.8$; Associative of multiplication **25.** $x = 1$; Multiplication of one **27.** –23 **29.** 0 **31.** 31.0 **33.** 5 **35.** $(4 + 3 \times 4) + (4 + 2) = \frac{16}{6}$ **37.** $(9 + 4 \times 6) + 3 - 2 = 9$ **39.** Whole, integer, rational **41.** Rational **43.** Whole, integer, rational **45.** Answers may vary. 4 + 3 + 2 + 1 **47.** Answers may vary. A sample is given. $6 \times (4 + 2 + 8) + 2 \neq (2 + 3) \times (3 + 3 + 20) + 2$ **Explore Math** **49.** (9 – 5) + (7 – 3) = 1; (9 + 7) + (5 + 3) = 2; (9 – 3) + (7 – 5) = 3; (9 – 3) – (7 – 5) = 4; (9 + 3) + (7 – 5) = 5; (5 + 3 + 7) – 9 = 6; 9 – [(7 + 3) + 5] = 7; (9 + 7) + (5 – 3) = 8; (7 + 5) – (9 + 3) = 9; (5 + 9) – (7 – 3) = 10

Pages 494-495
1. p – $0.40 **3.** –27 **5.** 2 **7.** $3 - y$ **9.** $-(p + q)$ **11.** $n + 1\frac{1}{10} - 2\frac{1}{5}$ **13.** –1 **15.** 8.25 **17.** $n - 3$, 3 less than a number is always smaller than 2 less than the number. **19.** $3,644

Pages 496-497
1. m + $9.90 = $12.65; m = $2.75 **3.** $n - 18\frac{7}{10} = 4\frac{1}{2}$; n

$= 23\frac{1}{5}$ **5.** $a = -9.8$ **7.** $a = 8.4$ **9.** $r = -15.10$ **11.** $a = -\frac{1}{5}$ **13.** $c = 17\frac{1}{10}$ **15.** $c = -5.6$ **17.** $n = 26.5$ **19.** $q = -10.66$ **21.** $x = 1\frac{1}{4}$ **23.** $m = -5$ **25.** $x = 11\frac{1}{8}$ **27.** Estimates may vary. $16,600 **29.** Yes; no; no; you must solve the equation 58 x 3 + $r \leq 250$. (58)(3) + 20 = 194, is less than 250, but (58)(3) + 80 = 254 and (58)(3) + 100 = 274 are both greater than 250. **Skills Review 1.** 21 **3.** 125

Pages 498-499
1. 12 x 6 **3.** $\frac{\$5.25}{t}$ **5.** 6 **7.** –5.4 **9.** 11 **11.** 7 **13.** 11 **15.** $\frac{1}{9}$ **17.** –10.5 **19.** 1 **21.** 6 **23.** –6 **25.** 0.95 x x

Pages 502-503
1. a; $s = 95$; 95 copies **3.** $t = -14$ **5.** $t = 1\frac{2}{3}$ **7.** $n = \frac{-5}{8}$ **9.** $x = 1\frac{1}{2}$ **11.** $x = -4$ **13.** $s = 42\frac{2}{3}$ **15.** $n = \frac{2}{5}$ **17.** $n = -14$ **19.** $u = -0.3$; C **21.** $x = 54$; M **23.** $n = -310$; M **25.** $y = \frac{7}{16}$ **27.** $\frac{2n}{3} = 24$; $n = 36$ **29.** $\frac{n}{-6} = 2\frac{1}{2}$; $n = -15$ **31.** $\frac{4x}{5} = 20$; $x = 25$ **33.** 760 posters **35.** $275.50

Pages 504-505
1. 450.5 mi/h; 40 mi/h **3.** 4,302 mi **5.** 13.2 mi/h **Choose a Strategy 7.** 120 mi **9.** First train: 160 mi; second train: 180 mi

Pages 506-507
1. Add 4 to both sides; divide both sides by 10. **3.** Subtract 13 from both sides; multiply both sides by 4. **5.** $a = 19$ **7.** $x = 4$ **9.** $x = 21$ **11.** $y = 50$ **13.** $m = 5$ **15.** $s = 12$ **17.** $x = 100$ **19.** $c = 52$ **21.** $z = 8$ **23.** $x = 7$ **25.** $x = 5$ **27.** $n = 64$ **29.** $x = 12$ **31.** $x = 2$ **33.** $x = -8$ **35.** $t = 5$ **37.** $n = 87$ **39.** $x = 1\frac{1}{9}$ **41.** $2b + 2.5 = 6.3$, $b = 1.9$ point

Pages 508-509
1. 100 **3.** $F = 212°$ **5.** 58.33% **7.** 100% **9.** $b = 136$ **11.** They differ by 8.

Chapter 15

Pages 520-521
1. a **3.** b **23.** $0 < y < 125$ **25.** $d \geq 3$

Pages 522-523
1. (0, 2) **3.** (–3, 0) **5.** *G* **7.** I **9.** IV **11.** *y*-axis **23.** The lengths of the sides in ΔDEF are twice as large as the lengths in ΔABC. The area of ΔDEF is four times the area of ΔABC.

Pages 524-527
1. (9, 5) **3.** $A^{I}(-1, 5)$, $B^{I}(2, 1)$, C^{I} (2, 5) **5.** $A^{III}(-7, 5)$, B^{III} (–4, 1), C^{III} (–4, 5) **7.** A^{V} (–1, 10), B^{V}(2, 6) C^{V} (2,10) **9.** $A^{VII}(-1, 4)$, B^{VII} (2, 0), C^{VII} (2, 4) **11.** *A*(–4, 1); *B*(0, 1); *C*(0, 5); *D*(–4, 5) **13.** *A*(–2, –2); *B*(2, –2); *C*(2, 2); *D*(–2, 2) **15.** *A*(–5, –4); *B*(–1, –4); *C*(–1, 0) *D*(–5, 0) **17.** *A*(1, 0); *B*(1, –5); *C*(5, –5) **19.** *A*(1, 5); *B*(1, 0); *C*(5, 0) **21.** *A*(0, 5); *b*(0, 0); *c*(4, 0) **23.** Horizontal; left **25.** Answers may vary. Add –5 to both coordinates. **27.** *P'*(1, 8); *Q"*(4, 19) **29.** *x* + 3, *y* – 4) **Skills Review 1.** E **3.** D **5.** A **7.** 8,432; C **9.** –56,916; C **11.** –56; C **13.** $-1\frac{1}{4}$; M **15.** $\frac{4}{5}$; M **17.** –2; P **19.** –13; –16; 1; b< a < c **21.** 4; –8; 16; b < a < c **23.** $-\frac{1}{6}; \frac{1}{6}; \frac{-5}{6}$; c < a< b **25.** 1; 10; -10; c < a < b **27.** $\frac{2}{21}$; $1\frac{11}{21}$; 10.5; a < b < c

Pages 528-531
1. (3, 4) **3.** *M* '(1, –1); *N* '(3, –3) **5.** (3, –7) **7.** *M* '(1, –1); *N* '(5, –1); *P* '(4, –2); *Q* '(2, –2) **9.** *D* '(–1, 4); *E* '(-3, 1), *F* '(-6, 3), and *G* '(–4, 6) **13.** c **15.** b **17.** a **19.** b **21.** Yes **23.** Yes **Explore Math 25.** An expression of words and or numbers that reads the same in both directions. **27.** Answers may vary.

Pages 532-535
1. *A* **3.** *A* **5.** *A'* (-1,–2), *B'* (-3,-4), *C'* (-5,-2), *D'* (-2, -1) **7.** *F* '(–1, 2), *G* '(–5, 2), *H* '(–4, 1), *J* '(–2, 1) **9.** b **11.** Rotation **13.** Rotation of 180° or two reflection (over the *x*-axis and *y*-axis or vice versa). **15.** b, d **17.** yes

Pages 538-539
1. a; rotation and translations **5.** Yes **7.** Yes **9.** Yes **11.** Yes **13.** The triangle tessellates, Methods may vary.

Pages 542-543
1. –5; –3; –1; 1 **3.** No. In exercise 2 *y* decreases. **Explore Math 27.** The larger the multiple of *x*, the steeper the slope.

Pages 544-545
1. (–3, 2) **3.** (3, –4) **5.** (1, 6) **7.** (2, 1) **9.** no solution **11.** (2, 7) **13.** (0, 4) **15.** No solution **17.** No solution **19.** (–1, 1) **21.** (5, 2) **25.** The lines are parallel. No Parallel lines do not intersect. There is no solution.

Pages 546-547
1. $C = 2x + 10$ **3.** (10, 30) **5.** Best Bites **7.** 50 miles

Pages 548-549
1. 250 tickets **3.** 450 tickets **Exercises 5-9,** method choices may vary. **5.** When each club is visited 4 times **7.** When visited fewer that 4 times **9.** The City Health Club; answers may vary; example shown. . . one club may be more conveniently located than the others.

Index

ACKNOWLEDGMENTS

Design

Cover and Special Features: SHELDON COTLER + ASSOCIATES Lipman Hearne, Rosa + Wesley Design Associates, Jack Weiss Associates

Photographs

Cover: Richard Chesnut, Fred Schenk xi (tl): Tony Freeman, PhotoEdit xi (tr): Bob Daemmrich, The Image Works xi (cr): Tony Freeman, PhotoEdit xi (br): Brent Jones xii (br): California Institute of Technology xiii (bl): NASA xiii (br): GEOPIC™, Earth Satellite Corporation xiv (l): Pamela Price, The Picture Cube xv (t): Courtesy International Business Machines Corporation xvii (t): Richard Hutchings, InfoEdit xvii (b): Tony Freeman, PhotoEdit xviii: NASA xix (tr): Eric Carle, Stock Boston xix (cl): Bill Gallery, Stock Boston xix (br): Stacey Pick, Stock Boston xx (t): Doug Menuez, Stock Boston xx (b): Chris Bjornberg/Science Source from Photo Researchers 1 (t): Bob Daemmrich 1 (b): MacDonald Photography, The Picture Cube ScottForesman photographs by: Richard Chesnut 14, 36–37, 50, 51, 65, 86, 87, 220, 221, 265, 268–269, 300–301, 313, 378–379, 392, 393, 415, 435, 443, 462, 504, 505, 536, 558, 559; Arie deZanger 300–301, 312, 435, 559; unless otherwise acknowledged, all photographs are the property of ScottForesman. Ovak Arslanian: 268–269 Art Resource: Erich Lessing 95 The Bettmann Archive: 473 Alice J. Belling: 478 Lee Boltin: 304 Cameramann Int'l: Milt and Joan Mann 488–489 Woodfin Camp & Associates, Inc.: Michael Friedel 450–451 Webb Chappell: 60, 96 Cliak/Tony Stone Worldwide: Bob Daemmrich 430; Alan Smith 431 Bruce Coleman: John Elk III 9 Duomo: David Madison 300–301, 334–335 Ellis Wildlife Collection: Gerry Ellis 186–187 FPG: 414; M. Rothell 2–3; Bill Stanley 300–301; Willinger 2–3 Focus on Sports: 405, 454 The Image Bank: Steve Dunwell 418–419; Heintz Fischer Kenny 112–113; Michael Melford 36–37; J. Vogt 418–419 Philip M. Isaacson: 349 Catherine Koehler: 397 Renee Lynn: 72—73 David Madison: 334–335, 518–519 Larry Maglott: 212, 238, 308, 310, 311 Tom Magno: 89, 157, 270, 290 Magnum Photos: Michael Nichols 186–187 Egyptian Expedition of The Metropolitan Museum of Art, Rogers Fund 1930: 232 Doug Mindell: 56, 196, 198, 199, 218, 219, 289, 324 Museo Nazionale de Villa Guila, Rome: 152 Museum of the American Indian, The Heye Foundation: 532(r) NASA: 476 Ken O'Donoghue: 74; 240, 248, 252 Odyssey Productions: Robert Frerck 211, 305, 307, 336, 349, 396 Carol Palmer: 272 PhotoEdit: David Young-Wolff 38 Courtesy Pulsar LaBean Enterprises: 488–489 Jeff Rotman: 450–451 Frank Siteman: 38, 40, 248, 320 From *Magnificent Macrame* by Marie-Jeanine Solvit, © copyright 1979 by Sterling Publishing Company, NY. Photos by Philippe Jolladaud and Patrice Veres: 169 Stock Boston: Peter Menzel 306 The Stock Market: Daniel Aubry 2–3; David Barnes 72–73; Jeffrey 334–335; Garry Gay 112–113; David W. Hamilton 36–37; Gill C. E. Blackman 300–301; James Blank 86; Dave Brown 282; Dave Davidson 537; Steve Elmore 264, 265; Stephen Green Armytage 2–3; Brownie Harris 418–419; Chris Jones 488–489; Charles Krebs 334–335; Harvey Lloyd 450–451; Tom Marfin 418–419; Bill & Jan Moeller 518–519; Roy Morsch 15, 186–187, 283, 334–335; Stan Osolinski 186–187; Gabe Palmer/ Mug Shots 2–3 H. Mark Weidman: 154–155 Helmut K. Wimmer: 154–155

Illustrations

Elizabeth Allen, Jean Bailey, Diane Bennett, David Biedrzycki, Marty Braun, Tom Briggs, Robert Burger, Robert Cline, Dan Collins, Jose Cruz, Susan Dodge, Cecile Duray-Bito, Cameron Eagle, Andrea Eberbach, Janice Freid, Bill Gerhold, Brad Hamann, Gerry Hampton, Peter Harris, Lipman Hearne, Steve Henry, Monica Incisa, Dave Joly, Dave Jonason, Bob Jones, Mike Jones, Robert Jones, Robert Korta, Jack Lefkowitz, Andy Levine, Roger Leyonmark, Brenda Losey, Judith Love, Chuck Ludeke, Jeff Mangiat, Susan Mills, Mike Muir, Eileen Mueller Neill, Sharon O'Neil, Brenda Pepper, Jada Rowland, Bruce Sanders, Linda Schiwall-Galio, Elaine Sears, Judy Seckler, Dan Siculan, Suzanne Snider, Barton Stabler, Maria Strosier, Carol Stutz, Peggy Tagel, Julia Talcott, Heather Taylor, Bill Thompson, John Trotta, Paul Vaccarella, John Walter Jr.

Data

pp. 108–109, Courtesy *Compton's Encyclopedia,* 1986, a division of Encyclopedia Britannica p. 488, *The World Book Encyclopedia*

SCOTTFORESMAN STAFF

ScottForesman gratefully acknowledges the contributions of the following individuals.

Editorial

Karen Usiskin, Janice Ziebka, Therese Smith, Clare Froemel, Nancy Baty, Greg McRill, Jean Tucknott, Mary Schaefer

Design

Barbara Schneider, Virginia Pierce, George Roth, David Dumo, Tom Gorman

Production

Mary Lou Beals, Joy Kelly, Barbara Albright, Kathy Oberfranc, Lois Nelson, Fran Simon, Sally Buehne

Marketing

Cathie Dillender, Nan Simpson, Muffet Fox

Business

Elizabeth A. Dietz, Elizabeth R. Semro

Picture Research/Photo Studio

Nina Page, Rosemary Hunter, John Moore, Phoebe Novak

Photo Lab/Keyline

Marilyn Sullivan, Mark Spears, Madeline Oton-Tarpey, Gwen Plogman